CULTURE AREAS:

I. Chibcha
II. Andean
III. Antillea
IVA. Amazon
IVB. Eastern Brazilian Highlands
V. Chaco
VI. Patagonian
VII. Araucanian
VIII. Fuegian

TRIBAL GROUPS:

1. Carib
2. Arawak
3. Jivaro
4. Mundurucú
5. Apinayé
6. Inca
7. Aymara
8. Sirionó
9. Botocudo
10. Tupinamba
11. Araucanians
12. Ona
13. Yahgan

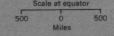

Scale at equator

500   0   500

Miles

SOUTH AMERICA

Anthropology: The Study of Man

Anthropology: The Study of Man

Fourth Edition

E. Adamson Hoebel

Regents Professor of Anthropology
University of Minnesota

McGraw-Hill Book Company

New York   St. Louis   San Francisco   Düsseldorf   Johannesburg   Kuala Lumpur   London
Mexico   Montreal   New Delhi   Panama   Rio de Janeiro   Singapore   Sydney   Toronto

Anthropology: The Study of Man

Library of Congress Catalog Card Number 71-37097

07-029137-3

    3 4 5 6 7 8 9 0 D O D O 7 9 8 7 6 5 4 3 2

*This book was set in Helvetica by Black Dot, Inc., and
printed and bound by R. R. Donnelley & Sons
Company. The designer was Judith Michael; the
drawings were done by Russ Peterson. The editors
were Janis Yates and Helen Greenberg. John F.
Harte supervised production.*

Cover photo: Remojadas clay standing figure, A.D.
*300–900, Veracruz, Mexico. The Museum of Primi-
tive Art. Photo: Lisa Little.*

To Irene

Contents

Part 5 *Symbolic Expression*

Part 6 *Anthropology Today and Tomorrow*

Preface

The revision of an anthropology text has become a formidable task. Anthropology, like every other science, has been expanding, modifying, and reconstituting itself at an ever-increasing speed. Thus, of the approximately 900 works cited in this book, more than a third were published between 1960 and 1972. Continuous reexamination and restatement of basic data, methods, and theoretical orientations is imperative for the author who wishes to help students achieve a grasp of this exciting field of knowledge. What is attempted here is an updated, reasonably consistent, and comprehensive statement of a coherent series of concepts, propositions, and theories about the past and present nature of man, culture, and society supported by factual information from the whole range of anthropology. At the same time, doors are opened and the paths to alternative paths of exploration indicated.

All elements of the previous edition have been thoroughly examined and reworked. I believe this has resulted in an improved theoretical consistency in the treatment of human and cultural evolution as interacting processes. Part 2 ("The Evolution of Man and Culture") incorporates the latest significant findings on fossil man and prehistoric culture, plus more material on American and Asiatic prehistory, reflecting the growing tendency among archaeologists to work within the framework of culture theory. The chapter on human variability has been reconstituted to deal with the approach of clinal distribution and genetic viability. In Part 3 ("The Material Base of Culture") increased emphasis has been given to ecology and to a more functional treatment of housing and handicrafts. Economic and political anthropology have been given more specific treatment in the analysis of social structure in Part 4 ("Social Structure"). In keeping with current developments in anthropology, Part 5 ("Symbolic Expression") has been introduced as a new section in which religion, language, and art have been rephrased as symbolic expressions of cultural systems. The final chapters focus on the great transformation in which all mankind is now being caught up: the passing of civilization and the emergence of surbanization, the culture of the Atomic-Space Age.

When a task of this magnitude is finished, one thinks with gratitude of all those who have played a part in its completion. This book is dedicated to Irene, my wife, because she upgraded the content with research, creative thought, and writing of her own.

She sustained me in the whole endeavor and worked long hours on many nights. I also salute those professional colleagues who gave me the benefit of their ideas and who responded to the publisher's request for expert evaluation and criticism of the manuscript. I wish to acknowledge especially the contributions of Robert F. Spencer, and Everett L. and Janet O. Frost.

The creative work by the Frosts in preparing the *Instructor's Manual* and by Prof. Stanton K. Tefft and the Frosts in writing the *Study Guide* to accompany this work will greatly enhance its usefulness to student and teacher alike.

The high quality of the bookmaker's art, which is evident in the tranformation from manuscript to finished volume, deserves this author's expression of deep gratitude. Janis Yates, Senior Editor, Helen Greenberg, Editing Supervisor, Jack Harte, Production Supervisor, Judy Michael, Designer, and Sam Holmes, Photo Consultant, as well as others too numerous to name, have completed this complex and taxing undertaking with skill, patience, and, I suspect, anxiety occasioned by my own delinquencies.

Thanks to all—and love!

E. Adamson Hoebel

Anthropology: The Study of Man

Part 1   Introduction

Anthropology: The Study of Man

It is a characteristic of being human that man wishes to know himself. Therefore, if for no other reason than to bring satisfaction to our probing curiosity, mankind deserves study for its own sake. Yet, there are further possibilities in the study of man. An improved understanding of ourselves, by ourselves, may enhance our ultimate capabilities to direct our futures with greater intelligence concerning where we want to go and how to get there. Thus anthropology, like any other reasoned study, not only satisfies the human intellect; it can serve larger ends as well. By knowing man we can more effectively understand man's problems and how to cope with them.

Anthropology has few final answers, but it sheds the light of fact and reason on many pressing questions.

Are there, for example, any universals in mankind's behavior? Is the family necessary? Are there "better", i.e., happier, ways for people to mature and to rear children than those the contemporary nuclear family offers? Is there a better way for man to use his environment and natural resources than the one we are witnessing toward the end of the twentieth century? Is it wise to promote more efficient agriculture, modern health and sanitation measures, advanced technology, monogamy, family planning, and higher education in areas and societies which have long

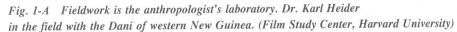

Fig. 1-A   Fieldwork is the anthropologist's laboratory. Dr. Karl Heider in the field with the Dani of western New Guinea. (Film Study Center, Harvard University)

existed without them? Are there common denominators in human values and systems of social control which make the ideal of a world law possible? Or is there some basic aggressive instinct, "territorial imperative," or other deep-seated factor which makes the achievement of such a goal totally unfeasible? Is violence ubiquitous? Is war inevitable? As man starts out to colonize new worlds in space, are there any rules or values from the Ice Age past and the chaotic present —the two million years of human experience —he should carry with him? If so, which ones?

Anthropologists have now developed quite definite knowledge of what the earliest human beings looked like; even a good deal about their thought processes, their creations, their "religion," if you will. Is it to be expected that the future will see equally radical changes in man's physique, physiognomy, brain power? Or is man now biologically "complete," "finished"? Has he "gone about as far as he can go," evolutionarily speaking?

Incidentally, what is man? A "naked ape," as a noted zoologist calls him?[1] What sets him apart from the rest of the animal world? His use of tools? His development of language? His penchant for religion? Or the curiosity about himself which we noted in the first sentence of this book?

The Uses of Anthropology

If it is presumptuous (and it is!) to claim that only anthropologists seek the answers to such questions or that anthropology provides definitive answers to all of them, it is not too much to state that all of these are basic concerns of anthropology, and further, that it is impossible to reach any satisfactory answers without some understanding of anthropological findings.

The helpfulness and relevance of anthropology to the broad quest for deeper knowledge about man's nature and behavior may be seen in the rapid growth of anthropology as an academic discipline. Until World War II, only a handful of universities and colleges had anthropology departments, and a small number of others offered merely a course or two. In 1970 there were more than 200 recognized departments giving anthropology degrees, and courses dealing with anthropology are increasingly being offered in junior colleges, adult education programs, high schools, and even grade schools.

Further, both the methods and the concepts of anthropology have had a noticeable impact on natural and physical sciences, social sciences, businesses, and government. Such terms as "primitive culture," "cultural relativity," "comparative method," and "culture shock" are no longer the special property of anthropologists. It is perhaps not widely known that Ruth Benedict's wartime study of Japanese culture and character unquestionably influenced, with beneficial results, the successful policy of United States relations to Japan at the end of World War II.[2] Better known is the more recent Peace Corps emphasis on steeping its volunteers in the basic cultures of the peoples they seek to aid. With the emergence of independent, developing countries from the erstwhile empire holdings in Asia and Africa, the practitioners of law, political science, and economics have become actively interested in the indigenous cultures of these parts of the world. Technical-assistance programs and schemes for economic development, agricultural projects, military missions, even missionary activities—all, it is now recognized, can be successful only insofar as they relate meaningfully to the fundamental cultures of the peoples involved. Planners, administrators, and business men, either within the separate new nations or acting as consultants or entrepreneurs from other countries, give increasing attention to this basic premise.

[1]D. Morris, *The Naked Ape.*

[2]R. F. Benedict, *The Chrysanthemum and the Sword.*

The expansion of public health programs to all parts of the world has had a like effect in stimulating close cooperation between anthropology and the practice of medicine. Cultural anthropology is now widely accepted as indispensable to the training of public health professionals and has recently been recognized by the United States National Institutes of Health as a basic, medically related science.[3] To change a society's food-raising methods, its eating habits, its sanitation practices, and the size of its ideal family are not projects to be undertaken lightly, even for such lofty goals as increased longevity, better health, and less physical suffering. Such changes are not easily accomplished, either! Anthropology offers clues as to why.

But anthropology has other roles, functions, and pleasures than furnishing guidelines for those who would change the world. Basically, its goal is to explore the nature of man as an evolving, culture-bound creature, living in organized societies—each different from every other and yet similar in many ways. Anthropology tells us what the known limits to the range of human experience to date are and what the common denominator of being human is—what is shared by all mankind. The primary task of this book is to set forth the underlying facts and essential theories of anthropology as they now stand.

The Distinctive Qualities of Anthropology

Man is a part of nature—of the universe with all its phenomena. The study of man called *anthropology* (Gr. *anthropos,* man + *logia,* study), when followed in accordance with the principles and methods of science, is consequently a natural science. One of its branches is concerned with the evolutionary origin, the physical structure, and the physio-logical processes of man. This branch is traditionally known as *physical anthropology,* or sometimes as *human biology.* But anthropology involves a good deal more than just the study of the natural history of man's physical nature, for man is also a culture-producing animal. Therefore, anthropology is the *science of man and culture.* As such it is a major social and behavioral science, and more, for in its concern with the arts and in the anthropologist's efforts to sense and communicate the total life-ways of specific peoples, it is also a *humanistic discipline.*

Anthropologists study man wherever they find him—in arctic snows or desert wastes; in temperate prairies and woodlands; and in verdant jungles. They search out his remains in prehistoric sites, and they carry on living field studies in primitive villages and in the urban settings of modern civilizations. Anthropology is concerned both with fossil men and living peoples. It, in the words of Clyde Kluckhohn, "holds up a great mirror to man and lets him look at himself in his infinite variety."[4] For many years the thrill in anthropology for Western man was the discovery of new and undreamed-of (by him) customs and societies. Anthropologists were busy gathering the worldwide inventory of human social and cultural invention—filling in the image of man that would be reflected in the mirror. That task is now nearly done. There are but a few remaining societies to be discovered and reported on. The record is nearly in, although many problems wait to be solved.

The frontiers of anthropology are shifting from survey reports to in-depth analysis of what lies behind the image, to questions of human evolution, motivation, social structure, and function. Descriptions of the variations of life styles which have been observed in one society after another are basic grist to the anthropological mill, and the student of anthropology will find much of descriptive interest as he progresses in his study. But he will also find that description serves to

[3]B. D. Paul, "Teaching Anthropology in Schools of Public Health," in D. G. Mandelbaum, G. W. Lasker, and E. M. Albert (eds.), *The Teaching of Anthropology,* p. 503.

[4]C. Kluckhohn, *Mirror for Man,* p. 11.

provide the facts for explanation of human social behavior, which has become the major concern of anthropology today.

However, many other sciences and disciplines are also concerned with one aspect or another of man or his works. What, then, is so special about anthropology that it should be named "*the* science of man"?

The Study of Mankind as a Whole   First of all, anthropology sets as its goal the study of mankind as a whole. Political science studies man's government; economics studies his production and distribution of goods; neurophysiology, his nervous system; architecture, his housing and building; musicology, his music; and sociology, his society. But none of these, nor any of the other specialized disciplines one might name, such as geography or history, professes systematically to research all the manifestations of the human being and of human activity in a unified way.

Man is a culture-creating and culture-bound animal. As evolving creatures, hominids (see pages 120–121) reached a level of development of the nervous system which enabled them to invent many new ways of behaving which were not preset in their genetic codes. This began to be manifest some two million or more years ago. Since that time all human behavior has been simultaneously biological *and* cultural. The basic premise flowing from this fact has been well put by the anthropologically oriented geneticist Theodosius Dobzhansky: "Human evolution can be understood only as a product of interaction of these two developments."[5] Herein lies the biological and social unity of man. A fundamental proposition of anthropology is that no part can be fully, or even accurately, understood apart from the whole. And conversely, the whole—man and the total of all his manifestations—cannot be accurately perceived without acute and specialized knowledge of the parts. To understand

any aspect of human sexual behavior, for example, one must examine it in terms of genetics, physiology, climatic features, the value system, and the technical, economic, kinship, religious, and political structures of each human society. Anthropology touches upon, draws from, and feeds into virtually any field of knowledge one might care to name. The skills of the anthropologist must be highly diversified, but the unity of the discipline is maintained by concentration on the holistic character of man and culture.

The Concept of Culture   A second distinguishing feature of anthropology is its development of the concept of culture and the importance of this concept in anthropological thought. *Culture is the integrated system of learned behavior patterns which are characteristic of the members of a society and which are not the result of biological inheritance.* Culture is not genetically predetermined; it is noninstinctive. It is wholly the result of social invention and is transmitted and maintained solely through communication and learning.

These are the essential components of the concept of culture as the term is currently used by most anthropologists. Other phrasings are, of course, possible. Thus, Kroeber and Kluckhohn, after review and evaluation of some five hundred phrasings and uses of the concept, gave the following definition:

Culture consists of patterns, explicit and implicit, of and for behavior acquired and transmitted by symbols, constituting the distinctive achievements of human groups, including their embodiments in artifacts; the essential core of culture consists of traditional (i.e., historically derived and selected) ideas and especially their attached values; culture systems may, on the one hand, be considered as products of action, and on the other as conditioning elements of further action.[6]

Every separate society has its distinctive culture. The consequent effect is that the

[5]T. Dobzhansky, "Evolution: Organic and Superorganic" (*The Rockefeller Institute Review*, vol. 1, no. 2, 1963), p. 1.

[6]A. L. Kroeber and C. Kluckhohn, *Culture: A Critical Review of Concepts and Definitions"* (Papers of the Peabody Museum of American Archaeology and Ethnology, Harvard University, vol. 47, 1952), p. 181.

characteristic behaviors of the members of one society are in some respects significantly different from the characteristic behaviors of the members of all other societies. Anthropology has demonstrated that the distinctive behavior of different human populations race differences, for example, is overwhelmingly the product of cultural experience rather than the consequence of genetic inheritance. The importance of the cultural concept in anthropology is so great that most of the rest of this book is devoted to a consideration of its nature and its manifestations in human behavior.

The Use of the Comparative Method A third hallmark of anthropology is its deep-rooted and long-standing commitment to the use of the *comparative* method.[7] The anthropologist is not like the careless thinker who pronounced that all Indians walk single file, and when challenged for evidence, declared, "Well, the one I saw did!" The anthropologist refuses to accept any generalization about human nature that emerges from his experience with his own society alone, or even with two or three other societies, especially if these are a part of the same cultural tradition in which he has been brought up. If one is going to talk about man and human nature, one needs to know what the whole range of human biology, human behavior, and human social forms actually is. To acquire this knowledge, the physical anthropologist studies and compares the widest possible range of human populations, ancient and modern, to determine the common and the unique biological qualities of man. The cultural anthropologist studies and compares the widest possible range of human societies, primitive and civil-

ized, in all parts of the world, to determine the common and the unique social and cultural features of man's behavior. The general anthropologist tries to relate the physical and cultural manifestations in all their variety.

The importance of comparative cross-cultural testing for another behavioral science has recently been stated by an eminent psychologist:

. . . [A]nthropological evidence has been, and can continue to be, of invaluable service as a crucible in which to put to more rigorous test psychology's tentative theories, enabling one to edit them and select among alternatives in ways which laboratory experiments and correlational studies within our own culture might never make possible.[8]

Fieldwork as an Equivalent to the Experimental Laboratory A fourth distinctive feature of anthropology is its long-standing emphasis upon fieldwork for obtaining its data and testing its hypotheses. When a scientist, such as a chemist, is confronted with a problem, he works out an experiment designed to test the validity of the hypothesis about which he is concerned. The method of laboratory experimentation is to manipulate and thereby control the quantity and action of certain known factors in order to determine how they influence one another or an unknown x factor. This fundamental tool of the physical sciences is ordinarily not available to the social sciences, which must to a great extent limit themselves to observation of existing situations rather than of those which may be experimentally designed to suit their needs. Anthropologists, however, have found a highly useful substitute in the combination of field studies with the comparative method. Faced with a problem to be solved, the modern anthropologist seeks a society or a series of societies that already contain the combination of factors necessary for a testing of the theory or hypothesis in question. He may

---

[7]One of the very earliest anthropological studies, written by the French missionary Joseph François Lafitau, compared Iroquois and Huron Indian cultures with those of Greece and Rome. It was based upon Lafitau's fieldwork as a Jesuit missionary in western New York between 1712 and 1717 and was called *Moeurs des sauvages Ameriquains, comparées aux moeurs des premiers temps* (Customs of American Savages, compared with Customs of Early Times). See Chap. 3.

[8]D. T. Campbell, "The Mutual Methodological Relevance of Anthropology and Psychology," in F. L. K. Hsu (ed.), *Psychological Anthropology*, p. 334.

search for the data in preexisting field reports in anthropological libraries, or he may plan a fieldwork expedition to study an appropriate tribe or society.

Margaret Mead's Study of Adolescence in Samoa Margaret Mead's famous study of adolescence in Samoa is a classic example of this procedure. What adults consider teen-agers' turbulent emotional state and propensity to rebellion has long concerned psychologists and educators. In the United States during the 1920s, the storm and stress of adolescence were generally accepted as natural parts of the process of growing up. This view had the scientific imprint of the authoritative work of the psychologist G. Stanley Hall.[9] Dr. Mead had her doubts, entertaining an alternative hypothesis that the emotional disturbance suffered by adolescents in American and Western European society is a psycho-

[9]G. S. Hall, *Adolescence.*

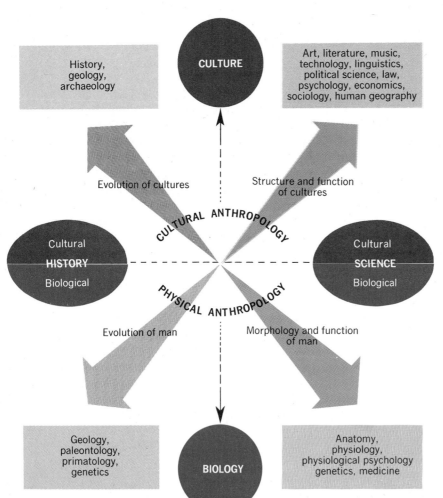

Fig. 1-1   Anthropology: its subdivisions and related sciences in terms of its historical-scientific and biological-cultural orientations.

logical reaction to specific stresses built into American and European cultures. If a society could be found in which these stress conditions were absent (and in which no hidden variables were present that could also produce the emotional upset), that society should reveal an absence of adolescent disturbance and the presence of an easy transition from childhood to adult life. Such a conclusion, then, would point to the cultural determination of adolescent behavior. Familiar with the ethnographies of the South Seas (Polynesia), Dr. Mead believed that the culture and social organization of Samoa, which was also reasonably accessible, probably would provide the requisite "controlled" conditions. She therefore chose Samoa as her first laboratory. Her field observations, as reported in *Coming of Age in Samoa* in 1928, fulfilled the expectancy, or prediction, and demonstrated the invalidity of Hall's theory.

The Subdivisions of Anthropology

Anthropology is so diversified that in order to achieve precision, its practitioners must of necessity specialize. The two major aspects of the subject are the biological and the cultural; the two main subdivisions are therefore (1) physical anthropology and (2) cultural anthropology. Each, in turn, has a number of specialized subdivisions of its own. This structure is illustrated in Figure 1-1.

Physical Anthropology   Man is first of all a biological organism and only secondarily a social animal. The study of the nature of the human organism through physical anthropology is therefore basic to understanding the nature of man. The aim of physical anthropology is to develop an exact body of knowledge concerning the biological characteristics of human populations, ancient and modern. It is, of course, only through the study of living or recently deceased people that physical anthropologists can learn about

the structure, growth, and physiology of the human body in any very detailed way. They have developed ingenious instruments and special techniques for precisely measuring innumerable ratios of size, composition of the body, dental patterns, hair form and color, skin color, blood pressure, blood groups, basal metabolism, and so forth. Because physical anthropologists are interested in the characteristics of populations, they customarily deal with large masses of measurements which are statistically processed. Physical anthropologists are commonly the most practiced statisticians among anthropologists. Their field is also closest to physiology, anatomy, and zoology among the collateral sciences.

The evolution of man is also the special concern of physical anthropology. Evolution raises two questions: "What happened?" and "How did it happen?" The first is answered largely through the comparative study of fossils, including those of the monkeys, apes, and man, known as *paleontology* (Gr. *palaios,* old + *onta,* living things + *logia,* study). The answer to the query "How?" is derived largely from human genetics and the study of biological adaptation to environment—both the province of the physical anthropologist.

A "new" physical anthropology has developed since World War II. Its major quality is a shift of emphasis from measurement and classification of human types toward a much greater concern with the influence of genetics on stability and variation in human populations. Experimental and field studies are carried out on adaptation to climatic extremes. Physical anthropologists have also, since 1960, become increasingly involved in field studies of primate behavior (especially of baboons, chimpanzees, and gorillas) in an effort to obtain insight into protohuman social behavior as an aspect of evolution (see pages 96–99).

Archaeology   Civilization began after the domestication of plants and animals and the rise of cities some nine thousand years ago (see Chapter 10). History began with the invention of writing, after the dawn of civilization. Civilization, which means the culture of cities, is a degree of complexity of culture. Civilized cultures are more complex than are primitive cultures, but they are not necessarily "better" or more "moral." By "primitive," anthropologists mean those peoples, cultures, or societies which have not acquired writing: hence, they are preliterate in an evolutionary sense, or nonliterate. All cultures that existed before the invention of writing were preliterate and prehistoric. As will be seen later, the spread of literacy and its accompanying urban mode of life has been steady and inexorable, but nonetheless slow. Only five hundred years ago, the vast majority of all human cultures were without writing, and therefore primitive. Until the moment of discovery by travelers and explorers from Oriental and Western civilizations, they remained nonliterate and prehistoric.

Cultural anthropologists, traders, missionaries, and government administrators who have written about still nonliterate peoples brought the latter within the ken of history, although it may have taken them somewhat more time before they learned and adapted a written language to their own uses.

What has all this to do with archaeology? Archaeology (Gr. *archaios,* ancient + *logia,* study) is concerned with filling out the human record by stripping the mantle of the earth from the buried remains of ancient cultures and the skeletal remnants of man and his associated plant and animal life (see Figure 1-2). It tells us all we know of prehistoric man and cultures. The importance of prehistoric archaeology to anthropology is manifest in the fact that most of the data covered in Part 2 of this introduction to anthropology are derived from the work of prehistoric archaeologists.

Classical Archaeology Archaeologists who concentrate on the excavation and recon-

struction of classical civilizations, such as those of Sumer, Egypt, Greece, India, and China, are more commonly thought of as classicists than as anthropologists. This is an expression of the fact that classical studies were central to European universities long before anthropology and its interests were established. Classical archaeology, dealing as it does with literate civilizations, serves to fill out the early historical record and it is less closely tied to prehistory than anthropological archaeology is. Nonetheless, the goals and functions of both prehistoric and classical archaeology are the same—to provide hard and tangible evidence of man and his past.

Although the field archaeologist has his own meticulous and refined techniques of excavation,[10] in his larger intellectual tasks of giving meaning to what he has found, he is no different from other anthropologists who are concerned with cultural history and developmental processes. The job is one of relating the facts to general principles that adequately explain what was taking place. A student of prehistory must understand cultures and cultural processes to breathe life and meaning into the dead bones and silent stones of the long-lost past.

Not only must a modern prehistoric archaeologist have full command of general anthropology, but he must also be well versed in geology and paleontology, in addition to possessing the special skills of archaeological techniques. Archaeology is an exacting specialization to meet the canons of modern science, but the archaeologist is first of all an anthropologist. It is significant that although a number of American universities give training in archaeology, none gives a degree in this discipline.

Cultural Anthropology That branch of anthropology which deals with learned behavior characteristics in human societies is known

[10]See B. M. Fagan, *Introductory Readings in Archaeology;* and F. Hole and R. F. Heizer, *An Introduction to Prehistoric Archaeology.*

as *cultural anthropology*. It, in turn, has many subdivisions, of which *ethnography, ethnology, social anthropology,* and *linguistics* are the most prominent.

Ethnography   The foundation of cultural anthropology is ethnography (Gr. *ethnos*, race, peoples + *graphein*, to write). Literally, the word "ethnography" means to write about peoples. As we use the term, it refers to the descriptive study of human societies. Early ethnographies were almost wholly derived from the reports of explorers, missionaries, traders, and soldiers. It was only toward the end of the nineteenth century that trained observers such as Franz Boas entered the field to study human societies directly. Now, most ethnographic work is done by trained anthropologists who have carefully learned participant-observer techniques calling for objective and penetrating observation and interviewing, empathic rapport with a people, and accurate reporting. Modern cultural anthropologists are expected to earn their spurs in ethnographic fieldwork before they are fully qualified as anthropologists.

All ethnographic monographs have some theoretical framework implicit in their organi-

Fig. 1-2 Archaeology recovers the material evidence of early man and past cultures. Archaeologists of the Middle Missouri Salvage Program race a reservoir's rising waters in the excavation of a prehistoric village site. (U.S. Department of the Interior, National Park Service.)

zation, but they do not deal explicitly with theoretical problems. They are, we may repeat, descriptive reports of data and are little concerned with comparison per se, hypothesis, or theory. Ethnography provides the building blocks for cultural anthropology, but it is necessary to look elsewhere for the grand design.

Ethnology Ethnology is the "science of peoples, their cultures, and life histories as groups."[11] It differs from ethnography in that as a science it seeks interrelationships between peoples and their environments, between human beings as organisms and their cultures, between different cultures, and between the differing aspects of cultures. As a science, ethnology strives to derive explanations that go beyond description, emphasizing analysis and comparison. Since each culture is clearly a changing continuum through time, ethnology is much concerned with the historical background of cultures. This aspect of ethnology is sometimes called *cultural history*. When its concern is with general principles of cultural development, it expresses itself as *cultural evolutionism*.

Ethnology, in turn, breaks down into a number of subdivisions in accordance with degree of specialization. Thus there are specialists in, and specialized studies on, primitive kinship and family life, economic activities, law and government, religion; material culture and technology; language, the arts of painting, sculpture, music, and dance; folklore and mythology—almost any major aspect of human cultural manifestations that one might think of.

Social Anthropology Ethnologists who concentrate on social relations, such as family and kinship, age groups, political organization, law and economic activities—in short, what is called *social structure*—prefer to be called *social anthropologists*. English anthropologists who accepted the position of A. R. Radcliffe-Brown deny the usefulness of historical studies in anthropology and wish to divorce cultural anthropology from history. They have established a separate subdivision of cultural anthropology under the rubric *social anthropology*, which they also at times call *comparative sociology*.[12] Social anthropology is nonhistorical, in their view, while ethnology is historical.

Linguistics Linguistics is the science of language. Many linguists look upon their discipline as a completely autonomous science in its own right, and there is a growing trend in American universities to establish independent departments of linguistics. However, languages are aspects of cultures, intimately interacting with all the other manifestations of culture, and are therefore best understood in the cultural context. Consequently, among the social sciences, the scientific study of languages is widely held to be a branch of cultural anthropology. In the United States, at least, all the larger departments of anthropology include linguistic analysis as a part of their programs. However, traditional language studies in archaic (Sanskrit, Greek, and Latin, for example) and modern Indo-European languages have been part of university activities in areas outside anthropology for centuries.

Anthropologists, once they had begun to base their studies on objective fieldwork, were forced to learn many primitive languages from scratch, with never a book of grammar to guide them. This proved to be a good thing. A universal system of phonetic writing had to be developed so that records could be kept of what native informants were saying in tongues for which no system of writing existed. This soon led to a realization that some cultures organize speech in accordance with grammatical principles very different from those which govern the old,

---

[11]A. L. Kroeber, *Anthropology* (2d ed.), p. 5.

[12]See Chap. 3 for a more detailed discussion.

familiar Indo-European languages. Some anthropologists, fascinated by their new discoveries, began to concentrate their efforts on recording and analyzing primitive languages, and linguistics as a specialized branch of anthropology developed in a way that revolutionized all language study (see Chapter 31).

Other Subspecialties of Cultural Anthropology
Every major field of human endeavor is cultivated as a special subfield of anthropological study. The adaptation of man to his total environment is the concern of the *ethnoecologist.*

Material culture is the province of the specialist in primitive technology. There are the fields of primitive dance, *ethnomusicology,* and primitive art. Since the time of Sir Edward Burnett Tylor[13] (1832–1917), primitive religion has been central to the interests of anthropologists, while specialists in social organization have focused on family and kinship. Political anthropology (the study of primitive and colonial political systems) has come into its own since 1950. Legal anthropology and primitive economics are burgeoning. Folklorists deal with oral traditions, and symbolic anthropologists try to fathom the social meaning and cultural functions which are indirectly expressed in the imagery of myth, art, and ritual.

There are medical anthropologists who try to interpret nonoccidental systems of medical thought and practice to Western medicine men, and there are a few *ethnobotanists* who specialize in primitive herbalism and vegetable stuffs. Although some anthropologists have studied ethnic populations in urban settings since the beginning of this century, it was out of the ashes of the summer riots and burnings in United States cities in 1967 that there has sprouted a new breed of specialists, called *urban anthropologists.* They strive to bring the unique attributes of an-

[13]See pages 66–67.

thropology to the study of subcultures in contemporary cities. Then there are the *applied anthropologists* who work as advisors to government, industries, and human relations organizations in the effort to put anthropology to work, today. Practically every chapter in Parts 3 through 6 of this book is an expression of the thought and findings of a special subfield of anthropology.

Area Specialization   Finally, all anthropologists specialize by geographic areas. One can be a North American archaeologist or cultural anthropologist, or a South American, African, Oceanian, South or East Asian, or Middle East specialist, as the case may be.

An anthropologist is expected to know about peoples in all parts of the world, but as an area specialist, he concentrates his fieldwork in one or two selected areas and he will undoubtedly know the published literature on that area in greater depth.

The Branches of Anthropology in Relation to Levels of Scientific Research

Figure 1-3 shows a schematic representation of anthropology and its main subdivisions according to four levels of generalization, or degrees of abstraction. On the first level, anthropometry, archaeology, and ethnography observe and record the primary facts of the human populations and prehistoric and recent cultures. On the second level, limited generalizations are formulated and tested by specialists in the designated areas of interest. On the third level, generalizations concerning human evolution, growth and development, and racial characteristics are formulated by the physical anthropologist, while generalizations concerning cultures are worked out and tested by the cultural anthropologist on the basis of the findings of the specializations on the second level. Finally, on the fourth level, the general anthropologist undertakes to synthesize the results of physical and cultural anthropology into a universal scientific interpretation of man and his works. However, it is important to know that these levels are only figurative. Ideas and information are in continuous flow between all parts, for, as A. L. Kroeber aptly put it, "In truly successful fundamental science, theory, method, and data are not stratified into a caste system but are integrated on one functional level."[14]

The overall view of man which is presented

[14]A. L. Kroeber, *Style and Civilizations* (2d ed.), p. 63.

in this text consists largely of the broadest general rules that scientific discovery has been able to formulate for man and culture, supported by reference to more special tests of theories and hypotheses on the third and second levels. These illustrative generalizations are based upon first-level observations, that is, descriptions of the biological traits of specific fossil men and modern populations and of the customs and institutions of living societies which make up the pith and substance of anthropology.

Fig. 1-3   Anthropology and the interrelation of its parts: The subdivisions of anthropology represent successive levels of generalization or abstraction. On the first level, anthropometry, archaeology, and ethnography are the empirical, or fact-finding, specializations. The second-level specializations are concerned with studies in depth of limited aspects of man or his works. On the third level, physical anthropology and cultural anthropology collate the findings concerning the human organism and human culture, respectively. Anthropology combines them all in a single discipline on the fourth level.

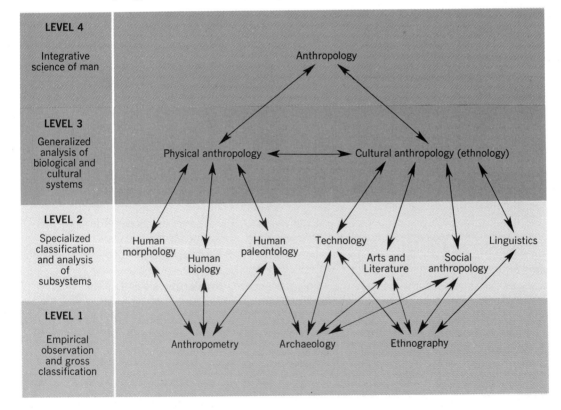

The Relation of Anthropology to the Social Sciences

Anthropology is usually organized as a social science in American universities, although it is clear from all that has been said thus far that anthropology is a good deal more than that. Nonetheless, its dominant identity among the social sciences is due to the fact that the bulk of anthropological work is focused upon culture and, within culture, upon social organization. We have discussed the features of anthropology that distinguish it as a discipline. Each of these bears on the question of the relation of anthropology to the sister sciences, and yet the often-asked question: "How does anthropology tie in to history, sociology, and psychology?" deserves a more specific answer.

History   Early in this century, the English anthropologist R. R. Marrett (1866–1943) declared that anthropology is history, or it is nothing. He did not mean that it is history in the formal sense; he was emphasizing that time is a basic dimension in all human experience. The stream of life is a continuous flow. All anthropologists grant this fact, but they differ over how much value there is to anthropology in history and historical research. Archaeologists are of course staunchly committed to the value of the historical component. Many social anthropologists, on the other hand, are apt to hold that it is sufficient to concentrate on the search for understanding of societies that currently exist, the "now" anthropology of today. Prehistoric and historic data, they aver, can never be obtained in sufficient detail or with sufficient validity to serve adequately the demands of science.

A balanced view of the relation of anthropology to history would hold that a comparison of directly observable societies does indeed put the study of man on a firmer scientific footing in terms of verifiable and vali-

dated results. Yet it would also agree that it is scientifically important to study the processes of the growth and change of cultures. Culture and society are not momentary things. They come out of the past, exist in the present, and continue into the future. What they *are* is the product of what they *have been,* worked upon by presently impinging conditions and influences. What they *will be* is the product of what they *have been* and *are,* worked upon by the conditions and influences that engage them today and will engage them in the future. Neither the present nor the future can be wholly understood without a knowledge, however faulty, of the past.

There are, of course, historians and historians, histories and histories. The historian is a social scientist when he undertakes to derive general laws of social change or to explain specific events by noting repeated regularities observed through time. Or he may be a philosopher of history if he strives to explain what took place at particular times in history in terms of an a priori scheme of interpretation. Or, if the historian's interest is no more than the "scholarly pursuit of special knowledge of particular fact," he is neither social scientist nor philosopher; he is simply an historian *sui generis.* His emphasis is then on the uniqueness of the situation. "History never repeats itself," he says. The time and the place and what happened then and there —stated exactly, accurately, and specifically —are what is important to the historian as a chronicler (see Figure 1-4).

In science, as opposed to history, a fact is not itself of central interest. The object of science is to relate a multitude of facts to one another so as to make valid, general propositions about the nature of things. The anthropologist's ways of organizing his knowledge are different from those of the historian, and his methods of operation are basically different also. The "field" for the historian is the library. His working unit is a document. His joy is the discovery of a long-lost packet of letters or reports. For the anthropologist, the "field" is a remote tribal group, a central-city population, or an archaeological site. His working unit is the person and a people. His joy is the discovery of a new type of social relation, fossil, or set of artifacts. A student of contemporary Africa puts it succinctly: "Africa has two kinds of history: the conventional kind to be studied through European accounts of exploration, settlement, and colonial rule, and an unconventional kind to be studied through anthropological accounts of indigenous economic and social organization."[15]

Sociology   Sociology and anthropology are the closest kin among the social sciences. It is for this reason that they are frequently to be found in the same department in American universities. Their similarity is in their interest in social organization and behavior. In these fields, the basic theoretical approaches have much in common; indeed, in many respects they are indistinguishable. But the specific interests of the sociologist and the anthropologist and their ways of going about their work may be very different. Sociologists do not usually receive the biological, archaeological, and linguistic training that is so important to anthropologists. Anthropologists work as participant-observers in small societies, supplemented by intensive, day-after-day, person-to-person discourse on cultural practices. Their emphasis is on people-in-culture. Sociologists usually work with larger samples of more limited aspects of society; hence their heavy emphasis on statistical data and procedures. The questionnaire and the census reports are likely to be the sociologist's major factual resource. Also, American sociology devotes a great deal of attention to problems of social pathology and social work: delinquency, crime, poverty, mental illness, and broken homes, as they occur in society. This has been a commitment of sociology in the United States from the very beginning.

Anthropology has only lately turned its conscious attention to social problems and administration.

Psychology   Anthropology and psychology are both concerned with behavior and hence have much in common. But whereas anthropology is interested primarily in group organization of behavior and the cultural patterning of behavior, psychology is more concerned with the behavior of the individual organism and how it responds to specific stimuli. Psychologists are much more oriented to the use of laboratory experiments, tests, and measurements and to statistical expression of their findings in an effort to achieve scientific precision in their field. The behavioral situations studied by experimental psychologists tend to be simplified and neat, that is, controlled experiments that are designed to eliminate extraneous variables. Anthropologists undertake to relate the simple but verified findings of psychology to the complexities of the real-life situations which they confront in going societies, where their findings are indeed less rigorously verified. Anthropologists as anthropologists study man. Experimental psychologists, although not all of them share this penchant, are more than likely to forsake man, with all his complexities, to study the more manageable mouse, rat, guinea pig, monkey, or pigeon.

While contemporary social psychologists also incline strongly toward laboratory experimentation, clinical psychologists and psychoanalysts are forced by the nature of their tasks to treat whole persons in the context of their total social settings. The deep probing of psychoanalysis into the hidden psychic processes has engendered a number of insightful concepts that have proved very useful to anthropologists in the interpretation of cultural systems and their relations to tribal personality types. The field of culture and personality (see Chapter 2) was one of the most active and productive areas of anthropology in the decades of 1930 to 1960.

[15]G. Dalton, "Traditional Production in Primitive African Economies" (*The Quarterly Journal of Economics*, August, 1962), p. 378.

Learning theory as developed in psychology is of course of great importance to anthropology; culture is acquired only through learning. Psychology probes the processes of how the human animal learns and how he learns to learn. Anthropology, in turn, teaches us what is learned in various societies, how it is taught, and what the rewards and punishments provided by each society for proper learning or failure to learn are. "Culture," as viewed by Miller and Dollard, ". . . is a statement of the design of the human maze, of the type of reward involved, and of what responses are to be rewarded. In this sense it is a recipe for learning."[16] Because cultures

[16]N. Miller and J. Dollard, *Social Learning and Imitation,* p. 5.

vary so widely, the conditions of human learning and human behavior vary widely. Anthropology offers psychology a wider factual base against which to test its theories and assumptions. This is recognized by the psychologist Donald Campbell in these terms:

Implicitly, the laboratory psychologist still assumes that his college sophomores provide an adequate base for a general psychology of man. . . . For social psychology these tendencies have been very substantively curbed through confrontation with the anthropological literature. Continued confrontation, however, will be required to prevent relapse. For the general psychologist, most of the lesson is yet to be learned.[17]

[17]D. T. Campbell, *op. cit.,* p. 334.

Fig. 1-4   The student beginning to study anthropology as a science first approaches the subject through the mastery of general principles. As he moves on to more specialized courses, he enters an area in which generalizations become narrower and the empirical data loom larger. As a graduate student, he masters the technique of empirical observation and research in the field and laboratory. As a professional anthropologist, he moves on to the formulation of specialized hypothesis and theory. Finally, he may formulate new and encompassing generalizations that are aimed at synthesizing all the empirical findings of the subspecializations of physical and cultural anthropology.

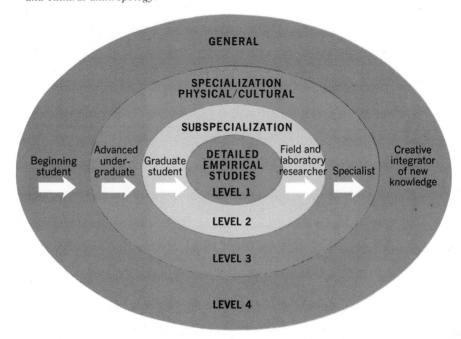

Law, Political Science, Economics, and Public Health Law is an aspect of any society's culture, and it is exceedingly important as a shaper of cultures, since it is explicitly devoted to discouraging certain forms of behavior while supporting others. Because legal anthropology places so much emphasis on the functions of law in total social systems, it has proved particularly fruitful in illuminating by comparison the foundations of our own law system. "Law," according to Bohannan, "is one of the best-studied subdisciplines of anthropology; the literature is small but of high quality."[18]

Only since World War II and the consequent emergence of independent, developing countries from the erstwhile empire holdings in Asia and Africa have economics and political science in the United States become actively interested in the indigenous cultures of these parts of the world. But now the economics and government of these areas have taken on extreme importance.

The expansion of public health programs to all parts of the world has had a like effect in stimulating close cooperation between anthropology and the practice of medicine.

It should be clear by now that anthropology in many of its aspects participates vitally in the dynamic complex of the social sciences. If we can refer to anthropology as the study of dead bones and live issues, we can also say that this live subject gets livelier by the year.

SUMMARY

Depending on the methods and goals of the anthropologist, anthropology may be a biological science, a social science—or a humanity. Because man is a part of nature, anthropology is a natural science with two major subdivisions: physical anthropology (or human biology) and cultural anthropology. Physical anthropology is concerned with the evolutionary development of man and with the present biological characteristics of human populations. Cultural anthropology is concerned with the customs and ways of living characteristic of human societies. When approached with the methods of science, cultural anthropology is a social and behavioral science. When cultures are studied with emphasis upon the feeling expressed in their art, literature, and beliefs, anthropology takes on the quality of the humanities.

Anthropology studies mankind as a whole; first, as a biocultural phenomenon in which culture is viewed as a means of continuing adaptation to the total environment—a means of survival and of definition and achievement of goals which are not genetically inherited; second, with the basic functional proposition that all parts of a culture are interrelated and that no part may be understood except as a component of a whole. Cultures and societies are systems.

Culture is the integrated system of learned behavior patterns which are characteristic of the members of a society and are not the result of biological inheritance. Each society has its own culture.

Anthropology has always been devoted to the use of comparative methods. It searches out all types of societies, in all times and places. It undertakes to formulate generalizations about man and human behavior based on the discovery of regularities found in all cultures (the least common denominator of culture), and it undertakes to discover the variations and the range of variation in human cultural systems.

Anthropologists refuse to make generalizations about man based on experience with one society only, be it European, Indian, Chinese, or American.

Consequently, anthropology uses fieldwork as its equivalent to the experimental laboratory of the physical scientist. When there is a special problem to be solved, the

[18]J. P. Bohannan, *Social Anthropology*, p. 284.

anthropologist seeks out a society which may be expected to have the desired combination of traits or variables. Under conditions of participant observation, it may be possible to determine what does actually take place.

Archaeology provides anthropology with information about men and cultures of the past. Prehistoric archaeology is devoted to the span of human existence before the invention and spread of writing (*ca.* 7,000 B.C.). Classical archaeology is concerned with early civilizations. Civilization is the culture of cities; it represents a high degree of complexity of culture, including agriculture as a food base, plus a written language. Primitive societies subsist by hunting, food gathering, or gardening; they have no writing and no cities. Primitive peoples leave no written records; hence, they are prehistoric, until such time as writing is brought to them: Ergo, the importance of prehistoric archaeology in pushing back the shrouding mists of time through recovery of hard facts for anthropological analysis.

Cultural anthropology has numerous subspecialties. Chief among them are ethnography, ethnology, social anthropology, and linguistics. Ethnography is the descriptive recording of the life-way of a particular people, as a result of field study. Ethnology is the comparative analytical science of cultures in time (historical) and space (ecological). Social anthropology concentrates on the organization of social groups, such as family and kin, political and economic structure. Anthropological linguistics identifies the characteristics of the spoken languages of all mankind. In addition, there are almost as many subspecialties of cultural anthropology as there are manifestations of culture: art, dance, folklore, botany, technology, politics, economics, law, medicine, religion, education, and child training. Anthropology overlaps all the social sciences and many of the biological sciences and thus is intimately related to each of them. Yet it retains its own

unique identity by virtue of the holistic orientation and its special theories and methods. The study of anthropology is essential to a knowledge of man and to a liberal education.

SELECTED READINGS

Beattie, J., *Understanding an African Kingdom: Bunyoro* (1965). A straightforward, short account of the technique and methods used in the field study of a given society.

Casagrande, J. B. (ed.), *In the Company of Man* (1960). Twenty distinguished anthropologists each offer a profile of the one key informant who has been central to his or her own anthropological fieldwork. In so doing, they convey the human aspect of teamwork between the scientist and his "subjects" in a way that is highly empathic.

Gillin, J. P., *For a Science of Social Man: Convergences in Anthropology, Psychology and Sociology* (1954). Seven leading American social scientists examine the interrelations of their various fields.

Golde, P. (ed.), *Women in the Field* (1970). Twelve North American women-anthropologists write about their personal field experience in all parts of the world.

Hammel, E. A., and W. A. Simmons (eds.), *Man Makes Sense* (1970). A reader in cultural anthropology in which part I, "The Personality of Anthropology," with articles by Arensberg, Maybury-Lewis, Lévi-Strauss, Kroeber, and Geertz, provides an extended introduction to the nature of anthropology.

Henry, J., *Culture against Man* (1964). A hypercritical look at American culture and society which should be read for an appreciation of the way in which the author combines the technique of the participant-observer with the use of anthropological theory to shed a flood of new light on aspects of American family life, schooling, mental illness, and treatment of the aged.

Mandelbaum, D. G., G. W. Lasker, and E. M. Albert (eds.), *The Teaching of Anthropology* (1963). Written by a number of anthropologists, primarily for teachers of anthropology, it covers all the subdivisions of anthropology and all the relations of anthropology to other subjects. Inquisitive students should find it interesting to see how their teachers go about deciding what to teach them.

Mead, M., *Anthropology: A Human Science* (1964). Selected papers on aspects of anthropology as a means of studying man, culture, and societies, written between 1939 and 1960. The scope of the papers is broad and the author's insights and understanding are penetrating and helpful.

Powdermaker, H., *Stranger and Friend* (1966). The personal growth and fieldwork maturation of a fine and sensitive anthropologist, who describes her early fieldwork in Lesu (Melanesia), a Mississippi town, Hollywood, and Zambia (Africa).

Shils, D. L. (ed.), "Anthropology" (*International Encyclopedia of the Social Sciences,* vol. 1, 1968), pp. 304–344. Six articles by anthropologists summarize the content and recent trends in cultural anthropology.

Chapter 2

Man, Culture, and Society

Once there was neither man nor culture. Today man threatens to crowd all other animals from the face of the earth, save only those which serve his purposes. Man has invented culture, and by means of culture he has domesticated himself and numerous plants, animals, and natural forces. He promises to "domesticate" the entire world before long. By means of his cultural achievements, he has begun to probe outer space, has left his footprints on the moon, and has junked the first auto driven on lunar soil. In the near future he may be capable of interplanetary travel.

The Culture-creating Capacity

How did man, the animal, become man, the human being, *Homo sapiens?* The process has been a prolonged and unceasing response to environmental situations in which the biological processes of natural selection, working upon genetic variations in living organisms, have produced biological, or organic, evolution. A million or more years ago, man had become sufficiently differentiated from the other animals so that we can now look back on him as representing a new form of life. A feature of this differentiation was the elaboration of his nervous system, the brain in particular, to the point where he could not only see, smell, and act but also symbolically represent a wide range of experience. He

acquired the capacity to think and to speak. He could experience things and situations vicariously, not in the instant act but "dramtized" within the nervous system. He learned how to communicate experience to himself and to others through those symbolic representations we call "concepts," or "thoughts," expressed in gesture, word, dance, and art.

Fig. 2-A   An Amahuaca child of the Peruvian rain forest is "covered" with banana gruel so that it may grow and ripen into a mature human being. (Robert Russell.)

The "animal" became contemplative. And thinking, he began a process of self-organization. He began to "see" the universe about him not only in terms of the immediately confronted stimulus but also in terms of what he "remembered," not just through conditioned habit but also through word representations of past experience. He acquired the capacity to project past experience into the future by thinking of what might be. He learned to create experience which had not yet happened and which might never take place at all. He began to shape a world of experience according to images of his own creation. He became imaginative.[1]

Along with the development of his thinking brain, this creature, man, also was broadening the range of his physiological processes and physical activity. But the great innovation lay in the degree to which he could organize a relatively small number of movements into large and various combinations. He acquired the capacity to invent new behavior.

As a result of biological evolution, man acquired the capacity to produce culture on the grand scale and in turn to become the product of his cultures. Culture, like life, began very simply and humbly. Like life, it has gradually grown and assumed a greater and greater variety of forms in an unbroken continuity from preexistent forms.

The Noninstinctive Nature of Culture   In the first chapter, culture was defined as the integrated system of learned behavior patterns that are characteristic of the members of a society and that are not the result of biological inheritance. It is the essence of the concept of culture that instincts, innate reflexes, and any other biologically predetermined forms of behavior are ruled out. Culture is therefore acquired behavior. But it is as much

a part of the natural universe as the stars in the heavens, for it is a natural product of man's activities, and man is part of nature.

Learned Behavior   That cultural behavior is learned behavior may be demonstrated by answering the question: "What would happen if a group of babies were cut off from all adult care, training, and supervision?" The answer is, of course: "They would die." Therefore, we must modify our question and put it in this form: "What would happen if a group of babies could be fed and protected without adult supervision or training and without any form of contact with adults? Would they manifest any of the special traits of behavior that were characteristic of their parents?"

Our answer cannot be based upon direct empirical observation; legend, mythology, and the testimony of honorable men notwithstanding, wolves, jailers, or scientific experimenters have not set up such a situation under conditions of control or observation that meet the elementary canons of scientific acceptability. But enough is known of infant physiology, learning, and psychology to justify an answer in unequivocal terms. Assuming the survival of the infants, they would eat, drink, defecate, urinate, and gurgle and cry. These would be direct responses to basic biological drives. But what they would eat, when they would eat, and how they would eat would not be according to the tastes and palates of any group of men we now know. It is quite unlikely that they would cook their food. Presumably they would sooner or later get up on their hind legs, and even before adolescence they would experiment in mating without benefit of incest tabus or any preferred approaches of courtship. They would communicate emotional states through gesture and sounds. But they would be devoid of language, utensils, fire, arts, religion, government, and all the other features of life that distinguish man from other animals. They would develop few of the traits which we characterize as "human."

---

[1]William Golding treats this process in a simple and empathic way in his novel *The Inheritors,* a fictionalized account of the last of the Neandertals.

In spite of their shortcomings, however, these hapless children would enjoy a kind of social life. They would constitute not only an animal aggregation but also an animal society. It is quite probable, however, because they are human beings, that they would very quickly begin the accumulation of incipient culture.

Instinctive Behavior　Many animals in addition to man have a social life and even social organization. Ant society has long been recognized for its well-delineated division of labor among drones, workers, fighters, males, females, and queen. The organization of the colony, with its living quarters and storage rooms for eggs, presents the picture of a well-ordered society. The ants interact with one another in an integrated, sustained set of relationships. These relationships are preset in the genetic organization of the ants. So far as is known, little if any of their behavior is learned from adult ants. If eggs are hatched without any adult ants being present, a host of new ants is produced, which, when they attain maturity, apparently reenact every single aspect of all the forms of social life that have characterized their species for untold generations.

The Dance of the Bees　The behavior of certain other insects is also highly social and involves the communication of information within the society. Honeybees have been studied with great care and with fascinating results in a series of experimental observations by Karl von Frisch, of Munich. Female "scout" bees search out the location of sweet, pollen-bearing plants. When she has found a good source, the scout determines the location, takes a fix on the sun, and returns immediately to the hive. She then executes a dance in which she moves along a straight line pointing toward the source. She circles back to the starting point, alternately to the left and right. The speed at which she makes her straight runs indicates approximately how far away the source of supply is. The smell of the pollen indicates the sweetness, or potential honey content. The workers fall in behind her in the dance, and when they have received the message, they take off unerringly to the right spot. Different species do different dances, but the basic pattern is the same.

This fascinating dance of the bees emphasizes the importance of communication in group living, but it does not represent cultural behavior. As von Frisch himself has written:

The brain of the bee is the size of a grass seed and is not made for thinking. The actions of a bee are mainly governed by instinct. Therefore, the student of even so complicated and purposeful activity as the communication dance must remember that he is dealing with innate patterns, impressed on the nervous system of the insects over the immense reaches of time of their phylogenetic development.[2]

Protoculture among Apes and Monkeys　On the other hand, we would be taking undue credit unto ourselves if we denied *all* culture-creating capacity to *all* subhuman creatures.

Monkeys and apes have been shown to be quite capable of solving a number of problems posed for them by experimenters. Chimpanzees show considerable intelligence and inventiveness. What is more, they are quite definitely capable of learning from one another through direct imitation. Apes ape each other.

Thus, when one of a group of experimental apes accidentally jabbed the end of a pole into the ground and found to his immense delight that he could hoist himself skyward, all the other members of the colony were soon searching for sticks; pole vaulting was the rage. Another discovered that by scattering bread outside the bars of his cage, he could lure unwary yard chickens in close, while he lurked with a stick with which to jab them in his hand. Annoying the chickens then became the current sport of the group. The alarmed squawks of the hens provided rich

[2]K. von Frisch, "Dialects in the Language of the Bees" (*Scientific American,* August, 1962; SA Reprint Series no. 130), p. 3.

simian diversion. These and other tricks were discovered by the apes without help from psychologists. When they had spread among the group, they had for the time being all the qualities of customs. But, alas, when interest wore off and enthusiasm waned, as it always did after a few days or weeks, each practice was forgotten, never to be performed again. Their destiny was that of fads; they did not endure to become customs.

However, the semiwild Japanese monkeys which are being carefully studied in their seminatural habitats by Japanese scientists clearly show that elemental discoveries are communicated within the group and do become established as cultural features. Direct observation of colonies of Japanese monkeys (*Macaca fuscata*) reveals, for example, that each troop has its own characteristic food prejudices. This, surely, is the most elemental of cultural universals.

According to Syuno Kawamura: "The monkeys of the Minno Ravine know how to remove the earth of the slope by scratching with their hands to get the roots of Boehmeria nivea, and also probably of Lilium spp. and Dioscorea spp., while those of Takasakiyama entirely lack such knowledge."[3]

Food habits are established among unweaned infant monkeys who, sitting by their mother, pick up the food she drops from her mouth. Without their mother's example, experimental infants of the same species find it hard to learn to take any food but milk.[4]

New foods have been experimentally introduced to troops of wild monkeys by the Japanese scientists with very illuminating results. When candy is introduced, the two- or three-year-olds are the first to take it up as a food. Later the mothers learn from their children to eat it. And once a mother has acquired a taste for candy, that taste is "handed down to her baby without exception." The adult males who supervise the young monkeys also soon learn to eat candy, but the young males who have little to do with juveniles take it up last of all. New culture traits spread differentially within the troop.

In another troop, the new habit of eating wheat was introduced by an adult male. His example was followed by the "chief" of the troop and from him was passed on to the "chief female," who in turn transmitted it to her offspring. Within four hours, wheat had been tried and accepted by the entire troop. Only half of another troop ever accepted the candy eating that had been introduced by a child, however.[5]

Incipient culture building is clearly within the province of primates other than man. Yet they evidently lack the capacity to express experience symbolically. David Kaplan has put it well in stating, "Some scholars would question whether the ability to symbolize is unique to man, but all would agree, I think, with [Morton] Fried . . . that 'only man, on this planet, engages in massive, systematic and continuous symboling.'"[6]

Symbolism and Culture

Many of the elemental behavior patterns that make up a culture may be learned directly, without reliance on symbolic content. This may be seen in the behavior of the deaf child who learns to master simple manual skills without the use of language and without the usual means of assimilating many of the more complex ideas which other children get at an early age. It is equally obvious just how much of his society's culture is shut off from such a child. Without skillful remedial education, available only in the most advanced cultures and societies, the congenitally deaf child can rarely share the thoughts, beliefs, or attitudes or acquire the reasoning skills of his people

[3]S. Kawamura, "The Process of Sub-culture Propagation among Japanese Macaques," in C. H. Southwick (ed.), *Primate Social Behavior,* pp. 83–84.
[4]*Ibid.*

[5]*Ibid.,* pp. 85–88.
[6]D. Kaplan, "The Superorganic: Science or Metaphysics?" (*American Anthropologist,* vol. 67, 1965), p. 961.

except on the crudest level. He will know only a little of his people's gods, music, folktales and legends, star lore, or magic. He will be barred from more than elementary comprehension of his people's kinship system, law, politics, and rules of inheritance and trade. He may learn to paint through imitation, but he will know little of the meanings of the designs he copies or the significance of the colors he uses. All these manifestations of culture, and more, will be beyond him, for his infirmity denies him the one truly distinctive attribute of man—language, the "purely human and non-instinctive method of communicating ideas, emotions, and desires by means of a system of voluntarily produced symbols."[7]

The clue to understanding the nature of language, that cultural product without which culture is limited, is to realize that language is the major device for *symbolizing*. A sound may be no more than a noise, a disturbance of the air that stimulates no discernible response in man or beast. A sound may also be a *signal* that evokes a response, such as the whistle that calls a dog to his master's side. On a higher level a sound may be a *symbol,* which is a signal or sign that stands for something. It has *meaning*. Languages are arbitrary systems of vocal symbolism, to which civilized cultures have also added visual symbols: writing. Symbols may also be tactile, such as the piece of sandpaper that is conventionally put on a bottle which contains poison so that it may be felt in the dark.

It is not necessarily a matter of conscious recognition among all peoples, but some, such as the Caduveo of Brazil, understand quite clearly the symbolic functions of their visible, artistic facial paintings. As reported by Claude Lévi-Strauss, "The Indians have replied for us. The face-paintings confer upon the individual his dignity as a human being: they help him to cross the frontier from Na-

ture to culture, and from the 'mindless' animal to the civilized Man."[8] Mythology and religion, with its ritual drama, exist as elaborated symbol systems, impressing and sustaining the cultural system of a people (see Chapter 29).

So it is that almost all aspects of culture come to be symbolically transmitted to the members of a society. So it is that the very way in which the members of a society see and understand the world in which they live is shaped by the symbol system that makes up their culture.

The Integration of Culture

The members of a society never exhibit *all* the behaviors of which we now know human beings are capable. This is one of the great lessons that modern anthropology has taught us. Many people around the world think that what they were brought up to do is *ipso facto* an expression of human nature. Little do they realize that other human beings have found quite different ways of doing the same thing. Or perhaps they do not do it at all. In the succeeding chapters of this book, the main varieties of known culture patterns are examined. The range of variability is surprisingly wide.

The Imperative of Selection   As each society builds its culture through the ages, it ignores or rejects many of the potential behavior patterns of which men are capable. Of course, this is partly due to the fact that the majority of these potential patterns remained undiscovered by most of the isolated societies of the past and hence were not available for inclusion in their cultures. Yet even if they had been available, many of them would necessarily have been excluded. Social behavior must be predictable within a range of limited leeways. Expectancies must be realized, if men are to gauge their actions in terms of

[7]E. Sapir, *Language,* p. 7.

[8]C. Lévi-Strauss, *Tristes Tropiques,* p. 176.

experience. Men in society are men interacting. If everyone were to go off behaving in any one of the multitudes of ways in which human beings are capable, the result would be bedlam and disaster. Society is possible only in terms of a limiting order.

Limitation of ways of behaving is not only a social necessity but also an individual necessity. Experimental animal psychology, as well as psychiatry, has demonstrated that habit formation and habitual rewarding of psychological responses are necessary for individual mental health.[9] Behavior must be integrated to a high degree for effective functioning of personality.

Further, many behavior patterns are mutually contradictory and inherently incompatible. A people cannot enjoy free sexual license and at the same time practice celibacy; no one has yet discovered how to eat his cake and have it too. This principle applies to thousands of other aspects of culture and is the basis of the *imperative of selection,* as summed up by Ruth Benedict:

The culture pattern of any civilization makes use of a certain segment of the great arc of potential human purposes and motivations. . . . The great arc along which all the possible human behaviours are distributed is far too immense and too full of contradictions for any one culture to utilize even any considerable portion of it. Selection is the first requirement.[10]

Fundamental Cultural Postulates The selection of the customs that go to make up a culture is never wholly random and haphazard. Selection is made with reference to a set of deep-lying assumptions, or postulates, about the nature of the external world and the nature of man himself. These assumptions as to the nature of existence are called *existential postulates.* There are also deep-lying assumptions about whether things or acts are good and to be sought after, or bad and to be rejected. These are called *normative postulates* or *values.*

For a brief example of what is meant here, consider the following Trobriand Island existential postulate, first noting that the Trobrianders, who live in the South Pacific, are socially organized in matrilineal clans. At the foundation of Trobriand life is the following self-evident (to the Trobriander) proposition:

Pregnancy results from the entry by a spirit (*baloma*) of a dead matrilineal clan ancestor into the body of a woman.

From this flow two corollaries: (1) the father is not genetically related to the child; and (2) a person belongs only to the clan of his or her mother. Any Trobriander knows this "as a matter of course." This is elemental Trobriand truth. Many Trobriand specifics of social life and feeling are understandable only in these terms.

Both existential and normative postulates are the reference points which color a people's view of things, giving them their orientation toward the world around them and toward one another.[11]

The basic assumptions of a culture are generally consistent among themselves, although there are usually some exceptions. If a society is to survive, the gears of its culture must mesh, even though they may growl and grind.

In selecting its customs for day-to-day living, even in little things, the society chooses those ways which accord with its thinking and predilections—ways that fit its basic postulates concerning the nature of things and what is desirable and what is not. If these ways are consistent with the basic postulates, and if these in turn are consistent with one another, integration is achieved. The culture is then a harmonious working whole.

To recapitulate:

1. Every culture represents a limited selection of behavior patterns from the total of human potentialities, individual and collective.

2. The selection tends to be made in ac-

---

[9]S. J. H. Masserman, *Principles of Dynamic Psychiatry,* pp. 126–129.

[10]R. F. Benedict, *Patterns of Culture,* p. 237.

[11]For fuller exposition of several systems of fundamental cultural postulates, see Chapter 28, on culture and world view.

cordance with certain postulates (dominant assumptions and values) basic to culture.

3. It follows that every culture exemplifies a more or less complete and coherent pattern, structure, or system of actions and relationships.

"The quality of a society," observes Otis Lee, "will vary with the quality of its basic values . . . with their suitability to its needs and circumstances, and with the consistency and thoroughness with which they are worked out."[12]

Some of the basic postulates of a culture may be explicitly stated by the people who hold them. Others are not explicitly stated, either because they are so taken for granted or because the people are so unused to reflecting about their beliefs that they are not themselves able to state them. In anthropology, when the social scientist is thoroughly familiar with the observed behavior of a society in all its aspects, he may generalize as to the principles that underlie the behavior; thus he identifies the postulates for them,[13] like the linguist who analyzes a primitive language and formulates the rules and principles of grammar. The people who speak the tongue know only that one form is right and another is not, without being able to express the principles in so many words. There are striking parallels between general cultural and linguistic processes which are discussed in Chapter 31.

Configurations of Culture   Although a culture is built up of elements and traits, the significance lies less in its inventory of traits than in the manner of their integration. For this reason we have phrased the definition of culture in terms of the "integrated system of learned behavior."

Benedict, who introduced the configurational idea into modern anthropological thought, has written of culture: "The whole, as modern science is insisting in many fields, is not merely the sum of all its parts, but the result of a unique arrangement and interrelation of the parts that has brought about a new entity."[14]

This is a sound principle for the understanding of the nature of cultures and the uniqueness of divergent societies, for it is theoretically possible for two societies to possess identical inventories of culture elements and yet so arrange the relationships of the elements to one another as to produce two quite unlike societies. By simple analogy, two masons may take two identical piles of bricks and equal quantities of mortar. Yet, with these materials, one may build a fireplace while the other builds a garden wall, depending on the way they integrate the bricks. The configuration of a culture is its distinctive and characteristic form that derives from the special relationship of its parts to one another. It presumes internal integration in accordance with some basic and dominant principles or value systems underlying the whole scheme. Thus, Pueblo culture is characterized by collectivistic, ritual emphasis under priestly direction, while Plains Indian cultures emphasize individual self-realization through aggressive fighting against outsiders and hallucinatory vision experiences. (See pages 547–551.)

Cultural Relativity   All cultures differ in their basic postulates at some points. Each has general features in common with all others, but in specifics every culture is different from every other in some respects. Some are very different. "Mankind is one. Civilizations are many," the great anthropologist Franz Boas used to say. The anthropological realization of this fact has led to the establishment of the

---

[12]O. Lee, "Social Values and the Philosophy of Law" (*Virginia Law Review*, vol. 32, 1946), pp. 811–812; reprinted in O. Lee, *Freedom and Culture*, pp. 89ff.

[13]A detailed description of how basic cultural postulates are expressed in Cheyenne culture may be found in E. A. Hoebel, *The Cheyennes: Indians of the Great Plains*. Other examples may be found in J. A. Hostetler, *Amish Society*, and, for traditional (pre-Communist) China, in F. L. K. Hsu, *The Study of Literate Civilizations*, pp. 61–71.

[14]Benedict, *op. cit.*, p. 47.

concept of cultural relativity, which is closely related to the intensive anthropological use of the comparative method.

The concept of cultural relativity states that standards of rightness and wrongness (values) and of usage and effectiveness (customs) are relative to the given culture of which they are a part. In its most extreme form, it holds that every custom is valid in terms of its own cultural setting. In practical terms, it means that anthropologists learn to suspend judgment, to strive to understand what goes on from the point of view of the people being studied, that is, to achieve empathy, for the sake of humanistic perception and scientific accuracy. The anthropologist undertakes to assume the role of detached observer rather than that of apologist, condemner, or converter. He learns to laugh with people, not at them. He must have a real respect for human beings, whoever they may be. The student who lacks this trait—who cannot put aside all chauvinist ethnocentrism, that is, the habit of uncritically judging other peoples' behavior according to the standards set in his own culture—can never become a first-rate cultural anthropologist.

The Functional Nature of Culture

The fact that each culture is made up of a multitude of selected traits integrated into a total system means that all parts have a special relationship to the whole. Each part may have its specific *form* as, for example, a bow, a canoe, a pot, a marital arrangement, or a legal process. No one of these elements of culture exists in a vacuum, however, or stands as an isolated unit. It plays its part in contributing to a total life-way. The way it and all the other parts relate to one another and influence or affect one another forms the *structure* of the culture. The contribution that each part makes to the total cultural system is its *function,* in contrast to its form.

Thus the bow, whose form may be ex-

(a)

Fig. 2-1   Culture patterns situations, but patterns vary by cultures. Greetings symbolize social relations: (a) *a Japanese student keeps physical distance and bows deeply to his professor;* (b) *two Arabs rub noses;* (c) *the Latin American* abrazzo *emphasizes emotional expressiveness.* [(a) *Marc Riboud, Magnum;* (b) *Courtesy of the American Museum of Natural History;* (c) *Reni Burri, Magnum*]

pressed in measurements and pictures, may function in meeting the needs of food getting and defense, in ritual symbolism in the religious and governmental systems, in fire making, and in musical activities. To understand all the functions of the bow in any culture, it is absolutely necessary for the anthropologist to follow through all its relationships to every other related aspect of the culture. He must do this for each unit of culture, to see finally how all units work to maintain the total life-way of the people he is studying.

A strange custom may seem meaningless

(b)

(c)

and incomprehensible, or tantalizingly exotic, at first acquaintance. Within its cultural setting, and in relation to the basic postulates of those who practice it, and in terms of its functions within the system of which it is a part, the significance of the custom becomes scientifically meaningful. It is no longer a queer custom, but a socially significant act—always with reference to the system or structure of which it is a part. (See Figure 2-1).

Functionalism emphasizes the dynamics operating within a culture. It is concerned with a good deal more than the mere description of habits and customs.

A. R. Radcliffe-Brown (1881–1955), who was one of the early exponents of functionalism and who contributed a good deal to its development, has used a biological analogy to make its meaning clearer. In his words:

An animal organism is an agglomeration of cells and interstitial fluids arranged in relation to one another not as an aggregate but as an integrated whole. For the biochemist, it is a complexly inte-grated system of complex molecules. The system of relations by which these units are related is the organic structure. . . . [T]he organism *is not* itself the structure; it is a collection of units (cells or molecules) arranged in a structure, i.e., in a set of relations; the organism *has* a structure. Two mature animals of the same species and sex consist of similar units combined in a similar structure. The structure is thus to be defined as a set of relations between the entities. . . . As long as it lives the organism preserves a certain continuity of structure although it does not preserve the complete identity of its constituent parts. . . . Over a period its constituent cells do not remain the same. But the structural arrangement of the constituent units does remain similar. . . . [T]he life of an organism is conceived as the *functioning* of its structure . . . a cell or an organ has an *activity* and that activity has a *function.*[15]

[15]A. R. Radcliffe-Brown, "On the Concept of Function in Social Science" (*American Anthropologist,* vol. 37, 1935), pp. 394–395; reprinted in A. R. Radcliffe-Brown, *Structure and Function in Primitive Society,* pp. 178–187. See also B. Malinowski, "Culture" (*Encyclopaedia of the Social Sciences,* vol. 4, 1931), pp. 621–646.

The functions of each part are found in the contributions the part makes to maintenance of the life process of the whole organism. So it is with culture. The functions of each custom and of each institution are found in the special contributions they make to the maintenance of the life-way that is the total culture.

Malinowski emphasized that the interrelatedness of all parts of a culture means that the modification of any single part will inevitably produce secondary changes in other parts. Missionaries and officials of governmental technical-aid-and-development programs have often overlooked this simple principle, with the result that their efforts have had many an unforeseen and unwished-for consequences. But even with the most intelligent awareness it is exceedingly difficult to foresee the ultimate social consequences of any act of induced cultural change.

The Components of Culture   Cultures are built up of *behavioral norms,* or *customs.* They are sometimes identified as *culture elements,* which may be combined as *culture complexes.* Complexes may in turn constitute *institutions.* Norms may be classified according to the scope of applicability to the members of a societal population, namely, as *universals,* *alternatives,* and *specialties.* All these concepts are useful in the analysis of culture.

Behavioral Norms and Patterning   Cultural behavior is organized and patterned. This means that it is ordinarily not random but repetitive and fairly consistent. It is customary. For analytical reasons social scientists prefer to think in terms of *norms* rather than *custom,* for "custom" has too many popular meanings. A norm is the average or modal behavior of a given type that is manifested by a social group. Statistically, it means either the average or the greatest frequency of a variable. If variation is observed in a certain type of behavior on the part of a population, a count may be made of the number of times each

variation occurs in a given sample. The variations may be ranged in a continuous series in accordance with their degrees of likeness, with the most unlike forms at the two ends, or poles, of the scale. This gives the *range* of variability in the behavior. Next, the number of times each class of behavior occurs is plotted along the range of variability. This gives the *frequency distribution.* The frequency distributions may then be transferred to a graph which has the range of distribution as its base line and the frequency incidence for each class produces a *frequency-distribution curve* (Figure 2-2).

In most situations, the curve shows a high point with a slope away on either side. This is a *bell curve.* In some situations, variation away from the high point will be in one direction only. This is a *J curve* (Figure 2-3). A norm is a statistical expression of the most common class, called the *mode;* the average class, called the *mean;* or the middle class, called the *median,* in the total frequency distribution.

Customs are social norms statistically identified. They are that which is normal. When feasible, analyses of social behavior should be statistically based. Anthropological experience has shown, however, that it is not usually feasible to make rigorous statistical studies of all kinds of behavior. Consequently, when an anthropologist describes a custom, he is usually stating what appears to be the modal behavior. Only in extremely rare cases does he make an actual statistical count of all behavior over a given period of time to determine an arithmetically accurate distribution. Such precision may be ideally desirable but under the given situation either impossible or impractical. Modern canons of anthropology do insist on observation of the behavior described whenever possible. Yet sometimes it is not possible to observe what is recorded, since the behavior may have died out or may be secret, or the field worker may not be around at the particular time the event occurs. Therefore, to find out whether a given habit is modal or not, we frequently must take a people's word for it. They say this is what they always do, usually do, or would do if they did it at all (the hypothetical ideal).

Culture Elements, Complexes, and Institutions A *culture element* is a pattern of behavior (or the material product of such behavior) that may be treated as the smallest unit of its order.

Anthropologists often speak of *culture complexes*. A complex is a network of closely related patterns. For example, the activities of a dance taken together form a dance complex; the activities of the hunt form a hunting complex; the activities of child training form a child-care complex.

The complexes that are woven together in relation to the basic interests of social living are called *institutions*. For example, those concerned with subsistence activities and the production and distribution of goods are called *economic institutions;* those concerned with sex, reproduction, and kinship are called *kinship institutions*.

Universals, Alternatives, and Specialties Norms that apply to every member of a society, such as the use of the fork among adult members of Western societies, are called *universals*. Although certain kinds of behavior may be required of everyone in a society, most cultures allow some degree of choice between norms for specific situations. These are known as *alternatives*. A Cheyenne warrior, for example, could make a personal choice between a bow and arrow, a spear, or a club wherewith to smite the Crow. Each is a norm, but one does not exclude the other within the culture as a whole.

The traits that are restricted to a particular subgroup, such as the common tabus of medicine men or the hairdos of married women, are *specialties*.

The specialties of one group may be known to the other members of the society and yet not used by them, because they are not patterns for their behavior. Many American adult men know the Boy Scout salute, having once

been scouts, but they do not use it as a form of greeting after they have left scouting behind. In a complex society, however, most

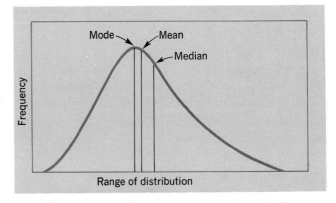

Fig. 2-2 Three kinds of norms in a skewed frequency-distribution curve.

Fig. 2-3 Model of a J curve. Hypothetical frequency distribution of homicides per male in an Eskimo community.

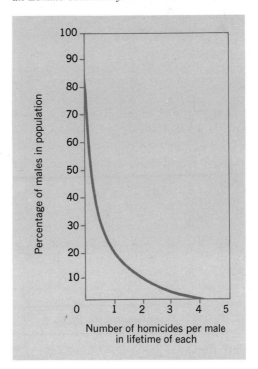

specialties remain unknown to most of the people. This may be because the specialties require unique aptitudes or a rigorous course of training which is undertaken by only a few, or it may be that the specialties are the secret and hidden knowledge of a few, kept within their closed circle for the benefits that may be derived from secretiveness. The result is that no individual can ever acquire or manifest in himself all the elements of his society's culture. It means also that no anthropologist, even the most assiduous, can ever make note of, to say nothing of record, all the aspects of any culture, even the simplest known to man.

This, then, provides one answer to the question, often asked: "How can one speak of American culture when there is such a difference between the culture of New Yorkers and that of Kentucky mountaineers?—between the Italians of Lower Manhattan and the Scandinavians of Minnesota?—between the Yankees of Vermont and the *paisanos* of Monterey?" The universals shared by all Americans are the common binding and integrating elements of American culture and society. The specialties of the different regional groups and socioeconomic classes are internally differentiating elements which, when taken together, are referred to as subcultures.

The cohesive strength of a society is in part a product of the relative proportion of *universals* to *specialties*. In any analysis of a society and its culture, it is absolutely essential, in the interests of clarity and accuracy, never to generalize from the norms of a subgroup to make statements about the society as a whole, unless it has been observed that the norms of the subgroup are also characteristic of the whole. Americans who live west of the Hudson River and north of the Long Island Sound can appreciate the meaning of this injunction if they will reflect on their feelings about European authors who write about America after a visit to New York City.[16]

[16]The analytical concepts of universals, alternatives, and specialties were introduced into anthropology by Ralph Linton (1893–1953). See his *Study of Man*, pp. 272–275.

Culture as Construct or Reality

Do cultures really exist, or do they exist only in the imagination of the social scientist? This is a question of epistemology, or the nature of knowing. The culture whole, or *the* culture of a society, is an abstraction of a high order. When we speak of a culture, we talk as though it were a neatly taped-off entity, when in point of fact each culture is woven into other cultures at many points of intersocietal contact.

The Culture Construct   Cultures are constantly changing and modifying. Yet in anthropology we investigate a society on a field trip of greater or less duration, after which we write up a monograph describing its culture. In so doing, we fix for the moment those main lines of characteristic behavior that have been perceived and noted as though they were all taking place at any given moment. It is as though a fast-moving action had been stopped with a high-speed camera shutter to obtain an instantaneous picture. We get the main contours of the action frozen for an instant in what Linton called the *culture construct*.[17] It is a statement that lumps together descriptions of modal behavior, in which each mode typifies or represents what is actually a variable range of behavior produced in the members of a society by a given stimulus.

The Real Culture   It should be realized, then, that what we deal with in anthropology is the *culture construct* rather than the *real culture* itself. The culture construct presents the real culture as accurately as scientific methodology permits.

The real culture is what all the members of a society do and think in all their activities in their total round of living, except for truly idiosyncratic behavior. The real culture, however, is never sensed by anyone in its entirety. It can be only partially perceived as it is or-

[17]R. Linton, *The Cultural Background of Personality*, pp. 43–46.

dered and translated into understandable terms by the anthropologist, the philosopher, or the novelist. This is why such radically different accounts of the same society and culture can be formulated by different reporters. Reality is never known raw, for it is always processed through one's instruments of knowing. A scientific knowledge of culture can never give us the real culture; it professes only to bring the culture construct as close to the real as the most advanced and reliable methods of anthropological research make possible.

The Ideal Culture   *Ideal culture* consists of a people's verbally expressed standards for behavior, which may or may not be translated into normal behavior. Ideal norms are generally selected and phrased in terms of group well-being, and they are often violated when individual self-interest induces another course of action or even when hidden, or covert, values stimulate contradictory behavior.

An outstanding example of the clash between public and private interests is found in Malinowski's account of clan incest among the Trobriand Islanders:

If you were to inquire into the matter among the Trobrianders, you would find that . . . the natives show horror at the idea of violating the rules of exogamy and that they believe that sores, disease and even death might follow clan incest. . . . [But] from the point of view of the native libertine, *suvasova* (the breach of exogamy) is indeed a specially interesting and spicy form of erotic experience. Most of my informants would not only admit but actually did boast about having committed this offense or that of adultery (*kaylasi*); and I have many concrete, well-attested cases on record.[18]

The Trobriand native manages to get away with it, provided he keeps it from becoming a publicly recognized scandal, because the Trobrianders have a system of magic which ensures immunity from the threatened diseases if a person has the proper charms. One

[18]B. Malinowski, *Crime and Custom in Savage Society*, pp. 79 and 84.

segment of the culture provides the means for making a mockery of the other. Preservation of the clan is a social interest loudly acclaimed. Intercourse with a clan cousin is an individually motivated sport that is a genuine custom.

We need not discuss here the gaps that exist between our own ideals of democracy and our practices that negate them. It is because of such ever-present gaps between the thought and the deed, between the ideal and the action, that the realistic social scientist will not take a people's say-so as valid evidence of the real behavior norm.

The Relation of Society to Culture

Society and culture are not one. A human society is made up of people; a culture is made up of the behavior of people. We may say that a person belongs to a society, but it would be wrong to say that he belongs to a culture; he manifests a culture.

Society Defined   Although a society is made up of people, it is more than just a human aggregation. It is a population or a group of individuals united by some common principle or principles.

A society occupies an identifiable space, for it is territorially localized even though its boundaries may not be marked by an Iron Curtain or a Great Wall of China. Its members interact in a centripetally oriented network of relationships. Even though they may have numerous contacts with the members of other societies, the majority of their activities are in relation to each other. Further, their relationships are far from random. They are patterned and ordered according to learned norms of conduct and belief which differ in some respects from their counterparts as manifested by other populations. In short, the patterns of relationships in a society are distinctive, culturally defined, and limited. Finally, the members of a society are affectively bonded by common linguistic and symbolic representations. They speak a common language, even though there may be wide dialectic variations or even two or more distinct languages present. They are emotionally stirred to a consciousness of kind by common life experiences, myths, rituals, and other symbolic identifiers: clothing and ornaments, foods ("as American as apple pie"), totemic and tribal markers. The discovery of how fabulously intricate, imaginative, and effective the systems of symbolic representations can be in so-called primitive cultures continues to delight and interest the best-informed of anthropologists. And in our contemporary days of challenge, the alienated counterculture revolutionary strikes sensitive social nerves by turning societal symbols upside down.

In sum, a human society is: (1) a spacially identifiable population, (2) interacting in a centripetally oriented network of relations, (3) which are culturally patterned and limited, (4) distinctive in some respects from their counterparts in other cultures, and (5) affectively bonded by common linguistic and other forms of symbolic representations.

Culture and Societal Maintenance Cultures develop as answers to the problems of individual and group living. One imperative of living is to keep alive, and all surviving biological forms are so built that a sufficient number of the species stays alive long enough to reproduce a succeeding generation. Living forms, therefore, have a built-in survival capacity relative to the environments they have experienced in the past. Cultures consist, on the one hand, of set ways of meeting the survival needs of individuals. Because of the prolonged dependency of the human infant, a stable societal and group relationship is a biological prerequisite to continuance of the species. Cultures provide individuals with ways in which to hunt and fish, make fire and tools, defend themselves, relate to other members of their society, cure their illnesses, and assuage their fears and anxieties. Cultures provide the individual with "proved"

ways to meet the needs for food, shelter, safety, reproduction (sex), relaxation, and psychic security.

Societies, too, have their needs which must be met by each culture if the societies are to survive. These have been identified as the "functional prerequisites of societal survival and continuity." The anthropologist John W. Bennett and the sociologist Melvin M. Tumin identify six such prerequisites:

(1) To maintain the biologic functioning of the group members; (2) to reproduce new members for the group; (3) to socialize new members into functioning adults; (4) to produce and distribute goods and services necessary to life; (5) to maintain order within the group, and between itself and outsiders; and (6) to define the "meaning of life" and maintain the motivation to survive and engage in the activities necessary for survival.[19]

Every cultural system therefore includes established ways of providing food, shelter, and health and of organizing sex relations, enculturation of individuals, the economy, technology, trade, government and law, war and defense, and meaningful world and religious views. (Parts 4 and 5 of this book are organized in terms of these institutions.)

It is not enough that a people *know how* to do things, however. It is also imperative that they find satisfaction in doing what they are to do. Men must *want* to eat, drink, and mate. Motivation on this level is so elementally physiological that societies have no great difficulty in eliciting such engagement from their members. The rewards of reproduction and enculturation of children are much less direct, however, and require adequate cultural provision. Not to work is easier than to work. To work in order to procure enough food is an automatic animal response to food deprivation. But if people are to be induced to work to satisfy secondary and derived wants in terms of self-gratification and social duty, there must be very special cultural rewards. Each society must learn how to

[19]J. W. Bennett and M. M. Tumin, *Social Life*, pp. 45–59.

provide the rewards that keep its workers working.

Cultures vary in the quality of the institutional devices they provide for societal survival. Traits that are ineffective or less effective in meeting the demands of the functional prerequisites reduce the efficiency and survival capacity of the society. Although cultural relativity teaches us that each custom or usage is valid in terms of its own cultural context and therefore should not be judged morally good or bad, the fact remains that one type of trait or another may be more or less effective in serving societal ends. Societies that invent and do not control lethal customs are doomed. Thus, if the notion that sex is evil and incompatible with the pure life were spread to all the members of a society, resulting in the practice of enjoined celibacy, that society would soon be extinguished because the secondary prerequisite, that of reproduction of new members for the group, would not have been met. Today, the great danger which threatens us all is the development through technology of the potentially lethal trait of uncontrolled use of atomic energy in war.

Cultures are man's means of improved survival, but cultures are limited by biological and social imperatives. They need not be implicitly successful.

Finally, the most human of all the functions of culture is to define the meaning of life and to maintain the motivation to keep going. The humanities are called "the humanities" because they search for the humane in man's work—that which provides the psychological commitment to life and society on the part of the animal being who has reached the state of development wherein he can demand to know: "What is it all about?"

Personality and Culture

Societies are made up of individuals, and cultures, while manifest through the behavior of individuals, set patterns for individual behavior which exist before the individual is born and persist after he has died. All cultures change through time, but they have an enduring continuity that supersedes the mortal span of the person. Some anthropologists have held that culture exists *in* personality. Yet, considering how much more than the individual personality culture actually is, this view seems to be too narrow. Culture, with roots in individual behavior, is superindividual. The problem, then, in considering man, culture, and society, is to see how man and culture interrelate. Thus, we approach the problem as one of personality *and* culture.

A personality is the integrated system of behaviors, learned and unlearned, that are characteristic of an individual. A culture is the integrated system of learned behavior patterns that are characteristic of the members of a society. The interrelations of the two have posed three kinds of problems for mutual study by psychologists and anthropologists: (1) How does culture affect personality? (2) How does personality affect culture? (3) How does personality response to specific cultural experience influence other aspects of the culture, or in what sense are individual personalities intermediary links in a chain of cause and effect between different parts of cultures?

Determinants of Personality A given personality is the product of many interacting factors, which may be classified under four main categories: (1) the constitutional characteristics of the individual (his biology, neurophysiology, endocrine system, body type, etc.); (2) the nature of the physical environment in which the individual lives; (3) the culture in accordance with which the individual lives; and (4) the unique, or idiosyncratic, biological-psychological-social experience or history of the individual. These components are fused in the creation of each personality.

Constitutional Characteristics The most obvious, although not necessarily the most important, factors in the determination of personality are the physical and mental capacities with which the individual is endowed at birth. These are the traits which are frequently termed "inherited" or "innate," although these labels are in themselves misleading and open to a variety of interpretations. Included are such factors as body build, intelligence, neurological make-up, presence or absence of deformities, and the like.

Morphological factors which can be readily seen as having a direct influence on personality are stature, weight, and physical appearance. The personality of a dwarf cannot be that of a giant. We must keep in mind, however, that the social meaning of a physical characteristic is culturally determined. In Western culture, big men are expected to be dominant in ascendant-submissive relations. Differing cultures attach individual and often widely differing meanings to such physical attributes as larger-than-average size.

To illustrate this point, we may contrast American behavior with that of the Trobriand Islanders with respect to identification of physiognomy among kinsmen. In American society a newborn baby is carefully evaluated by relatives and friends to see whether it looks like the mother or the father, or this uncle or that aunt, or this grandfather or that grandmother. Americans have a real obsession to find points of resemblance to kinsmen. Maternal kinsmen project maternal identities upon the infant. Paternal kinsmen project their counterparts. If the physical traits are definitely identifiable with those of one line or the other, the stimulus value is quite marked, and the role behavior may be influenced one way or the other.

In the Trobriands, on the other hand, the dogma of the culture is that children do not and cannot resemble the mother or her kin in spite of the Trobrianders' theory of procreation. To hint as much is offensively bad taste. Yet resemblance to the father is always assumed and affirmed. Physical aspects of the father as well as aspects of his personality,

but not those of the mother, are thus imputed to the children.

A queerer quirk in Trobriand culture is the dogma that brothers never look alike. Malinowski once suggested, apropos of some Trobriand Islanders' remarks about how much a group of brothers looked like their father, that it followed from this that the brothers must look like one another. The natives made it plain that they thought he had very crude manners to make such a gauche remark.[20] Syllogistic reasoning could not stand in the face of culturally controlled perception. From the Trobriand point of view, any fool can see that brothers just never do look alike.

Physical Environment Anthropogeographers of the nineteenth century attempted to explain national character in terms of physical environment. Mountain dwellers are ruggedly individualistic, it was suggested. Enjoyers of temperate climates are creative and vigorous. Dwellers in the tropics are indolent and sexually precocious, and so on through a long list of stereotypes. Most early anthropogeographic work was so facile and superficial that it was tossed out, along with the concept of race as a determinant of psychological and behavioral characteristics, by twentieth-century anthropologists. Nonetheless, the mineral content of diet can and does affect the endocrine system of whole populations. Whether a people must adapt to an arctic, desert, or rain-forest environment is a factor of significant influence. Differences in the altitudes at which people live and the characteristic barometric pressures to which they must adjust are not without personality effects. Such matters are therefore not to be overlooked, and the imaginativeness of Professor John Whiting in seeking a causal relation between male initiation practices, multiple marriages, and climate is a good example of taking the environmental factor into account (see page 385).

[20]B. Malinowski, *The Father in Primitive Psychology*, pp. 87–92.

Cultural Determinants   Cultural determinants set the patterns and limits for normal behavior within any society. In Miller and Dollard's phraseology, culture is "...a statement of the design of the human maze, of the type of reward involved, and of what responses are to be rewarded."[21] The operation of these determinants, together with the feedback effect of personality responses to them, constitutes the subject of the rest of this chapter.

Idiosyncratic Features of Individual Experience
Every individual has a unique personal history. Not all aspects of the society's culture are open to all persons, and differences in status mean differences in social opportunity and experience. These mean differences in status roles and personalities. Even more important, however, is the fact that persons of identical status nevertheless do not have the same experiences. The mother prefers one child over the other. One child burns his finger; another does not. One woman has an automobile accident; another does not. One infant falls in the river; another does not. No two persons ever have the same social experience, not even identical twins. From psychoanalysis we have learned how important the fortuity of history can be in shaping the direction of personality development.

Culture tends to standardize personalities by channeling the experience of all individuals along the same broad stream. But life is made up of so many instances, so many situations, such rich variety of experience, that absolute standardization can never be realized.

A Comprehensive Classification of Personality Determinants   Personality is therefore to be understood as a behavioral synthesis of an individual's physical (including neural and glandular) constitution, the physicochemical

character of his environment, the patterns of his culture, and his internalization of, and reactions to, his total life history in relation to people and things. These four categories are drawn on the basis of *levels within the natural order* and the nature of the individual's experience.

A hint of the immense complexity of interacting factors that should ideally be understood may be obtained from trying to imagine all the steps which would be involved in getting all the data for just one person—to say nothing of a representative sample of a society. The model that accounts for this classifies determinants in terms of the criterion of *degree of universality among human beings.* The four categories based upon this principle are (1) the *universal*—those determinants which are relatively constant for all mankind, whatever the environment, culture, or race; (2) the *communal*—those determinants which are relatively constant and unique for all the members of a given society as opposed to the members of other societies; (3) the *role*—those determinants which are linked to different statuses within a society; and (4) the *idiosyncratic*—those determinants which are uniquely individual, in either constitution or life history. Combining these with the four determinants based upon the level of natural order gives fifteen major components of personality (Table 2-1).

This framework points the way for sifting out "group personalities." Thus the universal determinants, which apply to all mankind, produce what there is of "human nature" the world over. The communal traits lead to national or societal character types. The role determinants shape the distinctive personalities of persons belonging to various age, sex, occupational, class, and caste groupings within societies. The idiosyncratic determinants guarantee the uniqueness of every individual as long as men endure.

Clyde Kluckhohn and Henry A. Murray expressed the foregoing epigrammatically in their well-known quotation:

[21]N. Miller and J. Dollard, *Social Learning and Initiation,* p. 5.

Table 2-1 The Components of Personality*

	Determinants based on degree of universality among human beings			
Determinants based on level of natural order	Universal	Communal	Role	Idiosyncratic
Cultural	Incest tabu, kinship systems, property, magic, religion, housing, time reckoning, etc.	Special forms of kinship, property, magical and religious beliefs, etc.	Special roles culturally differentiated for status groups within each society	Fortuitous experiences in social relations
Social	Group life, child care	Size, distribution, density of population, etc.	Play groups, congeniality groups, cliques, etc.	
Biological	Birth, death, hunger, thirst, metabolic action, skeletal-muscular structure, basic drives, etc.	"Racial" variations of universal traits, health conditions of society at large, etc.	Age and sex differences, racially based class and caste	Individual peculiarities of stature, physiognomy, glandular functions, etc.
Physical environmental	Atmospheric pressure, gravity, earth, sun, moon, stars, clouds, water, wind, precipitation, etc.	Local climate, topography, wild plant and animal life, other natural resources, etc.	Differential access to material goods by different status groups	Unique relations to flood, storm, lightning, and other physical phenomena

*Modified from C. Kluckhohn and O. H. Mowrer, "Culture and Personality" (*American Anthropologist*, vol. 46, 1944), pp. 1–29.

Every man is in certain respects
a. like all other men,
b. like some other men,
c. like no other man.[22]

Child Training and Personality

"As the twig is bent, so grows the tree." A major factor in the development of the child as a person is the accumulation of innumerable pressures, most of them subtle, others not so subtle, that shape his images and his feel of the surrounding world. He strives to act in accordance with these understandings (Figure 2-4). The child's feel of the world and his gradually growing perception of what that world will give and what it demands serve as his guides for getting on.

All these perceptions must be explored and tested. At the instant of birth, the world is nothing for the newborn infant. It is sensed only as a rude and sudden change from the all-encompassing perfection of the womb to the coldness of the air that first strikes him. His first response is a wail and not a laugh.

The world that awaits the child is a world of people who already have a multitude of cultural commitments concerning how to behave—people with culturally colored emotions, expectancies, and anxieties. It is a world of many physical things, some beneficial, even essential to human existence; some inexorably destructive; some now one and then the other. Of these the infant is blankly ignorant. Of all these he must in time become knowledgeable.

Investigations of human adults show that much of their behavior consists of patterns derived from processes of conditioning in early childhood. Under ordinary circumstances the child's first experience, and his experience for some time thereafter, is in the

[22]C. Kluckhohn and H. A. Murray, "Personality Formation: The Determinants," in C. Kluckhohn and H. A. Murray (eds.), *Personality in Nature, Society, and Culture,* (1949), p. 35.

primary conjugal family. This is his world. Margaret Mead, for one, has shown how this world differentially puts the imprint of its finger on him:

The Arapesh [of New Guinea] treat a baby as a soft, vulnerable, precious little object, to be protected, fed, cherished. . . . When the mother walks about she carries the child slung beneath her breast in a bark-cloth sling, or in a soft net bag in which the child still curls as he curled in the womb. Whenever it is willing to eat . . . it is fed, gently, interestedly.

Among the neighboring Iatmul head-hunters:

From birth the baby is handled as if it were a separate little entity capable of a will of its own. . . . As soon as the Iatmul child is a few weeks old, the mother no longer carries it everywhere with her . . . but instead places it at some distance on a high bench, where it must cry lustily before it is fed. . . . [T]he sense of the mouth is built up as an assertive, demanding organ, taking what it can from a world that is, however, not unduly unwilling to give it. The child learns an attitude towards the world; that if you fight hard enough, something which will treat you as strong as itself will yield—and that anger and self-assertion will be rewarded.

And again:

The Mundugumor [another New Guinea tribe] women actively dislike child-bearing, and they dislike children. Children are carried in harsh opaque baskets that scratch their skins, later, high on their mother's shoulders, well away from the breast. Mothers nurse their children standing up, pushing them away as soon as they are the least bit satisfied. . . . Here we find a character developing that stresses angry, eager avidity. In later life love-

(a)

(b)

(c)

Fig. 2-4   Cultural patterning of behavior: New Zealand Maoris threatened enemies and thieves with far-out tongues and popeyed look. (a) *The pattern is portrayed in the image of a protective spirit carved in the panel of a Maori food storehouse;* (b) *Maori war dancers live it; and* (c) *Maori small boys practice it. (Courtesy of the American Museum of Natural History.)*

making is conducted like the first round of a prize-fight, and biting and scratching are important parts of foreplay.[23]

Child training encompasses a good deal more than consciously directed education. As a biological organism, each individual is moved by a mass of impuses or drives. Many of these are innate, that is, inherent in the neurophysiological make-up.

Enculturation   The ways in which these needs may be satisfied are always limited and standardized in every culture. No society permits its members to eat any which way at any time they please. No society permits its members to urinate and defecate whenever or wherever they get the urge. Sphincter control is always demanded. No society permits unlimited expression of the sex drive; on the contrary, all societies exert considerable social control in this matter.

Each person must learn what kinds of responses to drive pressures lead to goal achievement and need satisfaction. Antisocial responses—that is, culturally prohibited behavior—are punished through social efforts to extinguish them. The individual must learn to inhibit his impulse to act in prohibited ways and to habituate his behavior to culturally indicated ways.

The total process is called *enculturation,* which is defined as conscious or unconscious conditioning occurring within that process whereby man, as child and adult, achieves competence in his culture. A well-adjusted personality is one that successfully gratifies his personal urges within the allowable expectancies of his social environment. In social psychology and sociology, the term of long-standing use that is synonymous with enculturation is *socialization.*

Human life is lived in a state of continuous tensions that may only be minimized, never permanently eliminated. The battle between inner urge and the channeled limitations allowed by culture is unending. "Inner psychic conflict would seem to be of the very essence of man."[24] Maturity in personality represents an acceptance of the terms according to which life can and must be lived in any given society. When a growing child has adjusted his behavior to the patterns of his culture, when its pertinent values, beliefs, and modes of action have become a normal part of his thinking and behavior, he has *internalized* his culture and has become thoroughly enculturated. His personality has matured.

Along the way he will have acquired many drives and attendant goals that were not in him at birth. These drives are not *basic* but are, rather, *acquired* or *secondary.* They are extensions of a more elemental need for warm social response. The goals are culturally symbolized in the social rewards that go with prestige status. Most men in most societies struggle to achieve and shape their personalities in accord with the demands of such acquired drives with as much intensity of action as the basic drives evoke.

Primitive Education and Enculturation   Education, as opposed to child training, implies the more formal efforts of adults to mold the personalities of the young, but among primitive peoples the gap is nowhere as great as it is in American society, for example. Primitives never make an issue over "education for life," as our school people do. In a tribal group, education *is* life. The father does not work in a factory or an office the child never sees. The child is not shut up in a school away from the home for hours and days on end. In the simple camp or village, he is around and underfoot while all the fundamental activities of adult life take place. He can play with a bow and arrow until he is old enough to tag along on the hunt and learn by precept in action just

[23]M. Mead, *Male and Female,* pp. 65 and 68–69. By permission from William Morrow and Company, New York.

[24]A. I. Hallowell, "Psychological Leads for Ethnological Field Workers," in D. Haring (ed.), *Personal Character and Cultural Milieu,* p. 296.

(a)

(b)

(c)

Fig. 2-5   Acceptance, rejection, and sibling
responsibility in childhood experience: (a)
Wisconsin father and son; (b) Alorese infant
among adults; (c) a Balinese preadolescent caring
for two younger siblings. [(a) and (c) Photographs
by Ken Heyman from Margaret Mead and Ken
Heyman's Family, The Macmillan Company,
New York; (b) Courtesy of Cora DuBois.]

how to handle it expertly (Figure 2-6). He can play around the older boys who are watching the herds until he is ready to herd himself. He can see and imitate the dancers until he himself is admitted to the dance (Figure 2-7). He can listen to the tales of tribal lore and myth as they are told until he knows them by heart (Figure 2-8). Most knowledge comes as a byproduct of living, with one or another of the family members as a natural, nonprofessional instructor. And much is learned from play with other children who are just a bit older.

Formal learning is usually limited to the more esoteric or specialized aspects of religion and magic. Where tribal initiations are held, they almost invariably involve formal instruction in these affairs.

C. W. M. Hart has pointed out that in most primitive societies, the education of children before puberty is left to the informal ministrations of parents and other relatives. In many societies, however, the boys are hauled off to a "bush school" at puberty to be put through a severe course of discipline and training in esoteric knowledge covering the "value system of the culture, its myths, its religion, its philosophy, its justification for its own entity as a culture."[25] Hart continues: "The initiation schools are directed at imparting instruction that cannot be given in the home, under conditions as unlike home conditions as possible, by teachers who are the antithesis of the home teachers the boy has hitherto had."[26]

Initiation Education among the Tswana An example of the scope of such initiation education, from the Tswana, is provided in the following paragraph by Professor Schapera:

All the eligible boys were initiated simultaneously in groups, kept secluded in one or more special "camps" (*mephatô*) away from all the villages for three months or so. The details of the ceremony

were kept a profound secret from women and all other non-initiates, who were forbidden under penalty of severe assault and even death to approach too near to the camp. At the camp the boys were first circumcised in order of tribal precedence. They were then systematically taught a number of secret formulae and songs, admonishing them to honour, obey, and support the Chief; to be ready to endure hardships and even death for the sake of the tribe; to be united as a regiment and help one another; to value cattle as the principal source of livelihood, and so herd them carefully; to attend the *kgotla* regularly, as this was the place for men, and to look after its fire; to honour and ungrudgingly obey old people; and to abandon all boyish practices. Much of this instruction dealt also with the important topic of sex, the boys being taught the physiology of sex relations, the duty of procreation and other rules of conduct in married life, and the dangers of promiscuous intercourse with ritually "unclean" women. They were further taught tribal traditions and religious beliefs, and the tribal songs of war and self-glorification, and were made to participate in symbolic dances of many kinds. They were, moreover, subjected to starvation and blows, discomfort and actual torture, and rigorous and irksome taboos of many kinds, and were made to participate in strenuous hunting expeditions, all with the object of hardening them.[27]

The rituals of priests, and often of shamans, must ordinarily be taught on an apprenticeship basis, for these are frequently so complex, as well as secret, that they can be imparted only under isolated conditions which encourage students' strict attention and rigorous study.

On the whole, it is safe to say that primitive children find their education less irksome than ours do. It demands less of them, and they can readily see the utility of what they learn because it is evident all about them in everyday living (Figure 2-9). They use their knowledge as they acquire it; they do not have to learn in a vacuum things that they will not have a chance to put to use for some years to come—or, perhaps, never.

[25]See C. W. M. Hart, "Contrasts between Prepubertal and Postpubertal Education," in G. D. Spindler (ed.), *Education and Anthropology*, p. 141.
[26]*Ibid.*, p. 140.

[27]I. Schapera, *A Handbook of Tswana Law and Custom*, p. 106. By permission from Oxford University Press, London.

Theoretical Systems of Culture and Personality

The first anthropological studies on personality and culture were Malinowski's *Sex and Repression in Savage Society* and Margaret Mead's *Coming of Age in Samoa*. Malinowski tested Freud's theory of the Oedipus complex against the facts of Trobriand society. In the matrilineal system of social structure of the Trobriand Islanders, authority over children is exercised by the maternal uncle (mother's brother), rather than the father. Malinowski asked the question: "In this type of social setting does a boy have incestuous desires for his mother and 'hate' his father as an authority figure and rival for the affections of the mother?" After analyzing Trobriand behavior and Trobriand mythology, Malinowski concluded that the answer is "No." It is the uncle who is resented and the sister (particularly the clan sister) who is the object of intrafamilial sexual interest. Therefore, the basic principle of the Oedipus complex exists, but its manifestation alters with the cultural complex.[28]

Mead's work in *Coming of Age in Samoa* was discussed in the first chapter as an ex-

[28]B. Malinowski, *Sex and Repression in Savage Society;* also *The Father in Primitive Psychology.*

Fig. 2-6   The Amahuaca child of the Peruvian rain forest learns to make and use arrows in direct association with his father. (Cornell Capa, Magnum.)

ample of the use of the comparative method in anthropology as a substitute for laboratory-controlled experimentation to test hypotheses. It will be remembered that Mead's conclusion was that Samoan adolescents do not go through the period of psychological stress that characterizes American adolescence because Samoan culture is free of certain stress-producing features.

Neither Malinowski nor Mead expressed an

Fig. 2-7   Patterning of behavior: learning to dance in Bali. The teacher does not demonstrate by precept but guides each movement. The Balinese does not learn by watching but by kinesthetic sense. (Henri Cartier-Bresson, Magnum.)

explicit theory of culture and personality at that time (1926 and 1928, respectively). In 1934, however, Ruth Benedict (1887–1948) published her famous *Patterns of Culture,* which became the theoretical prototype for a number of later "configurational studies." Subsequently, Abram Kardiner, a psychoanalyst, with the cooperation of Ruth Benedict, Cora DuBois, Ralph Linton, and other anthropologists, developed and published a "theory of basic personality structure" for handling questions of the effect of culture upon personality and vice versa. This, too, became the model for a number of studies. All these theoretical systems rest on intensive psychocultural analysis of one or a few tribes. John Whiting, a former colleague of G. P. Murdock in the initiation of the statistical method of cross-cultural studies, entered the lists in 1953 with the publication of a broader theory of culture and personality, in which specific hypotheses are put to correlational tests that are statistically devised.

Each of these theories will now be considered.

The Configuration of Culture and the Ideal Personality Type   The central thesis of Ruth Benedict's approach to this problem was that the ideological contours of a tribal culture are impressed upon individuals in terms of an ideal personality type. Each society has a more or less clear idea of what constitutes the "good man" and the "good woman," the kind of person an individual ought to be.

In Benedict's analysis, the precepts, maxims, rewards, and punishments are all directed toward molding all men in the image of the ideal. He who approximates the ideal is an object of social cynosure. The character of this ideal personality is equated with an abstracted tribal character structure.

In *Patterns of Culture,* Benedict purported to demonstrate the empirical validity of the theory by detailed descriptions of what she called the "Dionysian configuration," represented by the Kwakiutl Indians of the Northwest Coast of North America, and the "Apollonian configuration," exemplified by the Zuñi Indians of New Mexico.

Dionysian-Apollonian Configurations   The Dionysian and Apollonian concepts were phrased as follows:

The basic contrast between the Pueblos and the other cultures of North America is the contrast that is named and described by Nietzsche in his studies of Greek tragedy. He discusses two diametrically opposed ways of arriving at the values of existence. The Dionysian pursues them through "the annihilation of the ordinary bounds and limits of existence"; he seeks to attain in his most valued moments escape from the boundaries imposed upon him by his five senses, to break through into another order of experience. The desire of the Dionysian, in personal experience or in ritual, is to press through it toward a certain psychological state, to achieve excess. The closest analogy to the emotions he seeks is drunkenness, and he values the illuminations of frenzy. With Blake, he believes "the path of excess leads to the palace of wisdom." The Apollonian distrusts all this, and has often little idea of the nature of such experiences. He finds means to outlaw them from his conscious life. He "knows but one law, measure in the Hellenic sense." He keeps the middle of the road, stays within the known map, does not meddle with disruptive psychological states.[29]

The factual validity of Benedict's characterizations of Kwakiutl and Pueblo society is open to serious challenge.[30] She drew her configurations with the artistic license of a poet, rather than with the exactitude of a scientist. Nonetheless, her beautifully written exposition of her configurational theory has exerted great influence on anthropology, education, and public thinking from 1934 to the present. It is the most popular book on anthropology written thus far in the twentieth century.

A much clearer, if less lyric, presentation of ideal personality types may be found in Aztec literature, and may aid in understanding Benedict's hypothesis.

Aztec Ideal Personality Types   Not every society formulates these ideals explicitly, but the Aztecs did in terms that seem simultaneously

[29]R. F. Benedict, *Patterns of Culture*, pp. 78–79. By permission from Houghton Mifflin Company, New York.
[30]See V. Barnouw, *Culture and Personality*, pp. 41–48, for a bill of particulars.

Fig. 2-8   Enculturation. Young Bushman boys, with youths, learn the band's traditions from an elder as they sit around the campfire. (From Jens Bjerre's Kalahari, *Hill and Wang, New York)*

familiar and quaint. As stated in the Floren-tine Codex, the ideals for father and son are as follows:

One's father [is] the source of lineage, the begin-ning of lineage. [He is] the sincere one. One's father [is] diligent, solicitous, compassionate, sympa-thetic; a careful administrator [of his household]. He rears, he teaches people; he rears, he teaches others. He advises, he admonishes one. He is ex-emplary; he leads a model life. He stores up for himself; he stores up for others. He cares for his assets; he saves for others. He is thrifty—he saves for the future, teaches thrift, looks to the future. He regulates, distributes with care, establishes order.

One's bad father [is] lazy, incompassionate, negligent, unreliable. He is unfeeling, neglectful of duty, untrustworthy; a shirker, a loafer, a sullen worker.

One's good son [is] obedient, humble, gracious, grateful, reverent. [He is] one who shows rever-ence, who obeys, humbles himself, is thankful, shows appreciation, resembles [father or mother] in body and character, [and] in way of life.

One's bad son [is] perverse, wicked, rebellious; a vile brute—mad, deranged, disobedient; one who ignores commands; a fool, lewd, gaudy, vain, un-trained; a dunce who accepts not, who receives not the counsel of mother [and] father. Training, teach-ing, reprimands, corrections go in one ear and out the other. He belittles; he is disrespectful, bold, defiant, agitated, impetuous, rash, fitful.[31]

Guidelines for mother and daughter as well as for a host of other persons, are spelled out with the same specificity.

Like culture, the ideal personality type is a construct. While it suffers from dangers of oversimplification, it nonetheless offers a fun-damentally useful approach. For example, when we speak of the "national character" of a people we are really speaking of a collective ideal personality type. The French national character is different from the British, and the British is in turn different from the German. Plains Indians' personalities are typically strikingly unlike those of Pueblo Indians. The Benedict approach has pointed up and driven

home the theory that the personalities of the majority in any society are largely reflections of the ideal personality presented by that society's culture.

The collective actions of a nation are to a certain degree the reactions of the ideal per-sonality type to given stimulus situations. Accurate analyses of national character can aid in understanding national conduct. The problem from the point of view of social sci-ence is to see that such characterizations are validated by adequate empirical data and critical checking.[32]

Basic Personality Structure and Cultural Projection Although the concept of basic personality structure developed by Abram Kardiner originated in the concept of the ideal personality type, it developed from the latter and is not identical with it.[33]

Whereas the use of the concept of ideal personality type demonstrates the close inter-relation between culture and personality, it presents a characterization that is essentially descriptive and nongenetic. It describes a type of personality without attempting to probe deeply into questions of how it got that way.

Kardiner, a psychoanalyst by training and in practice, focused interest on the psycho-dynamics of personality and culture. The unique aspect of his approach is the way he undertakes to determine the effect of social institutions upon personality and of per-sonality upon institutions.

Out of the interaction of this generalized psychoanalytic proposition that social insti-

[31]C. E. Dibble and A. J. O. Anderson, *Florentine Codex: Book 10, The People*, pp. 1–2.

[32]The March, 1967, issue of the *Annals of the American Academy of Political and Social Sciences* is devoted to "National Character in the Perspective of the Social Sci-ences." It provides a good, up-to-date overview of the subject.

[33]A. Kardiner, *The Individual and His Society;* and A. Kard-iner et al., *The Psychological Frontiers of Society.* A con-cise summary of the historical development of the concept may be found in Kardiner's article, "The Concept of Basic Personality Structure as an Operational Tool in the Social Sciences," in R. Linton (ed.), *The Science of Man in the World Crisis*, pp. 107–122.

Fig. 2-9 (a) *Small boys of the Dani tribe in western New Guinea (West Irian) practice spear throwing in a game called "Kill-the-hoop."* (b) *As adults they face their enemies in serious battle.* [*Photo* (a) *by Samuel Putnam and* (b) *by Karl G. Heider.* © *1968 by the Film Study Center, Peabody Museum, Harvard University, from* **Gardens of War** *by Robert Gardner and Karl G. Heider, Random House.*]

(a)

(b)

tutions and personality do affect each other, and from the anthropological materials on cultural determinism have emerged these constructs: (1) Certain culturally established techniques of child treatment, called *primary institutions,* shape basic attitudes toward parents; these attitudes exist throughout the life of the individual. (2) The "group of nuclear constellations" of attitudes and behavior formed by the culturally standardized patterns of child treatment in any society, and persisting among the adults, is the *basic personality structure* that is characteristic of that society. (3) By means of the mechanisms of projection, the nuclear constellations derived from primary institutions are subsequently reflected in the development of other institutions such as religion, government, and mythology. Institutions derived as a result of projective systems are called *secondary institutions.*

The Kardinerian system is a limited system that attempts to establish two things: (1) the identification of the basic personality structure and the process of its formation as a reaction to child-care customs; and (2) the carry-over effect of the basic personality patterns into certain of the larger institutional structures of the society.[34] In other words, Kardiner is striving to show how one phase of culture shapes personality and how the resultant personality in turn shapes other phases of the culture. He is really probing the interrelation between culture and personality, not just the influence of culture on personality.

The method in its present stage of development is avowedly self-limited. It does not attempt to discover how the primary institutions, the child-care complexes, came into

being. "The primary institution is treated as the taking-off point for the individual, not for the culture."[35] Furthermore, it assumes that various elemental aspects of culture, such as certain technologies (for example, basket making), may have no direct bearing on the basic personality structure. And yet further, it acknowledges that in many cultures certain institutions lie outside and are independent of the projective system.

On the positive side, a precept of psychodynamics which is essential to the whole scheme, and which we have not yet mentioned, is that the individual is not wholly the passive receptor of his cultural system. Culture is transmitted through learning, but the individual works emotionally upon what he experiences and what he is taught.

The point is that [direct] learning processes do not account for the integrative character of the human mind in so far as the emotional relationships of the individual to his environment are concerned. . . . In addition to direct learning processes, the individual builds up a highly complicated series of integrative systems which are not a result of direct learning.[36]

In a dynamic situation of cultural change, such as the present, a new "youth culture" which is not the result of parental enculturation may result. The effect is a generation gap.

Alorese Culture and Basic Personality Structure
It is quite impossible to convey the meaning of an operational application of the basic personality structure with anything like reasonable adequacy here. Yet a skeletal sketch will portray the idea better than none at all. We have selected Alor for the purpose, since it is the only one of the primitive cultures on which Kardiner has published results of psychodynamic analysis based upon adequate data.[37] All his other analyses of primitive cul-

[34]Note that Kardiner's secondary institutions are institutions in the ordinary sociological sense. However, his primary institutions are what anthropologists usually call *trait complexes.* In a strict sense they are not institutions at all. This leads Kardiner in his later work to amend the concept of primary institution to read: "primary institution or related practices, whether institutionalized or not." (*The Psychological Frontiers of Society,* p. 25.)

[35]*Ibid.*
[36]A. Kardiner, "The Concept of Basic Personality Structure as an Operational Tool in the Social Sciences," *op. cit.,* pp. 109–110.
[37]C. DuBois, *The People of Alor.*

tures (Marquesan, Tanala, Comanche) must be recognized as experimental probing; the conclusions drawn from such probing must be treated as wholly provisional and indicative of potential results rather than final fact.

The Alorese, who live on the island of Timor in eastern Indonesia, are gardeners; their environment is that of the tropical forest. For women, the main cultural activity is gardening; for men, it is an endless round of wealth exchanges, the making and collecting of loans. Money, which in Alor consists of pigs, Javanese bronze vessels (*moko*), and gongs, is lent out at interest with tight bonds of obligation that bind the debtor to his creditor. Marriage and death, among other occasions, call for extravagant consumption of pork along with tremendous exchanges of *moko* and gongs. The heavy burdens of these occasions force the principals deep into debt.

Capitalism in Alor is primarily a vehicle for egotistical dominance over one's fellow men. In the family, the internal tensions and hostilities of the Alorese household fail to gratify the security needs of the infant child. Alorese culture is integrated about the basic insecurity of the individual. Dominance through credit control is an attempt at compensatory adjustment.

In like manner, Alorese wars in the past rested not upon any military interest.[38] War was only a means of getting even, a sort of irritable gesture expressed not in any art of warfare but in a series of long-drawn-out feuds marked by cowardly assaults carried out by trickery and stealth. Women, as well as men, were the victims.

The Alorese child is neglected. He is wanted, not rejected, but he is neglected. The mother works, and works hard, in her scattered fields. After the fourteenth day following his birth, she has little time for her child. The father is away from home much of the time. The hunger pangs of the infant are irregularly and inconsistently met. The mother does not take the child to the fields with her; someone else around the house must tend him—the grandmother, an older child, or the father, if he is home. Several women may nurse him now and then; he is given gruel and premasticated bananas almost from the outset. His hunger cravings are physiologically met, but no consistent image of any person upon whom he can depend for relief of hunger tensions is developed. Premasticated food may be given by anyone who wants to stop the infant's incessant bawling, but rejection and spitting out of such food, which is often observed, indicate that food thus given does not relieve the emotional tensions of the child. Hunger is more than an empty stomach.

Although the child is not left alone and is usually lugged around half-sitting in a shawl, he is not fondled or caressed by his parents to relieve his tensions. The mother or elder brother or sister, or whoever else is paying any attention to the infant, masturbates him to calm him down. This is merely a distraction and does not help to build the child's ego, for it is no more than an absentminded gesture.

In the primary institutions of Alor child feeding, there is no possibility of production of a parental image as a reliever of tensions. The intermittent appearance of the mother makes of her a tantalizing object who gives but inadequately the satisfactions so desperately needed.

Early childhood illnesses are indifferently treated and are aggravated by rough handling and irritating medication. The child learns to walk without assistance or encouragement. Again no one is available to enter into a relationship eliciting trust and dependence in response to receiving security and abetment. Defecation and urination are not brought under any particular coercive control. In this respect, Alorese child neglect is of a slight psychological benefit to the growing child. No anal eroticism is produced.

When weaning comes, the rejection of the child by its mother and mother substitutes, while not abrupt, is damaging. The breast-seeking child is pushed away or slapped. Then jealousy and rage are deliberately evoked by taking another child to the breast. Food is promised but not given. The adults think this is very funny.

These are the main lines of the primary institutions. What is the basic personality structure?

As children the Alorese are shy and reserved—they do not expect favorable response—but they readily fly into tantrums and become vituperative. Because they cannot obtain their desires or rewards in a direct way, they steal and forage as a regular thing. Aggression becomes canalized and predatory. The child, in turn, may reject his family by running away from home to live with some more remote relative.

This is the most extreme gesture of defiance and independence that the child is permitted and offers both a safety valve for pent-up aggressions and an opportunity to sustain the hope that the child may find in one of its other relatives the long-sought-for kind parent.[39]

None of the childhood patterns builds toward emotional solidarity within the family.

The ego development and social conscience of the adult are very weak. There is little self-confidence or sense of responsibility to others or to society. The adult male's relations to women are a projection of his almost complete defeat, as a child, in his relations to his mother. Husband-to-wife relations are bitter and nonintimate. Woman is the economic provider, and the male is dependent upon her. He cannot really dominate her. Compensation is found in the elaborate activity of loans and exchanges, the functions of which are essentially to gratify the psychological rather than the production-consumption needs of the economy.

Warfare and religious institutions in Alor bear quite clearly the impress of the projective system. War is disorganized, fitful, and vengeful. Religion falls within the category of ancestor worship, as is characteristic of the cultures of this part of the world. But the ancestors are neither exalted nor revered. Their powers for good are not exaggerated, and the Alorese feel no desire to assuage them by suffering or renunciation in their names. Because there is no interest in, possibility of, or benefit to be derived from getting back in their good graces, there is no restitution by penance. One expects no more from the ancestral gods than one expects from parents.

Ancestors, however, want to be fed. Their descendants' failure to feed the gods makes them angry—failure to feed the child was the supreme frustration. Angry gods punish their descendants. With great reluctance and only under the duress of misfortune, the Alorese make sacrificial food offerings to the ancestral spirits.

Religious art is careless and slipshod. Gods are projected "fathers" and "mothers." With no idealization of parents in the culture, there is no idealization of the gods. Representative carvings of ancestral deities are carelessly made, perfunctorily used, and quickly discarded. The dead are projections of the powerful and insistent creditors who bedevil adult life. In short:

The basic personality in Alor is anxious, suspicious, mistrustful, lacking in confidence, with no interest in the outer world. There is no capacity to idealize the parental image or deity. The personality is devoid of enterprise, is filled with repressed hatred and free floating aggression over which constant vigilance must be exercised. The personality is devoid of high aspirations and has no basis for the internalization of discipline. Individuals so constituted must spend most of their energy protecting themselves against each other's hostility. Cooperation must be at a low level and a tenuous social cohesion can be achieved only by dominance-submission attitudes, not by affection and mutual trust.[40]

Alor is a society with an old culture. It has survived for quite some time. This means that

[39]A. Kardiner et al., *The Psychological Frontiers of Society*, p. 156.

[40]*Ibid.*, p. 170.

it has made the necessary minimal adjustments to the physical and biological imperatives. Yet that it is a precarious adjustment cannot be doubted; the continuance of the society must hang on a very thin thread. One of its strengths has been that the protection of island isolation has sealed it off from too much external competition.

As an object lesson in the interaction of culture upon personality and of personality upon culture, however, it is superb.[41]

The Whiting-Child Theory and Correlational Method   J. W. M. Whiting, Harvard anthropologist, and I. L. Child, Yale psychologist, have combined Kardinerian-Freudian theory; the learning theory of Dollard and Miller, Skinner, Hull, and others; and the cross-cultural statistical techniques of G. P. Murdock to produce a different and an intriguing approach in *Child Training and Personality*. Although many hypotheses derived from psychoanalytic thought are used in this theory, the emphasis of the approach is on hypothesis testing—something in which psychoanalysis has been weak. The data for testing the hypotheses are drawn from the Human Relations Area Files (page 73).

Essentially, Whiting and Child set the following propositions:

1. Child training is universal: "In all societies the helpless infant . . . must be changed into a responsible adult obeying the rules of his society."[42]

2. Societies differ in their rules and in their methods of teaching conformity to the rules. These differences have differential personality effects.

3. Specific qualities of personality effects are projected on adult institutions and influence their content.

So far, this is no different from Kardinerian theory. Now behavioral theory comes in.

4. Adults reward responses that correspond to culturally established patterns of behavior. Positive sanctioning (positive reinforcement) increases the tendency to repeat the approved response. Responses that do not correspond to culturally established patterns of behavior are not rewarded and may be punished. Negative sanctioning (negative reinforcement) decreases the tendency to repeat the unapproved response.

5. The intensity of negative sanctions and the ages at which they are applied contribute to socialization anxiety. Approved responses bring drive reduction or satisfaction. Because they are rewarded, each successful repetition intensifies the satisfaction potential of the behavior.

6. Excessive frustration or excessive gratification in socialization results in negative or positive fixation. Fixation means that events of a certain kind have greater or lesser psychological importance for someone who has had the fixating experience than for someone who has not.

7. Illness is anxiety-producing. Explanations of illness, or causes to which illness is usually attributed, are fantasy-colored by projection of fixations customarily established in the members of a given society by child-training experience.

For example, oral fixations will produce such "causes" of illness as eating and drinking (especially "poisonous" foods) or curses and other magical spells. Anal fixations will generate explanations of illness in terms of failure to hide one's feces or other personal waste.

A number of special hypotheses were refined for testing. The method consisted in giving numerical values on a scale of rating for degree of severity of socialization of oral, anal, sexual, dependent, and aggressive behaviors. This was done wherever possible for fifty selected societies. (Interestingly enough, middle-class practices in Chicago, which represented the United States in the sample, rated very high in severity and low in indul-

[41]In this context, the analysis of the Mandan Indian Okipa ceremony, given in Chap. 29, is relevant.
[42]J. W. M. Whiting and I. L. Child, *Child Training and Personality*, p. 63.

gence in virtually every measure of early child training. Americans, it seems, are severe with, and demanding of, their children.) Each society was also classed, if the data warranted it, as *having* or *not having* oral, anal, sexual, dependent, or aggressive explanations for illness. Correlations were statistically derived between negative and positive fixations on the one hand and type of "disease theory" on the other.

The study established high correlations for the effect of severe, or negative, sanctions in producing illness projections. Positive fixations were not shown to be effective in influencing adult theory of disease causation.

Additional Social and Cultural Correlates of Child-training Practices Extensions and modification of the Whiting-Child theory and method have subsequently been worked upon by Whiting and his associates, as well as by independent investigators.

Games John M. Roberts and Brian Sutton-Smith have studied the occurrence of types of games relative to quality of child-training practices in a cross-cultural sample of fifty-six societies. Tribal societies possessing *games of strategy* (in which the outcome is the product of rational choice among several courses of action) are societies which emphasize and reward obedience, while punishing disobedience on the part of children. Such societies are relatively more complex in culture and social organization. Societies with a cultural emphasis on *games requiring physical performance skills* pay less attention to obedience in child training while rewarding achievement. Societies in which preadolescent children are shouldered with the responsibility of tending their younger siblings show a cultural preference for *games of chance.*

Games provide models for cultural participation. Strategy games prepare one for finding one's way in a complex cultural setting, while the associated child training conditions one to role conformity. Games of physi-

cal skill prepare one for individual initiative and extroverted activity and are indicated as linked to hunting types of societies. Games of chance take control of life out of the hands of the player, whose role is passive.

The studies also show that, across the board, "[T]here are consistent differences cross-culturally in the training of boys and girls. Boys, for example, are given higher achievement training, while girls are given more consistent obedience and responsibility training."[43]

Parental Rejection and Adult Personality Traits A recent cross-cultural statistical study by R. P. Rohner indicates that parental rejection of children, as manifest in an absence of doing things to please the child, enjoying it, playing, singing, plus other failures to exhibit warmth and affection, generates children who are "anxious, hostile, insecure, and who devaluate their feelings of self-worth." Further, "adults who were rejected as children tend to devaluate their feelings of self-esteem and self-adequacy (low self-evaluation) . . . to be dependent, emotionally unresponsive and to evaluate the world negatively, . . . lacking in generosity."[44] Whether children are deprived of food, or fed generously, is indicated not to be a major correlate of the type of personality syndrome indicated above.

Evaluation of the Whiting-Child Method This method stands or falls on the true randomness of the ethnographic sample on which any particular study rests and on the validity of the value-rating judgments (coding) made by the evaluators of the descriptive ethnographic reports. The evaluations are usually subjective and often rest on inadequate ethnographic data. Yet the judgments are

[43]J. M. Roberts and B. Sutton-Smith, "Child Training and Game Involvement" (*Ethnography,* vol. 1, 1962), p. 176.
[44]R. P. Rohner, "Parental Rejection, Food Deprivation, and Personality Development: Tests of Alternative Hypotheses" (*Ethnography,* vol. 9, 1970), p. 421.

processed as though they were "hard" quantitative units. Those who feel that a science must have numbers applaud the effort. Those who are skeptical of the value of the results are apt to think of it as "the method of putative precision." It does, however, produce a provocative new look at the materials.

SUMMARY

Culture is essentially a human phenomenon. Other creatures are capable of some cultural behavior on a very elemental scale, but only man creates and utilizes symbolic conceptualizations (the essence of culture) on a massive, systematic, and continuous scale.

A culture is not a thing, nor is it a precise entity. Nevertheless, it is conceived of as having an existence and as being distinctive. It is expressed in individual behavior and exists only in the actions of people. Yet it transcends the individual, for the culture according to which the individual lives existed before his birth and continues its existence after his death. It consists not only of all the learned behavior manifested by the members of a society but also of patterns *for* the behavior of members of a society. Language and symbolism are major attributes of all cultures.

Anthropology demonstrates the vast range of behavior of which human beings have proved themselves capable. Yet no society could exist if its members were to indulge in all these behaviors. Some are directly contradictory to others and consequently are incompatible. Aside from this, sheer diversity of possible actions would make behavior so unpredictable that social conditions would be chaotic. To organize people's activities, the establishment of major lines of standardized behavior is a social imperative. Thus cultures are selecting and limiting.

Integration, the establishment of internal consistency in norms, is also an essential characteristic of cultures. Integration is achieved with reference to certain basic propositions or postulates about the nature of things and acts and about their goodness or badness.

The formulation of a culture by the anthropologist is a *construct,* an abstraction from the *real culture,* which itself can be perceived only partially. The *ideal culture* is a people's formulation of the standards of behavior it believes should prevail.

The components of culture are *culture traits, culture complexes,* and *institutions.* They are also identified as *universals, alternatives, specialties,* and *idiosyncrasies.* The elements and complexes of a culture are functional in that each part tends to be related to the others in ways which contribute to the operation of the whole culture. The differing ways in which variant culture traits are related to one another lend to each culture its configuration.

Culture consists of set solutions to problems; it is the major adaptive device used by man.

Society and culture must not be confused. A society is people: a population which occupies an identifiable space. The relations of its members are culturally patterned and distinct from those of other societies, and its members are emotionally bonded by common linguistic and other forms of symbolic representations. If a society is to survive, its culture must satisfy certain functional prerequisites.

The personality of the individual is analogous to the culture of a society in that it is a sum of integrated behavior traits. The bodily constitution, physical environment, culture, and unique personal experience, as reacted to by the individual, combine to produce the total personality.

Enculturation encompasses all the processes by means of which the individual learns to internalize the norms of his culture.

Basic drives result from biological needs that must be met. All cultures provide means of satisfactory drive reduction by presenting patterns for goal achievement. The growing individual must learn to adapt his behavior to the expectancies of his society and to its peculiarities. The person who fails in this is a deviant and, under mental stress, may become neurotic or psychopathic. Mental abnormality, however, is a relative thing.

Ruth Benedict showed how *ideal personality types* reflect differing configurations of culture. Abram Kardiner developed the concept of *basic personality structure*, a modal personality syndrome developed in response to child-training practices. Secondary institutions are held to be in part projections of basic personality structures.

A recent trend in anthropology has been to attempt to establish statistical correlations between formal aspects of culture and cultural features of child training and experience.

SELECTED READINGS

Aberle, D. F., *The Psychological Analysis of a Hopi Life-history* (Comparative Psychological Monographs, vol. 211, no. 107, 1951). A systematic interpretation in terms of general personality and culture theory of what took place in the life history of Sun Chief, the Hopi Indian whose autobiography was edited by L. Simmons (see below). Aberle's contribution is highly suggestive of illuminating examples. It should be read in connection with *Sun Chief.*

Barnouw, V., *Culture and Personality* (1963). Useful as a general introduction to what has been done in the field and the methods that are used in relation to theory.

Benedict, R., *Patterns of Culture* (1934). The classic formulation of the idea of cultural configuration in relation to ideal personality types. Persuasively written in fine literary style, it should not be taken as a reliable ethnography of the cultures discussed, although its major theme is acceptable.

Haring, D. (ed.), *Personal Character and Cultural Milieu* (2d ed., 1956). A well-balanced anthology of technical papers written by professionals for professional reading. It will be hard going for the beginning student, but it is rewarding for those who want to go further into the subject.

Kardiner, A., et al., *The Psychological Frontiers of Society* (1945). Contains a general statement of the Kardinerian theory, with description and analysis of the Comanche, Alorese, and a midwestern United States community.

Kroeber, A. L., and C. Kluckhohn, *Culture: A Critical Review of Concepts and Definitions* (Papers of the Peabody Museum of American Archaeology and Ethnology, Harvard University, vol. 47, 1952). An encyclopedic survey and analysis of the concept of culture. Possibly not of much interest to the beginner, but a very useful guide nonetheless. Now available in a paperback edition (1964).

Mead, M., *Male and Female* (1949). Dr. Mead's provocative summing up of the interplay of culture and individual psychology in the shaping of men and women in seven primitive societies and the United States.

———, and M. Wolfenstein (eds.), *Childhood in Contemporary Cultures* (1955). Applies culture and personality theory to growing up in a number of contemporary societies. Includes a number of interesting chapters.

Middleton, J. (ed.), *From Child to Adult* (1970). Contains selected articles on enculturation and education in a variety of societies, mostly primitive.

Opler, M. K., *Culture, Psychiatry and Human Values* (1956). Mental illness and culture expertly interrelated.

Simmons, L., *Sun Chief: The Autobiography of a Hopi Indian* (1942). A fascinatingly rich and revealing document of personal experience. Not only does it give the inside view of what it means to grow up as a Hopi, but it also lays bare the severe personal conflicts caused by the need to integrate a single personality while living under two incompatible cultures.

Singer, M., "Culture: The Concept of Culture" (International Encyclopedia of the Social Sciences, vol. 3, 1968), pp. 527–543. Summarizes and compares the competing theories of culture and social structure in anthropology.

Spuhler, J. N.: *The Evolution of Man's Capacity for Culture* (1959). A symposium discussing factors relating to the development of the capacity to create and maintain culture.

Whiting, J. W. M., and I. L. Child, *Child Training and Personality* (1953). Spells out the theory, method, data, and results of their application of the correlational technique and use of cross-cultural data.

Chapter 3

Anthropology: Its Growth and Methods

Anthropology as an organized body of knowledge, with a theory and with a corps of specialized thinkers, is now in its second century, for it may be said to have been born in the decade following 1860. The seeds of anthropology were planted during the Renaissance in Europe; then followed a long period of germination during the fifteenth and sixteenth centuries. The roots were formed during the seventeenth and eighteenth centuries, as the age of discovery resulted in growing curiosity, on the part of European political philosophers, concerning the meaning of the many strange societies of uncivilized men that explorers and travelers were encountering. Philosophies of history were popular during this period. Then, during the first half of the nineteenth century, something that could be differentiated from philosophies of history began to take shape, until, between 1860 and 1871, anthropology emerged full-flowered as an eagerly cultivated field in its own right.

In 1860 appeared Bastian's first book; in 1861 Maine's *Ancient Law* and Bachofen's *Mutterrecht.* The burst in the first dozen years was phenomenal: Jacob Burckhardt, 1860; Fustel de Coulanges's *Ancient City,* 1864; McLennan's *Primitive Marriage,* 1865; Tylor's *Researches,* 1865; Lubbuck's *Origin of Civilization,* 1870; Morgan's *Systems of Consanguinity,* 1871; Tylor's *Primitive Culture,* 1871.[1]

By the turn of the twentieth century, great anthropological collections had been established in the major museums of natural history, chairs of anthropology were being established in various universities, and an-

thropological societies were flourishing in England, on the Continent, and in the United States. Systematic fieldwork in ethnology and archaeology was well under way. Professional journals devoted to anthropology were firmly established. The nineteenth-century

Fig. 3-A Illustration from the Florentine Codex. (From Bernardo de Sahagun, General History of the Things of New Spain: The Florentine Codex. *Translated by Arthur J. O. Anderson and Charles E. Dibble. Published by The School of American Research and The University of Utah. Illustration from Book IV. Copyright 1957 by the University of Utah)*

---

[1] A. L. Kroeber, "The History and Present Orientation of Cultural Anthropology: 1950," in *The Nature of Culture,* p. 144.

evolutionary edifices of Tylor, Morgan, Frazer, and others were being subjected to serious critical challenge, as the young science showed signs of maturing in methods and thought.

The years between 1900 and 1925 marked the period of Boasian historical reconstructionism in the anthropology of the United States and of diffusion theory and research in Germany and Austria. In France, this was the period when the foundations of functionalism and the social structure approaches to anthropology were being laid by Émile Durkheim and his associates. During these decades, ethnographic fieldwork techniques were perfected and modern anthropology reached its first phase of maturity.

From 1930 to 1940, functionalism as developed by Bronislaw Malinowski and A. R. Radcliffe-Brown dominated the scene in both Britain and the United States. Anthropology was temporarily destroyed in Germany by the Nazi terror and, except for prehistoric studies, was more or less dormant in France. The old Boasian movement in the United States was being transformed by the infusion of psychological interests, wedded to functionalism. The years following World War II brought a veritable explosion of anthropology around the world, not only in terms of professional developments but also in the areas of university response, public interest, and practical applications of anthropological findings.

This chapter traces the main outlines of the course of this growth and development, not by spelling out each and every happening or by discussing every contributor to anthropology, but by dealing only with movements that have had a major influence on anthropology today. The final chapter of this book will undertake to look to the future.

Anthropology in Classical Thought

Anthropology is one branch of knowledge that does not claim to have its origin among the Greeks. The Greeks, to be sure, were much interested in social organization, especially in political structure, but their thought on the subject was philosophically concerned with ideal systems, and they had little interest in studying living social and cultural systems or in comparing the ways in which various societies actually dealt with human problems. As noted by John Rowe: ". . . [T]he ancient Greeks for the most part held that the way to understand ourselves is to study ourselves, while what others do is irrelevant."[2] In their exuberant discovery of the potentials of the human mind for intellectual and artistic expression, the Greeks denied that there was anything to be learned from "barbarians," the non-Greeks. All their wisdom notwithstanding, they had not grasped "the essence of the anthropological point of view is that in order to understand ourselves we need to study others."[3] Herodotus (484–425? B.C.), it is true, is sometimes credited with being the father of anthropology because of his comments on customs of peoples other than the Greeks in the fifth century B.C., but his observations were neither systematic nor firsthand. They seem to be derived mostly from Persian sources, but of these no original documents remain.

Tacitus (*ca.* A.D. 55–120), a Roman historian living five hundred years after Herodotus, wrote a tract on the origin and locality of the Germans that is much referred to as an early ethnography, and it does stand out as a rare, early source of some anthropological significance.

Herodotus and Tacitus notwithstanding, there was no body of literature and no systematic thought or discourse concerned with societies of the outer world; indeed, there appears to have been very little interest in such societies. There is little basis for a claim that anthropology had its origins in classical antiquity.

[2]J. H. Rowe, "The Renaissance Foundations of Anthropology" (*American Anthropologist*, vol. 67, 1965), p. 2.
[3]*Idem.*

Anthropology in the Age of Reason

Anthropology is a child of the Enlightenment. The Renaissance did not give birth to anthropology per se, but it did establish a comparative point of view. Renaissance man looked to the past rather than to contemporary primitives, but:

The Renaissance scholars . . . treated antiquity as a different world from the one they knew, remote but accessible to all through its literature and its monuments. The Renaissance education of their time spread the view that the ancients were both different and worthy of study. Men trained in this tradition were better prepared than any of their predecessors to observe and record contemporary cultural differences when the opportunity presented itself.[4]

The opportunity came with the opening of the New World by Columbus's discovery of America and the subsequent exploratory voyages that girdled the globe. For many decades, the journals of explorers and the accounts of the more literate conquistadores —such as Bernal Diaz del Castillo, who fought with Cortez and left vivid pictures of Mexico and the Aztecs as he saw them in 1519, and Cook and Bougainville, who wrote many descriptive passages dealing with peoples of the Pacific—provided fragmentary and episodic accounts of diverse races and customs and set men to further thinking. Such bits and snippets of information did not constitute "anthropology," but they did stir men's minds. The *Jesuit Relations*, a vast body of reports from the Jesuit fathers working in North and South America which covers a century and three-quarters, from 1610 to 1791, contains much material of ethnographic interest in its seventy-three published volumes. This, too, was cumulative grist for the anthropological mill, but it was not yet anthropology.

Nonetheless, the first true anthropology was done by two Catholic missionaries, the first a Spanish Franciscan, Fray Bernadino de Sahagun (1499–1590), who worked in Mex-

ico between 1529 and 1549, and the second a French Jesuit, Joseph-François Lafitau (1681–1746), who worked at the Jesuit mission of Sault Saint Louis among the Iroquois and the Hurons of western New York.

Sahagun's *General History of Things in New Spain* Tenochtitlán, the capital city of the Aztecs, was destroyed in 1521. Sahagun arrived eight years later to participate in the conversion of the Indians of Mexico. Before long he was engaged in a full-fledged ethnographic scheme to record the beliefs and customs of the Aztecs in a systematic manner. He trained young Aztecs of the nobility— those who would have become Aztec priests under the old order—to write their native tongue, Nahuatl, in Spanish script. He himself traveled about questioning local informants, who provided answers, accompanied by hieroglyphic paintings in the old Aztec manner. With the glyphs as the framework of a codex, he pursued his questions with his "research assistants," who carefully wrote out the answers in their native tongue, recording a true "inside view" of Aztec culture.

The Florentine Codex The text covers a diverse range of subjects, one after the other: "The Gods"; "The Ceremonies"; "The Origin of the Gods"; "Soothsayers and Omens"; "The Sun, Moon, and the Stars"; "The Binding of the Years"; "Kings and Lords"; "The Merchants"; "The People"; "The Conquest of Mexico." The book on "the people" spells out the ideal role performances for every kinship status and all other recognized statuses in Aztec society, and it describes their polar opposites by detailing the traits of the "bad" performer in each status. (See pages 45–46, above.) Parallel to the Nahuatl text, Sahagun added his own loose, running Spanish translation and commentary. The range and details of material are remarkably rich and fascinatingly objective, a trait which we admire today but which was not well received by Sahagun's superiors at home. Publication of the codex was suppressed; then it was lost or forgotten, at last to be rediscovered after nearly three hundred years. Only between 1947 and 1965 was the translation of the full Nahuatl text undertaken and this unique gift made available to modern anthropology.[5]

In the century following Sahagun, many Spanish chroniclers wrote on the customs and government of the conquered Indian nations. Some of these were official "intelligence" reports, and some were the products of personal scholarship. Of all, the four-volume *Historia del Nuevo Mundo*, written between 1650 and 1660 by the Jesuit, Father Bernabé Cobo, is judged most useful, being both clear and accurate in content and scientific in its approach.[6] Ethnography was gaining definite substance, but it was still far from becoming a reliable and orderly discipline.

Sahagun's work is straight, descriptive ethnography of a high order but contains no reflective analysis of Aztec customs or society. As a matter of fact, the good priest, who undoubtedly had his eye on the Inquisition, would not have dared to make a dispassionate analysis of Aztec usage even had he been so inclined. For the record, he declared: "My tears fall like hailstones as I think on the multitude of lies by which people here in New Spain were led into error."[7] It was, he said, the work of Satan.

Lafitau's Comparative Ethnology Father Lafitau wrote a century later, in France, in a different religious and cultural climate. His work is a continuation of Renaissance classical interests carried forward with new information. The very title of his book bespeaks his intent and purpose. Lafitau's two-volume

work was published in Paris in 1724 and was called *Moeurs des sauvages Ameriquains, comparées aux moeurs des premiers temps* [Customs of the American savages, compared with customs of early times]. Just as Greece and Rome represented an earlier stage of civilization than eighteenth-century Europe, so too, he reasoned, the cultures of the Hurons and the Iroquois represent an even earlier condition of mankind. Evolutionary theory was taking shape.

Three Anthropological Principles Lafitau gave clear expression to three additional principles that have since become basic in anthropology: (1) contemporary primitive cultures throw light on ancient cultures, and vice versa; (2) possible historic relations between cultures cannot be speculatively established but are determinable only on the basis of careful content analysis that demonstrates significant similarity of specific traits; and (3) alien cultures must be evaluated on the basis of the total conditions under which they operate, not in terms of European standards (the principle of cultural relativity).[8]

How far a cry from the cultural snobbery of Greece and the dogmatic intolerance of Sahagun's Spain! Lafitau's mind was cleared for new thinking, and thinking anew, he could see facts to which men had previously been blind. So it was that he discovered the Iroquoian form of bifurcate-merging kinship system. His powers of ethnographic observation and description were notable, and the example given by Sol Tax is worthy of reproduction:

Among the Iroquois and the Hurons, all the children of a Cabin [long house] regard their mothers' sisters as their mothers, and their mothers' brothers as their uncles; in the same way they give the name of father to all their fathers' brothers and that of aunt to their fathers' sisters. All of the children on the side of the mother and her sisters and of the

[5]See C. E. Dibble and A. J. O. Anderson, *Florentine Codex: General History of the Things of New Spain* (in thirteen parts).
[6]J. H. Rowe, "Inca Culture at the Time of the Conquest," in J. H. Steward (ed.), *Handbook of South American Indians*, vol. 2, p. 194. See *ibid.*, pp. 192–197, for a critical evaluation of a number of early sources on Inca culture and history, for example.
[7]Dibble and Anderson, *op. cit.*, part II, p. 46.

[8]See W. N. Fenton, "J.-F. Lafitau (1681–1746), Precursor of Scientific Anthropology" (*Southwestern Journal of Anthropology*, vol. 25, 1969), pp. 173–187.

father and his brothers they regard as equal to brothers and sisters, but as regards the children of their uncles and aunts—that is to say, of their mothers' brothers and their fathers' sisters—they treat them only on the footing of cousins although they may be as closely related as those whom they regard as brothers and sisters. In the third generation the grand-uncles and grand-aunts become grandfathers and grandmothers of the children of those whom they call nephews and nieces. This continues always in the descending line according to the same rule.[9]

Robertson's Evolutionary Ethnology By the middle of the eighteenth century, the idea of a developmental progression of human society had wholly seized the minds of enlightened rationalists in Europe and North America. Voltaire, Montesquieu, Montaigne, and Condorcet, in France, and Hobbes, Hume, and Locke, in England, had all built political philosophies or philosophies of history on the comparative contrast of primitive societies and the current state of sociopolitical development. They used ethnographic data as arguments to buttress their social theories, but they did not contribute to the development of an anthropology except as they further improved the climate of thought that would nourish it.

The first modern, systematic anthropological theorist is not one of these more famous people, but the Scottish historian William Robertson (1721–1793). Robertson's *History of America*, first published in 1777, is not a good ethnography of the American Indians, but it advanced a remarkably rational and surprisingly sophisticated anthropological theory and methodology. He, not Morgan or Tylor, is the first modern formulator of cultural evolutionism and cultural determinism in systematic terms.

In common with the thought of the En-

lightenment, Robertson accepted the comparative evolution of human *society* as the essential fact of primary importance. In explanation of his concern with the American Indians, he wrote:

In order to complete the history of the human mind, and attain to a perfect knowledge of its nature and operations, we must contemplate man in all those various situations wherein he has been placed. We must follow him in his progress through the different stages of society as he gradually advances from the infant state of civil life towards its maturity and decline.[10]

Three Stages of Evolution In the organization of his material, Robertson used three stages of evolutionary typology: savagery, barbarism, and civilization, in ascendant order. Savages do not have writing, metals, domesticated animals, he noted, thus treating most of the New World tribes under the rubric of savagery.

In tracing the line by which nations proceed towards civilization, the discovery of the useful metals, and the acquisition of dominion over the animal creation, have been marked as steps of capital importance in their progress. In our continent [the Old World], long after men had attained both, society continued in that state which is denominated barbarous. Even with all that command over nature which these confer, many ages elapse, before industry becomes so regular as to render subsistence secure, before the arts which apply the wants and furnish the accommodations of life are brought to any considerable degree of perfection, and before any idea is conceived of various institutions requisite in a well-ordered society.[11]

Archaeological Evidence Robertson clearly enunciated the fundamental importance and priority of subsistence technology over other aspects of culture, which modern evolutionists and ecologists are apt to treat as a discovery of Morgan, Tylor, Marx, and White. Nor was his long-range view of human development derived from speculative philosophy. Robertson was acquainted with archaeo-

[9]J. F. Lafitau, *Moeurs des sauvages amériquaines*, vol. 1, pp. 552–553. Quoted and translated by S. Tax, "From Lafitau to Radcliffe-Brown: A Short History of Social Organization," in F. Eggan (ed.), *Social Anthropology of North American Tribes* (enlarged ed.), pp.445–446.

[10]W. Robertson, *The History of America*, vol. 2, p. 262.
[11]*Ibid.*, p. 176.

logical fact and explicitly recognized the significance of prehistoric stone artifacts a half century before Boucher de Perthes rocked Europe with his Abbevillian discoveries (see page 150). He gave temporal priority to lithic cultures over bronze and iron cultures three-quarters of a century before European prehistorians worked out the sequence in detail.

It is a doubtful point, whether the dominion of man over the animal creation, or his acquiring the use of metals, has contributed most to extend his power. The era of this important discovery is unknown, and in our hemisphere very remote. It is only by tradition, or by digging up some rude instruments of our forefathers, that we learn that mankind were originally unacquainted with the use of metals, and endeavored to supply the want of them by employing flints, shells, bones, and other hard substances, for the same purposes which metals serve among polished nations. Nature completes the formation of some metals. Gold, silver, and copper . . . were accordingly the first metals known, and first applied to use. But iron, the most serviceable of all, and to which man is most indebted, is never discovered in its perfect form; its gross and stubborn ore must feel twice the force of fire, and go through two laborious processes, before it becomes fit for use. Man was long acquainted with the other metals, before he acquired the art of fabricating iron, or attained such ingenuity as to perfect an invention, to which he is indebted for those instruments wherewith he subdues the earth, and commands all its inhabitants.[12]

Parallelism Robertson also established the principle of parallelism for use in evolutionary theory:

The character and occupations of the hunter in America must be little different from those of an Asiatic, who depends for subsistence on the chase. A tribe of savages on the banks of the Danube must nearly resemble one upon the plain washed by the Mississippi. Instead then of presuming from this similarity, that there is any affinity between them, we should only conclude, that the disposition and manners of men are formed by their situation, and

arise from the state of society in which they live. The moment that begins to vary, the character of a people must change.[13]

In addition, with perfect logical induction, Robertson predicted from known zoological and ethnographic facts the discovery that the Bering Strait had been used to cross from the Old World to the New, and it was his theory that the American Indians had come from Asia by way of Siberia.

Cultural Determinism In explaining behavioral differences among different peoples, Robertson discarded racism, which was the common explanation of cultural differences during his time and which, unfortunately, still is today in many quarters. His statement of enculturation expresses the fundamental postulates of cultural determinism in modern personality and culture theory:

A human being as he comes originally from the hand of nature, is everywhere the same. At his first appearance in the state of infancy, whether it be among the rudest savages, or in the most civilized nations, we can discern no quality which marks any distinction or superiority. The capacity of improvement seems to be the same and the talents he may afterwards acquire, as well as the virtues he may be rendered capable of exercising, depend, in a great measure, upon the state of society in which he is placed. To this state his mind naturally accommodates itself, and from it receives discipline and culture. . . . It is only by attending to this great principle, that we can discover what is the character of man in every different period of his progress.[14]

Finally, he contrasted the world views, personalities, and social institutions of the Aztecs and the Incas in terms of their distinctive "national character,"[15] the very words reintroduced into American anthropology after World War II in relation to such work as that of Benedict on Japan and of Mead and other personality and culture specialists as applied to modern nations.

---

[13]*Ibid.,* vol. 1, pp. 249–250.
[14]*Ibid.,* vol. 1, pp. 368–369.
[15]See *ibid.,* vol. 2, pp. 206–227.

[12]*Ibid.,* vol. 1, pp. 309–311.

With William Robertson, Presbyterian minister, principal of the University of Edinburgh, and Historiographer to His Majesty for Scotland, one can say that cultural anthropology was finally born.

Nineteenth-century Evolutionists

Archaeology moved ahead more rapidly than ethnology during the first half of the nineteenth century. Then, in 1860, ethnology suddenly came to life with a vigor that has never diminished.[16]

The great figures in the creative development of anthropology between 1860 and 1900 were, first and foremost, the evolutionist Sir Edward Tylor (1832–1917), Sir Henry Maine (1822–1888), and Sir James Frazer (1854–1941), in England; Lewis Henry Morgan (1818–1881), in the United States; and Johann Bachofen (1815–1887), in Switzerland. There were numerous lesser figures who played significant roles, but these were the master builders who shaped the growing subject during its early years.[17]

Charles Robert Darwin: *Origin of Species*
The *Origin of Species* (1859) is in no sense a work in anthropology, but it should be clear from the discussion to follow in Part 2 that it has had a profound and ever-increasing influence on anthropology. It established man's natural place in the biological world and confirmed the proposition of the Enlightenment that mankind is struggling upward from a primitive antiquity. The *Origin of Species* established the continuity of all life and demonstrated how natural selection working upon inheritable variations results in adaptive modifications in life forms, which in turn lead through speciation to radiating evolution. Although Darwin reserved his exploration of man in evolution for a second book, *Descent of Man* (1871), the *Origin of Species* made it clear that man is the product of biological evolution just as technology, the arts, and society are the products of cultural evolution. Even Robertson had been content to accept the biblical story of Genesis as "infallible certainty," but after Darwin this would never be true again of any anthropologist of major stature. He made it possible for prehistoric studies and zoological analysis to move forward to parallel the development of cultural anthropology.

It is amply clear that Darwin *did not* supply the idea for cultural evolution and that he cannot be credited with starting the great anthropological outburst of the decade that followed the *Origin of Species*. Bastian, Morgan, Maine, and Tylor were well along with their works when Darwin's epoch-making study appeared. Morgan and Tylor were clearly building on Robertson (although neither appears to have so acknowledged), and even Darwin attributed his inspirational stimulus to Thomas Malthus (1766–1834), who cited Robertson extensively in the three-volume second edition of his *Essay on the Principle of Population* (1803). Nonetheless, Darwin's stimulus clearly quickened the movement to work out in detail just how human societies did evolve. But more important for anthropology in the long run was the establishment by Darwin of man as a subject within the rubric of natural science. It was this fact which gave anthropology such a strong place in the developing museums of natural history and which turned cultural anthropology from a loose philosophy of history into an empirical science.

[16]For a review of the significant ethnographic developments that were occurring in the United States prior to 1860, see A. I. Hallowell, "The Beginnings of Anthropology in America," in F. de Laguna (ed.), *Selected Papers from the American Anthropologist: 1888–1920*, pp. 1–55.

[17]For discussions of some of the secondary figures, see H. R. Hays, *From Ape to Angel: An Informal History of Social Anthropology*, part I; and T. K. Penniman, *A Hundred Years of Anthropology* (rev. ed.), chap. 4. Nor should N. O. Lurie, "Women in Early American Anthropology," in J. Helm (ed.), *Pioneers of American Anthropology*, pp. 29–82, be overlooked.

Lewis Henry Morgan: *Ancient Society*   Morgan (1818–1881) and Tylor are the preeminent figures of nineteenth-century cultural evolutionism. Of the two, Morgan made the broader contributions and may be considered first. As a young lawyer in upstate New York, he converted his literary society into the New Confederation of the Iroquois at the inspiration of his Iroquois friend Ely Parker (later a general in the Union Army and a Grand Sachem of the League of the Iroquois). An amateur naturalist who had published a classic ethological study, *The American Beaver,* he became an ethnographer, and ultimately produced a very professional and enduring monograph on the Iroquois tribe in 1851.[18] Rediscovering the Iroquois classificatory system of kinship terminology, he sent comprehensive questionnaires on kinship around the world to get the comparative data which he presented in his monumental *Systems of Consanguinity of the Human Family* (1861), thus starting anthropologists on their favorite passion—the study of kinship systems and social structure. In the meantime, he turned his legal contacts into entrepreneurial capitalism and made a small fortune in railroad building and iron mining, whereupon he gave up law and business to become a full-time ethnologist and successful defender of Iroquois land rights.[19]

Lineal Evolutionary Theory   Morgan expanded his explanation of classificatory kinship systems as survivals of earlier stages of social organization so that it became a full-fledged evolutionary account entitled *Ancient Society, or Researches in the Lines of Human Progress from Savagery through Barbarism to Civilization* (1877). His thesis was well summed up in his own words:

Commencing, then, with the Australians and Polynesians, following with the American Indian tribes, and concluding with the Roman and Grecian, who afford the highest exemplifications respectively of the six great stages of human progress, the sum of their united experiences may be supposed fairly to represent that of the human family from the Middle Status of savagery to the end of ancient civilization. . . . So essentially identical are the arts, institutions, and mode of life in the same status upon all continents, that the archaic form of the principal domestic institutions of the Greeks and Romans must even now be sought in the corresponding institutions of the American aborigines. . . . This fact forms a part of the accumulating evidence tending to show that . . . the course and manner of their development was predetermined, as well as restricted within narrow limits of divergence, by the natural logic of the human mind and the necessary limitations of its powers.[20]

The essence of lineal evolution as summed up by Morgan is as follows: (1) Culture evolves in successive stages, which are (2) essentially the same in all parts of the world, from which (3) it is to be inferred that the order of the stages is inevitable and their content limited because (4) mental processes are universally similar among all peoples (that is, there is a psychic unity of man). In other words, when confronted with the conditions of stage A, men universally respond by inventing the cultural forms of stage B, in reaction to which they then produce stage C, and so forth through the ages. The only difference is in the rate of speed with which they move through the several stages.

Morgan took Robertson's three stages of savagery, barbarism, and civilization and elaborated on them by dividing savagery and barbarism into three substages each (lower, middle, and higher). He then identified specific technological traits as diagnostic for the identification of each successive era as follows:

1. *Lower savagery* represents the transitional state from ape to man, before fire and speech were used. No populations representing this stage have survived.

2. *Middle savagery* is marked by the devel-

---

[18]*The League of the Ho-dé-no-sau-nee or Iroquois.*
[19]See B. J. Stern, *Lewis Henry Morgan: Social Evolutionist;* and Hays, *op. cit.,* chaps. 2 and 5.

[20]L. H. Morgan, *Ancient Society,* pp. 17–18.

opment of speech, control of fire, and hunting and fishing subsistence. The Australian aborigines are cited as contemporary representatives of this stage.

3. *Higher savagery* is distinguished by the invention and use of the bow and arrow and, in Morgan's scheme, is represented by the Polynesians (an egregious idea, for reasons to be discussed below).

4. *Lower barbarism* is characterized by the invention and use of pottery and is exemplified by Morgan's own Iroquois.

5. *Middle barbarism* is marked by the domestication of plants and animals in the Old World and by irrigation and adobe-brick architecture in the New World; the Pueblo Indians and the high cultures of Mexico and Peru, for example, represent this stage.

6. *Upper barbarism* begins with the use of iron for tools and weapons, as in Homeric Greece.

7. *Civilization* is achieved when men invent writing. It is divided into ancient and modern substages.

Morgan's *Ancient Society* is essentially an effort to fill out the details of selected aspects of culture for each level. He wrote: "Each of these periods has a distinct culture and exhibits a mode of life more or less special and peculiar to itself."[21]

The Evolution of Kinship Morgan's major interest was in kinship, and hence his greatest effort was to reconstruct the evolution of kinship organization. In so doing, he seized upon the most fundamental aspect of primitive social organization. Nineteenth-century evolutionary theory has been called "mesological," meaning half-way logical; it worked loosely and without much critical rigor from a number of general assumptions to the establishment of many presumptive details. In kinship, Morgan and others began with the proposition that nonhuman animals are promiscuous and therefore the earliest transi-

tional protohumans must have been promiscuous. Highly civilized societies (i.e., European) are monogamous and narrowly restrict mating by means of the incest tabu; therefore, since evolution proceeds through gradual modifications, mating went through a series of successive steps during which the range of individuals with whom one might mate or whom one might marry was always narrowing. The evolution of mating is from promiscuity to monogamy; Part III of *Ancient Society*, for example, maps out the road that was presumed to have been followed.

Promiscuity The stage of sexual promiscuity is entirely hypothetical; no known or observed society permits it. The incest tabu is universal.

Tabu on Parents and Offspring The first limitations on sex occurred, Morgan posited, when mating between parents and offspring was tabued. It was still possible for all the males and females of a given generation to mate at will within the local group. Kinship terminologies were invented at this point, and although this condition of human social organization (which he claimed prevailed on the level of early middle savagery) has not been observed either, Morgan argued that he had found surviving evidence of it in the generational terminology of the Malayans. Because all males and females on the parental levels were presumed to have intermated, he said they were lumped under a single term, distinguished only by a sex prefix. All brothers and sisters and everyone else in one's own generation intermated; hence, there was but one kinship term for them. All offspring could have been sired by any male in one's own generation; hence everyone in the generation below was called by the same term. Morgan was perfectly aware of the fact that the Hawaiians, whom he used as his type example, however free and easy their sexual practices might have appeared, did not permit uncontrolled intrageneration sexuality. But, according to his theory, they must have done so in the not-too-remote past, and although their

[21]*Ibid.*, pp. 12–13.

social forms had changed, the kinship terminology was lagging behind as a surviving imprint of the second stage. Hence, the Hawaiians, with their tremendously sophisticated primitive culture, were placed at the next-to-the-bottom rung of the evolutionary ladder. (It does happen that they have no pottery, but that was an art they lost in their overseas migrations to volcanic and coral islands, where ceramic clays are scarce or absent.) Morgan succumbed too easily to the tyranny of his theory.

Tabu on Brothers and Sisters   To return to Morgan's sequences, the third limitation on promiscuity occurred when ancient man supposedly discovered the disgenic consequences in brother-sister mating and so forbade it. The rule of exogamy was invented. The tendency to joint marriage continued to prevail. Now, however, a group of brothers and cousins jointly married and shared a group of wives together. Their own sisters had to marry into an outside band. Bifurcation was thus introduced into descent; i.e., the children of brothers formed one descent group, and the children of their sisters formed another. Descent lines came into existence for the first time, and because children are biologically much more readily identified with their mothers than with their fathers, Morgan claimed that the first clans were matrilineal. Whereas material resources had previously been shared in common by all members of the community in a form of primitive communism, the introduction of the principle of lineal descent substituted joint ownership by matrilineal clans for communal ownership by all. A new kinship terminology replaced the Hawaiian to accord with the new kinship relationships. Bifurcate-merging systems of terminology of the Iroquois type (see Chapter 23, page 461), separating the offspring of brothers and sisters, evolved. All this first took place in the period of lower and middle barbarism, according to Morgan's formulation.

Pairing Marriages and Monogamy   Late in the period of barbarism, a tendency to *pairing marriages* is said to have occurred. A wife now belonged to a specific man, although he might have several of them. Why pairing was initiated is not explained by Morgan, but once established, man saw it as adaptively superior; hence its spread.

As long as subsistence was predominantly horticultural, the matriclan system could continue. On the other hand, cattle are closely identified with men. Morgan believed pastoralism was a later form, and he could see that it was associated with paternal descent. Since ancient civilizations were patriarchal, earlier descent systems had to be matrilineal—he thought. (This is a good example of mesological reasoning.) Therefore, with no other evidence, pastoralism and patrilineal clans were assigned a later position on the evolutionary scale. The shift from matriarchal to patriarchal descent occurred because men as stockholders objected to passing their herds to sisters' sons, to whom they felt less sentimentally bound than to their own sons. In the simple dogma of Friedrich Engels (1820–1895), Morgan's Communist popularizer, "Mother right had to be overthrown and overthrown it was," in a revolution by "simple decree"—"one of the most decisive ever experienced by humanity"—that initiated the "World historical defeat of the female sex."[22] Women became the property of their husbands, as did their children. Patriarchal power was established in the *patria potestas*, as it was known in Rome. Monogamy, in Engel's formulation, followed as a means of consolidating property holding by means of limited descent lines. Civilization was born.

Morgan's *Ancient Society* also traces the evolution of property holding and of the state as parallel manifestations of related evolutionary changes, but there is not sufficient space to follow these through in this book.

[22]F. Engels, *The Origin of the Family, Private Property, and the State in the Light of the Researches of Lewis H. Morgan,* pp. 49–50.

The nature of nineteenth-century cultural evolutionism should be clear from what has been presented.

Criticism of Morgan's Theory   On the positive side, Morgan was perfectly right in his basic assumption that culture has evolved out of nothing. He was also on solid ground in accepting the archaeological sequence of hunting and gathering followed by domestication of plants and animals, of preceramic followed by ceramic, of bow and arrow preceding iron, and of writing coming late in culture history. These are very simple expressions of what we shall detail in a general way in Part 2 of this book.

Reconstructing the evolution of social organization is a very different matter from tracing general developments in material culture, however, and this was Morgan's sole concern. He was an ethnologist rather than an archaeologist. Nor does the cultural evolutionist have the solid evidence to work with that is available to the student of biological evolution. The problem that faces the cultural evolutionist, in contrast to that facing the biological evolutionist, is that the latter has solid datable fossils, while the cultural evolutionist has only the meager vestiges of material culture which the archaeologist provides for him (usually not more than 1 per cent of the total material culture of a group). An organic fossil represents a much greater proportion of the original living entity than archaeological remains do of the once-living intangible culture. Therefore, cultural evolutionists such as Morgan are forced into *inferential reconstructions* of culture patterns and social structures that are to be associated with each evolutionary stage. Their major tool is the weak instrument of analogic inference, and if they try to produce very specific results, it is easy to demolish the product. It is extremely difficult to give detailed substance to a theory of general evolution. Morgan built his system on the concurrent evolution of subsistence technology, kinship, property, and government. Of these, only the first leaves significant archaeological evidence, and our discussions in Part 3 will indicate the limits of what is known even today. Lafitau established, it is true, the principle that contemporary primitive societies can throw light on prehistoric societies, but "throwing light on" is something less than establishing valid sequential details of evolution of nonmaterial culture.[23]

Evolution in Communist Theory   In the field of political philosophy, Karl Marx was greatly stimulated by Morgan's evolutionary thesis. He found the key to history, according to his close companion, Friedrich Engels, in the study of the American Indian. After Marx's death, Engels wrote a book based on Marx's notes and ideas, bearing the title *The Origin of the Family, Private Property, and the State in the Light of the Researches of Lewis H. Morgan.* Marx and Engels used Morgan's scheme of lineal evolution as the framework upon which to build an account of the linkage between private property, the monogamous "patriarchal" family, and the state as the exploitative institutions that, the theory holds, are responsible for the exploitation of workers and the degradation of women. It is this work which established Morgan and cultural evolutionism as official theoretical dogma in Communist thinking and which largely characterizes Soviet and some non-Soviet ethnology to this day.[24] The pen of Engels undertook to turn nineteenth-century evolutionism into an ideological weapon to speed the downfall of capitalism and to assure the triumph of the Communist proletarian society as the next logically inevitable stage of cultural evolution. Evolution was to make manifest destiny of *The Communist Manifesto.*

[23]See R. H. Lowie, *The History of Ethnological Theory*, pp. 54–67; and "Lewis Henry Morgan in Historical Perspective," in *Essays in Anthropology in Honor of Alfred Louis Kroeber*, pp. 169–181, for a fuller critique of Morgan's work.
[24]See, for example, the discussion of the Algonkian land-tenure controversy, pp. 274–275.

Henry Maine: From Status to Contract Sir Henry S. Maine was a highly specialized legal historian and cultural evolutionist who confined his theoretical writings to the subject of the evolution of law. He used not a shred of data from any extant primitive society. His comparative sources were almost entirely limited to Greece and Rome, although he did draw somewhat on his knowledge of the village community in India. Maine's value to anthropology does not lie in his specific series of evolutionary stages in law; this has long since been proved to be without substance and even more chimerical than Morgan's theory.[25]

Ideal Types as Polar Opposites Maine is important today because he established the theoretical use of *ideal types* of societies and institutions as *polar opposites* for purposes of comparative analysis in social science. In *Ancient Law* (1861), he formulated the contrast in terms of ancient (primitive) societies in which social relations were dominated by *status,* as opposed to "progressive" (modern) societies in which social relations are predominantly determined by *contract.* Status means that a person's kinship identity predetermines his legal position. Contract means that legal positions arise from free agreement among individuals. The contrast is that between obligations and identities which are *family*-centered and those which are *individual*-centered.

Today, this is the major functional-structural difference between the social systems of the undeveloped and Oriental countries in contrast to the Western, industrialized nations. Maine not only drew out the details of the contrasts but also tried to link the two poles in an evolutionary model, even as Morgan had done. He inserted the dimension of time and phrased it in a famous formula: ". . . the movement of the progressive socie-

ties has hitherto been a movement *from Status to Contract.*"[26] Maine also contrasted the dominance of private law in primitive societies with that of criminal law in civilized societies. Maine's very important functional analysis of the use of legal fictions and equity to achieve social change without structural destruction cannot be examined here. For students of sociology, we should note that many sociological theories have been built on foundations laid by Maine: Tönnies's *Gemeinschaft* versus *Gesellschaft,* Durkheim's "mechanical" versus "organic" solidarity, Redfield's "folk-urban" continuum. There is little question that Maine not only formulated ideas of lasting value for anthropology, sociology, and law, but that he first fashioned some of the basic tools of the modern social scientist.

E. B. Tylor and J. G. Frazer: The Evolution of Religion Morgan dismissed religion as a subject for evolutionary study, thus showing a degree of circumspection that he did not extend to kinship. He wrote:

The growth of religious ideas is environed with such intrinsic difficulties that it may never receive a perfectly satisfactory exposition. Religion deals so largely with the imaginative and emotional nature, and consequently with such uncertain elements of knowledge, that all primitive religions are grotesque and to some extent unintelligible.[27]

Morgan has been proved right to doubt the first point: no valid general evolutionary sequence can be established for religious forms. He was wrong on the second point, for all religions can be demonstrably understandable if the principles of cultural relativity are grasped and the basic postulates are perceived upon which strange religions are built, as our later discussions (Chapters 28 through 30) should demonstrate.

Morgan notwithstanding, Sir Edward Burnett Tylor, who has been called the "father of anthropology in all its British develop-

---

[25]See R. Redfield, "Maine's *Ancient Law* in the Light of Primitive Societies" (*Western Political Quarterly,* vol. 3, 1950), pp. 574–589.

[26]H. S. Maine, *Ancient Law,* p. 165.
[27]Morgan, *op. cit.,* p. 5.

ments,"[28] had already published his great two-volume work[29] from which the anthropological concept of culture is derived, and which is almost wholly devoted to the evolutionary development of religion in culture. Frazer followed through with his monumental twelve-volume classic on magical and religious developments.[30] The outlines of Tylor's theory of the evolution of religion from the invention of animism and the soul concept, through ghost and ancestor worship, nature worship, and on to polytheism and monotheism will be presented in Chapter 30, pages 574–576, and are consequently passed over here.

Frazer's task, as he set it for himself, was to trace the origins of magic and religion. The path he outlined was somewhat different from that presented by Tylor. Frazer identified both religion and magic as means of controlling natural forces, but he assumed that primitive man in the evolution of culture first invented magic, turning to religious belief only after experience taught him the fallibility of magic as a means to ends. Frazer's theory was wholly psychological, and he used the device of thinking as he believed primitive men must have thought in the dim, lost ages of the past. (Max Gluckman tells us that Radcliffe-Brown called this the "if-I-were-a-horse" method of evolutionary reconstruction, the method of the farmer whose horse has strayed from the barnyard. Before starting on an aimless search, he scratches his head, chews on a bit of straw, and asks, "Now if I were a horse, where would *I* go?"[31]) Thus, Frazer for an answer:

postulated a theory of intellectual development by placing on a time-scale institutions which co-exist [magic, religion, and science]. He worked out the stages on this scale by imagining how he himself would have reasoned had he been there: first, thinking he could control nature by associating like antecedents with like after-events [sympathetic magic]; by thereafter escaping from his keen-witted disillusionment [magic really does not work] into the belief that the powers were there but superior to him [religion]; and yet thereafter by escaping from his further disillusionment, this time with religion, to accepting a regularity and an immutability in nature of which man could avail himself, once he bowed to necessity [science].[32]

The evolutionary theory of *The Golden Bough* is an intellectualist dream without a wisp of reality in its form, and yet the book is a golden treasury of ethnographic and classical learning, a fascinating compendium of strange doings and fanciful beliefs, both primitive and classical, written in formally elegant English. It deserves to be read for generations to come, but not for its method or theory.

Twentieth-century Developments

At the turn of the century an important event for anthropology was an upswell of dissatisfaction with the substantive hollowness, however fascinating, of the schemes of the cultural evolutionists. This was to be the century of scientific thinking, and science is as impatient with meta-anthropology as it is with metaphysics. The reaction came first in the work of Franz Boas (1858–1942) and his followers.

Franz Boas: Historical Reconstruction The great achievement of the Boasian reaction is that it ushered in the era of modern, empirical anthropology by terminating the three-hundred-year philosophy-of-history phase of speculative evolutionism, and initiated the

[28]G. W. Stocking, Jr., "Tylor, Edward Burnett" (*International Encyclopedia of the Social Sciences*, vol. 16, 1968), p. 175. The entire article, beginning on page 170, is well worth reading.
[29]E. B. Tylor, *Primitive Culture: Researches into the Development of Mythology, Philosophy, Religion, Language, Art and Custom.*
[30]J. G. Frazer, *The Golden Bough: A Study in Magic and Religion.*
[31]M. Gluckman, *Politics, Law, and Ritual in Tribal Society*, p. 2.

[32]*Ibid.*, p. 5.

effort to develop reliable and objective methods of observation and recording in ethnography, physical anthropology, archaeology, and linguistics. It was Boas who introduced the practice of recording the statements of primitive informants in their own languages. To make this possible, he devised the American system of phonetic recording and set the pattern for all American graduate programs in anthropology that require intensive linguistic training of advanced students. He also laid the foundation for all American Indian language studies and for the present "modern" techniques of teaching foreign languages (emphasizing use of vernacular conversation rather than memorization of word lists and grammatical rules). He insisted on detailed reporting of ethnographic observations derived from field research. He developed statistical techniques for handling growth and development data in physical anthropology.

Boas was born a year before the *Origin of Species* was published. He was trained in physics and mathematics. His bent was for natural science, but his interest was the study of human beings; he measured their bodies with exactitude and strove to record their beliefs, myths, and ceremonies as they themselves stated them. He strove for the inside view. Kroeber said, and with truth: "It is perhaps Boas' fundamental contribution to science and civilization: to treat human data with rigorous scientific method on a scale unattempted before."[33]

Boas's aim in the period from 1890 to 1930 was to convert anthropology from the deductive speculativeness of the evolutionists to the inductive exactitude of natural science. This he did with marked success. We do not say that he made a science of anthropology; we say that he converted anthropologists in the United States to the orientation of the scientist in tackling the problems of anthropology.

[33]A. L. Kroeber, "Preface," in W. Goldschmidt (ed.), *The Anthropology of Franz Boas* (American Anthropological Association Memoir 89, 1959), p. vi.

Controlled Comparison and Areal Analysis   Boas's stance was by no means wholly negative. He maintained that universal laws of culture were to be found, but he insisted that they be extracted from painstakingly gathered facts, not from the philosopher's closet. He abhorred premature generalization—which in his time meant almost all generalization. Boas introduced the methods of both *controlled comparison* and *areal analysis* of the development of cultural forms through distribution of traits within a culture area.

Tsimshian Mythology   The development and application of these combined methods were presented by Boas in 1916, when his study of Tsimshian mythology was published.[34] A full body of Tsimshian myths is given in this work, and the myths are then classified and analyzed to lay bare the component motifs of which each is built up. Next, the distribution of each myth is plotted for the entire Northwest Coast culture area (here is the idea of controlled comparison: the environment is generally homogeneous, and the cultures likewise). The components of each myth throughout the Northwest Coast are also analyzed and plotted. From these data, the steps in the development and elaboration of the myths are reconstructed and the lines of diffusion of the components are plotted. The specific evolution of myths within the Northwest Coast environment was thus worked out with as much exactitude as is humanly possible. What is more, Boas took special pains to show how myths that have intercontinental distribution were changed by the Kwakiutl Indians to reflect Kwakiutl culture. He did not talk in terms of evolutionary adaptation nor of myth as symbolism, but he did demonstrate factually how specific cultural forms were adapted to the total environment—physical, cultural, and social.

Northwest Coast Art   Boas also analyzed Northwest Coast art, which, like all other aspects of culture, he viewed functionally in its full cultural context:

[34]F. Boas, *Tsimshian Mythology*.

This art style can be fully understood only as an integral part of the structure of Northwest coast culture. The fundamental idea underlying the thoughts, feelings, and activities of these tribes is the value of rank which gives title to the use of privileges, most of which find expression in artistic activities or in the use of art forms.[35]

The Aims of Boasian Methodology Boas's major objection to evolutionist methodology, to be more emphatically reiterated by Malinowski and Radcliffe-Brown, was that it tore traits out of context and built with gross disregard for cultures as meaningful wholes.

Myth, art, material culture, ceremonial organization, and social organization—all these were to be studied in depth, in context, within a culture area; distributions were to be plotted to determine which manifestations of a trait were universal within the area, which were special, and where the cultures of greatest complexity lay. *Then* one could say something about the developmental (historical) cultural processes for that area and the conditions it represented. He would go no further. When this had been done for a number of areas, it would be time to compare results to see whether higher levels of generalization with empirical validity were possible. Boas was not a young man in a hurry, and he made short shrift of those who were.

Boas's associates and followers in the first quarter of this century expanded the research in a program of their own. From his center in the anthropological division of the American Museum of Natural History in New York, Clark Wissler (1870–1947) sent out expedition after expedition to round out the ethnographic data on Plains Indian military clubs and the sun dance. Robert H. Lowie (1883–1957) put the results on military societies through the analytical mill, while Leslie Spier (1893–1961) did the same for the sun dance.[36]

These manifestations of the Boasian method are usually treated as though they were concerned solely with the reconstruction of historical fragments of cultures. It is often overlooked that the concern was not with chronology so much as with the dynamics of cultural process: how was the sun dance received and restated to fit the ends and purposes, the particular outlooks, and the cultural forms of each society—and what did they have in common?[37] Again, let it be stated, the aim was to specify the details of cultural adaptation, not in terms of a universal general formula, but in terms of variegated diversity of real cultures in specific environmental settings.

To sum up in Boas's own words:

In short then, the method which we try to develop is based on a study of dynamic changes in society that may be observed at the present time. We refrain from the attempt to solve the fundamental problem of the general development of civilization until we have been able to unravel the processes that are going on under our eyes.

. . . if we look for laws, the laws relate to the effects of physiological, psychological, and social conditions, not to sequences of cultural achievement.[38]

With Boas, anthropology came to be firmly grounded in empiricism. Primitive cultures were fast disappearing. The job was to get in the field and make objective studies before the sands of time ran out. As factual knowledge scientifically obtained began to come in and to be collated, the known errors in the current evolutionary schemes began to pile up.

As the recognized errors increased, so did the Boasian rejection of evolutionism as it was then practiced. To pull the pillars from under the edifices of lineal evolutionism was often a major interest of American anthro-

---

[35]F. Boas, *Primitive Art*, p. 280.

[36]R. H. Lowie, *Plains Indian Age Societies: Historical Summary* (American Museum of Natural History, Anthropological Papers, vol. 11, 1916), pp. 877–984; and L. Spier, "The Sun Dance of the Plains Indian" (*American Museum of Natural History, Anthropological Papers,* vol. 16, part 1, 1921).

[37]J. W. Bennett, "The Development of Ethnological Theories as Illustrated by Studies of the Plains Indian Sun Dance" (*American Anthropologist,* vol. 46, 1944), pp. 162–181.

[38]F. Boas, "The Methods of Ethnology" (*American Anthropologist,* vol. 22, 1920), pp. 316 and 328.

pologists, and in some extreme instances, the enthusiasm for the truth that Boas insisted upon was too readily converted into a scorn of all theory.

Scientific caution so hypertrophied to scientific negativism that in 1939 Kluckhohn reported the mental state of American anthropologists to be such that "to suggest something is 'theoretical' is to suggest that it is slightly indecent."[39]

R. H. Lowie's great work, *Primitive Society,* published in 1920, seemed to put the *coup de grâce* to Morgan. By 1925, English, American, German, and French anthropologists had turned completely away from any interest in the evolution of culture. In England and France, anthropologists were absorbed in functional analysis of living cultures. Evolutionism was dead and buried—so it seemed.

Diffusionism In Germany and Austria, an anthropological theory of diffusion of cultures on a broad scale developed as a second alternative to evolutionary anthropology. This theory held that intensive development of culture occurs only in a few select centers, from which it spreads outward through borrowing. Under the leadership of Father Wilhelm Schmidt (1868–1954), it flourished for several decades (from 1910 to 1940), but had little influence on the general development of anthropological method; it disappeared with World War II—at least, for the time being.[40] Discussion of the *Kulturkreislehre* (culture complex theory) will be waived, as will be that of the British diffusionist writers Elliot Smith and W. J. Perry, who set forth highly speculative diffusionist schemes that were quite devoid of method.

Functionalism and Social Structure In England, the major reaction to evolutionism

came in the form of a total rejection of culture history as a subject for anthropological study. In its stead, Bronislaw Malinowski and A. R. Radcliffe-Brown built a new approach to anthropology which emphasized cultures as social systems. Negatively, they took the position that, at worst, historical and cultural evolutionary studies are a futility: there are few verifiable facts to work with, and hence there are no chronological data from prehistory other than archaeological data for a science of anthropology to use. At best, they argued, historical reconstruction is a strategic waste of anthropological time—much richer results may be harvested by focusing on living societies that can be observed in action. Why strain so hard with even such a method as Boas's when it produces what Kroeber called "comparative sterility" because "It does not tell, and does not try to tell, why things happen in society as such."[41]

It is far better, they insisted, to see how societies work as complete systems; one will learn much more about what culture does and what it is used for from verifiable observation. In this they were correct; the payoff from functional research *is* much richer than that derived from the historical reconstructions of the heyday of Boasianism.[42]

Durkheim's Basic Contribution The forerunner of the functionalism of Malinowski and Radcliffe-Brown, and the intellectual ancestor of later British social anthropology, in particular, was the French social scientist Émile Durkheim (1858–1917). Durkheim and Boas were contemporaries, and both gave a new direction to anthropology at the turn of the century. Boas's influence was more direct during the first third of this century; Durkheim's was longer delayed, but since 1930 his influence has grown progressively.

Durkheim was professionally more a soci-

[39]C. Kluckhohn, "The Place of Theory in Anthropological Science" (*The Philosophy of Science,* vol. 6, 1939), p. 333.
[40]See C. Kluckhohn, "Some Reflections on the Method and Theory of the Kulturkreislehre" (*American Anthropologist,* vol. 38, 1936), pp. 157–196.

[41]A. L. Kroeber, "Review of R. H. Lowie, *Primitive Society*" (*American Anthropologist,* vol. 22, 1920), p. 380.
[42]Radcliffe-Brown's *The Andaman Islanders* and Malinowski's *Argonauts of the Western Pacific,* both published in 1922, opened the era of functional anthropology.

ologist than an anthropologist. Like Boas, he emphasized the importance of rigorous method and empiricism in building a scientific base for the understanding of society. Unlike Boas, he did not himself participate in, or contribute to, the development of ethnographic field studies. Nonetheless, he welcomed anthropological contributions to his highly influential journal, *Année sociologique* (1898 to 1914). His one avowedly anthropological book, *The Elementary Forms of Religious Life,* was less successful than his analysis of social interdependence in his *Division of Labor* and his development of the idea of the entity of society in relation to collective identity, particularly in his study *Suicide.*

The question of what holds a society together was of primary importance to Durkheim. As polar opposites, he analyzed what he called mechanical solidarity as contrasted to organic solidarity. *Mechanical solidarity* he held to be characteristic of small homogeneous types of societies—namely, the simpler primitive tribes and peasant groups. Such societies are bonded by an undifferentiated commonness of beliefs and sentiment —what Robert Redfield later came to call the *moral order.* (See pages 671–672.) Social values (normative postulates) are sustained by direct, collective group action. *Organic solidarity* is characterized by structural differentiation of status and roles (division of labor) within the society. Organic solidarity imposes the need for linking of subgroup systems of norms in effective functional relationships.

The function of a social institution, or usage, he held, is the relation between it and the needs of the social organism, the society as an entity. The very concept of "functional prerequisities for societal maintenance," which was presented in Chapter 2 (page 34), derives from Durkheim's notion of needs of the social organism. The idea of social function could be developed in differing ways, however, and this was done by Malinowski, Radcliffe-Brown, and their followers.

Malinowski's Theory and Method Malinowski's great contribution was the pattern he set for ethnological field research. A citizen of Polish Austria, he was "interned" at the outbreak of World War I while attending a meeting of the Anthropology Section of the British Association for the Advancement of Science, being held in Australia. He was permitted to spend the duration of the war among the Trobriand Islanders. Although he was trained as a mathematician in Poland, people and anthropology were his natural passion, and it was people living life that entranced him. This is what he looked for; this is what he reported. He, it will be remembered, was the first anthropologist to insist that what people *do* (no matter how seemingly trivial or irrelevant) is what must fill the ethnographer's notebook. What *they say they do* is important to record, to be sure, but it must not be taken as representing their culture in fact. Evidence is what the field worker can see; informants are to recite myths and roles but not to generalize customs, except as these express attitudes.

Beyond observing and reporting, Malinowski's credo was "the theoretical assumption that the total field of data under the observation of the field-worker must somehow fit together and make sense."[43] There are no such things as survivals, he argued. Every aspect of culture is functionally significant in its matrix.

The task of the social anthropologist is to dissect the culture with sufficient skill to reveal its workings: "The real mental effort, the really uphill work is not so much 'to get facts' as to elicit the relevance of these facts and systematize them into an organic whole."[44]

Three Manifestations of Function Malinowski's theory and method dealt with function as the organizing principle operating on three levels: (1) the effect of a custom or

[43]E. R. Leach, "The Epistemological Background to Malinowski's Empiricism," in R. Firth (ed.), *Man and Culture: An Evaluation of the Work of Bronislaw Malinowski,* p. 120.
[44]B. Malinowski, *Coral Gardens and Their Magic,* vol. 1, p. 322.

institution on other customs or institutions within the culture, (2) the goal-achievement effects of a practice as goals are defined by the members of a society, and (3) the part played by a custom or institution in promoting social cohesion (solidarity) and the continuance of a given way of life in a given environment. Whether an anthropologist correctly identifies the functions of culture traits and institutions is a subtle problem of validation. There is no foolproof methodology in functionalism, but it is frequently possible to demonstrate the interacting effects of the various aspects of the culture. Societies became living, pulsating, dynamic entities under the Malinowskian method of fieldwork and analysis. With history out the window, what was lost in the time dimension was gained in an understanding of the social physiology of living societies. The superb quality of field studies done by Malinowski-trained students in England and the United States is testimony to the marked advance made in anthropological methods under his stimulus. Malinowski found a way to give illuminating answers to people who want to know "why."[45]

Radcliffe-Brown and Structuralism   Radcliffe-Brown's organic analogy of functionalism was presented on page 29. It should be re-read at this point. Radcliffe-Brown and subsequent British social anthropologists, such as E. E. Evans-Pritchard, Meyer Fortes, Max Gluckman, and Raymond Firth, moved on from functionalism to concern with social structure, which has been the chief focus of British—and a number of American—social anthropologists since 1940. Functionalism was not rejected; rather, it was absorbed and became an implicit aspect of almost all Bri-

tish, French, and American cultural anthropology but no longer a primary emphasis.

Social structure is the network of ways in which individuals and groups within a culturally organized population are related to each other in their ongoing activities. It is the system of statuses (or "offices") which are held by individuals, and the roles (or ways of behaving) that are formally expected of the status holders.[46] In British social anthropology, however, the focus of interest is not on the whole gamut of social relations but upon the structure of corporate groups—lineages, clans, work groups, age classes, and territorial organizations—which have an enduring existence within a society. The concern is, for the most part, with the economic, political, religious, and ritual activities of such units of social organization.

In this introduction to anthropology we treat social structure as the organizational part of the total life-ways of human societies: social structure rests on and utilizes a technological base; it also reflects and is sustained by an ideological and symbolic system of knowledge and beliefs. In the pages to follow, Part 3, "The Material Base of Culture"; Part 4, "Social Structure"; and Part 5, "Symbolic Expression" deal with each of these aspects of culture in turn.

French Social Structuralism   British and American social structural studies are focused on field research in depth as applied to specific societies. Their aims and methods are strongly those of natural science—a movement *from* specific, empirical research *toward* general classification of types of societies and the formulation of cultural laws of social organization.

A contrasting approach by the French anthropologist Claude Lévi-Strauss (who is currently revered as the preeminent intellectual of Europe) has a much more abstractly math-

---

[45]Malinowski built a theoretical system on the relation of culture to the satisfaction of human organic needs, but as Gluckman points out, the biogenic endowments of mankind are sufficiently similar so that they cannot be a significant factor in accounting for varying social organizations. See M. Gluckman, *Politics, Law, and Ritual in Tribal Society,* pp. 29–30.

[46]See Chap. 18.

ematical foundation. It begins with theoretically conceived images (models) of societies which can then be compared to see what deep-lying rules might exist which govern the actual forms that societies do take. British social structuralism is largely inductive-deductive: it moves from specific observation to the use of general laws. French social structuralism is more deductive-inductive. It emphasizes the general principles which govern the overall organization of societies regardless of the specific forms they may take.

Although Lévi-Strauss's structuralism is exciting considerable interest among professional anthropologists today, it will not be explored or extensively used in the development of this text, for the reason that it is as yet too abstruse for beginning purposes.[47]

Culture and Personality Research The development of general theory in the study of the interaction of culture upon personality development and the feedback effect of personality types upon cultural institutions has been covered in Chapter 2. The nature of the work by Malinowski, Mead, Benedict, DuBois, Kardiner and Linton, and Whiting and Child, among many others, need not be restated here. Historically, it is interesting to note that while the linguist Edward Sapir personally provided much stimulus to the psychoanalytic interest in the *individual* in primitive societies on the part of Benedict and others, it was as Boas-trained anthropologists that Benedict and Mead gave culture and personality studies the impetus and theoretical start that made them the major interest of American cultural anthropologists from 1930 to 1950.

The great excitement created in the 1930s by the relating of personality psychology to the problems of anthropology has now calmed down, but so long as anthropology does not forsake the study of *man* for the study of dehumanized culturology or social structure as things *sui generis,* so long will culture and personality research continue to yield rich rewards in terms of interest and useful applications, both in psychotherapy and in cultural-development programs.

Cross-cultural Correlational Methods A major research resource for anthropology was created when G. P. Murdock initiated the Yale Cross-cultural Survey in 1937. The survey was designed as a classified repository of ethnographic fact. The data were indexed in such a way that anyone wishing to find what had been reported on almost any feature of culture could immediately select the cards bearing the index key for the subject of his interest. Each card contained a verbatim reproduction of what was written on the subject in a given book or article. The cultures included in the survey represented all the geographic areas of the world and all levels of development. The files served from the outset as a convenient reference source so far as the tribes covered by the survey were concerned. The value of the Yale Cross-cultural Survey was such that it was subsequently made an interuniversity project in the form of the Human Relations Area Files, which continues to expand and revise its ethnographic coverage.

By their very nature, the files invite statistical testing of anthropological hypotheses. It is usually relatively easy to determine whether certain types of culture traits are present or absent in a given culture. If this determination is made with reference to a trait in all the cultures, the relative frequency of the trait can be quickly determined. This then makes possible the substitution of a more exact expression of frequency than "rarely," "commonly," or "usually," which have so long been characteristic of anthropological generalizations.

---

[47]The student who wishes to explore this topic on his own is referred to C. Lévi-Strauss, *Structural Anthropology.*

In any science, relationships count for more than mere frequencies, and this is where statistical coefficients of correlations may be helpful. Does matrilineal organization correlate with horticulture or not? Does virilocal residence correlate with patrilineal descent? With progeny price? With pastoralism? The cultural anthropologist for years had to content himself with relying on as wide a memory retention of ethnographic fact as possible, on the basis of which he could formulate tentative hypotheses of relationships. When a hypothesis was put forward, other anthropologists would comb their memories to see whether they could think of contradictory cases, especially from the tribes they had specialized in. If there were not too many serious exceptions, the hypothesis would stand, accepted for the time being, at least. This is the *method of disproof by the crucial instance,* still the favorite methodological test of most anthropologists. Obviously, it has its weaknesses. How many facts from how many cultures can even the best-read ethnologist keep in his head?

Murdock's Statistical Study of Social Structure   In 1941, Murdock built up a checklist of significant facts on family, kinship, kin and local groups, and sexual behavior. The data from eighty-five tribes in the Human Relations Area Files were registered on the lists as indicating presence (+) or absence (−) of a given trait. Similar data lists were made for 165 additional societies not included in the files. Thus Murdock had data sheets on 250 cultures. By counting each occurrence or absence of a trait as a positive or negative unit, he was able to produce quantified four-cell tables for a large number of paired traits, on the basis of which coefficients of correlation could be calculated. For example, bilocal residence paired with generational-type (Hawaiian) kinship terminology produced the frequency distributions shown in Table 3-1.

Application of Yule's coefficient of association formula (the one used by Murdock) produces a Q (correlation) of +.65 with a 100 chi-square (X^2) level of confidence in statistical significance in this instance.

The correlation for five other groups of generational kinship terms in association with bilocal residence ranged between +.64 and +.75. Thus, the theorem that *bilocal residence tends to be associated with kinship terminology of the generational type* is validated. It changes from a hypothesis or theorem to a rule.[48]

In his epoch-making book *Social Structure,* published in 1949, Murdock ran statistical tests of correlations on twenty-six separate theorems derived from a fundamental postulate stating the factors which govern the grouping of kinsmen under a single relationship term (see Chapter 23) with mostly positive and statistically significant results.

Since then, strenuous efforts have been made by Murdock and others to refine and improve the method, which has several inherent difficulties. The first has to do with the representativeness of the sample itself. What, for instance, is a discrete culture, suitable for counting as a unit in the face of the known fact that culture traits diffuse through borrowing? If two historically related tribes show the same trait, does it count as one occurrence—or two? This is important when one is attempting to derive inferences as to the causal significance of an indicated relation between two traits. Should the sample be drawn from a universe of tribes, everyone of which has an equal chance of being included? Or should the universe be presorted into cultural clusters (some of which will include a number of related tribes) so that the sample will include a representative selection of clusters, by cultural type and geographic distribution?

These thorny questions (and others) have by no means been wholly solved. But in moving in that direction, Murdock first tested the statistical reliability of the sample used

[48]G. P. Murdock, *Social Structure,* p. 152.

as the basis of his book on social structure.

The statistical results differed sufficiently in each test so that he judged it necessary to select a larger sample that would represent culture types and areas. The product is the *World Ethnographic Sample* of 585 cultures coded according to subsistence, types of community, kinship organization, marriage, kinship terminologies, residence, social classes, and political integration as classified by Murdock himself.[49]

The *Sample* differs from the *Human Relations Area Files* not only in the societies covered but in the nature of its data as well. The *Human Relations Area Files* constitute a kind of specialized library in which everything of significance which has been published on a selected society is reprinted on cards—verbatim, but not in the page sequences of the original books. Rather, paragraphs and pages are indexed according to their content (such as "food getting") and filed accordingly. If a researcher wants to compare tribes for food getting, he draws out all the cards bearing the number "22" from each file for each culture. He then has all that has been written on the subject right in his hands, without thumbing through hundreds of books.[50]

In the *World Ethnographic Sample,* on the other hand, no original source material is reproduced. Instead, the original data have been processed by Murdock and coded into categories and subcategories such as:

Column 71:   *Slavery*

   H   Hereditary slavery present
   I   Incipient or nonhereditary slavery
   O   Absence or near absence of slavery
   S   Slavery reported but not identified as hereditary or nonhereditary

Such data give slight qualitative information about how slavery operates in any society.

The data have been reduced to a barebones minimum in the code. But the coded keys can be readily placed on computer tapes for quick counts and correlations of one culture element with another, or with geographical areas. It is a handy device for use in a very limited way. Not all manifestations of culture are amenable to coding: they are too ambiguous or too complex to be reduced to simple categories. All possible cross-correlations from the data in the *World Ethnographic Sample* are now tabulated in the handbook by Coult and Habenstein,[51] which has been drawn upon a number of times in our discussions of social structure throughout the text.

Finally, however, Murdock decided that sampling presents such difficulties that cross-cultural analysis should be based on a total universe of human societies. The formulation of the universe has been undertaken in his *Ethnographic Atlas,* first published in twenty-one installments in the journal *Ethnography,* between 1962 and 1967, and finally in book form (1967). The *Atlas* purports not to be a sample, but the "known cultural universe" of all the world during the past five hundred years. It is based on 863 societies

[51]A. D. Coult and R. W. Habenstein, *Cross Tabulations of Murdock's World Ethnographic Sample.*

Table 3-1   The Occurrence of Hawaiian-type Kinship Terminology in Relation to Bilocal Residence in Murdock's Original Sample of 250 Societies*

Hawaiian-type kinship terminology		*Bilocal residence*	
		Present (+)	Absent (−)
	Present (+)	33	9
	Absent (−)	187	11

*Residence patterns and kinship systems are discussed in Chaps. 20 and 23. They are shown here simply to demonstrate how the statistical analysis is used.

SOURCE: Data from G. P. Murdock, *Social Structure,* p. 152.

[49]G. P. Murdock, "World Ethnographic Sample" (*American Anthropologist,* vol. 59, 1957), pp. 664–687; also available in the Bobbs-Merrill Reprint Series in the Social Sciences, No. A-166.

[50]The index is published as the *Outline of Cultural Materials* by the *Human Relations Area Files,* Inc.

which are reduced to 412 cultural clusters to provide independent (nonoverlapping) cultural types coded like the cultures in the *World Ethnographic Sample.*

Certain of the data in the *Ethnographic Atlas* have been tabulated for frequency distribution according to geographic areas by Erika Bourguignon and Lenora Greenbaum and published under the title, *Diversity and Homogeneity: A Comparative Analysis of Societal Characteristics Based on Data from the Ethnographic Atlas.* This work, unlike Coult and Habenstein, does not include correlations.

It will be noticed in Parts 3 and 4 of this book, that sometimes data from the *World Ethnographic Sample* are used, and sometimes from the *Ethnographic Atlas.* Wherever Bourguignon and Greenbaum's tables provide relevant data, these are used in preference to Coult and Habenstein's results from the *World Ethnographic Sample.* Where Bourguignon and Greenbaum provide no data but Coult and Habenstein do, then results of the latter are retained, in spite of possible sample defects.

This means that we recognize that the statistical results from cross-cultural tabulation are not necessarily *absolutely* reliable or valid. But they may be quite helpful and illuminating —if conservatively used.

Cultural Evolution Today   Although social evolution as a method and theory seemed to have been dead and buried by 1920 (outside the Soviet Union), it has never been wholly defunct and now has a new vitality. After all, the data derived from archaeological research around the world demonstrate that, wherever local archaeology has any prehistoric dimension, cultures have "evolved." If the record goes back far enough, it shows the simple material technology of hunters and gatherers, who had no metals, no domesticated plants or animals, no weaving, no pottery, no writing, no permanent house structures, no public buildings—a culture of

illiterate people of meager development. Because of limited technology and food-getting techniques, such societies are limited both in numbers of people and in the elaboration of social institutions. In later archaeological levels, domesticated plants and animals appear, evidence of permanent housing shows up, weaving and pottery are apt to be present, and settlement patterns indicate an increase in sizes of populations. Everything points to some degree of elaboration of culture. Such people are classed incipient agriculturalists whose culture contains domesticated plants and animals and settled villages or homesteads, but no writing, cities, or monumental ceremonial centers. The highest archaeological levels reveal all this and a good deal more. They yield the remains of *civilizations:* societies whose cultures include agriculture and cities; diversified craft specialties, including metallurgy; monumental, ceremonial, and governmental structures; writing; and an inventory of innumerable additional items. Civilized cultures may or may not be more "moral" than precivilized, or primitive, cultures. In anthropology, the word "civilization" refers only to a degree of complexity of culture, although civilizations do show qualitative differences in social structure and the character of social relations when compared with primitive societies. Anthropologists reserve judgment on the ethical "goodness" or "badness" of the differences.

The primitive world was the world before the invention of writing. Most of the span of human experience occurred during this time. The archaeological record testifies to an orderly pattern of cultural development within the prehistoric era, that is, before the time of written records. By inference, patterns of social culture must also show some regularities of development. The task of studies in cultural evolution is to determine the content of such patterns, if possible.

The pendulum of Boasian antievolutionism had completed the swing of its arc by 1945, and a new look at cultural evolutionism became possible. Since then, three sorts of neo-evolutionism have emerged.

Specific Evolution A refinement of the idea of cultural evolution was introduced in 1960 by Marshall Sahlins, who calls it *specific evolution,* "the historic development of particular cultural forms . . . phylogenetic transformation through adaptation."[52] In specific evolution, the concern is with the sequence of changes in the cultural history of particular societies; for example, what actually happened in the development of American culture between 1776 and now? In what specific senses were these modifications responses to the potentialities of the North American continent and its mastery? Or how, specifically, were Pueblo Indian cultures changing and modifying between A.D. 100 and today? This is more than history, for specific evolution is concerned with more than a chronicle of events; it wants to know how the *cultures* changed. It is really cultural history or Boasian *historical reconstruction* under a new name in a theoretical framework more congenial to thinking in evolutionary terms.

Multilineal Evolution As developed by Professor Julian Steward, multilineal evolution searches for parallels in specific evolution. It does not attempt, at least in its present stage, to develop a comprehensive set of evolutionary principles to cover the growth of culture from earliest prehistoric times to the present. Rather, it deliberately narrows its scope to focus on parallel developments in limited aspects of the cultures of specifically identified societies. It undertakes to determine whether identifiable sequences of culture change occur in the same order in independent cultures. When such apparently similar sequences are identified, it then seeks to determine whether like causes have produced them.

Multilineal evolution is essentially a methodology based on the assumption that significant regularities in cultural change occur, and it is concerned with the determination of cultural laws. It is inevitably concerned also with historical reconstruction, but it does not expect that historical data can be classified in universal stages.[53]

Multilineal evolutionary studies aim to examine whole cultures in detail to see what specific social forms do in fact take shape on different levels, that is, degrees of complexity, of social integration. It expects great diversity in detail but assumes the probability of limited generalizations with respect to directions of evolutionary change.

General Evolution General evolution differs from multilineal evolution mainly in the level of its formulations. It attempts to establish evolutionary trends for culture *in toto* rather than for limited cultures of comparable types, as does multilineal evolution. Its formulations are consequently much broader in scope. They are of the type that V. Gordon Childe, Leslie White, Robert Redfield, Elman Service, and Darcy Ribeiro, among others, have formulated with respect to the great changes in culture that accompany the development from Paleolithic to Neolithic to Metal Age technological bases.[54] General evolution does not assume that every culture develops exactly comparable details in cultural patterns on comparable levels of technology. But it does hold that broad-scale trends in the succession of cultural forms are demonstrable.

To study the general evolution of culture is to examine the courses along which human

---

[52]M. Sahlins, "Evolution: Specific and General," in M. D. Sahlins and E. R. Service (eds.), *Evolution and Culture,* p. 43.

[53]J. H. Steward, "Evolution and Process," in A. L. Kroeber (ed.), *Anthropology Today,* p. 318.

[54]Or as indicated for legal evolution by the present author in "The Trend of the Law," in E. A. Hoebel, *The Law of Primitive Man,* chap. 12; see also L. Pospisil, *Anthropology of Law,* chap. 5.

societies have arrived at more distinct patterns of behavior to fulfill more distinct functions. In writing on the "reality of social evolution," MacIver has said: "The main interest of the evolutionary method is not the modification of specific form into specific form but the emergence of a variety of more specific forms from the less specific."[55]

Archaeology, Physical Anthropology, General Ethnology, Linguistics, and Applied Anthropology The significant trends and discoveries of these fields in the present era are all implicitly presented in the materials that make up the remainder of this book. They shall not, therefore, be singled out for separate discussion here.

SUMMARY

Classical Greece and Rome failed to develop any anthropological ideas because, believing there was nothing to be learned from barbarians, they were incapable of a comparative approach to human institutions.

Anthropology as an identifiable subject is a child of the Age of Reason, when thinkers of the Enlightenment began to form an evolutionary philosophy of history to account for the newly discovered primitive peoples revealed by the voyages of discovery. Comparative ideas had already been born in the Renaissance, however, as Europeans contemplated the ancient classical world. Sahagun's account of the Aztecs, coming early in the sixteenth century, is the first systematic ethnography of a non-European people. Early in the eighteenth century, Lafitau, the French Jesuit, published the first comparative ethnology—a study of American Indian cultures compared with those of Greece and Rome. **William** Robertson's *History of America* formulated a number of basic principles of evolutionary anthropology and laid the foundations for the evolutionary systems

that would mark the birth of anthropology as a full-fledged field, beginning in 1860.

Nineteenth-century evolutionism is best characterized in the work of L. H. Morgan, who attempted to correlate successive steps in the limitation of sexual relations from promiscuity to monogamy with stages of technological evolution. Kinship systems, social organization, and ownership of property were also inferred in progressive steps related to forms of marriage. The method was mesological, and the resulting evolutionary scheme collapsed when twentieth-century anthropologists proved that there is no demonstrable evolutionary sequence in types of kinship systems.

Tylor and Frazer formulated analogous schemes of evolutionary sequences for spirit beings, from animism to monotheism (Tylor), and for magic, religion, and scientific thought (Frazer). Maine treated the evolution of law as a progressive shift from primitive status-dominated cultures to civilized cultures, which he characterized as basing personal relations on individual contract. The two types of society resulting from such cultures were treated as polar opposites.

In the twentieth century, the American rejection of cultural evolutionism was initiated by Franz Boas, who emphasized the gathering of empirical data in the field and the methodological procedure of trait analysis of specific institutions within a culture area as a means of limited historical reconstruction.

In England, Malinowski and Brown rejected all historical goals for anthropology. Instead, they substituted the study of whole cultures as integrated systems as the type of anthropological research that they claimed would give the most rewarding results. Field studies should overlook nothing in the way of behavior or attitudes because every custom and act is functionally significant. The object of research is to discover the functions as a means of learning how societies hold together and achieve their purposes. Radcliffe-Brown moved from a concern with function

[55]R. M. MacIver, *Society: Its Structure and Changes*, p. 424.

to an emphasis on social structure, the organization of interpersonal relations within a social system. Structural theory and research have been characteristic of British social anthropology since 1940, and are also a major feature of contemporary French and American cultural anthropology today.

Cross-cultural correlational studies have been gaining a steadily increasing foothold in American anthropology since the establishment of the Yale Cross cultural Survey (now the Human Relations Area Files) and Murdock's use of coefficients of correlation to test a number of long-standing anthropological hypotheses. Murdock's *World Ethnographic Sample* and the continuing *Ethnographic Atlas* are providing a wide range of coded data for computer calculation of cultural correlations. This still-new area of cultural anthropology is expected to continue to gain in strength in the years ahead.

Interest in social and cultural evolution has revived in recent decades. Modern evolutionary studies take three major forms: (1) *specific evolution,* or the continuing modification of particular societies as they adapt to changing conditions; (2) *multilineal evolution,* or the study of parallel developments in societies at comparable levels of cultural development and environmental circumstance; and (3) *general evolution,* the delineation of "the grand scheme" in the development of human cultures and societies.

SELECTED READINGS

Brew, J. O. (ed.), *One Hundred Years of Anthropology* (1968). Excellent papers covering the growth of the field during the first hundred years of the Peabody Museum, Harvard University.

Hallowell, A. I., "The Beginnings of Anthropology in America," in F. de Laguna (ed.), *Selected Papers from the American Anthropologist: 1888–1920* (1960), pp. 1–103. A comprehensive account of the events which led to the establishment of anthropology as a science in the United States.

Harris, M., *The Rise of Anthropological Theory* (1968). A polemical treatment of anthropological theorists and their ideas. Although it is often obscured by the author's rhetoric and biases, the book contains much that is valid and informative.

Hays, H. R., *From Ape to Angel: An Informal History of Social Anthropology* (1958). The style is breezy (it reminds one of *Time* magazine), and theory is superficially treated, but it tells a lot about anthropologists and the intellectual temper of their times.

Heine-Geldern, R., "One Hundred Years of Ethnological Theory in the German-speaking Countries: Some Milestones" (*Current Anthropology*, vol. 5, 1964), pp. 407–429. Should be read to round out the history, which, as we have given it, concentrates on developments in English-speaking countries.

Helm, J. (ed.), *Pioneers of American Anthropology* (1966). Interesting biographical accounts of nineteenth-century anthropologists at work.

Kardiner, A., and E. Preble, *They Studied Man* (1961). Essays on Darwin, Herbert Spencer, Tylor, Frazer, Durkheim, Boas, Malinowski, Kroeber, Benedict, and Freud. More limited than Hays, but equally interesting and much more penetrating.

Lienhardt, G., *Social Anthropology* (1965). A historical summary of developments since 1860, written for the layman.

Lowie, R. H., *The History of Ethnological Theory* (1937). Should be used to fill in on the English and Austrian diffusionist schools.

Naroul, R., and B. Cohen (eds.), *A Handbook of Method in Cultural Anthropology* (1970). Not in the least intended for the beginning student, this compendium of fifty articles cannot escape mention simply because of its importance.

Penniman, T. K., *A Hundred Years of Anthropology* (rev. ed., 1952). Rather weak in its handling of ethnology, this book is chiefly valuable for its treatment of the development of archaeology and physical anthropology.

Ribeiro, D., *The Civilizational Process* (1968). A sweeping, contemporary formulation of general evolution.

Stocking, G. W., Jr., *Race, Culture, and Evolution* (1968). Exceedingly thoughtful and well-researched anthropological history. The coverage deals only with limited topics (mostly Boas), but the product is a model of scholarly depth and fairness.

Part 2   The Evolution of Man and Culture

Chapter 4

Man's Place among the Primates

Anthropologists might well recite the lines of Alexander Pope as the first incantation of their creed:

> Know then thyself, presume not God to scan,
> The proper study of mankind is man.[1]

This interest in man, however, does not keep anthropologists from studying apes and monkeys, either as fossils or as living social groups. For although it is true that if you want to learn about man, you should study man, it is also true that additional insights may be gained about man and his nature through knowledge of his near relatives and his ancestors. Consequently, anthropologists study primates and fossil man to unfold man's biological background, seeking what may be learned about the prehuman roots of social and physical existence. To this end, we discuss in this chapter the reasons for man's classification among the primates. We shall then summarize the facts of primate behavior as they bear on the problem of the evolution of man and culture. As we proceed in this chapter and later ones, many questions of classification arise. Hence, an understanding of classifications needs first attention.

Problems in Classification

It is important at the outset to understand that a system of classification is merely a tool of the human mind, *created by men in order to organize their knowledge.* A rational system of classification, called a taxonomy (Gr. *taxis,* arrangement + *nomia,* distribution), is based upon a set of principles which define the criteria in accordance with which the phenomena in question are to be classified and ordered.

[1]Alexander Pope, "An Essay on Man," epistle 2.

Criteria in Classification The criteria are (or should be) actual attributes of the phenomena. The ordering is (or should be) done according to a rational master scheme, or theory, of relationships between the classes. Similarities of structure, function, development, and evolutionary history all enter into the classification of organisms. *Structure* refers to bodily form, or *morphology; function,* to the manner in which an organ works in the maintenance of the organism as a whole; *development,* to the sequences in the growth process, or life history, of the individual organism; and *evolutionary history,* to the se-

Fig. 4-A   Gorilla mother and baby. (Copyright Elsbeth Siegrist.)

quences of development in the ancestry of the type.

Ideally, there should be no ambiguity in the classificatory criteria according to which an object is put into one category or another. In fact, there are all too often ambiguity, confusion, contradiction, lack of agreement, and battles of ink. What are seen as attributes of the subjects to be classified are influenced by one's preconceptions and one's tools and techniques. How good is one's microscope and how good is one in dissecting, staining, focusing, and seeing what is there? "The scale of observation creates the phenomenon," it is said.

Classifications as Mental Constructs   Fragmentary fossils of which there are few specimens do not offer many clear-cut diagnostic features for comparison and classification. A leading physical anthropologist warns us:

How do we decide at what taxonomic level to make the divisions we are discussing? Strange as it may seem to students and others who believe there are no ambiguous answers in science, or ought not to be, this decision is largely a matter of opinion formed from admittedly fragmentary materials. Some people prefer to emphasize distinctions, others continuities.[2]

Thus it is that in prehistoric paleontology, when a very primitive and fragmentary fossil of a new type of hominoid is first discovered, the cries go up: "It's an ape!" "It's a man!" "It's an ape man!" Sides are chosen. The battle lines of cephalic calipers and comparative morphology are drawn, and the war of words begins. The result has been dubbed the "chaos of anthropological nomenclature" by George Gaylord Simpson, who wryly but cogently observes:

It is of course also true that the significance of differences between any two specimens has almost invariably come to be enormously exaggerated by one authority or another in this field. Here the fault

[2]J. Buettner-Janusch, *Origins of Man,* p. 164.

is not so much a lack of taxonomic grammar as lack of taxonomic common sense or experience. Many fossil hominids have been described and named by workers with no other experience in taxonomy. They have inevitably lacked the sense of balance and the interpretive skill of zoologists who have worked extensively on larger groups of animals. It must, however, be sadly noted that even broadly equipped zoologists often seem to lose their judgment if they work on hominids. Here factors of prestige, of personal involvement, of emotional investment rarely fail to affect the fully human scientist, although they hardly trouble the workers on, say, angleworms or dung beetles.[3]

Many hominid fossils have been discovered or first identified by amateurs or semiprofessionals for whom the urge to convince the world that they have found a new form of man or ancestor of man is well-nigh irresistible. Each stakes his claim by posting a new genus, or at least a new species, label on his creature. Others counter with what they consider to be more suitable labels according to their judgments. And so a single find may receive a variety of Latin sobriquets, and a number of different finds which should properly be grouped within a single classification are put into separate pigeonholes with different names.[4]

The history of the first famous finds of Java man (see pages 140–141) is an example of what has too often taken place. His discoverer, Eugene Dubois, named the fossil *Pithecanthropus erectus:* genus, *ape man;* species, *upright.* Three decades later, a leading American evolutionist, Henry Fairfield Osborn, argued that the specimen was not an ape at all, but that he belonged to an ancient fossil hominid who had crossed the threshold of humanity without having evolved far

[3]G. G. Simpson, "The Meaning of Taxonomic Statements," in S. L. Washburn (ed.), *Classification and Human Evolution,* pp. 6–7. By permission of the Wenner-Gren Foundation for Anthropological Research, New York.
[4]J. B. S. Haldane complains, "We have overclassified the primates," in "The Argument from Animals to Men: An Examination of Its Validity for Anthropology" (*Journal of the Royal Anthropological Institute of Great Britain and Ireland,* vol. 86, 1956).

enough to be classed as *Homo;* therefore, he proposed to call him *Paleoanthropus trinilensis:* genus, *ancient man;* species, *of Trinil* (the locality of discovery). Today, the consensus of European and American specialists is to designate the type as *Homo erectus erectus:* genus, *man;* species, *upright;* variety, *upright.*

If, therefore, inconsistency and contradiction among the names and classification systems used in this text and among the nomenclatures of other authors occur, there is nothing to do except to understand the provisional nature of all classifications.

However, science struggles continually to supplant disorder with order, unreason with reason, and dogma with objectively sustained theory. In this process, zoologists have arrived at a logical international formulation of rules and methods for making scientific classifications.[5] In 1962, an international symposium was convened under the auspices of the Wenner-Gren Foundation for Anthropological Research in an effort to clean up the chaos in the storehouse of the science of human evolution. It was not the aim of the symposium to formulate a code of primate classification, but much debris was nonetheless cleared away, and we were provided with a nomenclature that should serve as a standard until such time as new knowledge and further accumulation of experience make changes necessary. The detailed results are to be found in the volume edited by S. L. Washburn, *Classification and Human Evolution.* The taxonomies of man used in this text follow the consensus accepted by the Wenner-Gren conference.

The Linnean System of Biological Classification

It is entirely possible to classify living organisms without reference to evolutionary

[5]N. R. Stoll et al., *International Code of Zoological Nomenclature,* and G. G. Simpson, *Principles of Animal Taxonomy.*

development, as did Karl von Linné (1707–1778), the great Swedish naturalist who devised the basic system of classification in use today. The Linnean system was synchronic: it treated all forms on a single time plane. Today, however, biologists use taxonomy to imply common ancestry as well as physical resemblances. Two separate ideas are involved in this statement. The first rests upon the zoological proposition that two or more animal forms showing a large number of significant similarities in form and function must be more or less closely related. The second proposition is that close relationship means common ancestry. Further, the greater the detailed similarity in form and function, the more definite is the commonness of ancestry. The Linnean system as now used not only groups organisms according to similarities but also implies a good deal about evolutionary relations between living forms in terms of common ancestral types and closeness of collateral relationships. In the system now in use, the category levels are ranked in descending order as follows:

kingdom
  phylum
    class
      group
        order
          family
            genus
              species
                variety

Intermediary categories are frequently established by use of the prefixes "super-," "sub-," and "infra-," for example,

  superfamily
  family
  subfamily
  infrafamily

The Taxonomy of Man   It is not difficult to identify man as to kingdom, phylum, and class. Each primate is clearly a member of the animal kingdom and not of the vegetable kingdom. Because of his spinal cord and nervous system, he belongs to the *phylum* of chordates. Man's spinal column of bony segments and the associated skeletal structure put him in the *subphylum* of vertebrates. His practice of nourishing the young on nutrient fluids generated by the female mammary glands gives him membership in the *class* of mammals. Because the unborn young are developed in the maternal womb, he qualifies for membership in the *subclass* of eutheria, within which he is identified as belonging to the *infraclass* of placentals, since the fetus is nourished directly from the bloodstream of the mother through the placenta.

Within the *order* of primates, taxonomists identify two *suborders:* (1) the anthropoid, which includes all apes, monkeys, and man, and (2) the prosimian, which includes the tarsier, lemur, and tree shrew—the most primitive in development of the primates.

Within the suborder of anthropoids there are two *infraorders:* (1) the catarrhines (Gr. *kata,* downward + *rhis, rhinos,* nose), the Old World anthropoids, whose nostrils are usually narrow and closely spaced, and (2) the platyrrhines (Gr. *platys,* broad + *rhis, rhinos,* nose), the New World monkeys, whose nostrils are usually flat and widely spaced. Man is clearly a catarrhine. The catarrhines in turn subdivide into two *superfamilies:* (1) the hominoids (man and the apes) and (2) the cercopithecoids (Gr. *kerkos,* tailed + *pithekos,* ape), which include baboons, macaques, vervets, and langurs.

The hominoids group into three *families:* (1) hominid, man; (2) pongid, the great apes; and (3) hylobatid, within which fall the gibbons and siamangs. The hominid family today has but one surviving *genus, Homo.* It also produced one other identified *genus, Australopithecus,* long since extinct. There are two living *genera* of pongids: (1) *Pan* and (2) *Pongo. Pan* is made up of at least two *species:* (1) the chimpanzees and (2) the gorillas. *Pongo* exists today only in the form of the orangutan, in Sumatra and Borneo. And finally, there is but one surviving *species* of man, *sapiens,* and but one surviving *variety,*

also called *sapiens.* For man, then, his taxonomic identity is:

kingdom—animal
 phylum—chordate
  subphylum—vertebrate
   class—mammal
    subclass—eutheria
     infraclass—placental
      order—primate
       suborder—anthropoid
        infraorder—catarrhine
         superfamily—hominoid
          family—hominid
           genus—homo
            species—sapiens
             variety—sapiens

For fun, one may say (and be quite correct) that man is a hominid, hominoid, catarrhine, anthropoid, primate, placental, eutherian, mammalian, vertebrate, chordate animal.

The Characteristics of Primates

We must now backtrack a little and ask: "When is a mammal a primate, or what is distinctive about primates within the mammalian class and placental group?"

There is no absolute answer, for as Le Gros Clark has put it: "It is peculiarly difficult to give a satisfying definition of the Primates, since there is no single distinguishing feature which distinguishes all the members of the group."[6]

The differences between primates and other mammals are relative; they exist mainly in degree rather than in kind. Among the lower primates, the major morphological differences are those which are associated with tree life; among the hominoids, they are those which result from adaptations leading to upright posture and intensified manipulation (see Figure 4-1). In major respects they are:

1. Brain: Increasingly complex as one ascends the primate scale.

2. Eyes: Located well forward on the skull,

---

[6]W. E. Le Gros Clark, *History of the Primates,* p. 45.

rather than back and toward the sides. The back of the eye socket is closed and encircled with a bony ridge, whereas in other mammals it is open at the sides and rear. Vision is stereoscopic and very acute.

3. Face: Snout and jaws are reduced in size. Olfactory sense and dentition are also reduced.

4. Hands: (*a*) Forepaws are prehensile. The five-toed characteristic of primitive mammals is retained, but the toes have a marked flexibility that makes extensive grasping possible. (*b*) Claws have become flat nails on the top of the digits. (*c*) Digits have soft, fleshy pads on their undertips, richly provided with sensory nerves. Primates can feel and manipulate.

5. Hind paws: Retain five flexible toes, while big toe is especially strengthened as a pincer. In hominids the foot is more clublike and acts as a weight-carrying base.

6. Forearms: Exhibit a high degree of flexion; that is, with the elbow steady, they may be rotated clockwise or counterclockwise through almost a full circle.

7. Reproductive traits: (*a*) Among adults there is continuous association of the sexes rather than only during well-defined rutting seasons. (*b*) Female normally bears but one offspring at a time instead of a litter. (*c*) Generally, the female has but two mammary glands. (*d*) Postnatal development is relatively much more prolonged.

Morphological and Functional Characteristics of the Hominoids   Man, as the most highly developed primate, possesses all the above characteristics in their most clearly distinguishable forms. This means that he has by far the largest and most complex brain, eyes set fully forward in completely enclosed sockets with the back walls of the orbits fully formed, the smallest jaw relative to the brain case, the fewest teeth, the most fully shrunken bony structure of the snout, the most flexion of the fore limbs, and the most upright posture of all primates. The special and distinctive modifications which man has developed

in his evolution away from the more primitive and generalized primate ancestral type are detailed as we proceed with the examination of the fossil and contemporary representatives of the hominids in succeeding chapters.

Less obvious similarities and distinctions among the primates have been identified as the result of increasingly refined laboratory techniques for blood and genetic analysis. The main results follow.

Fig. 4-1   Skeletal modifications in the shift from pronograde (horizontal) to orthograde (vertical) posture. The spine gets a double curve; the rib cage projects, rather than forming an underslung basket—thus the viscera are poorly supported in man, and the abdominal wall sometimes ruptures; the pelvis broadens and becomes bucket-shaped; and the skull balances delicately above the vertebral column.

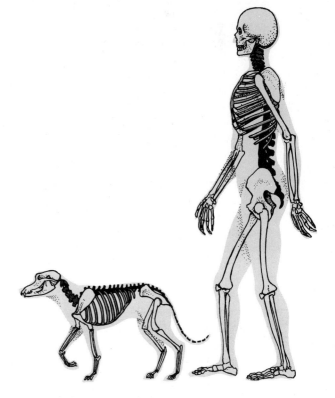

Blood Precipitates   Refinements in serology, or the study of blood, have given additional dimensions to the criteria of identification of man as a primate. Serum vaccines are produced by injecting foreign organisms into the bloodstream of a host animal, which produces antibodies specific to the alien organism. The white part of the blood, the serum, is extracted to be used as a vaccine for the specific. If dog blood is injected into a host, the resulting serum is specific for dog. When this antidog serum is mixed with dog blood, it produces a white precipitate. Weaker precipitation occurs when antidog serum is mixed with the blood of any canine, but no precipitate occurs at all if it is mixed with noncanine blood. *Only the blood of closely similar animals reacts to the vaccine serum of a member of its order.* Thus, antihuman-specific serum produces a white precipitate when mixed with ape blood and a weaker precipitate when mixed with the blood of monkeys, but no precipitates at all when mixed with nonprimate bloods. Even more specifically, the ape's reactions to ABO, RH, and MN blood-type serums of human beings are much the same as man's. It is evident that the chemical structure of human blood and of the blood of apes and monkeys is quite similar—and somewhat different from that of all other warm-blooded creatures.

Serum Protein Patterns   Current work is greatly refining the methods of serologic proof of man's relationships to other animals. By means of a process of electrophoresis, the proteins of various blood serums may be separated into from nineteen to twenty-five components showing characteristic shapes and patterns. In this process, a serum is mixed in a gel, which is placed between a positive and a negative electrode; an electric current flows between the electrodes and through the gel. The positively charged serum proteins move toward the negative pole, and the negatively charged proteins move toward the positive pole. The proteins move at differing

speeds, according to their molecular weights. A filter placed before each pole traps the proteins, collecting them according to their rates of motion. The similarities of serum protein shapes among man and the other primates are shown in Figure 4-2. Inspection reveals that the patterns of man, gorilla, and chimpanzee are very much alike, while those of the gibbon and the orangutan are distinctly different. Thus, serum protein analysis reaffirms that man is more closely related to the gorilla and chimpanzee than he is to the orangutan or gibbon. The serum patterns of other animals are found to be very unlike those of the hominoids. The cellular structure of blood protein thus confirms the more gross anatomical identification of man with the primates.

Chromosome Patterns   The genetic structures called *chromosomes* vary in number and in gross form among different plants and animals. The chromosome forms of man and the apes show close similarities, although the African chimpanzee and gorilla are more similar to man than the Asiatic orangutan and gibbon are. All are much more similar to one another than they are to any other animal chromosome forms.

Such similarities detail a close relationship among the primates as a whole and between man and the great apes in particular.

Ontogenetic Development: Baer's Rule   At various stages of human embryonic development, structures such as the notochord, gill arches, and gill grooves are present. They represent important features of certain early evolutionary forms that are not present in the fully developed human being. In broader terms, the human embryo passes through successive stages roughly similar to an undifferentiated cell mass, a coelenterate, a worm, and a generalized fish with the foundation of gill arches in its neck region. Finally, it takes on mammalian qualities and is ultimately born a human child (although even a proud parent frequently finds it difficult to agree that a

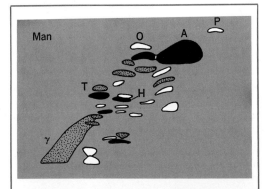

Man

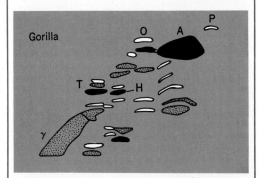

Gorilla

Chimpanzee

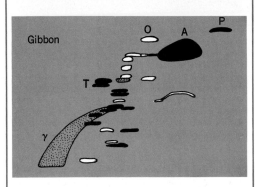

Gibbon

newborn infant really looks like a human being).

As first formulated by K. E. von Baer (1792–1876), these facts were expressed in the following proposition, called "Baer's rule": *The younger the embryos of different animals, the more alike they are; the older the embryos, the more distinctive they become.* Ernest von Haekel (1834–1919) subsequently reformulated Baer's rule into a "biogenic law," which states that the embryonic development of each individual is a compressed recapitulation of certain major features of the developmen of the species. This is the origin of the commonly stated principle, "ontogeny recapitulates phylogeny," or "each individual climbs its own family tree."

Overstatement of the theory by uncritical early evolutionists brought it into disrepute among some biologists. But the theory has some validity as is made clear by Dobzhansky: "Yet making allowances for overstatements and exaggerations, it remains true that many features of human ontogeny make no sense at all except on the assumption that they are retentions of the developmental patterns of remote ancestors."[7] More important for the question of taxonomy is the accepted fact that the successive stages of embryonic morphology of man and the apes and monkeys are very similar until quite late in fetal development when they begin to diverge significantly (Figure 4-3). In other words, the prenatal morphological similarity of man, apes, and monkeys reinforces their grouping in common categories.

[7]T. Dobzhansky, *Mankind Evolving: The Evolution of the Human Species,* p. 165.

Fig. 4-2   The close similarity of shapes of the proteins found in the blood serum of man and in that of the great apes is one type of evidence of their close evolutionary origins. (After M. Goodman, in S. L. Washburn (ed.), **Classification and Human Evolution.** *Aldine Publishing Co. Copyright © 1963 by the Wenner-Gren Foundation for Anthropological Research, Inc.)*

Evolutionary History:
The Fossil Record

Remains of ancient organisms are occasionally preserved in earth layers of different ages. Such remains are known as *fossils*. They may be reconstituted shells or skeletons that have become permeated with mineral materials from the surrounding deposits or metamorphosed by pressure and heat. Or they may be casts of imprinted molds left by the original organism. They may also be preserved specimens found in tar pits, logs, permafrost layers (permanently frozen earth), or glacial ice. The fossil record, as it has been fitted together, adds time depth to the biological picture. It frequently yields the actual ancestral types from which relatively similar living forms of organisms could have been derived. It provides the *diachronic* proof, or proof through

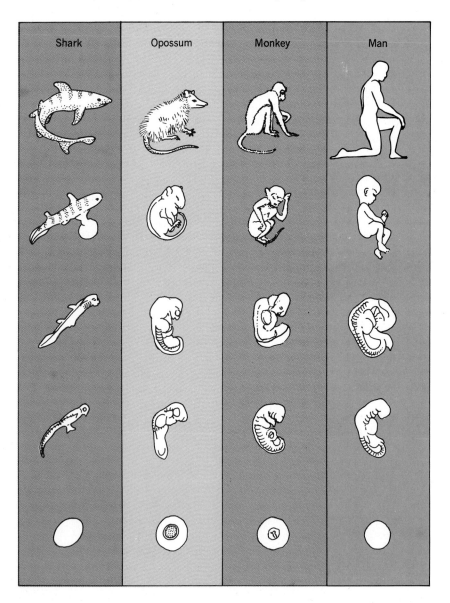

Fig. 4-3   Ontogenetic development in the shark, opossum, monkey, and man. Marked morphological differentiation among genera occurs late in fetal development. (Courtesy of the American Museum of Natural History.)

time, of common ancestry for common types by placing the solid evidence of gradual divergence from the common types before our very eyes. The fossils of prehuman primates and prehistoric man are described in the next five chapters.

The Living Primates

The fact that man and the living simians have so many detailed traits in common provides rational evidence of their common ancestry. However, this must not be taken to mean that the numerous kinds of monkeys, apes, and men have *one* common ancestor. The primates have enjoyed some seventy million years of evolutionary development as a distinctive order. During that protracted span, hundreds of primate genera and varieties have existed. It is therefore wrong to speak of any of these forms as *the* missing link, as though there were just one ancestral form. It must be realized at the outset that there are a number of series of links which make a complex pattern back to remote antiquity. Perhaps many of these links are still missing from the fossil record, but enough have been found to show the lines of development of the ancestors of primates. *There is no common ancestor, but many ancestral predecessors.* A complete family tree of man, the apes, and the monkeys would include a truly bewildering number of fossil ancestors.

All living higher primates carry some of their common heritage into the present, but the fact that the apes have certain traits today does not necessarily mean that man's early ancestors also had them. Apes, too, have evolved and changed during the past several million years, and they have developed their own distinctive specializations, such as the overgrown canine tusks, which were not characteristic of earlier primate ancestors. At no time, then, did man pass through an evolutionary stage in which he exhibited all the characteristics now displayed by the living apes or living monkeys.

Phylogenetically, one should not think of contemporary apes and monkeys as our ancestors. Instead, one should view them as related but modern animals differently adapted to different ecological situations. Apes and monkeys have similarities to man because, far back in time, they had common ancestors with man who, in that era, had made similar general adaptations to similar environments. Since that time apes, monkeys, and men have developed separately, each adapting differently to certain environments with different kinds of structures and behavior.

Our true ancestors can be known only from the fossils given up by the rocks of earlier Cenozoic times. Consideration of our fossil progenitors is reserved for the next chapter, however. We shall first take a brief look at the living primates to broaden our understanding of the order.

Prosimia: The Tree Shrew, the Tarsier, and the Lemur   A few shy species of surviving genera of the oldest of primate types survive in out-of-the-way places in the tropical belt of the Old World (Figure 4-4). Tree shrews are rather widely distributed throughout South and Southeast Asia. The tarsier is located in north-central Indonesia (Borneo, Celebes, and the Philippines). Lemurs survive only in Madagascar.

The Tree Shrew   The tree shrew is actually an insectivore and not a primate. Yet with his generalized incisor teeth, which are not of the gnawing type developed by rodents, his greater mobility of fingers and toes, his relatively larger brain, and his greater acuity of vision, he is—though still an insectivore—an insectivore that shows notable primate propensities. Indeed, in a number of details of skeletal and muscular construction, he shows specific lemuroid leanings. All in all, in the judgment of Le Gros Clark: "It seems very probable that the tree shrews represent in their general structure a tolerably close approximation to the earliest phases in the evolution of the primates from generalized mammalian ancestors.''[8]

[8]W. E. Le Gros Clark, *op. cit.,* pp. 43–44.

*Fig. 4-4   Living prosimia are the most primitive of all primates and the most similar to man's earliest primate ancestors. [After M. Wilson, in W. E. Le Gros Clark, **History of the Primates**. Courtesy of the Trustees, (British Museum) (Natural History).]*

The Tarsier   The tarsier, so named because of the extreme development of the tarsal bones in his heel, exhibits many of the general features of early primates, and in spite of his specializations, he could be very close to the original ancestral type. He is smaller than the lemur. He sports a small nose and large, goggly eyes—the better to see at night—and a free upper lip like that of monkeys and man, a lip that can be curled. He has full flexion of the neck, which can be swiveled in a complete half circle. These are all traits that point in the direction taken by the higher primates.

The evolutionary adaptation of the tarsier is all for the trees. Figure 4-5 shows a skeleton similar to his. He has developed round, platterlike toetips and fingertips with increased friction surfaces for clamping onto boughs (Figure 4-6). Like other primates, he does not have to dig in with sharp claws to climb and move about. Safe hand-and-foot contact is made much more quickly without claws, even though it may seem that squirrels and birds do all right in this respect. His most remarkable specialization, however, is the elongation of his tarsals. This gives him extra-effective leverage for sudden, propulsive jumping, while at the same time the toes at the end of his foot retain their prehensility for grasping.

The Lemur   The lemur looks rather like a little raccoon, except for his befingered hands and feet. His long snout, with its wet, doglike nostrils, is more generalized mammalian in character than it is primate, as are his large, movable ears and split upper lip. But the lemur's brain, his prehensile ''hands,'' and his flexible limbs distinguish him as a lowly type of pri-

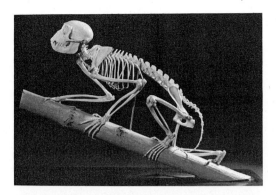

Fig. 4-5 *Skeleton of pronograde type adapted for tree-living. Note the arched spinal column, elongated pelvis, and grasping paws. (The Museum of Anthropology, University of Minnesota. Photo by Don Breneman.)*

the form of macaques, langurs, vervets, and baboons.

Of these the macaques are probably the most generally familiar, for they have by far the widest distribution. They cover a wide belt running all the way from Japan through China, Southeast Asia, India and western North Africa, to Gibraltar. (British tradition

Fig. 4-6 *The fronts of primate hands, showing relation of thumbs to fingers in the retention of prehensility. (J. Biegert, in S. L. Washburn (ed.),* **Classification and Human Evolution.** *Aldine Publishing Co. Copyright © 1963 by the Wenner-Gren Foundation for Anthropological Research, Inc. Courtesy of the author.)*

mate. He is a timid little animal who spends the greater part of his life in the trees and is active mostly at night. In evolutionary morphology, the lemur occupies an approximate midpoint between insectivores and monkeys. He is a primitive primate, but not the most primitive of the forms that we would place in the primate order.

The tree shrew, the tarsier, and the lemur are three examples of what the first Paleocene primate ancestors were like.

The Monkeys The living monkeys fall into two main infraorders within the suborder of anthropoids. These are the platyrrhines and the catarrhines, as already noted.

The Platyrrhines The platyrrhines are found only in the New World. They are notable mainly for their flat faces and long, frequently prehensile tails (Figure 4-7). Because they lead away from the main line of human evolution, we need not give further attention to them.

The Catarrhines The Old World catarrhines divide into two superfamilies: the hominoids, which include man and the great apes, and the cercopithecoids, which today are seen in

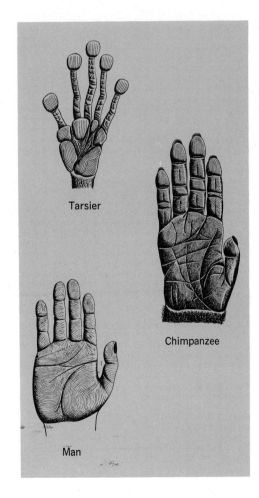

Tarsier

Chimpanzee

Man

has it that as long as the "Barbary apes" live on Gibraltar, the Rock will remain in English hands [Figure 4-8]). Over fifty species and hundreds of varieties of macaques are alive today, and there is no point in trying to describe them in general terms. Macaques can be seen in numbers in the monkey house of any zoo. They are usually equally at home on land and in trees.

Langurs are Asiatic monkeys, confined in their distribution to Tibet, India, and Ceylon and eastward to Java. Their territory overlaps that of the macaques, but it is more restricted, probably because of their more specialized adaptation to a vegetarian diet.

The baboons and the vervets (mandrills) are ground dwellers who have adapted their way of life to open country rather than to forests. With their large muzzles, quadrupedal gait, and moderate-sized tails, they are ana-tomically quite remote from man, in spite of the fact that they utilize a terrestrial habitat.

The Great Apes   The living pongids consist of the African gorilla and chimpanzee, along with the Indonesian orangutan. The Malayan gibbon and siamang are classed separately as hylobate.

Almost all the distinctive features of the gorillas and chimpanzees are related to the fact that they have become adapted to a semierect posture, combined with brachiation for food getting and quadrupedal knuckle walking and occasional bipedalism for locomotion. In their knuckle-walking mode of getting around, the gorillas and chimpanzees support themselves on the middle segment of the backs of the third and fourth fingers of their hands and on their plantigrade feet. They use this method of locomotion on the

Fig. 4-7   New World Capuchin monkey. The broad, flaring nostrils mark it as a platyrrhine. (Courtesy of the American Museum of Natural History.)

Fig. 4-8   Old World Colobus monkey. The narrow, downward-pointing nostrils mark it as a catarrhine. (Courtesy of the American Museum of Natural History.)

ground and in the trees. Gorilla brachiation is limited to lifting and lowering themselves by their arms through the trees in the search for the fruit that is a primary element in their diet, and to locate and build their nightly nesting areas. Chimpanzees sometimes brachiate, sometimes move bipedally, and sometimes knuckle-walk when they are in the trees, and often drop to the ground to knuckle-walk or walk bipedally.

The Asiatic great apes, the orangutan and gibbon, are highly adapted to arboreal existence in Southeast Asia (Figure 4-9). The orangutan does not knuckle-walk but instead walks quadrupedally with flexed or open palms facing down (palmigrade) in a pattern called quadrumanous. When in the trees (where they spend most of their time), orangs sometimes brachiate but often move about searching for fruit quadrumanously.

Many skeletal and muscular adjustments have accompanied this change from the climbing and leaping of the prosimians to the arboreal quadrupedalism of the great apes. The feet have lost some of their mobility and a considerable amount of their prehensility (Figure 4-10). The leg bones are much stouter and have much more pronounced dorsal ridges (the *linea aspera*) for anchoring the flexing muscles that run to the thigh and pelvis. The ilia in the pelvis have flared out, and the whole hip structure has become shorter and wider. The spine has become more massive and rigid, with fewer vertebrae. The shoulders have broadened, the chest has become more like a barrel and less like the prow of a ship, and the breastbone has become short and stubby.

The fore limbs of the apes have become enormously elongated and strengthened relative to the length of the body, for this pair of limbs bears most of the brunt in getting about in the trees. The apes have lost their tails—externally, that is, for a vestigial tail is still to be found in the coccyx, as it is also in man.

In the skull, the occipital condyles, the

(a)

Fig. 4-9 (a) *A five-year-old male orangutan thoughtfully regards his natural environment.* (b) *A brachiating gibbon and his partner resting in the crotch of a tree.* [(a) *Courtesy of Barbara K. Harrisson for Sarawak Museum.* (b) *Ylla from Rapho Guillumette Pictures.*]

(b)

hinges on which the skull articulates with the spine, have moved from a position far back on the occipital bone forward to an intermediary position. The related *foramen magnum,* or great opening, through which the spinal cord passes from the cranium as an appendage of the brain, has also moved forward and downward from a vertical orientation to one that forms an acute angle with an imaginary horizontal base line.

In adult males, especially, heavy chewing and neck musculature is attached to remark-able bony ridges that form sharp crests along the top of the skull and across the occiput.

Concerning dentition, the apes have cusp patterns for the upper and lower molars similar to those of man. The canine teeth of the apes are very different from man's, however, for the apes possess conical, daggerish canines projecting well beyond the surface level of the lower teeth and overlapping them.

The brains of these creatures, while far inferior to those of the hominids in mental capacity and development, are greatly superior to those of all other animals.

Primate Behavior

Before 1958–1960, very little was known about the behavior of wild chimpanzees and gorillas in their natural habitats. Now, however, the daily lives of wild chimpanzees and gorillas have been painstakingly scrutinized by trained observers.[9] Figure 4-11 shows their behavior in some typical situations. Little is still known scientifically about the comparable behavior of gibbons and orangutans.

In essence, research done in their natural habitat shows the great apes to be exceedingly timid and nonaggressive. It took Jane Goodall fourteen months of almost daily, quiet contact before the chimpanzees of the Gombe Stream Reserve on Lake Tanganyika would accept her presence without distur-

[9]See I. DeVore (ed.), *Primate Behavior: Field Studies of Monkeys and Apes,* for generalized comparative accounts of the studies and their results.

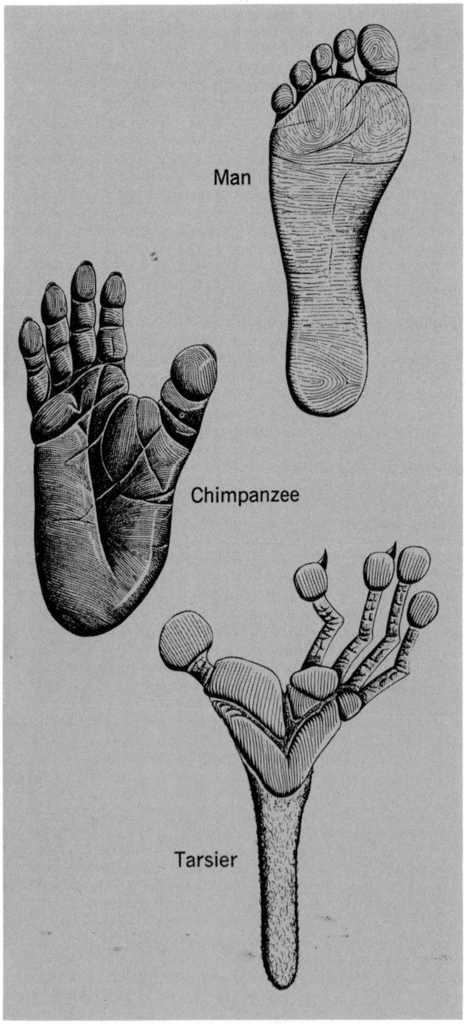

Fig. 4-10   The undersides of primate feet, showing strengthening of big toe, reduction of grasping powers, and solidification of the foot as a walking and standing base in man. (J. Biegert, in S. L. Washburn (ed.), **Classification and Human Evolution.** *Aldine Publishing Co. Copyright © 1963 by the Wenner-Gren Foundation for Anthropological Research, Inc. Courtesy of the author.)*

bance and flight.[10] Gorillas became used to the presence of a peaceful investigator in the vicinity more readily, however. African apes have apparently survived by keeping out of harm's way. Populations are small aggregations (sixty to eighty chimpanzees and two to thirty gorillas), divided into subgroups among which individuals readily transfer their membership. Each primary group focuses about a large, dominant adult male, who is clearly the leader. Males are dominant over females, and dominance hierarchies exist within the sexes; yet chimpanzees and gorillas are remarkably tolerant in personal relations, and there is little fighting to establish or maintain dominance. Accession to authority, mildly exercised, seems to be readily accepted.

The infant-mother dependency-protective relation is close and attentive for three years. Adults of both genera, but particularly gorillas, "gave one the impression of having an independent and self-dependent temperament, appearing stoic, aloof, and reserved in their affective behavior."[11] They are social creatures, but they are not sociable. Social organization is minimal and loose, and yet very cohesive in that individuals rarely tend to get very far apart. Communication within the proximate group is accomplished more by means of bodily and facial gesture than by sounds. On the other hand, subgroups that are out of sight of one another regularly indicate their locations by calls.

Goodall has emphasized the tool-using propensities among the chimpanzees under her observation. Wild chimpanzees prepare stems which they insert in termite holes until they are covered with insects, which they then bite off, and a chimpanzee in the Omaha, Nebraska, zoo was reported, in the press in 1968, as having learned by himself to pick the lock on his cage with a piece of wire which he kept hidden. Captive chimpanzees will occasionally throw sticks and stones, with very poor aim, at "enemies." The apes, in spite of their manifest learning capacities in circuses and in the laboratories of experimental psychologists (see pages 23–24), do not under natural circumstances produce very notable cultural contributions.

The eating habits of the apes are largely vegetarian, and six to eight hours a day are required to collect enough plants and fruit to sustain their large bodies. Goodall has seen an occasional chimpanzee devour a freshly killed baby monkey or infant antelope.

Antecedents of Culture   It is impossible for an outside observer to *know* what takes place in the mind of a chimpanzee, but Kortlandt may not be overimaginative when he observes:

The chimpanzees were unceasingly alert and curious. They seized every opportunity to bring variety into their lives, taking different paths down the hill on different occasions and continually changing their gait and their mode of locomotion. They were fascinated by everything new and unusual. They carefully examined all the objects I laid in their path and even collected some of them. Once I saw a chimpanzee gaze at a particularly beautiful sunset for a full 15 minutes, watching the changing colors until it became so dark that he had to retire to the forest without stopping to pick a papaw for his evening meal.

Another respect in which the animals resembled human beings was in their doubting and uncertain nature. They appeared to ponder such problems as whether to turn to the left or the right, or whether or not a papaw tasted good. Often, just like laboratory chimpanzees puzzling over a difficult problem in an intelligence test, the chimpanzees I observed scratched themselves elaborately while making these decisions.[12]

Man's ancestors surely had this capacity to ponder over problems in an even greater degree. This capacity for thought is the ultimate key to his culture-creating capacity. When fully flowered, it is the glory of man.

[10]*Ibid.,* p. 428.
[11]G. B. Schaller, "The Behavior of the Mountain Gorilla," in *ibid.,* pp. 345–346.

[12]A. Kortlandt, "Chimpanzees in the Wild" (*Scientific American,* May 1962), pp. 128–134.

(a)

(b)

(c)

(d)

Fig. 4-11   African apes, the chimpanzee and gorilla, are semiadapted to ground dwelling and more closely related to man. (a) At home in the trees, alerted to the presence of outsiders. The infant, grasping its mother for support, is in a position to climb on her back in case they decide to flee. (b) Chimpanzee "togetherness." A pongid sensitivity session of females and juveniles engaged in grooming and establishing mutual feelings of close interdependence. (c) Chimpanzees in upright and quadrupedal postures engaged in a tiff over possession of the infant, which is clinging to its mother's back in the normal carrying position. (d) A chimpanzee foraging for food on the ground. (e) The forest gorilla normally moves about on all fours, but when threatened (f) the males rise on their hind legs for defiant chest-thumping acts. [(a, b, c, d) copyright © 1969, Dr. H. Albrecht, Bruce Coleman, Inc. (e, f) reprinted from The Year of the Gorilla *by permission of the author, George B. Schaller, © 1964 by the University of Chicago.]*

(e)

(f)

Before we leave the living primates, however, it may be well to note four important and socially significant traits of apes and monkeys which are of fundamental importance for man: (1) group sociability and year-round association of the sexes; (2) prolonged infant dependency and protection of the females and their young by the males; (3) incipient food sharing; and (4) communication and rudimentary conceptualization, but without the capacity for speech.[13] These traits provided the basic behavioral elements for the first human societies and "culture."

Building upon this base, the hominids ultimately achieved (1) a transition to hunting and meat eating; (2) upright posture and regular reliance upon toolmaking and tool using; (3) family grouping with local bands; (4) outgroup mating (consciousness of incest sensitivities); and (5) speech. The first two of these hominid traits we derive from the fossil

record. The last three are inferred from our knowledge of primitive human societies. Let us now turn to the fossil record.

SUMMARY

Classification is man's way of simplifying his world of experience. Scientific classification is the process of identifying common characteristics inherent in a number of differing phenomena and of grouping them in categories. It is the search for the like in the unlike. Classifications are always arbitrary constructions of the human mind in that the taxonomist decides which traits are sufficiently alike and significant to be included among the attributes of a class. A good taxonomy must be empirically sound; that is, the traits that it uses for classification must be genuine characteristics of the subjects to be classified and not imputed by the prejudices of the observer. Nevertheless, there is always a subjective act of judgment in every assignment of a specimen to a given category within a system of classification. However, scientifi-

---

[13]See, especially, J. Van Lawick-Goodall, "A Preliminary Report on Expressive Movements and Communication in the Gombe Stream Chimpanzees," in P. C. Jay (ed.), *Primates*, pp. 313–374.

cally educated people accept the proposition that a living human being should be classified among the primates as an anthropoid, catarrhine, hominoid, and hominid.

Primates are mammals possessing highly complex brains, stereoscopic and sharp vision, a sense of smell and a snout that have been reduced in acuity and size, prehensile forepaws (with nails and fleshy pads), hindpaws that have become feet with a big toe, and forearms with total flexion. They have no rutting season, two mammary glands, usually one offspring at a time (normally there are no litters), and a long period of postnatal development.

In addition to such gross morphological and functional characteristics, which are shared by the prosimia, monkeys, apes, and men, a number of special common traits have been revealed through advanced techniques in scientific laboratories. These include blood precipitation reactions, serum protein patterns, chromosome patterns, and similarities in ontogenetic development.

Finally, the fossil record reveals many transitional forms that link the present fossils phylogenetically through geologic time.

The living primates are represented by the prosimia (the tree shrews, the tarsiers, and the lemurs) and by monkeys, apes, and men. The prosimia, which are the most primitive in form, are quadrupedal tree dwellers of small size. Monkeys exist in hundreds of varieties and more than fifty species. They, too, are mostly arboreal forest dwellers (particularly in Africa) and are quadrupedal, although the members of a number of genera, such as baboons and vervets, are terrestrial. The great apes are limited to only four genera —those to which the chimpanzee, gorilla, orangutan, and gibbon belong. These large, tailless creatures are forest dwellers, but the members of the African genera, the chimpanzee and the gorilla, spend more time on the ground than in trees, and they can walk in a semiupright position. When moving about in trees, they knuckle-walk or walk bipedally and lift by the arms.

All nonhuman living primates subsist on leaves, shoots, berries, and insects. Chimpanzees occasionally kill and eat the meat of the young of defenseless monkeys and antelopes, but man is the only modern primate who is a habitual meat eater. He alone is the great toolmaker and tool user, the talker and thinker, who lives more by culture than by instinct.

SELECTED READINGS

DeVore, I. (ed.), *Primate Behavior: Field Studies of Monkeys and Apes* (1965). A very useful summary of recent field studies of primate behavior written by a number of the people who have done the original research. The product of a cooperative project and conference held in 1962.

Goodall, J., "My Life among the Wild Chimpanzees" (*National Geographic,* vol. 24, no. 2, 1963), pp. 272–308. If you want to know what patience, resourcefulness, controlled courage, and skill it takes to do a really successful field study of chimpanzees, this article will tell you. Illustrated with excellent color photographs.

Jay, P. C. (ed.), *Primates: Studies in Adaptation and Variability* (1968). A continuation of developing studies in primate behavior, following upon that reported in DeVore (above).

Pilbeam, D., *The Evolution of Man* (1970). A well-reasoned and authoritative modern view of the subject.

Schaller, G. B., *The Mountain Gorilla* (1963). The most comprehensive account of gorillas in their natural habitat in the Belgian Congo (1959 to 1960).

Simpson, G. G., *Principles of Animal Taxonomy* (1961). An expert coverage of the subject.

Washburn, S. L. (ed.), *Classification and Human Evolution* (1963). The papers of the 1962 Wenner-Gren symposium on classification of the hominoids. The book contains a number of excellent papers by foremost students of the primates.

Chapter 5

Evolution and the Primates

Two thousand years ago, the Latin poet Lucretius gave us the classical version of the evolution of human culture and the concept of a lowly beginning for man, followed by the growth of material culture, social order, religion, and language.[1]

What the classical ancients dimly understood, we can now see in finer detail and clearer outline, for the last century of research in the physical, biological, and anthropological sciences has done much to dispel the misty fogs that have so long shrouded our past. No longer need we rely on myth and fancy to understand something of our origins.

[1]For a vivid, modern version, *Lucretius, The Way Things Are; The* De Rerum Natura of *Titus Lucretius Carus,* translated by Rolfe Humphries, is recommended reading.

With the tools of archaeology to provide the fossil evidence, the techniques of physics and botany to prove the antiquity of the fossils, and the science of genetics to reveal how evolution takes place, we have a firmer hold on the reality of the past than was the case a century, or even fifty years, ago.

The problem for science today is to reconstruct in more certain detail the lines along which man has developed in evolution from the simple, single-celled organism that first came into being in the Paleozoic era three billion years ago, and to determine the processes at work in shaping him.

In this chapter, we shall discuss certain factors of biological evolution as they relate to the primates, namely, the dating of fossils,

Fig. 5-A   Dr. Barbara K. Harrisson, anthropologist, with orangutan, Baho National Park, Sarawak. (Junaidi bin Bolhassan, for Sarawak Museum.)

Table 5-1   Geologic Eras, Beginning Dates, and Dominant Life Forms Developed in Each Era

Geologic era	Beginning date (before present)	Dominant life forms
Cenozoic	65,000,000	Man Primates Mammals
Mesozoic	230,000,000	First mammals Birds Dinosaurs
Paleozoic	6,000,000,000	Land plants Reptiles Fish Trilobites Oldest dated algae

Table 5-2   Epochs of the Cenozoic Era, with Dates and Newest Life Forms Developed in Each Epoch

Epochs	Beginning date (before present)	Newest life form
Recent	15,000	
Pleistocene	2 to 3,000,000	*Homo sapiens* *Homo erectus* Australopithecines
Pliocene	13,000,000	*Ramapithecus*
Miocene	25,000,000	Apes
Oligocene	35,000,000	Monkeys
Eocene	60,000,000	Small mammals, including first primates
Paleocene	65,000,000	Placental mammals

the mechanics of evolution, and the fossils of the prehominid primates.

Geology and the Antiquity of the Primates

Stratigraphy is the analysis of geological deposits in terms of discernible layers. Derivative time sequences are inferred from the relative positions of the strata, for the underlying strata are older than those overlying them—barring serious disturbances of the earth. In any local site, the relative ages of major geological strata are ordinarily clear. But in no single locality is one likely to find the entire sequence of major strata for all geologic periods. The master key is then built up by matching overlapping sequences. Once the key is established, the relative position of an isolated geological stratum can be determined by matching it to the homologous stratum in the key. Stratigraphy thus makes it possible to tell the relative ages of rocks and of the fossils and archaeological materials that may be contained within them. This in turn makes it possible to place the sequences of the evolutionary development of life forms in time by means of hard facts.

Geologic Eras and Periods   The time that elapsed from the beginning of our universe to the birth of the earth is *cosmic time*. *Geologic time* began with the laying down of the first sediments four to six billion years ago, and extends to the present. Major blocks of geologic time are called *eras*. Eras are brought to a close by drastic changes in earth conditions, called *revolutions*. The three geologic eras and their dominant life forms are indicated in Table 5-1. Minor changes in earth conditions, called *disturbances*, take place within eras, producing the subdivisions of eras, called *epochs* and *periods*. The evolution of the primates occurred entirely within the final geologic era, the *Cenozoic*. Within this era are seven epochs: the *Paleocene*, the *Eocene*, the *Oligocene*, the *Miocene*, the *Pliocene*, the *Pleistocene*, and *Recent* (see Table 5-2). The Miocene, Pliocene, and Pleistocene epochs are of critical importance for man's immediate antecedents, and Pleistocene geology is crucial for the study of man himself, for this is the period in which the hominids finally evolved.

The Pleistocene Epoch The Pleistocene was an unstable epoch of fluctuating cold and moderate warmth.

During spans of extreme cold, snow that falls in high altitudes or in high latitudes of the northern hemisphere does not melt off in the short, cool summers. It accumulates year by year, packed down by its own weight, until it is metamorphosed into ice. Although ice is a solid, it has a low viscosity which enables it to flow downgrade, scouring mountain valleys and spreading outward from the massive ice cap over vast areas. The locking of water in the ice, during *glaciations* (advances of ice sheets), lowers sea levels around the world by several hundred feet. The great glacial weight upon the continents and the lightened weight of the water in the ocean basins cause continental subsidence and changing of land contours. Temperate and tropical zones outside the frigid glacial areas shift and change, forcing extensive migration and new adaptations by plant and animal life. The unstable Pleistocene was thus a time that tested and stimulated the adaptive capabilities of man, and also hastened his evolutionary development.

The long heaps of debris left at the points where glacial advances ceased (called *morains*), outwash deposits, and river terraces all correlate with specific glaciations. Changes in flora and fauna also correlate with glacial and interglacial phases. Thus, the geochronology within the Pleistocene can be fairly precisely determined in many local areas of the world today. The major climatic cycles within the Pleistocene produced four primary advances of the ice sheets or glaciations. In Europe, these are named after Alpine valleys, while in North America they are called after the states in which their effects are most prominent.[2] For our purposes, it is suffcient to refer to them by numbers, using roman numerals for glaciations and arabic numerals for interglacials (Figure 5-1).

Recent research on the Pleistocene Epoch is based primarily upon the analysis of microorganisms and molluscs found in the cores of ocean-bed drillings. This research has revealed a prolonged cool period preceding the first actual glaciations. There

Fig. 5-1   The Pleistocene time scale, with European and North American nomenclature for major glacial phases. The prolonged second interglacial is sometimes called the Great Interglacial.

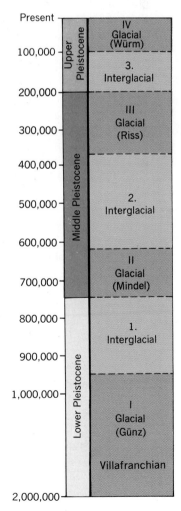

Present		
	Upper Pleistocene	IV Glacial (Würm)
100,000		
		3. Interglacial
200,000		
	Middle Pleistocene	III Glacial (Riss)
300,000		
400,000		
		2. Interglacial
500,000		
600,000		
		II Glacial (Mindel)
700,000		
800,000		
		1. Interglacial
900,000		
	Lower Pleistocene	
1,000,000		
		I Glacial (Günz)
		Villafranchian
2,000,000		

[2]Günz, Mindel, Riss, and Würm, in Europe; Nebraskan, Kansan, Illinoisan, and Wisconsonian, on the North American continent.

is no firm evidence as yet, however, that there was anything like the Alpine glacial advances before the Günz glaciation. There is general agreement that a million or so years of cold climate should be attributed to the beginning of the Pleistocene Epoch. This phase of the Pleistocene is known as the Villafranchian— the time in which the first modern genera of animals appear.

The whole span of the Pleistocene can be said to cover one and three-quarters to two, or possibly three, million years.

Dating Prehistoric Remains   Concern with evolutionary sequences makes it important to know which forms of life came after which. For these purposes, the *relative dating* of materials is sufficent. Often, however, it is not possible to link a deposit in one part of the world directly with another elsewhere so as to be able to say with certainty which is the older. This, then, may seriously inhibit the establishment of evolutionary sequences, if two crucial fossils or cultural deposits happen to be involved. In such instances, absolute dating is a great help. In *absolute dating,* exact or approximately exact years, integrated with our modern calendar, may be established. When such dates are available, relative ages are then readily determinable. Absolute dates for prehistoric remains are therefore always desirable, even if they are not always attainable.

Physicochemical Dating   Early in this century, Lord Rutherford and his coworkers at Cambridge Univeristy, England, demonstrated that uranium and thorium gradually disintegrate to become nonradioactive lead. Rates of decay were established and expressed in years of half-life. A *half-life* is the span of time necessary for 50 per cent of a given amount of uranium or thorium to disintegrate to lead isotypes. Table 5-3 shows the half-lives and the residual products of the five radioactive minerals known to occur in some rocks. In 1907, the idea was born that if the ratio of residual lead to radioactive elements could

Table 5-3   Radioactive Elements and Their Disintegration Products, with Their Half-lives (in millions of years)

Radioactive element	*Nonradioactive decay product*	*Half-life*
Uranium 238	Lead 206, helium	4,500
Uranium 235	Lead 207, helium	710
Thorium 232	Lead 208, helium	13,900
Potassium 40	Calcium 40, argon 40	1,310
Rubidium 87	Strontium 87	50,000

be determined in representative rocks, the age of the original formation of the rocks could be determined. For example, if the number of atoms of uranium 238 in a rock is equal to the number of lead 206 atoms, it means that one-half of the original uranium 238 has converted to lead 206; a half-life of uranium 238 has elapsed, and the rock is 4.5 billion years old (assuming no contamination or other upsetting factors). Recent derivations indicate a probable age of 4.5 to 6 billion years for the earth, and more than 6 billion years for our portion of the universe. In archaeology, potassium 40–argon 40 (K^{40}– A^{40}) readings are potentially important, since under optimum conditions they can fix dates between one hundred thousand and two million years by virtue of the relatively short half-life of potassium 40.[3]

Carbon 14 Dating   Immediately after World War II, a new possibility for dating archaeological materials was conceived by the nuclear physicist W. F. Libby. The method is based on the same principle of disintegration of radioactive elements, but instead of being applicable solely to rocks, it is usable with organic materials: wood, bone, and seeds and other forms of plant life. It works with the charcoal from prehistoric campfires, the remains of man's dinners (animal bones and

[3]H. Brown, "The Age of the Solar System" (*Scientific American,* April, 1957, S. A. Reprint 102); A. Knopf, "Measuring Geologic Time," (*The Scientific Monthly,* November, 1957), pp. 225–236. And see especially F. Hole and R. F. Heizer, *An Introduction to Prehistoric Archaeology,* 2d ed.), chap. 10.

seeds), and the bones of his very self, provided they are not too fossilized.

Carbon 14 (C^{14}) is formed in the stratosphere when neutrons freed by cosmic rays bombard atmospheric nitrogen. The nitrogen becomes transmuted to radioactive C^{14}. Atmospheric movements are assumed to mix C^{14} evenly throughout the earth's air. Plants absorb C^{14} from the air; animals absorb it from the plants they eat. When a plant or an animal dies, the absorption of C^{14} ceases, and its disintegration begins. The half-life of C^{14} is now calculated at 5,730 ± 40 years.[4] The number of radioactive emissions per minute, as measured by specially devised counters, indicates the amount of C^{14} still residual in a specimen. From this, its age may be calculated. Carbon 14 dating presents a number of technical problems, and its readings need to be used with care. It is also limited by the fact it is reliably effective only up to 30,000 years, although recent improvements in technique indicate that usable readings up to 70,000 years may be available.[5]

Palynology or Pollen Analysis   Under favorable circumstances it is possible to reconstruct general climatic conditions for a given time and place by taking core drillings for the soil and analyzing the pollen content from different levels. The principle is very simple. For example: birch grows under cold, wet conditions while beech requires a much milder climate. It is also known that late, post-glacial conditions were cold and wet. The presence of a large quantity of birch pollen, combined with an absence of beech (along with varying ratios of other selected plants) in a soil sample, suggests that the soil dates from a time when the climate was cold and wet, such as in the late Pleistocene.

The method is particularly useful for specifying local climatic conditions at given prehistoric sites dating from the end of the Pleistocene on. There are several conditions which must be met before a pollen analysis can be applied to an area. They include the necessity of environmental conditions at the area which will preserve the pollen; past environmental conditions that resulted in general, areawide vegetational changes rather than local, specialized changes; and finally, the establishment of a standardized pollen sequence near the area in a naturally deposited context such as a lake or swamp. The analyst must have a comprehensive knowledge of the ecology of the area he is studying. He must also be capable of distinguishing one magnified grain of pollen from another, and must be endowed with the patience of Job to count the number of grains of each type of plant in a standard-sized sample.

Coprolitic Analysis   Akin to pollen analysis, but not directly a dating technique, is the analysis of human and animal fecal remains that have been preserved in dry caves, a recently developed interest. Human fecal remains contain the undigested remnants of prehistoric meals: seeds, plant fibers, animal hair, bits of shells of nuts and molluscs. Not only do such remnants shed light on the diet of prehistoric men, but they also reveal something of the plant and animal life of the period in which the diners lived. This in turn provides clues to climatic conditions; hence, to geologic periods. Because the materials are so largely organic, they are eminently suitable for C^{14} analysis and dating.[6] As a further aid to reconstruction of environment and climate, animal coprolites can also be analyzed for organic materials that might suggest the nature of their food supplies and feeding habits.

Dendrochronology   Dendrochronology (Gr. *dendron,* tree + *logy,* study of), or tree-ring dating, exploits the fact that trees grow faster in wet years than in drought years, provided their roots are not waterlogged. This, in turn, shows in the annual growth rings of some types of trees, especially pine. The basic

---

[4]Libby's original figure was 5,568 years.
[5]See Hole and Heizer, *op. cit.,* for other less commonly used physicochemical methods.

[6]R. F. Heizer and L. K. Napton, "Biological and Cultural Evidence from Human Coprolites" (*Science,* vol. 165, 1969), pp. 563–568.

technique is very similar to that used in building a stratigraphic master key, except that instead of matching layers of types of rock, growth rings of comparable thickness belonging to trees that grew in the same area are matched (see Figure 5-2). The method is neat and precise, but it is applicable only in a limited number of environments. So far, keys going back 1,500 years in the American Southwest and 4,000 years in Nevada have been worked out. Efforts are being made to apply the method to Turkey and other semiarid regions.

Paleontology Paleontology (Gr. *palaios,* old + *onta,* existing things) is the study of past life through fossils. Associated flora and fauna add another dimension to chronological analysis. Woolly mammoths are Ice Age mammals, which do not occur in deposits laid down in warm Mesozoic times. Consequently, the mere presence of such fossils in a deposit indicates that the stratum is almost certainly post-Mesozoic and is likely to be of the Pleistocene epoch. In favorable instances, the total assemblage of fossil plants and animals may indicate rather clearly whether it is a Lower, Middle, or Upper Pleistocene deposit.

Taken separately, or in combination as circumstances permit, such techniques as those just presented help to take the guesswork out of prehistoric dating. As additional experience with physicochemical methods leads to greater precision and reliability, the replacement of inference with direct facts will be achieved. Having indicated the nature of the time scale within which evolution has taken place, we come to our next task, which is to review some of the major mechanisms by means of which evolution occurs.

Genetics and Evolution

How do new genera and species come into being through a gradual process of evolution over many generations of time? Only when this is understood can we begin to answer the more specific questions concerning the origins of man: "How did the primates de-

Fig. 5-2   The basic technique of dendrochronology. Matched annual growth rings in overlapping segments, beginning with one of known age, fix the date at which each beam was cut. (Modified from J. D. Jennings, **Prehistory of North America.** *Copyright © 1968 by McGraw-Hill Book Company.)*

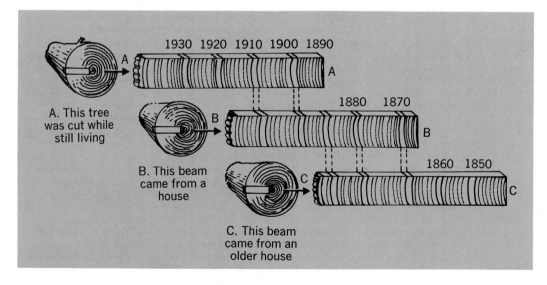

velop from simpler mammals?" "How did the different genera of fossil men derive from the primates?" "How do the many types of fossil and living primates—including man—relate to one another?"

The answers have been found in the biochemistry of the gene, the microbiology of cellular reproduction, the Mendelian laws of inheritance, and Darwin's principles of natural selection. Although anthropology is not directly concerned with the biochemical nature of the genetic code, it is very much concerned with the macro-level effects of Mendelian inheritance and natural selection—problems of population genetics. For this reason, a summary review of the more relevant genetic principles is in order here.[7]

Cellular Reproduction Up until 175 years ago, the idea of spontaneous generation of life, such as maggots, was commonplace in Europe and America. By the middle of the nineteenth century, however, microscopic study of living organisms was demonstrating that all organisms are communities of cells and that every cell is the offspring of preceding cells. The pattern of inheritance is different for uniparental and biparental organisms. Because primates are of the biparental type, only the second pattern need be considered here.

Mitosis The mature human body is made up of trillions of cells, all organized in an integrated system. Every one of these cells is the product of repeated reproduction of a single pair of sex cells (*gametes*). The fusion of a male gamete, or sperm, with a female gamete, or ovum, produces a *zygote,* or fertilized egg. At this point in an organism's life history, it receives the basic genetic materials that will largely determine the nature of the molecular

structure of all its subsequent cell development. The organism itself grows by multiplication of additional cells through cell division, or fission. In multiple-celled organisms, all cells contain nuclei, and each nucleus contains genetic materials in a substance called *chromatin.* The particular kind of cell division that occurs among metazoa is known as *mitosis* (Gr. *mitos,* thread) because it is characterized at one stage by the formation of threads out of the chromatin. The threads in turn break up into microscopically visible bodies of distinctive shapes, which are known as *chromosomes* (colorable bodies). The cells of man produce forty-six chromosomes in twenty-three pairs. In mitosis, chromosomes split longitudinally into two separate halves, which then migrate to opposite poles in the cell, whereupon the cell itself divides into two new daughter cells, each of which contains identical chromosomal complements of twenty-three pairs. By means of mitosis, each chromosome produces an exact replica of itself that is repeated in all the trillions of cells that subsequently mature to form the organism—except for the sex cells. Gametes go through a special process of self-reproduction called *meiosis* (Gr. *meioun,* to make smaller).

Meiosis The *diploid* state occurs when there is the normal chromosome complement of paired chromosomes characteristic of all but sex cells. Fertilization joins two gametes, which, if the sex cells were diploid, would double the chromosome count every generation. To prevent this from happening, sex cells have a special process of self-reproduction, in which a gamete receives only one of the chromosomes out of each pair. Human gametes have only twenty-three chromosomes. Whether it is the chromosomes inherited from the father or those inherited from the mother which go into any given gamete is apparently a matter of chance. As a result, there is *variation* among the offspring of any mating pair.

[7]Those who retain a good mastery of basic biology may overlook the next seven pages. For those who wish more detailed and authoritative background material, the following are recommended: I. M. Lerner, *Heredity, Evolution, and Society* (1968), and R. C. King, *Genetics* (2d ed., 1965).

Mitosis produces hereditary stability and is the basis of continuity of organic life. *Meiosis* ensures continuity but introduces an element of variation among offspring. *Variation is the first key to evolutionary change.*

Genes in Heredity Chromosomes are exceedingly gross units of hereditary reproduction, for they are constituted of an undetermined number of smaller units, called *genes*. Genes in turn are known to be constituted of combinations of deoxyribonucleic acid (the now-famous DNA), ribonucleic acid (RNA), and several types of proteins. Variations in the molecular structure of DNA constitute the hereditary determinants in genes. The DNA code, or molecular structure, sets the pattern for subsequent molecular synthesis in cell formation.[8]

A gene is thought of as that minimum part of a chromosome (1) which functions to control a single chemical synthesis in a cell; (2) which, when its own molecular structure changes (mutates), alters just one trait of a cell; or (3) which can separate from its own chromosome and transfer, or "cross over," to the other chromosome in the pair in a reproductive cell. In other words, a gene is a unitary segment of the continuous molecular chain that constitutes a chromosome. Traits are the products of the genes that an organism inherits. The traits that can be detected as characteristic of an organism develop, under the direction of genes, according to the DNA code in the genes interacting with the total cellular environment of the organism and the external environment that impinges on the organism. More briefly, organic traits are the product of gene patterns as limited by environment.

Mendelian Inheritance The Austrian monk Gregor Mendel (1822–1884), breeding peas

in the garden of the Augustinian monastery in Brünn, Austria (now Břno, Czechoslovakia), knew little of the cellular mechanisms outlined above, but he discovered laws for the inheritance of traits that hold for all living things. He noted that when two pure lines of unlike peas (for example, with smooth versus wrinkled surfaces) were crossed, all the offspring were smooth. But when the hybrid offspring were mated with one another, smoothness and wrinkledness showed up as distinct traits in a definite proportion of 3 to 1. Furthermore, in all subsequent hybridizations, the characteristics of smoothness and roundness were inherited independently and recombined in all possible ways (see Figure 5-3). Mendel also showed this to be true of other traits, such as color.

The Laws of Mendelian Inheritance In explaining his observations, Mendel reasoned that the sperm and the egg each contain "factors" that control the development of traits. These are the modern genes. Further, he reasoned, each plant must get at least one factor from each parent plant. Therefore, there must be two factors for each trait in the offspring. But only one factor can be passed on when the offspring mate, so there must be a reduction of the two factors to one in the sperm and egg. How it was done, he did not know, but he predicted meiosis as a process. He further noted that the redistribution of factors among the offspring was entirely random and also that differences in the effects of the factors influenced specific traits. For example, the factor for smooth skins is dominant over that for wrinkled skins when the two forms of this factor are combined in the cells of an offspring. Because the hereditary factors transmitted through reproductive cells are separable units and are inherited as such, Mendel's first law of inheritance is called the *law of segregation*. Phrased in modern terms, in which "gene" is synonymous with "factor" it states: "Genes do not blend, but behave as independent units. They pass intact from one generation

[8]The Watson-Crick model, which presents a theoretical concept of DNA molecular structure, is described in contemporary biology and genetics texts. A good exposition may be found in I. M. Lerner, *op. cit.,* pp. 75–92.

to the next, where they may or may not produce visible traits, depending on their dominance characteristics. And genes segregate at random, thereby producing predictable ratios of traits in the offspring."[9]

Mendel's second law expresses the fact that inherited gene pairs for a given trait are not influenced by the inheritance of, or the failure to inherit, any other specific genes *located on other chromosomes*. The genetic controllers of traits are independently assorted among offspring, and they express their traits independently of the location of other genes on other chromosomes. This is known as the *law of independent assortment*. It explains how each individual, except an identical twin, may receive a unique *total* combination of inherited traits. The possible number of gene combinations for any twenty-three hypothetical traits in man that are controlled by genes located on different chromosome pairs is 2^{23}, or more than eight million different gamete combinations. In fertilization, the fusion of two such gametes gives the mathematical possibility of $8,000,000 \times 8,000,000$, or more than sixty-four trillion gene combinations. Since many more than twenty-three different traits are controlled by genes located on different chromosome pairs, the number of possible total trait combinations is more than astronomical. Here, then, is a second major Mendelian source of variation.

The third law of Mendelian inheritance was discovered not by Mendel, but by T. H. Morgan (1866–1945), the first of the great geneticists at Columbia University, early in the present century. It is the *law of lineal order of genes;* namely, the genes for specific traits are located in regular sequences along a chromosome, and they are linked together by chemical bonds, so that they are all normally inherited as a chromosome group. When chromosomes match up in the zygote, they ordinarily bond in parallel strands. Some-

[9]P. B. Weisz, *The Science of Biology* (2d ed., 1963).

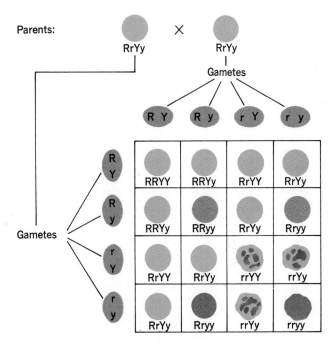

Fig. 5-3   Independent assortment and recombination of genes. In this model, each parental gamete contains a heterozygous combination of dominant and recessive genes for smooth (R) and wrinkled (r) shape and for yellow (Y) and green (y) color. In meiosis, the genes are segregated, independently assorted, and recombined, as indicated in the block diagram. (P. B. Weisz, **Elements of Biology.** *Copyright ©️ 1965 by McGraw-Hill Book Company.)*

times, however, they twist across each other, and a segment of each chromosome may become detached at the point of crossing-over (Figure 5-4). Each detached segment "joins" the chromosome of its opposite number, and a switch of chromosome segments is effected. The genetic code of each particular chromosome in the pair is thus altered. Although genes are independently assorted in inheritance, their relative positions on the chromosomes are important, for genes influence one another's effects in the development of traits. Crossing-over, by changing the proximity of specific genes, can alter their combined effects and so modify cell structure and somatic form, thus producing yet another source of variation.

Genotypes and Phenotypes   Each individual receives two matching genes of each type, one from each parent. The separate genes that match or pair with each other at the same chromosome locus are *alleles* (Gr. *allelon,* of one another). The total complement of genes transmitted to a zygote makes up its *genotype* (Gr. *gen,* to reproduce + *typos,* blow), or the genetic constitution of a given organism. When the pair of alleles for a given trait in an organism is the same (that is, both dominant or both recessive genes), the condition is called *homozygous* (Gr. *homos,* like + *zygotos,* yoked). The trait then directly manifests its genetic base. When the pair of alleles for a given trait in an organism is unlike (one dominant and one recessive gene), the condition is *heterozygous* (Gr. *heteros,* unlike + *zygotos*). The appearance of an organism is the sum of its traits; this is known as the *phenotype* (Gr. *phainein,* to reveal + *typos*). Because recessive genes are masked in heterozygous genotypes, their presence is not directly revealed in the phenotype and can be determined only by their known occurrence among the ancestors or descendants of a particular organism. This has certain evolutionary consequences of importance that are noted in the discussion of Genetic Drift on pages 112 and 113.

Mutations   The genetic variations occurring among individuals in the transmission of traits from one generation to another, discussed above under Mendelian Inheritance, all operate as a *sexual recombination of genes.* Additional variations also occur as a result of internal changes in the molecular structure of genes themselves. This is the alteration of the DNA code, which changes the control effect of the gene over cell growth. When such changes are sufficiently stable to be inherited in the genes of the offspring, they are called *mutations.*

The average frequency of mutations is estimated as possibly 1 in 100,000 genes. But because a single human gamete may contain some ten thousand genes, it is possible that one gamete in ten contains a spontaneous mutation.[10] A gene mutation that is lethal in its effect may cause the early death of the organism, as is often the case with the mutation that produces hemophilia. The individual then has no chance to reproduce, and the mutant gene is not passed on through heredity. Such mutations have no significant evolutionary consequences unless they are linked to other genes, which are consequently lost because of the lethal mutation.

If the mutant gene happens to be recessive, there will be no visible trait effect in the generation in which the mutation occurs. Its effects will show up in homozygous genotypes in later generations, in very low frequencies. If, on the other hand, the mutation is dominant and not lethal, and if it has an adaptive advantage, it may establish its phenotypic effects immediately. These same effects will be inherited by a majority of the organism's offspring. Since mutations, even

Fig. 5-4   Crossing-over as a form of genetic variation. Genes that are far apart in locus on their chromosomes are more apt accidentally to cross over and become "misplaced" than genes that are close together. (P. B. Weisz, **Elements of Biology.** *Copyright © 1965 by McGraw-Hill Book Company.)*

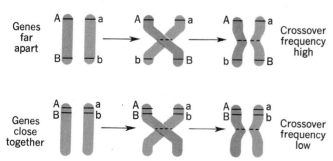

[10]King, *op. cit.,* p. 201.

though they occur wholly by chance, take place regularly and repeatedly, nonlethal forms may, under given conditions, become established in a *Mendelian population.*

Mendelian Populations and Gene Pools A Mendelian population is a localized grouping of members of a given species who interbreed mostly among themselves but occasionally breed with members of sister populations. All the genes possessed by all the members of the population constitute its *gene pool.* The gene pool is therefore the reservoir of genetic materials available to the population for the genotypic inheritance of the next generation. Because of the reproductive processes of mitosis and meiosis, the tendency is for the organisms of a particular species to convey the gene pool relatively unchanged to succeeding generations.

The Hardy-Weinberg law states that if mating within a population is random, if mutations do not occur, and if the population is large, the frequencies of genes in a gene pool will remain constant from generation to generation; a condition of genetic equilibrium will be maintained, and there will be no evolution. Such stability preserves the species and works against evolution. *Evolution means change in the gene frequencies of populations.* Phenotypic changes occur from generation to generation as a result, and the bodily forms and living processes characteristic of the population are modified thereby. But what lends direction to the change?

Variation, Natural Selection, and Adaptation
The factors that upset genetic equilibrium are (1) mutation, (2) natural selection, (3) population mixture, and (4) genetic drift. Of these, the first two are the most important as evolutionary processes. To Charles Darwin (1809–1882) and Alfred Wallace (1823–1913) goes the main credit for the first comprehensive formulations and systematic explanation of species origin in terms of developmental sequences. Darwin, in particular, demonstrated that inheritable variations are

differentially affected by the environment in which a population lives. In his own words:

It may metaphorically be said that natural selection is daily and hourly scrutinizing, throughout the world, the slightest variations; rejecting those that are bad, preserving and adding up all that are good; silently and insensibly working *whenever and wherever opportunity offers,* at the improvement of each organic being in relation to its organic and inorganic conditions of life.[11]

In modern terms, if, among individuals carrying new genes, some survive and have offspring of their own, the new genes are added to the gene pool, and the characteristics of the population are changed by that much. If, however, they fail to survive to reproduce because of the effects of the new gene in the local environmental setting, the new variation does not alter the gene pool, and no impact on its future results. If, in addition to surviving, the individuals who possess the new genes and their resulting traits survive with greater relative frequency than those who do not have them, the chances are they will increase the frequency of the new genes in the population from generation to generation.

Natural selection is the operation of any environmental factors upon genetic variations that result in *differential reproduction.* Those variant individuals which reproduce and survive most frequently are the best adapted to the environment; from generation to generation, they contribute a progressively larger proportion of descendants in the population. Eventually their genes may become preponderant in the population, and the modal phenotypes of the population will be altered. In such a situation, those gene carriers which are most positively responsive to the environment in terms of their reproductive capabilities have survived, and the population becomes better *adapted* to its environment.

In the evolutionary context, the important

[11]C. Darwin, *The Origin of Species* (Macmillan edition), p. 78.

questions to be asked about a mutation are whether its survival value is negative (lethal) or positive (adaptive) and, in either case, to what degree. *Population genetics* is the study through which gene frequencies and the *survival quotients,* or *reproductive potential,* of different genes in specific environments are mathematically determined. Such quotients are indicators of rates of evolutionary change. Obviously, a mutation has to have a high selective advantage and frequency, as well as the quality of dominance, to change the physical character of a population very rapidly in a stable environment.

The Effect of Population Mixture   Interbreeding between two populations with differing gene pools results in new combinations of genes in the offspring generations of the mixed populations. Although we have been talking as though each gene were responsible for a single trait, genes actually work in concert to influence the development of many phenotypic traits. The new phenotypes can become characteristic of the population either because of continued *hybridization* or because the hybrids have a higher survival and reproductive quotient than the nonhybrids. Eventually a new Mendelian population may result, as has been the case in recent centuries with the Afro-American and South African Colored populations (see Chapter 11).

The Selective Effect of Environmental Changes Environments as well as genes are to some extent unstable. Any environmental change will alter the selective effect upon the gene pools of all the populations inhabiting such an altered environment. Environmental variation is therefore just as important and necessary to evolution as genetic change. But an environment is also biological as well as geological. Any change in plant or animal life is itself an environmental change affecting everything else in the environment. Every evolutionary change has a feedback effect that produces environmental changes for other organisms. Hence, evolution has progressively speeded up from geologic era to geologic era, as the cumulative effect of organic changes is felt.

Adaptive Effects of Sickle-cell Anemia   Whether or not a given mutation has a selective disadvantage always depends upon the specific environment, or ecological niche, with which the population has to contend. An example which has excited much interest among geneticists and anthropologists is the discovery of a mutant recessive gene that causes a blood disorder known as *sickle-cell anemia,* so named because the defective red blood cell is sickle-shaped. The homozygous genotype is believed to be 100 per cent lethal, and homozygotes for this gene usually die in childhood. Few live beyond thirty years of age. However, in its heterozygous state, in which a person receives a normal dominant gene from one parent and the recessive mutant gene from the other, the genotype is not lethal. Heterozygous children do not die because of their single sickle-cell gene.

The factor which has intrigued modern scientists is that the heterozygotes have a special immunity to malaria. In the malaria zones of the Old World tropics, thousands of homozygous dominants die from, or are seriously impaired by, malaria. This disease is caused by various parasites which are carried by certain mosquitoes. The mosquito bite injects the parasite into the human blood stream. The red blood cells (hemoglobin) are then parasitically infected and the normal hemoglobic functions are impaired. Racking chills alternating with burning fever, combined with the weakness of anemia, result: the condition is called malaria. However, the red blood cells of persons who have inherited the sickle-cell gene are evidently not receptive to the malaria-producing parasite. It is thought that the virus becomes fixed on the surface of the hemoglobin, starves for want of oxygen, and is then destroyed by antibodies. So it is that heterozygotes with one recessive sickle-cell gene are malaria-resistant and get on much better in malaria-infested tropical lowlands than do those who do not carry the gene at all.

They suffer from neither anemia nor from malaria. They do suffer, however, from the probability of seeing at least some of their offspring waste away in intensely painful anemic deaths—if they inherit the sickle-cell gene from both parents.

In a malaria-ridden environment, it is thus advantageous for the population to have the sickle-cell mutant in the gene pool, even though it means that every child born a homozygote is doomed to an early death, a sacrifice necessary to the maintenance of the population. The mutation is a curse for the homozygote and a blessing for the fortunate heterozygote.

In tropical West Africa, one-fifth to two-fifths of the indigenous Negro populations are known to carry the sickle-cell trait. In the United States where it is estimated that approximately 30 per cent of the Afro-American gene pool is derived from European ancestry through black-white matings, the sickle-cell gene is carried by about 9 per cent of the Afro-American population. Although malaria ravaged populations of the South Atlantic coastal area of the United States in the eighteenth and nineteenth centuries, mosquito eradication eliminated it by 1910. There is no longer a survival advantage for sickle-cell carriers among blacks living in the United States. Yet, at the beginning of 1970, the sickle-cell gene meant certain premature death for the 300,000 sickle-cell homozygotes now living among the country's 22 million blacks. Now, however, there is hope. Medical research at the University of Michigan (announced early in 1971) indicates that small daily doses of urea, the main ingredient of urine, will check the disease. Intravenous injections suppress the crisis symptoms in advanced cases within a few hours. Urea is not yet known to influence the inheritance of the sickle-cell trait. It operates only on the

internal physiology to prevent the deterioration of hemoglobin.

Malaria eradication modifies the environment in such a way that there is no longer an advantage in the sickle-cell mutant; hence, the mutant has a very low frequency in long time nonmalarial zones as compared with those where the disease is still rampant.[12]

The presence of malaria works selectively to increase the recessive sickle-cell gene in a population. Therefore, evolution in the direction of sickle-cell anemia as a trait has been maintained among populations that live in malarial zones. But now a new dimension has been added to upset the biocultural ecology. Homozygotes for sickle-celling will not necessarily die (if the suppressive cure for its effects holds up to its promise). Many more will live to pass on their sickle-cell inheritance. Whether the percentage of such genes in the local gene pools will then increase or decrease will depend on other variables, such as the presence or absence of malaria.

Genetic Drift   It is also possible for an isolated population to experience a change in its original genetic composition without the effect of mutation or natural selection. This is the result of the *Sewall Wright effect,* named after the American geneticist who demonstrated the workings of *genetic drift.*

Suppose a small group of people (or any other organisms, for that matter) migrate to a new territory and subsequently lose contact with their ancestral group. Suppose, further, that in later generations more groups break off from the descendants of the original immigrants to make their homes elsewhere, and that they, too, become isolated as populations.

In a situation in which the gene frequency for a given trait is only 15 per cent for the original population, it could easily happen that by sheer chance no more than 5 per cent

[12]See A. C. Allison, "Aspects of Polymorphism in Man" (*Cold Spring Harbor Symposium in Quantitative Biology,* vol. 20, 1955), pp. 239–255.

of the migrants carry the gene. In the gene pool of the emigrant population, the frequency of this gene is automatically reduced by two-thirds. The gene pools of the original and the new societies are different by that much. Furthermore, in the absence of intermarriage, mutation, and changes in factors of natural selection, the change would remain constant indefinitely. Now suppose that in the course of time, a handful of descendants of the emigrants move on to new territories. There is only a 5 per cent frequency of the gene in the total pool of their parent population. By chance, it is possible that none of them will carry the gene. In that event, the gene would drop out of the population entirely. The new population would be absolutely different from its ancestors in the phenotypic trait that the gene in question effected.

Drift may also move in two or more directions simultaneously. Figure 5-5 is a simplified model of how this may take place. Let us assume equal frequencies of two alleles, x and y. In the model, each x and each y represents a gene frequency of 10 per cent in the total gene pool of the original population. Therefore, we begin with five x's and five y's.

Fig. 5-5   Hypothetical genetic drift (Sewall Wright effect) in a series of subdividing populations. The genetic character of two populations with a common ancestry may change without mutations solely by operation of the laws of chance in the distribution of genes.

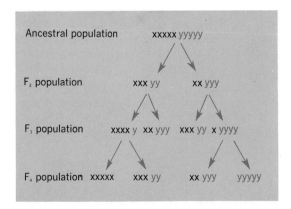

Ancestral population	xxxxx yyyyy	
F_2 population	xxx yy	xx yyy
F_3 population	xxxx y xx yyy	xxx yy x yyyy
F_4 population xxxxx	xxx yy	xx yyy yyyyy

Assume that the population divides equally; half the people pack up and move away entirely. By chance it hypothetically happens that one population contains three x's and two y's, and the other population two x's and three y's. Now, let us follow the three-x, two-y population. It inbreeds; then its children decide to split up, and half of them migrate. The chances are one in five that the migrating group will carry away a ratio of four x's to one y, leaving the home F_3 generation with two x's to three y's. The migrants inbreed; then half their children carry on the tradition of breaking away and moving on. The chances are one in five that the migrating group will carry away a ratio of five x's to zero y's, leaving the home F_4 generation with a ratio of three x's to two y's.

The third generation of isolating migrants has lost all its y genes. In the character that y determines, it has nothing in common with its racial ancestors. On the two-x to three-y side of the F_2 generation (the right of the model), similar splitting and isolating migrations can produce a population totally devoid of x. From the original equally heterogeneous ancestral population have come several new ones with varying proportions of x and y, one that is pure x, and another that is pure y. The ancestral group has spawned at least three races: a mixed one like itself, a pure x, and a pure y. All this has occurred without any changes in the original gene structures but through the roll of the genetic dice when group fission occurs and the resulting groups inbreed.

Speciation   We have already referred several times to "species." A *species* consists of one or more populations whose members are capable of intrabreeding among themselves. Simultaneously, they are either incapable of interbreeding with members of other populations, or they do not habitually do so. Genetically, species members exchange genes through reproduction. Nonspecies members do not.

Speciation occurs when two or more groups from an original population become isolated from one another and, in adaptation to their separate environments, go through sufficiently great genetic modifications that their genetic molecules are incapable of interacting on one another. This is the process that produces the branched-tree, or dendritic, effect on phylogenetic charts (see Figure 5-6, for example). The result is *differential evolution* through *adaptive radiation*. Most new species are formed in this manner. In limited conditions, however, such as on a small island, a species may change through time without producing additional species. A new species simply replaces the original through straight-line change, known as *transformation*.

In the evolution of the hominoids, the lines of man, gorilla, chimpanzee, orangutan, and gibbon were simultaneously radiating from a common ancestral species in the Oligocene era.

Extinction   The fossil record is replete with the eloquent testimony of species that had their day and survive no longer. Extinction is the outcome of failure to readapt to rapid environmental change. Again, remember that the appearance of new organisms in an environment is just as much a change as an alteration in climate or elevation of the earth's surface is. Extinction of one type of organism may open an ecological niche for a new organism to move into by its own means of adaptation.

Radiant evolution has progressively diversified the forms of life from its "simple" beginnings in the Paleozoic era. New forms have generally become more complex and more heterogeneous. The primates represent the most complex of all living orders. By virtue of his nervous system, man is the most complex creature of all. He is the product of the interacting forces that have just been summarized. Our next task is to trace out the phylogeny of the anthropoid branch of primates.

Fossil Primates from the Eocene to the Pleistocene

The opening epochs of the Cenozoic era were long, moist, and warm. The Eocene, lasting from sixty until forty million years ago, was a time of extensive forests that provided a rich habitat for myriads of unobtrusive, small, tree-dwelling primates, who evolved from the insect-eating, long-snouted, sharp-eared, ground-dwelling mammals of the order Insectivora. The prosimia proliferated.

Eocene Prosimia   The *prosimia* (before simians) were the earliest primates. Today fifty or sixty fossil genera of prosimia have been found in the northern hemisphere of the Old and New Worlds. Initially, the adaptive success of the prosimia was remarkable in the development of grasping paws for running on branches and of sharp vision for gauging jumping distances. Then they fell upon bad times. During the Oligocene, environmental changes were such that in North America and Europe they were "selected out"—extinguished. Perhaps they were outdone adaptively by the rodents, who could exploit the grasslands of the north more effectively and who could certainly outbreed any primate. However, the prosimia did successfully maintain themselves in Central and South America, where subsequent evolution produced the New World monkeys but no hominoids. In South Asia and Africa, the prosimia carried through the critical late Eocene and Oligocene periods to provide the ancestral stock for the anthropoid lines to come. It is presumed that tree living gave a selective advantage to those primates who varied in the direction of stereoscopic vision. The admonition to "look before you leap" was as valid then as now. Larger brains would also help in acrobatic judgment. Whatever the reasons, vision was becoming stereoscopic, and brains were growing larger.

The Oligocene Catarrhines We have no Oligocene fossil primates whatsoever from

Fig. 5-6   *A probable phylogenetic tree of fossil primates. (Adaptation by permission of The World Publishing Company from* Guide to Fossil Man *by Dr. Michael Day. Copyright © The World Publishing Company 1965 by Dr. Michael Day.)*

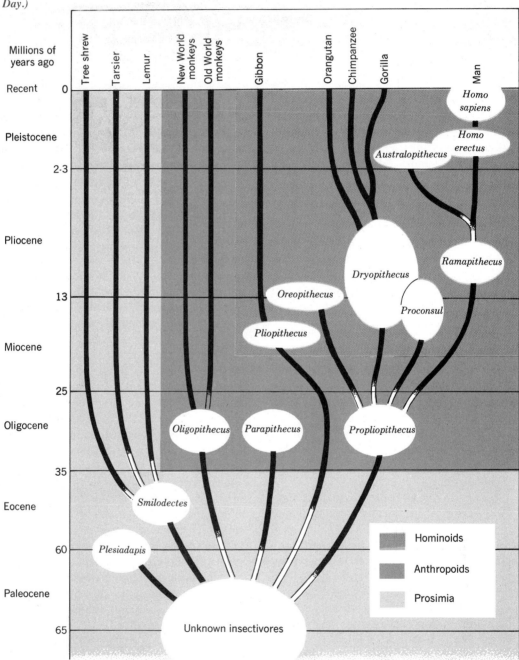

Europe. In Egypt, however, the story is very different. A famous fossil bed was laid down at Fayum, near Cairo, in early Oligocene times. The deposits are alluvial sedimentary strata related to the rise and fall of the Mediterranean shoreline.

Two jaw fragments and a few other bones, collected at Fayum at the beginning of this century, represent two Oligocene fossil genera, *Parapithecus* and *Propliopithecus*. On the basis of its dental pattern, *Parapithecus* has long been accepted as a true anthropoid, sufficiently generalized in its dental structure to have been of the type that could have been ancestral to the cercopithecoidal Old World monkeys. Since 1960, extensive excavations at Fayum by Yale University anthropologists have turned up parts of over two hundred primate individuals, which when fully studied should reveal a good deal more about the Oligocene anthropoids than is known at present. For one thing, the single *Propliopithecus* jaw had been thought for fifty years to represent a protohylobate, or gibbonoid, ancestor. Now it is evaluated as a generalized hominoid. This would make it a representative of the Oligocene ancestral pool from which man and all later apes evolved. It is generally accepted as representing one of the types from which all living hominoids—apes and man— are very probably descended.

A very important recent Fayum find is *Aegyptopithecus zeuxis,* estimated to be twenty-eight to thirty million years old. The several new fossils represent a small, monkey-like skull with pongid-like dentition. The skeletal material suggests that *Aegyptopithecus* was an arboreal quadruped with a tail. Its entire complex of traits has been interpreted as representing the earliest known dryopithecine and the possible antecedent to all the known hominoid forms.[13]

The Miocene Hominoids The twelve-million-year Miocene was an era of environ-

[13]E. L. Simons, "The Earliest Apes" (*Scientific American,* vol. 217, 1967), pp. 28–35.

mental conditions once again highly favorable to the arboreal primates. The climate was mild, generally moist, and wetter than today. Rain forests (a more elegant word for scientific use than jungle) covered much of Asia, Africa, and even Europe in the lower altitudes. Higher plateaus were richly grassed and sprinkled with open tree areas; they were pleasantly cool. Over wide spaces, the country was verdant and rich in vegetable foodstuffs. The cercopithecines were on hand, and the stage was set for the great primate evolutionary outburst that would produce the immediate hominoid precursors of modern apes and man.

The result, in the Miocene, was the production of the manifold genus of *Dryopithecus,* from which derive the pongids (orangutans) and members of the genus *Pan* (chimpanzee and gorilla). Another Miocene fossil ape, very closely related to the dryopithecines, was the African genus *Proconsul*. *Pliopithecus* is a third important Miocene fossil hominoid genus, and *Oreopithecus* is yet another.

Dryopithecus The first dryopithecine fossil fragment was described by the French paleontologist Edouard Lartet in 1856, three years before Darwin's *Origin of Species*. For many decades the one significant feature of the dryopithecine family that could be identified with certainty was its dentition, notably the much-talked-about "*Dryopithecus* Y-pattern" of the molars. As with some of the constellations of the heavens, it takes a good imagination to see the "pattern" to which the name applies. However, the molar teeth of Old World monkeys and baboons, when looked at from above, have four peaks, or cusps. The deep valleys between them are in the form of a plus sign. The molars of living hominids, on the other hand, usually have an additional fifth cusp, although this cusp has disappeared from some molars in modern man. The extra valleys made by the presence of the fifth cusp form a Y between cusps 3, 4, and 5 (Figure 5-7).

Any fossil ape having this pattern is sure to

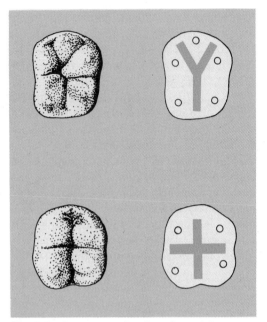

Fig. 5-7   Lower second molar of an adult
Dryopithecus, *showing the* **Dryopithecus**
Y-pattern formed by the fifth cusp (above). The
equivalent tooth of modern man, showing the
pattern formed by the four-cusp structure (below).
(Adapted from M. H. Day, **Guide to Fossil Man,**
World Publishing Company.)

be closely related to man and the modern apes. If he lived in the Miocene, he could easily be ancestral to all later hominids, extinct and living. Innumerable dryopithecine teeth and skeletal fragments have been found in Europe and Asia, but unfortunately no complete skulls or skeletons. Details of the genus's bodily structure are therefore lacking.

Proconsul   In Kenya, Africa (mostly on Rusinga Island, near the eastern shore of Lake Victoria), L. S. B. Leakey, who has devoted his life to the discovery and interpretation of prehistoric primates, has found several species of Miocene fossil apes of a single genus, called *Proconsul* in honor of a popular chimpanzee named Consul, a long-time resident of the London Zoo. *Proconsul* signifies "before Consul," which is certainly true enough, for K^{40}–A^{40} dates on two *Proconsul* fossils,

announced in 1970, are 18 and 19.7 ± .5 million years.

The nearly five hundred *Proconsul* individuals that have been discovered come in three distinguishable types, which Leakey has identified as separable species: *Proconsul africanus* (a small, gibbon-sized type), *Proconsul nyanzae* (a chimpanzee-sized form), and *Proconsul major* (who could match a gorilla for size).

Proconsul africanus is the best preserved and therefore the best known. It is small-brained when compared with man, but it had already achieved a cranial capacity that put it between the range of the gibbon and the chimpanzee (100 to 400 cc) (Figure 5-8). Its teeth are pongid. Its limbs, hands, and feet are considered to be those of a creature which could either brachiate in the trees or get about on the ground on all fours. It probably did both, but the fact that it could do either shows that the gorilla-chimpanzee pattern of life was already being established by these Miocene apes, who were beginning to exploit the ground as a possible habitat.[14] But more

[14]For details, see W. E. Le Gros Clark and L. S. B. Leakey, "The Miocene Hominidae of East Africa" (*British Museum Fossil Mammals of Africa*, no. 1).

Fig. 5-8   **Proconsul africanus.** *The reconstructed skull of a fossil Miocene ape as seen from the side. [From a drawing after J. T. Robinson, in W. E. Le Gros Clark,* **History of the Primates.** *Courtesy of the Trustees, British Museum (Natural History).]*

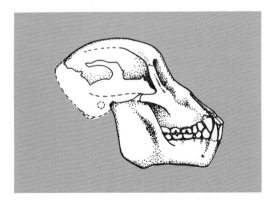

important in the Miocene stage of evolution is the apparent fact that *Proconsul* got about in the trees by swinging from the branches rather than by running along them, as all earlier primates had done. This is a primate adaptation that accompanies increasing body size in the direction of the hominoids. It, in turn, leads to adaptive radiation that selects for modification in the direction of hands rather than paws. The basis for manipulation and tool using was being laid. The earliest seeds of culture were about to be planted.

Oreopithecus   *Oreopithecus* is an Old World anthropoid who has graced the storage trays of European museums for over one hundred years. The type specimen, a jawbone with teeth, discovered in Tuscany (central Italy) in 1860, was for decades looked upon by most students as a fossil Old World monkey (cercopithecoid). A German specialist, G. Schwalbe, in 1916 argued that the teeth showed sufficient hominoid character to warrant identifying the type as an extinct genus of anthropoid ape. In 1958, *Oreopithecus* burst from the museum closet to make world news. Dr. Johannes Hurzeler, of Basel, Switzerland, had reopened the *Oreopithecus* question and had resumed digging in the lignite beds of the Pontine marshes in 1954. Within a few years, he had found the partial remains of at least four dozen individuals. But the great prize was the recovery on August 2, 1958, of an almost complete specimen in very good condition (Figure 5-9). Hurzeler hailed *Oreopithecus* as a primitive hominid and early ancestor of man. Considering the age (Upper Miocene–Lower Pliocene), this was news, indeed.

More sober evaluation, however, leads to a less ebullient conclusion. W. L. Strauss, Jr., has carried through a thorough comparative analysis of the original fossils. In his view, *Oreopithecus* is clearly a hominoid. Whether or not, within the hominoids, it falls in the hominid family is a moot question. Its teeth prove it to be definitely not pongid. But the

postcranial (from the neck down) skeleton is that of a brachiator, perhaps-quadrumanous climber. Most specialists now accept the idea that *Oreopithecus* is not a hominoid. G. G. Simpson, to whose judgment most scientists give great weight, has examined the *Oreopithecus* teeth himself and is convinced that they have too many nonhominid peculiarities to warrant putting them in the hominid class. He sees *Oreopithecus* as an early ape that separated from a *Propliopithecus* ancestral base during the Oligocene to evolve in a hominid direction along its own separate course, becoming extinct in Pliocene times and making no direct contribution

Fig. 5-9   A complete and nearly perfect fossil of Oreopithecus. (Courtesy of J. Hurzeler, Natural History Museum, Basel, Switzerland.)

to modern apes or man.[15] This is the interpretation accepted in the phylogenetic pattern of primate ancestry diagramed in Figure 5-6.

Gigantopithecus   A recent expedition working in Middle Pliocene deposits in India has confirmed the actual existence of a giant ape long known only from teeth found among so-called dragon bones in a Hong Kong drugstore in the 1930s. The large, manlike teeth had been variously interpreted as those of a giant ape or a hominid ancestor to *Homo erectus* (see pages 140–149). The recent discoveries in India yielded four jawbones which date from at least five million years ago. The interpretation of the material now suggests that *Gigantopithecus* was a massive, 600-pound, 9-foot-tall ape who was probably descended from *Dryopithecus indicus*. The wear on the teeth of *Gigantopithecus* indicates that he probably lived in an open, woodland and grassland environment where he developed a specialized mode of feeding called "graminivorous"—meaning the eating of small, tough grass seeds and stems and rhizomes which require a great amount of grinding. This grinding of plant products is the trait which explains the wear pattern on the teeth. *Gigantopithecus* is distinguished as the largest known primate. However, his size did not guarantee his survival, and he was apparently extinct by early Pleistocene times.

The Pliocene Hominids   During the mid-1930s, a combined Yale–Cambridge University expedition carried out intensive explorations in the famous fossil beds of the Siwalik Hills along the northern border of India and West Pakistan. Among the finds were remains of numerous dryopithecines of several different types. One of these is of great potential significance—*Ramapithecus brevirostis.*[16]

Ramapithecus Punjabicus   The major piece of this specimen is a part of the upper right cheek (maxilla). It contains the root of the lateral incisor, both premolars, and the first two molars. Other fragments and teeth have also been found separately. These provide samples of all the *Ramapithecus* teeth except the incisors. Enough of the maxilla is present to allow quite accurate reconstruction of the upper jaw:

According to this reconstruction the palate is arched, as in man; the canine was no larger than the first premolar, and was thick mesiolabially as in man, instead of spatulate, as in apes; and the ratio between the sizes of the front teeth (premolars and canines) and those of the cheek teeth (premolars and molars) is roughly the same as in man, and not as in the apes, which have relatively large front teeth. Enough of the maxilla is preserved to show that the upper jaw was more manlike than apelike in its depth and degree of prognathism.[17]

The dental complex of *Ramapithecus* has recently been analyzed by C. J. Jolly to suggest that it represents dietary changes leading away from the arboreal, quadrupedal, fruit-eating adaptation of *Dryopithecus* in the direction of a bipedal, terrestrial, seed-and-small-object-eating adaptation. Such a terrestrial adaptation would have been in response to environmental changes during the Miocene that were reducing the forests and expanding the grasslands. The dryopithecines who took to the ground developed the reduced canine, incisor patterns, and increased molar sizes which we recognize as characteristic of the hominids and first see in *Ramapithecus*. In short, the first adaptation which differentiated the hominid line from that of the hominoids (dryopithecines) was a ground-dwelling, seed-and-small-object-eating adaptation that led to frontal dental reduction and bipedalism.[18]

---

[15]See G. G. Simpson, "The Meaning of Taxonomic Statements," in Washburn, *op. cit.,* pp. 21–22.

[16]Rama is a legendary Hindu culture hero. Other closely related dryopithecine types discovered in the Siwalik beds and named by G. E. Lewis were *Sivapithecus, Bramapithecus, Sugrivapithecus,* and *Paleosimia.* Siva and Brama are

highly revered Hindu gods. Sugri is a monkey god. Taxonomically, these names are neutral. Culturally, they are in questionable taste.

[17]C. S. Coon, *The Origin of Races,* p. 205.

[18]C. J. Jolly, "The Seed-Eaters: A New Model of Hominid Differentiation Based on a Baboon Analogy" (*Man,* vol. 5, 1970), pp. 5–26.

The conclusion to be drawn from this is that *Ramapithecus* had developed dental features that point strongly in the direction of man. If additional finds at some future date show a skull with an adequately protohuman cranium and a pelvis indicating at least partially upright posture, then we could be quite sure that in *Ramapithecus* we have an early ancestor of man, as distinct from the pongids, in Pliocene India.

Africa has turned up a close cousin of *Ramapithecus* in the discovery by Leakey, in 1961, of a similar fragment of upper right maxilla containing a couple of molars and premolars. A canine tooth was found separately. This specimen has been dated at fourteen million years by $K^{40}-A^{40}$ analysis and falls within the Early Pliocene range. So far as presently reported, there is nothing to distinguish it as a separate genus from *Ramapithecus*.[19]

SUMMARY

The accumulation of facts by biology in all its branches and by paleontology, geography, and anthropology overwhelmingly demonstrates that the earth and all its living forms have been undergoing persistent evolution.

The antiquity of human antecedents is established through stratigraphy and geochronology based upon the rates of disintegration of radioactive elements, pollen analysis and tree-ring counts, and chemical content of fossil materials. Life began some 3 billion years ago in unicellular form. The evolution of life has consisted in the continuous development of greater and greater complexities and varieties of cell aggregations. The process is the result of genetic variation and adaptation to specific environments through natural selection. The continuity of life is maintained by cellular reproduction involving mitosis, which is the process wherein chromosomes are formed and split longitudinally into two halves, each of which goes to a new daughter cell, thus replacing the original cell with two exact replicas. In bisexual reproduction, however, gametes, as a result of meiosis, receive only half the usual number of chromosomes, so that when male and female gametes join, the fertilized egg, or zygote, will have the normal complement. Which chromosome goes into which gamete is a matter of chance. Thus all individuals are unique genotypes, and variation occurs. Genes are the units of DNA molecules that determine specific traits. They have a standard alignment along the chromosome body. But in the formation of new chromosome pairs, parts of chromosomes may be realigned through crossing-over. When this happens, more variation results.

In addition to variation produced by gene recombination in bisexual reproduction (Mendelian variation), gametic variation is produced by mutation, population mixture, and genetic drift.

Evolution occurs whenever natural selection acts upon genetic variations to produce differential reproduction, that is, when organisms possessing certain genes are more able to survive and reproduce themselves than other organisms in the population. A Mendelian population is a localized group of species members who interbreed (exchange genes). Enduring changes in the gene pool of a population caused by natural selection produce adaptation to the environment on the part of the population. When two or more groups from an original population become isolated and adapt to different environments to the point where they can no longer interbreed, speciation has occurred. Evolution has then produced two new organic species. This is the process of adaptive radiation, through which branching, leading to more and more living forms, has taken place.

The ancestry of all primates goes back to

[19]Leakey, whose dedicated enthusiasm has led him to the discovery of more important precursors of man than any living scientist, also (overenthusiastically, some think) tends to give each of his new local finds at least a new species status, if not that of a new genus, too. In this case, he has done both. Hence, he calls his specimen *Kenyanthropus wickeri*, after Kenya and Mr. Fred Wicker, on whose farm the fossil was found. See L. S. B. Leakey, "A New Lower Pliocene Fossil Primate from Kenya" (*Annals and Magazine of Natural History*, vol. 14, 1961), pp. 689–696.

some primitive Late Mesozoic mammal from which the prosimia of the Eocene period of the Cenozoic era were derived. The prosimia radiated over both hemispheres, but under Oligocene conditions most types became extinct. Modern prosimia are represented by living tree shrews, lemurs, lorises, and tarsiers, among others. In Late Oligocene times, anthropoid precursors evolved in Africa (and probably Asia) and are known in part from the fossils of *Propliopithecus* and *Parapithecus.*

Cercopithecoids evolved separately from one another in the Old and New Worlds after the Oligocene, and New World monkeys have only a remote relationship to man. Old World monkeys are more closely related to man, but they are not in themselves ancestral. In Miocene times, the protohominoid *Dryopithecus* came into existence. *Proconsul* is an African Miocene ape with the dentition, the brain, and apparently the brachiating equipment to qualify him as a close ancestor to the ancestral type. *Ramapithecus,* as representative of our Pliocene precursors, is apparently sufficiently human in dentition to indicate that hominid ancestors were already distinguished from the pongids in Miocene times, twelve to fourteen million years ago. *Oreopithecus* might have sired an entirely unique stem of men or apes if the genus had survived the Middle Pliocene, which it did not.

A gap of 3.5 to 8.5 million years exists between *Ramapithecus* and the appearance of the first man-creatures in the Late Miocene or earliest Pleistocene.

SELECTED READINGS

Aitken, M. J., *Physics and Archaeology* (1961). A professional handbook on the application of physics to problems of archaeological dating.

Clark, W. E. Le G., *The Antecedents of Man: An Introduction to the Evolution of the Primates* (1960). A detailed and thoroughgoing anatomical summary. Neither overtechnical nor overeasy to read, but sound and understandable.

Dobzhansky, T., *Mankind Evolving: The Evolution of the Human Species* (1964). Presents the latest findings and expresses Dobzhansky's humane reflections on "whence and whither mankind."

Hole, F., and R. F. Heizer, *An Introduction to Prehistoric Archaeology* (2d ed., 1969). A guide to archaeological methods, prepared for the nonprofessional, that includes excellent sections on stratigraphy and dating.

Lerner, I. M., *Heredity, Evolution, and Society* (1968). Elucidates the mechanics and products of evolution and heredity and their meaning in human thought and affairs. Especially clear diagrammatic materials.

Pilbeam, D., *The Evolution of Man* (1970). For a more detailed and comprehensive presentation of man's antecedents.

Scientific American, *Human Variation and Origins. An Introduction to Human Biology and Evolution* (1967). Collected papers by distinguished authorities expressing current thought on human evolution. All are well written and excellently illustrated.

Simpson, G. G., *The Meaning of Evolution* (1965). An outstanding contemporary exposition and interpretation of organic evolution.

Chapter 6

The Australopithecines and the Transition to Man

The moist and moderate Miocene provided the seedbed for the proliferating growth of the prehuman anthropoids. The Pliocene tested their survival capacities to the utmost, for it was a time of climatic catastrophe for all Africa. The Miocene rains had all but stopped, and for more than ten million years an incredible desert, which very likely linked the Sahara of the north and the Kalahari of the south, smothered the vast continent in searing heat and choking sand and dust. It imposed an even more excruciating survival test on the evolving primates than would the freezing climates of the north in the Pleistocene epoch, which was to follow.

In the high hills flanking the southern shoulders of the Himalayas of India, and perhaps on the flanks of the high equatorial mountains of Africa, there was, however, sufficient moisture to sustain the grasses, shrubs, and trees necessary for a primate environment. Thus the protohominids survived until the resumption of rains and snowstorms in the Pleistocene, when in Africa verdure again returned to the lowlands and water filled the lakes and streams.

The significant effect of the Pliocene climate on primate evolution would seem to have been the shrinkage, and even disappearance, of the Miocene forests and the resultant premium placed upon genetic adaptability to terrestrial living. Those primates which could come down from the trees and move about on the ground with sufficient agility to get from grove to grove in search of food and security would have had, by and large, the best chance to survive and perpetuate their kinds. What actually happened in the Pliocene can be only inferred, for the 3.5- to 8.5-million-year gap between *Ramapithecus* and the next higher fossil hominid remains for the time being a lost chapter in the history of the primates. By the very end of the Pliocene, however, the earliest known form of hominid had evolved. Their remains have been found in Early Pleistocene deposits in Africa and Indonesia. These are the australopithecines.

Fig. 6-A Skull of adult **Australopithecus africanus.** *(Cast. Museum of Anthropology, University of Minnesota. Photo by Don Breneman.)*

Australopithecus:
One Genus with Two Species

The "Austral" in *Australopithecus* refers not to Australia but to the south. As Australia is the southern continent, *Australopithecus* is the southern ape.

Although the several discoverers of the various australopithecine fossils at first enthusiastically named four or five different genera from their finds, in addition to a couple of further species, the consensus of scientific opinion now recognizes but one genus, *Australopithecus,* and two species, *Australopithecus africanus* and *Australopithecus robustus.*[1]

Differences in Adaptation *Australopithecus robustus* is pictured as a somewhat slow, plodding primate who went poking about with a digging stick or with his bare hands, prizing out roots and eating berries, seeds, and fruit in a rather pleasant, if slightly dampish, stream and lake environment. He lived from Late Pliocene to Middle Pleistocene times (5,500,000–700,000 B.C.), as did *Australopithecus africanus*. *Africanus* was habituated to somewhat drier environments and he probably had little love for groves and vines. *Robustus* was not adverse to a bit of meat, but the fossils associated with him show that he took the easy pickings and was no great hunter. His life was essentially that of the graminivorous gatherer not unlike that which Jolly reconstructs for *Ramapithecus*. *Africanus's* life-way, on the other hand, was that of the small-game hunter and seed and vegetable gatherer.

Clearly, these two species represent divergent branches of some ramapithecine ancestral stock which had probed the open areas between the forests for living space in Miocene times. The skull structure of each

[1]Consensus does not mean unanimity. Differences of opinion, interpretation, and naming continue to exist among some specialists.

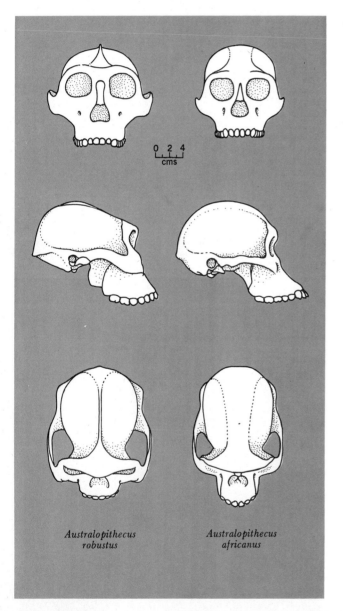

Australopithecus robustus

Australopithecus africanus

Fig. 6-1   The heavy facial and skull structure of **Australopithecus robustus** *contrasted with that of* **Australopithecus africanus.** *Both specimens are females. (After J. T. Robinson, in F. Clark Howell and Francois Bourliere (eds.),* **African Ecology and Human Evolution.** *Aldine Publishing Co. Copyright © 1963 by the Wenner-Gren Foundation for Anthropological Research, Inc.)*

species is shown in Figure 6-1. *Africanus* is more advanced phylogenetically, as will be spelled out in the pages to follow, than *robustus* is. *Robustus* was still largely a vegetarian, but he had achieved uprightness. *Africanus* shared the upright trait, but in addition to being a seed eater, he had become a carnivore with hominid dental and cranial features. He was evolving rapidly in the direction taken by man. He had also become a bone-tool user, if not a maker of stone tools. He definitely had acquired culture. Both *robustus* and *africanus* had made the critical evolutionary adaptation of bipedalism. They had fully freed their hands for potential tool using. But only *africanus*, through his more varied response to the potentialities of savanna life, made the shift to include fairly extensive meat eating in his diet.

Australopithecus africanus carried forward the new mode for which the ground had been laid by *Ramapithecus's* early adaptation to eating seeds and small objects in Miocene times (called Phase 1 of hominid evolutionary adaptation by Jolly).[2] The adaptive change added by *Australopithecus africanus* was his taste for meat along with vegetables, which seems to have been a critical factor in early human history, for it is associated with tool production and use. *Africanus* entered upon the exploitation of tools and weapons as extensions of the arm and so started our ancestors on the road to cultural adaptation (Phase 2). If Dart's interpretation of the bones and jaws found with the South African *africanus* fossils is correct (and the case he has made is impressive), *africanus* had killing and cutting tools in profusion. Whether he "made" them or simply used them is beside the point. If they served his purpose well, they were an effective *cultural* adaptation sufficient for survival at that time and place. What is to the point is that henceforth all hominid evolution is simultaneously biological and cultural. "Human evolution," to repeat Dobzhansky's

dictum, "can be understood only as a product of interaction of these two developments."[3]

Thus, the emphasis on meat eating in the diet of *africanus* placed a greater premium on tool using. Tool using is enhanced by superior intelligence, and a selective factor in favor of those with greater brainpower was probably operative on the australopithecine populations.

Grover Krantz suggests that just as important as tools could have been the capacity to stalk and pursue the quarry for hours and days at a time, as did Shoshone and Tarahumara Indians in the last century. This would have required a large brain and the capacity to keep one's mind on the long-range goal without distraction. Krantz calls it *persistence hunting.*[4] J. T. Robinson views the higher and lateral developments of the frontal area of *africanus* skulls, as compared with those of *robustus* skulls (see Figure 6-2), as evidence of

[3]T. Dobzhansky, "Evolution: Organic and Superorganic" (*The Rockefeller Institute Review*, vol. 1, no. 2, 1963), p. 1.
[4]G. Krantz, "Brain Size and Hunting Ability in Earliest Man" (*Current Anthropology*, vol. 9, no. 5, 1968), pp. 450–451.

Fig. 6-2   The fossil skull of the juvenile **Australopithecus africanus,** *discovered by Raymond Dart at Taung. Most of the calvarium had broken away, leaving exposed the natural cast of the brain. (Courtesy of the American Museum of Natural History.)*

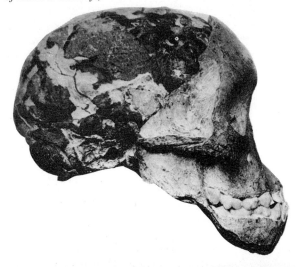

[2]C. J. Jolly, "The Seed-eaters: A New Model of Hominid Differentiation Based on a Baboon Analogy" (*Man*, vol. 5, 1970), pp. 19–22.

africanus's response, for the frontal lobes of the brain are the locality of the "associational" and "thought" processes.[5] This, in turn, if one follows the reasoning of E. A. Hooton, would have contributed to the further reduction of the canine teeth, along with a simultaneous shortening and broadening of the jaw. Enlargement of the brain broadens the calvarium, spreading the condyles apart at the rear. Reduction of the snout requires reduction of the canines for purely mechanical reasons, if for no other.[6]

The social consequences of the new dietary adaptation of *africanus* held tremendous implications for the future evolution of hominid temperament and relationships. Although present-day foraging monkeys and apes move about their territories in groups, each individual is independent in the plucking of fruits and shoots to feed himself. The operation is collectively organized largely in terms of mutual protection against outside aggressors. With their unweaned infants clinging tightly to their furry bodies, females forage exactly as do the males, who feed only themselves. Hominid hunters and foragers must, however, act differently. Their hands have been freed to fashion and use tools and weapons, and hunting has elicited a further bisexual differentiation in food getting. The role of females in hunting is functionally limited. The mother (with her young) gathers seeds and vegetables near a home base. The active male brings home his kills to share with his mate and offspring. The freeing of woman's hands for tool using has been accompanied by the prolongation of infant dependency, which is related to the protracted postnatal growth of the increasingly complex brain. At the same time, the human species was losing its body hair. There was nothing for human babies to

cling to as the mother moved from place to place, and babies lost their instinctive ability to cling. In the transitional stages of cultural development, the mother had to carry her young in her arms. Later cultural adaptations have provided net, woven, and fur slings, or even more specialized cradleboards, but still women do not actively hunt.

So it is that, even as among predators, the mothering female became interdependent with the male for sustenance, and the male evolved in the direction of external predation. *Australopithecus africanus* made the big break which opened the path in this direction for mankind.

Australopithecus africanus In 1924, Raymond A. Dart, professor of anatomy at the University of Witwatersrand, Johannesburg, South Africa, reported the find of a nearly perfect juvenile primate skull in the quarries near Taung, South Africa. Its association with numerous extinct Pleistocene fossils, including monkeys, made its antiquity apparent. The specimen was six years old at death, as indicated by its teeth. Its face, as well as the frontal region of the calvarium, was intact. The larger part of the brain case had been dislodged and lost in the mining operations, but a perfect fossil endocranial cast revealing the size and shape of the brain itself was attached to the face (see Figure 6-2).

The anatomical character of the first known *Australopithecus* as a type was difficult to determine with certainty because diagnostic characteristics are somewhat indefinite in the young; much surer comparisons can be made with adult skeletons. Nonetheless, Dart felt safe in identifying a new genus of hominoid to which he gave the name with which we are now familiar. Subsequently, in 1936 and thereafter, other *Australopithecus* fossils were found at Sterkfontein, Makapansgat, Swartkrans, and Kromdraai—all in southern Africa—and the validity of the first Taung specimen as representative of a new genus

[5] J. T. Robinson, "Adaptive Radiation in the Australopithecines and the Origin of Man," in F. C. Howell and F. Bourliere (eds.), *African Ecology and Human Evolution*, pp. 410–413.

[6] E. A. Hooton, *Up from the Apes* (rev. ed.), pp. 163–167.

was thoroughly established.[7] The Sterkfontein site produced the almost complete cranium of a sixteen- to eighteen-year-old, plus another fragmentary skull. Makapansgat has produced three fragmentary crania. About two hundred australopithecine teeth have been recovered from the South African sites, and the remains of approximately sixty-five different individuals are represented. The sample is quite good.

Morphology of the Cranium   The skulls of *Australopithecus africanus* present a generally hominid quality, with small brain cases and protruding, chinless jaws (Figure 6-3). Within the small cranium of *Australopithecus africanus*, the brain assumes moderate proportions, varying from about 450 cc. to a maximum of 700 cc. Gorilla brains run from around 300 cc. to a recorded maximum of 685 cc., while the chimpanzee–orangutan range is 290 cc. to 475 cc. The average brain of *Australopithecus africanus* was thus larger than that of the average chimpanzee but similar to that of gorillas. Relative to body size, however, the brain of *Australopithecus africanus* is distinctly larger than that of the massive gorilla and somewhat larger than those of the chimpanzee and orangutan. Figure 6-4 shows various cranial capacities in contrast.

A question may be raised as to the validity of comparisons based on mere brain size, since it is well established that no correlation exists between brain size and mental ability within the present human species except in pathological cases of microcephaly and mac-

rocephaly. Nevertheless, among the several primate genera and in comparison with even lower animal forms, brain volume, cortical surface area, and the relative development of the different parts of the brain are determinable and significant indicators of relative mental capacity and degree of environmental adaptability—including, of course, the ability to produce culture. It will be seen that the higher fossil hominids all have relatively large brains; in the case of modern man, the minimal size (except for microcephalics) is 1,000 cc., whereas the largest nonpathological brains run to 2,000 cc. The human mean is approximately 1,500 cc. for males and 50 cc. less for females. Males do on the average have more brains than females, but this does not mean that they are smarter. Within the species, brain size within the normal range has no functional significance. Males have larger brains because their bodies are generally bulkier (sexual dimorphism).

Fig. 6-3   Restored cranium of an adult **Australopithecus africanus.** *Fossilized fragments are dark colored; restored areas are white. (Cast. Museum of Anthropology, University of Minnesota. Photo by Don Breneman.)*

[7]The first Sterkfontein find was made by Robert Broom in 1936. Broom named it *Plesianthropus,* but it is clearly an *Australopithecus africanus.*

When Dart discovered the remains of a fossil man ape at Makapansgat in 1951, he thought it was somewhat different from his Taung *africanus,* and he misinterpreted the coloration of the associated animal bones as being due to burning. Although there was no direct evidence of the use of fire by the man ape, Dart ebulliently named him *Australopithecus prometheus,* "bringer of fire." Subsequently, *A. prometheus* has been more soberly relegated to *A. africanus,* which is distinction enough.

The skull of *Australopithecus africanus* presents a high, fairly rounded cranial vault when compared with that of the gorilla. The next feature that excites interest is the low position of the occipital ridge for the attachment of neck muscles. This phenomenon is distinctly hominid rather than apelike. The mammalian skull hinges on the atlas (the first cervical vertebra) by means of two bulbous knobs, the occipital condyles. In quadrupeds these are located on the vertical rear wall of the

skull. In apes they are at the back of the skull but moved forward and oriented on a slanting plane. In *Homo sapiens* they are well under the skull, beneath the auditory *meatus,* and horizontally oriented. The position of the occipital condyles of *Australopithecus africanus* approximates their position in man and is therefore hominid rather than pongid in quality. The position of the occipital condyles is functionally related to the orientation of the *foramen magnum.* It follows that in this fea-

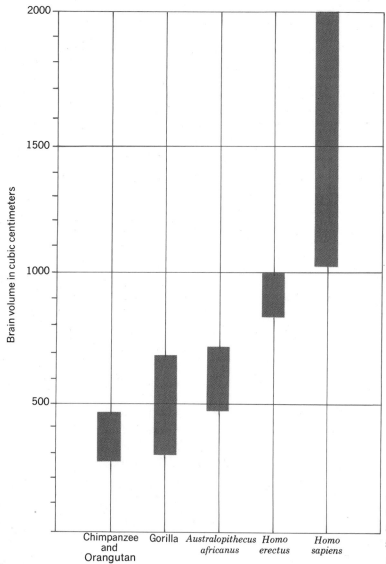

Fig. 6-4   The ranges of cranial capacities of the great apes, **Australopithecus africanus, Homo erectus,** *and* **Homo sapiens.** *The progressive increase in minima and maxima is evident.*

ture, too, the australopithecines are hominid. In apes the mastoid structure is weakly developed, if at all. In man and the australopithecines, it juts down as an inverted pyramid. The australopithecines may well have been the first sufferers of mastoiditis, or infection of the mastoid sinuses, although there has been no report as yet that any of the extant skulls show pathology of the region.

All these traits combine to indicate that in spite of the apparent general primitiveness of the cranial appearance of *Australopithecus africanus* and the relative puniness of his brain, the structure of his cranium exhibits generalized hominid features and predicates upright posture like man's.

When we look at the lower facial structure and the jaws of *Australopithecus africanus,* we note that the snouty protrusion of the face combined with the small cranium presents a general apelike quality. Attention to certain details, on the other hand, gives a different impression.

The dental features of *Australopithecus africanus* also link the creature to man. The alveolar arch is rounded and short instead of being narrow and deep, as is the ape's. The canine teeth are much reduced in size and do not flare out or project beyond the cutting edges of the incisors and premolars, as do the tusklike dental weapons of the pongids. The incisors and premolars (the cutting teeth) are relatively larger than are the molars (the grinding teeth) when compared to those of the vegetarian apes. This is very much a manlike feature. In details of cusp form and root structure of the teeth, *africanus* points toward man. More than this, the immature fossils of *Australopithecus africanus* indicate a tendency toward early replacement of the deciduous teeth by the permanent dentition—a trait which is characteristic of the hominids and which is progressively more marked the higher one goes in the primate order. This development is a function of the growth period relative to the total lifespan.

The Pelvis and Upright Posture   On the evidence from the skulls of *Australopithecus africanus* and their teeth alone, we are probably confronted with an upright, ground-living creature who was less ape than man, in spite of his small brain. But then, it takes more than just brains to get up and walk. It requires a proper skeletal and muscular structure to do so with even moderate efficiency.

Among the earliest hominoids, it was the spine-chest-shoulder-forearm complex that first underwent marked modification through adaptation to brachiation. Then, as the australopithecine ancestors of the hominids took habitually to the ground, the next great segment to be generally modified was the pelvic–lower-limb complex. Modification of the jaw-face-cranial complex (particularly the great enlargement of the brain) came later in the phylogeny of man and *Homo sapiens* precursors.[8] It is now held, with sound evidence, that the complex of features related to upright posture is the most important morphological characteristic of the hominid line and the preliminary condition for the later mental development that came to characterize the genus *Homo.* "The total morphological pattern of the limbs and pelvis in the known representatives of the Hominidae thus presents a criterion by which these are distinguished rather abruptly from the known representatives of the Pongidae."[9]

What of the pelvis and legs of the australopithecines? Twenty-three years after Dart's discovery of the infant Taung skull, the Sterkfontein site yielded a pelvic bone amid a welter of other skeletal remains which fortunately also included a thighbone (femur) and a shinbone (tibia). The next year (1948), the site at Makapansgat produced a pelvic bone of an adolescent (presumably belonging to

[8]S. L. Washburn, "The New Physical Anthropology" (*Transactions of the New York Academy of Sciences*, vol. 13, 1951), pp. 298–304; also "Tools and Human Evolution" (*Scientific American,* vol. 203, 1960), pp. 62–75. See also W. E. Le G. Clark, *The Fossil Evidence for Human Evolution,* pp. 11, 13–14, 123.

[9]Le G. Clark, *op. cit.,* p. 14.

the teen-ager whose jaw had previously been discovered in the same spot). In 1953 a complete pelvis was dug out at Sterkfontein. Even a quick glance at Figure 6-5 shows how hominid the fossil pelvis is. The adaptive modifications of the pelvic configuration that make it functionally effective for upright posture and walking (see Figure 6-6) are basically as follows:

1. The extension of the lateral attachment of the gluteal musculature of the buttock in a broadening of the ilium. This produces an adequate balancing effect for the upper portions of the body, which rest on the sacrum.

2. The downward swing of the iliac crest in the sacral area. This places the point of attachment of the *gluteus maximus* behind (instead of lateral to) the hip, improving the effectiveness of its extensor function in erect walking.

3. The shift of the sacrum (on which the spinal column now rests) upward and closer to the hip socket (acetabulum). This improves stability in transmission of the weight of the trunk to the hip joint and also provides a certain amount of basinlike support for the internal organs which now rest in the abdominal-pelvic basin.

4. The new ruggedness of the anterior iliac spine. This provides a first rooting for the ligament (the iliofemoral) that extends to the femur to provide countertension to the *gluteus maximus* in erect standing.

5. The shortening of the distance between the ischial tuberosity and the acetabulum. This brings the anchorage of the upper end of the hamstring muscles into a position behind the hip joint rather than under it, a further aid in the maintenance of upright posture.[10]

The *Australopithecus* leg bones also show conformity to the demands of upright posture. The creature stood more like a man than an ape. In the words of Coon:

[10]*Ibid.*, pp. 151–152. For a good summary discussion of the associated musculature, see J. Buettner-Janusch, *Origins of Man: Physical Anthropology*, pp. 138–141.

. . . as far as the femur is concerned the Australopithecus from Sterkfontein, at least, could have either walked or run erect, as he pleased, and if his ancestors had ever brachiated in the trees, no trace of the brachiating type of adaptation remained on their femurs once they had become anatomically suited for life on the ground."[11]

In addition to the pelvic and leg-bone materials, the australopithecine finds include many fossilized bones of the hands and feet. One group from Olduvai Gorge includes twelve of the major bones of a single foot so perfectly preserved that the details of the foot are readily reconstructable. Although it is much smaller than a human foot, the metatarsal, which is the key bone to the arch, is hominid and the big toe is structured and positioned like a man's. That is, it is *big,* points forward, and is not splayed out. It is the lever that bears the thrust of the forward stride as each step is completed and the next one started.

The skeletal structure of *Australopithecus africanus* reveals a small, 50- to 90-pound individual who stood and ran on his hind legs. This and his mode of life tell us that he

[11]C. S. Coon, *The Origin of Races*, p. 246.

Fig. 6-5   The ilium of Homo sapiens sapiens *(left) compared to that of* Australopithecus africanus *(right). (Museum of Anthropology, University of Minnesota. Photo by Don Breneman.)*

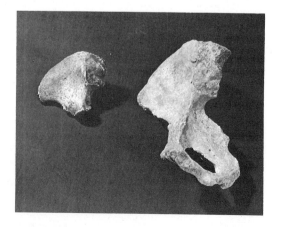

was probably agile and quick-footed, so that some anthropologists, with his discoverer in mind, call him "the South African darter."

Life and Culture of **Australopithecus africanus** It is not enough to know from the skeleton that *Australopithecus africanus* had risen to the potential of early manhood. One wants immediately to ask, "Did he use or make tools? Is there evidence that he had a culture?" We have already answered "yes," although these questions cannot be answered unequivocally. Prehistoric cultures, especially those of Pleistocene hunters, may be reconstructed in only their thinnest outlines. So much rests on inference from limited facts that enthusiastic opinion and intellectual prejudice frequently run far beyond the reasonable limits of the evidence. This leads to a surprising amount of argument over the tool habits of the australopithecines.[12]

Dart has stoutly claimed since 1949 that *africanus* was not only a "darter" but also a "basher." In Biblical times, Samson is said to have slain a thousand Philistines with the jawbone of an ass. Dart has quite convincingly demonstrated that *africanus* was a slayer of baboons and other game and that he used a thighbone of an antelope as a bony bludgeon. He may, somewhat like Samson, even have used half the lower jaw of an antelope.[13]

Africanus's environment was that of the moderately well-watered savanna, a country of scattered shrubs and trees among lush grasses. It was prime grazing country and

was well stocked with game, but it had little to attract a large tree-dwelling primate. *Australopithecus africanus* was not a tree dweller —his hands were freed by upright posture, he could run quickly, and his teeth, like those of *Homo sapiens*, were those of a meat eater.[14]

Africanus may have started to eat meat when he scavenged for carrion in competition with vultures and hyenas, but he was far beyond that by the time he left his own bones in the caves of South Africa. *Africanus* seems to have been a wily predator. He had crossed the Rubicon from prehominid herbivorousness to hominid carnivorousness.

On behalf of these South African australopithecines, Dart stoutly argues that they used weapons in a patterned way—not *stone* tools, to be sure, but clubs of bone. How else could

[14]If a meat-eating skeptic asks: "Are the teeth of vegetarian Brahmins in India any different from ours?" the answer will be no, but the Brahmins have not been off a meat diet for more than a hundred or so generations, and they do not have to chew raw roots and uncooked bulk greens.

Fig. 6-6   The human (**Homo sapiens sapiens**) *pelvis viewed from the front and above, showing the basinlike structure and rounded, flaring ilia. (Museum of Anthropology, University of Minnesota. Photo by Don Breneman.)*

[12]The conflict is well summarized by D. L. Wolberg, "The Hypothesized Osteodontokeratic Culture of the Australopithecinae: A Look at the Evidence and the Opinions" (*Current Anthropology*, vol. 11, 1970), pp. 23–38.

[13]See R. A. Dart, "Predatory Implemental Technique of the Australopithecines" (*American Journal of Physical Anthropology*, vol. 7, 1949), pp. 1–16; "The Predatory Transition from Ape to Man" (*International Anthropological and Linguistic Review*, vol. 1, 1953). The argument for *Australopithecus africanus* as killer is given in great detail and with no little vehemence by Robert Ardrey in his *African Genesis*, especially chaps. 7, 9, and 10. Per contra, see S. L. Washburn, "Australopithecines: The Hunters or the Hunted?" (*American Anthropologist*, vol. 59, 1957), pp. 612–614.

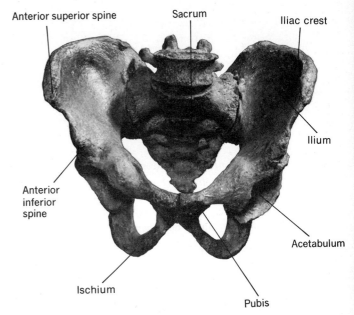

Anterior superior spine   Sacrum   Iliac crest

Anterior inferior spine

Ilium

Acetabulum

Ischium   Pubis

one account for the numerous clobbered baboon skulls in the caves in which *Australopithecus africanus* is found? Out of one collection of fifty-two *Parapapio* skulls, forty-eight, or 92 per cent, had fractured crania. Most of the fractures are on the left frontal region of the baboon skulls, and many bear the imprint of a dual point of impact. Using the reasoning of an expert in forensic medicine testifying on a case of presumptive criminal homicide, Professor Dart argued that the circumstantial evidence shows death by frontal attack with a double-knobbed crusher wielded by a right-handed killer.

A count of the more than a million fossil bones taken from the *Australopithecus* breccia of the cave of Makapansgat shows that 11.2 per cent are thighbones of antelope. This is far above the normal proportion of thighbones in ordinary collections of fossilized antelope skeletal material, and of these thighbones, 90 per cent are pieces from the knee end (the joint that has double-knobbed condyles). This end most readily serves as a club. Halves of antelope jaws with their sharp molar teeth (a vicious weapon) are also found in numbers out of proportion to reasonable expectancy, had they not been brought into the cave.

These were apparently the weapons of *Australopithecus africanus,* the lively hunter, for no stone tools have been found in the lower, or early, australopithecine breccia of the South African sites. This, however, is not the problem that some prehistorians make of it. As adaptive devices, the saw-toothed jawbones and knobby bone clubs of *Australopithecus africanus* in South Africa could certainly have served their needs more efficiently than the Oldowan pebble tools associated with the australopithecines in East Africa (see pages 134 and 135).

Further, quantities of bone flakes of the sort that are produced only by cracking and twisting a "green" longbone indicate the activity of a two-handed manipulator engaged in the search for edible marrow. Longbones with spinal fractures bespeak the same testimony. Some longbone splinters from Makapansgat look very much as though they could have been used as half-round gouges or scoops. Unlike the two-knobbed bashers, however, they would have left no permanent marks or impressions on other bones or permanent materials; consequently, this possibility of tool use remains only a loose guess.

Although simple stone tools have been found in the same cave deposits which have yielded australopithecine fossil remains in South Africa, they are not yet firmly accepted as the products of australopithecine hands.[15] In any event, no stone tools have been found in the lower, or earlier, australopithecine breccia of the South African sites (East Africa is a different matter). The industrial complex of the South African *Australopithecus africanus* is pre-Paleolithic and has been given the somewhat stupendous label of *osteodontokeratic* (Gr. *osteon,* bone + *dontos,* tooth + *keratos,* horn) to signify that those first hominid hunters worked with bone, teeth, and horn. Presumably, they would also have used wood, but no tools of this material have as yet been recovered. Wood is too perishable.

Australopithecus robustus The creature first discovered by Broom at Swartkrans in 1948 and called *Paranthropus* (Gr. *para,* near + *anthropos,* man) is today recognized as *Australopithecus robustus.* He is bigger, bulkier, and more muscular, and above all, he has larger molar teeth.

The cranial bones of *robustus* are thick and the brain case itself is not larger than that of *africanus.* Instead of the rounded forehead of *africanus,* however, *robustus* has a sloping forehead, which leads back to a sagittal ridgepole, a medial crest like a gorilla's (Figure 6-2). This makes it clear that he was heavy-jawed, for the sagittal crest anchors the thick muscles that work the jaws. The lower jaw is indeed made of massive bone. Concomitantly, the nasal area of the face is flat.

Robustus's teeth also fit the same picture.

[15]J. T. Robinson and R. J. Mason, "Occurrence of Stone Artifacts with *Australopithecus* at Sterkfontein" (*Nature,* vol. 180, 1957), pp. 521–524.

The chewing and grinding teeth (premolars and molars) are very large, larger than human teeth and those of *africanus*. His incisors, or biters, are smaller than those of *africanus*, however. His immense molars have enamel 3 millimeters thick, three times as thick as in *africanus* and man. They are worn down and pitted, as if from chewing gritty food. J. T. Robinson, who statistically analyzed over 375 teeth of *Australopithecus robustus*, concludes: "All the features of *Paranthropus* [*Australopithecus robustus*] dentition, as far as size and proportion are concerned, may be explained on the assumption that selection has retained as large a chewing area in the grinding teeth as is consistent with reducing jaw size at the expense of the less important teeth (incisors and canines) in a large vegetarian."[16]

Finally, *robustus* has added a unique sixth cusp to his molars. It is rare among hominids, but invariable with *robustus*. It may turn out to be an important diagnostic feature for linking him to fossils elsewhere, whatever its functional significance was for the living creature.

The pelvic remains are similar to those of *africanus*, but larger. The longbones indicate a much heavier body size (100 to 150 pounds, as against 50 to 90 pounds for *africanus*).[17]

The Olduvai Australopithecines

Our knowledge of the australopithecines was opened by the discoveries in South Africa. It has been given new dimensions and fitted into a larger picture by the rapidly accumulating discoveries at Olduvai, Tanzania, in East Africa, and in the Koobi Fora area east of Lake Rudolph, in Kenya.

Olduvai Gorge Olduvai Gorge has been called "the Grand Canyon of human evolution." It is not so awe-inspiring to see, but it is

Fig. 6-7   Excavations in progress in Bed III at Olduvai Gorge in 1963. Acheulean hand axes left in situ may be seen protruding from the face of the cut directly above the heads of the workers. (Courtesy of R. I. Murrill, University of Minnesota.)

stupendous in its yield of fossil man and prehistoric cultures, extending from the earliest Pleistocene times toward the end of the period. Figure 6-7 gives an idea of the exploratory work there. The gorge is cut from west to east into the west wall of the Great Rift Valley. It is now a dry canyon in wild country, lying midway between Lake Victoria and fabled Mt. Kilimanjaro, 150 miles by air southwest of Nairobi. Here a series of water and wind-laid strata rest upon a bed of volcanic lava. The restless earth in this territory elevated the land surface in Late Pleistocene times, and a prehistoric river cut through the strata, exposing them from bottom to top. The weathering faces of the canyon continually expose the buried fossils and artifacts.

The stratigraphy of Olduvai presents five major strata, or beds. Bed I contains Lower Pleistocene fossil fauna such as the modern elephant, the one-toed horse, the cow, and a number of Pliocene survivors such as three-toed horses, mastodons, and antlered giraffes. It was laid down in the first African pluvial during a time of rising and falling lake levels. Some strata are lake bottoms, with fish, crocodile, and hippopotamus remains. Others are land surfaces. Both lakes and land were periodically showered with volcanic ash. Bed

[16]J. T. Robinson, "The Dentition of the Australopithecinae" (*Transvaal Museum Memoirs*, no. 9, 1956), p. 149.

[17]For a more detailed comparison of the anatomies of *Australopithecus africanus* and *Australopithecus robustus*, see J. T. Robinson, "The Origins and Adaptive Radiation of the Australopithecines" in G. Kurth (ed.), *Evolution and Hominization*, pp. 120–140.

I varies from 18 to 105 feet in thickness. The upper strata of Bed I indicate a time of interpluvial dryness and subdesert.

The K^{40}–A^{40} (potassium 40–argon 40) dates indicate an approximate age of 1.9 million years for the lowest sections of Bed I, and one million years for the upper portions.

Between Beds I and II is a *disconformity*. This means that the upper surfaces of Bed I were eroded away and that Bed II was laid down at a later date—in this case one hundred thousand to several hundred thousand years later. Bed II is a thick (60 to 80 feet), wet-climate layer of clay and silt lake deposits. Upper Bed II represents the mid-Pleistocene pluvial in Africa. Then comes another disconformity caused by geologic faulting. Bed III represents a time of violent erosion (indicating sporadic runoff of heavy occasional rains in a generally dry country, such as occurs in New Mexico and Arizona today). Bed IV is another layer of lake deposits, with fish, crocodile and hippopotamuses. It represents a Late Pleistocene pluvial phase, possibly equivalent to the fourth glacial. Figure 7-9 (page 153) shows a diagrammatic cross-section of the Olduvai beds. All these beds are rich in fossils and artifacts.

Fossil and Cultural Remains at Olduvai   Bed I is a hominid deposit. In 1960, L. S. B. Leakey and Mary Leakey discovered fragments of a child consisting of three pieces of the calvarium, parts of the mandible with all teeth, an upper molar tooth, and a set of hand bones. On the same floor with the child, crudely chipped stone tools of quartz rocks had already been discovered. This is the famous Oldowan pebble (or chopper) culture, which extends all the way through Bed I and into Bed II and which is also widespread elsewhere in Africa and in Asia.

The Oldowan Bed I Pebble (Chopper) Culture   There is not much to describe in this oldest of known lithic (stone) industries. In Leakey's summing up:

The Oldowan culture has from time to time been referred to as a "pebble culture," and this description is to some extent correct, for the vast majority of the implements of this culture are in fact made from water-worn pebbles. It must, however, be clearly understood that other forms of raw material were also used by the makers of this culture. Specimens occur which have been made from nodules of chert, and others from rough irregular lumps of quartz and quartzite, and there seems to be little doubt that sites containing assemblages of this

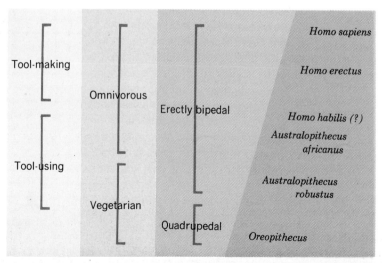

Fig. 6-8   Diagrammatic representation of the prevailing theory of the evolutionary relations of hominids (australopithecines) and hominins (**Homo**). Posture, diet, and toolmaking and tool using are shown as operative factors correlated to primate types. Note that the threshold between the quadrupedal and bipedal stages is a major one and that the break in the line marks off two essentially discontinuous zones. Note also that this is not a family tree, but an adaptive grid. (Modified from J. T. Robinson, in F. Howell and F. Bourliere (eds.), **African Ecology and Human Evolution.** *Aldine Publishing Co. Copyright © 1963 by the Wenner-Gren Foundation for Anthropological Research, Inc.)*

culture might be found where tools made of actual water-worn pebbles were entirely absent.

The commonest tool type of the Oldowan culture is a crude chopper, varying in size from about the dimensions of a ping-pong ball to that of a croquet ball. The chopping edge is made by removal of flakes in two directions along one side of the pebble or other lump of stone which has been chosen, the intersection of the flake scars resulting in an irregular jagged cutting edge.[18]

The most important feature of the tools is that they are, indeed, intentionally constructed (Figure 6-9). There is a plan and a purpose, an idea and its execution, in these simple worked stones. A hominid was coordinating mind and hand to improve his means of achieving his goals. If one definition of man is *a primate who is capable of the manufacture of definite tools,* then there were indeed manlike creatures at Olduvai when Bed I was being deposited. His pebble tool was a kind of hacking knife—a chopper of sorts—used in all likelihood to cut up meat, which was eaten raw. (There is no evidence of the use of fire in the Bed I deposits.)

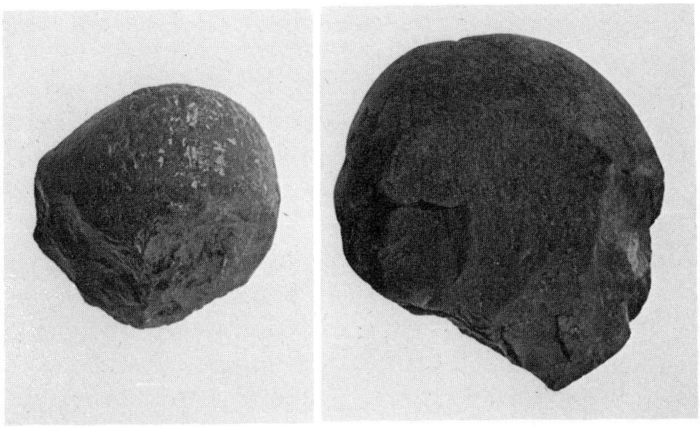

Australopithecus africanus or *Homo habilis?*

In addition to the juvenile, remains of several other individuals of a similar type have been found by the Leakeys in Bed I, plus a very fine specimen of an adult *Australopithecus robustus* skull.[19] There is a real division of opinion over the interpretation of the non-*robustus* fossils from Bed I. Most paleontologists and prehistorians accept the Bed I group tentatively as a local population of *Australopithecus africanus,* but Leakey and his two associate physical anthropologists, P. V. Tobias and J. Napier, have claimed membership in the genus *Homo* for the little Olduvai Bed I hominids on the following grounds: (1) Their estimated cranial capacity of 643 to 724 cc. gives a mean of 80 cc. more than the largest known capacity of the australopithecines; (2) their

Fig. 6-9   Oldowan pebble (or chopper) tools from Bed I at Olduvai Gorge. (Museum of Anthropology, University of Minnesota. Photo by Don Breneman.)

small teeth and cranial contours give a "total pattern more markedly hominized than that of *Australopithecus*"; and (3) they indubitably produced the Oldowan tools.[20] They therefore named this population *Homo habilis* (L. *habilis,* apt, skillful), the "handy man." This position holds that any hominid who has achieved the psychocultural-organic level is *ipso facto* to be welcomed into the brotherhood of man. However, whatever anthropologists choose to call the Bed I hominids does not alter the facts one way or another, and the ultimate taxonomic decision will reveal more about our state of mind than it does about the early Olduvai fossils. It is simply a matter of how broad-minded we become in defining the qualifications for membership in the genus to which we assign ourselves.

The facts, in short, are that an improved form of australopithecine, akin to *africanus,* lived at Olduvai early in the Pleistocene, at least 1 million and possibly 1.85 million years ago. He almost certainly made the simple Oldowan stone tools and an occasional bone tool;[21] for food he ate a variety of bits of small game and tortoises—and, of course, vegetables.

---

[18]L. S. B. Leakey, *Olduvai Gorge,* p. 34.

[19]This is the specimen that Leakey first called *Zinjanthropus* (Arabic *Zinj,* East Africa + Gr. *anthropos,* man). It is frequently referred to as such in the literature, but there is general agreement that this particular individual is an australopithecine.

[20]P. V. Tobias, "Early Man in East Africa" (*Science,* vol. 149, 1965), p. 27. See also S. Tax (ed.), "The Origin of Man" (*Current Anthropology,* vol. 6, no. 4, 1965), pp. 342–438.

[21]See S. Cole, *The Prehistory of East Africa* (rev. ed.), p. 212.

New Discoveries in Africa

Since 1965, the established age of the oldest known australopithecines has been pushed back an additional four million years to Pliocene deposits dated at five and a half million years B.C. This startling result is the product of a Harvard expedition to Kenya where an arm-bone fragment of *Australopithecus,* believed to be four million years old, was found in 1965. Two years later, the expedition recovered a fragment of a lower jaw of an *Australopithecus* individual in deposits dating to 5.5 million years in a formation near Lake Rudolph, Kenya. At the same time (and also in 1968) a joint French-American expedition to the Omo Valley, north of Lake Rudoph, in Ethiopia, discovered a series of hominid teeth along with mandible fragments in deposits which range from two to four million years in age. The Omo remains seem to have come from both *Australopithecus africanus* and *Australopithecus robustus.* "If these attributions are confirmed," notes Clark Howell, "then the hominid samples from the Omo Beds would indicate the co-existence of (at least) two australopithecine taxa through much of the range of Pliocene/Pleistocene time."[22]

Other Australopithecines

A possibly more advanced species of *Australopithecus* seems to have existed among the australopithecines of South Africa, where J. T. Robinson has sorted out some distinctive bones from the trays containing *robustus* remains from Swartkrans. They are in his view different from both *africanus* and *robustus.* They include upper and lower jaw pieces with teeth (apparently from the same skull), a nearly perfect lower jaw from another individual, and some cranial fragments. In 1961, Robinson and Leakey were both convinced that the fragments represented an advanced hominid of the same grade as the Olduvai Bed I form.[23] Another apparent representative of the group was found in 1961 at Lake Chad in West Africa; it is probably of Lower Pleistocene age.

Australopithecines in Asia   No australopithecines have ever been found in Europe, and considering how intensively the prehistory of Europe has been explored, it is not very likely that one ever will be.

It is otherwise in Asia. Two fragments of lower jaws were found in 1941 and 1952 in Lower Pleistocene beds in Java at Sangiran. They are large and thick. In size and other characteristics the teeth are australopithecine. Particularly significant is the identical cusp pattern, including the sixth cusp of *Australopithecus robustus.* Von Koenigswald, who made the first discovery, felt he had a human type in his hands and named it *Meganthropus* (Gr. *mega,* large + *anthropos,* man) *paleojavanicus* (Gr. *paleo,* ancient + *Java*). The consensus, however, is that these Java individuals are australopithecines of the *robustus* type. Thus, the *robustus* species of *Australopithecus* had a wide African distribution and a foothold in Asia.

SUMMARY

The australopithecines of South and East Africa are the first upright, bipedal hominid fossil primates consisting of two recognized species—*Australopithecus africanus* and *Australopithecus robustus.* Morphologically, *africanus* is rather small (50 to 90 pounds) and agile. His calvarium is smooth and broad, with a rounded frontal contour, and it housed a brain varying from 425 to 700 cc.—larger than any ape's, but smaller than the minimum

---

[22]F. C. Howell, "Remains of Hominidae from Pliocene/Pleistocene Formation in the Lower Omo Basin, Ethiopia" (*Nature,* vol. 223, 1969), p. 1239.

[23]This is the form that Robinson named *Telanthropus* (Gr. *tele,* far, remote + *anthropos,* man). J. T. Robinson, "The Australopithecines and Their Bearing on the Origin of Man and of the Making of Tools" (*South African Journal of Science,* vol. 57, 1961), pp. 3–13.

for *Homo sapiens.* His dentition consists of canines and molars that are relatively much reduced in size, combined with enlarged incisors and premolars. He had the dental equipment of a meat eater, which the fossil animal bones associated with his own fossils show him to have been. He had evolved from normal primate vegetarianism through rama-pithecine graminivorousness to become a predatory hunter, who apparently in South Africa used bone clubs and antelope jaws as smashers and slashers, and at Olduvai pro-duced a stone-tool industry (the Oldowan). From his use of such tools, we infer that he had a genuine culture.

Australopithecus robustus normally grew to almost double the size of *africanus.* His heavy jaw housed massive masticatory mo-lars, which were worn down by chewing gritty roots and vegetables. His forehead was low and recessive, running back to a strong sagit-tal crest.

At Olduvai Gorge, Tanzania, a number of australopithecine fossils have thus far been found. Those in Bed I are associated with an Oldowan lithic industry; they were unques-tionably toolmakers and meat-eating hunters. Except for the *robustus* specimen of Bed I, the others are small and of a brain size that is estimated to run up to 725 cc. by Tobias, who, with Leakey and Napier, takes the position that these forms should be classed as *Homo habilis* on the basis of their purported tool-making dexterity. This view has not won general acceptance, however; most pre-historians prefer to look upon the Olduvai Bed I toolmakers as *Australopithecus,* and probably *africanus.* Whatever the ultimate taxonomic outcome, the australopithecines of Africa (excepting, perhaps, *robustus*) had the essential attributes of man—upright pos-ture, a brain larger than those of apes, a taste for meat, and a hunter's culture including the tools with which to hunt, fight, and butcher. They were at least protomen, if not already men, and they had given evolution a new direction for the hominids.

SELECTED READINGS

Cole, S., *The Prehistory of East Africa* (rev. ed., 1963). Chapters 1 to 4 provide the best popular in-troduction to the setting and background of the Olduvai australopithecines.

Coon, C. S., *The Origin of Races* (1963), Chapter 7 (pp. 217–304). Covers the physical anthropology of the australopithecines in great and judicious detail.

Dart, R. A., "Cultural Status of the South African Man-Apes" (*Smithsonian Institution Annual Re-port,* 1955), pp. 317–338. Dart's summation of the case for *Australopithecus africanus* as a bone-tool user.

Day, M. H., *Guide to Fossil Man* (1965), pp. 118–136, 161–210. Photos and specifications of australo-pithecine fossil remains.

Hockett, C. F., and R. Ascher, "The Human Revolu-tion" (*Current Anthropology,* vol. 5, 1964), pp. 135–168; reprinted with critical evaluations by a number of specialists in M. F. A. Montagu (ed.), *Culture: Man's Adaptive Dimension* (1968). A highly stimu-lating presentation and discussion of possibilities in the biocultural adaptations, including speech, that could have effected the transition to man.

Leakey, L. S. B., "Very Early East African Homi-nidae and Their Ecological Setting," in F. C. Howell and F. Bourliere (eds.), *African Ecology and Human Evolution* (1963), pp. 448–457. A brief statement of Leakey's views on the subject in 1962.

Pilbeam, D., *The Evolution of Man* (1970).

Robinson, J. T., "Adaptive Radiation in the Aus-tralopithecines and the Origin of Man," in F. C. Howell and F. Bourliere (eds.), *African Ecology and Human Evolution* (1963), pp. 385–416. Presents a succinct summary of the probable origins and rela-tions of the two types of australopithecines. Robert-son persists in clinging to the designation *Paran-thropus* instead of adopting *Australopithecus ro-bustus.*

Tax, S. (ed.), "The Origin of Man" (*Current Anthro-pology,* vol. 6, no. 4, 1965), pp. 342–446. Contains a detailed account of the K^{40}–A^{40} (potassium 40–argon 40) method of dating, plus results for Olduvai Gorge and elsewhere, plus eleven additional arti-cles on the australopithecines and *Homo habilis* (mostly reprints). A handy but highly technical compendium of data and viewpoints.

Tobias, P. V. "Early Man in East Africa" (*Science,* vol. 149, 1965), pp. 22–33. Presents the case for the *Homo habilis* taxonomy for the Olduvai Gorge Bed I australopithecines and gives a compact summary of the finds.

Wolberg, D. L., "The Hypothesized Osteodonto-keratic Culture of the Australopithecinae: A Look at the Evidence and Opinions" (*Current Anthropology,* vol. II, 1970), pp. 23–38. Judiciously describes and assesses the pro and con positions on *Australopithecus* as a tool user.

Chapter 7

Homo erectus and the Lower Paleolithic Age

The evolutionary development of the earliest, large-brained, fully upright-walking primate was accomplished in the Old World by first interglacial times—some two-thirds of a million years ago. The first fossil man to be discovered (in 1891), Java man, was a representative of this taxon, which is now known as *Homo erectus* (upright man). *Homo erectus* stands midway between the australopithecines and modern man, *Homo sapiens,* in the sequential order of hominoid development. Although the opinion is still provisional, the dominant view among human paleontologists is that *Homo erectus* evolved rather rapidly out of the *Australopithecus africanus* gene pool. It should be kept in mind that the australopithecines were widely dispersed over Africa, the Middle East, and South Asia, and that not all populations would necessarily be evolving at the same rate. Some could have changed to bring forth one or more hominid features of *Homo,* while yet other populations produced other new features. Still other populations might, at the same time, have changed little genetically, or not at all.

Eventually, however, under generally like environmental conditions, the new surviving genes would tend to spread. For a long while australopithecine populations that had become noticeably *Homo*-like would exist simultaneously (but in different areas) with those which remained australopithecine. Thus, fossil remains of *Homo erectus* and *Australopithecus* are found in geological deposits of the same geological age. In Java and Africa, fossil australopithecines and the earliest representatives of the genus *Homo* are both found in Lower or Early Middle Pleistocene beds. By the end of the Middle Pleistocene both *Australopithecus africanus* and *Australopithecus robustus* were no more. They had become extinct; they were replaced by *Homo erectus* who was now their successor, for their roles in the drama of evolution had been played out.

Fig. 7-A   Acheulean hand ax.

Homo erectus erectus

When first discovered in Java, the original fossil representative of earliest man seemed to be as much ape as man in the opinion of its discoverer, the Netherlander Eugene Dubois. Hence, it was named *Pithecanthropus erectus* (Gr. *pithecos,* ape + *anthropos,* man; L. *erectus,* upright) or ape man who stands erect. By 1930, some specialists were convinced that the type was sufficiently human in form and abilities to be viewed as a man, albeit not yet *Homo.* Not until 1960 were the majority of physical anthropologists willing to agree among themselves that the fossils should be brought within the family of man as *Homo erectus.*

The discovery of the first *Homo erectus* was made in sandstone and conglomerate deposits in the valley of the Solo River near Trinil in Central Java. It came as the result of a deliberate search for primitive fossil man on the part of Dubois (not by "two boys," as the *New York Herald Tribune* once reported it).

Dubois first recovered a fossilized and very primitive calvarium of a hominoid (Figure 7-1) along with some primate teeth. A year later, he found a fossilized primate femur at the same level, 15 yards away. For at least two decades, skeptics expressed doubt that the femur and calvarium belonged to one individual and that a being with so primitive a skull could walk on his two hind legs, head up. By 1920, however, the validity of association of the leg bone and skull was generally accepted, and the fossil was viewed as the long-sought "missing link" between ape and man.

For nearly half a century Java man stood alone. Then in the mid-1930s, the efforts of G. H. R. von Koenigswald brought forth a rich harvest of further finds in Java, all confirming the validity of Dubois's original contribution and expanding our knowledge of many aspects of the total morphology of Java man. Between 1936 and 1941, when the Japanese invasion put a stop to von Koenigswald's work, six new representatives of Java man were found at a place called Sangiran in close proximity to the old Trinil site. In addition, the fossil skull of an infant was found at Modjokerto, in eastern Java. Von Koenigswald's assemblage of Java fossils includes a skull (the Modjokerto infant), two complete and two partial calvaria, an excellently preserved upper jaw and teeth, three fragmented lower jaws, and a number of miscellaneous teeth.

Morphology of Java Man   On the basis of the abundant assemblage, it is now possible to be quite specific about the human qualities of Java man.

Cranial Characteristics   The Java cranium (Figure 7-2) is quite unlike that of the australopithecines. Instead of the relatively high and rounded cranial vault which characterizes *Australopithecus,* Java man has a flat, receding forehead that slopes back from beetling browridges. The supraorbital torus is massive. The temporal regions behind the orbital area are very constricted and narrow, and the greatest breadth of the skull is far back toward the occiput and low down in the temporal area. Although there are no sagittal and occipital crests such as are found in the adult male chimpanzee and gorilla, the roof of the

Fig. 7-1   A cast of the calvarium of the first specimen of **Homo erectus erectus,** *found by Eugene Dubois in Java in 1891 and originally known as* **Pithecanthropus erectus.** *(Smithsonian Institution.)*

skull is markedly gabled, and the occipital region is angular. The mastoid process is only slightly developed, while the foramen magnum is far forward under the skull, much as it is in *Homo sapiens*. These are indicative of at least semiupright posture combined with heavy neck and jowl musculature to support a powerful jaw.

The palate is huge and there is a strong facial prognathism conforming to massive jaws with recessive chin devoid of the human dental eminence (prow). At the same time, it does not show the slightest trace of a simian shelf. The teeth are intermediate in size between those of apes and those of *Homo sapiens*, but they are preponderantly hominid. Their pongid features are the presence of a slight canine-incisor diastema, or gap, in some but not all individuals, and the large size of the molar teeth relative to those in the front of the dental arch.

The exact cranial capacities of the Java skulls are not known, since none of the skulls is complete. However, the adult range is from 775 cc. to approximately 975 cc. This puts the Java man well above the apes and australopithecines but somewhat below the normal minimum for *Homo sapiens*, whose range of brain volume is 1,000 to 2,000 cc. The average brain volume of modern man is 1,500 cc. for males and 1,450 for females. Endocranial contours of the Java skulls indicate a relatively weak development of the frontal lobes. The largest cortical areas are localized in the parietal, or motor-control, regions.

The Femur The first-discovered femur of Java man excited particular interest and won for him the species designation *erectus* (see Figure 7-3). In all respects it is a human type of leg bone, one that goes with bipedal, orthograde posture: it is long and slender and has a ridge (the *linea aspera*) running down the dorsal side for the anchorage of the hamstring muscles, which are so important in the upright position.

Recent fluorine analysis confirms the con-

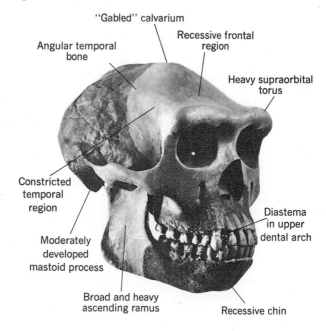

Fig. 7-2   Restored skull of **Homo erectus erectus** *(Java skull no. IV). The dark areas represent the original fossilized sections; the light areas are restorations. (Courtesy of the American Museum of Natural History.)*

"Gabled" calvarium

Angular temporal bone

Recessive frontal region

Heavy supraorbital torus

Constricted temporal region

Diastema in upper dental arch

Moderately developed mastoid process

Broad and heavy ascending ramus

Recessive chin

Fig. 7-3   The femur of the original Java **Homo erectus erectus** *(bottom) compared with that of a modern* **Homo sapiens sapiens** *(top). Except for the tumerous growth caused by an injury during life, seen near the upper end of* **Homo erectus's** *femur, the two leg bones are essentially similar. Observe that the* **Homo sapiens** *bone also has a tumerous growth on the front center of the shaft. (Museum of Anthropology, University of Minnesota. Photo by Don Breneman.)*

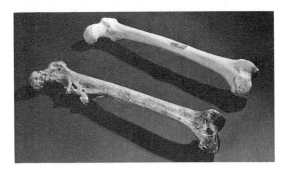

temporaneousness of all the femurs with the skull and with the extinct Pleistocene mammals that come from the same deposit. In addition, the later Pekin finds conform to the same kind of skull-leg complex.

These facts, plus the now well-authenticated fact that *Australopithecus* also was upright, indubitably establish the erect posture of Java man. Thus, he shared this human trait with *Australopithecus* but outdid him in brain capacity; hence, he is placed higher on the phylogenetic tree.

Early and Late Java Man   We mentioned that at Sangiran, Java, where von Koenigswald first worked from 1936 to 1939, two distinct geological strata are identifiable. The top layer is the same as that which had yielded Dubois's Java man at Trinil. Hence, it is called the *Trinil bed*. The Trinil animal fossils and geology show it to have been laid down in a mid-Pleistocene pluvial period, probably equivalent to the second glacial.

The lower stratum contains earlier types of fossil fauna identified as post-Villafranchian and therefore early Middle Pleistocene or, possibly, late Lower Pleistocene. Because they are older than the Trinil beds, these are probably first interglacial. These deposits are the *Djetis beds*.

This geological detail is important because two of the known Java skulls of *Homo erectus* come from the Trinil beds, and two from the older Djetis bed at Sangiran. It establishes the long continuity of evolutionary development in *Homo erectus erectus* in Southeast Asia. The somewhat more rugged quality of the fossils from the Djetis bed suggests that its type was morphologically, as well as temporally, more primitive than the *erectus* forms from the Trinil beds.

Cultural Evidences   No stone or bone artifacts have as yet been recovered in direct association with the remains of Java man. However, a stone-flake industry, called *Patjitan*, is best known from the upper portions of the Trinil beds in other parts of Java

(see Figure 7-4). The implements are crude, heavy scrapers or chopping tools with ⊔-shaped edges such as those which characterize adzes. The Patjitan choppers are early representatives in Java of the great Eastern *chopper-tool tradition,* which extends through Java, Burma, India, and Pakistan to the Valley of the Indus and north through China and into Japan.[1] Pointed "pebble" tools similar to those of the Oldowan are also included in the inventory of the tradition. It is reasonable to infer that Java man was a toolmaker. He has not left us such direct evidence of his hunting prowess as *africanus* has, for the locations of the Java finds are neither caves nor campsites. However, his later descendants in Java (Solo man) and his close relatives in China (*Homo erectus pekinensis*) were great hunters and evidently enthusiastic eaters of human brains (see pages 147–148). There is little doubt that Early *Homo erectus* in Java was a predator, as was *Australopithecus africanus*. He had the teeth of a meat-eating hominid as well.

Homo erectus pekinensis

To complete the introduction of known fossil representatives of earliest man, we return to Asia, where a more developed variety of *Homo erectus* has been found in profusion, not far from the capital of mainland China.

The great homesite of the original Pekin finds, called Choukoutien locus 1, was originally a vast cavern with a lofty ceiling 100 feet above the floor and one and two-thirds times as long as a football field. During its prolonged use through a time of relatively stable climate, it became filled from bottom to top with bones, tools, and muck. The great cave was one of those water-made limestone caverns, not unlike the South African australopithecine sites produced in pre-Pleistocene times. During the long Middle Pleisto-

---

[1]The Burmese form of the tradition is known as *Anyathian;* in Pakistan it is the *Soan;* in China it is the *Choukoutienian.*

cene it was a refuge as well as a refuse dump for *Homo erectus*.

Between 1924 and 1939, in the years preceding the Japanese invasion of China, fourteen different skulls, some facial bones, quantities of teeth, and eleven limb bones were recovered here—the remains of forty or more individuals. The diggings also showed ample evidence of the use of fire and yielded a plentiful supply of simple stone tools and other evidences of cultural activities. Of Pekin man we know a good deal, although as usual not as much as we would like. The fossils were all lost in the Japanese invasion of December 1941.[2] Fortunately, Franz Weidenreich had sent excellent casts to the United States before World War II, and his detailed monographs on the fossils make the total loss

of the original fossils less of a catastrophe.

Once the war was over and the revolution which followed completed, the new Chinese government continued the fine tradition established by the old Chinese Geological Survey. The recovery of fossil man in China goes on through the work of the Institute of Vertebrate Paleontology and Paleoanthropology in Peiping. Since 1949 there have been numerous additional discoveries of *Homo erectus* as well as of fossilized early *Homo sapiens* and some forms which appear to be transitional between *erectus* and *sapiens* in China.[3]

The evidence shows that Pekin man had at least four characteristics that went beyond those of his south-country cousin in Java. He had a distinctly larger cranial capacity. He had fire—which was one reason he could live in caves. He had better tools and weapons;

[2]W. W. Howells tells the story in some detail. For the interesting facts of this intriguing tragedy, see his *Mankind in the Making,* pp. 166–168.

[3]Kwang-chih Chang, "New Evidence on Fossil Man in China" (*Science,* vol. 136, 1962), pp. 749–760.

Fig. 7-4 Patjitan chopper tools from the upper Trinil beds in Java. (Courtesy of the American Museum of Natural History.)

and he seems to have had a penchant for eating other Pekin men.

Morphology of Pekin Man Comparison of Figures 7-2 and 7-5 shows the superficially observable similarity and the singular differences between *Homo erectus erectus* and *Homo erectus pekinensis.*

Cranial Characteristics There is the similar heavy supraorbital torus, the recessive forehead, the constricted frontal region, the angular occiput, the protruding face, and the massive jaw with a weak chin. In *pekinensis,* however, there is no diastema of the upper dental arch. The most significant difference is in the size and contour of the calvarium. There is a marked expansion of the brain itself, and the brain case has enlarged and rounded out to accommodate it. The cranial capacity of Pekin man overlaps that of Java man but attains volumes well above that of the latter. The Pekin cranial vaults run from 850 to 1,300 cc. capacity with a mean of about 1,075 cc. Pekin man has thus far outstripped the great apes and *Australopithecus.* His smallest-brained members had cerebrums nearly as large as those of the most brainy Java man, and the cerebrums of his "big domes" equaled those of the average modern man. *Pekinensis,* as his culture reveals, was a hominid of reasonable intelligence and abilities.

The relative geographic isolation of Pekin man shows up in a number of highly peculiar osteological characteristics. The first of these is the so-called Mongoloid shovel-shaped incisor, which is scoop-shaped on the posterior surface. This produces a ridge across the back of the cutting edge and down the sides. Java man entirely lacked this characteristic, but it has survived as a diagnostic feature of modern members of the Mongoloid race, including many American Indians. All the grinding teeth (molars and premolars) have enlarged pulp cavities extending downward into fused roots, a condition known as *taurodontism* (Gr. *tauros,* bull + *dontos,* tooth). This feature is not exclusively distinctive of

pekinensis, however. European Neandertals have it, as do many American Indians, Eskimos, and South African Bushmen. The Pekin canine teeth are large but, as is true of the rest of the teeth, they are definitely human.

Two other features of the mouth are notably distinctive of *pekinensis.* One is the mandibular torus, a heavy bony ridge inside the lower jaw from the canine to the first molar on each side (the lingual surface). It is a common characteristic of subarctic peoples; more than half the Eskimo population has it, and prehistoric Japanese, Chinese, and Scandinavians, among others, reveal the trait in proportions running from one-fifth to two-thirds of their populations. In all likelihood, these peoples were heavy skin chewers, as Eskimos are known to be; skin chewing is a technique that keeps wet boots and clothing from becoming unwearably stiff. The heavy, deep, but polished, wear, characteristic of all adult Pekin teeth, may indicate the cultural pattern of heavy chewing of soft, but tough, materials.

The other mandibular feature is the presence of multiple *foramina mentalia,* the openings in the lower jawbone beneath the first and second premolars, through which pass the nerves and blood vessels serving the muscles and other tissues of the chin and lower cheeks. Most human beings have only one *foramen* on each side of the jaw—not so *pekinensis.* In the seven recovered inferior maxillae of Pekin man, all have from two to five such openings. Among all the hundreds of known fossil men, none but *Homo erectus pekinensis* and the fossil men of Ternifine, Algeria, and of Heidelberg, Germany (Figure 7-7), have more than one. This could have been a special adaptation to the hearty use of masticatory muscles, particularly for distribution of the facial blood with less crowding of the major veins and arteries.

Bodily Characteristics The body and limb bones of *pekinensis* have a few distinctive features of the kind characterizing some local populations as against others, that is to say, racial differences. Yet, taken as a whole, the skeleton is indistinguishable from that of *Homo sapiens* today. Just as the australopithecines developed upright posture and other bodily changes far in advance of their cranial development, so *Homo erectus* achieved the modern level of bodily development while he still had a moderately primitive brain, teeth, and face. The evolution of the postcranial (below the skull) skeleton of man was thus completed 500,000 years ago. *All subsequent morphological evolution, except for minor racial variations, has been concentrated in the brain and head.* This is to be expected, for once the hominid had risen to the psychocultural-organic level, his organic adaptations became concentrated primarily in his culture-creating apparatus, the brain.

Homo erectus *in Africa*

Recent finds in Algeria and at Olduvai Gorge add new dimensions to the picture of Lower Pleistocene Early Man and his accomplishments. At Ternifine, Algeria, during the second glacial, there was a watering hole where men and animals congregated for their dawn and evening drinking. The men waylaid antelope, zebras, and giraffes; they feasted on elephants, rhinoceroses, giant baboons, and hogs; and they contested with the saber-toothed tiger. In 1954 and 1955, at the site of this ancient watering and hunting spot, C. Arambourg found three human jaws in good condition and part of a human parietal bone among the animal bones. The human materials are too fragmentary to give definitive results, but the expert view is that the heavy jaws and the teeth have much in common with those of Pekin man, while at the same time exhibiting some similarities to features of *Australopithecus robustus*. As is so common with the discoverers of new fossils, Arambourg was convinced that he had a new genus of man. He named it *Atlanthropus mauritanicus*. However, Professor William Howells predicted in 1959: "It seems probable that most people will accept Professor Arambourg's assertion that the Ternifiners are

closely related to Pekin and Java man, and will therefore reject his new genus."[4] The contemporary consensus of professionals is expressed in the summing up by Bernard Campbell for the 1962 Wenner-Gren Foundation conference on classification: ". . . it seems clear that, together with other Middle Pleistocene N. African fossils,[5] they may represent a variety of the species *Homo erectus* which can reasonably be associated as a single subspecies."[6] This species or variety is now named *Homo erectus mauritanicus,* and it is the Western counterpart of *Homo erectus pekinensis.*

In 1960, in the middle of Bed II at Olduvai Gorge at a level which yields many stone tools

[4]W. W. Howells, *Mankind in the Making,* p. 180.
[5]That is, the 1953 discovery in the quarry of Sidi Abd er-Rahman at Casablanca; the Smugglers' Cave discovery in 1935 at Temara, Morocco; and the Rabat skull of 1933.
[6]B. Campbell, "Quantitative Taxonomy and Human Evolution," in S. L. Washburn (ed.), *Classification and Human Evolution,* p. 66.

Fig. 7-5 Skull of **Homo erectus pekinensis.** *(Courtesy of the American Museum of Natural History.)*

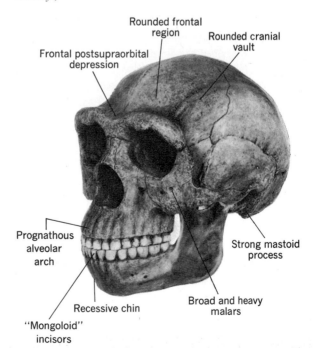

Rounded frontal region

Rounded cranial vault

Frontal postsupraorbital depression

Prognathous alveolar arch

Strong mastoid process

Recessive chin

Broad and heavy malars

"Mongoloid" incisors

and a $K^{40}-A^{40}$ date of 500,000 years, Leakey found a fossil skull that shows "certain superficial characters such as a very large brow ridge and relatively low vault, which recall the Pithecanthropicines."[7] Although Leakey seems to prefer not to think of the new find from Bed II as *Homo erectus*, most anthropologists do, pending detailed analysis of the skull. It is presumed to be an East African representative of *Homo erectus mauritanicus* and the Olduvai successor to the australopithecines.

Aspects of the Life and Tradition of Pekin Man

There is no way of knowing whether Pekin man habitually made the Choukoutien caves his home base or whether he just periodically visited them, but that he camped out in the caves again and again is clear. Deliberately broken and split bones of animals are found by the thousands throughout the deposits; ashes and scorched bones give testimony of the first-known hearths of mankind. The quantities of worked choppers show the continuation of the australopithecine tool tradition.

Pekin man dined mostly on venison. Two-thirds of the animal bones with which his personal and cultural remains are intermingled are those of two species of the fallow deer. The deer obviously did not walk into the caves themselves, nor would they have been dragged into them in such numbers by the other predators with whom man struggled for possession of these sites. Other game that graced his menu included sheep, antelope, roebuck, small horses, and camels. But *Homo erectus pekinensis* was clearly a more wily and ferocious hunter than this inventory alone would indicate. Making up another sizable part of the solid remains of his gar-

bage are the bones of elephants, rhinoceroses, bison, and water buffalo—creatures which would have left him alone if not bothered and certainly would not have invaded the caves themselves. He could have killed these huge beasts by means of fire drives, stampeding them over cliffs in wild panic before deliberately set grass fires or lines of men, women, and children waving flaming brands. He might also have trapped them individually in pitfalls, or, like the Congo Pygmy, he might even have brought down the great elephant by hiding near the game trails and leaping up under the belly of the lumbering beast, thrusting fiercely into the vitals of the soft underbelly with a fire-hardened wooden spear, and dodging to safety behind sheltering rocks or trees. Or, again like the Pygmies, he might have collected the carcasses of the big game which had stumbled to their death through disease or old age.

As for the monster cave bears, saber-toothed tigers, leopards, and giant hyenas, whose fossil bones—also burned and sometimes split—are mingled throughout the debris, it is hard to believe that he fought them face to face, although he might have. He had the brains to be cunning and the courage to drive these great predators from the caves to make room for himself. Masai and other East African hunters have traditionally proved their manhood in this century by provoking a lion to charge and awaiting the final leap crouched upon the ground, holding a spear aslant with butt planted to receive the shock as the lion impales himself upon the point. Pekin man could well have done the same. True, he had no iron spearheads, or even flint, but he did have the fire with which to harden a wooden point, and with his chopper tools he could skin any beast and hack up its meat.

Lithic Industry   The chopper tools of Pekin man did not reach the level of technical excellence attained by *Homo erectus* at the same time in Africa and Europe, where the Chel-

[7]L. S. B. Leakey, "East African Fossil Hominoidea and the Classification within This Superfamily," in Washburn, *op. cit.*, p. 43.

lean-Acheulean tradition was well under way. The Pekin, or Choukoutien, industry, as described by Kenneth Oakley,

. . . consists principally of roughly broken pieces of quartz, with a few crudely flaked pebbles of greenstone, quartzite and cherty rocks. . . . only a small percentage of the pieces are recognizable as tools, but these include chopper-like cores and flakes trimmed as points and scrapers. The industry proved to be practically uniform throughout the thickness of the . . . deposits. . . . Most of the raw material was evidently collected from the bed of a nearby stream, but crystals of quartz with well-formed facets were found among the tools, and these must have been sought by Pekin Man in the granite hills some miles away to the north-east or south of the Choukoutien caves.[8]

It is as though the cultural adaptation of Pekin man stabilized as an adjustment to an unchanging environment and he had little impulse to improve his stone-tool industry. Another possibility, of course, is that he may have concentrated on wooden weapons. More probably, however, in terms of what we know of the dynamics of culture growth, the stability of his long interglacial environment, and his relative geographic isolation from what was going on among other peoples (he was living on the very eastern margin of the human world of his time), shielded him from changing selective pressures and isolated him from new ideas generated elsewhere.

Cannibalism Lastly, there is the matter of cannibalism. Cannibalism, or *anthropophagy* (Gr. *anthropos,* man + *phagos,* to eat), is of three kinds, classified according to the dominant motivation.

The first is *ritualistic* and *incorporative*. It involves the idea that the special qualities of the victim are contained in a bodily essence, which the feaster may incorporate into his person by eating the bodily substance. In some cultures the transference may be made without cannibalistic ingestion. Head-hunting, such as that in Melanesia or among the

Ifugao of Luzon in the Philippines, is practiced to secure the head, which contains the "soul stuff"; this is incorporated in the souls of the slayers through ritual transference.

The second form of cannibalism may be called *gustatory*. Men eat men because they think they are good eating. This kind of sentiment and practice had a sporadic but widely scattered distribution in recent times. It was common in Oceania and parts of Africa, especially among the Congo tribes. In both places, prisoners were penned and fattened for the feast, like the hand-stuffed geese of France. Gustatory cannibalism occurred also in parts of South America, but not among the North American Indians.

The third form of cannibalism is *survival cannibalism*. It is a final recourse of starving people. Eskimos practiced it without pleasure. In the words of a King William Island Eskimo speaking to the great Knut Rasmussen:

Many people have eaten human flesh, but never from any desire for it, only to save their lives, and that after so much suffering that in many cases they were not sensible of what they did. . . . But we who have endured such things ourselves, we do not judge others who have acted in this way, though we may find it hard, when fed and contented ourselves, to understand how they could do such things. But then again how can one who is in good health and well fed expect to understand the madness of starvation? We only know that every one of us has the same desire to live.[9]

In 1847, a wagon train of emigrants from Illinois, the famous Donner Party, became snowbound at the foot of the Sierra Mountains in Nevada. As starvation took its toll, a few rose to heights of heroism in snowshoeing across the mountains to bring aid from California; others turned to eat their own dead.[10] It can happen here.

There is no way of knowing what kind of cannibalism Pekin man indulged in, but that he ate human brains and the marrow of the

[8]K. P. Oakley, *Man the Tool-maker,* p. 113.

[9]K. Rasmussen, *Across Arctic America,* pp. 223–224.
[10]Grippingly described by George Stewart in *Ordeal by Hunger.*

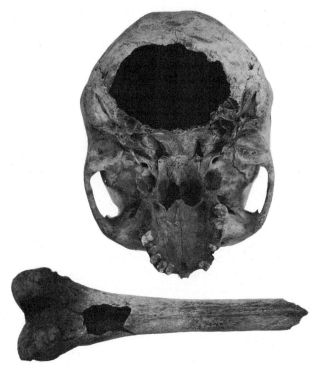

More significant is the fact that in all five of the skulls of Pekin man, the foramen magnum at the base of the brain case had been artificially enlarged so that it would admit a fist. The operation was the same as the one performed on a number of skulls of Middle Pleistocene *Homo sapiens* (see page 168) and in much later times by the producers of the Blackduck culture of prehistoric Minnesota (Figure 7-6). The Minnesota Indians, however, worked with more finesse than Pekin man. Rather than smashing the long bones, they did a neat surgical job and buried bones and skulls together. The interment indicates that this was probably a case of ritual cannibalism.[11]

Homo erectus (heidelbergensis)

As a footnote to the discussion of *Homo erectus,* the variety of man discovered in 1907 in Lower Pleistocene sands at Mauer, near Heidelberg, Germany, needs mention. It is represented by a massive lower jaw (Figure 7-7) with a perfectly preserved set of teeth more similar in size and character to those of *Homo sapiens* than other *Homo erectus* specimens. The jaw itself bespeaks *Homo erectus,* the teeth hint at evolution beyond that level. But no other remnants of Heidelberg man have ever been found, either at Mauer or elsewhere. Without facial or cranial bones to round out the picture of the type, there is no way of knowing whether this is a local European variant of *Homo erectus erectus* or whether it might have come from a population which had already crossed the *Homo sapiens* threshold in first interglacial times.

Fig. 7-6   Prehistoric American Indian skull (above) with basal hole for extraction of the brain. Portion of human femur (below) with hole for removal of the marrow. Both are from the Minnesota Blackduck culture. (Museum of Anthropology, University of Minnesota.)

long bones of his fellow men seems quite evident. First, the recovered bones of *Homo erectus* in the Choukoutien caverns were found scattered helter-skelter throughout the deposits, just as were most of the animal bones; both kinds of bones are fractured and split. This might have been done to produce tools, but most of the bones are unworked and unused. Nor are these river-terrace deposits, in which the bones could have been scattered by running water. The bodies of men and animals had been dismembered, and the bones smashed and tossed aside by those who crouched and cooked about the campfires.

[11]As late as 1900, five Winnebago Indians in Wisconsin, seeking to prove their manhood and to obtain supernatural war power, went on the warpath by train to kill a Potowatamie Indian, whose heart they cut out, cooked, and ate. See Paul Radin (ed.), *Crashing Thunder: An Autobiography of an American Indian,* chap. 22.

Homo erectus (vertesszöllös)

In 1965, a fossilized occipital bone of man, plus several teeth, was found in association with living floors, hearths, stone artifacts, and Pleistocene mammalian remains in a stratified site at Vertesszöllös, in northern Hungary. The deposits, which date from 400,000 B.C., are of the second glacial period. That the people were hunters is evidenced by the remains of rodents, deer, wild cattle, rhinoceros, and several carnivores. In addition to the hearths, the cultural remains include the kind of chopper tools that are found at Choukoutien in association with *Homo erectus pekinensis*. Nor are they unlike some of the choppers found in certain of the industries in the Oldowan tradition of East Africa.

Although the teeth are similar in form to those characteristic of the Asiatic forms of *Homo erectus* (hence, the provisional classification with *Homo erectus*), the rounded character and other details of the occipital bone suggest affinities with the later European *Homo sapiens steinheimensis*, the early form of *Homo sapiens* found in second interglacial deposits in Europe. It could be that in the Vertesszöllös find we have discovered a *Homo erectus* in transition to *Homo sapiens*. Time will tell.

The Life and Industries of Homo erectus

We have now seen that the earliest known type of mankind had established itself throughout much of the Eastern Hemisphere in Middle Pleistocene times (CA. 700,000 to 200,000 B.P.).[12] His fossil remains have been found in North and East Africa, southwestern Europe, and Southeast and East Asia. He was clearly a wanderer who pushed to the outer limits of the available land areas of the Eurasiatic heartland. Northern Europe and Asia were evidently climatically too intemperate for most of these warmth-loving creatures. With greater adaptability than the australopithecines, he pressed his range of occupation somewhat further north than had his hominid predecessor. In his living habits, *Homo erectus* had continued the first thrust of *Australopithecus africanus's* biocultural innovations. He mastered walking, specialized toolmaking, and hunting. To these he added the controlled

[12] B.P. means Before Present.

Fig. 7-7   Heidelberg jaw (left) compared with the jaw of a chimpanzee (center) and the jaw of a modern man (right). (Courtesy of the American Museum of Natural History.)

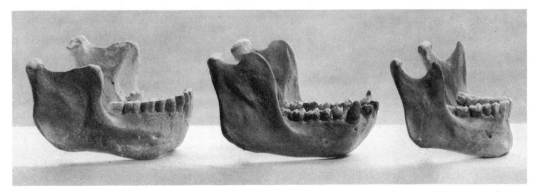

use of fire, thus passing well beyond the limits of ordinary animal life.

In the words of Sherwood Washburn,

The capacity for bipedal walking is primarily an adaptation for covering long distances. Even the chimpanzee can run faster than a man, and any monkey can easily outdistance him. A man, on the other hand, can walk many miles, and this is essential for efficient hunting. According to the skeletal evidence, fully developed walkers first appeared in the ancient men who first appeared in the Old World from 500,000 [700,000] years ago to the middle of the last glaciation. These men were competent hunters, as is shown by the bones of the large animals they killed. But they also used fire and made complicated tools according to clearly defined traditions."[13]

Tools of the Middle Pleistocene Hunters   In the West, including North Africa,[14] and as far east as the Indus Valley in Pakistan, the basic tool tradition of *Homo erectus* is known as the Acheulean, after the type station (original site) at St. Acheul, in France. The Acheulean is a lithic tradition focused upon the hand ax or *coup de poing*, in the terminology established by French archaeologists in the last century. Although the hand ax is the dominant diagnostic artifact of the Acheulean, varieties of flake tools such as scrapers and knives were also important parts of *Homo erectus's* tool kit.

Hand Ax   The hand ax was made by selecting an oblong nodule of flint. Such nodules have a smooth, irregular surface more or less like the skin of a russet potato. This is the *patina*. When flint has been freshly dug, it fractures quite easily. Flint that has been exposed to the air for some time is more untractable. Using a round igneous rock, 2 or 3 inches in diameter, as a hammerstone, the flint knapper strikes sharp blows around the outer surface of the nodule. In the Acheulean

tradition, he kept turning the nodule over and over as he removed flakes from both sides. The core could be held in the hand or rested on the worker's knee or on a log. More flakes were removed from one end of the nodule than from the other. The result is an almond- or pear-shaped tool with a broad butt end which fits comfortably into the fist. Projecting below the grip is the pointed working edge of the artifact. As a weapon, it was serviceable as a skull crusher of beasts in hunting or of men in fighting. As a tool, it served for hacking limbs from trees, butchering large game, and cracking bones for marrow. In view of the tens of thousands of Middle Paleolithic hand axes recovered in the past hundred and fifty years, it must have been that no early man or woman was ever without one—except by accident.

The perfection of the learned skills of flint knapping as applied to the hand ax continued steadily from its earliest manifestations during the crude Abbevillian and Chellean phases of the Acheulean tradition in second glacial and early second interglacial times. By the time of the third glacial advance, control of a hammerstone percussion technique had been much improved. In addition, the introduction of a method of using bars of hardwood or antlers with which to deliver sharp blows for the removal of thinner and smaller flakes resulted in beautifully shaped and finished hand axes of the Upper Acheulean types (Figure 7-8). The evolution of technological skills of tool production, extending from the Chellean through the Acheulean, spanned 500,000 years and more than 20,000 generations! Early man could pattern and retain the mental blueprint of his learned behavior. He could communicate and transmit his slowly won mastery of new achievements to other members of his group and from group to group, so that the tool traditions became part of an intercontinental cultural pool. But the rate of technical growth and diffusion over half a million years was minuscule. Compare, in contrast, the technical and social innovations

[13]S. L. Washburn, "Tools and Human Evolution" (*Scientific American*, vol. 203, 1960), pp. 65–67.
[14]J. D. Clark, *The Prehistory of Africa*, p. 78.

which have been added to the cultural inventory of man since James Watt first invented the steam engine eight generations ago.

Flake Tools The Acheulean inventory included, in addition to the hand ax, nicely retouched and especially shaped stone flakes for cutting, planing, and scraping the flesh off hides to be made into leather, and awls to punch holes for sewing.

A few rare finds of ends of sharpened wood staffs prove that *Homo erectus* provided himself with spears for hunting and fighting, and digging sticks (dibbles) for root, grub, and rodent gathering. The pointed stick as dibble was probably the woman's tool, while the

Fig. 7-8   Acheulean hand axes. Almond-shaped (upper left) and discoidal (lower right). (Specimens on left, courtesy of the American Museum of Natural History; on right, Museum of Anthropology, University of Minnesota. Photo by Don Breneman.)

pointed staff as pike was a weapon in the hands of men. At least, such is the basic division between the use of these implements by males and females in contemporary hunting and collecting primitives.

The Acheulean Tradition at Olduvai Gorge
The relationship of the hand ax traditions to the Oldowan pebble-tool tradition of the australopithecines is neatly exhibited at Olduvai (Figure 7-8). In 1960, Leakey found a *Homo erectus* skull and numbers of Chellean (Early Acheulean) artifacts in the middle of Bed II at a level which yields a $K^{40}-A^{40}$ date of 500,000 years. At the very bottom of Bed II, half the artifacts are "indistinguishable from the types found in Bed I, and in appearance characteristic of the Oldowan culture."[15] However, the other half of the artifacts represent a distinct evolutionary advance over the types of tools found in Bed I and are hand axes of the Chellean I type. "Some of these crude hand axes," writes Leakey, "are made of large pebbles and others are made of lumps of quartz and lava, but all of them agree in having, as an essential characteristic, flaking in three or four different directions and the intersection of two jagged cutting edges . . . in a point at one end."[16]

At a second level, 10 to 15 feet above the base of Bed II, the hand axes have taken on a specialized quality: the butt ends are thick and massive and usually with a marked flattening on the lower face. Running along the upper face is a steep ridge, which is usually more or less central in the anterior part and curves markedly—but irregularly—from about the center of the butt end. On the lower face, the flattening, which is so marked in the posterior half, is sometimes carried forward the whole length of the specimen, but in other examples is replaced by a sharp ridge formed by the intersection of flat scars in two directions at a steep angle.[17] Still within Bed II and

[15]L. S. B. Leakey, *Olduvai Gorge*, p. 34.
[16]*Ibid.*
[17]*Ibid.*

20 feet above the horizon that yielded the implements just described above are found

. . . large thick hand axes more or less triangular but sometimes roughly oval in outline when viewed from above. The lower face is remarkably flat . . . due to careful flaking which usually extends over the whole inferior face. The upper face has a more or less defined central keel anteriorly, so that a section through the anterior part of the specimen is roughly triangular.[18]

At Olduvai Gorge most of the broad features of the technological evolution of the hand ax are revealed in firm stratigraphic sequence. Yet, this is by no means the full story of the Acheulean traditions in Africa; rich Middle Pleistocene sites with deep stratigraphy covering tens of thousands of years have been exposed all over Africa except for heavy rain-forest areas of the Congo basin.[19] A majority of the African Acheulean industries, however, represent highly developed (rather than more primitive) forms of the tradition.

Of the ecological preferences of Acheulean *Homo erectus* bands Grahame Clark writes:

Indications from Africa are that Acheulean culture was adapted to the Savannah. Camping-places were normally set within easy reach of water. For example, at Olorgesaile in Kenya, Acheulean man lived like his forebears of Bed I at Olduvai on alluvial flats surrounding a lake. The banks of the lake itself seem to have been avoided, possibly on account of mosquitoes or in order to avoid disturbing game. The locations chosen for actual occupation were commonly sandy patches along the courses of seasonal runnels; these would have been free of vegetation and no doubt water could have been secured from them by scooping into the bed. . . . The areas of occupation at Olorgesaile were sharply defined as if to suggest that they were limited by some form of shelter or possibly even by a thorn-brush hedge.[20]

The Use of Fire   The Late Acheulean men of Africa also possessed fire, but it is at the open

site of Torralba, in Spain, that we learn of the importance of the first use of fire in hunting. Although no fossil remnants of the men themselves have been found in the extensive excavations undertaken by F. Clark Howell in 1961, many Acheulean tools attest their presence in the locale 300,000 years ago. The site itself lies in what is now open, undulating Spanish farm land in the valley of the Ambrona River, northeast of Madrid. The end of the Lower Pleistocene was a time of marked climatic variability in this region. The Ambrona valley served as a passageway for herds of the great (and now extinct) straight-tusked elephant (*Elephas antiquus*), deer, aurochs, horses, and many lesser beasts. There, men armed with Acheulean weapons awaited them. But they were also armed with the controlled use of fire, as evidenced by the random appearance of charred pieces of wood and charcoal throughout and around the great kill sites. The sites themselves, as soil and pollen analyses indicate, were bottomland bogs into which the herds were stampeded, quite possibly by setting fire to the dry, late summer grasses. The racing flames would then drive the animals deep into the muck from which there was no escape. Armed with heavy hand axes and wooden spears, wary and courageous *Homo erectus* males could then move in for the kill—after the beasts had worn themselves out in fruitless struggles against the sucking embrace of the deadly swamp[21] (see Figure 7-10). The vast numbers of helter-skelter skeletons, well-preserved (but few complete), reveal that they were butchered on the spot, with such

[21]For a comparative study of the use of fire drives and their ecological consequences, see O. C. Stewart, "Fire as the First Great Force Employed by Man," in W. L. Thomas (ed.), *Man's Role in Changing the Face of the Earth*, pp. 115–133.

Fig. 7-9   Sequence of lithic industries represented by Oldowan pebble-tool chopper and Acheulean hand axes at Olduvai Gorge, Kenya, correlated to geologic strata and fossil remains of hominids. (Tools after L. S. B. Leakey, Olduvai Gorge, I, *Cambridge University Press.)*

[18]*Ibid.*
[19]See F. Bordes, *The Old Stone Age,* pp. 64–76, for a handy summary of the African sites. For more technical treatment, see S. Cole, *The Prehistory of East Africa.*
[20]G. Clark, *The Stone Age Hunters,* pp. 36–37.

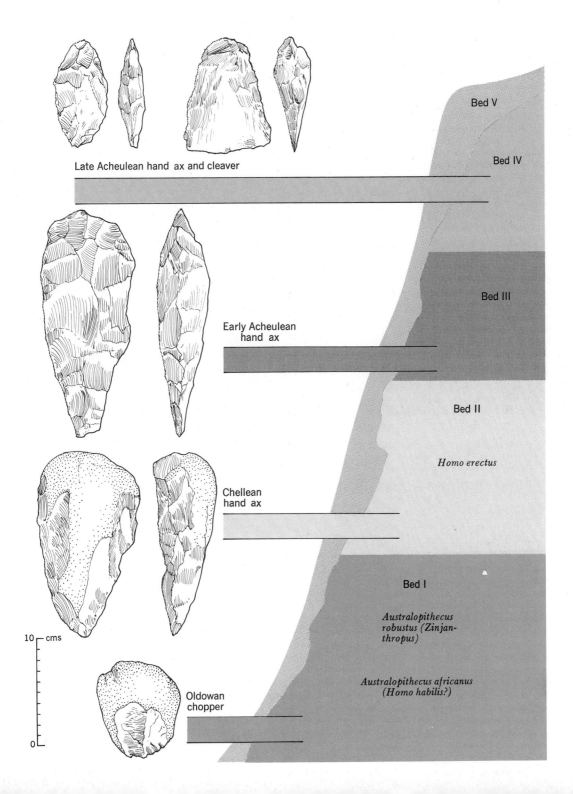

Late Acheulean hand ax and cleaver

Bed V

Bed IV

Early Acheulean
hand ax

Bed III

Bed II

Homo erectus

Chellean
hand ax

Bed I

*Australopithecus
robustus (Zinjan-
thropus)*

*Australopithecus africanus
(Homo habilis?)*

10 ⌐ cms

Oldowan
chopper

0 ⌐

parts as could be carried away to the campsites stripped and hacked off. The skeletal bulk remained where the beast had died.

One can imagine the gluttonous gorging that followed such a kill. Even if *Homo erectus* had taught himself how to sun-dry or smoke meat for preservation, he had no means for transportation of food stores beyond what he and his women could carry. He was a migratory hunter, living from hand to mouth and day to day. Like Eskimos who, after a big whale kill, can and do eat as much as 10 pounds of meat each at one sitting, so the Torralba hunters may have similarly indulged themselves a half million years ago.

Consumption of game in such quantities also meant that man had learned the rudiments of cookery. Knowledge of the art of outdoor barbecuing is surely among the most ancient marks of being human. Our long ancestry of primate vegetarianism did not equip us with the correct hormonal digestive input to handle large amounts of uncooked meat. Cooking effects the chemical and physical transformations necessary to give the digestive process a prestart before ingestion.

It may be too much to attribute the success of *Homo erectus* to his mastery of fire, but there is good reason to believe that this was a key factor in his ecological adaptation. The Greeks well knew the importance of fire to mankind. Prometheus dared as *Homo erectus* dared. According to the myth, fire was the cherished possession of the gods and was not meant for men. When Prometheus stole it from the lightning of Zeus and gave it to man, the gods could not take the gift away, but they condemned Prometheus, the firebringer, to the torture of the damned, chaining him hand and foot to a rock, belly exposed to the tearing beak of a vulture. The Greeks were not alone in seeing fire as a divine possession that man could steal by his wits alone; the myth is one of the primeval basic conceptions of all mankind. The story of the theft of fire is told in one form or another in

Fig. 7-10   The close of an elephant hunt. Except that they possess iron-headed, rather than flint-pointed, spears, and that the environment is semitropical rather than glacial, these Mandari hunters of the eastern Sudan, Africa, could be reenacting a Paleolithic mammoth hunt. (From P. Molloy, **The Cry of the Fish Eagle,** *Michael Joseph, Ltd.)*

virtually all societies, primitive and civilized.[22]

Pekin man, like *Homo erectus* in the West, was probably a "fire stealer" rather than a fire maker. At any rate, no fire-producing instruments have come from his caves. Lignite and coal beds, which lie close to the surface and could have been subject to spontaneous combustion, lie near to Choukoutien. And, of course, lightning sets fire to trees. The precious tending of the "eternal ember" of the household fire was surely a matter of great concern and could well have been the focus of simple, basic, ritual anxiety.

SUMMARY

With *Homo erectus* the evolutionary development of upright posture, enlargement of the brain, and basic technology had reached levels unequivocally acknowledged as human. This phase of early humanity was achieved more or less simultaneously in Africa, Europe, and Asia during Early Middle Pleistocene times. It continued with minor biological modifications and cultural improvements for something like a half million years.

Homo erectus erectus is represented by fossil materials from Java, Olduvai Gorge, and possibly Heidelberg, Germany. Java man is found in two distinct strata (the Djetis and Trinil beds) of the Lower Pleistocene age. Java man had a maximal cranial capacity just short of the minimum for *Homo sapiens*, while his own minimum cranial capacity exceeds that of the most capacious australopithecine skulls. His skull is angular, with a recessive forehead behind heavy browridges. The jaw is massive, but the teeth are more hominid than otherwise. The structure of the femur indicates upright posture.

No cultural remains have been found in the same deposits with Java man fossils, but the presence of chopper tools in the Trinil

beds of Patjitan in Java implies the continuation of the pebble-chopper tradition begun by the australopithecines.

In Africa and in Europe, *Homo erectus* developed stone-tool traditions distinguished by the hand ax, or *coup de poing,* but also containing a number of specialized varieties of flake tools for cutting and scraping. He had become an upright-walking big-game hunter with the mental capability of sustained concentration on a single goal, such as is necessary for persistent hunting. The site at Torralba, in Spain, shows that he also used fire in animal drives and in cooking. At Torralba, human skeletal materials are lacking, but the Acheulean industry and Middle Pleistocene dating associate the site with *Homo erectus.*

The evolution of the Chellean-Acheulean hand ax tradition at Olduvai Gorge is associated with a fossil skull of *Homo erectus* in Bed II.

While Western *Homo erectus* was building the hand ax tradition, Pekin man (*Homo erectus pekinensis*), who evidently indulged in cannibalism, diversified the Patjitan choppertool tradition into that of Choukoutien. This did not, however, represent an advance in stone technology to any great degree. Although Pekin man shared the cultural control of fire with Western *Homo erectus,* it is interesting that a basic Oriental-Occidental cultural differentiation was manifest in second glacial and interglacial times.

SELECTED READINGS

Bordes, F., *The Old Stone Age,* pp. 51–97. Fairly detailed general summary of the Abbevillian and Acheulean traditions in Europe and Africa, compared to Lower Paleolithic industries in Asia.

Clark, J. D., *The Prehistory of Africa* (1970). Contains the most up-to-date coverage of *Homo erectus* in Africa.

Clark, W. E. Le G., *The Fossil Evidence for Human Evolution* (1955), chap. 3. The analysis of the Java and Pekin fossils contained in this chapter will fill in many additional details not included in our dis-

[22]See "Suŋ Snarer" in M. Leach (ed.), *Standard Dictionary of Folklore, Mythology and Legend,* vol. 2, p. 1089.

cussion. The writing is fairly technical, but still understandable by the nonprofessional. Clark classifies the two forms of *Homo erectus* as *Pithecanthropus erectus* and *Sinanthropus pekinensis,* but this should produce no difficulties if the nature of the synonyms is kept in mind.

Cole, S., *The Prehistory of East Africa* (rev. ed., 1963), chap. 5, "The Hand-ax Makers." Covers a number of manifestations of the Chellean in Africa, with an interesting account of the fabulous site of Olorgesaile.

Coon, C. S., *The Origin of Races* (1963), chap. 9, "Pithecanthropus and the Australoids," and chap. 10, "Sinanthropus and the Mongoloids." Much detailed comparative data on all the *Homo erectus* finds.

Day, M. H., *Guide to Fossil Man: A Handbook of Human Paleontology* (1965), pp. 65–69, on the Heidelberg jaw; pp. 101–115, on *Homo erectus mauritanicus* remains; pp. 137–143, on *Homo erectus* calvarium from Bed II at Olduvai Gorge; pp. 221–237, on the Java finds; and pp. 250–258 on the Pekin "Lower Cave" remains. Good photos and concise summaries of osteological character-istics, associated fauna, cultural remains, geological strata and dating, and taxonomic identities. Additional primary bibliographic references also listed.

Howell, F. C., and the Editors of Time-Life Books, *Early Man* (1968), pp. 76–100. Interesting for its photos of excavations in progress at Torralba and for the imaginative paintings of the daily life of *Homo erectus* (except that in the great scene of the fire drive of mammoths, the wind is blowing in the wrong direction so that the fire would drive the men, not the elephants, before it!).

Leakey, L. S. B., *Olduvai Gorge* (1951). A handsomely illustrated work on the evolutionary sequences of the hand axes at Olduvai. Unfortunately, it ignores the flake-tool components of the Chellean-Acheulean complex and therefore gives a distorted impression of the tradition as a whole.

Oakley, K. P., "On Man's Use of Fire, with Comments on Tool-making and Hunting," in S. L. Washburn (ed.), *The Social Life of Early Man* (1961), pp. 176–193. A good summary of the data on the first evidences of man's use of fire and the implications to be drawn therefrom.

Chapter 8

Prehistoric *Homo sapiens* in the Middle Paleolithic Age

The evolutionary progression that resulted in *Homo sapiens* was slow but accelerating. The accompanying development of culture proceeded at a like pace. Nearly two million years elapsed from the time that pebble tools were first used to the threshold of the Upper Paleolithic Age. The process had been started by the australopithecines and consolidated in Africa, Asia, and southern Europe by *Homo erectus*. In the Middle Paleolithic, it was carried forward by *Homo sapiens*.

As in earlier times, hunting and gathering were still the source of human sustenance, but the techniques were slowly changing, and man's mentality was changing even more rapidly. Upright posture was no longer his predominant feature. Man's brain caught up with, and surpassed, his morphological development. He was becoming more and more the toolmaker and the thinker.

By the middle of the long second interglacial period, the mental development of man had expanded to the point where, for the first time, present-day paleontologists are willing to classify his fossil remains as those of *Homo sapiens* (Gr. *homo,* man + L. *sapiens,* intelligent). In this group are the Steinheim, Swanscombe, and Fontechevade forms of early *Homo sapiens*. They were the forerunners of Neandertal man and the later *Homo sapiens,* who would introduce the advanced hunting cultures of the Upper Paleolithic.

Homo sapiens steinheimensis The Steinheim fossil fragments were discovered in southwestern Germany, not far from Stuttgart, in the summer of 1933. They came from second interglacial gravels containing ex-

tinct Pleistocene fauna such as mammoths, rhinoceros, and bison. The skull and face are well preserved, although twisted and compressed by the pressure of the overlying gravels or possibly by a crushing blow. Nonetheless, they are in good enough shape to allow for clear identification of their qualities.

Fig. 8-A Neandertal man, side view, Restoration by Dr. J. H. McGregor. (Courtesy of the American Museum of Natural History.)

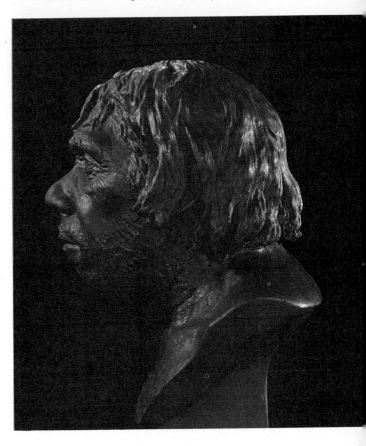

The forehead is moderately recessive behind marked supraorbital ridges. The occipital region is less angular and more rounded than that of Pekin man; it has a very slight occipital torus, and the mastoids are small but sharp. The cranial capacity of 1,150 cc. is at the lower end of the range for modern man. The face is relatively small, and the overall dental configuration is human. It is the skull of a *Homo sapiens* who antedated the Neandertalers and modern forms of *Homo sapiens* by 250,000 or more years.

The Swanscombe Skull No artifacts have been found at Steinheim, but at Swanscombe the situation is very different. The Swanscombe fossil comes from a second interglacial terrace of the Thames River. These terraces yielded the first-known Lower Paleolithic hand ax, a beautiful Acheulean specimen found at Gray's Inn Lane, London, in 1680. The terraces have for generations constituted a happy hunting ground for relic hunters and dealers in stone "spearheads," who have looted tens of thousands of Lower Paleolithic tools from these deposits. The usual early, interglacial boreal forest fossil fauna (including *Elephas antiquus, Elephas primigenius, Cervus* (Merk's rhinoceros), and *Megaceros* (bison and horse) abound to prove, along with analytical geology, that the terrace gravels were laid down in second interglacial times.

A sample of the men who hunted these beasts, roughed out the hand axes with which they were killed, and knocked off the stone flakes with which they were butchered was finally found in 1935 and 1936 by Alvan T. Marston, who had been keeping close watch on the removal of the gravels from the site since 1933. Marston first found a human occipital bone embedded in the face of the gravel workings 24 feet beneath the present ground surface. Nine months later, after the gravel had been worked back 8 yards, the left parietal of the same skull was found at the same level. And again, in 1955, the right pari-

etal of the same individual was discovered about 50 feet from the first fragment. Fluorine analysis has proved the bones to be as old as those of the extinct associated Pleistocene mammals. Here is unimpeachable evidence of the nature of early man in Britain.

Because the muscular markings are light in comparison to the size and thickness of the skull, it is inferred that the individual was a female. The estimated cephalic index of 78 indicates a medium-rounded head; the occipital diameter is very broad. Within the thick-boned cranium was housed a brain of approximately 1,325 cc., just about the modern female average. Even more significant is the modern complexity of cortical convolutions shown on the endocranial cast. The foramen magnum is located well under and forward on the cranium. The Swanscombe woman was upright and human-brained. Although we have no evidence concerning her face, teeth, or bodily structure, she is certainly a member of the genus *Homo;* and, indeed, Morant concluded after detailed study, there is nothing about the fragments that would justify excluding her from the species *sapiens.* By the same token, Weiner and Campbell have demonstrated through multivariant statistical analysis that she does not qualify as a member of the variety *sapiens* (namely: *Homo sapiens sapiens*), to which contemporary modern man belongs.[1] She is a British representative of *Homo sapiens steinheimensis.*

The Fontechevade Specimens The portions of two skulls found at Fontechevade in southeastern France in 1947 by Miss G. Henri-Martin are also *Homo sapiens steinheimensis.* Associated with a Late Clactonian industry called *Tayacian,* and separated from an overlying Mousterian level by a seal of limestone,

[1] G. M. Morant, "The Form of the Swanscombe Skull" (*Journal of the Royal Anthropological Institute,* vol. 68, 1938), pp. 67–97; and J. S. Weiner and B. G. Campbell, "The Taxonomic Status of the Swanscombe Skull," in C. D. Overy (ed.), *Swanscombe—A Survey of Research on a Unique Pleistocene Site* (1964).

these skulls are clearly interglacial, possibly Mindel-Riss rather than Riss-Würm. The Fontechevade cranial capacity equals the modern average: 1,460 to 1,470 cc. The skull is long, broad, and low, but in the words of Henri Vallois, who analyzed the Fontechevade finds:

The essential fact is the absolute absence of a supraorbital torus: the glabella and the brow ridge are less developed than in the Upper Paleolithic Europeans, or even the majority of Europeans today. They recall, in their general configuration, skulls of female Europeans; there is no nasion depression, and the brow ridge does not extend down to the upper border of the orbit.[2]

The inference to be drawn from these large-brained Lower Pleistocene fossils is that the evolution of man had achieved its present biological plateau in Europe and Africa by second interglacial times. Populations of *Homo erectus* were still present, but sufficient genetic modifications were widespread, so that many individuals were clearly becoming *Homo sapiens* phenotypes. Keeping in mind the principles of genetic variation, natural selection, and adaptive radiation (Chapter 5), it is only reasonable to hold that there would be just a few manifestations of sapienization at first among predominantly *erectus* populations. Gradually, as the selective advantages of *sapiens* traits began to take effect, higher percentages of genes of the *sapiens* type would be established, until at last they characterized whole populations. This was fully achieved by the time of the third interglacial but was well under way in second interglacial times.

Homo erectus had very nearly completed the skeletal adaptation to upright posture. After the achievement of full human cranial capacity by *Homo sapiens steinheimensis*, the major changes are in the face and dentition.[3]

[2]H. V. Vallois, "The Fontechevade Fossil Men" (*American Journal of Physical Anthropology,* vol. 7, no. 3, 1949), p. 352.
[3]See C. L. Brace and M. F. A. Montagu, *Man's Evolution,* pp. 255–264.

The facial and dental adaptations of man that occur with *Homo sapiens* appear to be closely related to his improving skill as a hunter, toolmaker, and user of fire, and ultimately, to drastic changes in dietary habits. The possible mechanics of these changes are discussed a bit later, after a consideration of the actual cultural developments that occurred.

Middle Paleolithic Cultures

The Acheulean Tradition   It is hardly probable that Steinheim man developed the Acheulean hand ax industry that is found in such profusion in the Thames second interglacial terraces. This development possibly occurred in East Africa. When Steinheim man followed the retreating Mindel-Riss glaciation into western Europe, he brought knowledge of the hand ax and flake-tool techniques with him.

At Olduvai, the evolution of the hand ax had continued through Bed III (third pluvial) and into Bed IV. In these later deposits, the hand axes were produced by application of a much more controlled flaking technique than was used earlier. This involved a finishing process whereby, instead of a blow being struck directly on the core with a hammerstone to remove flakes, it was struck with the round edge of a stick, bone, or horn. The force of such a blow is diffused so as to remove thinner flakes in the desired direction. This method of flake removal is called the *cylinder-hammer technique.*

The invention of the cylinder-hammer technique made possible the manufacture of thin, symmetrically refined hand axes of the Acheulean type such as the samples shown in Figure 7-8 (page 151).

Above all, the material effect of these developments was economy of raw material. Not that there was necessarily any shortage of raw rock, but the more suitable cores had to be searched for, and it was more economical to produce a lasting and more efficient tool by use of improved techniques than to bang out a new hand ax with crudely removed flakes whenever one was needed. In addition, if early *Homo sapiens* was psychologically similar to modern craftsmen, both primitive and civilized, he undoubtedly found creative satisfaction in producing a beautiful job well done.

Flake Tools as a Part of the Chellean-Acheulean Complex Although archaeologists write of the "core-biface hand ax complex," it must not be forgotten that man has never confined himself to the manufacture and use of only one type of weapon or tool. Thus, although Leakey himself has contributed to the common distortion of the image of the core-biface hand ax complex by discussing hand axes only in his beautiful monograph on Olduvai Gorge, Professor Hallam Movius, Harvard's distinguished Old World archaeologist, properly notes:

In the immediately overlying beds [Bed II at Olduvai] pointed chopping tools appear which are regarded as the forerunners of the true bifacial hand-axes that have been reported from the next series of deposits, *in association with various types of massive flake tools*. . . . In Bed III the pointed hand-axes of Middle Acheulian type are associated with cleavers . . . *and proto-Levalloisian flakes*. This developmental sequence culminates in the Late Acheulian of Bed IV, where, in addition to the finely made pointed hand-axes, there are rectangular-shaped cleavers *and a fully developed Levalloisian flake industry* [italics added].[4]

The maker of a hand ax *ipso facto* produces quantities of flakes. He has no interest in most of them, and a workshop floor near a good source of raw materials will be littered with thousands of unused chips and flakes. Nonetheless, the flintworker and his women would not be human if they failed to pick up appropriately shaped flakes suitable for cutting meat and scraping wood and hides. The

[4]H. L. Movius, Jr., "Old World Prehistory: Paleolithic," in A. L. Kroeber (ed.), *Anthropology Today*, p. 177.

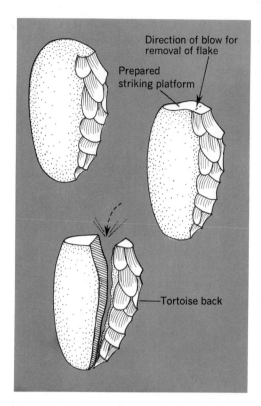

Fig. 8-1   The manufacture of a Levalloisian flake. After the surface is shaped and a striking platform is prepared, the flake is removed with a single blow. Edges may be resharpened after use. Such a tool, which is ready for immediate use without further preparation, was probably used as a skinning knife or skin scraper.

evidence is perfectly clear that the early bands of *Homo sapiens* who produced the hand axes also used many flake tools.

The Levalloisian Flake-tool Tradition The very special technique of producing a highly serviceable flake implement, known as Levalloisian (after the type site at Levallois, France), appeared in western Europe during the second interglacial period, and at Olduvai, in East Africa, in Bed III. The pattern and technique for producing Levalloisian flakes are sufficiently significant to require special attention. The important point is that Leval-loisian flakes are not simple fragments of sharp rock that are by-products of hand ax production and subsequently convenient to use. They are the primary object of the flint-worker's intention when he picks up a flint nodule to begin his task. The procedure is called the *striking-platform-tortoise-core tech-nique*. It involves the following steps, which are illustrated in Figure 8-1.

1. An oval-shaped flint nodule is flaked around its edge to remove irregularities and to give it symmetry.

2. The patina is removed from one side by a series of blows directed along the edge toward the middle so that the surface of the nodule resembles the surface of a tortoise shell, rather than that of a potato. When this task is completed, the worker gets ready to remove the flake from the core.

3. A striking platform is next prepared by removing a flake from one end of the nodule roughly at a right angle to the long axis of the nodule. In terms of our own experience, we might think of the way in which we knock off one end of a boiled egg with a sharp blow of a table knife. The end of the egg becomes flat; likewise, the end of the nodule. This flat plane forms the Levalloisian-prepared strik-ing platform, or facet (Figure 8-2).

4. The tortoise back is removed with one clean blow delivered obliquely to the striking platform. The flake comes off in a single piece which is tortoise-shell-shaped on the back-side and smooth on the front. The cutting edges are finely resharpened by the removal of small flakes from the outer edges, not by striking but by firm application of pressure against the edge, using a bone or antler to get the job done.

In southern Europe, Africa, and the Middle East, the Levalloisian method of producing flakes was joined to the Acheulean hand ax tradition. Hence, in that part of the world, during the times of *Homo sapiens steinheim-ensis*, it resulted in the Acheulean-Levalloi-sian tool complex.

The Clactonian Flake-tool Complex Although the hand ax complexes clearly dominated in Africa, western Europe, the Middle East, and Southwest Asia, the chopper and flake-tool complexes of Asia spread in a broad band along the northern edges of the Chellean-Acheulean territory (see Figure 8-3). In France, as reported by François Bordes, there are strata dating from the Middle Pleistocene which yield "Clactonian" flake-tool assem-blages in which there are no hand axes.[5]

The Clactonian complex is named after the English resort of Clacton-on-the-Sea, where it was first discovered and recognized early in this century. The most spectacular diagnostic tool of the complex is the so-called Clacton-

[5]F. Bordes, *The Old Stone Age*, p. 92.

Fig. 8-2 A late Acheulean-Levallois flake showing the prepared dorsal surface and striking platform at the top (left). The lateral view of the same artifact shows the smooth, curved fracture plane which forms the ventral side of the flake. The bulb of percussion, formed at the point of impact of the blow which removed the flake, may be clearly seen on its upper right edge. (Museum of Anthropology, University of Minnesota. Photo by Don Breneman.)

ian flake. This is a large flake which consistently shows an oblique 130-degree angle from the striking facet to the bulb of the re-

Fig. 8-3   Developmental relationships of the major tool traditions of the Paleolithic Age in the Old World. All the Paleolithic complexes began in the Villafranchian pebble-tool tradition. The Acheulean (Chellean-Abbevillian) hand ax-flake tradition and the Clactonian developed separately and fused in the Mousterian traditions. The Asiatic chopper-tool traditions remained separate.

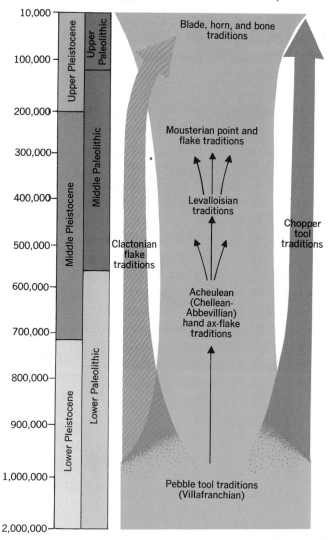

moved face. Clactonian flakes are prepared by steps more or less similar to those used in the Levalloisian technique, except that the tortoise-back effect is not produced, and the flakes often have broad chopper edges. Such chopping tools are the functional equivalent to the Acheulean hand ax.

However, the Clactonian complex must not be thought of solely in terms of its type tool. Clactonian hunters, like those who carried the Acheulean tradition, had a number of tasks to perform and they made specialized tools to carry them out. The four varieties are shown in Figure 8-4. The endscraper is not too different from the Upper Paleolithic tool produced by *Homo sapiens sapiens*, shown in Figure 9-3 (page 181). It was probably used as a bone and woodworking gouge. The so-called denticulate tool has a saw-tooth cutting edge that could be usable on meat or fresh softwoods. The sidescraper could have served as a knife, but its primary use was undoubtedly intended for scraping down the fleshy sides of hides to be used as clothing and for utensils. No such hides have been found, but men living in the subarctic climate of glacial times very likely wrapped themselves in fur robes and slept under fur coverings. The nicest of Clactonian specialties is the allpurpose tool called the bill hook. It is a combination sidescraper, spokeshave, knife, and drilling tool—the original Boy Scout knife. The spokeshave would have been well adapted for shaping the wooden spear point which has survived through 500,000 years or more in the Pleistocene deposits at Clacton.

Seasonal Migrations and Housing of Middle Paleolithic Man   In the last chapter, we discussed the use of fire by the men of Torralba and Ambrona, in Spain. The suggestion of Clark Howell that the sites be assigned to *Homo erectus* was followed. In the absence of actual fossil remains of man himself at Torralba and Ambrona, however, such a judgment remains wholly tentative. The producers of the sites could have been either *Homo* *erectus* or *Homo sapiens*. Both species lived in Europe throughout the Middle Pleistocene and they shared essentially similar Acheulean hand ax traditions. Technology is independent of race.

In the case of the seasonal seaside Mediterranean homesite, which we are now about to discuss, the choice has been made to present it within the context of this chapter (rather than the preceding one) simply because it falls within the larger ecological zone which produced the Steinheim and Fontechevade fossil representatives of *Homo sapiens*. On the other hand, the only known *Homo erectus* fossil from the same zone is that of Heidelberg man. It comes from first interglacial deposits and is hence too early in time to be linked to the site. Torralba and Ambrona are contemporary to the Terra Amata site with which we are now about to be concerned, but they are on the other side of the Pyrenees in a different eco-area.

We know that Middle Paleolithic man was a big-game hunter who regularly used fire. Some bands were cave men, but others roved the forests, tundra, and open plains far from caves, building themselves real houses. They were not palaces, to be sure, but when we realize that a third of a million years ago springtime migrants built 50-foot-long gabled houses on the shores of the Mediterranean, we cannot but be impressed. This knowledge comes as the result of a great discovery made in October 1965 in the heart of Nice, France.[6]

Nice is now a fashionable resort city with a fine harbor. It can also claim the oldest remains of housing known to man. The discovery came as a result of bulldozing for a new construction site on an ancient sand beach that lies well above the present mean level of the Mediterranean. The beach was formed at the end of the second glaciation, as determined by the fauna, flora, and tool assemblages uncovered by the blades of the

scrapers. When fossils and hand axes began to be exposed in numbers, construction work was temporarily halted and a crash archaeological salvage program launched. Three hundred workers, mostly volunteers, went to work under professional scientific supervision. Because of their efforts, the site, now known as Terra Amata, yielded 35,000 archaeological objects, but more importantly, 21 house sites.

Postholes in the compacted sands show the oval outlines of the houses. Circles of boulders around the postholes lay in place as sometime reinforcements. A line of large

Fig. 8-4 Clactonian flake tools. The classic Clactonian chopper flakes are at the bottom. Characteristic special flakes are shown above. (Museum of Anthropology, University of Minnesota. Photo by Don Breneman.)

[6]H. deLumley, "A Paleolithic Camp at Nice" (*Scientific American,* vol. 220, 1969), pp. 42–50.

postholes down the center of the elongated floor marks the location of the uprights which supported the ridgepole. Each house faced the sea, where the southern sun shone through the doorway. Inside the doorway, where ventilation would be best, lay a small, scooped-out hearth. And on the northwest side of each hearth was a loose wall of stones to shield the fire from the drafts that blew along the floor. Evidently, the walls were not too windproof. The floor on the east side of each dwelling shows a clear area surrounded by myriads of flint chips. Here squatted the master toolmaker of the household, preparing and repairing the hand axes and flake tools for his band of hunters and food processors.

Two Early Acheulean cultural traditions were evidently represented by the bands which frequented the spot. The more primitive is seen in a pebble-tool assemblage consisting of choppers and a small number of rock scrapers and projectile points (evidently intended to be hafted on spears). The producers of these Oldowan-like tool kits built their cabins closest to the shore of the Pleistocene Sea which they were frequenting.

The second tradition is associated with the cabin floors which were located higher up from the ocean edge on the prehistoric sand dunes. The assemblages here combine Early Acheulean hand axes with Clactonian choppers, along with a few worked bones.

Because no human fossils were discovered, it is not possible to say anything about the species identity of the early populations at Terra Amata. Nor can one tell whether they were closely contemporary or not, although the similarity in their house forms would seem to indicate it.

Coprolitic analysis (see page 105) of human feces found in the same sand strata as the floors of the cabins (but always outside them) show that these people only visited Terra Amata for brief periods in the spring. Their main homes were elsewhere, as yet undiscovered. We know this because the coprolites contain undigested pollen such as is shed by plants in the late springtime. It could be that these early nomadic hunters came down to the warm coast mainly to eat their fill of fresh greens after a long winter of heavy meat protein and carbohydrate diet. While on the coast, they also dined on fish and shellfish. Yet this alone could not have been their reason for the seasonal visits to the coast, because seafood is available the year around, and the coprolites indicate the migrants stayed only as long as the spring plants were fresh.

It is clear, however, that these meat eaters did not go vegetarian in the spring. Fossil remains of *Elephas meridionalis* (southern elephant), Merk's rhinoceros, stag, ibex, ox, and wild boar show that the house builders were true Paleolithic big-game hunters who yearned for a little variety in their diets.

Finally, it is evident that they were an industrious people given to activity. They stayed at Terra Amata for only a few weeks in the spring. Yet on arrival they built themselves noteworthy houses, both for comfort and, one might surmise, as functional expressions of their band unity and their humanness. They were clearly conscious of being different from mere animals.

The pattern of the domicile is very likely that of a joint family household. The family was probably bilateral (see pages 443–444), since there was little inheritable property to stimulate the development of unilateral descent. Most likely, these people practiced the incest tabu, which forced a male to seek his mate from outside the family and household (see pages 397–400). Because subsistence was predominantly by hunting, it may be inferred that residence was with the band of the husband rather than with that of the wife (see pages 426–428). This means that the composition of the band would have consisted of an older male or two, one of whom would be the household headman, their wives, their sons and the sons' wives, plus children. The whole group could number, say, from ten to thirty people living in one house. Related households might have formed a hamlet, made up of a somewhat larger composite band, but probably not numbering more than 100 persons.

It is also possible, but there is no way of knowing, except by inference from the practices of hunters and gatherers such as the Shoshone Indians and Australian aborigines, that households which were scattered on the nomadic hunt during most of the year gathered briefly for ceremonial rites and sociability in the spring. It would be the "human" thing to do.

Homo sapiens neandertalensis

The first Neandertal[7] skull was found on Gibraltar in 1848. It was viewed as an interesting specimen, but its significance struck no responsive chord until a second fossil, after which the Neandertal subspecies is named, was found in a cave in the Neander Valley near Düsseldorf, Germany, in 1856, three years before the publication of Darwin's *Origin of Species*. The discovery was made just in time to take its place in the excited debates over human evolution which enlivened the latter half of the nineteenth century. The evolutionists hailed the find as an example of intermediary, submodern fossil man. The conservatives sourly held that he was nothing but a pathological freak, probably a peasant. It was even suggested that he

might have been a "stupid" Roman legionnaire of the less soldierly kind who crawled off in the cave for twenty winks and liked it so much that he stayed there. However, the discovery of two more skulls of the same genre at Spy, Belgium, in 1887 put an end to all such scurrilous reflections on the character of the man of the Neander Valley. It then became clear that an order of man different from all modern races had been in Europe in earlier times and, further, that he was the producer of certain of the Old Stone Age cultures, the antiquity of which had been established earlier through the efforts of the French archaeologist Boucher de Perthes.

Immediately after the turn of the century, Neandertal men, women, and children began to rise from their graves in profusion—from France and Spain to the Crimea, and later from Palestine and North Africa, until there was no doubt that Neandertal man had been a very important figure who had really gotten around in his time.

Neandertal Man and Modern Man For nearly a hundred years an incredible amount of confusion was engendered by the "Neandertal problem." The problem is: What is the evolutionary (phylogenetic) relation of Neandertal man to modern man?

For half a century (*ca.* 1890 to 1935), the dominant theme was that Neandertal man is a distinct species of the genus *Homo,* and that this species evolved rather directly from the pithecanthropine forms of Asia. It produced the Mousterian culture of the Middle Paleolithic Age, and meanwhile, somewhere, somehow, in Asia Minor or North Africa, modern man of the species *sapiens* evolved and developed the basic Upper Paleolithic culture (Châtelperronian), moved into Europe during the middle of the fourth glaciation, and proceeded to exterminate the Neandertals with pestilence and war in the span of a few millennia. Finally, it was held that because "Neandertal" traits are so rare in skeletons of the late Upper Paleolithic and thereafter,

---

[7]The original spelling of this word was "Neanderthal." However, early in this century in Germany an imperial commission of philologists, with authority to streamline the language in the interests of Teutonic efficiency, recommended that since German is quite consistently spelled as it is pronounced, the unsounded *h* should be dropped from all *th* combinations except in *der Thron.* (For a group of professors to tamper with the seat of the Emperor would be lese majesty. Less respectful German wags said they were afraid that the monarchy might collapse if the *h* were removed from the throne.) Be that as it may, prehistorians love antiquities and many of them still cling to the archaic *h* in "Neanderthal." See also H. Vallois, "Néanderthal-Néandertal?" (*L'Anthropologie,* vol. 55, 1952), pp. 557–558.

species differences must have made racial interbreeding impossible. This is the "theory of hominid catastrophism."[8]

One thing is certain. The Classic Neandertal type disappeared from the scene around 40,000 years ago.

In the 1930s, two events set in motion a reevaluation of the whole question of the historical relation of Neandertal man to modern man.

The discovery of the Swanscombe and Steinheim fossils showed the existence of a type of man in Europe in second interglacial times with "little indication of specifically Neanderthal morphology."[9] Mid-Pleistocene man in Europe and North Africa is not a Neandertal prototype in a narrow sense. Next, the characteristics of a number of fossil individuals discovered in Palestinian caves by Dorothy Garrod were published. On Mt. Carmel, near the Sea of Galilee, two sites yielded Early and Middle Mousterian cultural inventories in association with several dozen human skeletons, or rather, parts of skeletons.

The remarkable aspect of the Mt. Carmel population is its variability. From the lower levels of the Tabun Cave came a girl who is similar to the Swanscombe-Steinheim variety of *Homo sapiens*. In the upper levels of the cave were genuine *Homo sapiens sapiens* (contemporary modern men) and others with mixed Neandertal and *Homo sapiens sapiens* traits. At Shkūl, a rock shelter not far from Tabun, a Mousterian burial plot yielded remains of ten persons who possessed skeletal features varying from Neandertaloid to distinctly *sapiens* (see Figure 8-5). These fossils are of the early last pluvial in the Middle East, contemporary to the Neandertals of the first part of the fourth glacial epoch in Europe. In the light of the then-prevailing theory, the

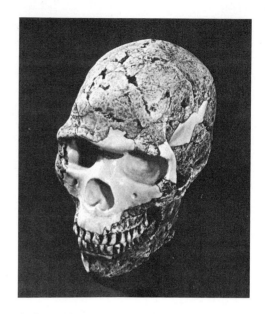

Fig. 8-5   The reconstruction of Shkūl V, a late Pleistocene Homo sapiens sapiens *from Palestine showing variation in the direction of Neandertaloid traits. (Cast, Museum of Anthropology, University of Minnesota. Photo by Don Breneman.)*

discovery of primitive *Homo sapiens* types, of fossils with mixed Neandertal-modern *Homo sapiens* traits, and of fossils that were similar to the Cro-Magnon type of *Homo sapiens sapiens* was extremely surprising (see page 175).

Theodore McCown and Sir Arthur Keith proposed at the time that a basic Neandertal population was evolving into modern man.[10] They examined and rejected an alternative hypothesis that the Mt. Carmel population represented the hybridization of a population of Neandertals with a population of *Homo sapiens sapiens*, both having originated separately elsewhere (the place being left undetermined). The possibility that evolutionary divergence and polymorphism were occurring simultaneously seems to have been ignored. At any rate, it was held that both

[8]See C. L. Brace, "The Fate of the 'Classic' Neanderthals: A Consideration of Hominid Catastrophism" (*Current Anthropology*, vol. 5, no. 1, 1964), pp. 3–46.

[9]F. C. Howell, "The Evolutionary Significance of Variation and Varieties of 'Neanderthal' Man" (*The Quarterly Review of Biology*, vol. 32, no. 4, 1957), p. 334.

[10]T. D. McCown and A. Keith, *The Stone Age of Mt. Carmel*, vol. II (1939).

modern types and Neandertals were present in the Holy Land 45,000 years ago.

In 1957, excavations by Ralph Solecki in Shanidar Cave in Iraq showed that what had happened in Palestine was no fluke. Seven rather complete Neandertal skeletons were found, along with a rich Mousterian tool assemblage. One skeleton was that of an infant; the others were adults. The famous first skeleton of Shanidar is that of a smashed forty-year-old male upon whom the roof had literally caved in 44,000 years ago, according to carbon 14 dating. All the Shanidar individuals looked like "modernized Neandertals."

More recent finds in central and eastern Europe, including the remains of as many as eighteen individuals in a single site, confirm the implications of the Middle Eastern finds.[11] It is now clearly established that there is a wide range of variability in the cranial and postcranial (trunk) features of Middle Pleistocene Neandertals. Traits characteristic of Classic Neandertal men of western Europe appear alongside traits held to be characteristic of *Homo sapiens sapiens*, both in individual fossil specimens and within fossil populations from single sites. *Homo sapiens sapiens* fossils from the same areas overlap the Neandertal fossils in time, and they also show great variability, including features characteristic of the much earlier *Homo sapiens steinheimensis*.

Put into contemporary perspective, the "problem" of Neandertal man does not disappear. It takes on different and broader dimensions. Originally it had a narrow and misleading focus, because the type was for so long known only in the highly specialized form found in western Europe—the so-called Classic Neandertal. In this form the diagnostic physical traits of the Neandertal skeleton appear in their most pronounced manifestations (see Figure 8-6). Yet it is now recognized

that West European Neandertals drew for their ancestry on the same generalized *Homo sapiens* gene pool as did those of Africa and the lands to the east. Human evolution, from 400,000 to 30,000 years ago, was going through a fairly volatile phase of adaptation under widely varying ecological conditions—both in space and through time. Mousterian hunters were wanderers who mixed genes from local population to local population throughout the whole Euro-Afro-Asiatic heartland. The West European bands, how-

Fig. 8-6   Profile and three-quarter front views of the restored skull of a Classic Neandertal, "The Old Man of La Quina" (cast). The capacious cranium with marked supraorbital and occipital ridges also reveals a strong mastoid process. The dental arch is moderately prognathous above a slightly recessive chin. (Museum of Anthropology, University of Minnesota. Photo by Don Breneman.)

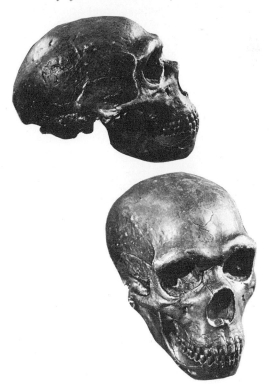

[11]J. Jelínek, "Neanderthal Man and *Homo sapiens* in Central and Eastern Europe" (*Current Anthropology,* vol. 10, no. 5, 1969), pp. 475–503.

ever, seem, under conditions of extreme glaciation, to have been more isolated than most and to have shared in the greater gene pool of *Homo sapiens* to a lesser degree. Hence, they intensified the radiation of their genetic changes away from the more generalized characteristics of man that were developing among other *Homo sapiens* populations. They are recognized as a distinct variety of *Homo sapiens* but not as a species in their own right.

Homo sapiens soloensis and Homo sapiens rhodesianensis   The first of these two special varieties of *Homo sapiens* was found in the Ngandong beds, which overlie the Djetis and Trinil beds in Java. Eleven fragmentary skulls and two tibia of Solo man were found just 6 miles from Trinil, on the Solo River, in 1931 and 1932. The geological matrix places the fossils in the Upper Pleistocene.

Every one of the skulls had been subjected to postmortem butchery. In all but one instance, the face had been hacked off entirely, and no lower jaws were found at all. In all but one skull, the foramen magnum had been enlarged by a stick or bone that was inserted in the hole and then pressed upon. Apparently, Solo man was keeping up brain cannibalism. The skulls all lay bottom up, which means that they had been carefully placed. They were not water-rolled, which means they were found where they had been left. And they were in such good condition, apart from intentional mutilation, that the absence of any loose teeth or other parts of the body, except for the two shinbones, indicates they had been carried in their butchered condition to the river bank. For a feast, or as ritual sacrifices? Who can say?

Viewed superficially, Solo man is a Neandertal-like *Homo sapiens*. The skulls are thick-boned. The browridges are heavy but do not form a massive, continuous shelf. The range of the Solo cranial capacities is from 1,035 to 1,255 cc., with an average, combining both sexes, of about 1,100 cc. This places the type in the lower ranges of *Homo sapiens*.[12]

Rhodesian man represents another Upper Pleistocene variety of *Homo sapiens*. Like *soloensis*, he has heavy Neandertaloid browridges, discontinuous over the nose; a recessive, low-domed calvarium with a strong occipital ridge and angular roof, weak mastoids, and a cranial capacity of 1,280 cc. The lower face projects to a prognathous upper alveolar arch, a feature that indicates possible ancestry to later African populations.

Morphology of Homo sapiens neandertalensis   Keeping in mind the wide range of variability, the more distinctive skeletal features of the Neandertals are specifically:

1. Long, low, wide, and capacious cranium (1,300 to 1,600 cc.)
2. Cranial base acutely oriented upward with tilted foramen magnum
3. Bun-shaped or angular occipital profile
4. Large facial area
5. Semicircular supraorbital ridges fused above the nose and with the temporal regions
6. Convex curvature of the upper jaws, fusing directly with the cheekbones without forming a suborbital depression (canine fossa)
7. Short, massive spinal column
8. Long, vertical dorsal spines on the cervical vertebrae
9. Limited forward curvature of the cervical and lumbar areas of the spine
10. Heavy, short upper arm (humerus) with a massive head
11. Pronounced curvature of the radius (bow bone in the forearm)
12. Short forearm relative to upper arm
13. Broad, flattened ilia in the pelvis
14. Highly curved thighbone of massive structure
15. Short shinbone
16. Very short leg in proportion to thigh

[12]B. Campbell, "Quantitative Taxonomy and Human Evolution," in S. L. Washburn (ed.), *Classification and Human Evolution*, p. 66.

In appearance the Neandertal was short, massive-chested, powerfully armed, large-bodied, beetle-browed, broad-nosed and large-headed.

The Mousterian Culture of Homo sapiens neandertalensis

The basic subsistence of Neandertal *Homo sapiens* was not appreciably different from that of the pre-Mousterian big-game hunters of the Steinheim type. The Neandertal time-span ran from the very end of the third inter-glacial through the first half of the fourth glacial, when it came to an abrupt end. The Mousterian complex began approximately 100,000 years ago and ended around 35,000 B.C.

The Mousterian Complex   The distribution of tool assemblages of the Mousterian com-plex is vast—Europe, Africa, and all South and East Asia. But variety in the local assem-blages is also considerable, for men were now becoming able to recognize and put into effect more and more alternative possibilities in their basic technologies. In the main, it may be said that Neandertal man's Mousterian stone technology continued the evolutionary trend which had been slowly developing through all the Lower and Middle Paleolithic. However, a definite shift from the production and use of hand axes to more and more em-phasis on varieties of flakes marks the general trend (see Figure 8-7). Thus, in what Bordes calls *Mousterian of Acheulean Tradition,* the frequency of hand axes in early (so-called Type A) sites varies from 8 to 40 per cent of the lithic assemblages, with the mode falling between 10 to 15 per cent. Such hand axes as there are diminutive when compared to their Acheulean antecedents. In later levels (Type B), hand axes are rare (less than 8 per cent) and these are usually small and crudely made.

In the *Typical Mousterian,* hand axes have

all but disappeared, while points (probably attached to spears) are common and well made. Levallois flaking continues in this

Fig. 8-7   Representative Mousterian tools. Top row (left to right): Typical Mousterian convex sidescraper, Levallois point, and sidescraper. Second row: Levallois point, Quina-type sidescraper, and discoidal scraper. Third row: Mousterian of Acheulean tradition endscraper, and denticulate flake. Bottom: Mousterian of Acheulean tradition hand ax, point with thinned butt, and denticulated concave scraper. (Museum of Anthropology, University of Minnesota. Photo by Don Breneman.)

tradition, as well as in the two additional Mousterian traditions which Bordes identifies for Europe. Two special traditions, the *Quina-Ferrassie* and the *Denticulate Mousterian,* contain few or no hand axes and are diagnostically distinguished by their different components of flake tools and points.

In Africa, Typical Mousterian assemblages are found in Egypt and along the Mediterranean Coast. South of the Sahara, an Acheulean derivative called *Sangoan* extends from Kenya to southern Rhodesia. Here, hand axes continue, with the addition of a special adaptation in the form of large biface picks, plus large flint gravers or planing tools. It is thought that these were special woodworking tools developed by forest-dwelling peoples. In South Africa, heart-shaped hand axes give way over time to increasing numbers of flake tools in the local manifestations of the Mousterian complex.[13]

Bone-tool Inventory   Like *Australopithecus,* Neandertal man made extensive use of bone implements. It has always seemed reasonable to suppose that early man surely made as much use of wood and bones for tools and weapons as he did of stone. Rare fragments of worked wood are proof of wood use, but the loss of most pieces through decay gives little idea of what the relative importance of wooden artifacts may have been. The situation with respect to bone is different. Bone fossilizes better than wood and many more fragments have been preserved in and about human living sites. Few archaeologists have given more than scant attention to analysis of bone assemblages for possible tool use, however. Beginning in 1959, an English archaeologist, James Kitching, undertook to rectify this defect.

Kitching concentrated on an osteodonto-

keratic assemblage from Mousterian deposits in the English site known as Pin Hole Cave. Only seventy-three Mousterian stone tools were yielded, but hundreds of used bone flakes. Except for the teeth of rabbits, which the Pin Hole Neandertalers extracted to use as sharp punches, the skeletons of small animals were not used as sources of bone artifacts. Large animals were treated differently. Carcasses of reindeer, bison, bears, hyenas, and wolves were dragged bodily into the cave, probably with much grunting and gesticulation. Horses, woolly rhinoceros, and giant deer were usually butchered where killed and only selected bony parts were taken back home. These parts were commonly antlers, teeth, and jaws—all most serviceable as tools.

Half jaws of carnivores, with their projecting canines, were used as ripping tools. Antlers, shoulder blades, jawbones of reindeer, and leg bones of rhinoceros were used as splitting wedges and hammers. Split and trimmed ribs of reindeer and bison, and spirally broken splints of leg bones served as knives. Shoulder blades of rhinoceros and reindeer were trimmed and used as spades for digging. Rounded bone flakes from large leg bones, the hip blade (ilium) of rhinoceros, the shoulder blades of reindeer, bison, and horses were all used as skinning tools. Other bones were put to use as hide scrapers. A really nice adaptation was the use of the large hip socket of the rhinoceros as a pounding bowl or mortar. And for pestles with which to grind and pound, what could be better than the foot bones (carpal and tarsal) of rhinoceros? The brain case of reindeer made a cup or scoop, as did the hip socket of the rhinoceros. Kitching also thinks that the hollow humerus (shinbone) of the rhinoceros, with the marrow removed, served as a prepottery tankard.[14] The hardware of a Neandertal household was plentiful.

---

[13]For a comprehensive, more detailed, but still not too technical, comparison of the major manifestations in the Old World, the best treatment may be found in F. Bordes, *The Old Stone Age,* pp. 98–146.

[14]J. W. Kitching, *Bone, Tooth and Horn Tools of "Paleolithic Man."*

Housing Most known Mousterian homesites have been found in caves. In the more extreme fluctuations of cold in the fourth glaciation, caves were clearly appealing to Neandertal man for the shelter they offered. So also were overhanging rock cliffs, especially those which formed rock shelters on the north side of a river valley. The noonday sun provided welcome reflected solar heat which continued to radiate into the cold night. Yet no more than his pre-Neandertal *Homo sapiens* predecessors was Neandertal man exclusively a cave man.

One example of Mousterian open-plains housing comes from Molodova, in western Russia. A ring of huge mammoth bones, lying close together, surrounds a floor which is clear of bones and 18 feet in diameter (Figure 8-8). Within the floor are the remains of fifteen hearths. This Mousterian home was probably made of supple tree trunks inserted at the base into hollow tubes of mammoth leg bones, which were found buried upright in the ground. Animal skins would have covered the frame. The piles of bones around the circle are believed to have served as weights to help hold the structure in place and especially to keep the skins tight against the ground so as to shut out wintry blasts along the floor. Outside a break in the bone ring, to the northwest, is an accumulation of mammoth bones left from butchering operations. The large number of hearths within the tent space could indicate that the basic materials were left "on

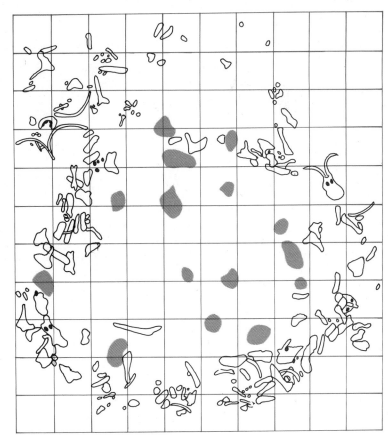

Fig. 8-8   Ground plan of site of Mousterian dwelling on the open plains of western Russia at Molodova. The small dark dots represent mammoth teeth; the larger dark areas are hearths within the original hut and indicate repeated occupation. (After F. Bordes, **The Old Stone Age,** *p. 143.)*

0   1m

location," so to speak, for seasonal use by a wandering band that returned for the hunt from time to time.

Ritual and Death   If "hearth and home" had come to have emotional meaning for the Neandertaler, so too, the evidence tells us, had living and dying. Of the prerequisites for the maintenance of human society suggested in Chapter 2 (page 34), the most uniquely human is a definition of "the meaning of life" which maintains the motivation to survive and engage in the activities necessary to survival. This concept is expressed in symbolic representations of feelings and ideas.

To date, there is little evidence of material art produced by the Neandertalers. On the other hand, two expressions of human feeling do stand out: burial of the dead and a ritualized bear cult. Interment of the dead was an established practice of the Mousterian Neandertals. A good many of the recovered fossil skeletons of Neandertal man have been found carefully bedded in shallow pits and accompanied by flint tools and occasional bones. One Neandertal was buried in Shanidar Cave, Iran, on a bed of pine boughs and flowers, according to the pollen concentrated in the earth surrounding his skeleton. Whatever this might or might not lead us to infer about belief in immortality and a continued spiritual existence apart from the body, it does show concern for the individual as a person. Even newborn infants were stylistically (we mean to say, in a planned pattern) buried in the cavern of La Ferrassie in France.

The evidence of a bear cult among different groups of Neandertal man is ample. Bear burials have recently been discovered in the Cavern of Regourdon, in southern France, confirming the importance of the bear-skull cache from the Dragon's Lair (the Drachenloch) in Switzerland, where a stone-lined pit, or cist, held a collection of packed bear skulls, including the lower jaws. The hole was closed with a large stone slab. The Drachenloch also yielded a bear skull without a lower

jaw but with the right thighbone of another bear pushed between the cheekbone (malar) and the brain case (calvarium) on the right side. This device was found placed upon two shinbones (femurs) from still two other bears.

Variations in cults are so tremendous that it would be foolhardy to try to reconstruct even by speculation what the Neandertal cave dwellers were up to. However, the possibilities may be sensed in the Bear Dance, and its accompanying mythology, as it is still performed every spring among the Ute Indians of Colorado and Utah. It commemorates the emergence of the bear from his long hibernation and his confrontation by a legendary Indian who learned the dance from a bear. When the Utes perform "his dance," they are sure that the friendship of the bear for human beings is secured. They are confident that it makes hunting safer.[15]

SUMMARY

In the second interglacial period, sapienization, i.e., modification of skeletal traits and mental capacity in the direction of those characteristic of modern man, transformed *Homo erectus* into *Homo sapiens*. The Middle Pleistocene forms of *Homo sapiens* are represented by the fossils from Steinheim, Swanscombe, Fontechevade, and other sites.

The culture of early *Homo sapiens* continued the big-game subsistence patterns of *Homo erectus*. Likewise, the technology in Europe and Africa showed no developmental break. The production of hand axes was refined by the invention of the cylinder-hammer technique and pressure retouching. Increasing variety in the flake tool kit was achieved through invention of the Levallois flaking technique and the spread of the Clactonian tradition. All were fused in varying degrees

[15]J. H. Steward, "A Uintah Ute Bear Dance, March 1931" (*American Anthropologist,* vol. 34, 1932), p. 265. See also A. I. Hallowell, "Bear Ceremonialism in the Northern Hemisphere" (*American Anthropologist,* vol. 28, 1926), pp. 1–175.

by different populations of early man as local manifestations of the Acheulean complex.

The great new development, on the basis of present evidence, was sophisticated housing, sufficiently large to shelter a small composite band. Such bands were probably the basis of social life.

The evolutionary history of man and culture continued without revolutionary mutation through the rest of the Middle Pleistocene, into the fourth glacial epoch. The product was Neandertal man (*Homo sapiens neandertalensis*) and the Mousterian cultural complex.

When compared to the earlier Steinheim type of *Homo sapiens,* Neandertals first appeared to be a primitive regression, except for their very large cranial capacities. Later discoveries at Mt. Carmel (in Israel), at Shanidar Cave (in Iraq), and elsewhere have demonstrated that the rugged Classic Neandertals are a specialized variation within a broad polymorphic range of *Homo sapiens* including, at the other extreme, noticeably modern individuals.

The Mousterian tool complex, which is intimately associated with Neandertal man, is found in many combinations of component elements throughout the ice-free parts of Europe, the Middle East, Africa, and Asia. In general, it is characterized by a decline in frequency and functional reliance on the hand ax. Concomitantly, specialized varieties of flake tools increased. Recent research at Pin Hole Cave in England also shows how important the use of bone for tools probably was in Mousterian times.

Although most known Mousterian sites exist in caves and rock shelters, work in Czechoslovakia, Hungary, and South Russia shows that Neandertal man had also adapted himself to life in the open. At Molodova in the Ukraine, mammoth bone tent-rings outline the floors of open Neandertal homesites. Human burials and bear-skull interments give hints of a growing concern with individual personality and symbolic representation of belief and "meaning in life" through ritual expressionism.

SELECTED READINGS

Bordes, F. *The Old Stone Age* (1968). Chapter 8, "The Mousterian Stage in Europe," is highly recommended for more (and lucid) detail on the specifics of the several varieties of the Mousterian complex. Chapters 9 and 10 provide useful summaries of the Mousterian in Africa and Asia. An authoritative account, handsomely illustrated.

Brace, C. L., "The Fate of the 'Classic' Neanderthals: A Consideration of Hominid Catastrophism" (*Current Anthropology,* vol. 5, no. 1, 1964), pp. 3–46. A strongly colored, but highly informative, coverage of the question: What were the Neandertals and what happened to them?

Chard, C. S., *Man in Prehistory* (1969), pp. 92–124. Emphasizes ecological factors in Middle Pleistocene developments.

Howell, F. C., and the Editors of Time-Life Books, *Early Man* (1968). A popular account, with heavy pictorial emphasis. The primary author is an outstanding authority; the text is informative and reliable, if sketchy. Color photos of artifacts are excellent; numerous sketches, helpful; and artists' colored paintings of imaginatively reconstructed scenes of prehistoric activities add life to the story.

Howell, F. C., "Observations on the Earlier Phases of the European Lower Paleolithic," in J. D. Clark and F. C. Howell (eds.), "Recent Studies in Paleoanthropology" (*American Anthropologist,* vol. 68, no. 2, part 2, Special Publication, 1966), pp. 88–200. A definitive and tough synthesis of extant knowledge on the subject. While too difficult for the beginning student, it is well worth examining to see how meticulous archaeological interpretation can be. It should be taken as a neutralizing antidote to the possible overenthusiasm of the kind of book written by Pfeiffer.

Pfeiffer, J. H., *The Emergence of Man* (1969), pp. 112–220. A highly readable survey of Neandertal man and his culture, with emphasis on the human-interest aspects of prehistoric archaeology.

Chapter 9

Homo sapiens and the Upper Paleolithic Age

Thirty-five thousand years ago the era of Neandertal man had run its course. Modern man, *Homo sapiens sapiens,* took over the scene midway through the fourth glacial period, and the biological development of man as he exists today was at long last completed. Thereafter only one genus, one species, and one subspecies, *Homo sapiens sapiens,* remained on the scene to continue the story of mankind. There is no reason to suppose that biological evolution has come to an end, yet the burden of change has, since the

Fig. 9-A   Upper Paleolithic wall painting in the cavern of Lascaux. (Photograph by Hans Hinz, with permission of Caisse Nationale des Monuments Historique.)

beginning of the Upper Paleolithic, been carried increasingly by cultural innovation rather than by genetic modification.

The Origin of Modern Man

It is unlikely that modern man originated in any very precisely localized spot. There was no Garden of Eden, except in an allegorical sense. Although Aleš Hrdlička, of the Smithsonian Institution, argued that modern man evolved directly from Neandertal man, and although this same thesis has lately been revived by C. L. Brace, its probable validity is not so very great. Neandertal man enjoyed an intensive but limited distribution in the West. Third interglacial, non-Neandertal *Homo sapiens* existed over a wide area of the Old World. Of modern man, Dobzhansky writes: "*Homo sapiens sapiens* was from the beginning a wanderer and a colonizer. . . . [T]oward the end of the Pleistocene he is already a cosmopolite who appeared in eastern Asia, Australia, Africa and America."[1]

Modern man represents a continuing evolution of Middle Pleistocene *Homo sapiens,* with a certain amount of gene flow between various populations. Geographic isolation and differential natural selection were sufficient to produce different populations, but there was apparently enough genetic intermixture so that *Homo sapiens sapiens* was developing as a subspecies all through Africa, Asia Minor, and the outer edges of Asia more or less simultaneously.

Modern man does not appear to have developed in Europe where *Homo sapiens nean-*

[1]T. Dobzhansky, *Mankind Evolving,* p. 180.

dertalensis held the stage through the first advance of the fourth glacial. But he does, indeed, displace Neandertal man during the milder interstadial phase following the first crest of the fourth glaciation. In view of the very limited persistence of any distinctive Neandertal traits in subsequent Late Pleistocene populations, it does not seem that the Neandertals had much of a chance to contribute to the enduring gene pool.

European and American writers have, in the past, been prone to think of early *Homo sapiens sapiens* in the image of Cro-Magnon man (see Figure 9-1). The first fossil remains of the Cro-Magnon variety of *Homo sapiens sapiens* were discovered in a grotto behind the present Hotel des Cro Magnons, in Les Ezies, France, in 1868. These remains looked so modern, and so little was then known about human prehistory, that the mayor of Les Ezies had them reburied in the local cemetery! Later they were disinterred for scientific study. Because he lived in Europe, produced excellent art a good 20,000 years ago, was so large-brained, high-domed, upright, and so much more obviously like a northwestern European in appearance and capabilities than *Homo sapiens neandertalensis,* it was easy for European scholars to say he *is* modern man.

The fact is that the Cro-Magnon fossil group is but one manifestation of *Homo sapiens sapiens* (Figure 9-2). It is not the only type that lived in the Late Pleistocene and produced a manifestation of Upper Paleolithic culture, nor is it the earliest. There are also the local varieties of Late Pleistocene *Homo sapiens sapiens,* found as fossils at Grimaldi, Combe Cappelle, and Chancelade, in France, and at Brno and Predmost, in Czechoslovakia. In southern Africa, there is the Boskop type. In Southeast Asia, there is the Wadjak predecessor of later Australoids and the 40,000-year-old fossil skull from Niah Cave in Borneo. And in China, the fossil man of the Upper Cave at Choukoutien is also a *Homo sapiens sapiens* as are a number of other more recently discovered Chinese specimens. These finds by no means exhaust the list.

Hereafter, when we speak of modern man, we shall refer to *Homo sapiens sapiens* in all his varieties.

The Morphology of Modern Man

What, in generalized terms, are the morphological traits of modern man?

His skeletal features are different from those of his *Homo sapiens* predecessors only in those traits which are associated with the final attainment of upright posture. The long bones of the legs lose their curvature and become characteristically more slender and less robust. The iliac wings of the pelvis become more smoothly rounded and tilted more

Fig. 9-1 Skull of Cro-Magnon man, a Late Pleistocene Homo sapiens sapiens. *Its thoroughly modern characteristics are evident in its smooth-contoured cranium with high forehead, rounded occiput, and large volume. Also to be observed are its strong nasal bridge, prominent malars (cheekbones), and generally recessive face above a strong, jutting chin. (Cast. Museum of Anthropology, University of Minnesota. Photo by Don Breneman.)*

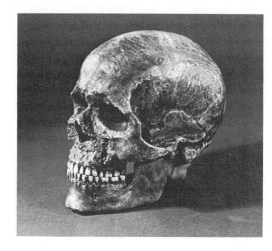

toward the rear. The radius in the forearm is much less bowed, and the humerus becomes relatively longer and generally more delicate. The scapula broadens out at the top and is relatively less elongated.

The modifications of major significance leading to *Homo sapiens sapiens,* however, are found in the brain and the skull. It is, after all, the brain that is the generator of the culture-creating capacity, and it was with the emergence of modern man that the slow-moving Lower Paleolithic cultural experience suddenly became activated and civilization was at last created.

Modern man exhibits a globular brain case and a marked reduction of the face and lower jaw (see Figure 9-1). The new forehead makes room for the enlarged frontal lobes of the brain. The supraorbital ridges virtually disappear; the occipital torus becomes residual. The mastoid process is more pronounced as a muscular anchor. The foramen magnum is horizontally oriented and well forward under the brain case.

Mastication, except in the special circumstances of Eskimos, has become, for man the cooker, functionally much less significant. The molars are persistently smaller, and the old *Dryopithecus* Y-pattern of five cusps is frequently replaced with a four-cusp structure that produces a + pattern.[2] Smaller teeth are set closely in a reduced dental arch embracing a smaller palate. A broadening of the skull increases the relative width of the span between the maxillary condyles. The more active tongue (modern man is "the great talker") requires maneuvering room within the jaw. At the same time, the bowed region of the lower jaw (symphysis of the inferior maxilla) must remain strong. The modern jaw is subject to a great stress of lateral compression by the inward pull of the pterygoid

muscles, which run from the condyloid processes to the upper walls of the palate. The two sides of the jaw could easily crack where they are joined together at the chin. The jaw in *Homo sapiens sapiens* is reinforced in the thickening of the symphysis.

Another feature of modern man that relates to a reduction of the chewing function is the diminution of the temporal muscles. The zygomatic arches bridging the temporal bones of the face are reduced and the face is narrowed, Eskimos excepted. The whole face is drawn back under the frontal part of the cranial vault as well as being reduced in size. The eye sockets are located under the bulb of the frontal bones rather than under the ridge of a supraorbital torus. Finally, of course, the nasal bridge is pronounced to a greater or lesser degree, depending on the racial variety.

The stature of some varieties becomes notably larger than that of any premodern populations. Further, the brains of all forms of modern man are large (1,000 to 2,000 cc.) and have complex cortical surfaces.

The Taxonomic Inventory of the Hominids
The classification used in this text is that formulated by Campbell for the international symposium on "Classification and Human Evolution" held at Burg Wartenstein, in Austria, in 1962.[3]

In this system, shown in Table 9–1, there are two genera, four (or five) species, and eight subspecies of man, fossil and living. All are now extinct except *Homo sapiens sapiens.*

Upper Paleolithic Cultures

The Upper Paleolithic Age and *Homo sapiens sapiens* made their first appearances togeth-

---

[2]C. S. Coon, in *The Origin of Races,* pp. 360–364, gives details on the relative frequency of the + in lower and upper molars (the first, second, and third molars differ) by populations.

[3]B. Campbell, "Quantitative Taxonomy and Human Evolution," in S. L. Washburn (ed.), *Classification and Human Evolution,* pp. 66–69.

er, in Southwest Asia and Europe, around 35,000 B.C. The earliest known manifestations of the Upper Paleolithic are found in Iraq (Shanidar Cave), Afghanistan (Kara Kamar), Israel (Mt. Carmel), and Cyrenaica, North Africa (Haua Fteah). The earliest C[14]-dated Upper Paleolithic sites in western Europe fall about 2,000 years later, at Arcy-sur-Cure in the Yonne department of France. Some prehistorians suggest that this implies an origin of the Upper Paleolithic culture complex in Asia Minor, followed by rapid diffusion westward via migrating *Homo sapiens sapiens*. More reliable dates are needed before jumping to such a conclusion, however.

Yet one thing is certain. The Upper Paleolithic lasted from 35,000 B.C. to 8,000 B.C., when the first great cultural revolution of human history began. Upper Paleolithic men were still living in the tradition of the meat-eating predators. The hand ax almost wholly disappeared from their working kits but flake and blade tools directly traceable to earlier forms abounded. In the latter phases of the Upper Paleolithic, as reindeer became relatively more numerous than the rhinoceros and elephant, harpoons carved from antlers became the chief weapon. This was a new invention, but it was still only a refinement of what had existed for several hundred thousand years—the stone-pointed spear. The spear thrower (called *atlatl* after the Aztec name for the tool) was introduced early in the Upper Paleolithic, however. It was indeed something new, but again it was hardly revolutionary, for all it really accomplished was to extend the arm as a lever. Efficiency and force were thus increased, but Neandertal and Steinheim men had been throwing spears for thousands of years before *Homo sapiens sapiens* invented the *atlatl*.

What modern man, the Paleolithic hunter, did do was to bring the Stone Age hunting tradition to a climax. To an improved material technology he added a fabulously imaginative intellectual culture. With sympathetic magic he enhanced his faith in his own likelihood of success and survival. Because he was now man, he was capable of worry and fear of things and events which had not yet come to pass. In short, he developed imagination. Out of this was generated his remarkable cave art of multicolored wall paintings and low-relief murals, plus etchings and engravings on bone, and very "modernistic" sculpture. The forms of the art and its implications will be discussed later in this chapter.

Table 9-1   The Taxonomic Inventory of the Hominids

Genus	*Species*	*Subspecies*
Homo	*sapiens*	*sapiens*
		neandertalensis
		steinheimensis
	erectus	*rhodesianensis*
		soloensis
		pekinensis
		mauritanicus
		erectus
	habilis(?)	
Australopithecus	*robustus*	
	africanus	

SOURCE: B. Campbell, "Quantitative Taxonomy and Human Evolution," in S. L. Washburn (ed.), *Classification and Human Evolution*, pp. 66–69.

Fig. 9-2   The known types of man. (Skull drawings adapted from S. L. Washburn, "Tools and Human Evolution," Scientific American, with permission of publisher.)

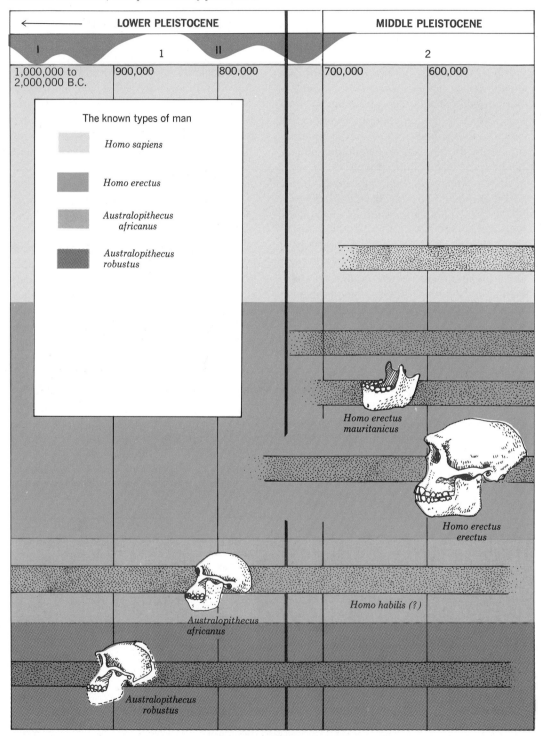

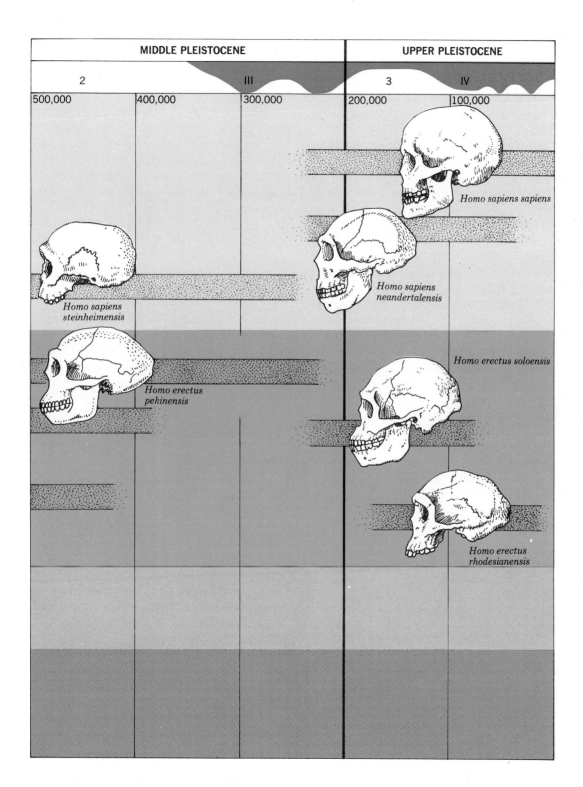

2

III

3

IV

500,000

400,000

300,000

200,000

100,000

Homo sapiens sapiens

Homo sapiens neandertalensis

Homo sapiens steinheimensis

Homo erectus pekinensis

Homo erectus soloensis

Homo erectus rhodesianensis

Upper Paleolithic Traditions in Europe It is now well understood that the relative frequencies of different types of flake tools, etc., vary from site to site as local manifestations of a general tradition vary from prehistoric population to population. They also vary through time. However, for purposes of orientation only the major general traditions of the Upper Paleolithic will be discussed, each with its distinguishing characteristics.

The Early Upper Paleolithic consists of the Châtelperronian (also called Lower Périgordian), Aurignacian, and Gravettian (also called Upper Périgordian) traditions. A brief, somewhat alien, interlude, the Solutrean, constituted the Middle Upper Paleolithic. It was followed by the Magdalenian tradition of the Late Upper Paleolithic. Keeping in mind that none of these traditions began or ended in a given year, the sequence and the probable duration of each are given in Table 9-2.

The Châtelperronian Tradition: 32,000 to 28,500 B.C. This incipient Upper Paleolithic tradition is not very richly represented among known archaeological assemblages, and there is a diversity of opinion as to whether it may have evolved locally in France or was developed in Southwest Asia, from whence it may have diffused westward. The latter alternative is perhaps the most probable. The

Châtelperronian does not show the high degree of specialized elaboration that marks the succeeding Upper Paleolithic cultures. Nor does it include the elongated flake blade that is the hallmark of the Upper Paleolithic. The distinctive Châtelperronian blade has a curved cutting edge. The back edge, on which finger pressure would be applied in use, is blunted with fine transverse chipping (see Figure 9-3*c*). Simple, pointed bone tools were also produced, but there was none of the art that became so important in the Gravettian and Magdalenian, later on.

The Aurignacian Tradition: 28,500 to 22,000 B.C. Unlike the Châtelperronian industry, which is sparsely distributed, Aurignacian industries are numerous in southwestern France and Central Europe. Their distribution, which ranges from France, where it appears quite suddenly, through Hungary to the caves of Israel, Iraq, and Afghanistan, strongly suggests a point of origin in Southwest Asia. The occurrence of a hybrid Mousterian-Aurignacian tradition, known as the Szeletian, in Hungary, Slovakia, and Moravia, testifies to the probable fusion of an indigenous Middle Paleolithic population and migrating Upper Paleolithic men from the southeast.

In Europe, as in the Middle East, Aurignacian man was usually a dweller in rock shelters and cave mouths. He had fire and was an avid hunter and skin dresser. His tool kit was characterized by elongated, parallel-sided flakes which were triangular in cross-section and retouched to give steep, rounded working ends (Figures 9-3*a* and *d*). Also included were tools known as *gravers*, or *burins* —elongated blades with one end coming to a sharp-pointed chisel edge. These tools were used for working wood, bone, ivory, antler, and soft stone. Burins are the implement of the carver. They also could have served as leather punches or awls for sewing skins into clothing and hides into tent covers, although fine, highly polished bone awls were more likely part of the woman's sewing kit. Hump-

Table 9-2 Upper Paleolithic Cultures and Their Durations

Radiocarbon dates	Tradition
B.C.	
15,000 to 8,000	Magdalenian
18,000 to 15,000	Solutrean
22,000 to 18,000	Gravettian (Upper Périgordian)
28,500 to 22,000	Aurignacian
32,000 to 28,500	Châtelperronian (Lower Périgordian)

SOURCE: After Grahame Clark, *World Prehistory*, p. 51.

Fig. 9-3   Upper Paleolithic stone tools. (a) Aurignacian endscraper; (b) Châtelper-ronian double-concave scrapers; (c) Châtelperronian backed blade and graver (burin); (d) Aurignacian gravers; (e) Gravettian backed blade; (f) Gravettian gravers (side and top views). (Museum of Anthropology, University of Minnesota. Photo by Don Breneman.)

backed "nosed scrapers" were also produced from small cores. Aurignacian blades lack the transverse fine flaking that blunts the back edges of Châtelperronian and Gravettian blades—a small feature that demonstrates how large little cultural differences can loom. Finally, the makers of the Aurignacian assemblages produced bone "javelin heads" having fine, sharp, piercing points and cleft bases for fixing the bone heads into wooden shafts (Figure 9-5).

The Gravettian Tradition: 22,000 to 18,000 B.C. The Gravettian tradition flourished during a brief amelioration of the frigid climate of the fourth glaciation. In East Europe, the interstadial climate softened sufficiently to permit the creators of the Gravettian cultures to live in skin tents or oval huts on the loess plains of Hungary and South Russia. Although Gravettian blades have some features in common with the Châtelperronian (and for this reason French archaeologists hold that the one is an outgrowth of the other, both together constituting what they call the Périgordian), the gap in time between the end of the Châtelperronian and the onset of the Gravettian makes it unlikely that the Gravettian tradition was an outgrowth of the Châtelperronian.

Gravettian flintworkers produced delicate, slim blades with dull back edges which are so refined that they are often likened to penknife blades (Figures 9-3*e* and *f*). Burins were produced in large variety, and Mousterian-like triangular points appear, with the added feature of biface retouching (i.e., the removal of flakes from both faces of the artifact). A further innovation can be seen in points worked down to a tang at the base. The tang, like that on modern knives, was probably for hafting a handle to the blade.

Gravettians not only relied on flintworking, but applied their flint carving tools to ivory, bone, and antlers to make awls and lanceheads, spatulas (perhaps used to beat snow from clothes and tents?), scoops, and shovels. They also produced decorated pins and bracelets of ivory, plus beads and pendants of clay, bone, iron, and stone to be worn about the neck by both men and women. These decorative objects were incised with rows of dots and parallel lines in complex geometric designs. The Gravettians were truly skilled artisans. More than that, they were artists who modeled small animals in clay and carved excellent stylized human (mostly female) figurines in ivory and sometimes, in baked clay. They planted the seeds of artistic creativity that were to flower so gloriously in the Magdalenian of France between 15,000 and 10,000 B.C. The Gravettians added to the practice of burying the dead the extra flourish of arraying the bodies in full clothing and personal ornaments and sprinkling red ochre over all.

The Solutrean Tradition: 18,000 to 15,000 B.C. Immediately overlying the Gravettian strata in some parts of France is a distinctive culture named after the site of Solutre. Its main feature is the biface laurel-leaf point, which in its most developed form is the apogee of the flintworker's technique (Figure 9-4). Solutrean workers also produced excellent barbed and tanged arrowheads, delicately worked over both surfaces (like the laurel-leaf points) by means of carefully controlled pressure flaking. They also made bone and ivory pendants, beads, bracelets, and long-bone pins. For the first time, "eyes" were put in awls; the needle was invented 18,000 years ago! The presence of red, yellow, and black pigments indicates the probability of body painting and ornamentation in the Gravettian manner. But although some examples of sculpture and paintings have been found in Solutrean deposits, it appears that the Solutreans had little interest in representative art. Nevertheless, it may be said of Solutrean man that he was a true artist in flintworking. At the height of his technique, the Solutrean workman gave form, rhythm, and symmetry to his products beyond the needs of utilitarianism. The best of his willow-leaf and laurel-leaf points are the results of highly skilled effort.

The distribution of true Solutrean sites is

Fig. 9-4 Solutrean points. Laurel-leaf types on the left. Willow-leaf types on upper right. Shouldered or tanged projectile points, lower right. (Museum of Anthropology, University of Minnesota. Photo by Don Breneman.)

The Magdalenian Tradition: 15,000 to 8,000 B.C. The Magdalenian tradition elaborates the boneworking propensities of the Gravettians, producing an intriguing series of barbed harpoons out of the bone javelin point. In the Lower Magdalenian, harpoons were fashioned with a single row of barbs carved along one side only. In the Upper Magdalenian, the barbs were fashioned to alternate along both sides, and a "swallowtail" base was developed to facilitate hafting into the wooden shaft which held it (Figure 9-5). Magdalenian man also invented the dart thrower, or *atlatl*, mentioned earlier.

Flintworking went into an abrupt decline. Biface points disappeared as they were replaced by the staghorn harpoon. Aurignacian-type tortoise-backed scrapers, or push

Fig. 9-5 Evolution of the Upper Paleolithic harpoon. At the left are two Aurignacian plain bone harpoon heads with cleft bases. On the right are a single-row barbed harpoon of Early Magdalenian, followed by the more developed double-rowed barbed harpoon with swallowtail base. (Museum of Anthropology, University of Minnesota. Photo by Don Breneman.)

limited to France west of the Rhone River. The origin of the Solutrean tradition remains a mystery; its demise was sudden and is as yet unexplained. Bordes suggests that the Solutrean might be a belated Mousterian extension in which flintworking was carried to its climax for the prehistoric Old World.[4] The Solutrean correlates in time with a very cold phase of the fourth glacial. It seems to be an aberrant Upper Paleolithic culture that intrudes as a brief, alien interlude in the Gravettian-Magdalenian sequence. In its interaction with the Gravettian, it may have provided a kind of stimulus—a challenge that gave impetus to the Gravettian trends which flowered in the rich exuberance of the Magdalenian.

[4]F. Bordes, *The Old Stone Age*, p. 158.

planes, also disappeared. Scrapers became rare, perhaps replaced by bone fleshers. Crude knives, made mostly of splinters of flint rather than of blades, became the dominant tool of the day. Except for the *atlatl* and harpoon, the Magdalenians had but minor interest in technology. They did what was necessary in tool production, but little more. Their interest had shifted to a new form of environmental control—magical art.

Paleolithic Art Painting, engraving, sculpture, and modeling were familiar media of expression, and Upper Paleolithic man (except the Solutreans) were skilled in all these fields. Their art began in experimental crudeness and developed steadily to the sure technique of masters. It offers a rich field for the study of developmental processes in art because the sequences in improvement are clearly discernible in archaeological series.

Although they represent different techniques, engraving and painting were closely integrated by the Gravettian-Magdalenian artists. They developed hand in hand to produce closely similar forms of expression. It appears that when an engraving was made first, its incised lines were always painted in afterward. Sometimes a wall surface was given a paint wash, after which the engraving was incised. The effect was to set out the engraving in fresh contrast to the painted background.

Early Gravettian engravings and paintings were no more than crude, stiff outlines. Later Gravettian pictures became more accurate representations, and in the Lower and Middle Magdalenian, skill in composition, contour, and the use of polychrome were achieved. Some comparative examples of Gravettian-Magdalenian art are given in Figure 9-6.

Sculpture does not show such a progressive trend, since most of the known examples reveal reasonably good technique, whatever the phase. Mural sculpture was wall engraving developed to produce medallion types of low and high relief. The best work, however,

was done in sculpturing in the round on bone, antler, and ivory, and in shaping such articles as dagger grips and dart throwers in animal and bird forms. The most famous example of plastic modeling is a family group of a bison bull, cow, and calf from the cavern of Tuc d'Audubert.

Much light is shed on the beliefs and mentality of Upper Paleolithic man by the art that he produced. If ever an art reflected the spirit of its culture, it was this. There have been argumentative exchanges of opinion between utilitarian-minded anthropologists and those who insist that art be evaluated as an end in itself. Aesthetes have held that it manifests the essential artistic and creative genius of its makers. Anthropologists have insisted on the magico-religious utilitarianism of the art, for they see the cultural functions of art as more significant than the aesthetic aspects alone.

Upper Paleolithic art had the gross purposes of filling men's stomachs and of maintaining the population by serving as a magical aid in hunting and procreation. But besides being a means to these ends, it was also an end in itself. The Upper Paleolithic artist produced not merely images, but beautiful images. He not only strove to produce magically efficacious representations of the goals of his desires but also developed artistic skill for the intrinsic pleasure it gave him. For his sculpture, he deserves to be called "the Paleolithic Greek," and because of his painting, it is not hyperbole to call the cavern of Lascaux "the Sistine Chapel of the Ice Age."[5]

It is likely, however, that magical purposes never left his mind. This is especially evident in the case of his mural art, which is rarely found where it may easily be seen. The Upper Paleolithic artist did not adorn the walls of his home or the entrance to a cavern. On the

[5]In 1956, I visited Lascaux at Christmastime and had an hour alone in the cave with its discoverer, Henri Ravidat. A week later I visited the Sistine Chapel. *My* feeling is that it would not be amiss to call the Sistine Chapel "The Lascaux of the Renaissance."

contrary, his works of art are found deep in the earth's bowels, in the dark, mysterious caverns where the artist worked by the fitful smoky flare of a stone lamp. There he drew his animals: the woolly mammoth, bison, reindeer, wild cow, bear, woolly rhinoceros, horse, and ibex—most of them now long since extinct in Europe. Again and again he painted red gashes on their bodies, gashes dripping with blood. He often showed projectile points piercing their flesh, and in some instances streams of red blood are painted flowing from nostrils and mouth. Diagrammatic scenes of log-covered pits into which mammoths are crashing have been found in such sites as the cavern of Font de Gaume. All

these expressions of realism are acts of wish fulfillment through compulsive, mimetic magic (see also pages 578–581).

The psychology and the act must have been not unlike that of Navaho Indian sand painting today. The sand paintings are highly stylized, but together with their accompanying image-filled chants, their effect in curing or crop growing is compulsive. There is firm faith that the act guarantees the result. An even more apt analogy is spelled out in the autobiography of a Winnebago Indian, written in the first decade of this century. Crashing Thunder tells of a very holy hill in Wisconsin in which there was a cave wherein lived twenty spirits, called *Those-who-cry-like-babies.*

Early Gravettian

Late Gravettian

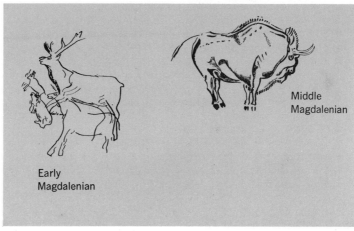

Early Magdalenian

Middle Magdalenian

Fig. 9-6 Four phases of Upper Paleolithic art.

My father had control of them and when he wished to bless a man he would take his bow and arrows and, holding them in his hands, lead the man around the hill and into the lodge (*i.e.,* into the hill). There he would look for a stone pillar, and upon it, at about arm's length, he drew the pictures of a number of different animals. My father possessed only one arrow, but that one was a holy one. Then dancing around the stone pillar and singing some songs, he finished by breathing upon the pillar. Finally he walked around it and shot at it and when

Fig. 9-7   An Upper Paleolithic masked deer dancer, commonly known as The Sorcerer. A male-animal fertility figure, 29½ inches high, painted over engraved outline, and located high on the wall of the most inaccessible recess of the Caverne les Trois Freres, Ariege, France. (After the tracing and restoration by H. Breuil.)

Fig. 9-8   Deer and antelope dancers, San Ildefonso pueblo, New Mexico. Modern (1908 – 1909) water color by Alfredo Montoya. (Courtesy of the School of American Research, Santa Fe, N.M.)

he looked at the stone, it had turned into a deer with large horns which fell dead at his feet. . . . My father was a very famous hunter and my brother wished to be like him.[6]

Rarely did Upper Paleolithic artists portray themselves. Sometimes, however, cave paintings do present anthropomorphic figures such as the famous "Sorcerer of Les Trois Frères," in France, shown in Figure 9-7. The Sorcerer was probably a medicine man endowed with deer-hunting power. He wears a wolf's tail and a deerhead mask and is pranc-

[6]P. Radin (ed.). *Crashing Thunder*, pp. 27–28.

Fig. 9-9   The Venus of Willendorf. A Gravettian goddess of fertility. She represents the idealization of a reproducing mother. (Courtesy of the American Museum of Natural History.)

Fig. 9-10   The Venus of Brassempouy, a stylistically "modern" fragment from Upper Paleolithic times. The hairstyle is quite different from that of the Venus of Willendorf. (Courtesy of the Musée des Antiquités Nationales.)

ing in a ritual dance similar to the Deer Dance performed by Pueblo Indians today (Figure 9-8).

Some magic may be wholly beneficent. This is particularly true of fertility magic. The Gravettians were especially fond of statuettes of pregnant women of whom the Venus of Willendorf (Figure 9-9) is the most famous. The parts of her torso which swell with pregnancy are given lavish exaggeration and virtually every line is a segment of a perfect circle: the apotheosis of the feminine curve. The face, arms, legs, and feet are ignored. The artist has composed her with selective interest. The detail of her coiffure and that of the Venus of

Brassempouy (Figure 9-10) show that the hairdo had its social, and probably cult, significance 20,000 years ago and that the hairdresser existed as an artisan long before our era.

Whether the charming statuettes, which stand only 2 to 6 inches high, were talismans to be carried by the woman who wished for a child, or whether they were worshipped by men and women alike as mother-goddess idols, cannot be known. It seems possible that they represent a cult of this goddess, for in the Mesolithic and Neolithic Ages to follow, there is no question of the importance of worship of the mother goddess in the Middle East.

We may conclude by saying that the Upper Paleolithic art of Europe and North Africa was a vividly representational art—an art of flesh, blood, and hope—a functional art which aided in survival, an art which was eagerly used by a hunting people in a glacial age as a symbolic expression of their major interests.

The Paleolithic Age in Africa and Asia   The distribution of the archaeological remains of the Paleolithic tradition reveals that the basic culture complex as an entirety must have brought about an efficient environmental adjustment. Aurignacian complexes are found throughout the Middle East, in the Crimea, and into Siberia, where they are associated with remains of semi-subterranean houses (Figure 9-11). Eastward, these complexes extend into India to the boundary of the old Acheulean and East Asian chopper- and flake-tool complex. Aurignacian and Gravettian traditions also occur in East Africa and the Mediterranean coastal areas as the Capsian tradition.

In Africa, the Middle Paleolithic Acheulean traditions went through a number of local developments, but a general Upper Paleolithic complex, called the *Sangoan,* spread over East Africa and the Congo basin. Related local traditions of South Africa and the Cape regions are known as *Fauresmith* and *Still-*

bay, respectively. As a forest tradition, the Sangoan could not do away with the hand ax, as the Upper Paleolithic traditions of Europe did. Thus, in the Sangoan, the hand ax of the preceding Acheulean tradition was elongated to take on the form of a pick, or broadened along the cutting edge and narrowed at the butt to become very similar in form to a modern steel ax. The chipped-stone type is called a *tranchet* (Fr., cutter). The more generalized hand ax evolved into two specialized artifacts in the Sangoan. The Sangoan equivalent of the Mousterian point consists of elongated biface lance heads that are analogous to Solutrean blades far to the north. The Sangoan also included tanged and shouldered points resembling those found in the Solutrean tradition. In other words, the Upper Paleolithic traditions of most of Africa evolved in much the same directions as those of Europe and Asia Minor, while at the same time developing certain distinctions.[7]

As for East and Southeast Asia, Movius's concise summary may still be sufficient:

Uninfluenced by contemporary innovations in Africa, Europe, and western Asia, the archaic and very primitive tradition of making implements of the chopper and chopping-tool varieties either on pebbles or roughly tabular blocks persisted in the Far East as long as the practice of making stone tools survived.[8]

During the time of low sea levels, when Siberians were first crossing into North America, Upper Paleolithic men from South Asia were pushing down into what is now the Indonesian archipelago and into Australia. They may have needed rafts at points, but they reached Australia around 33,000 B.C.[9] The absence of big game and good flaking stone reduced their technology to crude

[7]For details, consult S. Cole, *The Prehistory of East Africa*, pp. 183–199, or J. D. Clark, *The Prehistory of Africa*.
[8]H. L. Movius, Jr., "Old World Prehistory: Paleolithic," in A. L. Kroeber (ed.), *Anthropology Today*, p. 181.
[9]J. P. White, "New Guinea: The First Phase in Oceanic Settlement," in R. C. Green and M. Kelly (eds.), *Studies in Oceanic Culture History*, vol. 2, pp. 45–52.

choppers and flakes, with reliance on wood spears, dibbles, and simple utensils. A way of life developed which remained little changed for millennia after the rising postglacial seas cut the prehistoric Australians off from Asia.

Ancient Man in the New World

Toward the end of the fourth glacial period, men out of·Asia following the big-game trails through the grasslands, pressed eastward across the land bridge connecting Siberia to North America. Even today, the gap across Bering Strait is not so great but that it is actually possible, if foolhardy, to get from Siberia to Alaska by leaping from one ice floe to another. It was done in the 1920s by an ex-whaling captain who wanted to prove the point. But at times in the Late Pleistocene epoch the so-called land bridge was in fact a broad plain of rich grasslands over 1,000 miles wide. The lowering of the sea level because of water locked in the continental glaciers and the compensatory uplift of land between the continents caused by the weight of billions of tons of ice on the continental land masses produced an open interconti-nental causeway, lasting from about 26,000 B.C. to 8,000 B.C. The indications are, how-ever, that the availability of open land routes between the extremes of the Canadian ice mass and those of the mountain glaciers

varied from time to time. The archaeologist Chester Chard, writing in 1968, states that the ice-free corridor through which wander-ing hunters could have passed was open only from 26,000 B.C. to 23,000 B.C.—a brief 3,000 years. Then the ice barrier was closed until 10,000 B.C.—13,000 years in which the first handfuls of migrants were totally cut off from the fountainhead of their origins in Asia and Alaska. After 10,000 B.C., new migrations into the heartland of North America could be resumed in earnest.[10] On the other hand, J. D. Jennings, whose contributions to our knowl-edge of early American prehistory are out-standing, also writing in 1968, accepts as most probable the thesis that 18,000 B.C. to

[10]C. E. Chard, *Man in Prehistory*, pp. 141–142.

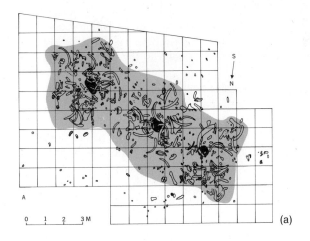

(a)

(b)

B

Fig. 9-11 **(a)** *Ground plan of an Upper Paleolithic (Pushkari I) joint family homesite on the open Russian plains. The three hearths down the middle of the long tent could have been the foci for individual families within the joint family establishment. The debris consists mostly of mammoth tusks, teeth, and bones. (From A. Mongait,* **Archaeology of the USSR,** *p. 79.)* **(b)** *An ethnographic reconstruction of the dwelling. (By V. D. Zaporozhaskaya, in Mongait, ibid., p. 80.)*

10,000 B.C. "would seem to bracket man's entry into the New World . . . with some certainty."[11]

It is not possible to specify the first peopling of the New World with fine detail for the period before 15,000 B.C. But that the first arrivals came sometime between 25,000 and 10,000 B.C. is highly probable.

Early Fossil Men in America   Nearly a score of fossil finds of hominid skeletons possibly of the Late Pleistocene age have been found in North and South America. None of them is claimed to be older than the fourth glaciation and only two of them were excavated and reported with sufficient care that their geological setting is beyond doubt. The one sure find is that from Midland, Texas, discovered in 1954. The skull, which was crushed and fragmented by overlying deposits, is sufficiently complete to allow for reconstruction of the cranium. It, along with the body bones, indicates a true *Homo sapiens sapiens*, as can be readily seen in the photo in Figure 9-12. The stratigraphy, radiocarbon and fluorine analyses, plus comparative evidence, indicate a probable date of 18,000 B.C., and a minimal date of 10,000 B.C., for the specimen. Associated animal fossils include Pleistocene horses, bison, and antelope. Miscellaneous flint chips, scrapers, and knives from the same level as the skull suggest that the Midland woman (for the features of the fossil are female) died at a lakeside or streamside campsite.

Other possible American ancient man fossils, such as that of the Tepexpan man from Mexico and the Brown's Valley and Pelican Rapids fossils from Minnesota, are sufficiently similar to the Midland fossil to indicate that the latter is not an aberrant specimen.[12]

Finally, it is important to note that there is absolutely no evidence of Neandertaloid elements in the genetic heritage of the migrants of the New World. Late Pleistocene men in northeastern Asia and in North America were not very different from the generalized forms of later American Indians.[13]

The Chopper-tool Complex of Early Man in America   Many enthusiastic searchers for Early Man in North America have recovered thousands of chopper tools and scrapers from sand blowouts and exposed high beaches and terraces in desert areas of the western United States where glacial lakes and rivers once lapped. On the basis of these artifacts, it is held by some that the earliest migrants brought the Asiatic chopper tradition with them and that this tradition is antecedent to all else. The trouble is that *all* the chopper implements have been surface finds. They could be simply heat-cracked rocks or even unfinished artifacts which had been roughed out at a quarry and carried to the spots where they are found. There is no stratigraphic identification for any of them. Their true age is, therefore, wholly a matter of guesswork and an expression of faith. In dry country, light soils and sand are blown away by strong winds; small stones remain where they originally lay, and as the sand blows out from under them they gradually settle lower and lower until at last they rest on a resistant soil base. Water action from cloudbursts can have the same effect. The stones covering a desert floor, the so-called desert pavement, may originally have been scattered throughout the whole thickness of a once-overlying layer representing thousands of years' difference in time. Now they all lie together and there is no way of telling which is the older.[14]

[11]J. D. Jennings, *Prehistory of North America*, pp. 43–44.
[12]H. deTerra, J. Romero, and T. D. Stewart, *Early Man in Mexico* (1949); A. R. V. Arellano, "Some New Aspects of the Tepexpan Case" (*Bulletin of the Texas Archaeological and Paleontological Society*, vol. 22, 1951), pp. 217–225; on the Minnesota girl (Pelican Rapids), see E. A. Hooton, *Up from the Apes* (1947), pp. 405–407 and 648.

[13]T. D. Stewart, "A Physical Anthropologist's View of the Peopling of the New World" (*Southwestern Journal of Anthropology*, vol. 116, no. 3, 1960), p. 269.
[14]Cf. F. W. Sharrock, "Prehistoric Occupation Patterns in Southwestern Wyoming and Cultural Relations with the Great Basin and Plains Cultural Areas" (*University of Utah Anthropological Papers*, no. 77, 1966).

Tough-minded archaeologists insist that until such a day as a chopper assemblage is found in a stratigraphic setting indubitably ascribable to the earlier phases of the fourth (Wisconsin) glacial epoch, the chopper-tool phase remains problematic, and little can be said about the cultures of the very first Americans.

The Lithic- or "Big Game-projectile"–Traditions   After 15,000 B.C. it is a different story. Since 1925, a number of sites yielding the fossil skeletons of mammoths and bison in direct association with skillfully made projectile points have been found in the High Plaine and Plains, while assemblages of similar projectiles without the fauna have been found all the way to the east coast.

The Llano Tradition: 11,500 to 11,000 B.C.   The earliest of these lithic traditions is labeled the *Llano,* after the Llano Estacado, or Staked Plains, of Texas and New Mexico. Llano sites date from 15,000 to 8000 B.C. This was a time in which Pleistocene paleontologists see a cool, moist climate in the North American heartland beyond the reaches of the ice sheets. Here there were vast expanses of grass and lightly forested parklands. Lakes and marshes, the products of rain and glacial runoff, abounded. Here teeming herds of mammoths, great-horned bison, elk, giant beaver, antelope, horses, wolves, and many lesser mammals fed and watered. It was a paradise for meat-eating men. There is no direct evidence of fire drives such as were employed at Torralba in Acheulean times. But at the Lehner site in Arizona, nine mammoths were found to have been slaughtered, as well as some horses and bison. The Llano men definitely used fire for roasting their kills, however, as a concentrated charcoal-bearing hearth area bespeaks.

The hallmark of the Llano industries is the channeled or fluted projectile point known as Clovis (see Figure 9-13, top). The fine flaking and elongated shapes of the Clovis and all subsequent Big-Game tradition points are reminiscent of Solutrean, rather than Aurignacian or Magdalenian, techniques. The highly skilled flint-flaking capability of the big-game hunters has little in common with the crudity of the chopper tools which had supposedly been made earlier. Another interesting note is that, whereas no specialized flake tools have been found with the choppers, the Llano industry includes scrapers, knives, burins, and choppers. It is a well-rounded too kit.

The Folsom Tradition: 11,000 to 10,000 B.C. While the Folsom industry is not the oldest in North America, it was the first to be discovered (1920 to 1927) and the most famous. In the original site at Folsom, New Mexico, twenty-three bison had been slaughtered and nineteen of the deeply fluted Folsom points left in the flesh between the ribs of some of the beasts. At another Folsom site near Fort Collins, Colorado, the fossil bones of a hundred or so of the same species (*Bison antiquus*) of giant longhorn bison lay in a heap where the animals had been stampeded over a river bank. A dozen and a half points of the Plainview variation of the Folsom type (Figure 9-13) were found among the fossil bones.

Fig. 9-12   The oldest authenticated American. The Midland skull viewed from the right and above. In cranial capacity and structure, it is in every respect a **Homo sapiens sapiens.** *(Courtesy of the Museum of New Mexico.)*

Clovis fluted points
Llano tradition

Folsom fluted points
Folsom tradition

Sandia points
Folsom tradition

Cody knife   Eden point
Plano tradition

Folsom men focused on longhorned bison (the mammoth had become extinct), and rounded out their meat diet with camels and elephants, all Pleistocene mammals that have been extinct since the last glacial retreat.

The Plano Tradition: 10,000 to 5000 B.C.   The Paleolithic Big-Game traditions of the western High Plains played themselves out with the final disappearance of the Pleistocene fauna. Over the final millennia many local variations of the projectile point-hunting complex were developed, but the way of life remained essentially what it had been 10,000 years earlier. The material inventory was limited. "It is characterized by a number of projectile points or knife blades showing a considerable variety of form, although the fine flintwork and the generally lanceolate form of the Llano and Folsom complexes persist. However, the fluting is entirely lost as Folsom disappears."[15] The special, localized varieties of Plano points and knives are too numerous to summarize here; Jennings' *Prehistory of North America* provides a clear treatment for those who are interested in more detail.

In Plano times, the big game was changing from greater big game to lesser, from the mammoth elephant and giant longhorn bison to the modern bison and antelope. The ecology was becoming modern—drier and temperate, with shorter grasses on the plains and fewer lakes, bogs, and marshes.

[15]J. D. Jennings, *op. cit.,* p. 95.

Fig. 9-13   Artifacts from the Big-Game, or Lithic, traditions of the Late Upper Pleistocene epoch in North America. A high skill in flintworking is revealed in the Clovis (Llano) and Folsom fluted points shown in the top row. Quite different but truly beautiful expressions of the artisan's skill are the Cody knife and Eden point of the Plano tradition shown in the bottom row. (Museum of Anthropology, University of Minnesota. Photo by Don Breneman.)

The time was at hand for the culture of the foragers to take over, providing the base for the next stage of cultural evolution: that based upon the *domestication* of plants and animals. This is the subject of the next chapter.

After 5000 B.C., hunters persisted in and around the Plains of North America, the marginal savannas of Africa, in some forests of the major continents and the arctic wastes of Eurasia and North America—but the Big-Game Stone Age way of human life, beginning in the Lower Pleistocene a million or more years ago in Europe and Africa, played itself out at long last on the plains of northern Mexico and the United States.

SUMMARY

As the Glacial age approached its final climax, man was evolving toward his present state.

Homo erectus had already become *Homo sapiens* during the course of the long second interglacial in Europe. The earliest transitional form is represented by *Homo sapiens steinheimensis*. Neandertal man evolved from the basic *Homo sapiens* pool to produce a specialized subspecies of *Homo sapiens* (*neandertalensis*) in the West. *Homo sapiens sapiens,* modern man, emerged outside Europe during the third interglacial and was fully established in Africa, Asia Minor, and South Asia by the beginning of the fourth glaciation. He arrived in Europe during the fourth glacial interstadial, quickly replacing the Neandertal subspecies.

Homo sapiens sapiens quickly developed inventories of specialized flake and horn or bone artifacts all over the northern half of the Western Hemisphere. He dropped the hand ax tradition. In Africa, refined and specialized axes were developed in the Upper Paleolithic Sangoan.

In Asia, east of India, the chopper-tool and flake complex continued quite unmodified as long as the ancient Paleolithic hunting traditions survived.

It is reasonable to infer that the tribes of the Upper Paleolithic had fully developed cultures on a level comparable to that of any recent society of skilled hunters such as the Bushmen, Eskimos, or nomadic Plains Indian tribes. They had the full mental equipment for development of religion and magic, familial and kinship systems, government and rudimentary law, folklore and mythology, and dance, painting, and sculpture. Although they are thought of as cave dwellers, they also built semi-subterranean houses.

Wherever he went, *Homo sapiens* took fire and fire making with him. The remains of his art and his consistent burial of his dead give evidence that his imaginative intellect had achieved the humanistic level. Although organically he was an animal, he had unconditionally climbed to the level of the *psycho-cultural-organic.*

He quickly spread out to inhabit the entire world, peopling the South Pacific and the Americas. He was finally ready to move beyond direct dependence on wild plants and animals as a savage hunter and gatherer. In his more germinal centers of cultural creativity, he was ready to domesticate plants and animals and to revolutionize his life as a farmer and a founder of towns and cities. He stood on the threshold of civilization.

SELECTED READINGS

Bordes, F., *The Old Stone Age* (1968), pp. 147–241. Excellent brief account of the Upper Paleolithic stone industries. Many helpful line drawings of typical artifacts.

Breuil, H., *Four Hundred Centuries of Cave Art* (n.d.). Profusely illustrated, with descriptive analysis of the total range of Upper Paleolithic mural art by the great master of European prehistory.

Clark, G., *The Stone Age Hunters* (1967), pp. 43–90. A popular summary containing excellent color plates of Upper Paleolithic art and tools.

Clark, G., and S. Piggott, *Prehistoric Societies* (1965). Chapters 4 through 6 summarize the most modern view of the cultures of the Upper Paleolithic in the context of the cultures of recent hunters and fishers.

Coon, C. S., *The Origin of Races* (1963). Page 472 to the end of the book catalogs and describes all the Upper Pleistocene fossils from Asia, Europe, and Africa.

Jennings, J. D. *Prehistory of North America*, pp. 39–108. The best comprehensive introduction to the question of Early Man and Upper Pleistocene cultures of the New World.

Movius, H. L., Jr., "Old World Prehistory: Paleolithic" in A. L. Kroeber (ed.), *Anthropology Today*, (1963), pp. 163–192. An authoritative summary of what is known of Old World manifestations of Paleolithic culture.

Chapter 10

The Dawn of Civilization

Homo erectus had lived as a predator and simple toolmaker. The predatory way of Stone Age life was raised to a high level by *Homo sapiens sapiens* in the Late Pleistocene period of Europe, Siberia, Africa, and North America. Then, with the waning of the glaciers, man became a gatherer of small foodstuffs, fish, shellfish, and game, rather than a roving big-game hunter. Around 9000 B.C., in the Middle East and in parts of the New World, he shifted from hunting and food gathering to intensive foraging and hunting, in which a band focused upon seed and vegetable collecting supplemented by hunting

and fishing. Vegetation became a primary source of sustenance once again in human affairs. Big-game hunting continued in some parts of the Old World, as it did in the Plano complexes east of the Rockies in North America, but the diminution of many of the great Pleistocene mammals and their final disappearance from numerous areas of habitation forced most groups of men to change their living habits. They settled down in more or less permanent locations and developed the *Mesolithic Era of Intensive Foraging* as their form of adaptation to new environmental situations.

Fig. 10-A Stonehenge, Salisbury Plain, England.
(George Rodger, Magnum.)

Intensive foraging led to the domestication of plants and animals and to the establishment of settled farming communities. In their early phases (*ca.* 7500 to 4800 B.C., in the Middle East), these developments produced the *Early Neolithic Era of Incipient Agriculture.* As the complex was expanded and refined through time, it became the *Full Neolithic Era of Developed Agriculture* (4800 to 3800 B.C., in the Middle East). In time, ceremonial and market centers became towns and cities. Bronze was accidentally invented, and the first metallic tools and weapons were produced. Writing evolved from pictographic notations (see pages 637–641), while specialized artisans made diverse quantities of goods. Priests and kings organized religion and government. The urban revolution was on, the world of primitive man was being transformed, and the first civilizations were taking shape in the *Bronze Era of Regional Development and Florescence* (3800 to 2000 B.C., in the Middle East). In due course, organized states struggled for dominance and survival throughout a *Bronze and/or Iron Era of Cyclical Conquests* (2000 B.C. to A.D. 1 in the Middle East, continuing to the fall of Rome, A.D. 450, in Europe). South Asia and Middle America were following parallel courses at roughly the same time, but whether they did so independently or in interaction is a much-investigated and often-debated question.

The Mesolithic Era of Intensive Foraging

In Africa, Europe, Asia Minor, and Asia, the lithic hallmark of Mesolithic technology is the microblade (Figure 10–1). Microblades were minute to small flakes of more or less geometric form that were set in a row along a piece of wood or bone to give a durable cutting edge to harpoons, swords, and, above all, sickles. Braidwood and Willey have summed up this distinguishing feature

of technology as "the ecumenical. . .spread of the habit of producing microliths or bladelets for the making of composite tools."[1]

Equally important to the complex was the introduction of milling stones for grinding seeds. They may be of either the mortar-and-pestle type or the hollow-slab-and-rubbing-stone. In America, this latter-combination is called by the Mexican-Spanish names *metate* and *mano*. In English usage, *quern* or grinding stone is the preferred term (Figure 10–2).

Mesolithic populations, like their Paleolithic predecessors, were still hunters and food gatherers, but they lived by stalking and trapping deer, wild boars, and many lesser animals while relying heavily upon wild seeds, berries, nuts, and roots, and in special places, upon fish and shellfish. Their subsistence base became much more diversified than that of the Paleolithic big-game hunters. It was a mode of life more conducive to experimentation and elaboration of culture. The result was wide local and regional diversity leading to a degree of cultural and social change far beyond any previously experienced in human history. For this reason, it is not feasible in this study to follow in detail the prehistoric manifestations of the Mesolithic and subsequent cultural stages in their development around the world—in the Middle and Far East, Europe, Africa, North and South America. Instead, our emphasis will focus on major complexes and developmental processes characterizing the cultural courses toward and into civilization.

The Natufian Tradition: 9000 B.C. to 7000 B.C. The Mesolithic of the Middle East is at present best known through the Natufian complex of Palestine (Israel and Jordan of today), even though earlier assemblages of Mesolithic traditions exist in the Zagros

[1]R. J. Braidwood and G. R. Willey, "Conclusions and Afterthoughts," in R. J. Braidwood and G. R. Willey (eds.), *Courses toward Urban Life*, p. 333.

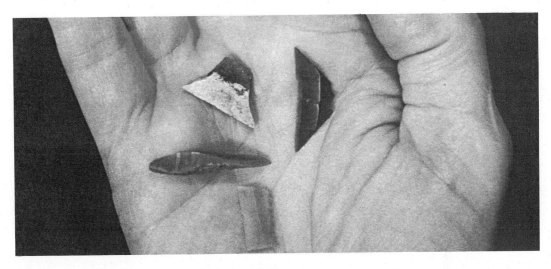

*Fig. 10-1   Microlithic blades from the European Mesolithic Age;
a minuscule punch and three geometric cutting blades.
(Museum of Anthropology, University of Minnesota.
Photo by Don Breneman.)*

Mountains, east of the Tigris River in Iran. The Natufian lithic assemblage contains flints of which 80 per cent are microliths.

Fig. 10-2   Metate and mano. (Museum of Anthropology, University of Minnesota. Photo by Don Breneman.)

The rest are familiar survivors from the Upper Paleolithic—backed blades, awls, scrapers, and picks. Sculpture in stone, bone awls, needles, and harpoon heads are particularly reminiscent of the Solutrean and Magdalenian work of an earlier age. So also is the inset blade "machete" with its animal-head hilt, shown in Figure 10–3. Other stone artifacts include metates, basalt pestles, hammerstones, and net sinkers. Bone fishhooks are also numerous. A distinctive sheen on many microliths results from the abrasive effect of thousands of stems of grass upon the surface of flint. A flint edge may crush and sever the cellular structure of a stem of long grass or wheat, but each living stem in turn takes its microscopic toll from the crystalline structure of the blade.

Although the Natufians of Palestine lived in caves and rock shelters where these were available, they were true village dwellers, constructing settlements of round, stone-walled pit dwellings. At Eynam, a stratified Natufian site in Israel, three early Natufian villages, one above the other, have been excavated. Each contained roughly fifty dwellings compacted into a tight little hamlet covering about 2 acres. The circular floors of the houses were dug several feet into the ground. Then a plastered stone wall around the pit raised the solid interior room walls another 3 feet. Over this wall a perishable reed or mat dome probably completed the shelter, which could be up to 21 feet in diameter. The ground between the houses was pocked with clay-lined storage pits, or caches, indicative of seasonal surpluses of seeds held for later use. Some pits were re-used for burials, and in some instances burials were beneath the floors of the houses (Figure 10-4).

Fig. 10-3   Natufian "machete" with inset microlith blades. [After K. P. Oakley, **Man the Tool-Maker.** *By permission of the Trustees, British Museum (Natural History).]*

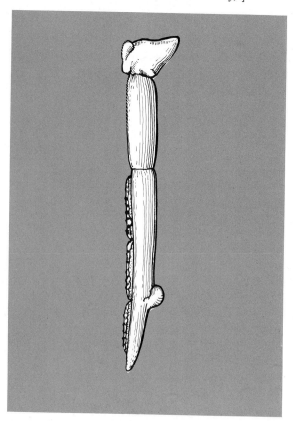

The technique of sinking the floor of the house into the ground before raising the superstructure above is adapted to the conditions of temperate climates with cold winters. For obvious reasons, it never occurs in the tropical areas where the ground is too wet. There, houses are apt to be built on piles to get them off the ground (see Figure 14-6, page 292), a technique that requires considerably developed technological experience. The semi-subterranean house has two advantages: (1) It is easier to keep warm, and (2) it can be made roomy without raising high side walls. The first reason is the functionally effective one, since many primitive people have solved the problem of getting sufficient inside height when building above ground.[2]

Inasmuch as no actual foodstuffs have as yet been found in the storage pits at Eynam, one cannot say with certainty that the Natufians had domesticated plants. Yet, like the Shoshone Indians of the western deserts (see pages 256–258), and the Ojibwa wild-rice harvesters of the Great Lakes region of North America, they clearly foraged intensively for seeds and other wild plant edibles. In addition to the storage pits, the numerous sickle-blade microliths and the bone sickles in which they were set attest to harvesting techniques which have gone well beyond the more primitive method of beating the ripened seeds into a pouch or basket with a flat stick or woven fan. The presence in Natufian assemblages of basaltic manos and metates, as well as mortars and pestles of the same igneous rock, is suggestive of a diet in which stone-ground meal was cooked for porridge and gruel, very possibly flavored with bits of fish or meat. Pottery was not yet invented, but solid stone bowls and carved drinking mugs (beakers) ground out of basalt are found in numbers. They were clumsy but serviceable.

Quantities of bone fishhooks and notched

---

[2]See pp. 304–305, for a discussion of modern pit dwellings and their ethnographic distribution.

stone sinkers, plus the presence of shells of fresh-water snails and mussels, testify to the exploitation of lakes and streams. The bones of wolf, boar, fox, hyena, cattle, deer, gazelle, rabbit, rodents, and birds at Eynam, plus bear, leopard, and horse in the Natufian strata at Mt. Carmel, give continuing evidence of the importance of hunting in the Mesolithic. In sum, as Jean Perrot, speaking of the Natufian tradition, tells us:

Fig. 10-4 Ground plan of a part of Eynam with circular houses and storage pits for cereals, some of which have been reused as graves.
(From Mellaart, **Earliest Civilizations of the Near East;** *drawn by Gillion Jones after Perrot. Reproduced by permission of Thames and Hudson, London.)*

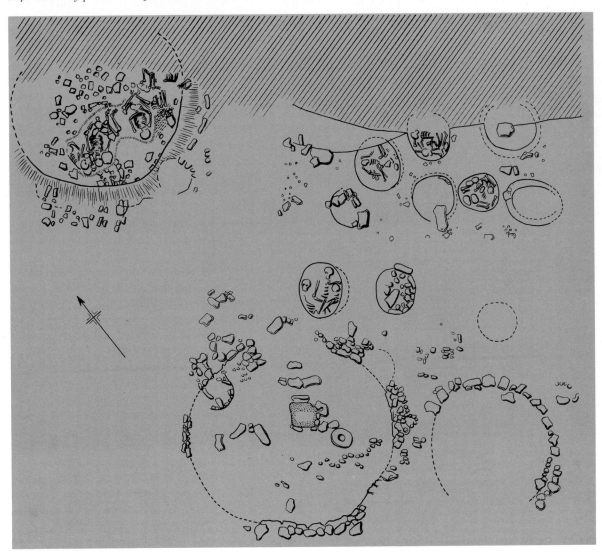

This assemblage conveys the impression of an economy still essentially based on hunting and fishing and, by comparison with the preceding assemblages, on the intensified collection and consumption of seeds (including probably wild wheat and barley). We have no clear evidence of cultivation, but, from the subsequent development in Jericho, it is not unreasonable to infer that the economy of late Natufian times was already oriented toward the cultivation of cereals in the zone of their natural habitat.[3]

The Khartoum Tradition in Africa The Mesolithic complex took many forms in varying local situations as it diffused south, east, north, and west. Four thousand years after the Natufian, it was well established along the upper reaches of the Nile in the form of the Early Khartoum, of which Desmond Clark says:

In the mesolithic so-called Early Khartoum culture [5000–4000 B.C.] we see a group of very specialized food collectors, dependent upon food resources derived from the Nile and living in large "village" settlements along the river banks. The stone industry, which is adapted to both hunting and fishing, is based on small blades and tools and includes some microliths and large crescents, the crescent adze-flake, bone harpoons, net sinkers, and grindstones. Although these people grew no crops and had no domestic animals, their pottery, with its characteristic wavy-line decoration, is a good indicator of a sedentary type of life.[4]

Note that the introduction of pottery here, as in a number of other places, antedates the domestication of plants and animals.

Marginal Mesolithic Manifestations in Northern Europe When the microlithic tradition became established north and west of the Middle East, it included special adaptations to the forest environments which had replaced the glaciers. Mesolithic microlith traditions became established along the river deltas and lake shores of North Europe around 5000 B.C. The small flakes were set in harpoons or were used as arrowheads, rather than as sickle teeth, for these people harvested berries, which need no cutting, rather than grasses; they were men of the forests and "There are no mortars, pestles, or any stone implements other than such items as flint points and scrapers to suggest the exploitation of plants."[5]

A more characteristic tool is the straight-edged ax. The axhead, called the *tranchet*, was shaped by symmetrically chipping a flint nodule and partially smoothing the surfaces with an abrasive polishing stone while giving it a well-ground cutting edge. Later, similar axheads were ground wholly from small unflakable igneous rocks. Such a polished stone axhead is called a *celt*. The finished stone axhead was then glued into a socket formed of the soft antler horn of a stag (Figure 10–5). This, in turn, was hafted into a wooden or antler handle. The finished and hafted ax was a great improvement over the old Lower Paleolithic hand axes, for the energetic force of the blow was increased many times—not only because of the leverage of the handle but also because the blow could be swung harder without risk of injury to the hand, which had been a danger when the axhead had been held in the hand itself.

Barbed bone or antler-headed spears were used as in Upper Paleolithic times, but the really new hunting invention was the bow and arrow. No longer was it necessary to rely on the *atlatl* for projectile force. Maglemosean (Great Bog) bows, of which original elmwood specimens have been found, are simple, so-called self-bows, which means that they are unreinforced slats of wood without reflex curves. The bows are tapered at the ends, as are modern bows, broadening out in the middle area but constricted in the handgrip area. From their invention in Mesolithic times until the invention of gunpowder, the bow and arrow were destined

[3]J. Perrot, "Palestine-Syria-Cilicia," in Braidwood and Willey (eds.), *op. cit.*, pp. 150–151.

[4]J. D. Clark, "Africa South of the Sahara," in Braidwood and Willey (eds.), *op. cit.*, p. 14.

[5]H. T. Waterbolk, "The Lower Rhine Basin," in Braidwood and Willey (eds.), *op. cit.*, p. 233.

to become the prime projectile and hunting weapon.

The presence of skeletons of domesticated dogs is a possible indication of the intensive nature of the hunting aspect of the culture. Man and dog may already have entered into a mutual-aid relationship as a hunting team. If not, they were at least keeping company. At any rate, the predatory facet of the Paleolithic cultures continued in the Baltic specialization of the Mesolithic. Dugout canoes hewn from solid logs were another adaptive device. They made it possible to penetrate the swamps for hunting and to get from one shore settlement to another.

The man of the lake and river cultures of the European woods was not exploiting farinaceous plants because he was a forest dweller; hence he had no use for the equipment of the grassland peoples far to the south. Yet he

. . . was no longer a migrating, nomadic hunter. He had become specialized as a hunter of *Standwild* [nonmigratory animals] and as a fisherman who rounded out his diet with fruits; he operated from relatively solid huts, which could not readily be disassembled and re-erected farther along the route, and thus was inhibited, just as by the dugouts, from transportation over a wider region.[6]

The European northerner was making no contribution to the agricultural revolution by domesticating new plants or animals. Nonetheless, he was working out a settled pattern of environmental exploitation of the woodland habitat to the limits of his Mesolithic capabilities. In so doing, he shaped a way of life that was to be important to the men of the northern latitudes for a long time to come.

India and China to the east took up their manifestations of the Mesolithic, apparently independently of the Middle Eastern tradition.[7]

[6]H. Schwabedissen, "Northern Continental Europe," in Braidwood and Willey (eds.), *op. cit.*, p. 260.
[7]K. –C. Chang, "The Beginnings of Agriculture in the Far East" (*Antiquity*, vol. 44, 1970), pp. 175–185.

The Mesolithic in North America While Late Upper Paleolithic big-game hunters were still searching out their prey in Europe and parts of Asia, seed-gathering foragers were already at work in North America laying the foundations for their horticultural revolution. New World archaeologists now lump the hundreds of local manifestations of the foraging pattern of existence under the rubric *Archaic*.

The Western Archaic, found in the Great Basin (Utah and Nevada), the Southwest, (New Mexico and Arizona), and the Pacific Coast regions, is well known from a number of dry cave sites. Its earliest manifestations are firmly dated from around 10,000 B.C. It continued with very little change right into the nineteenth century in the living cultures of the Shoshonean-speaking Indians of the Great Basin. The Western Archaic was adapted to many-sided exploitation of a predominantly desert environment.

The Eastern Archaic was adapted to an even richer and more complex exploitation of the more luxurious environment of the woodlands east of the Mississippi. The

Fig. 10-5   Maglemosean ground-stone axheads set in staghorn sockets. (Museum of Anthropology, University of Minnesota. Photo by Don Breneman.)

big-game hunters of the Lithic stage still existed between the Rockies and the woodlands at this time. The Eastern Archaic did not get underway until around 6000 B.C. in the Middle West, although on the Atlantic Coast it was well differentiated from the Lithic a thousand to fifteen hundred years earlier (7500 to 7000 B.C.). The focus of the Eastern Archaic subsistence techniques is identified as "forest efficiency," a skillful combination of woodland hunting of deer, smaller animals, and migratory birds, and the harvesting of plentiful nuts, berries, wild seeds, and roots.

The Desert Tradition   J. D. Jennings, who defined the Desert tradition early in the 1950s, summarizes its traits as follows:

. . . cave and overhang locations for settlement, bark or grass beds, seasonal gathering, intensive exploitation of resources, small-seed harvesting and special cooking techniques, basketry (twined predominant), netting and matting, fur cloth, tumpline, sandals (moccasins rare), atlatl, pointed hardwood dart shafts, varied (relatively small) projectile points, preferential use of glassy textured stone, flat milling stone and mano, a high percentage of crude scraper and chopper tools, digging stick, firedrill and hearth, bunt points, wooden clubs, hornshaft wrenches, tubular pipes, use of olivella and other shells, vegetable quids.[8]

The presence of deer-hoof rattles and medicine bags is evidence of shamanism (see pages 583–586). Most significant, however, is the use of shoulder-blade grass cutters as the analogue of the Old World microlith sickle. The presence of grinding stones in all sites further confirms the fundamental importance of seed harvesting in the new life of postglacial man in the New World and the Old. Hunting of small animals rounded out the subsistence diet of these early Americans. In Utah and Nevada (the Great Basin), climatic variations did not seriously alter the

ecology, which remained consistently marginal desert around the fluctuating lake shores. Population has always been sparse and meager in this area, which is incapable of supporting grasses outside the limited edges of fresh-water basins and high mountain valleys. Hence, the desert culture remained virtually unchanged from 9000 B.C. to A.D. 1850 and did not contribute appreciably to the development of agriculture in the Western Hemisphere.

In the nineteenth century, the Gosiute, Paiute, Bannock, and Shoshone Indians were living in small local groups of 50 to 200 people. Each local group was known by the name of the food which it foraged most intensively (Fig. 10-6). Thus, the band which occupied the Snake River Desert of southern Idaho called itself *H3kandika. H3k* is a desert grass seed. *Dika* means "eater." The people are the Seed Eaters. Other Shoshone bands are the Root Eaters, Pine Nut Eaters, Groundhog Eaters, Rabbit Eaters, Mountain Sheep Eaters, Fish Eaters, Salmon Eaters. Could anything speak more eloquently of the importance of foraging in tribal life?

The living example of the Shoshonean way of life as food gatherers is detailed in a later chapter (pages 256–258). We may, if we wish, have a good basis for imagining very similar activities taking place in the same desert area some 11,000 years ago.

Fig. 10-6   Desert-Culture foragers. Southern Paiute seed gatherers on the Kaibab Plateau, north of the Grand Canyon, in 1873. The women (left) wear basketry hats and carry baskets on their backs, while they hold seed-catching baskets in their hands. The girls (right) carry basketry water bottles sealed with pitch pine and slung across the forehead with tumplines. (National Anthropological Archives.)

[8]J. D. Jennings, "The Desert West," in J. D. Jennings and E. Norbeck (eds.), *Prehistoric Men in North America*, pp. 154–155.

The Mid-continental Archaic Traditions The archaeology of the Eastern Archaic stage is much too complex (and lacking in adequate systematic comparative analysis) for us to consider more than the characteristic features of one spectacular manifestation which may at least give the feel of what was happening in cultural adaptation and evolution.[9]

We select the manifestation which unfolded at Indian Knoll, a hunting and shellfish-gathering site in the valley of the Green River, in western Kentucky. Here, from around 4000 B.C. to the time of the birth of Christ, forest foragers returned again and again. Their debris of shells, bones, tools, burials, and dirt built a compacted 2-acre mound 8 feet in thickness. (Fortunately for archaeologists,

[9]Readers who are interested in a very useful overall summary by subregions should refer to J. D. Jennings, *Prehistory of North America*, pp. 108–163, or G. R. Willey, *An Introduction to American Archaeology*, vol. 1.

prehistoric men left littered campsites and did not worry about pollution.) Excavations over a number of years have yielded some 26,000 animal bones, uncounted mollusc shells, 55,000 artifacts, and 1,200 (more or less) burials of human beings, together with a score of domesticated dogs.

Packed clay floors with fire-reddened hearth areas reveal the location of homesites, some of which have postholes for fire screens before the hearths. The absence of permanent dwelling structures is notable. Numerous charred hickory, walnut, and acorn shells around the fireplaces testify to the gathering proclivities of the denizens of the site. Ninety percent of the thousands of animal bones are those of deer—the Big-Game Hunter tradition lingering on. The rest are those of small, modern, nonmigratory forest mammals such as raccoon and opossum.

Flaked projectile points by the hundreds

also continued from the lithic tradition. *Atlatl* weights and ends show that the bow had not yet been introduced. Bone fishhooks reveal that the foragers of Indian Knoll took not only shellfish from the river. Ground stone pestles and metates indicate the milling of seeds, nuts, and probably of dried deer meat to produce *pemmican,* or jerky, for winter use.[10]

Splintered bone awls and chipped flint drills, knives, and scrapers speak of hide dressing, clothing, and skin shelters. Shell beads, pins, rings, and gorgets provided personal jewelry, while the painting of the dead with red ocher probably signifies that body paint was important to the living. Of the numerous burials in the living mound, somewhat more than half the bodies were found in round pits, flexed on their sides or backs in the fetal position, but whether this represented a symbolic return of the dead to the "womb of the Earth" or the fact that it required less work to dig a round pit than a long grave, who can say today? But it could be significant that prone burials were not put in graves. They were laid out on the ground, painted red, and mounded with earth.

Other Archaic sites yield fragments of coiled baskets, used to collect and store seeds, berries, and roots. Nets for trapping fish, rabbits, and birds were woven—and sandals to lessen the damage to feet. Weaving and netting (see pages 321–323) are new technological achievements added in the Mesolithic Era of Intensive Foraging. The knapping of flint tools and weapons was no longer a dominant handicraft activity. Culture and technology were beginning to show signs of noticeable diversity.

The Mesolithic foraging complex of the New World developed quite independently of that of the Old World, so far as one can tell.

The situation seems to have been one of parallel development. Small bands of men were settled in favorable locales near good sources of water and were squeezing their land for all it was worth in terms of plants and readily accessible fish and small game. As Emil Haury has written, "The long and intimate experience of a wide range of plant life undoubtedly saved them during adverse climatic shifts, for changing the dependency from desirable to less-desirable, and perhaps hardier, plants was made relatively easy."[11]

In the Middle East, in Mexico, and perhaps in Southeast Asia, such intimate environmental knowledge led to the domestication of plants and animals: the phase of cultural development known as *Incipient Agriculture,* which occurred during the Early Neolithic Age and is the immediate prelude to the dawn of civilization.

The Early Neolithic Era of Incipient Agriculture

The domestication of both plants and animals was a gradual process that took place in a number of different parts of the world along independent lines. Domestication consists merely in controlled cultivation and husbandry. A domesticated plant is one that is useful to man and is cultivated by him. (Dandelions are noxious weeds in the lawn to most persons, but cultivated dandelions are sold at usual salad prices at vegetable stands in city areas settled by Italian-Americans.) The first steps in plant cultivation were probably taken in the process of weed elimination (a weed is any plant that is held to be undesirable). A patch of wild plants was tended, and weeds were cut or uprooted. Kwakiutl Indians, for example, cared for their wild-clover patches. Clover beds were the properties of specific families who dug them for their roots. The main roots, however, were never taken

[10]Later American Indians, especially on the Plains, hung thin slabs of meat on racks to sun-dry. The dried meat was then pounded to shreds which were mixed with berry pulp and formed into cakes. The cakes were stored in transportable rawhide envelopes (*parfleches*). The pemmican could conveniently be added to boiled nut or seed meal for a basic soup or gruel at any time.

[11]E. W. Haury, "The Greater American Southwest," in Braidwood and Willey (eds.), *op. cit.,* p. 112.

out, and pieces of root that were not considered suitable for food, if they had been dug up, were replaced in the ground for future growth.[12]

Real domestication began, however, when seeds, roots, or shoots were deliberately planted or stored from one season to the next for later planting. Not only did this call for foresightedness and self-restraint (you cannot eat your seed and plant it, too), but it also required dry storage to prevent mildew and rot and to ensure security from rats and mice (a good reason for domesticating cats). There was also the very difficult task of preparing the soil and selecting those particular plants which would yield the largest or the most easily harvested and processed seeds. The idea of plant domestication was hard to come by, but once established, the concept quickly caught on, and it spread over all continents and the isles of the Pacific in a matter of 8,000 years. Even before the Age of Exploration, during which European traits were disseminated around the world, the bulk of mankind's societies had already become pre-agricultural gardeners.

Lightly forested upland grass areas may strike the reader as strange places for the origins of primitive gardening, but new evidence does not support the old theory that gardening first began in irrigation oases of the arid river valleys of the Old and New Worlds. Irrigation comes later, and it is where the grasses grew naturally but not too densely that the process of plant domestication began. Primitive wild wheat and barley grow in a natural state at elevations of 2,000 to 4,300 feet above sea level in the Anatolian highlands of modern Turkey and on the hilly flanks of the Fertile Crescent, which swings from the Nile along the eastern edge of the Mediterranean and down the Tigris and Euphrates Rivers (see Figure 10-7). In Mexico, at the site of the earliest known manifestation of plant domestication (see pages 212–214),

pollen analysis indicates a semidry climate supporting mesquite and grassland.

Çatal Hüyük   *Hüyük* is Turkish for a mound built up by generations of village or town life on a given spot, such as the one Schliemann found at Troy. Ever since excavations were begun at one such *hüyük* in southern Turkey in 1961, under the direction of James Mellaart, the picture of Early Neolithic culture has been undergoing rapid change. The first three years of work (1961 to 1963) were sufficient to establish that barley, wheat, lentils, and peas were thoroughly domesticated and were producing surplus yields in Anatolia by 6385 B.C. $\pm$ 101 years. Sheep were domesticated and sheared for wool, which was woven into fine cloth. Cattle were domesticated by 5800 B.C. $\pm$ 92 years. An amazingly rich inventory of specialized handicrafts included beautifully worked wooden bowls and boxes; baskets; obsidian and flint daggers, spearheads, lance heads, arrowheads, knives, scrapers, awls, and sickle blades; jewelry of bone, shell, and copper; obsidian mirrors; and bone awls, punches, knives, ladles, spoons, clay bowls, spatulas, bodkins, belt hooks, toggles, and pins. This was a creative and well-off people.

The town itself (for that is what existed at Çatal Hüyük) was a solid community structure of adjoining rooms not dissimilar to the Indian pueblos of the southwestern United States. Like the pueblos, the rooms had to be entered through an entrance in the roof, which also served as a smoke vent for the fires in the hearth and oven on the floor beneath. This structure made a defensive citadel of the community house, and the doorless and windowless walls of mud brick gave added protection from flooding by the river on whose banks the prehistoric town stood.

Numerous shrines are scattered throughout the complex, with full-sized clay cattle heads protruding from the walls, some with statuettes of a fertile mother goddess (Figure 10-8), as well as of a bearded consort god

[12]E. S. Curtis, *The Kwakiutl,* p. 43.

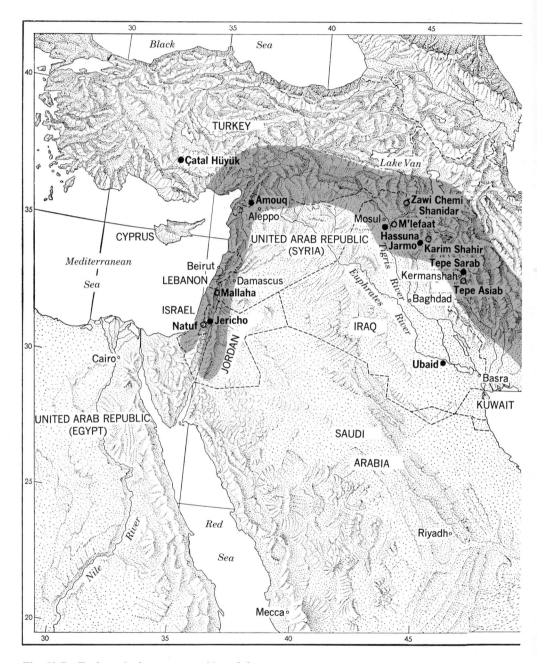

Fig. 10-7   Early agriculture communities of the Middle East. The major known sites in Anatolia and the Fertile Crescent. (Adapted from R. J. Braidwood, "The Agricultural Revolution," **Scientific American.**)

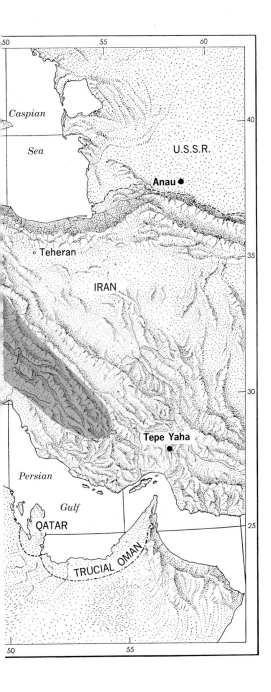

seated on a bull. Layer after layer of religious murals, painted on the walls and then plastered over to make way for the next painting, bespeak a vital and highly developed cult and religious-belief system, much concerned with the mystery of life and death. Life-associated scenes, done in symbolic red paint, are on the west walls of the shrine rooms. Death scenes created in black paint are on the east side (Figure 10-9).

Mellaart expressed puzzlement after the conclusion of the 1963 dig that no workshops had been exposed among the 200 rooms that had by then been excavated:

> Somewhere in the mound there must be the workshops of the weavers and basketmakers; the matmakers; the carpenters and joiners; the men who made the polished stone tools; the beadmakers . . . the flint and obsidian knappers . . . the merchants of skin, leather and fur . . . the workers in bone . . . the carvers of wooden bowls and boxes; the mirror makers; the bowmakers . . . the merchants and traders who obtained all the raw material; and finally the artists—the carvers of statuettes, the modelers and the painters.[13]

It could well be, however, that the town itself was a ceremonial and administrative nucleus for a number of farmsteads and cottage industries dispersed about the countryside—a regional community. Future excavations will provide the answer.

Mellaart's view that the city's wealth depended on its control of a well-organized trade carries conviction. The heart of the trade appears to have been the obsidian that came from the volcanoes some fifty miles away—obsidian that found its way to Jericho and Jarmo (discussed a few paragraphs later) and to Cyprus in the Mediterranean. Clearly, the social, political, and theological structure of Çatal Hüyük and the environs over which it held sway was strong. It would seem that the people of the town were too specialized in trade, politics, and religion to have spent much time in farming. They hunted

[13]J. Mellaart, "A Neolithic City in Turkey" (*Scientific American*, vol. 210, no. 4, 1964), p. 99.

for sport and for game food; bones of wild animals are profuse in the refuse dumps, and excavations in 1965 and 1966 uncovered wall paintings of hunts containing hundreds of human and animal figures. But compact as it is, it hardly seems likely that a town which covered only one-twentieth of a square mile (32 acres) could have housed so diversified a productive system within its confines.

The town at Çatal was burned out and rebuilt a number of times between its Early Neolithic founding *ca.* 6500 B.C. and its final abandonment in the Hittite period *ca.* 1900 B.C.

One cannot help being impressed, on the basis of what is now known from the excava- tions at Çatal Hüyük, at how rapidly the transition from Paleolithic hunting bands to regionally organized communities occurred, once the domestication of plants and animals —the food revolution—had taken place in the Middle East. The swiftness with which the cultural explosion occurred indicates how much more fully *Homo sapiens* was utilizing his intelligence potential than he had in Late Paleolithic times. Once man had evolved a nervous system capable of producing language and culture on anything more than the most rudimentary level—and this was achieved in the *Homo sapiens* of third interglacial times—cultural adaptation was henceforth the product of cumulative experience, limited mostly by the productive potential in food and energy control that could be marshaled. This has been true for at least the last 100,000 years of human experience. There is little indication, which can only be indirect, of genetic change in man's nervous equipment during all the time that cultural development has moved on apace.

Jericho   During the 1950s, prior to the discovery of what lay beneath Çatal Hüyük, Jericho and Jarmo were two sites of intense interest and excitement. Jericho is actually the Biblical city that rested on top of Tell es-Sultan (*tell* is the Arabic equivalent of the Turkish *hüyük*).

Underneath the 70 feet of debris and dirt, the English expeditions, directed by Miss Kathleen Kenyon, uncovered an early Neolithic town at 600 feet below sea level, where an ancient spring created an oasis. On the bedrock are the clay-paved floors of Natufian huts whose burned posts have given a carbon 14 date of 7800 B.C. ± 210 years.

In later levels, the huts had been superseded by semi-subterranean houses with stone foundations and adobe brick walls surmounted by domed wattle-and-daub roofs. Walls and floors were mud-plastered for cleanliness and coolness. The later town covered 10 acres and was surrounded by a

Fig. 10-8   A mother goddess from Çatal Hüyük giving birth while seated on a "divine" throne of two felines. (From Mellaart, Earliest Civilizations of the Near East, *with permission of Thames and Hudson, London.)*

stone wall 6 feet thick and 12 feet high, with a 30-foot tower at one point (and possibly at others not yet excavated). The oasis was a valuable spot and thus a mark for marauders, and it was heavily defended. The village, or a section of it, was burned out, and its charcoal has been given a carbon 14 date of 6850 B.C. ± 210 years. It is thus several centuries older than Çatal—assuming the carbon 14 dates to be comparably correct.

Although actual grain from Jericho has not been reported on, serrated sickle blades and a specialized wedge-shaped metate attest to its well-established use as food. Beautifully modeled reproductions were made of heads of the deceased (Figure 10-10) and were buried in clusters. Yet in spite of their skill in ceramic sculpture, the Jerichoans made no pottery, and their technological inventory was in no way comparable to that of Çatal to the north. Jericho was marginal to the centers of early domestication of plants and animals.

Fig. 10-9   A mortuary ceremony at Çatal Hüyük performed by priestesses of the vulture cult. The large bull-heads, wall paintings, room shape, and human remains are just as excavated. The vulture priestesses are artistic reconstructions. (From Mellaart, Earliest Civilizations of the Near East, with permission of Thames and Hudson, London.)

Jarmo   Jarmo, a small village–farming community of some 200 inhabitants, located in northeastern Iraq, was brought to the center of the stage by Robert Braidwood of the Oriental Institute and Department of Anthropology at the University of Chicago. Braidwood has enlisted the able collaboration of expert geologists and biologists in his study of the total cultural and ecological setting as it existed around 5600 B.C., when domesticated wheat and barley had just been established in this area. Jarmo is but one of dozens of Early Neolithic village sites showing the pattern of incipient agriculture in the countryside of Iraq. Its significance derives from the fact that it was the one selected for intensive excavation.

Braidwood and Howe give a summary of Jarmo's revelations:

1. It does yield positive traces of a village–farming community way of life; several-roomed rectangular houses within villages of some degree of permanence; the remains of at least domesticated wheat, barley, probably the dog and the goat, and possibly even the sheep, with the pig appearing in the upper levels; the conventional artifactual traits of the "neolithic," with pottery appearing before the phase is completed. As they pertain—by reasonable but *not* absolutely guaranteed interpretations—to food production, these artifacts are querns and rubbing stones, mortars and pestles, flint sickle blades with sheen, occasional subfloor storage pits, a peculiar form of oven, possibly for the parching of grain, a few large celts (hoes?), and an occasional large pierced stone ball (digging stick weight?). Overwhelmingly, however, it is the demonstrated presence of the plant and animal domesticates and the apparent year-round permanence of a village of perhaps twenty-five well-built houses that make Jarmo impressive for our present purposes. It should remain clear, however, that a very significant portion of the Jarmo subsistence pattern still depended upon collected foods.

2. Jarmo does indicate firm traces of longer-range trade, especially evidenced by the great bulk of obsidian (closest natural flow near Lake Van in Anatolia) in its chipped-stone category. We suggest that this first indication of a bulk carrying trade—

Fig. 10-10   Skull of an early Neolithic man from Jericho with face modeled in clay. (Photograph by K. Kenyon, from K. Kenyon, **Digging up Jericho,** *Ernest Benn, Ltd., London. Courtesy of the Jericho Excavation Fund.)*

with its implications of attendant exchanges of ideas—may well presage a reversal of the above-mentioned trend toward regional specialization and localized intensification.[14]

Conspicuous among artifacts from Jarmo are the pecked and abraded stone mortars, pestles, and grinding stones—the millers for the wheat and barley that the Jarmoans had tamed. Compared with the dwellers of Çatal Hüyük, the hill villagers of Jarmo were somewhat "backwoods"; their culture was a good 500 years behind that which was being enjoyed at Çatal. Comparisons of Çatal, Jericho, and Jarmo indicate the rapid establishment of village and town settlements based upon an incipient agricultural foundation, with

[14]R. J. Braidwood and B. Howe, "Southwestern Area beyond the Lands of the Mediterranean Littoral," in Braidwood and Willey (eds.), *op. cit.,* p. 138. (By permission from the Wenner-Gren Foundation for Anthropological Research, New York.)

specialization sustained by trade in which the villages served as regional market centers. Such comparisons also indicate that the domestication of plants probably occurred first in Anatolia rather than on the hilly flanks of the Fertile Crescent (see Figure 10-7), as had been previously thought.

The Domestication of Wheat and Barley Charred kernels of wheat and barley and impressions of kernels in clay are the proof of domestication of plants at Çatal and Jarmo. The wheats at Jarmo are wild einkorn (*Triticum aegilopoides*), which has a single seed per spikelet, and domesticated einkorn (*Triticum monococcum*). Wild einkorn is still a common grass in many parts of Asia Minor, and domesticated einkorn is still cultivated in hilly regions with thin soils in the Middle East, although it is much inferior to the free-threshing strains of hybrid wheat which have been found at Çatal and which were introduced into Europe from Anatolia during the sixth millennium B.C.[15]

Two-row barley (*Hordeum spontaneum*) is present in quantity at Jarmo. Six-row barley, a less primitive form, occurs further south and also at Çatal Hüyük. Barley is usually found associated with wheat throughout the Old World Neolithic and later phases of culture. Wheat, however, is the foundation crop and "staff of life" for all the Middle East and European village-farming communities and civilizations. Barley is an adjunct. Carbonized field peas, lentils, and vetchling at Çatal and Jarmo reveal that these early horticulturalists also had the wherewithal for basic vegetable soup, and the remains of their pottery show that they had the vessels in which to cook it.

The Domestication of Animals The animal remains at Jarmo include the skeletons of wild goats, sheep, cattle, pigs, horses, and asses, all of which originally inhabited the highland in a wild state. Dogs had already been domesticated elsewhere during the

[15]J. Mellaart, *op. cit.,* p. 97.

Mesolithic, but there is no certain evidence that they were at Jarmo, although pottery models of doglike figures with upturned tails could indicate the canine presence. Changes in the shape of the horns of goats at Jarmo show that these animals were domestically bred, and the fact that goat skeletons make up 80 per cent of all those found at Jarmo tell us that these people were no longer dependent upon hunting. The high proportion of butchered young billy goats is further indirect evidence that the goats at Jarmo were domesticated. Immature males were evidently slaughtered for eating, while only a few were kept to mature as breeding studs. Females were allowed to grow up for breeding and possibly for milking. Milk would have provided a very good food supplement for the lean preharvest seasons.

The kind of ecological specialization that leads to pastoralism has recently been discovered at Tepe Sarab, a herder's campsite of the same age as Jarmo, which lies about a hundred miles to the southeast at an elevation of 3,000 feet. It has goats, but no metates or manos. The Tepe Sarabians apparently traded goats and possibly cheese for meal in the lower-lying farm villages.

Early Neolithic Manifestations in East and Southeast Asia The dim outlines of the Neolithic transformation in the Far East are only just beginning to take shape as new archaeological findings are newly reported. The discovery of pottery with carbon 14 dating of 8000 B.C. from the Jomon culture of Japan indicates an early start on some of the technical aspects of post-Pleistocene development in that part of the world. But even more important is the discovery, by the University of Hawaii archaeological expedition to Thailand in 1967 and 1968, of nuts, oil seed, spices, water chestnuts, cucumbers, beans, and peas in strata dating (C[14]) from 10,000 to 6000 B.C. This would indicate that when the facts are finally in and evaluated, it may be proven that the Asians had made the transition from hunting to gardening before the Middle Easterners.[16]

Kwan-chih Chang interpolates the following summing up of the patterns of emergent gardening in Southeast Asia:

1. Most of [the] earliest cultivators of tropical and subtropical southeast Asia inhabited estuarial plains and low terraces and engaged for subsistence mainly in fishing. In their habitat were abundant wild plants, which because of the topographical complexity were highly diversified. These fishermen led a settled, stable life and were familiar with their plant resources and the nature and uses of many plants. Utilization of select plants gradually gave way to their control and cultivation as a perhaps minor but essential means of subsistence.

2. Wild and initially-domesticated plants in the fishing-hunting cultures of southeast Asia were probably first used mainly for containers (e.g. bamboo trunks and bottle gourds) or for cordage for use in fishing (nets, fishlines, and canoe-caulking material); or were herbs with various uses, or poisons. Man's dependence upon plants for these and other uses, plus the obvious food value of many aquatic plants, wild fruits, berries, roots, and tubers, were among the strong reasons for their continued and growing use and eventual cultivation.

3. Under these circumstances the first wild but utilized plants that became the cultigens in southeast Asia probably included bamboos, the bottle gourd, fruit trees, some aquatic plants, and such roots and tubers as the taro and the yam. There is almost general agreement that in southeast Asia root, tuber, and fruit plants were cultivated much earlier than cereal plants. Among the cereals millet, sorghum, and Job's-tears are thought to have been used before rice.

4. The initially-cultivated crops probably played a minor role in the total subsistence system of the inhabitants, supplementing a diet derived mainly from fish, wild animals, and shell-fish. Food cultivation was at first probably a small-scale undertaking in little patches near the individual homes. Only small peripheral forest clearings were necessary, and no tool more elaborate than a digging stick was used.[17]

[16]See K. -C. Chang, "The Beginnings of Agriculture in the Far East" (*Antiquity*, vol. 44, 1969), pp. 175–182, and W. G. Solheim, II, "Reworking South Asian Prehistory" (*Paideuma*, vol. 15, 1969), pp. 125–139.

[17]K. -C. Chang, *op. cit.*, p. 180.

Parallel Developments in the New World

While the hillmen of the Near East were taming wheat and barley, and subsequently chick peas, beans, lentils, rye, flax, and sundry vegetables, and so laying the foundations for the first civilizations of Mesopotamia and the Nile, the American Indians of the highlands of southern Mexico were engaged in the same process at almost the same time.

During the first half of this century, it was believed that corn was wholly the product of the crossing of one or another of two tassel grasses (teosinte or *Tripsacum*) with an unknown wild grass. No wild corn had ever been discovered. In the 1950s, however, the picture suddenly changed when the pollen of wild corn was unexpectedly discovered in borings of 80,000-year-old soil taken from the prehistoric lake bottoms where Mexico City now stands. Corn did exist before man came upon the scene.

The oldest known corn at the time had been uncovered in Bat Cave, New Mexico, in 1948. It had a carbon 14 date of from 2000 to 3000 B.C. The Bat Cave corn was primitive when compared with the corn Indians were growing when the Spaniards first arrived, but it was far from being wild corn, and it was obviously by no means the earliest domesticated corn.

Ten years later (1958), R. S. MacNeish began a dedicated and systematic search for the natal place of corn. Two years of searching out caves and rock shelters in the Guatemalan and Honduran highlands and the hill country of Chiapas in southeastern Mexico brought no results. But in 1960, the thirty-ninth cave tested in Puebla, Mexico, paid off handsomely. Minuscule corncobs, bearing kernels that were best studied under a magnifying glass, were found. They were the product of wild corn. Their carbon 14 date goes back to 5000 B.C. This was not cultivated corn, but the Mesolithic foragers of Mexico were definitely harvesting the parent of modern corn 7,000 years ago.

The culture sequence in the valley of Tehuacán sketches out the first headings of the story of incipient agriculture in that part of the New World (Figure 10-11). The sequences are as follows.

From 6700 to 5000 B.C., foragers had domesticated mixta squashes and avocados. They also collected wild beans, chili, and amaranth, but they had no corn.

Between 5000 and 3500 B.C., corn was domesticated, as were amaranth, the jack and common bean, chili, black and white zapotes, maschata squash, and the water-bottle gourd. The populations of this period were not assiduous farmers, for these foods appear to have constituted only about one-tenth of their total diet. For the rest, they hunted and trapped small game.

By 3400 B.C., a marked change is seen; settlements of pit houses (see page 302) had replaced caves and rock shelters. The farming village was established in America, and one-third of the food of the inhabitants was made up of garden produce, including the plants previously mentioned as well as runner beans, and the dog.

Eleven hundred years later (2300 B.C.), a number of varieties of hybridized corn and pumpkins had been bred, and the first pottery was made. (Note how much earlier it was present at Çatal Hüyük and Jarmo.) Irrigation agriculture began slightly later, at about 700 B.C. By A.D. 700, true cities, under dynastic Mixtec rulers, were flourishing in the valley of Tehuacán, and 85 per cent of all food was agricultural in origin.

This is the sequence for only one valley in Mexico.[18] Variations in the pattern and dates for first appearances elsewhere may be dis-

[18]R. S. MacNeish, "The Origin of New World Civilization" (*Scientific American,* vol. 211, no. 5, 1964), pp. 29–37.

Fig. 10-11 Stages in the evolution of corn in the valley of Tehuacán, Mexico. Wild corn (top), first discovered in 1960, dates from ca. 5000 B.C. Successive improvement of breeds through domestication and crossbreeding is revealed in (middle) early hybrid corn, ca. 3500 B.C., and (bottom) early modern corn, ca. 1500 B.C. (Courtesy of R. S. MacNeish.)

covered in the future. Nonetheless, the essential story is there. Squashes, beans, and maize were domesticated, in that order—and all between 7000 and 5000 B.C. They became the "triumvirate that forms the basis of much of American Indian agriculture."[19] They pro-

[19]G. F. Carter, "Origins of American Indian Agriculture" (*American Anthropologist,* vol. 48, 1946), p. 1. There is new, as yet unpublished, evidence, however, that the Maya relied heavily on the nut of the ramon tree as a basic food source.

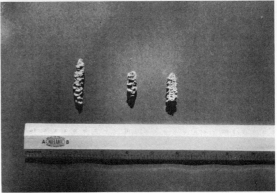

vided the nutritional source for the energy that went into building the civilizations of the Olmecs, Toltecs, and Aztecs, as well as those of many lesser-known groups.

In South America, the domesticated potato became the staple for Andean peoples, while in the Amazonian rain forests, techniques for growing and processing manioc were developed to meet special environmental conditions (pages 263–264), much as the Southeast Asians developed rice culture in lieu of wheat and barley as their special adaptation of agriculture to the requirements of their physical environment.

New World cultures did not build extensively upon domesticated animals until the Spanish introduced horses, sheep, and cattle. Andean tribes domesticated the llama and alpaca—whose wild ancestors were native American camels—and the guanaco and vicuña. The llama was bred and used largely as a beast of burden, and the alpaca largely for its wool. Guinea pigs, those gentle little beasties, were domesticated for food in the Andes. The earliest known American domesticated dog was unearthed from an Archaic site near Eldred, Illinois, in the summer of 1970. It had been deliberately buried and is dated at approximately 7000 B.C.

The independent domestication of cotton in the semitropical parts of Asia and the Americas produced a new source of fiber for weaving. Cotton was substituted for the flax that was domesticated earlier in the Middle East as a source of thread for weaving, in addition to the fleece of goats and sheep.

The Full Neolithic Era of Developed Agriculture

The Full Neolithic—the phase of cultural evolution in which man depended mainly on gardening and the exploitation of domesticated animals for food and sustenance—came out of the simple beginnings of the previous era as prehistoric men experimented

with selective breeding and domestication of more plants and animals. Communal life focused in the village or town, and although it may have been necessary to move the villages periodically as fields became exhausted, except for full pastoralists and marginal hunters, the nomadic way of life was gone.

Domesticated Plants and Animals Wheat and barley, plus the goat, sheep, and dog, as already indicated, had been domesticated by the end of the Era of Incipient Agriculture. During the Era of Developed Agriculture, the remaining basic cereals, rye, flax, and millet, were added to the list of domesticated plants of Asia Minor, western Asia, Africa, and Europe. Wheat, however, remained the fundamental foodstuff.

In Southeast Asia, the cultivation of rice was developed as the staple food source for Neolithic societies located in the rain forests of the Eastern Hemisphere, where wheat and barley will not grow. Yams and taro were also added.

Wild Late Pleistocene cattle (*Bos primigenius*) provided the stock from which, by 3500 B.C., the humped domestic cattle of India and Mesopotamia were derived. The cult of the sacred cow, already established at Çatal by 5500 B.C., spread with domesticated cattle in a great arc from eastern Africa through Egypt and Mesopotamia and into India.

The pig did not fare so well, and it was not domesticated at Çatal. It was hunted in Mesolithic times and has continued to be sought throughout historic ages. But the pig is nonmigratory, and can be herded only by thoroughly settled farmers. As Zeuner writes: "It is indeed difficult to imagine how a nomadic community, and even tribes that changed their habitations twice annually according to the season, could cope with the art of pig-driving, since the animal is notoriously unaccommodating in this respect."[20] Neolithic

[20]F. E. Zeuner, *A History of Domesticated Animals*, p. 260.

farmers achieved domestication of the succulent pig at the same time that they domesticated the cow, however.

Although wild horses were of much interest to Upper Paleolithic artists, no horses were domesticated in Mesolithic times. Horses are free-spirited and skittish. There is nothing timid about them, and taming a wild horse is no gentle operation. Possibly the first domestication of the horse occurred in the steppe country of southwestern Russia and Asia, where gardeners saw their lands becoming desiccated and therefore combined sporadic gardening with horse nomadism. This took place around 2500 B.C. As a way of life, it swept across the steppes and spawned the later Mongol hordes of historic times.

Other domesticates of the Neolithic Old World are the buffalo and yak, elephant, camel, ass and mule, cat, ferret, mongoose, rabbit, and dormouse. It is not likely that birds were domesticated in Neolithic times.

Artifacts   In contrast to Paleolithic hand axes, Neolithic adzes and axes were generally hafted to a handle. Wooden drills and wet sand were commonly used to drill holes through stone axheads into which the handle could be fitted (Figure 10-12).

War clubs and maces became differentiated from industrial axes. In the Middle East, they were pear- or ball-shaped. In North Africa and the Danube region, disk-shaped club heads were more prevalent. This type spread to the north in Middle Neolithic times.

A prevalence of flint arrowheads throughout all Neolithic deposits, except for those of the Lower Neolithic in the Balkans and parts of the Near East, attests to the wide use of the bow and arrow for both hunting and war. In the area where the bow was little used, baked-clay sling pellets show that the weapon with which David felled Goliath was not just a Hebraic device, by any means. Daggers of flint (Figure 10-12) and bone, as well as the familiar scrapers and blade sickles, continue well into the Bronze Age.

Fig. 10-12   Neolithic drilled ground-stone axhead and pressure-flaked flint dagger. (Courtesy of the American Museum of Natural History.)

Perhaps most significant of all is the manifold development of pottery, which fits in with the making of gruel, so important to the diet of Neolithic man. Early Neolithic pottery is usually plain and undecorated, and the forms are simple and clean-lined. The body color of the clay varied from area to area, according to the nature of the natural clay and the additives put into it (see pages 318–320, on the techniques of pottery making). Although plain ware continued to be used for kitchen purposes, painted and decorated pots were usually developed quite rapidly. The possibilities for distinctive variations led to numerous local types (see Figure 10-13). Thus, Grahame Clark describes the Late Neolithic pottery of Tell Halaf, in Assyria, as:

. . . outstanding on account of the variety of its forms and above all of its painted decoration and because of the excellence of its firing; but it was still hand-made, and there is no reason to think it was necessarily or even probably made by whole-time potters. In addition to dishes and flasks the forms included bowls with sharp-shouldered bodies and flaring necks and bowls and flasks on hollow stands. The decoration comprised geometric patterns like triangles, chevrons, lozenges, chequers, stars, Maltese crosses, quatrefoils and rosettes; stipples, including egg and dot; and stylized representations of men and animals, including designs based on the bull's head. It was applied to a buff or cream slip by glaze paint. At the climax of the industry the decoration was polychrome; red, orange, yellow and black paints being used, sometimes highlighted by white spots. The pottery was apparently fired to temperatures up to 1200° C. in great domed kilns with rectangular annexes. . . .[21]

The Urban Revolution More important than pottery or artifacts were the new gardening techniques that were developed in the Full Neolithic in the great river valleys of Mesopotamia (the Euphrates and Tigris), Egypt (the Nile), and western Pakistan (the Indus). In the fertile floodwater lowlands, it was possible to carry on intensive gardening to the extent that continuous settlements could develop along the Nile, while in Mesopotamia and Pakistan, full cities emerged. The development of towns into cities changed the

whole scheme of life for more and more of humanity from that time onward. Civilization means "city making." Where civilization took over, the primitive tribesman moved into town and became an urbanite (of whom the most sophisticated were "urbane"), or he remained on his land as a satellite peasant villager. Of the first towns and cities, the essential characteristic described by Henri Frankfort is worth noting:

Now one may say that the birth of Mesopotamian civilization, like its subsequent growth, occurred under the sign of the city. To understand the importance of the city as a factor in the shaping of society, one must not think of it as a mere conglomeration of people. Most modern cities have lost the peculiar characteristic of individuality which we can observe in cities of Renaissance Italy, or Medieval Europe, of Greece, and of Mesopotamia. In these countries the physical existence of the city is but an outward sign of close communal affinities which dominate the life of every dweller within the walls. The city sets its citizens apart from the other inhabitants of the land. It determines their relations with the outside world. It produces an intensified self-consciousness in its burghers, to whom the collective achievements are a source of pride. The communal life of prehistoric times became civil life.[22]

Although in America the Maya built a civili-

---

[21]G. Clark, *World Prehistory*, p. 86. (By permission from Cambridge University Press, Cambridge, England).

[22]H. Frankfort, *The Birth of Civilization in the Near East*, p. 48.

Fig. 10-13   Early Neolithic pottery from Halaf. (Courtesy of the University Museum, Philadelphia.)

zation without cities, and although Egypt, too, achieved a civilized level before it developed cities, it is reasonable to hold with the great English prehistorian V. Gordon Childe that the food-producing revolution of the Mesolithic and Early Neolithic Ages laid the basis for the urban revolution of the Late Neolithic Age and the Bronze Age. The urban revolution fostered the aspects of civilization that have been of enduring significance for humanity.

The Urban Culture of Mesopotamia: Al Ubaid and the Sumerian Civilization   The events that took place in the Tigris-Euphrates Valley serve as a good model of the process of urban evolution in its early phase, and of the making of cities and the development of civilized ways of life. For this reason, the major aspects of the emergence of Sumerian civilization (4000 to 500 B.C.) are surveyed in the next pages.

The Ubaid Period   The alluvial delta of southern Iraq offered neither timber nor stone, but it was rich in soil and water. At Al Ubaid, an early village, located on a low rise of land near the Euphrates, was settled around 4000 B.C. by Iraqi highlanders who brought a well-developed subsistence economy of developed agriculture into the river bottoms with them. They had microlithic sickles and a new type of sickle made of hard-fired clay. They made themselves simple wattle-and-daub-walled huts with palm-stalk frames. They also made Quonset-type huts of reed bundles set vertically and arched to meet along the center top, a type of construction that survives in the Euphrates delta to this day. But elsewhere more impressive Ubaid towns were constructed of adobe bricks, such as those used at Çatal Hüyük, thirteen hundred years earlier.

The coming Bronze Age was adumbrated by the presence of a few cast-copper tools and axes and more numerous fired-clay copies of them. Forecasting a most important feature of the early civilizations were the sizable temple structures of the Ubaid towns.

Monumental public works of a religious nature were the most visually prominent feature.

The Sumerian Protoliterate Period   As the name of this period indicates, it is marked by the appearance of the earliest form of writing. The evidence has been found in the temples in the form of clay tablets bearing signs and pictograms incised with reeds (Figure 10-14). The predynastic texts have not yet been deciphered, and the contents of those of the early dynasties are prosaic and hardly religious. Yet they shed a flood of light on the role of the temple priests as organizers of work and society. It must have been they who prepared the tablets listing wages paid and goods received, and often including lists of names. Religion was obviously of extreme importance, as attested by the very large temples constructed on artificial mounds.

Pottery had for some time been turned on a wheel and produced commercially in quantity for daily use. Copper and silver bowls and dishes were now wrought for ceremonial use or display. Statues were carved and used in

Fig. 10-14   Stages in the development of cuneiform writing. Visual symbols impressed in clay gave the first permanence to the spoken word. (Courtesy of the University Museum, Philadelphia.)

association with the temples (see Figure 10-15). Clearly, a vigorous cultural flowering was under way.

The Sumerian Early Dynastic Period: Full Civilization (3200 to 2800 B.C.) Technologically, the most significant development is the harnessing of the ass and oxen to solid-wheeled chariots and to plows and carts. Agricultural efficiency was reaching a peak, while trade and wars were spreading. Each citizen, whether artisan, fisher, or soldier, was, in the early phases of development, also a part-time farmer. As the culture expanded, some soldiers and governmental officers became full-time professionals, as were a number of the priests and traders.

The city was the political unit in relations with the outside world. In the protoliterate phase, it had governed itself in matters of war and intercity relations through a democratic town council. Matters of boundary conflicts, safe conduct, and irrigation were its main concerns. Internal organization of town activities focused on the temples. Each city "belonged" to a god, and every citizen belonged to a temple district and served the god of his temple. Allotments of land, work assignments, and raw materials were designated by the head priest-administrator of the temple district. Each workman had to deliver a specified amount of produce; anything beyond this was his own. Some goods went to maintain the priests, and much was redistributed among the producing populace. Thus, the division of labor and the economic exchange necessary to effective civilization were achieved—in this case without an internal market system. A fair part of the Sumerian cities' output was exported in exchange for precious stones, metals, and incense for the temples and for necessities for the people. The head priest-administrator of the temple of the god of the city distributed major tasks among the various temple units. In this way the walls were maintained, as well as the irrigation systems that were being elaborated for more effective food production.

In Sumer, in the early dynasties, the system of exaction of labor was not particularly exploitative. People were in effect taxed by not being allowed to keep all they produced. But

Fig. 10-15 . A group of alabaster Sumerian temple statuettes from the Abu Temple in Tell Asmar, Iraq. In the theocratic system of Sumerian civilization, the gods and their priests were of first-rank importance and were given visual manifestation. (Courtesy of the Oriental Institute, The University of Chicago.)

through highly organized effort, each received or retained a good deal more than he could have produced on his own or than his Mesolithic progenitors had been able to enjoy. He was induced to play his part by acceptance of an elaborate theology of catastrophism and beneficence. Floods and pestilence were common disasters. Anxieties born of human insecurity and intellectual concern with cause and effect had elaborated the supernatural element in the explanation and relief of tensions. Gods properly served could benefit rather than punish man, the Sumerian believed, and he apparently served willingly.

Every urban civilization must find some way of inducing farmers and workers to produce surpluses. Otherwise, a society could never build above the lowest Mesolithic levels. Many later civilizations used force and gross exploitation, but in Sumerian cities this was not the case. The symbols on seals and in art all referred to the gods, and the gods, as Frankfort says, "were also symbols of a collective identity. Each city projected its sovereignty into the deity which it conceived as its owner."[23] Yet even in Sumer at the city of Lagash, the priests were in time so enriching themselves that the political arm had to put a rein on them. In turn, some political heads (*ensi*) became extorters themselves.

Characteristics of Early Civilization In this account, Sumer serves the purpose of epitomizing the process of the urban revolution that followed hard upon the food revolution. It exemplifies the ten characteristics of early civilization specified by Childe:[24]

1. The great enlargement of an organized population means a much wider level of social integration (organized social interaction) than ever occurred in any prehistoric tribal society of food gatherers and hunters.

2. Social means for collections of "surplus" production of farmers and artisans are

[23]*Ibid.*, p. 57
[24]V. G. Childe, *The Dawn of European Civilization; What Happened in History; Man Makes Himself.*

Fig. 10-16   The development of cast bronze axheads. From left to right, observe the increasingly deep grooves in the sides to secure the shaped haft, plus the addition of the nib to secure the haft lashing. In the most highly developed ax (far right), the side ridges have been closed to form a full cup and the knob has been modified to form an eyelet in which to tie the haft lashing. (Museum of Anthropology, University of Minnesota. Photo by Don Breneman.)

devised to produce a central accumulation of goods for "managed" use.

3. Specialization of production among workers is instituted, along with systems of redistribution and exchange of goods.

4. Specialization and exchange are expanded beyond the city in the development of far-reaching trade.

5. Monumental public works in the form of temples, palaces, storehouses, and irrigation systems are constructed and maintained through the centrally organized use of surplus productive time not devoted to food production or basic manufactures.

6. Highly developed art forms give expression to symbolic identification and aesthetic enjoyment.

7. The art of writing is developed to facilitate the process of organization and management. It is later expanded to other uses, especially theological and protoscientific.

8. Arithmetic, geometry, and astronomy

are developed as rational thinking techniques. This constitutes the initiation of exact, predictive science.

9. Well-structured political organization comes about in which membership based on residence replaces political identification based on kinship.

10. A privileged ruling class of religious, political, and military functionaries organizes and directs the whole system.

All this, as we have described it for the first thousand years of Sumer's evolution (Ubaid through the early dynasties), took place in what Julian Steward identifies as a regular phase of civilizational development in early times, and labels *the era of regional development and florescence.*[25] It is a time in which the first magnificent realization of the human potential is seen, the first era of cultural creativeness on the grand scale.[26]

The Bronze and Iron Era of Cyclical Conquests Once well established, the early

Fig. 10-17   Ornaments of the late Bronze Age. Neolith north woodsmen of the Baltic region creatively expressed their aesthetic interests in gold and bronze jewelry, among which bracelets and pins were important. (Photo by Lennart Larsen of the Danish National Historical Museum, Copenhagen.)

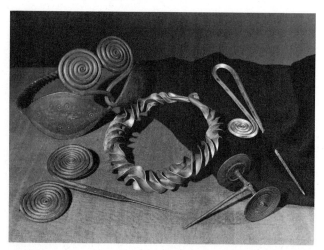

civilizations consistently turned to war and conquest, as characterized in the last 2,250 years of Sumerian history (2800 to 550 B.C.).

The diagnostic features of this era, according to Steward, are the emergence of large-scale militarism, the extension of political and economic domination over wide areas (empires), a strong tendency toward urbanization, and the construction of fortifications. In the social structure, priest-warriors constituted the ruling groups, usually under a divine monarch, whose importance is revealed in elaborate status burial. Social classes now tended to become frozen into hereditary classes, in contrast to the society of the previous era, which probably permitted individuals some upward mobility through personal achievement. Gods of war became prominent in the pantheon of deities.

There were no important technological changes in the era of cyclical conquest. Bronze appeared in Peru, Mesopotamia, and Egypt, and was used for weapons and ornaments. Figures 10-16 and 10-17 show the artistry attained in working bronze. But the metal contributed little to the production of food or other goods and added no new forms of energy to the culture. Iron, though not an Iron Age culture, appeared in China. The principal change in manufactures was a strong trend toward standardization and mass production, with a concomitant sacrifice of aesthetic freedom and variety. Large-scale, trade within the empires, and even beyond, brought the beginnings of a special commercial class, but coinage and an efficient monetary system were not yet developed.

Civilizations rose and fell, prospered and faltered. Conquerors raged back and forth across the lands with sword and fire. Some

[25]J. H. Steward, *Theory of Culture Change,* p. 195.
[26]The details of the specific regional development of other Mediterranean civilizations, plus those of the Indus Valley, China and Southeast Asia, Mexico, Middle America, and the Andes, become at this point too complex for the scope of this book. Hence, Sumer is allowed to stand as the prototype. However, see the list of selected readings at the end of this chapter for further leads.

of the more peaceful activities are illustrated in Figure 10-18. Artisans learned how to smelt iron to make better weapons and improved plowshares and pots. In the New World, there was no smelting of iron, and there were no horses, but the cycles of conquest ran their courses there, too, until the great civilizational edifices of Middle America and the Andes were brought down in crashing ruins by the conquistadores of Spain early in the sixteenth century. But here we bring our studies of prehistory to a close, for in the Era of Cyclical Conquests writing was developed (see pages 637–641) and history begins. The classicist takes over from the anthropologist.

SUMMARY

The end of the fourth glaciation brought a new type of adaptive response from *Homo sapiens sapiens.* He shifted from predominant reliance on predatory hunting of big game to intensive exploitation of the vegetative and small-game and fish potentials of his local environment, developing thereby the Mesolithic Era of Intensive Foraging. In the Mediterranean, the Natufian tradition is the best-known exemplification of the Mesolithic. In Africa, it is the Khartoum, and in North Europe where a forest environment prevailed, it is the Maglemosean. In North America, a specialized form of the Mesolithic existed from 10,000 B.C. to A.D. 1850 in the Desert Culture west of the Rocky Mountains. The Mesolithic of the Archaic traditions in the eastern woodland areas developed regional and local manifestations of rich variety, with a focus on "forest efficiency." The mano and metate are the hallmarks of the era (except in the Maglemosean of the North European forests), plus the introduction of woven fibers for baskets and nets.

The Mesolithic Era of Intensive Foraging evolved very quickly (over the span of a few thousand years) into the Early Neolithic Era of Incipient Agriculture, which rested upon hoe cultivation of newly domesticated plants

and the transformation of wild beasts of prey into household domestics.

Old World domestication led to the development of a number of farinaceous cereals, of which wheat and barley were first and basic. In the New World, the focus was on maize, amaranth, squashes, and beans. The Old World also developed its own legumes. The dog was domesticated in both hemi-

Fig. 10-18   Bronze Age pictographs from Sweden showing domestic cattle used in plow agriculture; a "Viking" crew with a big chief; and a charioteer with his team of horses.

spheres, but the Old World provided more domesticable animals, such as cattle, sheep, goat, pig, cat, and horse; and hence, pastoralism emerged as an important secondary environmental adjustment there.

Over a span of several millennia, the small, settled farming village of the Era of Incipient Agriculture gave rise to towns as centers of political and religious operations, staffed by priests and chiefs, along with their subordinates. Specialization in crafts contributed to the development of the towns as market centers. As efficiency of production was stepped up through the Era of Regional Development and Florescence, cities emerged in many parts of the Mediterranean, South Asia, and China. The urban revolution was on, and civilization was achieved. Complex social structures on a broad level of integration produced a new order of living for man. Writing was invented, and the replacement of the prehistoric tribal world of nonliterate, hunting, and gathering primitive men by the historic world of simple gardeners and urban handicrafters, organized and managed by a literate elite of priests and military leaders, was underway. Civilization was born and mankind was caught up in the first great cultural transformation since australopithecine times. Today, he is caught up in the second, and greater—the transformation from the Age of Civilization to the newly born Atomic Space Age, the emergent opening phase of which we shall call the Era of Surbanization (see pages 678–685).

SELECTED READINGS[27]

Adams, R. M., *The Evolution of Urban Society: Early Mesopotamia and Prehistoric Mexico* (1966). Parallels and deviations in evolutionary patterns in the urban revolutions of the Old and New Worlds.

Braidwood, R. J., and G. R. Willey (eds.), *Courses toward Urban Life* (1963). Contains many excellent

[27]Titles marked with an asterisk (*) are paperback reprints of abridged and updated chapters from Stuart Piggot (ed.), *The Dawn of Civilization: The First World Survey of Human Civilization in Early Times* (1961).

papers covering the manifestations of the eras of intensive foraging and incipient agriculture in all parts of the world. Each paper is written by an outstanding, pioneering expert in the field.

*Bushnell, G. H. S., *The First Americans: The Pre-Columbian Civilizations* (1968). Magnificently illustrated in color, with brief, simple text.

Childe, V. G., *The Dawn of European Civilization* (6th ed., rev., 1958). The classic statement of Childe's thesis.

Clark, G., *World Prehistory: A New Outline* (2d rev., 1969). A comprehensive description of many specific cultures that manifest the transition to the Early Neolithic. It is clearly written and recommended as a more extensive treatment of the subject than could be provided in this introduction to anthropology.

Flannery, K. V., "The Ecology of Early Food Production in Mesopotamia" (*Science,* vol. 147, no. 3663, 1965), pp. 1247–1256. Collates data and new theory in a useful synthesis.

Frankfort, H., *The Birth of Civilization in the Near East* (1951). A scholarly treatment that relates classical archaeology to Braidwood's researches. More up to date than Childe's work.

Jennings, J. R., *Prehistory of North America* (1968). Highly recommended for its treatment of the Late Paleolithic big-game hunters, the Archaic foragers, and the formative stage (Neolithic Era of Intensive Agriculture) as manifest in Mexico and the United States.

Kenyon, K., *Digging up Jericho* (1957). Exactly what the title says.

*Lloyd, S., *Early Highland Peoples of Anatolia* (1968). Richly illustrated, brief summary of the Bronze Age civilizations, especially the Hittite in Turkish Asia Minor.

MacNeish, R. S., "The Origin of New World Civilization" (*Scientific American,* vol. 211, no. 5, 1964), pp. 29–37. A popular and well-illustrated account of the discoveries in Tehuacán Valley, Mexico, and the cultural series that led to emergent civilization in the New World.

*Mallowan, M. E. L., *Early Mesopotamia and Iran* (1965). Chapter 3 (pp. 59–71) presents a clear description of Sumerian writing on clay tablets. The riches of Ur are well portrayed.

Meadow, R. H., "The Emergence of Civilization," in H. L. Shapiro (ed.), *Man, Culture, and Society*, (rev. ed., 1971), Chapter 5. A somewhat more detailed summary than that presented in this text.

Piggot, S. (ed), *The Dawn of Civilization: The First World Survey of Human Civilizations in Early Times* (1961). A luxury volume with full texts covering early civilizations of the Mediterranean, the Indus, China, Southeast Asia, and America, written by England's leading specialists.

Ribiero, D., *The Civilizational Process* (1968). A new and sweeping formulation of trends and types of civilizations in an evolutionary synthesis from the first agricultural revolution to the Atomic-Space Age. A modernization of V. Gordon Childe's book.

*Watson, W., *Early Civilization in China* (1966). From the Paleolithic through the Bronze and Iron Ages in China.

*Wheeler, M., *Civilizations of the Indus Valley and Beyond*. From Mohenjo-daro and Harrapa to the Persians and Greeks in the Indian subcontinent.

Willey, G. R., *An Introduction to American Archaeology*, vol. 1 (1966). Authoritative, simple, and elegant. Chapter 3 (pp. 78–177) is particularly recommended for those who wish to follow through on the development of civilization in Middle America.

Zeuner, F. E., *A History of Domesticated Animals* (1963). Discusses the basic facts relating to the domestication of each variety of animal all across the board, including birds, fishes, and insects.

Chapter 11

Human Variability and Race

All the living members of the hominid family form one genus and one species, named *Homo sapiens.* Within this single species there are no two individuals (except for identical twins) who are exactly alike in genetic make-up. Attend any gathering of human beings and it is easy to observe that there is much variability within the general similarity of all those present. Beyond the variability of a local group, any world traveler can observe different clusters of physical traits in different populations. Such populations are what are commonly referred to as the races of man-

kind, or, in taxonomic terms, as subspecies within the species *Homo sapiens.*

Reasons for Studying Human Variability

Anthropologists study human variability and the geographic distribution of human genetic traits for several reasons. First, since the clusters of variations, called "races," seem to be central to many of the world's social and political problems, it is desirable to separate

Fig. 11-A United Nations leaders at the UN General Assembly. (United Nations.)

the biological aspects of race from the cultural ones. Only then can the two aspects of human variability be rationally analyzed and sensibly controlled. The well-being of man requires this consideration at the very least. Second, by determining just what the biological variations of human populations actually are, anthropologists and human biologists hope to be able to learn what the population mechanics are which differentiate individuals and groups from one another. Third, by studying the geographic and ethnic lumpings and the distributions of variable traits, the natural and cultural processes leading to the prominence of certain traits over and against others in human populations may be discovered.

In Chapter 5 the mechanisms which produce genetic variability in persons and populations were summarized as the foundation of organic structure and evolution. We are now interested in what it is that produces differences in species subgroups within *Homo sapiens sapiens*.

Closed and Open Genetic Systems: Species and Subspecies

In Chapter 5 a Mendelian population was defined as a localized grouping of members of a species who interbreed mostly among themselves but occasionally with members of sister populations within the species. A species was defined as one or more populations whose members are capable of intrabreeding among themselves, while at the same time they are incapable of interbreeding with members of other species, or they do not habitually do so. Put in other words, this involves: (1) community of inheritance among the members, (2) capacity of the genes to spread throughout the group, and (3) inhibition of the gene spread to other groups.[1]

[1] I. M. Lerner, *Heredity, Evolution, and Society*, p. 16.

Each species is, therefore, genetically isolated from all other species. It is a *closed genetic system*. Members of the species *Homo sapiens* are incapable of interbreeding with any other animal.

Within a species, however, populations may be found which possess gene pools in which certain genes occur in frequencies different from the frequencies of these in other populations. These populations may be distinguished as subspecies, or races. They have same differing inheritances, or gene pools. However, the members of the two populations are not incapable of interbreeding and exchanging genes. They are *open genetic systems* (Figure 11-1). Within a species, genetic systems by their very nature can be readily altered by genetic inputs from other populations; they can also initiate their own genetic changes which are not just the result of mutations.

If the changes within a gene pool of a subspecies population accumulate to the point where exchanges of genetic materials can no longer take place with other subspecies populations, then the two populations have become, by definition, separate and distinct species. There is no evidence that any such genetically isolated subgroups of *Homo sapiens* have existed since Middle Pleistocene times, and that is why we can say there is only one species of man, *Homo sapiens*.

When it is realized that there are no closed genetic systems within a species, the problems of classifying patterns of human variation can be conceived of as two-pronged. First, there is classification of human beings into categories according to genetic traits that seem to cluster coincidentally with geographic and/or ethnic limits of populations. This kind of classification results in the identification of subspecific, or racial, groups. The other line is to define and determine the geographic distribution or gradients of single-trait variants as such without regard to any defined population groupings, geographical or ethnic. The process of trait-variant mapping is called *clinal* identification, and it represents a new anthropological approach to the study of human variability.

Natural Selection and Clinal Distribution

Natural selection is only one process by which the composition of gene pools may be altered. It is, however, the major process by which populations achieve more efficient adaptation to specific environments. Some genes in a Mendelian population are either selected for, and hence retained in the gene pool, or they are selected against, and hence are greatly reduced in frequency or eliminated altogether. Naturally selected genetic traits may or may not coincide in distribution with the geographically localized populations which are called races. For example, although sickle-cell anemia (pages 112–114) has much the highest gene frequency in the African and Afro-American populations, it also occurs in other populations living within 15 to 30 degrees on either side of the equator. The frequency distribution of sickle-cell genes is clearly related to the prevalence of malaria and is not exclusively a Negroid trait. It cuts across a number of geographically defined racial groupings.

Three Rules of Bodily Adaptation to Geographical Environment There are other traits which have variable manifestations in greater or lesser degrees of distribution and which are believed to be linked to adaptive functions through natural selection. They include pigmentation, body size, and relative prominence of protruding body parts. These relations are generalized in Gloger's, Bergmann's, and Allen's rules.

1. *Gloger's rule.* "In mammals and birds, races which inhabit warm and humid regions have more melanin pigmentation than races of the same species in cooler and drier re-

gions; arid regions are characterized by accumulation of yellow and reddish-brown phaeomelanin pigmentation."

2. *Bergmann's rule.* "The smaller-sized geographic races of a species are found in the warmer parts of the range, the larger-sized races in the cooler districts."

3. *Allen's rule.* "Protruding body parts, such as tails, ears, bills, extremities, and so forth, are relatively shorter in the cooler parts of the range of the species than in the warmer parts."[2]

Gloger's Rule and the Skin Color of Man Do tropic dwellers in fact have more melanin pigment than those who inhabit colder and drier climates?

Most human beings have relatively light-colored skin, which, if not covered by clothing, tans in strong light as a response to natural ultraviolet radiation. Those exposed constantly to sunlight become quite dark the year round. Those who live in middle latitudes go through an annual cycle of skin coloring, tanning in the summer and bleaching in the winter. In order to ascertain the standard (unmodified) skin color of a person, skin-color tests must be taken on the underside of the upper arm, near the armpit.

Dark skin color results from high melanin content. It is fairly constant and subject to little or no seasonal variation. The original geographic distribution of this genetic trait is along the tropic regions of the Old World within 10 to 20 degrees of the equator (Figure 11-2).

Of several hypotheses which have been advanced to provide functional explanations of racial skin color among human populations, the one that applies the physiological effects of vitamin D is the most impressive.

Vitamin D is necessary to the absorption of calcium from the human intestine. Calcium is necessary to bone building and maintenance. Vitamin D deficiency results in soft

[2] C. S. Coon, "Climate and Race," in H. Shapley (ed.), *Climatic Change*, p. 14.

bones and rickety bodies. Ordinary diets do not of themselves provide enough of the vitamin to maintain calcium absorption at an adequate level. Prior to the discovery of vitamin D enrichment of foods, the only possible way to overcome a dietary insufficiency of this vitamin was the manufacture of it by the human body itself, stimulated by absorption of ultraviolet rays from sunlight. However, too much vitamin D (hypervitaminosis D) causes calcification of soft tissues as well as being contributory to skin cancer. The latter attribute should have no effect on natural selection, however, since it usually operates late in life after the reproductive period is ended. Calcification of the soft tissues could eliminate those people who are overreactive to ultraviolet radiation in vitamin D production, and their kind could be selected out of populations living in areas of intensive sunshine. It is hypothetically suggested that "in equatorial latitudes the danger was in too much, rather than too little, absorption of ultraviolet rays and therefore in too much vitamin D production.[3]

In the nonforested regions of the tropics, the functional adaptive usefulness of black or near-black skin under the high and constant equatorial sun is clear. However, much of the equatorial region in which the black peoples live is gloomy rain forest and has been so in the past, at least in postglacial times. Much larger areas of the world are open parkland, desert, and water. It is here that the adaptation of black skin was probably effected, rather than in the jungles. In the Americas, the Amazon valley is jungle, and the more open areas of the western equatorial region have a heavy, permanent cloud cover. This, and the fact that the local populations have not been very long in these regions, should account for the absence of black pigment in the aboriginal New World.

At the opposite extreme of the color spectrum is the sunburning, nontanning variety of skin that is confined to a very small minority of the world population which is located in the cloudy areas of northwestern Europe. For them, the prehistoric conditions of natural selection were reversed. Those who did not get enough ultraviolet rays because of dark skin color became undercalcified. They did not survive to pass their genetic heritages back into the gene pool. Northland populations thus became progressively less pigmented as those whose melanin production was lower survived at a higher ratio.

Bergmann's Rule and Human Body Size Bergmann's rule for warm-blooded animals expresses the fact that the smaller the skin area relative to total body volume, the lower the

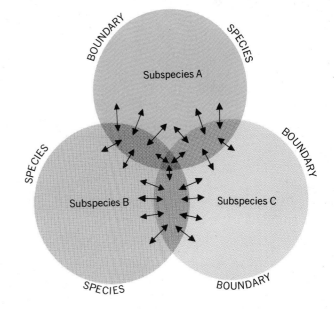

Fig. 11-1 A species is a closed genetic system. Its members are incapable of interbreeding with those of other species; therefore, it receives no genes from any other species. On the other hand, the Mendelian populations which constitute subspecies, or races, are open genetic systems. Although the members of a subspecies usually intrabreed, they are capable of interbreeding within the species; hence some genes are transmitted from one subspecies to another.

[3]I. M. Lerner, *op. cit.*, p. 32.

loss of body heat, and vice versa. A short and stocky Eskimo physique conserves body heat, while the long, lanky physique of the Nilotic Negro (Figure 11-3, right) helps to dissipate it. Here in the United States, stature may differ by race (see Figure 11-4). Differences in the numbers of sweat glands and capillary control of blood flow are also significant factors. Bergmann's rule applies with moderate consistency to human beings. Heavier populations are concentrated in the north, while slighter ones are found in equatorial regions (except for Pacific Islanders, who bask in the very comfortable trade winds).

Allen's Rule and Human Bodily Extremities   The shape of the protruding parts of the body facilitates or inhibits heat loss and heat retention. Populations in hot climates do have larger extremities. Desert Negroes as well as desert Caucasoids have long limbs and slim torsos. The forehead and hands are the concentrated sweat areas. A long, narrow head and long hands function to effect heat dissipation, which is especially important for the brain. Negro populations are uniformly long-headed and long-handed. Heat control in the hands and feet is more than a matter of sweating, however. The capillary system in the hands acts like the thermostat at the head of the engine block in a water-cooled automobile, which controls the flow of water to the radiator according to temperature. In high temperatures, arterial blood returning to the heart flows through the close-to-the-

Fig. 11-2   Worldwide distribution of intensity of pigmentation (color) of skin, according to Biasutti. (Adapted from Coon, **The Living Races of Man,** *with permission of A. Alfred Knopf.)*

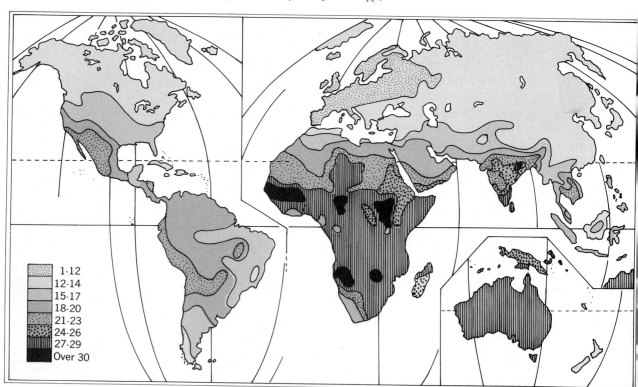

1-12
12-14
15-17
18-20
21-23
24-26
27-29
Over 30

Fig. 11-3   The long-limbed Batutsi of Burundi (right), with their small torsos, exemplify bodily adaptation to hot climates. This body shape produces the largest heat-dissipating skin area relative to total body volume. On the other hand, the short-limbed Arctic Mongoloids, such as the Chuchki female (left), with their large, heavy torsos, exemplify bodily adaptation to cold climates. This body shape produces the smallest skin area relative to body volume. Surface radiation is minimal and body heat is more effectively preserved. (Right, United Nations; left, courtesy of the American Museum of Natural History.)

surface veins on the back of the hand. When the temperature drops below a critical threshold, vasoconstriction shuts down the flow to the surface arteries, while vasodilation opens it to the deeper-lying ones. Thus internal heat, carried in the blood, is conserved. Recent experiments indicate population differentials related to environment in this respect.

The cranial features of Mongoloid populations are all thought to be adaptations to the extreme cold: round heads; flat cheekbones; small, flat noses; heavy layers of subcutaneous fat; and fatty double eyelids, which produce the characteristic Mongoloid internal epicanthic fold, or almond-shaped eye (see Figure 11-5). Theoretically, these adaptations took place among the Northeast Asian populations during the Upper Pleistocene. They are, of course, highly characteristic of Eskimos and many other North Asian local populations.

Thus, a number of kinds of human variability have been tentatively associated with the effects of selective adaptation in relation to the ecological characteristics of the differ-

Fig. 11-4   The statures of Navaho and white American girls of college age compared. Although there is overlapping in the stature of individuals, white girls are taller on the average than are the Navaho.

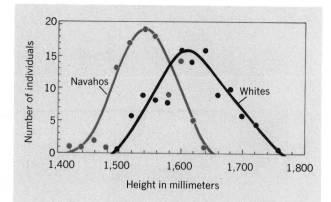

ing environments of various populations.[4] It is also true that experimental observations have thus far been too limited, and research techniques too underdeveloped, to make it possible to account for all geographically patterned distributions of human variations in terms of naturally selected traits. Further, some naturally selective forces are not necessarily limited to one, or even a few, restricted geographical locations. Consequently, the traits they might select for (such as the malarial influence on the distribution of sickle-cell anemia) cannot be used as distinguishing traits for continentally (or even less broadly) distributed major geographic races.

In summary, one of the mechanisms which produce variation in gene frequencies between populations *is* the process of natural selection. This process can produce geographically patterned variation of the type associated with geographic races, if the selective factors occur in geographic patterns. But at the same time, some population variations which are due to environmentally selective factors may not coincide with geographic differences between, or within, continents. They may be found in geographically isolated populations which otherwise are referred to as separate races.

Clinal Studies, the Nonrace Theory, and Selective Trait Patterning In *clinal study* individual traits are analyzed and the geographic distribution of their variants is mapped. Figure 11-2 offers an example of this method. It shows the worldwide distribution of intensity of epidermal pigmentation (skin color) as plotted by the Italian geographer R. Biasutti. The lines, which are called *clines,* are smoothed curves connecting geographic locations from which similar degrees of skin color have been reported. In conception, it is similar to a conventional weather map with its isobars which run through

[4]See P. T. Baker, "The Biological Adaptation of Man to Hot Deserts," in T. W. McKern (ed.), *Readings in Physical Anthropology,* pp. 174–185.

weather stations reporting similar baromet-ric readings. There are two related purposes to a clinal approach.

Clinal distributions of several traits can be mapped all together to determine if sev-eral traits have coincidental geographical distributions of their variants. Such cluster-ing might be the product of geographically related forces of natural selection acting in unison on the variants of several traits. So far, analysts, such as the physical anthropol-ogist Frank Livingstone, seem to think that no such coincidental clusterings have been de-termined and that this fact demonstrates the lack of significant correlation between geographically distributed populations and naturally selected traits. In one sense this implies that there are no significant Men-delian populations within *Homo sapiens. The logical extension of this point of view would be that biologically there are no races of man-kind.* Rather, it would hold that humanity constitutes one large, intraspecific gene pool.[5]

The implications of separating the con-sideration of naturally selective trait pattern-ing (revealed in the correlation of clines to environments) from the identification of geographically located Mendelian popula-tions must then be understood as a product of two processes which cause trait patterns. First, naturally selected traits can produce geographical patterning in human variation. Second, nonrandom breeding patterns of Mendelian populations can produce genetic drift (pages 113–114) in the patterning of human variation which shows geographic manifestions. It is important to perceive the two patterning processes separately. For this reason geographic racial classifications must be viewed as analytic tools to isolate and describe *general* patterns of population variations. Also, clinal studies isolate and

describe *single* trait patterns of human pop-ulation variation. Combinations of the two kinds of studies can aid in analyzing the processes which produce and pattern var-iation. Racial classification is not a scien-tific end product but rather a tool for analy-sis.

Geographic Races

The kind of population commonly meant when people talk about race is an aggre-gation of people who have inhabited in the past, and who still do inhabit to a great ex-tent, a given continent or a large section of a continent. The effect of geographic bar-riers on prehistoric populations can be seen in Figure 11–6. Such populations tend to be sufficiently isolated from the inhabitants

Fig. 11-5   Adaptation to extreme cold climate in the Arctic Mongoloid face. A Greenland Eskimo with heavy subcutaneous fat covering the cheeks, the flat nose, and heavy double eyelids. (Courtesy of the American Museum of Natural History.)

[5]F. B. Livingstone, "On the Non-existence of Human Races" (*Current Anthropology*, vol. 3, 1962), p. 297; and C. L. Brace, "On the Race Concept" (*Current Anthro-pology*, vol. 5, 1964), pp. 313–314.

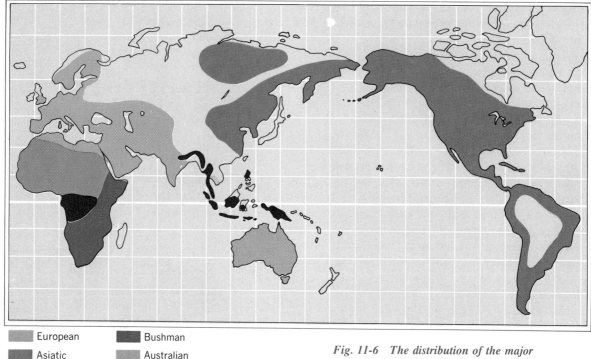

European Bushman

Asiatic Australian

African Pygmy

Fig. 11-6   The distribution of the major macrogeographic races of mankind in the Mesolithic age about 9000 B.C. The presence of glaciers limited the distribution of mankind while the interior of South America had not yet been populated. (Adapted from W. W. Howells, "The Distribution of Man," in W. S. Laughlin and R. H. Osborne (eds.), **Human Variation and Origins.***)*

of other continents so that they have more common ancestors among themselves than they share with other populations on other continents.

In current anthropological usage, such races are called *geographic races.* A geographic race is a human population that has inhabited a continental land mass or an island chain sufficiently long to have developed its own distinctive genetic composition, as compared with that of other continental populations. A modern classification of geographic races is given within the next few pages.

Local Races   Within a continent, there may be barriers to easy intermixture of the continental population. Thus, the people of the North Baltic area interbreed among themselves to a much greater extent than they do with the people of the Mediterranean belt of southern Europe. They can be distinguished as subpopulations, localized over broad areas *within* a continent or island chain. This produces a lower-level classification of races, such as the Nordic, Alpine, and Mediterranean within the European. Some physical anthropologists would push the analysis further and distinguish even more narrowly defined local races in the Balkan area, for example, where an unusual cranial shape, called "sugarloaf," and certain other physical features are common, thus identifying a so-called Armenoid race. The Basques of the Pyrenees are another good example of a local race. There is no agreement on just how many local races one could identify in the world. Garn and Coon suggest that the number might be about thirty.[6]

A Modern Classification of Geographic Races In 1950, Coon, Garn, and Birdsell proposed a classification of races based upon the idea of geographic races identifiable as Mendelian, or inbreeding, populations.[7] Garn subsequently refined the application of the concept and presented a classification of living races in nine major categories:

1. European: population of Europe, North Africa, and the Middle East, and their world-wide descendants
2. Indian: population of the Indian subcontinent
3. Asian: population of Siberia, Mongolia, China, Japan, Southeast Asia, and Indonesia
4. Micronesian: population of the western Pacific Islands from Guam to the Marshalls
5. Melanesian: population of the western Pacific Islands south of Micronesia, extending from New Guinea to Fiji
6. Polynesian: population of the eastern Pacific Islands from Hawaii to New Zealand and Easter Island
7. American: population of "Indians"
8. African: population of Africa south of the Sahara
9. Australian: population of aboriginal Australians

Garn has also formulated a classification of living local races,[8] which we have regrouped under their geographic races and renumbered as follows:

I. European
   1. Northwest European: population of Scandinavia, northern France and Germany, the Low Countries, the United Kingdom, and Ireland
   2. Northeast European: population of Eastern Baltic, Russia, and modern Siberia
   3. Alpine: population of central France, southern Germany, Switzerland, and northern Italy, to the Black Sea
   4. Mediterranean: population surrounding the Mediterranean, eastward through Asia Minor

II. Indian
   1. Indic: population of India, Pakistan, and Ceylon (Note: Garn calls this race Hindu, but inasmuch as Hindu properly identifies a religion, we feel that Indic is more appropriate.)
   2. Dravidian: aboriginal population of southern India

III. Asian
   1. Classic Mongoloid: population of Siberia, Mongolia, Korea, and Japan
   2. North Chinese: population of northern China and Manchuria
   3. Turkic: population of western China and Turkestan
   4. Tibetan: population of Tibet
   5. Southeast Asian: population of South China through Thailand, Burma, Malaya, the Philippines, and Indonesia
   6. Ainu: aboriginal population of Japan
   7. Eskimo: population of northern maritime fringe of North America and ice-free fringes of Greenland
   8. Lapp: population of arctic Scandinavia and Finland

IV. Micronesian (no local races distinguished)

[6] S. M. Garn and C. S. Coon, "On the Number of Races of Mankind" (*American Anthropologist*, vol. 57, 1955), pp. 996–1001. Also S. M. Garn, *Human Races*, chap. 2.
[7] C. S. Coon, S. M. Garn, and J. B. Birdsell, *Races: A Study of Race Formation in Man.*

[8] S. M. Garn, *Human Races*, pp. 127–132.

V. Melanesian
1. Papuan: population of mountain highlands of New Guinea
2. Melanesian: population of coastal area of New Guinea and most of the other islands in the Melanesian archipelago

VI. Polynesian
1. Polynesian: aboriginal population
2. Neo-Hawaiian: nineteenth- to twentieth-century blend of Polynesian, European, and Asiatic

VII. American
1. North American (Indian): aboriginal population of Canada and the continental United States
2. Central American (Indian); population of the Southwestern United States, Mexico, and Central America to Brazil
3. South American (Indian); population of South America except Tierra del Fuego and populations included in (2)
4. Fuegian: population around the Straits of Magellan
5. Ladino: new Latin-American population resulting from blending of Mediterranean, Central and South American (Indians), Forest and Bantu Negroes.
6. Afro-American: Colored eighteenth- to twentieth-century population blended of Northwest Europeans and Africans living mostly in North America

VIII. African
1. East African: population of the East African Horn, Ethiopia, and Nilotic Sudan
2. Sudanese: population of the Sudan, except for Nilotics
3. Forest Negro: population of West Africa and most of the Congo
4. Bantu: population of South Africa and adjacent parts of East Africa
5. Bushman-Hottentot: surviving post-Pleistocene population in South Africa
6. Pygmy: small-statured population living in the equatorial rain forests, sporadically scattered throughout Africa, Southeast Asia, Indonesia, and New Guinea
7. South African Colored: population of South Africa produced by a blend of Northwest European and Bantu, plus some Bushman-Hottentot

IX. Australian
1. Murrayian: aboriginal population of southeastern Australia
2. Carpentarian: aboriginal population of central and northern Australia

Salient Features of the Geographic and More Important Local Races

European (Formerly Caucasoid)   The European race is not actually white. It belongs to the group possessing varying pigmentation. Eye color varies from light blue to dark brown. Hair is blond to black and of fine to medium texture; it may be straight, wavy, or curly, but it is rarely kinky and never woolly. The males tend to grow hair on their chests, arms, legs, and faces as well as on their heads. The nose is narrow and high, rarely broad or flat. Although the forehead is usually sloping, the face is not prognathous. Chins tend to jut, and lips are thin. Stature is medium to tall.

Northwest European (Formerly Nordic). This population is low in pigmentation. Hair is blond, ranging from a flaxen color to light brown; eyes are blue, gray, or hazel. Head form is dolichocephalic (narrow- and long-headed); the face is also narrow and angular. Jaws and chin are usually prominent; the nose is narrow and usually high. Hair is sparse on the body and thin on the head, and it usually falls out in adult males. In form the hair is straight or wavy but seldom curly. The body is tall and slender; the torso is relatively small, and the legs are long. The chest is usually shallow and flat.

Alpine   These people are brachycephalic (roundheaded) and have broad faces with sharp, square jaws. They are brunets; eyes and hair are brown to black, and the skin is olive-hued. The nose is well padded with adipose tissue at the tip, and it tends to be broad. The body is usually solid and heavy, rarely exceeding medium stature. Alpine men grow fine dark beards, and if hair on the chest indicates masculinity, they have more of what it takes than any other Europeans.

Mediterranean   The Mediterranean is also a brunet, but unlike the stocky Alpine, he is usually small of stature. He tends to be slight in youth and fat in maturity (this applies to the female also). The race is dolichocephalic, with narrow, high foreheads unmarked by any protrusion of a supraorbital ridge. Hair is black or dark; it is usually wavy and is rarely straight. Although luxuriant on the head, it is sparse on the face, limbs, and body. Eyes are brown; the skin is light brown or pale olive. Noses are narrow and high-bridged.

Northeast European   This is a roundheaded, broad-faced population, with thin lips; gray-blue eyes; straight, light-colored hair; and light-colored skin. Stature is short and the body heavy.

Indian   The fact that India is a subcontinent isolated from the rest of Asia by vast mountain ramparts qualifies its population for consideration as a geographical race. The population is, in fact, made up of hundreds of local races and microgeographic races. Tribal and caste endogamy has split the population into numerous intrabreeding groups separated by great social distances that are more inhibiting than geographical distances. However, two major categories of local races are identified: the Indic and Dravidian.

Indic   In the north of India, skin color is variably light. In the south, it may be very dark. Stature is short, except in the extreme northwest, where there has been much European (mostly Mediterranean) intermixture.

Most Indians are brunets, and the hair is usually wavy. Body hair on males is moderately frequent. The head is almost always dolichocephalic. Eyes are dark brown and large. Body build is gracile.

In traditional classifications by anthropologists, the Indics are grouped within the Mediterranean race.

Dravidian   This population is heavily pigmented, with dark brown skin, brown eyes, and black, wavy hair. The head is dolichocephalic; the face is narrow. Stature is short (mean of 5 feet 2 inches), and the torso is slight in build. Dravidians are believed to be the archaic inhabitants of India and remotely related to the Australians.

Asian (Formerly Mongoloid)   The most outstanding Asian physical trait is the almond-shaped eye, effected by the internal epicanthic fold. The infants frequently have a unique feature, the "Mongoloid patch," which is a purplish, triangular area of skin at the base of the spine. Skin color is brown or yellowish-tan. Eyes are brown or dark brown, and the hair is black. It is very coarse and straight, growing long on the head and scarcely at all on the face or body. Most Asian populations are brachycephalic. The cheekbones are broad and high, while the nose is squat and low-bridged, thus giving a somewhat flat-faced appearance. While their body trunks are fairly long, heavy, and broad, they are usually short and squat in stature because of the shortness of their legs.

Micronesian   This population resulted from a blending of Southeast Asians and Melanesians. It is medium-statured, brown-eyed, and dark-skinned. Hair is black and frequently frizzy. The head is brachycephalic to mesocephalic.

Melanesian (formerly Oceanic Negro)   The peoples of the "Black Islands" are blackish in skin color (some are brown) and hair color. The hair is long and frizzy, head is usually dolichocephalic, and the nose is high and broad (sometimes called Semitic). Eyes are dark and set in a very prognathous face, which has notably thick lips. Body hair is scanty. Stature is medium and the body well formed.

Polynesian   When, at some future date, miscegenation blends all the races of man into one standardized variety, that variety may reasonably be expected to look somewhat like the aboriginal Polynesians. The Polynesians of today are predominantly Indic mixed with Melanesian and Southeast Asian stocks. The race is very similar to the Malayo-Indonesians except that the stronger Mediterranean heredity gives a wavy form to the hair, elongates the face and body, lightens the skin, and produces a high nose. African traits show up in a tendency to fullness of lips. The dominant roundheadedness of the Asian characterizes most Polynesians. Hair grows luxuriantly on the head, but, as is to be expected in an Indic-Asian-Melanesian mixture, it is scanty on the face and body. As well-fed islanders, they have developed large and powerful bodies.

American (formerly Amerind)   The Indians of the Americas are highly variable in stature, head form, and details of facial features. In general, however, they reveal their Asian ancestry in a predominance of brachycephaly; brown eyes; black, usually straight hair; thin lips; broad, high cheekbones; occasional internal epicanthic fold; and yellow or reddish-brown skin covering a broad and heavy body. Blood-type frequencies differ markedly from those of the Asian, however (see pages 238–239).

Afro-American   The Afro-American population (called North American Colored, by Garn) is less than 300 years old. Yet it is significantly different in its genetic composition from any existing European or African population. Although its gene pool is predominantly African in origin, its European component is high. According to the estimates of I. M. Lerner, "It seems highly probable that about 30 percent of autosomal genes in the current American Negro population is of European origin, and that the American Indian contribution is negligible."[9]

African (formerly Negro)   Africans are the possessors of the darkest pigmentation of all mankind; nevertheless, few Africans are actually black. Most are dark brown or brownish-black in skin color. Hair is prevailingly black, coarse, wiry, and tightly curled, kinky, or woolly. With few exceptions, heads are long and narrow. The occipital region juts out, as does the lower portion of the face, which in appearance is accentuated by the everted mucous membrane that forms the lips. The African nose is broad, with flaring wings and a broad, deeply depressed bridge. The hair on the head, though thick, is short in length, while the male beard is sparse; body hair is rare. Stature is medium tall. The forearm is long, and the legs tend to be thin (i.e., the calves do not ordinarily develop thick musculature).

East African   The East African is notable among Africans for his slender body build and tall stature and for his high, narrow head and straight nose.

Bushman-Hottentot   This remnant population has a dolichocephalic to mesocephalic head with a smallish, triangular face. The nose is very low and broad, beneath a low, sloping forehead. The eyes frequently have an internal epicanthic fold. Skin color is yellow-brown. The hair grows in tight "peppercorn" spirals close to the scalp. Stature averages only 5 feet. The body is slight and prone to fatty buttocks (steatopygous).

Australian   The Australian aboriginal population developed in relative isolation directly

[9]I. M. Lerner, *op. cit.,* p. 233.

from Late Pleistocene migrants. There is a strong reddish cast to the Australians' dark skin. The hairiness of their heads and bodies and the waviness of their hair indicate a strong possibility of archaic Dravidian relations.

The Australian forehead slopes back from the heaviest supraorbital ridges to be found in any surviving race. The skull is narrow and houses a brain that is notably smaller in volume than that of any other living race. The face juts forward, and the dental arches do so even more. Dark-brown eyes are set beside a deeply depressed nasal root, below which is a broad, thick nasal tip. The whole face is compressed from symphysis to nasion. The Australian is neither very short nor very tall (adult male mean, 5 feet 6 inches). He grows a slender, short body on a pair of pipestem legs.

This descriptive typology does not cover all the local races or spell out all the descriptive details, but it should serve in distinguishing the more notable populations of the world.

As Figure 11-7 shows, the European, Asiatic, and African races dominate the world scene in the twentieth century. European emigration to the Americas has largely swamped the original American population except in Middle America and central South America. Emigration has had a similar effect in Australia. Asiatics have expanded into the once-glaciated areas of their continent and southeast into Indonesia. African migration into the southwest Pacific has all but completed the extinction of the Pygmies in that part of

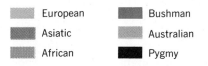

European	Bushman
Asiatic	Australian
African	Pygmy

Fig. 11-7   Distribution of the world's peoples in the twentieth century. (Adapted from W. W. Howells, "The Distribution of Man," in W. S. Laughlin and R. H. Osborne (eds.), **Human Variation and Origins.***)*

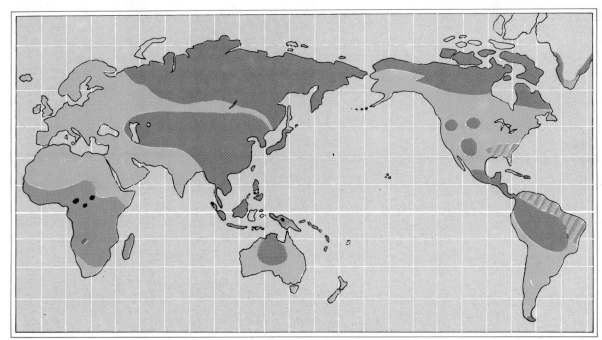

the world. The southward migration of Negro Africans in Africa has reduced the Pygmies and Bushmen to small, barely surviving remants. The world does change.

Blood Groups and Geographic Races

Almost everyone is familiar with the existence of the O, A, B, and AB blood types. Blood is classified according to its agglutinative reactions, i.e., according to whether the hemoglobin (red blood corpuscles) clump together when mixed with alien blood. Two classic blood clumpers, A and B, were the first to be isolated. They are antigen A and antigen B. Type O blood is immune to the effect of both antigens; hence it can ordinarily be used in transfusions to any other basic blood type. (O-type persons are universal donors.) Type A can be transfused to types A and AB, but not to type B. Type B can be transfused to types B and AB, but not to type A.

Soon after blood types were discovered, it was noticed that the percentage frequencies of the four types were not the same for different phenotypic races. First, it was observed that most European populations run from 40 to 50 per cent O, from 30 to 40 per cent A, from 8 to 12 per cent B, and from 1 to 6 per cent AB. In sharp contrast, some American Indian tribes revealed almost all O, little A, and virtually no B. The Utes, for example, run 98 per cent O, 2 per cent A, and zero for B and AB. As against Europeans, here is surely a clear-cut hereditary population difference. Among the Mongoloids of Asia, the samples thus far tested show roughly around 30 per cent each of O, A, and B, with a small residue of AB. Local populations within the larger geographic populations just mentioned vary in O, A, B, and AB distributions to some extent, but the major differences tend to run as indicated.[10]

The advantage of blood types as genetic criteria of race is that they are discrete traits. A type is either present or absent in a person. It is neither ambiguous, as is "olive skin," nor continuously variable, as is stature. Therefore, the gene distribution in the population for a number of blood types can be precisely calculated.

In addition to the classic blood types, numerous other agglutinators have been discovered. These include the M and N types and the Rh negative and positive, as well as several subtypes—the Lewis, Lutheran, Kell, Duffy, Kidd, and others. The distribution of the major blood-group systems, by geographical race, is shown in Table 11-1.

The A antigens have been found to fall into two subtypes, A_1 and A_2. It is significant that the A occurring in American Indians, Asiatics, Pacific Islanders, and Australoids is all A_1.

Rh-negative genes occur in about 15 per cent of Europeans. They are absent among the Asians, Australians, Pacific Islanders, and American Indians who have been tested to date. Once again, the Mongoloid affinity of the American Indian has apparently been confirmed.

Beyond blood groupings, not much progress has thus far been made in isolating easily identifiable genes for use in racial classifications. A peculiar and interesting gene is the one that determines the ability to perceive a bitter taste in phenylthiocarbamide (PTC).

The allele for tasting ability (T) is inherited as a Mendelian dominant over the nontasting allele (t). Seventy per cent of the population of the United States are tasters, and 30 per cent are nontasters. In terms of gene frequency, this means that 55 per cent of the United States population carry the t gene.[11] Within a sample of Navaho Indians, on the other hand, the proportion of nontasters is only 2 per cent. The frequency of the t allele in this Navaho population is $\sqrt{0.2}$, or 14 per

[10]For the method of calculating gene frequencies in a population, see H. H. Strandskov, "Genetics and the Origin and Evolution of Man" (*Cold Spring Harbor Symposia on Quantitative Biology,* vol. 15, 1951), pp. 1–11.

[11]The frequency of a recessive gene in the gene pool is equal to the square root of the genotypes for the recessive gene in the population: $\sqrt{0.30} = 0.55$.

Table 11-1   Distribution of Major Blood-group Systems in the
Geographic Races

Blood-group system (alleles in parentheses)	Description of phenotype frequencies
A, B, O (including A_1 and A_2)	O most common group; over 50% of individuals in most populations are of this type. B nearly absent in aboriginal America and Australia, and progressively more common in Europe (15%), Africa, India, and Asia (up to 40%). A_2 practically limited to Europe.
MNS, U (or S^u)	American Indians almost exclusively M. N most common in Australia and the Pacific. MS and NS absent in Australia. U negative rare and apparently limited to Africa.
Rh (R_1, R_2, R_0, r', r, etc.)	Rh-negative individuals (Rh) rare or absent in most of the world, but approximately 15% of Europeans are Rh-negative. Of the Rh-positive alleles (R_1, R_2, etc.), the R_0 form is found primarily in Africa (up to 70%).
Duffy (Fy^a, Fy^b, Fy)	Most Australians and Polynesians and 90–99% of Asians are Duffy-positive (Fy^a). 90% of Indics, 85–90% of most American Indians, 65% of populations of England and America, and 27% of Afro-Americans. Fy^a very low in Africa, but the gene Fy extremely common (>80%).
Diego (Di^a, Di^b)	Diego-positive (Di^a) individuals limited to Amerindians (2–20%) and Asians. Di^a absent in Europe, Africa, Australia, Micronesia, and Polynesia and in Eskimos.
Kidd (Jk^a, Jk^b)	Kidd-positive (Jk^a) most common in West Africa and Afro-Americans (>90%), North American Indians (70–90%), and Europeans (approximately 70%) and least common in Chinese (50–55%).

SOURCE: S. M. Garn, *Human Races*, p. 47.

cent. This is definitely a significant racial difference. Although not enough different populations have as yet been tested for T, t, the indications are, according to Boyd, "that the results for the tasting gene parallel in general what has already been observed for the Rh negative and A_2 genes, that is, that European populations tend to differ rather strikingly from Mongoloid populations. In both cases there is insufficient information about the Africans."[12]

In summary, on the basis of gene-frequency occurrences for various blood types and PTC, Boyd suggests five major contemporary races similar to those commonly identified by bodily traits (morphological phenotypes). These are the Caucasoid, Negroid, Mongoloid, American (Indian), and Australoid. The American is phenotypically linked to the Mongoloid in polygenic traits, but the presence of the B agglutin gene among the Mongoloids and its absence among American Indians suggest sufficient racial differentiation of the American Indians since their migration to the New World to warrant a separate racial category in genetic terms. Conversely, if races were to

[12]See W. C. Boyd, *Genetics and the Races of Man*, p. 281. F. S. Hulse, *The Human Species*, chap. 12, provides a comprehensive summary of blood-type distributions as of 1963, including a number of useful maps.

be established on the basis of specifically single-locus genes only, such as blood-group genes, the phylogenetic relation of the American Indians to the Mongoloids would never have been established.

Race and Cultural Capacity

In 1777, when the American Colonies were struggling to win their war of independence, William Robertson, the clearest thinker of the eighteenth century in terms of modern anthropology, wrote in Scotland:

A human being as he comes originally from the hand of nature, is everywhere the same. At his first appearance in the state of infancy, whether it be among the rudest savages, or in the most civilized nations, we can discern no quality which marks any distinction or superiority. The capacity of improvement seems to be the same and the talents he may afterwards acquire, as well as the virtues he may be rendered capable of exercising, depend, in a great measure, upon the state of society in which he is placed. To this state his mind naturally accommodates itself, and from it receives discipline and culture. . . . It is only by attending to this great principle, that we can discover what is the character of man in every different period of his progress.[13]

Time has not altered, nor the doctrines of racism impaired, the clarity of this simple truth.

In this century, there have been numerous efforts, beginning with the first intelligence tests administered to American soldiers in World War I, to test the validity of the proposition that there are (or are not) significant differences in the behavioral potentials of different races. After fifty years of ingenious, and also ingenuous, efforts in psychological measurements, the evidence from psychology is largely inconclusive.[14] It does, however,

demonstrate several points: (1) So-called intelligence tests measure innate skill plus cultural experience. No test has yet been evolved that can eliminate the cultural factor, and differential ratings of the various races in intelligence tests must be critically evaluated. (2) Aptitude tests do reveal racial differentials in visual, motor, and vocal skills, but these too are subject to cultural influences that have not been eliminated in tests and measurements. (3) Many skills of intelligence and aptitude definitely change when the cultural environment changes.

The whole result of scientific race psychology has been to throw the explanation of significant behavior differences among people of different races over into the field of cultural experience. The findings of psychology harmonize with those of anthropology and history, which we treat simultaneously in the next section.

Race and Culture History   It is the judgment of anthropologists that all races are equally capable of cultural development and that culture operates independently of racial heredity. How, then, it is often asked, can it be that some races are culturally more advanced than others? How does one account for the fact that the Africans did not attain civilization until it was brought to them by Europeans? Is it not true that the highest modern civilizations have been developed by the European whites?

Three principles must be grasped in formulating the answers to these questions: (1) Although all cultures are fundamentally similar in their nuclear cores, the range of cultural variability as manifested by human societies is truly remarkable. Limits to the range of culture are imposed by the physical nature of man. These limits are so basic and so generalized, however, that they are common to all races of man. The forms of variation are the result of the processes of culture growth, not of racial predisposition. (2) The behavior and cultural ingenuity of different peoples within any given race are so variable that obviously

---

[13]W. Robertson, *History of America*, vol. 1, pp. 368–369.
[14]See especially the comprehensive article by the geneticists W. F. Bodmer and L. L. Cavalli-Sforza, "Intelligence and Race" (*Scientific American*, vol. 223, 1970), pp. 19–29, who conclude (p. 29): ". . . currently available data are inadequate to resolve this question in either direction."

the racial factor can be of little importance. (3) The same people may exhibit astounding cultural energy at one period of their history and be almost wholly devoid of it at another. Peoples who have been culturally quiescent for centuries suddenly burst into a veritable fury of cultural development without any determinable change in racial composition. The Japanese are the most spectacular example in modern times.

It is easy for North Europeans and their descendants to forget how late they came to the forefront of civilization and cultural development. The centers of cultural invention did not shift to northern Europe until the Renaissance, only 500 years ago. During the Dark Ages, the Maya Indians of Central America showed greater cultural accomplishments than the European whites.

The history of the Uto-Aztecans is also pertinent. The Aztecs, Comanches, and Shoshones are all Indians who speak similar languages indicative of a common historical background. They are racially quite similar, and 700 years ago they stood as lowly hunters and gatherers at the bottom of the cultural scale, living in the western deserts of North America and possessing a meager cultural inventory. Historical events radically altered their basic characters and cultural development.

The Aztecs wandered southward until they settled in what is now Central Mexico among several long-established high cultures. In A.D. 1325, they founded Tenochtitlán (the present Mexico City), and 175 years later they were overlords of the land: maize growers, road builders, astronomers, artists, and possessors of a city with public buildings of cut stone so magnificent that Cortez cried out that in all Andalusia there was nothing to compare with the glory of this city.

The Comanches wandered into the southwestern plains at a somewhat later date. There they acquired Spanish horses and guns and came into contact with the warlike tradition of the Plains tribes. They became truculent, nomadic robbers and fighters, so vio-

lent that to this day the plainsman's saying, "as wild as a Comanche," is still heard in the West.

The Shoshones, who retained the attitudes and culture once shared with the Comanches, obtained neither guns nor horses. They were regularly mauled by the Blackfeet, who had guns and horses, so they timidly hid out in the desert—peaceable, because they dared not make war. They developed a strong inferiority complex, and they are the only Indians the author has ever worked with who welcomed the coming of the whites. "If the white man had not come, there would be no Indians left," they said. By Indians, they meant themselves.

As circumstances found them, the Aztecs and Comanches had become definitely achieving people, and the Shoshones miserable by any man's count. But race was a constant element. The accidents of culture history had frowned upon the hapless Shoshones.

What causes cultural spurts is a complex and difficult question that must be analyzed in terms of cultural process. Outstanding among the multitude of factors is cross-fertilization of cultures, the stimulation of new ideas and new ways of coping with the environment. Isolated peoples always stagnate, whether they are Asian, African, or European. But the bent of the culture is important too—a backward-looking, ancestor-worshipping culture is not readily amenable to change and further development. The physical environment is also influential. All these can be shown to be active factors. But since it cannot be shown that races differ in the possession of hereditary mentality and capacities, because the performance of different groups within a single race ranges from high to low, and because the performance of a single racial group varies so markedly through time, it becomes evident that race per se is of small moment in cultural achievement. Culture, not race, is the molder of human societies.

The UNESCO Statement on Race   In conclusion, we can do no better than cite the closing paragraphs of the *Statement on Race,* formulated in 1950 by an expert panel of physical anthropologists and geneticists convened in Paris by the United Nations Educational, Scientific, and Cultural Organization. It reads as follows:

We have thought it worth while to set out in a formal manner what is at present scientifically established concerning individual and group differences.

(*a*) In matters of race, the only characteristics which anthropologists have so far been able to use effectively as a basis for classification are physical (anatomical and physiological).

(*b*) Available scientific knowledge provides no basis for believing that the groups of mankind differ in their innate capacity for intellectual and emotional development.

(*c*) Some biological differences between human beings within a single race may be as great as or greater than the same biological differences between races.

(*d*) Vast social changes have occurred that have not been connected in any way with changes in racial type. Historical and sociological studies thus support the view that genetic differences are of little significance in determining the social and cultural differences between different groups of men.

(*e*) There is no evidence that race mixture produces disadvantageous results from a biological point of view. The social results of race mixture, whether for good or ill, can generally be traced to social factors.[15]

SUMMARY

All mankind constitutes a single species. Species are closed genetic systems in that while all normal members of the species population are capable of interbreeding, they cannot interbreed outside the species. Within the species there may be Mendelian populations which are localized groupings of species members who interbreed mostly among themselves but occasionally with members of sister populations. They represent open genetic systems.

There are two lines of approach to the study of variation in human traits. The oldest and commonly known one is to classify geographically localized populations according to clusters of genetic traits. This results in the identification of subspecies, or races. The other method is to determine the geographic gradients of isolated genetic traits according to clines. A cline is a line on a map connecting similar values of a measured trait—such as intensity of skin color, or degree of epidermal pigmentation.

Natural selection is the major process by which populations achieve more efficient genetic adaptation to specific environments. Gloger's rule states that in mammals and birds, pigmentation is more intense in warm and humid regions and lessens as one moves toward the poles. Bergmann's rule states that the warmer the range, the smaller the populations of a species are in physical size, compared to those which live in cooler regions. Allen's rule states that protruding body parts are relatively shorter in the cooler areas of a species' range than in the warmer ones. These rules appear, in general, to apply to the races of men.

However, some contemporary physical anthropologists hold that clinal mapping of several genetic traits of man do not show coincidental distribution of their variations. If this is indeed true, then it would follow that there are in fact no significant Mendelian populations within *Homo sapiens* and that there are biologically no races of mankind. The idea of race would exist as a cultural concept and a biological chimera.

Nonetheless, most physical anthropologists believe that geographically based, subspecies clusterings of populations do exist and that these may be identified as geographic and microgeographic (local) races.

The relative frequency and, in some cases, the total absence of genes for the several known blood types (for example, most Ameri-

[15]For the entire statement, see H. L. Shapiro, "Revised Version of UNESCO Statement on Race" (*American Journal of Physical Anthropology,* vol. 10, 1952), pp. 363–368.

can Indian groups are almost entirely O, with little A, and virtually no B) indicate that there *are* subspecies Mendelian populations within *Homo sapiens,* even though the influence of natural selection and geography in the distribution of most blood-group types is not yet known.

Finally, there is no scientifically demonstrated relationship between race and innate intelligence. The possibility exists theoretically, but culture history seems to demonstrate that the capacity to develop culture is quite independent of race and is the product of a number of convergent factors, particularly cross-cultural stimulation.

SELECTED READINGS

Boyd, W. C., *Genetics and the Races of Man* (1950). A thorough book by a pioneer authority in the field.

Buettner-Janusch, J., *Origins of Man* (1966), part 2 (pp. 345–624), offers a thorough and authoritative discussion of the mechanics of human biology and race.

Coon, C. S. (with E. E. Hunt, Jr.), *The Living Races of Man* (1965). The most comprehensive and interesting work on the origin, character, and distribution of contemporary races.

———, S. M. Garn, and J. B. Birdsell, *Races: A Study of Race Formation in Man* (1950). An easily understandable, short examination of selective adaptation and its effects in producing races.

Count, E. W., *This Is Race* (1950). A comprehensive selection of writing on race from all parts of the world.

Dobzhansky, T., *Mankind Evolving* (1962). Chapters 9 and 10, "Polymorphism, Class, and Caste" and "Race," are excellent discussions of race building and racial classification.

Garn, S. M., *Human Races* (1961). The most clearly written, authoritative treatment of the subject.

———, *Readings on Race* (2d ed., 1968). The readings provide clear and interesting examples of the effects of natural selection, gene flow, and genetic drift in the evolutionary development of present-day races.

Hulse, F. S., *The Human Species* (rev. ed., 1971). A good general summary with reasonable detail. Particularly useful for its summary of blood-type distributions among the populations of the world.

Kuttner, R. E., *Race and Modern Science* (1967). Particularly part 2, "The Races of Man and Human Genetics," by C. P. Oliver.

Shapiro, H. L., *Race Mixture* (1953). A genuinely authoritative treatment of the findings of science on the results of racial interbreeding.

UNESCO, *The Race Concept* (1952). A balanced evaluation of the idea of race: what it is and what it is not.

Part 3   The Material Base of Culture

Chapter 12

Food Getting

Man eats to live. The cravings of hunger are sensory stimuli which provoke the organism into food-getting activities. Ingestion of food is an absolute necessity to the maintenance and functioning of every living organism. Food as fuel to be released as energy is necessary to bodily action. Food as repair material to replace the continuous loss of substance from the body is necessary to bodily maintenance. True foods are either energy yielders or nonenergy yielders which supply inorganic materials for body replacement. Man must get an adequate intake of both. In addition, he must take in indigestible materials, called roughage, to assist the passage of true food and its residues through the alimentary canal.

Food getting is a physical imperative; subsistence, a fundamental interest; and hunger, a diffuse primary drive.

Any society which fails to develop at least minimal subsistence techniques is doomed. The ghost of Malthus haunts all mankind. In the ghastly light of the twentieth-century population explosion, the ghost becomes ever more restless.

The subsistence resources available to a people depend upon three factors: natural environment, population, and culture. People who subsist by gathering roots, berries, seeds, and insects are for the most part directly dependent upon what the natural environment offers for the taking. People who have acquired the techniques of planting, cultivating, and harvesting crops, or of the husbandry of animals, and who have mastered methods of cooking or otherwise changing the chemicophysical substance of natural products so as to make them useful or more desirable as foods, are less directly dependent upon the natural offerings of their physical environment. As man learns to expand his food-producing resources through cultural techniques and devices, he pushes back the specter of starvation and lays the base for the expansion of society, but only insofar as food production can keep ahead of population increase.

Fig. 12-A   Andaman Islander, located in the Indian Ocean, fishing with bow and arrow. (Courtesy of the American Museum of Natural History.)

Cultural Ecology

Ecology is the study of the reciprocal relations between organisms and their environments. What does a specific environment offer in mineral resources, water, air temperatures, surface features, and plant and animal life? What biological equipment does the organism in question possess? How well- or ill-adapted is it to the environment in which it finds itself? In other words, what are its relations to the environment in ingesting air, water, and minerals (foodstuffs), and what is its effectiveness in converting them into life-maintaining energy (the metabolic process)? What are its spatial arrangements relative to the physiographic characteristics of the environment and to all other living things which impinge upon it, directly or indirectly? With whom does it cooperate for mutual aid (symbiosis)? With whom and with what must it contend for survival as exploiter or exploited?

Organic evolution, we know, has produced many highly specific plant and animal adaptations to particular and peculiar ecological niches. Even man, as we have seen in the last chapter, shows intraspecies adaptations to intense environmental selective pressures. These are manifest in body form, skin color, the presence or absence of sickle-cell genes, specific blood types, and varieties of diseases —to name only a small handful of several hundred possibilities. Increasingly, however, as man has progressed through time, he has interposed culture as an intermediary adaptive mechanism by means of which he links himself to his environment. *Human ecology* is concerned with the ways in which man relates to his surroundings and the effect his activities have on the natural and social environments.[1] In the current crisis of potential overpopulation with its severe environmental strains, exacerbated by stepped-up industrial exploitation and negative feedback of wastes into the environment, human ecology has suddenly become a popular issue, taking on the emotional overtones of a holy war.

Environmental Determinism   Culture works on environments, but environments impose limits on cultures. For example, the natural environment does not absolutely determine the type of housing a people will employ, but it does define their possibilities. Igloos are not built on deserts; nor are thatched-palm pile dwellings found in the arctic. In a positive sense, as will be seen in Chapter 14, certain types of housing do correlate with particular kinds of environment. The same is true of basic subsistence techniques. The natural environment limits but does not wholly determine the nature of the foodstuffs a human population can enjoy. The complexity and efficiency of each technological culture are of tremendous significance. Ingenuity in fishing, for example, is apparent in the traps on the Congo River (Figure 12-1). In a stable adjustment to the limits of marginal desert living, the prehistoric food foragers of the Desert Culture in the Great Basin of North America eked out a meager but surviving existence for 11,000 years. In that limiting environment, both the technology and the social organization of these people, as well as all other aspects of their culture, remained simple and undeveloped. Yet, prehistoric Pueblo Indians, equipped with domesticated plants and sophisticated gardening techniques, were able to penetrate, and establish themselves in, some parts of the Great Basin.[2] Given a sufficiently developed technology and the elaborated social system to go with it, deserts can be made to bloom, hothouses can be maintained in the arctic, and ice cream can be frozen on a Pacific isle.

---

[1]O. C. Stewart, for example, has shown how the Indians' practice of setting fire to the prairies drove back the forests in North America. See his "Fire as the First Great Force Employed by Man," in W. L. Thomas (ed.), *Man's Role in Changing the Face of the Earth,* pp. 115–133.

[2]A. L. Kroeber, in *Cultural and Natural Areas of Native North America,* provides an excellent and detailed analysis of the geographic areas of North America and the varieties of aboriginal cultures found in each of them.

The Navaho and Pueblo Indians The cultural ecology of the Navaho and Pueblo Indians aptly illustrates the significance of total cultural character and focus in a people's use of their environment. These tribes share the same part of the southwestern desert in New Mexico and Arizona. They have been neighbors ever since the Navahos moved down from Canada some 1,000 years ago. Both tribes practice gardening and pastoralism, and yet their utilization of the environment and their social systems are very different. The Pueblo Indians of today live in compact masonry villages housing 100 to 1,500 people (see pages 302–305). Most of their villages have remained stationary for centuries. They garden with intensive proficiency and exhibit more interest in religious and ceremonial control of weather and crop fertility than they do in the mechanics of gardening itself. Dominance of the group over the individual is tight and relentless. The political system is that of a totalitarian theocracy.

The Navahos, on the other hand, live in widely dispersed hogans (semisubterranean earth lodges; see pages 290, 305), and their main interest is fixed upon sheep. They also garden, but in only a minor way. They do virtually nothing about weather control or crop fertility. Their interests in the supernatural rest in the maintenance of personal health. Until recent times,[3] they had no centralized government, nor even chiefs. Their social system is loose and highly atomistic. Navahos and Pueblos in personality, life styles, and social organization, are as unlike as night and day, despite their identical physical environment.

Both are limited in their gardening to natural water courses, since the annual rainfall is meager. Both do some hunting, but neither could make hunting a major subsistence source, for game is too sparse in their environment. Obviously, neither tribe makes or uses boats or does any fishing. But these are negative examples of environmental limitation. The number and degree of differences, and especially the elaborate richness of Pueblo culture, however, show how much more important in cultural ecology are the quality and degree of development of the culture itself than the mere physical environment.

Levels of Subsistence Techniques: The Evolutionary Sequence

In Part 2, as we followed the evolutionary development of man and culture, we saw how the australopithecines and Early Man lived by hunting and gathering for two million years of Paleolithic existence throughout the Ice Age. Then, shortly after the end of the Pleistocene, when *Homo sapiens sapiens* was fully established, he quickly shifted to intensive foraging

Fig. 12-1 Fish traps at Stanley Falls on the Congo River, near Stanleyville, Congo. Elaborate, reinforced scaffolding of lashed poles to support the basket weirs attests to a high degree of cooperative organization and technical skill. (Courtesy of the American Museum of Natural History.)

[3]Under the influence of the Indian Reorganization Act of 1934 (the so-called New Deal for Indians), the Navahos organized as a federally chartered corporation and have operated under a tribal council since that time.

as a new way of life in the Mesolithic Era. Out of the new preoccupation with seeds and symbiotic animals, the Neolithic Era of Incipient Agriculture, with its domesticated plants and animals, quickly followed. The urban revolution was generated and social organization was transformed from primitive to civilized. Subsistence was on a new base. In the following Bronze and Iron Ages, draft animals were linked to the newly developed plow. At this time, intensive agriculture supplanted incipient agriculture (hoe culture or gardening).

In areas not readily adaptable to gardening, some peoples intensified their reliance upon domesticated animals as a source of food energy, thus inventing pastoralism as a way of life. As a subsistence base, pastoralism is neither earlier nor later than incipient agriculture in evolutionary emergence. (Remember that Tepe Sarab was a herders' campsite of the same age as Jarmo, only 100 miles to its east; see page 211). Pastoralism is an alternative form of ecological adaptation designed for a specialized environment.

Each successive food-producing system has, in the main, increased the food energy available per capita in inverse ratio to the amount of work energy expended in producing it. This means that increasing surpluses of energy are made available for other social uses. Whether these surpluses will be utilized, and how, will depend upon the values and goals which come to characterize a people's culture. But, in general, stepping up the ladder of subsistence technologies does result in increased levels of social complexity and heterogeneous integration, and in diversity of specialized functions, functionaries, and organization. The simpler societies are more primitive in that the subsistence techniques on which they rely were the first to be developed in prehistoric times. They are also more primitive in their relative lack of complexity and internal differentiation. These are in turn functions of the size of the population supportable by existing subsistence resources.

The levels of subsistence techniques arranged from bottom to top in the order of their evolutionary priority *and* increasing complexity of cultural integration can be summarized as follows:

4. Intensive agriculture (plow culture)
3. Incipient agriculture (gardening/hoe culture) and pastoralism
2. Intensive foraging
1. Hunting and gathering

Modern Distribution of Subsistence Technologies   In 10,000 B.C. all human populations were hunters and/or gatherers.

By 7000 B.C. intensive foraging had taken hold in North Africa, Asia Minor, and South Asia, in the Old World; and in the Desert and Archaic Cultures of the New World.

By 3000 B.C. civilizations based upon incipient agriculture were well underway in the Mediterranean and the South and East Asiatic belts of the Old World; and in Nuclear America (the area of high cultures which extended from northern Mexico to the southern Andes).

After A.D. 1500, when Columbus had opened all the world to European exploration, Murdock estimates, perhaps only 15 per cent of the earth's surface was still occupied by hunters and gatherers.[4] There were no hunting and gathering *or* foraging peoples left in Europe or the Mediterranean areas. On the edges of Greenland, Eskimos clung to their precarious hunting existence. The Lapps had become intensive reindeer pastoralists. Across the north of Siberia, the Yukaghir, Samoyed, and Tungus continued as hunters who also herded reindeer.

Africa was given over wholly to pastoralists and food-growing peoples, except for the Bushmen, Congo Pygmies, and a few other scattered groups. All Indonesians, except for a few small groups, were gardeners or agriculturalists.

Agriculture in the Old World attained a

[4]G. P. Murdock, "The Current Status of the World's Hunting and Gathering Peoples," in R. B. Lee and I. de Vore (eds.), *Man the Hunter*, p. 13.

continuous distribution from Europe, around the Mediterranean and well into Africa, and across India and South Asia.

In North America, although hunting and gathering predominated, all the prairie and eastern woodland tribes south of the Great Lakes and the St. Lawrence River raised some maize, beans, and squashes. The Indians of the Southwest were intensive gardeners and growers of maize.

Even in the Great Plains, settled villagers gardened in the river bottoms, and there were few hunting tribes on the far reaches of the Plains themselves. Hunting and foraging were characteristic of California, the Great Basin desert, the woodlands of Canada, and the arctic wastes inhabited by the Eskimos. Texas and northern Mexico were still mostly exploited by food foragers, but most of Central and South America was given over to horticulture.

Throughout the Pacific the islanders were gardeners and fishers, except for natives in Australia and Tasmania and small enclaves of Pygmies. Only in Australia did hunting and gathering survive as the dominant form of food getting. However idyllic the "natural existence" of the primitive hunter and gatherer may seem to the city-bound romantic, human beings have readily abandoned it for more reliable food sources whenever the cultural opportunity has been offered. (See also Chapter 10.)

By the nineteenth century, Neolithic and Iron Age gardening and agricultural techniques had so diffused around the world that, of the 863 selected cultures in Murdock's *Ethnographic Atlas,* analyzed by Bourguignon and Greenbaum,[5] only a residual 26 per cent were "heavily dependent" on hunting, fishing, and gathering as a combined subsistence base. In contrast, nearly 72 per cent were gardeners or agriculturalists who used these modes of production for 25 per cent or more of their subsistence. Even more im-

portant, two-thirds of all the cultures of the world had become dependent on horticulture or agriculture for more than half their subsistence requirements. We emphasize this because Americans are apt to be misled by their image of American Indians as representative of non-European peoples in the world at large. Nine out of ten North American cultures were still those of hunters and gatherers, while this was true of seven out of ten South American cultures. In spite of the high cultures based on intensive agriculture in Middle America and the Andes, the New World was clearly lagging far behind the Old in the development and spread of advanced subsistence techniques.

Animal husbandry definitely shows up as a secondary, rather than a primary, food source. A mere 2 per cent of the 863 cultures were pastoral to the degree that they relied on herds of domesticated animals for three-fourths or more of their food. All but one of these cultures were concentrated in the Mediterranean and Asiatic areas. On the other hand, virtually every African culture included the care and use of some domesticated animals for food. In Oceania, the care of domestic animals in the form of pigs and water buffalo (in Indonesia) was ancillary to fishing or gardening in more than three-fourths of the subsistence economies. In the New World, in post-Spanish times, horses came to be herded by a quarter of the North American tribes, but by very few in the continent to the south.

None of the categories of subsistence techniques, it must be emphasized, is absolutely exclusive. All food economies are mixed, to a greater or lesser degree. Gardeners still hunt and fish. Pastoralists raid or exchange meat for flour. Even an atomic, industrialized society such as ours includes agriculture, pastoralism, fishing, and hunting within its activities. When we identify a subsistence economy as agricultural or pastoral, it means only that this is the predominant food source. A hunting and gathering economy is just that, however.

[5]E. Bourguignon and L. Greenbaum, *Diversity and Homogeneity,* tables 1 to 9, pp. 23–31.

Hunting

We have distinguished hunters from foragers in that the former are predominantly predatory carnivores in their subsistence habits. Man is omnivorous by nature. This more than any other single trait distinguishes him from his vegetarian hominoid relatives. The revolutionary meat-eating habit first took hold in the evolutionary development of the australopithecines. Yet hunters always rely to some extent upon berries, nuts, and roots to round out their diet. The Cheyenne Indians, for example, were great meat eaters, like other nomadic Plains Indian tribes. Nonetheless, it was the women's task to gather roots, seeds, and berries to cook with the meat. Some sixteen varieties of wild fruit, a dozen or more kinds of vegetable stalks and buds, plus eight to ten varieties of roots, were regularly included in their diet.

Weapons   It is difficult for man to down his animal victims without the aid of tools. In almost all hunting situations, he relies upon some inventive device to assist him in bringing down his quarry. Thus he uses clubs, spears, darts, arrows, deadfalls, pitfalls, snares, nets, weirs, hooks, axes, knives, and poisons to accomplish his ends. He may enlist the aid of a dog, or mount a horse or camel. He may fashion a boat to carry him (Figure 12-2). Whatever device he may use, his hunting techniques are those of assault (shooting, spearing, clubbing, axing, stabbing), trapping and snaring, the pitfall, and poisoning. Shooting, while the most commonly preferred technique among recent primitives, was probably the last of these methods to appear in human prehistory. The bow was not invented until late Paleolithic or early Mesolithic times. Paleolithic man had clubs, spears, and hand axes. While there is no direct evidence that he utilized traps and snares or pitfalls, it is likely that he had invented simple devices of this order. We know that he used fire drives in Middle Pleistocene

times, half a million years ago (pages 152–155). There is no way of knowing whether he wittingly used poisons or not.

Because it is so efficient a weapon, the bow had attained almost worldwide distribution by the seventeenth century. The skill of most primitive hunters in tracking game to bring it within bowshot is so well known as not to bear repeating here. Devices of disguise are cleverly used in some tribes. Bushmen artists have depicted disguised bowmen stalking the unwary ostrich. Western Indians were wont to wear antelope skins to approach that fleet and shy beast. To down eagles on the wing, Cheyennes hid under grass in a pit from which they slowly rotated a stick with a bit of cloth on the end. This aroused the curiosity of the king of birds, who warily soared lower and lower until the patient hunter could spring from his blind for a shot. Cheyennes also caught eagles barehandedly by luring the eagle to land on a pit blind, where he could be seized by the legs.

In the jungles of Malaysia and South America and in the woodlands of the southeastern United States, the blowgun with dart is often preferred for the hunting of small game and birds. The blowgun is a hollowed-out tube of bamboo or wood (sometimes 8 or 10 feet long), used exactly like a beanshooter. The heavy jungle growth inhibits any long-distance shooting, and in such a setting darts are often more effective than arrows, especially in South America and Indonesia, where they are poison-tipped.

Communal Hunts   Most primitive hunting involves sustained, organized group effort by bands of men, although it may engage the participation of all able-bodied women and children as well. Among Plains Indians individual hunting of bison and antelope was permitted during the fall and winter seasons, when game was hard to come by and people were widely scattered in small camps. In the late spring and summer, however, the bands came together for the great tribal ceremonies, such as the sun dance. Then they moved en masse to seek out the huge herds of buffalo. Scouts went ahead to find the herds, and the whole line of march was policed by the members of a military society. When a herd was discovered, all the hunters approached in a line from down wind, with the soldiers keeping them in order. At last, upon signal from the hunt chief they would ride out to surround the herd in an enveloping circle. If the circle was successfully closed, the bison could be run down and shot between the ribs from the right side by a bowman shooting to the left from across the neck of his rushing steed.

The Ritual of the Hunt The hunting of large animals is not usually a matter of technique pure and simple. Ritual and magic are evoked to reinforce the hunter, whose anxiety for personal safety and fear of failure are overriding. Much of the cave art left by Cro-Magnon man is eloquent, if mute, evidence of this (pages 184–187).

The Cheyenne Antelope Hunt Although the secular, soldier-policed hunt sufficed for the buffalo surround on the plains, the skittish antelope required different methods. For killing it a magic technique was used.[6] A shaman who had received his power from antelopes in vision experiences directed the hunt. Guns and bows and arrows were forbidden; only clubs could be used, indicating great antiquity for this type of hunt. After an all-night ceremony to activate his power, the shaman led the people to the open prairie. Two highly esteemed virgins were given sacred wands; they then set out in the direction of the antelope along each arm of a V path. The shaman used his power to draw the antelope into the V. After a while, two young men on fast horses rode forth on the

paths of the virgins. As they overtook the girls, they received the antelope wands, like relay runners. Behind the leaders a line of hunters on their fastest horses followed along the routes to post themselves at intervals on the sides of the V.

As soon as the horsemen were on their way, the women and children formed a circle at the foot of the V, with the shaman in the center. After several miles, the lead riders would have reached the herd; they crisscrossed behind it and rode back outside the lines of hunters. Other riders drove the antelope down the V and into the waiting circle of women and children. While the medicine man directed the movements of the animals caught within the circle, the women and children waved blankets and branches to keep them from breaking through. As panic and exhaustion immobilized the befuddled creatures, the hunters moved in with clubs to kill them. One such hunt, observed by the frontier

Fig. 12-2 An Eskimo carving in ivory portraying a kayak hunter. On the deck before the harpooner is the harpoon head ready to be fitted into the shaft at his right. The line, which is fastened to the harpoon head, is coiled around a reel from which he can pay out the line as the whale or seal dives. The large object behind the hunter is an inflated sealskin float which he will use as a drag when following his submerged game. (Private collection. Photo by Don Breneman.)

[6]The magic surround was widespread throughout the Plains, the Great Basin, and the Southwest of North America. See R. Underhill, *Ceremonial Patterns in the Greater Southwest*, pp. 28–34.

trader George Bent in 1858, produced a kill of over 600 antelope at one time.[7]

The Alaskan Eskimo Whale Cult Whaling a-mong the Eskimos and certain Northwest Coast Indians is assuredly one of the bravest and most technically skillful hunting-by-assault accomplishments of any primitive people. However, in order to reinforce his hunting skills, to give social recognition to the outstanding hunter, and merely in con-sequence of his belief in the spirit nature of whales and all the denizens of the animal world, the Alaskan made of whale hunting not only a hunt activity but also a cult of magical and religious observances.

Lantis's analysis of the Alaskan Whale Cult[8] has revealed it as a complex of techno-logical, economic, sociopolitical, magico-religious elaborations. The Whale Cult is only one example among the many that come to our attention when we observe actual sub-sistence activities by means of fieldwork.

Whale hunting, then, in addition to the actual chase, which involves skilled use of boats, paddles, harpoons, lines, and floats to locate, trail, attack, destroy, and land the great sea monster (Figure 12-3), is worked into a web of behavior and beliefs that in-cludes the following chief elements:

1. The headman of a whaling crew is a headman of the local group. Whaling leader-ship is integrated with social leadership.

2. Distribution of the parts of the whale is regulated by customary usage in accordance with which the boat owner, harpooner, and others hold particular rights.

3. Initiation into the Whale Cult is through a long, arduous period of instruction in which the young whaler learns the rituals and songs and seeks a vision.

4. Special amulets to ensure good luck are used in the whale hunt and are hidden

away in a secret cave between seasons. Knowledge of such caves and of the use of the amulet is passed from father to son.

5. Whaling songs are sung. They are pri-vate incorporeal property (see pages 284–285).

6. The season of whaling is a special ceremonial and tabu season. The whalers are isolated from the main village. They are unclean, must sleep in the open, and (in northern Alaska) must not eat raw meat.

7. Whalers must be sexually continent before and during the whaling activities.

8. All those left in the village during the actual hunt must neither sleep nor work.

9. The wife of the chief whaler must re-main quietly at home without eating, "in order to draw the whale to her."

10. Corpses or parts of the bodies of de-ceased whalers are used in ceremonial pre-paration for the hunt or are carried in the whale boat.

11. All gear must be repaired and cleansed before the onset of the whaling season; other-wise the whale will be offended.

12. When the whale is hauled ashore, it is given a symbolic drink of water by the whaler's wife.

13. As the whale is cut up, certain parts of its body are ceremonially handled, and very special rituals are performed to return the whale's spirit to the sea unangered. It is given food, and no disturbing noises are permitted.

14. The length of the ritual period following a whale killing is the same as for a human death (three to five days).

This is only a brief sketch of the Whale Cult complex, but it indicates how much more there is to hunting than tracking and killing.

Intensive Foraging

Foraging differs from gathering in the in-tensity of the dependence upon wild seeds, fruits, and roots. Instead of using wild plant life to supplement a predominantly meat

---

[7]G. B. Grinnell, *The Cheyenne Indians*, vol. I, p. 288.
[8]M. Lantis, "The Alaskan Whale Cult and Its Affinities" (*American Anthropologist*, vol. 40, 1938), pp. 438–464.

(a)   (b)

Fig. 12-3   The whale hunt.
Point Hope (a) (Alaska)
Eskimos attack with hand
harpoon; the detachable
head is lashed to a line
which leads to an inflated
seal-bladder float. (b) The
flukes of a harpooned
bowhead whale show as it
sounds for the depths; the
line float in the water
marks the position of the
submerged mammal.
(c) The exhausted 34- to
40-foot-long prey is
dispatched with a spear
thrust to its vitals. The
highly maneuverable, but
fragile, skin umiak is used
for this hazardous
operation. (Courtesy of the
American Museum of
Natural History.)

(c)

diet, the forager relies upon hunting to supplement a predominantly vegetarian diet, but he has not yet domesticated plants.

To illustrate the subsistence techniques of a group of hunters and foragers, we might describe the activities of one or another Australian tribe (Figure 12-4) or the Tasmanians, Semangs, Andaman Islanders, African Pygmies, or African Bushmen. Any of numerous California tribes would do equally well, as would one of the three main tribes of Tierra del Fuego. However, we take the Great Basin Shoshones as our exemplars.

The Shoshones of the Great Basin   The Shoshoneans (speakers of Shoshone, a linguistic family within the Uto-Aztecan stock) lived in small local groups thinly distributed throughout the Great Basin. We have already made note of them as carriers of the Desert tradition of North American Mesolithic for-

agers (pages 202–203). Each band was named for the food with which it was most intimately associated.

Bands were bilateral and very loosely organized. There were no chiefs, but each had a headman, called tɛgwoni, "good talk thrown out to the people." The headman knew fully the ecology of the area, directing camp movements to where the ripened seeds and roots were to be found at appropriate times. Every morning he ritually warned his people not to waste food and not to forget that hard times and food shortages were surely ahead.

In 1860, Abbé Domenech noted of the Great Basin Shoshones: "According to the season, they emigrate from one place to another to seek miserable roots, which form their only nourishment; even animals are seldom to be found there."[9] It is because of their root-

[9]E. Domenech, *Seven Years' Residence in the Great Deserts of North America,* vol. 1, p. 242.

Fig. 12-4   Central Australian intensive foragers winnowing dried root meal. (Courtesy of the American Museum of Natural History.)

grubbing activities that the Shoshonean food gatherers are known throughout the Western states as *Diggers*. Julian Steward lists over 100 species of seeds, roots, and nuts known to have been eaten by the Shoshones.[10] Roots were extracted with a simple, pointed digging stick, or dibble. Seeds were collected with the aid of a woven basket and a fanlike beater with which to knock the grass seeds into the basket. Of all the delectable seeds offered by the desert, those of the sunflower were the most prized. Roasted lightly and ground on a stone metate, they were reduced to an oily paste which tasted, according to the Shoshones, "just like peanut butter." In my own fieldwork among the older members of the H3kandika (Seed Eater) Shoshones, who live on Bannock Creek in Idaho, gallon jars of peanut butter made most acceptable presents, apparently stimulating memories of olden days. Pine nuts also played a great part in the social economy of the various Shoshones—with results that we shall look into when discussing land ownership in Chapter 13.

Not only was the environment exploited for roots, berries, and nuts, but insects were looked upon as an epicurean delight. Regular communal grasshopper drives were organized. A sizable pit, 3 or 4 feet deep and 30 to 40 feet across, was laboriously prepared. Then men, women, and children formed a large circle, which converged slowly on the pit as they drove the grasshoppers before them with brush beaters. A good drive netted countless grasshoppers, which could then be roasted to provide a feast of plenty.

Ants were a more favored delicacy because of their pungent flavor when properly prepared. In March, when the ants had left the larva stage but were not yet up and around, a woman would scoop up an entire ant nest in her large, scallop-shaped winnowing basket. With dextrous and wonderful manipulation, she shook the basket so that the ants gathered

in its heel, while the sand and dirt bounced off the outer edge. When only ants remained, she scooped up hot coals with the basket. Rapidly jouncing them in the air, she kept the coals and ants turning together and the basket from burning up. When at last the legs were burned from the ants and their bodies properly toasted, her motions were deftly altered; the ashes bounced off the edge of the basket, while the ants once again foregathered in its heel. They were then dumped upon a grinding stone, rolled out, and reduced to a delectable paste—from the Shoshone point of view.

Small rodents were trapped by means of simple deadfalls. Rabbit hunting took the form of a great communal hunt under the direction of a hunt chief.[11] Nets were set up, and beaters drove the quarry into the waiting meshes. Soft robes were plaited from thin strips of rabbit fur for winter use. Antelope were occasionally hunted in much the same way, but with the addition of magical lures and antelope disguises worn by the hunters. A fence of brush supplanted the nets of the rabbit hunt.

Deer, mountain sheep, and mountain goats were sometimes pursued alone by the most energetic hunters. A hunter with much endurance would chase a deer or sheep for two whole days until exhaustion of the quarry made it possible for him to get close enough for a shot. Should this seem like incredible exertion, perhaps the motivation can better be appreciated if we quote Lewis and Clark on the meat hunger of the Shoshones. One of the expedition's hunters had killed a deer on Friday morning, August 16, 1805. The Shoshones accompanying Captain Lewis, after a pell-mell race to the spot where Lewis's man had dressed the deer,

. . . all dismounted in confusion and ran tumbling over each other like famished dogs; each tore away

---

[10]J. H. Steward, *Basin Plateau Aboriginal Socio-political Groups* (Bureau of American Ethnology, Bulletin 120, 1938), pp. 21–32.

[11]Communal rabbit hunts extend down through the Southwest into the pueblos, where participation is not only a lark but also a religious duty, and into the various groups of the Gila River area.

whatever part he could, and instantly began to eat it; some had the liver, some the kidneys, in short no part on which we are accustomed to look with disgust escaped them; one of them who had seized about nine feet of the entrails was chewing at one end, while with his hands he was diligently clearing his way by discharging the contents at the other.[12]

This method of eating "sausage" was still remembered by my Shosone informants in 1934.

Shoshone deer hunting was much like that of the Tarahumara Indians of Mexico, of whom Bennett and Zingg report:

Hunting deer consists of chasing the deer for two days—never less than one day. The Tarahumara keeps the deer constantly on the move. Only occasionally does he get a glimpse of his quarry, but he follows it unerringly through his own uncanny ability to read the tracks. The Indian chases the deer until it falls of exhaustion, often with its hoofs completely worn away.[13]

Fear of starvation constantly haunted the Shoshones. Like the Eskimos, they sometimes took a desperate last resort in cannibalism. But cannibals were feared and hated, and occasionally lynched.[14]

It would be an error to conclude from the above remarks that the Shoshones were devoid of all fastidiousness. They would and will eat neither dogs nor coyotes, for Coyote is a supernatural culture hero—a lovable rapscallion who figures in many a myth as an Indian equivalent of Tyll Eulenspiegel. He is the younger brother of Wolf, whom some Shoshones look upon as the Supreme Deity.[15] To kill a coyote or his cousin the dog is unthinkable; to eat them, impossible. Modern Shoshones, in 1934, were even loath to eat

the surplus Navaho sheep sent them by the government. Skinned sheep look too much like flayed dogs.

Bands of food gatherers are necessarily seminomadic. They must cover wide areas to skim off sufficient provender to keep them alive. But a given band tends to stay within its own familiar territory because (1) any animal may secure food and water more efficiently if it knows the land; (2) all human groups practice some storage of food; (3) they may also practice conservation of food resources; (4) their movements are hindered to a certain extent by their possession of material goods; and (5) property concepts are universal among mankind; tacit agreement allocates to each group its landed property unless the equilibrium is upset by war and migration.[16]

Incipient Agriculture: Hoe Culture or Gardening

Rainfall and the seasons control the basic patterns of primitive agriculture outside the tropical rain forests. There are four major crop complexes that have been developed by man. Two are basically adapted to dry uplands and seasonal variation in climate; two are adapted to tropical rain forests. One of each type is found in the Old World and the New. Thus, a suitable agricultural combination exists for all environments except those which are too extremely cold or too sere and dry to support intensive plant life.

The Old World upland-seasonal complex is the old Neolithic one of Asia Minor centered on wheat, barley, flax, rye, and millet. These crops are fall-sown, make a large part of their growth of stalk and leaf in cool weather, and complete their maturity during the long summer days of warmest weather. These climatic adaptations made easy the diffusion of such plants into northwestern Europe. In the

[12]M. Lewis and W. Clark, *History of the Expedition of Captains Lewis and Clark, 1804–05–06*, vol. 1, p. 401.
[13]W. C. Bennett and R. M. Zingg, *The Tarahumara*, p. 113.
[14]E. A. Hoebel, *The Political Organization and Law-ways of the Comanche Indians* (American Anthropological Association, Memoir 54, Contributions from the Laboratory of Anthropology, 4, 1940), p. 141.
[15]R. H. Lowie, *The Northern Shoshone* (American Museum of Natural History, Anthropological Papers, vol. 11, part 2, 1909), pp. 233ff.

[16]J. H. Steward, "The Economic and Social Basis of Primitive Bands," in *Essays in Anthropology in Honor of Alfred Louis Kroeber*, p. 332.

European lands, there was still the same condition of a cool, moist starting period, although the start was shifted to spring, and maturity still took place during the long days of midsummer.[17] Old World cereals are sown broadcast. New World plants are individually planted in hills.[18] Threshing may still be a primitive process among certain peoples (Figure 12-5).

The Old World wetland complex centers around rice cultivation or the growing of such tubers as yams or taro. The New World dryland-seasonal plants are the maize-beans-squash complex and in the Andean region, also the potato. The New World tropical-wetland complex centers on the cultivation and processing of manioc.

Forest Horticulture Lightly forested highlands may strike the reader as strange places for the origins of gardening. Clearing forests is hard work, and it would seem at first careless thought that open country would be more suitable. However, two factors militate against horticultural origins in open lands. Deserts are deficient in water, even if the soil is friable. Archaeological evidence does not support the thesis that gardening first began in "irrigation oases" of the arid river valleys in the Old and New Worlds. Grasslands are impenetrable to planting by peoples who do not have heavy plows. Even our own pioneers avoided the heavily sodded prairies, until special sod-breaking plows were developed (which was not so long ago). Although the best grain-producing lands in the world are the American and Russian prairies, they have become so only under modern conditions. Tropical rain forests could have been made to support gardens by primitive men, but the environment was not conducive to the first efforts at plant domestication. Archaeological evidence and botanical facts do not indi-

[17]C. Sauer, "American Agricultural Origins," in *Essays in Anthropology in Honor of Alfred Louis Kroeber,* p. 285.
[18]The modern use of long rows, or drills, is a modified improvement on this practice.

Fig. 12-5   Anuak tribesmen of Sudan thresh millet with hand flails on a raised platform. The loosened grain falls through the floor of the platform to the ground below. The chaff blows away during the fall. Thus the seeds are separated from stalk and chaff by a method that, in this part of the world, probably goes back to the prehistoric Neolithic Age. (United Nations.)

Fig. 12-6   Garden hoe made of the shoulder blade (scapula) of a bison and a rake made of a deer antler; tools of the Mandan Indians of the middle Missouri River in South Dakota. In the eighteenth century the Mandans prospered by trading surpluses of corn to nomadic tribes for furs, which they in turn exchanged with French traders for European goods. (Museum of Anthropology, University of Minnesota. Photo by Don Breneman.)

cate great antiquity for domesticated jungle plants.

Slash and Burn Clearing   Clearing the forest for planting requires energetic labor; it is not for lazy men. But for people who are not rushed for time, it can be effectively done with primitive tools by the "slash and burn method." Each tree is girdled by cutting a ring through the bark and cambium layer. Death follows. The dead trees may then be burned out or left standing. Their leafless branches no longer shade the ground. The weedless floor of the virginal forest is a light rich humus, and the gardeners simply plant among and around the dead stumps (Figure 12-7). Stumps are a serious nuisance only to the farmer with a plow.

Fig. 12-7   Typical yam garden in the tropical rain forest of the Central Highlands of New Guinea; the standing stalks are banana plants on which the yam vines will climb. The carefully constructed fence is to keep out the wild pigs, which would root up and eat the yam tubers. In the center of the picture is a new, partially cleared plot, already fenced but not yet planted. The large trees have not yet died and are not ready for burning. (Photo by E. A. Hoebel.)

Dry-rice Cultivation in the Old World: Borneo
As practiced by the Siang Dyaks of central Borneo, whose methods are typical of dry-rice cultivation, each man selects a sloping plot for clearing and planting. If it is a new one, he cuts partially through the trees on the lower side of the slope. Large key trees at the top of the plot are then felled so as to smash down the lower trees. All are trimmed, left to dry, and, after several weeks, burned. In all this he is usually helped by neighbors, whom he must help in turn. Work parties often get drunk on rice wine at lunchtime, when the party phase washes out the work aspect of the joint undertaking.

Planting is done by poking holes in the ground with a pointed stick, after which a couple of grains of rice are dropped in (Figure 12-8). Weeding is done occasionally, but it is so disheartening a task that most gardeners prefer to clear a new field every two or three years. In Borneo, where culture is primitive and communities are small, there is still more than enough land to support this method of land use.[19]

Maize Cultivation among the Maya   High cultures that support large populations may enjoy no such margin of safety. The *milpa* system, as it is known among the Mayas, was (and still is)[20] basically similar to the *ku*, *kaingin*, or *jhum* system, as it is known in Borneo. In J. E. Thompson's account in *The Civilization of the Mayas*, we read that:

The Maya system of agriculture was primitive. Land suitable for agriculture was prepared by burning off trees and undergrowth. After the first rains, the sower, with a bag of seed and a sharp-pointed stick, crossed and recrossed the field, making a hole with his stick in the ground at every pace, and throwing a few grains of maize into the pit. . . . At the end of the season the field was abandoned, and next year the Maya farmer marked out a new piece of land to be cleared and sown. In the course of time and with the large increase of population that undoubtedly occurred, the Mayas must have been driven farther and farther afield in search of virgin soil. The exhausted soils nearer home must have been resown after shorter and shorter periods of recuperation. In time the yield of the district would have fallen below the level of consumption, and, faced with evacuation or starvation, the people chose the former.[21]

In this we have one of the theories to account for the decline and abandonment of the great centers of the Old Empire of the Mayas (A.D. 320 to 890). Morley has advanced the theory that intensive slash and burn gardening by the ancient Mayas resulted in the invasion of grasses that converted the tropical forest of southern Yucatán to tough sod savanna. With their primitive dibbles, they were unable to pierce the sod, he thinks, and so by the natural consequences of their own efforts, they were driven from their cities.[22] Thompson's view, however, relies on less direct factors than the effect of *milpa* farming on

the soil or vegetation. Old Maya cities were not urban centers of population concentration. They were religious and court centers supported by small farms more or less evenly distributed for miles around, not clustered like European peasants' homes beneath the walls of citadels. Such a pattern requires a pacifistic society. It is quite possible that the upset of the delicate social balance by the introduction of war forced the abandonment of Mayan centers in southern Yucatán around A.D. 900.[23]

Yam Cultivation in the Old World   Throughout all the tropical rain forests of Africa, Melanesia, and New Guinea, the yam is the staff of life. Clearings in the rain forest provide growing space for the yam tubers and their vines. Giant yams can grow to 20 pounds,

[21]Field Museum of Natural History, Anthropology Leaflet 25, 4th ed., 1942, p. 15.
[22]S. G. Morley, *The Ancient Maya*, pp. 71–72.

[23]J. E. S. Thompson, "A Survey of the Northern Maya Area" (*American Antiquity*, vol. 2, 1945), pp. 2–24. The whole problem of the possible causes of the decline of the Mayan society of the Old Empire is being subjected to restudy by prehistorians and ecologists. It has also been convincingly demonstrated in the fieldwork of Dennis Puleston that the protein-rich nut of the ramon tree was the subsistence resource for the peasant Maya gardeners. Maize was the highly valued ritual food of the managerial priestly classes.

Fig. 12-8   Slash and burn horticulture in Borneo. The jungle has been felled and burned to open a gardening space. A cooperative work group of Dyaks, planting dry rice, is using dibbles to make holes for the seed rice among the fallen logs and remaining stumps. (Courtesy of William W. Conley.)

while their vines lace across the ground or climb stakes and trees (Figure 12-7). In both Africa and Melanesia, yam growing, processing, and eating evoke intense cultural passion and provide a focal point for numerous socio-magico-religious rites.

The Trobriand Islands For no people has this been more explicitly and meticulously documented than for the Trobriand Islanders by Bronislaw Malinowski in his classic two-volume study, *Coral Gardens and Their Magic.* A few of Malinowski's observations are quoted to convey the meaning of gardening in this one people's lives:

The gardens are, in a way, a work of art. . . . A considerable amount of energy is spent on purely

aesthetic effects, to make the garden look clean, showy and dainty. [Page 80]

As to the varieties of yam, taro and taytu, they have literally hundreds of names for each of them. [Page 76]

It may be said that among the forces and beliefs which bear upon and regulate gardening, magic is the most important, apart, of course, from the practical work. [Page 62]

Garden magic . . . is in the Trobriands a public and official service. It is performed by the garden magician . . . for the benefit of the community. [*Idem.*]

To each village community this magic . . . is a very precious possession and a symbol of its social integrity as well as of its standing in the tribal hierarchy. [Page 68]

Food is displayed on all occasions—at death and at dancing, at marriage and at mourning feasts. [Page 82]

Accumulated food is to them a good thing—its absence is not only something to be dreaded, but something to be ashamed of. [*Idem.*]

The crops harvested each year . . . are . . . the economic foundation of public and private life, of most institutions and pursuits in the Trobriands. [Page 83][24]

The richness of practice and belief, of which these statements are but the driest essence, is truly an expression of the human capacity to invest mundane survival activities with meaning and purpose.

Wet-rice Culture in the Old World Wet-rice irrigation was probably developed in India some 3,000 or more years ago, whence it spread into China, Southeast Asia, and western Indonesia. Prior to its penetration of Indonesia, yams, taro, and millet were the staple crops of this part of the world. In the central islands of Indonesia (the eastern Lesser Sundas and the southern Moluccas), American maize, introduced in post-Columbian times, has won out over rice as the staple crop; but in the extreme east, where Indonesia merges into Melanesia, sago prevails. Rice cultivation belongs to the Asiatic, not the Oceanic, province.

Wet-rice culture requires extensive water

Fig. 12-9 Ifugao rice terraces in the valley below Benaue, a modern town, in the Northern Province, Luzon, the Philippines. Neolithic-type wet-rice culture in its most intensive form. (Courtesy of Fred Eggan.)

[24]B. Malinowski, *Coral Gardens and Their Magic* (vol. 1, 1935).

control and irrigation systems (Figure 12-9), which sustain and require heavy population density combined with societies that are confined to specific localities because of the work required to build and maintain the systems. Some of the most populous areas of the world are those of wet-rice-growing societies in the Orient.

The economic organization of irrigation cultures is too complex for us to attempt to analyze here. Barton has given us a useful study of the Philippine Ifugaos,[25] to which the reader may refer, and Linton also published some illuminating materials on the social adjustments that were forced when a primitive dry-rice culture changed over to wet-rice techniques in Madagascar.[26]

Manioc Culture in the New World   Manioc, also called cassava, is a New World plant whose tuberous roots are rich in carbohydrates. It is the source of tapioca. The use of manioc as a basic foodstuff by Amazonian Indians reveals a genuine ingenuity. Sweet manioc, which grows wild, gives relatively small yields. The domesticated forms with large yields contain much poisonous prussic acid. This necessitates a leaching process of some complexity before the manioc tubers can be converted to edible cassava. The roots, after being dug, must be sliced and fermented to free some of the poisons. Next they are pulped on hand graters and then wrung dry of liquids (Figure 12-10). The dried pulp must then be ground to a flour or meal and heated to free the remaining volatile poisons. Only then is it safe for use.

The Kuikuru of central Brazil grow eleven varieties of manioc, all of which are poisonous. Yet manioc makes up 80 or 85 per cent of their diet, according to the estimates of

Robert Carneiro, who has given us a thoughtful analysis of their system.[27] The heavy rain forest is opened for gardens exactly as we

[27]R. L. Carneiro, "Slash and Burn Cultivation among the Kuikuru and Its Implications for Cultural Development in the Amazon Basin," in *The Evolution of Horticultural Systems in Native South America: Causes and Consequences— A Symposium, Anthropologica Supplement No. 2, Caracas, 1961.,* pp. 47–67.

Fig. 12-10   Manioc processing in the Amazonian rain forest. The pulp of the manioc is squeezed free of poisonous juices in a woven tube which contracts when stretched lengthwise by the bar being pushed down. (Photo by Cornell Capa, Magnum, from M. Huxley and C. Capa, **Farewell to Eden,** *Harper & Row, New York.)*

[25]R. F. Barton, *Ifugao Economics* (University of California Publications in American Archaeology and Ethnology, vol. 15, no. 5, 1922).
[26]R. Linton, "The Tanala," in A. Kardiner, *The Individual and His Society;* also *The Tanala: A Hill Tribe of Madagascar* (Field Museum of Natural History, Anthropological Series, vol. 22, 1933).

have described. Before 1900, stone axes and the jaws of the piranha were used to girdle the trees. Now trade axes, machetes, and brush hooks are used. Plants are allowed to grow for one and one-half years to get a maximum starch output, although they could be harvested in half a year. From their fixed village, the Kuikuru cultivate about 95 acres from among the 13,500 acres of rain forest that are available to them. Men do the gardening and have to put in only two hours at agricultural labor and an hour and a half at fishing, daily. The remaining ten to twelve waking hours are spent in dancing, wrestling, loafing, or other informal means of recreation. They could grow much more food as surplus with the available time and land. But the jungle has not favored extensive trade, so no more

is raised than is required to eat well. There is no population pressure or other immediate reason to dig in harder. Carneiro emphasizes that the mere possibility of food surplus is not enough to engender the work that produces a surplus and a concomitant elaboration of other parts of the culture and an expansion of its scope and complexity.

Intensive Agriculture: Plow Culture

The development of plow culture combined the two basic inventions of the Neolithic Age —domestication of plants and domestication of animals—into a synthesized productive unit (Figure 12-11). The hand hoe was enlarged and changed from a hacking tool to a scarifier dragged through the earth by one or two harnessed draft animals yoked to the service of man. The most common animals used were oxen in the West and water buffalo in the East; horses and camels have done field service, too. Plow culture enhanced the limited energy input of the primitive hoe wielder with the greater energy input of the grain- and grass-eating draft animal. The result was basic to the urban revolution and the support of city artisans and cadres of priestly and military managers and landowners.

Fig. 12-11   A contemporary Bolivian Indian at work in his fields in the Altiplano of the Andes. In ancient times, a wooden scarifier was yoked to the draft animal. Thus man brought animal energy under control for his own purposes. (United Nations.)

Origin and Spread of the Plow   Whether the plow was first developed in the Middle East or in Asia, or in both areas more or less simultaneously, is not yet established. In any event, it came late in human history. The oldest extant evidence of the plow goes back to Mesopotamian cylinder seals and Egyptian paintings, both from their respective early Dynastic periods in the fourth millennium B.C. —a good 3,000 years after the first development of horticulture in the Old World. After 3000 B.C. the plow is known in Cyprus, Greece, and India. Fifteen hundred years later, plows were in use in Bronze Age northwestern Europe. At the other end of Eurasia, China did not receive the plow until 300 B.C.

In Africa, the Sahara desert and the tough grasslands of the Sudan were evidently barriers to the southward diffusion of the plow. No native cultures of Africa south of the Sahara were, in modern times, based upon plow agriculture, even though 82 of 116 African societies in Murdock's *World Ethnographic Sample* were horticultural. In contrast, forty-nine of seventy-eight Mediterranean societies included in that sample practiced plow agriculture.

In Asia, fifty-four of eighty-five societies in Murdock's sample used the plow and a mere five were still gardeners.

The spread of plow agriculture in 5,000 years is phenomenal testimony to its productive efficiency, especially when combined with fertilizing.

Yet in all that time, no American Indian ever invented the plow, nor did it diffuse to the New World. No culture, however high in other arts, ever rose above the gardening level in North or South America.

Pastoralism

Pastoralism, the term applied to cultures whose major subsistence technique centers around the herding and husbandry of domesticated animals, is, as we have seen, a specialized adjustment to specific ecological factors. Primitive dwellers in heavy grasslands or deserts cannot readily become gardeners, and as the original peoples in these areas moved from hunting and foraging to higher levels of economic development, they became herders, relying primarily upon their animals for food and trade with which to sustain their societies. Historically, this occurred in the Neolithic Age, at the same time that incipient agriculture was developing in regions more suitable to the raising of crops.

Pastoralism is preeminently an Asian-African economic complex. In Africa it covers the whole Sahara, where it centers on the camel and the horse, as it also does in eastern Arabia. In the northern Sudan and most of

East Africa, it combines with hoe culture, and in the extreme south, the Hottentots and Hereros live on their cattle. The great Asian steppes, from the east shores of the Caspian to the boundaries of China and from the Himalayas to the arctic wastes, support such eminently pastoral peoples as the Kazaks, Tartars, Altai, Kalmucks, and Mongols with their herds of horses, sheep, and cattle.

It should be mentioned that the possession of animals is not the exclusive prerogative of pastoralists; all gardeners keep some domesticated animals—pigs, goats, and dogs being the most common. Such animals may or may not be eaten. Many are not. Indeed, so frequent is the abjuration of the flesh of domesticated animals among their primitive masters that Lowie concluded that "the original reasons for keeping animals were not practical ones."[28] Domesticated animals are seemingly kept as pets, for emotional reasons, or as objects of religious sacrifice as often as for food.

It should also be noted that pigs, goats, and dogs, even when not eaten, are not as economically useless as is often imagined. Hambly notes that goats, for instance, are ubiquitous and neglected in Africa; they are neither milked nor used extensively as a meat supply. But "goats pick their own food supply, and since they are almost omnivorous in their selection of vegetable food, there is no cost of maintenance."[29] What Hambly failed to note is that in their omnivorousness, goats are good garbage disposers. So are pigs and dogs, a fact that has led Ashley Montagu to suggest this as the original reason for the domestication of dogs in Neolithic times.[30]

The known practical uses to which domestic animals can be put are, according to Forde, (1) consumption of their meat and

[28]R. H. Lowie, *An Introduction to Cultural Anthropology*, p. 52.
[29]W. D. Hambly, "Source Book for African Anthropology" (*Field Museum of Natural History, Anthropological Series*, vol. 26, part 2, 1937), p. 596.
[30]M. F. A. Montagu, "On the Origin of the Domestication of the Dog" (*Science*, vol. 96, 1942), pp. 111–112.

blood; (2) use of their hides; (3) use of their hair or wool for weaving or felting; (4) milking and dairying; (5) load carrying or pulling; and (6) riding.[31] To these should be added the use of their dried dung for household fuel, especially in India, and their value as media of exchange and reciprocity.

Yet most primitive peoples ignore or fail to take advantage of one or several of these practical uses. In East Africa south of Abyssinia, the art of riding was totally unknown to the native people. In Africa beef is eaten only ocassionally. Women may toil under heavy loads, but cattle must not be burdened or set to pulling loads. So, although the cult of the cow is the dominant theme of most East African cultures, the use of this animal falls far short of full realization of all its potentialities, and in India the religious tabus which surround it severely limit its utility.

Of course, we, in our use of horses, reverse the situation. We ride them, make them haul burdens, and pet them. But we neither milk nor eat them. The mayor of New York City in 1943 insisted that the eating of horse flesh is "immoral and uncivilized," and upon these lofty if ethnocentric principles he forbade the sale of horsemeat as a wartime measure to relieve an acute meat shortage.

The failure of most pastoralists to make maximum use of their chief economic resource, their animals, has baffled many observers and scientists in addition to Lowie. The rejection of most dairy products by both the Chinese and the East Africans has presented one such puzzle. It has long been known that Chinese pastoralists do not milk their cattle, nor do they eat cheese or other dairy products (although they are not averse to beef as food). Similarly, most East Africans drink little sweet milk, although they draw cattle blood to drink and make a cult of sour milk. For all their familiarity with sour milk, few Africans have developed the art of cheese making, and butter is less often eaten than

used in dressing the hair or applied as a cosmetic for lending the body a glossy sheen.

Until 1966, the Chinese aversion to all dairy products, and that of Africans to sweet milk, seemed to be a deep-seated cultural fixation. New medical research now suggests that it has a genetic base. Lactase, an enzyme produced in the small intestine, is necessary to the digestion of milk sugar, or lactose. Medical studies now indicate that most adult Chinese, Asiatics, and American Indians, and 70 per cent of Afro-Americans and West African Negroes, are unable to digest milk. Most, but not all, whites have no difficulty. The symptoms of lactase deficiency are abdominal bloating, cramps, and diarrhea after drinking more than a glass of milk. By implication, European populations have developed genes for lactase production. Most Asians and Africans have not. It appears that, except for infants, not everybody needs milk. Not everybody can stand it. After all, the possibility for human access to dairy products is not more than 8,000 years old.[32]

Pastoralism in Africa   It is well known that in India the cow is considered sacred, but in East Africa it is the heart and core of life. "First, last, and always the role of cattle in Karamojong life is to transform the energy stored in the grasses, herbs, and shrubs of the tribal area into a form easily available to the people."[33] The cattle do not represent wealth; they *are* wealth. As Elizabeth Marshall Thomas has written of the pastoral Dodoth of East Africa, among whom the women are millet growers:

For the Dodoth, cattle are the warp of life. They are the only wealth, the foundation of economic and social stability, the origin of all human ties. . . . Cows give milk. This is drunk daily, and churned into butter, and curdled with cow's urine into a

[31]C. D. Forde, *Habitat, Economy, and Society,* p. 401.

[32]Shi-Shung Huang and T. S. Bayless, "Milk and Lactose Intolerance in Healthy Orientals" (*Science,* vol. 160, 1966), pp. 83–84.

[33]R. and N. Dyson-Hudson, "Subsistence Herding in Uganda" (*Scientific American,* vol. 220, 1969), p. 78.

salty cheese. Oxen give their blood. . . . People drink the blood raw after squeezing it with their fingers to break the clots, or they cook it with green millet flour into a delicate delicious pudding, as airy as a soufflé. Cowhides make sleeping mats and clothing. Cow dung makes flooring. Fresh cow urine, in its sterile stream, washes dirty hands or cleans utensils or softens leather or curdles milk for clabber or speeds the making of ghee. The first morsel a baby eats in his life is a drop of butter. From then on, he will be involved with cattle; every day and night of his life his nostrils will be filled with their sweet odor, his ears with their vibrant voices; and when he dies, if he dies at home, his body may be wrapped in the hide of one of his oxen and buried in the soft earth of their pen.[34]

This passage conveys a small touch of the significance of cattle for African pastoralists, but the intensity of emotional identification of a man with his cattle, although it may be written about, cannot really be sensed by an outsider. An indication of the complexity of exchange of cattle at marriage may be found in the example concerning the Nuer tribe on pages 347–349.

In the New World, only the Navahos became pastoralists—and then only in modern times with sheep acquired from the Spanish. In the southern Plains, such tribes as the Comanche became herders, but not pastoralists, in the mid-nineteenth century. Their horse herds numbered in the thousands, but horses were eaten only occasionally, were never milked, and were used mostly for riding in war and hunting. As mounted cavalry, the Comanches overwhelmed the sedentary horticultural Apaches of the South Plains and drove them out of Texas. Horses were also useful in trade and as prestige tokens akin to the war bonnet. A man identified so completely with his favorite horse that the killing of such an animal was treated as murder. It required a revenge killing of the horse killer, even as a man would avenge the death of his brother.

[34]E. M. Thomas, "The Herdsmen" (*The New Yorker*, May 1, 1965), p. 52. (By permission from *The New Yorker* and Alfred A. Knopf, Inc., New York.)

Transhumance   Transhumance is pastoralism linked to sedentary agriculturalism. Basic subsistence is derived from cultivation, but is rounded out by the work of shepherds who take the sheep, goats, and cattle to upland summer ranges for grazing.

The Jie of Uganda   The Jie of northeastern Uganda, as reported by Phillip Gulliver, are an excellent example of this mode of subsistence. In Gulliver's summary statement:

The life of the Jie is based on a mixed economy; but although agriculture provides the bulk of the staple food—sorghum for porridge—the Jie themselves give major importance to the care and value of their livestock, particularly cattle. . . . Unlike agriculture, livestock have a significance beyond food production. They have a notable aesthetic value, and they are essential to the rich complex of rituals that would be thought ineffective without the slaughter of oxen [page 159].

Permanent settlement is limited to a small area in the middle of the country. . . . Here in fixed homesteads [see Figure 14-15, page 301] arranged in stable communities live some four fifths of the population—women, children, and most of the men. . . . The bulk of the herds are kept in separate mobile camps in the pasture lands and are tended by youths and young men subsisting directly off the livestock [pages 161–162].

The pastoral cycle is briefly as follows: by about the middle of the rainy season the stock camps are all located in the eastern region, where, by that time, new grass has grown sufficiently and surface water collects in pools and stream beds. Camps are scattered throughout the region. Dairy herds are at their largest in the homesteads, and milk supply is at its peak. As the dry season sets in, both grass and water quickly become exhausted and camps must shift westward. There is an irregular migration of the camps, for it is entirely the responsibility of each herd owner to determine the timing and direction of movement as he assesses the situation. At first in the western region water supplies are sufficient to allow a wide spread scatter of camps, but as the time of the last rains recedes, surface water dries up and camps are compelled to converge on one or another of the half-dozen permanent watering places for the remainder of the season. The choice of watering place is a matter for each herd owner to decide, although usually he tends to put his camp near the same one each year. Nevertheless, some readjustment of locations does occur each dry season when some places tend to become overcrowded or when men decide to shift for personal reasons. With the onset of the next rainy season it again becomes possible for camps to scatter through the western region as fresh grass and water are available. Then there is a shift back to the east, where the rains come a little later [page 162].[35]

Transhumance is essentially an Old World phenomenon.

Pig Culture in Melanesia

Throughout the southwest Pacific the raising of pigs on a share-crop basis is a focus of motivational energy in striving for prestige by men in most societies. Gardening provides the yams that are the staple food, but pigs are wealth, and a big man is the one who can put a "call" on hundreds of pigs for slaughter and distribution when he wishes to dedicate a new men's meeting house, settle a dispute, or appease his ancestors. When pigs are slaughtered, cooked, and distributed among the guests, it may be that only a minute portion is actually eaten. The slabs of pork may pass through a number of hands, like worn currency, in payment of debts or as gifts, imposing new obligations on others, until at last, in rancid decay, their usefulness is over.[36]

SUMMARY

An elemental feature of every culture is a complex of techniques for production, consumption, and distribution of food. The physiological need for anabolic replacement of used-up energy in the body imposes a biologic imperative on every society to organize its culture so that at least minimal food requirements are met. Otherwise, the society and its culture will not survive. The ecological adjustment of a culture to the physical environment in which it operates is therefore of prime importance. Consequently, the culture areas of the world are, in large measure, also food-getting or subsistence areas.

Environments limit but do not determine the content of cultures. Thus cultures as diverse as those of the Pueblo Indians and the Navahos, each influenced by a separate historical background of culture, can exist side by side in the same geographic area, sharing an identical physical environment.

The prehistoric evolution of subsistence techniques resulted in four primary levels of food getting. They are: (1) hunting and gathering, (2) intensive foraging, (3) incipient agriculture (gardening/hoe culture) and pastoralism and (4) intensive agriculture (plow culture). By the nineteenth century, only a small minority of the world's societies were still based on hunting and foraging. Half had evolved to gardening; a few were pastoralists; and approximately a fifth had achieved plow culture, which provides the foundation for urban civilizations.

Thus, the vast majority of recent primitives shared in the great Neolithic complex of gardening. Pastoralism represents a specialized adjustment to physical environments that are not suitable for gardening by people who possess only primitive horticultural techniques, or it may be joined to gardening in a mixed economy.

Most peoples reinforce their rational food-production methods with religious and magical practices which function psychologically to strengthen their sense of assurance that the food quest will not fail disastrously, and so they allay the ever-present gnawing anxiety that their means of survival may not suffice. Many of the rituals also serve to reinforce, symbolically and in action, the interdepen-

---

[35]P. H. Gulliver, "The Jie of Uganda," in J. L. Gibbs, Jr. (ed.), *The Peoples of Africa.* Copyright © 1965 by Holt, Rhinehart and Winston, Inc. Used by permission.
[36]See Chap. 17, *Economic Organization*, pp. 346–347, for a more detailed description of the pig-exchange networks.

dence and group solidarity of the members of a society and its lesser collective units.

Forest gardening involves temporary clearing of woodlands by means of the slash and burn technique. Few forest gardeners fertilize their plots; hence, gardens are allowed to return to the forest after a few years as new plots are opened up.

Plow agriculture (prior to the modern overseas expansion by Europeans) was confined to Asia Minor, North Africa, Europe, and South and East Asia. Although 80 per cent of human societies had not acquired plow agriculture before the modern era, most of the world's population was concentrated in the civilized societies of the north temperate belt of Eurasia in which subsistence by intensive agriculture was concentrated.

Although there remains a possibility that the idea of the domestication of animals and the cultivation of plants may have spread from the Old World into the New, the only domesticated animal brought from the Eastern Hemisphere into the Western in pre-European times was the dog. Because the specific plants cultivated by American Indians were (with the possible exception of cotton) entirely indigenous to the Western Hemisphere, and because the techniques of cultivation used in the New World were quite unlike those established in the Old World, we infer that New World horticulture (and, hence, the New World Neolithic complex) developed independently of Old World influence.

Pastoralism, as a dominant mode of subsistence, is an alternative ecological adjustment to dry or semiarid grassland environments. Transhumance combines gardening with limited and subsidiary herding.

SELECTED READINGS

Barth, F., *Nomads of South Persia* (1961). Middle East pastoralism, based on sheep, described and analyzed by an outstanding social anthropologist.

Coursey, D. G., *Yams* (New York, 1969). The ethnobotany of yam culture in Africa presented with detail and imagination. Includes an account of the modern production of yams in Mexico and China, for their yield of steroids from which are synthesized the hormones of "the Pill."

de Schlippe, P., *Shifting Cultivation in Africa: The Zande System of Agriculture* (1956). A modern study based on anthropology and agronomy, with very enlightening results.

Ekvall, R. B., *Fields on the Hoof* (1968). A culture case study of the pastoral complex of a remarkable people, the nomads of Tibet, who have adopted yak culture (with subsidiary animals) to the maintenance of human society at altitudes of 16,000 feet. The culture is being subjected to doctrinaire destruction by modern China as incompatible with the teachings of Mao.

Forde, C. D., *Habitat, Economy, and Society* (1937). Contains condensed descriptions of the subsistence activities of a number of tribes and the relation of their social structures to such activities. Also presents a general comparative summary of the subject.

Klima, G. J., *The Barabaig: East African Cattle Herders* (1970). A culture case study of a pastoral tribe.

Nelson, R. K., *Hunters of the Northern Ice* (1969). A systematic study of traditional and modern techniques of hunting on sea ice and of the life of the Eskimos of the Arctic coasts of Alaska.

Netting, R. M., *Hill Farmers of Nigeria* (1968). A modern ecological–social anthropological study (1960 to 1962) of a contemporary intensive-gardening society in Northern Nigeria, West Africa.

Richards, A. I., *Land, Labour, and Diet in Northern Rhodesia* (1939). How the Bemba tribe makes its living.

Steward, J. H., *Basin Plateau Aboriginal Socio-political Groups* (1938). The ecology and livelihood of the peoples of the Great Basin desert.

Chapter 13

Land Ownership and Personal Property

Property is a universal feature of human culture. However, from the anthropological point of view, the concept of property embraces a far larger inventory of possessions, both tangible and intangible, than the twentieth-century man of the West is likely to realize. The land upon which the social group is located and from which it draws its sustenance, the beasts that rove upon it wild, the animals that graze upon it tame, the trees and the crops, the houses that men erect, the clothes they wear, the songs they sing, the dances they execute, the charms they incant, these and many more are objects of property. Men tend to bring within the scope of property whatever they rely upon for the maintenance of life or value for other reasons. So it is that property is as ubiquitous as man, a part of the basic fabric of all society.

The Nature of Property

People may relate to property in various ways: individually (to personal property), by groups (to joint property), or by the society at large (to communal property). Property may be fixed and immovable (real estate), or it may be movable (chattel). It may be material and concrete, or it may be an idea or a way of acting (incorporeal). It may be transferable by gift, barter, sale, inheritance, or confiscation, or it may be inalienable. It may or may not be protected by law. It may be reinforced by ritual or protected by magic. Or it may be sustained as customary usage sanctioned without the aid of either law or the supernatural. Many people habitually think of property only as a thing or as things. Yet the thing itself is but one aspect of property, for the essential nature of property is found in its qualities as a social institution. Property lends formal expression to social structure. It specifies and allocates access not only to concrete necessities such as land and food supplies, but to items of symbolic value such as a feathered headdress, house decoration, and honorific titles.

Property: A Social Creation Property in its full sense is *a web of social relations with respect to the utilization of some object (material or nonmaterial) in which a person or group is tacitly or explicitly recognized to hold quasi-exclusive and limiting connections.*

As an illustration, a stone conveniently shaped for use as an axhead lies unnoticed and unused for years on the surface of the ground. It is not property. It is, in legal terminology, a *res nullius:* a nothing. A wandering tribesman finds it, takes it, and uses it as a hand ax. This in itself makes the stone merely an object of possession. If the social practices of the possessor's tribe are such that any other person could appropriate this tool at will, it would still be a mere matter of possession. But if the custom is such that his fellow tribesmen recognize that he has special *rights* in possessing that piece of rock and that all others have a *duty* to desist from using or taking it, then it is an object of property. The stone has not changed, but the social pattern with respect to it has. It is the special and peculiar set of social relations which has transformed the rock into an object of property. Thus, we have two irreducible aspects of property: (1) the object, and (2) the web of social relations that establishes a limiting and defined status relationship between persons and the object.

This limiting relationship is often referred to by lawyers and economists as an *exclusive right of use.* It is exclusive insofar as it excludes nonowners from legitimate use without the express or tacit approval of the owner. However, the right is rarely, if ever, so absolutely exclusive that the owner may utilize the object in any way his whim may dictate. His rights of use are always limited to some extent by the demands of society. After all, society, not the individual, creates and maintains the institution of property. This is not to say that society created the *object.* The point of emphasis is that an object does not become property until the members of the society at large agree to bestow the property attribute upon it by regulating their behavior

in a self-limiting manner. This is done because social experience has led to the conclusion that social benefits are derived from granting "exclusive" rights to individuals and groups with respect to certain classes of objects that they have created or acquired. By the same token, men always limit the extent of that exclusiveness in accordance with their conception of the needs of social good. Property—a social creation—is consequently always subject to social limitations, even in the most individualistic societies. Thus it is that as social concepts change from time to time, the specific content of property concepts undergoes alterations. The form and content of property notions are not the expression of immutable instinct or of any im-

Fig. 13-A   A Yurok canoe owner and family.
(Peabody Museum, Harvard University.)

agined laws of nature. Property in the United States today is not what it was in the mid-nineteenth century, nor what it will be at the dawn of the twenty-first.

Yurok Canoe Ownership   As an example of the way in which property is constituted, we may briefly analyze canoe ownership among the Yuroks of California—a highly individualistic people. A Yurok boat owner nominally possesses his canoe as private property. It is his. He has a series of demand rights against all other **persons** not to molest or damage his boat. **He has** the privilege right to use it upon the public waters. He does not have to sell it or give it away. These are all marks of exclusive rights. Yet he is also subject to a series of well-recognized duties which limit his exclusive prerogatives. For one thing, he is obligated to ferry any traveler over the river when called upon to do so. Failure to perform this duty gives the traveler a demand right for legal damages equal to one dentalium shell.[1] On the other hand, if the owner suffers injury because of the service he has to render, the traveler is subject to damages. Thus, when one canoeman's house burned down while he was in midstream, his passenger had to pay for it.

This is what Cook meant when he said, ". . . ownership . . . is found to consist not only of an indefinite number of rights in the strict sense of claims available against an indefinite number of persons, each of whom is under a corresponding duty, but also a large and indefinite number of privileges, powers and immunities. . . ."[2]

Property and Law   Finally, we should take note of the relation of property to law. In the modern world, it is a fact that a vast proportion of the law of the state is devoted to the definition of the relationships between owners of property. Much of the activity of our courts and police is concerned with maintaining and enforcing these relationships. Government feeds and grows on the complexity of property in a heterogeneous industrial civilization.

But to state that property rights "exist only because government recognizes and protects them"[3] is an expression of an amazingly myopic point of view. Property rights are tacitly and explicitly recognized and upheld by all forms of social sanction, legal and nonlegal alike. And in the case of primitive society, the recognition and support of property institutions are in fact more frequently nonlegal than legal. Even when legal in nature, primitive property law falls predominantly within the area of private law, which operates independently of the formal governmental machinery.

Land as Property in Primitive Cultures

Land is a *sine qua non* of human existence. It is therefore the most important single object of property. All societies are territorially based,[4] and most sustenance is drawn from the soil, either directly or indirectly.

Land Tenure among Food Gatherers and Hunters   Most human societies claim property rights in land as communities. The Australians, African Bushmen, the Veddas of Ceylon, and the Tasmanians recognize clearly discernible natural boundaries as marking off local group territories. Each resents un-

---

[1]A narrow, tubelike seashell, harvested by the Nootka tribe, traded and used as shell money among other tribes of the Northwest Coast of North America. See P. Drucker, *Cultures of the North Pacific Coast,* pp. 151–152, 177–178.
[2]W. W. Cook, "Ownership and Possession" (*Encyclopaedia of the Social Sciences,* vol. 11, 1933), p. 521.

[3]R. M. MacIver, "Government and Property" (*Journal of Political and Legal Sociology,* vol. 4, 1946), p. 5. For an opposite point of view refer to A. I. Hallowell, "The Nature and Function of Property as a Social Institution" (*Journal of Legal and Political Sociology,* vol. 1, 1943), pp. 115–138, especially pp. 130ff. Above all, every student should read the article by W. H. Hamilton and I. Till, "Property" (*Encyclopaedia of the Social Sciences,* vol. 12, 1934), pp. 528–538.
[4]One notable, possibly the only, exception to this is the case of the Orang Laut, the Malayan sea gypsies of the Java and Flores Seas. These tribes are autonomous units, living a roving existence entirely in boats.

invited or surreptitious incursions—usually reacting with recourse to war or to regulated expiatory combat. Recognition of communal possession as a true communal property right is seen in the Australian practice whereby one band sends an emissary to another to ask permission to collect certain foods on the lands of the second community. It is up to the band elders to consider and grant or reject the request.

In addition to the obvious economic reasons for exclusiveness in the use of their land, some Australian tribes have a vital, mystic relation to the land. The land is tied up with their dead ancestors; they cannot migrate from it because that would break an immutable tie to the ancestors, and neither do they wish to have upsetting strangers poking around their sacred territory.

Special Sharing of Resources Although Shoshone Indians of the Great Basin identified local groups with their home territories, they freely moved into one another's domains under certain conditions.

Steward has given an admirable explanation of the situation in terms of ecological factors. The uncertainty and variability of the pine-nut and wild-seed crops are so great that territories exploited by different groups shifted widely from year to year. When there were good crops in any locality, they ripened so fast and fell to the ground so quickly that the people who ordinarily lived in the area could not possibly gather them all. When a good harvest was promised, they therefore spread the news abroad so that people whose crops had failed could come to share their harvest with them. "Under such conditions," asserts Steward, "ownership of vegetable food resources would have been a disadvantage to everyone."[5] Nonetheless, the Shoshones held a country they called their own—they owned it and shared it among themselves.

An almost identical practice existed in Australia. There, certain tribes were dependent upon a fruit known as *bunya-bunya,* which, like pine nuts, is uneven in its yield. A territorial group which anticipated a large yield in a given season might send out messengers carrying invitation sticks to other groups, sometimes as far as 100 miles away, or they might raise smoke signals. The visitors were under no circumstances permitted to hunt in the hosts' territory, but they could harvest to their hearts' content for about a month and a half. One observer counted more than twenty tribes, speaking different languages, amicably gathered at a single bunya-bunya harvest.[6]

Among the Eskimos, land is not considered property in any sense, nor is local group sovereignty applied to territory. Anyone, whatever his local group, may hunt where he pleases; the idea of restricting the pursuit of food is repugnant to all Eskimos (except for some groups in western Alaska, who were influenced by the very property-minded Indians of the Northwest Coast).

Eskimo interest is in game per se. Land is ignored and not conceptualized as property, in spite of the fact that each local group is identified by the territory in which it lives.

Such exceptions as these indicate that territorial exclusiveness is by no means universal. However, it is perfectly correct to say that the vast majority of food-gathering and hunting tribes do hold their land in common. Any member of the tribe may hunt where he will; as Neighbors once wrote of the Comanches: "No dispute ever arises between the tribes [bands] with regard to their hunting ground, the whole being held in common."[7]

Land as Joint or Individual Property On the other hand, a few hunting peoples have developed practices of joint, and even individual, ownership of hunting and fishing areas. Notable among these are the Algonkian (for-

[5]J. H. Steward, *Basin Plateau Aboriginal Socio-political Groups* (Bureau of American Ethnology, Bulletin 120, 1938), p. 254.

[6]J. Dawson, *Australian Aborigines,* p. 22.
[7]R. S. Neighbors, *History of the Indian Tribes of the United States,* vol. 2, p. 131.

merly spelled "Algonquian") tribes of Canada and certain Indians of California and the Northwest Coast.

The Kwakiutls of British Columbia partitioned coastal areas of water as private property for fishing purposes. All intruders were driven off. In a similar vein, the California Yuroks exhibited a partial private proprietary right to ocean areas. Kroeber told of a Yurok family that "owned" a portion of the sea off the beach extending about four miles in either direction from their house site. Other people could fish there, but they had to surrender the flippers of all sea lions taken within the area.[8] Dentalium beds beneath the ocean were also owned by families. No others could harvest them.

The Algonkian Land-ownership Controversy
The question of whether the Algonkian Indians in the eastern woodlands of Canada practiced joint-family (or even individual) ownership of hunting territories has interested American anthropologists for half a century. Recently, Marxist-oriented theorists such as Marvin Harris[9] and Harold Hickerson[10] have stirred the embers of the issue into the flames of dogmatic controversy. According to Hickerson:

The idea of primitive communism was an important part of the social evolutionary theory of Morgan. More than that, it was the foundation for Marxian historical materialism in its broadest reference to the development of human society. . . .

The notion of private or familial ownership among the Algonkians, still in the upper stage of barbarism, would refute Morgan's idea that communism was the first stage in the development of forms of ownership. . . .

The descriptions by Speck, Eiseley, Cooper,

Hallowell, Landes, and others of a particularistic Algonkian social order . . . entail an assault, at times made explicit, on Morgan's evolutionary theory of human sociocultural development, an assault which has the more significance because of the threat, tacit or otherwise, to the theory of the priority of collective norms of the Marxists.[11]

It would almost seem that the survival of the Communist ideological world hinges on whether Algonkian Indians practiced non-communal ownership of land in their pristine state of pre-Columbian "barbarism," or whether the practice was a product of contact with European "exploitive mercantile and industrial systems." Be that as it may, the concern of the earlier Algonkian specialists was with Morgan the evolutionist, and not with Marx and Engels the communist social theorists.

The discovery of family-held hunting territories among the Algonkians was the work of Frank G. Speck (1881–1950), the outstanding fieldworker in the area prior to A. I. Hallowell. In a classic paper, called "The Family Hunting Band as the Basis of Algonkian Social Organization,"[12] Speck undertook to demonstrate that (1) the family group was a fundamental social unit among the hunting tribes of the northeastern woodlands; (2) hunting territories were held by, and inherited within, such groups; (3) there were effective ecological reasons for the usage; and (4) the practice was already in existence at the time Europeans first arrived on the scene. Speck subsequently mapped out family hunting territories for several Algonkian tribes.

Speck granted that family hunting territories as he found them among the Algonkians were an exception to the general rule of tribal ownership among hunters. This was possible, he proposed, because the Algonkians relied on nonmigratory fur bearers, such as the beaver and muskrat, for most of their meat and skins. Speck demonstrated that Algonkians actually husbanded their

[8]A. L. Kroeber, lecture, "Seminar in Psychological Approaches to Culture" (University of California, Spring, 1941). An interesting legal case arising from failure to surrender the flippers is analyzed in E. A. Hoebel, *The Law of Primitive Man*, pp. 54–55.
[9]M. Harris, *The Rise of Anthropological Theory*, pp. 357–359.
[10]H. Hickerson, "Some Implications of the Theory of the Particularity, or 'Atomism' of Northern Algonkians" (*Current Anthropology*, vol. 8, 1967), pp. 313–327.

[11]*Ibid.*, pp. 315, 316.
[12]*American Anthropologist*, vol. 17, 1915, pp. 289–305.

colonies of these animals. Each man knew how many beaver houses and occupants there were in the ponds owned by him. He took care to harvest only as many as would not exhaust the breeding stock. Strangers trapping a pond or stream could quickly exterminate the beaver. Strictly enforced private property rights worked against this danger.

In 1939, John M. Cooper, another Algonkian specialist, reviewed the whole question, concluding: "In a word, previously to and independently of the [European] fur trade, the furbearers were of very great value to the northern Algonquians, as meeting their needs in food, clothing, and [inter-tribal] trade."[13] Hence, it was unlikely that competition for furs to trade to Europeans had generated the system.

Two contemporary anthropologists have returned to the empirical data to argue that Algonkians subsisted on moose rather than beaver prior to the introduction of the European fur trade,[14] or that family hunting territories were functionally impossible—people would have starved to death on them.[15]

So, after half a century, the question of the pre-Columbian existence of the Algonkian joint-family hunting territory remains unresolved. If the problem were a simple anthropological issue of fact, it would have been buried and forgotten long since. The issue is not one on which archaeology can be of help. Property consists of social behavior which leaves no concrete remains. There is nothing of relevance for the archaeologist to recover. History is silent, for the first historical notes on Algonkian land ownership were written well after the European fur trade was estab-

lished. No social anthropologist was on the ground to observe and record. In short, there is no way in which anthropological science can resolve the problem; there is not enough for it to work with. The issue survives as one of political dogmatics which, like militant theology, is more prone to generate polemics than rational objectivity.

Land Tenure among Pastoralists Among pastoral herders, there is a notorious "carelessness as to land." The Comanches, for instance, who were horse herders and hunters of game, had no concept of land. "Land was a matter of unconcern for them, being held neither individually, jointly nor communally."[16] Buffalo herds could be found anywhere, and pasturage for their horses was unlimited.

Even among people whose grazing resources are limited, the tendency is to treat the pasturage as public domain. Notable exceptions have, nevertheless, been reported for the Tungus reindeer herders of Siberia and the Kazaks (or Kirghiz, as the Russians call them to avoid confusion with the Cossacks) of Central Asia east of the Caspian Sea.

Although the Chukchi and Samoyed, neighbors of the Tungus, do not subdivide their pastures within the tribe, the Tungus treat the pastures as the common property of a group of cooperating and intermarrying clans, from which they exclude other groups and their herds by force, if necessary. In some instances, a territory is divided among clans as such. In recent times, individual families have utilized customary grazing grounds somewhat exclusively and irrespective of clan ties.[17]

Kazak practices are even more distinctive. These excellent horsemen subsist on large

---

[13]J. M. Cooper, "Is the Algonquian Family Hunting Ground System Pre-Columbian?" (*American Anthropologist*, vol. 41, 1939), p. 87.

[14]E. Leacock, *The Montagnais "Hunting Territory" and the Fur Trade* (American Anthropological Association, Memoir 78, 1954).

[15]R. Knight, "A Re-examination of Hunting, Trapping and Territoriality among the Northeastern Algonkian Indians," in A. Leeds and A. Vayda (eds.), *The Role of Animals in Human Ecological Adjustments*, pp. 27–42.

[16]E. A. Hoebel, *The Political Organization and Law-ways of the Comanche Indians* (American Anthropological Association, Memoir 54: Contributions from the Laboratory of Anthropology, 4, 1940), p. 118.

[17]C. D. Forde, *Habitat, Economy, and Society*, p. 361.

flocks of sheep and a few goats and camels. As is so often the case in primitive economy, they vary their life and social organization according to the seasons. It is their custom to summer in the lowlands, where they graze their herds at will in the tribal territory. In April, each household sneaks out of the winter village in an attempt to get to good pasturage before the others. In midsummer, drought so parches the land that constant movement from one grass spot to another is necessary. The families and clans do not lay claims to any piece of the country at this season, for the richness of the herbage varies greatly from year to year. Winter camps are fixed settlements conveniently located near a well-protected pasturage amid the trees in a deep river valley. Each lineage or family group has its winter grazing sites established with natural boundaries or rock piles and stakes.

Land Tenure among Gardeners   Land as property is seen in quite a different light in societies based on gardening and agriculture than in those we have previously discussed. Since full-fledged gardeners and farmers are more or less intimately bound to the soil, it is hardly surprising that they show greater interest in it.

For the most part, primitive gardeners work their lands individually, by lineages or by clans, and occasionally by clubs, but the ultimate title to the land commonly rests in the community. This makes it necessary to draw a clear distinction between proprietary title and *rights of use*. The basic principles of land ownership and use in Indonesia clearly exemplify the distinction.

Land Tenure in Indonesia   In Indonesia, among the indigenous rice growers, we find the relationship between communal ownership and individual holding clearly delineated. In the autonomous villages of the independent tribes, all land belongs to the village, which is made up of a core of related clansmen. The solidarity of the group is strong and mystically

symbolized in the possession of a common temple and sacred relics. The deceased village ancestors are buried in the soil, which contributes to the group's feeling of sacred intimacy with its land. Any member of the community may reclaim and cultivate from the unused communal land as much ground as he can handle, provided he first informs the headman, obtains his consent, and makes a ritual sacrifice. Then he alone is entitled to cultivate that land as long as he works it and keeps it clear. He has continuing rights of use. Among some Indonesians, however, if he neglects to prepare the field at the start of any season, he may be confronted by someone else who wants to take it up. Then he must set to work or let the field go. Generally, however, if he abandons a field, he retains his rights of use until the jungle has reclaimed it. Then it reverts wholly to the community domain. If he has built dikes, it may be that his hold remains unimpeded until all traces of the dikes have disappeared.

He may borrow goods or money on such lands as he holds by pledging the land as security. But he may never "sell" the land, nor can a creditor ever obtain a complete foreclosure. There is no possibility of alienation. Land belongs forever to the community.

Outsiders may acquire use of land from the community domain by arranging for payments to the local headman. The contract is in theory for one year only and must be renewed annually. The importance of inalienability to survival of native life was recognized by the Dutch in the last century when they forbade the selling of Indonesian land to nonnatives and limited the duration of leaseholds by Europeans and other aliens.

Among the inhabitants of a village, the rights of use are inheritable within the family line, but if a line dies out, the land reverts directly to the community domain for redistribution by the headman.

An interesting aspect of the close social bond between the community and its land is seen in the event of a secret murder of an outsider on community land. If the murderer cannot be found, the community owning the land must indemnify the victim's kinsmen. After all, he died on their common property, so it is assumed that he was killed by someone in that group.[18]

Ifugao Land Tenure   In the Philippines, the Ifugaos reveal a pattern basically similar to the one just generalized for Indonesia at large. The Ifugaos are extreme individualists, however, and have no organized villages. Terraced rice fields belong to families, with rights of use inherited by both males and females as a part of their marriage portions. *Camote,* or sweet potato, fields are hewn from the public domain in the mountainside forests by man and wife together and are owned by them jointly as long as they are cultivated. Soil depletion in *camote* fields is so rapid, however, that they are abandoned after several years. Still, the title remains with the clearers of the fields until the second growth of underbrush has reached the thickness that prevailed before clearing.

Abandoned rice fields may be taken up without permission by a person other than the owner for a period equal to the exact number of years they have lain unused. After that, the title of the original owner becomes active once again. This certainly seems to be a sensible safeguard against withdrawal of needed land from production by overlanded gentry.[19]

The rule that a person must work lands recently acquired from the public domain in order to retain title is a general and basic one among primitive gardeners the world over. It effectively guards against one of man's besetting social evils—land hoarding by a wealthy few and the closing of the doors of opportunity to the land-hungry.

Pueblo Indian Land Tenure   How fundamental and widespread the Indonesian land-use principles are in the primitive gardening com- plex can be seen from Titiev's comment on the Hopi pueblo of Oraibi in Arizona:

> The village chief is the theoretical owner of all his town's lands; these lands are divided among the clans residing in his pueblo; and each individual farms a specified portion of his clan's holdings. In addition, there is a large piece of unassigned land, part of which may be used by any villager with his chief's consent. Under such a system land is never bartered or sold, and only rarely exchanged. Ownership is restricted to the privilege of use, but this right is so carefully recognized that if a man decides to allow some of his fields to lie fallow, no other farmer may use them without the specific permission of the owner.[20]

Grazing land for sheep, goats, cattle, and horses is communally shared. The Hopi practice is characteristic of all the pueblos of New Mexico and Arizona.

The rights of use in pueblo land are, however, contingent upon the fulfillment of obligatory duties toward the maintenance of the well-being of the pueblo as a whole. These duties are many, including participation in ceremonial dances. For failure to fulfill these duties the members of a Sia Pueblo family, who had been converted to the Pentecostal faith, were exiled from the pueblo and their rights of use in the land, which had been inherited by the family for generations, were revoked. They received no compensation for their houses, for these were made of the earth and stone belonging to Utset, the Mother Creator, and through her assigned to the pueblo forever.[21] Persons and families receive their rights of use contingently from the pueblo.

Land Tenure in African Tribal States   On a higher level of political development, as seen in a number of West African tribal states such as that of the Ashanti of Ghana, all land "belongs" to the paramount chief, or king. He

[18]B. ter Haar, *Adat Law in Indonesia*, pp. 81–127.
[19]R. F. Barton, *Ifugao Law* (University of California Publications in American Ethnology and Archaeology, vol. 15, 1919), pp. 40–44.

[20]M. Titiev, *Old Oraibi* (Papers of the Peabody Museum of American Archaeology and Ethnology, Harvard University, vol. 22, no. 1, 1944), p. 181.
[21]The case is described in full in E. A. Hoebel, "Keresan Pueblo Law," in L. Nader (ed.), *Law in Culture and Society*, pp. 112–116.

assigns it to various chiefs; they allocate it to clans, whose headmen assign individual plots to each gardener. In return, the land-working populace owes fealty to the chiefs and above all to the king. They must do public work, pay taxes, and perform military service. As long as they are loyal and faithful in their duties and as long as they are not involved in serious crime, they may not be ousted from their lands. The privilege of use passes down through the family. However, a man may not transfer or sell his plot outside the family without approval of his clan elders. Often the family would pawn or sell a member into slavery in order to avoid alienation of its hold on the land. Since the services which are called for from landholders are general public duties, they are actually services to the king only in theory. The king's ownership of all land is therefore largely ideological. The kingship serves as the symbol of community unity, and landed property is phrased in terms to fit the ideal.

The symbolic and emotional overtones of the relation of men to their lands are nicely expressed in the words of Max Gluckman:

The secular value of the earth lies in the way it provides for the private interests of individuals and groups within the larger society. They make their living off particular gardens, pastures, and fishing-pools; they build their homes, make their fires, and eat their meals on their own plots of ground; they beget and rear their children on the earth. Their ancestors are buried in the earth. Men and groups dispute over particular pieces of earth to serve these varied ends. But men live, work, dance, breed, die, on the earth in the company of other men. They obtain their rights to earth by virtue of membership of groups, and they can only maintain themselves by virtue of this membership. To live on the earth they require friendship with other men over a certain area. The earth, undivided, as the basis of society, thus comes to symbolize not individual prosperity, fertility, and good fortune; but the general prosperity, fertility, and good fortune on which individual life depends. Rain does not fall on one plot, but on an area; locust swarms and blights and famine and epidemics bring communal disaster, and not individual disaster alone. With this general prosperity are associated peace and the recognition of a moral order over a range of land. In West Africa men worship the Earth, and in this worship groups who are otherwise in hostile relations annually unite in celebration. In Central and South Africa kings, who symbolize the political unity of tribes, are identified with the earth: the Barotse word for king means 'earth'. And in some African tribes there is a dogma that the king must be killed when his physical powers decline, lest the powers of the earth decline simultaneously. Among the Nuer, the ritual expert who is connected with the earth, in its general fertility, and who therefore symbolizes the communal need for peace and the recognition of moral rights in the community of men, acts as mediator between warring sections.[22]

General Principles of Land Tenure among Primitive Peoples Primitive gardeners assign the rights of use to individuals or families. In some instances, title is vested in the clan, but usually ultimate ownership is vested in the community. In parts of Africa, this communism is transformed into a type of feudal monarchy, where the king symbolizes community entity. Unused land is public domain from which enterprising individuals may carve their plots, with or without official approval, depending on tribal practice.

On the whole, primitive peoples overwhelmingly treat their land resources as a communal asset. In this sense, they are preponderantly communistic. Pastoralists are, for the most part, land communists because the necessity to rove makes individual ownership impractical. In the case of the hunters and gatherers, there is also little impulse to private ownership of land, since so far as the hunters are concerned, most animals are free-ranging, and it is more advantageous to rove at will when on the chase. When the habits of prized animals made it feasible, such peoples as the Algonkians and Northwest Coast Indians were quite ready to abandon land communism for vested rights. Primeval man is not "by nature" a communist. But he

[22]M. Gluckman, *Custom and Conflict in Africa*, pp. 16–17.

responded to ecological and economic factors which usually made communal land ownership the most feasible means of allocating access to basic food resources.

Theories of social evolution which assume "primitive communism" as the first mile on man's rough road thus have some foundation, as far as use of the land resources goes.

Those who take the institutions of private property for granted are prone to point to the widespread communism of primitive man as proof of the "advanced" quality of private-property institutions. Communism, they hold, is representative of a primitive state, and the spread of modern Communism is a reversion to a condition of savagery.

With equal lack of balance, Marxists see the land communism of the primitives as proof that communism is the "natural" and therefore the proper and manifest condition for all human society.

The anthropologist notes that the real estate practices of primitive peoples are not properly to be conceived as a justification for any particular economic forms in modern civilization. These varying property practices merely demonstrate that men can, and usually do, adjust their social institutions to the special needs of their subsistence technologies and natural resources.

Property Rights in Consumables

Food is undoubtedly one of the most basic property interests of omnivorous man. Land may seem important, but that is largely because it is the chief original source of the food supply. We have already seen that some foodstuffs are in some societies free goods, as is the air we breathe. But elsewhere and oftentimes access to food is limited; the ethics of food use fluctuate. The sense of the necessity of mutual aid and a realization of the inescapable interdependence of men struggle eternally with the self-assertive urges of barebones survival (when resources give

but slim pickings) and selfish gratification of desires. Selfishness corrupts altruistic ideals; mutual aid tempers the harshest self-interest. Property rights in food are the formal crystallization of each society's struggle to regulate the distribution and use of this essential commodity.

Property Rights in Game Wild plants and animals on communal lands are communal property, but the slaying of game and the collection of plant stuffs alter the economic condition of these goods, subjecting them to altered property statuses. So it is that, while the general principle of collective ownership of free-running game and unharvested plants holds good, we find that in most instances the expenditure of work in reducing the game and plants into consumable food stocks converts them into private property. All peoples recognize private ownership of food. Yet inasmuch as private ownership never entails absolute exclusiveness, and since among hunters and gatherers food is derived from communally owned resources, the communal claim upon privately owned foodstuffs is insistent.

Among the Comanches, anyone coming upon a hunter who had just made a kill could claim the choicest quarter of the animal merely by placing his hand upon it. If four different people happened on the unfortunate hunter, they took everything except the hide. This, custom decreed, he could retain by hanging onto the tail of the beast. Far to the north, Boas recorded, the following was typical for the Baffin Land Eskimos: "Who first strikes a walrus receives the tusks and one of the forequarters; the next man, the neck and head; the following, the belly; and each of the next two, one of the hindquarters."[23]

Again, in the practice of the Comanches, any hunter returning to the camp with game was obliged to come in openly and share his

[23]F. Boas, *The Eskimo of Baffinland and Hudson Bay* (American Museum of Natural History, Bulletin No. 15, 1907), p. 116.

spoils with all who came to his lodge for a portion of it. "If a man won't give it away, they camp on him until he does."[24] To frustrate this social lien on the products of their individual efforts, some families camped alone during hard times.

After the communal antelope hunts of the Plains Indians, the meat was equally divided among all participating families, for the whole project was a gigantic cooperative undertaking. In communal bison hunts, after the acquisition of horses, all Plains tribes allowed each man whose marked arrow had killed a bison to keep the meat. But even so, the old and infirm who could not hunt and the wives of luckless hunters received their shares from those who had made a kill, and it was the usual thing to teach a boy to give away all his first kill of any large game animal.

Food Sharing   Sharing of food, even though the food is privately owned, is the basic virtue of almost all American Indian tribes and of most of the primitive hunters of the world. To be generous with food—that is the ideal. But as Lowie has pointed out, etiquette which demands that all comers be fed from a man's private larder is something quite different from actual communal ownership of a common hoard by all the members of the group.[25] The psychological and social response to private beneficence results in a different order of social prestige ranking from that which is produced by common ownership.

The successful hunter reaps prestige from his beneficence as a public provider. In return for food, which does not come easily, he is accorded a leadership position among his people. His rewards, beyond what he may eat himself, are sociopsychological. He is motivated to extend himself as a hunter not only that he may eat but also that he may enjoy the pleasures of socially recognized achievement. There is real survival value for a marginal subsistence society in this arrangement. The African Bushman headman known to Elizabeth Thomas is a perfect example of this common pattern among hunting peoples:

Toma flourished as a young man and became an excellent hunter with tireless legs, tireless eyes, and a deadly aim, and it was said of him that he never returned from a hunt without having killed at least a wildebeast, if not something larger. Hence, the people connected with him ate a great deal of meat and his popularity grew.[26]

Outright pooling of food occurs less commonly among the hunting and collecting peoples than among the gardeners. In the South Pacific, it is associated with prestige competition between local groups and tribes. Great quantities of produce are offered to the chief to be used in feasting rival tribes. The chief's storehouses among the Maori, for example, were the people's storehouses, for the people identified his needs as their needs. They were regularly fed from the great storehouses, but above all, their great concern was that the chief should be able to entertain visitors munificently. Should he fail in this, their outraged pride would make them ashamed before the world. Eating was to the Maori the supreme pleasure, and only by the joint efforts of all could it reach the great heights they so cherished.

Communal pooling of certain foods is also characteristic of American Pueblo Indians. Annual rabbit hunts are held every fall, and all men must participate as a religious duty. The dried rabbits are offered to the head priest-chief of the pueblo, who stores them in his house to be used in ceremonial meals and to be doled out by him to the poor and hungry families of his pueblo in time of need.

Individual Property Rights in Game   At the opposite extreme, certain Algonkian hunters of

[24]E. A. Hoebel, *The Political Organization and Law-ways of the Comanche Indians*, p. 119.
[25]R. H. Lowie, *Primitive Society*, pp. 207–210.

[26]E. M. Thomas, *The Harmless People*, p. 182; see also J. H. Dowling, "Individual Ownership and the Sharing of Game in Hunting Societies" (*American Anthropologist*, vol. 70, 1968), pp. 502–507.

North America, such as the Ojibwa, demonstrate the ideological lengths to which rugged individualism in food procured from wild game can go. Says Landes:

The game and fish that a man catches in the winter are his private property. When he returns with them to his lodge . . . he decides what to do with them. . . . When he gives game to his wife . . . he has lost all claim to it. It is never said that he gives game to his wife for her use in making food and clothing for the family; but they phrase it that a man gives game to his wife and therefore the game belongs to her to do with as she pleases. . . . The wife now employs "her" property in the manufacture of food and clothing. She gives the finished product to her husband, immature children, and herself. When these gifts have been given, they become the property of the recipients.[27]

Among many hunting tribes, animals having a fixed abode, such as a hibernating bear, a bee, or an eagle, are often seized upon as objects of private ownership, even where all other claims to animals are communal. The Nama Hottentot places a few broken twigs before a wild beehive, and a Sia Indian publicly announces the location of bee trees which he has discovered—not to invite others to find the way to the delicacy, but to warn them off. Eagle nests are privately owned among all the Pueblo Indians, so that eagles born in the nest belong to the owner of it. A Pueblo hunter who finds a bear's den marks it, and the bear is his to take in the spring.

Similarly, wild fruit trees in Indonesia and among many peoples of the South Pacific may be blazed or otherwise marked by an individual so that he alone may harvest the tree's yield. In the Melanesian area, the tree is guarded by a magic charm that brings foul diseases to any violator of the property right of the owner. Ownership of such trees is usually divorced from the land upon which the tree stands. In some places, it is even possible to own a tree that stands on another man's land.

[27]R. Landes, "The Ojibwa of Canada," in M. Mead (ed.), *Cooperation and Competition among Primitive Peoples*, pp. 90–91.

Property Rights in Garden Produce   Ownership of foodstuffs produced by gardening tends generally to be vested in individuals or family households, but the lines are not drawn with universal consistency. Since most garden plots are worked under individual rights of use or outright ownership, and since most of the expended effort is individual effort, harvests are commonly individually owned. Polynesian practices in contravention of this usage have already been noted, however. Among the Keresan-speaking Pueblos, just as rabbit hunts are communal duties, so are the planting and cultivating of the cacique's, or chief's, garden. The harvest is stored in the cacique's house for communal use.

Matrilateral practices in Melanesia require that a man raise his crops on his sister's behalf. Since his sister's household is not his own household, he must in effect transfer the yams from his garden to the storehouses of her husband. His storehouses in turn are filled in part by his wife's brother. What a man produces does not necessarily remain his own property.

Property Rights in Livestock   The word "chattel," which means any object of personal ownership, is derived from the Old French word *chatel*. The modern Anglo-American word "cattle" has the same origin. *Chatel* has its ultimate etymology in the Latin word *caput,* meaning "head." *Chatel* in ancient France referred to property of the greatest value, head property. Cattle were so much the chief form of property among our pastoral ancestors that our specialized word for personal property grew from the same root. And the word "pecuniary" (pertaining to money) derives directly from the class of movable property known as *pecunia* in Roman law, where the term was itself derived directly from the Latin word *pecus,* meaning "herd."

This small fragment of word history formulates the universal principle of stock ownership among all primitive peoples. Cattle are chattels. They are privately owned. The one great known exception occurred in that remarkable precursor of the totalitarian socialist state, the Inca Empire. Among the Incas, private citizens could own up to ten llamas, but the vast majority of the beasts were state property. The wool collected from the state herds was stored in government warehouses, to be distributed annually in equal allotments to each family head.[28]

Grazing land among migratory primitive pastoralists does not economically lend itself to subdivision. Hence, as has been noted, it is usually communally held and used. But livestock comes in individual units to which individuals may readily attach themselves. Undoubtedly, there is a deep emotional impulse underlying this tendency. Domestication begins in a symbiotic relationship between man and animal which is fundamentally personal. It is most clearly seen in the affectionate relation between man and his dog, the first of the domesticated beasts. It runs through all herders in greater or lesser degree. Nuer men, when they have nothing more pressing to do, spend hours in sensuous contemplation of their cattle.[29]

[28]J. H. Rowe, "Inca Culture at the Time of the Spanish Conquest," in J. H. Steward (ed.), *Handbook of South American Indians*, vol. 2, pp. 219, 267.

[29]E. E. Evans-Pritchard, *The Nuer.* pp. 16–50.

Fig. 13-1   Livestock are chattel. Karamojong pastoralists of Kenya, in East Africa, placing their property mark on one of their animals. (Courtesy of **Natural History** *and Rada and Neville Dyson-Hudson.)*

"Some men," said Post Oak Jim, of the Comanche herders of 1850, "loved their horses more than their wives." Favorite horses among most Plains Indians were treated almost as family members. Among the Solomon Islanders and other Melanesians, pigs are the chief objects of value.

In the history of mankind, the domestication of animals has undoubtedly been a great stimulus to the development of private-property institutions. Thus the *World Ethnographic Sample* shows wealth to be a significant factor in the social differentiation of freemen only among pastoralists (phi = 0.157).[30]

[30]A. D. Coult and R. W. Habenstein, *Cross Tabulations of Murdock's Ethnographic Sample*, p. 518.

Property Rights in Artifacts

Weapons and implements for individual use are ordinarily owned either by their creator or by their user. Primitive women ordinarily own the pottery they have modeled. A man owns the spear or ax he has shaped himself. There is to some extent an identity between the artisan and his creation, as though it were an extension of his personality. Most of mankind has recognized this identity and respected it by establishing protective devices in the form of personal-property institutions. The stimulus to individual effort which is activated as a result contributes to the adaptive success of the society in self-maintenance.

Fig. 13-2 A Digo, Kenya, magical protector of the garden. A thief will be pursued and punished by its power. (Courtesy of Luther P. Gerlach.)

Trobriand Canoe Ownership Joint and mixed ownership of artifacts is also common. Thus, among the Trobriand Islanders, each canoe is nominally "owned" by one man; yet others, who make up its crew, have proprietary rights in the use of the vessel.

All these men, who as a rule belong to the same sub-clan, are bound to each other . . . by mutual obligations; when the whole community go out fishing, the owner cannot refuse his canoe. He must go out himself or let someone else do it instead. The crew are equally under an obligation to him . . . each man must fill his place and stand by his task. Each man also receives his fair share in the distribution of the catch as an equivalent of his service. Thus the ownership and use of the canoe consist of a series of definite obligations and duties uniting a group of people into a working team.[31]

Incorporeal Property

It no longer surprises anthropologists that nonmaterial things of value are objects of property in primitive society.[32] It never would have surprised us at all if our grandfather's generation and its predecessors had not been so smugly self-assured that uncivilized men were of childlike mentality and that Europeans alone were capable of mental abstraction.

However, the better to understand the nature of incorporeal property, consider the case of a Plains Indian visionary who has fasted and sought supernatural power. A bear has appeared to him in a dream; it spoke to him and taught him four new songs, and it also instructed him in the preparation of a rawhide shield to be painted with a bear symbol and other devices. The bear in the vision also instructed his tutelary that a shield made in accordance with the instructions would provide immunity in battle if the four songs were sung before an engagement began. The visionary has made a shield as instructed; he has sung the songs; his comrades have heard the words; and he has deliberately exposed himself to the missiles of the enemy, coming through unscathed. The value of the shield and the songs has been publicly demonstrated. The shield, as Lowie has made clear, is a material object that is clearly personal property.

But the shield as such, in the culture of the Plains Indians, is of little value. What is of value in conjunction with the shield are the songs and the mystic power which the two engender together. The incorporeal property is the thing of worth. The complex of shield, song, and power may be transferred as a gift to son, nephew, brother, or friend. (In at least one Comanche case, which the author has recorded, the transfer had to be followed by the recipient's having a vision before the mystic power would become operative, however, and this may frequently be the case among other tribes.) Or this same complex may be sold in a commercial transaction having the qualities of a contractual sale. In either case, the recipient may use the complex if he has properly acquired the rights through regularized transfer, but not otherwise. The consequence of unauthorized use of the shield and songs is that the usurper will most certainly be killed by enemy missiles because of the punitive action of the supernatural power. But there is no reason to believe that the true owner may not recover the shield if it is stolen, and with it his enjoyment of the songs.

Certainly we have here a sufficiently large aggregate of rights denoted by ownership so that we may properly speak of them as incorporeal property. Thus, we find again and again that magic rites and charms, songs, dances, and names are the property of persons and groups of persons. Myths and legends may belong to lineages, as among the Indians of the Northwest Coast. These are

[31]B. Malinowski, *Crime and Custom in Savage Society*, p. 18.
[32]See R. H. Lowie, "Incorporeal Property in Primitive Society" (*Yale Law Journal*, vol. 38, 1928), p. 551; and *Primitive Society*, pp. 235–243. See also E. A. Hoebel, *The Law of Primitive Man*, pp. 60–63.

objects of property in exactly the same sense as are our copyrights, patents, and "good-will." After all, if a people is capable of creating intangible patterns for behavior, such as magic and songs, it is not a great step into the abstruse to attach protective social rules to these abstractions when and if they become objects of value.

Likewise, the hereditary right to work is a traditional incorporeal property right for certain groups in India, and the available work is distributed accordingly. N. S. Reddy writes of the Madiga caste of leatherworkers in Madras: "The right to work is inherited as any other piece of property, and the quantum of employment that accrues to the individual holder is upheld by the community at large."[33]

SUMMARY

The essential nature of property is to be found in social relations rather than in any inherent attributes of the thing or object which we call *property*. Property, in other words, is not a thing, but a network of social relations governing the conduct of people with respect to the use and disposition of things. Each member of a society has a social position in relation to the property object. These positions are associated with customary ways of behaving (roles), which determine each person's rights to use the object, on the one hand, or which forbid or limit his use of it, on the other.

If any object can be used by anybody or everybody, it is not "property" but a free good. If it is thought by the members of a society to be equally accessible (even though only in theory) to all the members of that society, we have *communal property*. If the statuses (or social positions) of the members of a group, such as a family, lineage, or association, are predominantly similar in relation to the use of an object, we have *joint property*. If the position of an individual in relation to

the object is such that he alone has predominant priority in its use and disposition, we are confronted with *private property*. Property relations, however, are so complex that such labels must be used with great restraint, for any given manifestation of property may be compounded of qualities of all three orders. Property can properly be analyzed only in terms of the detailed norms of behavior that exist in each culture.

Such analysis does, however, show that certain kinds of objects have a tendency to become communal, joint, or private property, according to the nature of the subsistence culture.

Land is the most basic form of property. Among most primitive peoples, the ultimate title to land is vested in the tribe, although a few hunters, like the Eskimos, have no concept of land as property. Among the Algonkian tribes of the woodlands of eastern Canada, who focused on the trapping of small game, hunting lands were held by families or even by individual owners. Whether or not these exceptional practices extended back into pre-Columbian times is uncertain. The issue has taken on a strong theoretical color because of the importance of primitive land communism in Marxist evolutionary theory.

Pastoral people, in particular, tend not to establish property claims in land, although they have highly refined individual or lineage property rights in their herds. Gardening tribes vest rights of use in family lines, which in turn assign the land to individuals, or else village headmen assign plots periodically, acting on behalf of the tribal chief, who symbolically is the owner for all the tribe.

Food is usually private property, but its use and distribution may often be subject to complex customs which express a social claim requiring a sharing of food through exchange, tribute to a chief, or hospitality. Tools, weapons, clothing, and ornaments are generally private property.

Primitive peoples are, in general terms, neither more nor less communistic than civil-

---

[33]N. S. Reddy, *Transition in Caste Structure in Andrah Desh with Particular Reference to Depressed Castes*, p. 61.

ized peoples in ownership of property, except that land is more consistently held in common and landlordship is rare.

Romantic notions that all primitive societies are marked by the free sharing of all necessities are dispelled by examination of ethnographic facts. Ownership as defined by various primitive groups is remarkably complex, often rigidly structured, and sometimes bewilderingly varied. Primitive societies frequently extend the concept of ownership to intangibles (ideas, songs, rituals, arts) as well as to concrete objects. Thus, there may actually be less free access to the "good things in life" than in our own society; certainly, there is more formalized exclusivity than idealists often suppose.

SELECTED READINGS

Gluckman, M., *The Ideas in Barotse Jurisprudence* (1965), chaps. 3, 4, and 5. Presents and analyzes the concepts and uses of a South African tribe with respect to status and rights in land, immovable property, and chattels. A thorough and sophisticated piece of work.

Goody, J., *Death, Property, and the Ancestors* (1962). Part III (pp. 273–327) is an excellent conceptual analysis of property in primitive and civilized cultures. The entire book is a masterful study of mortuary ceremonies and property transmission and of their functional relation to social structure in two African tribes.

Hallowell, A. I., "The Nature and Function of Property as a Social Institution" (*Journal of Legal and Political Sociology*, vol. 1, 1943), pp. 115–138. The most thorough anthropological treatment of the subject currently available.

Herskovits, M. J., *Economic Anthropology* (1952), part IV, "Property." An extensive treatment of the subject.

ter Haar, B., *Adat Law in Indonesia* (1948), chaps. 2 and 10, "Land Rights" and "Inheritance." A comprehensive survey of adat law among the many tribes in this area of Southeast Asia.

Thurnwald, R., *Economics in Primitive Communities* (1932), chap. 10, "Ownership and Property." A very brief statement of general principles.

Chapter 14

Housing

The need for shelter has long been recognized as one of the basic requirements of mankind. Yet a survey of the way in which both primitive and civilized men have housed themselves through the ages leads to the conclusion that the majority of humanity has never (not even today) enjoyed comfortable or more than minimally healthy housing. This is not to say that most people have been dissatisfied with their forms of shelter, for acute discontent usually produces change. It is merely that man's great inventive genius seems to have been focused more on other technologies and arts than on the amenities of his own housing.

Consider the Navaho in his simplest of houses making intricate sand paintings and performing his nine-day chants, the Australian, with only his bush windbreak for shelter, putting on elaborate initiatory rites, or the earth-lodge Pawnee (Figure 14-1) with his complex hako ceremony to ensure long life.

It must be concluded that the need for shelter is so physically elemental that it is

Fig. 14-A   Taos pueblo, New Mexico, (Collections in the Museum of New Mexico. Photo by Wyatt Davis.)

easily and simply satisfied, while the feelings of insecurity and inadequacy that myth, magic, and religion strive to overcome are so deep and diffuse that elaborate cultural inventions are devised to relieve them. Further —and possibly, most important—man's earliest childhood experiences are closely associated with the particular type of dwelling possessed by his family. Basic habits are linked to a definite form of dwelling, and changes in housing patterns mean changes in individual personality and, indeed, in family and kinship structures and function. More than that, changes in house form may very well necessitate changes in the entire social structure.

Basic Cultural Values

The state of technology in a given society, the skill with which men have learned to build structures, might be assumed to be a key factor in the kind and quality of the homes to be found in a given society, but examination fails to reveal a satisfactory correlation. The majority of New Guineans live in simple thatched huts, but the Sepik River men's clubhouses (*Haus Tambaran*) are imposing, highly decorated structures with great gabled roofs rising sometimes to heights of more than 100 feet (Figure 14-2). As Herskovits points out, the term "dwelling" is by no means synonymous with shelter or building. "The magnificent Central American structures, or those of the 'lost' civilizations of Malaysia were not dwellings at all. They symbolized the power of the ruler, the splendor with which the gods were worshipped."[1] It is all too abundantly clear that a similar dichotomy between building skills as applied to monuments, cathedrals, commercial skyscrapers,

[1]M. J. Herskovits, *Cultural Anthropology,* p. 131.

Fig. 14-1   A Pawnee Indian earth-lodge village on the Loup River in Nebraska in 1871. (Smithsonian Institution, National Anthropological Archives.)

etc., and building skills as applied to peoples' *homes* has chronically existed among literate and advanced civilizations as well as in non-literate societies (Figure 14-3). Only in the last century have Western men turned their architectural attention to developing comforts and convenience in their own homes. The goal of "adequate housing for all" is no more than a few decades old and abysmally far from view, even in affluent America.

Fig. 14-2 Entrance (below) and decorated facade (above) of men's clubhouse (Haus Tambaran) *of the Maprik District, Middle Sepik River, New Guinea, showing details of its monumental structure and the elaborate magico-religious symbolism of its painted facade. The colors are orange, yellow, brown, black, and white. (Photo by E. A. Hoebel.)*

Fig. 14-3 The monumental edifice and simple dwelling. A Catholic church and Samoan house, Savaii, Western Samoa. Since Christianization in 1821, the Samoans have turned much of their energy to competitive building of innumerable churches while still retaining their traditional, joint-family, open-sided thatched house. In this scene, the mats which may be let down in time of storms have been dropped around the side toward the church. (Photo by E. A. Hoebel.)

Factors Influencing Housing   A strange conservatism marks the entire development of housing. Certainly men have not concentrated interest or attention on the problem of providing functionally sound housing with anything like the degree of assiduity with which problems of myth making, religion, art, song, and dance have been treated.

Despite a wide variety of housing forms around the world and across time, we find again and again that man has modified his dwellings not at all or only with the most perverse obstinacy, even when opportunities for "improvements" were well known or close at hand. The Navaho in his crude wood and dirt hogan (Figure 14-4) has lived for a thousand years in close proximity to the sophisticated adobe apartment houses of the Pueblos without manifesting the slightest revision of his own house style. Obviously, the materials and the know-how for sturdier, better-insulated shelter have long been readily available, yet consistently rejected. More is at stake than a change in house forms. If the Navahos were to give up their widely scattered and separated hogans for the consolidated, communal dwellings of the pueblo, they would have to reorganize their lives and stop being Navahos as they now know themselves.

They could not continue their present amorphous system of social organization or nurture their individualistic separateness.

Thus, whether people build and live in scattered single-family dwellings, joint-family households, or communal structures will closely tie in to social structure and even model personality types.

Caves as Homesites

We have seen that caves and rock shelters have served as homes for some men since the earliest Pleistocene times (Figure 14-5). If not too damp, they function as comfortable refuges from beasts, weather, and prowling enemies. Archaeologists always probe cave sites when looking for remains of ancient man because the chances of finding some human refuse in a cave are always good. Not that there is the least evidence that primitive men suffered from agoraphobia—the morbid fear of being in an open space. Nor is there much empirical evidence to support the psychoanalytic notion that our earliest ancestors preferred caves because, in the snug, enveloping darkness of the cavern, these unsophisticated people subconsciously re-

Fig. 14-4   The semi-subterranean dwelling of the Navaho Indian, a "forked-stick type" hogan. The weaver is using a vertical-frame hand loom. (Courtesy of the Smithsonian Office of Anthropology, Bureau of American Ethnology Collection.)

captured an ineffable sense of security once enjoyed in the prenatal state—even as an English author, contemplating the atomic bomb, has declared, "In these parlous times, what I want is a womb with a view!"

Although caves have served man well as homes (and the time may again come when any number of us will be grateful for a good, deep cave), caves are few and men are many. There never were enough to go around. More than that, caves have a number of serious disadvantages as homesteads. They may not be well situated with respect to water and game. They cannot be moved around, and in consequence they inhibit the nomadic tendencies which are characteristic of hunters and gatherers. They are always unhealthy spots. Garbage accumulations are bothersome. If dampness is present, arthritis threatens, as well as rheumatic fever.

No, even Old Stone Age man preferred an open campsite, climate permitting, and by and large, mankind has favored building shelters and houses to curling up in nature's holes in the ground. After all, even our primate relatives do not patronize dens. Every one of them sleeps above ground. There never really was an Era of the Cave Man. Most people live in houses, however humble. To this we now turn our attention.

Environment and House Types

The walls and roofing of primitive houses are variously made of snow, thatch, bark, mats, hides, felt, mud, planks, or stones. In the arctic, the Eskimos use snow blocks for their well-known igloos. What is used depends partly on availability of materials, the exigencies of climate, and on culture-bound predelictions. We have already seen some evidence of how selectively climatic conditions have worked upon man in biological evolution (Chapter 11). Would it not be remarkable if men failed to make functionally effective cultural adaptations in meeting the need for shelter?

Taking the world as a whole, the most readily available building material is, of course, wood and vegetable fiber. Poles have formed the framework for houses since

Fig. 14-5 Contemporary French peasant dwellings built into the face of the rock shelter of Laugerie Bas, Les Ezies, France. The rock shelter was used as a homesite by Neandertal and Upper Paleolithic man. The houses rest on the original prehistoric sites. (Photo by E. A. Hoebel.)

Lower Paleolithic times. In the arctic where wood is scarce, however, the ribs of whales served prehistoric peoples in the construction of their summer houses.

Forest peoples, contending with frequent rain, roof their houses with thatch or slabs of bark. Thatch is also effective in providing numerous pockets of dead air to serve as insulation against the heat of the overhead

sun. In the rain forests of Southeast Asia, the Pacific, and South America, the raising of the house floor on stilts (the pile dwelling) provides dryness and improved circulation of air for better health and comfort. In the coastal areas of the Melanesian Islands, pile dwellings are commonly built over the waters of lagoons (Figure 14-6), just as the Neolithic lake dwellers of Switzerland built their homes on the shores of the sub-Alpine waters.

Heavy mud or baked-clay roofs provide maximum heat capacity (heat insulation) for the searing temperatures of desert dwellers. The same holds true for the walls of homes. But earth cannot be used for home construction in areas where rain is heavy and frequent.

Stone houses were built only by extremely sophisticated primitives—Mayas, Aztecs, Incas, and other groups in Central and South America; Pueblo Indians in the Southwest; and the early predecessors of Mediterranean civilization.

Subsistence and House Types

If environment influences the choice and availability of materials suitable for housing, the food-getting activities of peoples constitute a second important factor. Nomads and hunters on the move can be readily seen to have different housing demands from those of more settled farmers—just as the contemporary camper may recall settling for very makeshift accommodations for one night,

Fig. 14-6   Pile dwellings in the new village of Peri, Manus Island, New Guinea. Above, the old people's homes standing over the shallow waters of the lagoon, as they did before World War II. Below, the relocated modern village with street and square established on the island itself. Peri is the village made famous by Margaret Mead in **Growing up in New Guinea** *(1930) and* **New Lives for Old** *(1953). (Photo by E. A. Hoebel.)*

while building more elaborate arrangements if he plans on remaining for any length of time.

One interesting generalization that may be made is that the houses of wanderers are likely to take the form of a *circle,* while those of permanent settlers are usually *square* or *oblong.* This difference is not a matter of mere happenstance. Living habits and geometry combine to produce the following results.

Marginal Foragers: The Windscreen Contemporary foragers live in marginal environments. The productive grasslands which first gave rise to foraging in Mesolithic times have long since been given over to agriculture and pastoralism. What remained in recent centuries for the small and dwindling handful of humanity that clung to foraging as a way of life were deserts and deep jungles—places where technologically more advanced people did not press in.

Fig. 14-7 The Bushman brush shelter provides daytime shade and some protection from the wind, the prime necessities for life in the Kalahari Desert of South Africa. It also identifies the family base, even though it is minimal in architectural sophistication. (Photo by John Marshall.)

The shelter of such people is usually the simple windscreen. Such dwellings are little more than temporary nests (Figure 14-7). Murdock describes the usual Tasmanian shelter as "a simple windbreak, constructed of interlaced boughs or strips of bark in the form of a crescent and open on the leeward side."[2] This is the exact counterpart of the Shoshones' windbreak used in summer wanderings. The natives of Patagonia huddled before similar shelters made of skins. For more permanent settlements, beehive-shaped grass houses, called *wickiup,* were the Shoshones' highest attainment in housing.

The Arunta *wurley* is no more than a lean-to constructed of leafy branches laid against a horizontal pole, which in turn is supported in the crotches of two upright sticks set into the ground 6 to 8 feet apart. In the jungles of the Malay Peninsula, Negrito Pygmies build lean-tos of palm leaves on a frame very much akin to the *wurley.* The hut of the African Bushman is simply a dome of light sticks not more than 5 feet high and thatched with straw.

All these people wandered in search of food. None of them had domesticated animals capable of carrying house materials from campsite to campsite. Therefore, they built no more than was minimally necessary, something that could be abandoned with little loss of labor expended.

Hunters and Herdsmen: The Tent Hunters who have dogs or horses, such as the Plains Indians, and hunters whose food supply is sufficiently adequate that they need move only seasonally, have developed something better than the windscreen. They rely on the tent as their form of dwelling. The same is true of nomadic herdsmen (Figure 14-8). Although modern technology makes rectangular, roofed tents feasible, primitive tents are rarely of this type. They are either dome- or cone-shaped: the floor plan is round or elliptical. The tent is indeed a "structurally brilliant invention . . . light in weight, com-

[2]G. P. Murdock, *Our Primitive Contemporaries,* p. 5.

posed of small members and easily erected, dismantled . . . [which] if we judge it by the modern structural criterion of 'the most work from the least material' (like all tension structures), ranks as a very advanced form of construction."[3] Compared with other structures, the tent offers maximum resistance to strong winds, exposes the least surface area against wind, heat, and cold, and requires the least structural support for the volume of enclosed space (Figure 14-9). And it is portable. Yet few people live in tents if they can help it.

Gardening and Agriculture: Fixed Dwellings

Recent examination of housing patterns and subsistence activities results in an interesting correlation between ground plans of housing and food-getting practices. As summed up by Michael Robbins,[4] cross-cultural statistical tests demonstrate that circular ground plans tend to be associated with relatively impermanent settlements, occupied by small populations who hunt or practice only incipient (hoe) gardening. Rectangular ground plans tend to be found in relatively sedentary settlements with larger populations and the practice of intensive gardening or plow agriculture (Figure 14-10). Since less than 20 per cent of recent societies subsisted by hunting while only 13 per cent were pastoralists, we may deduce that the vast majority of humanity houses itself in square or rectangular dwellings.

Oblong, gabled structures are formed by joining two lean-tos at the ridge. The gabled structure is almost always raised on walls (Figure 14-11). By such simple means, the internal cubage, or volume of usable living space (especially head room), is greatly increased. Not only is more space made available, but a tighter roof and stronger walls can also be produced. These improvements are bought, however, at the price of firmly em-

bedded house posts and an elaborate superstructure of tie-beams and trusses. A great deal of additional work is required—work which will not be expended unless the house is going to stay in place for at least some time. People with cultivated fields are those most likely to be stable in their residence; therefore, it is not surprising to find the more costly (in time and energy) rectangular houses associated with agricultural economies.

From the Neolithic Age onward, this pattern has been true of most of humanity. More space means more work, and only settled peoples find it worth the effort.

Fig. 14-8   The nomadic Rendille of Kenya transport the framework and covering of their beehive-shaped tents by packing the parts in a traditionally standardized way on the backs of donkeys. (East Africa Tourist Agency.)

[3]J. M. Fitch and D. P. Branch, "Primitive Architecture and Climate" (*Scientific American,* vol. 207, 1960), p. 136.

[4]M. C. Robbins, "House Types and Settlement Patterns: An Application of Ethnology to Archaeological Interpretation" (*The Minnesota Archaeologist,* vol. 28, 1966), pp. 1–25.

Social Organization and Domicile

In recent years, there has been some concern expressed about the physical isolation of the American family in its private home or apartment unit, and the ways that this affects relations between children, their aunts and uncles, and their lonely elderly grandparents (see pages 463–465). Yet, the intimate and subtle relations between house forms and the functional manifestations of individual, familial, and kinship behavior and the more general aspects of social and economic institutions have been largely neglected in both anthropological and sociological literature.

Morgan's Theory   Almost a full century ago, Lewis Henry Morgan attempted a pioneer study in the relation between house form and social living.[5] His keen mind perceived the possibility of close interrelations, but his study was vitiated by his preconceptions. His analysis of house forms and house life was tailored to fit his assumptions. The pertinent presuppositions were: (1) The gens (clan) was universally "the unit of social organization and government, the fundamental basis of ancient society."[6] (2) Since food and house hospitality was universal among American Indians, it follows that the law of hospitality implies common stores and communistic living in large households.[7] (3) "These and

[5]L. H. Morgan, *Houses and House Life of the American Aborigines* (Contributions to American Ethnology, vol. 4, 1881).
[6]*Ibid.,* p. 2.
[7]*Ibid.,* p. 61.

Fig. 14-9   After the buffalo hunt, 1870. Nomadic Plains Indian women scraping buffalo hides, which have been pegged out on the ground for treatment. Slabs of buffalo meat are drying in the sun on racks stretched before the skin tipis. (Smithsonian Institution, National Anthropological Archives.)

other facts of their social condition embodied themselves in their architecture.''[8] From these premises, Morgan attempted to demonstrate that the housing of the Iroquois, the Pueblo Indians, and the Northwest Coast tribes were manifestations of primitive communism. The individualistic Ojibwas in their one-family huts gave him a momentary pause. They certainly were not practicing communal living in the nineteenth century, but he thought they must have done so in ancient times.

In all this, Morgan grappled with some truth and a large amount of error. Social organization and type of dwelling *are* interrelated.

[8]*Ibid.,* p. 105.

Emphasis upon kinship tends to gather relatives under a common roof. This, however, is not necessarily a communistic unit. It may be merely a joint-family household. And the clan, as we shall see in Chapter 22, is not characteristic of the more primitive levels of human society.

Family Attitudes and Living Patterns It is difficult to make valid general statements about the many nuances of the relation between household structure, attitudes, and living patterns. Malinowski, however, provided a good capsule summary in the following terms:

Fig. 14-10   The settlement pattern of Sia pueblo, seen from the air. The pueblo is on the top of a mesa which falls away toward the dry bed of the Jemez River (top right). The compact nature of the housing, which encloses the ceremonial dance plaza, can be readily seen. Just above the village, looking like gas tanks, are the ceremonial chambers (kiva) of the Squash and Turquois moieties. Below the village (on the left) are corrals for horses and sheep. At the extreme lower right are irrigated fields and irrigation ditch. (Photo by Harvey Caplin.)

The isolated homestead distant from all others makes for a strongly knit, self-contained, economically as well as morally independent family. Self-contained houses collected into village communities allow of a much closer texture in derived kinship and greater extent of local cooperation. Houses compounded into joint households, especially when they are united under one owner, are the necessary basis of a joint family or *Grossfamilie*. Large communal houses where only a separate hearth or partition distinguishes the various component familes make for a yet more closely knit system of kinship. Finally, the existence of special clubhouses, where the men, the bachelors or the unmarried girls of a community sleep, eat or cook together, is obviously correlated to the general structure of a community when kinship is complicated by age grades, secret societies and other male or female associations and is usually also correlated to the presence or absence of sexual laxity.[9]

Within the dwelling, the place of the hearth and attitudes surrounding it are of great importance. "Hearth and home" were once inseparable.

In the Trobriand Islands, for instance, the hearth has to be placed in the center, lest sorcery, which is mainly effective through the medium of smoke, should be carried in from outside. The hearth is the special property of women. Cooking is to a certain extent tabu to men and its proximity pollutes uncooked vegetable food. Hence there is a division between storehouses and cooking houses in the villages. All this makes the simple material arrangements of a house a social, moral, legal and religious reality.[10]

The positioning of sleeping places relates to sexuality and parenthood, to incest tabus, and to sexual segregation based upon notions of pollution of male virility.

Separation of Men and Women In some parts of the world, sexual segregation produces individual "family" houses for each woman, her unmarried daughters, and her prepubescent sons. The adult males, however, live together in jointly owned clubhouses. This basic pattern is widespread in Melanesia, especially.

The Enga Among the Enga-speaking peoples of the Central Highlands of New Guinea, for example, the men's house is a meeting and sleeping center only. It holds no ritual activities. By the time a boy is six years old, he is expected to have left his mother's house to take up life in a men's house whose members belong to his own patrilineage. In a demographic survey done by M. J. Meggitt in the 1950s, 309 men and boys were found to live in 57 men's houses. Associated with these were 155 women's houses for 235 women and 266 girls (under fifteen years of age) and little boys—plus 9 men who "were elderly or poor, and their behavior was

Fig. 14-11 Construction of an Amahuaca Indian rectangular house with raised gabled and thatched roof. Amazonian region. (Photo by Robert Russell.)

[9]B. Malinowski, "Culture" (*Encyclopaedia of the Social Sciences*, vol. 4, 1930), p. 632.
[10]*Idem.*

thought to be eccentric."[11] Linked to this separateness is a pervading belief among men that women are dangerous to their powers and that their polluting effect must be reduced through minimal contacts.

In Africa generally, partial residential segregation of adolescent boys is usually practiced. However, the total segregation of adolescent boys of warrior age into settlements of their own is marked among such tribes as the Masai and Kipsigi of East Africa, and the Nyakusa further south.

Joint-family Households   In contrast to the dispersed settlement pattern just described for the Enga, the notorious headshrinking Jivaros of eastern Ecuador reveal sexual segregation within a communal joint-family household.

The Jivaro Indians   The unit of Jivaro social organization is the patrilineal family group living under a single roof. "Such a household is quite independent and self-sufficient, being subservient to no one."[12] The typical Jivaro house (*jivaria*) is about 75 feet long and some 40 feet wide, elliptical, with parallel sides and rounded ends. The walls are made of 10-foot laths of palm or bamboo lashed vertically to the frame. The roof is thatched. At each end of the house is a door of heavy planks, which must be lifted and set aside to gain entrance. These doors are barred from the inside. An interesting sexual dichotomy reserves one door for men only and the other for women. In like way, one-half of the interior is for men, and the other half for women. Each man has his private sleeping platform against the wall on his side; each woman has her platform on the women's side. Women's platforms are enclosed with mat walls but the men seek no such privacy. Thus, within

the *jivaria* separation is based upon sex. Although several conjugal families may be living in a single house, they are not spatially separated on a family basis. Lamentably, we know little about interpersonal relations within the household group or about how the Jivaros manage their sex lives.

In Jivaro society there are no clans, villages, or other forms of social organization beyond the isolated household, except a loose and amorphous federation of five or six households under a common war leader.

The Iroquois Long House   In the long house of the Iroquois Indians we find an internal organization more typical of joint-family households. The structure of an Iroquois long house was something like that of a Quonset hut. A roof consisting of slabs of dried bark was laid on vertical walls. The house could be enlarged or shortened merely by adding or removing sections at either end. Doors were at the ends, with an open passage down the entire house, which in one instance was 110 yards long—more than the length of a football field (Figure 14-12). On either side of the passage were cubicles about 12 feet wide and 6 feet deep, closed on the sides but wide open to the passageway, like the long corridor of bedrooms in the Palace of Versailles. Down the center of the passage were spaced the fireplaces (Figure 14-13). As has been observed by Lafitau:

Along the fires there extends on each side a platform of twelve to thirteen feet in length by five or six in width and nearly as high. These platforms, shut in on all sides except that towards the fire, serve as beds and as chairs to sit down upon; on the bark which forms the floor of the platform they spread rush mats and furs. On this bed, which is hardly a fit support for the effeminate or lazy, they stretch themselves without ceremony, wrapped in the same clothes that they wear during the day. . . .

The base of the platform, on which they sleep, is elevated at most one foot from the ground; it is given this elevation to avoid the dampness, and it is not greater, on the other hand, to avoid the inconvenience of the smoke which is insupportable in

[11]M. J. Meggitt, "Male-Female Relationships in the Highlands of Australian New Guinea" (*American Anthropologist*, vol. 66, no. 4, part 2; Special Publication, 1964), p. 207.
[12]M. W. Stirling, *Historical and Ethnographical Materials on the Jivaro Indians* (Bureau of American Ethnology, Bulletin 117, 1938), p. 38.

the cabins when standing erect, or even a little raised.

The bark which covers the platforms above and which forms the ceiling of the bed, serves them as a closet and larder, where they place, in the view of every one, their dishes and all the little utensils of their household. Between the platforms are placed large chests of bark, in the form of tuns, and five or six feet high, where they put the corn when shelled. . . .

While it is possible to walk back and forth in the cabins on either side of the fires between the hearths and the mats, it is nevertheless not a comfortable place for a promenade; moreover, the savage, wherever he is, unless he is actually travelling, is always either seated or lying down, and never walks.[13]

Who lived in this big building, and what were their arrangements? Each long house "belonged" to a lineage of related women. At the head of the long house was an influential older woman. The household certainly included all her daughters and their husbands and children. It usually also included her sisters and their families, as well as the fami-

[13]Translation from the French by M. L. LeBrun in L. H. Morgan (H. B. Lloyd's ed.), *League of the Ho-dé-no-sau-nee or Iroquois*, vol. 2, appendix B, pp. 290–291.

Fig. 14-12 Recent excavations have revealed the vast dimensions attained by the Iroquois long house at the height of its development. The length of this joint-family dwelling exceeds that of a football field by 30 feet. The stakes, set by the archaeologists, mark the location of postholes. The small round house on the right probably housed a sublineage. A second long house was located behind the round house. (Courtesy of J. A. Tuck.)

Fig. 14-13 The ground plan of a "five-fire" Iroquois long house according to Lafitau's description, from L. H. Morgan's League of the Ho-dé-no-sau-nee or Iroquois.

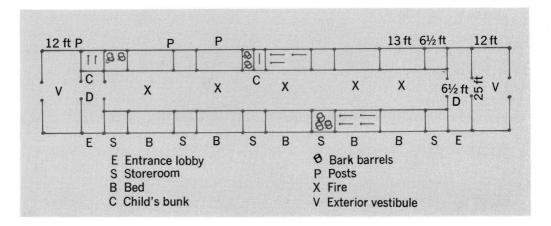

lies of her married granddaughters. All the women of the long house, in theory at least, belonged to the same clan. The long house bore the name and clan insignia of its dominant matrilineal family (except in the case of the Seneca tribe). Married men were supposed to move into the long house of the wife, but the son of an influential mother married to a girl from a family of less account might choose to stay in his mother's home.

And since the Iroquois were given to adoption of captive enemies as replacements for dead relatives, there were always some of these in the household.

The women could throw their husbands out at any time. For the dispossessed divorcé, there was nothing to do but pick up his gear and leave. He had no legal claim on children or home.

The social organization of the Iroquois long house was that of a joint matriarchate (see the discussion of the composite unilineal family, pages 434–435). Segregation within the long house was not, as among the Jivaro, by sexes but rather by conjugal families. Each woman had her cubicle, which was shared by her husband and children. Eating was partly a joint-family, partly a separate-family, affair. Each conjugal family shared a cooking fire with the occupants of the opposite compartment. Down the center of the passageway lay a hearth for each pair of families.

An Iroquois village consisted of several to many long houses within a protective palisade. A number of villages together made up a tribe. The six original Iroquois tribes made up the Iroquois nation. Loyalties reached out far beyond the lineage group in the long house. Further, the Iroquois were militant expansionists. They could release their internal tensions in outward aggression.

As the cultural environment of the Iroquois changed under the impact of white colonization of their country, the long-house organization began to break down, giving way to log houses of smaller dimensions, until by 1800, the long house as a dwelling form was no more.[14]

In Southeast Asia, where long houses are common, they tend to be associated with clans.[15] Where the village unit is formed on

Fig. 14-14   An oasis settlement of round houses with domed, reed roofs resting on dry-masonry walls with associated animal pens built entirely of reeds. In Chad, western Africa. (Photo by Emil Schulthess, Black Star.)

[14] W. N. Fenton, "Locality as a Basic Factor in the Development of Iroquois Social Structure," *Symposium on Local Diversity in Iroquois Culture* (Bureau of American Ethnology, Bulletin 149, 1951), pp. 35–54.
[15] E. M. Loeb and J. O. M. Broek, "Social Organization and the Long House in Southeast Asia" (*American Anthropologist,* vol. 49, 1947), pp. 414–425.

territorial rather than kinship bonds, as in Java and the Philippines, each family has its own separate house. The lineage and joint family do appear to go together. Morgan had a certain amount of truth to back him up. But lineages and clans do not by any means always live in long houses, while some clanless people do. The relationship is not absolute.

The Compound Homestead of African Pastoralists   The joint households previously described are those of gardeners who live in wooded areas where long timbers are available and where the main problem is protection of human, not animal, life. African pastoralists give a different form to the joint-family homestead. In their ecological setting, materials for large buildings are frequently rare, and a major need is to protect both people and stock from raiders (Figure 14-14). The homestead of the Jie, whose seasonal cycle was described in a previous chapter, may be taken as generally typical (Figure 14-15).

A Jie homestead ordinarily contains the families of from six to eight men, all descendants of one grandfather. The social base of the household is therefore the patrilineage (see pages 466–468). Families are polygynous (see pages 429–431). All the wives, their children, and the married sons with their wives and children live within the compound —thirty to forty people in all. The compound is a palisaded pole brush fence in which the only openings are small apertures 3 feet square. Anyone entering must crawl on his hands and knees, presenting his head for a death blow in case he is not welcome.

Ringing the inner side of the wall is a series of fenced yards—one for each married woman. Here she has a small thatched hut with no windows, which is used only for sleeping in rainy weather. Otherwise, sleeping, cooking, and eating are done in the open yard, although some wives build themselves a kitchen hut with open sides. Every woman's yard also contains a small house for young cattle, and this is used as an emergency kitchen if there is no regular one. Each yard also

has at least two large plastered baskets on stilts for storage of grain. The yard of each wife is her own domain. Although the yards of the co-wives of a common husband are adjacent to each other, no door leads directly from one to another. It is necessary to go out into the cattle pens to achieve passage to any other yard. The cattle and goat pens (kraals) take up about half the interior courtyard of the homestead. Here the livestock are

Fig. 14-15   The ground plan of a Jie household. The yards lettered A belong to the wives of one man; the Bs are the yards of the wives of a brother; and the Cs, the yards of yet another brother, and so forth. The entire homestead is physically and socially a tight unit, discrete among all the other homesteads of the tribe. (From **The Family Herds** *by P. H. Gulliver, Routledge & Kegan Paul, Ltd., London, 1955. By permission.)*

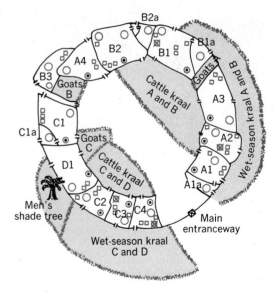

⊣⊢ Palisade fence and doorway

〰 Brush fence and gateway

○ Main house

▫ Granary basket

○ Hut for calves

⊕ Kitchen   Total population of homestead: 56

Usual number of residents: 40-45

herded at night, except in the rainy season, when they are kept in outside kraals.

The homestead is the base of a corporate lineage which inherits and owns all the cattle in common. The unity of the lineage as against all the rest of the world is clearly symbolized and reinforced by the very nature of the homestead.[16]

Pueblos: From Pit House to Communal Apartment House From the pit house to the great five-storied apartment buildings of the Pueblos of the Southwest United States is a great distance to travel in the span of a millennium.

Three main archaeological patterns of prehistoric culture have been found in the Southwest. The first is the Anasazi, of which the contemporary living Pueblos are a part. Because of its geographic localization on the high plateaus of northern Arizona, New Mexico, southern Utah, and Colorado around the Four Corners,[17] it is sometimes referred to as the *Plateau Culture*. It must not be confused with the ethnologist's Plateau Culture area, which is located on the Columbia River Plateau. The second cultural pattern is the Hohokam, also called the *Desert Culture* because of its location in the central and southern Arizona deserts. The third is the Mogollon-Mimbres, also known as the *Mountain Culture* because of its association with the mountainous area of southeastern Arizona and southwestern New Mexico. In their earliest known phases (about 2,000 years ago), each of these cultures included pit houses as the dwelling type.

The Pit House The technique of sinking the floor of the house into the ground before raising the superstructure above it represents a distinctly different line of development in house forms. This technique is adapted to the conditions of temperate climates with cold winters. For obvious reasons, it never occurs in the tropical areas where the ground

is too wet. The semisubterranean house has two advantages: (1) it is easier to keep warm, and (2) it can be made roomy without raising high side walls. The first reason is the functionally effective one, since many primitive people have solved the problem of getting sufficient inside height when building above ground.

Among recent primitives, the pit house has found greatest favor with numerous peoples of western North America and North Asia. The description of the pit houses seen by Lewis and Clark just below the Dalles of the Columbia River could very well have applied to the Campignian house types of 14,000 years ago:

They are sunk about eight feet deep, and covered with strong timbers, and several feet of earth in a conical form. On descending by means of a ladder through a hole at the top, which answers the double purpose of a door and a chimney, we found that the house consisted of a single room, nearly circular and about sixteen feet in diameter.[18]

Almost identical words describe a traveler's view of the pit dwellings of the Samoyed tribes of Siberia: "They lived in little, half underground lodges, with circular upper parts and without windows. In the middle of the latter there is a hole, through which smoke and people pass."[19]

Here we have the parallel occurrence of two similar culture traits on separate continents. In this case, they do not represent independent inventions, however, for the combination of facts covering their archaeological distribution and details of structure indicates clearly that this mode of dwelling, which was in frequent use in Late Pleistocene Siberia and survived into the present century among the sedentary fishing cultures of that land, was carried into western North America by early migrants from the Asian mainland.[20]

---

[16]For more detail, see P. H. Gulliver, *The Family Herds.*
[17]The only place in the United States where four states touch one another.

[18]M. Lewis and W. Clark, *History of the Expedition of Captains Lewis and Clark, 1804–05–06*, vol. 2, pp. 253–254.
[19]Olearius, *The Description of a Journey in Moscovia*, pp. 167–168.
[20]See W. Jochelson, "Past and Present Subterranean Dwellings of the Tribes of North Eastern Asia and North Western America" (*Proceedings of the 15th International Congress of Americanists*, 1907).

The Anasazi Tradition The evolution of the Anasazi begins with what is known as the *Basket Maker period* (A.D. 100 to 500). Basket Maker houses were constructed of inclined posts, poles, and twigs laid horizontally to form a dome around and above a saucerlike pit 10 to 20 feet in diameter. The frame was plastered over with mud. Individual houses were built in small groups, either within shallow caves or in the open.

In the succeeding Modified Basket Maker period (A.D. 500 to 700), pit houses still prevailed. They now consisted of a framework of four or five uprights supporting a flat roof. Entrance was gained either through the smoke hole over the fire pit or through a projecting passageway on the south side of the house. A low ridge of mud separated the south from the north half of the house. A new feature that marked this period, however,

was the long, flat-roofed structure of poles and mud that contained two rows of contiguous rooms. Some of these buildings were in the shape of crescents. Two lines of architectural development had emerged.

In the period of the Modified Basket Maker, the pit houses were used for ceremonial and dwelling purposes. The multiroomed surface houses were apparently used mostly for storage. Later, in the Pueblo periods, the pit house evolved into the underground ceremonial chamber, or *kiva*. The aboveground storage rooms became the multiple apartment houses for which the Pueblo Indians are justly famous. The climax was reached between A.D. 1000 and 1300 in the Pueblo III period. To this period belong the famous cities in the caves, including Cliff Palace in Mesa Verde National Park (Figure 14-16). Of the open sites of this period, Pueblo Bonito

Fig. 14-16 The Cliff Palace at Mesa Verde, in southwestern Colorado, was constructed nearly a millennium ago. The many round ceremonial chambers, called kivas, *are indicative of the complexity of religious organization in this multiple dwelling that housed an entire village. (Courtesy of the American Museum of Natural History.)*

in Chaco Canyon, New Mexico, is the best known. These buildings contained hundreds of rooms built of coursed masonry walls rising often to four stories. The modern pueblos are merely shrunken survivals of the Great Period.

The Configuration of Pueblo Culture   There is a close nexus between the communal houses of the Pueblos and the general configuration of Pueblo culture. The pueblos of the Great Period were defensive citadels as well as domiciles. The outer ground-level walls of the open-site pueblos were blank surfaces with no doors or windows. To enter a house, one had to climb to the roof and go down the smoke hole, as in the pit house. To the hostile outer world the pueblo turned its back. It faced inward upon the court, in which the public dances of its rich ceremonialism occurred. The great building formed a compact, architecturally integrated, in-turned whole (Figure 14-17). The members of the pueblo were forced to live in the closest intimacy with one another; not just the members of one household, each of which had its own apartment of one or several rooms, but all

families, all clans were piled together in a great heap. The cooperative emphasis of Pueblo life was required by the nature of their housing, if nothing else. And, of course, their housing could not have come into being had they not simultaneously been developing cooperative values.

We would agree with the conclusion of Steward in speaking of the Basket Maker and Pueblo I cultures: "It is difficult to reconcile the division of the early villages into small house clusters with any other social unit than the unilateral lineage or band."[21] Steward and Titiev[22] both suggest that a movement of consolidation of independent clans or bands in Pueblo II times resulted in the building of communal houses. "The formerly separated small groups are amalgamated, but do not lose their social and ceremonial integrity."[23] And because these formerly discrete groups did not lose their integrity when compressed

[21]J. H. Steward, "Ecological Aspects of Southwestern Society" (*Anthropos*, vol. 32, 1937), p. 99.
[22]M. Titiev, *Old Oraibi* (Papers of the Peabody Museum of American Archaeology and Ethnology, Harvard University, vol. 22, no. 1, 1944), pp. 96–99.
[23]Steward, *op. cit.*, p. 96.

Fig. 14-17   A plaza in Taos pueblo, New Mexico. The compact mode of pueblo living is clearly evident. On the roofs, behind the chimneys where the wind will not blow away the flour, are mano and metate for grinding corn, and in the plaza are Spanish-type beehive ovens for baking bread. (Collections in the Museum of New Mexico. Photo by Parkhurst.)

into the larger pueblo units, plus the irritability engendered by too close living, vindictive factionalism is an inherent aspect of Pueblo life. The crowded intimacy of Pueblo living seems also to have left its impress in the form of excessive touchiness, quarreling, backbiting, and fear of witchcraft—centrifugal forces which led again and again to the breakup of pueblos and the establishment of new settlements. The hundreds of ruined pueblos which make the Southwest an archaeologist's paradise are rich testimony to the long Pueblo struggle to adjust their house forms to their social conservatism.

Well-integrated religio-ceremonial structures have to a great degree counteracted the tendency toward breakup in Pueblo society. In the political sphere, however, the Pueblos have failed in the development of governmental mechanisms which combine reasonably centralized authority with flexibility in the handling of divergent interests. This is, of course, the eternal problem of healthy government. In the case of the Pueblos, their compact form of housing contributed to an intensification of the imperative need for political skill.

Earlier in this chapter we remarked that the Navahos could not adopt the Pueblo house form and remain Navahos in spirit and action. We have seen something of the difficulty the Pueblo Indians themselves have had to reckon with in the solution of their housing problem. Those who have wondered how it is possible for the Navahos after centuries of contact with the Pueblos—centuries in which they have absorbed much of Pueblo ritual, imagery, and arts—to live even yet in wretched log and mud hogans, when they have for so long had the exemplar of Pueblo masonry houses before them, may find the answer in the Navaho's devotion to his form of social organization. Present-day Navaho social forms are undoubtedly much closer to those of the society that was enjoyed by the Basket Maker and Pueblo I peoples than the modern social forms of the Pueblo Indians are. The

scattered Navaho communities of individual hogans are not greatly different from the ancient open-site pit-house villages of the Anasazi.

SUMMARY

All cultures contain patterns for the physical establishment of a home. House types are variable in structure, depending upon the nature of the local climate and materials, the kind of subsistence economy indulged in, and the nature of the social organization of the society and the kinds of aggressive threats it must face from enemies.

Nomadic peoples, hunters and gatherers, ordinarily throw together simple, temporary shelters. Nomadic pastoralists produce technologically more elaborate structures. The ground plans of the homes of wanderers are usually round, for this type of layout produces the largest volume of living space for the least expended effort. Domed houses and tents are capable of withstanding more wind pressure for the amount of material used than are any other forms of structure.

Sedentary peoples build rectangular houses with vertical walls. These require more work in construction but can be built larger than the round houses.

Dwelling patterns are intimately related to social structure as well as to physical environment. Sexual segregation in New Guinea is expressed in separate small houses for males and females. As a different arrangement, the Jivaro communal house separates the men and women within one common structure.

In societies built around the joint-family or localized lineage, such as the Iroquois, a single housing unit may serve as a common dwelling. Such joint-family houses found in many cultures, both prehistoric and contemporary, exemplify the close interrelationship between social and architectural forms.

The fact that the Navahos rely on the individual hogan and the Pueblo Indians use the communal apartment house, even though both tribes have simultaneously inhabited the same area for 1,000 years, illustrates the effect of general cultural configuration upon architectural forms. Small family huts consolidated within a compound reflect a nice adjustment of the requirements of a lineage type of social organization to a pastoral ecology.

SELECTED READINGS

Beals, R., P. Carrasco, and T. McCorkle, *Houses and House Use of the Sierra Tarascans* (1944). A study of the relationship between architectural and social forms in highland Mexico.

Fortes, M., *The Web of Kinship among the Tallensi* (1949), chap. 3, "The Homestead and the Joint Family." A model study of the functional interrelation of home and family.

Loeb, E. M., and J. O. M. Broek, "Social Organization and the Long House in Southeast Asia" (*American Anthropologist,* vol. 49, 1947), pp. 414–425. A useful analysis of the relation between lineage and homestead.

Murdock, G. P., *Our Primitive Contemporaries* (1934). Sections in each chapter devoted to the ethnography of a tribe describe a variety of house types.

Roberts, J. M., *Three Navaho Households* (Papers of the Peabody Museum of American Archaeology and Ethnology, Harvard University, vol. 40, no. 3, 1951). An intensive study of the membership, possessions, and household activities of the occupants of three representative Navaho hogans.

Steward, J. H., *Theory of Culture Change* (1955), chapter entitled "Ecological Aspects of Southwest Society." Includes a highly suggestive historical treatment of the relation of dwelling patterns to social organization.

Waln, N., *The House of Exile* (1933). A beautifully written novel giving the inside view of life in a traditional Chinese compound household.

Chapter 15

Tools and Handicrafts

In discussing the evolution of man and culture in Part 2, emphasis was laid upon the significance of the development of the tool-making capacity by the hominids. Man, we recognized, is the toolmaker. Indeed, the prehistoric ages of man are identified by his lithic technologies.

Tools are devices for transforming, transmitting, or storing energy. In this they are similar to domesticated plants and animals. The energy theory of culture (pages 676–683) holds that the cultural and social complexity of a people is directly related to the energy-utilization capacities created by their tech-

Fig. 15-A   Throw-net fisherman working from a dugout canoe along a coastal lagoon, Dahomey, West Africa. (Courtesy of United Nations, Food and Agricultural Organization.)

nology. Thus far, we have given attention to the larger food-getting and subsistence activities engaged in by human beings: hunting-fishing-gathering, foraging, gardening, animal husbandry, and intensive agriculture. (Industrialism has not been included as within our specific purview.) We have studied them as systems. We have not, however, explicitly given attention to the artifacts which make the operation of these systems possible (except for the Stone Age hunters).

Basic Tools and Weapons

When we speak of the technologies of a people, we are referring to the man-made elements in culture that have a physical existence of their own. Because of this, they form the greater part of ethnographic museum collections.

It is a strange feature of contemporary anthropology, however, that cultural anthropologists tend to show little interest in the study of primitive tools, weapons, and clothing. This, in spite of the fact that it is the rage to talk about "ecology" and man's use of his environment on the one hand, while on the other hand, the quasi-Marxist evolutionary school of Leslie White's followers makes technology a first cause in determination of all other aspects of culture. Around the turn of the century, when more anthropologists were attached to museums than to universities, it was otherwise. Material culture was their forte, and they were fascinated with material forms and processes. But, since World War II, there appears to have been a diminishing anthropological interest in "handicrafts," i.e., how man makes the things which distinguish him from animals. Yet, man cannot be understood without some comprehension of *what* he has used to extend his energies and increase his efficiency, and *how*—in the simple societies—he has manufactured these items. Therefore, we shall take a brief look at some of those items of his

material culture which are most commonly found among primitive peoples.

Even the simplest societies use a surprising number of tools, most of them employed directly in the task of obtaining food or in protecting themselves, but others designed for ceremonial uses. In analyzing 400 items of material culture among the Ingalik Indians of central Alaska, Osgood categorized the items as follows: primary tools, lines, containers, miscellaneous manufactures, weapons, fishing implements, snares, deadfalls and other traps, clothing, cradles and personal ornaments, shelters, caches and racks, travel implements, dyes and paints, tags and games, puberty paraphernalia, funerary objects, and religious and ceremonial objects.[1]

"Primary tools," which would include axes, awls, knives, scrapers, points, and mauls, might be used for numerous purposes, as we have already speculated in examining the earliest human cultures. Other artifacts might be quite limited in function; this would be especially true of those connected with ceremonial use. Not all societies would show such an elaborate inventory, and habitat has a clearly limiting effect on the materials used in manufacture, as we shall see in descriptions of basketry and pottery particularly. Weapons such as axes, wooden clubs, *atlatls,* bows, and spears have been previously described. In defense against them, shields of wood, leather, wicker, and metal were used almost worldwide among pregun peoples (Figure 15-1).

Similarly, we have seen the development of garden tools from simple digging stick to hoe to plow (to tractor and combine). As subsistence methods became more efficient, food surpluses required containers for storage, cooking equipment, utensils for eating, transport for trading. Methods of transportation by land included the travois, or drag cart, and later the wheeled cart, which was in-

---

[1]C. Osgood, *Ingalik Material Culture* (Yale University Publications in Anthropology, no. 22, 1940).

Fig. 15-1   The Igorot warrior of northern Luzon in the Philippine Islands equipped himself with a wooden shield, a barbed, iron-headed spear with which to down his enemy, and an iron beheading ax to bring home a human trophy for ceremonial transfer of the "soul-stuff" of the dead man to himself, thereby increasing his own strength. (Courtesy of the Museum of Natural History, Smithsonian Institution.)

vented during the Neolithic somewhere in the Mediterranean culture sphere. Interestingly enough, although a few rare wheeled "toys" have been found in prehistoric Middle America, so far as is known the wheel was never put to work as a tool or mechanical device by any American Indian until it was introduced from Europe. The wheel used in wagon and chariot was an implement of the male. When applied to pottery making as an element associated with plow culture, potting shifted from being a woman's task into the hands of the male throughout Eurasia. But when the wheel was adapted to spinning in the technically advanced areas of the Old World, women still held on to the production of homespun thread and cloth. The potter's wheel was male; the spinning wheel, female.

"Machines" Herskovits has pointed out that the machine, a contrivance by which energy is converted from one form to another, is "by no means unknown to nonliterate peoples," and cites wedges, levers, rollers, bellows, looms, drills, etc., as examples of simple machines which maximize man's strength. [2]

Even peoples whose equipment is of the simplest, who have no machines such as these, employ mechanical principles that are quite complex. The boomerang of the Australian, the heavy knobkerrie of the South African Bantu, the spear-thrower—all show a shrewd utilization of physical forces that give the individual added flexibility and power in using his physical capacities. The use of the principle of the spring in the manufacture of the compound bow is another instance of this. Even the simpler type of bow, made of one piece of wood, recognizes and allows for the elasticity of wood, while the bow-string compounds the same principle, and the feathered arrow insures better aim. [3]

Certainly, in examining the material culture of primitive societies, one cannot but be struck by the ingenuity and resourcefulness of the toolmakers. It is an observable fact that many modern hand tools vary little from their ancient models except in materials and method of production; the basic principles, and often the design, are identical. Obviously, a comprehensive cataloging of all of man's technological devices is impossible. Many have already been referred to in the discussions of hunting, agriculture, housing, clothing, development of trade, etc., and others will be touched upon in later chapters, for

[2]M. J. Herskovits, *Cultural Anthropology*, pp. 119–120.
[3]*Ibid.*, pp. 120–121.

wherever man is found, there, also, are the products of his hands and the implements with which he has made them.

Traps Traps and deadfalls have been previously mentioned as primitive food-getting devices. In the common springtrap, the animal puts his head into a noose to get the bait, releases the trigger, and is hoisted, if not by his own petard, at least in consequence of his own action. Deadfalls are a form of trap in which the animal who tugs at the bait releases a trigger that literally brings down the roof on his head.

Fish weirs, commonly used on the west coast of North America, in South America, and in the African Sudan, consist of fencelike obstructions across a river or lagoon, and are designed to lead the fish through a funnel into a large basket or crib (see Figure 12-1). Although he can wriggle into the funnel, the poor fish cannot reenter the narrow spout.

Probably all recent primitives have utilized some means of trapping or snaring animals. It is also likely that man in the Early Paleolithic was already catching his animal brethren with crude but carefully prepared snares.

Materials

Before the recent invention of plastics, the materials from which instruments could be made were limited mostly to stone, bone, horn, shell, wood, hide, animal and vegetable fibers, gold, copper, bronze, and iron. Virtually all the basic uses of these materials, prior to the invention of the steam engine, had been worked out by the end of the prehistoric Iron Age and diffused to a large part of mankind.

Stone Almost all primitive peoples were dependent upon stone as the material from which to make cutting and scraping implements. The greater part of the prehistoric span of man's existence in Europe occurred in the Stone Age. In North and South America, while the peoples of high culture knew metallurgy, it is proper to say that all the Indians were Neolithic people as were all the Oceanic peoples of the Pacific, although it must be remembered that on coral islands rocks other than flint had to be used. Africa south of the Sudan was given over to tribes with lithic technologies, while many of the Sudanese Negroes were well advanced in ironworking and bronze casting.

Although the course of European Paleolithic and Neolithic cultures has already been indicated, a review of stone artifacts may be in order.

The most fundamental classification of stone implements is the one that draws a distinction between chipped and abraded (polished) artifacts. Method of production is the criterion. We have already seen that chipping was the exclusive stoneworking technique of the Old Stone Age. Although it seems most reasonable to suppose that Early Paleolithic men must have experimented with abrasive techniques, the economy of effort found in chipping was sufficient to win preference for that method for hundreds of thousands of years.

Flint, chert, and chalcedony are preferred materials because of their fracture qualities. By percussion delivered by means of a hammerstone, which is a round or ovoid igneous or metamorphic rock held in the hand, a fresh nodule of flint may be forced to yield flakes from its surface. Since the outer edge of the flake (the one farthest from the point of percussion) is almost always thin and sharp, many flakes may be used as crude cutting or scraping tools with no further preparation. The residual core of the nodule is also suitable for use as a crude ax. Thus are formed the two basic subdivisions of chipped implements, flake and core. The addition of pressure flaking permits skilled workmen, possessing high-quality flint, to elaborate specialized forms of flint artifacts. The basic flake implements of almost all primitives are scrapers, points, and awls. Scrapers are used mostly in the preparation of skins or in the shaping of wooden shafts for weapons and tools. Points are used as penetrating heads for various kinds of projectiles (darts, arrows, spears), or as knife blades (Figure 15-2). Cores may also be worked into scrapers and points, but generally they are shaped to form hand axes or celts.

Abrasion is used to shape rocks that fracture poorly or with great difficulty. The use of wet sand or sandstone is almost an essential for the process. The outer surface of an intended artifact may be worn into shape by being rubbed on sandstone or with a piece of sandstone held in the hand. Tough stone is even sawed in two by using thin slabs of sandstone or by pouring wet sand under a piece of wood that is rubbed back and forth. Sawing, however, is relatively rare.

Drilling through solid stone has been within the capabilities of most primitive peoples since Neolithic times, and the process of drilling a hole in a stone hammer head is actually the most advanced technique for hafting purposes. The simplest form of hafting is to bind a strip of sapling around the stone. Elaborations of this technique, using cord or rawhide, occur in all parts of the world. An advantageous improvement is to groove the axhead by grinding or pecking in order to give a firmer setting to the head. Staghorn sockets were developed by Neolithic Swiss lake dwellers to form a type of compound hafting for their celts (Figure 10-5, page 201). Elaborate compound haftings are characteristic of eastern New Guinea, where, in the Mt. Hagen district, hafted stone axes are wildly exaggerated (Figure 15-3).

Mauls of stone differ from axes only in that they are intended for crushing or driving and therefore have round or blunt edges. Axes are intended for chopping and therefore have sharp edges. What appear to be grooved mauls, yet have no abrasion scars from use as mauls, are apt to be either loom or snare weights or fishnet sinkers.

Bone, Shell, and Horn   The skeletons of vertebrates and the shells of crustaceans find their uses in primitive material culture. Unworked shells make serviceable if not durable scrapers and saucers. Caribbean Indians

Fig. 15-2   An obsidian-bladed dagger from Manus, in the Admiralty Islands off the northeast coast of New Guinea. The blade is hafted in an incised baked-clay handgrip. (Private collection. Photo by Don Breneman.)

Fig. 15-3   Polished stone ax from the Mt. Hagen district, New Guinea. An example of artistic overelaboration of a utilitarian object. (American Museum of Natural History collection. Photo, courtesy of the Museum of Modern Art.)

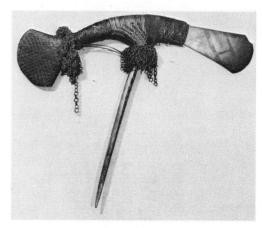

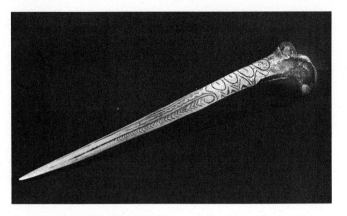

Fig. 15-4   A decorated ritual bone "pointer" made from a human tibia (shinbone). New Guinea. (Private collection. Photo by Don Breneman.)

Fig. 15-5   Horn (mountain goat) ladles used in ceremonial feasts of the Haida Indians of the Northwest Coast of North America. The carved figures on the handles are totemic crests of the chiefly lineages of the owners. Each figure symbolizes an ancestor or mythological event in the ancestry of the owner. (Courtesy of the American Museum of Natural History.)

rubbed heavy seashells into polished celts like those of stone. The long bones of birds and animals, splintered and polished to a smooth point, have always found favor as perforators and awls, and the earliest needles were made of slivers of bone (Figure 15-4). Fishhooks made of bone occur almost everywhere. Harpoon heads of bone, antler, or ivory were characteristic of Magdalenian man and Eskimos alike (Figure 9-5, page 183).

One of the most interesting bone implements is the garden hoe produced by Indians in the eastern Plains area from the shoulder blade of the bison (Figure 12-2, page 253). The scoop-shaped scapula was lashed at right angles to a wooden handle and used exactly as we use a hoe today. Alaskan Eskimos use whale scapulas as handleless snow shovels, and ivory tusks for many purposes. The horns of cattle and goats can be worked into beautiful and serviceable implements (Figure 15-5).

Wood   It seems certain that Paleolithic man relied as much upon wood for artifacts as he did upon stone. This statement, however, is based on inference from recent primitive cultures rather than direct archaeological evidence. Wood is perishable, and yet all primitives make considerable use of it. Eskimos use relatively less than most peoples, for the simple reason that trees do not grow in the arctic. Northwest Coast Indians, endowed as they were with excellent workable cedar, turned wood to an unusually great number of uses. A Northwest Coast inventory would include plank houses, wooden totem poles, adze handles, canoes, paddles, clubs, bows, arrows, helmets and slat armor, bowls, dishes, spoons, boxes, rattles, batons, and masks in a profusion of carved and painted varieties.

Eastern Woodland Indians preferred to use the bark of the birch for canoes, boxes, and housing. Plains Indians seized upon hides. Pueblo Indians use wood only sparingly, for, skillful in pottery making, they prefer utensils

Fig. 15-6 (Left)   Carved wooden Kaydebu dance shield. Trobriand Islands, Southwest Pacific. (Private collection. Photo by Don Breneman.)

Fig. 15-7 (Right)   Wooden fighting sword with saw-tooth edges. Trobriand Islands. (Private collection. Photo by Don Breneman.)

*Fig. 15-8   **Kundu,** or carved wooden drum, with snakeskin head from New Guinea. (Private collection. Photo by Don Breneman.)*

of clay and homes of adobe and stone. Tropical tribes in Africa, Oceania, and South America, who find themselves in rain forests with plenty of wood at hand, use it extensively (Figure 15-6). Polynesian wooden clubs are a sophisticated transformation of the cave man's bludgeon as is the Trobriand Islanders' double-serrated wooden fighting sword (Figure 15-7). Other examples of decorative woodcarving are shown in Figure 15-8.

With stone-bladed adzes as weapons (Figure 15-9) and as woodworking tools, the Oceanic peoples of the South Pacific shaped wood to their own ends and purposes as they made the ocean and its far-scattered islands their own (Figure 15-10).

The Drill Because of the extreme significance of the controlled use of fire in man's cultural development, it may be well to underline the universal and fundamental use of

Fig. 15-9   Battle adze with characteristic Maori curvilineal decoration. Maori, New Zealand. (Courtesy of the University of Pennsylvania Museum.)

wood in firemaking. Wood is widely used as a fire starter around the world, and most primitive societies appear to have developed some form of drill to assist in this process. It was already a part of the cultural inventory of the Desert Culture of North America 10,000 years ago.

By setting the drill in a wood socket and pouring dry tinder about it, it is possible to generate enough heat by friction to start a fire. Hand-rotation, strap, bow, and pump methods are all used. The fire plow is a simpler but less efficient device. Named the "stick and groove method" by E. B. Tylor, the implement consists of a grooved board lying on the ground and a blunt stick which is pushed back and forth with vigorous pressure until friction-generated heat kindles fire—a method concentrated primarily in Polynesia. In Indonesia the fire saw, a variant form, is preferred. In this method, a piece of split bamboo is sawed so rapidly that the dust ignites.

Most primitive peoples, we have seen, have been able to drill through solid stone since Neolithic times. The drills are ordinarily simple wooden rods or tubes rotated between the hands or by mechanical means. Wet sand does the actual cutting. But think how many drills must be used to go through a 2-inch piece of basalt. Although rotation between the hands was unquestionably the most primitive and earliest drill technique, it is probable that Neolithic man hit upon the bow drill, since he had the bow and arrow. Also, in later Neolithic times he produced many polished axheads with drilled transverse haft holes. However, in modern times hand drilling has had a much wider distribution than use of the bow drill, even among peoples who pos-

Fig. 15-10   Samoan master boatbuilders at work, hand-hewing a curved plank to be fitted to the wood keel behind the boy at upper right. Note the Stone Age type adzes they are using. (Photo by E. A. Hoebel.)

sess the bow and arrow; thus it by no means follows automatically that the one leads to the other. The trick of the bow drill, as every Boy Scout who has passed his fire-by-friction test knows, is to wind the bowstring once around the drill, hold the top of the drill in a hand socket, and then saw back and forth with the bow like a cello player. The Eskimo takes a bite on the socket instead of a hand-grip. The strap drill works on the principle of the bow drill, except that there is no bow. The ends of the working thong are simply held in the hands and drawn back and forth. A clever refinement is the pump drill. By first winding up the string on the drill shaft and then push-ing the crossbar down, a spin is imparted to the drill. The momentum given to it by the stone or pottery flywheel automatically re-winds the string. Another downward push keeps it spinning.

Metals Metallurgy is scarcely a simple craft, for it requires the kind of technological knowledge that is more closely allied to civili-zation than to savagery. Yet preliterate people did acquire metalworking skill. This was probably true of the Europeans, as well as of the peoples of the Mediterranean and Asia, during the prehistoric Bronze and Iron Ages. It was true of many Africans, and also of the Peruvian Indians and Indonesian peoples. All were close to the threshold of civilization.

The beating out of gold nuggets or chunks of pure copper does not constitute metal-lurgy. Indians in the copper-rich regions of Lake Superior made tubular arrowheads and spearheads of beaten native copper. Copper pieces are found in mounds of the prehistoric Hopewell culture of Illinois and Ohio. Eski-mos fashioned a few rare tools out of the iron residue of meteorites found on the frozen surface of the ground. But not a single North American Indian knew how to smelt a metal.

The Mexicans, who knew how to melt gold nuggets with the aid of blowpipes, came close to the secret of the reduction of ores. The Peruvians found the secret in the smelt-ing of copper and tin, which were mined from hills looked upon as sacred shrines. Inca metalworking processes included smelting, alloying (bronze), casting, hammering, re-poussé, incrustation, inlay, soldering, rivet-ing, and cloisonné. Skill in goldworking by the highly honored profession of goldsmiths was the bait that brought the gold-greedy conquistadores down upon the hapless Indi-ans.

The Africans have concentrated upon the more prosaic tools of the blacksmith's forge. From iron smelted in little clay blast furnaces with hand bellows, they shape such utilitarian tools as knives (Figure 15-11), adzes, axes, and hoes; even the most mundane tools may be shaped with artistic love when they are to be endowed with symbolic value. Bronze casting in West Africa reached a peak of artistic perfection in the work of the Bina at Benin that has made the Benin masks pre-cious collectors' items. The Benin method of casting is the "lost-wax," or cire-perdue, technique, in which a model is first made of wax and then covered with clay. The wax is then melted out to make room for the molten metal. When the clay molds are broken, the casting is freed (Figure 15-12).

Containers

All human beings use artificial containers. Skin pouches or bags may serve to meet this need. Primitive containers may also be made of wood or of plastics, such as clay. But of all these possibilities, baskets, which are con-tainers made of interwoven reeds, grass, or shredded bark (bast), have by far the widest distribution.

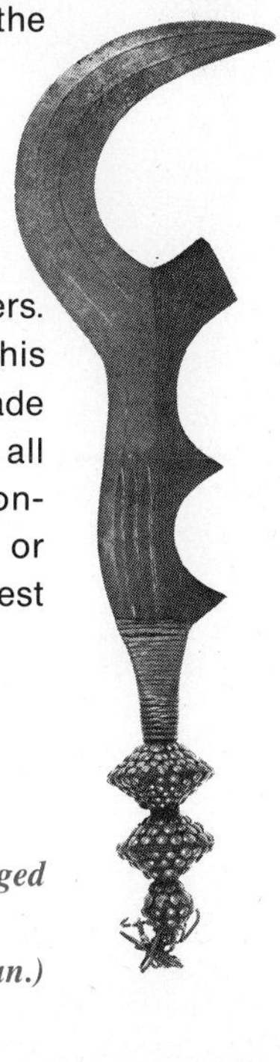

Fig. 15-11 Multi-edged West African hand-forged fighting knife. (Museum of Anthropology, University of Minnesota. Photo by Don Breneman.)

Bags and Baskets   Basket making is a truly ancient craft. Direct archaeological evidence yields basketry remains from the Neolithic sites of Europe and the Archaic Desert Culture of the United States. In the Southwest, elaborate basketry skill gave the name Basket Maker to the potteryless pre-Pueblo inhabitants of the area.

The simplest basketry container (made by the marginal food collectors, the Fuegians and other southern South Americans, the Australians, and Bushmen) is a loose, open-weave bag such as that used to package onions and oranges in the United States.

Bags of genuine netting are not so much

Fig. 15-12   The bronze casters of Benin (Yoruba tribe, Nigeria) produced complex compositions by first modeling in wax over which a clay mold was pressed. Molten bronze, poured on the wax, melted and replaced it, thus taking on the form of the mold. (Courtesy of the Brooklyn Museum.)

woven as worked out in crochet patterns. *Knotless netting,* as this technique is called, occurs throughout a large part of the Western Hemisphere and in Oceania and Australia.[4]

A basket differs from a bag in that it is at least semirigid, if not actually stiff. It is built upon its own frame, or its foundation is formed as it is made. The body is produced by the interlocking of long strips or threads of fibrous materials such as dried reeds, grasses, split cane, or shredded bark. Basketry materials can be found in all environments inhabited by man. Several of the basket-making techniques, described below, are illustrated in Figure 15-13.

Plaiting   The simplest basket-making method is that of wickerwork or plaiting. Every reader of this book has done plaiting with strips of paper in kindergarten. It is the alternating over-and-under technique. However, virtuosity such as that displayed by the Hopi of Third Mesa[5] in producing wicker trays of sumac and rabbit brush is not kindergarten work. In method, plaiting and wickerwork are alike, except that plaiting is done with very soft and pliable materials, and wickerwork with stiff materials.

Twilling   Twilling is plaiting with variations. Instead of plaiting in and out, over one under one, the basket maker goes over two or more strands and under two or more. Each row is offset from the one next to it, so the effect produced is that of a series of staircases or slanting lines.

Wrapping   Wrapping utilizes a slightly different technique. The foundation of the basket consists of stiff parallel rods. A pliable strand is turned or wrapped once around each rod in a continuous series. It is used relatively little.

[4]D. S. Davidson, "Knotless Netting in America and Oceania" (*American Anthropologist*, vol. 37, 1935), pp. 117–134.
[5]The Hopi villages are located on three mesas in northeastern Arizona. From east to west, the mesas are named First, Second, and Third.

Twining This is a more complicated basket-making method. In its simplest form, two strands of pliable material are simultaneously woven in and out between parallel foundation strands. As each strand is passed between two foundation strands (from over to under, and vice versa), it is given a half twist (Figure 15-13). The foundation strips are thus firmly bound on both sides in a way that gives much strength to the weaving. Soft grasses or strips of rabbit fur twined in this way produce a clothlike material. In fact, twined rabbitskin robes to be worn in the winter were the sole clothes of many peoples of the Great Basin and California.

Coiling This is the most sophisticated and painstaking of all basketry methods. As a technique it has little in common with plaiting, twilling, and twining, except the use of a foundation of one or more rods or a bundle of grass. Presumably it represents a distinct inventive idea. A spiral coil of the foundation material is built up like rope coiled on the deck of a ship by a careful sailor. It is permanently bound by a strand of pliable material wrapped around the bundle that is to be sewed into position. A hole is then punched through the outer edge of the coil already in place. The binding strand is pushed through this hole and back up around the outside coil to hold it in place. Figure 15-13 shows this method better than words can describe it.

Coiled basketry has a sporadic distribution about the surface of the globe that suggests independent invention in several areas. A continuous distribution occurs from Northeast Asia through Alaska, down through the Mackenzie-Yukon area into the Great Basin, California, and the Southwest. In extreme isolation, the Labrador Eskimos and the Tierra del Fuegians also make it. In the Old World, the coiling technique occurs in Africa, Indonesia, and Australia.

Twined and coiled baskets are used to hold not only dry stuffs but also water when they are closely woven and sealed with clay or pitch. The Shoshone Indians make their

drinking-water baskets slightly permeable, like Western water bags. Enough liquid seeps through to keep the water cool by evaporation, and a gentle flavoring from the pine gum used as the sealing agent makes a delectable desert drink.

Fig. 15-13 *Basketry techniques: open twining, close twining, plaiting, and coiling. (After C. Wissler,* **The American Indian.***)*

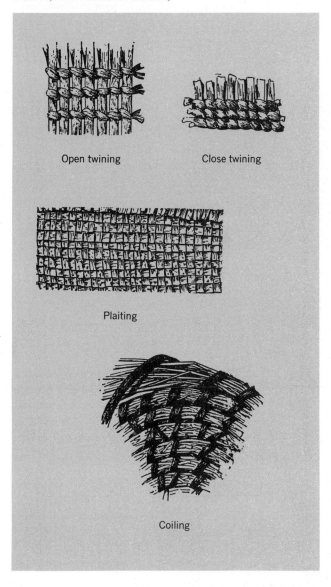

Open twining   Close twining

Plaiting

Coiling

In North America there is a close association between tightly twined and coiled basketry and stone boiling as a method of cookery. Preheated stones are grasped with wooden tongs and held in the basketful of water. The heat of the stones brings the water to a boil. In the Plains area, a pouch of skin suspended on four stakes was used in the same way.

Conversely, where pottery is well developed, basketry is not used for cooking purposes. Once the techniques are known, pottery is quicker and easier to make than baskets. More than that, it is more efficient for cooking purposes, since it may be put directly over the fire.

The Pomo Indians of California are acclaimed as the world's finest basket makers. Not only did they use the three basic basket-making techniques (plaiting, twining, and coiling), but they also practiced five kinds of twining (plain, diagonal, three-strand, three-strand braided, and lattice). Coiling was done on a one- or three-rod base. The variety of forms, however, is too great to describe here (Figure 15-14).[6]

There are also many modifications on the basic patterns practiced by various people in different parts of the world. The reader interested in the details should go to the classic work of Mason on American Indian basketry.[7]

Pottery The making of pottery is one of the higher accomplishments of primitive life. Paleolithic man never achieved it. The first pottery was not invented until Mesolithic times. The earliest migrants to North America left Asia before the technique of pottery making had spread to Siberia. There are no shards associated with the earliest prehistoric finds on this continent. Not until the Modified Basket Maker period (A.D. 500 to 700) did the people of the Anasazi culture, who were later to become such skilled potters, start to make ceramic vessels.

In Central America and the Andean region, archaic pottery making began earlier. It is most likely that pottery was independently invented in one or another part of this area, whence it spread out to other parts of the New World. Patagonians and Tierra del Fuegians never received the invention, while basket-making Californians and Shoshones rarely found the urge to copy their neighbors in the Southwest. Northwest Coast Indians were satisfied with their baskets and wooden boxes, and the Indians of the Canadian woodlands utilized bark utensils.

All peoples of Africa make some pottery, but it has received scant attention as an artistic craft on that continent, where woodworking, metalworking, and weaving are of more interest to the native populations.[8]

The potter's art extended across Asia through Indonesia into the Pacific. Good pottery was made in Melanesia and Guam, and in Palau and Yap in western Micronesia, but to many Micronesians and the Polynesians it became a lost art even before the introduction of European alternatives. Polynesians hit upon the substitute device of the stone pit oven for cooking purposes.

In general, except for the gap just mentioned, the distribution of primitive pottery follows the distribution of gardening and agriculture. Food gatherers and hunters are too far removed from the centers of pottery invention to have received the art by diffusion, or, because of their nomadic life, they have rejected clay pots as too burdensome.

Pottery-making Techniques A primitive potter must successfully complete six steps in the making of even the simplest pot:

　1. He (or she) must know where to find

[6]See S. A. Barrett, *Pomo Indian Basketry* (University of California Publications in American Archaeology and Ethnology, vol. 7, 1908).

[7]O. T. Mason, *Aboriginal American Basketry* (United States National Museum, Report, 1904), pp. 171–548. For a discussion and analysis of ethnological problems in basketry, see G. Weltfish, "Prehistoric North American Basketry Techniques and Modern Distributions" (*American Anthropologist*, vol. 32, 1930), pp. 454–495.

[8]Omitted from the scope of this statement are the ancient civilizations of the Lower Nile and Asia Minor.

decent clay. Surely the reader, as a child, has hopefully made at least one crude clay vessel, only to have it crack and crumble upon dry-ing. Clay is a disintegrated rock consisting essentially of hydrous aluminum silicate with various impurities. The relative proportions of silica and aluminum oxide, plus the nature and quantity of the impurities, determine the quality of the clay for pottery purposes.

2. The clay must then be prepared. Most primitive potters first dry the clay and then pulverize it so that coarse extraneous mate-rials may be sifted out. Clay of homogeneous texture is thus procured. The mechanical and chemical composition of the clay is usually corrected by the addition of tempering mate-rials, which may be powdered shell, mica, quartz, sand, or even crushed potsherds. Tempering serves to give the clay a workable and binding consistency. It also prevents cracking and checking on drying. Archae-ological specimens indicate that the earliest Neolithic potters did not add artificial temper to their clay. The clay must also be moistened to a proper working consistency.

3. The clay must next be shaped into a vessel.

4. After this is completed, the pot must be air-dried.

5. Decoration, if any, is applied before or after drying, depending upon the nature of the decorative process. Glaze may be added at this point.

6. The final and critical step is the firing of the pot.

Modeling   Steps 3, 5, and 6 deserve to be discussed in some detail. There are three possible methods of shaping pottery vessels, all of which were known to primitive man. The least used, but possibly the oldest, is to mold the clay about a basket or gourd, which becomes burned out in the firing process. This method is wasteful of labor and baskets: truly a long way to a pot. Modeling may be done either from a solid lump of clay or from built-up coils that have been rolled out like long snakes. Either process may be per-formed with or without a paddle and dolly. And either method may be used with or with-out a potter's wheel.

The Potter's Wheel   The potter's wheel

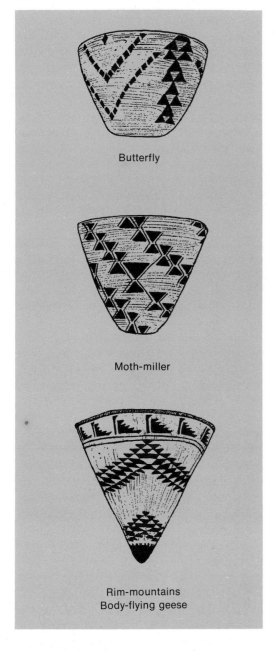

Fig. 15-14   Basketry designs of the Maidu Indians, neighbors of the Pomo of California. (After Boas.)

Butterfly

Moth-miller

Rim-mountains
Body-flying geese

need not be a true wheel; i.e., it does not have to be round in circumference. It can be a square platform—or octagonal. But it must embody the basic principle of the wheel, namely, a plane rotating on an axle. No American Indians, not even the sophisticated Mayas, Incas, or Aztecs, were ever able to discover this principle for themselves. Hence, all American Indian potters were wheelless.

In the Old World, the potter's wheel appears to have been invented in Egypt some five thousand years ago. It spread throughout Bronze Age Europe and eastward through India. In using the wheel, the lump of clay is centered directly over the axle, and in the hands of a skillful worker, the revolving mass seems miraculously to grow up and out into a vase.

Coiling   In the coiling of pottery, a piece of clay is always first laid down as a base. Pueblo Indians start the bottom coils in a tray or pottery bowl to provide a support and a turning base. Other peoples invariably use a flat rock or piece of board. If the pot is to be a large one, it must be set aside to dry for a while when the side walls are half built so that it will become stiff enough to hold its shape. When the whole pot has dried to a leathery consistency, it is pressed smooth with the worker's fingers or with a rounded dolly of stone or clay held against the inside wall while the outer surface is patted or rubbed into shape.

Decoration   Attractive corrugated ware for household use was made by prehistoric Pueblo Indians, who, instead of obliterating the coils, pinched or pressed down the outer rounded edges.[9] A much more primitive decorative device was to pat the surface of the pot with a cord-wrapped paddle, imparting to it a textilelike surface.

In the European Neolithic, cord imprints were applied in horizontal series to create what the Germans have called *Schnurkeramik*. The other great class of European Neolithic pottery was produced by scratching in bands of incised lines or punctate dots, the so-called *Bandkeramik*. More sophisticated artisans obtain decoration through slip, painting, method of firing, and sculpture. A slip is a surface wash of very fine clay which, when baked, produces a smooth finish. Use of a clay of different composition from the body produces a different exterior color. Painted designs are put on before firing. The paint changes color in baking.

Firing   All primitive pottery is baked or fired, but a kiln is not necessary for this purpose, and few primitive potters have them. Several pots are fired at once to save labor. They are simply piled up in inverted fashion (the bottom ones resting on rocks) and covered with a heap of wood or dry dung, if that is available. The latter makes a very hot fire; even without the use of bellows, temperatures of 1200 to 1700°F are produced.

If the potter wants to turn out creamy ware or shades of buff, brown, orange, or red, he does not inhibit or smother the fire. He knows air produces those colors according to the chemistry of the clay. All combustible materials in the clay are oxidized. If he wants black pottery, he smothers the fire with wet grass, peat, wood, or powdered dung. The oxygen in the clay is thus driven out by reduction, and carbon deposited by the smoke produces black coloration.

Glazing was known to few primitives. It is attained by applying a slip or painted design of lead oxide, silica, or salts in solution. At high temperatures, they fuse and impart a glassy luster.

The final technical step in pottery making (porcelain) was never attained by any primitive people. Invented by the civilized Chinese, who developed it into a high art imitated by Europeans, chinaware is nothing but very thin pottery made of pure pipe clay (kaolin) fired at such high temperatures that it fuses throughout.

[9]See R. Bunzel, *The Pueblo Potter* (Columbia University Contributions to Anthropology, vol. 8, 1929), for a comprehensive analysis of an important pottery complex.

Fabrics

Weaving is an outgrowth of netting and basketry. Its product is textile fabric. It differs from basketry in that the strands are so pliable and fine that they must be worked on a loom,[10] which is a device for holding the warp[11] threads taut. Such strands are string or thread made of animal or vegetable fibers. They may also consist of strips of fur, although woven fur robes are not considered to be true cloth.

Twine   The manufacture of twine is universal in human culture. In the simplest method, fibers are simply rolled between the palms or between the thigh and the hand. Spindles were independently developed in Egypt, and much later in Central and South America. The primitive spindle is a long, narrow stick with a stone or pottery collar near one end which serves as a balance wheel and keeps the thread from running off. A rough string of fiber wound several times about the spindle and held taut with the left hand is tightly twisted and simultaneously wound around the spindle, which is spun with the right hand (Figure 15-15). Several spinnings are needed to produce an even thread.

Weaving   In spite of the fact that cord or thread making is universal, weaving is not. Although an ancient art in the Mediterranean area, India, Indonesia, and prehistoric Europe, it did not extend deeply into the tropical forests of Africa (although it is practiced in the Sudan), nor was it known to the Bushmen. It was a lost art in most of Polynesia, where its absence was adequately met by bark cloth (as it was in the African Congo). In Melanesia and the Micronesian Caroline Islands, a limited

amount of weaving was done, but here, too, the preference was for bark cloth. There was no weaving in primitive Australia.

In the Americas, the Andean region around A.D. 1200 became the center for some of the finest and most complicated handwoven fabrics the world has ever known. The direction of the textile industry became one of the most important interests of the Inca government, which levied taxes, fines, and tribute in cloth. Great stores of perfect cloth, well preserved in the high, dry climate, have been recovered by modern archaeologists and collectors.

Fig. 15-15   A Guatemalan woman, wearing a homewoven blouse and skirt, spinning thread with a hand spindle. (Photo by Esther Bubley for PepsiCo International.)

---

[10]Knitting and crocheting are special forms of close netting, not weaving.

[11]The *warp* is the group of parallel-lying foundation threads over and through which the *weft*, or *woof*, is woven at right angles.

The Loom   Archaeological stratigraphy gives a clear sequence for the development of looms in this area. The belt loom was the earliest (Mochica culture, A.D. 600 to 700). It was followed by a horizontal frame loom supported on stakes, which is to this day preferred by Aymara Indians. Finally, it was followed by a vertical four-pole frame loom built against the wall.

From the Inca center, true loom weaving is distributed north and south along the Andean cordillera, and up through Central America and Mexico into the Southwest (Figure 15-16). Simple frame weaving is done in the Amazonian basin, as is belt loom work; frame weaving occurs in the Gran Chaco and the pampas, but disappears completely in the extreme south. Native American cotton is the chief material used from the Southwest down through South America.[12]

Weaving was absent in California and the Plains area, but very primitive suspended-warp weaving was done on the Northwest Coast and in the woodlands of the Mississippi Valley and the Southeast.

[12]See L. M. O'Neale, "Weaving," in J. H. Steward (ed.), *Handbook of South American Indians*, vol. 5, *The Comparative Ethnology of South American Indians*, pp. 97–138.

Suspended-warp weaving is done without a true loom. It calls for finger weaving without the aid of a heddle. Chilkat blankets from the Northwest Coast are the most famous product of this kind of weaving (Figure 16-2, page 328). The warp of shredded cedar bark is suspended free-hanging from a horizontal pole supported on two uprights. The weaving is done from top to bottom, as the weaver works the woolen weft in and out with the fingers.

True looms must meet two needs: (1) they must keep the warp taut, and (2) they must have some arrangement whereby a whole group of warps can be lifted at once, so that the weft may be passed through the *shed* (the open space between the lifted warps and the dormant ones) in one movement. When the lifted warps are released, the shed closes as they fall back into place, and the weft falls automatically into its over-and-under position.

The device that performs this function is known as the *heddle*. The most primitive heddle is a simple stick, which need be only a little wider than the *web* (the breadth of the warps). One heddle is passed under every other warp. The remaining warps are manipu-

Fig. 15-16   A Navaho woman starting a blanket on a suspended frame loom. Ganado, Arizona. (Courtesy of the Museum of the American Indian, Heye Foundation.)

lated by means of one or more additional heddles. By alternately lifting each heddle, the warps can be shifted to speed up the weaving. After the weft is passed through the shed by means of a *bobbin,* it is hammered tightly against the woven material with a flat stick (the *batten*) or a comb. Design patterns are woven in by use of more than two heddles or by laying in differently colored wefts and warps.

The belt or waist loom solves the problem of warp tension by tying one end of the loom to a pole and the other to a belt around the weaver's waist. Larger looms may have a four-pole frame, or the warp poles may be lashed to ceiling or floor.[13]

Felting   Weaving and spinning are two ways to interlock fibrous materials to form a compact cloth covering; felting, in which animal wools are matted together by wetting, beating, forming in sheets, compressing, and drying, is another.

Because of the relatively greater complexity of the weaving process, it was at one time assumed that felt was the earlier invention. But the world-wide distribution of weaving as against the limitation of felting to Asia and Europe makes it clear that felting is a special and later invention. For all their skill in weaving, and in spite of the fact that they possessed an excellent supply of wool in the llama and alpaca, the Andean Indians never felted at all. Of course, felting is possible only where woolly animals provide a source of materials.

Bark Cloth   In such tropical areas as Indonesia, Oceania, Central Africa, and Central and South America, bark fibers are used as equivalents of wool. The principle underlying the manufacture of felt and bark cloth is the same: a sheet of material is produced by matting fibers so tightly that they adhere permanently. However, geographical distribution and analysis of the complexes make it

Fig. 15-17   Samoan bark or tapa cloth. White with reddish brown design. (Private collection. Photo by Don Breneman.)

quite clear that bark-cloth manufacture was independently invented and not derived from felting or vice versa.

A full comparative study of bark-cloth techniques in all parts of the world is yet to be done.[14] But in general the process is the same everywhere. The fibrous inner bark of a suitable tree, such as the paper mulberry (which is cultivated for the purpose in Polynesia), is stripped, scraped, and beaten out with a grooved wooden mallet or paddle on a wood anvil. It may or may not be soaked in water as a part of the preparatory process. Where it is, there is no limit to the size of the cloth that can be made, since one piece may readily and effectively be "felted" into another.

Indonesians and Polynesians decorate their *tapa* cloth with stamped designs carved into

[13]See C. Amsden, "The Loom and Its Prototypes" (*American Anthropologist,* vol. 34, 1932), pp. 216–235.

[14]An excellent prototype of such a study was done by Raymond Kennedy, who demonstrated that the internal congruity of technical steps and linguistic terminology associated with bark-cloth manufacture in Polynesia and Indonesia is such that it must be inferred that Polynesian bark-cloth manufacture originated in Indonesia. See his "Bark Cloth in Indonesia" (*Journal of the Polynesian Society,* no. 172, 1934).

wooden blocks and printed over the surface of the material in brown vegetable dyes (Figure 15-17). Polynesian block-print designs have been fashionable for some time in sports shirts and casual clothes in the United States.

SUMMARY

Tools are artifactual extensions or substitutes for human limbs and other features of the body. With tools, man adapts his activities to a more efficient exploitation of his environment without reliance on genetic changes to achieve the result. This is the reason why some biologists, as, for example, Julian Huxley, think that biological evolution has finally come to an end with modern man. We adapt through culture rather than through biological changes of our bodily inheritance.

Stone and wooden tools are as old as man. Bone implements date from the Old Stone Age and are found in all parts of the primitive world. Pottery and weaving represent high arts not developed until Neolithic times, but they subsequently spread to virtually all humanity. Felting and the production of bark cloth are interesting specialized primitive methods of producing fabrics used as body covering.

We can say that an age of handicrafts began in the Paleolithic Age and lasted until the industrial revolution in Europe. For most of humanity that age is dying only now; yet the demise is to be hastened by the great technical-assistance programs for so-called underdeveloped countries. These programs are designed to supplant handicraft technologies with modern industry, for handicrafts, although they have served humanity well for a million years, do not greatly increase man's energy output. They require a heavy output of time and effort for a relatively small return in food or other consumable goods. Except as handicrafts survive as specialized arts in advanced civilizations, handicraft technology is synonymous with a primitive mode of livelihood, but it is one that often reveals remarkable ingenuity and technical skill combined with high aesthetic quality.

SELECTED READINGS

Amsden, C. E., *Navaho Weaving* (1949). From sheep to blankets in all their varieties among the Navahos.

Blackwood, B., *Both Sides of Buka Passage* (1935), chap. 10, "Useful Crafts." Material culture and its social uses among a Melanesian people.

Bunzel, R., *The Pueblo Potter* (1929). A comprehensive analysis of an important handicraft complex.

Mason, O. T., *The Origins of Invention* (1895). A classic study of how tools came into being, this work is now available in a 1966 reprint.

———— , *Aboriginal American Basketry* (1904). A complete survey of American Indian basketry.

Osgood, C., *Ingalik Material Culture* (1940). One of the most thorough and meaningful treatments of the tools and handicrafts of a hunting people.

Sayce, R. U., *Primitive Arts and Crafts* (1933). Succinctly summarizes the field of primitive handicrafts.

Singer, C., E. J. Holmyard, and A. R. Hall (eds.), *A History of Technology*, vol. 1, *From Early Times to the Fall of Empires* (1954). Encyclopedic and detailed in its coverage, it is a mine of fact and information.

Spier, R. F. G., *From the Hand of Man* (1970). A simply stated overview of the gamut of primitive tools.

Trowell, M., and K. P. Wachsman, *Tribal Crafts of Uganda* (1953). Comprehensive, well illustrated, and especially good on musical instruments.

Chapter 16

Clothing and Ornaments

Few human beings accept their appearance as biological evolution has fashioned it. In all times and climes, man undertakes to effect what he believes are improvements upon his bodily appearance. His cosmetic accomplishments, both primitive and civilized, are wonderful if not always beautiful to behold. The time and effort that have gone into painting, pricking, scarring, puncturing, and otherwise mutilating and deforming the human body for aesthetic and status reasons are beyond all calculation. We shall leave it to sociologists and economists to calculate how many billion dollars are spent per year on clothes and cosmetics in the most advanced civilizations of today.

The gradual denuding of the human body from hairy to "naked ape" has posed many still unsolved problems of explanation. It is not easy to formulate a general theory of biological adaptation which will adequately account for all aspects of the phenomenon.[1] Man, in a way, seems to have stripped himself

[1] See D. Morris, *The Naked Ape*, pp. 13–49, for a summary discussion of some of the competing theories.

Fig. 16-A   Facial tattoos and earrings of a Bororo girl. Niger. (Marc Riboud, Magnum.)

defenseless, shorn of natural bodily protection. He has no body shell, except the residual finger and toe nails. He has no scales, except figurative ones over his eyes. He has no fur except for skimpy body patches of hair.

Basically, this denuding adaptation seems to have been in the direction of functional dissipation of excess body heat generated by hunting in tropical or semitropical areas. (Most primates forage in a slow and leisurely manner. For them, getting enough to eat produces no sweat.) When man moved into more frigid climes he built shelters and had fire with which to warm himself at night. He also learned to utilize animal hides as a substitute for his own deficiency, thus compensating for a specialized biological adjustment by using his brainy, cultural, inventive capacities. If man had lost his natural coat, he had become capable of inventing clothing.

However, the invention of clothing for insulation was not the only culturally adaptive alternative. In the mountains of New Guinea today, a thick coating of pig grease holds in body heat during the chill, dank night and foggy morning hours.[2] Prehistoric man could have done the same. And this may well have provided one foundation for overall body paint, the grease forming a natural medium for pulverized dry pigments, such as red ocher, which was all the Tasmanians commonly wore.

Protection against the elements, however, is but one of the factors which underlie the impulse toward clothing, and in view of the fact that clothing is often ill-adapted to a specific environment, it may not be the primary motivation. A sense of modesty or shame, the need for visible distinctions between classes and social groups, and a desire for display and adornment all come into play in greater or lesser degree. There is considerable uniformity of dress (or undress) and style within each primitive society, but almost universally there are distinctions between the costumes of men and women, children and adults, leaders (kings, chiefs, headmen) and commoners. As far back as the Neolithic period, when it is known that clothing was in widespread use, it is assumed that these factors, as well as weather protection, were already at work.[3]

The Undressed Man

People who wear little or no clothing in no way contradict what has just been said. Be he ever so unclothed, man is seldom unadorned. If he wears not so much as a G-string, he certainly sports a nose, ear, or lip plug, or bears his tattoos or scarifications, or paints his face, or curls his hair, or cuts it off, or blackens his teeth, or knocks them out, or perhaps merely files them to a point. Thus, the Central Australians, for example, seem never to have hit upon the idea of wearing animal skin for clothing. For the men, a conspicuous pubic tassel suspended from a belt of human hair and armbands of twisted fur sufficed. A woman was "dressed" if she had a string of beads around her neck.

People who dwell in the tropical rain forests tend to get along with a minimum of clothing. This is true in Africa, the Americas, and Oceania. Generally, however, the men wear some sort of pubic covering, a suspensory or supporter. It is hardly necessary to seek magical reasons for the widespread use of this device, as such reasons were sought by the early anthropologist Waitz (1821–1864),[4] and after him by Sumner (1840–1910).[5] Notions of mystic shielding of the male sex organ from evil influences are more likely to be secondary developments. Certainly, the conspicuous coverings of gleaming shells, gourds, bark,

[2]Many an auto engine has come to grief because New Guinea workmen have drained the crankcase for body oil.

[3]L. Spier, "Inventions and Human Society," in H. L. Shapiro (ed.), *Man, Culture, and Society*, p. 228.
[4]F. T. Waitz, *Anthropologie der Naturvoker*, vol. 6, pp. 575–576.
[5]W. G. Sumner, *Folkways*, pp. 432, 456.

hide, cloth, or grass do not serve to divert attention but rather to attract it. To conceal is often to reveal, as the bikini designers well know.

An alternative to the rigid sheath is a small apron of leather, grass, or cloth worn in front, or fore and aft, or between the legs and about the waist. Such a garment is frequently worn by women as well as men. It is the basic, and often the only, bit of clothing worn by most primitive peoples.

The Sense of Modesty   Modesty is a habit, not an instinct. The discomfiture that is felt when one's sense of modesty is disturbed is a diffused, neurophysiological upset of a large part of the nervous and organic system, shock-stimulated by a behavior situation that contrasts sharply with those to which a person has been habituated. And of course, there is more than the element of mere habit in the total situation. There has also been a strong, ideational indoctrination that penalties, social or supernatural, accompany any departure from the habituated pattern. Apprehension of dire consequences contributes much of the tone of fear and anxiety that colors the feelings of immodesty. As late as 1936, for example, old-timers among Comanche males felt acutely uncomfortable and indecent if they thoughtlessly went out without a G-string, even though fully clothed in pants and shirt.

A favored tale among anthropologists is that of Baron Nils E. H. Nordenskiold (1877–1932) who in his Amazonian travels undertook to purchase the facial plugs of a Botocudo[6] woman who stood all unabashed in customary nudity before him. Only irresistible offers of trade goods at long last tempted her to remove and hand over her labret (Figure 16-1). When thus stripped of her proper raiment, she fled in shame and confusion into the jungle. After all, the close identification between the Botocudo as a person and the *botocudo* as a plug is such that to become unplugged is most un-Botocudo.

Such circumstances make it clear that the use of clothing does not rise out of any innate sense of modesty, but that modesty results from customary habits of clothing or ornamentation of the body and its parts.

The Use of Robes   When warmth is needed, something more must be added. Most races of mankind are relatively so hairless that they need artificial insulation. Hence, we rob the animals of their hairy covering—skin and all. The trapper flays the beast and prepares the hide, the tailor shapes it, and the lady of fashion slips the skins of animals over her own when she makes her winter excursions. Wool coverings are also produced at the expense of animals, but not necessarily by lethal methods.

Fig. 16-1   Lip and ear labrets displayed by a Suia male, Brazil. (Emil Schulthess, Black Star.)

[6]"The *Botocudo* owe their name to the large cylindrical wooden plugs worn by men and women alike in the ear lobes and lower lips. These cylinders, of light wood (*Chorisia ventricosa*), were 3 to 4 inches (7.6 to 10 cm.) in diameter and 1 inch (2.5 cm.) thick. The ears were perforated at the age of 7 or 8, the lips a few years later." A. Métraux, "The Botocudo," in J. H. Steward (ed.), *Handbook of South American Indians*, vol. 1, *The Marginal Tribes*, p. 534.

Shoshones wove rabbit-skin robes, as did the early prehistoric Basket Makers. African Bushmen provide themselves with skin cloaks. The Yahgan of Tierra del Fuego wore a small sealskin, sea-otter, or fox cape as the sole protection against a nasty subantarctic climate—except for a small pubic covering worn by women. The Ona of the same area and the nearby Tehuelche sported longer and larger capes. The Tasmanians wore no conventional cloak, but the men were given to draping and tying sundry strips of fur around their shoulders and limbs.

When we turn our attention once again to South America, we find that the fur mantle is worn by Patagonians and Indians of the Gran Chaco in inclement weather. The famous woven wool ponchos of the Andean Indians are undoubtedly a cultural elaboration of more primitive covering.

In North America, the artistically woven Chilkat blankets of the Northwest Coast Indians (Figure 16-2) made in four colors of dyed goat's wool and cedar-bark thread were totemically elegant versions of everyday robes woven of cedar bark only.

In the Plains, the buffalo-hide robe was also a form of cape, a large one, later to be replaced by the trader's blanket, which is to this day the symbol of the conservative Indian, the "blanket Indian," who clings to the old ways. Even in the rugged Northeastern woodlands, the draped robe was the chief item of winter clothing, besides leggings and moccasins. In the Southeastern Woodlands, the natives went naked except for a loincloth. When cold did sweep down from north they, too, cast on a loose robe or cape of fur.

Fig. 16-2   A Chilkat Indian chieftain from the Northwest Coast of North America. The face and eye design, seen in both the carved wooden helmet and the blanket, is highly characteristic of the art of the Northwest Coast. The woolen weft of the blanket is woven on a warp of shredded cedar bark. (Courtesy of the American Museum of Natural History.)

The Tailored Man

We may conclude, then, that tailoring was not one of the more widely esteemed human arts. Most of mankind, including such sophisticates as the Greeks and Romans, have done quite well without it. The feature that is unique about tailoring is that by means of sewing, clothing may be made more or less to fit the human frame. The very idea of tailoring is "fit," and "well-tailored" means more fit rather than less. In temperate and arctic climates, it is functionally advantageous to have tailored clothes. The insulating efficiency of clothing is greatly enhanced by the closed, tubular effect of the tailored garment, which gives little room for the play of chilly breezes upon the body. In the tropical rain forest or torrid desert, the very advantages of tailored clothing become its disadvantages.

Two factors, therefore, combined to limit the pre-Columbian distribution of tailored clothing to Europe, northern Asia, and the northern half of North America: (1) selective adjustment to climatic factors, and (2) the fact that tailoring is an advanced technique, which the Fuegians, who certainly could have used warm garments, failed to invent.

That cultural improvements are not *ipso facto* beneficial is incidentally demonstrated in the debilitating effect of the introduction of European clothing among the Yahgan, of whom Cooper wrote:

The clothing of the *Yahgan* seems to us utterly inadequate, given the climatic conditions—temperatures commonly around and well below freezing point in winter, high winds, frequent snow, hail, sleet, and cold rain—but in view of the seeming role played in their decline by introduced European clothing and their relative good health prior thereto, perhaps their clothing was reasonably well-adapted to the environment.[7]

In this case, we would observe that it is not so much that their clothing was reasonably well adapted (which it was not) as that they were physiologically well adapted to a *specific* environmental situation. The adjustment was more biological than cultural. The introduction of tailored European clothing and other elements was a cultural modification that so altered the total environment of the Yahgans as to disturb disastrously the biological balance between them and their physical world. Inexorable extinction apparently stalks them.

This, of course, has been a common consequence of culture contact when very primitive peoples find their environment drastically unsettled by incursive elements emanating from a suddenly presented, unlike, and higher culture.

The Diffusion of Tailoring   Tailored clothing was made originally among the arctic and subarctic peoples of Siberia and North America and the ancient Chinese. The distribution in North America, as Wissler pointed out,[8] was coterminous with the distribution of caribou; in Asia the association was coterminous with the reindeer. Although the Northwest Coast Indians could easily have adopted the tailoring technique (they did sew boxes together), they did not do so. The northern bison hunters of the Plains did, however, make loosely tailored shirts and dresses of the modified poncho type.

Real tailoring is done by the Eskimos and Indians of the Canadian woods. Coats are fitted with genuine sleeves and necks. Eskimo garments with the fur turned in and the outer skin dyed and decorated are not only functional but also aesthetic (Figure 16-3).

The diffusion of tailoring in prehistoric times raises several unsolved problems. Did it spread from the ancient civilization of China to the Siberian barbarians, and from there to the east and west? Or did the primitive skinworkers of northern Asia develop it, from whence it came to the Chinese?

The westward diffusion into Europe proper did not occur until a number of centuries after the conquests of Caesar. And finally, since the bursting of the confines of Europe in modern times, when tailored clothing became the symbol of the European conqueror, human creatures in all parts of the world have now enclosed their bodies in suits and dresses. The lovely tapa sarong of the Polynesian has given way first to the missionary's Mother Hubbard, and now to conventional Western garb. But, having "civilized" the Polynesian out of the sarong, we moderns have taken its charms for our own.

Footgear

Fashion in all cultures is a top-to-toe concern; head and feet, as well as the body proper, usually receive attention, too. However, among primitive peoples, footgear is more

[7]J. M. Cooper, "The Yahgan," in J. H. Steward (ed.), *Handbook of South American Indians,* vol. 1, *The Marginal Tribes,* p. 87.

[8]C. Wissler, *The American Indian* (3d ed.), p. 62.

common than headgear. The status functions of headgear can be served readily enough by hairdos. The protective functions of hats are also notably less important than the protective function of shoes. Here again, the physical environment is an important factor in influencing the adoption of an element of material culture.

The problem of fabricating a foot covering that will stand up under the wet rot of the tropical jungle is practically insoluble. Even the best contemporary efforts, with all the resources of science, are still not very satisfactory. Jungle primitives prefer to go barefoot. An unshod foot dries more quickly and comfortably than one encased in a soaking and muddy moccasin. For this reason, the highly sophisticated Indians of the Northwest Coast rain forest went barefoot, even in southern Alaska.

Even more important is the simple fact that it is easier to walk barefoot on mud-slick trails, especially on hills and mountains. Flexed toes in the mud can get a grip which corrugated soles or cleats cannot—the latter clog up and encase the feet in a gooey ball.

Yet, however calloused the soles of unshod feet may become, cuts can be seriously crippling through opening the system to parasitic diseases, and, in the case of leprosy, where the feet lose all sensitivity, embedded stones and thorns cause putrefying infections (Figure 16-4). Consequently, if the climate does not discourage it, most peoples have provided themselves with sandals, moccasins, shoes, or boots.

Sandals   In reasonably mild, not too wet, temperate parts of the world such as the Mediterranean area and its cultural extension into South Asia, the sandal is the type of footgear that finds most widespread use. In its simplest form, it is a piece of leather roughly fitted to the sole and held firm by thongs passing over the foot.

Sandals with woven fiber soles were very popular with prehistoric Southwestern and Great Basin Indians. Wissler noted, "In eastern North America moccasins were discarded when walking in the rain, in wet grass, or upon moist ground."[9] This was also true of the Incas with their rawhide-soled sandals, which would become soft and squishy when wet, and then hard and out of shape when dried. Wissler thought he detected a link between the wearing of sandals and the wearing

Fig. 16-3   The tailored skin clothing of the Eskimo hunter makes life in the Arctic humanly possible. The fur of the skins is worn on the inside for maximum insulation and preservation of body heat. Not only is the clothing a highly efficient form of adaptation, but its pleasing decoration expresses a strong aesthetic drive and artistic technique. (Courtesy of the American Museum of Natural History.)

[9]*Ibid.*, p. 65.

of woven clothing in both the Old World and the New. The fact is, however, that in prehistoric North America, the production of woven sandals antedates the weaving of cloth by thousands of years. Such sandals are an aspect of the making of baskets, not of textiles.[10]

Moccasins and Boots The simplest footgear is a piece of hide folded about the foot. When tailored, it becomes a moccasin of the type made famous by the North American Indians. Further development of this form produced the boot. The so-called arctic boot which extends well above the knee, is an adjunct of true tailoring. This is not at all surprising, since anyone skilled enough in cutting and sewing to make a boot is *ipso facto* skilled enough to tailor clothing, and vice versa. Further, the same climatic circumstances that lend to tailored clothes their functional value do the same for boots. People who have to plod around in snow and cold find high tops more comfortable. Who enjoys walking through the snowdrifts in oxfords? However, we have learned in anthropology not to expect that necessity necessarily mothers invention. The Indians of the North American boreal forests (the Canadian woodlands), who make tailored clothing and are confronted with heavy snows, make

[10]*Ibid.,* p. 64.

Fig. 16-4   Health propaganda for shoes in New Guinea. Leprosy of the foot is aggravated by stone bruises which cannot be felt because of deadened nerves. An educational sign in pictures and pidgin English tells New Guinea highlanders: (1) Man he has leprosy; he walks about barefoot; (2) Now a big sore comes up; (3) He goes along to the hospital and gets plaster (cast); the plaster stops the sickness; (4) Sore it dries up (finish); (5) Now whenever (altogether) he walks about, he puts a shoe on his leg. (Photo by E. A. Hoebel.)

moccasins instead of boots, in spite of the fact that the more northerly of these Indians have contact with boot-wearing Eskimos. The boot of the Eskimos, worn from Greenland to Alaska, was undoubtedly borrowed from the Siberian herders and hunters. It is quite definitely an Asian trait.

The high, thigh-length, cavalier-style riding boots of the Tehuelche Indians of the Patagonian pampas (whence comes its name, the "Patagonian boot") are apparently a post-Columbian adoption. The early, horseless "foot Tehuelche" wore a kind of moccasin stuffed with straw.[11] Because of its association with the horse, a post-Columbian acquisition, the Patagonian boot is hardly to be

[11]J. M. Cooper, "The Patagonian and Pampean Hunters," in J. H. Steward (ed.), *Handbook of South American Indians,* vol. 1, *The Marginal Tribes,* p. 144.

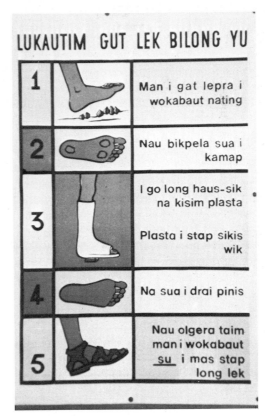

considered an independent primitive invention. But it is interesting to note that similar boots were not adopted in the Amazon, where the natives still prefer to go barefoot, or in the Andean region, where the prehistoric sandal holds sway.

Hairdo and Headgear

It appears that one of mankind's most intense and ubiquitous concerns is with the coiffure. We do not know when the earliest prehistoric men and women first began to play with the cranial hair, but archaeological evidence from the Upper Paleolithic in Europe demonstrates that Cro-Magnon man and his contemporaries already laid great emphasis upon the female hairdo. In the Gravettian statuette of the Venus of Willendorf (Figure 9-9, page 187), no facial features were carved by the artist. But the pattern of the hairstyle is meticulously incised. This trait of the Venus of Willendorf in the Gravettian epoch, more than 20,000 years ago, appears not to have been a mere accident but a strong feature of the culture, for a similar degree of care was lavished upon the hair pattern of the female head from the Grotte du Pape at Brassempouy (Figure 9-10, page 187).

Add to this the fact that all recent peoples, whatever their level of culture, primitive or civilized, give attention to the dressing of hair, and we may conclude that concern about hairdo is a universal trait in human culture.

Hairstyles and Social Status   The trimming and arrangement of the hair are not merely matters of decoration and ornamentation; in culture after culture, such treatment serves to symbolize social position (Figure 16-5). The most basic status represented in the treatment of the hair is that of sex. Males and females within any given society almost without exception have different ways of fixing the hair.

Hairstyles are also used to indicate age status. Omaha Indian boys had their heads shaved close, with isolated tufts of hair left here and there. Men either wore their full head of hair lying loose or shaved it off, except for a continuous roach along the sagittal line. At one time in American society, young girls wore their hair down until after adolescence, when they were privileged to put it up.

Among the Omahas, the shaved heads of the boys indicated more than just age status, for the patterns of the remaining tufts were different for the boys of each clan. "The cutting of the hair was done, it was said, in order to impress on the mind of a child, as in an object lesson, the gentes [patrilineal clan] to which a playmate'belonged."[12] This selfsame practice is widespread among Sudanese West Africans. There the pates of children are divided into patterns of diamonds and squares formed by parting the hair and gathering it into tightly tied tufts. In Africa, the various patterns indicate different social affiliations. Some of the styles, the tightly braided tufts all over the head, for example, can be seen on small children among Afro-Americans, who have long since lost all vestiges of African clan organization. Current styles of hair length and grooming (plus moustaches and beards, in the case of men) offer eloquent clues to attitudes regarding main-stream culture and the "counter-culture," particularly —but not exclusively—among adolescents and young adults.[13]

Headgear   While attention to hair is virtually universal, the wearing of hats and caps is not. It is probably safe to say that only in the coldest regions do we find headgear related to the exigencies of climate. The fur-lined parka of the Eskimo is so well adapted to frigid temperatures that it has long been copied by other contemporary dwellers in cold winter areas. The Angmagssalik Eskimos of East Greenland developed gorgeous

[12]A. C. Fletcher and F. LaFlesche, *The Omaha Tribe* (Bureau of American Ethnology, Annual Report 27, 1911), p. 198.

[13]Hairstyle and social status are, of course, what the rock musical *Hair* is all about.

some parts of ancient China, and among the Indians of the West Coast of North America. Huge leaves are sometimes employed as "umbrellas" in the Trobriand Islands and other parts of Melanesia, both for rain and shine protection, but they can scarcely be labeled "hats." Throughout most of Africa south of the Sahara, Polynesia, South America, and Melanesia, however, despite the almost constant heat and glare of the sun, no protective head-covering is routinely found.

Head covering for purposes other than protection is another matter. Almost every material available in the environment or procurable by trade is employed in the construction of the highly decorative creations with which

Fig. 16-5   Elaborate hair and bodily decoration of the wife of a Makere chieftain, northeastern Congo, Africa. (Belgian Government Information Center.)

Fig. 16-6   Another example of beauty and efficiency in Eskimo skin clothing. The white foxskin cap with embroidered leather visor is from the Angmagssalik Eskimos of East Greenland. (Courtesy of the American Museum of Natural History.)

caps made of foxskin with visors of embroidered sealskin—works of elegance which went far beyond purely utilitarian requirements (Figure 16-6). Fur hats were also common in Mongolia and among Labrador Indians. Along with eyeshades attached to the parka, some Eskimo tribes developed primitive snow goggles made of wood with a narrow open slit to protect hunters from snow blindness.

Aside from the frigid zones where total covering is an absolute necessity, head covering is more a matter of pure beautification, status identification, or ceremonialism than of comfort (Figure 16-7). Most societies in the tropics use neither sunshades nor sun goggles. Basketlike hats or sunshades are found in the Philippine Islands, Tibet, and

primitive men and women have adorned their heads: feathers, furs, reeds, grasses, leather, hair, teeth, shells, insect wings, bones, seeds, beads, fibers, metals, flowers, tusks, and more. Seldom is only one material used. A rattan basketry crown may be embellished with animal teeth, bone hairpins, and feathers. Masks for special occasions may be a complementary and necessary part of the hat. Headdresses are sometimes donned only for specific rituals.

Feathers are among the most widely distributed head decorations; their use ranges from a single feather stuck in the hair or headband to the elaborate Plains Indian war bonnet, an intricate construction of hide, beads, fur, horns, and eagle feathers which may trail from the crown of the head to the heels of the wearer—6 feet long!

In most societies, the type of headgear

and/or hair dressing provides instant social identification. Headgear attains particular importance in leadership roles. The chief, king, priest, medicine man, or other leader is usually literally "topped off" by some symbol of his headship. As primitive societies became acquainted with Europeans and European fashions, the hat of the foreigner was often the most envied article of apparel, and the chief frequently abandoned his traditional "crown" for the visitor's top hat (Figure 16-8). In Australian New Guinea, those indigenes assigned leadership tasks were given caps or hats to symbolize their authority, and they are now called "hat-men."

In all the foregoing discussions, certain parallels with contemporary civilizations will immediately come to mind. Specialized roles, particularly those denoting authority, often call for specialized garb: the doctor's white coat, the policeman's cap and badge, the priest's vestments. Usually footgear is the most utilitarian article of clothing, headgear the least, and body covering a mixture compounded of protection, status identification, tradition, current fashion, and other nonutilitarian variables.

Fig. 16-7   Decorative garb of the wives of Asari "Big Men" in the Western Highlands of New Guinea. Their varicolored headdresses are made of tropical birds. The crescent shells suspended from their necks are shimmering gold in color and represent great wealth—three months of hand scraping to get the thinness which produces the gold color. (Photo by E. A. Hoebel.)

Ornaments and Ornamentation

Man's passion for self-embellishment may perhaps be best seen by examining the attention he gives his body exclusive of clothing, which sometimes, at least, increases his comfort. Jewelry and cosmetics serve no such purpose; both are purely decorative. They are "luxuries," based on no obvious biological need. Yet to obtain them, Americans spend some 5 billion annually, and in primitive societies men and women not only expend vast amounts of energy and time but undergo agony, torture, and discomfort to achieve the gratification of being properly turned out. The intensity of focus on such adornments has baffled many scholars. One eminent anthropologist has noted,

In fact, so universal is this urge to improve on nature that one is almost tempted to regard it as an instinct. Aside from such fundamental drives as those for food, love, security, and the expression of maternal solicitude, I can think of few forms of human behavior that are more common to mankind as a whole . . . [the] impulse to draw attention to the body finds an outlet among the civilized sophisticate equally with the untutored savage."[14]

Cosmetics   Lotions, pastes, powders, pigments, perfumes, and synthetic essences to alter the texture, color, feel, and smell of the external surfaces of the human body are neither primitive nor civilized but, rather, universal cultural responses to the basic human need for favorable response. They are designed to heighten the stimulus intensity of the physical presence of one person upon the touch, smell, sight, and perhaps taste of others. Those others are usually members of the opposite sex, but not exclusively so. If personality is the social stimulus value of an individual, then cosmetics serve to intensify personality.

Body Paint   Rouge is the most common cosmetic for two reasons: (1) red ocher (iron oxide) occurs in many places and is readily procurable, and (2) red is the primary color with the longest wave length perceptible to the human eye, the color with the greatest natural stimulus value. When mixed with grease, it may be harmlessly applied to the human body. Yellow, black, blue, and white are the other favored colors.

Body painting among primitive peoples is for the most part limited to special occasions. Such occasions are, of course, usually ritual and ceremonial. These events are out of the ordinary, and painting changes the individual from an ordinary person to a man of distinction. War paint is usually linked to magical potency and serves less to frighten the enemy than to bolster the faint heart of its wearer.

[14]H. L. Shapiro, "From the Neck Up" (*Natural History,* vol. 56, 1947), p. 456.

Thus, much of primitive cosmetic practice takes on symbolic values.

Tattooing   The trouble with paint and cosmetics, as every woman knows, is that its application is not lasting. The solution hit upon by many peoples is tattooing. In North America, light tattooing is found among the Eskimos, continuing down the West Coast and into South America. The two high centers

Fig. 16-8   The Light, an Assineboin chieftain, as portrayed by the artist George Catlin in 1832. In trailing eagle-feather headdress, painted robe, and fringed shirt, he is dressed for his trip to visit the President of the United States. On his return to his homeland, he had changed to a new kind of splendor—the regalia of an officer of the dragoons, bestowed upon him in the capitol. (Courtesy of the Smithsonian Institution.)

of the art, however, were Polynesia and Japan. Curiously, the status associations of tattooing in Polynesia and the civilized world are just reversed. Among Americans, soldiers and sailors in the lower ranks, longshoremen, unskilled laborers, and Hell's Angels are usually the persons who get themselves tattooed. Among people of higher status, it is considered *déclassé*. But within the lower classes it serves as a symbol of masculinity and toughness. In Polynesia, the higher the social status, the fuller the tattooing. It extended over face, body, and limbs, and in some overenthusiastic cases, even to the tongue. The process was long drawn out, and painful, but socially rewarding.

A tattoo is made by puncturing the skin with needles carrying an indelible dye— usually carbon black. This posed a problem for the Africans and Australians. No white dye for tattooing was ever discovered by them. The solution hit upon in Africa and Australia was to incise the skin instead of puncturing it. Then by rubbing ashes, grit, or other irritants into the wounds, scar tissue can be encouraged to form, so that a series of raised lumps remain in a permanent visible pattern.

Scarification   In Central Australia cicatrization, or *scarification,* as the process is called, is a part of the adolescent initiatory rites for boys. The patterns are simply parallel rows of lines on the chest and back, but they are absolutely necessary to manhood. So important are they as symbols of manhood that individuals voluntarily repeat the operations in later life to keep their scars large and fresh.

In Africa, scarification (Figure 16-9) among the Congo Bantus is usually part of the initiatory rite.[15]

Traditional German corps (fraternity) students and university men gave great kudos to dueling scars, which reputedly had much sex appeal. A wound that did not fester and leave

[15]See pp. 381–385, for a discussion of cicatrization, circumcision, and clitoridectomy as important symbols of status transition through initiatory rites.

Fig. 16-9   Traditional and modern manifestations of culture in Chad, Africa. A highly cicatricized student of electromagnetics at work in the teaching laboratories of the Accelerated Vocational Training Center (**Centre de formation professionelle rapide**), *Fort Lamy, Chad. (UNESCO/Paul Almasy.)*

a glaring scar was a dead loss. So important were the duel-born scarifications that persons who had no such scars were known to slash themselves with razors and rub salt in the wounds to create the impression that they, too, bore the scars of honor.

Decorative Deformations and Mutilations
Tattooing and scarification are only superficial ornamental embellishments impressed upon the body. Piercing of the nasal septum, the lips, or the ears, so that sundry bones, feathers, shell, wood, or metal ornaments may be shoved through them, extends from the most primitive to highly civilized peoples (see Figure 16-10). The invention of the screw and spring clip has only recently obviated the need for ear puncturing among

American women, who find the functionally atrophied external ear a convenient appendage from which to dangle pretty baubles.

Incas, in South America, and Bagandas, among others in Africa, gradually extended the ear lobes to receive thin disks as much as 6 to 8 inches in diameter. Inca nobility wore disks of gold. Separation of the cervical vertebrae and extension of the neck in ringed brass collars by Burmese women is another familiar distortion.

Cranial deformation was much esteemed as a mark of beauty by various Northwest American Indian tribes (viz., the Flatheads of Idaho) and also by the Incas and other Andean peoples, who bound a flat board against the frontal region of the head of a baby in the cradleboard in order to produce a recessed

Fig. 16-10 Punan girl, Borneo, with beribboned hat and slit ear lobes distended by heavy decorative brass rings. (Courtesy of W. W. Conley.)

forehead and a high, peaked occipital. Binding with cloth to produce long heads was also practiced.

Circumcision, subincision, and clitoridectomy are not so much mutilations for ornamentation as they are mystical and status operations. The one is the removal of the foreskin of the penis; the second, a slitting of the skin and urethra along the length of the male sex organ, while the third is the surgical excision of the clitoris. Among the Central Australians, the first two operations, which are often fatal, symbolize masculinity in a male-dominated and ideologically masculine society; like scarification, they are performed without anesthesia and with flint knives on adolescent boys as a part of initiation into manhood. About half of the sub-Saharan African tribes also circumcise at adolescence, and for similar reasons. Circumcision is an absolutely required status mark of the Islamic male and orthodox Jew.

Filing or knocking out of incisor teeth occurs in scattered distribution from Australia up through Melanesia and Indonesia, and over into Africa. Prehistoric Europeans and American Indians spared themselves this mark of distinction.

As this discussion has shown, what is lost physically is gained socially. Mind triumphs over matter. No matter if the psychic satisfactions are not rational. The need that is met is elemental. The fashion and jewelry industries, the cosmetic manufacturers and purveyors, and the beauticians may rest secure that their services have a future—one that is as long as all mankind's.

SUMMARY

Wherever man is, or has been, found, he has shown a tendency to dress himself—if not in conventional clothing, at least in some kind of bodily decoration. Few, if any, peoples appear content with their bodies "as is." Body painting and jewelry found in burial sites dating as far back as the Upper Paleolithic attest to the antiquity of this practice.

The factors underlying this tendency are multiple, and there is little unanimity as to their relative importance. Protection from the weather is one clear motivation; however, except in arctic and desert zones where adequate covering is necessary for survival, the clothing of primitive peoples is often ill-suited to the environment. Where insulation against cold is vital, man has usually stripped animals of their coats to provide fur or hide robes for himself. A heavy body coating of grease is another means of conserving warmth. Bark, grass, woven reeds, and wool, depending upon which materials are provided by the habitat, are also used to make protective capes or robes. Tailored, or tubular, fitted clothing was a fairly recent Chinese or Siberian invention which diffused to northern American Indians without reaching the tropics of Middle and South America.

The sense of modesty, or shame, is postulated as another reason for clothing and bodily ornamentation. All societies have clear norms as to what constitutes proper dress, and all peoples do seem to feel modest about something. However, the "somethings" about which they are modest vary widely from culture to culture. In many societies nakedness is customary for one or both sexes, but propriety demands a particular headdress, lip plug, or piece of jewelry. Modesty is clearly a habit rather than an instinct; people feel uncomfortable in any social situation where they are shorn of habit-ingrained clothing, decoration, or deportment.

Sexual enhancement, the display of wealth, and identification between social groups are other factors which assume significance as one examines patterns of clothing, jewelry, hairstyles, or body decoration. All attributes of dress are seemingly invested with deep emotional gratification, quite apart from utility or comfort—which qualities, indeed, are often quite lacking.

Footgear is generally more utilitarian and functional than other aspects of dress. Tropi-cal people usually go barefoot, while the sandal is worn in temperate and desert areas. The crude moccasin, a piece of hide folded about the foot, is even simpler to make than the sandal, but it is not ordinarily worn where rainfall is frequent. Moccasins may have been the first form of self-shodding which Paleolithic man developed north of the Mediterranean in glacial times. When tailored (fitted), it becomes the American Indian type of moccasin, and when the sides of the moccasin are extended up the leg in the form of a tube, it becomes the arctic boot.

The artificial hairdo is a universal human cultural attribute as old as Upper Paleolithic man. Different patterns of hair arrangement signal tribal, clan, band, sex, and age identification, as is also true of hat styles. However, while hairdos are ubiquitous among human beings, headgear tends to be limited to persons of higher rank, and in many cultures no form of headgear may be found at all.

Body painting is usually symbolic, while tattooing and scarification may combine symbolism with status identification. Bodily mutilation in the form of filing and knocking out front teeth, piercing the nose, ears, and lips for the insertion of ornaments, chopping off segments of fingers, and artificially deforming the cranium are all sporadically distributed about the globe. Circumcision is especially a Mediterranean and North African feature. With subincision and clitoridectomy, it also appears in Sub-Saharan Africa and Oceania, while, interestingly enough, no forms of genital mutilation were known to any American Indians.

SELECTED READINGS

Elwin, V., *The Tribal Art of Middle India* (1951). For illustrations and descriptions of bodily adornment.

Erikson, J. M., *The Universal Bead* (1969). Provides a general survey, not detailed, of historical and ethnographic materials on beads and their forms, uses, and meanings.

Hambly, W. D., *The History of Tattooing and Its Significance* (1925). A broad survey.

Roach, M. E., and J. B. Eicher, *Dress, Adornment, and the Social Order* (1965). A rich collection of writings on the sociocultural significance of bodily adornment. Contains an excellent annotated bibliography for use in further research.

Roediger, V. M., *Ceremonial Costumes of the Pueblo Indians* (1961, reprint). Illustrated. A descriptive account of the materials used in Pueblo dance costumes, plus the relation of costumery and decoration to the dances themselves.

Wissler, C., *The American Indian* (3d ed., 1938), chap. 3, "The Textile Arts." A brief summary.

Part 4   Social Structure

Chapter 17

Economic Organization

In the previous chapters we have been concerned with the concept of culture in its several manifestations: the evolution of man and culture, the races of mankind, the subsistence base of society, technology and the material manifestations of culture, and ownership of property. We now turn to the organization of society and to that part of anthropology which is known as *social anthropology,* the study of social structure and relationships.

Social Structure

By *social structure* we mean the patterned ways in which groups and individuals are organized and related to one another in the functioning entity that is society. The culture of every society includes a figurative "manual" that lays out the major tasks to be performed, the job definitions of key personnel, and specific directions for carrying out the assigned functions. The tasks to be performed (as values) constitute what Malinowski called the *charter of social institutions.* The job definitions and the assignment of specified persons to carry them out may be called *social statuses.* The directives for accomplishing various tasks may be called *roles.*

Social Institutions An institution is a network of procedures centered upon certain focal interests. Economic institutions, for example, comprise the characteristic behaviors that center upon the production, the allocation and distribution, and the use and consumption of goods. Economic institutions include behavioral networks of food production and the manufacture of artifacts; gift exchange, trade, sale, preemption, and in-

heritance; utilization, hoarding, and consumption; and ownership, possession, and rights of use—everything which focuses upon production and utilization of goods and services. Marital institutions focus upon organization of intersexual relations, particularly the stabilization of mating, the nurture and enculturation of the young, household economic activities, the establishment and maintenance of mutual aid between kinship

Fig. 17-A A Kirdi market in central Sudan, Africa, east of Lake Chad. (P. W. Haeberlin.)

groups, and the legalizing of inheritance. Religious institutions focus upon the conceptualization of the supernatural, the formulation of effective ritual for dealing with the supernatural, and symbolic representation of the social entirety. All institutions within a society overlap and interweave. That is why we have emphasized "focused upon" in stating the central interests or goals of given types of institutions. Institutions are far from being mutually exclusive.

The Charters of Institutions   The charter of an institution consists of "statements" explaining why the institution exists and for what purpose. Myths, legends, beliefs, and judgments give sanctity and authority to the choices and commitments a society has made; they state why things are as they are and why they must be as they are, and they state why individuals must commit themselves to the goals as the goals are given.

Institutional charters, social statuses, and social roles may or may not be explicitly spelled out in any given culture. Most of them are not; they are implicit in customary, or normalized, action.

Symbolic art, music, ritual, and dance express and reinforce with emotional overtones the structural relationships between persons and groups which constitute the institutions.

The Personnel of Institutions   All institutions have personnel. Institutions represent stability and order established by the traditional past; yet they exist only in present action—in the behavior of functioning persons. The groups of people who carry out the roles of any institution constitute its personnel. Institutionally organized groups in preliterate societies are recognized as *kinship groups* (family, extended family, ramage, lineage, clan, phratry, and moiety) or *associations* (age sets, clubs and fraternities, cults, corporations, work groups, guilds, and the state). The personnel of an association consists of *members* and *specialists* (functionaries or officials).

Economic Organization in Social Structure

In determining the link that relates social structure to the material base of life, we first turn our attention to economic organization: the special ways in which goods and services are exchanged and redistributed within the social system. We treat economic organization as a link between the material base and social structure because it is concerned on the one hand with the products of technology, and on the other, with their differential distribution: the modes of exchange. In no society is everything up for grabs. Economic order, in one form or another, is a functional prerequisite to societal survival and continuity (page 34). As such, it is a universal aspect of culture, for if there have been societies which have failed to motivate men and women to work and production, and which have failed to develop effective systems of distribution of the products of work input, such societies have failed in adaptation to the circumstances of life. They have not survived for our study!

Primary and Secondary Consumption

A notable difference between primitive and civilized economic systems is that in simple primitive societies a high proportion of food and goods is consumed by the producer and the members of his own family or household. The consumption is *primary* and no exchange outside the primary group is necessary. A man literally "brings home the bacon"—and not from the market, or from some other farmer's enterprise, but from the bush. A man not only does his own hunting, his wife her own gathering, but he makes his own spear, his own bow and arrows, his own house, etc. But as soon as it becomes customary to share food with members of other primary groups, as soon as it is recognized that another man can make better arrows and specialized division of labor sets in—then a system of exchange is created. Exchange systems involve *secondary* consumption: food and goods are used by persons who are not members of a primary group of the original producer. Secondary consumption, as shall soon be demonstrated, occurs in primitive societies and sometimes to a high degree. However, in civilizations (particularly those of urban dwellers), primary consumption is very low. Just consider what, if anything, of the food, clothing, shelter, and other goods which you are using this day, you have produced any part of! Primary production may be the woof of the fabric of civilization, but exchange to effect secondary consumption is its economic web.

How do exchange systems work?

Three Modes of Exchange

The economist Karl Polanyi (1893–1964) brought into focus three contrasting modes of cultural channeling of ultimate access to valued goods in human societies. These are: (1) reciprocal exchange, (2) redistributive exchange, and (3) market exchange.[1]

Reciprocal exchange consists of obligatory gift giving and countergiving of goods and services between persons (and groups) of specific statuses (see pages 362–365) within a social system. A Trobriand Islander, for example, raises yams on land which is assigned to him in his own village. All but the poorest of these he carries to another village where his married sister lives with her husband. There they are shown in ceremonial display, and then carefully packed in thatched-roof storehouses made of horizontally laid logs through which the yams may be seen and continually admired until they are consumed. No man sells best-quality yams to another. Nor does he trade them to just anybody. Lesser-quality yams and melons he may trade for fish with an exchange partner, but he cannot walk up and down the beach

looking for any random fisherman with whom he may strike a good bargain. *This is not a market economy.*

From his sister's husband, a Trobriander receives return gifts, but most important of all, he gets his sister's sons, who leave their father to live with a maternal uncle, well before the onset of puberty. They become the uncle's helpers, are trained and educated by him; they also become his heirs and successors to his rights of use in land, his magical formulas, his wealth and prerogatives—as well as membership in his matrilineal clan. The prime yams, which a man laboriously produces and ostentatiously gives to his sister's husband, are well repaid by services received from the latter.[2]

Redistributive exchange occurs when a holder of economic or political office—a hereditary chief or monarch, or a priest, for instance—is vested with the power to exact goods or services as tribute. These are first funneled into the "royal" or cult holding centers. After the governing elite has creamed off what custom or its power enables it to use for its own consumption, a portion is redistributed to the populace. Redistribution may or may not be equitable. The basic handicraft producer is apt to get less in return than he puts out. Yet, over all, he and other members of his society may collectively benefit from the higher levels of production which result from their combined, élite-directed efforts. Such systems are characteristic of a number of state-organized, preliterate horticultural societies (see Inca, below) and early civilizations.

Market exchange is based on direct barter (the more primitive manifestation) or on sale and purchase through use of a commercial medium of exchange: money. Where markets

[1]K. Polanyi, *The Great Transformation.*

[2]B. Malinowski, *Coral Gardens and Their Magic*, vol. 1, The Customary Law of Harvest Gifts," pp. 188–217.

Author's note: In 1967 when I visited the Trobriand Islands, I found the yam gardens, storage houses, and exchange system virtually unchanged from Malinowski's descriptions of 1914–1917. In the case of this primitive society it is, therefore, quite proper to use the present, rather than the past, tense.

exist within the economic systems of tribal societies, they are usually peripheral; i.e., the goods available for exchange or sale through the market do not include "everything" available through the production system—especially land and labor. In other words, the bulk of exchange is reciprocal or redistributive, although markets do exist.

In cultures in which *most* exchange of goods and services is effected through transfer of symbolic tokens of unitary value (money), *market exchange* dominates. In a market economy all money uses are related to "free exchange"—free of kinship requirements, fealty to overlords, personal friendship, and other status limitations. In the free market, there are but two questions: do you "own" what you have to offer? and do you have the money (or the money credit) to make the payment? The market is impersonal. You can buy from anyone. You can sell to anyone. In reciprocal and redistributive exchange the relations are absolutely a matter of personal status.

Reciprocal Gift Exchange Within many primitive societies gift giving which builds into gift exchange marks every important crisis period in the individual life cycle or any other change of personal status. Birth, puberty, marriage, death, entrance into a club, or assumption of an office is called to public attention by the bestowal of gifts. The famous potlatches of the Northwest Coast Indians, with all their lavish expenditure of gifts, center around such occasions. Contractual arrangements such as marriage call for immediate two-way exchanges, often extending over months.

Gift exchange of economic significance may border on trade. Yet it may be merely symbolic in nature when the rule of equivalence is strong. The person who views our ceremonial gift exchanges on the occasion of the Christmas festival only in terms of the usableness of the gifts measured against cost and effort naturally thinks the whole business is silly. But he, poor soul, misses the point.

Quite true, we all end up with a number of things we neither need nor want. Quite true, it would be more rational to offer gift certificates or even money to one's friends or family so that they could buy what they want and need. But how flat are such gifts! Their donors confuse the social function of gift giving with utility. They forget that the gifts are symbolic of a social bond between giver and receiver. Gifts represent a state of social relations and a set of emotions, not only business.

The Andaman Islands On the lowest level of culture, the Andaman Islanders, in the Indian Ocean, nicely exemplify gift exchange. Movables were all privately owned by these people, and yet no one could possess a particular article for long.

When two friends meet who have not seen each other for some time, one of the first things they do is to exchange presents with one another. Even in the ordinary everyday life of the village there is a constant giving and receiving of presents. A younger man or woman may give some article to an older one without expecting or receiving any return, but between equals a person who gives a present always expects that he will receive something of equal value in exchange. At the meetings that take place between neighbouring local groups the exchange of presents is of great importance. . . .

Almost every object that the Andamanese possess is thus constantly changing hands.[3]

Pig Exchange in Melanesia In like manner, the elaborate extremes to which Melanesian "Big Men" go to operate exchange networks of pig-growing and pig-giving indicate clearly that there is more than just the utilitarian production and distribution of pork involved (Figure 17-1). In it one sees the very weaving of the fabric of societal interdependence. Margaret Mead's account of the Arapesh of New Guinea will help give some feel for the meaning of pig exchange in Melanesia:

We must now turn from the organization of everyday economic life to the organization of large-scale

[3]A. R. Radcliffe-Brown, *The Andaman Islanders,* pp. 42–43.

feasts. Here again, no matter how large the undertaking, it is phrased as one individual acting for a hamlet, or even sometimes for a cluster of hamlets, taking the responsibility of organization, while the others merely help him. It is a chain organization grouped around a leader who is called the *trunk* or *base* of the enterprise. The organization of feasts makes a man a "big man," but the Arapesh conceive this as an onerous duty which is forced upon him by community recognition of his ability to organize and lead, a duty which he fulfills without real enthusiasm and from which one retires as soon as one's first child reaches adolescence. In addition to organizing specific feasts centering about initiation, the exhumation of the bones of the dead, or the importation of some ceremonial dance complex from the Beach, the "big men" stand in a continuous exchange relationship with exchange partners, theoretically members of the opposite moiety, and always members of a different clan. These exchange partners call each other *buanyin*, are hereditary, usually in the male line, but not necessarily in the direct line. Old buanyin partnerships which have been unsatisfactory, that is, unequally matched, may be abandoned and new ones founded at any time. Such new ones again become hereditary. The buanyin relationship is modeled upon the relationship of brothers-in-law and the relationship which continues from it in the next generation, the cross-cousin relationship. Buanyins are conceived as members of autonomous groups, and engage in exchanges one with the other. But whereas between relatives and between trade friends, cost accounting, dunning, reproaching in economic terms are regarded as disgraceful, between buanyins there is a frank accounting system. Each one is expected to initiate exchanges with the other, and they are expected to insult one another publicly and to goad one another on to economic activity. The major exchanges between buanyins are of meat, and an exchange is initiated usually by the present to one of the buanyins of big game—wild pig or cassowary —or a domestic pig which has been trussed to a pole ready to be killed. If the man who now has become the temporary owner of the meat does not wish to use it, he gives it to his buanyin. He cannot refuse it, and will owe a return of the same amount to his buanyin in the future. If he has no pig or game with which to repay, he will have to rear domestic pigs in order to return the gift. Giving meat to a buanyin is therefore a way of banking. When a man receives this large present of meat from his buan-

yin, he in turn distributes it to his relatives, who are thus obligated to help him make returns to his buanyin when necessary. Buanyins give each other feasts, at which neither buanyin eats, but each distributes food to his helping friends and relatives. . . . When the time for the final feast is set, each dog [cooperating pig partner] gives back a whole pig, representing the three-quarters of a pig which he has received, plus other food. The trunk thus has all his negotiable wealth in his hands at once, and exchanges it either for dance ceremonial or for other pigs, or arranges for a return feast in another community which has similarly been organized around a trunk.[4]

Exchange of Cattle in Africa   The joining of families by marriage affords a major means of reciprocal distribution in most primitive societies. Since in much of Africa the cow is the principal unit of value—indeed, it has been written that the transfer of cows "has

[4]M. Mead, *Cooperation and Competition among Primitive Peoples*, pp. 32–34. (By permission of McGraw-Hill Book Company.)

Fig. 17-1   Slaughtered and roasted boars being distributed by a Chimbu "Big Man" in a ceremonial exchange of sixty-seven pigs in settlement of a dispute over land. Near Goroka, East Central Highlands, New Guinea, 1967. (Photo by E. A. Hoebel.)

had the function of making concrete certain already existent social relationships"[5]—it is not surprising that weddings involve complicated transactions in cattle.

Distribution of Marriage Cattle among the Nuer To illustrate the complex and highly ritualized socioeconomic aspects of progeny price, we may turn to the Nuer, a tribe of cattle raisers living on the upper reaches of the White Nile. Here, each marriage ideally calls for the transfer of forty head of cattle. Of these, twenty go to members of the bride's primary composite family, ten to her father's primary composite family, and ten to that of her mother. The distribution is as follows (see Figure 17-2):

1. *Primary family of the bride:* To the bride's father (*a*), eight head, specified as three cows and their calves and two oxen; to her brother born of another mother (*b*), two cows; to her brother born of the same mother (*c*), two oxen, three cows, and a cow and its calf (seven head); to her mother (*d*), a cow and its calf and a heifer.

2. *Siblings of the bride's father:* To the bride's father's elder brother by the same mother (*e*), a cow and its calf, a calf, and an ox (four head); to the bride's father's younger brother by the same mother (*f*), a cow and an ox; to the bride's father's sister (*g*), one heifer; to the bride's father's brother by a different mother (*h*), a cow and its calf and an ox.

3. *Siblings of the bride's mother:* To the bride's mother's elder brother by the same mother (*i*), a cow and its calf, a cow, and an ox; to the bride's mother's younger brother by the same mother (*j*), a cow and its calf; to the bride's mother's sister (*k*), one heifer; to a brother of the bride's mother through a different mother (*l*), a cow and its calf and an ox.[6]

In addition to these specific rights to cattle, every patrilineal relative of the bride, even though the relationship be so remote as that of descent from a common ancestor six or seven generations back, may claim a small

[5]P. G. Gravel, "The Transfer of Cows in Gisaka (Rwanda): A Mechanism for Recording Social Relationships" (*American Anthropologist,* vol. 69, 1967), p. 322.

[6]These figures represent the ideal norm among the Eastern Nuer as reported by Evans-Pritchard, "Nuer Bride-wealth" (*Africa,* vol. 16, 1946), p. 4. In the real culture, they vary by circumstance and district within the tribe. See P. P. Howell, *A Manual of Nuer Law,* pp. 101–124.

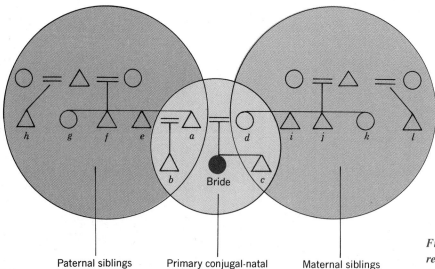

| Paternal siblings | Primary conjugal-natal family of the bride | Maternal siblings |

Fig. 17-2 Identification of relatives in Nuer progeny price distribution.

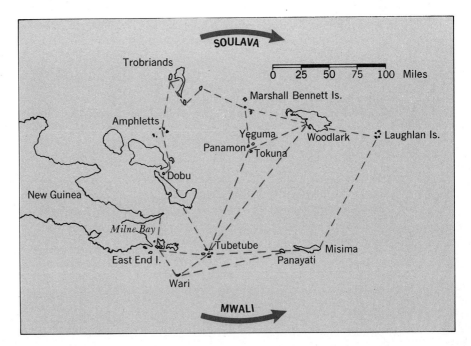

Fig. 17-3 The kula ring of the southwest Pacific. Lines show overseas trade routes. Arrows indicate directions in which necklaces (soulava) and armbands (mwali) are traded. (Adapted from Malinowski.)

gift from the groom's kinsmen. Special symbolic gifts of cattle may be called for in the name of ancestral spirits of the bride, of her "father's best friend, of an age classmate of her father, of her father's fireplace, and to the priest who performs magic rituals for enhancement of the bride's fecundity."

All this should make it very clear how much more than just a commercial transaction is the transfer of bride wealth.

The Kula Without doubt, the most elaborate and exciting system of reciprocal exchange yet noted for the primitive world is the *kula* of northwestern Melanesia. Malinowski's thorough description of the *kula* will continue to stand as a classic of anthropological economics for many years to come. The *kula* enterprise is a vast complex of trade, magic, ceremonial exchange, overseas travel, and pleasure seeking that involves the enterprisers of tribes many miles apart. The framework through which the whole organization

is expressed is the exchange of white shell armbands, called *mwali,* and long necklaces of red shell, called *soulava.* Exchange is intertribal and interisland. *Soulava* are always traded in a clockwise direction. *Mwali* go counterclockwise (Figure 17-3). There is no exception to this rule.

Each of these articles . . . meets on its way articles of the other class, and is constantly being exchanged for them. Every movement of the Kula articles, every detail of the transactions is fixed and regulated by a set of traditional rules and conventions, and some acts of the Kula are accompanied by an elaborate magical ritual and public ceremonies.

On every island and in every village, a more or less limited number of men take part in the Kula—that is to say, receive the goods, hold them for a short time, and then pass them on. . . . Thus no man ever keeps any of the articles for any length of time in his possession. One transaction does not finish the Kula relationship, the rule being "once in the Kula, always in the Kula," and a partnership between two men is a permanent and lifelong affair. . . .

The ceremonial exchange of the two articles is the main, the fundamental aspect of the Kula. But associated with it, and done under its cover, we find a great number of secondary activities and features. Thus, side by side with the ritual exchange of armshells and necklaces, the natives carry on ordinary trade, bartering from one island to another a great number of utilities, often unprocurable in the district to which they are imported, and indispensable there.[7]

Although the nonutilitarian nature of the *kula* exchange has been much emphasized, the *kula* expeditions are also seized upon as opportunities to engage in free barter for various artifacts. Such activity, which takes on the character of market exchange, is recognized as being different in quality and function; hence, the Trobriander knows it as *gimwali.*

Redistributive Exchange In redistributive exchange, "surplus" goods and labor are channeled as gifts, tribute, or corvée into the hands of a ruling or managerial class which usually keeps some for its personal use, but which also redirects a portion (often large) to "general" social goals.

Redistributive Exchange as the Foundation of Complex States In discussing the dawn of civilization in the evolution of culture (Chapter 10), we have already noted some aspects of redistributive exchange. As agricultural efficiency increased so that not all working time went into food production, specialized labor developed, and assignments of both tasks and the necessities of life were directed by strong governmental leaders.

Sumerian Civilization What we wrote in Chapter 10 of Sumer in its early dynastic period (3200 to 2800 B.C.) illustrates the significance of this mode of exchange.

Allotments of land, work assignments, and raw materials were designated by the head priest-administrator of the temple district. Each work-

man had to deliver a specified amount of produce; anything beyond this was his own. Some goods went to maintain the priests, and much was redistributed among the producing populace. Thus, the division of labor and the economic exchange necessary to effective civilization were achieved—in this case without an internal market system [page 219, above].

Mayan Civilization Far to the west, in Mesoamerica two thousand years after Sumer, the same type of redistributive exchange developed quite independently. Of the Maya civilization of 1000 B.C., Eric Wolf has written:

A man is buried at Kaminaljuyú in a mound 20 feet high, and set to rest surrounded by 400 pots, jade, marble greenstone vessels, jade-incrusted masks, pyrite mirrors, and ornaments of shell and bone. This man is the priest, set off from common humanity by dress, deportment, and skills, as well as by his vision of the universe and his dedication to the realization of this vision. . . .

The dominant figure of this new social order was the religious specialist. . . . These specialists . . . were not only devotees of the supernatural; they were also devotees of power, power over men. In them, society had developed a body not only of full-time religious practitioners but also of specialists in organization, capable of exacting labor and tribute as well as worship from the mass of men. . . . As servitors of their gods they also administered the many goods made as offerings to the deities. The temple centers became veritable storehouses of the gods, where costly produce accumulated in the service of the supernatural.[8]

Redistributive Exchange in Tribal Societies Lest one get the impression that redistributive exchange is characteristic only of civilizations and class-exploitative societies of more modern times, let us note that it also exists on the tribal level.

The Pueblos As cultural outposts of the great Mesoamerican cultural tradition, the southwestern Pueblos thinly reflect its qualities, even today. Apart from the universal obligation to participate in ceremonial dances,

[7]B. Malinowski, *Argonauts of the Western Pacific*, pp. 81–83.

[8]E. R. Wolf, *Sons of the Shaking Earth*, pp. 70, 78–79, 81.

every able-bodied man in the Rio Grande Pueblos of New Mexico is required: (1) to help cultivate and harvest the field set aside for the head priest-chief, or cacique; (2) to join in the communal rabbit and deer hunts to fill the cacique's storeroom; (3) to join in the labor of cleaning and repairing the irrigation ditches; (4) to sweep the pueblo plaza in preparation for ceremonies; and (5) to help replaster the Catholic mission church once a year.

The cacique drains off very little of the economic goods for his own use. His house is as undistinguishably modest as any man's in appearance. He wears the same clothes and eats no more, nor any less, than others. He is freed, however, from tilling the gardens, herding, and hunting. He concentrates all his efforts on "thinking good thoughts" and on ritual activity. He is freed to serve as the symbolic vessel of the pueblo's "collective soul," its full-time intercessor between his "children" and the manageable forces of the universe. In addition, he feeds ceremonial participants and redistributes meat and vegetables to widows, orphans, and the aged poor.

Trade and Market Exchange   The essential difference between trade and gift exchange is in their relative functions. In trade, the emphasis is on economic redistribution. In gift exchange, the emphasis is on social relationships. Trade rests on and fosters social interaction, but its main concern is with the distribution of goods. Gift exchange distributes goods, but its main concern is with personal relations.

Within small tribes, there is little trade. Gift exchange suffices for the most part. The level of culture is also a factor of some influence. Simple cultures with little specialization of labor do not call forth much intratribal trade. It is primarily the high cultures with large populations that are capable of considerable specialization of effort among their members. Services and products are then available for exchange and trade.

However, virtually all societies, large and small, engage in intertribal or international trade. Every society has its unique goods or possesses natural resources from which to supply materials not available elsewhere. Salt-water shells find their way hundreds of miles inland in New Guinea and North America. In the Bronze Age, copper from Cyprus followed trade routes all over Europe. Beeswax flint from Grand-Pressigny, France, found wide use over all western Europe in Neolithic times. Melanesian inlanders trade vegetables for fish with the coastal dwellers. Interisland trading is suggested by the chart (Figure 17-4).

Specialization based on custom rather than limitation of resources induces a good deal of trade. In New Mexico, Sia Indian women make excellent pottery. The pueblo of Jemez, less

Fig. 17-4   Micronesian navigator's chart made of split bamboo and cowrie shells. The shells represent islands; the curved sticks, currents. (Smithsonian Institution.)

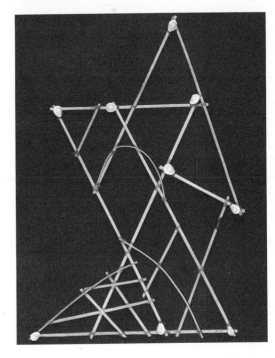

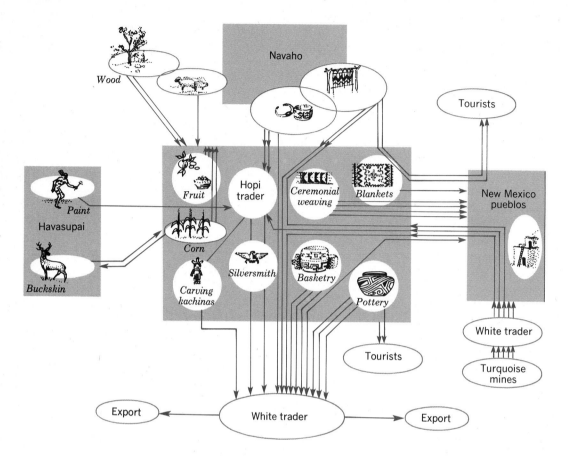

Fig. 17-5 *Hopi craftsmen trade finished products to Navahos and
Havasupai Indians in exchange for raw materials, paint, and blankets.
From white traders and New Mexico Pueblos they get industrial products.
(From L. Thompson and A. Joseph,* **The Hopi Way,** *p. 23.)*

than ten miles away, made none for many
centuries, although the same clays are available to both. Jemez exchanged corn for Sia
pots in the old days. Hopis trade maize with
the nearby Havasupai for buckskins and
paint, and maize for wood and wool with the
surrounding Navaho (Figure 17-5). But
within the Hopi tribe, only the women of the
pueblos on Second Mesa make coiled baskets; those who live on Third Mesa make them
of wicker, and painted pottery is produced
only on First Mesa.

The Crow Indians of the Plains were capable of growing tobacco. Indeed, they had a
ceremonial organization, the Tobacco So-

ciety, whose interest centered around the
growing of tobacco as a sacred ritual. Nevertheless, the nicotine plant was not grown for
use, and common tobacco had to be obtained by trade with other tribes.[9]

In western Melanesia, the Southern Massim own large seagoing canoes similar to the
one shown in Figure 17-6. They do not manufacture these boats themselves, although
they could. Instead, they obtain them in trade
from the tribes of the Northern Massim district.

Within the small group of Trobriand Is-

[9] R. H. Lowie, *The Crow Indians,* pp. 274ff.

lands, local specialization is very marked. Two towns alone produce the red shell disks so valued in the *kula* exchange. The people of the island of Kayleula make canoes and trade with the inhabitants of the western D'Entrecasteaux Islands for betel nuts, sago, pottery, and turtle shell.

To the east of the Trobriands, the natives of Woodlark Island produce homogeneous greenstone for tools and the best carved ebony of the area; both products are valued objects of trade.[10]

Dumb Barter It shocks many people to discover that businessmen carry on trade with enemy nations. A high command will deliberately spare certain enemy plants because by means of trade through neutrals, it is possible to secure products of those plants. Enemies not infrequently find it advantageous to let economic interests override their antagonisms.

This is the basis of the dumb barter, or silent trade, among certain primitives. The pygmy Semang of Malaya, for example, exchange forest products for goods offered by their enemies, the Sakai. Neither group sees the other party during the transaction. The Semang place their goods in a customary place and retire. When the Sakai find the offering, they appropriate it and replace it with whatever they wish to exchange. Later, the little Semangs come back to pick up the goods before retiring to their jungle fastness. In like manner, the Mountain Vedda of Ceylon trade game for iron arrowheads with the Singhalese smiths. They lay their game in front of the smiths' huts at night, to come back the next night to gather the returns.

Herodotus describes how Carthaginian merchants carried on dumb barter with the natives of the northwest coast of Africa. The Carthaginians placed their goods on shore and retired to their ships, sending up a smoke signal. The natives came and replaced the goods with gold. They got what they deemed

necessary, for the natives knew that if the mariners were shortchanged they would not return.[11]

A modernized version of dumb barter was practiced in the Ozark Mountain country of Arkansas into the 1930s, where "moonshine" corn whiskey could be bought as "stump liquor." As a means of avoiding revenue officers, it was the practice to leave one dollar on a known tree stump. During the night, a gallon of corn whiskey would replace it, to be picked up by the purchaser in the morning. The moonshiner did not have to expose himself to possible arrest.

Markets Open trade is naturally much more convenient, and primitive peoples have often developed elaborate machinery for this purpose. In Nigeria, huge market towns of great antiquity are in existence. Native artisans bring their brasswork, pottery, mats, baskets, leatherwork, and foodstuffs many miles to

[11]W. D. Hambly, *Source Book for African Anthropology* (Field Museum of Natural History, Anthropological Series, vol. 26, part 2), p. 650.

Fig. 17-6 Overseas outrigger trading canoe off the coast of Manus, Admiralty Islands, southwest Pacific, in 1967. The vessel carries a platform above the hull and outrigger. (Photo by E. A. Hoebel.)

[10]B. Malinowski, *Argonauts of the Western Pacific*, chap. 1.

these trading centers (Figure 17-7). The Kede tribe of northern Nigeria act as river transporters of trade goods, for the Kede are the consummate canoemen of the Niger. They carry kola nuts and palm oil north from Nigeria, bringing back gowns, mats, fish, rice, horses, and potash from the Hausa and Nupe tribes.[12]

African Markets   In Africa, the marketplace is often under the magical protection of some great native chief, whose super-

natural authority evokes the "peace of the market" so that enemy tribes may trade in safety. Chiefs frequently provide police and courts for markets in their districts, as well.

Bohannan points out that African markets in tribal subsistence economies are "peripheral"; that is, the markets are not essential to the economic livelihood of the societies because the number of people who actually derive their living from the markets is small. The economic function of African markets is but one part of the whole picture. Markets are public meeting places and communication centers for dispersal of gossip, news, and

[12]S. F. Nadel, "The Kede," in E. E. Evans-Pritchard and M. Fortes (eds.), *African Political Systems,* p. 169.

Fig. 17-7   Woman traders in a Digo market, Kenya, Africa. (Courtesy of Luther P. Gerlach.)

official pronouncements. Entertainers use markets as fairs are used in the United States —as places where audiences are gathered without effort. And markets, like fairs, are ready-made festivals. "The market day," observes Bohannan, "usually falls off into a beer drink."[13]

American Indian Markets European traders found a strong trade network already in existence among the Indians of the northern Plains of North America when they first arrived at the Mandan, Hidatsa, and Arikara villages on the Missouri River, in the middle of the eighteenth century. The village tribes grew surpluses of corn and squash which they traded to the nomadic tribes. They also tanned fur robes and painted hides and ornamental clothing. These they traded with the Assineboin, Cheyenne, and Crow for meat and skins. Spanish trade goods also found their way to the Middle Missouri along the intertribal trade routes from the Southwest by way of the Cheyenne, who in turn got them from the Kiowas, who got them from the Comanches and Mexicans.

When French and British traders introduced the gun and metal utensils, after 1738, and horses were acquired from the Southwest, the flow of new materials along the old trade networks drastically altered the cultures of the nomadic tribes. The great flowering of the buffalo-hunting cultures suddenly occurred. Within a hundred years, the same forces which had created them—European trade, the horse, and the gun—destroyed them in an epic tragedy.

Primitive Money Not all trade among primitive peoples is by means of direct barter. Various media of exchange are known in several parts of the world. Shells serve most commonly as a species of money: cowrie shells in the Pacific area and in Africa, and dentalium shells among the Indians of California. Wampum beads were used in exchange among the eastern Indians, and the

early Dutch in New York treated wampum as good cash. Importation of poor counterfeits caused the city council of New Amsterdam in 1650 to pass an ordinance pegging the exchange value of good-quality beads at six white and three black per *stiver* (a Dutch coin). Poor wampum was pegged at eight and four, respectively.

Iron hoes have served as a medium of exchange in parts of Africa, but perhaps the strangest of all primitive moneys were the huge limestone wheels of the Island of Yap in Micronesia (Figure 17-8).

Fig. 17-8   The great stone wheels of the islands of Yap in Micronesia were not intended for vehicles. They were prestige forms of wealth— "tokens" of great value—which have often been referred to as money. The stone was quarried on the island of Palau, some 500 sea miles away, and transported across the open ocean in sailing canoes. Approximately ten thousand of these wheels are found throughout the Yap district. (United Nations.)

[13]P. Bohannan, *Social Anthropology*, p. 242.

Inheritance

The transfers of goods which have been discussed thus far are "across the board," so to speak. They consist of lateral exchanges between the living. The continuity of society, however, requires that there be an orderly flow of property statuses in goods and incorporeals from one generation to the next. This constitutes inheritance.

Inheritance, in the words of G. D. H. Cole, "is the entrance of living persons into the possession of dead persons' property."[14] That is one way of putting it. This, however, leaves much unsaid. In a preceding chapter, property was identified as consisting of (1) an object (material or incorporeal), and (2) a web of social relations that establishes and maintains a limiting and defined relationship between persons and that object. This web of relationships consists of the roles or patterns of behavior that are associated with certain statuses, which are in turn related to the object of property. Ownership, therefore, is a complex of statuses and roles that allows certain persons the socially recognized privilege-right of limited control of the use or disposition of objects. These rights of control, though limited, establish the owners' active and positive relations to the object. Nonowners are under a duty to refrain from use of the object, or they are at least subject to much more restrictive access to its use. In other words, the statuses and roles of A with respect to property are distinct and special as against those of X, Y, or Z.

Analyzed in terms of culture theory, inheritance is not transfer of possession; it is the transference of statuses. And although much inheritance involves transfer after death, many statuses may be transferred *inter vivos*, during life. Nyakyusa sons of chiefs "inherit the country"; i.e., they assume the chieftainship, while their fathers still live. Ifugao children inherit the parental rice fields on mar-

riage. But obviously not all transfers of status are what we recognize as inheritance. Cheyenne peace chiefs on the Council of Forty-four were replaced every ten years by selection, not inheritance. The Presidency of the United States involves a transfer of status every time we change administration, but the office is noninheritable.

Inheritance, therefore, means a transference of status based upon a preexisting relationship between the predecessor and the successor. The relationship is personal and, usually, traditional.

Radcliffe-Brown, in his survey of patrilineal and matrilineal succession in primitive societies, came very close to realization of this when he concluded: "In general, though there are a few exceptions, transmission of property follows the same line as transmission of status."[15] The reason is that transmission of property *is* transmission of status. It follows that if most kinds of status are transmitted down one line or another, property statuses will follow along the same line. Therefore, a close correlation of type of social organization and devolution of property will naturally occur.

Effect of Unilineal Descent   In the event that a death is followed by a sororal or levirate marriage (see pages 408–409), the movable property of the deceased spouse stays right in the household of the surviving spouse, and the landed property remains in the relation to the survivor that it exhibited before the death of the spouse. But this is only because of the coincidence of identity of status between the deceased spouse and the one who replaces her (or him) in the household. The inheritance runs from deceased wife to her sister who replaces her, not from deceased wife to husband to his second wife.

Inheritance of rights of use in land follows fairly clear lines. Among matrilineal gar-

[14]G. D. H. Cole, "Inheritance" (*Encyclopaedia of the Social Sciences,* vol. 20, 1935), p. 286.

[15]A. R. Radcliffe-Brown, "Patrilineal and Matrilineal Succession" (*Iowa Law Review,* vol. 20, 1935), p. 297; also in his *Structure and Function in Primitive Society,* pp. 32–47.

deners, where women till the soil, inheritance runs from mother to daughters. If the picture is complicated with matrilineal organization coupled with virilocal residence (see pages 426–428) and male gardening (as in the Trobriand Islands), inheritance runs from mother's brother to sister's son. In parts of Melanesia, although land is inherited matrilineally, fruit trees privately owned by males are inherited patrilineally.

Whether matrilineal or patrilineal organization prevails also strongly influences the lines of inheritance of movable and incorporeal property. Patrilineal societies favor filial inheritance. Matrilineal societies favor inheritance from maternal uncle to sister's son. It is quite possible for a tribe to subject some forms of property to the avunculate and other forms to paternal succession. It is not necessary that the inheritance system be absolutely consistent with one principle or the other.

The sexual equivalence of brothers in marriage arrangements is reflected in their equivalence in relation to property. Thus *collateral inheritance,* or inheritance by brothers or sisters from brother or sister in preference to the children, indicates that the members of a fraternity have a solidarity that supersedes that of the conjugal-natal family. Plains Indians applied this rule to the inheritance of horses especially. The generation tie outweighs the filial or avuncular. This may well be reinforced in political inheritance of chiefship, where it is advantageous to avoid letting the mantle of leadership fall on a callow youth.

Incorporeal properties, especially magic formulas and medical powers, must be partially transferred before death if they involve secret knowledge. A man may transfer his charms or songs to son or nephew as a gift, without anticipation of his departure from life. This would be a gift *inter vivos,* not properly a matter of inheritance. Or it may be that the necessary knowledge is taught to the beneficiary without transfer of the right of use until after the death of the donor, which would be

a true case of a gift *causa mortis,* a gift made in the prospect of death and properly an aspect of inheritance.

Distinctions by Sexes   In general, it may be said that husband and wife do not inherit from each other in the primitive world. This is an easily understood consequence of the nature of marriage as an alliance of two kinship groups.[16] What is left by either spouse is more than likely to revert to the family or lineage from which he or she came. Men's goods are inherited by men, and women's by women. Two factors that are present on the primitive level are responsible for these conditions. The first is the absence or undeveloped state of a free market and money economy. Goods cannot be divorced from use with any appreciable degree of ease. They are not readily convertible into fluid capital. Therefore, they must be possessed by a competent user; the sexual division of labor bars inheritance of sex-linked property across sex lines. Second, in all primitive societies a person is more closely tied to his or her kinship group than to the marriage partner. The claims of surviving kinsmen outweigh the claims of the surviving spouse.[17]

Testamentary Disposition   In instances in which an individual wishes to transfer his property status to another person who is not specifically defined as an heir in custom or law, *testamentary disposition* may be allowed for. This is what we know as "making a will." The power of testamentary disposition probably exists in most primitive societies, although this matter has not been subjected to systematic investigation. In those societies in which it does exist, it does not apply evenly to all forms of property. The disposition of garden plots, for example, is usually governed

[16]See R. F. Barton, *Ifugao Law* (University of California Publications in American Archaeology and Ethnology, vol. 15, 1919), p. 26, for the Ifugao exemplification of this rule.
[17]See R. F. Benedict, "Marital Property Rights in Bilateral Society" (*American Anthropologist,* vol. 38, 1936), pp. 368–373.

by strict rules of inheritance not subject to individual meddling. At the same time, a man or woman may be quite free to alter the normal lines of inheritance of personal property in movables by use of the will. In some instances, the spoken will is inviolable; in others, it may be set aside by the living as contrary to law and custom. What is proper and what is improper at this point may often be as troublesome a question for primitive peoples as it is for us.

A case occurring among the Ashanti of Ghana in 1942 is a good example. Inheritance of land among the Ashanti runs down the maternal line; it should go from a man to his brother (who belongs to the same maternal clan) and then to a sister's son, but not to a son of either man, for this person belongs to a different clan.

A man when on his death-bed made a dying declaration giving one of his cocoa-farms to his son, and swore an oath enjoining his brother, who was his successor, to see that the gift was honoured. "If you do not give it to him," said the dying man, "I shall call you before the ancestors for our case to be judged."

. . . The man died and his brother succeeded to the property, but refused, with the concurrence of the other members of the family, to give the cocoa-farm to his deceased brother's son. Three months later a fire broke out in the village. The surviving brother fell from a roof while helping to put out one of the fires, and sustained an injury to his leg from which he subsequently died. Before he died, he told his family that he believed his deceased brother was summoning him to the spirit world to answer for his conduct in not honouring his brother's deathbed declaration. The general belief was that his death was due to his failure to carry out his deceased brother's instructions. The next successor to the property duly gave the cocoa-farm to the son to whom it had been left.[18]

Contrary to the sophisticated Ashanti, in the simplest societies inheritance is poorly developed. Nomadic hunters and collectors have few goods, and most of these are per-

sonal working equipment. Because of the universality of belief in an afterlife, many primitives assume that the deceased want and need their goods. (Figure 17-9). The result is, as Radcliffe-Brown has noted:

With us one of the most important aspects of succession is the transmission of property by inheritance. Yet in some of the simplest societies this is a matter of almost no significance at all. In an Australian tribe, for example, a man possesses a few weapons, tools, utensils, and personal ornaments, things of little value or permanence. On his death some of them may be destroyed, others may be distributed among his relatives or friends. But their disposal is of so little importance, unless in relation to ritual, that it is often difficult to find any rules of customary procedure.[19]

The same may be said of the African Bushmen, the Andaman Islanders, the Semangs, the Eskimos, and the Shoshones.

Primogeniture In societies of growing populations given to gardening or agriculture on limited land resources, there is always the problem of dispersal of the family holdings through inheritance by too many heirs. Primogeniture is the solution hit upon by some peoples. All property devolves upon the eldest son, who then has the duty to support the other members of the family in exchange for their labor. "A family must have a strong center," say the Ifugaos. Primogeniture more often applies to inheritance of chiefship and office, however, than to landed property. The mana of the Polynesian chief passes to the first-born son in an unending line. So strong is the primogeniture rule among the Maoris of New Zealand that on occasion a first-born woman may take a man's name and acquire the status of a first-born son.

Primogeniture can be a force in an expansionistic movement. Power and glory are available to second-born sons who sally forth to gain new land, wealth, and rank and who

[18]K. A. Busia, *The Position of the Chief in the Modern Political System of Ashanti,* p. 43.

[19]Radcliffe-Brown, "Patrilineal and Matrilineal Succession," *op. cit.,* p. 286.

found new lineages by leading a group of colonists to unsettled territory.

The evidence is clear for the Maori, and we may infer that primogeniture was a force in Polynesia that worked to drive younger sons out on overseas expeditions of exploration and colonization.[20]

How much of the brunt of empire building was borne by the younger sons of Britain who were shut out at home by the laws of primo-

geniture? In the classical laissez-faire economics of nineteenth-century England, primogeniture was hailed as a double-acting social device: it avoided inefficient division of the family inheritance, and it forced the younger members to fend for themselves, thus enriching society by their efforts. Those primitives who practice primogeniture recognize the first of these benefits, but it is unlikely that the second ever entered their conscious thoughts. Primogeniture is not much favored in the Western world today. Feudalism is gone, and enterprise capitalism is not favorable to primogeniture.

[20]B. W. Aginsky and P. H. Buck, "Interacting Forces in the Maori Family" (*American Anthropologist,* vol. 42, 1940), pp. 195ff.

Fig. 17-9 The ultimate disposition of the dead and their residual property in an unidentified Plains Indian tribe. Three members of a family lie in bundle burials with their grave goods on a scaffold. In the background the poles of their abandoned tipi stand stark against the sky, marking the undistributed remainder of their possessions. (Collection of the Minnesota Historical Society.)

Ultimogeniture   There are a few tribes that turn the tables completely about. By means of *ultimogeniture,* the youngest son inherits the greater portion of the family estate. Among certain peoples of India, Asia, and Africa, the elder brothers are set up with herds or households in part by family resources used in progeny price. What is left over at the father's death tends in cases of ultimogeniture to go to the youngest of them all on the grounds that he is the least likely to be well set up in life.

In concluding a discussion of primogeniture and ultimogeniture, a note of caution should be sounded. The vast majority of societies adhere to neither of the set rules.

Destruction of Property   In the instance of the Comanches:

In the disposal of a deceased's property there is but one rule which stood out with constancy: *upon the death of a person all effects of his (or her) personal usage were destroyed.* This included clothing, weapons, saddles, tools, paraphernalia, and horses customarily ridden by the deceased. . . . Further, even the tipi in which the dead person, man or woman, lived was totally destroyed; also for a child, but not for a baby. Articles of intimate personal usage were buried with the corpse. Other less important articles were burned. Possessions with medicine powers were either destroyed by throwing them into the river, or by placing them in an unfrequented tree where they could rot.[21]

All Plains Indians had similar rules. Surpluses were variously handled. The Comanches passed the residual estate to the widow, who in turn was obliged to pass some of it on to her husband's friends and relatives, and especially to nonrelatives, who hung around as enthusiastic mourners; they mourned and mourned until they were given sufficient gifts to stop them. Inheritance by nonrelatives was, in point of fact, characteristic in the Plains

[21]E. A. Hoebel, *The Political Organization and Law-ways of the Comanche Indians* (American Anthropological Association, Memoir 54: Contributions from the Laboratory of Anthropology, 4, 1940), pp. 120–121.

area. A family that went the whole way in mourning made itself destitute, until in due time friends and relatives reoutfitted them with gifts.

On the lower levels of culture, it is difficult to generalize inheritance rules with accuracy. Often there is no single rule of inheritance controlling all situations, or any single line of practice under any of the legal rules. Our canny Cheyenne informant, Calf Woman, cautioned: "Some families did differently than others."

SUMMARY

As human society rests on reciprocity in social relations, the flow and exchange of goods among peoples are important aspects of life. Exchange exists both within and between societies. The giving of gifts is the most elemental and ubiquitous mechanism of exchange there is. Gift exchange symbolizes in concrete form the existence of mutual interdependence between individuals and groups. Its function is both utilitarian and social. Gift giving which is obligatory because of the status relationships between persons and groups characterizes most simple societies. Such a system is, following the economist Polanyi, called *reciprocal exchange.* The bride wealth complex of cattle exchange in Africa is one highly institutionalized form of reciprocal exchange. Pig exchange in Melanesia is another.

Redistributive exchange occurs when a managerial elite of chiefs (kings) or priests receives goods and services from farmers and artisans. From these donations they draw off some wealth for their own use and that of the community as a whole. The governing bureaucracy, temples, palaces, city walls, irrigation systems, armies, and ceremonies are all supported by "surpluses" of the workers. Presumably, the sense of community wellbeing is adequate recompense for the individual workers.

Market exchange involves the free exchange

of goods without the limitations of kinship structure or the exactions of rulers. In primitive societies, market exchanges are usually managed through barter and trade rather than by use of a purchase-and-sale mechanism involving the use of money; they are also "peripheral" markets, since the marketeers in primitive and peasant societies do not usually derive their main living from buying and selling.

The worth of goods is determined not only by their materialistic usefulness and real scarcity but their symbolic qualities as well. In any event, value is culturally determined, except for the basic necessities without which existence is impossible.

The devolution of statuses with respect to goods from deceased persons to living survivors is what constitutes the inheritance of property. Communal goods cannot be privately inherited, but all forms of joint and private property may be. In many cultures, however, some types of personal property are buried or destroyed at the death of the owner, for their spiritual essence remains tied to their immortal owners.

The most fundamental and general rule governing primitive inheritance is that a person can inherit only those kinds of goods which he or she may customarily use. Thus, "men's goods" may not be inherited by women, and wives are barred from inheritance of such of their husbands' property. The same rule holds in reverse for women's goods.

In matrilineally organized societies, because each man's kinship status is determined by his affiliation with his mother's kinship group, most of his inherited property status must come from male members of that group—his mother's brothers or his own brothers—rather than from his father.

Primogeniture gives precedence to the first born as a means of preventing dispersal of basic property. Ultimogeniture gives precedence to the last born. Where it holds, it is usually in conjunction with the existence of progeny price.

SELECTED READINGS

Bohannan, P., and G. Dalton, *Markets in Africa* (1962). A modern analysis based on good anthropological accounts of indigenous trading centers.

Bunzel, R., "The Economic Organization of Primitive Peoples," in F. Boas, et al., *General Anthropology* (1938), chap. 8. A useful general summary.

Codere, H., "Exchange and Display" (*International Encyclopedia of the Social Sciences,* vol. 5, 1968), pp. 239–245. A brief and concise discussion of primitive exchange systems.

Dalton, G. (ed.), *Tribal and Peasant Economies: Readings in Economic Anthropology* (1967). A rich selection of materials representing modern research and thought.

Herskovits, M. J., *Economic Anthropology* (1952), part III, "Exchange and Distribution." Provides an extensive descriptive and theoretical analysis.

Mauss, M., *The Gift: Forms and Functions of Exchange in Archaic Societies* (1954). The classic study of the social functions of organized gift exchanges in primitive societies and classical civilizations.

Thurnwald, R., *Economics in Primitive Communities* (1932), chaps. 5–9, "Barter," "Trade," "The Market," "Purchase," and "Distribution of Goods and Wealth."

Chapter 18
Status and Role

Fig. 18-A   A Melanesian "Big Man" and his associate. Two Chimbu men of wealth and power, Goroka, New Guinea. (Photo by E. A. Hoebel.)

From this point forward, this book will be largely concerned with the characteristic patterns of statuses and roles in a number of institutional contexts such as family, kinship, clubs, classes, politics, law, and religion. However, a preliminary general overview of the manifestations of status and role should be useful; such is the intent of this chapter.

The Nature of Status

An individual's status is his social position with reference to the other members of his society as determined by a cluster of attributes or the generalized summation of all his attributes. Thus, every person has a number of statuses simultaneously. He has, in the most specific and narrow sense, as many statuses as there are recognized characteristics of the individual in his culture. Such characteristics are age, sex, bodily traits, and specific social experiences and affiliations. On the next level of abstraction, he has the more commonly recognized statuses that derive from the possession of certain combinations of traits, for example, the wisdom, courage, kindness, generosity, and even temper that characterize the Plains Indian peace chief. Finally, each person may have the generalized sort of status that is referred to as "social" status. This last sort of status identification calls for gross stereotyping of individuals. It seizes upon a small number of obvious criteria for lumping individual personalities into an undifferentiated class. The first sort of status identification, in contrast, calls for knowledge of numerous attributes of the individual and thus leads to a greater concern with the uniqueness of his personality.

Therefore, it should be kept in mind that status can be either specific or generalized and that there are varying degrees of generalization.

Ascribed and Achieved Status The statuses that an individual holds are attained in various ways. They may be sought through striving and competitive mastery of the roles linked to the various statuses. Such statuses in the terminology suggested by Linton are called *achieved*.[1] MacIver calls them *functional determinants* of social position.[2] Other statuses devolve upon the individual by virtue of innate biological characteristics such as sex, age, and race or by virtue of his preexisting social affinities, such as the statuses of his parents and kinsmen and the involuntary associations into which he is born. These statuses are *ascribed* to the individual by his social system, and there is little he can do to escape them or to alter them.

It is important to note that achieved statuses are attained only by first mastering the roles. As Barton has observed of the Kalinga in northern Luzon: "Elevation to rank and power in the community is a gradual process of emergence in which power is attained before the rank is acknowledged by the people."[3] When the role is finally mastered, the status flows from this fact. A master hunter must first master hunting.

In the case of ascribed statuses, on the other hand, the status comes first, and the roles are mastered subsequently. It is even possible to inherit ascribed status without mastery of the roles. There are betimes unkingly kings, ignoble nobles, unladylike ladies.

Ascribed status distinctions based on age, sex, the premarital state, childbearing, and kinship are the universal foundations of human social structure.

Achieved status criteria that are ubiquitous to all societies are those based on technological skill or artisanship (all peoples make tools), supernaturalism (all peoples have magico-religious specialists), the marital state, fecundity, and political leadership.

Nonuniversal ascribed statuses include caste-determined occupations, inherited supernaturalism, inherited possession of wealth, inherited possession of various religious and social perquisites and paraphernalia, and inherited political position (i.e., royalty) (Figure 18-1).

Nonuniversal achieved statuses include those based upon hunting skills, skill in games and dances, bravery and skill in war, skill in head-hunting, storytelling ability, possession or distribution of wealth, bodily mutilation, and membership in various specialized associations. (This list is not exhaustive.)

The functional importance of all these different statuses rests in the fact that they limit and influence the degree and direction of cultural participation and the manner and amount of interaction for individuals and groups. No one person ever manifests all the behavior characteristic of his culture because, for one reason, no one person ever embodies in himself all the statuses existent in his culture.

The greater the number of achievable statuses in a culture, the greater the opportunity for full participation (potentially, at least) by all members. The more extensive and rigid the ascribed statuses, the more constrained are the individuals in their culturally prescribed roles.

Cultures that emphasize achievable status are marked by internal social mobility, social striving, and (on the whole) competitiveness and individualism. Emphasis is placed upon "fulfillment of self" and assertiveness. The

[1] R. Linton, *The Study of Man*, pp. 113–114.
[2] R. M. MacIver, *Society,* pp. 78–79.
[3] R. F. Barton, *The Kalinga,* p. 148.

social gain is ideally a greater ultimate efficiency because capable persons are not barred from effective performance in those capacities for which they have adequate aptitudes. Conversely, caste and rigid class systems are socially wasteful because they ascribe roles to people who are not necessarily well suited to their performance, while at the same time they bar potential adepts.

On the other hand, the advantages of social systems that emphasize ascribed statuses lie in reduced strain and anxiety for the participating members of the society. Competitive insecurity is presumably reduced. Frustration born of failure to achieve a sought-after status is avoided.

When ascribed status systems begin to lose their authority, however, and persons in statuses of marked social disability begin to aspire to achievable statuses, their frustration and the anxiety of those in the threatened ascribed positions become acute and difficult to tolerate, in the way that marks interracial relations in the American population today.

Status Hierarchy: Rank The status system of every society involves also a certain amount of ranking. But, it should be noted, status and rank are not the same. "Status" is a neutral term, which refers only to position. "Rank" refers to hierarchical status—higher or lower with reference to other statuses. The rank order of a society is its system of status gradations. A high status is one that carries prestige; i.e., the attitudes associated with it are those of deference, reverence, submission, and subordination on the part of those of lower status. Prestige translated into action means power—the capacity to influence or direct the behavior of others. A low status carries little prestige; there is little power capacity associated with it.

The range embraced in a rank order will be wide or narrow depending upon the disparities in power structures formed by the culture. In simple democratic hunting and gathering societies, such as that of the Eskimos, the range is narrow. In complex, class-organized societies, such as that of the

Fig. 18-1 Procession of brass miniatures of chief and servants. Dahomey, West Africa. Cast brass figurines represent the chief, who is carried by two porters and is accompanied by a man holding the umbrella of state, drummers, a cymbalist story teller, a talkman, dancers, and food bearers. (Smithsonian Institution.)

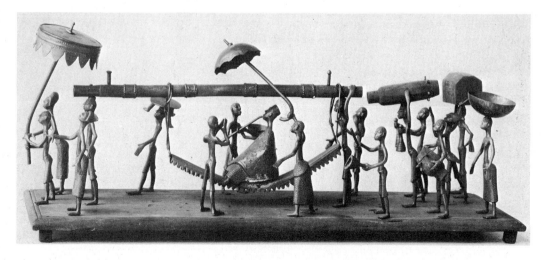

Fig. 18-2   *Differentiated status in ancient Nigeria. This Yoruba bronze plaque portrays a monarch mounted upon a decorated donkey and attended by armed bodyguards and holders of the royal sunshades. (Courtesy of the Museum of Primitive Art.)*

Yoruba, the range between slave and king is great (Figure 18-2).

The Nature of Role

Role is the customary complex of behavior associated with a particular status. Every man is to some degree a poseur. All are actors, for life in society is a playing of roles.

The command, "Just be your natural self," does not mean what it says. It really means, "Suppress your conscious awareness of the roles you must enact." A person's behavior is "natural," is free of posing, only when he has become so habituated to all his roles that he does not register awareness of them while performing them. Newborn infants in their first hours have no acquired roles as complements to their statuses. No one expects much of them, either.

Because every person has multiple statuses, he also manifests many different roles. A married professor behaves differently with his family (the husband and father roles) from the way he does in the classroom (the professor role). And if he is a volunteer fireman, he behaves quite differently when engaged in "firemanic" activities of either a fire-fighting or a social nature. At different times, therefore, different roles come to the fore. Several roles may be operative simultaneously, but the intensity of their effectiveness is variable.

At times, various roles may be held in abeyance or inactivated. A Pueblo Indian, while cultivating his fields, holds his dancing roles as a member of the Flint society in abeyance.

A person's roles could be likened to his wardrobe, from which he selects the costume suitable for each occasion, with many quick changes called for. Roles are therefore *latent,* except when they are being activated or made *manifest.*

Sexual Statuses and Roles

Sex dichotomy is a biological fact upon which culturally determined statuses are built. But what is biological and what is cultural in sex differences are not established with certainty for all types of activity. True, certain physiological functions are sex-linked. Females produce ova, while males produce sperm. Females have specialized sex organs for the nurture and incubation of fertilized ova;

males do not. Females are capable of parturition; males are not. *Homo sapiens* is a bisexual animal in which the basic reproductive roles are biologically fixed. So long as babies are born of women, differential statuses of male and female will be recognized and culturally reflected. The real social revolution will come when perfected biogenetic techniques make possible the fertilization and incubation of the human ovum outside the womb.

But even this impressive possibility will evidently be bypassed in favor of *cloning*. In this process a whole new organism will be grown from a single body cell of an already existing organism. The new individual will be an exact genetic replication of the genitor, for every normal body cell contains the genetic code for the entire organism within its nucleus. Human reproduction will then be accomplished without the medium of sex. There will no longer be a biological need for males and females. Sex will be obsolete, and so, in all probability, will be status differences between men and women. Responsible biologists, such as J. B. S. Haldane and Lord Rothschild see cloning as a reality in the very near future.[4] In the meantime, however, every society assigns different roles to males and females, as in the following instance.

San Ildefonso Pueblo

In San Ildefonso there is a sharp line between men's work and women's work, and in the respective attitudes of the sexes towards their work. Men's work on the whole tends to be cooperative. The ditches are dug by the male community in the spring; the fields are tended as a group enterprise. . . . Among women, on the contrary, work has tended to become competitive; women seldom carry on any of their activities as a group. . . . Theoretically, at least, women play comparatively minor roles. San Ildefonso men do work which elsewhere is frequently the task of women. Their special province is called "outside work." Traditionally they hunt, dress the skins of the animals they kill, cut and sew moccasins for themselves and for the women, weave baskets, and weave and create their own

dance costumes. . . . Men till the fields and the gardens, plant and reap, cut and haul firewood. Within the village itself they build the houses, care for the kivas, and clean the plaza before fiestas and dances. . . . Women's work is "inside." They care for the household, grind the grain, cook, and tend their children. They make and fire the pottery, and if there is no man in the family who can decorate it, the women may decorate their own.[5]

Lesu, New Ireland   Of Lesu, a gardening, fishing, and pig-raising society in Melanesia, Powdermaker wrote: "It is the sexual division of labour adhered to so rigidly that first strikes the ethnological observer. Men have one kind of work and women another, and a third kind may be done by either one of them or jointly."[6] The division of labor is set forth in Table 18-1.

Sexual Division of Work Roles   Although each society divides men's work and women's, what is distinctly men's work in one society, however, may be women's work in another. As obvious examples we may note that the weaving of Navaho blankets is women's work, while among the neighboring Hopi, both spinning and weaving are confined to men (Figure 18-3). In nineteenth-century America, boys were supposed to be able to swim, and girls were not; yet among the Yahgan of Tierra del Fuego, women are the swimmers. Among the Pueblo Indians, most garden work is done by men; among the Iroquois, hunting and fighting were for men, but tilling was for women only. Among the Maricopa Indians of southern Arizona, pottery making was "wholly a woman's occupation and a year-round task."[7] Weaving was properly men's work. Women harvested and ginned the cotton, which was grown exclusively by the men, and both sexes spun the yarn.

Because of such facts, anthropologists

[4]See G. R. Taylor, *The Biological Time Bomb*, pp. 22–30.

[5]W. Whitman, *The Pueblo Indians of San Ildefonso*, pp. 99–100.
[6]H. Powdermaker, *Life in Lesu*, p. 161.
[7]L. Spier, *Yuman Tribes of the Gila River*, p. 104.

Table 18-1   The Division of Labor in Lesu, Melanesia

Masculine	*Feminine*	*Joint*
Clearing ground for new garden and building garden fence Planting trees Getting sago Fishing	Planting taro and yams; weeding; gathering crops and carrying them home Catching crabs on the reef	Catching the sea worm, *beta*
Hunting wild pig and phalanger Cutting firewood; making the *liga;* bringing the leaves for cooking	Feeding domestic pigs Drawing water	
Preparing pigs, fish, and sago to be cooked Burying bananas in the sand Housebuilding and repairing	Preparing taro and yams to be cooked Sweeping the house and keeping it in order	
Making of masks, canoes, *malanggans,* fishing-nets, spears, ornaments	Carrying heavy burdens with the exception of fish and pigs	Making baskets and mats. Taking care of children. Medicine and magic. Making "paint" for the hair

SOURCE: After H. Powdermaker.

have learned to reject all generalizations such as that women are "naturally" housekeepers or that they are more "peaceful" or more "religious" than men. But anthropology has also established that throughout the world, certain kinds of work activities are quite consistently assigned to men and other kinds to women. In three-fourths of all societies, the tasks of food and fuel gathering, grinding seeds and grain, preparing foodstuffs for preservation, weaving, and manufacturing pottery, baskets, and mats are assigned to women. These are all jobs that, except for the gathering of foodstuffs, can be carried on in the immediate vicinity of the hearth and infant.

World Distribution of Division of Labor by Sexes Hunting, on the other hand, is exclusively men's work in all societies covered in Murdock's *Ethnographic Atlas,* except in Siam (now Thailand). Fishing is largely, but not exclusively, a male activity (in 84 per cent of the 717 societies in which fishing contributes to subsistence). Cattle herding in the Old World is almost exclusively limited to men, but no clear division of labor by sex is discernible with respect to other kinds of domesticated animals in other parts of the world.

Participation of men and women in gardening and agriculture varies from region to region. Women predominate in sub-Saharan gardening in Africa. Around the Mediterranean, men carry on most plow agriculture. In Asia men and women gardeners work side by side, while in the South Seas, gardening responsibilities are held by women in one-third, by men in one-fifth, and by both sexes in nearly half of the societies.[8]

In sum, the anthropological position is that

[8]E. Bourguignon and L. Greenbaum, *Diversity and Homogeneity,* p. 12.

Fig. 18-3   A Hopi weaver with suspended war loom. Among the Hopi and other Pueblo Indians, weaving is a male responsibility, while among the Navaho, use of this skill is woman's work. (Smithsonian Office of Anthropology, Bureau of American Ethnology Collection.)

certain sex-linked behaviors are biologically based, although subject to cultural modifications within limits. The roles in any society must be empirically observed and objectively recorded.

Age Statuses and Roles

From a gross biological point of view, life may be reduced to a simple formula: to be born, to mature, to reproduce, and to die. However, even the biologist will acknowledge that at least a few other events of significance occur along the way. Man embroiders upon the fundamental pattern.

Age statuses are recognized in all societies. The universal minimum includes at least three categories: child, adult, and old person, or, respectively, those not yet ripe for full social participation, those who perform the major maintenance activities of the society, and those who are beyond the stage of active participation and responsibility. Generally, recognized age statuses are more numerous. Thus, the Comanches recognize five ages: baby, preadolescent, unmarried "brave" or girl, grown person, and old man or woman. Each age has its separate, specific appellation. Young children may be highly valued as objects of desire, but they never have prestige merely by virtue of their status as infants. In the exceptional instances in which infants do enjoy high status and prestige, it is always as a consequence of some special factor other than age, as in the case of a princeling by birth or a twin with imputed supernatural qualities (as among the Dahomeans).[9]

Youths and persons of middle age rarely enjoy favored status by virtue of their age, as such, although prowess and wealth may bring prestige status to them.

Adulthood means full participation in the responsibilities and privileges of the society. It means marriage and parenthood and political, religious, economic, and club life, all to

[9]M. J. Herskovits, *Dahomey,* vol. 1, pp. 263, 270-272.

be spelled out in detail in the remaining chapters.

As for the aged, they have almost always enjoyed statuses of respect, reverence, and privilege because of the attributes that are ascribed to them by virtue of their being old.[10] It is not just being old that brings prestige; it is the accumulated wisdom and lore of the oldsters—the association of ancient custom with ancient people. As has been said of the Haida Indians of Queen Charlotte Island on the Northwest Coast: "They had great respect for the aged, whose advice in most matters has great weight."[11]

In the primitive world, the oldsters are "elders" in politics and government, magicians and priests in supernaturalism, and owners of property in some systems of economic organization. These are sources of power. Since such sources are more available to men than to women, old men usually have higher status than old women.[12] The positions of the aged are more secure in the settled horticultural tribes than among hunting and collecting peoples, especially those who live in the arctic and its fringes, where old people are unable to participate in primary productive activities to any extent.

The support of the aged is a luxury which many marginal societies find themselves unable to sustain in times of stress. Senilicide used to be general among the Eskimos. Old people might be blocked up in a snow hut to be abandoned to cold and starvation, or they might be killed by more violent means when they themselves requested it.[13] However, of the seventy-one societies tabulated by Simmons, only two (both Eskimo) violently remove the aged; seven abandon or expose them to natural elements to hasten their deaths.[14] This does not mean that in these

seven societies, all old people are destroyed when their powers wane. It depends upon individuals and circumstances.

Almost all observers remark that old people are respected in the tribes they have visited. Only the Bushmen of South Africa and the Witotos of South America are said definitely to withhold respect from aged men. Eight of the seventy-one tribes studied by Simmons deny deference to old women.

The Andaman Islands provide anthropologists with a favorite example of age as a status determinant. Kinship, which is so important in most primitive societies, is here somewhat muted. Rather:

The duties that one person owes to another are determined much less by their relation to one another by consanguinity and marriage, than by their respective ages and social status. . . . There is very little of any special customs relating to conduct towards different kinds of relatives. Corresponding to this we find very few terms to denote relationships and a considerable development of terms which denote age and social status.[15]

Older persons had many food privileges denied to the young. Gradually, and with elaborate ritual, the food tabus were removed for the growing youth, until at full maturity he could enjoy all the delicacies permitted for his sex. Younger persons had to defer to the older ones in all matters.

In Australia, where, as in the Andaman Islands, we find some of our most primitive peoples, seniority reached its greatest significance—so much so that Australian social organization is dubbed *gerontocracy,* "the rule of elders." The preeminent domination of the Australian local group by old, grizzled men gave birth and impetus to the nineteenth-century notion that the primeval condition of man was that of browbeaten youth frustrated by the hoary patriarch. Australia, however, represents a special elaboration of age status in a way not universally characteristic of the hunters and gatherers (in contrast are the African Bushmen and American Shoshones).

[10]L. Simmons, *The Role of the Aged in Primitive Society,* p. 79.
[11]A. P. Niblack, *The Coast Indians of Southern Alaska and Northern British Columbia* (Board of Regents of the Smithsonian Institution, Annual Report, 1890), p. 240.
[12]Simmons, *op. cit.,* pp. 47–49.
[13]E. A. Hoebel, *The Law of Primitive Man,* pp. 76–79.
[14]Simmons, *op. cit.,* table 6.

[15]A. R. Radcliffe-Brown, *The Andaman Islanders,* p. 81.

In stable societies, accumulated experience is valuable. Elders really do know more than youngsters, and what they know holds good. But in a rapidly changing culture, accumulated knowledge often becomes quickly shopworn. What was valid in the youth of the aged is no longer so. Wisdom based on outdated knowledge is, alas, of little use to him who clutches it as a source of prestige.

Changing Statuses: Transition Rites   Early in this century, Arnold van Gennep (1873–1957) published the classic work known in English as *The Rites of Transition*.[16] Van Gennep demonstrated that changes of status are frequently apprehended as crisis situations. In the transition from one basic status to another, as a person moves through the developmental stages of life, he must be detached from his previous status and incorporated into the new one. In the "in between" (liminal) phase the transient is viewed, and looks upon himself, with anxiety. The transient is leaving his familiar roles and has not yet acquired his new ones. He is unpredictable, dangerous—a threat to himself and his associates. Hence he is, in many societies, isolated and quarantined—sometimes even ritually "killed." At the climax of the transition rites he is then reborn (a neophyte)[17] as a new and more mature person, well-schooled in his new roles, ready to be reincorporated into community life.

To take an example from Western society, when old-time Army sergeants bullied and insulted rookies, they were not being merely sadistic, nor were they necessarily working off personal frustrations. Although sergeants may not be aware of any principles of functional anthropology, they do know that recruits have to be made over and put through a quick transition rite. A first act is the destruction of civilian ways and civilian thoughts:

"You're in the Army now." Induction means death of the civilian, and the "top kick" is the executioner. Completion of basic training means resurrection in a new status—General Issue.[18]

Torture in the puberty rites of Australian and many African tribes rises to heights of sheer cruelty. Yet beneath it can usually be found a functional rationalization. In Australia, circumcision and subincision, painful and dangerous surgical operations when crudely performed with stone knives (Figure 19-4), are but symbolic acts signifying the sexual and social completeness of the males in a type of society that rejects and culturally suppresses the significance of women.

In all cases, transition is the main theme—transition from the limited and undeveloped state of childhood to that of the adult endowed with the wisdom and privileges of a mature person. Thus, death and resurrection are recurrent themes of stepped-up puberty rites: death means the destruction of the childhood personality, and resurrection means that the person is restored to the community in a new status with new roles. The boy who retires to the hidden initiatory school in the bush, secreted from the eyes of all females and preadolescent boys, is "dead." When he returns to the camp of the band, circumcised, subincised, and cicatrized, with a few teeth knocked out and with new knowledge of totemic mythology, he is a new man.

In like manner, Gerlach and Hine, in their studies of contemporary movements of social change, such as the Black Power and the Pentecostal, note that one basic feature is, *"Personal commitment* generated by an act or experience which separates the convert in some significant way from the established order (or his previous place in it), identifies

---

[16]Written in French, the original title was *Les Rites de Passage* (1909). The English version appeared in 1960.

[17]Note that the very word means "produce anew" (Gr. *neos*, new + *phytos*, grown).

[18]It will be highly instructive to see what happens to the United States Army following its "humanization" of the indoctrination program for new recruits and the implementation of its 1971 slogan, "The Army wants to join you!" The slogan itself failed as a recruiting device and was dropped before the year was out.

him with a new set of values, and commits him to changed patterns of behavior."[19] Transition rites are not things of the past.

Functions of Transition Rites   Crisis periods are times of critical uncertainty when the fate of the individual or the group seems to hang in the balance. At such times men are not inclined to leave the outcome to chance or unbridled circumstance. Natural and supernatural forces may be controlled in fact and in belief. Therefore, positive techniques of rational assistance are employed, along with magic and ritual ceremonialism, to frustrate destructive and disruptive supernatural powers or to encourage and invoke positive and helpful forces. Through ritual and ceremony, a bridge is thrown across the yawning chasms of fear and doubt that carries men over transitional states to a safe arrival and a firm footing in the new status awaiting them on the other side. Their very enactment also serves another purpose. For those who participate and those who watch, the scene and the ceremony provide reassurance that like the neophyte, life and society shall be reborn through unending cycles of regeneration.

The next chapter, on the life cycle, deals in more detail with the transition rites encountered in birth, puberty, marriage, and death.

Aptitudes and Status

Not all statuses, by any means, are linked to the biological phases of the life cycle. The division of labor and functions worked out in each culture is always reflected in the status system of social relations.

If skill is a joy to any man, it should also be true that skill in any function valued by a society brings prestige and high status to the expert. By and large, anthropological data support this supposition. Proficiency in craftsmanship usually brings moderately high status among primitive people, but it tends to rank below military prowess, supernaturalism, political leadership, and wealth manipulation as a prestige generator. Polynesians, among all recorded primitives, gave the most conscious and organized recognition to craftsmanship. The *Tuhunga*, or "great adept," of the Tonga tribe in Polynesia was highly revered whether he was a master of oratory, tribal lore, house building, or canoe manufacture. Only by virtue of much mana (see page 577) was it possible for a man to excel in anything. And all Polynesians were impressed by mana.

At the other extreme, occupations linked to inferior castes in Africa, India, and Japan bring no kudos to their practitioners, no matter how skilled the craftsman. A Masai blacksmith is doomed for life to subordination, for that is the status his culture ascribes to blacksmiths. Among Japanese, the *Eta* form a polluted caste of hereditary butchers, or in some instances fishermen, whose pariah pollution is unmodified by the importance of their work or their skill in performing it.[20]

Wealth and Status

There are definite limits to the amount of goods that roving collectors of food are able to carry around with them. It is not possible for such people to accumulate wealth; there are no rich men. The possession of wealth is not, for the lower primitives, a status determinant of great significance.

The giving away of food and goods is another matter, however. Food claims are communal in nature in almost all hunting societies. Prestige and leadership go to hunters who have food to dispense, hides to bestow, arrows to give, and (among Plains Indians) horses to lavish upon favored friends, wayfaring visitors, and indigent neighbors. Plains

[19]L. P. Gerlach and V. H. Hine, *People, Power, Change,* p. xvii; see also pp. 110–158.

[20]E. Norbeck, *Takashima,* pp. 113–114.

Indians recognized as families of good standing those whose tipis were well kept and decorated and whose industrious men and women kept their lodges well supplied with victuals, fine robes, and handsome clothes; but above all, they respected those who gave freely of what they possessed. Fluid wealth brought high status in its train. Hoarded wealth brought only contempt. This is what settlers on the Indian frontier could not understand when silent Indians appeared at the cabin door expecting a ready handout.

Reciprocal-exchange systems are not likely to generate wealth distinctions: they tend toward reciprocal equality in goods. Yet, the organization of wealth as carried out by the "Big Men" in Melanesia (pages 350–351) links economic and political activities in status determination. To rise through the various degrees of the all-important men's club of the Banks Islanders calls for the payment of heavy initiation fees. Only the richest can afford to purchase the higher degrees. Indeed, as Lowie has summarized the data:

> It is only the man of wealth who can reach the highest degrees and thus acquire prestige. Yet the aboriginal conception is not that of avariciously hoarding wealth but rather of displaying one's greatness by exhibiting contempt for property. So a man of the loftiest status in the club may still promote his renown by providing the lavish entertainment associated with certain festivals; nay, a suggestion of niggardliness on these occasions would go far to destroy his influence.[21]

The Potlatch of the Northwest Coast Indians of North America   Among the tribes of the Northwest Coast, elaborate honorific status distinctions were ascribed through family and clan inheritance. At the same time, they had to be validated and kept up through ostentatious display and manipulation of wealth in the most conspicuously ostentatious manner possible. This was done in part by means of showy totem poles and the potlatch—an elaborate institution of feasting

accompanied by the lavish distribution of presents by the host and his kinsmen to guests of another lineage or tribe (Fig. 18-4). Its primary function was to serve as a demonstration of the family and individual statuses of the hosts. The guests were witnesses to the hosts' claims to certain statuses. Although accumulations of wealth were necessary for potlatching, it was not the wealth that gave status; it was the legitimate possession of honorific prerogatives, which were linked with specific names and titles, which were inheritable, but which could not be used until publicly assumed at a potlatch given for the purpose. To use a name not publicly notarized at a potlatch was a shameful presumption, and to address a person by a name he had inherited but not yet validated was an insult to his standing.[22]

Record of a Tsimshian potlatch that took place around 1930 illustrates the old principle with some modern touches. It is the story of the chief of the Gitlan tribe and a member of the Wolf clan. When Gusgai'in, chief of the Gitlan, died, his nephew announced that he would take up his uncle's name at some later date. Before this could be done, he and a Wolf clansman jammed their motorboat between the piles of a bridge. They were hung up when the tide flowed out from beneath them. This would be enough to cause any good boatman chagrin, but when they were badgered with the remark, "We saw a Wolf hanging up under the bridge," the status of all Wolves was impaired.

A potlatch was necessary to rehabilitate their position, and so they undertook to give a traditional ceremony, the family Feast of the Early Snow, commemorating the exploit of the ancestral chief, Gusgai'in, whose name was now to be assumed by his descendant. This ancestor had passed beneath a glacier in his flight from enemy captors, so with poetic flavor the *pièce de résistance* of the commemorative banquet was to be a native

[21]R. H. Lowie, *Primitive Society*, p. 277.

[22]See P. Drucker, "Rank, Wealth, and Kinship in Northwest Coast Society" (*American Anthropologist*, vol. 41, 1939), pp. 55–65. Occasional potlatches are still given.

sherbet made of snow mixed with olachen grease, berries, and crabapples. In keeping with the times, however, ice cream was served instead at this potlatch. A heaping dish of ice cream, more than he could possibly eat, was placed before each person who had taunted the Wolves.

Gorging a guest and then making fun of him was a favorite form of ridicule and provided much amusement for the guests. . . . When the feast and hilarity were over, the chief arose and explained the mythological background for the feast they were giving. He thanked the guests for coming and announced that, in so far as he was able, he would fill the position of his late uncle. Then La'is, the senior Wolf of the Gilustsa'u tribe, arose as the chief's spokesman and said that, as the chief had been publicly addressed as Gusgai'in, the latter was hereby acknowledging the name and assuming the position. . . . Spokesmen for each guest chief affirmed Gusgai'in's right to the name and welcomed the new chief as a brother. They also acknowledged that the bridge incident and other slurs would be forgotten. Much of tribal history was narrated during the speeches and many compliments were paid the host and his lineage.

Gifts of food and handkerchiefs were then distributed among the guests. Dancing ended the potlatch.[23]

The potlatch serves to affirm the status of the host; and the protocol of seating, serving of food, and distribution of gifts does the same for the guests. Invariably the giving is in order of rank. The person with the highest rank is called upon to come up first to receive his allotted share, and so on down the line. The position of each person with respect to every other is rigidly determined by the nature of the validated titular prerogatives he holds. The mere giving of a potlatch does not validate a person's claim to status. The real validation comes when he is called forth to receive his gifts when he is a guest at other potlatches. Only if his hosts call him forward at the moment warranted by the position he has claimed is his claim validated.

[23]V. E. Garfield, *Tsimshian Clan and Society* (University of Washington Publications in Anthropology, vol. 7, no. 3, 1939), pp. 205–206.

Fig. 18-4   *A Northwest Coast Indian potlatch around 1910.* (above) *Ready for the display and distribution of food and blankets (in the trunks).* (below) *A chief orates before the pile of Hudson Bay blankets which he is bestowing upon his rival. (Courtesy of the American Museum of Natural History.)*

Be it noted, too, that the recitations of tribal history reaffirm and perpetuate the institutional charters of Tsimshian society.

Kinship and Marital Statuses and Roles

Marriage is a universal phenomenon at all levels of cultural development. Premarital, marital, and postmarital statuses are therefore ubiquitous. The roles of husband and wife are of such extreme importance in any society that marriage and the family are subjects requiring special treatment in separate chapters (Chapters 20 and 21).

Kinship, which consists of networks of reciprocating statuses and roles, is also of such fundamental significance in all societies that it too will require special chapters (Chapters 22 and 23) for exposition and analysis.

SUMMARY

The concepts of status and role are fundamental to the understanding of all social systems. Statuses are specified positions within the system of social structure. Roles are the characteristic ways of acting that go with specific statuses. Statuses give rise to standardized behavioral expectancies. Social structure consists of sets of statuses and roles organized in institutions: networks of behavior patterns focused upon specific goals and interests. Social behavior is the behavior of persons performing their appropriate roles according to the statuses which have been ascribed to them or which they have achieved by mastery of the roles. Institutional personnel consists of persons who fill the statuses identified with the institution.

Age, sex, marital, and kinship statuses are fundamental and universal in human societies. At each stage of the journey through life, human beings have made a social issue of the transition crises. Each crisis marks a change in social status. Transition rites usually involve rituals of detachment, isolation, and reincorporation. They are practiced particularly at birth, adolescence, marriage, and death. Life is never wholly drab for any group of people. Ritual and ceremony, anticipation and anxiety, and preparation and performance all color and lend zest to the act of living. Each person in turn fulfills his roles and plays his parts. None can escape the beginning and the end. Most mature and reproduce as they traverse the whole cycle of birth, adolescence, maturity, and death, and work out their potentialities within the framework permitted by the cultures of the societies within which they are destined to live and die. Achieved, aptitudinally based statuses are also universal, but which aptitudes are valued and built into the status system is a variable factor. The statuses of religious specialist and political leader are universal, but, again, the degree to which they are emphasized and elaborated is highly relative.

SELECTED READINGS

Drucker, P., and R. F. Heizer, *To Make My Name Good* (1967). A contemporary reexamination of the potlatch as practiced by the Kwakiutl Indians.

Giffen, N. M., *The Roles of Men and Women in Eskimo Culture* (1930). Treats the division of labor by sexes in a simple culture.

Goodenough, W. H., "Rethinking 'Status' and 'Role': Toward a General Model of the Cultural Organization of Social Relationships," in M. Banton (ed.), *The Relevance of Models for Social Anthropology* (1965), pp. 1–22. Presents a somewhat different conceptualization of the terms "status" and "role," and demonstrates their application to the analysis of kin behavior among the Truk Islanders of Micronesia.

Kuper, H., *An African Aristocracy: Rank among the Swazi* (1947). Royalty and commoners in a South African tribe.

Mead, M., *Male and Female* (1949). An insightful and informative cross-cultural study of sexual roles in a changing world.

Chapter 19

The Life Cycle

Birth, maturity, reproduction, and death are the four basic and universal crises in the completed life cycle. In the earthly span of the human organism, every individual who fulfills his biological destiny must pass through each of these peaks in the cycle of life. Therefore, in no human culture are these critical periods wholly ignored. They may, however, be approached and surmounted with varying degrees of intensity. Some peoples are habituated to treat one or another of the life crises in a matter-of-fact manner. Others exhibit much anxiety. In the latter situation, there is considerable cultural emphasis on the crisis situation.

Conception

The life cycle begins with conception. Yet no primitive peoples have a scientifically accurate knowledge of the nature of conception. This ignorance is not too surprising, if we keep in mind that even civilized man has acquired a sophisticated knowledge of genetics only in the last hundred years, and there is still a good deal of talk about storks in our society.

However, most primitive peoples can recognize causal sequences with sufficient astuteness to be able to associate the act of sexual intercourse with conception. Some

Fig. 19-A   Zulu initiates in transition. With their white-painted bodies and the grass masks shielding their faces from the world, these dancing adolescent boys are in the limbo phase of the tribal puberty rite. They are marked as set apart from the living community but not really among the dead. (United Press International Photo.)

are acute enough to recognize that the male semen plays a role in the generation of life. Yet the naive notion that the male plants a seed, which the female nurtures, is the closest primitive man can come to reality.

Explicit notions of miraculous conception abound in the primitive world. In its most common form, the belief is expressed that a child is the reincarnation of an ancestral spirit who has slipped into the womb of the mother to be regenerated.[1] In Australia, this belief is raised to the status of a dogma so strong that the natives deny any relation between the sex act and conception other than to admit that the womb must first be opened so that ancestral spirits may enter.

The Physiology of Paternity   Earlier anthropologists took the Australoid denial of the physiology of paternity at face value. Modern anthropologists see it as a cultural suppression of recognizable fact, the purpose of which is to sustain the shibboleths of the social system.[2] Ancestor worship and totemism are important themes in Australian culture. The continuity of the totemic group is sustained by means of the doctrine of spiritual reincarnation. To give expression to the fact of physiological paternity would be a subversive undermining of the sacred institutions of Australian social life—it would be definitely un-Australian.

The matrilineal (see page 446) Trobriand Islanders say that the male plays no role in conception. Rather, the spirit of a dead clan ancestor (called *baloma*) enters the womb when the woman is wading in the lagoon. It grows and becomes a child. The nearby Dobu, who believe that semen is voided coconut milk, which, when it enters a woman, causes the blood within her womb to coagulate and form a fetus, say bluntly that the Trobriand Islanders lie. The point is a sore

one. So many angry words have been exchanged over this moot issue in the past that nowadays when Dobus and Trobriand Islanders meet, they tacitly avoid the touchy subject. Fortune's Dobu companions scolded him for broaching the subject on a visit to the Trobriand Islands.[3] Not without reason is anthropology sometimes called the "study of rude cultures by rude people."

The Dobu notion that babies are formed by the coagulation of blood is shared by many primitives sporadically distributed about the globe. They reason from the observed fact of cessation of menstruation during gestation. By inversion, they say that the clotting of the blood to form the baby stops the regular flow.

Pregnancy   Life begins with conception, and conception produces pregnancy. No matter how they may envision conception, all peoples recognize pregnancy in empirical physiological terms. There are a number of externally observable biological alterations that occur in mothers of all races. More notable among them are enlargement of the breasts and nipples, exudation of colostrum, cessation of menstruation, abdominal enlargement, and frequently, nausea.

From the little that has been written on this subject by anthropologists, most peoples seem to focus on one or two of the symptoms as signs of coming events, although it is probable that they make note of all of them. Cessation of menstruation is the one universally recognized sign. A fair percentage of the tribes even calculate the expected birth at ten lunar months after the last period.

Various Oceanic and African tribes make note of breast changes; the Arunta of Australia, the Pukapuka of Polynesia, and others have been put on record as noting "morning sickness." Others have told field workers that a significant clue is diminution of appetite and a tendency to become lazy.[4]

---

[1]See, for example, B. Malinowski, "Baloma; The Spirits of the Dead in the Trobriand Islands," in *Magic, Science and Religion and Other Essays*, pp. 125–227.
[2]See M. F. Ashley-Montagu, *Coming into Being among the Australian Aborigines*.

[3]R. F. Fortune, *Sorcerers of Dobu*, pp. 238–239.
[4]C. L. Ford, *A Comparative Study of Human Reproduction* (Yale University Publications in Anthropology, No. 32, 1945), p. 44.

Prenatal Tabus Pregnancy is the foreshadowing of birth. It is, therefore, in itself a crisis condition, or a preliminary phase of the critical event of giving birth. Most peoples seize upon the gestation period as calling for a cultural relief of their anxieties. Chief among these anxieties are fear that (1) the child will not develop ideally, (2) the fetus will miscarry, and (3) the birth will be difficult. Pregnancy tabus and injunctions are supposed to bring freedom from these fears.

Thus Ray reports for the Sanpoil Indians of Washington that a childbearing woman and her husband could not eat trout, lest the child shake like that lively fish. They could not eat rabbit, lest the child get weak legs. They could not eat "fool hen," lest the child be a moron. More than this, the mother-to-be had to rise before sunrise, stay awake through the day, swim in cold water, walk and run, and ride horseback to strengthen her for the ordeal to come.[5]

It may reassure some contemporary mothers, and induce some husbands to more indulgent understanding, to know that queer food preferences in pregnancy are not silly whims. Quite a number of peoples recognize that the pregnant woman has a craving for peculiar foods. Ford notes, however, that there do not seem to be any particular kinds of foods that are craved. The desire is for *variety*. What the basis of this desire may be we do not know.[6]

Childbirth

It is strange, perhaps, that most of the anxiety over the crisis of childbirth comes before the event, not during it. Magic, ritual, and tabu dominate the prenatal period; yet when the moment of birth is reached, the obstetrical problems are, in normal cases, handled with matter-of-fact effectiveness, free of mumbo

jumbo. For the most part, birth is strictly a woman's affair. However, a few tribes permit or require the husband to assist or to be present. Generally, however, the expectant mother retires into the house with one or two older female relatives to assist her. Midwife specialists are called upon among some peoples.

A widely accepted falsehood is that childbirth is easy for primitive women. It has even been anthropologically maintained that just as domestication increases birth difficulties for animals, so increasing domestication through civilization makes birth progressively more difficult for the civilized mother. There is little evidence for this idea. On the contrary, there is much empirical evidence in the record to prove that primitive women often suffer much agony and difficulty in childbirth; the multifarious magical provisions designed to assure an easy birth are surely ample evidence of the primitive's fear of hard delivery.

Practically all peoples have special emergency medical practices to call into play when birth is unusually difficult. In easy cases, there is little use of magic at the time of birth, but in drawn-out labor, medicine men and women are hastily invoked. The Cheyennes sent for a medicine man who had derived power from the otter. Otters make a delightful sport of sliding down mudbanks. This is the way the baby should behave and an otter medicine man could bring it about—so they say.

The Couvade A truly quaint custom is the *couvade*. On the birth of the child, the mother gets up and goes about her affairs, while the father goes to bed, apparently to recover from the effects of childbirth. During the period of his confinement, he is subjected to many tabus. This may be variously interpreted as a demand for attention on the part of the male, as a symbolic assertion of the father's identification with the child, or as a form of magical assistance in the establishment of the child in the everyday world. But it is hardly, as some young fathers might think, a consequence of sheer exhaustion. That it is the symbolic as-

[5]V. F. Ray, *The Sanpoil and Nespelem* (University of Washington Publications in Anthropology, vol. 5, 1932), p. 124.
[6]Ford, *op. cit.,* p. 48.

sertion of identification of father and child seems to be the likeliest possibility.

As a matter of fact, not many cultures have produced the couvade. The Caribs and various of their South American neighbors are the outstanding couvadists. The Ainus of Japan and also the Chinese of Marco Polo's time should be included, as well as certain tribes of South India. In the northern mountains of the Iberian peninsula, the couvade was practiced until very recent times.

According to Seed Eater Shoshone informants, they also practiced a real couvade in the old days.[7] When the expectant mother retired to her birth hut, the father went into a retirement hut of his own made for him by his mother. There he stayed isolated for five days, until the umbilical cord dropped from the newborn babe.[8] He observed all the tabus that normally applied to a menstruating woman. No meat or soup could be eaten, only cereals. On the day of birth, his mother came to him, and he rubbed himself with sage. If she said, "You have a boy," he took a long walk in the mountains—where the game abide—but he did not hunt. If she said, "You have a daughter," he walked down into the valleys, where the wild seeds grow. Thus he magically associated his child with its future occupation. When the five days were up he bathed, and then, when he killed his first game, he gave it away to the people.

The four widely scattered centers of the couvade (East Asia, the Pyrenees, northeastern South America, and the Plateau area of North America) indicate independent development and elaboration of the father's role in the birth crisis in these areas.

[7]E. A. Hoebel, *Shoshone Field Notes* (unpublished, 1934); also R. H. Lowie, *Notes on Shoshonean Ethnography* (American Museum of Natural History, Anthropological Papers, vol. 20, part 3, 1924), pp. 265–270.

[8]"A striking instance of numerical imposition is the frequent relationship between the sacred number of a group and the day on which the umbilical cord 'falls off': in Bali, where the mother is in a special state for the first three days after birth, the cord falls off in three days; in Iatmul, where the magic number is five, it falls off in five." M. Mead, "On the Implications for Anthropology of the Gesell-Ilg Approach to Maturation" (*American Anthropologist,* vol. 49, 1947), p. 74.

Naming and Presentation of the Child   The mere fact of birth does not necessarily complete the transition of the child from the status of fetus to that of a member of the community. Many people feel that there must be a formal presentation to the people and the spirits. Many people feel that until this act is completed, mother and child must remain in isolation. The mother is contaminated by her blood and by the dangerous forces of the birth crisis. This is the putative rationalization. Practically, of course, it is a good thing for the mother to have a chance to rest.

Postnatal Isolation   The Hopi child and mother, although visited by relatives on the day of birth, remain isolated for twenty days. On the twentieth day, mother, father, and child are bathed many times over. Relatives of every clan give the infant at least one name associated with their individual clan. Then as the sun rises, the infant is carried out to be held before the Sun God, who is told all the names of the child.[9]

The Seed Eater Shoshone mother and child were isolated even longer—forty days. The birth hut was built by the woman's mother a long way from the camp. When the baby's umbilical cord dropped off after five days, the hut was moved closer to the camp. All menstrual tabus were observed, but, in addition, the maternal grandmother prepared each day a bed of grass over hot coals for the mother to lie upon. (Today a hot-water bottle is used.) Throughout the day, the mother worked busily at weaving and other small tasks. Few friends came to visit her. After six weeks, she and the child rejoined the village.

Naming Ceremonies   The Omaha Indian child was touchingly introduced to the entire cosmos in a traditional ritual always performed by a priest of a given subclan. On the eighth day after birth, the priest was sent for. When he arrived, he took his place at the door of

[9]A fascinating autobiographical description of the entire birth ritual may be found in L. Simmons (ed.), *Sun Chief,* chap. 1.

the lodge in which the child was born. His right hand raised, palm up to the sky, he intoned this beautiful invocation in a loud, ringing voice for all the world to hear:

Ho! Ye Sun, Moon, Stars, all ye that move in the
  heavens,
  I bid you hear me!
Into your midst has come a new life.
  Consent ye, I implore!
Make its path smooth, that it may reach the brow
  of the first hill!

Ho! Ye Winds, Clouds, Rain, Mist, all ye that move
  in the air,
  I bid you hear me!
Into your midst has come a new life.
  Consent ye, I implore!
Make its path smooth, that it may reach the brow
  of the second hill!

Ho! Ye Hills, Valleys, Rivers, Lakes, Trees, Grasses,
  all ye of the earth,
  I bid you hear me!
Into your midst has come a new life.
  Consent ye, I implore!
Make its path smooth, that it may reach the brow of
  the third hill!

Ho! Ye Birds, great and small, that fly in the air,
Ho! Ye Animals, great and small, that dwell in the
  forest,
Ho! Ye Insects that creep among the grasses and
  burrow in the ground.
  I bid you hear me!
Into your midst has come a new life.
  Consent ye, I implore!
Make its path smooth, that it may reach the brow of
  the fourth hill!

Ho! All ye of the Heavens, all ye of the Air, all ye of
  the Earth,
  I bid you all to hear me!
Into your midst has come a new life.
Consent ye, consent ye all, I implore!
Make its path smooth—then shall it travel beyond
  the four hills.[10]

Yet even this ritual did not make the child a real member of the tribe, for a baby did not complete its transition until it could walk. Then it went through a "turning of the child

ritual," wherein it discarded its baby name and got new moccasins. Baby moccasins always had a hole cut in the sole so that if a messenger from the spirit world came to claim the infant, the child could answer, "I cannot go on a journey—my moccasins are worn out!" New moccasins without holes were an assurance that the child was prepared for the journey of life and that its journey would be a long one.

Presentation: Becoming a Tribal Member In Africa, the Ashanti entertained similar notions. The child was not ceremonially named and publicly presented until eight days had passed. Then it became a genuine human being. Should it die before that time, its little corpse would be casually thrown on the garbage heap, for it was believed to have been but the husk of a ghost child whose mother in the spirit world had pawned it off on a living mother for a short period while she went off on some jaunt or other. On returning from her undertaking, she recalled her little spirit baby.

Further to the south in Africa, a Swazi baby, until the third month of life, is described as a "thing." It has no name, it cannot be handled by the men, and if it dies, it may not be publicly mourned. It is recognized as being very weak and vulnerable (infant mortality is tragically high), and the parents perform various rituals to protect it against dangers emanating from animals, humans, and nature herself. In the third month, the infant is shown to the moon and symbolically introduced to the world of nature. It is entered into the category of persons and is given a name, which may be sung to it in its first lullaby.[11]

Not all societies undertake a formal presentation, but most of them, including Western Christianity with its christenings and baptisms (Fig. 19-1), seem to do so. Virtually all societies do isolate mother and child for periods of time varying from a few days to several months.

[10]A. C. Fletcher and F. LaFlesche, *The Omaha Tribe* (Bureau of American Ethnology, Annual Report 27, 1911), pp. 115–116.

[11]H. Kuper, *The Swazi*, p. 50.

Naming, incidentally, is a universal human practice. Shakespeare to the contrary, there is much in a name. It symbolizes the individual's personality and often indicates some aspects of his social status. The name is usually bestowed at the end of the seclusion period. If the name is ceremonially bestowed, this is usually done by a near relative; otherwise, the most common practice is for the mother to decide what her child is to be called. Names that are associated with good luck or great deeds tend generally to be preferred. Thus the Menominee discarded their original names if they were chronically sick, in the hope that a new name would bring a healthier state of being.

Change of names or acquisition of additional ones often occurs in the course of the individual's lifespan in many primitive societies, as new names are assumed to indicate new statuses.

Childhood

Producing, rearing, and educating children to take their role in the full life of the community are prime motivations in all societies. We have already seen in Chapter 2 (pages 38–42) that a wide variance exists in attitudes toward and handling of children. The momentarily popular myth that all primitive peoples treat their children gently, with a maximum of bodily contact and a tender indulgence of all behaviors, is, alas, only a myth. Some do, some don't. Primitive peoples are primarily concerned with the eventual readiness of their children to assume their proper place and responsibility in their particular social order. Grandparents and other relatives frequently assume major parenting responsibilities. In some parts of Polynesia adoption is frequent and casual, and parenting is diffused among older siblings and numerous members of the extended family.

It is probably safe to say that no primitive society is marked by the "child-centered family" as it is known in the contemporary United States. Children are valued primarily for their potential roles as members of the lineage or clan. They spend their childhood learning these future roles. While not participants in most adult activities, they are free to watch much of what occurs. Imitative play is a major medium of all children's learning. In some societies boys are removed from their mothers' homes at about six years of age, and their education is more formally structured after the habits of men. In most instances, however, all children remain with their parents and with no particular sex segregation of siblings until puberty. Helping with tasks begins relatively early and progresses gradually as strength and skill permit.

Puberty

The second crisis in the life cycle is adolescence or puberty. Puberty, like birth, is a manifestation of a basic alteration of the biological state of the individual. It is the time of maturation of the secondary sexual characteristics and the final growth to functional capacity of the sex organs. Puberty marks the twilight of youth and the dawn of adulthood.

Puberty Rites and Transition of Status   In both boys and girls, puberty is not an abrupt transition, but an accelerated development extending from about the eleventh to the sixteenth year. Body hair does not sprout overnight on boys; the lengthening of the vocal cords, with embarrassing sound effects, is not instantaneous; and the relative broadening of the shoulders is a process of adolescent growth as much as the activation of the testicles and the production of fully formed seminal fluid are.

In the female, the majority of puberty changes, including emergence of body hair, broadening of the hips, increase of subcutaneous adipose tissue (especially on the hips and breasts), and development of the sex organs, all occur over a period of months. One function alone, however, first manifests

Fig. 19-1   Naming and presentation of the child. Romany gypsies offer their infants for baptism and blessing. (Sabine Weiss, Rapho Guilumette.)

itself at a particular moment. The onset of menstruation quite definitely signals the attainment of puberty for the female.

The Cultural Definition of Puberty The transition from adolescence to adulthood is fundamentally a biological phenomenon. Yet for human beings it represents also a sociological transition. Because social status is culturally defined, adolescence is for most peoples more a cultural than a biological problem. The first fact to note is that some cultures handle adolescence most casually.[12] The second is that some ritualize it for one sex or the other or for both, with most cultures placing heaviest emphasis on adolescence rites for boys. The third factor is that puberty rites do not necessarily synchronize

Fig. 19-2   Infancy and maturity. Liberian mother and child. (United Nations.)

[12]For example, in Samoa, "Adolescence represented no period of crisis or stress, but was instead an orderly development of slowly maturing interests and activities. The girls' minds were perplexed by no conflicts, troubled by no philosophical queries, beset by no remote ambitions." M. Mead, *Coming of Age in Samoa*, p. 157.

with biological pubescence. They occur when, sociologically, childhood is left behind and adulthood is entered.

Negatively, this principle is admirably demonstrated in the case of the Alorese in the East Indies. For boys, the attainment of adulthood is a long-drawn-out process calling for extensive economic enterprising. Because of this, and since there are no men's clubs and no secret societies, there are no rites of transition, no tribal initiation. Instead, ". . . at about sixteen the boys begin to let their hair grow long. At this time they begin to acquire male dress ornaments: sword, shields, areca basket, wide belt, bow, combs, and head plumes. This is ridiculed by the women, who hoot the men, and scoff at this manifestation of masculine vanity."[13] The boys also file their incisors halfway down and blacken their teeth.

Quite another type of ritual occurs in Tanzania, as illustrated in Figure 19-3.

Incision of the foreskin (supercision) was practiced by some of the Polynesian societies, but by no means all. Among the Marquesan Islanders the operation was performed after a man had reached twenty-five years of age, and it might be postponed even until fifty. It had nothing whatsoever to do with puberty. And then again, among the Tongans, although boys were usually supercised between the ages of twelve and sixteen, it could be done as early as six. Adolescence was not important, but the status symbol of manhood was. As Gifford has written:

Supercision was regarded as a sign of manhood and any youth who declined to be operated upon would be forbidden to eat with the other members of the household, could not touch another's food, and would be spurned by the girls. An uncircumcised person is called *kou* or *taetefe*.[14]

Among the warrior tribes of the Plains and eastern North America, there were no puberty rites per se. But at adolescence young men set out on vision quests to obtain the supernatural power that was believed so essential to a successful life. However, vision vigils were carried on by adults too, so it cannot be said that any great emphasis was placed upon puberty by these people. In the same manner, they treated the adolescence of girls casually. Although all the tribes isolated the menstruating woman, nothing much was made of the first menses, except that the Cheyenne father proudly stood in the door of his tipi shouting the good news to the whole camp and celebrated his daughter's womanhood by a giveaway of a fine horse to some poor oldster.

But the Northern Shoshones and other peoples of the Columbian Plateau made a real crisis of the event for the girl. The pubescent Shoshone girl was isolated just for the period of her flow, but she had to be very busy so that she would not become a lazy woman. "Whatever she does then lasts for life." She could eat no meat and could not scratch herself except with a special stick. At the end of her first isolation, she was brought new clothes by her mother—women's clothes.

Northern Shoshone attitudes were but a pale attenuation of those of the Carrier Indians to the north of them. As Benedict says: ". . . [T]he fear and horror of a girl's puberty was at its height. Her three or four years of seclusion was called 'the burying alive.' . . . She was herself in danger and she was a source of danger to everybody else."[15]

In such societies as those of Africa and aboriginal Australia, both peoples who place much emphasis on age grading (see Chapter 24), adolescence rites become genuine "tribal initiations." This is especially true where men's secret societies are of great importance. Consequently, boys' initiations are also striking in many parts of eastern Melanesia.

Andaman Island Rites   As an example of the more dramatic forms of puberty rites, we

---

[13]C. DuBois, "The Alorese," in A. Kardiner and associates, *The Psychological Frontiers of Society*, p. 139.

[14]E. W. Gifford, *Tongan Society* (Bernice P. Bishop Museum, Bulletin 61, 1929), p. 187.

[15]R. F. Benedict, *Patterns of Culture*, p. 28.

may quote from Radcliffe-Brown's account of the Negrito Andaman Islanders. These pygmy people had no secret societies or other associations, but they did place great emphasis upon age status. To be marked and accepted as an adult, each boy and girl had to go through specific ceremonies. Beginning early in childhood, both sexes were gradually scarred over their entire bodies with small incisions "to help them grow strong," but the culmination was reached at puberty in the following manner. At the first sign of her menses, the girl was wept over by her mother and other female relatives. Such weeping did not express sorrow but rather marked an occasion of importance. The lass then plunged into the ocean for a two-hour bath—an act of ritual cleansing—after which she was tastefully decorated with pandanus leaves and clay.

Thus covered with leaves the girl must sit in the hut allotted to her, with her legs doubled up beneath her and her arms folded. . . . The girl sits thus for three days. Early every morning she leaves the hut to bathe for an hour in the sea. At the end of the three days she resumes her life in the village. For a month following she must bathe in the sea every morning at dawn.[16]

When the friends and relatives of a boy decided that he was old enough to have the incisions made on his back, a dance was held throughout the night and the next morning.

The boy kneels down and bends forward until his elbows rest on the ground in front. One of the older men takes a pig-arrow and with the sharpened blade makes a series of cuts on the boy's back. Each cut is horizontal, and they are arranged in three vertical rows, each row consisting of from 20 to 30 cuts. When the cutting is finished the boy sits up, with a fire at his back, until the bleeding stops. During the operation and a few hours following it the boy must remain silent.[17]

Immediately upon completion of the puberty rites, a number of food tabus were imposed upon both sexes. These were gradually

[16]A. R. Radcliffe-Brown, *The Andaman Islanders,* p. 93.
[17]*Ibid,* p. 95.

removed in a series of formal ceremonies over a period of several years. Neither a boy nor a girl became a full-fledged adult until all the tabus had been removed.

If the whole ritual cycle is viewed as an entity, we see again that adolescence rites do

Fig. 19-3   Puberty ceremony for young boys of the Wagogo tribe, Tanzania. For a period varying from ten days to three weeks, initiates virtually become women. They are attended by women and often dress as girls. Then they are blindfolded and, except in the privacy of the ceremonial huts, they do not see the world again until the masks are removed after circumcision. The masks vary in design. These are of reeds decorated with guinea fowl feathers. (George Rodger, Magnum.)

not represent a fixed biological phenomenon so much as a social event roughly correlated to the biological.

West African Rites   West African initiatory rites are frequently extremely elaborate and impressive. Of the Kpelle of Liberia, where initiation is into the tribal secret fraternity, the Poro, James Gibbs writes:

While a boy is in the Poro bush, he is instructed in tribal lore: farming, house building, crafts, the use of medicines, dancing, warfare, history, the treatment of women, and deportment before chiefs and elders. Physical ordeals, hazing, and the meting out of harsh punishment not only ensure that he learns well but that he acquires a deeply ingrained willingness to submit to authority because it is authority.

When a Poro initiate enters the bush it is said that he is "eaten" by ŋamu. By the time he comes out, he has acquired a lɔi laa or "bush name," by which he is known thereafter. The uninitiated person has died, and a new person has been born in his place. His new status and rebirth are also evident in the cicatrices on his back and chest, said to be the teeth marks of the Great Masked Figure imprinted in the process of disgorging the initiate at his rebirth. Circumcision is usually arranged individually before the boy becomes an initiate.[18]

Relation of Puberty Rites to Other Factors

Becoming a man or a woman means finding one's adult place in the social system. It means accepting ascribed statuses and winning those which may appropriately be achieved. Psychologically, it means internalization of a self-identity that is adequately related to the social system in which one must function. It means anchoring of the self primarily within the kinship group or, alternatively, to social units outside the kinship group. In either case, since every society is larger than the nuclear family (see pages 442–443), it becomes universally necessary to detach the individual to some degree from his family of birth.

The Factor of Social Independence   Yehudi Cohen classifies two types of societies: (1) those which train for social independence, i.e., those in which anchorage and identification are in the nuclear family, and (2) those in which children are brought up for sociological interdependence, i.e., anchorage of the individual in wider kinship groups such as lineages and clans (see Chapter 22). Statistical correlations based on data from sixty-five societies show that type-2 societies overwhelmingly (36 to 1) use initiation ceremonies as a part of the socialization process. Among the type-1 societies in Cohen's sample, the ratio is only ten with initiations to eighteen without.[19] Societies that train for family identification use other means than initiatory techniques.

Circumcision and Personal Identity in Relation to Other Culture Traits   In pre-Columbian times circumcision was exclusively an Old World culture trait of which the American Indians knew nothing. Not one single Indian tribe was found to practice it. In the Old World, it has been predominantly a feature of the Mediterranean area—an expression of Semitic and Arabic cultural symbolism. Thus, 68 per cent of the Mediterranean societies in the *Ethnographic Atlas* are found regularly to practice circumcision or some other surgical modification of the male genitals. Among the Negroes south of the Sahara, slightly more than half (56 per cent) of the societies circumcise or subincise their boys. In Asia, only a handful of peoples (17 per cent) mutilate male genitals, while in Oceania the proportion is somewhat higher (one-fourth).[20]

Whiting and his associates have engaged in an intensive search for the whys and wherefores of circumcision as a part of transition rites. They discovered that the circumcision of boys, particularly when it occurs as a part

---

[18]J. L. Gibbs, Jr., "The Kpelle of Liberia," in J. L. Gibbs, Jr. (ed.), *Peoples of Africa*, p. 222. Copyright © by Holt, Rinehart and Winston, Inc., publishers. Used by permission.

[19]The correlations read: $X^2 = 26.44$, $T = .64$, $p < .001$. Y. Cohen, *The Transition from Childhood to Adolescence*, p. 114.

[20]E. Bourguignon and L. Greenbaum, *Diversity and Homogeneity,* table 35, p. 57.

of initiation rites, is strongly associated with three other cultural phenomena: (1) the custom of having a mother and baby sleep together, while the father sleeps separately; (2) a tabu of a year or longer on resumption of sexual relations between parents after the birth of a child, the so-called postpartum tabu; and (3) virilocal residence, in which a married couple resides with the husband's kin. The first two customs result in strong mother-son identification, and the third intensifies the ultimate claim of the father's kinsmen to the boy's social allegiance or identification. Hence, the severe hazing at puberty serves to break the mother-son tie and to transfer the boy into the world of men (Figure 19-4).[21]

Female Puberty Rites In a representative ethnographic sample of sixty societies drawn from Murdock's *World Ethnographic Sample,* Judith Brown found that approximately one-half observed mandatory puberty rites for girls between the ages of eight and twenty. Cross-cultural correlations shed some light on which types of societies initiate girls and which do not. In sum, if girls bring their husbands to live with them in their mothers' homes (uxorilocal residence), the chances are greater that the culture will include female puberty rites. By implication, removal of a girl from her parental home to her husband's sufficiently signals the status change from unmarried to married. If the girl remains at home, a ceremonial "booster shot" is helpful in effecting the personal identity transfer from mother (and her family) to the husband (and his). Brown also found that most female initiation rites are not painful. The relatively few societies (30 per cent of those which initiate girls, or 15 per cent of the total sample) which do inflict pain, such as in clitori-

dectomy (the female analog to circumcision), tend to be societies in which little girls sleep after birth with their mothers to the exclusion of their fathers. They first identify with the mother; later, they must move into a male-dominated domestic unit. Painful initiation imprints the status transfer. Finally, the greater the woman's contribution to subsistence activities, the more likely her society will be to emphasize her passage from the child's to the woman's statuses and roles. What is important in life tends to be signalized.[22]

There are a number of ancillary functions tied up with puberty ceremonialism. Cicatrization and the filing or knocking out of front teeth serve as both decorative elements and status identifications and also as tests of the neophyte's ability to endure physical pain.[23] Strict discipline imposed during the rites works to fix the authority of elders. The instruction in etiquette, mythology, and magic that usually accompanies puberty initiations embraces education and training in a practical sense and enhances ties or individual loyalty to the institutions of the tribal society. Yet under and through it all is the basic fact of transition—a transition that is fundamentally biological but often elaborately cultural —the transition to maturity.

Maturity

Adulthood in every society means full participation in the responsibilities and privileges of that society. It means marriage and parenthood, as well as economic, political, religious, and club life. As new roles are acquired in each of these areas, various transition rites are again observed to note the passing into new life phases and new behaviors. Maturity

---

[21]J. W. M. Whiting, R. Kluckhohn, and A. Anthony, "The Function of Male Initiation Ceremonies at Puberty," in E. E. Maccoby, T. M. Newcomb, and E. L. Hartley (eds.), *Readings in Social Psychology,* pp. 359–370. See also the discussion of Professor Hart's thesis concerning prepubertal and postpubertal education on p. 42 above.

[22]J. Brown, "A Cross Cultural Study of Female Initiation Rites" (*American Anthropologist,* vol. 65, 1963), pp. 837–853.
[23]When Elizabeth M. Thomas acknowledged to a Dodoth of Kenya that Americans do not pierce the lower lip so as to be able to wear a labret, he said, "That is cowardly."

(a)

(b)

Fig. 19-4   Puberty rites of Australian aborigines.
(a) *Initiates lying upon their ceremonial
sponsors undergo circumcision.* (b) *After further
instruction in totemic mythology and religious
symbolism, the continuity of totemic membership
is symbolized in the act of letting blood run from
the arm of the sponsor to flow over the initiate's
body.* [(a) *Fritz Goro,* **Life Magazine,** © *Time,
Inc.* (b) *From Jens Bjerre's* **The Last Cannibals,**
William Morrow, N.Y.]

is what most of the remainder of this book is about as we spell out marriage and family, kinship, club life, law, politics, religion, and art. The management and the maintenance of a society are in the hands of those who have proven themselves in age and skills.

Death

For the individual, death is the last of the life crises. Every person lives with awareness of his own death, and every society has evolved some method for coping with the death of its individual members. "Death, like birth or marriage, is universally regarded as a socially significant event, set off by ritual and supported by institutions. It is the final *rite de passage*."[24] Death has no absolute finality for any primitive people. All of them believe in the immortality of the soul.[25]

Yet all men well know that death marks the end of corporeal existence. Belief in the transition from the carnal to a wholly spiritual existence at death comes through faith and imagination, a projection of life from a tangible and material state to an ethereal illusory condition sustained in the dogma of culture. Because the dead are no longer constantly among the living but appear, or make their influence felt, only indirectly, they are almost always relegated to another state of being in human cosmogony. Hence, one societal task associated with death is that of assigning new relationships between the deceased and the survivors. The new status of the deceased (spirit) may be viewed as hostile or benign, and the new behavior of the living may range from excessive fear, with attempts to placate, to idolatrous worship. In any event, the need for transition rites is clear, and such rites are usually highly circumscribed.

In Middle Paleolithic times, Neandertal man was the earliest human being to have left tangible evidence of concern over death. He deliberately buried his deceased fellow tribesmen—a boon to archaeologists and an indication that he had developed imaginative intelligence to the point where the soul concept had become possible. All later men have consistently worked into their cultures some form of disposal of the corpse. A great variety of methods has been recorded. A partial listing by Kroeber includes: "burial, cremation, water burial, setting away in vaults or canoes or houses, scaffold burial, exposure or simple abandonment, cremation with eating or drinking of the ashes by the relatives, temporary inhumation with either reburial or preservation of the bones—not to mention previous mummification, dismemberment, and other related practices" (Figure 19-5 and 19-6).[26] As we have seen from archaeological evidence in former chapters, even burials were handled in a wide variety of ways, with bodies stretched out, curled up, richly adorned, undecorated, etc. Regardless of how the deceased body is disposed of, similar variations in preparation occur, and all are accompanied by a greater or lesser development of transitional funerary rites.

Death Rites: Funerals and Mourning   Death is ritualized in two directions. The first deals with the deceased, the separation of the spirit from the body, and the disposal of the corpse: the funeral. The second focuses on the bereavement of the survivors (Figure 19-7), the transfer of property rights and other statuses from the dead to the quick, and the reincorporation of the bereaved into the ongoing community: mourning.

Cheyenne Death Practices   To illustrate these facets of the social management of death, let us take a summary look at the nineteenth-century Cheyennes, nomadic hunters of the Plains:

[24]J. W. Riley, Jr., "Death and Bereavement" (*International Encyclopedia of the Social Sciences,* vol. 4, 1968), p. 19.
[25]See Chapter 30 for a discussion of the soul concept.

[26]A. L. Kroeber, *Anthropology* (2d ed.), p. 402.

For the Cheyenne there is no Hell or punishment of any sort in after-life; no Judgment or Damnation. Although Cheyennes sin when they commit murder and they often do wrong, murder is expiated in the here and now, and wrongdoing builds up no burden of guilt to be borne beyond the grave. For the Cheyenne there is no problem of salvation; goodness is to be sought as rightness for its own sake and for the appreciative approval of one's fellow man. When at last it shakes free of its corporal abode, the Cheyenne soul wafts free and light up the Hanging Road to dwell thereafter in benign proximity to the Great Wise One and the long-lost loved ones. Only the souls of those who have committed suicide are barred from this peace.

In spite of the happy destination that awaits the dead, death is clearly a traumatic experience for the surviving relatives. Each individual is highly valued, for the population is small, and every loss is keenly felt. This is why revenge drives are so strong against enemies who kill Cheyennes.

The corpse of one who has died in camp is quickly disposed of, for people feel that its ghost will not start its journey to the Milky Way until the body has been removed to its final resting place. In other words, the spirit does not take leave of the tribe until the final act of physical separation is complete. It is believed, further, that ghosts like company on their journey and that some of them try to take the spirit of a living person with them, and, hence, if the

Fig. 19-5   Death. Crow Indians preferred above-ground disposition of their dead, either in trees or on scaffolds (see Fig. 17-7). (Courtesy of the Museum of the American Indian, Heye Foundation.)

Fig. 19-6   Prehistoric Anasazi Pueblo burial with grave offerings, Alkali Ridge, Utah. (Peabody Museum, Harvard University.)

body is not disposed of with alacrity, someone may die. Children are especially susceptible to this danger.

Cheyenne burials are bundle burials. Relatives and close friends dress the body of the deceased in its finest clothing. They wrap it, extended full length with the arms at the sides, in a number of robes lashed round about with great lengths of ropes. The burial bundle is transported by travois (a vehicle made of two trailing poles supporting a platform) to its place of deposit some distance from the camp. It may be placed either in the crotch of a tree or upon a scaffold. Or it may be covered over with rocks on the ground. The owner's favorite horses are shot and left at the grave along with his weapons, or, in the case of a woman, her utensils. A man's shield and war bonnet are usually left to his son or best friend; a woman's flesher is left to her daughter. Everything else is given away, usually to nonrelatives who come to the survivor's lodge to mourn until everything has been disposed of, including the lodge.

The mourning customs fall most heavily on the women. Female relatives, especially mothers and wives, cut off their long hair and gash their foreheads so that the blood flows. If the dead one has been killed by enemies, they slash their legs so that they become caked with dried blood; sometimes the blood is not washed off for many weeks. Widows who wish to make an extravagant display of their bereavement gash themselves fearfully and move off alone to live destitute in the brush. The isolation may last a full year, until relatives begin gradually to camp around her, slowly reincorporating her into kin and community life. In these instances the death of a husband means the almost total severance of social bonds for the survivor.[27]

[27]E. A. Hoebel, *The Cheyennes*, pp. 87–88. It should be understood that most of these practices are no longer followed.

In this description, the transitional isolation of the bereaved, with the ultimate aim of re-incorporation into the living society, is made clear. The Cheyennes were a hunting society in which most statuses were achieved rather than ascribed. There was, therefore, not much to pass on through inheritance. Hence, the mourning requirements were actually few and simple.

Death Practices of the Siuai Conversely, in societies where social structure is more complex, we expect the probability that funeral

Fig. 19-7 Old age and mourning in the jungle market of the Gururumba of the Eastern Highlands of New Guinea. An elderly widow, wearing the white clay paint of mourning, displays her net bag of garden produce for sale or exchange. (Courtesy of the American Museum of Natural History.)

rites and mourning will be more highly elaborated.[28] Certainly this holds true for many societies, such as the Lo Dagaa peoples of West Africa, for whom we have the most thorough study of death and its societal consequences.[29] It holds true, also, of such Melanesian peoples as the Solomon Islanders studied by Douglas Oliver, whose results we briefly summarize.

The Siuai of Bougainville are sharers of the Melanesian cultural tradition of "Big Men," reciprocal pig exchange, and shell money. They are horticulturalists. Status ranking is of great significance. "The death of a child or young person occasions smaller funerals, and an infant's dying is usually a matter for near relatives alone. On the other hand, the death of a high-ranking leader gives rise to a more elaborate train of events and the funeral may be attended by hundreds of persons."[30]

If a leader dies in the prime of life, it is assumed a sorcerer had a hand in his death. Few primitive societies have a conception of death due to natural causes; most assume supernatural or magical reasons. (See Chapter 28.) At the moment of death, his nearest kin crowd around his corpse and wail loudly. The largest slit gong in the men's house to which he belonged is sounded. The news is out! After an hour of keening, the men withdraw to make plans, and more female relatives crowd into the house to carry on the crying.

After consulting with the widow, a son gives valuable shell money to his paternal uncle and mother's brother's son (matrilateral cross-cousin). An even larger amount of shell money is then distributed among other relatives and friends to pay them for the pigs they must contribute to the funeral. Enough pigs

are required to feed all who will be invited to attend from other villages. The bigger the man, the more villages to be invited. Relatives keep arriving throughout the day to join the wailing.

During the next day a funeral pyre is built and delegations continue to arrive between sunset and midnight. There is much ritualistic weeping.

Before dawn the corpse is prepared and placed on the pyre, which is then lighted. The bereaved members of the family cling close to the burning heap as long as they can stand the heat, loath to let the moment of separation come. By dawn, most of the hundreds of visitors have drifted away. The widow and son gather up unburnt bits of bone, dispose of them, and purify their hands in a final act of separation. The funeral is over, but the period of mourning goes on. For some days, no work is done by the kin. Little is eaten. No one washes, for this would remove the mourning clay. It used to be (before Australian administration suppressed revenge expeditions) that an ally and his henchmen symbolically killed the sorcerer during this phase. After a week or two, the kin resume normal activity. Phase 1 of mourning is ended.

Phase 2 ends several weeks later when every relative who has received shell money brings in his reciprocating pigs. The pigs are butchered and strips of pork are carried to all the villages whose members had attended the funeral.

Seclusion and separation continue for months for the widow—and many widowers undertake this voluntarily, in honor of their wives—until some relative or friend presents a "bringing-out" gift of a pig or shell money. Thus, the last of the mourners is incorporated once again into normal social life.

Yet a form of symbolic exclusion, or separation, may linger for years in the gardens, forest, or parts of rivers which are "set-aside" —tabued in memory of the deceased. For a child, it might be only a corner of a garden. Reincorporation of a "set-aside" area requires a feast and a formal release of the

---

[28]This proposition has not, in fact, been subjected to extensive cross-cultural testing and no satisfactory general theory has been developed to account for the wide range of variation in form and intensity of death rites. A generation or two ago, death and mourning in the United States, for example, were more seriously observed than they are today. Does this relate to a qualitative change in American social structure?

[29]J. Goody, *Death, Property and the Ancestors.*

[30]D. L. Oliver, *A Solomon Island Society,* pp. 214–215.

ghost of the dead from its guardianship of the space.

Functions of Mortuary Rites   Thus it may be seen that as transition ceremonies, funeral rites serve five basic functions. (1) Participation in mortuary ceremonies, by habitual dramatization of the faith in immortality, prepares the living for the death that awaits them. "The belief in immortality," wrote Malinowski, "lived through ritually . . . makes him cherish more firmly the belief in his own future life. . . . Thus the ritual before death confirms the emotional outlook which a dying man has come to need in his supreme conflict."[31] (2) Funeral rites serve magically to assure the separation of the soul from its body, to guide the deceased through the supreme transition safely and properly. (3) The rites serve to readjust the community after the loss of a member and to regularize the emotional disturbances resulting from the upset of affective habits in connection with the deceased. Death usually evokes grief. (4) Where feasting and property giveaways are involved, mortuary rites effect a redistribution of wealth and statuses. (5) Finally, the rites lend color, richness, and depth to life through the drama of their performance. They are often somewhat theatrical, and may be seen as having a certain entertainment function.

SUMMARY

Human beings do not accept the salient points of the life cycle solely in biological terms. Birth, maturity, reproduction, and death—each is conceptualized and handled in cultural terms as well as physiological ones. The degree of cultural intensity in dealing with such changes of life varies from culture to culture. Some people treat one or another of the phases of the cycle quite matter-of-factly; yet most human beings are haunted by anxieties. In response, they apprehend the transitional phases as life crises, developing specific ritual practices and correlative techniques for handling each situation. Anthropologists identify such practices as transition rites, or *rites de passage.*

All peoples have a theory of conception, although most such theories cannot qualify as scientifically sound. A few, such as those of the Australian aborigines and Trobriand Islanders, deny the physiology of paternity altogether, attributing conception to spirit behavior. Many peoples attribute conception to the growth of a seed implanted by the male in the female, but a few believe the fetus is caused by coagulation of the female blood initiated by the sex act.

Once pregnancy is perceived, the mother certainly, and the father probably, is commonly subject to a number of tabus designed to forestall abnormal development of the child and miscarriage, or difficult labor. The birth itself is usually handled in a routine manner, although postnatal isolation of the mother and child is common. In a few widely scattered parts of the world, the father simulates childbirth and postpartum recovery in a practice known as the couvade, evidently a form of symbolic identification in the generation of the infant.

Merely being born a *Homo sapiens* does not make one a human being. Formal rites of naming and presentation to the world complete the transition into humanity.

Adolescence produces the second crisis of the life cycle. Puberty rites mark the transition to adulthood, especially for boys, in many cultures. Yet, in some societies, such as the Polynesian, where boys are closely associated with the men from the outset, there are no ceremonies whatsoever to mark the transition through puberty. The same was true of Plains Indians in North America. Intense and painful puberty rites are more definitely Old World phenomena. Such rites appear to be associated with early (in life) mother-son identification and virilocal residence; their function is to weaken "momism" and to effect a psychological identification with the

[31]B. Malinowski, "Culture" (*Encyclopaedia of the Social Sciences,* vol. 4, 1931), p. 641.

world of men. Conversely, if upon marriage the newlyweds live with the bride's parents, there is a greater likelihood that the girl will have to go through puberty ceremonies than if the residence is virilocal. Girls are much less likely to be mutilated or hazed in their rites than boys are.

Maturity marks full participation in the responsibilities and privileges of full social life. It means marriage and parenthood, and economic, political, religious, and club life in many different manifestations.

All primitive and most civilized peoples believe in some form of the soul (or souls) and its immortality. Mortuary rites effect the transition of the dead from their carnal life to their spirit existence. More than that, however, they also reassign and effect the transfer of the statuses of the deceased with respect to social responsibilities and property. Thus, there is the funeral, which disposes of the corpse and separates spirit from body. Then there is bereavement; the placing of the kin in limbo, so to speak, and finally reincorporating them into the community with reconstructed relationships and the torn web of life repaired.

SELECTED READINGS

Cohen, Y. A., *The Transition from Childhood to Adolescence* (1964). Undertakes to distinguish pre-pubertal and postpubertal rites of separation of the child from its family and to correlate each type with specific social orientations.

Erikson, E. H., "Life Cycle" (*International Encyclopedia of the Social Sciences* (vol. 9, 1968), pp. 286–292. A very compact and useful statement of the attributes of the major (eight) psychosocial crises in the individual developmental cycle.

Ford, C. L., *A Comparative Study of Human Reproduction* (Yale University Publications in Anthropology, no. 32, 1945). Summarizes primitive natal attitudes and birth practices.

Goody, J., *Death, Property and the Ancestors* (1962). The most comprehensive analysis available of the death practices and their functional significance in a primitive culture.

Jocano, F. L., *Growing Up in a Philippine Barrio* (1969). Written by a native of the Philippines, this book details the ways in which infants become adult members of a society, fulfilling their roles as bearers of their village culture.

Read, M., *Children of Their Fathers* (1968). The life cycle among the Ngomi tribe of Malawi, East Africa.

Simmons, L., *The Role of the Aged in Primitive Society* (1945). A general survey of the status of old people.

Van Gennep, A., *The Rites of Passage* (1960). First published in French in 1909, this is the classic foundation for all anthropological research in puberty rites.

Chapter 20

Mating and Marriage

The prolonged dependence of the human individual on adult nurture, character shaping, and culture transmission, tied in with the peculiarities of relations within the conjugal-natal family, which is a nearly universal form in all human societies, makes untrammeled expression of sexuality socially impossible. Thus, all societies impose rigorous limitations on sexual activities and undertake to steer such sexual activity as is allowed in certain clearly defined directions. There is no such thing as a promiscuous human society. To be human is, in the nature of things, to be subject to sexual inhibition. The amount of inhibition and the forms it takes vary, as does everything else, from culture to culture. Anthropological examination of the cross-cultural record shows that American society imposes and engenders a greater degree of inhibition than is usual, although in recent times it appears to be moving away from this distinctive position as reproduction becomes less and less an urgent social need, as education is more and more of a public function, and as access to economic resources is increasingly managed by the welfare state.

Murdock's comprehensive survey of kinship institutions among the representative sample of 250 societies in the Yale University Cross Cultural Survey led him to estimate: "From available evidence . . . it seems unlikely that a general prohibition of sexual relations outside of marriage occurs in as many as five percent of the peoples of the earth."[1] From this it can be seen that the American position is highly atypical. Nevertheless, it still remains true that all societies impose a number of limitations on sexual activity and attempt to regulate reproduction and mating.

[1]G. P. Murdock, *Social Structure*, p. 264.

Mating

Mating is *the pairing off of individuals of opposite sex under the influence of the sex drive.* It is preponderantly a psychophysical phenomenon, basically instinctive in nature. But among human beings it is definitely influenced by various culture patterns that control the forms of its expression. The purpose of this chapter is to describe the nature of the cultural channeling of mating and to explain it as far as is possible.

Mating implies more than mere sexual intercourse; a degree of permanence is in-

Fig. 20-A   Kana courtship. Waghi Valley, Central Highlands of New Guinea. (Laurence LeGuay.)

volved in the association of the mated pair. However, mating is not to be confused with marriage; intimately related though the two may be, they are not inseparable. As in the case of nonhuman animals, mating can occur on a purely biological plane, without benefit of marriage. Conversely, marriages can occur without mating.

Marriage is a social institution determined by culture. Marriage is *the complex of social norms that define and control the relations of a cojoined pair to each other, their kinsmen, their offspring, and society at large.* It defines all the institutional demand rights, duties, privileges, and immunities of the pair as husband and wife. It shapes the form and activities of the association known as the *family.*

Premarital Mating   Taking human societies as a whole, the majority accept premarital sexual experimentation without serious disapproval. Of the 863 societies in Murdock's *Ethnographic Atlas,* 67 per cent impose little restriction on premarital sexual behavior. The greatest proportion (75 per cent) of permissive societies is found in the Pacific area, thus supporting the romantic image of the permissive Pacific brought back by nineteenth-century sailors. The most restrictive area of the world is the Circum-Mediterranean, the home of the Semites and Muslims. Here only 41 per cent of the societies are found to be tolerant of premarital sexual behavior.[2]

Malinowski's description of the Trobriand Islanders exemplifies, perhaps in a somewhat extreme fashion, the pattern. In his words:

Chastity is an unknown virtue among the natives. At an incredibly early age they become initiated into sexual life, and many of the innocent looking plays of childhood are not so innocuous as they appear. As they grow up, they live in promiscuous free-love, which gradually develops into more permanent attachments, one of which ends in marriage.[3]

In the absence of the severe guilt feelings that traditionally color premarital sex activity among our youthful population, premarital activity may function among primitives to prepare young people for marriage. It can provide an intimate test of the compatibility of mating pairs before they actually enter into marriage, with all its social and economic responsibilities. This is Malinowski's principle of the *social function of premarital sexual activity.*[4] There is little doubt that the purpose to which Malinowski calls attention may so be served in some societies, but it seems more likely that societies are apt to permit the free play of the biological drives, outside the limits of the incest tabu, before marriage because of indifference to the effects of such activity.

This set of attitudes is well exemplified by the Kadara of the Nigerian plateau, a gardening and hunting people who practice infant betrothal. The young groom, after his fiancée has become three or more years of age, labors in his betrothed father's gardens for a set number of days each year until, after ten years, he may claim his wife. Marriages, however, are very brittle and are expected to last only through the births of the first three offspring. These children belong to the husband and his kinship group. What is valued are the children *per se,* not the family or the chastity of the bride. "It is fairly common," writes M. G. Smith, "for unmarried girls to be impregnated or to give birth to children by youths other than their betrothed. Offspring of such premarital pregnancies are members of the patrilineage of the girl's betrothed and are welcomed as proofs of the bride's fertility."[5]

Restrictions on Premarital Mating   At any rate, not much emphasis can be placed upon the

[2]E. Bourguignon and L. Greenbaum, *Diversity and Homogeneity,* p. 54.
[3]B. Malinowski, *The Argonauts of the Western Pacific,* p. 53.

[4]B. Malinowski, "Culture" (*Encyclopaedia of the Social Sciences,* vol. 4, 1931), p. 630.
[5]M. G. Smith, "Secondary Marriage among Kadara and Kagoro," in P. Bohannan and J. Middleton (eds.), *Marriage, Family, and Residence,* p. 113.

function of premarital experience as a factor in mate selection in the vast number of primitive societies in which the boy and girl have very little to say about whom they marry. It will be shown later to how small a degree marriage in primitive society is concerned with sexual gratification and personal compatibility on the basis of romantic love. Primitive societies are much more concerned with (1) the biological perpetuation of the group, (2) the perpetuation of the culture and social existence of the group through proper nurture and training of the oncoming generation, and (3), last but not least, the furthering of immediate special interests in prestige, property, and prerogatives of the *extended families* of the pair to be joined in marriage; i.e., the transmission of social status.

This last point is well illustrated in the practices of the Philippine Ifugaos, who permit free premarital sexual activity only for members of those classes in which there is not much at stake in property and prestige. Each night, adolescent boys of the lower and middle classes must seek the congenial comfort of the house of a widow, which also serves the regular purpose of a dormitory for unmarried adolescent girls, who, by custom, are not permitted to sleep under the family roof. In the deep of the night, the boys try their luck at lovemaking. Much experimentation in different dormitories ultimately leads to a permanent attachment to some one girl— a form of companionate marriage that eventually blossoms into a fully accredited marriage, after numerous exchange gifts have been made and family rituals of marriage have been observed.

Upper-class Ifugaos, however, behave in quite a different manner, since the parents do not care to run the risk of permitting their children to mate in accordance with mere amatory whim. The society of the Ifugaos rests on a subsistence base of wet-rice culture in paddies that have been carved in rugged mountainsides (see Figure 12-9, page 262) through the prodigious efforts of untold generations of labor. Possession of rice fields is a precious heritage: a necessary means to wealth, prestige, and upper-class status—the cherished goal of the Ifugao. Because family status rests heavily on property, marriage is a useful instrument for augmenting the status of the next generation by combining the resources of two families of property. To have a scion find a compatible but propertyless bride in the damsels' dormitory is, for the upper-class Ifugao, an economic calamity. To avert such an eventuality, rich children of the Ifugaos are betrothed in infancy, or even before birth. Figure 20-1 shows such a contract marriage. A contract marriage is arranged by the parents, who guarantee the amount of land and other goods to be conveyed to the bride and groom. Throughout childhood, the boy and girl take turns living in each other's parents' homes until they establish a home of their own on marriage, shortly after adolescence.[6]

The illustrations cited above indicate that economic factors can influence the imposition of checks on free premarital sexual activity. This must have played an increasingly important role in the unfolding of human history as societies built up more and more property. Mating became more than a simple expression of biological drives. Controlled by marriage, it tied reproduction to allocation of property and its transference from one generation to another.

While economic determinism has a sturdy finger in the pie, other factors must also be recognized. Religious belief is pervasive. In the area of sex control, its power cannot be overestimated. Inca maidens dedicated to serve the sun in the nunneries of Cuzco were required to remain virgins until they were married off to a worthy dignitary, who was the recipient of royal favor from the demigod, the Great Sun, the ruling Inca. Rome had her vestal virgins. And the military societies of the

[6]R. F. Barton, *Philippine Pagans;* also *Ifugao Law* (The University of California Publications in American Archaeology and Ethnology, vol. 15, 1919), pp. 15–22.

Cheyenne Indians each had four honorary virgins to perform ritual services in the society ceremonies. An active sexual life is often incompatible with religious specializations.

Shamans are generally devoted to this principle. Unless they are engaged in fertility rites to bring on a crop of babies or corn, they almost universally submit themselves to temporary celibacy when they are about to invoke their mystic powers. The belief is that the female physiology is itself charged with a mystic power of great potency. In this man-dominated world, the unique female power is interpreted as evil and dangerous, dangerous especially to the mystic powers of men. Contamination of a male's supernatural power by the negative power of the female is believed to result from sexual association. When this attitude is exaggerated, it leads to the sexual asceticism of some of the Late Classical cults and early Christianity, an asceticism that survives in the celibacy of the Catholic clergy and the Puritan distrust of sex embedded in much of our culture. Such intense elaboration of sex asceticism is only another example of the principle of skewed elaboration of culture. Sociology can adduce few good functional reasons for its existence. Psychiatry and psychology can adduce manifold instances of malfunctioning as a result of it—the psychotic and neurotic quirks of the repressed personality.

Fig. 20-1   An Ifugao boy and girl married couple at their elevation to the rank of **kadangyang**—*the highest social class. The boy wears a headdress and has a white chicken hanging from his belt. His contracted wife stands next to him, with a chicken in her left hand. (Lowie Museum of Anthropology, University of California, Berkeley.)*

Various combinations of one or more of the considerations just mentioned have led a slight majority of contemporary primitive societies to inhibit, or at least to try to check, premarital sexual activity among their young. The Trobriand Island instance represents a minority situation. The primitive societies that do impose a check on adolescent premarital sex experience do so for the most part not because they view such activity as inherently evil, but rather because economic and other social interests have priority over sex. Ubiquitously, however, *every society prohibits sexuality between brother and sister at all ages.* This is the consequence of the universal prohibition of incest.

The Prohibition of Incest

Mating with any person who is *culturally defined* as a member of one's kinship group is commonly forbidden. Any such prohibited mating is incestuous. The prohibition of sex relations between culturally identified relatives is therefore known as the *incest tabu.* It automatically follows that marriage between persons subject to this rule is also forbidden.

Incest tabus are universal among all peoples. The universality of incest prohibition and the fact that it is concerned with a basic biological act have led to the common view that it is instinctive. Universality, however, is not in itself any evidence of instinct. We might as well say that fire making is an instinct, since all peoples practice it. The weight of the evidence is on the other side. Incest prohibition is not instinctive; rather, it is rooted in a social, not a biological, basis.

Exceptions to the Incest Tabu   Let us observe how this works. *The tabu on the mating of brother and sister occurs everywhere, as does the tabu on mating between parent and child.* The exceptions that bar absolute universality are few and far between, nor do they in any case apply to the entire popula-

tion of any society. The exceptions to the brother-sister rule are the famous cases of the royalty of Egypt, Hawaii, and the Incas. In these instances, marriage between brother and sister of royal lineage was required in the belief that the supreme royalty was divine and that marriage with mortals was a corruption of the divinity. But alas for ideals! Cleopatra, although she married her twelve-year-old brother, saw to his murder while she mated with Julius Caesar and Mark Antony. Whether because of the example of the Ptolemies or as a result of other historical causes, brother-sister marriage as a means of keeping property within the family was evidently not uncommon in Egypt during the period of Roman rule following the death of Cleopatra.[7]

Another special and very peculiar exception to the brother-sister tabu exists among the Balinese, who suppose that boy and girl twins have been too intimate in their mother's womb. The penalties for incest are severe in Bali, but in the case of baby twins, temporary banishment of the parents and the "erring" twins, followed by a ceremony of purification and atonement, negates the sin. This makes it permissible for the mating in the womb to be completed as a true marriage in later life.[8]

Ordinary brother-sister marriages are said to have been permissible among the aboriginal Ainus of Japan, but the evidence for this is merely mythological, and myth is not good historical evidence. It has also been reported that the Lamet tribe of Southeast Asia countenances brother-sister marriage if the pair have been raised in separate households, i.e., are not sociologically members of the same family.[9]

Edmund Leach has recently reported another tribe of Southeast Asia who permit half

---

[7]R. Middleton, "Brother-Sister and Father-Daughter Marriage in Ancient Greece" (*American Sociological Review,* vol. 27, 1962), pp. 603–611.

[8]J. Belo, "A Study of a Balinese Family" (*American Anthropologist,* vol. 38, 1936), p. 30.

[9]K. G. Izikowitz, *Lamet, Hill Peasants in French Indochina,* pp. 134–135.

brothers and sisters to marry under certain circumstances. In calling attention to the Lakher, he writes:

They consider that the child of a properly married man is exclusively his and that his divorced wife has absolutely no rights in the child whatsoever. It follows that if a woman has a son and a daughter by two different husbands the children are deemed unrelated to one another. Therefore they may marry without restraint. In contrast, the son and daughter of one man by two different mothers stand in an incestuous relationship to one another.[10]

In ancient Hawaii, title to chieftainship rested on high-ranking descent and inherited supernatural power, called *mana* (see pages 566–577). Incestuous marriage in the royal lines (called *pi'o*) intensified the inherited *mana* and the accompanying sacredness of the royal heir beyond that held by either of his or her parents. Such marriages occurred not only between brother and sister but also between uncles and nieces, aunts and nephews.[11]

The Penalties for Incest The punishments, or negative sanctions, for the violation of the incest tabus vary greatly from one society to another, but a definite regional distribution of characteristic reactions is discernible. In Australia, where kinship is a subject of intense interest, most tribes punish incest with death. Plains Indians, on the other hand, do not consider incest either a crime or a sin. They simply look upon it as impossible behavior, so inconceivable that only insane persons indulge in it. Yet the punishment was mild in the few rare cases that have been recorded. A Dakota father of an incestuous brother and sister proclaimed, "Now I am the father of dogs!" Comanche informants cannot remember a single actual case of incest among their people, nor can they stretch their imaginations sufficiently to give a specific

statement of what the public reaction would have been had such a case occurred, except to say that the people would have shunned them and called them *keshuant* (crazy).

In ancient Bali, the punishment was symbolic and devastating. The hapless couple were adorned with yokes customarily worn by pigs. They were then made to crawl on all fours to drink from the swill trough of the hogs. After this humiliation, they were banished forever from the village, and their lands were confiscated. No other village would take them in for fear of ill luck and disaster. They were doomed to a fearsome existence alone in the jungle.[12]

The forensic Ashanti of the West African Sudan give vivid reasons for the imposition of the death penalty for incest. According to them, if the sinful crime were to have gone unpunished, ". . . hunters would have ceased to kill the animals in the forest, the crops would have refused to bear fruit, children would have ceased to be born, the '*Samanfo* (spirits of dead ancestors) would have been infuriated, gods would have been angered, *abusua* (clans) would have ceased to exist, and all would have been chaos (*basa basa*) in the world."[13]

Biological Explanations of the Incest Tabu
It has been argued by Westermarck[14] and Morgan,[15] among earlier anthropologists, that primitive man became cognizant of genetic deterioration resulting from close inbreeding. They averred that on this basis, humanity preserved its genetic health by preventing close inbreeding through the establishment of incest prohibitions. This is the popular belief of most people in the United States. The fact is, however, that inbreeding does not necessarily produce physical deterioration. Inbreeding does no more than in-

---

[10]E. R. Leach, *Rethinking Anthropology*, p. 14.
[11]W. Davenport, "The Hawaiian Cultural Revolution: Some Political and Economic Considerations" (*American Anthropologist*, vol. 71, 1969), p. 7.

[12]J. Belo, "A Study of a Balinese Family," *op. cit*, p. 29.
[13]R. S. Rattray, *Ashanti Law and Constitution*, p. 304.
[14]E. Westermarck, *The History of Human Marriage*, vol. 2, pp. 218–241.
[15]L. H. Morgan, *Ancient Society*, p. 424.

tensify the phenotypic traits that the inbreeding population possessed at the outset. Recessive traits have a better chance of obtaining somatic realization where inbreeding is marked. If undesirable recessives are in the stock, they may well come to the fore, and deterioration may then result. Nevertheless, it is equally true that inbreeding intensifies the influence of dominant traits. A stock with desirable dominants becomes stronger. The end result may be good or bad; it all depends on the distribution of traits with respect to dominance and desirability. Cleopatra, the last of the Ptolemies and the product of twelve generations of brother-sister marriages, was hardly a specimen of physical degeneration.

In the long run, however, modern population genetics makes it quite certain that the effect of gene mutations in such a slow-breeding animal as man would be powerfully negative. This comes about because deleterious and lethal mutations are many times more frequent than are those which are adaptively advantageous. In small populations such as those of primitive tribes, there would be small margin to allow for selective culling out without extinction of the whole group. The danger would be intensified by the fact that the closer the inbreeding, the greater the relative frequency of homozygous inheritance: hence, the greater probability of destructive mutations wreaking their effect and endangering survival. The incest tabu, whatever its specific cultural content, inhibits close inbreeding. We can now feel certain, on sound scientific grounds, that its effects are genetically beneficial for mankind.

Westermarck's Instinct Theory Westermarck also stated that human beings raised in the intimacy of the same family circle have an instinctive aversion to sexual relations among themselves. He held that the social rules prohibiting incest lend cultural expression to a biologically natural repugnance.[16] Most an-

[16]E. Westermarck, *op. cit.*, p. 192.

thropologists of today have wholly rejected this hypothesis on the ground that there is too much evidence of an actual proclivity for sexual relations with those who are conveniently at hand; it is to suppress this tendency in favor of structural solidarity of the basic kinship groups that the strong anti-incest rules exist, they maintain. Indeed, they ask, if an instinctive aversion exists, why the heavily sanctioned social rules to prohibit an act that would not occur anyway?

Adopted Sister Marriages in Taiwan Nonetheless, support for Westermarck's position has recently been revived by Arthur Wolf through his study of two forms of marriage among Chinese settlers in Taiwan. The prestigious form of marriage is the "grand" or "major" marriage, called *ta-hun*. It binds an alliance between two extended families, establishing important interfamily obligations, along with payment of dowry and progeny price (pages 410–412). Such marriages, which were common before 1930, were arranged by the elders, and the bride and groom did not see each other until their wedding day.

The "minor" marriage was also common (40 per cent of all marriages from 1900 to 1925). This type, however, was "socially despised." The minor marriage pattern, used only by disadvantaged families, worked in the following way: poor parents adopted a baby girl to raise as a future wife for a son, thus obviating the need to pay out the progeny price which would have been due for the bride if she had come as a mature member of another kinship group. And by giving away their own baby daughters to other families, they also eliminated the raising of dowries for them when their time came to marry.[17] In other words, by accepting the idea that minor marriages were despised, they acknowledged the claim of the propertied classes to the social prestige and power derived from property manipulation in conjunction with marital

[17]A. P. Wolf, "Adopt a Daughter-in-law, Marry a Sister: A Chinese Solution to the Problem of the Incest Taboo" (*American Anthropologist*, vol. 72, 1970), pp. 864–874.

alliances. Possessing little property, they dropped out of the social game and arranged marriages without property exchanges. Yet they seemed to think that the stigma of propertyless marriages could be reduced by effecting the betrothal through infant adoption years before the marriage would occur. How does this affect the Westermarck argument?

Professor Wolf proposes that if Westermarck's hypothesis is right, then couples who were raised together would find that sexual aversion persisted after marriage and would permanently mar their marital relations; they "should be less intimate and more prone to marital discord." With data that are unusually good, he shows that "minor" marriages resulted in 33 per cent fewer children than did the "major" variety, along with a relative frequency of divorce and/or adultery of 4½ to 1.[18] Wolf believes his data establish that there is "some aspect of childhood association sufficient to preclude or inhibit sexual desire" in the "minor" marriages. There is no question but that such marriages produced fewer children and were less enduring than the ideal "grand" marriages.

But the question still remains: are these facts the indices of lesser sexuality in "adopted sister-brother" marriages in Taiwan? Or do they indicate only that in the old Chinese society there was less at stake socially in the prestigeless and disdained "minor" marriages, and that there was less commitment to the structural form of marriage when there was less to win or lose by maintaining such marriages? For reasons that will unfold as our discussion of marriage and kinship develops in the succeeding pages, we believe the answer will still be found in sociopsychological rather than purely psychological causes.

The Relation of Social Structure to the Incest Tabu Although the incest tabu may well serve eugenic ends, there is much about the specific manifestation of the principle of incest prohibition that can be explained only in sociocultural terms. The fact is that although parent-child and sibling sex relations are almost universally prohibited, the incest tabu is often extended far beyond the membership of the conjugal-natal family. No Chinese, for example, may marry another who bears the same surname, even though they come from far-separated parts of China with no family contact whatsoever. The assumption is that they have a common clan ancestry, and between clan members there may be no marriage.

Marriage with known cousins is tabued in two out of every three cultures.[19] In a notable number of social systems, however, sex relations with cousins who fall outside a person's kinship group are allowed, and marriage with these particular cousins may even be socially encouraged or prescribed.

Cross-cultural anthropological research amply demonstrates that the degree of genealogical closeness is irrelevant to the application of the incest tabu. Rather, the specific identification of the individuals who are brought within the scope of the incest tabu is a function of the forms of kinship organization that prevail in a given society.

The Effect of Kinship Terminology on the Scope of the Incest Tabu Modes of addressing relatives reflect the structure of the kinship groups in any society (see Chapter 23). American Indians, when talking to whites, may speak of "my sister" and "my Indian sister." What is the distinction? In standard American terminology, a sister is a girl born of the same parents as oneself. However, Catholics do stretch the term to include nuns, and members of a sorority extend the term to include one another. When the Indian of today makes the distinction between "sister" and "Indian sister," he is trying to make clear that the Indian concept of "sister" is somewhat different from the standard American concept. If the speaker is

[18]A. P. Wolf, "Childhood Association and Sexual Attraction: A Further Test of the Westermarck Hypothesis" (*American Anthropologist,* vol. 72, 1970), p. 506.

[19]Bourguignon and Greenbaum, *op. cit.,* p. 53.

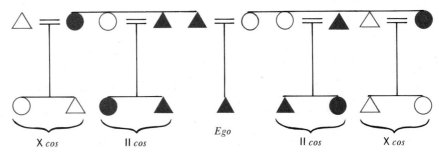

Fig. 20-2   Genealogical separation of cross- and parallel-cousins.

a Seed Eater Shoshone from Idaho, the term "sister" in its native sense means not only "daughter of my own mother" but also all female cousins through both father and mother. Relationship terms may be taken quite literally; therefore, a girl called "sister" *is* a sister and must be treated as such in all respects. Sex relations and marriage with all "sisters" are therefore automatically tabued.

This broadening of relationship categories has been aptly called *lumping*.[20] It is the usual characteristic of relationship systems that are identified as *classificatory*. Because most primitive systems are classificatory, many individuals are embraced within the incest prohibitions by the simple fiat of a social system that dubs them "father," "mother," "brother," or "sister," when in biological fact they are not actually such. (See pages 457–459 for a more detailed discussion of this phenomenon.)

The Terminological Distinction in Types of Cousins
The Shoshones and the Hawaiians, for example, lump all cousins in a single sibling (brother and sister) category. Many other peoples' indulge in a form of discrimination that intensifies the impression of arbitrary disregard of biological reality. A certain type of cousin is classified as brother or sister, but another type of cousin is regarded as not being a kinsman at all. The first type of cousin we call *parallel-cousins* because the parents

[20]R. H. Lowie, "Kinship" (*Encyclopaedia of the Social Sciences*, vol. 3, 1931), pp. 568–572.

through whom they are related are of like sex. The other type of cousin we call *cross-cousins*, not because of temperamental peculiarities, but because the parents through whom they are related are of opposite sex; there is a crossing over from one sex to the other in the genealogy of relationship (Figure 20-2). In any tribe in which cross-cousins are distinguished from parallel-cousins, cross-cousins are never reckoned as belonging to the same kinship group. In the dogma of the social system, they are not kinsmen. The logic of such a premise produces a biological absurdity, but the biologist protests in vain. To marry a parallel-cousin may be incest, and to marry a parallel-cousin who is a member of one's own clan *is* incest. However, to marry a cross-cousin may be the accepted thing to do; it may even be the required thing to do. Thus, one is forbidden to marry a first cousin of parallel relationship, whereas it is good form to marry a first cousin of cross relationship. Both are equally close in genetic kinship, but the second is no relative at all in *culturally determined* kinship.

Functional-Structural Explanations of the Incest Tabu   There are two types of functional-structural theories in explanation of the incest tabu. One rests primarily on psychological principles and emphasizes the potentially disruptive effect of sexual competition within the kinship group. The fullest statement of this theory came from Malinowski. The other emphasizes principles of social structure and the importance of marital alliances as a means of broadening the scope of social integration. Sir Edward Tylor, Leslie White, and Claude Lévi-Strauss are major proponents of this view.

Both schools of thought, however, were anticipated by Lord Bolingbroke, who rejected the idea that incest aversion is the expression of an innate moral sense, as was argued by eighteenth-century Scottish moral philosophers. Bolingbroke baldly stated that far from being instinctive or innate, "the abhorrence of incest, as well as other forms of sexual modesty, is wholly artificial." Rather, he argued, exogamy works "to improve sociability among men, and to extend it as wide as possible, in opposition to that insociability which is so apt to grow up between distinct families and states." Lord Bolingbroke anticipated Malinowski's psychological-functional theory of incest prohibition by holding that an additional effect of the incest tabu and exogamy was to prevent the destruction of the foundations of society. Children who marry their parents, he reasoned, will have less respect for them as the chief magistrates of the family; and what weakens the family weakens the greater commonwealth.[21]

The Psychological Theory   Malinowski posited the proposition that sexual affection is anteceded in the development of the individual by strongly conditioned parental and fraternal affection, based on intimate family associations, which occurs before the maturation of the sex drives. These are the affective emotions that cement the bonds of family and kin and give solidarity to the foundation group of any society—the group of immediate kinsmen. The family is founded in part upon the sexual association of spouses, between whom the sex drive may have legitimate play. But sex is a dangerous element. From its drives arise powerful emotional disturbances

of great disruptive potentiality. In preadolescence, the sex drives are unmatured; they are not yet dangerous. On maturation under unrestricted conditions, however, gratification of the sex drives would frequently be sought with those nearest at hand, toward whom one already has affection—the members of one's own household. This would naturally lead to mating between siblings and parents and offspring. The violent emotions engendered by sexual affection would blast and disrupt family unity built upon the earlier established filial-fraternal affections.

A house divided against itself cannot stand; it will become all one thing, or all the other. Overt sexual rivalry within the functioning kinship group cannot be permitted. The solidarity of the foundation unit of society is protected against its disruptive effects through the universal incest prohibition and its variant extensions.[22] Promiscuity and the family cannot exist side by side; sex relations, except for those of the father and mother, must be barred within it. Thus the preservation of the kinship group, the foundation unit of society, is maintained.

The Alliance Theory   In its very simplest form, the alliance theory holds that by marrying out of the kinship group primitive men avoided conflict and widened their chances for survival and prosperity (Figure 20-3). It was put baldly by Sir Edward B. Tylor: "Again and again in the world's history, savage tribes must have had plainly before their minds the simple practical alternative between marrying-out and being killed-out."[23]

The earliest extant ethnographic account of this principle in action is found in the Bible, Genesis 34 (King James version). Jacob had migrated with his flocks and his followers to new territory. There his daughter, Dinah,

[21]For further details, see A. O. Aldridge, "The Meaning of Incest from Hutcheson to Gibbon" (*Ethics*, vol. 61, 1951), pp. 309–313.

[22]B. Malinowski, "Culture" (*Encyclopaedia of the Social Sciences*, vol. 4, 1931), p. 630.

[23]E. B. Tylor, "On a Method of Investigating the Development of Institutions Applied to the Laws of Marriage and Descent" (*Journal of the Royal Anthropological Institute of Great Britain and Ireland*, vol. 18, 1888), p. 267.

had been seduced by the son of the prince of the city of Shalem. Her brothers were spoiling for blood. Hamore, the ruling prince of the town, however, sued for Dinah's hand in marriage to his son and proposed a general marital alliance: "And ye make marriages with us, and give you daughters to us, and take our daughters unto you. And ye shall dwell with us: and the land shall be before you; dwell and trade ye therein [Gen. 34:9–10]." The advantages in the alliance through marriage were clear-cut; but the outcome of the event drives home the lethal alternative. Jacob's sons accepted the offer with the proviso that all the men of the city must be circumcized like themselves. This was done,

and while they were convalescing, Simeon and Levi killed them all, recovered their sister, took the surviving women and children as captives, plundered the city, and made off with the flocks [Gen. 34:14–29]. Indeed, the alternative to marrying-out may be being killed-out, but the marrying-out cannot be based upon misplaced trust.

Exogamy

Exogamy (Gr. *ex*, outside + *gamos*, marriage) is defined as *the social rule that requires an individual to marry outside of a culturally defined group of which he is a member.* The con-

Fig. 20-3 *In India an important role in arranging marital alliances is played by the* **gor**, *or marriage broker, who works adeptly to balance each family's effort to maximize its gains and minimize its losses in rank, wealth, and the welfare of its child. In the marriage ritual shown here, the* **gor**, *seated before the bride and groom, is bringing the alliance to its conclusion. (Photo by Bhupendra Karia.)*

jugal-natal family is, with the few exceptions already noted, always exogamous. Whether other kinship groups are exogamous, and in what manner, is a reflection of the particular social structure that prevails in the society.

Simple Exogamy When the prohibition against marrying a kinsman is applied without discrimination to all known genetic relatives, exogamy is simple or undifferentiated. Two-thirds of the societies in the *Ethnographic Atlas* practice simple exogamy, as indicated by the existence of a tabu on marriage to any kind of cousin whatsoever.[24] Generally speaking, simple exogamy occurs in societies in which kinship is organized bilaterally; i.e., without the presence of lineages or clans. Hence, the occurrence of simple exogamy is unevenly distributed around the world. It was highest in North America (83 per cent), where 65 per cent of the Indian tribes were bilaterally organized. It was (and still is) lowest in the Mediterranean area (34 per cent), where only 31 per cent of the societies are bilaterally organized.

Restricted Exogamy   Restricted exogamy is selective. It is the residual consequence of the cultural development of the alliance principle when applied to lineages and clans within a society. In this form, marriage is forbidden with certain categories of kinsmen, while at the same time it is preferred or required, as the case may be, with other categories of genealogic relatives who are not culturally defined as being kinsmen. These persons are almost always one kind or another of cross-cousin. This calls for marriage to a mother's brother's child *or* a father's sister's child (Figure 20-4) among first cousins, or to their equivalents if the preference applies to second or third cousins or beyond. Such cross-cousin marriages are *symmetrical*.

In the *Ethnographic Atlas*, 20 per cent of the societies forbid marriage to parallel-cousins but make it permissible with either kind of cross-cousin (defined as *duolateral cross-cousin marriage*). A mere 4 per cent (32 out of 762) prescribe marriage of a male to a mother's brother's daughter (*matrilateral cross-cousin marriage*), and less than 1 per cent (4 in 762) require marriage to a father's brother's daughter (*patrilateral cross-cousin marriage*).[25] Such cross-cousin marriages are *asymmetrical*.

Lévi-Strauss's Theory of Matrilateral Marital Exchange Why should cousin marriage, especially cross-cousin marriage, be so frequently preferred? And why should so many peoples prefer the symmetrical to the asymmetrical form of cross-cousin marriage? Why are matrilateral cross-cousins preferred as wives three times as often as patrilateral cross-cousins? The distinguished French anthropologist Claude Lévi-Strauss argues that cross-cousin marriage exists because it promotes social integration through regularization of group interdependence in the exchange of women.[26] He builds on the theory of his predecessor, Émile Durkheim (1858–1917), to the effect that the expansion of human society involves specialization and division of labor; such specialization requires stabilization of interdependence, if the society is not to come apart at the seams. The basic function of exchange and trade is to promote interdependence and social solidarity. Women, holds Lévi-Strauss, are the most highly valued scarce commodity because it is through them that children, the continuers of the group's survival, are born. Therefore, exchange of women is of prime importance in ordering interdependence. In duolateral, or symmetrical, cross-cousin marriage, woman swapping is practiced in all directions; it may tie closely related groups more tightly to one another, but it does not produce a strong integrating principle. Lévi-

---

[24]Bourguignon and Greenbaum, *op. cit.,* pp. 51, 53.

[25]*Idem.*

[26]C. Lévi-Strauss, *Les structures élémentaires de la parenté,* (*The Elementary Structures of Kinship*).

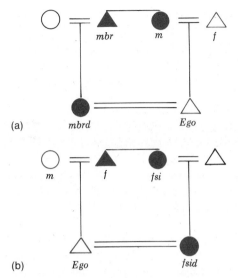

(a)

(b)

*Fig. 20-4   (a) Matrilateral
cross-cousin marriage in a patrilineal
society. A male ego marries his
mother's brother's daughter (mbrd),
who does not belong to his
patrilineage. (b) Patrilateral
cross-cousin marriage in a
matrilineal society. A male ego
marries his father's sister's daughter
(fsid), who does not belong to his
matrilineage.*

Strauss demonstrates that matrilateral cross-cousin marriage in a society with matrilineal descent groups results in group A's giving its women to group B, which gives its women to group C, which gives its women to group A. The three groups, which constitute a society, are thus bound to one another in a closed circle (Figure 20-5).[27] This presupposes that matrilateral cross-cousin marriage is prescriptive, or required, rather than merely preferential. Lévi-Strauss argues that matrilateral cross-cousin marriage in matrilineal societies is a "best" way of producing social solidarity.

Lévi-Strauss's theory is built on the proposition that the needs of social solidarity pro-

duce asymmetrical cross-cousin marriage (a structural argument). However, the empirical fact that so few societies have incorporated matrilateral cousin marriage as a preferred form indicates that although the system logically leads to social solidarity, it obviously is not a necessary condition for societal maintenance. Most societies survive quite well without it, and there is no empirical evidence that societies with circulating matrilateral cross-cousin marriage are in fact more solidly bound than others.

Endogamy

Endogamy (Gr. *endo*, within + *gamos*, marriage) is the converse of exogamy. It is *the social rule that requires a person to marry within a culturally defined group of which he*

*Fig. 20-5   The circulation of women through
prescribed matrilateral cross-cousin marriage
creates a closed circle of interdependence,
Group A gives women to B and receives them
from C; B gives to C and receives from A;
C gives to A and receives from B. Progeny
price, dowry, and gift giving are means of
more direct, complementary equivalence; so,
B receives women from A and gives other
items of value to A in exchange.*

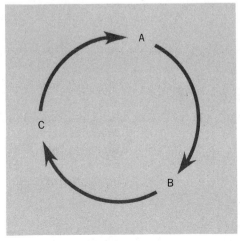

---

[27]Of course there may be more than three kinship groups in the system.

is a member. Endogamy is much less common than exogamy. Unlike exogamy, there is no particular universal type of social group to which the endogamous rule applies. Nevertheless, endogamy is found to some degree in many societies, although the rule is not always explicit and verbalized. It frequently expresses itself as a tendency, without actually being a requirement. It may also apply to any kind of social group. The discussion of incest prohibitions has shown, however, that because of the prevalence of exogamic rules, the application of endogamy to family or clan is most exceptional. Rules of exogamy and endogamy are contradictory and cannot apply simultaneously to the same social group. Endogamous groups must always contain at least two exogamous subgroups within them.

The world's most famous system of endogamy is the caste organization of India, with its two thousand or so castes and subcastes, between which marriage was formally prohibited on the ground that contact with lower castes is ritually polluting for members of upper castes. The new constitution of India attempts to apply Mahatma Gandhi's principles of democratic equality and brotherhood through the legal abolition of castes and caste rules of endogamy, but, as with racial integration in the United States, India still has a long way to go to achieve Gandhi's ideal.[28]

Slightly less than 10 per cent of the world's societies are organized in *demes,* or village communities which tend to be endogamous. The highest proportion of such units of community organization are found in the rain-forest areas of South America. In North America, intravillage endogamy is almost an absolute must among the Pueblo Indians.

While castes are explicitly endogamous, social classes are prone to exhibit similar tendencies without recourse to explicitly prescribed rules. We are all familiar with many

subtle manifestations of this. Its roots are in the desire to retain the exclusive and distinctive qualities of self-regarding in-groups. Intermarriage is a leveler and universalizer of culture and race. In-groups who implicitly feel that their values are too dear to leave open to competition raise the barricade of endogamy. Orthodox Hebrews may not marry Gentiles on pain of banishment from synagogue and family, followed by the performance of mourning rituals for the dead. Stumbling blocks are put in the path of marriage between Catholic and non-Catholic.

Parallel-cousin Marriage   The marriage of a man to his father's brother's daughter is a unique exception to the usual rule of lineage and clan exogamy. It originated among the biblical Semites, who were patrilineal pastoralists; it became firmly fixed among the Arabic Muslims (followers of Islam, the religion founded by Muhammed in the seventh century) and later converts to Islam, such as the Muslims of India and Pakistan. As a preferential, and sometimes prescribed, form of marriage, it requires selection of a wife from within the kinship group. Thus in the King James version of the Old Testament (Num. 36:8–9), it is stated: "And every daughter that possesseth an inheritance in any tribe of the children of Israel, shall be wife unto one of the family [patrilineage] of the tribe of her father, that the children of Israel may enjoy every man of the inheritance of his fathers. Neither shall the inheritance remove from one tribe to another tribe."

And so it was that Jacob, when he followed the orders of Isaac, his father, that he not take a wife from among the daughters of Canaan (where his sons later slaughtered the newly circumcized menfolk of Shalem), but rather marry a daughter of his mother's brother, was marrying within his own patrilineage. The fact that Leah and Rachel were cross-cousins (mother's brother's daughters) was incidental and irrelevant. The significant fact can be readily seen if Jacob's and his

[28]M. Gallanter, "Law and Caste in Modern India" (Asian Survey, 1963), pp. 544–559.

wives' ancestries are traced back to Terah and his sons, Abraham and Nahor. Abraham is Jacob's father's father, through Isaac. Jacob's wives, Leah and Rachel, are direct patrilineal descendants of Terah through Nahor, Bethuel, and Laban (Figure 20-6). Jacob married his father's father's brother's son's son's daughters—all members of the same patrilineage derived from Terah (Gen. 12-30).

Among some Arabs, a man has an absolute right to marry his father's brother's daughter; a girl must marry her father's brother's son unless he explicitly waives his preferential rights in favor of another. For this waiver of his right to his parallel-cousin, he can demand and receive a good payment. What is more, if a girl marries another man without her cousin's permission, he may undertake to kill her or her father, his uncle, if the uncle is the one who arranged her illegal marriage. In West Pakistan, refusal to assent to such a marriage frequently produces intense conflict between brothers. Leach is quite right in suggesting that the Islamic legal specification of large rights of inheritance for a daughter runs counter to the patrilineal principle and that parallel-cousin marriage serves to keep her share of the property within the lineage.[29] R. F. Spencer, and Murphy and Kasdan, suggest that parallel-cousin marriage is a consequence of a low level of political organization among fighting, pastoral predators, who in the absence of a centralized tribal authority need all their manpower and herds to counter the assaults of competitive local lineages. By marrying within, they intensify the solidarity of the fighting male cadres.[30]

Barth demonstrates that among those Kurds who have developed a feudalistic political structure in addition to the lineage one, parallel-cousin marriage is statistically much less frequent. Where moderately adequate politico-economic institutions of a different type supplement the Arabic lineage structure, parallel-cousin marriage becomes functionally less significant and, in fact, much less frequent in occurrence.[31] Patai's report shows that modernized city Arabs, for whom the lineage increasingly loses its significance, are rapidly reducing the practice of cousin-right to a vestigial custom, as its functional reasons for existence dissolve.

The powerful insistence on parallel-cousin marriage among the Muslims reinforces the

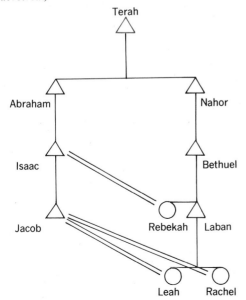

Fig. 20-6   Patrilateral parallel-cousin marriage among the pastoral Hebrews of the Old Testament. The patrilineage of Terah, showing the prescribed marriage of Isaac to his patrilateral cousin Rebekah, and of their son Jacob to his parallel-cousins Leah and Rachel. (This diagram is limited to the male offspring through whom the line of descent devolved.)

[29]E. R. Leach, *Rethinking Anthropology*, p. 110.

[30]R. F. Spencer, "The Arabian Matriarchate: An Old Controversy" (*Southwestern Journal of Anthropology*, vol. 8, 1952), pp. 481–490; R. F. Murphy and L. Kasdan, "The Structure of Parallel Cousin Marriage" (*American Anthropologist*, vol. 61, 1959), pp. 17–29.

[31]F. Barth, "Father's Brother's Daughter Marriage in Kurdistan" (*Southwestern Journal of Anthropology*, vol. 10, 1954), pp. 164–171.

principle that the incest tabu is largely non-biological in nature. When there are impelling reasons for marriage within the culturally defined kinship group, they may even negate the normal exogamic tendencies.

Affinal, Substitution, or Continuation Marriage

Much more pervasive than the general rules of endogamy are the rules of preferential marriage that bring about exogamous marriages between in-laws, hence called *affinal marriages,* or marriages to relatives through marriage. To identify such marriages as affinal, as is the usual practice of American and English anthropologists, is to emphasize the form of the marriage. The Dutch anthropologists, who have given more weight to the functional aspects of such marriages, call them *substitution* or *continuation marriages,* for their function is to continue the relationship between the two kinship groups of the original marriage partners and to hold the children of the original marriage within the extended family.

The Levirate   Marriage of a woman to her brother-in-law, known as the *levirate* (L. *levir,* brother-in-law), is the most popular affinal marriage form among the peoples of the world. Under the simple levirate, the marriage occurs only after the death of the husband, when the widow is inherited by the dead man's brother. In the case of the *junior levirate,* only a younger brother may be the inheritor. This practice occurs in all parts of the world among peoples of the most diverse levels of cultural development. The Stone Age Australians made it a rule; the biblical Hebrews approved of it; and the civilized Incas provided for the inheritance of all a man's secondary wives by his younger brother or perhaps by his sons. An Inca first wife never remarried. She was supported by the state, if necessary, with a widow's pension proffered by an effective social security system.

Whether the young man who finds himself with his brother's widow on his hands likes it or not depends partly on personalities but also on cultural determinants. The Comanche inheritor of a widow was apt to look on this inheritance as a right and a privilege, especially since the widow might not marry another man without that person's obtaining a quitclaim from the heir. And that required a consideration—a horse or two, or perhaps some blankets. In other cases there is no element of choice for the collateral heir. The woman is his, willy-nilly. Her family has a claim on him as much as he has a claim on her. His family also has a voice, as in the case of a Shoshone Indian who in 1933 was forced to divorce the wife of his own choice in order to marry his dead brother's wife. His people wanted to keep the girl in the family, and the laws of Idaho do not permit a man to have two wives.

The purpose of the levirate is not hard to discern. It effects a continuation of the link between the two kinship groups that was established through the original marriage. It is a manifestation of the intergroup character of marriage in that the defunct husband's kin have the privilege and right to prevent the widow from leaving their group. Her obligation is not only to the man she married but also to his kin. Of equal importance, in view of the fact that in primitive society the children usually follow the mother when a home is broken, the children are not lost to the father's group. On the other hand, the claims of the widow's kin upon the group of the defunct husband are maintained in the substitution of a brother. The situation is one of balanced reciprocity.

The Sororate   As in the levirate, where a living brother takes the place of the dead father in a bereaved household, so in the sororate a sister is substituted for the mother. Therefore, in the sororate a bereaved husband marries his deceased wife's sister. From the woman's angle, a girl marries her dead sister's husband.

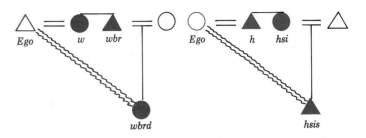

Fig. 20-7   Left, wife's brother's daughter marriage in a patrilineal system represents the secondary affinal marriage. Wife and wife's brother's daughter belong to the same lineage. Right, husband's sister's son marriage in a matrilineal system. Husband and husband's sister's son belong to the same lineage.

The sororate goes hand in hand with the levirate; each is the complement of the other. It is observed by virtually every tribe of North America outside of the Pueblo area and is widely distributed throughout the world.

The common mistake of confusing the sororate with *sororal polygyny* should be avoided. Under the true sororate, a man is married to only one sister at a time. Under sororal polygyny, he does not wait for the death of his wife to marry her younger sister; he takes her when she becomes of age.

Extended Affinal Marriages   In a few societies, if a sibling is not directly available within the immediate conjugal-natal family for substitution for a husband or wife and if there is not an available cousin who stands in the brother or sister category, a substitute from an older or younger generation may be taken. This results in such practices as (1) marriage of a man to his wife's brother's daughter, (2) marriage of a woman to her father's sister's husband, and (3) marriage of a woman to her husband's sister's son (see Figure 20-7). Wife's-brother's-daughter marriage is an extension of the sororate principle to another generation. Such extensions are limited to societies in which the unilineal principle of descent is strong, and each type of marriage is closely related to the kind of unilinealism that prevails.

Thus, in a patrilineal system, a girl automatically belongs to the same clan as her father's sister (her paternal aunt). She has the same clan identity as her aunt, and her individuality is submerged in the corporate identity. She

steps up to represent her unilineal group in the continuation of the marital alliance.

On the other hand, in a matrilineal system, a boy automatically belongs to the same clan as his mother's brother (his maternal uncle). He has the same clan identity as his maternal uncle, and his individuality is submerged in the corporate identity of the maternal kinship group. He steps forward to represent his unilineal group in the continuation of the marital alliance (see Crow Kinship System, pages 462–463).

Marriage with extended affinal relatives is not common; only a small minority of societies find it worth bothering with or necessary to fall back upon. But in a strong unilineal system inclined to generalize the principle of clan identity, such marriages follow logically enough.[32]

Modes of Marriage

We have thus far been concerned with the matter of whom one may or may not marry. The next question is: "How does a man get a wife, or a woman, a husband?" Very few societies leave it to individuals who are to be married to decide for themselves. The near-anarchy of American practice in this respect is most exceptional, although it represents a discernibly increasing trend in many parts of the world as the acids of "modernity" corrode the old kinship bonds. Most marriages

[32]See L. A. White, "A Problem in Kinship Terminology" (*American Anthropologist*, vol. 41, 1939), pp. 569–570.

either are still arranged by the families concerned or involve family consent and participation. For this reason, to understand marriage at all, and primitive marriage especially, it is necessary to grasp this basic principle: *marriage constitutes an alliance between two kinship groups in which the couple concerned is merely the most conspicuous link.* Every man learns, sooner or later, that when he marries the "one and only," he marries not only her but all her relatives as well. Brides, of course, have the same experience.

In spite of what aspirant youth may feel about it, marriage is not a concern of the marrying pair alone. Society at large has its stake in the affair and what ensues from it. The families of the principals to a marriage have their very direct interests in its many ramifications.

Thus, of the seven formalized modes of acquiring a wife, only two (marriage by capture and marriage by elopement) do not heavily involve the active participation of the kinship groups of the bride and groom. The seven modes are (1) by progeny price, or bride wealth; (2) by suitor service; (3) by gift exchange; (4) by capture; (5) by inheritance; (6) by elopement; and (7) by adoption.

Progeny Price   In the primitive world, the formal exchange of goods of value for the offspring a woman is expected to produce is the normal, or most usual, method of getting a wife. *Progeny price* was found to prevail in virtually all tribes of Negro Africa, where 214 of 238 (90 per cent) of those listed in the *Ethnographic Atlas* practice it, usually in the form of payment of cattle, called *lobola* after the Bantu term. Taking the world as a whole, well over half (58 per cent) of all societies in the *Atlas* expect progeny price to be paid to the family of the bride by the kin of the groom.

It must not be assumed that the payment of progeny price for a woman means that women are degraded slaves to be sold from the auction block of a marriage mart—a sordid

commercial commodity.[33] A commercial element necessarily colors the institution, for, after all, a family with five daughters and one son for whom a bride must be acquired is economically better off than the family with one daughter and five sons to be provided for. But women are not fluid goods in a free market.

Nor does the occurrence of progeny price mean that the position of woman in terms of prestige, privilege, power, and labor is necessarily high or low. It does mean, however, that women as progenitors have value as members of the kinship group. The value of a woman in terms of progeny price is determined by a compound of the social and economic status of the groom's family balanced against that of the bride's family. In some instances, the personal qualities of the bride and groom may also be factors.

The social prestige of a married woman is directly influenced by the amount of the progeny price that has been paid on her account. A twenty-cow wife in East Africa has a definite advantage in any argument with a woman on whose account only ten cows have been given. Among the Yuroks of California, this was so fixed that the social status and wergild of a man were determined absolutely by the progeny price paid for his mother.

Progeny price may be in part compensation for the loss of the girl by her kinship group, but it is much more an act of compensation to that group for its loss of a legal claim to the children that she will bear. Two facts make this clear. The transference of progeny price is closely correlated with patrilineal-descent systems and residence of the married couple with the groom's kin. Again referring to Murdock's comparative data, we learn that of 217 societies demanding progeny price, all but 18 are virilocal. Of the 18 nonvirilocal

---

[33]The Native Administration Act of 1927, Union of South Africa, in recognition of the importance of progeny price in native society, expressly forbade any court from setting aside *lobola* or *bogadi* as "repugnant to natural law." J. Lewin, *Studies in African Native Law,* p. 57.

societies, only 6 are uxorilocal.[34] Clearly, the loss of the woman's children from the residential seat of her kin is a factor that must be balanced by reciprocal payment of other items of value. But beyond this, there is the circumstance that virilocal residence tends strongly to generate patrilineality. Although the wife does not become a member of her husband's unilineal group, her children do. In patrilineal societies, therefore, each marriage of a woman means that her lineage suffers a loss of all the progeny that may be born through her. For this sacrifice, it expects and receives redress. Patrilineal kinship groups and progeny price show a high phi correlation at 0.412, while matrilineal kinship groups and progeny price show a negative correlation of −0.112.

That it is in exchange for a quitclaim, so to speak, on posterity rather than for the bride herself that the progeny price is demanded may be seen more clearly in the fact that an implicit warranty of the fertility of the bride is part of the transaction. It is therefore a common expectancy among Africans that the bride's family must substitute a younger sister without charge if no issue is forthcoming from the first daughter for whom they have received progeny price. As an alternative, the sum of the progeny price must be refunded. This is often difficult, however, because the capital received in payment for the daughter may already have been invested in the purchase of a wife for a son. Thus, it has been reported (for the Thonga, for instance) that the family may be required to surrender their son's wife to their son-in-law in lieu of their barren daughter. These same requirements hold if the married daughter deserts her husband, who has paid for her.

Establishment of Jural Rights   Linton's report on the Vezo Sakalava of Madagascar shows

to what extent progeny price is actually the establishment of a jural, or a legally effective, right to children among these people. In the case of divorce, neither a refund of the cattle paid nor the substitution of another woman is socially permissible. The divorced wife may remarry, but only with her former husband's permission. This will be forthcoming upon agreement by the wife and her new husband-to-be that the first children born to them (up to the limit of three) will be deeded over to the first husband, who is the one who paid the progeny price to her family. The woman nurses and keeps the children until weaning, whereupon they are turned over to her first husband and become his legal heirs without the formality of adoption.[35] All this illustrates another basic principle to be referred to in more detail later on: *among primitives, jural fatherhood is generally of more significance than biological fatherhood.* A nice Sakalava refinement is that although legally a divorced husband may demand a refund, good form does not countenance it. That would be putting material values above human values. Such a man would put cattle above children.

Finally, among the Bavenda of South Africa and other tribes, if the progeny price is paid in installments, the children do not pass to the husband's kinship group until the sum is paid in full.

An interesting twist to progeny price as a means of obtaining offspring is found among the Dahomeans of West Africa. Here a married woman may arrange for a second wife for her husband as a means of providing him with children. These children call their sire's first wife "father" because she, after all, is the one who paid for them.[36] This may seem to be carrying the principle of sociological father-

[34]A. D. Coult and R. W. Habenstein, *Cross Tabulations of Murdock's World Ethnographic Sample*, p. 378. The phi for progeny price/virilocality is 0.391; for progeny price/uxorilocality, it is 0.192, and for avunculocality, 0.055.

[35]R. Linton, *The Tanala* (Field Museum of Natural History, Anthropological Series, vol. 22, 1933). For numerous like examples from Africa, see M. D. W. Jeffrys, "Lobola Is Child-price" (*African Studies*, vol. 10, 1951), pp. 145–184.
[36]M. J. Herskovits, "A Note on 'Woman Marriage' in Dahomey" (*Africa*, vol. 10, 1937), pp. 335–341. The term "father," incidentally, in its more exact meaning, should be understood as "person who paid the progeny price."

hood a bit far, but who can deny that it is logical? In one form or another, this practice is not uncommon among the patrilineal tribes of Africa.

Progeny price as a social institution cannot be comprehended unless it is viewed also in terms of its functional effects in cementing the links in the web of kinship that makes possible the expansion of the scope of society.. Social groups are often in opposition to one another, disputing, quarreling, even feuding and fighting. Intermarriage imposes a check on the disruptive tendencies of intergroup conflict. Marriage alone tends to exert a tranquilizing effect in this direction, but it takes more than marriage in and of itself adequately to achieve cohesion. Progeny price involves a number of kinsmen in a network of economic obligations and expectancies. Many more than just the husband, on the one side, and the bride's parents, on the other, are drawn into the activity. The distribution of marriage cattle among the Nuer, previously discussed under "Economic Organization," is a concrete example of the broad network of persons involved. Figure 17-2 shows the range of relatives concerned with the progeny price (see page 348).

Suitor Service   A cheap, but not easy, way to obtain a wife and rights to her children is to work for them. Jacob put in seven years of labor to win the hand of Rachel, plus seven for Leah, who was not part of his bargain. Among the Siberian Chukchi, Koryak, and Yukaghir tribes, service for the bride is the regular practice; it seems to have replaced progeny price, which was the earlier form for acquisition of a wife.

Scattered tribes in all parts of the world have been found to require service in the bride's household as the price the groom must pay (77 out of 565 cultures).[37] Many of these tribes allow no alternative, but in others, suitor service is simply a substitute for pay-

ment of the progeny price, similar to the arrangement by which a vagrant washes dishes to pay for his meal.

The obligation of a son-in-law to work for his wife's parents may be an enduring responsibility. Although the Comanche Indians did not require outright suitor service, a son-in-law was expected to send a good share of the game he slew to the tipi of his mother-in-law. This was why parents wanted their daughter to marry a good hunter. A son-in-law did not have to do this, but he was a good son-in-law if he did and a poor one if he did not. His reward was a younger daughter as his second wife. But no meat, no second daughter.

Gift Exchange   In cultures in which descent is not exclusively vested in any particular line of kinsman (i.e., bilateral descent), there is little likelihood of payment of progeny price (phi = −0.349). Equivalent exchanges of gifts between the families are an alternative possibility.

When gift exchanges are customarily equal, no one comes out ahead. This is the case with the Cheyenne Indians. A boy who has set his heart on a particular girl talks it over with his family. If they think the choice is a good one, after taking into consideration not only the qualities of the girl but also the character of her family, they muster their nicest transferable possessions to place at the disposal of the young swain. These are carefully loaded on a fine horse. They then call upon a respected old woman to lead the horse to the tipi of the girl's elder brother. There she stakes it out for all the camp to see, while she enters the lodge to press the suit of her protégé. The elder brother calls in his cousins for a family conclave. If they decide that the proposal is acceptable, they unload the horse and distribute the gifts among themselves, the brother taking the horse. All then disperse to their separate lodges to rustle up what each will offer as a return gift. Each is expected to bring back in the next day or two

[37]Coult and Habenstein, *op. cit.,* p. 424.

something equal in value to what he has received. In the meantime, the bride is made beautiful, and when all is ready, she is mounted on a good horse, the presents are loaded on another, and the old woman is called upon to lead the bride and the gift horse back to the groom's tipi. There she is received by all his family, and her accompanying gifts are distributed among them in accordance with what they gave. So far as economic value goes, they are exactly where they were before.

Perhaps we can understand the social function of such activity better if we reemphasize the elaborate American gift exchanges at Christmas. The amount of energy, trouble, and effort that goes into acquiring and distributing suitable gifts is immense, and the results are frequently discouraging. As often as not, we end up with a collection of items we would just as soon do without. Nevertheless, in the exchange we reaffirm and bind anew the friendships and relationships we value or find desirable.

It may come as a shock to those who enter into the elaborate wedding gift giving institutionalized in American culture to learn that equivalent exchange of gifts at marriage is actually the rare exception, not the rule. Only 82 out of 860 cultures provide for it.[38] The fact that it is negatively correlated with patrilineal (phi = −0.014) and matrilineal (phi = −0.007) societies reinforces the point that progeny price is compensation for loss of jural rights over the children who are to be forthcoming from a marriage. (Because gift exchange is so infrequent, however, the phi correlations given here have low levels of statistical significance.)

Capture Novelists and romanticists formerly wrote of the days when the cave man was supposed to beat his beloved into insensibility with a knobby club and then drag her by her flowing hair to his lair, where she forthwith became his loving wife. When

anthropology was young, serious consideration was given to this fantasy as the earliest method of getting a wife. Indeed, marriage by capture was the first premise underlying the theory of social evolution put forth by the Scottish anthropologist J. F. McLennan a hundred years ago.[39] Suitors' trials and sham battles at marriage were thought to be symbolic survivals of the scuffles that accompanied the abduction of the feminine prize.

Mock capture is a real and not uncommon practice. When a young Bushman and his bride are to be married, the folk gather from all around to join in the wedding feast. In the midst of the meal, the groom seizes the bride. This is the signal for all her relatives to grab their dibbles and set to beating him. A minor battle royal takes place among the guests while the groom receives his drubbing. If he can keep his hold on the girl, he succeeds in his marriage. If he lets go under the hail of blows, he loses her.[40]

The African Bahima subject the bride to a tug of war between her clan and the groom's, which always wins. When the final pull is given in the groom's favor, the bride is hustled to a cowhide and lifted from the ground by the groom's cohorts, who rush off with her, chased by friends and relatives.[41]

Of course, the hilarious horseplay that climaxes our own weddings and the escape of the bride and groom in a cloud of exhaust smoke (provided a spark plug has not been removed) are cut of the same cloth. If this is not a survival of bride capture, what then is it? Modern anthropology prefers a functional to a pseudo-historical explanation. More properly, it is to be understood as a symbolic expression of latent and repressed hostilities of the two marrying families. True, they are to be allied in marriage, but alliance is possible only where differences exist. Alliance always involves a measure of antagonistic

---

[38]Bourguignon and Greenbaum, *op. cit.*, p. 3.

[39]J. F. McLennan, *Primitive Marriage.*
[40]G. W. Stow, *The Native Races of South Africa,* p. 96.
[41]J. Roscoe, *The Northern Bantu,* vol. 2, p. 256.

Fig. 20-8 Marriage is an incorporation rite among the Karamojong, Kenya, in East Africa. The groom presents at least one animal—a cow, sheep, goat, or donkey—to each of the bride's close relatives. In return, he receives their pledge of future support for himself and the family he is about to found. After the bartering, the bride is dragged, with mock protestations, from the hut where she has been hiding (top left). At the groom's village, the co-wives and sisters-in-law of the bride each present a neckwire to the bride, then smear her with milk fat (top right). The bride is hazed by the women, including the girls of her huband's group (bottom left). She carries a ridiculously small pot which she must steady on her head as if she were a clumsy novice who cannot carry a pot as a proper wife should. To emphasize her low status as the newest female member of her affinal group, the pot is repeatedly knocked from her head with sticks. A mock attack with switches upon the bride and her attendants by the boys of the groom's village completes the ritualistic pattern (bottom right). (Rada and Neville Dyson-Hudson, **Natural History.***)*

cooperation. Common interests must dominate any alliance, or it will not be forged. Yet the antagonisms are felt, unconsciously or otherwise. The bride-giving family resents the successful intrusion of the suitor, and they are given the ritual opportunity of letting him know it in a harmless way. Thereby, the deep emotions of resentment are drawn off. Likewise, any feeling that the swain is considered unworthy of the precious daughter may be dispelled by forcing him to prove his worth.

All this is not to contend that marriage by capture does not exist. It does. But we must realize that it could never have been *the* prevailing technique in any supposed stage of human history. Rather, it is a supplementary way of getting a wife. Its advantage is that it is cheap and adventuresome, if risky. On the other hand, its disadvantages, aside from risk, are heavy. Since marriage is an alliance between kinship groups, capturing a wife brings none of the advantages that are to be derived from such an alliance. There are no wife's relatives to back a man up or contribute their share of property. The man who captures his wives will therefore be at a disadvantage, compared with the man who has gotten his by reciprocal means. His children will not have the advantages and status that his wife's family might bestow, and if his sole wife is from an alien tribe, his children will not be raised in the pure tradition of his own culture.

Plains Indian warriors, like the men of many another primitive tribe, did capture and mate with alien women. Many are the nations who have considered women the legitimate prize of war. However, unless a man is poorly off, he first marries a girl of his own tribe in the regular manner. His captured wives are secondary additions to his household: his concubines and his wife's household drudges. Here, as elsewhere, the position of the captive woman may be closer to that of a slave than of a true wife.

Again and again, we find that the abduction of women is the cause of bitter wars and annihilations. Helen of Troy may be the most fa-

mous such *bella causus belli*, but she was neither the first nor the last among her sex.

Inheritance Inheritance of widows through the operation of the levirate and filial inheritance is of course of extreme importance as a form of marriage. However, nothing further need be added here to what we have already said on this subject except to note that the Palvic and Bura tribes of northern Nigeria allow a man to inherit his grandfather's wives.

Filial Inheritance Attention has already been called to the Inca practice of permitting a brother or a son to inherit the secondary wives of a dead man. Inheritance of the wives of his father, none of whom was his uterine mother, is also known to have been practiced by the Caribs of South America and by a number of African tribes. Filial inheritance is obviously possible only where there is polygamous marriage. It also serves to keep the women in the family.

Elopement Elopement is a safety valve. It is one of those saving cultural forms whose function is to provide an acceptable byroad for escape from the dictates of formal custom. Marriage, as we have seen, is never left open to the untrammeled choice of the marrying individuals. There are incest and exogamic prohibitions; there are the limitations of preferential mating; and there are the personal prejudices of family members to be considered. On the other hand, there is love. Few people are so given to romantic love as Americans, who in individualistic sentimentalism exalt the ideal of marriage based on love—that mysterious psychophysiological reaction. Although many primitive cultures do not allow very much weight to love in marriage (indeed, many seem to ignore it entirely), the fact is that all primitives have their amorous likes and aversions, too.

From the evidence, it would appear that elopements take place in every known society. When familial or social disapproval blocks a fervently desired marriage, or when a planned marriage with a distasteful partner is about to be forced on the unwilling one, elopement is a way out. The tribes which require that elders and relatives seek the consent of marriageable youths to the arrangements they plan for them are surely a minority among mankind. This makes a general human necessity of the path of elopement.

Of course, the existence of a formal rule does not mean that it will always be insisted upon. Cheyenne men held the legal right to dispose of their sisters as they wished. But as Calf Woman put it, "Kindhearted brothers always found out how their sisters felt about it before they promised them to any man."

It is difficult to formulate a generalization concerning the status of elopement marriages. Among the Cheyennes, the elopement would ultimately be recognized as a marriage and be validated by gift exchanges only if the pair ran off before the girl had actually been engaged by her brother to another man. It was a different matter if the promise had already been made. In several Cheyenne cases, brothers committed suicide when their sisters eloped after they had been promised to someone else.[42]

In parts of the Pacific area, the tendency to *cultural orthogenesis* resulted in elopement becoming the *regular* way of getting married. This was the situation in a number of Australian tribes. According to the reports of Howitt,[43] elopement became the *reductio ad absurdum* of overdeveloped marriage rules among the Kurnai tribe. Broad rules of exogamy combined with narrow rules of localized mating (i.e., the mate had to be taken from a specific band) to narrow strictly the field of legitimate choice. Old men dominated the society and had the first choice of young girls. Matters were so carefully controlled that a boy could scarcely find a girl whom he would be permitted to marry. Fortunately for the

Kurnai, they made "pretend rules" of these principles. Most marriages of young couples were by elopement, and customarily medicine men were expected to help them escape. What then? The righteous citizenry (most of whom married in just this way) were terrible in their anger. A posse of vigilantes set forth to do social justice. The couple fled to a traditional asylum. If they were overtaken, they were cruelly wounded and could be killed. Once at the place of asylum, however, they were safe. They stayed there until a baby was born. Then they could return home to face a softer music, for they would merely be given a beating and then be accepted as legitimately married.

Adoption   In Indonesia and modern Japan, a man may obtain a wife by being adopted into her family.[44] It is a device by which a patrilineally organized family may maintain its line when there are no sons. By legal fiction, the son-in-law thus becomes a "son" in his wife's family, and his children belong to her family and not his. A peculiar aspect of this device is that technically the groom's bride becomes his own "sister." It is necessary that the people close their eyes to this bit of logic, for that, of course, would be incest. Convenience masters logic, and the husband is a "son" of his father-in-law for purposes of reckoning descent. The adoption of a girl to become a son's wife in Taiwan has already been discussed in detail.

Fictive Marriage

Forms of fictive marriage occur occasionally. Among them are the special practices of the Kwakiutl and the Nuer. In the case of the Kwakiutl the inheritance of chiefly prerogatives passes from a titled man to his grandson through his son-in-law, the grandson's

[42]K. N. Llewellyn and E. A. Hoebel, *The Cheyenne Way*, chap. 9.

[43]A. W. Howitt, *The Native Tribes of South-east Australia*, pp. 273ff.

[44]B. ter Haar, *Adat Law in Indonesia*, pp. 175–176; and J. F. Embree, *The Japanese Nation*, p. 162.

father. It is not possible for the titles to pass to succeeding generations through the chief's sons directly. If there are no daughters, such inheritance could be blocked for lack of a son-in-law. Boas wrote:

In such a case a man who desires to acquire the use of a crest and the other privileges connected with the name performs a sham marriage with the son of the bearer of the name. . . . The ceremony is performed in the same manner as a real marriage. In case the bearer of the name has no children at all, a sham marriage with a part of his body is performed, with his right or left side, a leg or an arm, and the privileges are conveyed in the same manner as in the case of a real marriage.[45]

The son-in-law acquired the titles and then begot children by a second wife. These children were able to inherit from their jural grandfather.

In the Trobriand Islands the leader of a chiefly clan (*guyau*) who wishes to link a commoner clan (*tokay*) to himself may, in the absence of a suitable girl, "marry" a man, who becomes known as a *tokwava* (male wife). Through him the customary *urigubu* payments of yams[46] can be made in redistributive exchange (see pages 346–349).

We have already seen how strong the ties of kinship are among the Nuer, as expressed in progeny-price exchanges. So important is the maintenance of lineage inheritance that the Nuers often rely on what they call *ghost marriage* to give offspring to a male, man or boy, who has died without begetting heirs. For it is necessary to "keep green" the name of a man whose position in the lineage structure is important. In such an instance, one of his "brothers" (from a kinship line that is overstocked or less important) marries a woman on behalf of the dead man or, as they say, "to the name of his brother." This man lives with the woman as in any ordinary conjugal family

except that *he* is not married to her. The children that he begets take their place in the lineage as the offspring of their ghost father; they inherit accordingly and receive and give progeny price and wergild in like manner.[47]

The Nuer also have a form of "wife marriage" that differs from that already noted for the Dahomeans (page 411). Among the Nuer, a woman who is beyond childbearing age may sometimes use the cattle that belonged to her dead husband to set up a marriage between a man and woman in the name of her husband and herself. The children of such a marriage then belong to her deceased husband and herself, and they inherit accordingly.

In another Nuer variant, an old woman whose lineage is about to die out because she has no living paternal relatives may, if she has the requisite cattle for the progeny price, marry a woman to the name of a dead man of her lineage. Then she invites some unrelated male to have intercourse with the "ghost bride," thus legally establishing a line of heirs.

Pushing the use of fiction to its ultimate, the Nuer give a barren woman the status of a male. After all, has she not demonstrated that she is lacking in the essential attribute of the female? In exceptional cases, then, a wife may be married to her name. That is, a marriage between a man and woman is arranged in which the *man* is the legal substitute for the barren woman in question. The children belong to her name, which means, because she is accorded the status of a male, that they take their patrilineal descent from her, so closing a link in the patrilineal lineage.[48]

---

[45]F. Boas, *Social Organization and Secret Societies of the Kwakiutl*, p. 359.

[46]H. A. Powell, "Competitive Leadership in Trobriand Political Organization," in R. Cohen and J. Middleton (eds.), *Comparative Political Systems*, p. 177.

[47]Compare the ancient Hebrew practice spelled out in the Old Testament: "If brethen dwell together, and one of them die, and have no son, the wife of the dead shall not be married without [the lineage] unto a stranger: her husband's brother shall go in unto her, and take her to him as a wife, and perform the duty of a husband's brother unto her.

"And it shall be, that the first born which she beareth shall succeed in the name of his brother which is dead, that his name be not put out of Israel" (Deut. 25:5–6).

[48]P. P. Howell, *A Manual of Nuer Law*, pp. 74–75.

Fig. 20-9   Wedding preparation for a Masai girl in Kenya. Iron wire, prepared by Masai blacksmiths, is wound around her left leg to complete her married status decorations. The coils on her arms and the right leg have already been put on. (Courtesy of the American Museum of Natural History.)

Professor Paul Bohannan prefers that these arrangements not be viewed as marriages at all, since in some instances no man is joined with a woman.[49] This is true of the Kwakiutl case and of several of the Nuer practices that emphasize the importance of passing jural and property rights from one generation to another through the production of jural offspring. In these situations, however, the arrangement is treated as if it were a marriage, and the social and legal consequences of a regular marriage flow from it even though the marriage be fictive.

Divorce and the Dissolution of Marriage

In spite of the desire of kinsmen to retain the marriage link, primitive marriages are brittle

[49]See P. Bohannan, *Social Anthropology*, p. 77.

things. Romance and individual desire may not play so great a role in determining the choice of a first partner as they do with us, but they are permitted more sway in the shifting of mates after marriage. Only a small proportion of marriages among primitives are for life.

Hobhouse, Wheeler, and Ginsberg found in their study that of 271 tribes, only 4 per cent forbid divorce; 24 per cent allow it for specific causes; 72 per cent permit it on the basis of mutual consent based on incompatibility or whim.[50] The sample may not be statistically perfect. Nevertheless, the results just quoted are probably not too far from accurate fact.

Aside from the economic arrangements that may have to be untangled where a high progeny price was paid or a rich dowry given, divorce does not entail such difficulties among the primitives as it does in Western society. The first reason rests in the fact that although religious ritual may enter into the marriage ceremonies, marriage is hardly a religious affair. In addition, the problem of the care and disposition of the children is more easily handled. Ordinarily, they go with the mother. It has already been noted that sociological fatherhood is more significant to primitive man than biological paternity.

There is little evidence on record to indicate that when the primitive mother remarries, the emotional transition for the children is difficult. If the mother does not remarry right away, it is easy for her and her brood to settle among her relatives, for the tribal community is small and she has not been far from her kin at any time. If she is a captive from an alien tribe, she probably remarries without delay. Unmarried adult women are unthinkable to most primitive people.

The prevalence of wife stealing is another important unsettling factor. In societies in which sexual competition among the men is a means of attaining social status, no home is

[50]L. T. Hobhouse, G. C. Wheeler, and M. Ginsberg, *The Material Culture and Social Institutions of the Simpler Peoples*, p. 164.

truly safe. Eskimos may cooperate economically, but they engage in violent competition for women. To steal another's wife and get away with it proves the abductor a better man than the loser. The risk is great, however, because the husband, if half a man, will attempt to murder the absconder. A would-be wife taker often anticipates this by killing the husband first and marrying the widow afterward.

In the 1920s, Knud Rasmussen visited a village of Musk Ox Eskimos in Canada. He found that every adult male in the community had been involved in a murder centering about wife stealing.[51]

Special practices, such as the licensed wife stealing of the Crow Indians, may also break up the family. This is a phase of competition between two rival military associations, the Foxes and the Knobby Sticks. Each spring one or another of the fraternities is privileged to capture any wife of a member of the other fraternity, provided she has had premarital sexual relations with the captor. The husband may not resist the abduction or take his wife back. The triumph of the kidnaping fraternity is supreme.

Cheyennes and other Plains tribesmen considered it a great feat ceremonially to throw away wives at a special dance. The Cheyenne warrior tossed a stick among the male spectators, and whoever was struck by it had to marry his wife, if only for a day.

Until recently, anthropologists were of the opinion that men were allowed more leeway than women in the matter of divorce. However, a cross-cultural survey by Murdock invalidates this conclusion. Among forty objectively selected cultures from all parts of the world, it was impossible in three-fourths of the sample for Murdock to detect any substantial difference in the rights of men and women to terminate an unsatisfactory marriage. Six cultures, it is true, stack the cards in favor of the men. But on the other hand, four cultures allow superior privileges to the women as regards divorce. Insofar as the right to get divorced is concerned, Murdock concludes that "the stereotype of the oppressed aboriginal woman proved to be a complete myth."[52] Matrilineal descent, plus residence in the locality of the wife's kin, strengthens the hand of the woman. Among the highly matrilineal Hopi and Zuñi, where women own the houses, a woman can divorce her husband simply by setting his gear outside the door. Any man who comes home and sees his pile of belongings outside the door knows just what it means. It is time to go home to mother.

The causes of divorce and the grounds for it may be two quite different things. Yet it may be illuminating to close this chapter with a listing of what the Ifugao of Luzon consider grounds for divorce:

1. A bad omen of the bile sac of the sacrificial animal at any one of the four feasts of the marriage ritual

2. A bad omen of the bile sac at any of the three principal rice feasts of either family during the first year after the completion of the marriage rituals

3. Barrenness

4. Death of several offspring

5. Permanent sexual disability

6. Unwillingness to perform the sexual act

7. Neglect in time of sickness; "failure to cherish"

8. Insulting language by an in-law

9. Reduction of the area of fields agreed on in the marriage contract

10. Selling of a rice field for insufficient reason and without consent of the other spouse

11. Continued refusal of a father-in-law to deliver the fields called for in the marriage contract when the couple reaches a reasonable age

12. Incurring of unreasonable debts[53]

[51]K. Rasmussen, *Across Arctic America*, p. 250.

[52]G. P. Murdock, "Family Stability in Non-European Cultures" (*The Annals of the American Academy of Political and Social Science*, vol. 272, 1948), pp. 195–201.

[53]R. F. Barton, *Ifugao Law*, pp. 23–24.

SUMMARY

The regulation and channeling of the sex drive and its effects have been of universal and fundamental concern to all human societies. Most societies are not concerned about premarital mating, but all societies limit sexual activities and define sexual and social obligations in marriage.

As a starting point, the prohibition of sexual relations and marriage between culturally identified relatives is universal. It is known as the incest tabu. Except for a few special cases such as permitted incest between divine royalty, brother-sister and parent-child incest is wholly tabu everywhere. Beyond the confines of the conjugal-natal family, the boundaries of the tabu vary with social structure.

Biological explanations of the incest tabu propose that close inbreeding results in eugenically deleterious or even lethal traits. In the operation of natural selection, inbred populations would decrease survival possibilities. Thus, human populations which failed to develop or adopt an incest tabu became extinct. Westermarck offered a more specific version: that children raised in a common household have an instinctive aversion to sexual intimacy with each other. Instinct theories have been rejected by twentieth-century anthropologists largely because they do not satisfactorily account for the variable extension of the incest tabu outside the immediate conjugal-natal family. However, modern population genetics has established that very close inbreeding in a species with slow reproduction rates would result in the production and homozygous establishment of many more deleterious than advantageous mutant genes. Consequently, whatever the original cause for the introduction of the incest tabu, its genetic effects are positive.

The first differentiating effect of social structure on the extension of the incest tabu may be seen in the identification of cousins. When all cousins are classified by the same terms as brother and sister, the tabu extends to them. On the other hand, when kinship terminology distinguishes between parallel- and cross-cousins, marriage with parallel-cousins may be tabued, while marriage to certain cross-cousins may be preferred or required. Cross-cousins are never members of the same lineage or clan; therefore, they are not culturally defined as members of one's kinship group. They need not be tabued. Parallel-cousins may be members of one's kinship group, and when they are, they are tabued.

Malinowski's theory of the incest tabu holds that sexual competition within the family and larger kinship units engenders emotional hostility which is disruptive to kinship solidarity. The tabu exists to prevent destructive disruption of the foundation units of any society. The alliance theory, which finds high favor among anthropologists today, holds that the incest tabu results in exogamy—marriage outside the group. Exogamy, in turn, produces reciprocal ties between kinship groups, enlarging their security base and the scope of their social interaction. Exogamy is necessary to the expansion of society.

Restricted exogamy forbids marriage to certain types of cousins, while permitting (or requiring) it with others. Matrilateral cross-cousin marriage, according to the theory of Lévi-Strauss, enhances social solidarity by relating the kinship groups in a closed circle linked in regular marital alliances of woman givers and woman receivers. Few societies actually practice this kind of preferred marriage, however.

Endogamy runs in the opposite direction from exogamy. It works to preserve social uniqueness by requiring marriage within a defined group—kinship or otherwise. Castes, classes, and religious and racial groups may practice endogamy. *Demes* are local communities which are predominantly endogamous. Parallel-cousin marriage as practiced by the biblical Hebrews and extended into modern times by the followers of Islam is the most notable manifestation of kinship endogamy.

Continuation marriages exist to maintain the alliance bond between two affinal groups of kinsmen. The levirate (marriage to a brother-in-law) and the sororate (marriage to a sister-in-law) are its major forms. Other varieties are marriage to a husband's sister's son, to a wife's brother's daughter, and filial inheritance.

In the acquisition of wives, over half of all societies require the transfer of valuables to the bride's family as progeny price. This compensates her family for the release of their claim to her children as heirs. In virtually all societies practicing progeny price, the children belong to the lineage or clan of the father, and a married woman lives in the abode and location of her husband. In a few instances, suitor service may substitute for progeny price. Reciprocal gift exchange is found in a few bilateral societies.

Wife capture, fantasy notwithstanding, is a rare practice, although dramatized bride capture as a symbolic expression of affinal tensions does have its occurrence in a number of wedding rituals.

Finally, fictive marriages are sporadically entered into in order to provide continuity of inheritance of a family line or to make possible kinship alliances when a person of the proper sex status is not available.

Although there is almost always a strong emphasis on alliance continuity, virtually all societies allow for personal incompatibility and the expression of postmarital preferences through divorce.

SELECTED READINGS

Bohannan, P., and J. Middleton (eds.), *Marriage, Family, and Residence* (1968). A book of readings. Part I, pp. 1–46, consists of two very useful papers on the incest question.

Dumont, L., "Marriage Alliance" (*International Encyclopedia of the Social Sciences*, vol. 10, 1968), pp. 19–23. Provides a more detailed but not overly technical view of the theory of marital alliance.

Evans-Pritchard, E. E., *Kinship and Marriage among the Nuer* (1951). An authoritative study based upon detailed knowledge of a tribe of cattle raisers in the African Sudan.

de Josselin de Jong, J. P. B., *Lévi-Strauss's Theory of Kinship and Marriage* (1952, 1970). A much more detailed précis of Lévi-Strauss's theory, expressed in reasonably understandable terms.

Marshall, G. A., "Marriage: Comparative Analysis" (*International Encyclopedia of the Social Sciences*, vol. 10, 1968), pp. 8–19. A brief, contemporary statement.

Radcliffe-Brown, A. R., and D. Forde (eds.), *African Systems of Kinship and Marriage* (1950). Synoptic analyses of nine African marriage and kinship systems.

Schapera, I., *Married Life in a South African Tribe* (1950). Old and new ways in the setting of South Africa.

ter Haar, B., *Adat Law in Indonesia* (1948), chap. 9, "Marriage Law." Gives a straightforward exposition of basic marriage forms as they occur in Indonesia.

Westermarck, E., *The History of Human Marriage* (1925). Although the theoretical system of this work has been long outdated, it contains a wealth of very useful descriptive material on marriage practices around the world.

Chapter 21

The Family

Marriage establishes the conjugal-natal family, a group consisting of mated spouses and their offspring. Marriage defines sets of statuses and related roles and expectancies governing the relations of the conjugal-natal group as spouses, parents, offspring, and siblings. It defines their statuses and roles in relation to wider groups of kinsmen and to the wider world of nonkinsmen. Marriage, it will be remembered from the previous chapter, is the institution; the family is the group, or body of personnel, whose actions are designed to fulfill the aims of the institution.

Functions of the Family

M. J. Levy, Jr., and L. A. Fallers suggest that the functions of the family may be grouped in four categories: (1) sexual, (2) reproductive, (3) economic, and (4) educational.[1] More explicitly, the functions of the family may be stated as follows: (1) The institutionalization of mating and the channeling of sexual outlets, thus establishing a legal father for a woman's children and a legal mother for a man's children; each acquires a "monopoly" in the sexuality of the other. (2) The nurture and basic enculturation of the young in an atmosphere of intimacy, preparing them to accept the statuses that will come to them as the jural heirs of their established parents and kinsmen. (3) The organization of a complementary division of labor between spouses, allocating to each certain rights in the labor of the other and in such goods or property as they may acquire through their individual or joint efforts. (4) The linkage of each spouse and the offspring within the wider network of kinsmen: the establishment of relationships of descent and affinity. These functions are universally performed by the family as a social unit. Other social arrangements may also exist wherein these functions are performed, such as the matrilateral group (pages 435–436), in which the mother's brother either displaces the father or takes on some of the functions normally performed by the father in the conjugal-natal family. Matrilateral groups are, however, relatively rare.

The family, in one form or another, is the primary unit of human culture and sociality. In the words of Marion Levy, Jr.:

1. There is no known case of a society lacking families as subsystems thereof.
2. There is no known society in terms of which initial placement of individuals fails to be in family terms—and almost certainly overwhelmingly, if not exclusively, in family terms.
3. There is no known society in terms of which not only initial but a substantial part of the basic learning—that is, the learning institutionally expected to be shared by all or virtually all the members of a given society—is not learned in a family context for the vast majority of the members of the society.[2]

In many societies, the sex drive may be legitimately satisfied prior to marriage; in such cases, there would be no reason for the individual to take on the responsibilities of marriage if sex gratification alone were a function of the family.

The care of infants and children is the matter of overriding concern. The rather casual interest of primitive societies in the

---

[1] M. J. Levy, Jr., and L. A. Fallers, "The Family: Some Comparative Considerations" (*American Anthropologist*, vol. 61, 1959), pp. 647–651.

[2] M. J. Levy, Jr., "Notes on the Hsu Hypothesis," in F. L. K. Hsu (ed.), *Kinship and Culture*, p. 34.

question of actual biological fatherhood has already been sufficiently emphasized. But that some man or group of men must be tagged with the responsibility of performing the adult male activities necessary to keeping the young ones alive, growing, and learning is universally recognized as of the utmost importance. There must be jural fatherhood to regularize transference of statuses from one generation to the next. In meeting the requirements of infant care and child development, the sex differences of male and female are such that a cooperative division of labor makes for greater efficiency and skill in the work that is to be done. Childbearing can still be done only by women, the prospects of

asexual reproduction from body cells (cloning) in the laboratories (see Chapter 18, page 370) notwithstanding. Nursing ties women down, while men have greater freedom of movement. Mobility, combined with greater strength, inevitably allows men to become more efficient hunters. Many skills can be performed equally well by either sex, but inasmuch as practice makes perfect, each sex is more likely to develop high skills if it concentrates on certain tasks and relies on the opposite sex to do likewise with certain others; so the spouses and the children all harvest greater benefits from such an arrangement.

The basic functions of the family may be

Fig. 21-A   An American conjugal-natal family. (Photo by John Brook.)

performed with varying degrees of effectiveness from culture to culture, and the details of the ways in which families within different culture systems carry out these functions produce the remarkably different individual personalities of children and adults, as was indicated in Chapter 2. At this juncture, the most relevant fact is that evidently no substitute can serve the functions of child development as well as an intimate kinship group, family or otherwise. Those anthropologists who have paid especial attention to the relations of culture to personality formation by means of direct observation of primitive societies agree that anthropological data give universal significance to the conclusions drawn from recent studies of children in institutions. Margaret Mead sums it up:

It has been . . . effectively demonstrated that children do not thrive, in spite of good physical care, if kept as young infants in impersonal institutions, and that separation from the mother—especially at certain periods—has serious deleterious effects on the child. Retardation, failure to learn to talk, apathy, regression, and death all appear as accompaniments to institutionalization when no mother surrogate is provided.[3]

Substitute, or surrogate, mothers may, if the relationship is personal and within the intimate setting of the family circle, provide that direct emotional response with which the human infant must be provided. Nursing involves more than the imbibing of mother's milk. The surrogates may in many instances be direct substitutes for the biological mother or father, as in the operation of the sororate and the levirate, or they may be collateral surrogates who play the parental roles on a less intensive level. A Navaho child may find himself cared for, and nursed by, a number of clan sisters of his mother, whom he learns to call "mother" under the Navaho system of kinship terminology and who, for their part, call him "son" from the beginning. The family

is not necessarily the small, nuclear family, isolated in its separate dwelling unit; it may be this, but it may also exist as a regular cell-like feature of a larger familial structure.

Thus, although the independent conjugal-natal family of the Euro-American form occurs in all societies, it is the sole form of familial unit in about half of them. In the other half of the world's societies, the nuclear family is encysted within some kind of composite extended family, a larger kinship group that includes more than a single set of spouses and their children.[4]

The Conjugal-Natal Family

Every individual who is legitimately born and not forthwith orphaned, and who ultimately marries, is a member of a primary and a secondary conjugal-natal family: that of his parents, into which he is born, and that which he founds with his spouse in wedlock. In the first he is an offspring; in the second he is a progenitor (Figure 21-1). Viewed from the outside, the two families are alike in terms of form and function. The statuses of the given individual within the two families are very different, however, and his role experiences in each are quite unlike.

The conjugal-natal family is limited both in scope of membership and in duration. It can include no more persons than a mated pair can produce or adopt, and it cannot endure for more than the lifespan of two generations: the lifespan of the founding spouses, and the lifespan of the children who are born into their marriage. The lone surviving founder of an independent conjugal-natal family, in societies such as the American, can face a bleak and lonely old age. Each conjugal-natal family gradually wastes away as death takes its toll, until at last it is no more. This type of family is a discontinuous social unit.

[3]M. Mead, "Some Theoretical Considerations on the Problem of Mother-Child Separation" (*American Journal of Orthopsychiatry,* vol. 24, 1954), p. 474.

[4]E. Bourguignon and L. Greenbaum, *Diversity and Homogeneity,* p. 49.

Each such family is born and destined to die within the span of a century.

This is a consequence of the universal incest tabu, for if parent could marry child and brother could marry sister, a conjugal-natal family could be continued indefinitely through internal replacement as the original members died off. Perpetuity of the conjugal-natal family is forgone, however, in the interests of societal stability. The individual family sacrifices itself as an entity in the interests of maintenance of the stability of the whole society, for this is of more fundamental importance.

However much the independent conjugal-natal family may be cherished as a social unit, it has certain functional disabilities. In the first place, the conjugal-natal family is very unstable. There is the constant possibility of divorce, and where divorce is not countenanced, emotional disturbances arising from the incompatibility of the father and mother can easily destroy the affective solidarity that is so important to good family functioning. If a primary purpose of marriage is to fix the biological father of the children with the economic and social responsibility of providing for them, his ability to perform this essential social function is seriously impaired when he divorces or leaves the mother. True enough, the consequences of a conjugal-natal family breakup are not so serious in a primitive society, where the mother is securely embedded in the protection of her extended family and where remarriage is easier than it is in urbanized Western civilization.

Also, the conjugal-natal family is a temporary association. It begins with the union of the married pair and ends with the dispersal of the children. Furthermore, upon marriage, a person enters a new conjugal-natal family, and his loyalties are split. From our own experience, we know the tensions that can result from the pull of loyalty to our husbands or wives as against our fathers and mothers. The instability of the conjugal-natal family and its short lifespan also limit its usefulness as a

means of inheritance of property and perquisites.

Nonetheless, R. T. Smith notes that sociologists such as Talcott Parsons maintain, and probably rightly, that

the family system of the urban United States is not a denuded form of a more "normal" or "natural" family system but is itself a highly specialized form that articulates most satisfactorily with a highly differentiated economic and political system and with institutionalized values that stress achievement rather than inheritance. It is argued that the smallness and relative isolation of the family from other kinship ties is an adaptation that makes possible the spatial and status mobility of its members.[5]

(See, also, the discussion of the American kinship system in Chapter 23, pages 463–465.)

Monogamy and Family Structure   The independent conjugal-natal family is possible only

[5]R. T. Smith, "Family: Comparative Structure" (*International Encyclopedia of the Social Sciences*, vol. 5, 1968), p. 311.

Fig. 21-1   The dual nature of the conjugal-natal family. Each family is a conjugal family for the spouses who establish it and a natal family for the offspring who are born into it.

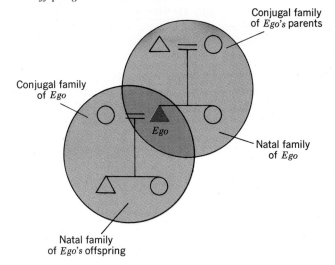

Conjugal family
of *Ego*'s parents

Conjugal family
of *Ego*

Ego

Natal family
of *Ego*

Natal family
of *Ego*'s offspring

when marriage is monogamous, but monogamy is the sole permitted marital form in only a minority of human societies (in one in six societies).[6]

The normal state of affairs is to allow polygamy, especially among men in positions of power and social leadership. Still, it is important to realize that what is *permitted* in a culture and what *prevails* in fact may be two different things. Thus, it is usual to refer to societies whose cultures permit multiple marriages as *polygamous;* yet it is unlikely that more than a few marriages in any society will actually be polygamous, since a number of factors limit multiple marriages.

First, there is the relative balance of the sex ratio. Approximately equal numbers of males and females are born. Unless some selective factor operates in favor of one sex and against the other, there will be an approximate equality in the numbers of adult males and females available for marriage. If this is the case, whenever one man has two wives, some other man in the tribe has to do without. There is, of course, the possibility that the short-wived men may band together to share one wife among themselves, but such polyandrous arrangements are very rare.

If it is the current practice for a man to settle in the household of his wife, he obviously cannot live with all his wives simultaneously unless they are sisters. Uxorilocal residence[7] discourages the polygynous form of polygamy. Beyond this, the attitudes of his in-laws will discourage marriage with women from other kinship groups, especially if the society is matrilineal and the wife's relationship group is in a strong position. Marriage is a kinship-group alliance, and a son-in-law whose affinal allegiances are multiple is apt to be less desirable than one whose affinity is to one group alone.

Few precise statistics are available, but all reports indicate that monogamous marriages actually predominate in most societies that permit polygamy. Contrary to the notions of nineteenth-century anthropologists, monogamy most definitely is not the end product of an evolutionary series narrowing down from primitive promiscuity to civilized monogamy. The very primitive Andaman Islanders and the Semangs of the Malay forests limit themselves to one wife apiece, but the Semangs marry again and again in serial monogamy, Hollywood style. Inca commoners were forbidden to marry more than one wife, but a man might receive a concubine as a gift in reward for faithful service to his overlord. The occurrence of prescribed monogamy among the matrilineal, uxorilocal Iroquois in New York and the equally matrilineal, uxorilocal Hopi and Zuñi suggests that in these instances, monogamy is correlated with female-dominated residence and economy. Monogamy prevails among all the Southwest Pueblos, but among the Eastern Pueblos of New Mexico, where female dominance fades out, it is impossible to tell whether this is due to ancient Pueblo custom or whether it has been brought about by the influence of the Catholic Church. Among the Zuñi and Hopi monogamous marriages are very brittle. Among the Keresan Pueblos, however, the Catholic injunction against divorce is rigidly adhered to. Clandestine relations outside marriage occur among all these people.

Exclusive monogamy is not correlated with any stage of culture. Its absence among pastoral nomads, who are predominantly patrilineal, is nevertheless a notable fact.

Residence Patterns   A conjugal-natal family almost always has a home. Because of the sentiments that suffuse the family relationship, "home" connotes a good deal more than "house." A long-abandoned dwelling is a house, but it was once also a home. We sing fondly of "home, sweet home," but it is unimaginable, for reasons that are clear enough, that we would ever, within the family circle,

[6]Bourguignon and Greenbaum, *op. cit.,* p. 49.
[7]The practice whereby a married couple settles in the locale of the wife's parents.

burst into heart-moving song over "house, sweet house."

The rules of exogamy require that a man and wife come from separate conjugal-natal families and separate households. Upon marriage, the first question to be settled is: "Where shall we live?" In most societies, this issue is resolved ahead of time and therefore does not call for debate or allow much room for individual preference. The custom of the society may be *virilocal* (L. *vir*, male + *locus*, place), according to which the newlywed couple settles in the locality of the husband's primary conjugal-natal family. Or it may be *patrilocal* if most of the husband's paternal relatives customarily live in the same camp, neighborhood, village, or district.

On the other hand, the custom of the tribe may be for the couple to settle in the locality of the wife's parents, in which case it is called *uxorilocal* (L. *uxori*, wife + *locus*, place).

Following Murdock, we may call the practice *matrilocal* if the couple settle in the locality of the wife's matrilineal kinship groups.

A few tribes with little fixed property and weak social organization give the couple free choice on whether to settle in the locality of the bride's or the groom's primary conjugal-natal family. This practice is known as *bilocal* or *ambilocal* (L. *ambo*, both + *locus*, place) residence.

A small number of matrilineally oriented societies expect the couple to settle in the locality of the male's mother's brother. In this situation, we have *avunculocal* (L. *avunculus*, mother's brother + *locus*, place) residence.

Finally, some social systems, such as the Euro-American, provide for independent establishment of residence without too much reference to the prior location of the primary conjugal-natal families of the newly married pair. This condition bespeaks *neolocal* (Gr. *neos*, new + L. *locus*, place) residence, which is in effect an absence of restrictive rules of residence, leaving the options open for the newly founded, independent conjugal-natal household.

There are, then, five basic varieties of residence: (1) virilocal (with patrilocal), (2) uxorilocal (with matrilocal), (3) avunculocal, (4) bilocal (or ambilocal), and (5) neolocal. In most societies, one rule alone prevails for the married life of a couple, although some may use combinations of two or more. Thus, among the nomadic Plains Indians, a couple's first tipi was usually set up beside that of the bride's parents for a year or so. Then, when the new household was well established, the young couple was likely to camp beside the groom's family. Among the Dobuans, a couple alternated residence in each other's village every other year. And in some complex primitive societies, such as the Ashanti in Ghana, where the ideal rule is virilocal, there may actually be a good deal of informal variation from case to case.[8] Furthermore, it is not a simple open-and-closed matter as to whether a given household represents one kind of residence pattern or another, if it contains a mixture of several conjugal-natal families. It may also remain a moot matter as to how to classify a society as a whole, when two or more residential patterns are found to exist with equal frequency.[9]

A glance at Table 21-1 will quickly show that a great majority of human societies are male-oriented in residence patterns. The average for the world sample in the *Ethnographic Atlas* is 69 per cent virilocal and patrilocal. But in the continental Old World the ratio rises to over 80 per cent, while in North and South America the figures are 58 and 41 per cent, respectively. Conversely, female-focused marital residence is virtually non-existent in the Mediterranean area and in Negro Africa, thus reflecting the importance

[8]M. Fortes, "Time and Social Structure: An Ashanti Case Study," in M. Fortes (ed.), *Social Structure*, pp. 54–84.
[9]Cf. W. H. Goodenough, "Residence Rules" (*Southwestern Journal of Anthropology*, vol. 12, 1956), pp. 22–37, for a very pertinent exemplification of these problems in the study of the social organization of Truk in the Micronesian Islands.

of intensive agriculture and pastoralism as subsistence bases in that part of the world. In the New World, women hold a better power position. Over a third (40 per cent) of the South American societies in the sample are uxorilocal or matrilocal—still not as many as are viri/patrilocal but an impressive figure, nonetheless (Figure 21-2).

It should be immediately obvious that the nature of residence patterns strongly affects the internal quality of the family unit and its extensions. If residence is uxorilocal, the woman is in constant daily interaction with *her* parents and sisters. The children of sisters grow up together, and the children of brothers do not. Husbands are "aliens" in a new setting. Sisters are grouped in a continuing solidarity. The opportunity for women to exert a solid front is enhanced, and their position in the direction of social affairs is stronger. With virilocal residence, just the opposite occurs.

Another factor that affects the quality of the family is whether marriages are based on village exogamy or endogamy. If the marriages take place within the local group or village, the differentiating effects of residence rules are much reduced. In spite of virilocality,

if the home of the bride's parents is only 100 yards away, the continuity of her tie to her primary conjugal-natal family is not so seriously strained as it is when she is transported to another village; concomitantly, the influence of the paternal group cannot be so strong.

The Composite Conjugal-Natal Family

Within polygamous marriages, we have been drawing a distinction between polygyny and polyandry. *Polygamy* means multiple marriages; *polygyny* means multiple women and *polyandry* means multiple men. Polygyny is therefore that form of family in which a husband has more than one wife at a time. *Bigamy* is the more special form of polygamy in which the husband limits himself to two wives, or a woman to two husbands. In societies where there may be more than one husband or wife in a family at the same time, the conjugal-natal families are not independent but are, rather, segments of a *composite conjugal-natal* family. The latter is therefore a family consisting of two or more conjugal-natal family segments.

Table 21-1   Relative Frequency of Dominant Patterns of Marial Residence, according to Geographic Areas

Dominant residence pattern	*All societies* $n = 859$	*Sub-Saharan Africa* $n = 237$	*Mediter-ranean* $n = 96$	*East Eur-asia* $n = 94$	*Oceania* $n = 126$	*North America* $n = 218$	*South America* $n = 88$
Viri/patrilocal	69%	82%	80%	82%	62%	58%	41%
Uxori/matrilocal	13%	2%	0%	11%	14%	21%	38%
Avunculocal	4%	10%	2%	0%	3%	3%	2%
Neolocal	5%	5%	13%	2%	4%	5%	9%
Bilocal	8%	4%	4%	3%	14%	14%	10%
Husband/wife living separately	1%	0%	1%	1%	2%	0%	0%

SOURCE: Data adapted from E. Bourguignon and L. Greenbaum, *Diversity and Homogeneity*, table 28, p. 50.

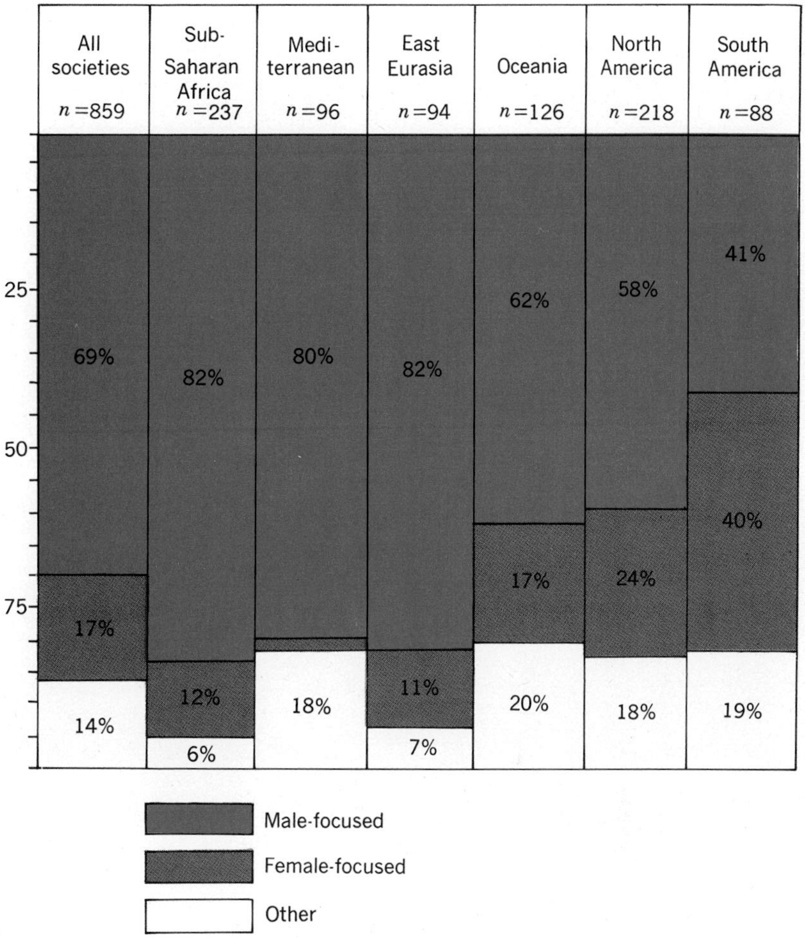

	All societies	Sub-Saharan Africa	Medi-terranean	East Eurasia	Oceania	North America	South America
	n =859	*n* =237	*n* =96	*n* =94	*n* =126	*n* =218	*n* =88
	69%	82%	80%	82%	62%	58%	41%
					17%	24%	40%
	17%	12%	18%	11%	20%	18%	19%
	14%	6%		7%			

Fig. 21-2   *Relative frequency of male-focused and female-focused residence patterns, according to geographic areas. The male-focused pattern represents viri/patrilocal; the female-focused one, uxori/matrilocal, plus avunculocal. (Data from Table 21-1)*

Male-focused

Female-focused

Other

Polygyny In spite of the Judeo-Christian insistence upon monogamy, this practice is a cultural emphasis shared by a relatively small number of societies (16 per cent of the sample in the *Ethnographic Atlas*). Nearly half (44 per cent) of all societies hold the polygynous family to be the norm, while nearly as many permit polygyny but do not attempt to make it the regular thing. Almost all African societies are emphatically polygynous (see Figure 21-3), enough to readily block a zealous effort to have polygyny declared contrary to fundamental human rights in the United Nations Commission on Human Rights in the early 1950s.

Functions of Polygyny There are a number of social motives underlying polygyny as an institution. If a man has the means to support several wives, he is able to present a richer and better-equipped household to the world. More women can prepare better clothes and food. If women's handicrafts are marketable or suitable for exchange, his household wealth will be increased. When the Blackfoot Indians found a lucrative outlet for tanned hides in the Canadian fur trade, women as tanners became an economic asset, and polygyny grew to an extent unprecedented in the Plains. Bride price went up, and the age of marriage for girls went down, while the

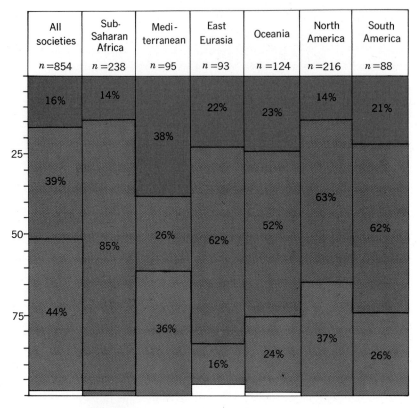

All societies	Sub-Saharan Africa	Medi-terranean	East Eurasia	Oceania	North America	South America
n=854	n=238	n=95	n=93	n=124	n=216	n=88
16%	14%	38%	22%	23%	14%	21%
39%	85%	26%	62%	52%	63%	62%
44%		36%	16%	24%	37%	26%

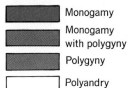

Monogamy
Monogamy with polygyny
Polygyny
Polyandry

Fig. 21-3   Relative frequency of monogamy, monogamy with polygyny, polygyny, and polyandry as expected marriage forms, according to geographic areas. (Data adapted from E. Bourguignon and L. Greenbaum, Diversity and Homogeneity, Table 26, p. 48)

age of marriage for men was set back; well-established Blackfoot entrepreneurs cornered the available women, and it took young men a longer time to acquire enough capital to purchase wives.[10]

Polygyny may also serve as a mechanism for competitive status in the sexual field when to have and to hold several wives against all comers is a dangerous task, as among the Eskimos.[11]

[10]O. Lewis, *The Effects of White Contact upon Blackfoot Culture, with Special Reference to the Role of the Fur Trade* (American Ethnological Society, Monograph 6, 1942), pp. 38–40.
[11]E. A. Hoebel, *The Law of Primitive Man*, pp. 75–76.

Strange as it may seem to some, it is repeatedly reported that in many tribes the women do not object to their husbands' taking on additional wives. This is most apt to be true when additional wives are co-workers or "chore wives," as among the Comanches of the Plains. A secondary wife may be desired because she will perform special functions, as with the African Baganda, among whom a second wife is chosen from the husband's paternal grandmother's clan. This wife is charged (among other things) with the responsibility of caring for her husband's hair and nail clippings in order to protect him against sorcery.

On the other hand, instances are on record of primitive women who have shown extreme jealousy when their husbands brought home a new wife. A Cheyenne woman hanged herself because her husband took a Pawnee captive to wife, but her own grandmother remarked, "She was foolish to hang herself over such a little thing."

Most primitives aver that polygyny works out best when a man's several wives are sisters. This is psychologically reasonable, inasmuch as sisters are more used to one another's ways than unrelated women are; they are subject to the influence of emotional loyalty acquired in childhood as members of the same conjugal-natal family. As representatives of the same marriage group, their nonpersonal interests in the marriage are identical, which is not the case with unrelated women. *Sororal polygyny* is in effect an anticipation of sororate privileges. A man does not wait for the death of his wife before he marries her younger sister. Instead, as among the Comanches, he has an expectation that if he performs his son-in-law obligations to his wife's parents, they will reward him with his wife's younger sister when she becomes of age.

Where exchange marriage between two families prevails, the levirate will also work to produce sororal polygyny, for example, when brothers have married sisters and a man inherits his deceased brother's wife.

Various household arrangements are made as adjustments to the requirements of the multiple-wife family. The Angola practice is probably typical of Sudanese African tribes. Hambly tells of an Angola headman with eleven wives, each of whom has a separate hut in his compound. The husband customarily sleeps with each wife four or seven successive nights, as his personal habit may be.[12] Among the Jie, it will be remembered (pages 301–302), each wife in a polygynous unit within a joint-family household has her own fenced-in yard and sleeping hut. If a Co-

manche had less than four wives, they usually shared the same tipi. More than four wives necessitated at least two tipis for the household.

Within composite families, there is usually a firm hierarchical distinction between the wives. The first-married wife is given a No. 1 position of authority, so that even though she may be displaced by a later wife as a sexual favorite, she still has the gratification of priority in formal status. The Comanches, again, definitely made such distinctions, for secondary wives were "chore wives" who had to do household work under the direction of No. 1. No wonder the busy wives of great chieftains were usually quite willing to have their husbands marry extra housekeepers. It helped lighten their load.

Polyandry   The actual marriage of several men to one woman is as rare (occurring in 4 of the 854 cultures in the *Ethnographic Atlas*) as the marriage of several women to one man is common. Tibetans and the Todas and other tribes of India are the most famous polyandrists.[13] The Toda polyandrous union is usually, but not necessarily, fraternal.[14] Some polygynous marriages also occur, and quite a few monogamous ones. Children are ordinarily betrothed in infancy, and the boy makes progeny-price payments twice a year all through his childhood. He also has to provide a buffalo to help pay funeral expenses of members of his betrothed's family. Just before puberty, the girl is deflorated by a man from some clan other than her own. Then she is ready for marriage. Right after puberty, she is given a dowry and taken to the home of her husband. Although she may have been betrothed to just one man, it is understood that she is also the wife of all his brothers. Even a boy yet unborn may become her husband, along with his elder brothers, when he becomes of age.

[13]See G. D. Berreman, "Pahari Polyandry: A Comparison," in P. Bohannan and J. Middleton (eds.), *Marriage, Family, and Residence*, pp. 147–167.
[14]Called "adelphic polyandry" in British social anthropology.

[12]W. D. Hambly, *Source Book for African Anthropology*, pp. 418–419.

All the brothers live together and share their wife without friction and supposedly without jealousy. When the wife becomes pregnant, one of the brothers goes through a ritual of "presenting the bow." This makes him the jural father of the ensuing child and the next couple of children to be born. There is no concern over whether he may be the biological sire or not. After he has his share of offspring to sponsor, another brother "presents the bow," thus making himself the father of the next group of children, and so on.

This disregard of biological paternity in favor of ceremonially established sociological fatherhood is also manifest in a way reminiscent of Sakalava progeny-price privileges mentioned previously (page 411). Occasionally, a Toda woman may leave her legitimate husbands to live with another man without official approval, or she may take a concubitant, who pays her husbands for the privilege; in either case, her subsequent children still belong to the man (her husband) who performed the bow-and-arrow ritual.[15]

Polyandry in the Darjeeling district of India is restricted to the younger brothers of the man who performs the wedding rite with the wife. If the elder brother dies and the common wife has no children, she may break the polyandrous bond by first tying a string to a finger of her No. 1 husband's corpse and binding it to one of her own fingers. Then by severing the string, she symbolically destroys the marriage tie.

Tibetan and Eskimo polyandry have been attributed to the practice of female infanticide. While it is quite true that both peoples practice infanticide, census figures do not indicate a surplus of adult men in Tibet, and reliable censuses of the primitive Eskimo indicate that women outnumber men in almost all Eskimo communities, in spite of the common destruction of baby girls.

Although rare, polyandry is more common

(at least in a modified form) than was thought to be the case a few decades ago. A form of polyandry has been reported from at least two East African tribes, leading us to expect that there are probably several other unreported instances. Among the Bahima of Ankole, where progeny price is high, a poor man may call on his younger brothers to contribute cattle to his cause.[16] All the brothers who have contributed take turns living with the bride until she becomes pregnant; she then lives with her "husband." Whoever the sire may be, the resultant child is the jural offspring of the elder brother who married the girl.

Property and Polyandry   Edmund Leach has proposed that fraternal, or adelphic, polyandry is "intimately associated" with inheritance of land through males only, combined with virilocal residence and dowry. In the South Asian cases, a woman who marries patrilocally may surrender her dowry but receive movable goods from the husband in its stead. Brothers jointly pay the dowry, thus obtaining a joint interest in the sexual prerogatives of the husband.[17]

Extensions of Brotherhood   Leach's hypothesis is appropriate to the South Asian data, but it does not fit the facts for North America. While economic factors may be at the bottom of polyandry in some societies, there appear to be other motivations elsewhere. Both the Shoshones and the Eskimos practice polyandry, and yet neither show much concern with property considerations. These are bilateral societies in which a man must depend on his brothers (and cousins) for security and survival. In Shoshone and Comanche kinship terminology, there is no separate word for "brother-in-law" or "sister-

---

[15]W. H. R. Rivers, *The Todas*, pp. 477–480.

[16]J. Roscoe, *The Banyankole*, p. 123; "The Cow Tribe of Enkole in the Uganda Protectorate" (*Journal of the Royal Anthropological Institute of Great Britain and Ireland*, vol. 37, 1907), p. 105.

[17]E. R. Leach, *Rethinking Anthropology*, pp. 104–113.

in-law." All female sisters and cousins of a wife are addressed by a single term, *kw3h3*. A woman addresses all her husband's brothers and cousins by the term for "husband," *kumaxp*. The polyandrous emphasis is on the mutuality of the bond of brotherhood.

"A man loves his brother; he knows that if his brother dies, no one can replace him; he gives him everything he can," explained That's It. "A brother therefore sends his wife over to him occasionally as a gift. She cannot go of her own free will or meet him secretly, or her husband will be angry." It was also expected that when a man was on the warpath, his brother could sleep with his wife.[18]

This notion of the sexual equivalence of brothers crops up in the quaint Shoshone and Comanche custom whereby an aggrieved husband courteously addresses an adulterer who has made him a cuckold as "brother." Men who have had sex relations with the same woman are "brothers," even though unrelated and even while the husband is prosecuting the adulterer for damages.

Comanche young men frequently enter into a relation of institutionalized friendship with a chosen "chum," called *haints*. They usually marry sisters, whom they freely lend to one another as wives. Shoshones and Comanches had to rely on "brothers," real or putative, in war and in law, in love and in play.[19] Their adelphic polyandry expresses the structural-functional significance of "brotherhood" as the keystone of their social life.

That such attitudes are not mere aberrations of the Comanches is fully attested by Murdock's findings to the effect that nearly two-thirds of the 250 societies in the Yale Cross Cultural Survey for which data are available permit postmarital sexual intercourse between a man and his brother's wife (anticipatory levirate) or between a man and his wife's sister (anticipatory sororate).[20]

Eskimo polyandry is of the same order as Shoshone, except that the putative brother with whom an Eskimo normally exchanges wives does not usually live in the same village. A traveling Eskimo needs a woman to dry his fur clothes and chew the hides to keep them soft, among the more necessary amenities of arctic living. Most Eskimo men have at least one regular partner in each village, who will make his wife available on a basis of amicable mutuality. At the same time, he needs someone at home to look after his own wife when he goes off traveling. A good friend will normally agree to take on the task with all its responsibilities and sexual amenities.[21]

Wife Hospitality The widespread primitive practice of men sharing their wives with certain other men on specific occasions is closely related to the institution of polyandry. Most commonly, a host deems that proper social form requires him to offer the hospitality of his wife to an overnight guest. An early white trader on the upper Missouri River, Jean Baptiste Trudeau, took note that "So true is this, that husbands, fathers and brothers, are importunate with the white men who visit them, to make free with their wives, daughters and sisters, particularly those who are most youthful and pretty. . . ."[22]

Wife hospitality was practiced because a man who accepted the woman for the duration of his stay in the village became a putative son-in-law or brother of his benefactor. Such arrangements helped to establish a network of trade in the eighteenth and early nineteenth centuries throughout the upper Plains. French, English, and American traders solidified their business interests with various Indian tribes by becoming "kinsmen" through sexual sharing.

Similar concepts of hospitality have been noted in all parts of the primitive world by

---

[18]E. Wallace and E. A. Hoebel, *The Comanches*, pp. 138–139.
[19]*Ibid.*, p. 132.
[20]Murdock, *Social Structure*, p. 268.

[21]For more detail, see R. F. Spencer, "Spouse Exchange among the North Alaskan Eskimo," in P. Bohannan and J. Middleton (eds.), *Marriage, Family, and Residence*, pp. 131–144.
[22]G. H. Smith, "J. B. Trudeau's Remarks on the Indians of the Upper Missouri, 1794–95" (*American Anthropologist*, vol. 38, 1930), p. 567.

countless explorers, travelers, and lay observers, as well as by anthropologists.[23] As an institutionalized practice, wife lending is functionally analogous to *blood brotherhood,* "a pact or alliance formed between two persons by a ritual act in which each swallows the blood of the other. The pact is one of mutual assistance and is backed by powerful sanctions."[24] The formal exchange of wives is analogous to intimate exchange of "magical" personal essence. At any rate, it should be clear that wife hospitality in societies that emphasize kinship obligations and privileges of brotherhood is not an act of immorality in the context of those societies. It serves as a means of broadening and strengthening social bonds.

Leach's hypothesis and that offered above are not incompatible or contradictory. Each explains special sets of circumstances. Fraternal polyandry in South Asia and that in North America are alike in that a group of brothers share sexual privileges in a wife or wives, while the woman's offspring are jurally the heirs of a specific male. Although the social reasons (structural and functional) for this are quite different in the two cases, the unlike conditions have produced similar results. This is called *convergence:* separate lines of development have led to a single point.

The Composite Unilineal Family

In following the extensions of polyandry beyond the immediate limits of the patrilateral, composite conjugal-natal family, we were led into considerations of "brotherhood." Let us now return to an examination of some ways in which the concept of the family may be extended to incorporate a group of closely related conjugal-natal families into a single property-holding, residential group. Such units are usually called the *joint family* or the *composite unilineal family.* Half the world's societies in the nineteenth century organized their family residential units in this way.[25]

The essential difference between the composite conjugal-natal family and the composite unilineal family is that the former involves only one spouse with several mates, while the latter involves married kinsmen living together in a single household, each with his or her own distinct spouse and offspring.

The Tanala Joint Family Linton's description of the patrilineal joint family among the Tanala of Madagascar presents a good example of the smaller version of the composite unilineal family. A Tanala joint family begins with a single conjugal family. When the sons grow up and marry, they build new houses for themselves close to their parental home. The father, as head of the joint family, directs all its activities concerning clearing and cultivating the fields for dry-rice culture, caring for the family cattle, and similar tasks. All earnings of the male members are placed in his hands for investment in cattle and for dispersal for progeny price and such little cash needs as the sons may have. As long as his father lives, a man has little chance to accumulate any wealth in his own right. The joint family is a cooperative work group and a corporate unit in dealing with other members of the society.

As long as the founder lives, his male lineal descendants are bound to the joint family, and it is not uncommon for a patriarch to have a dozen or more able-bodied sons and grandsons under his control. Upon his death, the process of fission starts. Although the family continues to live and work together under the leadership of the eldest son, his brothers do not have to put their earnings into the common holding unless they wish to. When he, in

---

[23]See E. Westermarck, *The History of Human Marriage,* vol. 1, pp. 224–230, for a more detailed body of references to the custom.

[24]E. E. Evans-Pritchard, "Zande Blood-brotherhood," in *Essays in Social Anthropology,* p. 131.

[25]Bourguignon and Greenbaum, *op. cit.,* p. 49.

turn, is at last succeeded by his eldest son, the joint family begins to break up. The third-generation leader is younger than most of his uncles, who become restive under his leadership. Moreover, it is likely that the group will have grown too large for its land holdings. Then one or more men split off to found a new joint-family household elsewhere.[26] The functional significance of economics for the joint family is shown by Linton's analysis of the breakdown of the joint family resulting from the introduction of wet-rice culture among the neighboring Betsilio tribe.[27]

Balkan and Asian Joint Families   Among gardening and pastoral peoples, the joint family appears as a corporate landowning entity, made up of the descendants of at least two siblings or cousins living in a single dwelling or in closely spaced houses that form a household. Archaic Indo-European peoples commonly favored this type of setup, which is known among the peoples of the Balkans as the *zadruga,* such as was visited some years ago by Louis Adamic.

. . . we were guests in the home of a family counting sixty-eight members. It was one of the few remaining family *zadrugé,* or collectives, in Serbia. We met about forty of the members, including the *stareshina,* or head of the family, a patriarch of seventy and absolute ruler of the group. The enormous household, with a considerable tract of ground and a twenty-room house, was all but self-sufficient economically. Every member above ten had his or her special duty to attend to. Six women and girls, supervised by the *stareshina's* wife, did nothing but cook and bake. Eight other females only spun, weaved, sewed, and embroidered. Five men and boys attended to all the sheep, goats, buffaloes, cattle, and horses. One man was the family shoemaker. And so on. Eleven families lived under the same roof. The husbands were all the *stareshina's* brothers, sons, and grandsons; their wives had married into the *zadruga* from near-by villages.[28]

In India and Pakistan, the patrilineal joint family, called *kumbah* in Pakistan, is still a vital form even in the urban setting. In such large cities as Karachi, a joint family will occupy a single five- or six-story house, with the parents on the lower floor and each son establishing his secondary conjugal-natal family on succeeding floors in order of seniority—the youngest having the most flights to climb. Even fully trained professional men, if conservatively oriented, turn their salaries over to the household father and mother to administer on behalf of the group as a whole.

If the extension of kinship is on matrilineal lines, the joint family will be matriarchically organized, as is the Iroquois joint family, whose dwelling structure is described in Chapter 14.

The Matrilateral Group

Some societies utilize the brother-sister relationship as a means of counterbalancing limitations of the conjugal-natal family. The result is a social unit that may be called the *matrilateral group,* which consists of a woman, her brother, and her offspring or a conjoint combination of lineal descendants of a female.[29]

Thus, among the Dobu of Melanesia, the conjugal-natal family is the household unit; i.e., its members live together. After a man marries, he never again enters his sister's house; consequently, the *susu,* as the matrilateral group is called in Dobu, has no household base. However, children cannot eat food grown in their father's fields; all fishing gear, including canoes, is used jointly and is inherited only by members of the *susu.* Consequently, the *susu* has an economic base, and the conjugal-natal family does not. Emotional security is found only in the *susu,* and not in

[26]R. Linton, "The Tanalas of Madagascar," in A. Kardiner, *The Individual and His Society,* pp. 189–192.
[27]*Ibid.,* pp. 282–290.

[28]L. Adamic, *The Native's Return,* p. 215.
[29]It has also been called the *consanguineal family.*

the conjugal-natal family. All Dobuans believe that all other Dobuans except those of their own *susu* are their magical enemies. Husband and wife, coming as they do from different *susus*, are hostile at marriage and all their days thereafter. Each believes the other is trying to destroy him by foul magic. The *susu* inherits the corpses and skulls of its members. It bestows personal names and social status in relationship terms. Widows, widowers, and the children of a dead person may never enter the village of the deceased spouse or parent, but *susu* relatives of a dead person may enter the village of the surviving spouse or children.[30]

The Zuñi Household   The differentiation and interrelationship of conjugal-natal family and matrilateral group are also strikingly revealed by the Zuñis of New Mexico, of whom Benedict wrote:

To the women of the household, the grandmother and her sisters, her daughters and their daughters, belong the house and the corn that is stored in it. No matter what may happen to marriages, the women of the household remain with the house for life. They present a solid front. They care for and feed the sacred objects that belong to them. They keep their secrets together. Their husbands are outsiders, and it is their brothers, married now into houses of other clans, who are united with the household in all affairs of moment. It is they who return for all the retreats when the sacred objects of the house are set out before the altar. It is they, not the women, who learn the word-perfect ritual of their sacred bundle and perpetuate it. A man goes always, for all important occasions, to his mother's house, which, when she dies, becomes his sister's house, and if his marriage breaks up, he returns to the same household.

This blood-relationship group, rooted in the ownership of the house, united in the care of sacred objects, is the important group in Zuñi. It has permanence and important common concerns. But it is not the economically functioning group. Each married son, each married brother, spends his labour upon the corn which will fill his wife's store-room. Only when his mother's or sister's house lacks male labour does he care for the cornfield of his blood-relationship group. The economic group is the household that lives together, the old grandmother and her husband, her daughters and their husbands. These husbands count in the economic group, though in the ceremonial group they are outsiders.[31]

The Nayar Taravad   Of the matrilineal type of joint-family household, that of the famous Nayar caste of Kerala, on the Malabar coast of southern India, has long held the interest of anthropologists.

The Nayar are supposed to have been the ruling class of the aboriginal society predating the Hindu influx. Today they form the third-ranking caste of a complex caste society. Above them is the erstwhile royal house of great wealth and power, which may have emerged long ago from the Nayars themselves. Beneath the royal house (but far above the Nayars in sublimity) is the caste of Nambudiri Brahmans, whose sacred families are patrilineally organized on a strict basis of primogeniture. The Nayars are a closed caste of landowners and professional soldiers, who in contrast to the Brahmans are strictly matrilineal and matrilocal. The household, or *taravad,* is a joint organization housed under one roof. The eldest woman is the titular head of the household, but the house, lands, and joint property are administered by the eldest brother for the benefit of the group. All the males (brothers, sons, and grandsons) contribute to the maintenance of the *taravad* and draw their support from it. The offspring of the women belong to the *taravad* and are maintained within it. The men mate with women of other *taravad* without obligating themselves to any legal duties toward these "wives" or children, who live with their mothers.

Marriage by members of the *taravad* is often no more than a ritual bow to Hindu convention. If a ceremony is performed, it

[30]R. F. Fortune, *Sorcerers of Dobu,* pp. 5–30.

[31]R. F. Benedict, *Patterns of Culture,* pp. 75–76.

may soon be followed by legal divorce, even though the couple continues an enduring relation as mates. For unlike most joint-family practices elsewhere, the Nayar male may not live in the joint-family household of his mate. The couple merely visit together, and out of these visits come the children who people the *taravad* of the mother.

Both men and women may have several mates simultaneously, since mating involves no formal obligations. Younger sons of the Brahman class may enter into sexual alliances with Nayar women, but they still remain outside the *taravad,* and their children remain irrevocably fixed within it.

Under changing economic and social conditions, the Nayar matrilineal joint family has been gradually dissolving, and patrilineal tendencies have become increasingly strong.[32]

The matrilateral group exists because it offers certain advantages in which the conjugal-natal family is weak. Yet the conjugal-natal family is definitely preferred over the matrilateral group. The conjugal-natal family is universal; the matrilateral group is not.

What is defective or objectionable in the matrilateral group? The answer will be found in the incest tabu. The basis of the matrilateral group is the sibling bond of brotherhood and sisterhood. Yet all societies find it necessary to tabu sex relations between brother and sister, often manifesting extreme anxiety over the consequences of incestuous relationships. The matrilateral group encourages emotional and functional ties between a pair who must never become sexually involved with each other. This is dangerous business, so much so that many societies apparently prefer to make it impossible for such a situation to exist. In Dobu, for example, a man may not enter his sister's house. Another disadvantage of the matrilateral group is that the splitting of loyalty between it and the conjugal-natal family may produce personal and cultural conflicts that are difficult to resolve. Meyer Fortes observed: "Ashanti discuss the subject interminably, stressing especially the inevitability of conflicting loyalties. For a woman the conflict turns on the difficulties of reconciling attachment to her mother with her duty to her husband."[33]

In a social system in which the matrilateral group is an important functioning unit, the woman who has few sisters and many brothers is certainly more apt to be better off than a woman who has several sisters and only one brother, for as Malinowski has written of the Trobrianders, ". . . the more brothers the merrier for each sister, the more sisters the less endowment for them."[34]

Communes

The idealistic urge to break away from family exclusiveness is old in Western civilization. We have seen that family and kinship have predominated as the almost universal means of internally organizing human societies and of allocating status and accessibility of privilege, power, and consumable resources. With advancing civilization, kinship recedes in relative importance, while more universalistic modes of social identity come to the fore. Still, down to the nineteenth century in the West, and to the twentieth century in China, the family and the extended kinship group remained the virtually unchallenged vehicle of living, reproducing, and inheriting.

Until the Russian revolution of 1917, challenges to conventional family organization came from small prototype movements of limited success and duration, engendered by intellectual idealists, both religious and sectarian. The Shakers of Mt. Lebanon, New York, founded in 1787, lived in "family" units

[32]K. Gough, in D. M. Schneider and K. Gough (eds.), *Matrilineal Kinship,* chaps. 6 and 7.

[33]M. Fortes, "Time and Social Structure: An Ashanti Case Study," in M. Fortes (ed.), *Social Structure,* p. 75.
[34]B. Malinowski, *Coral Gardens and Their Magic,* vol. 1, p. 189.

of fifty or sixty "brothers" and "sisters," housed by sex in two separate buildings and maintaining themselves by gardening, fruit preserving, and craftwork. The Shakers, however, suppressed sexuality and allowed for no matings among their members. New members were added through adult conversion and the adoption of children. Other notable family communes with a religious focus are the Amana, Hutterites, Harmonists, Zoarites, Perfectionists, and United Order.[35]

[35]See D. W. Douglas and K. du P. Lumpkin, "Communistic Settlements" (*Encyclopaedia of the Social Sciences,* vol. 4, 1931), pp. 95–102.

Current hippie and other communes of the counterculture movement are more in the stream of the socialistic utopias of New Harmony, founded by Robert Owen in Indiana, Ohio, and New York between 1820 and 1828. They all represent withdrawal from urban industrialism to bucolic romanticism. The socialistic communes of the last century placed high value on work and common sharing. Contemporary youth communes seem more to emphasize common intimacy of feeling and being, with little value placed on work. It is too soon to tell whether they foreshadow a new trend in organization of family life or whether they will be no more than a marginal fad of passing historical in-

Fig. 21-4   The commune kitchen at The New Buffalo, a New Mexico "family" of three dozen members in 1970. (Dennis Stock, Magnum.)

terest. In the last chapter of this book we shall return to this subject as we look beyond today's civilization.

SUMMARY

Marriage is the social institution which defines the statuses and roles governing the relations of the members of the conjugal-natal group to one another, their kinsmen, and their nonkinsmen. That is, it defines the family.

The universal functions of the family are: (1) the institutionalization of mating and the establishment of legal parents for a woman's children; (2) nurture and enculturation of the young; (3) organization of a complementary division of labor between spouses; and (4) the establishment of relationships of descent and affinity.

The conjugal-natal family has two overlapping forms from the point of view of any individual. The natal family is that into which ego is born; it was founded by his parents. The conjugal aspect is the family he founds with his spouse at marriage. In the natal family, ego is an offspring; in the conjugal, he is a genitor. In a large sense, "my family" usually includes both aspects; hence the term, *conjugal-natal*. The conjugal-natal family as an independent residential unit exists in about half the societies of the world. Residence patterns greatly influence the character of the conjugal-natal family; they also reflect the dominant orientation of the kinship system in a society. In virilocal residence, a married couple lives in the locale of the husband's natal family; if this locale includes an aggregation of the husband's patrikin, marriage is recognized as *patrilocal*. When a couple settles in the locale of the wife's natal family, residence is *uxorilocal;* if the locale includes an aggregation of the wife's matrikin, marriage is recognized as *matrilocal*. When kinship is matrilineally oriented, but power is focused in the men, residence may then be in the locale of the husband's mother's brother. In this case, it is called *avunculocal*.

Relatively few societies (16 per cent) insist on monogamy. Half the known societies set up the polygynous (two or more wives) composite conjugal-natal family as the norm. The polyandrous composite conjugal-natal family of two or more husbands is an interesting but very rare form of organization, centered mostly in northern India. Attenuated polyandry occurs as a result of emphatic *generation equivalence* among brothers, i.e., brothers are merged into a single status for the entire group.

The composite unilineal family consists of joint households of kinsmen related through either their fathers or mothers. It is a corporate socioeconomic enterprise in which kinship overrides individual separatism.

To compensate for the relative fragility and lack of durability of the conjugal-natal family, some cultures use the matrilateral group to perform some functions which might otherwise be carried by the family. The matrilateral group consists of women and their children, plus the women's brothers. Examples are the Dobuan *susu,* the Zuñi natal household, and the Nayar *taravad*. The major inhibiting factor for the matrilateral group is, of course, the universality of the brother-sister tabu. The matrilateral group may have potentially everything that marks the family, except for one thing. It cannot function as a unit of mating and reproduction.

Communes are efforts to found and maintain composite living groups devoid of kinship and private property. Thus far in human history such modes of organization have been rare and marginal to the societies in which they occur. They have interesting possibilities, however, which will be discussed in the closing chapter of this book (pages 682–683).

SELECTED READINGS

Belo, J., "A Study of a Balinese Family" (*American Anthropologist,* vol. 38, 1936), pp. 12–31. An account based upon firsthand observation.

Bohannan, P., and J. Middleton (eds.), *Marriage, Family, and Residence* (1968). An excellently chosen collection of papers by a number of leading contemporary anthropologists. The most useful single supplementary source for the subject of this chapter.

Fortes, M., *The Web of Kinship among the Tallensi* (1949), chaps. 6 and 8, "Husband and Wife in the Structure of the Family" and "The Relationship of Parent and Child." An excellent study.

Geertz, H., *The Javanese Family* (1961). A modern descriptive account of life within the family circle, with an analysis of the family within the kinship structure.

Goody, J. (ed.), *The Developmental Cycle in Domestic Groups* (1958). The product of joint examination by a group of anthropologists of what happens in families and other domestic groups during the natural history of the family group. Covers a variety of societies.

LaBarre, W., *The Human Animal* (1954). Brilliantly written, this book presents a biosocial theory of the development and essential nature of family relationships.

Mead, M., *Male and Female* (1949). A provocative and interesting synthesis of the author's field studies and views on family relationships in seven primitive cultures and in the United States.

Schneider, D. M., and K. Gough (eds.), *Matrilineal Kinship* (1961). Although this book is focused on kinship rather than on the family *per se,* it contains a good deal on family structure in matrilineal societies.

Chapter 22

The Extension of Kinship

One of anthropology's most fascinating discoveries is that the seemingly simple matter of descent and kinship can be so variously perceived, so intricately defined, and assigned so central a role in the ordering of many total cultures. Yet, the contemporary Western cultural bias toward individually achieved identity seems to produce a general impatience with the anthropological stress on the many forms and complexities of kinship relations. It is a hard fact, however, that

it is simply impossible to understand the workings of most societies without grasping their approach to kinship—kinship systems, kinship functions, kinship terms. (Many unsuccessful economic, political, and developmental missions attest to this truth.) Therefore, we begin to look in detail at how kinship operates.

The family tie nowhere ends with parents and children, for parents have their parents, grandparents, uncles, aunts, brothers, sisters,

Fig. 22-A   An American extended family. Joseph and Rose Kennedy with their children and sons- and daughters-in-law. (Paul Schutzer, Life Magazine, © *Time, Inc.)*

and cousins to whom the bond of kinship extends. In all societies, the cementing effect of these bonds is strong enough to produce a network of special relations between relatives that makes the relationship group distinguishable as an entity within the larger society.

In primitive societies and most non-Western civilizations, the kinship bond is likely to override all others. Behavior toward relatives is not the same as behavior toward non-relatives. Rich uncles win special deference. A person always has certain obligations to his kinsmen. The status of a relative is unique, compared with that of the rest of mankind.

As a striking manifestation of this fundamental fact, E. E. Evans-Pritchard observes:

If you wish to live among the Nuer, you must do so on their terms, which means that you must treat them as a kind of kinsmen and they will treat you as a kind of kinsman. Rights, privileges and obligations are determined by kinship. Either a man is a kinsman, actually or by fiction, or he is a person to whom you have no reciprocal obligations and whom you treat as a potential enemy.[1]

Because we live in an industrialized society of great social mobility, in which we depend to a great degree upon our own efforts and those of mutual-aid associations (insurance and benevolent societies), unions, and philanthropic and governmental agencies to provide social security, rather than our relatives, it is hard for most of us to comprehend the importance of kinsmen in simpler societies. In primitive society, most of these responsibilities rest with the kinship group.

The contrast is philosophically stated by an old Pomo Indian of California, who soliloquized:

What is a man? A man is nothing. Without his family he is of less importance than that bug crossing the trail, of less importance than the sputum or exuviae. At least *they* can be used to help poison a man. A man must be with his family to amount to anything with us. If he had nobody else to help him, the first trouble he got into he would be killed by his ene-

mies, because there would be no relatives to help him fight the poison of the other group. No woman would marry him. . . . He would be poorer than a new-born child, he would be poorer than a worm. . . . The family is important. If a man has a large family, . . . and upbringing by a family that is known to produce good children, then he is somebody and every family is willing to have him marry a woman of their group. In the White way of doing things the family is not so important. The police and soldiers take care of protecting you, the courts give you justice, the post office carries messages for you, the school teaches you. Everything is taken care of, even your children, if you die; but with us the family must do all of that.

Without the family we are nothing, and in the old days before the White people came, the family was given first consideration by anyone who was about to do anything at all. That is why we got along. . . .

With us the family was everything. Now it is nothing. We are getting like the White people and it is bad for the old people. We had no old people's home like you. The old people were important. They were wise. Your old people must be fools.[2]

In India a Hyderabad farmer repeats the refrain more succinctly, "Without castemen and kinsmen to support him, a man is as good as dead. No one will marry him; no one will help him in times of trouble; no one will complete his karma when he dies."[3] And among the Mossi, a proverb-loving tribe on the Upper Volta River in West Africa, the folk saying runs, "A chicken isn't very big without his feathers," meaning "Always have some relatives with you in court."

Kinship provides a major category of building blocks as the foundation of all hitherto existing societies.

Principles of Extended Kinship

The conjugal-natal family, although it is the seedbed of society, is itself always embedded

[1] E. E. Evans-Pritchard, *The Nuer*, p. 182.

[2] B. W. Aginsky, "An Indian's Soliloquy" (*American Journal of Sociology*, vol. 46, 1940), pp. 43–44.
[3] P. G. Hiebert, *Konduru*, p. 13. *Karma* is a person's destiny or "fate" which has been determined by his acts in a previous incarnation.

within a larger series of kinship groupings. These are the *kindred*, the *ramage*, the *lineage*, the *clan*, the *phratry*, and the *moiety*. Many societies, including those of Europe and their derivatives in North and South America, and such societies as the Eskimo, Ifugao, and Comanche, extend kinship only so far as the kindred. Many more build on the lineage and clan; a smaller number combine lineages and clans within moieties and phratries. What are these groups and how are they organized?

The basic division rests on the distinction between the *bilateral* and *unilineal* principles. A *bilateral* kinship group is one in which members receive their identity through the bond of descent reckoned from both parents. A *unilineal kinship group* is one in which members receive their identity through the bond of descent reckoned asymmetrically through lines of males or females. If descent is reckoned from father to sons to son's sons, etc., the system is patrilineal. If descent is reckoned from mother to daughter to daughter's daughter, the system is matrilineal. A *unilineal kinship system* is one in which all the kinship groups are either matrilineal *or* patrilineal. If patrilineal *and* matrilineal kinship groups exist side by side within the same society, the system is one of *dual* or *double descent.*

Bilateral, or Cognatic, Kinship: The Kindred

The kindred expresses the bilateral principle in its most direct and undifferentiated form. In the largest sense, one's kindred includes every person to whom one can trace a genealogical bond. It includes all one's *cognates*, i.e., everyone who can be traced as related through a common relative, whether ancestral or contemporary, whether male or female. It spreads in all directions, and in a small tribe, pushing a bilateral genealogy to its ultimate limits could result in the inclusion of every member of the tribe as a relative. Comanche Indians, for one people explicitly,

recognized this and gave it as a reason for not identifying as members of their kindred those cognates who lay beyond the bilateral degree of second cousin.

A kindred as a functioning unit never organizes such a heterogeneous crowd as all potential relatives. Because cognate relationships ramify in all directions and multiply geometrically, their boundaries are too inclusive. They become so thin at the farthest edges that the definition of relationship is lost in the mists of uncertainty and vagueness. Consequently, anthropologists have found it very difficult to identify the actual, functioning kindreds in the societies where they are significant. The kindred is rather like a pool of personnel from which groups of individuals coalesce for specific cooperative activities, such as work parties, revenge groups, exchange groups, households, and transition rites. The composition of the actual kindred shifts and changes, dissolving and reappearing in altered form, depending on who among the kinsmen counts himself in for the occasion. Kindreds are flexible cells which are highly adaptable to fluid and relatively unstructured situations. They tend to be characteristic of simple hunting and gathering societies with limited resources, on the one hand, and of industrialized, free-market, urban civilizations, on the other.

Murdock describes the kindred very well for America:

In our own society, where its members are collectively called "kinfolk" or "relatives," it includes that group of near kinsmen who may be expected to be present and participant on important ceremonial occasions, such as weddings, christenings, funerals, Thanksgiving and Christmas dinners, and "family reunions." Members of a kindred visit and entertain one another freely, and between them marriage and pecuniary transactions for profit are ordinarily taboo. One turns to them first for aid when one finds oneself in difficulties. However much they may disagree or quarrel, they are expected to support one another against criticism or affronts from outsiders.[4]

[4]G. P. Murdock, *Social Structure*, pp. 56–57.

While the bilateral kinship system appears to work satisfactorily in those societies which use it, it does have inherent limitations and disadvantages, which have been summed up by Murdock as follows:

A particular disadvantage of the kindred appears in the instances in which an individual belongs to the kindreds of two other persons and thereby becomes involved in conflicting or incompatible obligations. If they get into serious difficulties with one another, for example, he may be required to avenge the one and yet to defend the other. If they become estranged, both are likely to turn to him for support and to subject him to emotional conflict and strain. The reader can supply numerous examples from the rankling family quarrels in our own society.[5]

The Occurrence of Bilateral Kinship Because we are so accustomed in Western society to reckoning our kinfolk or relatives bilaterally (we are equally "related" to our paternal and maternal families), it is easy to assume that this type of family pattern is universal and/or best. On the contrary, only about one-third of all human societies build their social structures on this foundation.

In Sub-Saharan Africa, where most tribes are gardeners or pastoralists, only one in twenty societies is based on the kindred. By contrast, two-thirds and three-fourths of the tribes of North and South America, respectively, were (or are) bilaterally structured. (See Figure 22-1).

Nonunilineal Kinship: The Ramage The ramage is a blending of lineage organization in such a way that anthropologists have come to call the result *nonunilinear organization.* First, the ramage utilizes the lineage principle: a person claiming ramage membership must be able to trace unilineal descent from the putative founder of the ramage. This might seem to make the ramage a unilineal unit. But, second, a person may trace his descent *either* patrilineally or matrilineally, according

to convenience and the acceptability of the claim to existing members of the ramage. Some members of the ramage get their identity as members through their mothers, others through their fathers. Hence the paradoxical lineal nonunilineality of the system. Murdock calls *ramages* "ancestor oriented *ambilineal* kingroups."[6]

Ramages have a stronger corporate quality than do most kindreds. They own land and other valued prerogatives. Hence, explicit ramage membership can have more definite advantages for the individual. Conversely, the ramage is more inclined to be demanding on its membership and, at the same time, to be choosy about whom it acknowledges as rightful members.

To use the Samoan ramage as an example:

The Samoan *'aiga sa* is a descent group controlling garden land, house sites, and certain ceremonials. It is exogamous, since the incest taboo is extended to all known relatives. Associated with each *'aiga sa* is one or more titles, from the senior of which the group takes its name. Title holders are selected from among the eligible males participating with the group. Affiliation with a descent group is through either father or mother, and a married couple may affiliate with the groups of either spouse. A person is mainly associated with one group—that with which he lives—but he may participate to some extent in several. Living with and using lands belonging to a particular *'aiga sa,* as well as the right to speak at meetings of the group, are dependent upon the consent of its members, and this may be denied if there is doubt about a person's genealogical relationship to the group or if he has failed to fulfill his obligations to it. Here, too, indefinitely extended relationships through consanguinity become limited by the obligations of participation. Even though there is considerable overlapping membership, the number of potential affiliations is appreciably reduced by both remissness in obligations and failure to remember genealogical connections.[7]

[5]*Ibid.,* p. 61.

[6]G. P. Murdock, *Ethnographic Atlas,* p. 49.
[7]W. Davenport, "Nonunilinear Descent and Descent Groups" (*American Anthropologist,* vol. 61, 1959), p. 561.

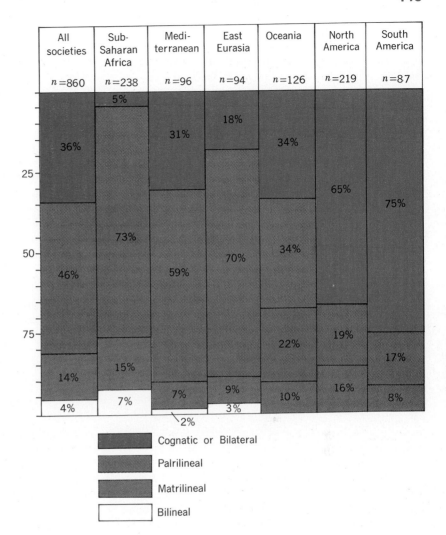

	All societies	Sub-Saharan Africa	Medi-terranean	East Eurasia	Oceania	North America	South America
	n=860	n=238	n=96	n=94	n=126	n=219	n=87

Fig. 22-1   Relative frequency of forms of kinship organization, according to geographic area. (Data from L. Bourguignon and E. Greenbaum, **Diversity and Homogeneity,** *table 29, p. 51.)*

Cognatic or Bilateral

Palrilineal

Matrilineal

Bilineal

The Samoan example is particularly apt, for half the societies in which ramages have been recognized are Oceanic. It could be that island ecology imposes limitation of available land for gardeners. Land is, therefore, highly valued. Thus, the exclusionary (yet flexible) membership qualifications, along with corporate land-holding, make the ramage a useful social response to the situation.

In spite of the great interest in nonunilineal descent stirred up among professional anthropologists since the late 1950s, the ramage is actually very rare. Only 31 of the 310 cog-

natic societies in the *Ethnographic Atlas* have ramages. And this is but 3.6 per cent (31 in 860 societies) of all the societies in the sample.

The Unilineal Principle of Kinship

The majority of human societies—two-thirds of those represented in the *World Ethnographic Sample*—are organized around the unilineal principle of kinship. One-third, including that of the United States, is bilateral (see Table 22-1). The popularity of the uni-

Table 22-1   Per Cent of Occurrence of Types of Descent Groups in a Sample of 505 Societies, Classified by Dominant Type of Subsistence Base

Type of subsistence base	*Bilateral*	*Patrilineal*	*Matrilineal*	*Duolineal*	*Number of tribes in sample*
Plow agriculture	32%	59%	8%	1%	117
Pastoralism	12%	77%	5%	6%	66
Developed agriculture	35%	35%	25%	5%	188
Incipient agriculture	45%	34%	15%	6%	33
Hunting and gathering	61%	19%	13%	7%	101

SOURCE: Data selected and converted to percentages from D. M. Schneider and K. Gough (eds.), *Matrilineal Kinship,* table 17-4, p. 677.

lineal principle indicates that as an adaptive invention, it serves well in overcoming some of the difficulties inherent in the kindred (vagueness of membership, unwieldy ramification, and competing obligations at times of conflict) and in the ramage (exclusionary practices and possible conflict of identity and loyalty). By figuring descent through one parental line, kinship becomes more clear-cut, and societies needing to rely on kinship groups to perform most of their basic functions are able to develop more predictable and reliable social patterns.

In a *patrilineal* system, the children of both sexes belong to the group of their father, which is, in turn, the group of his father's father, his father's father's father, and so on, as far back as genealogies are kept. The children of the man's sons and of the sons' sons, and so on, belong to the same group, as long as the line does not die out or break up.

In a *matrilineal* system, the children of both sexes belong to the group of their mother, which is, in turn, the group of her mother's mother, her mother's mother's mother, and so on, as far back as genealogies are kept. The relationship is *uterine.* The children of the woman's daughters and of the daughters' daughters, and so on, belong to the same group, as long as the line does not die out or break up.

Each unilineal kinship group is a collective body, a corporate entity, that endures through the ages. It may have a definite beginning, but it has the potential of unending endurance—unlike the conjugal-natal family. Unilineal kinship membership is therefore a matter of predetermined social heredity. One does not ordinarily join a unilineal group, for it is not a voluntary association. One is born into it perforce. The social fiction of adoption may make possible a change in unilineal affiliation, however. Unilineal group membership is discriminating and exclusive. It arbitrarily segments the population of a tribe; it separates genetic relatives into kinsmen and nonkinsmen. In compensation, it cements the genetic relatives who are included within the unilineal group into a firmer bond of kinship than is possible through bilateral extension of the family.

In a tribe segmented into lineages, sibs, or moieties . . . the individual knows exactly where he stands. . . . If both disputants are members of his own kin group, he is expected to remain neutral and to use his good offices to compose their differences. If neither is a member, the affair is none of his business. If one is a member but the other is not, he is expected to support his sibmate, regardless of the rights in the matter. In short, most conflict situations are simply and automatically resolved.[8]

[8]G. P. Murdock, *Social Structure,* p. 61.

In ceremony, economic activity, legal fracas and dispute, inheritance, and marriage, as these are related to kinship, the place and roles of members of unilineal groups are clear-cut.

A further consequence of the inclusive-exclusive character of unilineality is the sharp division it makes among cousins. Cross-cousins can never belong to the same unilineal group, although parallel-cousins may. This is what makes cross-cousin marriage possible.

Types of Unilineal Kinship Groups   The simplest type of unilineal group is known as the *lineage*. A lineage is an extended unilineal kinship group descended from a known ancestor, or founder, who ordinarily lived not more than five or six generations back. He, in the case of the patrilineage, or she, in the case of the matrilineage, is a real person and not a mythological or legendary figure. On the next level, above the lineage, there is the *clan*. A clan is an enlarged unilineal kinship group that rests on the fiction of common descent from a founding ancestor who lived so far in the distant past as to be mythological. When a tribal society is divided into two unilineal halves, each half is called a *moiety* (Fr. *moitié*, half), and the structure is known as *dual division*. Finally, there are *phratries*

(Gr. *phratria*, brother): linked groups of clans, where there are more than two such groups in the tribe. (If there were only two, they would be moieties.)

The possible extended unilineal groups are therefore (1) the lineage, (2) the clan, (3) the moiety, and (4) the phratry.

The Lineage   The lineage is the simplest form of extended unilineal kinship group in that it normally is limited to closely related agnatic (male descent line) or uterine (female descent line) kin and is rarely more than six generations deep. The "begats" of the Old Testament are the genealogies of the agnatic lineages of the pastoral Hebrews.

Lineages may be divided and subdivided into smaller segments. In such cases, they are called *segmentary lineages*. In a common African form, such as described for the Nuer by Evans-Pritchard,[9] each lineage is divided into two secondary lineages, which bifurcate into four tertiary lineages, which bifurcate into eight quaternary (or minimal) lineages. See Figure 22-2. When a minimal lineage fights with its opposite lineage (e.g., *a* versus *b*), no one else is directly involved except a local Priest of the Earth, who will evoke a settlement if anyone is killed. But if *a* becomes in-

[9]E. E. Evans-Pritchard, *The Nuer*.

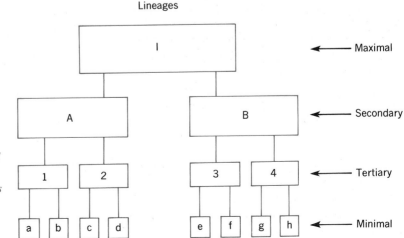

Lineages

Fig. 22-2   Bifurcating segmentary lineage relations. A and B are secondary segments of the maximal lineage, I. These in turn are segmented into two tertiary lineages each, which in turn segment into two minimal lineages each.

volved in a fight with lineages of *c* or *d*, then *a* and *b* join as segments of *1* to fight with *2*. If *1* gets into a dispute with *3* or *4, 2* will join it as a segment of *A* against *B*. But all will join together as a maximal lineage, *I*, against all other maximal lineages. Such intensive lineage activity prevails in segmentary societies with weak central governments.

In general terms, the subdivisions of any lineage segment may quarrel with one another but unite against all other segments on the same level.

Lineages may or may not reside as territorially based units. Localized minimal lineages usually form joint-family households or compounds.

Modern recognition of the lineage as a key structure in many social systems is due largely to the influence of A. R. Radcliffe-Brown and the work done in the field by anthropologists who were trained by him.

The Clan   Apart from size, the only essential difference between a lineage and a clan is that the members of a lineage can actually trace out their genealogies of common descent from a known ancestor, while clan members cannot. Nevertheless, if they belong to a given clan, people believe they have common descent, and their behavior is regulated accordingly.

Very often, however, the folklore of the clan includes a myth, as a part of its "charter," purporting to give a truthful account of how the clan came to be.

Dahomean Clans   Thus among the patrilineal Dahomeans of West Africa, one clan was founded by the son of a horse "who, bounding from the water in a fury of passion, lay with a woman on the bank of the river." Another clan is said to have descended from the "offspring of a woman and a pig, another from that of a woman and a toad, one from that of a woman and a dog, and the royal family . . . originated from the mating of a female leopard with the King of Adja." Another clan is said to have been created when a peanut was magically transformed into a man, who then mated with a poor woman who lived on roots. Dahomeans believe that the members of the Peanut clan lack the fine, smooth skin of other Dahomeans: "It is rough like the shell of a peanut." Further, the members of the Peanut clan are said to be recognizable on sight.[10] How this can be genetically possible in view of clan exogamy is a little difficult to understand, but ideological stereotypes can dogmatically color perception.

The members of a Dahomean clan have a rather special set of attitudes toward the animal or plant creature who begat their clan founder. All clans revere their clan founder and his descendants, who are their ancestors. All Dahomean clans except one abjure the flesh of the animal species associated with the founder, and many of them bear the name of the founder. All these features give the clans a totemic tinge.

Crow Clans   The usages of the Crow Indians illustrate a different kind of clan-origin legend. The clan names are taken from certain alleged exploits of the founders, after the manner of a Plains Indian warrior who bestows names on children memorializing outstanding events in his life. It would be quite a mistake to jump to the conclusion that members of the Crow "Greasy-inside-of-their-mouths" clan are slippery-tongued, for the name is actually honorific. The clan founder was such a provident hunter that he was always surfeited with rich, fat meat. It is said that his mouth was so coated with fat that when he spat in the campfire, his saliva flared up in the flames. Other Crow clan names memorialize alleged historical incidents or clan characteristics. The Piegan clan was originally called "They-eat-their-own-mucus." When some members of this clan once abandoned a wounded comrade in battle, they were dubbed "Piegan," meaning that they acted like the Piegan enemies, *not* a complimentary epithet from the Crow point of view.[11]

[10]M. J. Herskovits, *An Outline of Dahomean Religious Belief* (American Anthropological Association, Memoir 41, 1933), pp. 24–27.

[11]R. H. Lowie, *The Crow Indians*, pp. 15–16.

In all these instances, and in similar ones which could be drawn from a multitude of tribes, the actual origin of the clan is lost in the hoary past; this is not the case with lineages. Lineages may exist with or without clans. Clans may also exist with or without institutionalized lineages within them. Iroquois clans are made up of related groups of maternal lineages; the lineages are localized for the most part in long-house groupings. Very often lineage heads constitute the clan council, if there is one. In most parts of Indonesia, lineages are the basic functional group, for lineages or subclans form the localized village, while the clans have a more regional character.

The Moiety Reciprocity is the basis of all social relationships, for there can be no social relations without interaction. Human beings are so constituted that the isolated person is not a complete man. They are also so constituted that dependence without interdependence is not readily or for long accepted by the giver of services. He who gives would also receive. Through the building of a network of giving and receiving of services, a society expands its potentialities (see Reciprocal Gift Exchange, pages 346–350).

The principle of reciprocity is therefore operative in all societies. However, some societies are content to have it remain implicit in their cultures without placing much formal emphasis upon it. Others, such as the Trobriand Islanders and many other Melanesians, go to great lengths to institutionalize reciprocity and focus the spotlight of social awareness upon it.

One of the most effective ways of institutionalizing reciprocity is to organize the society on a moiety basis. Moieties are exogamous with few exceptions; each moiety supplies the other with its marriage partners. Other reciprocal services are invariably linked to the moiety alignments. Moieties thus effectively control certain types of behavior and serve to give concrete form to the reciprocity principle.

In cases where there are only two clans in a tribe, such as the Water and Land groups of the Central Miwok in California, clan and moiety are automatically synonymous. Multiple clans are the more common order, however, and when clans are linked to moieties, the moiety is the larger unit, and the clans are subdivisions of the moieties. Most of the Iroquois tribes have this kind of arrangement. Among the Seneca, to take a typical example, the Bear, Wolf, Turtle, and Beaver clans constitute one moiety, and the Deer, Snipe, Heron, and Hawk constitute the other. Originally, the moieties were exogamous, but in recent centuries they have lost their control over marriage, and only the clans have retained the exogamous rule. Each moiety performs the important mourning rituals on behalf of the other; the moieties compete against each other in the old Indian game of lacrosse, which is as much a ceremonial ritual as it is a sport. On the other hand, they do not enter into the political structure, although clans and lineages do.

Many American tribes possessing moieties associate them with the duality of the cosmos: sky and earth, water and land, winter and summer, red and white (war and peace). This may be seen as merely another way of objectifying the principle of reciprocity in the minds of the people.

The Phratry The clans in a phratry system retain their separate identities, but each clan in a phratry feels some sort of special identity to the others within its phratry. Moreover, they may have special obligations to fulfill toward one another.

The Hopi Indians have a large number of matrilineal clans, which are loosely linked into twelve exogamous phratries. The Aztecs, for their part, had four phratries embracing a number of clans among them. The Aztec phratries were important political and religious divisions in the structure of the empire, and they thus played a significant part in the social life of the people.

Nevertheless, it may be said that in general,

phratry organization is a relatively rare and functionally insignificant phenomenon. It does not usually control marriage, although Crow Indians think that it is better if members of the same phratry do not intermarry. Still, they have no prohibition against such action. For the most part, the phratry sentiment seems to rest either on a tradition of common origin or on common interests in ceremonial activity.

The Universal Functions of Unilineal Groups
Unilineal groups, except for the phratry, have two universal functions: (1) to broaden the base of the security group founded on the kinship bond by providing mutual aid and collective protection and liability in legal action and disputes, and (2) to regulate and control marriage.

Mutual Aid and Security   The lineage, clan, or moiety provides a large mutual-aid organization rooted in kinship. Man never stands alone. In seeking a firmer base for personal security than he can find without organization of his efforts and those of his fellow men, he casts about for some valid common interests that will serve to join him in social communion with others. There can be no doubt that the most generalized interest served by the clan is that of fulfilling the desire for security. The family, as we noted earlier, is the primary incubator of personal security. The clan expands this fundamental function of the family while at the same time tightening up the structure by reducing the diffusive effects of bilateral extension.

To meet the needs of security, lineages usually present a solid front to the rest of the world. In his personal interrelations with all persons outside the lineage, every lineage member must ideally be aided, abetted, and protected by all other members. This is the source of feuding in many societies and the primary defect of so many tribal legal systems.

As a complement of its united protection of individual members, the lineage or clan fre-

quently is collectively liable for the illegal acts of its own members against members of other clans or lineages. Thus, if a man commits murder, vengeance may commonly be taken on any member of the lineage, for even though he is innocent in fact, his person is legally merged with the persons of all his fellow kinsmen.

The Regulation of Marriage   The second universal function of the unilineal kinship group is to regulate marriage by means of exogamy. This, if we follow Malinowski's hypothesis, is a self-protective device that ensures solidarity by directing the sexual drive toward persons outside the essential kinship group.

We must not, however, overlook the fact that an additional security device is to be found in clan exogamy. Marriage imposes affinal obligations on the spouse's kin and clan. It tends to reduce overt aggression between the maritally allied groups; it also extends the base of support on which a man may depend (see Chapter 20, pages 402–403).

Secondary Functions of Unilineal Groups
In addition to the broad and universal functions mentioned above, clans carry responsibilities in the maintenance of culture. Both the nature of these responsibilities and the means of carrying them out vary from culture to culture. However, in general, these secondary functions cover a broad range of legal, governmental, economic, religious, and symbolic purposes.

Legal Functions   The lineage or clan commonly represents its individual members in lawsuits and is, conversely, responsible for their illegal acts. This function is discussed in detail in Chapter 26.

Governmental Functions   A function that the clan may or may not take on is that of government or law. The Aztec clan heads, called *speakers,* made up the Aztec tribal council. This group controlled ordinary political decisions, made war and peace, and as a judicial body decided disputes between clans and members of different clans. These same clan speakers sat on the grand national council, whose jurisdiction covered the most important law cases and election of the king. Aztec clans were grouped in four phratries, each of which had a captain-general, who served as a high-ranking military officer and who, in addition to his military post, served on the grand national council.

Many tribes have raised one clan to the position of royalty, and the hereditary chief must come from this clan. In Melanesia, this is true of the Trobriand Islanders; in Africa, the Dahomeans and the Ashanti are two examples among many.

Among the American Indians, the Winnebago of Wisconsin assigned political functions to seven of their twelve clans. The tribal chief was selected from the Thunderbird clan. In addition, this clan performed important functions connected with the preservation of peace (its governmental functions were mainly civil). The Warrior clan, as its name implies, provided war leadership; the village and hunt policemen came from the Bear clan; and the camp crier and aide-de-camp for the chief was always selected from the Buffalo clan. The Wolf, Water-spirit, and Elk clans had lesser political tasks. This was true not only of the Winnebago but also of the other highly organized Siouan tribes.[12]

Economic Functions   Among clan-organized tribes practicing hoe culture, the garden lands are almost inevitably owned or administered by the clans. Each Aztec clan owned its specific segment of the land. Assignments for use were made by the clan headman, who kept a record of all holdings. Every family head had the right to a plot of land (unless he had forfeited his clan membership by refusing to marry or carry out his clan obligations, in which case he became a common proletarian laborer). As long as a clansman was in good

standing, he could use his land or rent it to a fellow clansman (but not to an outsider). He could allot it to a clan descendant by testamentary disposition, but he could not alienate it (i.e., pass title to an outsider), for ownership of title was vested in the clan. He had what a lawyer would call a *possessory right of usufruct,* but not ownership. This same land-use system by clans prevails throughout Indonesia at this very time; it is also prevalent in Africa.

Clans may own other material goods in common, such as temples, meetinghouses, and sacred and ceremonial objects (see Chapter 13).

Religious and Ceremonial Functions   Clans or lineages may have their own supernatural beings and devices for controlling the supernatural world for their own ends, or they may possess certain ritual paraphernalia and ceremonies that they are expected to use for the well-being of the whole society.

Ancestor-worshiping Africans who have clan organization represent the first situation. The deceased clan ancestors are elevated to the status of clan deities. The clan head is usually the chief priest of the clan and the intermediary between his kinsmen and the ancestral spirits.

Among the Hopi and Zuñi, the all-important ceremonial organization is inextricably intertwined with the clan system; each clan must perform its part of the ceremonial activities for the benefit of the whole pueblo. Winnebago clans possess sacred bundles of religious paraphernalia used in ceremonial activity. These are examples of the second kind of situation.

Totemic Functions   Finally, clans may have totemic associations involving a feeling of identity with a plant, animal, or other natural object. This bond of emotional identity may extend from a mere feeling of kinship to actual reverence and worship. It may also lead to symbolic representation of the totemic object in clan fetishes.

[12]P. Radin, *The Winnebago Tribe* (Bureau of American Ethnology, Annual Report 37, 1923).

Dual (Double) Descent[13]

Prior to 1927, anthropologists thought that a society could embrace only one clan system, which had to be either matrilineal or patrilineal. Evidence to the contrary first came to the attention of English-reading anthropologists in R. S. Rattray's studies of the Ashanti, who were shown by this keen student of African tribes to have matrilineal clans called *abusua* and patrilineal groups called *ntoro*. The ntoro principle of inheritance is associated with the semen, and although the ntoro group is not organized, it, like the abusua, regulates marriage and sets certain incest prohibitions. It is totemic and imposes certain food tabus on its members.[14]

A subsequent report by Forde on another African tribe, the Umor, analyzes an even more precise system of dual descent.[15] The Umoran patrilineal, virilocal clan determines house and land affiliation and is called the *kepun*. There are twenty-two of these. At the same time, there are four *yajima* (plural form), which are matrilineal, nonlocalized clans through which movable property—principally livestock and currency—is inherited and marriage exchanges (progeny price and dowry) are made. "A man eats in his kepun and inherits in his lejima [singular form]," is the native adage. Murdock has put the phenomenon into focus by showing that double descent has a widely scattered distribution in Africa, India, Australia, Melanesia, and Polynesia.[16]

Ten per cent of the Oceanic tribes use double-descent systems, as do 7 per cent of the African societies; it is totally absent from the New World, giving a worldwide frequency of only 4 per cent.[17]

That it took English-speaking anthropologists so long to discover double descent shows how difficult it is for even carefully trained scientists to formulate conceptions necessary to the perception of new facts when those facts are completely alien to their experience and cultural background.

Lineage and Clan in Social Evolution

In the evolutionary theories of the nineteenth century, a major issue was whether matrilineal or patrilineal clans came first in the evolution of human society. Morgan, followed by Marx and Engels, argued that matrilineal systems took priority in a kind of communistic elysium. Patriliny, according to Marx and Engels, followed after the introduction of paired marriages, whereupon men were no longer content to pass their property collaterally to their sisters' sons. They established patrilineal inheritance, initiated private property in their domesticated herds, introduced slavery, and subordinated women to patriarchal domination. These practices resulted in what Engels called the first great social revolution and "the world-historical defeat of the female sex"[18] against which today's Women's Liberation Movement is contending. Bachofen also argued for the priority of the maternal clan in his work *Das Mutterrecht* (The Motherright). Others, such as McLennan, claimed that the patrilineal clan with patriarchal rule came first. In the Western world, the battle has long since been stilled,[19] but Communist anthropologists in Russia still hold faithfully to Engels' interpretation of Morgan.

---

[13]Also called *duolineal descent* and *double unilineal descent.*
[14]R. S. Rattray, *Ashanti; Ashanti Law and Constitution.* Dual descent as found in a neighboring people is explicitly examined in detail in a monograph by J. B. Christensen, *Double Descent among the Fanti.*
[15]C. D. Forde, "Kinship in Umor: Double Unilateral Organization in a Semi-Bantu Society" (*American Anthropologist,* vol. 41, 1939), pp. 523–553.
[16]G. P. Murdock, "Double Descent" (*American Anthropologist,* vol. 42, 1940), pp. 555–561. See also J. Goody, "The Classification of Double Descent Systems" (*Current Anthropology,* vol. 2, 1961), pp. 3–26.

[17]E. Bourguignon and L. Greenbaum, *Diversity and Homogeneity,* table 29, p. 51.
[18]F. Engels, *The Origin of the Family, Property and the State in the Light of the Researches of Lewis Henry Morgan,* p. 50.
[19]R. H. Lowie finally laid the issue to rest in his great synthesis of cultural anthropology, *Primitive Society,* published in 1920. See especially chap. 6.

Of course, there is no way of knowing from direct observation just what prehistoric social organization was like. Archaeological data can tell us what the technological traditions of a given locale were; they can reveal the outlines of settlement patterns; and they can yield exciting treasures of art, as well as the bones of men and animals. But in the absence of historical records, they tell us little of certainty about beliefs, values, marriage practices, kinship, inheritance, economic exchange, mythology, religion, ceremonialism, government, or law.

As for descent groups, bilateral, patrilineal, matrilineal, and double-descent extensions of the kinship group appear on *all* levels of cultural development and in all the major geographic areas of the world.

Among the most primitive or culturally undeveloped tribes . . . the Andamanese pygmies, the Paiute of the Great Basin, and the Yahgan of Tierra del Fuego are bilateral in descent, the Vedda of Ceylon, the Ramkokamekra of east central Brazil, and the Kutchin of northern Canada are matrilineal, and the Witoto of Amazonia, the Gilyak of Siberia, and the Miwok of California are patrilineal, while several native Australian tribes are characterized by double descent. All rules of descent are likewise well represented on the intermediate levels of culture, among agricultural and developed pastoral peoples. Even among literate peoples with relatively complex civilizations, our sample includes the bilateral Yankees and Syrian Christians, the patrilineal Chinese and Manchus, and the matrilineal Minangkabau Malays of Sumatra and Brahman Nayars of India.[20]

David Aberle has collated some very relevant data in which the societies represented in the *World Ethnographic Survey* are cross-classified by type (or level) of subsistence techniques and type of descent system.[21] Figure 22-3 shows the percentages of bilateral, matrilineal, patrilineal, and duolineal cultures that occur on each level of subsistence technology.

[20]G. P. Murdock, *Social Structure*, p. 186.
[21]D. F. Aberle, "Matrilineal Descent in Cross-cultural Perspective," in D. M. Schneider and K. Gough (eds.), *Matrilineal Kinship*, table 17–4, p. 677.

Descent Groups among Hunters and Gatherers   If hunting and gathering are taken as the most primitive food-getting techniques, such as were characteristic of the cultures of the Paleolithic era, we see that a majority (61 per cent) of such societies are bilateral and that there is no significant difference between the number that are patrilineal and the number that are matrilineal (19 and 13 per cent, respectively). Although 39 per cent of contemporary hunting and gathering cultures are unilineal or duolineal, it is not possible to say of any specific prehistoric culture whether it was organized bilaterally or not, except that the odds are 1.5 to 1 that it was.

Descent Groups among Intensive Foragers   Prehistoric intensive foragers marked the inception of the food revolution and the Era of Incipient Agriculture in the Neolithic Age. Among recent practitioners of hunting, fishing, and subsidiary gardening, there is a rise in the proportion of unilineal systems to 55 per cent. Patrilineality shows a marked increase. Thus, there is a slight trend toward lineages and clans, but it remains impossible to say whether any set of prehistoric foragers was unilineal or bilateral in a situation in which the odds are no greater than 5 to 4 in favor of unilineality over bilateralism.

Descent Groups among Developed Agriculturalists   On the level of developed agriculturalists, unilineality achieves a clear ascendancy: 65 per cent of the societies in the sample are unilineal, but there is no very great difference between matrilineal and patrilineal frequencies (25 per cent matrilineal, 35 per cent patrilineal). Matrilineal descent as a principle of social organization reaches its highest peak of frequency among developed agriculturalists, but even so, it is less common than either bilateralism or patrilineality. Gardening obviously encourages the formation of uxorilocal residence, for although women rarely hunt, they are the root and seed gatherers and, quite often, the gardeners. This is all work that can be done while tending a baby. Mothers and daughters work together, and men come to live with their wives. Only in such situations are matrilineal and matrilateral socioeconomic interests sufficiently strong to coalesce into matrilineages and matriclans; "matrilocality is a necessary but not a sufficient condition for the development of matrilineal descent groups. . . ."[22] Obviously, a rather unique and quite powerful combination of circumstances is required to overcome the more usual and effective factors that favor bilateral or patrilineal organization.

[22]Aberle, *op. cit.,* p. 659.

Descent Groups among Pastoralists The intimate relationship between males and livestock is dramatically reflected in the overwhelming patrilineality of pastoralism. Almost four-fifths (77 per cent) of all pastoral cultures are patrilineal.[23] ". . . [T]he cow "is

[23]This figure, as given in Figure 22-3, does not include Aberle's category of "New World pastoralists," which consists of societies that acquired domesticated livestock in post-Columbian times. There are 13 such tribes in the total sample of 565. Most of them are horse-herding hunters who were previously bilateral and who had acquired horses so recently that they did not have sufficient time to readjust their descent groups. Of the thirteen tribes, eleven (85 per cent) are bilateral, and two (15 per cent) are matrilineal. New World pastoralism is such an aberrant phenomenon that we have excluded it from the table.

Fig. 22-3   Inferred evolutionary trends in the occurrence of types of descent groups as revealed by the percentage of frequencies of descent groups in societies classified according to subsistence base. Pastoralism is not to be read as a higher evolutionary form than horticulture.

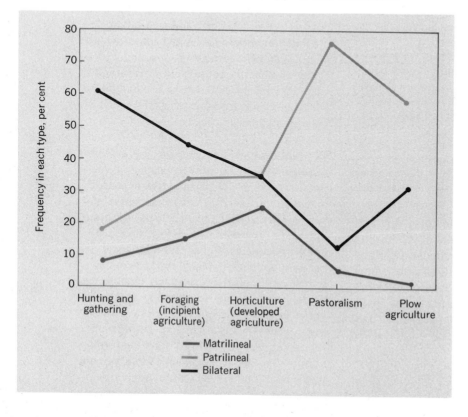

the enemy of matriliny, and the friend of patriliny."[24] This is the only safe generalization one could use in reconstructing the kinds of descent groups that were likely to have existed in any prehistoric stage of social evolution. And even this is of slight utility, since pastoralism is characteristic of a relatively minor proportion (12 per cent) of the cultures covered in the *World Ethnographic Sample.*

Descent Groups among Plow Agriculturalists

The hitching of the horse or oxen to the plow is the final step in precivilized evolution of subsistence techniques. It occurred in the Old World Late Neolithic Age. Plow agriculture subordinates the pastoralist's interest in animals to the horticulturalist's concern with farming. This is reflected in a reduction of the degree of frequency of patrilineality among pastoral societies as compared with societies with plow agriculture: from 77 per cent down to 59 per cent. There is a significant rise in bilaterality (12 to 32 per cent) as well as some increase in matrilineality and duolineal organization.

In Western civilization, the shift to bilateralism is a reflection of the influence of urbanization and the invention of the legal instrument of contract, whereby a person is able to stand as a self-determining, individual legal entity rather than as a unit in the corporate kinship group (see pages 517–518 for further development of this point).

As Figure 22-3 graphically reveals, most hunters and gatherers are bilateral, and as one "moves up" the evolutionary scale to developed agriculture, bilateralism declines. The patrilineal curve is the obverse to the bilateral. Matrilineality realizes its highest potential among intensive agriculturalists, but at no level does it ever exceed other forms of descent groups. On the highest level of food production (plow agriculture), it all but disappears.

Looking to the future, as the scientific,

industrialized technology of Western civilization is introduced all around the world, it is improbable that any unilineal systems of kinship organization will survive into the twenty-second century, except perhaps in a few peasant areas (see Chapter 34).

SUMMARY

The boundaries of kinship are never limited to the conjugal-natal family, for such a family is invariably embedded in a larger web of kinship. The major forms of kinship organization are bilateral, ambilineal, and unilineal (patrilineal, matrilineal, and double descent).

Bilateral extension of kinship produces the kindred. When extended beyond three degrees, it embraces so many persons that it becomes unwieldy in size. But even more difficult is the fact that each person must belong to a number of such extended groups, and is faced with the problem of conflicting loyalties.

A compromise form of the extended kinship group which partially overcomes these shortcomings is the ramage. The ramage allows for discretionary choice in identifying membership through either one's paternal or maternal descent from a ramage ancestor. Ramages are usually landholding groups in which membership is necessary if a person is to have access to gardening land. Combining two unilineal lines of descent within one structure, the ramage is ambilineal.

The majority of societies have found it expedient to utilize the unilineal principle for extended kinship reckoning. The unilineal principle has certain inherent advantages. It automatically reduces the number of potential members of the group by including only one-half of a person's relatives. Above all, it clearly establishes kinship identity and lessens the problem of conflicting loyalties.

Types of groups formed on the unilineal principle are the lineage, the clan, the phratry, and the moiety. Whether the matrilineal or patrilineal pattern prevails in a given culture

[24]Aberle, *op. cit.,* p. 680.

is strongly influenced by the residence customs: uxorilocal, virilocal, avunculocal, neolocal, or bilocal. Residence, in turn, is strongly influenced by the type of dominant subsistence base in a culture. Although among simple hunters and gatherers the bilateral principle of organization is dominant, unilineal groups are found in one-third of human societies on this level. Bilateralism progressively gives way to lineage and clan organization, as culture develops to foraging and intensive gardening. Its lowest frequency is found among the strongly patrilineal pastoralists. Patrilineality is relatively weak among hunters and gatherers; it becomes relatively stronger as cultures develop a horticultural base; it overwhelms all other forms among pastoralists; and it remains the dominant form among the protocivilized practitioners of plow agriculture. Matrilineality exists as a minor form of kinship organization on all levels of cultural development except the highest, where it completely disappears.

Generalizations concerning prehistoric kinship structures can be formulated only in broad, relatively unspecific terms. They may never be taken as statements of scientific laws; at best, they qualify as suggestive inferences drawn from contemporary primitive societies believed, on the basis of their material cultures, to be analogically similar to prehistoric societies whose material bases are known from archaeological data. Inferences about prehistoric social organization are never verifiable in specific content.

SELECTED READINGS

Bohannan, P., and J. Middleton (eds.), *Kinship and Social Organization* (1968). Parts II, III, and IV contain basic articles on unilineal, nonunilineal descent and bilateral systems by such authorities as Evans-Pritchard, Firth, Goodenough, Mead, Middleton, and Morgan.

Fortes, M., *The Web of Kinship among the Tallensi* (1949), chaps. 1, 5, and 11, "Kinship and the Lineage System," "Parents and Children in the Framework of the Lineage," and "The Web of Extra-clan Kinship." A masterful analysis of the complexities of kinship in an African tribe.

——, "Structure of Unilinear Descent Groups" (*American Anthropologist*, vol. 55, 1953), pp. 17–44. A most excellent exposition of the application of the unilineal principle in primitive cultures.

Fox, R., *Kinship and Marriage* (1967). Perhaps too advanced for the beginning student, but chapters 3, 4 and 5 will add much content to what has been outlined in the present book.

Goodenough, W. H., *Description and Comparison in Cultural Anthropology* (1970). Chapter 2, "Kindred and Clan," provides a clear-headed discussion of some current problems and thoughts in kinship analysis.

Lowie, R. H., *Primitive Society* (1920), chap. 6, "The Sib." Although this contains some discussions of problems that are no longer live issues in anthropology, the chapter is highly informative.

Murdock, G. P., *Social Structure* (1949), chaps. 3 and 4, "Consanguineal Kin Groups" and "The Clan."

Radcliffe-Brown, A. R., and M. Fortes (eds.), *African Systems of Kinship and Marriage* (1950). Descriptive analyses of a number of African examples of differing types of kinship organization.

Schneider, D. M., and K. Gough (eds.), *Matrilineal Kinship* (1961). An impressive work in which six anthropologists pool their efforts in ethnological examination of a series of matrilineal societies. Schneider proposes a set of hypothetical characteristics of matrilineal systems, Gough interprets the ethnographic data, and Aberle puts their propositions to the statistical test of cross-cultural validation on a broad scale.

Chapter 23

Kinship Systems and Terminology

Kinship behavior is not instinctive. The genetic code says little or nothing about how a man should behave toward his brothers, his father, his cousins, and his aunts. It says little or nothing about how a woman should behave toward her father, her sisters, her mother-in-law, her mother's sister, or any other genealogical relative. Kinship, we have seen, is a matter of social organization, and social organization is an aspect of culture, reflecting ecology, subsistence, ideology, and a host of other things.

Kinship relations consist of the interacting roles customarily ascribed by a people to the different statuses of relationship. Every culture includes a set of words, or labels, symbolizing each of its kinship statuses. These labels are called *kinship terms,* and the whole is called the *system of kinship* (or *relationship*) *terminology.*

The Classificatory Principle

The first important principle to grasp in the study of kinship systems is that *no system provides a separate and distinct term for every possible kind or position of genealogical relationship.* All systems equate, lump, or merge some relatives of different genealogical positions into one single category, which is identified by a specific term. For example, the Comanche Indians equate father, father's brother, and mother's sister's husband all under one term, *ap'.* Father's brother and mother's sister's husband (both of whom we call "uncle") are genealogically distinct from father, but to the Comanche they are merged

*Fig. 23-A   Tlingit totem poles in Alaska.
(Charles Mag. Black Star.)*

or equated under the same identifying term of relationship.

Kinship terms that result from merging are called *classificatory terms.* The effect of classificatory terminology is to merge lineal relatives (as one's father) with collateral relatives (as one's father's brother).

A kinship term that applies to a particular genealogical status and no other is called *particularizing* or *descriptive.* Anglo-Americans, for instance, tend to apply the terms "father" and "mother" only to actual progenitors when referring to relatives. However, as no system is ever wholly particularizing or classificatory, we also have certain classificatory terms, such as "cousin," "uncle," "aunt," "niece," "nephew," "grandfather," "grandmother," "grandson," and "granddaughter."

Our insistence on particularizing "father" and "mother" is sociologically significant, for it will be noted that in addition to this particularization, we use the words "son" and "daughter" to mean only our own children and not those of our brothers or sisters. Likewise, we use the terms "brother" and "sister" to refer exclusively to the siblings of our own primary conjugal-natal family. Other relatives of our own generation level we call "cousins." Our terminology thus places strong emphasis upon the exclusiveness of our primary conjugal-natal family; it rigidly distinguishes more remote relatives. This reflects the great social significance of our close relatives in the conjugal-natal family as against the rest of our larger kindred. Lineal relatives are more important to us than collateral ones.

In most societies, as we have noted, extended kinship groups play larger roles than is the case with the civilizations of Europe and the Western Hemisphere. In such societies, merging or lumping of relatives on a collateral basis is therefore much more likely.

Since kinship terms designate social statuses, what you must call a person ideally determines how you should behave toward him. Further, all persons who are called by the same kinship term should (and again, ideally) receive the same sort of treatment, since they enjoy ideologically identical statuses in the system of social organization.

Comanche Kinship Terminology   It will help to get the feel of kinship if we briefly explore the way in which relatives are grouped and identified in a few systems other than our own. To do this, we shall begin with a look at the way the Comanche Indians classify relatives.

Comanche social structure is bilateral and bilocal. Polygynous marriages were permissible until forbidden by the federal law of the United States. The Comanche kindred is exogamous; no one may marry a relative within three degrees of recognized relationship.

In treating any system of kinship terminology, it is necessary to have a starting point in a particular individual. This person is called *ego* (L. *ego,* I). In this example, we start with ego as a male, for it makes a difference whether a man or woman is speaking.

A Comanche male calls his mother *pia.* But there are also other female relatives called *pia,* namely, his mother's sisters, his mother's female cousins, and his father's brother's wife. *Pia* can thus be seen to mean not "mother" to a Comanche, but more exactly, "female relative of my mother's generation and kindred."

His father he calls *ap'.* But there are also other male relatives called *ap',* namely, his father's brothers, his father's male cousins, and his father's sister's husband. *Ap'* thus does not mean "father" to a Comanche, but "male relative of my father's generation and kindred."

The Comanche calls his mother's brother by a different term, *ara.* Thus, where we merge father's brother and mother's brother together as "uncle," the Comanche merges father and father's brother in one category, while distinguishing mother's brother in another.

The same thing is done with aunts. Mother and mother's sister are both classified as *pia,* but father's sister is distinguished as *paha.*

This practice is called *forked merging* or *bifurcate merging*.

| Father's brother | Mother's brother |
| merged with father | kept distinct |

Ego (speaker)

Members of the agnatic and uterine kindreds are thus kept distinct.

Within his own generation, all relatives are "brother" and "sister" to a Comanche; cousins are not identified as such. But relative age is, so the Comanche distinguishes between *paβi* and *tami*, "older male relative of my own generation" and "younger male relative of my own generation." A *paβi* may be ego's elder brother, father's brother's son, father's sister's son, mother's brother's son, mother's sister's son, and wife's sister's husband (if ego is a male) or husband's sister's husband (if ego is a female). *Tami* applies to all these categories if the person referred to is younger than ego.

A "son" to ego includes not only his own boys but also the male offspring of all his *paβi* and *tami*, the sons of his wife's sisters, and his sister's daughter's husband. All these are called *tua*.

A "daughter" includes his own female offspring and the female offspring of all his *patsi* (elder female relatives of his own generation) and *nami* (younger female relatives of his own generation), his wife's sister's daughters, and his sister's son's wife. All these are called *pedi*.[1]

The kinship terms that have been described here cover the members of ego's primary and secondary conjugal-natal families. Whereas Anglo-Americans use exclusive, descriptive terms that isolate the two conjugal-natal families, it may readily be seen that the Comanches merge such individuals within the larger kindred. For them, the kindred is the socially more important group.

All in all, the Comanches recognize thirty-six different kinship categories, each of which has a different kinship term. None of them is identical to the groupings or distinctions drawn by us in our kinship system. *The way in which any society identifies relatives is dependent upon the nature of its kinship groups.* These, in turn, are predominantly determined by the rules of residence and subsistence practices that prevail in the culture.

Principles of Kinship Identification

In a classic paper, Kroeber identified the following eight principles of kinship distinctions that may be utilized in shaping a kinship system.[2]

1. Difference in generation levels (father, son; grandparent, grandchild; etc.)

2. Difference in age levels within the same generation (elder and younger brother; father's elder brother; etc.)

3. Difference between lineal and collateral relationship (father, uncle; brother, cousin; etc.)

4. Difference in sex of relatives (brother, sister; uncle, aunt, etc.)

5. Difference in sex of the speaker (males and females may have two separate systems of terms)

6. Difference of sex of the person through whom the relationship is established (*father's* brother, *mother's* brother; *father's* father, *mother's* father; *father's father's sister's daughter's* daughter, etc.)

7. Difference between genetic relatives and those connected by marriage (mother; husband's mother, etc.)

8. Difference in status or life condition of

---

[1] For a full presentation of the Comanche system, see E. A. Hoebel, "Comanche and Hᵌkandika Shoshone Relationship Systems" (*American Anthropologist*, vol. 41, 1939), pp. 440–457. For a highly sophisticated transformational analysis of the Comanche system, the tenacious and stouthearted student might try E. A. Hammel, "A Transformational Analysis of Comanche Kinship Terminology" (*American Anthropologist*, vol. 67, part 2, 1965), pp. 65–105.

[2] A. L. Kroeber, "Classificatory Systems of Relationship" (*Journal of the Royal Anthropological Institute of Great Britain and Ireland*, vol. 39, 1909), pp. 77–84.

the person *through whom* the relationship is established (living or dead, single or married, etc.).

Few systems make use of all eight distinctions, but many use the first seven.

If the reader will carefully examine the Comanche terms that we have given, he will be able to identify each of the first seven principles in them. The Anglo-American system, on the other hand, utilizes only four of the eight (1, 3, 4, 7).

Types of Kinship Systems

It is a remarkable fact that although a very large number of differing kinship systems are theoretically possible, society after society classifies its kinsmen in essentially similar ways, so that the types of kinship systems that actually come into existence are few in number.

The classification (or typing) of kinship systems presents all the usual problems of selection of criteria that were discussed in an earlier chapter (pages 83–85). As is the case with races, fewer or more types result, according to the quality and number of criteria employed. The most significant criteria used by anthropologists for general classification of systems of kinship terminologies are of two orders: (1) the degree of merging and bi-

furcation of lineal and collateral kin in the parental generation, and (2) the degree of merging and bifurcation of collateral kin in ego's own generation.[3]

Kinship Systems Based on Classification of Parental Generation Use of the criterion of classification of lineal and collateral kin on the parental level produces four types of kinship systems: (1) generational, (2) lineal, (3) bifurcate merging, and (4) bifurcate collateral. (See Table 23-1.)

Generational Systems The emphasis in this type of system is on merging of all relatives on a given generational level. Thus, mother, mother's sister, and father's sister are all lumped under a single kinship term. The same is true of father, father's brother, and mother's brother.

Lineal Systems A lineal system emphasizes the distinction between direct ascendant and descendant relatives as separate from collaterals. Therefore, mother is distinguished from mother's sister and father's sister, who are merged, as in English "aunt." The same holds

[3]The first of these systems was formulated by R. H. Lowie and published in the fourteenth edition of the *Encyclopaedia Britannica*, in the article "Relationship Terms." The second system was formalized by G. P. Murdock, *Social Structure*, pp. 223–259.

Fig. 23-1   *The distinction of collateral and lineal kinsmen.*

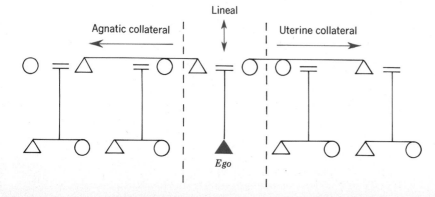

Table 23-1 Types of Kinship Systems according to Classification of Relatives in the Parental and in Ego's Own Generations

Type of descent group	*Classification of parental generation*		*Classification of ego's own generation*	
	Type	*Merging and bifurcation*	*Type*	*Merging and bifurcation*
Bilateral	Generational	[Mo = MoSi = FaSi] [Fa = FaBr = MoBr]	Hawaiian	[×Cos = ‖Cos = Sib]
Bilateral	Lineal	Mo ≠ [MoSi = FaSi] Fa ≠ [FaBr = MoBr]	Eskimo	[×Cos = ‖Cos] ≠ Sib
Matrilineal or patrilineal	Bifurcate merging	[Mo = MoSi] ≠ FaSi [Fa = FaBr] ≠ MoBr	Crow, Iroquois, Omaha	×Cos ≠ [‖Cos = Sib]
	Bifurcate collateral	Mo ≠ MoSi ≠ FaSi Fa ≠ FaBr ≠ MoBr	Sudanese	×Cos ≠ ‖Cos ≠ Sib

NOTE: The Hawaiian generational type merges all parents and all cousins; the Eskimo lineal type distinguishes parents and siblings from their collaterals; the three bifurcate-merging systems merge parents with collaterals of like sex and merge parallel-cousins with siblings, while distinguishing cross-cousins; the Sudanese bifurcate-collateral type distinguishes all parental kin and cousins.

KEY: [=] = merged categories; ≠ = distinguished or bifurcated categories; × Cos = cross-cousins; ‖ Cos = parallel-cousins; Sib = siblings.

for father and his collaterals, who are merged, as in English "uncle." Lineal systems are also associated with bilateral systems of descent groups.

Bifurcate-merging Systems Lineage systems of descent groups tend to produce bifurcate-merging systems of terminology, as will be demonstrated in the analysis of Crow terminology given below. Father's brother is merged with father, while both are distinguished from mother's brother. Put in another way, father and paternal uncle are lumped, and maternal uncle is distinguished. Likewise, mother and maternal aunt are lumped, and paternal aunt is distinguished. Members of the two descent groups are rigorously kept separate from each other.

Bifurcate-collateral Systems In this type of system, all collaterals on the parental generation level are bifurcated, or distinguished. Father, father's brother, and mother's brother all are called by separate terms of designa-

tion, as are mother, mother's sister, and father's sister. There is no significant correlation between bifurcate-collateral terminology and any particular system of descent groups, nor is there any adequate theory to account for the prevalence of this highly particularizing method of classification.

Relative Frequency of Systems Based on Classification of Parental Generation Approximately 44 per cent of the kinship systems in the *World Ethnographic Sample* are of the bifurcate-merging type. This happens because most descent systems are unilineal and automatically place mother's and father's brothers in different descent groups. Bifurcate-merging terminology reflects this simple fact.

Generational-type kinship systems go with bilateral descent systems and occur in 30 per cent of the cases. Bilateral systems do not separate mother's and father's kin, nor does generational terminology.

Lineal systems, which occur in approximately one-eighth of the cases, are strongly associated with the occurrence of bilateral descent systems.

Bifurcate-collateral types are fairly rare and do not correlate with any particular type of descent; they have not been adequately explained.

Kinship Systems Based on Classification of Cousins   Use of the criterion of merging and particularizing of siblings, cross-cousins, and parallel-cousins produces more refined results than analysis of the parental generation terminology alone. Therefore, Murdock has developed a typology of kinship systems based upon these criteria.

Murdock's classification sets up six types of kinship systems with respect to distinctions or lack of distinctions made in their terminologies for cousins. They are (1) the Hawaiian, (2) the Eskimo, (3) the Iroquois, (4) the Crow, (5) the Omaha, and (6) the Sudanese. These are actually the same as the generational categories, as can be seen from Table 23-1, except that the category of bifurcate merging is refined into the Crow, Iroquois, and Omaha types.

The Hawaiian System   This is the same as the generational system. Because of its emphasis on generation equivalence, the Hawaiian system draws no distinction between cousins and siblings, all of whom belong to the same kindreds.

The Eskimo System   The Eskimo system draws no distinctions between cross- and parallel-cousins but does distinguish cousins from siblings. Its emphasis is on the immediate chain of conjugal-natal families. The Eskimo system is familiar to all speakers of the English language, for this is the system used in Anglo-American culture.

The Iroquois System   In the Iroquois system of terminology, siblings and parallel-cousins of the same sex are usually equated under one term, whereas cross-cousins are distin-

guished by different terms. Iroquois terminology is almost nonexistent among bilaterally organized tribes. It is weakly correlated (phi = 0.135)[4] with matrilineal and duolineal descent groups and appears to be the product of a weak matrilineal, uxorilocal system of social organization.

The Crow System   The Crow system is based on a social structure that contains strongly developed matrilineal lineages and/or clans.

In cousin terminology, cross-cousins are distinguished from each other (i.e., there are separate terms for father's sister's son or daughter and mother's brother's son or daughter); these are also distinguished from parallel-cousins and from siblings. But paternal cross-cousins are merged with father and father's sister, according to sex.

It is in this last lumping of father's sister's daughter with her paternal aunt that the lineage emphasis is made clearest. Hocart has shown us how earlier anthropologists were trapped into false conceptions of kinship by thinking of such classificatory terms as "father" as meaning an extension of fatherhood.[5] Thus, Lowie translated the Crow Indian term *birupxe* as "father." *Birupxe* is the term applied to ego's father, father's brother, and father's sister's son (when ego is a male). Properly understood, it means not "father," but "male of my father's matrilineal lineage or clan." For the same reason, the term used in reference to ego's father's sister means "female of my father's matrilineal lineage or clan." The term for "mother" means "woman married to a male of my own matrilineal lineage or clan." Figure 23-2 diagrams this clearly.

Because father, father's brother, father's sister's son, and father's sister's daughter's son are all lumped together under one term as members of the same matrilineage, ego's

[4]A. D. Coult and R. W. Habenstein, *Cross Tabulations of Murdock's World Ethnographic Sample*, p. 512.
[5]A. M. Hocart, "Kinship Systems" (*Anthropos*, vol. 32, 1937), pp. 345–351.

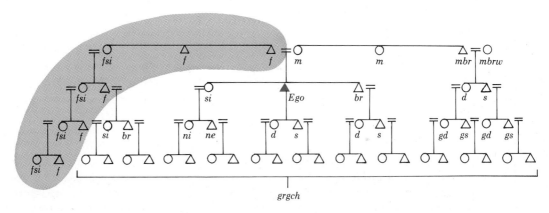

Fig. 23-2 *Crow-type identifications. Note that the male patrilateral cross-cousin may marry ego's mother and is called by the same term as father. The female patrilateral cross-cousin is merged with father's sister. Ego may marry his maternal uncle's wife; matrilateral cross-cousins are called by the same term as son and daughter.*

mother is called "wife" by all of them. She may marry any one of them in secondary affinal marriage. Therefore, levirate and husband's-sister's-son marriages are preferential forms in systems of marriage related to strong matrilineal descent systems and Crow terminology. Conversely, a man may marry his mother's brother's wife. The effect of all this on cousin terminology is that patrilateral cross-cousins are called by the same term as that used for father, and matrilateral cross-cousins, as children of the woman ego calls "wife," are designated by the same term as that used for son and daughter. It should be noted, however, that although these secondary affinal marriages are permissible, they are not reported as preferred marriages in all cultures in which Crow-type terminology occurs.

The Omaha System   The Omaha system is the patrilineal obverse of the Crow system. Mother and female matrilateral cross-cousin (mother's brother's daughter) are merged under one term that means "female member of my mother's patrilineage or clan." Father's sister's daughter (patrilateral cross-cousin) is merged with sister's daughter under a term that means "daughter of a female of my father's patrilineage or clan." (See Figure 23-3.)

The Sudanese System   This type is at the opposite pole from the Hawaiian in that its terms are emphatically particularizing, or descriptive. Consequently, it has separate terms for each type of cousin, for siblings, and for aunts, nieces, uncles, and nephews.

The Anglo-American Kinship System   The Anglo-American kinship system is of the Eskimo type. It lumps all cousins, but distinguishes them from brothers and sisters. In the absence of lineages and clans, it shows no lineal emphasis except within the primary and secondary conjugal-natal families. These are sharply set off from the kindred by the exclusive limitation of terms like "father," "mother," "brother," "sister," "son," and "daughter" to those who actually belong to the two conjugal-natal families.[6]

Monogamy is reflected in the fact that the words "father," "mother," "husband," and "wife" can apply to only one person within

[6]T. C. Parsons, "The Kinship System of the Contemporary United States" (*American Anthropologist*, vol. 45, 1943), p. 24.

the kinship system. When these terms are used within the church system, they imply and evoke certain filial responses and behaviors that carry over from the kinship system, but no one makes the mistake of assuming that they imply genetic relationship. We see this also in the use of "brother" and "sister" terms among members of social and religious clubs and movements.

One thing that is genuinely distinctive about the Anglo-American kinship terminology is the abundance of alternative terms used in addition to "mother," "father," "husband," and "wife." For "father" these are "dad," "daddy," "pop," "pa," "old man," "boss," "pater," and "governor." None of these carries the respect connotations, however, of the word "father." Their use varies in accordance with the authority roles acknowledged to the father by his children within the particular family, and they reflect the flexible nature of American family patterns. By and large, the term "daddy," widely used by youngsters, is dropped by boys as they grow

up, although it is often retained by daughters for many years. Father-son relations become more restrained and formal, whereas there is much evidence to support the inference that the persistence of the use of the word "daddy" by girls expresses a continuance of preadolescent affectivity between father and daughter.

A parallel series of terms exists for "mother": "mom," "mommy," "mummy," "ma," "mama," "mater," and "old woman." Very similar role qualities are ascribed to these terms as to the alternatives to "father." Both boys and girls tend to shift from use of informal mother terms to the more formal "mother" as they grow up. Boys, in other words, do not keep the familiar term for "mother" the way girls carry on with "daddy."[7]

Affinal relatives are all distinguished by means of the "in-law" suffix. However, a

[7]D. M. Schneider and G. C. Homans, "Kinship Terminology and the American Kinship System" (*American Anthropologist,* vol. 57, 1955), pp. 1195–1199; also, R. M. Burling, "American Kinship Terms Once More" (*Southwestern Journal of Anthropology,* vol. 26, 1970), pp. 15–24.

Fig. 23-3   Omaha-type kinship identifications. The relatives within the shaded area are members of ego's mother's patrilineage. Females identified as "m" are all classified with "mother" under a term which means "female member of my mother's patrilineage." Their brothers are all classified "mbr" under a term which means "male member of my mother's patrilineage." Note the differentiating terminologies on all generation levels.

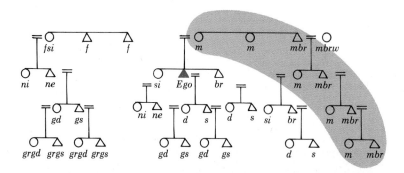

device of *teknonymy,* the practice of calling an adult by the name used by his child, is often used to soften the stiffness of the "in-law" term when addressing a mother-in-law or father-in-law. This is managed by identifying with the offspring and addressing spouses' parents as "grandmother" and "grandfather." They are lineal kin to the children, and so by this fictive device are drawn into the lineal family group.

Except for a slight linguistic emphasis given to the patrilineal line through patronymy, the consequences of which are more attitudinal than structural or behavioral, the system is symmetrically multilateral. All ramifications extending out from the immediate lineal line are treated with equal weight (or lack of it). Such distinctions in emphasis as do occur are the result of personal preferences or aversions and proximity of residence, not the consequences of any systematic emphasis.

Social Effects of the American Kinship System
The lack of structural cohesiveness outside the inner circle of families in lineal descent in the Anglo-American kinship system reflects the weak role kinship groups play in this society. This emphasizes the independence of separate conjugal-natal family units. Many problems concerning marriage and the family rise directly or indirectly from this fact. Parent-child conflict is generated because children must develop independence to be able to found their own economically independent families with separate households.

Much of the erratic behavior of adolescents, so baffling or frustrating to adults, may be traced in part to the insecurity of the emergent boy or girl, who is in transition from the bonds of his primary family of birth to the expectant secondary conjugal-natal family he or she must soon found. Insecurity in old age is the lot of many parents whose secondary conjugal-natal family has been pared down until only they are left. When one of them dies, the survivor is at sea, with no comfortable base in which to harbor. Old people's homes and old-age security legislation are the palliative social consequences.

Few of the social relations of children are predetermined by kinship status outside the immediate conjugal-natal family. Children are thrown into open competition for social status; some are rewarded with success and prestige, and others find only frustration and insecurity.

Marriage in the United States rests heavily on the bond of love and affection, for there are no absolutely ascribed preferential matings to solve the problem of mating, nor is there much family control of mating, as in Asia and France. These are only some of the upsetting consequences of our open, weak kinship system.

The advantages of this system are those which derive from individual freedom of action in social and economic relations: freedom to choose one's friends within or without the relationship group, freedom to choose one's mate, freedom to find an occupation fairly untrammeled by kinship status, and freedom to live where one wills according to a self-determined life style.

In America today, the individual couple is largely on its own, to stand or fall as a unit according to its ability to surmount the hazards of the loose, and weakening, kinship group, and to utilize the freedoms of a mobile and rapidly changing society. The divorce mills grind for those who fail, and rebellious youth share "pads" and seek a substitute for the rejected extended family in experimental communes of peers—creating new, fictive kin groups.

SUMMARY

Systems of kinship terminology reflect the forms of kinship grouping in the social organization of any culture. The kinship terms of address or reference are tags or labels symbolic of each relative's status in relation to the speaker of the term. Each status has its customary roles, or norms of behavior, and the behavior of relatives is generally standardized according to status.

No kinship system distinguishes each separate genetic relationship. On the contrary, the tendency is to lump relatives of unlike genetic status into categories of like kinship status. Systems that lump relatives extensively, merging lineal and collateral relatives in common categories, are called *classificatory;* systems that emphasize genetic distinctions are called *descriptive* or *particularizing.*

Kroeber's eight principles of kinship distinctions reveal the possible factors that may be used in developing kinship categories of terminological identification.

Lowie introduced a system for classifying kinship terminologies according to *merging* or *bifurcation* of the parental level of kinsman. This results in a four-class system: *generational, lineal, bifurcate merging,* and *bifurcate collateral.* Murdock's system classifies kinship terminologies according to merging or bifurcation of siblings and cousins. It produces a sixfold set of primary classes, which are identified with the names of the tribe (or area, in the case of the Sudanese) in which the type was first described at length. They are the Hawaiian, Eskimo, Crow, Iroquois, Omaha, and Sudanese.

The Hawaiian type of terminology, which equates all relatives of each generation level, is the most highly classificatory. Hawaiian and Eskimo terminologies are associated with bilateral social structure. At the other end of the pole, Crow and Omaha terminologies are associated with strong matrilineal and patrilineal social structures.

The American kinship system is bilateral, with an Eskimo lineal type of terminology. Beyond the conjugal-natal family, there is only the kindred, and this in weak form. Alternative kinship terms, used by Americans, reflect differences in degree of respect and familiarity between relatives on an individual basis, and in this there appear to be psychologically and socially significant differences on a sex basis. Kinship systems are reflected in relationship terminologies. Kinship dominates all relationships in most non-Western societies.

SELECTED READINGS

Bohannan, P., and J. Middleton (eds.), *Kinship and Social Organization* (1968). Part I, pages 1–148, presents eight landmark papers in the development of kinship theory and method. These are not really for the introductory student, but they are worth knowing about.

Eggan, F., *Social Organization of the Western Pueblos* (1950). This will not be easy reading for the beginner, but it is one of the finest comparative studies of kinship systems.

———— (ed.), *Social Anthropology of North American Tribes* (2d ed., 1955). Contains highly informative articles on the kinship systems of six American Indian tribes.

————, "Kinship: Introduction" (*International Encyclopedia of the Social Sciences,* vol. 8, 1968), pp. 390–401. A useful supplement to the Lowie article, cited below. Contains an excellent, comprehensive bibliography on the anthropology of kinship.

Lowie, R. H., "Kinship," (*Encyclopaedia of the Social Sciences,* vol. 3, 1931), pp. 568–572. The elements of kinship systems clearly presented.

Murdock, G. P., *Social Structure* (1949), chaps. 6 and 7, "Analysis of Kinship" and "Determinants of Kinship Terminology." Requires hard thinking, but analysis of kinship systems is never easy.

Schusky, E. L., *Manual for Kinship Analysis* (1965). A helpful handbook for identification and analysis of kinship systems.

Chapter 24

Associations, Clubs, and Age Groups

Although kinship regulates and controls a large part of the life of primitive peoples, it would be an error to assume that all areas of activity are confined to, or determined by, the kinship group, or by the class, caste, or geographical community. The urge to form voluntary associations, friendship groups, or clubs, is not exclusively a trait of contemporary, or even civilized, people. Most primitive societies, also, make some provision for voluntary, nonkinship groups, using them as a way to make life more intriguing, colorful, and meaningful, as well as to carry out certain functions not handled by other segments of the social system.

Such groups are frequently based on the common denominator of sex or age, or they may derive from shared experience or com-

Fig. 24-A   Masked spirit figures give oracular answers to questions in the initiation ceremonies of a men's tribal secret fraternity on the Fly River, Papua, New Guinea. (Courtesy of the American Museum of Natural History.)

mon skill. Although many of them have a recreational factor, with feasting, drinking, dancing, story telling, etc., incorporated into work or ceremonial activities, they usually serve important basic functions necessary to the welfare of the total society. Whether temporary and ad hoc, as in the case of a one-time job requiring a larger number of participants than a family can muster, or permanent and lifelong, as in the case of the tribal fraternities with responsibility for education and enculturation of the young, these associations transcend kinship groups and have the effect of creating bonds between nonrelatives.

The Nature of Associations

We may define an association as "a group organized for the pursuit of one interest or of several interests in common. Associations are usually contrasted with involuntary groupings serving a greater variety of ends, such as kin groups, castes, social classes and communities."[1]

Although "associations" are differentiated from "involuntary groupings," they are not, among primitive peoples, completely "voluntary." In few cases is membership a matter of wholly free choice. Some of the associations we shall examine embrace all the adults of a given sex in their membership; others include all males or females in a given age range; others invite only those with special characteristics, skills, or wealth. Kinship and locality may also play some part in determining these affiliations.

In general, associations, clubs, or sodalities, as some anthropologists call them, may be characterized as follows: They are not based primarily on the kinship factor; they have an exclusive membership within the

larger society; they possess a formal institutional structure; and they engender a discernible feeling of congeniality among the members along with *esprit de corps,* or the "we-feeling." Although many of these associations are traditionally known as "societies," (Plains Indian "military societies," Pueblo Indian "curing societies"), it may help to eliminate confusion if, in this chapter, we do not use the word "society" as a synonym for club or association, reserving it for its larger meaning. The term *fraternity* is traditional anthropological usage for a men's club in those instances where clubs promote the social fiction of brotherhood among their members. Those associations which include all the men or women of a given age range are known as *age grades, age classes,* or *age sets.* Even where membership is not based on age per se, a certain amount of age grouping is found in most associations. The latter fact is true, also, in our own culture.

Functions of Associations   As an illustration of how associations enhance tribal life, Banton cites the Blackfoot Indians of the North American Plains, whose primary subsistence pattern was based on buffalo hunting. During the winters when pastures were meager and the buffalo roamed in small, dispersed herds, small bands of Blackfoot kinfolk were adequate for the task of hunting, while larger encampments could not be fed from the small herds. However, with the lush grasses of springtime, the buffalo gathered in enormous herds. At that time:

The Blackfoot bands also combined, forming social and economic units that could most efficiently hunt the great herds. Most men were members of societies that included men of similar age. These societies organized the encampments, maintained order, and coordinated hunting operations during the summer migrations. The societies also performed dances and ceremonies. Quite apart from the explicit ends served by these associations, they brought men from different bands into relations of solidarity. Although a young man might choose

[1]M. Banton, "Voluntary Associations: Anthropological Aspects" (*International Encyclopedia of the Social Sciences,* vol. 16, 1968), p. 357.

which society he would join, it was hardly conceivable that he should belong to none.[2]

Whereas the Blackfoot organized their associations around economic need, the Tswana of Bechuanaland have utilized their highly structured associations to further the ends of political unity. Here, age is the sole basis of membership, and the groupings are called "age-regiments." The regiments are formed every few years, and all the eligible boys and girls between about sixteen and twenty years of age are initiated at the same time; there are separate regiments for the men and women. Schapera notes:

Since every adult in the tribe must belong to one, a regiment consists of all tribesmen of the same sex and of about the same age. The initiation ceremonies they undergo simultaneously, the name given to their regiment and identifying it ever afterwards, their organization into a single body under the leadership of some member of the royal family, and the numerous activities they as a body are subsequently called upon to carry out, give them a strong feeling of group solidarity cutting across the parochial loyalties of family, ward, village, and tribal community. The regimental organization serves, therefore, as an effective means of binding together people on a tribal rather than a local basis. Next to the Chieftainship, it is perhaps the most conspicuous means of integrating the members of the tribe into a unified whole.[3]

A regiment may be called on at any time to work for the chief or for the tribe. Any kind of public work may be required: building roads, making dams, searching for lost children, rounding up criminals, etc. Women's regiments may be called upon to thatch a roof, gather wood, or weed the fields for the chief's wife. Women are called on less often and given lighter work. The lengthy and torturous initiation ceremonies which formerly were an important function of the regiments have been replaced by simpler and more benign rites. However, the regiments do have re-

sponsibility for inculcating their members with appropriate values and suitable behaviors, and it is the mates in one's own regiment who punish, by fines or thrashing, any member's transgressions in conduct or failure to work.

Explicitly or implicitly, many clubs and associations assume a variety of educational functions. "Bush schools," initiation ceremonies, and preparation for specialized leadership tasks are conducted by clubs or fraternities. These associations may also, either overtly or covertly, assume police, legal, or judicial functions. In recent years, as primitive societies have begun moving toward industrialization, associations have assumed increasing importance, taking on many of the roles carried in the United States by public welfare, labor unions, settlement houses, ethnic clubs, and credit unions. Opportunities for self-expression, fellowship, increased self-esteem, heightened status, and honor (frequently including elaborate ranking systems and honorific titles) often accrue from club membership, and these, too, serve a purpose—not only for the individual but also for his society.

Club Life and Sex Roles   Despite a long-held stereotype that women in American society are more active in club and organizational life than men are, and that, therefore, women are more "sociable" than men, there is considerable doubt as to which sex spends more time in social or civic associations. In the primitive world, however, there is no question but that men are the devotees of club life and women are not. The organizational woman of the modern civilized world is one of the revolutionary developments of recent times. There was nothing like her in earlier human history.

The vast majority of all nonkinship-based social groups operate exclusively for men. Associations such as the Tswana Women's Regiments are rare. Sometimes women enter into men's organizations as auxiliaries. When

[2]*Ibid.,* p. 358.
[3]I. Schapera, *A Handbook of Tswana Law and Custom,* p. 104.

they do have clubs of their own, they are likely to be but weak counterparts of the vigorous organizations of the men. There are rarely all-embracing tribal associations of women, as there are of men.

Indeed, club life among primitive women is so undeveloped that Schurtz, who at the turn of the century gave anthropology its classic study of men's societies and age grades, advanced the theory that females are innately unsociable. They are inhibited in the formation of clubs, wrote Schurtz, because by instinct their activities and interests concentrate on reproduction, hearth, and home.[4]

This, of course, must be dismissed as androcentric prejudice. In its stead, a cultural-functional explanation that is nearer the facts of human experience may be advanced. First, the demands of family nurture have tended to isolate women and leave them little time for club activities. American experience of the last few decades shows that given time and the opportunity, women can readily take to club and public life. Second, primitive women, in addition to having little time for club activities, are in most male-dominated societies definitely discouraged from entering into the club systems set up by men, and the men do not look with favor upon female imitations of their organizations. This is found to be true especially in tribes that link secret men's clubs with religious activities. Revelation of the secrets of ritual to women (and uninitiated boys) meant death in Australia and West Africa, and even among the matrilineal Pueblos of the Southwest. A woman who accidentally witnessed the secret rites of Central Australian men's groups might possibly still be speared on the spot, as she would have been before the days of Australian governmental police and courts. The men's secret clubs of the Banks Islanders and certain other Melanesian tribes terrorize and bully the noninitiates (including all women).

When so much ado is made about the necessity of protecting the sacred secrets from women and when the sanctions imposed upon women who happen to penetrate the secrets are so fatal, is it surprising that women do not expose themselves to such risks by undertaking the formation of clubs along the lines so jealously guarded by the men?

The demands of family and the discouragement of male attitudes notwithstanding, women have not been totally deprived of club-affiliation possibilities. The Plains Indians often had women's clubs. Indeed, numerous tribal systems included a few female functionaries within the men's clubs. Each Cheyenne unit had four unmarried virgins who had ritual responsibilities and were called "sisters" by the members. There were craft guilds for Cheyenne women who had demonstrated special skills, such as the highly esteemed robe quillers club open to those who had quilled thirty buffalo robes with porcupine-quill embroidery.[5] The Crow Indians had a "deep-rooted belief that husband and wife were intimately associated in ceremonial activity, certain feminine disabilities to the contrary notwithstanding." Thus, husband and wife were usually jointly initiated into the highly important and prestigious Tobacco organization.[6] The function of the Tobacco cult was the ceremonial planting of tobacco, believed necessary to the welfare of the tribe.

Similarly, in Africa, the subjugation and exclusion of women, so noticeable elsewhere, are much attenuated. Although the tribal associations may be for men, they often include women. And what is more notable, women frequently have powerful clubs of their own. In Sierra Leone and Liberia, although some men's associations admit females, no women's clubs admit men. In view of the greater social power and prestige of the men's organizations, when absolute ex-

---

[4]H. Schurtz, *Altersklassen und Männerbünde (Age Classes and Men's Associations)*.

[5]G. B. Grinnell, *The Cheyenne Indians,* vol. 1, pp. 159–169.
[6]R. H. Lowie, *The Crow Indians,* p. 14.

clusiveness breaks down, there is more pressure from the women to penetrate the men's clubs than vice versa. An egalitarian attitude between the sexes is most evident when associations take over the functions of social service and economic aid as tribal members move into unfamiliar roles as industrial workers in urban settings of developing countries. This we shall see in ensuing discussions.

Types of Associations

In primitive social systems, club groups and associations are organized as variously as in our own society: by one or both sexes, according to restricted or inclusive age standards, for a multiplicity of purposes, openly or secretly, and so on. Here we can only review a few of the major types of associations most commonly found in primitive cultures. These include secret fraternities, both tribal and nontribal in membership, secular associations, and age classes.

Tribal Secret Fraternities   Secret fraternities that include all the adult men of a society are called *tribal fraternities*. The adjective "tribal" serves to distinguish them from the more limited type of associations that are open to only a privileged few. They are secret in that their meetings are not open to noninitiates and their lore and ritual may be revealed only to members (see Figure 24-1).

Tribal fraternities are a direct outgrowth of adolescence transition rites. Puberty rites, as we have seen (pages 380–385), serve to allay anxiety and reinforce societal values at the crisis period between childhood and maturity. Those who successfully complete the demands imposed by the puberty rituals do not necessarily organize into an association because of this fact. But because passage through puberty gives an exalted status of maturity and because puberty rites for boys and girls are almost always separate, all those men who have been made conscious of their

newly achieved status by the rites are apt to crystallize their special status in an organized association. The puberty rite then becomes an

Fig. 24-1   Interior of the house of a men's tribal secret fraternity on the Fly River, Papua, New Guinea. Ceremonial masks are stacked against the walls. (Courtesy of the American Museum of Natural History.)

initiatory rite. Not only is such an initiatory rite a transitional rite over a life crisis, but it also opens the door into the fraternity of men.

Such rites emphasize the destruction of the preinitiation personality of the neophyte. As Webster long ago noted:

Almost universally initiation rites include a mimic representation of the death and resurrection of the novice. The new life to which he awakes after initiation is one utterly forgetful of the old; a new name, a new language, and new privileges are its natural accompaniments.[7]

A new name and a new language are not in fact always forthcoming, but seclusion from the women and children followed by "rebirth" is a regular feature of primitive initiatory rites. In tribes where girls are initiated by the women, men and boys are rigidly excluded from their rites. Clearly, the process is one of intensification of sex-linked roles on either side.

The line to be drawn between puberty rites and tribal initiation ceremonies is not a sharp one. Whether we decide that a ritual falls into one class or the other depends on whether it leads merely to the status of adult or whether it brings adult status *plus* membership in a specific association of adults. Sometimes there is an intermediary borderline condition on which it would be most arbitrary to make a classificatory judgment.

Thus, in the case of the Andaman Islanders' puberty rites, we contemplate solemn and elaborate but nonsecret rituals that effect status shifts for boys and girls. Full-fledged men are distinctly separated from fledgling boys, and they enjoy many perquisities of adult status. They seem to be bound together by the bonds of consciousness of their common privileges and interests. Yet they do not seem to form a men's fraternity.

On the other hand, in the case of the Central Australian tribes, the initiated married men form a domineering, tightly knit group, possessed of much secret lore and enjoying many lordly privileges, all of which indicates without doubt that here we have true tribal associations.

Aside from Central Australia and certain Melanesian areas, the great center for the development of tribal fraternities is Africa, particularly West Africa from Sierra Leone into Nigeria, Cameroon, and the jungle region of the Congo.[8]

In West Africa, the *porro* and *bondu* fraternities and sororities of such tribes as the Mendi and Temne of Sierra Leone are most famous. All boys, upon completion of their puberty rites, enter the *porro;* the girls usually find themselves members of the *bondu.* Among the Kpelle, the *porro* is a central integrating and controlling feature of tribal life—family, religious, and political.[9] The chief officer (grand master) of the *porro* wields effective political power and social prestige. Membership in the fraternity is a prerequisite for marriage and for admission to all other clubs and offices. The *porro* is internally graded according to the general social status and ages of the members. On the other hand, many women no longer go through initiation into the *sande,* as the women's sorority is called in Kpelle.

Nontribal Secret Fraternities   Nontribal secret fraternities are secret in the same sense as the tribal ones. They differ in that their membership is definitely more limited and selective. Not all the men or women in the tribe can belong—not even all those of a given age group.

By far the most notorious of the widespread African nontribal secret fraternities are the limited and exclusive secret orders of the Leopard, Crocodile, and Snake, or of other beasts, reptiles, or birds. Of these, the Leopards are the most feared. *Egbo, Ekkpe,* and

---

[7]H. Webster, *Primitive Secret Societies*, p. 38.

[8]W. D. Hambly, *Source Book for African Anthropology* (Field Museum of Natural History, Anthropological Series, vol. 26, part 2, 1937), p. 498.

[9]J. L. Gibbs, Jr. (ed.), *Peoples of Africa*, p. 223; also, K. L. Little, "The Social Cycle and Initiation among the Mende," in J. Middleton (ed.), *From Child to Adult*, pp. 207–225.

Ngbe are but variant tribal names for the Leopard order. Human sacrifice and cannibalism gave a terroristic aura to the Leopards. They strike in the dark against their victims, who are selected because they have evoked the ire of the membership or merely because sacrifices are needed for fertility rites. The Leopard men wear leopard-skin cloaks. With wooden dies they make false leopard imprints in the earth to leave the impression that real leopards have seized the victims. With claw-like knives they mutilate and lacerate the flesh of their victims.

The terroristic activities of the Mau Mau among the Kikuyu tribesmen of Kenya in the 1950s was an aberrant development of the pattern of secret fraternities.

Functions of Secret Fraternities   The functions of African secret orders are by no means wholly homicidal. Their bloody activities are only incidental to deeper-lying interests. The associations are mutual-aid organizations that have taken on important social control responsibilities in addition to their magical, religious, and purely sociable aspects.

They counterbalance the power of the tribal king and work to keep royal power in check. Unquestionably, they serve at times as the people's solution to the trying problems that result from the need to temper anarchy with monarchy, which in turn must be stopped short of despotism. Within the framework of the tribal constitution, the secret orders are often cited as assisting the king in the application of the sanctions that uphold the tribal laws.[10]

As mutual-aid protective associations, the secret orders of West Africa pay special attention to the interests of their members as against those of the world at large. They collect private debts from delinquent creditors on behalf of their members, and they punish other transgressions against the brotherhood

as well. In some sections of Sierra Leone, the overextension of these practices into exploitative terrorism has caused violent public reactions, resulting in the outlawing of such clubs as the Leopard by the tribal chief.

Experience proves that secret orders are dangerous devices for use as instruments of government and social control. With the best intentions they may serve the public weal, but since the members are not publicly accountable for their acts, there can be no safe check on the inevitable temptation to use their heady power in their own selfish interests. Exclusive secret orders are inherently corruptible and corrupting in any society, be it *Egbo* in Liberia, *tamate* in the Banks Islands, or Ku Klux Klan in the United States.

Secret clubs of a purely congenial, ceremonial, or magico-religious nature are generally exempt from such strictures. Thus, in old Dahomey, where the power of the king appears to have become sultanistic in its strength, all secret orders were banned by royal edict. The king brooked no opposition or competition. There was, however, no objection to the banding together of men for mutual aid, as long as it was not done secretly. The Dahomean *gbe* was (and is) organized by a group of young men, not necessarily of the same age group. They socialize together, but the basic function of their organizations is to enable each member to make more impressive displays at weddings and funerals by calling upon the resources of all other members not in excess of a stipulated sum.[11] Women may belong to such clubs, or they may have separate clubs of their own. In effect, these secular nonsecret associations are exactly comparable to our own cooperative credit unions.

The various pueblos of the Southwest each have their several secret fraternities whose main functions are to perform masked *kachina* dances impersonating the gods and to carry out complex rituals according to calen-

[10]See Webster, *op. cit.*, p. 115–120; and R. H. Lowie, *The Origin of the State*, pp. 91–94.

[11]M. J. Herskovits, *Dahomey*, vol. 1, pp. 250–253.

dric cycles. The dances and rituals are performed for the benefit of all the people. Most of the ritual and accompanying liturgy is secret among the initiated members, but public dances are also presented. Thus, the village *cacique* (sacred chief) of Sia Pueblo calls upon the Flint fraternity to perform the stick-swallowing dance on behalf of the whole pueblo. The dancers shove sticks down their throats, imitating the poking of planters' dibbles into the ground, and the dance works to ensure a good spring sowing. Among the Hopi, secret fraternities join in a dramatic rain-making dance, shown in Figure 24-2.

The functions of such fraternities in the pueblos are largely religious, magical, and ceremonial. The high-ranking leaders of the secret orders form an ecclesiastical council

Fig. 24-2   Members of the Hopi Indian Snake and Antelope nontribal secret fraternities performing the rain-making Snake Dance. Snake fraternity members dance with live rattlesnakes in their mouths and hands, while cooperating members of the Antelope fraternity control the snakes with eagle-feather fans. (Courtesy of the Museum of Natural History.)

which is even today the ultimate source of governing power in most pueblos.[12]

Secret ceremonial associations also played an important role in the lives of the Indians of the Northwest Coast.[13]

Secular Associations   Purely secular organizations, given to furthering nonmystic interests and not concerned with terrorizing women and children, have no compulsive need to surround themselves with secrecy.

Such were the military and dancing clubs of the Plains Indians. These associations of warriors were fellowships for conviviality among men, whose warlike flame was sustained and fanned by the stories, the rituals, and the songs and dances of their lodges. Their basic interests were two: warfare and congeniality. Their enjoyment was derived not from roistering but from the quieter glow that builds up in companionate smoking of a pipe, huddled singing about a thumping drum, parading two by two in all their finery upon their best horses, or dancing for all the tribe to see.

Plains Indian Military Associations   Although the Plains Indian men's clubs are commonly called "military societies," they were military only in the sense that the American Legion is military—their members all were, or had been, fighting men. Rarely did these clubs go to war as units. They did not form regular segments of an army, for Plains Indian fighting was too individualistic for that, but they idealized and glorified war and labored to sustain the war ideal among their members.

Their officers were "chosen to die." In battle, they planted their insignia—a crooked spear like a shepherd's crook or a trailing shoulder sash that could be pegged to the ground—in the face of the enemy. They could not retreat from that spot unless a fellow

[12]See E. A. Hoebel, "Keresan Pueblo Law," in L. Nader (ed.), *Law in Culture and Society*, pp. 92–116.
[13]See F. Boas, *Social Organization and Secret Societies of the Kwakiutl Indians* (United States National Museum, Reports, 1895).

member dashed into the melee to pull up the peg or staff. Nominees for such offices were supposed to be bashful toward acceptance of the honor. Witness what Lowie was told by the Crow Indian Young Jackrabbit:

"All declined to smoke, then they came towards me. Some one asked them, 'Whom are you looking for?' They answered, 'Young Jackrabbit.' I was seated in the rear and tried to hide. They brought the pipe to me, but I refused to accept it. One of the pipe-carriers was my own older brother. He seized me by the hair, struck my chest, and said, 'You are brave, why don't you smoke the pipe?' He wished me to die, that is why he desired me to smoke the pipe. He said, 'You are of the right age to die, you are good-looking, and if you get killed your friends will cry. All your relatives will cut their hair, fast and mourn. Your bravery will be recognized; and your friends will feel gratified.' I took the pipe and began to smoke. They asked me whether I wished to have a straight or a hooked-staff. I chose the hooked-staff. My comrade also smoked the pipe."[14]

Thus were the chosen members recruited to these highly selective and exclusive positions.

Plains Indian men's clubs have been classified into ungraded and graded types. The ungraded, which occurred among the Crow, Cheyenne, Kiowa, Wind River Shoshone, and other tribes, were voluntary associations open to all men without regard to age (see Figure 24-3). A man needed merely a sponsor within the club; he also gave "presents" to the club upon his entry. There was no initiation.

The number of such ungraded clubs varied in different tribes. The Crows, in 1833, had eight. Toward the end of the century, these had been reduced to only two active ones, the Foxes and the Lumpwoods (Knobby Sticks).[15] The Cheyennes had six clubs: the Fox, Elk, Shield, Bowstring, Dog, and Northern Crazy Dog.[16]

Age Classes, or Age Sets We have defined age groupings as associations based on age and embracing within their membership all the men or women in a given age range. Usually, these age classes are defined and membership is determined when the individuals are at or near puberty. However, age classes are sometimes established at younger and also at older ages. Among the Plains Indians, age-graded associations occurred only among the Mandan, Hidatsa, Arapaho, Gros Ventre, and Blackfoot. Each of these tribes had a system of associations that were graded in a prestige hierarchy from young to old; age qualification was a prerequisite for membership in all cases. Normally, every member of a tribe, if he lived long enough, would pass through all grades. The higher grades naturally had progressively smaller membership, which, combined with the increasing age of the members, gave greater prestige.

Plains Indian Age Clubs Movement from one grade to another was by collective purchase of all the rights and paraphernalia of the club just above. Among the Hidatsa, for example, all the adolescent boys banded together and, aided by their families, made a great collection of hides, arrows, parfleches, etc. After indicating to the Kit Foxes, the lowest club, that they wanted to buy, arrangements would be made for ceremonial payment and transfer of the club to the upstarts. In addition, each neophyte chose a ceremonial father, or sponsor, who had to be a member of the neophyte's father's clan, from among the members of the Kit Foxes. To this man he offered gifts and entertainment—including the temporary favors of his wife if he had one. The ethics of ceremonial wife lending were mixed, however. The gesture had to be made, but most ceremonial fathers were "afraid" to use the privilege.

Thus, each candidate had to make individual payment to join an age society, but at the same time, it was absolutely necessary that his age group act collectively to acquire the rights to the club. Such clubs were there-

[14] R. H. Lowie, *The Crow Indians*, pp. 177–178.
[15] R. H. Lowie, *Societies of the Crow, Hidatsa, and Mandan Indians* (American Museum of Natural History, Anthropological Papers, vol. 11, 1913).
[16] K. N. Llewellyn and E. A. Hoebel, *The Cheyenne Way: Conflict and Case Law in Primitive Jurisprudence*, p. 99.

fore joint incorporeal property transferable only by sale (see pages 284–285). Northern Plains Indian age associations were not pure age grades or age classes, i.e., a series of groups each of which is automatically composed of all the persons of a given sex and approximate age. After an incumbent group of Hidatsa Kit Foxes sold their club to the next younger group, they were without any club organization until they succeeded in purchasing the Half-shaved Heads club from the group above them, who then had to purchase from the Dogs, who then had to purchase from the Lumpwoods. So it went up the line, until the oldest men entered the Bull club (see Figure 24-4).

The element of age grading in the Plains is a piece of fancy embroidery added by the more sophisticated sedentary gardening tribes of the Upper Missouri Valley to the simpler ungraded complex as seen among the nomadic tribes. From the Mandan and Hidatsa, the pattern spread to the Arapaho, the Gros Ventre, and ultimately the Blackfoot. The breakdown of aboriginal Plains culture came before the complex could spread farther.[17]

African Age Sets   Age grades, or age sets (as they are called by English anthropologists), occur in their most highly developed form in Africa, and according to the *World Ethnographic Sample,* three-fourths of all societies containing age classes are African.[18]

Nandi Age Sets   Keeping in mind what has already been said about the Tswana, we may take the Nandi of Kenya as an additional example. There are a number of grades of males in this tribe. The first grade is that of the uninitiated boys. For the scion of a wealthy

family, initiation may occur as early as at ten years of age, or a youth may be nearly twenty before he is put up by his family for initiation. Initiations, which occur every seven or eight years, are the highlight of tribal life and a rough time for the boys, who, as if circumcision were not enough, are beaten with stinging nettles and stung with hornets. The initiation includes military instruction, for, after initiation, the boys used to become warriors. The initiated group receives name emblems and ornaments. War formerly was their chief concern; they could play at love and enjoy sex, but they were not to be fretted with the responsibilities of marriage and children. After four years of experience, they were ready to "receive the country" from the elder grades. The age set above them, which was retiring from active warrior status, laid aside its warrior clothing, assumed the raiment of elders, and could then marry and settle down to connubial domesticity. This was not of an exclusive sort, however, since in formal custom each married man was expected to extend the hospitality of his home to any visiting classmate. Hospitality to a Nandi meant wife lending, a gratuity he would deny to all who were not members of his own age set. As a set advances in age, it ultimately enters the body of statesmen and tribal advisers.[19]

Swazi Age Sets   To the south, in Swaziland, the Swazi, a nation related to the better-known Zulus, reveal an age-set system remarkably similar to that just described. In the Swazi system, however, the whole organization was tightly controlled by the national king, who utilized the classes of fighting age as regiments in a standing army and as work corps in time of peace.

To this day, Swazi age sets, although shorn of their military reasons for existence, still carry on important tasks. In 1963, Hilda Kuper reported:

[17]Lowie worked out a classic age-area distribution study directed toward historical reconstruction of the development of such clubs. See his *Plains Indian Age Societies* (American Museum of Natural History, Anthropological Papers, vol. 11, 1916), pp. 877–984.

[18]A. D. Coult and R. W. Habenstein, *Cross Tabulations of Murdock's World Ethnographic Sample,* p. 27.

[19]A. C. Hollis, *The Nandi.* For an excellent detailed study of three variant systems of East African age sets, see A. H. J. Prins, *East African Age Class Systems.*

The age sets were more precisely organized in the days of intertribal warfare than at present, but much of the structure survives for other than military purposes, which they continue to fulfill. When the regiments were not fighting they served as labor battalions, particularly for the aristocrats, and this remains one of their major duties. Their most intensive work depends on the agricultural routine of plowing, weeding, guarding the corn against the birds, reaping, and threshing; they may also be summoned to gather wood, cut leaves and poles for building, move huts, drive locusts off the fields, skin animals, run messages, fetch and carry. No matter how arduous a task may be, work begins and ends with the *hlehla,* a dance song in the cattle pen. During the performance, which always attracts children and often the women of the homestead, individual workers dance out of the group and sing short songs of their own composition, boasting of some achievement or exhibiting their artistic virtuosity. . . .

The age classes are, however, still required for state ritual, and at the annual ceremony of kingship, designed to rejuvenate the king and strengthen the people, separate duties are allocated to the oldest regiments, to the regiment of men in full vigor of manhood, and to the youths who are considered sexually pure. Ritual is part of the educative process, a symbolic affirmation of certain social values, and in traditional Swazi society where specialized

Fig. 24-3   A Cheyenne Indian painting of the Bowstring fraternity honoring a distinguished leader of another fraternity, a crooked lanceowner, with the gift of a horse. The Bowstring insignia is the lance-headed bow. The scene is viewed from above at a 45-degree angle. (Private collection.)

Fig. 24-4 (a) *Plains Indian age grades; the Half-shaved Heads fraternity of the Mandans of the Missouri River earth-lodge villages, as painted by Carl Bodmer in 1833. (b) The dance of the Bull fraternity, the senior age grade of the Mandans. Spectators are standing on the roofs of the village earth lodges. Painting by Carl Bodmer. (Courtesy of the American Museum of Natural History.)*

(a)

(b)

formal educational institutions are nonexistent, the age classes serve as the main channels for inculcating the values of loyalty and group morality. The emphasis is less on the content of a curriculum, and the acquisition of new knowledge than on traditional values. In the past, special "old people" were appointed as instructors; teaching was not a separate career and learning was a gradual and continuous process of consolidation. The warriors are expected to master the main skills associated with adult life—in the barracks they even perform tasks normally left to women—and to develop the qualities of "manhood," specifically those related to the code of sexual morality. When a girl accepts a lover, she and her friends are expected to visit his barracks in special courting dress, which is brief but elaborately decorated with beads, and to sing and dance to make the relationship public. Should she on a subsequent visit find him absent, it is the duty of his agemates to try to see that she remains faithful to their friend. They find her accommodations and provide her with food. Lovers of other regiments are considered fair game, but the man who steals a girl of his own agemate is beaten and ostracized. In some other societies, sharing of women is a right of group membership; among the Swazi the emphasis on sexual monopoly over a particular lover is related to the ritual obligations placed on each member of an age group. In the main annual ceremony of the state, every individual of the unmarried regiment is responsible for contributing "pure strength" to kingship. At the present time, lover relationships are often not public and participation in state rituals is frequently evaded.[20]

Nuer Age Sets Age sets in Africa have been made to serve well as devices of social integration and efficiency. They cause greater internal segmentation, it is true, but it is a segmentation that promotes specialization of function along effective lines. It harnesses the energies of youth to the ends of the society and gives to each age group a strong awareness of its own status. In even so widely dispersed and scattered a population as the Nuer in the Nilotic Sudan, who have only the weakest of tribal structures in spite of the fact

that they number over 100,000 persons, the age-set system is one order of organization that runs through all divisions of the tribal society. Because of a generally undeveloped social and political structure, Nuer age sets are necessarily lacking in the qualities that distinguish their counterparts in Nandi and Swazi. As Evans-Pritchard reports:

The age sets have no corporate activities and cannot be said to have specific political functions. There are no grades of "warriors" and "elders" concerned with the administration of the country, and the sets are not regiments, for a man fights with the members of his local community, irrespective of age. In the rites of initiation there is no educative or moral training. There is no leadership in the sets.[21]

What then do they do? They fix and emphasize the status of all males in relation to other males as equals, juniors, and seniors. They are merely weak counterparts of the functionally more significant age sets to the south of them.

Nyakyusa Age Sets In sharp contrast to the weakly developed Nuer age sets are those of the Nyakyusa, who live on the northwest shores of Lake Nyasa. Little Nyakyusa boys of six to eleven years of age band together to herd their fathers' cattle, and for several years, they spend their waking hours together on the range. When they reach twelve or so, they leave off herding to take up the hoe in the gardens of their fathers; they then move into a village of older boys, no more to sleep at home. They return to the parental homestead for meals, but only when accompanied by a group of their age-mates. Boys should associate with boys even when visiting their parents. They live as members of a tightly knit juvenile gang, but without the element of gangsterism. They have no need to express hostility to the adult world. Their culture moves them steadily and early into the shouldering of the responsibilities of men through the concerted activities of youth.

[20]H. Kuper, *The Swazi: A South African Kingdom*, pp. 55–56. (Quoted with permission of Holt, Rinehart and Winston, Inc.)

[21]E. E. Evans-Pritchard, "The Nuer of the Southern Sudan," in *African Political Systems*, p. 289.

When the young men approach the age of twenty-five, one by one they marry. Each brings his wife into the age village of his peers, and what was once Boys' Town is gradually transformed into a family village of husbands and wives and their children. It is unique in that all the men of the village are of an age. Now each youth receives his own fields from his father, and he ceases to return to his parents' house for meals, eating instead, under his own roof, his food prepared by his wife rather than his mother.

In another ten years, when all the villages of a given age level within a district have matured, the formal government of the territory is ritually handed over to them, and they rule the land while their generation of sons begins anew the process, breaking off to start the formation of their own age villages-to-be.

In Nyasaland, the age set is more than an auxiliary to the kinship group or a segment of village life. While closely linked to his primary conjugal-natal family in many ways, the Nyakyusa boy begins the severance of the primary family strands long before he is ready to start a family of his own, and his age set becomes the core of the social structure of his entire society.[22]

Incidence of Age Sets The use of age as a basis of status identification is, as was pointed out in Chapter 18, a universal cultural phenomenon. The institutionalization of age groups into definite age sets is, on the contrary, exceedingly rare; it occurs in only 23 out of 547 cultures included in the *World Ethnographic Sample,* or 4 per cent of the sample. Sixteen of the twenty-three are located in Africa,[23] where the frequency of age grading (which even there equals only 15 per cent of the tribes) is clearly a result of diffusion, as it is among the Plains tribes of North America. But the sporadic distribution of age

grades around the world is good evidence of its independent invention in the several continental areas.

Eisenstadt's Theory of Age Groupings In a comparative study of age groupings, S. N. Eisenstadt developed the hypothesis that: "Age-homogeneous groups tend to arise in those societies in which the allocation of roles, facilities and rewards is not based on membership in kinship—or otherwise particularistically defined—units and criteria."[24]

This hypothesis is plausible, for it does seem reasonable to suppose that where desirable statuses do not flow from kinship ties, alternatives will be seized upon. Age groups would seem to be easily developed substitutes in view of the universality of age as a biological fact. However, the data of the *World Ethnographic Sample* raise serious doubts as to the significance of the hypothesis. There are too many societies that allocate roles outside the kinship system and do not develop age grades. Unidentified negative forces neutralize whatever tendency there might logically seem to be at work. Age grades are, it is true, very interesting to contemplate in themselves, but surprisingly they are not of as much significance in human affairs as anthropologists once thought.

Associations and Social Dynamics

No clear-cut relation of club occurrence and distribution shows up through such cross-cultural comparison as has been done to date. Obviously, however, one would expect these associations to occur more frequently in societies with larger, rather than smaller, populations, and with more complex cultures which provide for a greater differentiation of functions and interests. Urbanization and any other tendency which works to weaken the strength of the kinship bond will concomi-

[22]M. Wilson, *Good Company: A Study of Nyakyusa Age-villages.*
[23]Coult and Habenstein, *loc. cit.*

[24]S. N. Eisenstadt, *From Generation to Generation,* p. 54.

tantly contribute to a compensatory tendency to form clubs.

It is quite clear that associations flourish in rapidly changing, nontraditional social situations. Early in the nineteenth century de Tocqueville observed, "In no country of the world has the principle of association been more successfully used or applied to a greater number of objects than in America."[25] It will be remembered that Americans of that era, many of them migrants from either Europe or rural communities, were struggling to adjust to alien urban situations, separated from their kin, bewildered by new work and social roles, and frequently helpless in time of trouble. The multiplicity of voluntary associations of which de Tocqueville spoke was an adaptive response to new cultural circumstances. Just so, in a number of new African nations, voluntary credit unions among village and urban dwellers abound, and cooperative work groups and trade unions vie for members' loyalties, while helping to organize energy and resources for mutual improvement of their lot in life.

Professor A. L. Epstein, who pioneered the study of urbanization of mineworkers in Rhodesia, has penned an eloquently phrased summary of the process:

But as the urban communities themselves took root, new problems arose for which the traditional wisdom of the Elders provided no solution, and of which they were sometimes unaware. The need for new roads in the town, the need to seek avenues of employment for African women, the need in the towns for hostels for old people, the problem of discharged mine employees—these were some of the problems facing the new urban communities. They were drawing the attention of the younger and better-educated men in the Advisory Councils: they aroused little response among the 'Elders.'

The Africans who were led to join the Welfare Societies were of a younger generation, and were better educated. They were more conscious of the problems of urban life, and of the rapidly developing pattern of relations between the races. Significantly, the discussions of the Welfare Societies were conducted, and the minutes of their meetings recorded, in English. A District Commissioner had once sneered at the Welfare Societies as debating societies where the educated native had the opportunity to get up before his fellows and air his English. The District Commissioner did not appreciate that in using English at their meetings, the Africans were learning to handle one of the most important tools of the new culture. When Africans conversed together in English, they showed that they had interests in common which cut across tribal divisions. Furthermore, in the handling of novel concepts they were broadening their intellectual horizons, and making possible closer contact and acquaintance with the world outside. But more than this, in their professions of schoolteacher, of Christian minister of religion, and of clerk, they were actively engaged in pushing forward into a new form of society where clan affiliation or attachment to village headman and chief were no longer mechanisms of primary significance in ordering social relations. Through such organizations as the Welfare Societies, these people were beginning to stake out their claim to full membership in the new industrial society that was growing up around the mines.[26]

SUMMARY

Although kinship is the basis of social organization in all societies, groups whose membership cuts across kinship lines occur in numerous primitive, as well as all civilized, societies. These are *associations,* which are specifically organized to pursue special and limited interests. Such associations are also called *clubs,* or *sodalities,* and *fraternities.* If such associations include all the men or women of a given age range, they are known as *age grades, age classes,* or *age sets.*

Cross-culturally, the propensity to form and maintain clubs is predominantly a male activity. The demands of family nurture and the positive prohibition of women from club life in male-dominated societies account for the

[25]A. de Tocqueville, *Democracy in America* (1945), vol. 1, p. 198.

[26]A. L. Epstein, *Politics in an Urban African Community,* p. 84.

difference. Organizations for women are not totally absent, however. Many societies do contain women's clubs, sometimes organized around crafts or special skills, sometimes serving as auxiliaries to men's groups, often, but not always, established as age groupings. Both the Plains Indians and certain African societies provide for coeducational membership in some associations. As associations assume mutual-help functions in the modern world, the participation of women on an equal basis increases.

Tribal secret fraternities include all the men of the tribe, who by virtue of passing through the tribally required puberty rites, achieve manhood, and *ipso facto,* membership in the secret fraternity from whose esoteric knowledge and rituals women and uninitiated boys are barred—usually on pain of death. The possession of secret knowledge is used to keep women subordinate, while the acquisition of it in the initiation schools enculturates the youths to the tribal system.

Nontribal secret fraternities serve the vested interests of a more narrowly exclusive segment of the male population. Such fraternities may be largely secular and social, they may be primarily religious, or they may serve as units of military organization. In any event, they show a notable tendency to be involved in politics and government, often in terroristic ways, since they are not subject to open, public criticism and control.

Some Plains Indian societies are agegraded, as are a number of African systems. A group of boys enters the lowest grade as a body, progressing together to successively higher collective status as they move through life. Variations in the pattern are seen in the examples of Swazi, Nuer, and Nyakyusa.

Voluntary associations provide a means of social organization which may complement, or even displace, the fundamental kinship groups. They tend to be associated with increasing heterogeneity and size of population—along with an increasing complexity of culture—which engenders greater division of labor and diversity of function and interests.

Rapid social change and urbanization are conditions which appear to be conducive to "joining." America, since its early days, and Africa in modern times, exemplify the social resources which can be marshaled in the formation of clubs, work groups, and cooperatives.

SELECTED READINGS

Banton, M., "Voluntary Associations: Anthropological Aspects" (*International Encyclopedia of the Social Sciences,* vol. 16, 1968), pp. 357–362. A helpful, brief summary of the subject.

Eisenstadt, S. N., *From Generation to Generation* (1956). Particularly interesting in its comparative analysis of youth movements in Germany and Israel in relation to primitive age grading.

Epstein, A. L., *Politics in an Urban African Community* (1958), chap. 4, "Trade Unionism and Social Cohesion," pp. 86–156. Presents a rich account of this modern form of voluntary association as adopted by African workers in the copperbelt of Rhodesia.

Little, K. L., *West African Urbanization: A Study of Voluntary Associations in Social Change* (1965). An intensive study of associations in the shift from tribal to city life in new African nations.

Llewellyn, K. N., and E. A. Hoebel, *The Cheyenne Way: Conflict and Case Law in Primitive Jurisprudence* (1941), chap. 5, "The Military Societies." A case study of Cheyenne Indian men's clubs in operation.

Lowie, R. H., *Primitive Society* (1920), chaps. 10 and 11, "Associations" and "Theory of Associations." An excellent comparative discussion of clubs and age groups in several primitive societies.

Webster, H., *Primitive Secret Societies* (1908). An old but valuable work.

Wilson, M., *Good Company: A Study of Nyakyusa Age-villages* (1951). A truly fascinating account of a unique development of the age-grading principle.

Chapter 25

Social Classes and Castes

Wherever there exists an unequal allocation of goods and power throughout a society, there exists the possibility of social classes. Classes express social differences. However, the mere existence of differences does not necessarily give rise to a clear-cut class structure, on the one hand, or to a "class mentality," or class consciousness, on the other. Nor does the existence of class self-awareness necessarily instigate class conflict, or war. It may, or it may not.

All the problems of classification, which were discussed in dealing with the evolution of the primates and the transition to man (Chapters 4 and 5, especially pages 83–85), come to the fore once more when dealing with "social class." The question of whether a phenomenon is a concept (a classificatory idea) or a thing (a reality that exists as a discrete entity) plagued us in our consideration of race as a biological and social happening. With questions of social class, the same confusion and ambiguity compound our task to even greater degree. Even more than race, class has become freighted with overtones of social politics. Class consciousness and revolutionary class movements did not begin with the thought and writings of Karl Marx (1818–1883), but through Marx and his associates, especially Friedrich Engels (1820–1895), they received their modern ideological charter. This, in one form or another, has been developed into dogmatic Marxism as a sociopolitical creed, commonly called Communism.

The Communist doctrine asserting class exploitation of the landless by landowners, and of industrial workers by capitalists, and the accompanying dogma of class struggle leading to the ultimate establishment of a

Fig. 25-4   Caste and class in the land of the Incas today. An elite caste political spokesman with Indian leaders in a public meeting in Callejon de Hualas, Peru. Note the apparent differences in caste status symbols and attitudes in this scene. (John Collier, Jr., for the Cornell-Peru Project at Vicos.)

classless, socialistic society, pose one of the great challenges to contemporary humanity. The drawing of the Iron Curtain and the polarization of East and West Europe across the Berlin Wall in the cold war of 1946 to the present are but one manifestation of it. Under current conditions, to separate fact from dogma is especially difficult. Yet, a clear understanding of what social classes are and how they act in different types of societies is absolutely essential to a rational response to the Marxist challenge. To deal with the whole problem is more than we can assay in this introduction to anthropology. Nonetheless, we can bring the comparative findings of anthropology to bear on such questions as the following: Are there any societies that are classless? Is class differentiation the unique development of civilizations? Is exploitation an inherent feature of classism? Are classes in primitive society usually at war with one another? What of castes? And how does slavery fit into the history of human societies?

The Concept of Social Class

"The concept of class is concerned with the differentiation of social groups."[1] So far, so good. But that does not take us very far. Kinship groups are differentiated, often with refined, far-reaching, and arbitrary precision, as we have already seen. Associations are differentiated social groups. So are political parties and nations, religious sects and cults. Therefore, we must understand at the outset that "social class" as a concept actually has narrower denotations than the term literally suggests.

Marx defined class in terms of relation to the means of production, i.e., power over the use of productive resources and control over the disposition of products and access to consumable goods, both being backed up by the coercive power of the state.

The German sociologist Max Weber (1864–1920) accepted this economic criterion as a starting point. To this base he added two more factors: (1) standard of living, or sub-cultural life styles, and (2) prestige ratings of differing economic groups within the society. Virtually all non-Marxist social scientists have followed Weber's lead, although there is no agreement on the relative importance of the three criteria.[2]

To conclude these introductory remarks, let us recapitulate by quoting A. L. Stinchcombe on social stratification systems (higher and lower social classes):

The study of stratification systems involves three main topics: *the degree of inequality of rewards and privileges* (in wealth, power, and fame) in different societies and the causes and effects of different amounts and kinds of inequality; *the relation between the distribution of the good things of life and the solidarity of categories of people with different levels of reward* (such as social classes, ethnic groups, and regions within societies) and the causes and effects of different patternings of solidary groupings in relation to the distribution of privileges; and the *patterning of social relations between people of different levels of reward (conflict, domination, ritual equality, and so forth) and its causes and effects.* The pattern of a stratification system can be fairly well outlined if we know the amount of inequality in the distribution of rewards, the amount and patterning of solidarity among people at approximately the same level in the distribution, and the relations between "the rich, the wise, and the well-born" and the poor, the ignorant, and the lowly [italics added].[3]

R. M. MacIver (1882–1961) put it more directly and simply, with heavier emphasis on class attitudes:

We shall then mean by a social class any portion of a community which is marked off from the rest . . . primarily by a sense of social distance. Such a subjective character involves also as a rule objective

[1]P. Mombert, "Class" (*Encyclopaedia of the Social Sciences,* vol. 3, 1930), p. 531.

[2]For a general overview of theories of social class, see the articles on "Stratification, Social," by B. Barber, S. M. Lipset, A. L. Stinchcombe, and H. Rodman in the *International Encyclopedia of the Social Sciences,* vol. 15, 1968, pp. 287–315, 325–337.
[3]A. L. Stinchcombe, *op. cit.,* pp. 325–326.

differences, income levels, occupational distinctions and so forth, within the society. But these differences, apart from a recognized order of superiority and inferiority, would not establish cohesive groups. It is the sense of status, sustained by economic, political, or ecclesiastical power and by distinctive modes of life and cultural expressions corresponding to them, which draws class apart from class, gives cohesion to each, and stratifies a whole society.[4]

Social Class Defined   We may now specify a working definition of social class.

A social class is a category of persons within a society, who hold a number of distinctive statuses in common and who, through the operation of the roles associated with these statuses, receive differential rewards and privileges, and who, through a common life style, develop an awareness of their like interests in contrast to those of other such groups.

A social class can exist only with reference to other social classes. A one-class society is necessarily a classless society. Furthermore, if there is no consciousness of class, there can be no dynamics of class action. People must act in terms of class, if the *class concept* is to be functionally significant.

Finally, there are a number of things that a social class is not. It is not organized. Classes are not in themselves associations. But there may be, of course, associations that represent the interests of specific classes, as the AFL–CIO does for certain segments of the industrial workers in the United States or as the National Association of Manufacturers does for a portion of the industrial owners and manufacturers. Yet even in Russia, only a small part of the population of workers is organized within the Communist party and its affiliate associations.

Types of Class Systems

Inasmuch as social classes express themselves in attitudes associated with differences

[4]R. M. MacIver, *Society*, pp. 78–79.

in status and role, which in turn mean differences in authority, power, and access to goods, the characteristics of class systems exhibit marked qualitative differences from one type of culture to another. Obviously, simple hunters and gatherers who have no food surpluses to manipulate and who allocate food and other goods through balanced reciprocal exchange are not likely to develop social classes. On the other hand, post-Neolithic peoples who have a system of redistributive exchange with ultimate title to the land vested in a paramount chief or a king, with royal lineage or clan, will almost certainly have a highly institutionalized class system.

Yet it does not necessarily follow that sedentary horticulturalists will develop social classes, either. Title to Pueblo Indian land, for example, is vested in the pueblo, in perpetuity, and plots are equably assigned to clans and households in universal succession (page 277) with enduring rights of use. Everyone has equal access to the available economic goods of the society. There is no possibility of differentiation based on wealth. There are no social classes. Or are there?

In the pueblos, power is very unequally distributed. The priests who head the religious secret fraternities form a totalitarian oligarchy with power of life and death over all members of the pueblo. Their prestige is often awesome; and a good part of their life style, devoted as it is to the management of the esoteric ritual through which the universe is kept operating (see Chapter 28, pages 547–550), is different from that of ordinary commoners. In terms of religious and political power, they certainly form a class. In terms of food, clothing, and shelter, not at all. Therefore, Murdock codes the twelve Pueblos which are a part of the world sample in the *Ethnographic Atlas* as classless.

Cross-cultural Categories   Murdock's cross-cultural categories of social class systems are as follows:

1. *Classless societies,* which lack significant class distinctions among freemen (slavery is

treated as outside the class system), ignoring variations in individual repute that have been achieved through skill, valor, piety, or wisdom.

2. *Wealth distinctions,* based on the possession or distribution of property, which are present and socially important but not crystallized into distinct and hereditary social classes.

3. *Dual stratification* (a two-class system) in a hereditary aristocracy and a lower class of ordinary commoners or freemen, where traditionally ascribed noble status (high prestige) is at least as important as control of economic resources.

4. *Elite stratification,* in which an elite class derives and maintains its superior status by control over resources, especially land, in contrast to a propertyless proletariat or serf class.

5. *Complex stratification,* in which social classes are related to extensive differentiation of occupational status.

In sum, Murdock's classification presents two categories of classless societies (1 and 2, above), and three *types* of class systems (3, 4, and 5, above).[5]

Frequency of Social Classes   Taking the world at large, the majority (68 per cent) of the societies in the *Ethnographic Atlas* are classless. A third of these recognize socially important wealth distinctions (prestige) but have no hereditary social classes (2, above). One-fourth (24 per cent) of all societies have a ruling class which controls access to goods (types 3 and 4), and only one-twelfth (8 per cent) have multiple class systems (type 5). As shown in Figure 25-1, complex class systems are limited almost exclusively to the civilizations of the Mediterranean area and Asia. In the New World, only such pre-Columbian societies as the Aztec, Maya, and Inca qualified as complex. Eighty-seven per cent of all New World societies were classless! In

Sub-Saharan Africa and the Pacific, approximately two-thirds had no classes.[6]

The class phenomenon is Old World and civilizational—at least to this point in time.

The Organization of Class Systems

Having looked at the types of class systems and their relative frequency around the world, let us now examine just what is implied in various kinds of class or no-class societies. Some of the difficulties in assigning arbitrary labels will be readily noted as we observe that the lines between types 1, 2, 3, etc., are often blurred rather than completely clear-cut.

Plains Indians   Among the nomadic Plains Indians, whose cultures encouraged competitive status achievement, a nascent sense of class was noticeable. Grinnell wrote:

Family rank, which existed among the Cheyennes as among other Indians, depended on the estimation in which the family was held by the best people. A good family was one that produced brave men and good sensible women, and that possessed more or less property. A brave and successful man has raised his family from low to very high rank; or a generation of inefficient men might cause a family to retrograde.[7]

But there was no real social gap between good and not-so-good families, and the Cheyennes are considered classless. The poor, instead of being driven into servitude to the more prosperous by means of debt, wage dependence, or clientage, seem, rather, to have sponged upon the chief and the successful hunter.

Similar attitudes existed among the western Apache, who distinguished sharply between poor people and the rich. "Those who had little or no property, lacked the ability or desire and energy to accumulate it, and had

---

[5]G. P. Murdock, *Ethnographic Atlas,* pp. 57–58.

[6]Data from E. Bourguignon and L. Greenbaum, *Diversity and Homogeneity,* table 18, p. 40.

[7]G. B. Grinnell, *The Cheyenne Indians,* vol. 1, p. 129.

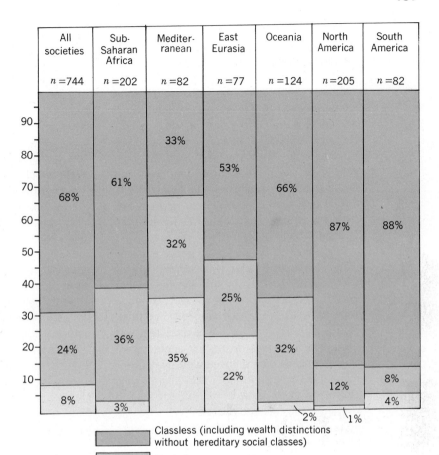

	All societies	Sub-Saharan Africa	Mediter-ranean	East Eurasia	Oceania	North America	South America
	n =744	n =202	n =82	n =77	n =124	n =205	n =82

Fig. 25-1   Relative frequency of social classes in percentages, according to major geographical areas. (Data from E. Bourguignon and L. Greenbaum, **Diversity and Homogeneity,** *table 18, p. 40.)*

- Classless (including wealth distinctions without hereditary social classes)
- Dual elite class stratification
- Complex class stratification

no social prestige were termed poor; the people with opposite traits were called rich.'' Poverty was pitied, and the wealthy person was expected to be generous with largess. For this he received public approval and attracted hangers-on among the poor who were then called *bidigishi,* meaning ''his incompetents'' or ''weaklings.''[8] The Apaches, however, also qualify as classless. In each of these instances, it is the fact of equal access to basic resources which leads us to so categorize them.

Yet out of such elemental recognition of

[8]G. Goodwin, *The Social Organization of the Western Apache,* pp. 541–543.

class differences, the Kiowa Indians of the Plains developed a strong sense of prestige ranking based on wealth and behavior.

Four classes were recognized by name: *onde, ondegupa, kɔɔn,* and *dapom.* The *onde,* who constituted about one-tenth of the population, were those whose family heads were ''handsome on a horse,'' wealthy and generous, proud in bearing, courteous in demeanor, and, above all, possessed of an outstanding war record. The *ondegupa* were the able artisans, hunters, herders, and medicine men, who had wealth, were generous, and were ''noble'' in character and behavior, but who lacked sufficient war credits. They made up one-third of the tribe. The *kɔɔn* were the common stuff, undistinguished in war or other accomplishments. They lived with their more illustrious kinsmen as poor relatives. Half the tribe was of this lower class. The *dapom* were simply *déclassé*. Shiftless and lazy, they filched and stole within the camp. Practically disowned by their own relatives, they were virtual outcasts. They imposed upon the generosity of the good people; theft was not looked upon or treated as a legal infraction. The *dapom* were not punished or extruded from the group. They were merely scorned and suffered to be borne.[9]

In general, all Plains Indian social systems were open and competitive, although there was a tendency, as in the Kiowa, toward wealth distinctions. Buffalo and antelope were there for all. In the nineteenth century, enemy horses were for the taking, and war was chronic. It was necessary only to have the "strong medicine" bestowed by "guardian spirits" (see pages 582–586) and the will, spirit, and skills—plus a little bit of luck—to move right up the social scale.

Northwest Coast Indians Class was more marked on the Northwest Coast of North America, where in every tribe a sharp division existed between freemen and slaves—unfortunates captured from other tribes. In the early nineteenth century, slaves constituted from 10 to 30 per cent of the total populations of various Northwest Coast tribes. They were in effect a depressed social group whose functions were to produce food for their masters by hunting and fishing, to do the menial work around the village, and to paddle the seagoing canoes. Whatever their rank in their own tribe, all slaves were reduced to the level of productive capital in the tribe of their masters. Just as any valuable good, such as a canoe or copper, could be

destroyed at a potlatch, slaves too could be killed to show their master's unconcern for wealth.

Most authorities have described the body of freemen in Northwest Coast society as consisting of two classes (type 3): nobles and commoners. Nobles were those men (and their wives) who had attained the rank of chieftain through the inheritance of chiefly titles, which they had validated by potlatching. Since most tribes held to primogeniture, the nobility consisted of the first-born, while subsequent offspring and nephews (in matrilineal societies) became commoners. Among the Tsimshian, according to Jenness, even finer distinctions were drawn. Intermarriage among the first-born children of the highest-ranking families of the nobility was reputedly obligatory, so that there was even an endogamous "royalty" within the nobility.[10]

Drucker, who has studied Northwest Coast culture at firsthand, takes issue with the orthodox view of Northwest Coast social classes. He flatly maintains that there was no class of nobility set off from a class of commoners, with slaves standing outside the class order, much less a threefold or fourfold class system. What actually occurred, as he sees it, was "that each society consisted not of two or more social classes, but of a complete series of statuses graded relatively, one for each individual of the group."[11] He argues that between high and low there were differences in degree but not in kind.

This particular conflict of interpretations is not resolvable; it merely points up the ambiguity of the concept of class in certain settings. It precisely parallels the situation that existed in the United States, when most Americans argued that we had no social classes at the same time that Warner and his

---

[9]J. Richardson, *Law and Status among the Kiowa Indians* (American Ethnological Society, Monograph 1, 1940); and B. Mishkin, *Rank and Warfare among the Plains Indians* (American Ethnological Society, Monograph 3, 1940).

[10]D. Jenness, *The Indians of Canada* (National Museum of Canada, Bulletin 68, Anthropological Series, no. 15, 2d ed., 1934), p. 337.

[11]P. Drucker, "Rank, Wealth, and Kinship in Northwest Coast Society" (*American Anthropologist*, vol. 41, 1939), p. 57.

coworkers were assiduously dividing us into upper upper, lower upper, upper middle, lower middle, upper lower, and lower lower (than which there are no lower) classes.[12]

Murdock, however, classifies the Tsimshian, Haida, Bellacoola, and Kwakiutl tribes, all of the Northwest Coast, as having dual stratification (type 3) rather than as classless with wealth distinctions.[13]

The Aztecs   Among the peoples of high culture in Central America and the Andean region of South America, class differentiation was strongly fixed as a classical system of complex stratification (type 5).

The Aztecs, in their meteoric rise and fall, developed from an apparently classless, unsegmented society with a rude material culture, prior to A.D. 1300, to an organized, sophisticated protocivilization in the fourteenth century. At the time of the arrival of the Spaniards in 1518, they were rapidly evolving a feudal aristocracy at the expense of the earlier clan socialism. The society then consisted of royalty, nobility, common freemen, propertyless proletariat, and slaves.

The core and largest part of the Aztec population was the body of free commoners, members of one or another of twenty localized "clans" (*calpulli*). Every married man enjoyed the right to cultivate a plot of clan garden land and to have a flat-roofed, one-room hut of adobe or clay-plastered wattle. He might become a craftsman, specializing in one of the many productive arts and trades. He had security and continuous employment and an obligation to perform military service. But he was hedged in by a code of sumptuary laws that reserved to the rich and to distinguished warriors and officials the rights of wearing fine cotton, jewelry, and particular hairdos. Presumption above one's rank was summarily and severely punished.

Class distinctions cut across kinship groups, for the class of honorary lords was recruited from all clans. They formed a nonhereditary order of merit with various grades conferred by the government as a lifetime reward for outstanding military accomplishment, service in civil office, service to the state as a traveling merchant-spy, or exceptional religiosity. They wore the beautiful and elaborate costumery depicted in Aztec art. They lived in the mansions of Tenochtitlan. They received homage and led a rich life apart from their common fellow clansmen. In theory, the huge parcels of conquered lands that they received as rewards for their services could not be inherited as family estates. All such rewards were to be redistributed to a new worthy after the death of the holder. This was always done, but, by a process not difficult to understand, a system of preference was crystallizing whereby sons of nobles were appointed to their fathers' positions of nobility. Inheritance of rank and landed estates was thus leading rapidly to the freezing of a hereditary aristocracy.

Above the nobles, in luxuriant splendor, stood the royal lineage, from among whose members the *tlacatecuhtli,* or king, was elected by the great council of lords.

Far below the royalty and nobles was the hapless proletariat. Aliens whose goods and lands had been expropriated by the state and Aztecs who had lost their clan privileges for failure to fulfill clan obligations eked out a meager and sweaty existence as burden-bearing laborers on the streets of the city and roads of the country, or they grubbed for their livelihood upon the estates of the lords. Taxes and feudal services left little to them.

Slavery was the lot of impecunious Aztecs who could not meet their bills. In like manner, criminals who could not make restitution for their thefts became the slaves of the freemen they had victimized. Children were sold into slavery by impoverished parents, and even adults among the proletariat might voluntarily sell themselves into servitude. Many

[12]W. L. Warner and P. S. Lund, *The Social Life of a Modern Community.*
[13]G. P. Murdock, *op. cit.,* column 67, p. 105.

slaves were alien boys and girls taken as tribute from conquered neighbors.

The society of the Aztec Indians was on the road to becoming the same type of pyramidal, exploitative society that existed in the flourishing days of the archaic Mediterranean civilizations. The Aztecs, however, had not hardened the inequalities of their society. Children of slaves were born free (into the proletariat). Slaves could not be killed or abused by their masters; they could even acquire property in their own right (although it is not likely that this opportunity meant much to many slaves); they could not be sold to another master except by self-consent; and if married by master or mistress, they became freemen.[14]

Melanesia   In the western and interior parts of New Guinea inhabited by the more primitive Papuans, social classes as such are practically nonexistent. In the eastern islands, where the Melanesian-speaking people predominate, differentiation into dual social classes is characteristic, even though there are many classless tribes, such as the Dobu. The actual governing of men throughout Melanesia is usually in the hands of a council of village elders, but there is frequently a class of wealthy "Big Men" who enjoy much social prestige by reason of their economic, ceremonial, and religious powers related to inherited prestige and a redistributional economic system (type 2).

Melanesian chiefs are often descendants of an immigrant group which has tricked the local populace into believing that its members have superior magical powers and control valuable rituals that will benefit the community. For this reason, it is considered only right that the chiefly class enjoy exalted sanctity and privileged superiority. The chiefs are also universally regarded by the people and themselves as a class of feast givers and

ceremonialists who reflect glory upon their people.

Polynesia   Traditional Hawaiian society (at and before the time of Captain Cook's arrival in 1778) was divided into a rigidly stratified, hereditary social class system composed of nobles (*ali'i*), commoners (*maka'āinana*), and polluted inferiors (*kauwā*).

The great majority of the society were commoners with specific occupational tasks: agriculture, fishing, crafts, etc. What they did not produce for themselves they traded for, or were given as recompense for their labors by the ruling chiefs. There were some variations in wealth and, therefore, in standards of living, and occasionally a paramount chief rewarded a commoner for special services by conferring "quasi-aristocratic" status on him.

Above the commoners were the *ali'i,* and from this aristocracy came the military forces as well as all important political officials. Their magnificent, feather-covered cloaks and helmets gave visible evidence of their social rank. This nobility was subdivided into a high, sacred group and a lower, nonsacred group, and there were rigid prescribed forms of deference which the lower order was obliged to follow in relation to the sacred group. Death followed any infraction of the rules, as when a commoner or a nonsacred *ali'i* failed to remain prostrate in the presence of the sacred, godlike *ali'i.*

Below the commoners was a small group of hereditary, segregated inferiors, similar to a pariah caste (discussed below). Marriage within each class was endogamous, but miscegenation with this class was especially abhorrent because of the fear of polluting family lines. Too little is known about this group to feel secure in calling them slaves, but there was an element of servitude and they were attached to masters.

In summary, Davenport writes:

... Hawaiian society was internally differentiated by hereditary ranked social classes. Because the classes tended to be endogamous, had occupa-

[14]G. C. Vaillant, *Aztecs of Mexico;* but especially see *The Florentine Codex* (A. J. O. Anderson and C. E. Dibble, trans. and eds.), book 8, *Kings and Lords,* and book 10, *The People.*

tional as well as ritual specialties, and were partially set apart by ideas of defilement, the society had some features of a true caste system.[15]

Caste

Caste is class hypertrophied. It represents hereditary freezing of the principles upon which class is based: differential and unequal distribution of goods and power; formation of social groups, each with its own life style, based on such distribution; and differential patterns of relation between caste groups.

Castes are always higher and lower in a hierarchical order. Castes are rigid: a person is born into his caste and can rarely escape from it; he must (usually) marry within his (or her) caste, and the offspring will remain in it. Castes usually have traditionally prescribed occupations within the productive and service system of the society. Caste behavior toward members of other castes is rigidly prescribed. In India, for instance, each caste refuses to drink water or food which has been handled by anyone belonging to a lower caste; to do so would be "polluting" and would acknowledge the equality or superiority of the handler. Although social intercourse between members of different castes may be highly circumscribed and severely limited, the intercaste relations form a functional social and economic network of interdependence in which even the lowliest and most economically deprived caste has its own autonomy and degree of independence. Caste members are not personal property; slaves are. Therefore, slavery and caste are separate social categories and are treated as such in all social science analyses.

Types of Caste Systems

Caste systems tend to be *simple* or *complex,* without much gradation between the two

types. A *simple* system has two or three castes. A *complex* system encompasses a multitude of castes.

Simple systems break down into two types:

1. *Pariah* castes: in which one or more hereditary occupational groups such as blacksmiths or leatherworkers are treated as pariahs (low, despised, outcast) by the general population, and are strictly endogamous. The Japanese butchers (*eta*), described on page 375, are a very good example of this type. Another example would be that of the Northern Somali of the East African Horn, of whom I. M. Lewis writes, with reference to all metalworkers: "Traditionally they are excluded from marriage with other Somali and have their own separate social organization modeled on and attached in subservience to that of their patrons."[16]

2. *Ethnic* castes: in which a socially superior endogamous caste (usually composed of conquerors) subordinates and holds down a socially inferior caste of conquered people or of foreign immigrants of different race and/or culture, barring them from equal privileges. The white/Negro ethnic populations of the United States still show residues of ethnic caste distinctions in spite of great strides toward equalization of economic, political, and social opportunities in recent decades.

The Simple Ethnic Caste System of Ankole
The African kingdom of Ankole as it existed in the late nineteenth century is a good example of a simple ethnic caste system combined with social classes.

The basic caste division in Ankole was between pastoralists, who called themselves *Bahima,* and gardeners, who were known as *Bairu.*[17] The Bahima were Hamitic or Hamiticized Negro cattle people, who came down the grassland corridor between Lake Victoria

---

[15]W. Davenport, "The 'Hawaiian Cultural Revolution': Some Political and Economic Considerations" (*American Anthropologist,* vol. 71, 1969), p. 4.

[16]I. M. Lewis, "The Northern Pastoral Somali of the Horn," in J. L. Gibbs, Jr. (ed.), *Peoples of Africa,* p. 338.
[17]In Bantu speech, the prefix "Mu" refers to a particular person; "Ba," to the tribe collectively; "Bu" to the tribal territory; and "Lu," to the language. Thus we have Bahima, Muhima, Buhima, and Luhima, and also Bairu and Mwiru.

on the east and the mountain and lake chain on the west. Their original home was probably southern Abyssinia. Racially and culturally, they were and are distinct from the Bantu horticulturalists, who had preceded them in occupation of the country. As they moved southward, the Bahima proved themselves as fighters to be superior to the Bantu-speaking Bairu and capable of effective enlargement of their social groups for politico-military ends. They conquered the Bairu and proceeded successfully to subjugate them without apparent difficulty, although the Bairu outnumbered them ten to one. The Bahima formed a dominant conquest-based caste; the Bairu were socially incorporated as a subjugated, inferior caste.

Unbreachable disabilities were imposed upon the Bairu:

1. All Bairu were forbidden to own fecund cattle. It is true that they were sometimes given barren cows or bull calves for services rendered a Muhima, but any Muhima could arbitrarily expropriate any productive cows found in the possession of a Mwiru.

2. While all Bahima males were liable to be called for military service, the Bairu were barred from bearing arms. They were kept militarily ineffective, and the chances of successful revolution kept at a low level.

3. There could be no intermarriage between Bahima and Bairu. Aside from the customary prohibition of intermarriage, the injunction against Bairu cattle holding was an effective bar. No marriage could be valid without progeny price in cattle, and the Bairu could receive no reproductive cows, nor did they have any to give.

4. Bahima men (especially chiefs) could take Bairu girls as concubines, but Bairu men had no equal right to Bahima girls.

5. No Bairu could hold high political office. At best, he might serve as district tax collector under a Muhima.

6. All Bairu had to work for, and pay tribute to, the Bahima chieftains, who in turn distributed the garden products and derivatives

to their fellows. The Bahima had no desire to kill the goose that laid the golden egg, however, and therefore the individual Muhima was barred from abuse of the Bairu, who was privileged to plead before a Bahima chief for compensation when ill-treated or exploited by an unauthorized Muhima.

7. When a Mwiru killed a Mwiru, that was a matter for retaliatory revenge among their own group. But if a Muhima killed a Mwiru, the law denied the right of direct action to the Bairu kinship group. The most its members could hope for was to be able to plead with the Bahima king that he obtain compensation on their behalf, and they were lucky if they got anything at all. But if a lowly Mwiru dared to kill a Muhima, the Bahima dispatched him forthwith.

Domination and exploitation in the Banyankole state was a direct, unabashed, and efficient process. It was an example par excellence of the oft-repeated story of the parasitic mastery of a sedentary people by nomadic herdsmen.

However, the caste structure was not the simple dichotomous arrangement we have thus far described. The Banyankole kingdom did not exist in a vacuum, and there were other Bahima kingdoms and tribelets in the area. Although racially self-conscious, the predatory Muhima was not averse to raiding alien Bahima. To put a stop to this, the kingdom of Ankole undertook the subjugation of various Bahima neighbors, who were then incorporated into the Banyankole tribal society as a separate tribute-paying class, known as *Abatoro*. They could intermarry with their conquerors, and they suffered no serious legal disabilities.

Yet a fourth class was the *Abambari*. Prohibition of intermarriage never prevents miscegenation. Out of the Bahima-Bairu concubine relations came half-caste offspring. Legally, the *Abambari* were classed as Bairu in the same way that mulattoes used to be classed as Negroes by American laws. But the personal interest of a Muhima father often mitigated the strict working of this rule. Those who had no legitimate heirs often raised the son of a concubine to the status of heir. Thus the exclusive separatism of the ruling caste was self-defeated and, ironically enough, to the greatest degree among the chiefly families and lineages. For it is just in this group that today a definitely larger percentage of dark Bantu Negroid physical types is found than occurs among the ordinary Bahima herdsmen in the more remote rural districts.

Lastly, there were the *Abahuku,* or slaves. Because of the convenience and effectiveness of the system of exploiting the Bairu and the limited economic possibilities in slavery when Bairu tools and gardening methods were used, slavery was never extensive. The slaves were Bairu taken in raids upon neighboring kingdoms. Ankole Bairu were never enslaved. Slaves were used as menials in the households of the very rich. They neither gardened nor tended the herds. They were chattels of their individual masters, and their ears were cut off to keep them from passing as Bairu if they succeeded in running away.[18]

The Complex Caste System of India   Identifiable castes in India number in the hundreds and the web of caste forms a richly detailed tapestry. Caste is ubiquitous in all matters of daily life, and the system is so refined in its ramifications, that some anthropologists propose that the term "caste" should be restricted solely to the Indian phenomenon. Most view the Indian system as the utmost, rather than the only, manifestation of complex caste organization. It is presented as such in this book.

The Idea of Varna   According to ancient Hindu belief, still very much alive, four so-called *varna* castes emerged from the body of primordial man. This was the beginning and

the ideological justification of the whole Indian caste system for more than 2,000 years.

From his mouth issued the Brahmins, who became priests and scholars. From his arms came the Kshatriyas, warriors and rulers; from his thighs came the Vaishyas, tradesmen, and from his feet rose the Shudras, cultivators. Traditionally, those in the Brahmin category are supposed to manage the culture through their control of religion, Kshatriyas to manage the society through their control of armed might, Vaishyas to manage the distributive economy through their control of trade, and Shudras to produce the economic wherewithal for the whole society.[19]

The four *varna* castes are all ritually clean and unpolluted, but the first three have superior purity and prestigious privileges because their male members are "twice-born." The "twice-born" go through a transition rite which symbolizes a second birth; hence, "twice-born." Each "twice-born" wears a sacred thread, called *dvija,* over his left or right shoulder, depending on his caste's rank. Shudras, who are *varna*-caste farmers, are but once-born; their rank is middling.

Harijan   Castes: The Untouchables   The *Harijan* castes are (were)[20] the untouchables. By the nature of their work, which puts them in close contact with "unclean" materials, they are considered polluted. As a result, great symbolic and actual social distance is maintained between the *varna* and *harijan* castes.

Jatis   Over all India the four *varna* castes and the *harijan* categories are divided into a thousand or more *jatis,* or specific castes. "A jati is an endogamous, hereditary social group that has a name and a combination of attributes."[21] The latter refers to the kinds of food which may be eaten or are prohibited, to

---

[18]K. Oberg, "The Kingdom of Ankole in Uganda," in E. E. Evans-Pritchard and M. Fortes (eds.), *African Political Systems,* pp. 121–162.

[19]D. G. Mandelbaum, *Society in India,* vol. 1, pp. 22–23.
[20]The constitution and law of India, since 1949, have abolished the social disabilities of the *harijans,* making their observance illegal. Old caste attitudes, though weakening, still persist, however.
[21]D. G. Mandelbaum, *op. cit.,* p. 14.

pollution versus purity and the relative degrees thereof, to sacred thread or no thread, and to learning and occupation, plus multitudes of lesser privileges and disabilities. *Jatis* are specified subsections of the *varna* and *harijan* categories.

Yet not every *jati,* nor even every *varna,* is present in every community. Thus, in Konduru, a South Indian village studied by Professor Paul Hiebert, thirty *varna* castes are found—but none of them is *Kshatriya* (warrior). Among the thirty are clerk, priest, merchant and moneylender, temple lamplighter, goldsmith, blacksmith, carpenter, brassworker, farmer, braceletmaker, tailor, weaver, potter, bodyguard, fisherman, courtesan, herdsman, winetapper, bodyservant, barber-surgeon, and washerman *jati.* Among the *harijans* are five *jatis* of priests, musicians, weavers, sweepers, and leatherworkers.[22] Special services are provided by itinerant members of other *jatis* who wander through the country as peddlers or entertainers.

The Jajmani System   Each *jati* has traditional relations to various other *jatis* in the rendering of their special occupational services. At the center of a web of such relations stands a hereditary landlord. At harvest time all of a landlord's, or *jajman's,* harvest of grain is piled in a heap on the threshing floor. The *jajman's* dependent field workers gather around, as do his "contracted" washerman, leatherworker, carpenter, barber, etc. The *jajman* presides like a lord, but the share each shall take is fixed, according to custom and service rendered. Each man comes forward to claim his share in order of caste rank—Shudras first. When the barber's turn arrives, for example:

The Barber measures out a gift share, four to six fans of grain, for shaving the household males and a *poli cherta* for ritual performances. He pulls aside his bonus (*addam dōsili*) "for showing the mirror" to his prosperous masters so they can have the privilege of observing their tonsure while it is taking place. Since the poor do not give a bonus at har-

vesttime, they are shaved without the benefits of soap or a mirror. The Barber does more than shaving, however; his knive is used at births to sever the umbilical cord while his wife assists in the delivery of the child. After funerals he shaves his clients at the time of their purification. But it is at weddings that he is most needed. He prepares the groom and is given small gifts of grain, liquor, coins, and the clothes that the young man had been wearing. He pares the nails of the couple during the ceremonies and claims the unhusked rice used in making the ritual designs. He arranges for a Barber band to play for the ceremony and also for the many processions that welcome the bridal party, that fetch the ceremonial pots and sacred earth, that accompany the wedding party to the temple, and that parade the newlyweds through town. Finally, on an auspicious day fixed by the family *purohit,* the Barber performs the ritual tonsure and receives the groom's turban as a symbol of his assumption of the jajmani rights over the new home.

When the Shudras have taken their share, the Leatherworker approaches for his: a gift share of a half pot of grain for repairing shoes and harnesses and a share for repairing the irrigation bucket at the well. He also claims the meat and one-half of the skins of the jajman's cattle that die throughout the year. The other half of the skins he must tan and return for the jajman's use. After the grain is cleared from the threshing floor, the Leatherworker sweeps up the tailings as his bonus (*danda kaṭṭu*). The biggest reward of the harvest often goes to the Leatherworker who has been a faithful worker during the past year. Such a man helps in the field work by drawing water before dawn to irrigate the rice, by sleeping in the fields to protect the harvest from wild pigs from the surrounding forest, and by guarding the cut grain from thieves. He beats the large leather-covered drum in his master's processions and sleeps before his door at night. The jajman rewards such a servant with a generous portion which can amount to ten pots of grain.[23]

A service caste worker may serve one or several *jajmans,* as the case may be.

In spite of the teeming millions in India's great cities, about 90 per cent of India's half-billion population live in rural villages in *jajmani* caste ordering. It may be a unique

[22]P. G. Hiebert, *Konduru*, pp. 17–28.

[23]*Ibid.,* pp. 87–88.

Table 25-1   The Distribution of Caste Systems by Total Frequency
and by Relative Frequency in Major Geographic Areas

Type of caste system	*All societies n = 819*	*Sub-Saharan Africa n = 216*	*Mediter- ranean n = 77*	*East Eurasia n = 81*	*Oceania n = 128*	*North America n = 219*	*South America n = 88*
Castes absent	86% (706)	82% (178)	48% (37)	73% (59)	98% (125)	100% (219)	100% (88)
Simple caste system: Pariah	8% (65)	12% (27)	48% (37)	— (0)	.08% (1)	— (0)	— (0)
Simple caste system: Ethnic	3% (24)	5% (11)	4% (3)	11% (9)	.08% (1)	— (0)	— (0)
Complex caste system	1.7% (14)	— (0)	— (0)	16% (13)	.08% (1)	— (0)	— (0)

SOURCE: Data compiled from G. P. Murdock, *Ethnographic Atlas,* column 69.
Note: Percentages above the figure "2" have been rounded off; totals do not equal 100% in all cases.

social system, but it embraces about one-twelfth of all mankind alive today!

The Frequency and Distribution of Caste Systems   Caste systems of social organization are relatively rare numerically. Of 819 societies in the *Ethnographic Atlas* on which there is sufficient information to make a judgment, only 103, or about 12.5 per cent, have castes of any type. Of these, simple pariah caste systems are most common (65, or 8 per cent of the whole), while simple ethnic caste systems are found in only 24 (less than 2 per cent) of the whole. Complex caste systems occurred in 14 societies.

In ethnographic distribution within the sample, caste organization is wholly an Old World phenomenon. The egalitarian societies of the American Indians were casteless.

Simple pariah caste systems occurred in half (48 per cent) of the 77 Mediterranean societies in the sample, and in one-twelfth of the 216 Sub-Saharan African societies.

Simple ethnic caste systems are found exclusively (with one exception) in the Mediterranean and African samples, but with relative frequencies of less than one in twenty.

Complex caste systems, conversely, are exclusively Asian creations. Thirteen of the 81 Asian societies in the sample (16 per cent) have complex caste systems. One Oceanic society in 128 (the Belu, on Timor, in Indonesia) had a complex caste system.[24]

The data on the comparative distribution of caste systems are summarized in Table 25-1.

Slavery in Primitive Societies

Slavery has entered several times into our discussion of class systems. Slavery has been one of the most important of human social institutions; it occurred in half the world's societies in the eighteenth and nineteenth centuries.

The Nature of Slavery   Contemporary democratic morality in industrial civilizations condemns slavery in such strong terms that we recoil from the idea of it in horror. It is now hard for us to conceive of involuntary servi-

[24]These data are compiled from column 67 of the *Ethnographic Atlas.*

tude as an implicit aspect of any society, and yet slavery has been an important part of human cultures for a far longer period of time than that during which civilizations have extirpated it from the social body.

Slavery is not in itself an absolute concept. In operation, it ranges from the complete degradation of a whole class of people by means of dogmatic denial of their humanity (slaves as chattels) to the inclusion of slaves as adopted members of the master's family and kinship group. Slavery, we are safe in saying, is a condition rarely welcomed by the slaves. There are few social advantages in being a slave and usually a good many disadvantages. The lot of the slave depends to a large degree on whether the tribe customarily utilizes its slaves as household servants or as field workers. In the former case, the relation of slave to master is unavoidably intimate, and slaves reap the benefit. If slaves are used as field workers, the owner's chief interest becomes one of economic exploitation, and, especially where there are great numbers of slaves, relationships become impersonal and harsh.

Slaves are derived both from within and from without a society. Internal slavery occurs only in the more advanced primitive societies with quasi-capitalistic practices of borrowing and lending. A borrower might pledge himself or a son or daughter as security on a loan. Default meant servitude. Or, as in the case of the Ashanti of Ghana, a man could pawn his brother's son to raise a sum. The boy then worked for the creditor until the loan was repaid; the labor he performed constituted the interest on the loan. Debt slavery did not ordinarily produce huge masses of slaves, nor were their positions inordinately harsh. A second internal source of slaves was the condemnation of criminals to servitude. This, too, is found only in the more highly advanced cultures, since a strongly centralized law system is a necessity.

The great source of slaves, however, was war and the exploitation of war captives, but war may or may not be waged to take captives. Slaves are in the tribe, but not of it. Without citizenship, slaves are outside the realm of jural personality, and their debased status does not contradict the slaveholders' notions of social equality—for themselves, exclusive of the slaves.

Frequency and Distribution of Slavery
Slavery is clearly associated with the evolution of culture; its origins appear to be very ancient. Table 25-2 shows the distribution of slavery according to the subsistence patterns of 565 cultures. Slightly more than one-fourth of the simple hunters and gatherers of recent times practiced slavery. The ratio drops to one-fifth among intensive foragers, rises to nearly half among horticulturalists and to more than half among societies predominantly based on plow agriculture or pastoralism. Slavery flourished in most preindustrial civilizations. After the Industrial Revolution, its economic usefulness disappeared, slavery was viewed as immoral, and it was legally rooted out as a social institution—but not until well into the nineteenth century.

Prior to the expansion of European cultures, slavery was unevenly distributed around the world (see Table 25-3). It was most rare in Oceania, where one-fifth of the societies practiced it. The Indians of North and South America had worked it into 30 and 27 per cent of their societies, respectively. The Old World was by all odds the home of slavery. More than half the societies of Asia and two-thirds of those around the Mediterranean took slavery for granted. But Africa was the true indigenous home of slavery. There, four-fifths of the societies included in the *Ethnographic Atlas* held slaves. The high incidence of pastoralism and developed agriculture might have contributed to the spread of slavery in Africa. Yet the presence of both these types of subsistence economies in high frequency in Eurasia and the Mediterranean regions did not produce nearly so much

Table 25-2   Frequency and Percentage Distributions of Slavery
in 565 Cultures, according to Level of Subsistence Base

Subsistence base	*Number of cultures with slavery*	*Percent of cultures with slavery*
Plow agriculture	59	53
Pastoral	27	55
Intensive gardening	103	47
Foraging	6	20
Hunting and gathering	27	27

SOURCE: Data from A. D. Coult and R. W. Habenstein, *Cross Tabulations of Murdock's World Ethnographic Sample*, p. 522.

Table 25-3   Distribution of Cultures with Slavery,
by Major Geographic Areas

Geographic areas	*Number of cultures by area* $n = 774$	*Number of cultures with slavery* $n = 363$	*Percentage of occurrence of slavery in each area*
Africa	204	160	78
Circum-Mediterranean	82	50	61
Eurasia	77	43	56
Pacific Islands	124	26	21
North America	205	62	30
South America	82	22	27

SOURCE: Data from E. Bourguignon and L. Greenbaum, *op. cit.,* table 19, p. 41.

slavery in those parts of the world. Future research into the structural-functional aspects of slavery may provide an answer to the African problem; little is available now.

SUMMARY

Social classes are the product of unequal access to economic goods and differences in economic, religious, or political power and rewards. A social class is a category of persons within a society who hold a number of distinctive statuses in common; who, through the operation of the roles associated with these statuses, receive differential rewards and privileges; and who, through a common life style, develop an awareness of their like interests in contrast to the unlike interests of other such groups.

Murdock classifies societies in five types: (1) classless (with no significant distinctions); (2) classless (with wealth distinctions); (3)

dual stratification (with a hereditary aristocracy and a class of commoners); (4) elite stratification (in which an upper class controls land and other important productive resources, while a lower class is propertyless); and (5) complex stratification (with multiple classes linked to extensive occupational division of labor within the society).

More than two-thirds (68 per cent) of all societies are classless, one-fourth have a dominant class controlling access to goods, and only 8 per cent have complex class systems.

Classless societies were most frequent among the American Indian societies of both the Northern and Southern Hemispheres. Complex classes existed almost entirely in the civilized areas of the Mediterranean and Asia, while dual stratification was highest in Sub-Saharan Africa. Simple hunters and gatherers, such as the nomadic Plains Indians, tend to be classless, as do those horticultural societies which rely on reciprocal economic distribution. Class is related to redistributive economic systems in which the upper class has prestige resting on supernatural power and sanctity, or controls the use of land. Hawaii represented this latter phenomenon. The Aztecs also manifested a complex class system.

Caste is class frozen by endogamy and hereditary ascription of membership. Simple caste systems are of two types: (1) *pariah,* in which one or more occupational groups is strictly endogamous and treated as low and despised; and (2) *ethnic,* in which a conquered people or foreign immigrants of different race and color are forced into an inferior caste and held down by the indigenous upper caste. Ankole exemplifies the latter. Complex caste systems encompass a great number of castes, graded and interwoven in a network of highly prescribed behavioral relations. Complex systems usually distinguishes between higher, "clean" castes and degraded, polluted, and polluting castes.

Within this dual division there will be many refinements of prestige and privilege relating to sanctity and caste separation. Not many societies (14 out of 819) have a complex caste system, but because of its presence in India, one-twelfth of all living human beings are locked into a caste order.

Until one hundred years ago, slavery was one of mankind's most important social institutions. It occurred in half the world's societies in the eighteenth and nineteenth centuries! In precivilized societies, slavery was generally not too harsh; slaves were frequently incorporated into the master's household and not seriously exploited as property. The development of intensive agriculture and the urban revolution made slavery economically profitable, however, and so it remained until the industrial revolution and a money economy made slavery less feasible.

In the absence of plow agriculture, pastoralism, and cities, only a few American Indian societies developed slavery, and Oceania was the least conducive to the institution. It flourished in the Mediterranean complex of civilizations and pastoralists, but still not to the degree that was manifest in Sub-Saharan Africa, where slavery occurred in 78 per cent of the indigenous societies.

SELECTED READINGS

Berreman, G. D., "Caste: the Concept of Caste" (*International Encyclopedia of the Social Sciences,* vol. 2, 1968), pp. 333–338. An expanded discussion of ways of looking at caste.

Hiebert, P. G., *Konduru: Structure and Integration in a South Indian Village* (1971). Presents a clear and understandable description and analysis of the dynamics of caste in relation to other forms of social organization in a specific village community of India today.

Kroeber, A. L., "Caste" (*Encyclopaedia of the Social Sciences,* vol. 3, 1930), pp. 254–256. A summary of the phenomenon.

Lipset, S. M., "Stratification, Social: Social Class" (*International Encyclopedia of the Social Sciences,* vol. 15, 1968), pp. 296–316. A very helpful survey of the different theories of social class.

Mandelbaum, D. G., *Society in India,* vol. 1 (1970), parts 1, 3, and 4. A complete overview of the *jati* system in India set in the theory of modern social anthropology.

Mishkin, B., *Rank and Warfare among Plains Indians* (American Ethnological Society, Monograph 3, 1940). The basis of class differentiation among some American Indians.

Oberg, K., "The Kingdom of Ankole in Uganda," in E. E. Evans-Pritchard and M. Fortes (eds.), *African Political Systems* (1940), pp. 121–164. For greater detail on the system described in this chapter.

Polanyi, K., and A. Rotstein, *Dahomey and the Slave Trade.* A historical, economic, and anthropological treatment of one of the great ports of trade in slaves.

Tuden, A., and L. Plotnicov (eds.), *Social Stratification in Africa* (1970). Contains eleven chapters on class, caste, or slavery as they have existed, or do exist, in African societies.

Chapter 26

Law and the Social Order

"If your subject is law, the roads are plain to anthropology. . . . It is perfectly proper to regard and study the law simply as a great anthropological document. . . . The study pursued for such ends becomes science in the strictest sense." Such is the judgment of one of the greatest jurists of the age.[1]

On a much more humble level, a Cheyenne Indian, High Forehead, after ruminating on my search for cases of grievance, dispute, and trouble and what was done about them, reflectively said: "The Indian on the prairie, before there was the White man to put him in the guardhouse, had to have something to keep him from doing wrong." Not only the Indian on the prairie, but every society has to struggle to maintain its social order, for society is a human creation. As such it is fallible and fragile. There is no instinct of social morality or law observance. Individuals must be induced to act within socially prescribed limits of behavior because they believe in the values of their society, or they must be constrained because some behaviors are ruled out.

Most societies include law within their systems of social control designed to achieve this end: "Anthropologically considered, law is merely one aspect of . . . culture—the aspect which employs the force of organized society to prevent, redress or punish deviations from prescribed norms."[2]

It was a common misconception until the beginning of the twentieth century to regard "law" in a rigidly limited manner: an invention of advanced civilizations, marked by written codes, legislation, and case decisions. Law was thought to consist of refined and consistently interlocking rules and formal doctrine, backed up by such machinery as arrest, subpoena, constables, police, courts, fines, jails, and prisons. Primitive peoples who lacked writing, formal legal codes, policemen, courts, and penal institutions were thus assumed to be without law. It is understandable, therefore, that "primitive law" was somewhat late in coming under investigation, and only since World War I has there developed a substantial body of literature on "legal anthropology," "anthropological jurisprudence," or the "ethnography of law"—some of the terms by which this specialization is called. Both lawyers with an interest in comparative legal systems and anthropologists concerned with systems of societal maintenance have contributed to the growing volume of work in this area.

It is now widely agreed that all societies, whether primitive or civilized—at least those which have survived for any study—have, or have had, some form of legal system. Further, there has been a radical shift of thinking about "the law." No longer is it conceived of in the static, formalistic "black-letter" law of written codes, statutes, and constitutions. Today law is seen through the behavioristic lens of legal realism, which holds that law consists of what people *do* in the realm of the legal—not what they say they do. The difference is that which we drew at the outset (pages 32–33) between ideal and real culture. Anthropologists today have learned to seek the norms of law in cases in action (the "trouble case" method), not in hypothetical rules.

Although the social ends sought and the outward legal appurtenances may differ

[1]O. W. Holmes, Jr., "Law in Science and Science in Law" (*Harvard Law Review,* vol. 12, 1899), p. 443.
[2]S. P. Simpson and R. Field, "Law and the Social Sciences" (*Virginia Law Review,* vol. 32, 1946), p. 858.

markedly from society to society, certain basic principles and functions appear to have universal applicability. Some of these differences, and, especially, the recurring similarities will be our concern in this chapter.

The Limited Significance of Courts and Legislation It is not legislation that creates law. Most primitive law is not legislated, and modern sociological jurisprudence and legal realism, from Holmes down, have made it perfectly clear that much of modern law is not legislated either.[3] English jurisprudence has long since given assent to this point of view, as witnessed by Salmond:

[3]O. W. Holmes, Jr., "The Path of the Law" (*Harvard Law Review*, vol. 10, 1897), p. 457.

But all law, however made, is recognized and administered by the Courts, and no rules are recognized by the Courts which are not rules of law. It is therefore to the Courts and not to the Legislature that we must go in order to ascertain the true nature of Law.[4]

The now classic formulation of this concept of the nature of law is Justice Cardozo's statement that law is "a principle or rule of conduct so established as to justify a prediction with reasonable certainty that it will be enforced by the courts if its authority is challenged."[5]

This behavioristic concept of law gives the anthropologist a handle he can grasp, but it

[4]J. W. Salmond, *Jurisprudence*, p. 49.
[5]B. N. Cardozo, *The Growth of the Law*, p. 52.

Fig. 26-A   An Ifugao, northern Luzon, ordeal by boiling water. The **monkalun,** *or go-between, is squatting behind the pot of boiling water. (Lowie Museum of Anthropology, University of California, Berkeley.)*

is still not enough. For if we think of courts in our traditional manner, i.e., as a formal sitting of professional judges, with bailiffs, clerks, and advocates, we must conclude: no courts, no law. This is what bothered Max Radin, who well understood the anthropologist's problem:

But there is an infallible test for recognizing whether an imagined course of conduct is lawful or unlawful. This infallible test, in our system, is to submit the question to the judgment of a court. In other systems exactly the same test will be used, but it is often difficult to recognize the court. None the less, although difficult, it can be done in almost every system at any time.[6]

Max Radin is right. But what sort of courts did he have in mind? Some courts are difficult to identify. Anthropologically, they may be regularly constituted tribal courts, such as the tribal council of an American Indian pueblo sitting in judicial capacity[7] or a court of the West African Ashanti, constituted of the chief, his council of elders, and his henchmen (see pages 515–516).

That type of primitive court is not hard to recognize. Any member of the American Bar Association would readily see it for what it is. But a more obscure type of court may be found in the Cheyenne Indian military fraternity. Consider the case of Wolf Lies Down, whose horse was "borrowed" by a friend in the absence of the owner. When the friend did not return from the warpath with the horse, Wolf Lies Down put the matter before his fraternity, the Elk Soldiers. "Now I want to know what to do," he said. "I want you to tell me the right thing." The fraternity chiefs sent a messenger to bring the friend in from the camp of a remote band. The friend gave an adequate and acceptable explanation of his conduct and offered handsome restitution to the complainant in addition to making him his blood brother. Then said the chiefs:

"Now we have settled this thing." But they went on, half as a legislature: "Now we shall make a new rule. There shall be no more borrowing of horses without asking. If any man takes another's goods without asking, we will go over and get them back for him. More than that, if the taker tries to keep them, we will give him a whipping."

Can anyone deny that the Elk Soldiers were in effect sitting as a court for the entire tribe? The test is, first, one of responsibility. That they knew. Second, it is one of effective authority. That they achieved. Third, it is one of method. Unhampered by a system of formal precedent that required them to judge according to the past, they recognized that the rule according to which they were settling this case was new, and so they announced it.[8]

Among the Yurok Indians of California, as typical of a less specifically organized people, the court was less definite, but it was nevertheless there. An aggrieved Yurok who felt he had a legitimate claim engaged the services of two nonrelatives from a community other than his own. The defendant did likewise. These persons were called *crossers* because they crossed back and forth between the litigants. The litigants did not face each other in the dispute. After hearing all that each side offered in evidence and argument, the crossers rendered a judgment on the facts. If the judgment was for the plaintiff, they rendered a decision for damages according to a well-established scale that was known to all. For their footwork and efforts, each received a piece of shell currency called a *moccasin*. Here again we have a court.[9]

On an even more primitive level, if an aggrieved party or his kinsmen must institute and carry through the prosecution without the

---

[6]Max Radin, "A Restatement of Hohfeld" (*Harvard Law Review*, vol. 51, 1938), p. 1145.

[7]E. A. Hoebel, "Keresan Pueblo Law," in L. Nader (ed.), *Law in Culture and Society*, pp. 92–116.

[8]For a full account of this case, see K. N. Llewellyn and E. A. Hoebel, *The Cheyenne Way: Conflict and Case Law in Primitive Jurisprudence*, p. 127.

[9]See A. L. Kroeber, "Yurok Law" (*Proceedings of the 22d International Congress of Americanists*, 1922), pp. 511ff. A dramatic presentation of a Yurok case-in-action is given in *The Ways of Mankind*, Series 1, Record 5, "The Sea Lion Flippers: A Study in Ethics."

intervention of a third party, there will still be a court, if the proceedings follow the lines of recognized and established order. There will be, then, at least the compulsion of recognized legal procedure, although the ultimate court may be the bar of public opinion. When vigorous public opinion recognizes and accepts the procedure of the plaintiff as correct and the settlement or punishment meted out as sound, and the wrongdoer in consequence accedes to the settlement because he feels he must yield, then the plaintiff and his supporting public opinion constitute a rudimentary sort of court, and the procedure is inescapably legal.

Consider the Eskimo dealing with recidivist homicide. Killing on a single occasion leads merely to feud, inasmuch as the avenger enjoys no recognized privilege of imposing the death penalty on the murderer of his kinsman with immunity against a counterkilling. A feud, of course, represents an absence of law, since blood revenge is more a sociological law than a legal one. But to kill again on a second occasion makes the culprit a public enemy in the Eskimo view. It then becomes incumbent upon some public-spirited man of initiative to interview all the adult males of the community to determine whether they agree that he should be executed. If unanimous consent is given, the leader then undertakes to execute the criminal, and no revenge may be taken on him by the murderer's relatives. Cases show that, in fact, no revenge is taken.[10] A community court has spoken. Such are the kinds of courts Max Radin had in mind.

The Nature of Law

We have seen in the above that lawmaking and a system of courts do exist in many primitive societies. Yet neither of these fea-

[10]For a report of such a case, see F. Boas, *The Central Eskimo* (Bureau of American Ethnology, Annual Report 6, 1888), p. 668.

tures defines what law is, or is actually fundamental to law. Law is obviously a complex of human behavior. The problem is: What kinds of behavior? What sets off legal behavior from that which is nonlegal or other than legal? What is it that makes law, law?

Law, Custom, and Social Control We have learned in earlier chapters that a culture is the integrated sum total of the learned behavior traits characteristic of the members of a society, embracing their total way of life—technological and ideological. Law is one aspect of culture, just as are kinship, subsistence patterns, language, and art.

Specifically, it has been stressed that, in every society, human behavior must be narrowed down from its full range of potential variety to a moderately limited body of norms, so that people can manage their lives with a reasonable degree of certainty that their own activities will evoke anticipated responses and results from their fellows. Social control is exerted to guide the learning process of all members of the society in the development of the appropriate behavioral customs. Law is one aspect of social control.

Yet it is useful to distinguish, if possible, between law and custom, and also between law and social control. We may say as a generalization: *Law is more than custom and less than social control.* What do we mean by that?

Custom consists of social norms (Chapter 2, pages 30–32), and all social norms are sanctioned. Behavior in accord with norms is usually rewarded. Behavior which departs too far from the norms is penalized. Social control consists of the entire gamut of rewards and disuasions. All child training, all education, all the unending responses of peers and associates throughout life are involved. Their positive responses range from the smile, the giving of food, the friendly pat, through consent to do something strongly desired, to bestowal of privileges, honors, and wealth. These are the positive sanctions that are constantly at work. On the other hand, there are negative sanctions which punish with a frown, a hateful word, a scornful curl of the lip, or a slap in the face (or elsewhere); by ostracism (social isolation); by deprivation of food, of clothing, or of other wanted things; by humiliation—all of these in everyday intercourse. They may be very effective, indeed. Yet their simple effectiveness does not make law of them.

So, too, the supernatural enters into social control. Ghosts, spirits, and gods may be believed to reward the moral and the just, just as they may punish the wrongdoer. Sin is the violation of a social norm which is negatively sanctioned by the supernatural.

Law consists of social norms, *plus*. Not all enculturation is effective for all individuals. Some ignore the norms now and then, or go beyond the limits of permissible leeway. Ordinary day-to-day social control has not worked in their cases. Then it is that law may be invoked. The pressure of the sanctions is stepped up and the penalties are no longer only psychological. The wrongdoer's goods may be confiscated: he is assessed damages or must pay a fine. Something valued is taken from him. Or he is physically injured or constrained: whipped, mutilated, incarcerated (a form of ostracism), exiled, or killed (the absolute form of ostracism, an irrevocable removal from the social scene). Such is the force of the law.

Three Basic Features of Law   Within the broad area of social control, then, we may say that law is set off from the general social norms by three characteristics:

1. The legitimate use of economic deprivation or physical coercion.
2. The allocation of official authority.
3. The element of regularity (consistency).

The Legitimate Use of Physical Coercion   The real *sine qua non* of law in any society is the legitimate use of physical coercion. The law has teeth, and teeth that can bite, although they need not be bared, for, as Holmes put it:

"The foundation of jurisdiction is physical power, although in civilized times it is not necessary to maintain that power throughout proceedings properly begun."[11] We would merely add to that declaration that it was not necessary to limit the latency of power to civilized times; primitive men often found that it was not necessary to display the power behind the law when the defendant acceded to proceedings carried through properly. Jhering has emphasized the factor of force in law: "Law without force is an empty name." Again, more poetically, we find: "A legal rule without coercion is a fire that does not burn, a light that does not shine."[12] In this we agree.

However, it is true that not all writers on law, especially primitive law, accept the criterion of force as an essential attribute of law. Professor Leo Pospisil, for example, holds that *how* a social obligation is enforced is less important than that it *is* enforced. "Is not the effect (social control, conformity) of a sanction more important than its form?" he asks. "Some psychological sanctions, although of nonphysical nature, perform as strong a control as do physical sanctions."[13] In this age of familiarity with brain-washing, no one will deny that. Nor will we deny the effective importance of "ostracism, ridicule, avoidance, or a denial of favors—sanctions that are sometimes very subtle and informal."[14] These, however, are (we believe) better viewed as other-than-legal forms of control.

The threat of the law is more often than not a sufficient deterrent; people wish to avoid the public exposure, the embarrassment, inconvenience, and ultimate risk of economic loss or physical coercion. Law has its effect of psychological deterrence. For law exists primarily not to punish but to channel behavior toward socially acceptable goals, thus

[11]O. W. Holmes, Jr., *McDonald v. Maybee* (*Supreme Court Reporter*, vol. 37, 1917), p. 343.
[12]R. von Jhering, *Law as Means to an End*, p. 190.
[13]L. Pospisil, *Kapauku Papuans and Their Law* (Yale University Publications in Anthropology, No. 59, 1958), p. 267.
[14]*Ibid.*, p. 267.

preventing the breach of social norms. But in the last resort, law deals in physical realities—the sanctions of forceful confiscation of property, if need be, or the use of direct physical compulsion.

The Official Element in Law   But force in law has a special meaning. Force means coercion, which in its absolute form is physical compulsion. There are, of course, as many forms of coercion as there are forms of power, and only certain methods and forms are legal. Coercion by gangsters is not legal. Even physical coercion by a parent is not legal if it is extreme in form. The essentials of legal coercion are general acceptance of the application of physical power, in threat or in fact, by a privileged party, for a legitimate cause, in a legitimate way, and at a legitimate time. This distinguishes the sanction of law from other social rules.

Private Law   The privilege of applying force constitutes the official element in law. In most primitive societies, this privilege is vested in the wronged individual or kinship groups. They must prosecute on their own behalf and exact the proper legal penalty. This is known as *private law*. If a public official is responsible for penalizing a breach of law, it is *public,* or *criminal law.* He who is generally or specifically recognized as rightly exerting the element of physical coercion is a fragment of social authority. It is not necessary that he be an official with legal office or a constable's badge. In any primitive society, the so-called private prosecutor of a private injury is implicitly a public official *pro tempore, pro eo solo delicto.* He is not, and cannot be, acting solely on his own, his family's, or his clan's behalf and still enjoy the approval or tacit support of the disinterested remainder of his society. If the rest of the tribal population supports him in opinion, even though not in overt action, it can mean only that the society feels that the behavior of the defendant was wrong in its broadest implications, i.e., contrary to the standards of the

society as a whole. Thus the behavior is in itself an injury to the society, although the group feeling may not be strong enough to generate overt and specific action by the group as a group and on its own initiative.

However, the private prosecutor remains the representative of the general social interest as well as of that which is specifically his own. This fundamental fact is ordinarily ignored in discussions of primitive law, and it is in this sense that we may say that the difference between criminal law and private law is a difference in degree rather than in kind, though there can be no doubt that some matters touch the general interest in fact and evoke group feeling much more vigorously than others in primitive law, e.g., sacrilege, homicidal tendencies, and, frequently, treason.

Public Law   When responsibility for initiating legal action against a wrongdoer rests not with the person wronged or his kinsmen, but rather is in the hands of a public officer—a headman, a chief, a bailiff, or a member of the chief's staff or royal household, or perhaps a shaman or a priest—then the offense is a *public wrong.* Public wrongs are traditionally called *crimes* in Anglo-American usage. Public law is the concern of government; private law operates apart from government. But it must be reemphasized that the actions of the private prosecutor have legitimacy (if he is acting in accordance with the provisions of the tribal system of private law) because the public at large supports the rightfulness of his action against the socially defined wrongness of the transgressor.

Regularity in Law   Regularity is what law shares at the core with social norms. Regularity is what law in the legal sense has in common with law in the scientific sense. Regularity means predictability. Yet, regularity, it must be warned, does not mean absolute certainty. There can be no true certainty where human beings are involved, and yet there is much regularity, for all society is based on it. In law, the doctrine of precedent (*L. stare decisis,* to adhere to decisions) is not the unique possession of the Anglo-American common-law jurist. Primitive law also builds on precedents, for new decisions rest on old rules of law or norms of custom. Regularity removes the threat of personal whim and caprice from law. Regularity lends to law its attribute of certainty. The norms of law make prediction of legal outcomes reasonably certain.

The characteristics of law are therefore *the right to apply economic sanctions or force (legitimate coercion), official authority,* and *regularity.* It is these qualities which distinguish law from custom or morals in any culture.

Law Defined

Thus we may form a working definition of law that fits primitive as well as civilized law in the following terms:

A law is a social norm of which it can be predicted with reasonable probability that its violation beyond the limits of permissible leeway will evoke a formal procedural response initiated by an individual or a group possessing the socially recognized privilege-right of determining guilt and of imposing economic or physical sanctions upon the wrongdoer.

We may further define *civilized law* as the law of societies whose cultures include writing; *archaic law* as the law of early civilizations; and *primitive law* as the law of nonliterate peoples.

Two other kinds of distinctions in law should be mentioned. These are the distinctions between *substantive* and *adjective* law, and between *organic* and *tyrannic* law.

Substantive Law and Adjective Law Legal norms are social norms that are reinforced by legal sanctions, as identified above. They are selected in accordance with their consistency in relation to jural postulates: the cultural assumptions that undergird the legal system.

Substantive Law Substantive law identifies the norms that are to be sanctioned by legal action. In most instances, substantive law undertakes to translate basic cultural postulates into social action by decision as to what particular behavior in a given instance may best be interpreted as conforming to the basic assumptions underlying the culture. Law implements the imperative of selection by saying implicitly: "In this society, this is permitted and that is not."

Adjective Law Procedural or *adjective law* designates the person, or persons, who may rightly punish a breach of substantive law; it also lays down the rules for prosecuting a case and fixes the customary penalties to be applied to each type of offense. In one form or another, the idea of due process of law exists in every society. Due process consists of the socially recognized right ways of carrying through a legal action once a plaintiff moves to act against an infringement of the substantive law. The "right ways" limit and channel the time and place of prosecution; the finding of evidence; the relevance of evidence; and the kinds and degree of coercion that may be used: what goods may be confiscated, or what physical sanctions are appropriate and allowable. The norms of *adjective law* institutionalize the sanctioning procedures. They separate right from sheer might. They are man's bulwark against the anarchy of strife and the terror of tyranny.

Organic versus Tyrannic Law Because of its element of coercion, law has its peculiar dangers. Out of control or in the hands of a vested minority, it can become a tyranny of terror directed not to the realization of the basic values of the society at large but to the subjugation of those who are not a part of the ruling clique, class, or caste.

When a law system is imposed on a people through conquest or by a minority which dominates through raw power not consensually allocated as a socially recognized privilege-right, that law system is *tyrannic.*

When a law system is self-developed by a people, when its rules and practices are generally accepted as in accord with commonly held ideas as to the nature of their society, its goals, and the legitimacy of its leaders and rulers—in sum, when the law system is in accord with the total social system—we can call it *organic law:* a vital system rooted in healthy soil. Most, but not all, primitive, tribal law systems have been of this order. And in the ensuing discussion, it will be of organic law that we speak, unless otherwise noted.

The Functions of Law

Law performs four fundamental functions essential to the maintenance of societies and their cultures. They are substantive, adjective, mediative, and readaptive in quality. These functions are:

1. The definition of obligatory relationships between the members of a society, so as to assert which activities are permitted and which are ruled out and to maintain at least minimal integration between the activities of individuals and groups within the society. This involves the culture-building process in response to the imperative of selection (substantive).

2. The allocation of authority and the designation of the person who has the socially recognized privilege-right to initiate and carry through legitimate corrective actions leading to economic or physical sanctions when substantive norms are violated, so that force is controlled and directed toward social goals (adjective).

3. The disposition of trouble cases as they arise; to clean up social messes (tangled claims, squabbles and fights, killings and woundings) so that people may get on about their business of everyday living with reasonable certainty and security (mediative).

4. The continuing redefinition of relations between individuals and groups as the conditions of life change, to maintain adaptability

and flexibility in both substantive and procedural law in response to shifting values and new technologies (readaptive).

A society may manage these functions with more or less skill; its legal system may function with sure effectiveness, achieving justice and order with a minimum of bungling and harshness; or it may be rigid and brutal, with order imposed by tyranny, and justice a fugitive in the land.

Case Law and the Settlement of Disputes

In his search for understanding of primitive legal systems and how they came into being, the anthropologist has benefited greatly from modern jurisprudence, which points up the fact that breach and disputes in conflicts of claims are the most constant source of the law. "Breach," says Seagle, "is the mother of law as necessity is the mother of invention."[15] On the authority of Holmes, we have it that ". . . a law embodies beliefs that have triumphed in the battle of ideas and then translated themselves into action." In the same vein, Pound has written: "The law is an attempt to reconcile, to harmonize, to compromise . . . overlapping or conflicting interests."[16] Law exists to channel behavior so that conflicts of interest do not result in an overt clash. It moves into action when interests do clash. New decisions are ideally so shaped as to determine which interests best accord with the accepted standards of what is good for the society. Of course, it is unfortunately true that tyrants, usurpers, and pettifoggers can and do pervert the ends of law to their own designs without regard to social interests or prevailing standards of what is right.

As a canon of realistic law, we may say that, regardless of the law that exists concerning a particular situation, an actual dis-

---

[15]W. Seagle, *The Quest for Law*, p. 35.
[16]R. Pound, "A Theory of Legal Interests" (*American Sociological Society, Publications,* vol. 16, 1920), p. 44.

pute must arise before the principles of the law can be tested; a law that is never broken may exist as nothing more than a custom, for one will never know the full implications of it until it is tested in a legal action.

The role of the claimant is the most important single factor in the development of law in primitive societies. Numerous writers have commented upon the relative absence of legislative enactment by primitive government. Lowie, who is distinguished among American anthropologists for his unique contributions to the study of legal phenomena, has offered a general statement that is fairly typical of the prevailing opinion: ". . . it should be noted that the legislative function in most primitive communities seems strangely curtailed when compared with that exercised in the more complex civilizations."[17] Salmond parallels this with the statement that ". . . the function of the State in its earlier conception is to *enforce* the law, not to *make* it."[18] Lowie continues: "All the exigencies of normal social intercourse are covered by customary law, and the business of such governmental machinery as exists is rather to exact obedience to traditional usage than to create new precedents."[19]

Now this would be true for wholly static societies, but, as Lowie would have been among the first to acknowledge, no society is wholly static. New exigencies always arise. One permanent thing about human society is its impermanence. Especially when unlike cultures come into contact do new materials, new ways of behaving, and new ideas enter into the cultural picture.

These new elements are not usually adopted simultaneously by all members of the society. The consequence is that when some members get new goods and new ideas, they have new interests for which the old lines of the culture have made no provision. Their use of their new acquisitions comes into conflict with the old standards held by others. New custom and new law must then be generated.

However or by whomever the judgment may be rendered in any dispute, it is the claimant and the defendant who lay the grounds of the claim and counterclaim or denial. If one or the other does it skillfully, soundly, and wisely, the basis of decision is likely to be found in his statement of his claim. No matter how selfish the motivation of a disputant may be, unless he is a fool indeed, he poses his claim against the background of "right" social principles, general rightness, and the well-being of the entire social group. How else can he gain enduring social acceptance of his position? Naturally, also, the more skillfully he argues his case in terms of the consonance of his claim with the well-established principles of social order, the greater the probability that he will shape the law as he wishes it to be determined.[20]

Evidence Any lawsuit or criminal trial involves at least two questions: "Is the alleged offense an illegal act?" "If so, is the defendant guilty of the offense?" The first is a question of law. The second is a question of fact. If the first can be brought to a negative answer, then there is no need to seek an answer to the second. The case must be dropped.

Assuming that there is a legal rule covering the alleged act, how are the facts then determined? On the lower levels of legal development, the question of evidence is not of great importance. In a small community, not much behavior is secret. As a Shoshone once commented to the author: "They just wait around. Sooner or later the facts will come out." In Comanche trials, the question of guilt or innocence was rarely raised. The usual point of argument was only the extent of damages.

[17]R. H. Lowie, *Primitive Society*, p. 358.
[18]J. W. Salmond, *Jurisprudence*, p. 49.
[19]Lowie, *op. cit.*, p. 358. (By "customary law" is meant "unwritten law.")

[20]Many examples of this process may be found in Llewellyn and Hoebel, *op. cit.*, or in J. Richardson, *Law and Status among the Kiowa Indians* (American Ethnological Society, Monograph 1, 1940). Because Cheyenne and Kiowa societies were undergoing rapid change during the period covered by these studies, the process of judicial lawmaking was more intensified than is the case in more stable cultures.

Judicial Hearings   In systems in which the administration of law is centralized in the hands of regular judges, the eliciting of evidence may be skillfully conducted. As an example, Max Gluckman's penetrating analysis of the judicial process among the Barotse of Rhodesia, in Africa, reveals in rich detail the institutional structure of the Lozi courts (*kuta*), made up of three sets of councilors: headmen or nonroyal chiefs, royal officers or stewards, and princes and prince consorts. Because the Lozi have no lawyers, ". . . the whole onus of eliciting and analyzing the evidence falls on the judges." Standards of judicial impartiality are explicitly strong: "A marked feature in all the judgments is the emphasis that the kuta decides by evidence and reasoning, and without favour."[21] Kinship allegiance should not enter.

The key concept here . . . is trial by due process of law (*tatubo kamulao*). The process is based on hearing evidence (*bupaki*) which establishes proof (also *bupaki*) on the facts (*litaba* = also things). Evidence itself is reduced by concepts of relevance (*bupaki bobuswanela*, appropriate or right evidence; *bupaki bobukena*, evidence which enters); of cogency (*bupaki bobutiile*, strong evidence); of credibility (*bupaki bobusepehala*); and of corroboration (*bupaki bobuyemela*). These types of evidence are tested as direct, circumstantial, or hearsay.[22]

When, through direct examination, the judges have elicited evidence sufficient to their needs, they enter a process of explicit formulation of a judgment. One after another, from the most junior judge up, in reversed order of seniority, the members of the *kuta* render their individual opinions, until the holding of the case is stated in the opinion of the senior chief:

Large parts of the judgments read like sermons, for they are all lectures on the theme "your station and its duties." The standards publicly stated for the parties are the norms involved in their social positions and relationships. . . . The essence of the judicial process is to state these norms to the world

and to assess against them the behaviour of the parties in a specific series of situations.[23]

Lozi judges are shrewdly appraised by the people, who express the reputations of individual judges in the following terms:

Kutalungusha—to be able to classify affairs;

kunyanyama—to be clever and of prompt decision;

sishongololi—a judge who relates matters lengthily and correctly;

muswanikisi—a judge who has good reasoning power and is able to ask searching questions.

Other words scorn poor reasoning:

kuyungula—to speak on matters without coming to the point;

kunjongoloka—to wander away from the subject when speaking;

kubulela siweko—to talk without understanding;

muyauluki—a judge who speaks without touching on the important points at issue;

siswasiwa—a person who gets entangled in words;

siyambutuki—a talker at random.[24]

Obviously, judges are themselves judged by severe standards of performance.

Supernatural Legal Devices   Generally speaking, however, the role of judges is much less significant in primitive legal systems than it is in the more developed legal orders of civilizations. Other devices used by primitive societies include resort to supernatural devices such as *divination, conditional curse,* and *ordeal.*

Extortion of confessions by third-degree methods occurs in a few tribes; for example, a Comanche husband could choke his wife or hold her over a fire until she named her lover. But more commonly the primitive man, when he could not get at the facts by direct means, had recourse to the supernatural.

Divination   *Divination* is the most common device. It is the process of evoking knowledge of some secret or hidden thing by mechanical or manipulative techniques. Thus an Eskimo shaman searches out answers by tying a

---

[21]M. Gluckman, *The Judicial Process among the Barotse of Northern Rhodesia,* pp. 82 and 61.
[22]*Ibid.,* p. 316.

[23]*Ibid.,* p. 49.
[24]*Ibid.,* p. 277.

thong to some reclining object such as a person, a bundle, or even his own foot. After inducing a spirit into the object, he asks it questions to which "yes" or "no" answers may be given. Then he tries to lift the object with the thong. If it is hard to lift, the answer is "no." If it raises easily, the answer is "yes."

Among many North American Indians, the still surface of water that has been put into the abdominal cavity of an animal reveals the image of the culprit. "Just as easy as reading a newspaper," said Post Oak Jim, the Comanche informant. Trobriand Islanders dug up a newly buried corpse to see what signs it might reveal. Maggots meant the lamented one was killed by the chief's sorcerer for having been too successful with women. If the lips were pursed, the same conclusion was indicated. Blotches of color on the skin meant he painted his house too ostentatiously for one of his social station, and so was done in by a jealous chief.

The Azande of Africa fed poison to a chicken, declaring repeatedly: "If this charge be true, let the chicken die. If this charge be false, spare its life." After the first chicken had responded, a second was given the test, but with the invocation reversed ("If the charge be true, let the chicken live; if it be false, let it die"). Thus, if the first chicken died and the second lived, the allegation was confirmed.[25]

Conditional Curse   Conditional curse enters into trial procedure among almost all peoples. It is the assertion that always includes or implies the sentence: "If what I say is not true, *then* may the supernatural destroy me." "You [Sun] saw me. May the one who lies die before winter."[26]

Even our own courts do not rely wholly upon our laws against perjury, since every witness must first swear a conditional curse: "So help me God." ("May God smite me if I lie.") Or is it, since the laws of criminal perjury are more recent than the conditional curse, that the courts do not have full faith in the efficacy of the curse?

Ordeal   Ordeal is peculiarly rare in the New World, which was to the good fortune of the Indians, to say the least. But most of the hideous forms known to medieval Europe were practiced with variations throughout Asia, Indonesia, and Africa. The ordeal by hot iron, with which Ibsen opens his historical play *The Pretenders,* had its counterpart in Ifugao. Various Philippine tribes used the old technique of tying up the two litigants and throwing them in a river. He who rose to the surface first was guilty. Ordeal by poison was popular in Africa. In Ashanti, the defendant in a trial could drink a poison brew. If he vomited, he was innocent; if he did not vomit, he died. And that is proof enough for any man!

Oath   Oath is merely a formal declaration that the testimony given is true. It may or may not imply the sanction of a supernatural power against falsehood. Often it is accompanied by a ritual act, such as touching the pipe to the lips among Indians, touching an arrow laid across the horns of a buffalo skull, or—as in American courts—placing one's hand upon the Bible.

Cultural Correlates of Conditional Curse and Ordeal   The virtual absence of appeal to the supernatural in legal disputes among American Indian tribes and its common occurrence in the Old World, especially Africa, shows how much it is an artificial, cultural invention. American Indians never thought up the idea of ordeal; a few of them knew and used the conditional curse. Somewhere in the Old World both ideas were hit upon, proved their social utility, and spread widely throughout the hemisphere.

A cross-cultural statistical survey undertaken by Professor John M. Roberts indicates that the use of conditional curse and/or ordeal as the means of settling issues of fact and simultaneously invoking supernatural

[25]E. E. Evans-Pritchard, *Witchcraft, Oracles and Magic among the Azande,* pp. 258–351.
[26]R. H. Lowie, *The Crow Indians,* p. 217.

punishment is rare among hunters and gatherers, important among pastoralists, but most frequent among peoples who rely on agriculture for subsistence. Also, the more highly stratified the society, the more likely the use of conditional curse and ordeals. Finally, the same holds with respect to political systems: the more centralized the government and the larger the community governed, the more likely the appeal to the supernatural in the legal settlement of disputes.[27]

What this means is this: in small tribal communities in which there is little differentiation in access to goods and resources, there tend to be fewer conflicts of property interests to generate disputes, and when disputes do occur, it is harder to hide the facts. Contrariwise, as populations become larger and more heterogeneous, as there are more goods to quarrel about, the task of the law becomes greater and more difficult. Direct and rational juridical devices fall short of meeting the demands of the law jobs in societal maintenance. Recourse is then had to the convenience of the supernatural, until in modern, rationalistic, and secularized civilizations the ritual oath loses its efficacy.

Representative Legal Systems

In order better to understand the nature of primitive law systems, it will be useful to sketch several thoroughly studied legal cultures, ranging from very simple and poorly developed types to highly developed ones that employ centralized governmental control. For this purpose we shall use the Eskimo, Comanche, Ifugao, Nuer, and Ashanti.

Eskimo Law The Eskimos provide a good example of law on the lowest levels of social organization. The small Eskimo local group

rarely numbers more than 100 members. Its organization is based on the bilateral family, beyond which there is nothing. There is no lineage, no clan, no clubs of either men or women, and no government. Each group has its headman: he who is "tacitly, half-unconsciously, recognized as first among equals"; he who is variously called *ihumatak,* "he who thinks (for others)"; *anaiyuhok,* "the one to whom all listen"; or *pimain,* "he who knows everything best." The headman leads, but he does not govern. He lends direction to his people's activity, but he does not direct. No Eskimo will give an order to another; therefore, the headman exercises no legal or judicial authority.

Prior to the imposition of Danish law in Greenland, of Canadian law in Canada, and federal and state law in Alaska, many acts prohibited under these legal systems were accepted as necessary by the Eskimos. Thus, certain forms of homicide were socially justified and legally permitted. Infanticide, invalidicide, suicide, and senilicide fell in this category. They are all responses to the basic Eskimo postulate that only those may survive who are able, or potentially able, to contribute to the subsistence economy of the community. Life is precarious in the arctic.

There were few legal offenses against property among the Eskimos because there was no property in land and free borrowing of goods made stealing pointless.

Eskimo law grew out of the aggressive status struggle that bedeviled the men. The society was wholly democratic, but prestige rivalry among the men was strong. Status could be gained through superior hunting skill and by stealing the wives of other men. The better the reputation of a man, the more likely he was to have his wife stolen. Wife stealing was not done primarily for sexual reasons. An Eskimo could enjoy sex without running the risks involved in home breaking. The motive lay in an attempt to outrank the man whose wife he took, if he could get away with it.

[27]J. M. Roberts, "Oaths, Autonomic Ordeals, and Power," in L. Nader (ed.), *The Ethnography of Law (American Anthropologist,* vol. 67, no. 6, part 2, Special Publication, 1965), pp. 186–212.

Wife stealing was not a crime, but most litigation arose from it. The challenge resulted either in murder or in wager of song, wrestling, or buffeting. Rasmussen found in the 1920s that all the adult males in a Musk Ox Eskimo group had been involved in murder, either as principals or as accessories; ". . . the motive was invariably some quarrel about a woman."[28] The fact that Eskimo husbands would lend their wives did not mean that they were free of jealousy. If a man lent his wife, he enjoyed the prestige of a giver of gifts. But if another man assumed sexual rights without permission, that was adultery and an assault on the husband's ego that could not go unchallenged. He would try to kill the wife stealer. But if he himself were killed, his murder had to be avenged, sooner or later. Since it was the usual Eskimo custom for the killer to marry his victim's widow and to adopt his children, a man might raise the boy who, when coming of age, would slay him in revenge for the murder of his father.

The alternative to killing an aggressor (and thus becoming involved in feud) was to challenge him to a juridical song contest. In the manner of Provençal troubadours of the thirteenth century, the two litigants scurrilously abused each other with songs composed for the occasion:

Now I shall split off words—little sharp words
Like the splinters which I hack off with my ax.
A song from ancient times—a breath of the ancestors
A song of longing—for my wife.
An impudent, black-skinned oaf has stolen her,
Has tried to belittle her.
A miserable wretch who loves human flesh.
A cannibal from famine days.[29]

He who received the most applause won. Thus was the issue settled without reference to the right or wrong of the case. But what was more important, the dispute was laid to rest.

Recidivist homicide, excessive sorcery (which is *de facto* recidivist homicide), and chronic lying were crimes punishable by death. Such was the nature of rudimentary law in the Eskimo anarchy.[30]

Comanche Law   Comanche Indian law-ways represented a somewhat higher development on the same general plane as Eskimo law.

The Comanches had chiefs, both civil and military. The band was larger than the Eskimo local group, and the Comanches had considerable property, especially in horses. They shared with the Eskimos a fierce drive toward male dominance and competitive rivalry among males for status by means of wife stealing. To this they also added the road of military glory. The Comanches recognized nine common legal offenses against the individual: adultery, wife absconding, violation of levirate privileges, homicide, killing a favorite horse, sorcery, causing another person to commit suicide (a form of homicide), failure to fulfill a contract, and theft.

Homicide called for the killing of the offender by the aggrieved kin of the dead man. This was a true legal penalty, for custom prevented the kin of the executed murderer from retaliating.

Adultery and wife stealing were handled variously, but in every case the aggrieved person was forced by public opinion to act. He could, and often did, proceed directly against the erring wife, killing her, cutting off her nose, or otherwise mutilating her hapless body. This was a husband's legal privilege. Or, if he preferred, he could collect damages from the male offender. This would be done by a direct demand. Whether or not he got what he first went after depended on how courageous the defendant was. If the aggrieved husband was not strong or fearless enough, he could call in his friends or kinsmen to prosecute for him. But then "the lawyers got the a' of it," for his helpers kept all the damages for themselves. Or, lacking

[28]K. Rasmussen, *Across Arctic America*, p. 250.
[29]K. Rasmussen, *Grønlandsagen*, p. 235.

[30]E. A. Hoebel, "Law-ways of the Primitive Eskimos" (*Journal of Criminal Law and Criminology*, vol. 13, 1941), pp. 663–683, or *The Law of Primitive Man*, chap. 5.

kin and friends, he could call upon any brave warrior to prosecute for him. Great braves were willing, for prestige reasons, to do this without any material recompense whatever.[31]

Ifugao Law The Ifugaos provide another example of law on the primitive level of organization. These mountain-dwelling headhunters of Luzon possessed no government worthy of being called such. Over 100,000 tribesmen live scattered throughout the deep valleys that crease their rugged homeland. Although there are clusters of houses in the more favorable spots, the Ifugaos have no true villages, nor do they have a clan organization. The bilateral group of kinsmen is tightly knit, however. In the course of centuries, the Ifugaos have carved the steep walls of their mountains into stupendous rice terraces fed by intricate irrigation systems. Their paddies are privately owned and protected by a complex body of substantive law. Ifugaos are capitalists who have many legal rules controlling credit and debt. In addition, they are litigious in the extreme, for each man is sensitive about his "face" and quick to take offense. Their list of possible legal wrongs was long indeed.

How did they handle a legal case prior to the establishment of American legal control around 1905, and, subsequently, of Philippine national law? A man with a grievance or a claim tried first to exact a satisfactory settlement from the opposite party. Failing this, he went to a *monkalun*, or "go-between," who was a member of the highest social class and who had a reputation as a man of affairs and a number of enemy heads to his credit. The *monkalun* heard his story and accosted the defendant with the charges. The defendant in turn pleaded his cause. Meanwhile, both plaintiff and defendant marshaled their fighting relatives—just in case. The *monkalun*

shuttled back and forth between the two parties, wheedling, arguing, threatening, cajoling—attempting to induce them to give ground so that they might meet on terms acceptable to each. Customary law made the penalties and obligations of both parties quite explicit for every conceivable offense, but first there had to be agreement on the exact nature and degree of the offense. Claim was balanced against counterclaim. Each side weighed the fighting strength and inclination of the other. But at long last, if the patience of the *monkalun* and the litigants endured, a settlement was reached and damages were paid (if it was an assault case), or the debt was satisfied (if it was an economic dispute). But if no settlement satisfactory to each disputant could be reached, the *monkalun* finally withdrew from the case. Then the plaintiff or his kinsmen undertook to kill the defendant—or any convenient kinsman of his. Feud was forthcoming. The legal machinery had broken down.[32] (See the photograph at the beginning of this chapter.)

The *monkalun* represented the public interest by his intervention. Yet he was only incipiently a public officer. He made no decision and enforced no judgment, but he provided the means, through his good offices, of bringing disputants to a resolution of their conflict. All Ifugao legal offenses were wrongs to be prosecuted by the aggrieved individual. There were no recognized crimes against society at large and, therefore, no public law.[33]

Nuer Law The legal system of the Nuer of the African Sudan was similar to that of the Ifugaos in many respects. The Nuer, like the Ifugaos, had no state. Unlike the Ifugaos, they were organized into segmented lineages (see page 447). The lineages represented the legal units that stood in opposition to one another. Evans-Pritchard saw them as a peo-

[31]E. A. Hoebel, *The Political Organization and Law-ways of the Comanche Indians* (American Anthropological Association, Memoir 54: Contributions from the Laboratory of Anthropology, 4, 1940), or *The Law of Primitive Man*, pp. 127–142.

[22]Ifugao procedure is dramatized in "The Case of the Bamboo-sized Pigs: Ifugao," in *The Ways of Mankind,* Series II.
[23]R. F. Barton, *Ifugao Law;* also Hoebel, *The Law of Primitive Man*, chap. 6.

ple who had no law because ". . . there is no constituted and impartial authority who decides on the rights and wrongs of a dispute and there is no external power to enforce such a decision were it given."[34]

According to Evans-Pritchard's analysis, feud and the threat of feud were the legal mechanisms by means of which adherence to norms was maintained. Violation of a norm could set off a feud between lineages. But among the Nuer, "A feud cannot be tolerated within a village and it is impossible to maintain one for a long period between nearby villages."[35]

We have already indicated that formal judges are not a necessary attribute of law. The Nuer, like the Ifugaos, employed the services of a mediator, the Priest of the Earth, to settle serious disputes. This is the priest who is especially related to the sanctity of the earth and who is also called the Leopard Skin Chief because he wears a leopard skin as an emblem of his office. Most Nuer offenses are legally settled by direct negotiation between the lineages without intervention of the Priest of the Earth. Bodily injuries gave rise to damages paid in cattle according to a definite and detailed scale commensurate with the degree of injury done the victim. Adultery and seduction of unmarried girls were also private wrongs for which compensation in cattle could be demanded and received. There were also suits over the return of progeny price after a divorce had taken place.

The Nuer are a proud and independent people, quick to resort to violence. Failure to pay the customary damages in cattle might bring deadly resort to the spear; then a feud could be launched and the equilibrium of the society seriously disturbed. But in spite of their truculence, the Nuer value good relations among neighbors and within the tribe.

According to P. P. Howell, who knew them well, ". . . the Nuer are, and always have been, acutely conscious of the need for unity and are always seeking someone by whom and through whom social disharmony can be averted."[36] Nuer traditions, he tells us, are full of references to great leaders:

Their principal characteristics are to be seen in the Nuer ideals: the desire and the ability to bind the people together; to mediate and to settle internal quarrels and disputes; to negotiate agreement with other tribes and peoples if they are to the advantage of the Nuer; to maintain good relations between neighbours; in fact, to check the process of fission which to the Nuer is highly undesirable. These qualities are stressed in Nuer tradition far more frequently than ability to lead the warriors into battle against the Dinka, and are more important than their sagas of great exploits and daring.[37]

Such men are called *ruic naadk,* "spokesmen of the people"; the Nuer have headmen of essentially the same quality as many other simple primitive people.

The killing of a Nuer by a Nuer resulted in the spiritual contamination of the murderer and all his household. The contamination, called *nueer,* was believed to bring disease and death unless it was ritually removed by the Priest of the Earth.

A killing, therefore, could entail the inconvenience of a feud, and it certainly entails (even today) the dangers and costs of *nueer.* A murderer would therefore seek asylum in the homestead of the Priest of the Earth. There he was secure against revenge while the priest arranged the payment of blood money by the killer's lineage to the lineage of his victim. If one or the other lineage held out unreasonably in agreeing to an acceptable settlement, the priest could threaten to curse them. If the curse were uttered, their cattle would sicken, their crops wither, and their people die—not a happy prospect! The ultimate sanction in Nuer law, therefore, was physical, albeit by

[34]E. E. Evans-Pritchard, "The Nuer of the Southern Sudan," in M. Fortes and E. E. Evans-Pritchard (eds.), *African Political Systems,* p. 293.
[35]E. E. Evans-Pritchard, *The Nuer,* p. 159.

[36]P. P. Howell, *A Manual of Nuer Law,* p. 33.
[37]*Ibid.*

supernatural means. When the blood money had finally been paid, the homestead, cattle, and body of the murderer were ritually purified in elaborate ceremony. Social relations between the two kinship groups were thus restored, and life could resume its course. The "social mess" had been cleaned up.

Ashanti Law   Finally, the Ashanti of West Africa may be cited as a highly advanced people who were well on the road toward civilized law by the middle of the last century. Today they are part of the nation of Ghana.

The Ashanti were a powerful nation who developed their own constitutional monarchy. Clan feuding was checked, and all private law was brought within the potential jurisdiction of the royal criminal courts. Any private dispute ordinarily settled between the household heads of the two disputants could be thrown into royal hands by the simple device of one of the quarreling persons swearing an oath on the Great Forbidden Name of a god that the other was guilty of an offense. In rebuttal, his adversary would swear on the same forbidden name that he did not commit the wrong. One or the other was then guilty of a false oath, perjury, which was a capital crime for which the liar lost his head.

Whoever heard the swearing had to arrest the two, for every citizen was the king's agent in such an event. He led them to a log kept for the purpose and chained them to it, after which he trotted off to the king's bailiff with the news. A day was then set for the trial. When hauled before the king and his council of elders, each litigant was called upon to tell his story. The stories were then repeated verbatim by the king's speaker, and each affirmed the accuracy of the repetition. So was the issue joined. Next, one or the other of the prisoners before the bar named a witness, who was brought forth to swear a deadly conditional curse that what he was about to say was the truth of the matter. In this the Ashanti placed implicit faith, for the whole trial hinged on what was now said. On the

testimony of the single witness, one party was freed and the other condemned to be beheaded—unless the king in deference to the needs of his treasury allowed the luckless one "to buy his head," i.e., pay a fine.[38]

Aside from this crude but remarkable device for extending the king's peace, there was also a great body of criminal regulations; the violation of any one of these would be pun-

---

[38]Ashanti procedure and the techniques of shifting a quarrel from the area of private law to that of criminal law are dramatized in "The Forbidden Name of Wednesday: Ashanti," *The Ways of Mankind*, Series II.

Fig. 26-1   Law in contemporary Ibo art. An Ibo couple of Nigeria publicly punished.

ished by death. These ranged from homicide —"only the king may wield the knife"—to carrying a chicken on top of a load. Even suicide was a capital offense, for it constituted a usurpation of the king's exclusive right to kill. The corpse of the suicide was hauled into court, tried, and ostentatiously decapitated. As a more practical gesture, his properties were also confiscated on behalf of the king's treasury.

Ashanti criminal law overreached the mark in much the same way as did the law of eighteenth-century England, with its 200 capital crimes. It is significant as an example of the way in which monarchy becomes the means of expressing the social interest in the maintenance of order by replacing of private law by criminal law. This is a genuine social advance over the chaos of societies that allow feuding.[39]

The Trend of the Law

It is a seeming paradox, on first thought, that the more civilized a society becomes, the greater is the need for law, and the wider the reach of law becomes. But it is no paradox, if the functions of law are kept in mind. Simple societies have little need of law, and on the earliest levels of human culture there were probably no legal institutions. In such groups as the Shoshones, Eskimos, Andaman Islanders, and African Bushmen, there is only a little of what we would call law. Almost all relations in the tribe are face to face and intimate. The demands imposed by culture are relatively few; child training is direct and comprehensive. Ridicule is keenly felt, for there is no escape in anonymity. Tabu and the fear of supernatural sanctions cover a large area of behavior. Special interests are few, for there is little accumulated wealth. Conflict arises

mostly in interpersonal relations. Hence, homicide and adultery are the most common legal focuses. Sorcery as a form of homicide always looms large as an illegal possibility, but among the simpler peoples, sorcery, which uses supernatural techniques, is usually met with supernatural countermeasures rather than with legal action.

Among the higher hunters, the pastoralists, and the ruder gardening peoples, the size of the group and the increased complexity of the culture make possible greater divergence of interests between the members of the tribe. Conflict of interests grows, and the need for legal devices for settlement and control of the internal clash of interests begins to be felt. Private law emerges and spreads. It exerts a restraining influence, but, like the clan, it has inherent limitations that prevent it from completely satisfying the need it must meet. As no man is competent to judge his own cause, procedure under private law leads too often not to a just settlement but to internecine fighting—to feud.

Feud and Law   Feud is a state of conflict between two kinship groups within a society, manifest by a series of unprivileged killings and counterkillings between the kinship groups, usually initiated in response to an original homicide or other grievous injury. Legal historians traditionally have seen primitive society as marked by a horrid and constant state of feud, rent by violent retaliation and blood revenge, and, in general, an arena of violence ruled by the law of the jungle and the retaliative *lex talionis* ("an eye for an eye, a tooth for a tooth, a life for a life"). It appeared that feud was the curse of primitive society from which men could escape only through law.

The fact is that there is very limited evidence for the actual occurrence of feud in primitive societies. Legal procedures or ritual devices such as regulated combat as a means of avoiding or terminating feud have been universally found to exist in such cultures. The

---

[39]This description applied a century ago. R. S. Rattray, *Ashanti Law and Constitution;* K. A. Busia, *The Position of the Chief in the Modern Political System of Ashanti;* and E. A. Hoebel, *The Law of Primitive Man,* chap. 9.

idea that feud is called for is widespread among primitives, but they actually prefer to accept damages rather than take blood revenge. An example would be the case of the Trobriand Islanders for whom Malinowski reported that although honor makes "vendetta" obligatory in cases of homicide, it was evaded by the substitution of blood-money (compensation). There was much Trobriand talk of feud, but Malinowski found not one specific case. In all anthropological reports, this is the rule rather than the exception.

But if there are strong grounds for doubting that feud occurs with anything like the frequency we have been led to believe, there is no question but that the folk belief in feud as a cultural expectancy, as both ideal and presumed behavior, is widespread. It is a folk phenomenon in its own right. The idea of feud, if not its reality, assumes importance.

Real feud is socially destructive and dangerous. When it does occur, it does represent a breakdown of peaceful resolution of conflict. As Drucker has written of the Northwest Coast Indians of North America, ". . . the threat of violence was always present if the claims of the aggrieved were disregarded. . . . Settlements of these conflicts were usually reached, but never easily. . . . And at times negotiations did break down and were followed by a period of bloody feuding."[40]

Law exists everywhere to preclude the recourse to bloody battles within societies. Law consists of procedures designed to obviate feud. Folk belief in the expected requirements of honor to engage in feud is customarily blown up to feed the fear of the effects of feud. It seems quite likely that this very fear of feud is one of the factors that nourishes and sustains primitive legal systems.

As the scope of commonality expands, as community of interest reaches out beyond the kindred and clan, beyond the local group and tribe, men gradually create the means to check internecine strife within the bounds of

the larger society through the expansion of the scope of law.

Experience in the development of other branches of culture is also accompanied by experience in the manipulation of the social-control phases of culture. Instruments and devices of government are created. To a greater and greater extent, private law is replaced by public law.

From Status to Contract: Sir Henry Maine
Sir Henry Maine, whose work *Ancient Law*, first published in 1861, remains a classic to this day, contrasting the importance of private law in primitive societies and the importance of public law in civilized societies.

If therefore the criterion of a *delict, wrong,* or *tort* be that the person who suffers it, and not the State, is conceived to be wronged, it may be asserted that in the infancy of jurisprudence the citizen depends for protection against violence or fraud not on the Law of Crime but on the Law of Tort.[41]

The state and its agencies corrode away the legal powers of the kinship group. The individual becomes increasingly free to make his own legal commitments independently of his kinship status. The trend was formulated by Maine as follows:

. . . [T]he movement of the progressive societies has hitherto been a movement from *Status to Contract.* . . . The individual is steadily substituted for the Family [kinship group], as the unit of which civil laws take account. . . . Nor is it difficult to see what is the tie between man and man which replaces by degrees those forms of reciprocity in rights and duties which have their origin in the Family. It is Contract . . . in which all these relations [of persons] arise from the free agreement of individuals.[42]

There are many limitations to Maine's generalization, but it is an evolutionary proposition of great significance. There is good reason to believe that the development of the abstract notion of contract, which was worked

---

[40] P. Drucker, *Indians of the Northwest Coast*, pp. 73–74.

[41] H. J. Maine, *Ancient Law*, p. 359.
[42] *Ibid.*, pp. 165 and 163.

out in Roman law, is the great inventive key to modern free society. It parallels the significance of abstract mathematical conceptualization, which is the key to modern science and technology.[43]

World Law The next development in law that may be foreseen on the basis of past trends and growing need is the freeing of the individual from the limitations of nationality and, concomitantly, the expansion of the scope of law to embrace a worldwide system framed and administered by a world commonwealth. Ultimately, it will be this or regression. Today, primitive law prevails between nations. What passes as international law consists of no more than normative rules for the conduct of affairs between nations as they have been enunciated and agreed upon from time to time by means of treaties, pacts, and covenants. In addition, a body of prevailing custom in international intercourse, recognized by tacit consensus or verbalized in arbitration, World Court awards, and United Nations decisions, provides the other main source of its substance. But this body of social norms for international intercourse is as yet no more than the bylaws of the subgroups we call nations. International law now consists of substantive rules without imperative legal sanctions.

The United Nations today, like the League of Nations of yesterday, because the power of universal coercive, absolute force is withheld from it, cannot make law of the international norms upon which it determines. Whatever the idealist may desire or the nationalist fear, force and the threat of force remain the ultimate powers in the implementation of law between nations, as they do in law within the nation or tribe. But until the use of force and the threat of force as now exercised by nation

against nation are brought under the socialized control of a world community, by and for world society, they remain not the sanctions of world law but the instruments of social anarchy and the constant threat to the survival of present societies.

The metamorphosis from primitive law to modern law on the plane of international intercourse awaits the emergence of the consciousness of world community by all men. If the fulfillment comes in our time it will be our happy destiny to participate in the greatest event in the legal history of mankind.

SUMMARY

Law is one aspect of the system of social control which is an implicit part of every culture. Social control consists of all those practices engaged in by the members of a society to reward and encourage culturally approved behavior and to penalize and discourage culturally disapproved behavior. Law is a part of the norm-selecting and norm-maintaining system relied upon by each society in its self-organization.

Law is more than custom and less than social control. Law, like custom, consists of social norms. Law shares with custom the element of regularity: that which is normally done (the *is*) and that which is expected to be done (the *ought*). Law sustains predictability in behavior.

Law, like custom, is sanctioned. Some deviation from social norms is usually allowed in most areas of behavior in most societies. Yet in many societies, deviation beyond the limits of permissible leeway in certain designated areas of behavior is negatively sanctioned by confiscation of economic goods or by the application of physical coercion. Economic sanctions are classed as *damages* or *fines,* depending upon who has legal authority and to whom the penalty is paid. In *private law* they are damages; in *public law* they are fines.

The difference between public and private

[43]See F. S. C. Northrop and H. H. Livingston (eds.), *Cross Cultural Understanding* (1964), especially chaps. 12, 13, 15, and 16, for further development of this point.

law depends upon who has the authority to initiate legal proceedings and impose the sanctions. This is *the element of officialdom.* The legal official is a person or group of persons who has the socially recognized privilege-right of acting against another person in accordance with the rules of due process of law. In most systems of primitive law, the wronged party, or his kinship group, is vested with the privilege-right of initiating a legal action and carrying it to completion by punishing the wrongdoer. This is called private law, but it has the backing of general social approval. On the other hand, if the legal action must be initiated by a headman, a chief, or a chief's representative (i.e., a governmental official), the offense is called a *crime,* and the whole process is in the area of public law. In both private and public law, however, the element of societal concern is to the fore.

A law is, therefore, defined as *a social norm whose violation will probably evoke a formal procedural response initiated by an individual or a group possessing the socially recognized privilege-right of determining guilt and of imposing economic or physical sanctions upon the wrongdoer.*

Substantive law consists of the norms to be enforced (the *what*). Procedural, or adjective, law consists of the norms which determine due process of law (the *how*). Law has four major functions: (1) to identify acceptable lines of behavior for inclusion in the culture and to penalize contradictory behavior, so as to maintain at least minimal integration between the activities of individuals and groups within the society; (2) to allocate authority and to determine who may legitimately apply force to maintain the legal norms; (3) to settle trouble cases as they arise; and (4) to redefine relationships as the conditions of life change, so as to help keep the culture adaptable.

The modern, realistic study of primitive law systems is based upon the analysis of actual cases of dispute and conflict. Law is what people do, not what they say they do.

Cases may be settled through direct negotiation between the disputants. This process may involve the use of a go-between or mediator; it may call for an arbitrator; or it may be put in the hands of a judge or judges.

In very small tribal societies, where most relations are face to face, the problem of evidence does not raise many difficulties. When the facts are not known, however, or the claims of the aggrieved party are denied by the defendant, recourse is usually to the supernatural powers by means of divination, conditional curse, or ordeal. In some rare cultures or situations, a simple oath suffices.

In the evolution of law, public law tends to gain in importance as societies become more complex. The trend of the law has been one of an increasing shift of responsibility for the maintenance of legal norms away from the individual and his kinship group to the agents of the society as a whole. In like manner, the individual tends to be allowed greater freedom in contractual determination of his social responsibilities. Concomitantly, there is less dependence upon ascribed kinship statuses in the more highly developed societies.

Feud has been viewed as an absence of law and as a breakdown of the legal machinery. The "law of blood revenge" was believed to be a common feature of many primitive systems. More recent studies indicate that although the idea of feuding is quite widespread, the more regular and frequent practice is to accept damages rather than seek blood revenge.

As society expands, so does the scope of the law, for unless the functions of law are adequately fulfilled, the existence of the society is endangered. The great modern problem of survival and cultural adaptation is the creation of an effective system of world law to meet the functional prerequisities of the new world society.

SELECTED READINGS

Barton, R. F., *Ifugao Law* (1969). The classic monograph on the Ifugao, now readily available in book form, is to be highly recommended.

Bohannan, P., *Justice and Judgment among the Tiv* (1957). An inside view of how a "stateless" West African society operates its law.

Gluckman, M., *The Judicial Process among the Barotse of Northern Rhodesia* (1955). How trouble cases are settled in an African tribe. Also, *The Ideas in Barotse Jurisprudence* (1965). A brilliant comparative analysis of Barotse legal concepts.

Hoebel, E. A., *The Law of Primitive Man* (1954). Presents a theory of law and society. Describes and analyzes the legal culture of seven selected primitive societies, followed by a functional interpretation of law in culture.

Llewellyn, K. N., and E. A. Hoebel, *The Cheyenne Way: Conflict and Case Law in Primitive Jurisprudence* (1941). Contains a number of case records of Cheyenne legal disputes and a systematic analysis of the law-ways of this remarkable Indian tribe.

Pospisil, L., *The Kapauku Papuans and Their Law* (1958). Particularly useful for its analysis of what this New Guinea people think their legal norms are and what they actually are according to the outcome of specific cases.

————*Anthropology of Law: A Comparative Theory* (1971). A theoretical and empirical treatment of law and society from an anthropological point of view which is both sound and informative.

Schapera, I., *A Handbook of Tswana Law and Custom* (1938). A very competent and thorough treatment of the social system and formal law of an African tribe.

Chapter 27

Political Organization and Politics

Politics is more than government and government is less than law. The political process performs much the same functions as have just been specified for law: (1) the definition of behavioral norms for acceptable conduct, (2) the allocation of force and authority, (3) the settlement of disputes, and (4) the redefinition of norms for conduct.

Political organization, and especially government, may well go beyond this, however. In addition, (1) it may organize group efforts for public works, such as tribal hunts, tending the chief's gardens, digging and repairing irrigation ditches, and building roads, temples, and pyramids; (2) it may carry ritual and ceremonial responsibility for religious control of the supernatural world and human conduct (see Sacerdotal Chief and Kings, pages 527–528); (3) it may organize and maintain markets and trading networks; and (4) it usually carries responsibility for defense of the home territory and the waging of war against enemy societies.

Law can exist without government in the form of private law. Much political activity does not express itself as law. Yet the very existence of law is itself an expression of political organization, for the legitimacy of the legal acts of a private prosecutor is an expression of public interest and public consensus.

Political organization is more than government as such, and it is not synonymous with the state, for the state is a specialized social phenomenon, while political organization is generalized. Government exists when there are specialized functionaries, or officers, designated and empowered to make and execute political decisions.

Fig. 27-A Andean woman voting in a township election in Bolivian highlands. (United Nations.)

The Nature of Political Organization

The only kind of society that could be said to be without political organization would be one consisting of a single bilateral extended family within which there were no organized subdivisions. Sex and age differences would be present, to be sure, and there would be one or two religious specialists. But the so-

ciety would be organized as a single large family operating under familial controls. All problems would be settled as family problems, and there would be no other divisive groupings within the community. Family and community would be one.

This kind of society was approximated among some of the simpler primitive peoples, such as the Shoshones, but it exists nowhere among men today, nor has it been observed to have existed since written records have been kept.[1]

Political organization comes into being wherever societies are segmented on the basis of kinship, economics, religion, sex, fraternities, or community. Where there are subgroups that are discrete entities within the social entirety, there is political organization—a system of regulation of relations between groups or members of different groups within the society at large and between one society and another.

Our earlier discussions of subsistence techniques and land tenure have indicated the importance of ecological relations, the patterns of adjustments of human populations to the territory in which they live. Because skillful exploitation of the immediate environment is absolutely essential to survival, man, like all other living creatures, develops an intimate relation to the soil and to its plants, to its lakes, rivers, and springs, and to its denizens. In cooperation with his day-to-day fellows, he works it for all that his technology enables him to win from it. The group molds its culture to the offerings of its territory, and although migrations are common, the general pattern is for a people to hold fast to the land they know—and have come to love.

Because the members of a community live together under a common culture, they share their patterns of living and ideas in common to a large extent. Community means commonality, in which diversity exists but unity prevails. Community means that the feeling of oneness—a sense of entity, an *esprit de corps* —extends to the whole territorial society. It means that the culture sets values that orient behavior in the direction of common as well as individual or subgroup interests. The common interests are what constitute political interests. The community is the polity. Political organization, therefore, is *that part of the culture which functions explicitly to direct the activities of the members of the society toward community goals.*

The State

It is quite possible to analyze political organization without any recourse to the concept of the state whatsoever. Indeed, the failure of political scientists to realize this until quite recently seriously handicapped the development of viable political theory beyond the realm of European types of government.[2] For a long time, thinking in terms of the state did more harm than good because it diverted attention from the broader, institutional aspects of political processes as they are woven through the entire weft of social life. This type of thinking kept both political scientists and anthropologists from paying attention to the political process in simply organized societies. Yet the state is so overpoweringly important in modern civilization, and is growing so steadily more so, that it cannot be ignored. Anthropologists now distinguish between stateless and state-organized societies.

The idea of a state embodies three elements: (1) a territory, (2) a culturally organized population, and (3) a centrally organized government with strong coercive powers.

The state is an institution among other

[1]"Among all known people—the autonomous, land-owning socio-political group is greater than the bilateral family." J. H. Steward, "The Economic and Social Basis of Primitive Bands," in *Essays in Anthropology in Honor of Alfred Louis Kroeber*, p. 333. A contrary view is advanced, however, by L. Sharp, "People without Politics," in V. Ray (ed.), *Systems of Political Control and Bureaucracy*, pp. 1–8.

[2]G. A. Almond and J. S. Coleman (eds.), *The Politics of Developing Areas.*

institutions within a given community's culture. It is not the society or the community; it is a complex of behaviors characteristic of the members of the community in one part of their lives—the political. Thus, as Linton observed, the tribe is a social entity marked by a sentiment of community due to common culture; the state is a subentity marked by common political organization with a well-developed government.[3]

Government is to be thought of as an executive instrument of political organization. The personnel of government are the specialists and functionaries who perform the state's business. They are the headmen, chiefs, kings, and council members, and their various aides.

Three Principles of Organization A political system may use one or more of three major units of social organization as the basis for its structure: (1) genealogical, or kinship, units; (2) geographical, or territorial, units; or (3) associational units.

Kinship Primitive societies, as has already been shown in previous chapters, generally rest most heavily on the kinship principle. Lineages, clans, phratries, and moieties may each have their headmen who not only are responsible for the regulation and guidance of affairs within their respective kinship groups but who also formally represent their groups vis-à-vis other kinship groups. Collectively, they may form the several levels of councils that act within or for the tribe in public affairs. How much of the structure and functioning of primitive legal systems is built upon kinship groups has already been made clear.

But note, on the other hand, that so far has the kinship principle fallen into desuetude in many modern states, and especially in the United States, that favoritism on behalf of relatives, called nepotism, is often

forbidden by law, although a new trend in equal employment opportunity for women is waiving the prohibition in favor of wives.

Territorialism On the other hand, since every community is a distinguishable territorial entity, every political system, both primitive and civilized, uses the geographical unit as a basis of organization as well. The smallest such unit is the *household*. The next largest is the *camp* (among nomadic hunters and gatherers) or the *village* (among sedentary peoples). The next largest is the *band*, comprising a number of camps (among the nomads) or the *district*, comprising several villages (among the sedentes). Above these is the *tribe* or *nation*, the largest group with a common language and culture. (Actually, a tribe may incorporate alien groups.)

Tribes may ally on a more or less permanent basis with other tribes to form a *confederacy*. This is usually done on a voluntary basis for mutual defense or aggression, and in confederacy each tribe remains self-determining in political matters to a greater extent than it yields decisive power to the confederacy. The only real difference between an alliance and a confederacy is in the development of more enduring and explicit institutions for determination of questions of mutual concern between the tribes.

When a tribe or confederacy incorporates the victims of its conquest into a permanent state system on a subordinate basis, the political system has expanded to become an *empire*.

All these forms of territorial organization were achieved by one or another primitive society.

Associations The use of special associations as a principle of political organization is, on the whole, relatively weak in primitive cultures, but nevertheless quite widespread. The heads of the secret religious fraternities form the tribal council in a number of pueblos. The military fraternities of the Plains Indians per-

[3]R. Linton, *The Study of Man,* p. 240.

formed major governmental functions, as do many of the secret societies of Africa and Melanesia. The age sets of other parts of Africa do likewise. In India, castes still operate as units of politics, although the modern constitution of India proscribes them.

The constitutional structure of the United States ignores the associational principle, but churches, labor unions, manufacturers' associations, and a host of other special-interest organizations have secondary political functions, of which lobbying is but one form of expression. One need only stroll the streets of Washington, taking note of the many stately headquarters maintained by a legion of organizations, to become aware of how true this is.[4]

Types of Political Organization

As a society emphasizes one or another principle of organization, or a combination of principles, it produces political organizations of different types. Some of these are structurally identifiable among primitive cultures as follows.

Stateless Systems   Stateless systems have no formal government embracing the entire society. Political functions are performed by subgroups and by functionaries whose political jobs are secondary to other interests and responsibilities. There is no person or group of persons with centralized authority applicable to the society as a whole.

Undifferentiated   In such cultures as those of the South African Bushmen, the Eskimos, and the Shoshones, kinship and political relations are one and the same entity. Small, local groups live as isolated, self-governing units, subject to no higher political power. Tensions between members of in-dividual families are settled directly without intervention of a band headman.

Segmentary Lineage   This is the uncentralized political system in which lineages rather than villages or bands form the significant units of organization. There is little or no common decision making for the tribe, nor is there much in the way of broadly integrative ceremony or ritual. The Nuer of the African Sudan are the classic example.[5] The segmentary lineage organization provides the structural framework. Such systems of political organization are very common in East Africa and in Melanesia, where the Kapauku and the Kuma are good examples.[6]

Age Set   Under this system, political matters are largely in the hands of age sets and their officers. The age sets cut across village and district boundaries and form the framework of political integration, as among the Nyakyusa. By virtue of the relatively limited distribution of age sets, this system is quite rare.

Village Council and Associations   In this type, there is no tribal government as such, nor do corporate lineages function in government, but authority is vested in village councils and men's fraternities. The Pueblos of the southwestern United States and such tribes as the Ibo of West Africa are representative.

Village or Band with Headman   Here, the tribe lacks overall government; each band or village, as the case may be, has a headman or chief endowed with mild political authority. Kinship may be important in many aspects of life, but it is not a major factor in political organization. Territorial identity and personal qualities of leadership on the part of a headman are the determining factors. For example:

---

[4]Even the American Anthropological Association maintains its headquarters in Washington, D.C.

[5]E. E. Evans-Pritchard's *The Nuer* became the model for a number of penetrating studies of this type of organization.
[6]L. Pospisil, *The Kapauku Papuans of New Guinea*, pp. 32–63; and M. Reay, *The Kuma*.

"The headman of a Chiricahua [Apache] local group can be thought of as a natural-born leader, one who earns the confidence and support of his neighbors. His influence is considerable, but it is of an informal nature."[7]

The leader is expected to speak on all important occasions. Among the Yavapai of Arizona, the headman was moderate in speech, stopped quarrels, and knew the best campsites. People followed him because his personality won their confidence. Of the Comanche headmen, That's It sagely observed: "I hardly know how to tell about them; they never had much to do except to hold the band together."[8] That's It put his finger on it. The headman in the primitive world rarely has explicit authority; his functions are so subtle that they defy easy description. Yet he is the focal point of the local group.

As Harrasser notes, among the Central Australians, the "chief is at most *prima inter pares* with few exceptions among the Dieri and in West Victoria."[9] Similar evidence comes from the Shoshones and the Eskimos. The Shoshone headman is called *tegwoni*, which in its fullest sense means "good talk thrown out to the people." In western Alaska, the headmen are those who "by their extended acquaintance with the traditions, customs and rites connected with the festivals, as well as being possessed of an unusual degree of common sense, are deferred to and act as chief advisers of the community."[10]

The simplest primitive societies are always democracies; rarely are they subject to dictatorial political leadership.

State Systems   State systems have chiefs, kings, or councils with authority over certain

spheres of social activity covering the entire society.

Chiefdoms   Complexity of social life sharpens the need for leadership and the delegation of responsibility. Societies that are developed enough to have a tribal state always possess chiefs. A chief is differentiated from the headman by degree of authority and social distinction. His position may or may not be inherited. His functions and powers are variable among different peoples.

In North America, it was unusual for a chief to have strong power. Great care was taken in many tribes to separate the offices of peace chiefs and war chiefs. Peace chiefs were the civil governors. Usually they were band or clan headmen elevated to the status of mem-

Fig. 27-1   West African chieftains. The Cameroons. (United Nations.)

[7]M. E. Opler, *An Apache Life-way*, pp. 233–234.

[8]E. A. Hoebel, *The Political Organization and Law-ways of the Comanche Indians* (American Anthropological Association, Memoir 54: Contributions from the Laboratory of Anthropology, 4, 1940), p. 18.

[9]A. Harrasser, *Die Rechtsverletzung bei den australischen Eingeborenen* (Beilageheft zur vergleichende Rechtswissenshaft, vol. 50, 1936).

[10]E. W. Nelson, *The Eskimos about Bering Strait* (Bureau of American Ethnology, Annual Report 18, 1899), p. 304.

bership in the tribal council. They supervised internal tribal relations and had judicial powers over a few classes of crime. Most legal offenses, however, remained in the area of private wrongs to be settled by the parties concerned. Sometimes, as in the case of the Cheyennes (see pages 532–533), Omahas, and Iroquois, the civil chiefs were explicitly chosen for limited tenure. War chiefs were the heads of military fraternities, or a war chief could be any man who had an outstanding war record. Naturally, such war chiefs could make their opinions felt in the tribe, but they had very limited constitutional powers in the operation of the camp in peacetime. The most militaristic American Indians were astute enough to realize that military dictatorship is the greatest of all threats to the democratic way of life.

Bantu Chiefs   The functional significance of chiefs in the Bantu tribes of South Africa may be sensed from Schapera's listing of their activities:

1. He attends habitually at his council-place where he listens to news, petitions, and complaints, from all over the tribe, and gives orders for whatever action is required.
2. Legislation has always been a recognized function of the chief.
3. He periodically creates a new age-regiment, and thus formally admits youths into the social category of adults.
4. He controls the distribution and use of land.
5. He also regulates the calendar of agricultural and certain other activities.
6. He organizes large collective hunts.
7. He mobilizes his people for defense and aggression.
8. He organizes religious ceremonies upon the due performance of which his tribe's security and prosperity are held to depend and which ensure that the rainfall is adequate.[11]

Small wonder that Tsonga proverbs say: "A tribe without a chief has lost its reason; it is dead. It is like a woman without a husband";

and "In a country without chiefs, the people devour one another."[12]

Ceremonial Chiefs   In some systems, the primary responsibilities of chiefs are not necessarily concerned with governing. Yet there is really nothing strange about this, if we consider the Queen of England. Her political functions have atrophied, but her symbolic and ceremonial functions evoke a stir of emotion in British hearts the world over.

In the primitive world, the Trobriand chief enjoys high status and many privileges. Tribute must be paid him, but he utilizes it mostly to put on ceremonial feasts on behalf of his people and his own renown, as well as to organize gardening and magically to control fertility and rainfall. This is true in greater or lesser degree for all Oceania (even in tribes where chiefs stem from conquerors), for as Forde observes:

The origin and development of chieftainship in Melanesia is by no means clear, but everywhere the chiefs claim the same essential rights and powers. They are nearly always real or alleged immigrants who make similar claims to sanctity, superiority and to the control of valuable ritual.

[The chiefs of the Sa'a people on the island of Mala, Solomon Islands, are aliens who] established and maintained their position by arrogance and determination. They are regarded, and regard themselves, as feast givers and the controllers of certain ceremonies. By the splendour of their feasts they enhance the prestige of their district and win the approval of the commoners who make gifts of food for yet more feasts.[13]

Exactly the same could be said of the Indians of the Northwest Coast of North America, with their potlatching chiefs.

Monarchy   Kingship results from the development of the hereditary tendency into a hereditary principle. Its main function is to introduce stability into the administration of govern-

---

[11] I. Schapera, *Government and Politics in Tribal Societies,* pp. 68–75.

[12] *Ibid.,* p. 105.
[13] C. D. Forde, *Habitat, Economy, and Society,* pp. 183 and 182. See also C. S. Ford, "The Role of a Fijian Chief" (*American Sociological Review,* vol. 3, 1938), pp. 542–550.

ment. Strong clans make for intratribal strife. Lineages and central government are inherently incompatible. Lineage autonomy must be superseded by a stronger law of the whole society. This can conveniently be the king's law and the king's peace. But the power of paramount chieftains is in itself a luscious prize for power-hungry men. With bloody intrigue and with turmoil in their struggles to project themselves into chieftainship, they can rend the peace of the tribe. Clearly defined hereditary succession puts a check on such social abscesses. Yet the oftentimes fatal defect of the hereditary principle is that the heir to succession may have no aptitude for the job. The king may be an indecisive weakling or, worse still, a dangerous egomaniac. In the one event, the state may fail to function effectively in times of crisis. In the other, tyranny supplants social justice, and men suffer under corruption.

Kingship is so common among advanced primitive societies that we must conclude that the need for centralized control outweighs the urge for democratic freedom at this level of social development. The resurgence of democracy comes later. But where democracy fails, the need for centralization produces dictatorship or fitful moves for the restoration of monarchy.

The hereditary principle is no thought-out device. It develops quite naturally and without conscious awareness. We can see this among those American Indian tribes which explicitly deny hereditary succession to chieftainship. In spite of the fact that any good man may become a chief, records show again and again that a chief is succeeded by one of his sons or maternal nephews. Chiefship runs in family or lineage lines. This arises from the fact that the training and high example set by the senior relatives engender chiefly qualities in the boys. People come to expect leadership from such lines. The boys assume that people will respond to their superior leadership—and they do. Eventually, the tendency may become a prescription.

In Polynesia and Africa, primogeniture often fixes succession upon the eldest son. Yet most tribes maintain functional flexibility by leaving succession open to selection from among the chief's heirs by the royal council or the matriarch (in Ashanti, the Queen Mother; among the Iroquois, the oldest woman in the lineage). This is a sound device except as it leads to palace feuds between the parties of the heirs who rely on the *coup d'état* to circumvent council deliberations. Civil war and temporary anarchy are the usual concomitants of the death of a monarch in many a Bantu kingdom. Indeed, as a precaution against this sort of thing, the death of the king is often kept secret until his successor is chosen and everything is ready for the coronation.

Sacerdotal Chiefs and Kings The skeins of religion and politics are composed of separate threads. Yet they are woven into the tapestry that is society, sometimes carefully separated, each forming its own design, and sometimes intertwined, joining church and state in one pattern. The warrior's sword and the magician's wand are different artifacts. A man may wield one or the other, but if he is skilled enough and if his culture permits, he may seize the sword in his right hand and the wand in his left. Then, indeed, he becomes an awesome power to cope with. The essential doctrine of separation of church and state in American democratic tradition is a needful defensive reaction to that power.

Shamans and priests are specialists in controlling the action of the supernatural; headmen, chiefs, and kings are specialists in controlling the actions of men. But the actions of men must be controlled in their relations to the supernatural as well as to their fellow men; the priest always has temporal influence. The politician uses religious means for political purposes when he is able to control religious power; the priest in turn is apt to use political means to attain religious ends when he has the techniques to do so. When either one has specialized his own peculiar techniques to a high degree and religious and political instruments are clearly developed, it sometimes occurs in the primitive world, as it so often does in the modern world, that rivalry and hostility between church and state are sharp. Among primitive men, however, a working agreement between the two often exists; for example, the Trobriand chief employs his hereditary sorcerer to destroy upstarts,[14] and the Yokuts-Mono chiefs in California connived with medicine men to mulct the guileless public.[15] On the other hand, use of supernatural power for self-advantage through black magic is almost universally treated as a deadly crime if carried too far.

In general, supernaturalism is so ubiquitous in the primitive world that it colors all government to a greater or lesser degree. Political officers almost invariably possess some magic power or religious sanctity. War making, legislation, and judicial procedure inevitably involve religious ritual.

In highly organized gardening societies of sedentary peoples dependent on fixed crops, the chief is usually the high priest of the rain, fertility, and garden cults. As he is the supervisor of politico-legal relations, so is he also responsible for the economic well-being and religious security of his folk. If his society is one of ancestor worshipers, as is usually the case in Africa and Oceania, he is also the ancestral viceroy on earth—his people's highest link to the ancestral spirits. He is himself a direct descendant of the gods and has godhood in him. In Africa, again and again, he symbolizes the tribal soul: a soul that must be hale and vigorous, or else the tribe wanes and dies. Hence, the fate of the king who became feeble or sickly was to be poisoned or strangled by his chief councilors.[16] It is

no unalloyed privilege to be a ruler. Eminence entails responsibility.

The extreme sacredness of the god-king limits his activities. In Tonga (Polynesia), the *tuithonga* may not walk abroad, for where he places his foot, the earth becomes tabu.

The Talking Chief "A White House spokesman announced today. . . ." The device of presidents is a possession of primitive chiefs and kings the world over. The Ashanti king or the paramount chief of a district rarely speaks in public. To do so is bad etiquette and policy on his part. He has his *okeyame* to serve as his mouthpiece. Most African kings have a court spokesman. In Samoa, each chief has his Talking Chief, who recites his chief's genealogy before every meeting of the native council. He speaks his chief's mind in debate. Kwakiutl and other Northwest Coast chieftains have their speakers at potlatches to extol the ancestry and virtues of their masters. Every Plains Indian peace chief had his crier, who announced decisions to the camp at large; his "loudspeaker," the Cheyenne interpreter, High Forehead, always called him.

The reason for these spokesmen is subtle but sound. When chieftains rise above the level of headmen, their power increases. He who wields powers of decision and enforcement must not be too familiar to the multitude. Some good men can maintain influence and fraternity simultaneously, but they are rare. It is a safer and surer technique to let a minion undertake the vulgar task of shouting to the masses.

The Council   The one universal instrument of government is the council. No tribe or nation does without it. No man can govern alone, nor is he permitted to. Monarchy, if taken literally, is a misnomer. Every king or chief operates within the network of his advisers and cronies. Some are helplessly enmeshed in it.

In small primitive bands and tribes, the council is a democratic gathering of adult

[14]B. Malinowski, *Crime and Custom in Savage Society,* pp. 85–86 and 92–93.
[15]A. H. Gayton, *Yokuts-Mono Chiefs and Shamans* (University of California Publications in American Archaeology and Ethnology, vol. 24, 1930), pp. 361–420.
[16]See J. G. Frazer, *The Golden Bough,* chap. 24, "The Killing of the Divine King."

males. In gerontocratic Australia, participation is limited to the elders. Elsewhere, it is mostly open to all males. Among American Indians, decision of the council had to be unanimous; one stubborn holdout could block action. Still there were neat devices for attaining unanimity. Tribal councils commonly consisted of all the band headmen. Among the Aztecs, for a special example, every family sent its headman to a clan council. Each clan council had a clan headman, a war chief, and a speaker. The speakers of the twenty clans formed the tribal, or national, council, which worked with the king and his executive officer, the Snake Woman (who was not a woman, but a man).

Among the great African monarchies, the king has the superficial appearance of an absolute autocrat. Yet he can rarely act without full approval of the council, and this is not forthcoming until the royal elders have sounded out tribal public opinion. Kings who abuse their power can generally be deposed; in the old days, they could be destroyed.

Monarchy, like every other social relation, rests on reciprocity. If the exalted ruler receives great social privilege, he must give service to the people in return. Some kings and dictators may ignore this precept, but it is difficult for them successfully to ignore for long the principle voiced in the Balinese proverb: "The ruler owes his might to the people."

Nonpolitical Associations in Government
It is an error to think of government solely in terms of the organs explicitly designed for governmental purposes. All government is pluralistic, and various extrastate organizations play their parts in determining and executing political policy.

The author for some years belonged to a small-town volunteer fire company. It is a closed fraternity, which elects its members by secret vote. It has all the trappings of a lodge: sworn secrecy, uniforms with gold buttons, rituals, dances, and ceremonial feasting. It also puts out fires as the occasion demands.

This firemanic fraternity is a private association, a true men's club. Yet it is an official branch of government under the laws of the State of New York. The costs of its fire-fighting equipment and meeting rooms are met by public taxation. It is regulated by public law and is controlled by publicly elected fire commissioners. It remains a club and yet is an organ of government, just as the Plains Indian military fraternities were, the social aspects of which have already been discussed in Chapter 24. Fraternity, feasting, dancing, and social enjoyment were the primary activities of such men's clubs, but they also took on police, judicial, and legislative powers when the need arose.[17] The tribal councils constitutionally

[17] R. H. Lowie, *Primitive Society*, p. 415; *The Origin of the State*, pp. 94–107; "Property Rights and Coercive Powers of the Plains Indian Military Societies" (*Journal of Legal and Political Sociology*, vol. 1, 1943), pp. 59–71.

Fig. 27-2   An Ethiopian tribal chief and his council meet with village family heads to proclaim and discuss a program of cattle vaccination. (United Nations.)

possessed all judicial and legislative powers covering criminal activity. However, the council chiefs were peace chiefs not given to coercive action. When coercive restraint or punishment was needed, they were not suited to the task. They were "fathers" to all the tribe, and Indian fathers do not punish their children. What was more natural than that the extragovernmental societies of warriors should take over policing the hunt, the rice harvest, and the great tribal ceremonials of the sun dance? This they did with vigor and dispatch. In later years, as the Plains tribes began to crumble before the onslaught of the white men, the Cheyenne military societies assumed more and more governmental power as crisis piled on crisis. But to no avail; they were overwhelmed.

In Africa, as we have already seen, various secret societies among certain West Sudanese tribes imposed peace, collected debts on behalf of their members, and, in the case of the Egbo society, punished wrongs.

In Melanesia, the numerous men's secret societies also directly and indirectly determine policy and operate as law-enforcing agencies.

Plains Indian military societies were not secret, and as a result their role in government was essentially democratic. It is quite otherwise with the exclusive secret orders of Africa and Melanesia. They are more akin to the Ku Klux Klan and other such cryptic groups that spring up in our midst to usurp the functions of the state and to corrupt democracy. That these extralegal bodies can sporadically attain a measure of success is testimony to the Hydra-headed nature of government in society.

The Political Process

Having briefly examined the major ways in which societies are politically organized, or structured, let us turn to the more intricate matter of how these structures work. According to the famous aphorism, "Politics is the art of who gets what, when, and how." Like all good aphorisms, this packs a good deal of truth in a few pithy words. But, again, like all aphorisms, it leaves out as much as it says. All role definition, which runs through every aspect of culture, defines activities and duties, expectancies and obligations. All norms of social organization spell out who does what, who gets what—when, where, and how. And politics is but one aspect of the cultural patterning and behavioral processes which are involved.

As we attempt to examine political processes in the anthropological context, it is important to keep in mind what has already been said on social structure in the preceding chapters, especially those on economic organization, the extension of kinship, clubs and associations, social classes and castes, and law. Every one of these facets of society has its political implications, and politics sinks its roots into each.

Politics, it must always be remembered, is not something discrete, an arena of life absolute unto itself. Politics is social behavior with an orientation, a slant, that gives it a coloring sufficiently different to warrant its own identity. But it is many-hued, and its colors, taken separately, are shared with other fields.

The Attributes of Politics

In the "Introduction" to *Political Anthropology*, the editors, Marc Swartz, Victor Turner, and Arthur Tuden, specify several qualities which identify the political process:

1. It is public rather than private: it is not an individual matter, nor familial. "An activity that affects a neighborhood, a whole community, a whole society, or a group of societies is unquestionably a public activity; whether it is *also* a political activity depends upon other characteristics—in addition to its being public." One of the important activities implied in this is achieving settlements that are

of a public, rather than merely a private, concern. Such settlements, to be public, "must concern a group as a whole, in a rather direct and immediate way."[18]

2. Politics is goal-oriented; it is concerned with ends and means—"What is it we want?" and "How do we go about doing it?" The political process always involves decision making—the selection of specified aims from among possible alternatives and the choice of administrative procedures. Politics is, like law, deeply involved in culture building, by defining social norms which it is believed will result in conversion of values (normative postulates) into social reality.

Politics involves public goals. However much vested groups within the society may strive and quarrel in pressing each its own interests as against those of others, the political decision relates to what goal shall be sought by the action of the community *as* community on the question at issue.

3. A third feature of the political process is that it allocates and focuses power. It assigns and specializes authority, either in decision making (as in the case of the law enforcers) or in directing activities (as in the case of the task-force leaders, whether in hunting, war, temple building, ritual, or whatever). Malinowski, in *Freedom and Civilization,* put it succinctly:

The principle of authority comes into being from the beginnings of mankind. . . . Political authority as we know it is indispensible even at primitive levels; we have defined it as the legally vested power to establish norms, to take decisions and to enforce them through the use of sanction by coercion.[19]

In small face-to-face hunting and gathering societies the power allocation aspect poses few problems. With his usual astuteness, That's It (the Comanche informant previously quoted) stated the reason for this:

"We were not like you white men. We didn't have to have an election every four years to see who would sit in the White House. A *paraivo* [band headman] just got that way. Everybody knew who he was." So clear and consensual were cultural goals and leadership requirements that leaders "emerged." When people no longer heeded a headman's ideas, he simply was no longer a headman.

On the other hand, in larger, more complex societies in which the decision-making powers of a chief, king, or president are far-reaching, control of the office assumes the utmost importance, and legitimation of the political administration is a matter of critical concern if tyranny is to be avoided.

Government: Law, Political Organization, and Politics It will be clear by now that there is a good deal of overlapping in the attributes of law, political structures, and political processes, and also in the manner in which each relates to government. Definitions are not easily arrived at, nor is there unanimous agreement on such definitions as are most commonly used. Implied in all of these concepts are the organization of activities for the general welfare, the establishment of norms, the use of coercion and the assignment of authority for the maintenance of these norms, and the acknowledgment of legitimacy of all these ends.

For our purposes, it is sufficient to say that the political sphere of social organization here means ". . . everything that is at once public, goal-oriented, and that involves a differential of power (in the sense of control) among the individuals of the group in question."[20]

The study of the formal designation of public offices with their established norms of statuses and roles is the study of *political organization,* or *structure,* a subdivision of social structure.

Government consists of the men and

[18]M. J. Swartz, V. W. Turner, and A. Tuden (eds.), *Political Anthropology,* p. 4.

[19]B. Malinowski, *Freedom and Civilization,* pp. 187–188 and 248.

[20]M. J. Swartz, V. W. Turner, and A. Tuden, *op. cit.,* p. 7.

women who hold designated statuses of authoritative leadership as decision makers and exercisers of power in the public sphere. It is expressed in the ways in which they exercise their powers and in the ways in which the governed respond to (and sometimes limit) their power.

The study of the ongoing maneuvering—pushing and hauling, wheedling, cajoling, arguing, threatening, punishing, and rewarding—by which the goals are agreed upon or set, and by which the people are led or shoved in the desired direction (or by which they resist and obstruct the "official" intent) is the study of *political processes,* or *politics.*

Modern (since World War II) anthropology, like modern political science, has become much more interested in the study of political *processes* than of political *structure.* And well it might, for this tells us much more of what is going on than does a formal comparison of the organization of different kinds of "chiefdoms" and "states."[21]

To demonstrate the operation of the political processes in their varied functional manifestations, let us look first at the Cheyennes, who represent the chiefdom type of political organization as integrated with both a tribal council and politically active military associations. Then, we shall summarize the structure and functioning of an African monarchistic state, using the Tswana of Bechuanaland in southern Africa.

Cheyenne Government and Politics   Professor John Roberts has recently extolled the old Cheyenne system for its outstanding quality in cultural self-management. Specifically, he comments on their excellence in respect to (1) "the·storage and retrieval" of traditional knowledge and information, (2)

their skill at problem solving on the tribal level, and (3) their effective implementation of decisions through "staff work" and "command responsibility."[22]

Tribal Organization   The Cheyennes had a bilateral family system with no lineages or clans. Beyond the family, there were uxorilocal kindreds, each headed by an active senior male. Related kindreds tended to camp together, thus forming the band, of which there were ten major ones. During the fall and winter months, when the buffalo herds were dispersed, the Cheyennes accommodated by scattering the band camps miles apart in protected river bottoms. Bands were then politically autonomous. In late spring, when the grasses were green, the Cheyennes all drew together for one of the great tribal ceremonies—the Sacred Arrow Renewal, the Sun Dance, or the Animal Dance. Throughout the summer the Council of Forty-four Tribal Peace Chiefs ruled supreme, assisted by the military associations.

Allocation of Leadership   Membership in the Council of Forty-four was for a term of ten years. Nominally, each band had four representatives on the council—and these chiefs were headmen in their own bands. They were chosen for their even tempers, energy, wisdom, courage, kindliness, generosity, and altruism. They were the "fathers" of everyone in the tribe and addressed as such. Although on page 486 we indicated that the Cheyennes recognized wealth distinctions, there was no class exploitation in the distribution of power. "Whatever you ask of a chief, he gives it to you. If someone wants to borrow something of a chief, he gives it to that person outright," old-time Cheyennes said over and over.

By combining the dual roles of band headman and tribal chieftain in the same person,

---

[21]For an excellent exemplification of this trend, see H. A. Powell, "Competitive Leadership in Trobriand Political Organization" (*Journal of the Royal Anthropological Institute,* vol. 90, 1960), pp. 118–45; reprinted in R. Cohen and J. Middleton (eds.), *Comparative Political Systems,* pp. 155–192.

[22]J. M. Roberts, "The Self-management of Cultures," in W. H. Goodenough (ed.), *Explorations in Cultural Anthropology,* p. 452.

the Cheyennes effected an efficient link between the kinship and local segmentary interests of the tribe and the tribal entirety. This is an absolute essential for maintenance of the tribe as an integrated whole.

The Role of the Chiefs Within the Council of Forty-four there were five sacred chiefs who represented the great spirits of the five directions. One of them held a supreme ritual position as the Sweet Medicine Chief—the personification of the culture hero who gave the Cheyennes their way of life. The legitimacy of the chiefs was chartered by the deepest of Cheyenne beliefs.

The Role of the Associations Alongside of, but subordinate to, the supreme and sacred Council of Forty-four, stood the ungraded military associations. They enforced the Cheyenne law against intratribal killing and violation of the rules of the communal buffalo hunt. They sometimes made new law (see page 502, above). They also interacted with the Council when important tribal decisions had to be faced, as the Comanche Peace Agreement of 1840 reveals.

Tribal Decision Making The customary way of making tribal decisions followed a pattern for the use of political power.

A war party of eight Cheyennes, on its way south to take horses from the Kiowas, Comanches, or Apaches, was stopping at a large [friendly] Arapaho camp. At the same time some Apaches came to visit Bull, an Arapaho leader. The Apaches told their host that the Kiowas and Comanches were seeking peace with the Arapahoes and Cheyennes. Bull took the opportunity to bring the eight Cheyennes together with the Apaches in his tipi; he filled his pipe and offered the smoke. The Cheyennes declined, Seven Bulls, the leader of the war party saying, "Friend, you know that we are not chiefs. We cannot smoke with these men, nor make peace with them. We have no authority; we can only carry the message. I have listened to what you say and tomorrow with my party I will start back [he has authority to call off his own raid,] to our Chey-

enne village, and I will carry this word to the chiefs. It is for them to decide what must be done. We are young men and cannot say anything, but we will take your message back to the chiefs."

When Seven Bulls reached the Cheyenne camp with his companions, he told of the Kiowa-Comanche proposition. That night a crier went about the camp calling for the chiefs to convene the next day. The big double-sized chiefs' lodge was pitched and early the next morning the chiefs all gathered there. Seven Bulls and his companions were sent for to deliver their message officially. The proposal was then on the floor.

After the first speakers had sat down, it was evident that there was no ready agreement at hand within the Council, so the proposition was made and accepted that the Dog Soldier Society should be asked to render a decision to the Council on the question.

High Backed Wolf, who was the directing head chief of the Council, sent one of the door-servants to bring in White Antelope and Little Old Man, the bravest chiefs of the Dog Soldier Society. When these two had been greeted in the chiefs' lodge, High Backed Wolf told them about the order of business, describing to them the state of opinion in the Council. "Now, my friends," he concluded, "you go and assemble your Dog Soldiers. Tell them about this matter and talk it over among them. Let us know what you think of it. Tell us what you think is best to be done."

When the Dog Soldiers had assembled, White Antelope laid the problem before them. "The chiefs are leaving this matter to us," he told his followers, "because we are the strongest of the military groups. It is my own thought that our chiefs are in favor of making peace. What do you all think about it?"

Said another of the Dog Soldier chiefs, "I think it best to leave the decision to you two, White Antelope and Little Old Man. Whatever you say will please us all." All the Dogs agreed to this with one assent.

The two men accepted it and declared for peace. Leaving their troop, they went back to where the Council was waiting for them, to tell the Council that they would make peace with the enemies. The chiefs all stood up at this and gladly said, "Thank you, thank you, Dog Soldiers."[23]

[23]K. N. Llewellyn and E. A. Hoebel, *The Cheyenne Way*, pp. 91–93.

The political process, we have said, is public, is goal-oriented, and allocates and focuses power. There can be no question of the public nature of this case. It was "official" and concerned the well-being of the entire Cheyenne tribe. It was also clearly goal-oriented: peace with the Comanches from whom the Cheyennes could obtain horses and a useful ally. Allocation of authority? Authority was designated clearly. The war-party leader said he could not speak for his people. He conveyed the message to a proper authority who convened the Council of Forty-four. The tribal chiefs knew they had the formal power to make a decision by themselves. But they also knew that without public support they could not make it stick. So *all* the military lodges were convened. Opinion was divided. So the Dog Soldier Society—the most powerful and prestigious of all the fighting associations—was delegated to "decide" the issue. The Dogs, in turn, knew that unending filibuster could prevent achievement of unanimous consent which was always required for action on a proposal. So they put it to their two bravest chiefs, the Door Keepers. The decision was for peace. Back up the line it went, as the military fraternities' recommendation to the Council of Forty-four who accepted the "decision" with thanks—and relief. Finally, the Sweet Medicine Chief announced it to the entire tribe *as the decision of the Tribal Council,* so giving the decision the seal of the highest authority. The soldiers had been co-opted, and no hothead would dare to lift a hand against the Comanche again. None ever did—from that day to this.

Such is the political process at its effective best.

Political Organization among the Tswana
The Cheyenne represented a simple form of state organization in a small tribe. The Tswana of Bechuanaland in southern Africa represent state organization on the level of monarchy in "large" tribal nations. Professor Schapera's lucid report on the Tswana provides us with one of the finest examples of how this is done.[24] It forms the basis for this summary.

The Tswana, or Bechuana, constitute an ethnologically identifiable group of tribes. Each tribe is a politically independent unit, although the more newly formed tribes recognize the seniority of the tribes from which they broke off. The population of the Tswana exceeds 100,000.

Tribal Organization   The integrating focus of the tribe is in the person and office of the chief, who is not only the supreme ruler but also "the visible symbol of its cohesion and solidarity." People may leave the tribe of their birth, and tribal citizenship is expressed by allegiance to a particular chief. Each Tswana tribe has a capital town (ranging in population from 600 to 25,000) and a number of smaller outlying villages.

Within the village or town, the households (which consist of one or more conjugal-natal families) are clustered to form the spatially distinguished family group. Closely related family groups live in a well-defined administrative unit, called a *ward*. All the wards together make up the tribe, except that in two of the larger tribes, the wards are grouped in sections.

A small hamlet may contain no more than one household. A small village may consist of a single family group. A larger village may have only one ward. A village, if large enough, may, however, embrace several family groups and wards. Each of these groups is a kinship-territorial-governmental unit of social structure.

Local Leaders   The leader of the household is the husband and father; for the family group, the leader is the senior male descendant of the common paternal grandfather whose name the group bears. His position is hereditary and ascribed. He directs the group's

[24]I. Schapera, *A Handbook of Tswana Law and Custom,* pp. 1–34 and 53–124.

activities and keeps the peace within his flock. In important matters, he acts in consultation with a family-group council of all adult males.

The headman of a ward holds his position by right of hereditary descent as the senior son of the preceding headman. He is not appointed by the chief except upon formation of a new ward. He does, however, act as his ward's representative to the chief, and he is responsible for the orderly conduct of his people and the execution of the chief's commands. He collects tribute for the chief and holds judicial authority in minor cases involving two family groups within his jurisdiction. He is also the leader of the men of his ward in their common age set.

The Council   A headman must act in consultation with a ward council made up of the senior members of his own family group and the leaders of the other family groups in his ward. If guilty of malfeasance in office, his own council will reprimand him or complain to the chief, who may then try to punish him through the Royal Court. Occasionally, the ward headman convenes all the adult males of the ward in a general folk moot for review of problems of wide concern. The headman carries many burdens of responsibility for which he receives little material compensation but great prestige and respect—providing he does his job well.

Each village, in turn, has its headman. If the village and ward are one, the ward headman and village headman are one and the same. Should there be two or more wards, the headman of the senior ward is the village head. His duties are similar to those of the ward headman, except that they are townwide in scope.

In those tribes which have districts, village organization remains the same as that described above, but the district will have, as a special representative to the capital, the headman of one of its more important indigenous villages (some outlying villages will consist of immigrant aliens).

The Chief (Monarch)   This brings us to the central tribal government organized around the hereditary chief, or monarch. He is chief of state (king) through primogeniture. *Kgosi ke kgosi ka a tsetswe,* a chief is chief because he is born to it. In succession, the direct line precedes all collateral lines; i.e., the sons of the king succeed, but his brothers and their sons cannot, although a brother of a dead king may serve as regent during the minority of the heir. If a monarch dies with no male issue, the chieftainship passes to his next senior brother.

Functionally, the Tswana chief "is at once ruler, judge, maker and guardian of the law, repository of wealth, dispenser of gifts, leader in war, priest and magician of the people."[25] He and his family take precedence in all things and receive high honors. Failure to obey his orders or to show him respect is a criminal offense. He is sustained by a royal coterie and with tribute.

In return, much is expected of him. His time is his people's. "Every man thinks he is the king's only subject" is a common folk saying. He must keep himself well informed of tribal affairs, be accessible to all who have complaints, organize and direct the army, sit as chief justice, preside over the tribal council, perform the major religious rituals, and above all be generous, redistributing most of the tribute that comes to him.

Other Functionaries   The male relatives of the chief form a nobility, a kind of privy council, with whom he must remain in close consultation. To maintain effective democratic control, the chief has an informally constituted body of confidential advisers (a "cabinet") drawn from among the important men of the tribe on whom he feels he can rely; they are usually, but by no means always, paternal relatives.

The government also includes a formal tribal council of all the ward headmen, who meet in secret executive session whenever convened by the chief.

[25]*Ibid.,* p. 62.

Schapera has published a translation of the condensed record of the promulgation of a Tswana enactment of partial prohibition in 1924. After discussing the problem of rowdy nighttime beer drinking with his council of senior uncles and getting their approval, Isang, king of the Kagatla tribe of the Tswana, convened the council of headmen. The "Congressional Record" reads as follows:

Chief Isang: "I do not say that beer should be prohibited, but that a law should be made about it."

Segale Pilane (chief's uncle and principal adviser): "We seek a plan for dealing with beer-drinking. Beer has ruined us; we have no children; we tried to educate them, but beer has spoiled them."

Komane Pilane (another senior uncle): "Let there be a law about beer-drinking, and let whoever violates it be punished."

Abel Madisa: "Let the sale of beer be prohibited." (Supported by Nasone Pilane, Montswe Rapalai, Mokalane Makgale, Pilane B. Pilane, Ramodisa, Klaas Segogwane, Antipas Sello, Masilo Ntsole.)

Chief Isang: "I endorse the suggestion that beer should no longer be sold. But now I ask, is there not some one who can suggest a law whereby beer may continue to be sold, but in such a way as not to cause trouble among the people?"

Maretele Mangole: "Let beer be sold, but the purchaser should go home to drink it."

Pule Mogomotsi: "Let it be sold, but on condition that it is no longer drunk at night."

Motshwane Pilane: "Let beer-drinking at night be prohibited, and also let beer be sold only for consumption at home."

Kgari Pilane: "Beer-drinking goes together with sexual immorality. You should not find fault with the boys alone, and ignore the girls. As long as beer continues to be brewed, immorality will be associated with it."

Mabuse Letsebe: "I say, let beer continue to be sold."

Segale Pilane: "Headmen, you have helped us; it is you who are the chief's policemen, and whoever breaks the law must be dealt with by you."

Chief Isang: "Let those who say that beer should not be sold raise their hands."

(85 men raised their hands; only two said that beer should still be sold.)

Chief Isang: "You are not of two opinions, you are unanimous. And what I say to you is that when you go astray and are turned back you should listen. To err is human, but to find fault with oneself is often lacking. Therefore I say: Beer must no longer be drunk at night. See to it that beer is brewed not by the girls but by their mothers. I shall allow the brewing and sale of beer from the beginning of June until December, and if there is no improvement I shall call you together again to kill the sale of beer. Women of the Maatlametlo age-regiment and downwards must not any one of them drink beer. Headmen, help to support the law."[26]

In this situation, the chief and his principal adviser put their problem to the headmen. Some of the latter advance a suggestion that does not immediately satisfy the chief, and he asks them to consider a more specific issue. After further discussion, during which several different views are expressed, a vote is taken on the original and more drastic suggestion. Despite almost unanimous agreement, the chief finally decides not to prohibit the sale of beer, but to try out a compromise for an experimental period. The two points that seem most important in the whole procedure are the method of consultation and the fact that the chief is guided but not bound by the views of the headmen; he actually follows the course that seems best to himself—in this particular instance, one less far-reaching than was generally agreed upon.

Affairs of great tribal import, although they are first taken up by the two preceding groups of advisers, cannot become official policy until they have been discussed and approved in open tribal assembly. To this all the headmen come and all adult men who want to make it their business.

Thus, although a chief is king because he is born to it, the Tswana have an even more fundamental proverb: *Kgosi ke kgosi ka morafe*, a chief is chief by grace of his tribe. The constitution of the state is such that he is subject to representative checks and balances. A self-willed chief does not last long.

[26]I. Schapera, *Tribal Legislation among the Tswana of the Bechuanaland Protectorate*, pp. 14–15.

Associations: Age Sets   There is yet another arm of the Tswana state to be mentioned. All Tswana men and women are initiated into sex-segregated age sets at puberty. These have important congeniality functions to perform, but they are equally important as units of political organization. An age set cuts right across the local segments of the tribe and counteracts the parochialism that inherently exerts a neutralizing effect on national integration. Each age set (which numbers from fifty to several hundred boys or men, depending on the size of the tribe) is headed by a commander, who is always a member of the royal family. In war, the age sets constitute regiments in the tribal army. The men of a given ward form "companies" within the regiment under the leadership of a son or close relative of their ward headman. In times of peace, the age sets serve as work brigades to perform any public service or job of construction that the king deems necessary.

Women's age sets also exist and are organized along the same lines as the men's. In the sphere of women's work, they also perform public services, though of a lighter nature.

A System of Checks and Balances   The Tswana system exemplifies how the state, as a political system in an advanced primitive society, weaves and balances kinship, territorial, and associational groupings into a harmonious whole. It shows how the functional prerequisite of allocation of authority to responsible leaders is checked and balanced with concomitant reliance on organized group consultation, through the provision of councils on each level of administrative structure, with a final check imposed through general assemblies at each level for consideration of all major or crucial decisions. Tswana political organization has the essential elements of monarchy, democracy, oligarchy, theocracy, and gerontocracy. It is each of these and all. It has no need for elective procedures and

spares itself a good deal of trouble and uncertainty thereby, for internal social mobility is limited and in this type of society the hereditary principle works well enough.

SUMMARY

Politics consists of those societal activities which (1) are concerned with public or community decision making; (2) are goal-oriented; and (3) distribute and allocate decision-making authority and the power to carry out the policies decided upon.

Political organization consists of the network of institutions that regulate relations between groups within a society and between one society and another. The units of political organization may be genealogical, territorial, or associational. The genealogical units, such as the family, kindred, lineage, clan, phratry, moiety, or deme, may or may not be subdivisions of territorial units. Territorial units range in scope from local group, band, village, district, and tribe up to confederacy, empire, and federation, or commonwealth.

The functions of political organization include definition of norms, allocation of force and authority, settlement of disputes (all shared with law), plus public works, ceremony and ritual control of the supernatural (shared with religion), economic activities (redistribution of goods and control of markets), and war (which may also be a private, nonpolitical matter).

Political organization may be stateless, but where government is added in the form of centralized authority for the whole tribe or society and endowed with specific (if even only part-time) functionaries, it becomes a state.

Government, from the most primitive to the most civilized, includes the council in one form or another. Very simple primitive societies vest leadership in headmen rather than chiefs. All adult males participate directly in decision making. Elemental primitive societies are essentially democracies. Chiefship is characteristic of the more developed primitive societies. Kingship exists in those in which chiefship has become hereditary. The chief or king is often the functioning symbol of the collective existence of the society; hence, his activities may be largely ritual and ceremonial. He is both priest or god and political head: the divine king.

The state is always multidimensional; it is made up of diverse elements. Governments can also consist of a variety of agencies that have nongovernmental aspects. Thus kinship groups and associations that exist primarily for other purposes may perform governmental functions and so exist as an integral part of the state system.

SELECTED READINGS

Cohen, R., and J. Middleton (eds.), *Comparative Political Systems* (1967). A reader which contains twenty long selections on a number of aspects of political organization and process in a wide range of tribes.

Evans-Pritchard, E. E., and M. Fortes (eds.), *African Political Systems* (1940). A symposium of excellent studies of political structure in a number of African tribes.

Fried, M. H., "State: the Institution" (*International Encyclopedia of the Social Sciences,* vol. 15, 1968), pp. 143–150. A succinct overall discussion of the state, anthropologically viewed.

Gluckman, M., *Politics, Law, and Ritual in Tribal Society* (1965). Especially for chapters 3 and 4, on stateless societies and on the state and civil strife.

Gluckman, M., and F. Eggan (eds.), *Political Systems and the Distribution of Power* (1965). Especially good for the article by Ralph Nicholas on factions in the political process in India and elsewhere, and for the analysis of differing types of African kingdoms by Peter Lloyd.

Lowie, R. H., *The Origin of the State* (1927). A stimulating pioneer study of the processes of state development among primitive peoples.

Mair, L., *Primitive Government* (1964). A general, nontheoretical description of the major types of government in African tribal societies. Contains an informative final chapter entitled "Primitive Government and Modern Times."

Rattray, R. S., *Ashanti Law and Constitution* (1927). A most valuable study of the historical development of the great federated monarchy of the Ashanti of the Gold Coast of Africa, now Ghana.

Schapera, I., *Government and Politics in Tribal Society* (1956). A comparative study of three South African tribal systems.

Southall, A., "Stateless Society" (*International Encyclopedia of the Social Sciences,* vol. 15, 1968), pp. 157–168. The concept structure, and functioning of stateless systems of political organization, briefly discussed.

Alur Society (1956). Subtitled *A Study in the Processes and Types of Domination,* this book analyzes the structure of a primitive political state embracing a multiple number of tribes.

Part 5   Symbolic Expression

Chapter 28

Culture and World View

Man faces the bewildering chaos of experience armed with mental artifacts of his own invention with which he organizes the natural phantasmagoria into a manageable and meaningful unity. He takes the inchoate mass of formless clay that is the experiential world and works it into a meaningful form according to his cultural preconceptions. He thereby assures himself of a reasonable amount of certainty and builds a base of understanding upon which to organize his life in comprehensible terms; absolute chaos is inconceivable, and if this is indeed a disorderly universe, man will impose order on it. He is "... endlessly simplifying and generalizing his own view of his environment; he constantly imposes on this environment his own constructions and meanings; these constructions and meanings are characteristic of one culture as opposed to another."[1]

[1] G. Bateson, quoted in C. Kluckhohn, "The Philosophy of the Navaho Indians," in F. S. C. Northrop (ed.), *Ideological Differences and World Order,* p. 356.

Fig. 28-A Navaho sand painting for the Male Shooting Way (Chant), a five- or nine-day curing ceremony. The black, star-studded masked god on the left is Father Sky. The blue, masked deity on the right is Mother Earth. Corn, squash, wheat, and another plant grow from her body. (Office of Anthropology, Smithsonian Institution.)

Again, as Kluckhohn has written:

Cultures or group life-ways do not manifest themselves solely in observable customs and artifacts.
There is much more to social and cultural phenomena than immediately meets the ear and eye.
If the behavioral facts are to be correctly understood, certain presuppositions constituting what
might be termed a philosophy or ideology must
also be known. The "strain towards consistency"
. . . in the folkways and mores of all groups cannot
be accounted for unless one postulates a more or
less systematic pattern of reaction to experience
as a characteristic property of all integrated cultures. . . . Each different way of life makes its own
assumptions about the ends and purposes of human existence, about ways by which knowledge
may be obtained, about the organization of the
pigeonholes in which each sense datum is filed,
about what human beings have a right to expect
from each other and the gods, about what constitutes fulfillment or frustration. Some of these assumptions are made explicit in the lore of the folk;
others are tacit premises which the observer must
infer by finding consistent trends in word and deed.[2]

The Nature of World View

The cognitive view of life and the total environment which an individual holds or which
is characteristic of the members of a society
is frequently referred to as *Weltanschauung,*
or world view. World view carries the suggestion "of the structure of things as man is
aware of them,"[3] and it is thus the life scene
as people look out upon it. It is the human
being's inside view of the way things are,
colored, shaped, and arranged according to
his cultural preconceptions. The planet we
live on, a world of physical objects and living
things, is by no means the same world to all
peoples. Indeed, a simple description of the
most basic observable components of this
world (the sky, the land, water, trees) by a
member of one culture might prove totally
unintelligible to a member of another. This

was well understood by a good friend, a Sia
Pueblo Indian, who stood beside me at the
ruin of Pueblo Bonito. "You see this bush,"
he said, pointing to a desert plant called
chamiso. "You may not understand this, but
that plant is I. I am it, and it is me and all my
ancestors. We call it '*wawshap.*'"

Juan was a member of the *wawshap* clan.
He was telling me that in his eyes and in his
deepest feelings, as he looked on that bush
or any other one of its kind, he was embodied
in it—he and all his clan ancestors. As an
anthropologist I had an intellectual understanding of what he was saying, but my world
view would forever prevent me from feeling
the same kind of emotional identification with
the plant. I could see the chamiso in botanical terms. I could think of its functions as a
symbolic representation of *wawshap* clan
unity in the maintenance of Durkheimian
organic solidarity of the social group (see
pages 70–71). I could analyze Juan's perception of the plant in terms of its moral effect in maintaining a vital sense of "the meaning of life." But I could not *be wawshap* as my
friend is. His world view is that of a Sian.
Mine is that of a rational, scientific, mechanistic Westerner. We live in the same world
but we view it differently. (Or, do our differing
views make it really a different world?)

Institutions, relationships, arts, and technology vary throughout the world in manifestly observable forms, but underlying them
are the existential postulates that orient a
people's particular slant on life and the ways
in which they organize their culture.

Etic, Emic, and Ethos   When seen from the
outside and reported by an observer who is
not, by training and living, thoroughly enculturated with the culture he observes and
writes of, the view is called "etic." The inside
view is labeled "emic." Regarding the
chamiso, Juan's view was emic; mine could
be only etic.

World view, as a concept, focuses on the
ways of knowing and identifying the component elements of the world—the existential

[2]*Ibid.,* pp. 357–359.
[3]R. Redfield, *The Primitive World and Its Transformations,*
p. 86.

and cognitive. Ethos expresses a people's qualitative feeling, their emotional and moral sensing of the way things are and ought to be—their ethical system.

Not all peoples or persons can by any means articulate systematically what their world view is. It is improbable that any Comanche could. At the same time, it is quite probable that many of the more reflective Aztec priests could have spelled out an Aztec world view quite clearly and consistently. This difference is in itself a cultural characteristic in its presence or absence. Usually it is up to the anthropologist or philosopher descriptively to analyze and formulate a people's world view from what he learns of their thinking, feelings, and actions. World view and ethos are found expressed in technology, personal relations, myth, song, dance, art, and religious and magical ritual in a multitude of gross and subtle ways. They are the reflected essence of a people's inner feelings and their ways of knowing "the way things are."

No world view is a given, in spite of the numerous peoples who believe that their way of life was bestowed upon them by culture heroes (such as Sweet Medicine and Erect Horns of the Cheyennes) or tribal ancestors (such as those of the Ashanti) or the divine revelation of prophets (such as the early Hebrews, Christians, and Muslims). World views grow with cultures. Generations of anonymous human beings contribute to the unending quest to make the unknown knowable, to transform meaningless bafflement into meaningful understanding.

We do agree with Andrew Lang and Paul Radin, however, that there are individuals in every society who are thinkers and systematizers, the idealists who crystallize the myths, shape the ceremonies, express the concepts in art—symbolic creators. But even they must work within the cultural framework.

To exemplify the nature of world view let us first listen to Alphonso Caso, the distinguished Mexican anthropologist, writing of the Aztecs. Then we shall explore the phenomenon more deeply by considering the Navaho, Hopi, Cheyenne, Ashanti, and American versions.

The World View of the Aztecs

In Aztec belief, man was created by the sacrifice of the gods and in turn was reciprocally bound to sustain them with the magical sustenance of life itself—the blood of human sacrifice (Figure 28-1).

The Aztec's Burden

Hence the pride of the Aztec, who looked upon himself as a collaborator of the gods, for he knew that his life was dedicated to maintaining cosmic order and struggling against the powers of darkness.

Fig. 28-1   Aztec sacrifice of a human heart to the sun. (From Bernardo de Sahagun, **General History of the Things of New Spain: The Florentine Codex.** *Translated by Arthur J. O. Anderson and Charles E. Dibble. Published by The School of American Research and The University of Utah. Illustration from Book II. Copyright 1957 by The University of Utah.)*

In a sense the universe depended upon him for its continued existence; upon him depended the food for the gods, upon him depended the beneficence of the gifts which they showered on mankind. Likewise, the light of the sun, the rain that formed in the mountains and watered the corn, the wind that blew through the reeds, bringing clouds or turning into a hurricane, all depended upon him. . . .

In addition to this cosmological ideal, the Aztecs also believed that they had an ethical ideal to attain. The struggle of the sun against the powers of darkness was not only a struggle of the gods, but it was also, above all, the struggle of good against evil. . . .

Opposed to this imperialistic and religious ideal there was always a feeling of pessimism in the depths of the Aztec soul. The Aztecs knew that in the end their leader, the sun, would be defeated . . . and then the powers of evil would prevail . . . and would destroy mankind.

Therefore, this life, for the Aztecs, was only transitory, and a feeling of pessimism and anguish appeared in their vigorous and terrible sculpture and a tinge of profound sadness in their poetry.[4]

Poetic Sadness   The Aztecs countered gloom with profusions of flowers and the beauty of songs as means of lifting the heart. Yet, their writers say that the surcease was fleeting and happiness elusive. The lord Xayacamach lamented that the pleasures to be found in flowers and song are as ephemeral as the psychedelic glories experienced by the Aztec eaters of the hallucinogenic mushroom in group religious rites. Indeed, they saw "marvelous visions, ephemeral forms of many colors, more real than reality itself. But afterwards this fantastic world fades like a dream, leaving man weary and empty."[5] Their despair appears in such songs as this:

Given over to sadness
we remain here on earth.
Where is the road
that leads to the Region of the Dead,
the place of our downfall,
the country of the fleshless?

Is it true that perhaps one lives
there, where we all go?
Does your heart believe this?
He hides us
in a chest, in a coffer,
the Giver of Life,
He who shrouds people in the grave.

Will I be able to look upon,
able to see perhaps, the face
of my mother, of my father?
Will they loan me
a few songs, a few words?
I will have to go down there;
nothing do I expect.
They leave us,
given over to sadness.[6]

Cultural Motivation   Driven by their sense of divine destiny, the Aztecs built monumental pyramids to elevate their temples of sacrifice; their armies reached out for many leagues to sweep up victims to be fed to the gods; their vast symbolic dramas reenacted the cyclical struggles to maintain life and the universe. Their compulsive and gloomy outlook on life was not the sole cause of their institutions and social organization, but it colored all they did. Without awareness of their world view there is no comprehension of their character or their society.

The Navaho World View

The Navahos, it will be remembered from the discussion of housing (Chapter 14), are an Athabascan-speaking people who migrated from Canada into the high, arid lands of the southwestern part of the United States some five hundred or more years ago. Originally hunters and foragers, they became gardeners in their new southwestern environment. After the Spanish brought horses, sheep, and goats, they also became pastoralists who were basically gardeners. The cultivation of

---

[4]A. Caso, *The Aztecs: People of the Sun*, pp. 93–95.
[5]M. León-Portillo, *Pre-Columbian Literatures of Mexico*, pp. 82–83.

[6]From *Cantares Mexicanos*, translated by M. León-Portillo in *op. cit.*, p. 85. (Quoted with permission of The University of Oklahoma Press.)

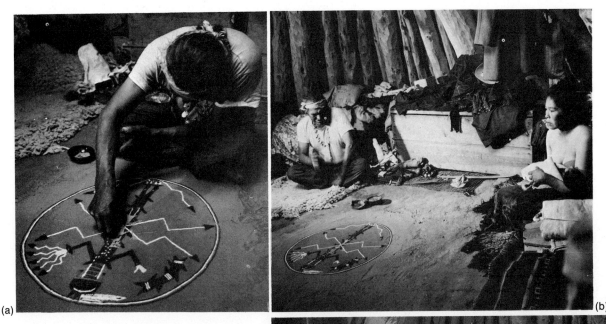

(a)

(b)

(c)

Fig. 28-2   A Navaho curing rite. (a) The sand painting is prepared on the floor of the hogan by the chanter. (b) The painting, which is itself a symbolic prayer, is vitalized by the priest with a hand-trembling chant. (c) As the chant continues, the mother and ailing child sit upon the sand painting to incorporate its holy and curative power. (Courtesy of the American Museum of Natural History.)

corn, beans, and squash was learned from the Pueblo Indians, as was much of their mythology and the visual imagery and technique of sand painting. In like manner, the Navaho system of matrilineal clans appears to have been copied from that of the Western Pueblos. But it has already been noted how the Navahos refused to consolidate in settled, compact villages of pueblo structure, preferring to live in scattered settlements of hogan camps. Their social organization is decentralized and quite amorphous. Clan exogamy is rigidly adhered to, but the sanction for incest is an obsessive urge to burn oneself to death—a fate that relatives try to forestall. The punishment is self-imposed. The Navahos hold elaborate ceremonies, known as chants, which are made occasions for social get-togethers; chanters must learn their rituals carefully (Figure 28-2). But chants are performed at the request of individuals or families to cure illness; they are not part of a cult cycle. Singers are individual practitioners, not members of religious fraternities. Clans are not corporate bodies set in segmentary opposition to one another.[7]

An Orderly But Dangerous Universe   The basic orientation of the Navaho is individualistic-familistic rather than collectivistic. He views the universe as an orderly but extremely dangerous place that must be treated with the utmost circumspection and caution.

The basis for this view is in the Navaho origin myth, which accounts for the history and character of the Holy People—the supernatural beings who belong to the sacred part of the world, as opposed to the Earth Surface People, who are ordinary human beings, living and dead. The origin myth tells ". . . The People that, from time immemorial, the universe has been a very dangerous place, inhabited by people who were untrustworthy, if not completely evil . . . [who] are forever present to Navaho consciousness as threats to prosperity."[8]

Earth Surface People, except for living relatives, are all potentially dangerous, and even slight contact with nonrelatives may cause serious illness. Anyone may be a witch, but especially anyone who becomes too prosperous. Witches are werewolves and ghouls who practice incest and who are the source of the greatest anxiety. But death, too, is horrible in the Navaho view, for ghosts are the witches of the world of the dead; they harass and plague the living with dire portents and unnerving teasing. Even the most forgiving friend may become a malignantly vengeful ghost bent on punishing some slight or neglect. Fear of ghosts makes even adult Navahos loath to face the dark alone.

Eight Fundamental Navaho Postulates   Against this background, Kluckhohn formulated

eight "keystones on which the Navaho view of the world appears to rest":

1. The universe is orderly: all events are caused and interrelated.
   a. Knowledge is power.
   b. The basic quest is for harmony.
   c. Harmony can be restored by orderly procedures.
   d. One price of disorder, in human terms, is illness.
2. The universe tends to be personalized.
   a. Causation is identifiable in personalized terms.
3. The universe is full of dangers.
4. Evil and good are complementary, and both are ever present.
5. Experience is conceived as a continuum differentiated only by sense data.
6. Morality is conceived in traditionalistic and situational terms rather than in terms of abstract absolutes.
7. Human relations are premised upon familistic individualism.
8. Events, not actors or qualities, are primary.[9]

These foregoing precepts expand into a world view with the following two major focuses.

The Compulsive Effect of Prayer and Ritual   The universe is mechanistically viewed as an interrelated system of cause and effect. The Holy People may indeed be spirit beings, but they are not free to act capriciously, for they are controlled by laws of their own making. Chant and ceremony are compulsive acts that control results rather than petition for gifts from the gods. Gladys Reichard, in writing of Navaho religion, spoke of prayer as the "compulsive word," which "functions properly because of its completeness and order," and whose "purpose is compulsion by exactness of word."[10]

So it is that mastery of an esoteric terminology, along with pragmatically tested, immediately apprehended sense data, gives one power. It is not mystic experience—

[7]The present tribal council was established under the aegis of the U.S. Office of Indian Affairs in 1923.
[8]C. Kluckhohn and D. Leighton, *The Navaho*, p. 125.

[9]Kluckhohn, *op. cit.*, pp. 359–360.
[10]G. A. Reichard, *Prayer: The Compulsive Word* (American Ethnological Society Monograph 7, 1944), p. 10.

neither visions nor ascetic self-torture—but *knowledge* (in Navaho terms) that gives power. Power, however, does not mean mastery over nature as Western man seeks it. Rather, the Navaho's basic quest is for harmony. "Individually acquired knowledge can assist in the restoration of harmony in one person's life, in that of the community, in that of the universe."[11] Everything in Navaho symbolism, verbal and visual, is in balanced pairs or quadruplets.

Disharmonic Forces   Disharmony, which is imbalance, means disorder manifest in flood, catastrophe, and, above all, personal illness. Every Navaho ceremony is a "cure" sung over a patient, even though some cures may also improve the state of the world. Witches are forever bent upon disturbing the harmony of things. The Holy People, and all people and things, witches excepted, are neither inherently good nor inherently evil. Good and evil are complementary and ever-present. If things stay in balance, a man and his family will do all right, but the universe is full of dangers. "Navahos," say Kluckhohn and Leighton, "seem morbid in the variety of threats from this world and from the world of the supernatural which they fear and name."[12] The compensatory mechanism of compulsive orderliness in behavior, art, ritual, and religion is their positive response. Complementary to formalism is the felt need to avoid risks. Excess of any sort is dangerous. Most acts are not immoral of themselves, but cause trouble if performed too intensively. "Stay within safe limits! Likewise," say the Navahos, "be wary of nonrelatives." Merely to touch a stranger can make one sick. The Enemy Way nine-day chant may be necessary to restore the order upset by the presence of a stranger. And where an American in a threatening situation may cry out, "Don't just stand there! Do something!" the Navaho canon is: "When in a new and dangerous situation, do nothing!"

In his response to the world as he sees it, the Navaho is an industrious individualist who works hard within the framework of the known. He devotes much time and effort to combating the disruptive forces that imbalance his world. He strives to be courteous, polite, and nonaggressive, avoiding trouble and witches, and seeking above all to have health and strength, to work and to acquire knowledge, to present a good figure with his clothes and jewelry, and to provide for his family—but not to acquire glory or the power to rule or govern men. There is no place for dominance over one's fellows in the Navaho world view.

The Hopi Way and the Pueblo World View

The Hopis are the nearest neighbors of the Navahos, and they are also the westernmost of the living Pueblos of the United States today. They are as typical of the different Pueblos of the Southwest as any Pueblo can be, although all Pueblos differ from others in some respects. A brief examination of the Hopi world view at this point will be useful because of the common historico-cultural base from which both Hopi and Navaho have drawn much of their ideology and because of the different orientation and more conceptual sophistication of the Hopi system.

The Hopis are intensive gardeners living in compact, permanently settled villages built of plastered stone houses set wall to wall around a central ceremonial plaza. Fields and houses are owned by women; the matrilineage is the bridge between household and strong matriclans. Kinship and economic life are female-centered, although men may own sheep. Ceremonial life and political life are male-centered and are organized around a complex system of secret religious fraternities (Figure 28-3).[13]

---

[11]Kluckhohn, *op. cit.,* p. 362.
[12]Kluckhohn and Leighton, *op. cit.,* p. 224.

[13]The best general summary of the Hopi social system is found in F. Eggan, *Social Organization of the Western Pueblos,* chap. 2, pp. 17–138.

An Intricate Balance of Parts   Laura Thompson summarizes the Hopi world view in these words:

Here we recognize an organic view of the universe. The cosmos is formulated as a living whole in which the subtly balanced relationships of the various parts to one another and to the multidimensional totality are similar to those which characterize living organisms. The parts and the whole are believed to transact for the good of all, according to a single, harmonious, immanent law. Man is a psychophysiological whole, differentiated from the rest of nature by his power of volition, which is an integral part of the scheme and is to be used for the commonweal. He cooperates with other men and with his nonhuman partners in fulfilling the law, through kinship and ceremonial groups. And the main mechanisms through which he expresses symbolically the cosmic process are ritual and art, reinforced by concentrated will-prayer.[14]

Expressing it more simply, a Sia Indian put it to me this way, "Yes, it's like the Hopi. If I would refuse the request to drum in the Fiesta, it would delay the answers to the people's prayers. There would be no rain. Or else too much rain would come and flood everything. It wouldn't come just right. It is a hard world that requires correct treatment."

Among all the Pueblos, as a matter of fact, this orientation of viewpoint is general. The

[14]L. Thompson, *Toward a Science of Mankind*, p. 189.

Fig. 28-3   A Flute Fraternity ceremony of the Hopi pueblo of Oraibi in which the members position themselves in a symbolic spiral pattern. (Peabody Museum, Harvard University.)

late Professor Edward Dozier, born and raised in Santa Clara pueblo, said:

> The dominant integrating factor of Rio Grande Pueblo culture is the view of the universe as an orderly phenomenon. People or things are not merely "good" or "bad." "Evil" is a disturbance in the equilibrium that exists between man and the universe, while "good" is a positive frame of mind or action that maintains harmonious balance.
>
> To keep man and the universe in harmonious balance, all must work together and with "good" thoughts. Unanimous effort of body and mind is not only a key value, but it is also enforced. . . . Any action, whether physical or verbal, which is construed by Pueblo authorities to be contrary to group concerns and unanimous will of the village is promptly and severely punished.
>
> Rio Grande Pueblo culture thus makes rigorous demands on the individual and fills him with deep anxiety and suspicion toward his fellow men. Not only is his personal behavior and social interaction strictly circumscribed, but his thoughts as well are rigidly harnessed. He is constantly plagued by an apprehension that he or his fellow man may break the harmonious balance of the universe and bring illness, famine, or some other form of dreaded disaster.[15]

Thus, for other Puebloans as well as for the Hopis, the most fundamental postulate premises the world as a complex, ordered system in which all parts are intimately interdependent on an essentially equivalent footing, each with its role to play in the maintenance of the harmonious working of the whole. Man is on the same footing as all other orders of phenomena—the birds, the beasts, the plants, the insects, the clouds, the mythic beings, the ancestors—all these and many more, each with its ordained function. The world in the Hopi view is tightly integrated and complexly organized, a delicately balanced mechanism.

The Human Role in the Universe   Unlike the Navahos, who view the world as dangerous, the Hopis see it as beneficent and predictable —except where human irresponsibility disrupts it. The nonhuman part of the universe is automatically controlled by the "correlativity principle." But man has a measure of willful self-determinism. He has a margin of choice. He may or may not carry out his functions according to the Great Scheme. If he does, the universe continues its orderly unfolding of events—healthily, happily, productively, satisfyingly. If he does not, crops fail, babies die, and famine, pestilence, and disaster sweep over the little community. Chaos and disorder reign.

A Hopi, in the Hopi view, must *want* things to go right. He must want this with all his being, which means that he must work industriously in his fields, at weaving, and at pottery or basket making, and that he must participate faithfully in all the ceremonies in which he has an assigned part by virtue of his statuses. In addition, he must concentrate all his psychic energy on "willing" or "praying for" (synonymous terms in Hopi) the result. He must think "happy" thoughts.

In other words, the Hopi must self-consciously keep himself committed to a positive minding of his role in the universe. Less than this constitutes failure as a human being, and such failure is heresy and treason. There is no room for the indifferent or uncommitted man in the Hopi scheme of things, nor is there room for the individualistic innovator who thinks he can improve on the Great Scheme. Such a person is a dangerous deviationist, even more immediately dangerous than the slovenly slacker. Each in his way is a saboteur of the order, the one because he does not make the effort to will enough, the other because he wills the wrong things. Each is *ka-hopi*, un-Hopi; each runs a great risk not only of being called a "two-heart" (a witch who stays alive by taking the lives of relatives), but also of being condemned and killed as a witch by the Kwan secret society. Hopi society is theocratic, collectivistic, and totalitarian.

Hopis fear witches, but in a way different from the way Navahos fear them. Navaho

[15]E. P. Dozier, "Rio Grande Pueblos," in E. H. Spicer (ed.), *Perspectives in American Indian Culture Change*, p. 122.

anxiety is diffuse, but witchcraft is directed toward individuals, as is ghost malice. Pueblo witchcraft is directed against the whole system. That Hopi witches kill individuals is incidental, for their major motive is to prolong their own lives by killing others, especially relatives.

To the Navaho, knowledge is power. To the Hopi (as to other Pueblo Indians), knowledge is not only power but also an obligation. Knowledge is a requisite to maintaining the balance of the universe; one must strain to know what is expected and needed, and one must will to make it work. But what one is privileged to know is ordained in the pattern. Roles for all persons and things are ideologically blueprinted, and to presume to roles that have not been assigned to one is *ka-hopi*. To know a ceremony for which one is not properly a priest means only that one will misuse it. Possession of unauthorized knowledge is feared by men and women throughout the pueblos, for to say of a person, "He knows something," is to mean that he is a witch.[16]

As an ideological adaptation to a harsh environment in which the Hopis have achieved a highly effective survival capacity, their world view unquestionably represents a high level of consistent integration that permeates their social structure, their art and ritual, and their personalities. Its demands upon the individual are severe, for each man is an Atlas, supporting the weight of the world upon his shoulders. There is little room for individualism, and there is no tolerance for the wayward. The Hopi socializes—or else. The world view of his society demands it.

[16]Thus Bandalier wrote of the New Mexican Pueblos: "[A cacique, the priest-chief,] can also be removed if the tribe so directs in general council, or if the war captain or the leading shamans so dispose. A degraded cacique seldom, if ever, lives long. There is too much danger in suffering him who is in possession of the most precious arts and knowledge to live while under a cloud. It is the war captain who, officially at least, attends to such executions." A. F. Bandalier, "Final Report" (*Papers of the Archaeological Institute of America*, vol. 3, 1890), p. 284.

The Mechanistic-Vitalistic Character of Navaho and Hopi World Views Although the Hopis and the Navahos posit the existence of spirit beings, and in this sense their world views are colored with animism, both are fundamentally mechanistic in their outlook. The Navahos assume that the acts of Big Holy People, Earth Surface People, and witches may be counteracted by compulsively effective ritual knowledge. The Hopis are even more mechanistic in their view of the universe as an intricately meshed set of systems, delicately interrelated in a total order that man must help to maintain by positive willing and correct role performance.

The Cheyenne Way as World View

Among yet another American Indian tribe a mechanistic view of the universe predominated but in essentially different ways from those of the Navaho and Hopi. Cheyennes talked about the Spirit Who Rules the Universe, the Spirit Who Gives Good Health, the Big Holy People Who Know Everything. They believed in Heammawihio, the all-knowing high god who lives above. *Wihio* means a high order of intelligence, like that of the spider who spins his web, seemingly walking on nothing. He knows more about how to do things than all other creatures. Heammawihio once lived on earth as a being, but ages ago retired to the sky where, symbolically represented by the sun, he lives remote from all things, now more an abstract principle of "knowing" than a being. All first offerings of the pipe or smoked cigarette were made to him. There were other big spirits such as Aktunowihio, the Wise One Below (in the earth), and the Thunder, Heammawihio's great bird who brings the summer rains. There were the innumerable animal and bird spirits who were sought on the vision quest, who appeared in visions and bestowed medicine power for curing, divination, or war on lucky women. Maiyunahu'ta, Spirits

Who Told Me in Sleep, they were called. All these were animistic beings, not in themselves mechanical forces. Yet they behaved mechanically. One offered them food, cloth, an enemy scalp, a piece of one's flesh, perhaps a chopped-off joint of a finger. "In a narrow sense," observes Robert Anderson, "it was giving; in a wider sense, simply doing, that which was valued by the supernaturals. . . . [T]he goal or response was a concrete return—health for oneself or kin, a wealth of horses, many coups on a raid, success in the hunt, or a shaman's powers."[17]

In Cheyenne ceremonies, the rites, not the words, were most important. The spirits, great and small, were like puppets who responded to the strings that were manipulated by compulsive ceremony and ritual.

The Theory of Limited Energy   Cheyenne wise men did not speak of an energy theory of the universe. Nonetheless, they subscribed to one; it was implicit rather than explicit in the tribal world view.

All Cheyennes knew that if a man wanted his son to mature as an outstanding person, he, the father, had to vow not to have sexual relations for seven, or fourteen, years after the boy's birth. All the father's "growth energy" had to be concentrated in that one child until he was mature.

If he had a colt which he wanted to become a fast, long-winded war pony, he asked a shaman with "horse medicine" to bless it with symbols of male sexual energy, while he himself vowed not to ride it at all for a given number of months. Then he rode it only in battle. Its energy had to be generated and stored for the special occasion.

Man and Ritual in Regeneration   Every year, the world had to be regenerated through the tribal Sun Dance or the Sacred Arrow Re-newal ceremony, for each year the world runs down, its limited amount of energy dissipated. But in the ceremonies, replete with imagery and symbolism of rebirth and growth of man, beast, and plant life, the energy quotient of the universe was renewed.

The Cheyenne myths tell that eons ago there was famine. "Vegetation withered, the animals starved, the land became barren and dry, and the ancient Cheyenne were on the verge of starvation, for they had no food but dried vegetation and their dogs of burden."[18] One of the two Cheyenne culture heroes, Erect Horns, went into the Sacred Mountain, where the spirits taught him the Sun Dance, which he in turn taught to the Cheyennes. In this ceremony:

At the time of the Lone-tipi, though everything is barren, the earth is beginning to grow. Now it has grown. Thus they make the earth, buffalo wallow, grease, wool, and sinew to make growth. By the time of the end of the lodge, things have grown, people have become happy; the world has reached its full growth, and people rejoice.[19]

By not wasting energy and by ritual knowledge of how mechanically to recharge it, the Cheyenne, in his view, could keep things going. The power of mechanical manipulation was learned from an instructor who was a priest, who had learned from a priest, who had learned from a priest, in an unbroken chain back to Sweet Medicine and Erect Horns, the mythical heroes who had been given the secrets of the universe by the Big Spirits themselves (Figure, 28-4).

The Cheyennes, like the Aztecs, believed that they bore a special burden of maintaining the universe for all mankind.[20] Unlike the Aztecs, they did not believe they had to feed the gods with human blood to renew their energy. They performed no human sacrifices.

---

[17]R. Anderson, "The Buffalo Men, A Cheyenne Ceremony of Petition Deriving from the Sutaio" (*Southwestern Journal of Anthropology,* vol. 12, 1956), p. 102.

[18]G. A. Dorsey, *The Cheyenne* I, *Ceremonial Organization,* p. 46.

[19]*Ibid.,* II, *The Sun Dance,* p. 57.

[20]This is still true; The Sun Dance is performed every year, culminating on the Fourth of July. The Sacred Arrows are renewed whenever there has been a murder in the tribe.

Cheyenne Personality Not all Cheyennes incorporated the Cheyenne world view with equal intensity. But many did, and these acted in accordance with moral and personal norms of behavior which clearly stamped the Cheyenne among other tribes.

Fig. 28-4 Cheyenne Sun Dance pledgers wearing the yellow paint of the First Day. Body paint changes with each day of the ceremony, as the symbolic focus progresses. (Courtesy of the American Museum of Natural History.)

Reserved and dignified, the adult Cheyenne male moves with a quiet sense of self-assurance. He speaks fluently, but never carelessly. He is careful of the sensibilities of others and is kindly and generous. He is slow to anger and strives to suppress his feelings, if aggravated. Vigorous on the hunt and in war, he prizes the active life. Towards enemies he feels no merciful compunctions, and the more aggressive he is, the better. He is well versed in ritual knowledge. He is neither flighty nor dour. Usually quiet, he has a lightly displayed sense of humor. He is sexually repressed and masochistic, but that masochism is expressed in culturally approved rites. He does not show much creative imagination in artistic expression, but he has a firm grip on reality. He deals with the problems of life in set ways while at the same time showing a notable capacity to readjust to new circumstances. His thinking is rationalistic to a high degree and yet colored with mysticism. His ego is strong and not easily threatened. His superego, as manifest in his strong social conscience and mastery of his basic impulses, is powerful and dominating. He is "mature"—serene and composed, secure in his social position, capable of warm social relations. He has powerful anxieties, but these are channeled into institutionalized modes of collective expression with satisfactory results. He exhibits few neurotic tendencies.[21]

The Ashanti World View

Ancestors are of no significance in Cheyenne thought. In many Asiatic and African belief systems it is quite otherwise, however. To exemplify a world view in which relations with ancestors are of paramount importance, that of the Ashanti, one of the great tribes of present-day Ghana, will be briefly presented.

When the Ashanti were conquered by the British in 1874, they had already united in a constitutional monarchy made up of a number of districts, each under a paramount chief and all bearing allegiance to the King of Ashanti, the Ashantihene. They lived in scattered villages and were ruled from seats of government situated in true towns.

[21]E. A. Hoebel, *The Cheyennes*, p. 90.

The Gods   The central theme of the Ashanti world view is ancestoralism, but the ancestors are no more than the most immediate of the numerous spirit beings that people the universe. The Ashanti's world is full of spirits; his world view may be labeled *vitalistic*.

Onyonkopon, the Supreme Being   The world is the creation of a high god, Onyonkopon, the Supreme Being. Although he originally lived close to men, low in the sky, he removed himself far beyond their reach because the activities of an old woman annoyed him. He is a person—aloof, remote, and uncensorious; all-powerful, he no longer exercises his power directly. He planned and created the universe, endowing it with a general order, and yet he sets no moral precepts and neither punishes human follies nor rewards human virtues. He is revered and looked upon with awe and veneration. Still, there are no priests who serve Onyonkopon; there are no rites or rituals of praise, petition, appeasement, or atonement. He gives nothing; he demands nothing. He is the pure, unifying principle of the universe—a personified abstraction, similar to Heammawihio of the Cheyennes, but more anthropomorphically conceived.

Abosom, the Executive Deities   The administration of the universe is in the hands of the great executive deities (*abosom*), the superintending gods of the major departments of nature—the rivers, the lakes, the sea, the clouds, and the earth itself. Beneath these secondary gods are the innumerable lesser spirits that animate trees, animals, and charms. Most ubiquitous, however, are the immortal ancestors—veritable busybodies who are concerned that everything be done right and morally. They are preceptors and censors of all Ashantis, from the humblest slave to the Ashantihene, who is their living viceroy in the administration of society.

Calling the Gods   Unlike the high god, the lesser gods have their priests and shrines.

In response to proper offerings and priestly incantations, a god may be induced to take up a temporary abode in one of his shrines—but then again, he may refuse or neglect to come. If he comes, he is beseeched to grant health, wealth, children, or protection from misfortune or witches. He grants or withholds according to his own willful disposition. The Ashanti does not conceive of controlling the gods; he views himself as dependent upon supernatural whim. Should a god respond, he speaks through his priest, either by possessing the priest himself, who then speaks in tongues while an assistant interprets, or by influencing the performance of various divinatory devices manipulated by the priest. Gods and spirits other than the Supreme Deity and ancestors are viewed instrumentally—as means to ends. Their popularity waxes and wanes as they are responsive or unresponsive to human demands.

The gods are treated with respect if they deliver the goods, and with contempt if they fail. . . . The Ashanti, like the other Akan tribes, esteem the Supreme Being and the ancestors far above gods and amulets. Attitudes to the latter depend upon their success and vary from healthy respect to sneering contempt.[22]

The Ancestors   A basic proposition underlying all Ashanti social structure is that the land belongs to the ancestors and the living enjoy only its use. The ancestral spirits therefore control the subsistence base that is administered on their behalf by the king, who in turn delegates its disposition to district chiefs, who parcel it out to lineage heads, who finally assign it to families.

The next fundamental postulate is that every person inherits his blood from his mother and this is the link from generation to generation. Through blood comes membership in the maternal lineage and clan (*abusua*). From clan membership flow the rights and duties of citizenship in law and in govern-

---

[22]K. A. Busia, "The Ashanti of the Gold Coast," in D. Forde (ed.), *African Worlds*, p. 205.

ment. Inheritance of property rights, goods, and titles to office derives from clan membership through blood. In dogma, clan membership means common descent from a mythical ancestress, exogamy, and bonds of mutual aid wherever clan members may be found.

Ashanti postulates undergird a double descent system, however. Everyone receives his spiritual essence (*ntorɔ*) through his father from his father's ancestral patriline. He belongs to an identifiable *ntorɔ* group, which has its own customs, usages, and rituals; from it he inherits his personal *sunsum*, "his ego, his personality, his distinctive character."

The Vital Soul   From the Creator the Ashanti receives his *kra*, his life force—the bit of animating spirit that returns to the Supreme Being when he dies. The *kra* is the soul, the undying part of him that continues its existence in the abode of ancestors. In short, in the Ashanti view, a man derives his social statuses through his mother's blood, his character through his father's spirit, and his life from the Supreme Being.

Social Control through the Ancestors   The gods, as viewed by the Ashanti, may give or withhold, but they do not punish. The ancestors, in contrast, protect their descendants and punish them if their behavior is reprehensible. Thus it is with reference to the attitudes toward gods that the Ashanti world view and religion are often said to have no ethical content. The morality imposed by the expectations of the ancestors is, however, strict and severe, for ancestors are not to be offended. Hence: "The Ashanti conception of a good society is one in which harmony is achieved among the living, and between the living and the gods and ancestors. . . ."[23]

The responsibility for maintenance of this harmony is vested in the chiefs. Each lineage has its sacred stool. The lineage chief, seated upon the lineage stool (throne) embodying the collective spirit of the ancestors, is the will

and voice of the ancestors, concerned with the conduct and well-being of lineage members. On the highest level, the royal stool of the king's lineage is the symbolic representation of all the ancestors of the Ashantis, and, as their intermediary, the Ashantihene governs the nation.

The postulate, "All contraventions of the will of the ancestors are sins," is fundamental to the Ashanti system of social control. Complementary to it is a related postulate: "The ancestors will punish the group as a whole if the group does not itself punish a sinner." From this flows the corollary, "All sins are crimes." All crimes are punishable by death because (postulate): "Men are endowed with conscious will." Therefore, a sinner is one who willfully defies the ancestors, forfeiting thereby his right to enjoy their protection and inclusion in their community of the living. Further: "The ancestors will judge and punish a man in the spirit world if he takes advantage of a miscarriage of justice here."

Great collective ceremonies honoring the ancestors occur every twenty-one days, and once a year all the categories of spirit beings are given simple offerings and asked for their continued help in ceremonies that extend for two weeks.

It can be seen from this description that the operative forces in the Ashanti universe are not mechanical, but wholly personal. As the Ashanti sees his task, it is not to achieve or maintain compulsive control over a balance of forces or to regenerate a dissipating store of energy. His duties are to remain on good terms with spirit beings (who are admittedly capricious but nonetheless inclined to lend a helping hand to mankind), and to maintain good relations with his fellows because the ancestors demand it.

The American World View

It may seem that the formulation of a descriptive analysis of *a* world view for the people of the United States is too great an undertaking. There are so many, and such diverse, cultural backgrounds represented in their recent immigrant origins; there is such a wide range in manifest belief, from atheism to devout religiosity; there is such a broad spectrum of interests in terms of occupation, recreation, and learning; and there are such vast differences between life in a tiny crossroads hamlet and life in New York's megalopolis, between the black separatist and white segregationist, between the middle-aged Kiwanian and the hippie countercultural revolutionist, that one may well wonder where lies the common denominator, or if one exists at all.

Yet outsiders generally agree that Americans are, by and large, highly standardized in outlook and manner. Relatively speaking, this is true. American society is marked by a very high degree of consensus and general agreement. There is little of the dogmatic in American ideology—certainly nothing that can be stated so succinctly as a Communist credo, for example. Nonetheless, a distinctive American world view does exist and may be stated in its bolder outlines as the anthropologist sees them. This, then, is how it appears—allowing for subgroup and individual variations, which are screened out in order that the major themes can be brought into clearer focus.

Rationalism and the Mechanistic View   Historically, the American world view is a derivative of the Judaeo-Christian–Hellenistic traditions as they were blended and modified through the Renaissance, the Reformation, and the industrial revolution in Europe. In the American setting, these traditions have taken on their own intensifications and selective qualities.

However much the Judaeo-Christian traditions may survive and influence the American life-way, American thought patterns are rational rather than mystic; the operative conception of the universe is mechanistic. The bedrock proposition upon which the whole world view stands is that the universe is a physical system operating in a determinate manner according to discoverable scientific laws. Thus, Americans use religion for purposes of social organization, but they rely relatively little upon prayer, ritual, or sacrifice to achieve their ends. Instead, they depend primarily upon basic scientific research and the technical application of the findings of science. Because they view the universe as a mechanism, Americans implicitly believe that man can manipulate it. He need not accept it as it is; he may work on it, and as he gains in knowledge and improves his techniques, he may even redesign it so that it will be more to his liking.

From this springs the conviction that the conditions of living are improvable: materially, biologically, and socially. Improvement means betterment; betterment means progress. Americans are progressive: neither revolutionary nor conservative, but progressive. Man can himself, in the American view, eliminate hunger and poverty, disease, and social injustice—if he sets himself to the task. This fundamental motivating postulate of contemporary American culture expresses itself in a focal value orientation of "effort-optimism." Because the world view is rational-mechanistic rather than mystic-vitalistic, it leads to action rather than contemplation, to aggressive engagement rather than passive renunciation. Americans "make war" on poverty, "stamp out" disease, "wipe out" illiteracy, and embark on the "conquest" of space, as their forebears "conquered" the wilderness. Such an action orientation makes for emphasis upon technology and science rather than upon philosophy and the arts. It has produced a mechanized agricultural-, industrial-, business-centered civilization rather than an ecclesiastical, scholarly, militaristic, or feudalistic one.

Pragmatic Empiricism   Concomitantly, the American cultural emphasis is pragmatic-empirical rather than theoretical-dogmatic. Americans are concerned more with "know-how" and "can-do" than with abstract wisdom or ancient knowledge, even, to a considerable degree, in science. In our universities and colleges, and in government grants-in-aid for research, this emphasis may be seen in the lopsided support for medicine, technology, and agriculture as against the humanities and social sciences.

The test of the validity of the American premise is, in the American view of things, continued expansion of the gross national product, ever-new medical breakthroughs, and continuous expansion of social well-being and opportunity. As long as the standard of living, expressed in wide distribution of consumers' goods, keeps rising, it is felt that things are going well. When the system temporarily collapsed in the Great Depression of the 1930s, Americans panicked and had to be reassured that "all they had to fear was fear itself." What unnerved them, however, was not unreasoning fear but the logical anxiety that the most basic premise of the American world view was an unworkable illusion.

Individual-centeredness When the American looks away from the universe and inward toward himself and his society, his focus of view is individual-centered, rather than kin-centered, class-centered, or collectivistically oriented, even though Americans are widely given to group organization. In the religious belief that has permeated much of the morality of the culture, it is premised that a man's moral responsibility rests in his private conscience. In the view of human nature held by Christianity, which is the dominant religion, man is inherently corrupt and sin-ridden by nature, and personal salvation (that is, purification from the moral stain of sin) is possible only in an emotional act of identification with God through Jesus (or his mother, Mary). Americans are therefore generally internally plagued with inner conflict and anxiety. Believing in the improvability of the self as an individual responsibility, and yet also holding (to a certain extent) that man is a sorry being,

they accept the proposition that inner psychic conflict is the very essence of human existence. Pastors are expected to be half counselor and half priest. To control the extreme consequences of inner conflict, there is less reliance upon religious or philosophic solutions than upon psychiatry and mental hygiene programs.

Rites of passage are weak or lacking, and the individual is left to wrestle with his own "identity crises." External values are weakly anchored in the America of today, and in the wildly swirling cultural revolution of the age many find it hard to get a grasp on meaningful standards.

Two-thirds of the American population are nominally religious in that they belong to some church. One-third are sufficiently uninterested in religion as to identify with no church. In contrast to the primitive world view, God, gods, spirits, ghosts, witches, and ancestors in the American world view are more residual than dominant.

Status and Social Mobility The individual-centeredness of the American world view, combined with its pragmatic action orientation, gives emphasis to status achievement and social mobility. Achievement-in-being is what counts, not an illustrious background. American egalitarianism and its proposition that all men are created equal derive from this combination of qualities. Every American has to prove himself to himself first and to his fellows second—to succeed in manifest ways. He sees himself in a fluid social organization that necessitates fluid status symbols whereby achievement can be tangibly expressed. In a business-based culture, money serves this function. Money is the measure of success; it validates one's efforts, and therefore oneself, by providing the means to purchase such external symbols of success as a college education, a discreetly selected foreign car, or a large house at a good address.

The world view of older, but contemporary, status-structured societies in Europe deprecates the materialism of Americanism. At the same time, a major feature of the revolutionary innovations of the postcolonial world since World War II has been the avid desire of the so-called underdeveloped nations to learn the mechanical-material techniques that have followed from the kind of world view that has had its most intensive development in the United States.[24]

The Counterculture Revolution   The countercultural revolution of the current younger generation rejects the traditional American world view as false-valued. It inverts the status symbolism of clothing—dressing in rags, Hollywood Indian style, romanticized workingmen's garb, gypsy and peasant dress, all in variations which ebb and flow in favor. It abhors regular time-clock-punching work and hopes to get along with little or no money.

It does not completely reject automobiles, but prefers beat-up cars to the latest models, and in housing it chooses a simply furnished pad rather than a "good address." It seeks social bonding in marriageless habitation, and searches for new substitutes for the rejected values in psychedelia, communes, mystical experiences (including the occult), mind expansion, back-to-nature experiments, etc. Personal guilt, ambition, and "success" are devalued, and emphasis is placed on honesty, intimacy, and sharing. The permanence of the movement and its impact on the ideological mainstream of American culture remain to be seen. (For further discussion, see Chapter 34.)

SUMMARY

World view, as stated by Redfield in one of his formulations, is the "insider's total vision

and conception of everything," his outlook on life.[25] As a science, anthropology might be content to work with reports on what the anthropologist as an objective observer sees and notes of behavior. Such observations must be so phrased that they are comparable within a scientific frame of analytical reference. Most of the chapters of this book have been presented from this point of view.

But as a humanity, anthropology must strive to tell us what the world looks like to a Navaho, a Hopi, an Ashanti, a Trobriand Islander, a Nuer, or an Ifugao. Such a task calls for the treatment of whole cultures and lifeways as viewed from the inside by the liver of the life-way. The aim is to feel and understand the universe not in scientific terms but in the terms, cognitions, and affects of the people concerned, who are not scientists at all. A complete anthropology requires both approaches.

Six world views have been sketched in this chapter. Obviously, the sketches are much too thin to convey how it feels to see the universe as a Hopi does—or as an American does. It is important, though, to sense the basic fact that cultures are not simply ways of doing, or of organizing societies. They also define the nature of the world, of man (existential postulates), and of what is to be sought after and what is to be avoided (normative postulates or values).

The Aztec peoples viewed the world as beset with manifold powers of darkness against which man and the gods struggled in perpetual effort. They fed the gods with human blood sacrifices in return for the gifts which were showered on man. The Aztec elaborated a fabulous ceremonial and social organization with which to wage the struggle but carried on with a pervading sense of impending and inevitable doom and sadness.

The Navaho world view builds on the assumption that spirit beings established the world as it is and endowed it with order; it is,

---

[24]It will undoubtedly have been noted in the foregoing description that, allowing for certain variations in the conception of the individual in relation to the state and in various degrees of coloration, the "world view" of the Russians is not so dissimilar from the American as is commonly thought.

[25]R. Redfield, *The Little Community,* p. 95.

however, a very dangerous and threatening world, but it may be controlled by compulsive symbolic acts. Individualism is to the fore, and social structure and material culture both reflect this basic fact. Disharmony and imbalance produce personal illness.

The Hopis intensify the concept of an orderly universe, and although they populate it with spirit beings, they tend to depersonalize it. All elements of the universe are grouped in large categories, which interrelate in an intricately delicate balance that is designed to operate beneficently for the well-being of all. Man, however, is endowed with will and he is required concentratedly to will the patterned maintenance of the system while he fulfills his ordained roles. Failure on either count disrupts the system and brings on social disaster as well as possible personal sickness. Individuals are consequently under extreme social pressure meticulously to conform to traditional patterns. On the other hand, the effect of ritual acts within the system is so impelling that unauthorized knowledge portends misuse, and the penalty for knowing what one has no right to know is death.

The Cheyennes viewed the universe as a spirit-peopled mechanical system charged with a limited quotient of energy. Like the Aztecs, they believed that it was their responsibility to keep the energy quotient at full charge. Unlike the Aztecs, they did not see this as feeding the forces of good to aid them in their struggle against the forces of evil. Rather, their basic theory was much more morally neutral. The world-maintenance energy runs down as it is used up. Therefore, it must be used carefully and annually recharged through ritual action in which the act itself is sufficient.

The Ashantis look out upon an anthropomorphized world of spirits. The order in this world is that sustained by the Supreme Being and the ancestors. The innumerable executive gods are unpredictable and willful; they are propitiated in hope of obtaining their favors, but eventually they are scorned if they fail too often to respond to human appeals.

The American world view is predominantly rational-mechanistic in its conception of an orderly universe operating according to discoverable scientific laws. The American approach to life is marked by effort-optimism, an activist conviction that the material, biological, and social state of the world is improvable through man's efforts. The social system emphasizes status achievement and individual self-validation through the winning of material tokens of success in which know-how is more important than contemplative wisdom. Individual responsibility, combined with a religious tradition of human sinfulness, contributes to internal anxiety and self-censure. At the same time, the democratic egalitarianism of Americans fits into the notion that every man should have an equal chance to show what he can do. It is a world view which looks forward to an always-changing future and which is concerned with the past largely as a key to what may be.

SELECTED READINGS

Forde, D. (ed.), *African Worlds: Studies in the Cosmological Ideas and Social Values of African Peoples* (1954). Nine studies of the world views of a selected group of African societies. Includes a very remarkable formulation of world view by a native informant from the Dogon of the French Sudan (pp. 83–110).

Geertz, C., *The Religion of Java* (1960). The world view of Javanese analyzed in terms of Hindu tradition, Islamic precepts, and indigenous beliefs.

Hamilton, E., *The Greek Way to Western Civilization* (1930). A sympathetic approach to Greek thought and action by way of Greek literature.

Hoebel, E. A., *The Cheyennes* (1960). Part I, "Ritual and Tribal Integration," and Part IV, "World View and the Cheyenne Personality," show how the Cheyenne view of the need to husband and renew the limited energy quotient of the universe is culturally expressed.

Hsu, F. L. K., *Americans and Chinese: Purpose and Fulfillment in Great Civilizations* (1970). An updated presentation of comparative contrasts of American and Chinese cultural orientations and their related behaviors. The account presents rich data and penetrating insights by an objectively knowledgeable American anthropologist of Chinese origin.

————, *The Study of Literate Civilizations* (1969). A handbook on the application of anthropological methods in the study of complex societies. Chapter 8, "Postulates as a Solution," succinctly states the underlying assumptions of the world views of China and the United States.

Leslie, C. M., *Now We Are Civilized: A Study of the World View of the Zapotec Indians of Mitla, Oaxaca* (1960). A penetrating and gracefully written expression of the world view of a Mexican people in transition from the old to the new.

Radin, P., *Primitive Man as Philosopher* (1927; rev. ed., 1955). This is the classic work that opened the door to the inside view of primitive thinking. It disposed of the condescending clichés that had prevailed about primitive simple-mindedness.

Redfield, R., *The Primitive World and Its Transformations* (1953). Chapter 4, "Primitive World View and Civilization," explores some implications of the concept of world view for modern life.

————, *The Little Community* (1956). Chapter 6, "The Little Community as an Outlook on Life," emphasizes the differences between the outside and inside views of cultures and the problems of investigation of the latter, plus the theoretical significance of world view.

Chapter 29

Religion and Myth: Symbolic Ideology

Throughout the history of mankind, world view and religion have been intimately intertwined, for both are expressions of ideational systems—products of human intelligence and emotional concern: expressions of the culture-creating ferment of the human mind.

World view, as we have just explored it, provides each people with its "set" toward the universe. Religion defines a part of that experience through the spirits and gods it creates; it clothes them with their own peculiar attributes of behavior, and provides men with guidelines for their own behavior in response to the presence and demands of the spirit beings with whom they must interact. Religion does more than this, however. Through ritual and myth, religion provides symbolic expression which subtly and pervasively impresses on participants and watching members of the society an emotional and

Fig. 29-A   The Foolish One. The being who symbolized untamed male sexuality in Mandan mythology as he was dramatized in the Okipa ceremony of 1832. (George Catlin's O-kee-pa, A Religious Ceremony and Other Customs of the Mandans, John C. Ewers [ed]. Copyright © 1967 by Yale University Press.)

intellectual commitment to the ordered belief system on which their lives rest.

In Chapter 2, "Man, Culture, and Society," we cited the sixth and most difficult functional prerequisite of society as defining the meaning of life and maintaining the motivation to survive and engage in the activities necessary to survival (page 34). This is the task of cultures at large, world views in general, and religions in particular. Atheistic cultures, such as those in modern Russia and China, deal with similar problems but without the use of religion. "The Thoughts of Chairman Mao" are specifically directed to this end, and judging from reports emerging from China, apparently quite successfully, for the present at least.

Anthropological Theories of Religion

Over a period of a hundred years, anthropology has worked to develop an objective understanding of religion in human cultures, an understanding that is free of dogma and separate from the value judgments that the religions of the East and West may have imposed on the intellectual climate of our times.

The earliest theories, those of the late nineteenth century, such as Sir Edward Tylor's, were primarily psychological; they undertook to explain the origins of religion in terms of mental responses to the puzzling aspects of life—dream experience and death in particular. They were directly and simply concerned with overt belief in spirit beings. The theory of animism, as it was called, dominated anthropological thought until challenged by the sociological theory of Émile Durkheim. Animism and related ideas will be examined in the next chapter. At this point it will be useful to take a brief look at Durkheim's contribution.

The Sacred and the Profane: Durkheim's Theory of Religion   Much religion is, indeed, a matter of individual experience, such as that of the North American Indian who must seek a vision in which a spirit bestows the power of medicine (supernatural power) upon him. Yet all religions build on the participation of the public, if only as spectators, in acts that not only affect the workings of extra-human forces but also express the solidarity of the group and at the same time internalize group loyalty and commitment to unified social purposes. This was the thesis of Émile Durkheim, Malinowski, and the functionalists. For Durkheim, to whom society was the supreme reality, to explain religion on the basis of dreams, as did Tylor, was to explain a reality by recourse to a fantasy.

Durkheim saw ritual participation as the true essence of religion. Man rises above the humdrum monotony of eking out his living and shares in the ecstasy of sacred experience obtainable only through periodic group dances and ceremonies, such as the *corroborees* of the Australian aborigines. Religion, for Durkheim, is an expression of social solidarity and collective beliefs. Man alone is as nothing. He realizes his significance and worth only as a member of a social group. Sacred rituals and beliefs symbolize society. Out of the ritual experience arises the difference between the sacred and the profane.

As phrased by Professor Lowie, the religious emotion expresses "a sense of something transcending the expected or natural, a sense of the Extraordinary, Mysterious, or Supernatural."[1] Religious belief is essentially mystical and subjective, whereas naturalistic belief emphasizes objective and rational determination of the facts.

This becomes clearer when put in terms of *profane* and *sacred,* as polarized by Durkheim.

The profane	*The sacred*
The sphere of the routine, mundane, taken-for-granted, workaday world.	The sphere of the unusual, extraordinary, not-to-be-taken-casually, "out-of-this-world."
Attitudes: blasé acceptance on a basis of common familiarity.	Attitudes: awe, sense of mystery, circumspection in dealing with something special.

[1] R. H. Lowie, *Primitive Religion,* p. xvi.

The terms "profane" and "sacred," so used, have meanings somewhat broader than ordinarily accorded them in common English usage, and care should be taken to keep this constantly in mind. The profane, then, is that which is viewed as natural; the sacred, that which is viewed as supernatural. The natural works in ways that are accepted as ordinary, as in accord with daily experience. The supernatural works in ways that are looked upon as unusual and special. The emotional connotations are consequently different. They are the product of human mental states.

Religion and magic therefore rest upon a belief in the supernatural, and they are basically matters of ideology and the kinds of feeling that accompany them. They require thought. Animals, although they certainly feel, do not engage in symbolic thought, as we have seen. Man alone symbolizes, and man's ideas about the supernatural are always symbolically expressed. So it is that on the subhuman level there is no religion or magic—no supernaturalism.

Today, anthropologists combine both the sociological and psychological approaches to religion in a kind of master theory which, while it embraces Tylor's simple animism, goes far beyond it in sophistication. In this and the following chapters, we shall present the essence of the modern view and then relate to it what is still relevant in the earlier theories of religion.

Anthropological Theories of Mythology

The questing mind of man has always asked the eternal "Why?" The creative minds of artists have always spun a literary web of answers in words and ideas. The human animal does not submit supinely either to the harsh demands of the physical world or to the ever-pressing demands of his society and its culture-bound limitations of individual freedom. Reasons are demanded. Reasons are given.

Myths, as distinct from folklore and legends, deal with sacred and semidivine beings in a time when the world was different and they tell how, through the activity of such beings, things came to be as they are. They instruct men in what must be done to avoid chaos— the state that man, individually and collectively, fears most.

In Malinowski's functional theory of myth, myth is more than idle speculation about the origins of things.

It justifies by precedent the existing order and it supplies a retrospective pattern of moral values, of sociological discriminations and burdens and of magical belief. . . . the [Myth] of magic [of religion, or of any other body of customs or single custom] is definitely a warrant of its truth, a pedigree of its filiation, a charter of its claims to validity.[2]

Myth believing is more than infantile self-deception; it is social reassurance—a device of education and learning, of culture maintenance.

Today, however, anthropological interests, while not ignoring function, relate myths more to symbolic transformations in which change and establishment of a new order of things is of more interest than origins. Victor Turner writes:

Myths relate how one state of affairs became another: how an unpeopled world became populated; how chaos became cosmos; how immortals became mortal; how the seasons came to replace a climate without seasons; how the original unity of mankind became a plurality of tribes or nations; how androgynous beings became men and women; and so on. Myths are *liminal* phenomena: they are frequently told at a time or in a site that is "betwixt and between."[3]

Myths are an important component of transition rites (see Chapter 19). They restate the first principles or basic postulates upon which a people's belief system and social structure rest. Myths phrase the nature of the

[2]B. Malinowski, "Culture" (*Encyclopaedia of the Social Sciences,* vol. 4, 1937), p. 640.
[3]V. W. Turner, "Myth and Symbol" (*International Encyclopedia of the Social Sciences,* vol. 10, 1968), p. 576.

personality a person must seek to transcribe in himself. Myths assist to "re-create or transform those to whom they are . . . told and alter the capacity of the initiand's being so that he becomes capable of performing the tasks of the new status ahead of him."[4] Because they are told in a sacred context and deal with sacred beings, myths are the timeless handmaiden of religion. They are the fertile seedbeds from which grew the sacred books of the great religions of later civilizations.[5]

A Comprehensive Definition of Religion
The anthropologist Clifford Geertz, a foremost contributor in this field, has recently defined religion as:

1. A system of symbols which acts to
2. establish powerful, persuasive and long-lasting moods and motivations in men by
3. formulating conceptions of a general order of existence and
4. clothing these conceptions with such an aura of factuality that
5. the moods and motivations seem uniquely realistic.[6]

What Geertz is saying is that religion is a system of transformation in which conceptions of order and the denial of chaos, along with a belief in justice and morality in the face of injustice and evil, are passionately affirmed as dominating reality in the face of contrary evidence. Through symbolic transformations, the inchoate human sense of order and moral rightness becomes convincingly affirmed for the believer who bears the imprint of the symbols.

We shall now try to make this clearer with a single interpretive example: the drama of the Okipa ceremony of the Mandan Indians of the upper Plains region in what is now South Dakota. Although the Okipa ceremony and its accompanying myths made up but one part of a fabulously rich myth-ceremonial system of the Mandans and explained only a part of their world and life to them, we believe it will serve our purposes, for it was indeed the greatest and most spectacular of all Plains Indian religious rites. It is necessary to present an extended account in this case, for only so is it possible to convey the sense of emic feel and etic analysis of the complex.

Mandan Culture

One may think of the Mandans as the Parisians of the Plains. Their villages were centers of cultural sophistication and intertribal trade for all the northern Plains area. Their archaeological tradition goes back a thousand years to the Initial Middle Missouri (River) version of the prehistoric Plains Village Tradition.[7]

The subsistence base of Mandan culture was, equally, intensive horticulture (maize, squash, and tobacco growing in the bottoms of the Missouri River and its tributaries) and buffalo hunting (without the aid of the horse). The climax of Mandan culture was reached between 1738, when the Assinneboines led LaVerendrye's party of French traders to the Mandan villages, and 1782, when a decimating series of smallpox epidemics began the destruction which Sioux attacks completed by 1860. Even before the arrival of the French with their European trade goods, the Mandans were prosperous producers and traders, exchanging surplus corn and beautifully dressed and ornamented hide robes for meat and furs brought in by foot nomads from farther south and west.

Nonetheless, theirs was a precarious existence. Their fixed villages of large earth lodges were well fortified against marauding attackers. Equally important, corn raising in North Dakota has always been unpredictable.

[4]*Ibid.*, p. 577.
[5]For example, see J. G. Frazer, *Folklore in the Old Testament.*
[6]C. Geetz, "Religion as a Cultural System," in W. A. Lessa and E. Z. Vogt (eds.), *Reader in Comparative Religion* (2d ed.), p. 206.

[7]See D. J. Lehmer, *Introduction to Middle Missouri Archeology.*

The Mandan had much to cope with, and in the course of a thousand years of experience developed the ideology and ritual to manage it.

Finally, we should note that Mandan social organization was based on matrilocal households, matrilineal clans, and a dual organization of a Sky and an Earth moiety, symbolizing the twofold nature of the subsistence base upon which their survival depended.

The Moiety Symbolism   The Earth People, also called Those-Below, People-Below, and Corn People, were believed to have once lived under the ground, later emerging from a hole in the earth, bringing the corn plant with them. Whenever an Okipa ceremonial lodge was built, the Earth People placed yellow corn under the postholes on their side of the Okipa lodge. They owned all the corn medicine bundles, which had power over growing plants, and also the priesthoods which carried secret knowledge of the origin myths and how to perform the elaborate corn ceremonies. The corn bundles and their accompanying priesthoods were *inherited* from priest to sister's son (matrilaterally) within the clans which were within the Corn, or Earth People, moiety. Without their intervention no corn would grow.

The Sky People [Those-Above] belonged to six clans named after birds and animals. They were symbolically related to the creatures of the animal world, and they planted mats of buffalo hair under the posts on their side of the Okipa lodge.

They owned all the animal medicine bundles, which had power over buffaloes, antelope, birds, etc. They owned the priesthoods which carried secret knowledge of the origin myths and how to perform the ceremonies which controlled the animal world. Thus the double-dual nature (above/below and animal/plant) of their mythically based concept of the universe and of their livelihood was fundamentally built into the social structure and the medicine bundles which controlled their tribal well-being.

The Mandan Theory of Power   The Mandan image of man was one of inherent lack of any personal aptitudes. "I claim no power for myself," a Mandan would say, "I have no power except what my sacred objects have promised me."[8]

Power could primarily be acquired from three sources: (1) inheritance and purchase of clan-owned medicine bundles and the priestly knowledge which went with them; this was the main road to prestige status; (2) the personal vision quest in which one fasted, chopped off segments of fingers, and cut out strips of one's own flesh as offerings to the spirit beings; and (3) "walking with the buffalo," an act in which a young man asked an older power holder to have ritual sex relations with the young man's wife. The woman, wearing a buffalo shirt, played the role of a female bison: the vessel of power from which a man could draw strength, ability, and success.

Like the Cheyennes (who surely got the idea from the Mandans), the Mandans believed that the energy available to any individual was limited and was steadily used up. A man went on only four war parties and went "walking" no more than four times—his powers were then exhausted.

Psychological Factors in the Power Concept   A few fortunate individuals received power through adoption by a supernatural being without being aware of it. This accounted for the rare successful achievers who had no important medicine bundles, inherited or individual. Thus the general power theory was not invalidated by their successes.

A Mandan was born empty. He had to strive and struggle hard to establish himself. His need for achievement exceeded that of *all* other tribal populations rated by David McClelland in his comparative analysis of achievement motivation.[9] For the Mandan male, the absolute test of his worthiness to

[8]A. W. Bowers, *Mandan Social and Ceremonial Organization,* p. 336.
[9]D. C. McClelland, *The Achieving Society,* p. 66.

succeed came in his performance in the torture rites of the Okipa.

The Male Syndrome The Mandan was born into a mother-dominated, semi-subterranean earth lodge in which his father was an outsider. His inherited bundles came from his mother's brother, and were paid for not by himself, but by his wife's brothers and sisters (lineage siblings). They owned his medicine bundles. He, in turn, had to pay them for his rights to the bundles. For everything he learned, every song, every technique, every ritual act, he had to pay in goods. Women did, too. Nothing came for nothing, either from parents or friends. With no striving to win the help of relatives and friends, with no uncanny trading and skillful hunting on his own part to get the goods to buy power, a Mandan remained—nothing. The Mandan male became the manipulator of goods, external things, and of medicine power which was usually not his own.

In actual purchases he had to surrender his wife to a ceremonial "father." Only so could he help his wife maintain a good home, keep his family in good health, and be himself successful in war and hunt. "The sexual act was tantamount to intercourse with the buffaloes. . . ."[10] So even when acting as a ceremonial father, the sexually giving male was nothing in his own right.

In the myths, the great supernaturals of Mandan society were born of virgins who conceived by supernatural means. The mate was not required in their procreation.

In psychodynamic terms, the Mandan male had to deal with a culturally engendered sense of worthlessness and self-hatred. Hostility to the father, who possessed his mother, is indicated. The ceremonial "fathers" who substituted for him as potent buffaloes with his wives, would be included; so also, his mother's brother, who had sexual rights in a maternal nephew's wife and from whom the younger man had to buy the hereditary medicine bundles on which his ultimate standing in the society would depend. Internalization of tribal values led to repression of sexual and aggressive aims in favor of manipulatory striving for externals—goods, medicine bundles, and priestly office. Repressed hostility and sense of self-worth found orgiastic outlet in the extreme sadism and masochism of the Okipa, to be described below.

For the male there were delayed rewards in fraternity membership in the graded societies, but not in war. Remember, after being used on four war parties his fighting power was normally depleted. He could become a village chief, but in this there was little political authority. Unlike the Comanche, he could find no rewards in the conquest of women. That avenue was not available to him. The greatest ultimate rewards were in the ritual and ceremonial roles that would come with bundle priesthoods, but these rewards were long deferred. And first there was the Okipa rite to be surmounted.

The Female Syndrome Woman's personal worth in Mandan society was clear. She was the generator of life and the transmitter of vital power upon whom her husband had to depend. A woman's kin bought a man's bundles for her husband—bundles, the rights to which he inherited through his mother's clan. Women were the owners of the houses in which men lived all their lives. The psychosymbolic implications of the lodge as earth-womb are strong and clear. Women were not only the corn growers; they were also the symbolic bison from whom men drew their war and hunting powers. The Mandan woman had little cause for self-doubt.

How, then, did these deep-lying factors project themselves into world view and religion? How was the religious system of myth, ritual, and action which support Mandan society translated into ". . . the ability of its symbols to formulate a world in which those values, as well as the forces opposing their realization, are fundamental ingredients"?[11]

---

[10]Bowers, *op. cit,* p. 336.

[11]C. Geertz, "Ethos, World View and the Analysis of Social Symbols" in A. Dundes (ed.), *Every Man His Way,* p. 309.

How did this complex system impel men to a manageable and effective adulthood?

The Okipa Myth

The essence of the sacred Okipa myth (distilled to its minimum) is as follows:

Lone Man wandered for a long time in an unconscious state. When he became conscious, his first thoughts were, "Who am I? Where did I come from?"

He retraced his steps until he came to a plant on which was a bug. Was the plant or the bug his mother? No answer. Later he came upon Coyote, the First Creator, who had made the world. They argued over their relative ages (Coyote won) and then they decided to fix up the earth, which was too sandy and wet. They made it as it is today and went their separate ways.

Lone Man met the first buffalo, from whom he received tobacco (the sacred herb).

After he had traveled all over the land, he decided it should have people on it. He created a man and a woman from the ends of his own ribs. In time, through intermarriage of their offspring, their number increased to form a large village, of which Lone Man was the protector-adviser. However, the people kept calling him back from his wanderings so much for advice that he said he would only send the South Wind to them instead of appearing himself.

Next, the Sky People arrived—and the Corn People (each event accounted for in separate myths)—until there were five separate villages.

Lone Man returned and liked what he saw, so he decided he should be reborn as one of the people. He picked a virgin to be his mother but failed to get into her womb as a seed of corn. Later, he made himself into the kidney fat of a buffalo, which she ate and so conceived. Lone Man grew up to be the Buffalo Spirit.

Another spirit man was born of a virgin in another village. This was Hoita, the Spotted Eagle. He grew up to be the Eagle Spirit and a rival of Lone Man. In anger at Lone Man, Hoita enclosed all the living animals and birds inside Dog Den Butte, which lies east of the Missouri River and north of Bismarck, North Dakota. The Mandans starved.

Lone Man got into the cave by various stratagems and learned the Animal (Buffalo) Dance, or Okipa, by means of which Hoita had called all the animals into the cave. He had a young Mandan, acting as his son, impersonate Hoita in the dance. Hoita released the buffalo and said that thereafter he would work with Lone Man for the good of the people.

Later, Lone Man got three turtle-effigy drums made of hide for the Okipa ceremony from the Great Turtle Spirit. To save the Mandan from the flood that would be sent by Maniga, a mythological chief of another tribe, Lone Man put a cedar post, symbolizing himself, in the center of the village in which he lived. He put a cedar plank palisade around it, like a fortification. The planks were tied with willow withes above which water could never rise. The post and palisade protected the village from floods.

Origin Myth of Oxinhede, the Foolish (Evil) One   A virgin Mandan girl was impregnated by a shadow (the Sun). She gave birth to a hyperactive black baby, called Oxinhede. Nobody could do anything with him. He was always jumping and running about. When he got to be a little older, he was given a bow and arrows. With these he killed the sacred snakes and many other holy things. He would not stay away from sacred things, always molesting them. He was known as the Foolish, or Evil, One. Although the people liked him, the Spirits of Sacred Things decided he had to be killed. And this was done.

The Okipa: A Ritual Drama in Three Acts and an Epilogue

The Okipa was first observed in 1832 by George Catlin, who painted his visual impressions and published his written observations in 1833, 1841, and 1867.[12]

The description of the Okipa which follows here is presented as a synoptic scenario, so to speak, of the great "Passion Play" of the Mandans, which took five days and nights to perform. It was put on every summer in each of the villages, if possible. The producer of each Okipa performance was a man of a wealthy family who had managed to accumulate large amounts of food and fine goods to be given away in connection with the rite. He was called the Okipa Maker. Primary roles were played by chosen impersonators of Lone Man, Hoita, and the Foolish One. Owners of appropriate bundles performed as Buffalo Bulls, Beavers, Wolves, Bears, etc. (all the creatures who controlled the animal powers on which the Mandan depended). Other officiants beat the three turtle drums. Two masked priests performed as surgeons. A score or more of young men played the roles of sacrificial initiates. Major bundle holders painted the actors.

Act I. The Father Figure: First Day   At dawn of the first day, the chiefs and medicine priests were called to the Okipa ceremonial lodge. At sunrise, the figure of Lone Man approached from the south. The Blackmouth fraternity met him at the village gate and reverentially led him to the lodge where he was solemnly received by the chiefs and priests. In an archaic tongue Lone Man retold them all the myths of his life when he was alive among the Mandan. That done, throughout the day he walked about the village, collecting bone knives with which the skin of the initiates would be pierced and their finger joints severed. In return he gave them buffalo meat. Women, children, and dogs were confined in their lodges, for this was the time of the male, the father figure. At various places around the

village, Lone Man gave orations on the origins of the people, their struggles against floods and starvation, reminding them of how he had given them all the things to make life better.

At dusk, he retired to the Okipa lodge. Soon after, the sacrificial initiates (boys from eight years of age to men of thirty-five) entered to begin their fasting, while Lone Man ate buffalo meat.

The meal ended, Lone Man transferred his pipe, the symbol of his power, to the Okipa Maker. Hoita was next called forward by Lone Man, who exhorted him to supervise the Animal Dance and see that it was performed exactly as it had been when Hoita kept the animals captive in Dog Den Butte. Lone Man's work was done; he quietly left to return to his home in the south. Immediately, the dancing began—in the lodge as it had in the cave in Dog Den Butte.

Interpretive Comment   Lone Man returned to the Mandan as an asexual, benign father figure, the designer of the Mandan life style, the bestower of buffalo, the bringer of all animal spirits from whom vital medicine power was derived. He brought the turtle drums on which the world rests. He reasserted the authenticity of all the symbolic acts which legitimated the Mandan view and way of life. With the transfer of his pipe, he bestowed his active power on the Okipa Maker, called upon Hoita to do his part, and so retired from the immediate affairs of men. He became an otiose deity who might be appealed to from afar, but who left the management of the affairs of the universe to lesser executive gods (Hoita and the Okipa Maker) and to human beings who were now on their own.

Act II. The Male Principle Conquered: Second, Third, and Fourth Days   Throughout the second day, the eight Buffalo Bull dancers emerged eight times from the lodge to dance in the plaza (see Figure 29-1). The Okipa Maker took a position at the plank wall around the Lone Man cedar post in the center of the

[12]The 1867 account, George Catlin's *O-kee-pa: A Religious Ceremony and Other Customs of the Mandans,* is now available in a 1967 reprint by Yale University Press. In this summary description, we rely mostly on Catlin and A. W. Bowers, *Mandan Social and Ceremonial Organization.*

plaza. There he wept and beseeched Lone Man to help the people. The presence of Lone Man was now an ungraven image—a faceless idol.

Throughout the morning the animal impersonators and sacrificians were being painted. Each was first prepared by an old man who tightly tied the prepuce over the head of each initiate's sex organ with sinew. Then he obliterated the whole genital area with clay plaster. The impersonators were then meticulously painted with symbolic designs over their entire bodies.[13]

The third day was called "Everything Comes Back Day." All the creatures who inhabited the earth with Lone Man and Hoita emerged from the lodge to do their mimetic dances along with the Bull dancers. "They all had some peculiar and appropriate songs, which they constantly chanted and sang during the dances."[14] Day and Night, as they were in Lone Man's time, danced, too.

In the meantime, in the lodge, the initiates were being prepared. Each one had selected a man from his father's clan to perform the operation. With a serrated knife to make a jagged wound, the clan father cut four holes over the shoulder blades or breasts and pushed two wooden skewers through the flesh. These were for the thongs by which the initiate would be suspended. More skewers were put into the legs; buffalo skulls would be suspended from them.

On the fourth day, the Bulls and other ani-

[13]See Bowers, *op. cit.,* pp. 131–132, for a detailed list of the impersonators.

[14]Catlin, *op. cit.,* p. 57.

Fig. 29-1   The scene in the village plaza during the Okipa ceremony. At the extreme left is the Foolish One, in spotted paint, with bald-headed staff. Bull dancers are performing in the foreground. At the center of the scene, the Okipa Maker may be seen leaning against the plank wall which surrounds the sacred cedar post. (Courtesy of the American Museum of Natural History.)

mal dancers "came out" to dance twelve times. The Okipa Maker was again at the Lone Man post, crying and praying to Lone Man.

In the course of one dance, a crazy figure appeared, leaping and running zigzag across the prairie from the west. He rushed in among the spectators as women and children scattered in shrieking alarm. It was the Foolish (Evil) One (Figure 29-A). His body was painted black with white circles. He had a grotesque phallus. He jumped over sacred paraphernalia. He burlesqued a buffalo bull in intercourse with a man masquerading as a woman. He advanced threateningly toward other women. They screamed in terror. The Okipa Maker left the Lone Man post, advancing deliberately, Lone Man's pipe in hand. Thrusting it in the Foolish One's face, he paralyzed him, while the crowd of spectators hissed and groaned at the sacrilegious one as the Animal Dance proceeded unheedingly. The Foolish One controlled, the Okipa Maker returned to his prayers and supplications at the cedar post.

Three times the Foolish One recovered and assaulted the women. Three more times he was subdued by the Okipa Maker. Each time the women became less terrified and began closing in on the Foolish One. After the fourth time, he turned his attention to the Buffalo dancers, simulating mating with four of them. His energy expended, one woman threw yellow ocher in his face. Others smothered him from all sides. The leader of the women took his mock phallus from him. He collapsed within himself, whimpered, and bolted for the prairie, pursued by hissing, screaming women, who pelted him with filth.

In triumph the women returned, escorting the woman who had deprived the Foolish One of his power. She mounted the entrance to the Okipa lodge and took command. In a long declamation she let it be known that *she* held the power of creation, the power of life and death over the people, and all control over the buffalo. They would come or stay away at her command, as *she* pleased.

She ordered the animal dancers to stop dancing. She directed the chiefs to go back in the lodge and witness the sacrifices of the young men which should now begin. She also demanded the most beautiful dress in the village, and this was dutifully given to her by the Okipa Maker.

Interpretive Comment   The turtle drums symbolized the eternal and deathless continuity of life. The dancing animals reaffirmed the constructive power of Lone Man and all associated with him. The lamentations of the Okipa Maker in his prayers to Lone Man reiterated the theme of dependency on the far-removed father figure.

Into this scene of variegated order came Chaos—the Black One, the Male Principle Uncontrolled. It is Foolish One, the sacrilegious scoffer at Mandan ethos. In his phallic grotesqueries, the unbridled male id, he terrified both women and children. Only the calm, controlled male power of Lone Man could master him.

Finally, the Female Principle boldly took over. With yellow clay signifying corn pollen and the People Below, women subdued Chaos and mocked him. In smashing the symbol of his exaggerated sexuality, they destroyed all his power and banished him from Mandan life, even as the spirit beings had killed him in the long ago.

The Female Principle was now dominant; even Lone Man (in the form of the Okipa Maker) was subordinate to the imperious control of the symbolic Mother of All.

Act III. In Limbo: Fifth Day   With all the initiates painted and ready, two of them were led to a position beneath the smokehole in the roof of the Okipa lodge. A war shield and four buffalo skulls were tied to the skewers in the skin of each one. By means of rawhide ropes fastened to the skewers in his chest or back, each man was drawn upward three or four feet off the floor—suspended in limbo betwixt heaven and earth, while his body was spun crazily around until he fainted (Figure 29-2).

Onlookers cried out, "Dead! Dead!" Lowered to the floor, the two initiates lay lifeless. On recovering consciousness, each made his way to a buffalo skull to offer his little finger in thanks. Others then went through the same process.

Thereafter, in groups of six, the revived initiates came out to run around the Lone Man post until the buffalo skulls, skewered to their legs and dragging on the ground, tore loose (Figure 29-3). Then, and only then, could they make their ways unassisted to their homes.

Interpretive Comment   The initiates had been in limbo since first they entered the lodge. Their sex had been neutralized with sinew and clay. They neither ate nor drank. They had retired from normalcy. Suspension betwixt heaven and earth is limbo. The rites of torture were clear in their intent—the ultimate

proof of worth and self-esteem. For the sacrificer, the masochism meant, "I surmount everything and achieve pleasure [goals]." For the priests and onlookers, the sadism of the act meant, "I triumph." With symbolic death the initiate's suffering was ended. The insufferability of life was made sufferable. He returned from limbo to creep back to the symbolic womb of his maternal earth lodge for recovery and reconstitution as a matured male, ready for marriage and the manipulation of the bundles he might now acquire.

Epilogue. Woman Triumphant: Fifth Night

The O-kee-pa having ended, and night having approached, several old men . . . perambulated the village . . . announcing that "the whole government of the Mandans was in the hands of one woman—she who had disarmed the Evil Spirit, and to whom they were to look during the coming year for buf-

Fig. 29-2   In the Okipa lodge. Suspended initiates are whirled with sticks while turtle drums are beaten at the right foreground. At the left, a performer is offering a finger joint for sacrifice. (George Catlin, **O-kee-pa, A Religious Ceremony and Other Customs of the Mandans,** *John C. Ewers [ed.]. Copyright © 1967 by Yale University Press.)*

faloes to supply them with food; . . . that the chiefs on that night were old women; that they had nothing to say. . . ."[15]

The Bull dancers and the priests of the Okipa were invited by the Chieftess to a Feast of the Buffalo before the Lone Man pole. Ten young women came with her. All other people had to remain secluded in their lodges. One by one, the women led the men onto the prairie to mate as buffaloes, until each man bought his release with a small payment. So ended the Okipa.

Interpretive Comment   It was driven home to all Mandans that this was indeed a matrilocal, matrilineal, matrifocal, matridominated society. Men were an integral but subordinate part, while the Female Principle was the locus

of power. Buffalo hunting was important to Mandan survival, but it was the female bison who was acknowledged as the major factor in the reproduction of the herds. Nonetheless, for the Mandans it was horticulture which most uniquely marked their character in the northern Plains. Anybody could hunt buffalo but only very special people could grow corn. And horticulture was associated with women and the Female Principle of life and social structure. This, all Mandans had to learn and accept. This was the central focus of Mandan religion. This was the message of the Okipa. From this there could be no departure.

As Victor Turner states for the closing of all mythological cycles, "The interstructural transition stage is over. Creative chaos has become created cosmos."[16]

[15]Catlin, *op. cit.*, p. 69.

[16]V. W. Turner, "Myth and Symbol" (*International Encyclopedia of the Social Sciences*, vol. 10, 1968), p. 581.

Fig. 29-3   The finale of the Okipa ceremony. Initiates are running and being dragged about the Lone Man post until their shields and the buffalo skulls tear loose. (George Catlin, **O-kee-pa, A Religious Ceremony and Other Customs of the Mandans,** *John C. Ewers [ed.]. Copyright © 1967 by Yale University Press.)*

SUMMARY

In its most comprehensive sense, religion is today viewed by anthropologists as a system of symbolic transformations of chaotic reality through which human beings provide themselves with conceptions of a general order of existence which they are moved to accept as true and real. The moods and convictions which are generated by the symbolic experiences of religion reinforce the general world views of each society and contribute to the motivational ethic of its people. Religion and its associated myths are directed toward stating the meaning of life and why and on what terms human beings should seek fulfillment.

Religion is much more than a belief in spirit beings—or gods, although these are an essential part of all religions.

Mythology is an intrinsic part of religion. It deals with the character and activities of sacred beings and tells how things were transformed by their acts from their primordial to their present state of being. Myth justifies the existing order of the universe and of society. It validates their truth. It specifies the charters of social institutions (in Malinowski's theory).

Myths are also important components of transition rites; they restate the basic postulates of the society; they tell what must be done, in limbo and in the reincorporated status of the new individual personality that is achieved after an act of transition is achieved.

In the Mandan Indian religion, which is used to exemplify the manifestation of myth and symbolic ritual as religious expression, the annual Okipa ceremony had the following features and background.

The Mandan had a subsistence base of buffalo hunting and intensive horticulture. Their social structure included matrilocal residence, matrilineal descent, with clans and moieties (dual organization).

The Mandan believed that men were born without any personal aptitudes. Capabilities were derived only from sacred objects contained in medicine bundles. Major bundles were inherited within the matriclan but had to be purchased with the aid of the wife's clanmates. Special powers could be obtained on the vision quest and through lending one's wife to a power holder ("walking with the buffalo"). Woman was viewed as the generator of life and as the symbolic source through which a man drew his power.

In the religious mythology of the Okipa, the world was created by Coyote. Lone Man, however, is the important figure. He created the first couple from whom the Mandan are descended. He left the Mandan and then rejoined them as a human being. When Hoita locked up all the animals in Dog Den Butte, Lone Man obtained their release, and with it the Animal Dance of the Okipa. Lone Man obtained the three turtle drums. He also overcame Maniga, the Flood Maker and killer of Mandans. When Lone Man left the people, he placed a cedar pole representing himself in the center of each village plaza. It had a plank wall which kept back the floods.

The Foolish One was born a sacrilegious prankster, for which he was killed by the Sacred Beings.

The Okipa reenacts all these mythic happenings, except that the Foolish One is destroyed by women in the Okipa. Lone Man is a remote, benevolent father figure. The Okipa Maker becomes his symbolic substitute for the duration of the ceremony. Hoita becomes Lone Man's "executive counterpart." The Foolish One symbolizes the male id running wild.

The initiates, who are symbolically desexed and hung in limbo, submit to torture and "death." They are killed as immature males, and return to their mothers' or wives' earth lodges to emerge, on recovery from their ordeal, as reconstituted adult males who understand and acknowledge things as they are.

The Okipa ends with the symbolic triumph of the woman who destroyed the Foolish One, followed by the Feast of the Buffalo in which the chiefs and medicine men of the tribe must give some of their power to the female dancers, who will pass it on to their husbands.

The Okipa ceremony established Mandan dependence on animals, while asserting the superior importance of horticulture and of women who were the gardeners and the mistresses of life.

SUGGESTED READINGS

Bascom, W. R., *The Sociological Role of the Yoruba Cult-group* (American Anthropological Association, Memoir 63, 1944). An excellent study of a West African manifestation of religious organization.

Bowers, A. W., *Mandan Social and Ceremonial Organization* (1950). Pages 111–163 present a somewhat disorganized, and therefore difficult-to-read, account of the Okipa ceremony. Nonetheless, it is an essential source.

Bunzel, R., *Introduction to Zuni Ceremonialism* (Bureau of American Ethnology, Annual Report 47, 1932). Gives an idea of how pervasive and complex a highly developed primitive religious system can be.

Catlin, G., *O-kee-pa: A Religious Ceremony and Other Customs of the Mandans* (1867; Yale University Press, 1967). The first eye-witness account of the Okipa, it also contains color prints of Catlin's original paintings. Should be perused in connection with this chapter.

Geertz, C., "Religion: Anthropological Study" (*International Encyclopedia of the Social Sciences,* vol. 13, 1968), pp. 398–406. A brief summary.

Lessa, W. A., and E. Z. Vogt, *Reader in Comparative Religion* (2d ed., 1965). Parts 3, "Myth and Ritual," 4, "Symbolism," and 12, "New Methods of Analysis" contain very valuable papers by Geertz, Kluckhohn, Lévi-Strauss, and others.

Turner, V. W., "Myth and Symbol" (*International Encyclopedia of the Social Sciences,* vol. 10, 1968), pp. 576–582. Offers a lucid analysis of myths and structural transformations.

Chapter 30

Supernatural Beliefs and Practices

Religion is manifest not only through symbolism and tribal ceremony. It also permeates the thought and feeling of individuals as individuals; it expresses itself through spells and incantations; it blends into magic and sorcery; it is managed by specialists—the shaman and the priest; and it may be organized into cults. Each of these manifestations will now be treated in turn.

Animism

Although the overall purpose of religion is, as presented in the last chapter, symbolic transformation of man's perception of the universe, thus creating a conviction of order and purpose to society and individual alike, all religions encompass manifestations of *animism* and *mana.*

Animism (L. *anima,* soul, spirit), as defined by the nineteenth-century English anthropologist Sir Edward Burnett Tylor, is the belief in spirit beings.[1] They are known by many names: plant and animal spirits, souls, ghosts, goblins, poltergeists, genies, trolls, sprites, elves, pixies, leprechauns, fairies, witches, demons, devils, angels, and gods. Their essential quality is their ethereal embodiment; they are beings without real flesh and blood—nonmaterial, but real enough for those who believe in them.

As spirits, they are uninhibited by the limitations of physical matter, by the weaknesses of human or animal flesh. They transcend matter, time, and space. They are supernatural. It is this that makes them wonderful, mysterious.

Tylor's Theory In his remarkable study (1871), Tylor examined many manifestations of animism among primitives, but he was interested in more than just describing its forms. Tylor was essentially an evolutionist. For him the ultimate question was: "How and why did human beings create the concept of spirit beings?" Somewhere along the line in prehistoric times, the human mind peopled the universe with spirits. What led it to do so?

Tylor saw the origin of animism in the phenomena of dreams, of life and of death. Dreams are a form of hallucination, an illusory experience. But that men dream is an empirical fact. In dreams we transcend reality. We soar to great heights of attainment and pleasure; we experience horrible happenings; we relive the past and anticipate the future; we visit places once visited and those where our feet have never yet been; we commune with the dead and departed or with the living who are far distant. Time, space, and limitations of the body do not hinder us—in our dreams.

Yet, in sleep or in coma, the body does not leave its resting place. We wake where we lie down to rest—except in the case of the unfortunate somnambulist. The body has not performed the miracles dreamed, but it is hard, even for the sophisticate, not to take dream experiences as real. To the primitive and, indeed, to many civilized men, the dream experience *is* reality.

The Soul Concept Primitive man reflected and concluded that there were two parts to man: the bodily self of mortal flesh and the spiritual *alter ego,* the soul. The soul concept is the root of animism. It is a universal concept.

The soul is, in itself, quite intangible. In the language of many peoples, the word

[1]E. B. Tylor, *Primitive Culture,* vol. 1, p. 424.

"soul" is synonymous with "shadow" or "shade." Intangible though it is, it is oftentimes perceptible in the image of the body it normally inhabits.

The soul is the vital force. Its presence animates the body; its departure stills it. It is in the stillness of sleep that the soul goes wandering. Man's restlessness is of the spirit, not the body.

The long sleep that is death comes when the sojourning soul does not return. The body that is the vessel for the soul has no further function once its soul has abandoned it. Disintegration follows. Illness is due to intrusive corruption of the soul or to soul loss.

This, according to Tylor, is the logic of the soul concept—in part.

Man does not live alone. The beasts of wood and field, the fowl of the air, and the fishes of the waters are also endowed with vitality. So too are the plants. By means of analogical reasoning, primitive man attributes souls to them also, as the cause of their vitality. Yet he does not do this completely by false analogy, for animals appear in dreams, even as do men. Thus, in most primitive belief, not only man but all living beings possess souls (Figure 30-1).

Souls after death may become ghosts or free spirits wholly disembodied. They live on in the world of man, within his very community or in a special realm, which the spirits of living men may on occasion visit or from which souls may come to visit the living.

Whether or not the concept of free spirits could arise only from the soul concept, as Tylor thought, or whether early man was imaginatively capable of creating the spirit concept out of mere nothingness, we shall

never know. It is enough that pure spirits inhabit the believing minds of people in all societies and that these imaginary beings are thought to be beyond the laws of nature. They and souls are living elements in all religions.

Nature Worship   The attribution of spirit qualities to plants and objects then produced, according to Tylor, what we call *nature worship*. From this came totemism and the creation of species deities, i.e., the deification not of persons (ancestor worship) but of animals

Fig. 30-A   A Plains Indian shaman in ritual regalia of medicine wands and fans, with bear cub apron and medicine herbs at his waist. (Painting by George Catlin, 1832. National Collection of Fine Arts, Smithsonian Institution.)

Fig. 30-1   A Tsimshian, Northwest Coast of North America, shaman's rattle. The raven who forms the body of the rattle possesses the secret of life, while the tongue of any creature contains the life spirit. The beaver, which stands on the stomach of a man who has just died, is receiving the supernatural power of the shaman. (Courtesy of the American Museum of Natural History.)

and plants (Figure 30-2). From these practices, Tylor derived the higher polytheism of the later barbarians, with its sky, earth, rain, thunder, lightning, fire, wind, water, sun, and moon gods, as well as gods of agriculture, hunting, birth, war, and death.

What ethnography has to teach of that great element of the religion of mankind, the worship of well and lake, brook and river, is simply this—that what is poetry to us was philosophy to early man; that to his mind water acted not by laws of force, but by life and will. . . .[2]

Tylor's notions on the origins of monotheism and the Supreme Deity will be noted in the discussion of High Gods at the close of this chapter (pages 591–592).

Of Tylor's anthropological theory of religion, it may be said that it suffers some inadequacies, but in the main we can concur with Lowie's judgment:

His theory is avowedly a psychological interpretation pure and simple, but inasmuch as it not only explains the empirical observations, but operates exclusively with facts like death, dreams and visions, all of which demonstrably exercise a strong influence on the minds of primitive men, it must be

conceded to have a high degree of probability. I, for one, certainly have never encountered any rival hypothesis that could be considered a serious competitor.[3]

Like all evolutionary theories that try to formulate the details of nonmaterial culture in prehistoric times, Tylor's theory is speculative and unverifiable. But, stripped of its evolutionary ordering of the data, it stands, as Lowie has said, as a valuable general analysis of a large part of the religious attitudes and behavior of men. Animism, however, is not the whole story. There is also *mana,* which calls for theoretical explanation.

Mana

Supernaturalism does not find its only expression in beliefs in spirit beings; there are also beliefs in the existence of supernatural forces that do not emanate from any kind of being. Such forces are expressed as special attributes of things, much as the force of gravity is related to objects that have mass.

[2]*Ibid.,* vol. II, p. 209.

[3]R. H. Lowie, *Primitive Religion,* p. 108.

Following the suggestion of another early student of primitive religion, R. R. Marett (1866–1943), anthropologists call it *mana,* a word derived from the languages of Melanesia where the concept of mana is strong and clear in native life.

Mana is a force, but not a vitalistic force. It exists as a supernatural attribute of persons and things. Above all, it is the exceptional power to do things that are unusual. Mana is therefore manifest in the unusual, when the unusual is not the work of spirits.

Extraordinary aptitudes of men are explained in terms of mana. The master craftsman in Polynesia excels in his skill because he possesses mana. The learned pundit excels in lore and knowledge because he possesses mana. The mighty warrior excels in the killing of men because he possesses mana. The outstanding healer, the expert canoeman, and any others who stand above their fellow men do so because of personal possession or control of mana. Mana, though it is an impersonal force, can be manifest in and through persons, as well as in stock and stone. The queerly shaped or unusually marked stone may be believed to possess

miracle-working power. This is its mana. The canoe that can outdistance all others, the song that heals, the war club that smashes more than a normal quota of skulls, the talisman that in itself brings good luck—all these have power, power that is mana.

The power that is extraordinary is not mundane force. It does not follow the regular laws of ordinary technologies or skills. Like the power of spirits, it transcends the natural. Mana is supernatural.

Religion and Magic

Man acts on the basis of his beliefs. Animism and mana are attributes of the subjective aspects of supernaturalism. Religion and magic are concepts based upon the ways in which man behaves in relation to the supernatural forces in which he believes. They constitute two forms of the external objectification of beliefs. The distinction rests on man's assessment of the motivating forces behind the supernatural. Is man subordinate to the caprice and will of the supernatural beings to whom psychological characteristics are at-

Fig. 30-2   Nature worship. In an Ainu village on Hokkaido, Japan, a family headman gives a prayer of thanks to the god of fishing for the first salmon of the autumn. (Ruiko Y. Ante.)

tributed? If his answer is "yes," his dealings with these beings, and theirs with him, will be religious in nature. Can man under certain conditions dominate and control the supernatural forces, be they animistic or manaistic? If his answer is "yes," his dealings with the supernatural will be magical in nature.

Prayer and magic are the two basic techniques of dealing with the supernatural. The first is a means of seeking spiritual rapport on a basis of subordination to animistic beings. The second is a technique of gaining external control over supernatural powers, animistic and manaistic. Between these poles, every possible form of interpersonal behavior may find its religious counterpart. As Benedict observed: "There is probably no customary behavior towards one's fellows that is not to be found somewhere as a religious technique."

The only limits on religion are the limits set by imagination and the human physical system. Both allow tremendous scope for variation and elaboration. Hunting is limited by ecology, animal habits, and the physical laws of mechanics in the development of weapons. There are few variants among hunting techniques the world over; not so the varieties of religious experience and practice.

The Religious Attitude   That which distinguishes religion from magic is neither the goodness of one nor the evil of the other, but the state of mind of the believer and his consequent modes of behavior. This is the distinction that was originally pointed out by Sir James G. Frazer.[4] In the religious state of mind, man acknowledges the superiority of the supernatural powers upon whose action his well-being depends. His attitudes are preponderantly those of submission and reverence. The Okipa Maker was a supplicant

to Lone Man throughout the ceremony, while the initiates, according to Catlin, ". . . began crying in the most heartrending tones to the Great Spirit; imploring him to enable them to bear and survive the painful ordeal they were entering on."[5] The objective behavior put forth is manifestly that of beseeching, petition, and appeasement in prayer, offerings, and sacrifice.

> Father have pity on me,
> Father have pity on me,
> I am crying for thirst,
> I am crying for thirst,
> All is gone—I have nothing to eat,
> All is gone—I have nothing to eat.

Such is the tenor of an Arapaho ghost-dance song, "sung to a plaintive tune, sometimes with tears rolling down the cheeks of the dancers."[6] It epitomizes the religious attitude, as does the Lord's Prayer, with its "Hallowed be thy name" (reverence); "Give us this day our daily bread" (petition); "Thine is the Kingdom, the Power and the Glory, forever" (subordination and awe).

"Oh spirits, here, humble in heart, I stand beseeching you" is the opening plaint of the Winnebago on a vision quest.

The Magical Attitude   The magician, on the other hand, believes that he *controls* supernatural power under certain conditions. He has power over power. He feels confirmed in his belief that if he possesses a tested formula and if he executes the formula perfectly, barring outside interference, he will get the results which that formula is specified to give. The supernatural power has no volition or choice of its own. It must respond. The magician works with a confidence similar to that of the student in the laboratory who knows that if he follows the manual instructions correctly, he will obtain a predictable result. The religious attitude and behavior

---

[4]See J. G. Frazer, *The Golden Bough,* chap. 4. Frazer argued a theoretical priority of magic over religion in prehistoric origins. This is a futile and irrelevant problem for which there are no empirical data upon which to base a conclusion.

[5]G. Catlin, *O-kee-pa* (1967 edition), p. 64.

[6]J. Mooney, *The Ghost Dance Religion and the Sioux Outbreak of 1890* (Bureau of American Ethnology, Annual Report 14, 1896), p. 977.

are devout; the magician works with a kind of arrogance—or, at the least, self-assurance.

Magic often does appear to produce the expected results. It seems to meet the pragmatic test. What works is so. At least, it must work in its initial applications, or the magical formula is usually rejected as false or worthless. When magic works, it does so for two reasons: (1) coincidence—if sufficient time is allowed, the desired event may well come to pass—and (2) psychological suggestion—when magic is directed against persons who suspect or fear that they are its objects, hysteria or compulsion grips them; they sicken and often die. Psychologists call this *somatic compliance* and *thanatomania* (the depression of the will to live to the point of extinction). The records of travelers and anthropologists abound with cases from the primitive world. Clinical records reveal many authentic cases among civilized men. Doctors well know the importance of the psychological state of the patient in crucial illness or injury.

Magic also serves its ends by giving the magician and his clients a needed psychological boost. As Malinowski reiterated, magic begins where mechanical technology ends. A Melanesian knows that magic cannot dig the soil in which he must plant his yams, so he does his own digging. He knows that he must hoe to keep down weeds, so he hoes. But he also knows that, no matter how great his skill, pests, foraging animals, and climate are beyond his technological ability to control. Yet these and unknown factors affect his crop for better or worse. He desperately needs a good crop. It is the object of his most ardent wish, so he endeavors to control the unknown element by magic or religion, and the confidence they give him quite definitely helps him to outdo himself in achievement of his wished-for goal.[7]

The warrior who believes he has magic invulnerability can surmount fear and leap to heroism far more easily than the man who confronts danger without such support.

Not only does magic actually help the magician is a canny prestidigitator. He simply deceives the credulous with skilled stage dogma of magic is strong, the practitioner often thinks the magical result has come to pass when nothing of the sort has occurred at all. Magic has much in common with daydreaming as a form of wish fulfillment.

Thus, magic, in some of its aspects, is similar to science. When the magician proceeds on the mechanistic assumption that the magical formula is a cause that must produce a given effect, his thinking parallels that of the scientist. His method, however, rests on fantasies. But it may be well to remind ourselves that much scientific belief, formerly useful but now discarded, also rested on similar unrealistic belief. It would, perhaps, be more accurate to call magic a technique based upon different premises.

Finally, it should be noted that magic often appears to work because the primitive magician is a canny prestidigitator. He simply deceives the credulous with skilled stage settings and sleight-of-hand artistry, some of which is really convincing.

It is thus possible analytically to distinguish magic from religion. The difference between the two methods of approach to the supernatural has tremendous social consequences. Religious emphasis on supernaturalism leads to subordination of men to gods and to the power of cult functionaries—the shaman and the priest. Religion is much more readily centralized and organized than magic, which is inherently more individualistic. Although organized religions always use a certain amount of magic in their rituals, churches are implicitly antagonistic to magic, since the magical attitude is incompatible with the religious attitude of submission. The conflict endures through the ages.

Because of its elemental kinship to science, magic is more susceptible to displacement by technological advances than religion is, and

[17] *Cf.* B. Malinowski, *Coral Gardens and their Magic,* vol. 10.

conversely, religion, with its element of personal dependence, is not so readily displaced by an advance in knowledge as magic is. Modern scientists may still hold to their religious faiths, but all will renounce magic.

The Blending of Religion and Magic Primitive man, however, does not greatly concern himself with the analytical distinction between magic and religion. Rather, he blends them as best he can to attain his ends.

The Plains Indian on his vision quest makes himself pitiable in the eyes of the spirits. If they favor him, they give power along with sundry paraphernalia and the ritual wherewith to invoke power. He acquires his power by means of a religious approach to the spirits. Once he has it, he uses it as a magic instrument of control over them. This is well illustrated in an account of the acquisition, use, and loss of supernatural power that a Bannock Indian headman, Running Water, gave the author in the course of his fieldwork in the Snake River Desert of Idaho in 1933:

"A long time ago the Indians around here learned to play poker. I decided I wanted to be able to win at that game, so I went out to seek *poha* [power].

"I went out into the mountains to a place where I knew there were lots of pack rats. I wore only my breechcloth. I ate no food and drank no water.

"Continuously I prayed to the pack rats, 'Oh, pack rats! Here I stand, a poor, helpless human being. Take pity on me! Wherever you go, you gather everything in. That's the way I want to be among my people. I want to be able to gather everything in when I play poker.' For three days and nights I fasted and prayed.

"On the fourth night a big pack rat, the grandfather of all the pack rats, appeared before me. 'Human being,' he said, 'I have heard your prayers. I am taking pity on you. I shall give you my power.

"'Now this is what you must do. When morning comes, scrape up the scale that is formed by our urine on the rocks. Make a small buckskin bag to put it in and wear this always around your neck.

"'Now I will teach you four songs. When you want to use my power wash yourself with dry wood ashes to remove all grease and paint.[8] Sing the four songs. Then when you go in to play poker, you will always win. You will be able to gather everything in, even as I do.'"

These things he did, and, according to his testimony, the power worked with great success until he got careless and cut in on a hand of poker right after doing a war dance—without washing off the paint with dry ashes. The effect nearly killed him, and his power was destroyed forever.

In this experience, Running Water was clearly using the approaches of the religious man. "Oh, pack rats! Here I stand, a poor, helpless human being. Take pity on me!" But he was also to become a magician. With the formula of the songs and the talisman of the urine scale, he automatically gained his ends at will—until he blew up the laboratory by carelessly failing to follow the formula.

Sorcery Sorcery is magic used for antisocial purposes. Magic is in itself amoral, neither good nor bad. It is the uses to which magic is put that determine its moral qualities. Thus, a medicine man or witch doctor, as one who has control over magic, may be thoroughly good in the eyes of his people, or he may be evil, or both. A Shoshone medicine man is called *pohagant,* meaning "one who has power." A sorcerer is called *tidjipohagant,* or "one who uses power evilly."

Sorcery is a form of aggression against fellow beings or their possessions that is not socially approved. Magic may also be used aggressively, but it is not sorcery if its use is a socially recognized privilege-right. This is

---

[8]Among American Indians, grease is held to counteract supernatural power. Thus, an automobile may not be parked too close to the house of an old-time medicine man on some Indian reservations even today.

clearly shown in the attitudes of the Kapauku and the Azande, to take two examples.

Kapauku Sorcery The Kapauku of the highlands of West New Guinea exemplify this clearly in their distinction between *kamu* (approved magic) and *kego* (sorcery). According to Pospisil:

From the functional point of view the broad categories of *kamu* can be divided into curative, preventive, countersorcery, rain-stopping, rain-making, profit-inducing, love-creating and war magic subcategories. The whole variety of these rites may be performed by any Kapauku man or woman. However, there are individuals who have acquired a reputation for being successful in white magical art. The people call these experts *kamu epi me* (lit.: "a man who knows white magic").[9]

Kego tai is the use of magical power to kill another Kapauku. Sorcerers (*kego epi me*) are feared, hated, ostracized, and sometimes executed by the relatives of their supposed victims.

Azande Sorcery Among the Azande of Africa, described by Evans-Pritchard, good magic is *wene ngua* and bad magic is *gbigbita*. Vengeance magic (*bagbuduma*) may be legitimately used to kill a person if the poison oracles used by the sorcerer's kin and those used by their chief both say the alleged sorcerer is guilty. *Pe zunga* magic, which may be used when the perpetrator of homicidal sorcery is not known, is also good. "It is regarded as a judge which seeks out the person who is responsible for the death, and as an executioner which slays him." In the words of the Azande, "it decides cases" and "settles cases as judiciously as princes." Even though its effect is to kill, it is socially approved because it will work only on behalf of a just cause. If there is no just cause, it will return to kill the person who evoked it. The Zande who wants to kill another without just cause can use a

number of forms of *gbigbita* magic, but if he is discovered, he will be executed.[10]

Tabu

Tabu is the inevitable negative element in religion. Supernatural power is implicitly dangerous. It is like fire or a heavy charge of electricity. When under control and directed toward desirable ends, it is beneficent. When out of control, it may well be disastrous. Man cannot get along without fire, and yet he must fight a constant battle against it. Modern civilization cannot function without electricity, but electricity must be handled with insulated tools and gloves.

Spirits and mana are deemed by most people to be absolutely essential forces in the human conception of the universe. They must be manipulated for human ends, but if improperly approached or used, they can react most dangerously. Running Water, the Bannock Indian, was nearly killed by his own pack-rat medicine because he became careless.

Supernatural power, it must be remembered, is above the realm of the ordinary. Because of this, it may not be approached or dealt with casually. It, too, must be handled with rubber gloves. Figuratively, tabus are great "Caution! Handle with Care!" signs. Tabu does not mean *verboten,* in the German sense. Rather, it carries the overtones of the French *défense de toucher.* The sense of awe that Professor Lowie saw as the important component of religion is intimately linked to the psychology that is responsible for the development of tabus.

In content, tabu consists of a series of negative rules, each of which states a form of behavior that will cause a supernatural power to backfire and injure the user. In reality, very few tabued acts are physically or socially

[9]L. Pospisil, *The Kapauku Papuans of West New Guinea,* p. 79.

[10]E. E. Evans-Pritchard, *Witchcraft, Oracles and Magic among the Azande,* pp. 388–389.

dangerous in themselves. This is why rationalistic attempts to explain the Hebraic or Islamic tabus on the eating of pork in terms of hygiene are really beside the point.

Typical of the irrelevance of most tabus was the injunction that went with the war bonnet of the famous Cheyenne chieftain, Roman Nose. His bonnet had the power to give invulnerability in battle. With it Roman Nose rose, unscathed, to fame on the western Plains. One of the rules of the bonnet was that its wearer must not eat any food taken from a dish with an iron utensil. If he did, a bullet or iron-tipped arrow could pierce him, just as the sharp metal pierced the meat, and the protective power of the hat would be nullified until restored through a long and elaborate ceremony of purification and atonement.

Just before the famous Beecher's Island fight with Colonel Forsyth's men on the Republican River of western Nebraska, in 1868, Roman Nose ate as a guest in the camp of the Sioux Indians. When it was pointed out to him that the wife of his host was using a fork in her cooking, he said, "That breaks my medicine." The battle began before Roman Nose could make atonement, so, like Achilles, he sulked in his tent. But under pressure, like Achilles, he donned his war gear, saying, "My food was lifted with an iron tool. I know that I shall be killed today." Roman Nose was killed by a bullet before he had a chance to strike a single blow in the battle.[11]

Violation of a tabu not only nullifies the positive power of medicine but may also bring disaster as a consequence.

The Functions of Tabu   The first function of tabu, as just indicated, is to sustain the awesomeness of the supernatural by reinforcing attitudes of care and mystery and by punishing attitudes of carelessness and profanity in dealing with the supernatural. It helps keep the sacred, sacred.

The second function of tabu is to set off the members of one social group from those of another and to strengthen their sense of solidarity. Just as a traditional hairdo may indicate that the social status of a married woman is different from that of an unmarried girl who has only reached puberty, or as men's hairdos used to set them apart from women, so adherence to special tabus may help set off the medicine man from the ordinary layman. Thus the Hebraic and Islamic tabus on pork help to identify membership in these religious groups, as did abstinence from meat on Friday by Catholics and as does the Mormon tabu on the use of tobacco and the drinking of coffee, tea, or alcoholic beverages.

Third, tabu is an essential ingredient of social control. In Polynesia, whence comes the word "tabu," high-ranking nobles possess mana because of their direct descent from the gods. So potent is their charge of mana that their very persons are surrounded with tabus, as is everything they touch. Sin, in Polynesia as elsewhere, is the violation of a tabu—an act punishable by supernatural sanction.

Not only is tabu applied to the requirements of care in handling supernatural objects, but it also can be, and is, applied to social standards of behavior which are not directly associated with the supernatural but in which, it is held, the supernatural takes an interest.[12] Incest, for example, is commonly subject to supernatural punishment as well as to mundane social sanctions, in most societies.

Religious Specialists

In every primitive society, all the people participate in some aspects of religious observ-

---

[11]A full account of the episode is given in G. B. Grinnell, *The Fighting Cheyennes*, pp. 267–282.

[12]For an excellent example, see A. I. Hallowell, "The Social Function of Anxiety among the Salteaux Indians," in D. G. Haring (ed.), *Personal Character and Cultural Milieu* (3d rev. ed.), pp. 389–403.

ances. Yet, because every society is internally segmented by sex, age, kinship, and marital groupings, access to religious power and the privileges of religious participation are not equally distributed. In the first place, years of experience and learning are necessary before an individual can know enough about basic religious beliefs to be in a position to master religious activities. Children always participate on a lower level.

Religion and magic are sources of power; they are means of influencing or controlling supernatural power, the greatest of all powers. Authority vested in adults is implicitly necessary to the perpetuation of culture. This is a special reason for keeping the heart of religious power in the hands of grownups.

Although women are not uncommonly shamans and priestesses, the centers of religious power are usually vested in men. Male-dominance tendencies lead men to keep access to the supernatural as a vested interest of their own sex. The matrifocal emphasis of Mandan religion was, as we saw, an expression of their matrilineal system and as such would represent a minority of human societies.[13] In more advanced, class-stratified societies, official religious power is almost inevitably an upper-class monopoly, while folk practitioners may operate on a lower level.

Shamans   Within the group of those who qualify for religious power, there are those who achieve an even more intimate access to the supernatural. They become religious specialists. Religion and magic are always so complex and, by their very nature, so extraordinary that the layman who is wrapped up in the day-to-day activities of making a living cannot penetrate very far into the realm of the sacred. To do this, a person must spend time away from the basic tasks of food production and must have an unusual personality and special aptitudes and skills. The men who have the time and the skills may become reli-

gious functionaries: shamans or priests. The shaman is the more primitive type of specialist. He exists in systems in which religion has not developed a church. *The shaman derives his presumptive power directly from a supernatural source,* either through mystic experience or through his ability to perform rites and his possession of paraphernalia as an individual. *The power of priests is derived from their office in a cult or church.*

Siberian Shamanism   A center of the most intensive development of shamanism in the primitive world is aboriginal Siberia. The very word "shaman" comes from a native Siberian tongue. Synonyms also meaning "shaman" are "medicine man" (usually applied to American Indians), "witch doctor" (usually applied to shamans of Africa and Melanesia), and *angakok,* in Eskimo.

The Siberian shaman is more definitely set off from his fellow men than his North Amer-

Fig. 30-3   A Bushman shaman in a trance. (Photo by Laurence K. Marshall.)

---

[13] See page 445.

ican counterpart is. For one thing, his personality is more clearly marked. For another, his "call" and training are more definite. Bogoras, the famous Siberianist, wrote of the Chukchi:

For men, the preparatory stage of shamanistic inspiration is in most cases very painful, and extends over a long time. The call comes in an abrupt and obscure manner, leaving the young novice in much uncertainty regarding it. He feels "bashful" and frightened. . . . The young novice, the "newly inspired," loses all interest in the ordinary affairs of life. He ceases to work, takes little food and without relishing it, ceases to talk to people, does not even answer their questions. The greater part of his time he spends in sleep.[14]

Bogoras observed that shamans were as a rule excitable and hysterical. He even opined that not a few of them were "half crazy." Psychiatry was not the vogue in Bogoras's day or he might have labeled the personality of the Siberian shaman "schizophrenic."

Becoming a Shaman   The personal experience of a Northern Paiute Indian, who lived in western Nevada, is more or less typical of the way in which an American medicine man received power. As recorded by Willard Park, it runs as follows:

When I was a young man I had dreams in which I doctored people. I did not take those dreams seriously. My uncle was an Indian doctor. He knew what was coming to me. He told me to be careful in talking, not to speak harshly [in order not to offend the supernatural spirits]. I did not become a doctor from these dreams. Finally, I decided to go to the cave near Dayton. I was about fifty then. My uncle did not tell me to go there. I just decided to do this myself.

I went into the cave in the evening. As soon as I got inside, I prayed and asked for power to doctor sickness. I said, "My people are sick. I want to save them. I want to keep them well. You can help me make them well. I want you to help me to save them. When they have died give me power to bring them back [return the lost soul]." I said this to the spirit in the cave. It is not a person. It comes along with the darkness. This is a prayer to the night.

Then I tried to go to sleep. It was hard to sleep there. I heard all kinds of noises. I could hear all the animals. There were bears, mountain lions, deer, and other animals. They were all in caves in the mountain. After I went to sleep I could hear people at a doctoring. They were down at the foot of the mountain. I could hear their voices and the songs. Then I heard the patient groan. A doctor was singing and doctoring for him. A woman with a sage-brush shoot in her hand danced. She moved around the fire jumping at every step. Each time she jumped she said, "hǝ,' hǝ,' hǝ'." Then the shaman sprinkled water on the patient with sage-brush. The singing and dancing went on for a long time. Then the singing stopped. The patient had died and the people began to cry.

After a while the rock where I was sleeping began to crack like breaking ice. A man appeared in the crack. He was tall and thin. He had the tail-feather of an eagle in his hand. He said to me, "You are here. You have said the right words. You must do as I tell you. Do that or you will have a hard time. When you doctor, you must follow the instructions that the animals give you. They will tell you how to cure the sickness. I have this feather in my hand. You must get feathers like it. You are also to find the things that go with it. Get dark beads. Put them on the quills of the feathers and tie a strip of buckskin to the quills. Also get a hoof of a deer, and down from the eagle. With these you can go to people to cure them. These are your weapons against sickness. You must get three rolls of tobacco. You can use them to tell your patients what made them sick and then you can cure them. The tobacco will also help you if you are choked with clots of saliva when you suck out the disease. With this you are beginning to be a doctor. You will get your songs when you doctor. The songs are now in a straight line [ready for use]. Bathe in the water at the foot of the cliff and paint yourself with *i • bi* [white paint]."

Then I woke up. It was daylight. I looked around but I could not see anyone. The man was gone and there was no sign of the animals or the people who had been singing and doctoring. Then I did as the spirit had ordered and waited to become a doctor. In about six years I had received enough instructions to begin to cure.[15]

[14]W. Bogoras, "The Chukchee: I Religion" (*Jesup North Pacific Expedition,* vol. 7), pg. 420.

[15]W. Z. Park, *Shamanism in Western North America,* pp. 27–28.

Another more or less typical way of becoming a shaman is described by Barton, concerning female shamans among the Ifugao:

The priesthood [shamanism] is almost entirely in the hands of women. Entry into it is always in answer to a "call" and is, in a sense, compulsory: the woman begins to sleep badly, has many dreams, grows thin, lacks appetite, believes that her soul has married an *anitu*[16] and that she can extricate herself from the condition only by becoming a priestess (*mangaalisig*). Or she may become conscious of the call from getting a stomach upset after she has eaten foods that are taboo to priestesses: eel, dog, certain fish, meat of the cow (but not carabao). She is said to be taught the rituals by the gods themselves, not by the older priestesses. But, of course, she has been watching and hearing these since she was a little girl and wondering whether fate would ever call her to be a priestess when she grew older.[17]

Suggestibility and a greater or lesser degree of emotional instability are essential traits of the shaman who obtains power by mystic experience. He or she must be capable of hallucinations. The person who cannot respond with visions and hallucinations to the pervading cultural suggestion that these form the road to power is out of luck if he would be a shaman. Crashing Thunder, a Winnebago Indian, was one of these. Even when he faked a vision and luck seemed to confirm his power, he knew in his inner self that his power was false. An extrovert whose aggressive personality demanded social prestige and the opportunity to amount to something, he was frustrated by his intellectual hardheadedness. Not finding the social means (supernatural power) to greatness open to him, he took the antisocial road —drunkenness, rowdyism, debauchery, murder, and fraud. Then when peyote at last reached the Winnebagos, the vision-stimulating drug brought visions and power to the tortured man. With power came the reorienta-

tion of his personality. He became a pillar of society, a moral leader, and a decent citizen—much to the relief of his fellow tribesmen.[18]

The evidence is clear that as far as becoming a spirit-endowed shaman is concerned, the odds favor those who belong to what might unkindly be called the "lunatic fringe." But the cultures of these people turn their peculiarities to account and make honored medicine men and women of them.

Shamanistic Magic   The shaman, as inheritor of magical power, is a different matter. True, the magician is the dupe of his own beliefs,

[18]P. Radin (ed.), *Crashing Thunder*. This book should not be missed by any student of anthropology.

Fig. 30-4   Shamanistic curing by a Zulu doctor of South Africa. The illness is caused by an intrusive element in the head which is sucked out through the ear with the aid of the horn. Herbs and other materials used in the ritual cure lie ready-to-hand on the blanket. (Ewing Galloway.)

[16]Soul of a deceased person.
[17]R. F. Barton, *The Kalingas*, p. 24. The calling of a Yurok girl to shamanhood is portrayed in "The Reluctant Shaman," in *The Ways of Mankind*, Series II.

but it is possible for him to work with cold calculation. Highly developed magic often involves sheer fraud, skill in prestidigitation, and the creation of optical illusions. Siberian and Eskimo shamans are skilled ventriloquists, using their tambourines so to deflect their voices that the listeners "after a few minutes . . . begin to lose the power to locate the source of the sound. . . . The song and drum seem to shift from corner to corner, or even to move about without having any definite place at all."[19]

The Algonkian Indian medicine man holds impressive séances in which the tent rocks and pitches violently upon the arrival of his "spirit." The tent is cleverly constructed to be manipulated mechanically with ropes and thongs.[20]

Pueblo Indian priests put on miracle dramas in which corn grows and ripens overnight and deer and bears materialize before the astounded eyes of uninitiated spectators. Some *kivas* are equipped with secret tunnels through which the props and actors are brought upon the scene.[21]

However, the deceit practiced by shamans may not always be such crass charlatanism as it at first appears. Eskimo shamans often disclaim their own skill, as did one of the best of them to Peter Freuchen: "This is nothing for a man like you to look at. I am only a big liar, and even if these idiots are stupid enough to believe me, I never expected you to stand for it. I am a foolish old man, and what happens here has nothing to do with the truth."[22] But the effect of his performance on the people in the igloo was ecstasy. People are not averse to being fooled if it gives pleasure. Be-

yond that, of course, credulous ones are duped without their being the wiser.

It is difficult to draw an accurate balance between the exploitative and the social-service activities of the primitive shamans. It is a false gesture to dismiss them solely as a class of exploiters. Yet it is true that they often turn their position and power to self-advantage. Eskimo shamans can impose almost any tabus they wish on individuals. They can sexually exploit women, married and unmarried, to gratify themselves in the name of spirits. Shamans can use their power particularly to consolidate the position of the elders as against the younger generation. But for this they must pay a price in self-denial of many things, for their work is dangerous in its own terms, and the burden of shamanism is often hard.

Priests

Priesthood is a manifestation of developed religion. It occurs in the more ordered primitive societies whose cultures are rich and complex. On the whole, it calls for an economic base of sufficient richness to support fairly large populations, plus some food and wealth surpluses. It is necessary to be able to organize and sustain permanent cults. The priest may have mana, but his power is less his own than the power resident in the office he holds. Unlike the shaman, he does not acquire his sacredness personally. He is vested in his succession to the *office* of priest. He becomes part of a religious corporation.

There are basically three kinds of priests: (1) those who serve inherited or enduring medicine bundles; (2) the family heads in ancestor-worshiping religions who serve as priestly intermediaries between the kinship group and the deceased ancestors; and (3) the priests who serve cult groups whose interests are directed toward special spirits or deities.

Incipient priesthood is revealed in Gulliver's account of a Jie rainmaking ceremony:

---

[19]Bogoras, *op. cit.*, p. 430.

[20]F. Densmore, "An Explanation of a Trick Performed by Indian Jugglers" (*American Anthropologist*, vol. 34, 1932), pp. 310–314.

[21]E. A. Hoebel, "Underground Kiva Passages" (*American Antiquity*, vol. 19, 1953), p. 76; and F. M. Hawley, "Jemez Kiva Magic and Its Relation to Features of Prehistoric Kivas" (*Southwestern Journal of Anthropology*, vol. 8, 1952), pp. 147–163.

[22]P. Freuchen, *Arctic Adventure*, p. 113.

At a ritual assembly, supplications are made by a leader, supported by the chorus of the other men present. The seniormost man present, holding a ritual wand, stands in the open space inside the cluster of seated men; he addresses *Akuj* [the High God] directly, explaining the reason for the assembly and seeking benevolent assistance. Interspersed in the monologue are communal supplications led by the standing man, in which his specific pleas . . . are echoed by the others' chorus. After the seniormost man, other seniors in turn take up the leadership. When a man begins to assume this role with the approval of his more senior associates he has achieved notable seniority [which includes the priestly role].[23]

It should be added that to achieve seniority and priesthood, he must have power from the High God, too.

Although in many primitive cultures there is a recognized division of function between priests and shamans, in the more highly developed cultures in which cults have become strongly organized churches, the priesthood fights an unrelenting war against shamans. Priests work in a rigorously structured hierarchy fixed in a firm set of traditions. Their power comes from, and is vested in, the organization itself. They constitute a religious bureaucracy. Shamans, on the other hand, are arrant individualists. Each is on his own, undisciplined by bureaucratic control; hence, a shaman is always a threat to the order of the organized church. In the view of the priests, they are presumptive pretenders. Joan of Arc was a shaman, for she communed directly with the angels of God. She steadfastly refused to recant and admit delusion, and her martyrdom was ordained by the functionaries of the Church. The struggle between shaman and priest may well be a death struggle.

Priestesses are much less common than female shamans, probably because the organization of associations tends to be correlated almost exclusively with the male sex in primitive societies.

Ancestor Worship and Cults of the Dead

Ancestor worship is by no means a universal form of religious expression, although belief in the spiritual immortality of the dead is. All cultures call for cognizance of ghosts, and all provide some means of dealing with them. The intensity of ghost awareness, however, and the amount of concern over the activity and feelings of ghosts are variable. In North America, the Pueblo Indians pay little attention to ghosts; the Plains Indians fear them, but their ghosts are not too prevalent; and the Navahos and Eskimos are bedeviled by ghost anxiety. They possess definite ghost cults, a body of practices and ritual observances associated with the propitiation or avoidance of ghosts.

Most traditional Plains Indians and the Navahos abandon any house in which a person has died. The ghost haunts the house and disturbs the inhabitants. Navahos, therefore, take a seriously ill patient who is about to die outdoors in order to save the house, or they rush him to the Indian Service Hospital, which is already heavily inhabited by ghosts: a house of the dead, not of healing. The Arizona desert is dotted with hogans abandoned because a death has occurred within. One of the author's Shoshone friends dismantled a log house that he had inherited from his brother, moved it a few hundred feet, and then reassembled it, after mixing up the logs to fool the ghost of his brother, who was then unable to recognize the new house. Ghost fear has long been a hindrance to Indian Service efforts to provide modern housing on some reservations. In the northern Plains, a workable expedient acceptable to the Indians in some places has been the fumigation of the house as an effective antidote to ghosts.

Eskimos believe that ghosts are harmful and relentlessly malicious as long as they remain in the memory of the living. On death, the corpse is not removed from the igloo by way of the door; this would make it too easy

[23]P. H. Gulliver, "The Jie of Uganda," in J. L. Gibbs, Jr. (ed.), *Peoples of Africa*, p. 188.

for the lingering ghost to reenter. Rather, a hole is chopped in the back, later to be re-filled after removal of the body. This baffles the ghost. Then, in case the ghost does find the entrance, knives are set in the snow floor of the doorway for three nights after burial. Such booby traps discourage ghosts. Among Eskimos, as with many other people, the name of the dead is tabued, lest it summon the reappearance of the ghost. Later, the name is given to a newborn child, reincarnating the name soul of the deceased ancestor.

Comanches also tabu names of the dead, but when they want to mention a defunct friend named Pork, for example, they call him Bacon. Ghosts are literal-minded, but people can get the idea.

Eskimos, like many other people, bury the dead with grave offerings—the personal equipment and gifts of friends and relatives to serve the ghost in the other world. These are "killed." They are broken to release the animate soul of the object. For it is the spiritual counterpart of the goods that obviously is used in the spirit world.

Plains Indians also sacrificed a warrior's favorite horse on his grave, as did medieval Europeans at times. This is no longer Occidental practice, but the officer's horse led behind the casket-bearing caisson with reversed saddle and upturned stirrups still follows the hero to his grave, only to be spared the final sacrifice.

Grave sacrifices were stepped up to extravagant heights for the royalty of Africa and India. Into the nineteenth century, Hindu wives were immolated on the funeral pyres of their princely husbands. In Dahomey in West Africa, whole corps of wives and retainers were slain to provide an adequate retinue for the deceased king. Shoshone and Comanche tradition has it that in ancient times, wives were killed to accompany their husbands' spirits, but in more recent days, the wives followed the general Plains Indian practice of self-mutilation and abnegation.

Ghost cults usually emphasize the malevo-

Fig. 30-5   An ancestral cult figure from the Sepik River of New Guinea. (Private collection. Photo by Don Breneman.)

lence of ghosts. The people of Manus in Melanesia are an exception. The ghost of the last deceased household head is the preceptor and protector of his family. He is addressed as "Sir." He punishes their moral derelictions, but above all he is busy thwarting the malignant efforts of other ghosts. All ghosts are malicious toward people not of their own kinship group. The social and economic rivalry that is characteristic of everyday Manus life continues in the afterworld through the jealousy and rivalry of the ghosts. Each ghost enjoys a brief span of immortal existence

Fig. 30-6   The cult of the dead in Tibet. Citapati, a disembodied Lord of the Graveyard, dances sightless with the wraithlike body of his once-living self and holding his eyeballs in his hand. (Courtesy of the American Museum of Natural History.)

while his skull adorns the doorway of his family hut. But the death of an adult male in the household is an indication that the family ghost has not been on the job. He has been negligent enough to permit a rival ghost to kill his descendant. He is no good. Therefore his skull is thrown out and replaced by that of his successor, who then rules as the Honored Ghost of the household until he, too, fails in his duty.[24]

Ancestor Cults   Ancestor worship is both an elaboration and an abstraction of the ghost cult. As an elaboration, it is best seen among the Bantu tribes of Africa. Every lineage and clan has its distinct ancestral deities, who are gods to their descendants but who are ignored by the members of other kinship groups. The gods of royal clans, because the heads of such clans must be honored by all the kingdom, are worshiped not only by the royal clan itself but also by all the subjects of the king. In ancestor-worshiping cults of this order, the eldest ranking member of the kinship group is not only its headman but also its priest. He stands nearest to the ancestral gods. He is the intercessor on behalf of his kinsmen. On the gods' behalf, he is the intermediary who is responsible for controlling the acts of his family or clan members. As in modern Japan, he has to keep the ancestral gods informed of the state of affairs within his domain. The Mikado had merely to make a ceremonial report at the ancestral shrine, but in Dahomey in West Africa, it was customary to execute a couple of victims to carry the royal message to the ancestors whenever the king had anything of moment to report.

Periodic elaborate feasts and sacrifices on behalf of the ancestral gods are characteristic of the western Sudan. In Dahomey, such cere-

[24]R. F. Fortune, *Manus Religion* (Proceedings of the American Philosophical Society, 1935); and M. Mead, "The Manus of the Admiralty Islands," in *Cooperation and Competition among Primitive Peoples,* pp. 210–239. But see M. Mead, *New Lives for Old,* for post-World War II changes in Manus religion.

monies are held by each clan every year, with litanies, dancing, offerings of food and libations of liquors, and sacrifice of animals. In the annual ceremonies of the royal clan, human victims used to be offered.

Voodoo Vodun,[25] among West Indies Negroes, is a syncretism of Dahomean ancestral rites and Catholicism.[26] The clan founders of Dahomey are known as *tovodun,* from whom the *vodun* cult is named. Vodun rites are fundamentally family rituals with offerings and sacrifices accompanied by chants and dances, in which various gods are impersonated and called upon to visit the ceremony. Dancers representative of specific gods are possessed in turn as each god is called with his drum *salute* (greeting). The trance behavior of the votaries and the ecstasy of the worshipers lend the eerie wildness to the performance that has given *vodun* its exotic reputation.

Ancestor worship as an abstraction of ghost worship occurs where gods are thought once to have been human beings but where the more recently deceased are not believed to be potent deities. This may be said to be true of Polynesian and Pueblo Indian religions. Maori chieftains are lineal descendants of gods through primogeniture. Honor is due these gods, but there is no cult of the dead. The masked gods, *kachinas,* of the Pueblos are vaguely thought of as ancestral beings, but dead ancestors are not worshiped as such.

Social conservatism is a characteristic feature of ancestor-worshiping religions. The ancestors as moral preceptors do not favor change from the social practices they knew as men. Since they punish moral lapses with death and illness and their standards are the old ones, the religious sanctions toward conformity are powerful.

[25]*Vodun* is the phonetically correct name for the cult complex popularly called *voodoo.*
[26]See M. J. Herskovits, "African Gods and Catholic Saints in New World Negro Belief" (*American Anthropologist,* vol. 39, 1937), pp. 635–643; and G. E. Simpson, "The Vodun Service in Northern Haiti" (*American Anthropologist,* vol. 42, 1940), pp. 236–254.

Nature Worship

Cults deifying various features of nature abound in the primitive world. Among agricultural and gardening peoples, sun, rain, and fertility deities are outstanding. Solstitial rites marked the annual crisis of the sun in the religion of the megalith builders of Neolithic Europe. Mysterious Stonehenge and Avebury in England and the cromlechs of Carnac in Brittany are aligned to the rising sun at the time of the spring solstice, as is the sun stone in the famous Sun Temple of Mesa Verde National Park, built by prehistoric Pueblo Indians 700 years ago. In ancient Rome, the solstice rites of the Mithraic cult gave way to the Christian Christmas celebration of the birth of Christ as the new light of the world. Each pueblo in the Southwest today has its priestly sunwatcher, who controls the ceremonial cycle with the movements of the sun. Pious people greet the sun with prayer each day.

All the religions in the great Central American culture complex made much of the sun. The Pyramid of the Sun near Mexico City is one of the truly great monuments of all the world. The Natchez of Mississippi and the Incas of Peru built theocratic states around the principle of sun divinity. The Natchez high chief was also high priest, called the Sun, or Brother of the Sun. The Inca of Peru was the personification of the divine sun. And until the disaster of 1945 induced the Emperor of Japan to deny it by imperial edict, he was supposed to be a divinity directly descended from the mythical sun goddess Amaterasu.

The sun figured greatly in Plains Indian religion. All tipis opened east, and tribal camp circles likewise. By the nineteenth century, the midsummer Sun Dance had come to be one of the most spectacular of Plains ceremonials.[27]

[27]See G. A. Dorsey, "The Cheyenne, II, The Sun Dance" (*Field Columbian Museum, Publication 103, Anthropological Series,* vol. 9, no. 2, 1905) for a good description of a typical sun dance with many illustrations. Volume 16 of the *Anthropological Papers of the American Museum of Natural History* contains descriptions of other tribal sun dances.

Although the sun looms large in the mythologies of the peoples of the Pacific area, it does not assume importance as an actual deity. This is true also of Africa and most of North America. Ancient Europe, the countries of the Mediterranean basin, and India were the great seats of sun worship.

In Africa and Polynesia, although the sun is not glorified, nature worship is not neglected. The entire universe is departmentalized among gods of the skies, earth, waters, trees, and thunder, with myriads of subdivisions among the specialized deities. On the less-than-god levels, all primitive religions include multitudes of nature spirits associated with particular spots, trees, volcanoes, mountains, rivers, lakes, and rocks.

To primitive man, the whole world lives. Souls, animate things, and whatsoever embodies the soul are spirit beings to be treated with religion or magic—or both.

The High God Concept

The time has passed when informed civilized men could think the primitive mind incapable of conceiving of a Supreme Being or High God. Tylor's greatest error was to infer that the High God concept could be only the end product of a long intellectual evolution, beginning with the soul concept and leading through ghost and ancestor worship to polytheistic nature worship and monotheism.[28]

Andrew Lang (1844–1912), before the turn of this century, proved that Australian, Polynesian, African, and American Indian notions of the High God were not derived from Christian teachings.[29] The indefatigable Austrian anthropologist Wilhelm Schmidt (1868–1954) confirmed it with his stupendous four-volume work, *Der Ursprung der Gottesidee.*[30]

The actual occurrence and distribution of the High God concept is now clearly delineated in the *Ethnographic Atlas.* It is rarest in Pacific Island religious systems, where only one-fourth manifest it. In East Eurasia and North and South America, somewhat less than half the cultures include the idea of a High God.

Among the Oceanic and American Indian tribes which did have the High God concept, he was usually otiose, on the whole unapproachable and disinterested.

Clearly, however, the center of the idea is the Mediterranean area, where 97 per cent of all cultures center around it. Judaism, Christianity, and Islam are its most evident manifestations, but the idea goes much deeper than that. In Sub-Saharan Africa 86 per cent of the tribal religions include the High God. There is a marked difference in the relation of the High God to societal ethos in the Mediterranean and Sub-Saharan areas, however. In Negro Africa the High God figures in the cosmology but he is not involved with human affairs or morality. What human beings do is their concern and that of their ancestral gods, but none of his. In Mediterranean religions, on the other hand, the High God is very much concerned with human affairs and morality (in 86 per cent of the cultures). He is a moral censor, rewarding and punishing according to strict behavioral codes. He is the apex of the system of social control.[31]

Outside of the strongly monotheistic Mediterranean religions, the acts of creation by the High God are only vaguely conceived in cosmological lore. Myths tell how he created departmental, executive subdeities charged with the responsibility for filling in the details of creation and running the universe. These are the gods men must appease and pray to. They are the ones who deliver or withhold the goods. Evil in life is due to their perversity or maliciousness. A common counterpart of the High God is a Trickster or Transformer, like Coyote among the western American Indians, who spoils or modifies the good work of

[28]E. B. Tylor, *Primitive Culture.*
[29]A. Lang, *The Making of Religion.*
[30]See W. Schmidt, *The Origin and Growth of Religion,* pp. 167–217, a condensed version of Schmidt's thesis.

[31]Data from E. Bourguignon and L. Greenbaum, *Diversity and Homogeneity,* table 23, p. 45.

the creator to burden man with death, sin, and travail. The Trickster is the equivalent of the serpent in the Garden of Eden.[32]

Lang's Theory Lang felt that the formulation of the High God concept was a consequence of contemplative religious thought. The corruption of this idealism and the creation of the less-pure deities he conceived as due to a "myth-making mood" and "the Old Adam" in man—his unsocial desire to obtain advantage over his fellow men. In this the Supreme Being is too ethical to lend a hand; hence, ghosts, spirits, and corruptible gods were formulated in playful and erotic fantasy, which is irrational and debases the gods. Thus, to Lang, when early primitive man was in an elevated mood, he was capable of systematic philosophic thought. Yet man also expressed his baser mood of selfish desire to elaborate the pantheisms of the savage world.

Religious reformers of Mediterranean civilizations have struggled long to suppress the supremacy of the second religious mood, striving to establish the Supreme Deity in absolute dominance.

Radin's Theory Paul Radin (1885–1963) modified Lang's notions in a way worth noting.[33] He abjured the notion of an original purity of the High God later corrupted. Instead, he posited two contrasting types of human mentality, idealist and realist. Idealists are men of intellectual and reflective temperament, men whom anthropological experience has shown to be present in small numbers among all peoples. They philosophize on the conundrum of life and the universe. Their thought seeks a direct, unified, orderly cause in explanation of the universe. The product of their thought is the Supreme Being. As idealists, they are little concerned with crass, material desires. Their god is free from the petty demands of men.

Pospisil's description of Kapauku religious ideology states Radin's case exactly:

Most of the Kapauku people do not ponder the nature of life and the universe around them. They are empiricists who are not inclined to speculate and philosophize. The topics that interest them do not concern the supernatural or metaphysics; indeed, they usually talk about such unphilosophical subjects as contemporary power relations, concrete monetary transactions, love affairs, or news concerning pig feasts and dancing. Philosophizing they leave to the few especially gifted individuals who make it their hobby to try to penetrate the nature of things beyond the barrier imposed by the human senses. Accordingly, the systematic and logically consistent philosophy that is described next is by no means the property of the Kapauku tribe as a whole; it belongs to a few very intelligent individuals from the southern part of the Kamu Valley who have elaborated their views of the universe into a logical systematic whole.[34]

The bulk of men, alas, are materialists. Their bellies, their health, wealth, and social power mean much to them. They develop religion in terms of gods and spirits, who control the means to satisfy these needs. When prayer, appeasement, and magic suffice to win the desired results, all goes well. But hunger, illness, failure, and death stalk the earth, for which the lesser gods and the forces of evil are responsible. Toward them man's emotions are ambivalent. The gods and spirits are both loved and feared. The emotional overtones of religion are mixed indeed. But taken in the main, the anthropologist cannot, on the basis of the facts, concur in the idealistic belief that religion in all its history represents solely man's striving for the highest values of life. Nor is it possible to derive religion from any single mainspring of motivation. Belief in souls, fear of ghosts, fear of fear, worship of ancestors, traffic with hosts of spirits, nature worship, and philosophical reflection all play their parts. Emphasis shifts from culture to culture, but religion is a growth with many roots and many fruits.

---

[32]Compare here the Mandan Okipa myth in its handling of Coyote as Creator, Lone Man as beneficent transformer, and the Foolish One as would-be destructive transformer.
[33]P. Radin, *Monotheism in Primitive Religion;* see also *Primitive Man as Philosopher.*

[34]L. Pospisil, *op. cit.,* p. 83.

SUMMARY

Animism, which is the belief in spirit beings, is the most basic and universal component of religious ideology. Sir Edward Tylor explained the origin of animistic thought as derived from early man's attempts to account for dream experience and death, separating the body from its spirit, or soul. After death, the disembodied soul was thought to live on as a ghost. Once the soul concept was developed, according to Tylor, men attributed spirits to natural phenomena and so developed *nature worship.*

Mana is a belief in supernatural attributes of persons and things which are not ascribed to the presence of spirit beings. Mana expresses the nonvitalistic idea of sacredness as that which is set apart and extraordinary. Unusual talents and extraordinary prowess, if not the gift of spirits, may be accounted for in this way.

Religion and magic are both aspects of supernaturalism. Their difference lies in the attitudes of the religious and magical practitioners. The religious person acknowledges his inferiority to spirit beings; the magician believes he has mastered a supernatural force through the possession of a compulsive formula.

Prayer is a supplication expressing dependence; an act of magic is an act of mechanical compulsion. Magic is basically moral and usually socially accepted. Magic used for antisocial ends becomes sorcery, socially feared and frequently punished by tribal law.

All religions involve *tabu.* Tabu is an expression of constraints designed to protect the sacred. It consists of prohibitions: "Thou shalt not's." Violation of tabus is *sin;* and the sanctions for sin are various forms of supernatural punishment.

Religious specialists are found in all societies. They are either *shamans* or *priests,* or a blend of both. Shamans receive their supernatural power directly from spirit beings, usually in a vision experience or through possession. Priests receive their power through the authority of their position in a cult or church. They are officers; shamans are not.

Ancestor worship as a special cult form represents an intensification of the ghost cult. The High God concept expresses belief in a creator deity who is a supreme being. Although this concept occurred in religions in all parts of the world, the idea of a Supreme Deity was lacking in most of the religions of Oceania and the New World. The High God who is concerned with human affairs and morality is primarily a feature of the Mediterranean complex of civilizations where Judaism, Christianity, and Islam were born and flourished.

SELECTED READINGS

Evans-Pritchard, E. E., *Nuer Religion* (1956). A penetrating field study of the concept and role of supernatural forces in a culture that lacks dogma, liturgy, sacraments (in a strict sense), and a developed religious cult and mythology.

Goode, W. J., *Religion among the Primitives* (1951). This book undertakes to scrutinize the interrelations of religion with other aspects of culture.

Howells, W. W., *The Heathens* (1948). A lively overview of primitive religious practices.

Hsu, F. L. K., *Religion, Science and Human Crisis* (1952). A case study of the uses of magic, religion, and scientific medicine in the folk response to a cholera epidemic in a Chinese village.

LaBarre, W., *The Ghost Dance* (1970). The origins of religions brilliantly analyzed and presented as a crisis phenomenon. The approach combines anthropology, psychoanalysis, and classical scholarship with great erudition, insight, and readability.

Lessa, W. A., and E. Z. Vogt, *Reader in Comparative Religion* (2d ed., 1965). Pages 253–559 contain a wealth of original articles and selections on the subjects of the present chapter.

Lowie, R. H., *Primitive Religion* (1924). Vignettes of several primitive religions, followed by a critical discussion of a number of anthropological theories of religion.

Norbeck, E., *Religion in Primitive Society* (1961). A concise and well-balanced general introduction to the subject of religion as a social phenomenon.

Chapter 31

Language

Without language, culture among men would be wholly impossible. All sentient animals communicate, and some, like bees and porpoises, apparently can do so extremely well. But it is only man who is able to generalize, to create explanations, and thus to build up the body of traditions which can be identified as human culture. What is not clear about animals other than man is the extent to which their patterns of communication are learned. The human being learns his language just as he learns his culture; man is not born with a language. Thus language is "a distinctly human system of behavior based on oral symbols" which is "used to describe, classify and catalogue experiences, concepts, and objects."[1] Language, therefore, is a special system of communication that is specifically *oral* and *symbolic*. And it is learned.

Anthropological Linguistics

An anthropologist, whether social or cultural, interested in penetrating the modes of life of different peoples around the world, is confronted with the problems of communicating with those peoples. He may observe what goes on, noting the patterns which arise in the day-to-day activities among the people whose culture concerns him. But he also needs to know the meaning of what goes on and how the people feel about it. This, it is evident, arises in the domain of language. The researcher must rely on an interpreter or learn the language himself. Ideally, to comprehend the ways of life of a people requires

This chapter was written with the collaboration of Robert F. Spencer.

[1] R. F. Spencer, "Language," in J. Gould and W. L. Kolb (eds.), *Dictionary of the Social Sciences*, p. 377.

more than the simple sentence or even the hints which may come from the use of a bilingual person who serves as an interpreter. Therefore, the conscientious field worker will probably undertake to use the language spoken by the culturally different group, whether Chinese or Hindi, Arabic or Eskimo. But quite apart from the need to communicate in an alien speech, to learn it and achieve some degree of mastery over it, an anthropologist quickly becomes aware that through a study of language new avenues of perception are opened, with unsuspected perspectives on human behavior reflecting special kinds of insights. Language, in other terms, not only underlies culture but offers a series of ways of penetrating culture and cultures.

Linguistics is a field of study in its own right. Here the specialist is not necessarily an anthropologist, although he may be. The linguist's interests lie in the many and varied forms of expression through language of which man is capable. The linguist may be concerned, for example, with differing grammatical structures or in the fact that one language may have very different modes of expression from another. He may be interested in the history of languages, in learning how one language is related to another, or he may analyze language and languages as structured systems and note how structures (or grammars) differ from one another. To the conventional linguist, the study of language and languages is often an end in itself. The anthropological linguist, however, while he may share these linguistic concerns, tends to add a somewhat different dimension. He is more interested in language as a phenomenon within cultures, to strive to understand the intricate problems of the ways in which language and culture relate to each other.

Anthropological linguistics grew out of the need of anthropologists to learn unwritten, exotic languages which are very different from anything that Europeans had previously known. Out of necessity, anthropological linguists like Franz Boas, Edward Sapir, and Leonard Bloomfield were in the forefront in development of ways of learning strange languages quickly and of reducing unwritten languages to writing by means of phonetic alphabets. Anthropology has always had an interest in language in itself. In recent years, however, the techniques and problems associated with language have been so refined that a virtually new discipline of vast proportions begins to emerge. As this book is being written, anthropological linguists are engaged in opening some suggestive and sometimes startling frontiers (see pages 607–608).

The Origins of Language Prehistoric archaeology, as we now know well, provides some evidence on the origins of culture, but we can find no artifacts that suggest when or how language might have come into being. Does the making of fire or a stone ax require language? Who knows? But the development of technological traditions over time implies that some sophisticated means of communication beyond mere imitation or emotive expression proved necessary. Around the turn of this century, scholars devoted considerable time to speculation about the origins of language. Then the question was abandoned as a fruitless pursuit, only to be revived in the present day as a realization of the ecological, social, and physiological preconditions of language has grown. Unquestionably of great importance is the existence of human society, plus the fact of the prolonged dependence of human young, as well as man's tendency to live in groups.[2]

It is an interesting fact that man has no organs which have evolved especially to produce speech. Most mammals can make sounds, and they have tongues, lips, teeth, larynx, and lungs, none of which has sound-making as a primary function. Yet men have these body parts so combined that they can produce the sounds of language. Apes, which are like men in their general facial and mouth structure, are capable of producing all the sounds that men make. Yet none of man's closest primate relatives has developed patterns of speech. How is it then that man can talk? The answer is that rather than any special adaptiveness to speech as such, the

Fig. 31-A Playback. An Amarakaeri tribesman listens to his tape-recorded speech. (Cornell Capa, Magnum, from Matthew Huxley and Cornell Capa's **Farewell to Eden;** *Harper & Row, New York.)*

[2]For a full and well-informed discussion of this matter, see C. D. Hockett and R. Ascher, ''The Human Revolution'' (*Current Anthropology*, vol. 5, 1964), pp. 135–168.

human being possesses a brain which makes speech possible. It is a matter of cortical control over the speech organs.

Perhaps it is here where language bridges the gap between the biological and the cultural. Any language is a learned system, it is true; but there is every indication that man's capacity for language is genetic, related to the growth of the forebrain and reflecting a neurophysiological breakthrough, or "tip-over," toward true speech. It is known that mammals and primates other than man possess calls in which meaning, a semantic element, may be present. But sounds or even meaning alone is not language. What man has achieved is to structure his utterances, giving them significant form and clothing them with an "aura of displacement," i.e., a quality of metaphorical allusion and abstraction in his verbalizations. To some extent, animals other than man can do this, and there is the laboratory evidence in the recent studies of the chimpanzee Washoe, who achieved mastery of some eighty signs, not verbal signs, but rather, signs of symbolic associations.[3] Yet Washoe cannot do what a human infant does; she cannot accord meaning to verbal cues and signs, form them by analogy, and so develop a series of speech patterns reflecting learning and a true mastery of language.

Beyond the level of the hominoids, the ability to achieve this sense of "grammar," or patterned structure, must have been slow in coming. A modern human being gets it early in life, and relatively quickly, receiving a neural "imprint." The human brain, like the man-made computer, has developed to the point where information can be stored and retrieved, patterned and reproduced at will.

Assuming that a genetic breakthrough to true language as a result of man's biological evolution took place in Lower Pleistocene times, it no longer becomes necessary to ask why the languages of men are so diverse. It is rather that the preconditions of human behavior which evoked language, social life,

[3] J. Bronowski and U. Bellugi, "Language, Name, and Concept" (*Science,* vol. 168, 1970), pp. 669–673.

and the use of tools appeared at various places wherever clusters of human populations arose. By the same token, man quickly produced and produces languages as finished systems wherever he does arise. This is why there is no such thing as a "primitive" language today. All languages (however much they differ) are matured speech systems.

Cues and Communication Many ways of communicating exist that do not utilize language. Cries of warning and aggression and "purrs" of contentment and affection are forms of communication not limited to men. Much progress has been made in the past decade by ethologists, the students of the comparative behavior of all living beings, toward the understanding of the circumstances under which various living species effect communication between themselves. The mating dances of various birds, the grooming and licking in which some species engage, and the establishment and defense of space by other species are all points suggestive of aspects of communication. Nor can man be excluded from ethological studies either. Men do use their bodies to communicate virtually as much as they employ formal language. What indeed can be more universal than the friendly expression of a smile? And yet such facial expressions, in themselves modes of communication, are also learned among men. There are happy smiles and sad smiles, smiles accompanying appropriate occasions. Even the smiling baby can become aware that his expression may carry with it an element of reward.[4] Yet the use of the smile is by no means universal. There are cultures where babies do not smile. Moreover, in such a facial gesture as the smile, muscles and movements are brought into play and controlled according to understandings which lie in learned behavior, i.e., in culture.

Kinesics and Proxemics We all know that languages may call for the use of the hands or

[4] R. L. Birdwhistell, *Kinesics and Context*, pp. 29–39.

the body as a means of conveying what the verbal sentence does not say. Gestures, in short, may become an adjunct of language and a vital factor in various kinds of social communication. The study of gestures (*kinesics*) is still in its infancy. By examining the nature of the message expressed through the use of gestures, one can perceive a good deal of the emotive, the psychological, direction of communication. Such gestures may be seen to relate to culturally defined habits. To an American, the nod of the head means "yes," but in the Middle East, a single nod of the head is a clear "no."

Some students of the communication problem have been concerned with *proxemics,* an area which may be defined as reflecting nearness or distance in human communication. The use of space in communication is also a culturally learned thing. North American businessmen in a conference may choose to sit or stand at a prescribed distance from each other, usually keeping a table between them; they may well be taken aback by a Latin American colleague who inclines to move in much closer in a conversation. To a Westerner, it is sometimes surprising to see two Arab boys walking hand in hand. Yet this is expected behavior in the Arab world and carries with it no sexual implication. American men usually walk closely side by side, while they permit women to precede them as a form of politeness. But among Shoshone Indians it is different; the clincher in an argument over my presence at a sun dance was, "He is one of us. He is not like those whites who hold hands with their wives. Haven't you seen how he always walks in front of his wife?" (An anthropological adage: When in Shoshone, do as the Shoshones do.)

These are only some of a vast range of cues in which men may engage. It is clear, however, that all social behavior depends on the understanding of cues: events or things that have a conventional meaning. The responder who "reads" a cue is in a position to act in a predictable manner within a given situation. The understanding of cues is absolutely es-

sential to effective participation in any social setting, be it animal or human. In order to have the inside view of a culture, one must know its cues like a native.[5] Language cues are *spoken* cues. They are able to rise to high levels of complexity—far beyond anything achievable in animal communication—because of man's capacity to generalize and abstract.

Parallels and Process in Language and Culture Culture and language, both learned, are the distinctive attributes of man. All men live in accordance with a culture, but the culture of the modern Englishman is not the same as the culture of a Zulu. This we already realize. Similarly, all men have language, but English is not the same as Zulu, Chinese, or Twi. As cultures vary, so also do languages.

But language and culture do not necessarily go hand in hand. There are peoples who speak mutually unintelligible languages who share in the same cultural traditions. In the American Southwest, for example, the town-dwelling Pueblo Indians, basically much alike in culture, speak languages related to four quite separate groupings. Unless a man from Zuñi learns Hopi, he cannot communicate with a Hopi, unless they both speak Spanish or English! Or, on the other side, peoples with very different cultures may be able to communicate through language across the barriers of cultural difference. Again, in the native American Southwest, the populous Navaho can converse quite readily with his Apache neighbor, even though the two have essentially different cultures. What is still more interesting is that both Navaho and Apache can make themselves understood in interior Alaska, thousands of miles away. The Athabascan speech family, to which both the Navaho-Apache and the interior Alaskan Indians belong, has apparently been spread

---

[5]This fact is demonstrated in a fascinating way in a popular book by E. T. Hall. He makes a point when he calls his book *The Silent Language,* but confuses the issue by so doing, because language is spoken. Communication may be silent.

fairly recently, so that some degree of mutual intelligibility remains. Clearly, too, the cultures of the southwestern desert dwellers differ from those of the peoples of the subarctic coniferous forest.

Culture and language may relate in special and subtle ways. The reason a people speaks the language that it does depends largely on the mere accidents of history, on such factors as isolation, contact, migration, or conquest. It does not follow that because a people has a certain kind of culture, it will speak a certain type of language. What appears to occur is that, as distinctly human phenomena, language and culture parallel each other processually, i.e., in the ways in which they *operate*. Thus, just as one may conceptualize a culture as an integrated system, a "whole" that is more than the sum of its parts, so also does a language assume a holistic character. It is, in fact, easier to delimit linguistic boundaries than it is to draw cultural ones. Where one language leaves off to be replaced by another, even though there may be blurring or bilingualism at the borders, is still easily seen. Great Russian, for example, a dominant language of the U.S.S.R., shades off in the western part of the country and is displaced by Ukrainian and Polish. Closely related to Russian though these languages may be, they are still quite distinct; there is no doubt in the mind of anyone familiar with them that a linguistic boundary has been crossed.

A culture, as we know, may incorporate borrowed elements; it may have inventions added to it; it changes gradually and organically through time. Language operates in the same way. Speakers of one language may borrow and incorporate, not only words, but also elements of grammatical structure from other languages. In English, for example, there is a vast number of *lexemes* (words, dictionary entries) drawn from languages all across the world. From Japanese come "typhoon" and "kimono," and from Carib, an American Indian language of the West Indies, there are "cigar," "hammock," and "hurri-

cane." English can invent as well, admitting new concepts to both the language and the culture. "Hi-fi," "generation gap," or "pot" would be pure nonsense words to Shakespeare. But just as some cultures accept change readily, others may resist change. The same is true of language where there can be striking conservatism. Unlike English, there are languages whose very structure is incapable of accommodating new terms or words. Chinese, to name one such, with its basic vocabulary made up of words of essentially a single syllable, cannot adapt to polysyllables. The result is the Chinese "loan translate" of a new item of technology; for example, the telephone is called "lightning speak." Yet the Chinese clearly understand this to mean the same thing as "telephone." Chinese evolves a whole series of single-syllable combinations which handle adequately the complexities not only of technology from the West, but philosophical ideology as well. The Navaho in the American Southwest, to cite another example, becomes quite anatomical in referring to the parts of an automobile; an engine is the car's "stomach," the fenders its "wings."

Some languages borrow not only words from others, but elements of grammar as well. In the Far East, there are the many languages classed with the Sinitic or Chinese grouping. To be sure, there are the different languages, sometimes erroneously called dialects, of China itself. But there are also Burmese, Thai, Vietnamese, Laotian, and many others that seem to share with Chinese the tonalities, the pitch of the voice necessary to communication. Although there may be a genetic relationship between these languages, it appears that they resemble each other primarily in the tonal pitch of the voice. And on the Northwest Coast of North America, the use of numerical classifiers, i.e., the categorizing of elements to be counted, reflects a concept which crosses the boundary of several apparently unrelated languages.

Language Fits Cultural Needs   What becomes clear from the foregoing is that each language is a completed system of symbols and abstractions. It once seemed quite reasonable to assume that one or another existing language might be more archaic or more primitive than another. Yet, as we have already said, this does not appear to be the case. Every language represents a finished product, a perfect system in the sense that each tongue is wholly adequate to all human situations. The ideas that a language can express are in some measure dependent on the interests and preoccupations of the society which develops it. It would be surprising to hear a discussion of logical positivism or cultural anthropology in Eskimo, but this does not mean that ideas of this kind cannot be expressed in Eskimo. English, similarly, must resort to circumlocutions to convey with exactness the subtleties of which Eskimo is eminently capable. Neither of these languages, nor any of the other 6,000 languages of the world, can thus be regarded as more archaic or primitive than another.

It has sometimes been contended that a language has evolved further than others if it possesses a larger vocabulary. But one of the knottiest problems confronting the science of linguistics is to define the "word." Even in English, is "the" a word? Is "the man" one word or two? The verb "do" might be regarded as a word, but what of "does" and "did"? The latter case, to be sure, involves changing forms of the same element, but the very fact that the form changes raises some further questions about language and its nature. The speaker of English uses only a small fraction of the dictionary, or more properly, of the language lexicon. Many unwritten languages are far more elaborate in terms of the number of words employed by a speaker in normal converse. By such a standard, English might be regarded as more primitive. If Arabic has over 1,000 words for "sword," something cultural and stylistic is implied; the culture stresses poetry, and thus

it is no surprise to discover an amazing array of synonyms and figures of speech.

Anthropologists are fond of pointing out that Eskimos have a large number of words for "snow," each denoting snow of a particular state of being, such as softly-falling-snow, dry-wind-driven-snow, drifting-snow, powder-snow, wet-packed-snow, dry-packed-snow-suitable-for-cutting-into-blocks (for igloo building), ice-crust-surface-snow, and so on. It is perfectly true that we can linguistically express different conditions of snow through the use of modifiers, but the point is that Eskimos, whose very survival depends upon snow conditions, do not view snow as "crystallized water vapor" or "that beautiful white fluffy stuff that falls from the sky on some cold days," but rather as a series of *different* substances.

The American city dweller does recognize snow, sleet, and slush as three distinctly different linguistic categories for crystallized water in different states of being—because this much, and no more, is culturally significant to his comfort and well-being. Since the birth of wide popular enthusiasm for skiing in the United States, however, a skier's vocabulary for snow, similar in its distinctions to that of the Eskimo, has been borrowed from the Austrian Tyrol because the state of snow is important to ski culture. Hence we hear the terms *Pappschnee* (wet, heavy snow), *Kornschnee* (barley snow that has melted under spring sunshine and frozen at night), *Pulverschnee* (powder snow), *Fernschnee* (broad expanse of breakable crust), and so forth.

In our own equestrian subculture of cowboys a comparable example exists. To most Eastern city dwellers a horse is a horse. Not so to the cowpoke. It is a mare, stallion, or gelding in denotation of its sex; a gray, sorrel, piebald, strawberry roan, palomino, or white face, in denotation of its color.

The basic principle illustrated by these examples is that every language is adequate to express the needs of its culture. As the culture expands, the language expands. If the belief or knowledge system embodied in the culture requires the expression of abstract ideas, the language will provide the means of getting those ideas across, regardless of what syntax is involved. If a culture stresses rhetorical style, oratory, folktale, or poetry, these cultural interests will find their linguistic expression. No existing language is so primary as to contain half-formulated grunted thoughts or so limited in expressions as to suggest that it exemplifies the dawn of human speech. English, it is true, like other European languages, accompanies a culture in which there is great diversity of occupation and activity. Since each specialty has its specialized vocabulary, no one person can command the whole lexicon of the language. But every culture has its specialties, occupational or otherwise. If anyone still has the notion, which was so common in the nineteenth century, that primitive languages are childlike and inherently incapable of expressing complex thoughts and ideas, this error should be dispelled.

The Universal and the Specific in Language
If language and its use represent a genetic "tip-over" passed sometime in the evolution of man as man, it follows that the resulting diversity in language is not unexpected. Moreover, it can be suggested that each language becomes a structured system in its own right. True, language changes in time and it is possible to trace language history, as where, for example, Latin of some 1,500 years ago swung toward a French, a Spanish, or an Italian variant. Similarly, English arose historically out of an Anglo-Saxon beginning, accepted a heavy overlay of Norman-French vocabulary after 1066, and so became fixed as a distinct and separate language as time passed. But these historic processes raise other questions than those connected with the comparison of languages as they exist today. It is important to look at each language as a structured whole, a functional system in

its own right. The implication of such a statement is that languages are relative entities; each one has to be seen in its own terms.

Cultural and Linguistic Relativism   The problem of cultural and linguistic relativism is a difficult one. What one culture may consider right, just, and beautiful, another may view as wrong, debased, and ugly. Similarly, in language, one tongue, such as Hopi, may be much involved with statements about *action* and *movement,* emphasizing verbs and stressing activity. Conversely, another language may be involved in discussing *things,* giving attributes to them, and thus be emphatically concerned with descriptive categories. The implication is that languages, by virtue of the kind of structure which they have brought out of the past, may be focused toward certain kinds and modes of expression.

Anyone who has studied another language than his own becomes aware of the problem. He begins to see elements of structure which do not wholly dovetail with what he brings from his own language, and he may find difficulty in making the full transfer. Certainly, one of the first and most obvious suggestions of difference is seen when one attempts to catch the meaning of a word in another language. The dictionary gives the equivalence, but somehow there is never a direct association. To look up the word for "hand" in an English-language, and in some other language, dictionary seems simple on the face of it. Yet where does the word begin and end? Does the language classify the hand as inclusive of the fingers? Does it include the wrist? Does the word refer to the back of the hand, the palm, or the whole hand with wrist and elbow? In other words, there are implicit classifications of experience and phenomena even in the use of apparently simple words. One might think that all men would agree on such seemingly basic issues, but the reverse is true.

But the relativistic suggestion may be carried further. Do all languages have verbs?

The answer is a guarded "yes," assuming that one can agree on what constitutes a verb, a noun, an adjective, or any other part of speech. It is sometimes said that relational words are the most difficult for an outsider. If a language lacks prepositions, with which English expresses such relations as "on," "above," "in," and so on, how does one express these basic ideas? "The on-ness of the flat object related to a suspended plane discerns itself me," sounds to an English-language speaker like a weird way for saying, "The book is on the table" or "I see the book on the table." Yet this kind of existential statement is demanded by the structure of some languages outside the English-speaker's experience. The result is that what to the speaker of one language may seem wholly logical is chaotic illogic to the speaker of another.

The Common Denominator of All Languages But if languages are relative systems, is there any common denominator among the languages of the world? Anthropological linguists have paid some attention to this question in recent years in the same way as cultural anthropologists have looked for universals in culture patterns. Languages in themselves are isolable, unique, idiosyncratic, but at the same time language is language—in itself a common human phenomenon. Thus a wholly relativistic perception of languages may be off the mark. Languages may differ markedly from each other but the difference is one of degree rather than of kind. All languages employ sounds, all accord meaning to symbolic utterances. Sound and symbol, it is true, may differ markedly from group to group and area to area. Men speak, however, and this is universally true.[6]

Writing and Language Some languages are written, some are not. Indeed, the term "primitive" is usually held to be synonymous with

[6]J. H. Greenberg, *Anthropological Linguistics*, pp. 137–154.

"nonliterate." But when the anthropological linguist gives his attention to the components of a language, he is concerned only with the oral system, or more accurately, with the oral-aural, the spoken and the heard. Writing is not a part of language in any vital sense. English could be written equally well with Chinese characters. As it happens, it uses a Latin alphabet. Systems of writing are inventions going back to relatively recent times, to the Bronze and Iron Ages. Language had been in existence long before. Nor should we think that because a language lacks writing it is slovenly or debased. On the contrary, it is more frequently the unwritten language which preserves oral tradition with fidelity, which stresses correctness and precision of speech. Current usage in written as against spoken English is an exception.

Some languages, such as Latin (in the past) and English, French, German, Chinese, and Russian, by virtue of writing and the accompanying transmission of elaborated traditions, have assumed greater importance in world affairs. While it is doubtful that the world will ultimately move toward universal use of English, Russian, Chinese, and Spanish because of their being fully dominant in certain world areas, languages with writing tend to be more encompassing. There are "great" languages, whose traditions and associations have taken on enlarged significance. Such languages are usually found in association with one or another of the great religious systems. There is Latin, for example, which, although "dead" in the sense that it has no living day-to-day native speakers, still retains importance in the total world of Roman Catholicism. Similarly, Hebrew, with its link to Judaism and its modern renaissance in Israel, and Arabic in the world of Islam, and Sanskrit in the religious traditions of India, and Chinese and its tie with Confucianism and Taoism, are all examples of the cultural effects of the written tradition in the functioning of "universalistic" religious ideology and practice.

When a language is not written, there is an

unfortunate tendency on the part of literate people to think of it as possessing limited worth. From the broad perspective of human history, this may be in a sense true, but from another standpoint, considering that any language serves the needs of the culture which speaks it, all languages appear to have equal value and function.

The Structure of Language

Whether English is spoken by Americans in the Midwest or in the Deep South, by the Englishman at Oxford, or the cockney cab driver in London, English still remains English. There are the dialects, to be sure, local turns of expression and sound variations which sometimes make it difficult for the speaker of one dialect to understand another, but the structure of the *language* remains consistent. A speaker of any language follows, and must follow, a definite structure in his speech. He has learned the basic structure of his language, and thus knows how to generate new utterances to suit the occasion and to transform mere words into *sentences* and *phrases of meaning* framed according to strict, "unconscious" rules. It is this knowledge, not words alone, which marks the great human achievement in speaking.

The Time Element in Linguistic Analysis

In regard to both culture and language *the major concern is with the predictable,* with the elicitation of pattern. Language, in fact, appears to offer a more convincing example of this than does culture for the reason that language, by its very nature, cannot admit so many variables. One can readily supply—or predict—the missing words in such a sentence as *John and Mary are___to the movies.* Here, whether one chooses the verbs *go, walk, drive, come,* or another among the host of choices, one can predict from the nature of the sentence that the verb will contain an *ing* ending. The precise structure of each language permits variations, but they differ according to the linguistic system.

In thinking about language, as in thinking about culture, one may ask initially how the system works. In doing so, we place language at a point in time with no concern for the origin of the finished product or for its relationships. The child learns the language of his group as it is spoken by those around him. The structure of English today is different from what it was in Chaucer's time, but the speaker of English need not know the history of the language. To see language (or culture) as a temporal end product and to ask how the system operates at a given time is to look at structure, at the parts which interrelate to make up the whole. This approach is structural, or *synchronic.* In synchronic studies, languages are analyzed as each exists at a given moment in history.

The historical, or *diachronic,* approach poses a very different kind of question. Rather than "How does it work?" we ask, "How did it get that way?" If the history of English as a language is the issue, then clearly, Chaucer's English and Shakespeare's English, as well as the earliest discernible forms of English, must be taken into account. Further, one wishes to see the parts of English which relate to the Germanic ancestor, to Latin, to Norman French, or to the great Indo-European family of which English, German, French, Latin, Russian, and the languages of modern India are also descendants.

Both approaches, the synchronic and the diachronic, have relevance for the understanding of language processes. The historical relationships of language may provide a clue to cultural relations. Similarly, to comprehend a language as it is spoken—not only to speak and understand it but also to see it as a structured entity—may provide some leads to a greater awareness of how cultures, too, are organized.

Synchronic, or Structural, Linguistics

Although any language contains a distinctive series of patterns, because language is oral and aural, the initial approach to a language is through its sound system by means of phonology (Gr. *phono,* sound + logy).

Phonology Every language has its own distinctive, idiosyncratic, and characteristic total series of sounds. A single sound in one language, or even a series of them, can appear in another. Taken as a total system, however, the sounds of a language offer a remarkable uniqueness. Linguistic science employs the term *phoneme* (Gr. *phonema,* a sound) to refer to these characteristic sound units in a given language. Some languages, such as Hawaiian, possess only a few basic sounds; others, such as Kwakiutl, may have considerably more. Rarely are there more than 45 to 50 basic sounds in any language.

A phoneme is thus the smallest sound unit of a language. But the sound alone, in isolation, is only a starting point. In the human speech mechanism, sounds, usually conventionally divided into vowels and consonants, not only appear in combination with each other, but in a given language, a sound is articulated or pronounced in a way peculiar to that language. The sound usually designated /t/ is pronounced by most speakers of English by placing the tip of the tongue on the gum just back of the front teeth (postdental). The sound is *stopped,* meaning that /t/, unlike /s/, cannot be continued, even though /s/ is pronounced in much the same position as /t/ in English. There are thus classes of sounds—those that are *stopped, continued, nasalized,* or *trilled,* along with possible combinations of these—as well as points of articulation—the use of the tongue, lips, teeth, vibration and resonance, and the various hard and soft parts of the oral chamber—to produce particular types of sounds. /t/ in English is not the same as /t/ in some other languages. In Tagalog, a Philippine language, for example, /t/ is pronounced with the tongue directly against the teeth. As between English and Tagalog this makes little immediate difference. But it could happen, and often does, that a language differentiates

between a postdental and a dental /t/, /s/, or /n/, and the result can be most confusing, at least to an English-speaker. Because he is used to a single postdental /t/, the English-speaker actually fails to hear the difference in the points of articulation. His own phonemes have not made him receptive to two, three, or four different tongue locations of /t/.

Sounds in a language also follow a pattern of arrangement. English /sk/ is wholly compatible with the sound structure of the language. But the same sound is impossible to pronounce in Spanish, where an initial vowel must enter before /s/ followed by any consonant, as Spanish *escuela* (eskwéla). Bantu languages in Africa build many words beginning with /ng/ (for instance, *ngbatu*). Not a single word in English starts so; it is against the English rule which requires that /ng/ may be used only at the end of a phonemic series. Similarly, no language incorporates all the phonemes that are in use among all the tongues of mankind. Strongly fixed motor habits in forming one's own speech make it extremely difficult to pronounce a foreign language like a native when it involves different habits. The difference between the English /z/ and /th/ is only a matter of a few millimeters in the placement of the tongue. In /z/, the tip of the tongue rests against the lower edge of the gums of the upper dental arch. In /th/, it is between the teeth themselves. But how many English-speaking Frenchmen and Germans never succeed in mastering that little shift!

It should be clear that even so apparently simple a system as the sounds of language is fraught with difficulties. True, the number of sounds a human being can make is limited, and a person learns to follow the linguistic patterns of his group. But when secondary phonemes, such as stress or accent, tone or pitch, length of vowel, presence or absence of resonance, throating, nasalizing, and many other possible factors, are added to the basic patterns, we can readily see that no language is a simple, phonetic system.

The sounds of a language, being adequate

for that language, are thus relative to that particular language as a system. Languages are culturally determined systems not only in their sounds but in the ways in which they put these basic elements together in structured order.

Phonemic Analysis   How is a phoneme recognized? The trained linguist brings his own judgment to bear, based on his knowledge of *phonetics,* the general science of sounds. Blessed with a good ear and through training and practice, he has acquired a sense of the general range of sounds which human speech has produced. In respect to a single language, the linguist looks for contrasts, for the differentiation of minimal pairs, /t/, for example, as against /d/. Both, as in English, may be aspirated; one is unvoiced, the other voiced. Both sounds thus stand out in English as distinctive phonemic elements. But in a language other than his own, even the trained linguist, unless he is an exceptional mimic, may do something wrong, failing to get the hang of a particular unit of articulation and making his utterance—often to the amusement of native speakers—with an atrocious accent. The linguist can generally tell what he is doing wrong; he can locate the uttered sound in its proper place and can describe it scientifically. But neither with mouth or mind can he replicate the action of the native speaker. Told that he has articulated an unaspirated, unvoiced dental stop, the native speaker's reaction may be, "So what?" All he knows is that this is the way one speaks in his language. For him that is usually enough.

But a kind of impasse is reached. There is nothing abstruse about a phonetic-phonemic distinction. One returns again in fact to the problem of the universal as against the specific. Yet it is this issue which has come to have some implications for the study of culture and which again suggests some analogies in process between language and culture.

Etics and Emics   Some years ago, the well-known descriptive linguist Kenneth Pike, in attempting to come to grips with the problem of the objective description of cultural perception by an outside student as against the awareness of the world held by a native, sought a resolution in his coining the terms *etic* and *emic,* drawn obviously from the linguistic terminology *phonetic* and *phonemic.*[7] Some anthropologists, examining both language and culture, have found the terms useful, suggestive of modes of analysis. *Etic* analysis brings the judgment of the observer to bear; he is making a statement about a people's behavior based on a broad comparative knowledge and is not emphasizing what the people themselves think or say. A formal analysis of kinship (Chapter 23) may provide a sense of the structure of social units; when a paternal uncle, the father's brother, is called by the same term as the progenitor, a specific structure comes to light. But of itself this does not tell what the user of this "father" term thinks or feels in regard to the persons so designated. The *emic* element takes this into account. How, in fact, does the native participant in a cultural system think of himself and the others as behaving? With culture as with language, one knows the "correct" grammar from the linguistic experience or the correct mode of action from the experience of the culture. A person may not be able to explain why he acts as he does; he knows merely that this is done. The meanings and associations of symbols, whether verbal or behavioral, may go deeper than the overt awareness of the individual. In language, phonetics and phonemics are two sides of the same coin; the crucial issue is the reference point of observation. And the same is true of cultural behavior viewed in terms of an etic-emic distinction.

Morphology and Syntax   It might be useful to compare a language to an organism. (Indeed, some anthropologists have treated culture in this way, although others are im-

---

[7] K. L. Pike, *Language in Relation to a Unified Theory of the Structure of Human Behavior,* parts 1–3.

patient with the analogy.) Suppose one considers a domestic cat. It is a mammal, of course, but it is also a specialized predator. It has, in addition to the features which permit assigning it to the class Mammalia, pointed ears, a set of rending and tearing teeth, a long tail used for balance, and padded paws with retractable claws, and it is capable of great speed. It makes characteristic sounds. In general, the familiar cat is a good example of adaptation in the animal world, one well equipped with the tools to meet its needs for survival.

Proceeding to the analogy, we may say that the cat is a whole animal, different from all other animals which are specialized in their own ways. The biological morphology, or structure, of the cat, the parts making up the whole animal, are meaningless outside the context of the animal in its entirety. Dogs and cats have some similarities—both are carnivores, for example—but there is a world of difference between them. A language is also a whole system. It too has a structure, or morphology. To take the analogy further, the parts of language, like those of the cat, may be assembled in a particular way and reflect a special kind of adaptation. Some languages, but by no means all, build their meaningful concepts out of verbs, forming names for things and concepts, i.e., nouns, from stems that reflect action. Arabic and Hebrew are good examples of such a process. Others, such as many of the European languages, appear to stress things rather than actions. In English, any verb may be made into a noun. In fact, the tendency in English is to teach children the names of things first—"mouth," "kitty," "doggie," and so on—and to introduce the child to verbs only later. Conversely, in Navaho, the child first becomes familiar with actions—"sitting," "running," "moving," and so forth. In Chinese, we can say that there are no nouns or verbs. Whether the concept expressed refers to a thing or an action (a noun or a verb) depends on its relations to other conceptual units expressed in an utterance. Just as animals differ in their mor-

phology, so language structures vary in the ways that their component parts are put together. Just as a relative difference exists between dogs and cats, so relative differences exist among languages.

Morphemes The basic element in any language is the phoneme, but phonemic units are put together in various ways to form the elements of *structure,* or the *morphology.* If phonemes are basic units of sound, *morphemes* (Gr. *morphe,* form) are basic units of structure. The synchronic linguist, interested in determining the facts of the structure of a language, reduces the language first to its bedrock of sounds. He then notes that sound arrangements follow a pattern, that a clustering of certain kinds of discernible elements occurs. These may be actual words, although again, the problem of what constitutes a word in a given language poses some difficulties. More often, these clusters are parts that form units which are set off by the secondary phonemic element of *juncture.* Junctures are simply the breaks between words. The sentence *The man is eating* suggests these junctures. Almost no break occurs between /the/ and /man/, indicating that when the definite article is used in English, it is almost a prefix, that is, something bound to the element following. Between /man/ and /is/ and between /is/ and /eating/ there is a slight rest, a tiny hesitation that sets each element off. In French, for instance, the junctures are less apparent; words flow together; other languages stress them more. The point here is that any language may have "free" morphemes (in this instance they equal words) or "bound" morphemes, that is, those which are in some way modified.

To illustrate what a morpheme is, let us take a closer look at the sentence given: *The man is eating.* /man/ is a primary morpheme with the bound /the/; /is/ refers to the state occupied by some singular person or object; /eating/ consists of two morphemes—the root form /eat/ and a suffixed bound form /-ing/ which in English refers to an action going on, continuing, proceeding. Again, a sentence such as *Birds fly* consists of several morphemes. /bird/ is made plural by a bound suffixed /z/.[8] /fly/ is a single morpheme, but since it is preceded by the plural noun /birds/ it is not the same as /fly/ in /to fly/; a third-person plural, present tense is understood. The linguist can treat this as a "zero" morpheme, one in which there is no inflection but in which a distinct environment, in this instance, agreement between noun and verb, is held to prevail.

Is such a way of looking at language really any different from the way in which many of us have studied and learned languages—the method of the paradigm, where one encounters such patterns as *I hit, you hit, he hits?* Indeed it is, since by listing and categorizing the morphemes of a language, one obtains a total perspective on the potential range of variations in the whole system. Because languages differ so markedly from each other in the ways they put their concepts together, it is necessary to "get the feel" of the system by means of the morphology. It is here that the understanding of language cues begins. Since languages do differ it is also necessary to obtain some sense of the meaning of the morphemes and the contexts in which they are used. Translation from one language to another is always difficult. Can one get all of the nuances, can one understand all that is conveyed in the oral-aural situation in a language that is not one's own? Morphemic analysis, which takes account of the language in its structural totality, offers a lead.

Morphemes and Meaning So far, little has been said about meaning in language. A morpheme, however, is a meaningful unit,

not only in the sense that it may be a word with the psychological and emotive reactions that words evoke, but because it appears in environments with other morphemes to create meaningful forms.

A few examples chosen from selected languages may illustrate the point.

To an English speaker, the sentence *When I was going to the store, I saw a dog* seems infinitely logical and simple. In Turkish, a Ural-Altaic language that originated in Central Asia, the same thought possesses a rather different structuring, using morphemes solely Turkish and not in any way suggestive of English. The Turkish sentence is: *Magasine gittiğim zaman bir köpek gördüm.*

English uses eleven word units, with several more morphemes, while Turkish employs only five. The Turkish morphemes are: /magasin/ which means "store," with a suffixed /e/ "place to which action is directed"; /gittiğim/ consists of a root morpheme /git/ "go," with a suffixed /*d(t)ik/ which is marked with an asterisk because it can never appear without some pronoun modification, but which refers to a continuous action in the past, and /-im/ referring to action by a first person "I," "my"; /zaman/ "time"; /bir/ "one," an indefinite single something; /köpek/ "dog," an indefinite noun (if the noun were definite, i.e., "the dog," the Turkish would be köpeği/, the /-i/ morpheme being used only where there is a definite direct object of a verb); /gördüm/ from a root morpheme /gör/ "see," plus /d(t)/ indicator of any part action, plus /-um/ action by a first person, again "I," "my."

In this case, what is the literal meaning of the Turkish sentence? One might render it into English, although meaninglessly: *To* (definite) *store my wenting time* (indefinite) *dog I saw.* Such a contrived rendition is scarcely necessary, since the Turkish sentence has much the same meaning as the English. We are simply attempting to convey the difference in the way in which concepts are put together.

Syntax A language, however, is much

---

[8]This also illustrates the problem of the change of a sound because of morphological factors. The rule in English is that if a noun ends in a vowel or a voiced consonant, i.e., a consonant which is accompanied with resonance, the suffixed /-s/ becomes itself voiced, i.e., /z/. A word such as *bee* /bij:/ takes its plural as /bijz/; *dog* /dawg/ becomes /dawgz/; but *cat* /kaet/ becomes /kaets/. This is true of any suffixed /-s/ in English, however variable the function of /-s/ may be. Its functions include: inflection of the third-person singular verb, present tense; possession; and designation of number, i.e., the plural.

more than a series of morphemes clustered haphazardly. Generally, morphemes, bound or free, follow some kind of ordered pattern. The pattern may be quite strict or fairly free. *Syntax* refers to *the arrangement of elements in phrases and sentences.* English, which has shed many of its inflections, or morphemic modifications, depends on a fairly rigid syntax. In the sentence *John and Mary to the movies went,* the hearer is at once aware of something wrong. But *John went the movies to Mary and* violates the rules of all English syntax and meaning.

When a language is more dependent on morphology, syntax may relax. In Latin, for example, the sentences *Canis ursum videt, Videt ursum canis, Videt canis ursum,* and so on through any other possible variations, all make good sense: *"The dog sees the bear."* The morphemic arrangement of /canis/ and /ursum/ make it completely clear that it is the dog which is doing the seeing and the bear which is being seen. Mandarin Chinese, and the Chinese languages generally, even more than English, have shed their morphology almost completely. For them, syntax has become a wholly necessary feature.

Languages thus vary tremendously in their structures, whether in sounds, in morphology, or in syntax. Some linguists have attempted to type languages according to the kind of morphology and syntax they possess, a process that is useful in showing the great potential range of human speech patterns. It also becomes eminently clear that one cannot read the structure of one's own language into another. What holds for English will not hold for even a closely related language.

Every language is bound by its own firm rules of grammar, and each speaker who wants to be understood must master the rules and abide by them. Language is a tyrant that does not permit much individual liberty, although there will always be great differences in individual skill in the use of a language.

One really intriguing point, however, is that although firm grammatical, that is, morphological and syntactic, rules control the use of language, the rules are not made by grammarians. They have been arrived at naïvely by generations of speakers who had no consciousness of what they were doing. Once certain elemental ways of shaping and combining morphemes were established, the mold for the future growth of the language was pretty well set. Rules of grammar give consistency to the tongue; they integrate the use of vocal symbols. Yet, the tyranny of grammatical rules notwithstanding, no primitive man can state the rules of his grammar. He can only tell you that a certain thing must be said this way and not that way. It is only the sophisticated linguist who can analyze a language into expressly stated rules. A bright informant working with a field worker may discover some elemental rules for himself, however. This happened when I asked a Shoshone Indian how to say: *my house, his house, her house, our house, their house.* /gani/ is the morpheme for "house." In the informant's responses each word contained *ngani* preceded by a different personal pronoun prefix. As I wrote down the words, a great light dawned upon him and he excitedly exclaimed, "Say! That /n/ in there must mean that something belongs to someone." On being assured that this was so (he had discovered the possessive infix), he marveled, "Well, what do you think of that? Here I've been talking Shoshone all my life and I never knew that /n/ in the middle of a word means it belongs to someone."

The rules of a language are unconsciously obeyed by its speakers. The normal way to learn any language is to become habituated to its unformulated rules through using the language, not by learning the rules. It has taken American language teachers a long time to learn this simple fact.

Transformational Grammars Grammatical transformations are the ways in which speakers combine and recombine strings of morphemes to form phrases and sentences.

There is considerably more to the concept of language as a total system than the mere rules of sound and structure. These are no more than the bare bones of a linguistic system. There is, in addition, an ordering that description alone cannot cope with. In English, for example, one cay say, "three big round red balloons," and there is no quarrel with the ordering of the adjectives. But suppose you modify this to, "three red big round balloons." The sense is changed, the adjectives are given a slightly different emphasis and the listener is clearly bothered. Go a step further and say, "red big three round balloons," and the listener will think you are nutty. On the other hand, the famous illustrative sentence coined by the linguist Noam Chomsky, "colorless green ideas sleep furiously," makes perfect structural sense, even though it lacks meaning; it "feels" all right—even good. But what gibberish to utter, "furiously sleep ideas green colorless!" This transformation of the word order is chaotic. It was awareness of problems of this kind that led Chomsky to a reformulation of some of the concepts of linguistics.[9]

The "transformational" model conceived by Chomsky stresses the element of syntactic structure. The model seeks to account for all the variations in a language system. These include not only the patterning of sound, but also the element of meaning. What Chomsky's transformational system does is to suggest that all elements in a total system should be specified, even if the totality of relationships in a given language system can be discerned only with difficulty. The point is stressed, however, that the goal of a transformational description is to elicit a formal statement (virtually mathematical) about the "competence" of a speaker and hearer of a language. As a speaker, one generates concepts in language by putting elements together in structured ways. Transformationalists are concerned with the "deep structures" of a language, not only the surface structures of sound and morpheme, but with the phrase

and the ways in which a speaker of a language rearranges the parts to form his sets of meanings. The semantic quality relates to the deeper structure of the language. The result is that in transformational grammars the way is opened for a much fuller understanding of language as a total structure. More than this, however, the transformational approach seeks to arrive at a uniform theory of language in terms of description and as a communicative device.

While the complexities of the transformationalist theory have at present little relevance for the parallels and analogies between language and culture, the refinements of the point of view, rapidly developing, may move in this direction. The theories of syntactic structure as put forth by Chomsky have drawn increasing attention from both anthropologists and linguists and may well be a highway to a broader and more comprehensive theory of the components of language.

Semantics: The Meaning of Meaning

Because the primary function of language is communication, the question of meaning is central. A linguist can, to be sure, look only at the structure of a language, noting the kinds of variety of verb forms or what happens to constitute a noun under varying sets of circumstances. But this is linguistics without meaning, an approach to language aimed solely at an analysis of the interaction of parts. It is not a treatment of the whole language. It is precisely this sense of the whole which the transformationalists are seeking, and they suggest that meaning lies in the "deep structure," vitally related to all other facets. The study of semantics is to some extent still in its infancy. As new modes of analysis are developing and as greater awareness of the symbolic nature of human behavior arises, some startling new insights are coming to light.

Initially, one may think of semantics when

[9]N. Chomsky, *Language and Mind.*

crossing from one language to another and from one culture to another.

Between languages, meaning is constantly a problem. This is true not only on the level of words alone but in terms of the basic definitions that are resident in the structure of language. It has been contended that because Russian and English employ different built-in concepts of time—that is, time is differently expressed in the structure of the two languages—there is a basis for much misunderstanding on the international level. Whether or not this is so in this particular case, it is probable that the varying structures of languages do inhibit cross-cultural understanding. A case in point is provided by the Keresan-speaking Pueblo Indians of New Mexico. Suppose a missionary were to bring to these peoples his particular brand of religion. In Keresan, no idea can be expressed without containing the morphemes indicating whether the action described depends on experience undergone by the speaker or whether the speaker has his information from hearsay. If the missionary tells his listeners in Keresan that in the beginning God created heaven and earth, he cannot use the experienced mode—*he* was not there. His remarks can only imply, "So I've been told."

But does one really need "meaning" in a study of language? On the face of it, the argument seems absurd. Yet, if one is considering structured units only, then the concern may be solely with structure, with phonology, morphology, and syntax. No one who takes the study of language seriously, however (unless the goal is a puristic structuralism), will wish to ignore the semantic issues. It is this kind of point which the transformationalists stress. Each of a pair of utterances, "occasionally it rains in May" and "it rains occasionally in May," generates a very different set of meanings. A perspective on a whole language seeks to answer both the question of structure and that of meaning as well. Increasing concern on the part of anthropologists with semantics suggests that there are

domains of the subjects which will require further exploration.

Emotional Quality in Meaning But what of meaning within a language? Every person, in any language, has his own *ideolect,* his particular style of speech, his favorite words and expressions, his particular set of images and thoughts which are evoked by words. Everyone can agree on the definition of "table"; what each hearer sees in his mind's eye may reflect a host of differing images, all of which, however, are acceptable tables. The field of psycholinguistics, which relates to the psychology of language, is as yet only in its infancy. Some breakthroughs have been made, to be sure, especially in the area of language learning. A speaker encodes an utterance, delivers it, and the hearer decodes it and responds. The linguistic system is internalized; the cues relate intimately to individual personality. It is clear from the experience of our own culture that some words are holy, some are obscene, some are proper for certain social occasions and improper for others. These distinctions indicate the continuing presence of the emotive quality of language. An expressed thought may be purely neutral, but it serves to relate the speaker to his cultural environment.

Meaning in a language poses some further problems. Just what does an utterance mean? The answer to this question depends in part on the social setting of the conversation, who is present, whether those present are men or women of superior or inferior statuses. The manner in which this problem is resolved depends on the demands of the cultural setting.

Getting away from the emotive element in meaning, we should mention the purely academic issue of just what words do mean. Does one really express his primary thoughts with any exactness? Actually not, since the word is accompanied by a host of other culturally determined nonlinguistic cues. I do not have to say precisely what I think. Indeed, in our own culture and in most others, care is necessary to avoid creating problems in social interaction. Some Americans prefer to say that a person has "passed away" rather than that he is "dead." And clearly, to say that he has "kicked the bucket" is in very bad taste. Meanings thus have social as well as psychological dimensions. Nowhere, perhaps, is the question of meaning so vital as in the specialized language of the law. Here exactness becomes imperative, a matter recognized by every society that has codified and verbalized its legal codes.

Culture and Language

Several ways in which language and culture may interact have been suggested. It seems clear that every language is in itself a cultural phenomenon. Language has absolutely nothing to do with biological inheritance; therefore, there is no inherent relationship between race and language. If, as is sometimes the case, a certain language is spoken solely by the members of a given race, it is only because the racial population, having been isolated from other populations, developed its own mode of speech. Once the isolation breaks down, this need no longer be so. Twenty million Afro-Americans speak only English, but their ancestors of one and two centuries ago spoke only one or another of the African languages.

The fact that it is extremely difficult for English-speakers to master some of the phonemes of other languages—ones that are used with ease by native speakers—does not mean that the native speakers have a natural proclivity to produce such sounds. It merely means, providing the adage is not taken too seriously, that "you can't teach old dogs new tricks." Once vocal habits are set, they become so firm that to break them is quite a task. There is nothing in the physical structure of the members of any race, however, that makes certain populations genetically suited to the pronunciation of some phonemes and not others.

Therefore, if the question "What is the relation between race and language?" is asked, the answer is, "None." On the other hand, if the question "What is the relation between culture and language?" is put, the answer is, "A great deal" (Figure 31-1).

Subgroup Dialects Most languages, although they are systems consistent within themselves, do have spoken variations that are used by different groups. Such groups may be localized, and in such instances the variety is recognized as a dialect or subdialect. Or such groups may be status groups within a society. Men employ certain speech usages that differ from those of women. In the same way, usages of adults differ from those of infants; those of professors from those of laborers; those of politicians from those of preachers. In Javanese, for example, socially inferior people address their superiors with one form of speech and are answered in another. Superiors use yet a third speech among themselves, while inferiors have still another.

The Sapir-Whorf Hypothesis: Language and Thought Habits Every language is adequate to the needs of its culture insofar as the speakers of the language can communicate to each other the ideas and feelings that their culture makes it possible for them to have. But the very structure of a language subtly molds the way in which people conceive of the nature of the world in which they find themselves. Philosophically, we know that man's idea systems are the screens through which he perceives reality. We saw in Chapter 2 how the basic postulates of each culture provide the assumptions about the general nature of things with which the members of each and every society view nature and themselves. Taken together, culture at large and language in particular grind the multiple lenses through which men view the world that surrounds them. Indeed, as Edward Sapir (1884–1939) was one of the first to perceive, in a real sense "language and our thought-grooves are inextricably interwoven, are, in a sense, one and the same."[10]

We say we have mastered a language, but only in the present generation have we begun to perceive that the language we are born to learn to speak in turn masters us.

How does this identity of language and thought-grooves become manifest? Perhaps two illustrations will suffice.

English- and Indo-European-language speakers confront time as a divisible entity that falls "naturally" into a past, the present, and a future. Until Einstein pushed the special language of mathematics and physics into a new sphere that could not be described by any of these conventional Indo-European distinctions, time could not be thought of by any of us in any other terms.

Benjamin Lee Whorf (1897–1941), a chemical engineer and fire insurance executive, became concerned with the problem of how English words betray people into burning down buildings. One example from Whorf's argument will do:

In a wood distillation plant the metal stills were insulated with a composition prepared from limestone and called at the plant "spun limestone." . . . After a period of use, the fire below one of the stills spread to the "limestone," which to everyone's great surprise burned vigorously. Exposure to acetic acid fumes from the stills had converted part of the limestone (calcium carbonate) to calcium acetate. This, when heated in a fire decomposes, forming inflammable acetone. Behavior that tolerated fire close to the covering was induced by use of the name "limestone," which because it ends in "-stone" implies noncombustibility.[11]

Shawnee Syntax and Conceptualization An example of the principles put forth by Whorf can readily be demonstrated by Shawnee, a lan-

[10]E. Sapir, *Language*, p. 232.

[11]B. L. Whorf, *Language, Thought, and Reality*, pp. 135–136.

Fig. 31-1   A mother tongue can easily become a symbol of social and personal identity. Panjabi speakers demonstrate for a separate Indian state. (Marc Riboud, Magnum.)

guage spoken by American Indians in what is now the southeastern United States.

Whorf confronts us with two English sentences:

1. I push his head back.
2. I drop it in the water and it floats.

The acts performed according to these two statements are quite unlike. In (1), the physical act is presented as the exertion of a force: subject → force → object. In (2), the emphasis is on an attribute of the object (it floats).

Shawnee language is so structured that in describing these same two events the Shawnee Indian sees and thinks of them in terms of similarity. How? To tell what happens in the first situation he says:

1. *ni*	*kwaškwi*	*tepē*	*n*	*a*
I	push back	on the head	by action of the hand	cause to a person

To tell what happens in the second situation, the Shawnee says:

2. *ni*	*kwašk*	*ho*	*to*
I	push back	at the surface of water	cause to an inanimate thing

Literally translated, (1) means, "I cause the head of a human being to be pushed back by action of my hand." Similarly translated, (2) means, "I cause an inanimate thing to be pushed back at the surface of water." Pushing against, a reverse force, is what Shawnee grammar induces the Shawnee speaker to see in *both* situations; not pushing and floating as separate phenomena. The Shawnee grammatical approach to what takes place is closer to the reality of the situation, as any student who learned Archimedes' principle in high school physics knows.

In other words, it is not always that "sentences are unlike because they tell about unlike facts" (although, of course, in some situations other than those just mentioned, they may be unlike in fact). In some cases, it may be that: "Facts are unlike to speakers whose

language background provides for unlike formulation of them."[12]

Limitations of the Sapir-Whorf Hypothesis The Sapir-Whorf hypothesis, as it has been demonstrated by the Shawnee example, is very suggestive and exciting. But like every body of theory, this point of view has its adherents and its opponents. Whorf's ideas have actually been somewhat misunderstood. He does not say that because of the particular slant of the language the associated cultural form is predictable. His contribution lies rather in calling attention to the kinds of reality which a given group creates for itself. In some degree, this is a linguistic feature. Decisions are made because of the traps which language itself sets, as Whorf's concern with the imputed qualities that language imparts to substances that may be flammable or nonflammable shows. People act according to the "realities" their language provides.

It might be argued that Whorf is not really dealing with language at all. Rather, he is relating behavior to factors of perception and cognition, areas which the psychologists call their own. The Whorfian hypothesis, suggestive though it may be, is extremely difficult to prove. The coloring of behavior through language may indeed be indirect; what constitutes reality in a human situation does vary; it can possibly be a function of the linguistic system. Although one can readily see that Shawnee, that any language, in fact, has its own peculiar ways of putting concepts together, we must recall that there are other Algonkian-speaking groups which share the world of the Shawnee, at least to the extent that their languages are related. Yet the cultures of the various Algonkian speakers are very different.

Whorf made a parallel analysis of the Hopi language in the American Southwest.[13] Here again, three other major language families exist among the Pueblo peoples. All are

---

[12]*Ibid.*, p. 235.
[13]*Ibid.*, pp. 51–64, 102–111, and 199–206.

generally similar in culture, yet all four languages, including Hopi, appear to be founded on differing conceptual bases. However attractive the Sapir-Whorf hypothesis may seem, language and cultural forms do not appear to dovetail on this level; when the hypothesis is subjected to rigorous analysis, the results seem to fail to hold up.

Cognitive Anthropology: Emic Classification and Folk Categories

More than three decades have passed since Sapir and Whorf formulated their perceptions of language structure and cultural perception. Since that time, however, there have been advances in respect to the interaction between the two. Psychology of language (psycholinguistics) aside, anthropologists in more recent years have been increasingly interested in the problem of the way in which a given folk perceives its world, how it classifies experience and the things of that world. In such investigations it is possible to return to the semantic question, to the apparent structures which emerge when the forms of such classification are analyzed, and finally, to the kinds of classification resident in a given culture in form, meaning, and category. The area of analysis is an exciting one and appears to hold considerable promise for the development, through language, of an avenue which sheds light on the nature of culture and cultural processes.

The emic approach noted above suggests that it is possible to free data from the categories which pure objectivity might seem to impose. In other words, can an anthropologist shed his own biases, those derived from his culture, and see the world through the eyes of the people with whom he is concerned? Perhaps he can; the question is, how can he do it?

Ethnosemantics An initial answer lies in the development of an *ethnosemantics,* a study of meaning and meanings resident in the system being analyzed. What, for example, does the speaker of a language perceive when he talks about the world around him? He possesses a *cognitive system,* that is, a built-in system of classifications. An example of such a human tendency to classify can be seen in the use of color words in various languages. English is very perceptive of color and there are perhaps 3,000 words dealing with all the possible shades of color —"red," "crimson," "scarlet," "cerise," "rust," etc. Another language, however, may limit the categories of color and be unable to express the subtle differences in color tones. A recent study has shown that all languages have terms for black and white. If there is a further distinction, it will predictably be red. Does this mean that the native speaker of a language fails to perceive the variations in color? Hardly; it is simply that the language limits the kind of classifications available to him, with the result that there are categorical limitations.[14]

Color terms represent a semantic domain for all languages. Any culture has a great variety of different domains which reflect the native taxonomy of the things as they exist in both nature and culture. All that is suggested here is that different peoples have different ways of dividing up the spectrum. When Navaho says "green," the language also means "blue" and also "purple." The Zuñi language embraces both "yellow" and "orange" in the single term it employs. Other semantic domains may encompass the terms used for the animal world, for plants, for foods, and so on through the categories which a culture perceives as significant. In English, for example, a "chair" describes a vast array of things on which people sit, from camp stools to reclining armchairs. Yet hassocks and sofas are not chairs, even if

---

[14]B. Berlin, "A Universalist-Evolutionary Approach in Ethnographic Semantics," in A. Fischer (ed.), *Current Directions in Anthropology,* vol. 3, no. 2, part 2 (1970), p. 8.

made to be sat on, while the difference between "chair" and "table" is certainly categorically and taxonomically marked.

A formal analysis, one which simply notes the classifications which are made, can thus be applied to the domains which any group of people establishes in language and culture. In language, an investigator seeks paradigms, the formal patternings of linguistic elements. Verbs may pattern out differently from nouns. So also in culture and meaning, there are always elements which go together (associate)—"tire" and "automobile" are related components; "automobile" and "ocean" are clearly not.

Componential Analysis   Componential analysis is a conceptual tool for the ordering of taxonomy and classificatory principles within a culture; it seeks to elicit the cognitive realms of the bearers of the culture in question.[15] These are essentially difficult concepts to get at, especially since the kinds of ordering and the classifications employed by the group may be on an unconscious level.

One important aspect of the contemporary concerns with componential analysis and ethnosemantics lies in studies of kinship and kinship terminologies as employed in different cultures. These are related not so much to the actual behavioral or structural implications of such a system as they are to the domains of semantic contrast resident in a kinship pattern. Floyd G. Lounsbury, for example, by applying principles of category and meaning to the sets of kinship terms in both the Crow and Omaha systems, is able to demonstrate the inherent classificatory relatedness of terms for relatives, suggesting that one system is a mirror image of the other and that there are semantic issues in generational designation which relate to the bases

of kinship classification.[16] The effect is to avoid the errors in categorization which arise when an outsider imposes his own formulation based on his own categories. In other words, the meaning of a structured system of kinship is one generated by the group employing it.

Ethnoscience   The upshot of these concerns with meaning lies in the development of an essentially newly conceived disciplinary focus—that of *ethnoscience*. In ethnoscience the purpose is to lay bare the semantic element, the kinds of taxonomies with which various linguistic, and by extension, various cultural systems are concerned. Just as in a grammar there is an elicitation of a series of paradigms and the formulation of a set of rules applicable to the specific language, so also in an ethnoscientific approach there is the concern with the paradigms of cultural behavior. The approach of Lounsbury and others working in this field stresses an economy of description. A grammar allows a tightly focused prediction of form and structure. An ethnoscience allows the same for a statement about culture. And by the same token, a grammar has its own sets of categories; the ethnoscientist does not impose his on the cultural situation but allows the cultural system to generate its own. The anthropologist as ethnoscientist is a neutral vehicle for the expression of the system in English or whatever other language he uses.

The Growth and Divergence of Languages

The origins of languages are lost in the distant past. The spoken word does not turn to stone—it leaves no remains for the archaeolo-

---

[15]See W. C. Sturtevant, "Studies in Ethnoscience," in A. K. Romney and A. G. d'Andrade (eds.), "Transcultural Studies in Cognition" (*American Anthropologist*, vol. 66, no. 3, part 2, Special Publication, 1964), pp. 99–131.

[16]F. G. Lounsbury, "A Formal Account of the Crow and Omaha-type Kinship Terminologies," in W. H. Goodenough (ed.), *Explorations in Cultural Anthropology*, pp. 351–387.

gist to unearth from an Eolithic or a Paleo-lithic site. Writing comes into being only after eons of language building have lapsed into the past. Words finally transcribed on stone or clay tablet, on papyrus, skin, or paper are manifestations of languages already millennia old.

Because all the people we can study have an already developed language, there is no way to reconstruct the multiplex processes by which a people hit upon agreement as to the grammatical principles that they begin with. But languages, in spite of their inherent stability, inevitably change through time.

Diachronic (Historical) Linguistics Scientific study of the patterns of change in given languages is possible and feasible. This may be done in two ways. Once a language is committed to writing, the changes that occur may be followed through a sequence of documents. The other approach is to push the history of related languages back into prehistoric times through internal analysis of homologous languages. The major principle underlying this second method is similar to that used in reconstruction of organic phylogenies; namely, that forms which have in common a number of functionally similar qualities that is greater than the level of chance occurrence are genetically related.

The Comparative Method The criteria used in historical linguistics are morphemic and syntactic identities. The quickest way to get an indication as to whether two languages are related is to compare their vocabularies, or word forms. (Thomas Jefferson, even while President of the United States, prepared word lists to be sent out to explorers and traders living among the Indians so as to get the answer to the question of American Indian origins and relationships.)[17] By sheer chance,

under the law of limited possibilities, they will possibly have some words in common. It is surely puerile to argue that two tribes are related because one can say that they share a handful of words. There must be a concurrence in a significant number of words and their associated meanings.

What constitutes significance? Two languages that are clearly unrelated and also phonemically unlike in structure will ordinarily share only 4 per cent of their total terms in like form and meaning. If it happens that the phonemic structure of morphemes in the two languages is similiar, then the concurrences may be double. It is therefore safe to hold that vocabulary identities of less than these percentages may be the product of nothing but chance, and the identities may not be taken as evidence of historical relationship. Conversely, it is the considered and well-supported judgment of linguists, as expressed by the American expert Professor Joseph Greenberg, that:

It can be safely asserted that a resemblance of 20 per cent in vocabulary always requires a historical explanation and that, unless similarity of phonetic structure leads to the expectation of a high degree of chance similarity, even 8 per cent is well beyond what can be expected without the intervention of historical factors.[18]

By means of mathematical comparisons among three or more languages, it is possible to work out even sharper determinations of possible genetic relations along the lines just indicated.

Languages are apt to include a large number of words borrowed from other languages (e.g., in English, *totem, canoe, tobacco, tabu, automobile,* and so forth). Fundamental words such as pronouns and those representing parts of the body are most likely to retain their identity with the morphemes of their ancestry. Free borrowing from unrelated languages

---

[17]Long vocabulary lists prepared by Jefferson are in the manuscript collections of the Library of the American Philosophical Society, Philadelphia.

[18]J. H. Greenberg, "Historical Linguistics and Unwritten Languages," in A. L. Kroeber (ed.), *Anthropology Today,* p. 270.

occurs more commonly in what are called the *cultural* (nonpersonal) *items*. Therefore, when the linguist is confronted by a group of languages that exhibit similarities greater than chance probability would account for in their *fundamental vocabularies,* while at the same time lacking similarities in their *cultural vocabularies,* he is certain that these languages were remotely derived from a common ancestor. If they had only recently come into contact with each other, the one would have borrowed words from the cultural vocabulary of the other before it would displace its own fundamental words with those from an alien source. Thus another device for establishing historical relations between languages is available.

Sounds change over time. This means that the phonemic system of a given language does not remain constant. In seeking relationships among languages, the linguist with historical interests again may return to the bedrock of the language in question, its phonology. In comparing sounds between one language and another that he assumes to be related to it, he may observe a distinct pattern, a systematic change through the phonology of both. This principle was first elicited in the nineteenth century by Jacob Grimm, the same scholar who along with his brother, Wilhelm, collected the famous fairy tales—not for purposes of entertainment, although that was a happy by-product of their efforts, but to see historical relationships in the distributions of the stories. Grimm's *law of phonetic change,* set forth in 1822, made possible the designation of the great Indo-European speech family. Taking Sanskrit, the language of ancient India, as a kind of prototype of Indo-European, the brothers Grimm observed that systematic changes took place from one language to another as time went on. For example, the Sanskrit word *pitar* became *patēr* in Greek, *pater* in Latin, *vater* in Germanic (*v* is pronounced *f*), and *father* in English. Similarly, Sanskrit *bhrata* becomes Latin *frater,* Germanic, *bruder,* English, *brother,* and Russian, *brat.* These, of course, are only some obvious examples of what emerges as a complex and predictable series of patterns of sound changes. It can be seen that earlier Indo-European *p* may become *f,* that a weak *b* (bh) may also move to *f,* and the *f* may move back to *b.* Other regular modifications are demonstrable among the numerous Indo-European tongues, and similar relationships have been established for many other language groups.

This means that in comparing vocabularies for identities, exact phonemic similarity is not to be expected. The linguist, however, comes to recognize phonemic correlates that should be treated as identical. In cases where written documents extending over a number of centuries are available for related languages, it is possible to validate directly the specific functioning of Grimm's law and its derivatives.

Languages may also be related by comparison of their morphological and syntactic features. Thus an isolating language, such as Chinese, which sets up its words as simple monosyllables, is hardly likely to be related to such an extremely polysynthetic language as Eskimo, which builds up single words with as many as a dozen or more morphemes. More refined criteria, such as the presence or absence of gender, or inflection, and so forth, are also relied on.

Looking thus at Indo-European, it becomes possible to suggest some ultimate relationships. The speech phylum (family) has grown over a period of thousands of years, presumably from a single geographic center. Dialect changed to language as mutual intelligibility ceased; groups moved, forming their own variations on themes of the original language. Once a parent language broke off from the main stem, it, too, was subject to further changes, giving rise to a kind of family language tree, with lesser branches off the main branches of the trunk. The process is analogous to genetic speciation and the radiating evolution of organisms, described in Chapter 5, except that language phyla cannot be traced back to one single original form, as is theoretically true of organic evolution. This comparative method has been applied to all the world's languages so that in a general way, it is possible to see wide relationships. In Africa, among the American Indian, in Asia and the South Seas, classifications suggesting historical relationships have been made.

Thus, although the Cheyenne Indians live far out on the western Plains, because their language is Algonkian, we know that they are an offshoot of the great Algonkian group of tribes that dominated the northeastern part of North America. The linguistic fact confirms Cheyenne legend that they came from the vicinity of a great body of water in a wooded land to the east. The fact that the Navahos and Apaches speak Athabascan dialects leads us to look for their original homeland far to the north in the woodlands of the MacKenzie-Yukon basin of western Canada, where all the tribes speak Athabascan.

Glottochronology The use of radioactive carbon counting as a means of reading the built-in "time clock" for the dating of archaeological sites is one of the really exciting techniques developed since 1947. Equally exciting is glottochronology, the recently developed method for calculating the approximate time of the divergence of two dialects or languages from a common mother tongue. Thus the date at which the speakers of the dialects separated from each other can be established.

The fundamental premise of the method is that the basic vocabularies of a language change at a given rate. A basic, or fundamental, vocabulary is one which consists of words referring to universal "culture-free" phenomena, such as air, cloud, sun, rain, hand, foot, and so forth. Standard word lists of 100, 200 or more terms are used for comparison and analysis. Judgments are made according to established principles of linguistic analysis as to whether the two forms of a given word are cognate (i.e., of the same stock or origin)

or noncognate. The relative number of noncognates to cognates is calculated. This provides a statement of the relative amount of change that has occurred since the two languages began to be separated from the original parent stock.

The rate of language change was first calculated on the basis of documented changes (noncognates) in a number of historic (written) languages. The replacement of terms in the fundamental vocabulary was measured at the rate of 19 per cent in a thousand years. The residue of cognates represents the rate of retention. The rate of retention actually varies among Indo-European languages from 86.4 per cent to 74.4 per cent per thousand years. This means that fundamental vocabularies may in fact change at rates of from 13.6 per cent to 25.6 per cent per thousand years. The average figure is 19.5 per cent, but, for convenience, 19 per cent is still used.

By use of a standard algebraic formula for computation of time depth, the number of years which have elapsed since the languages became separated can be calculated within a limited range of probability.[19]

In a number of applications of the principle, the dates derived through glottochronology coincide nicely with historically known dates from the archaeological sites of the presumed ancestral populations. Glottochronology has useful possibilities in giving a measure of time precision to historical reconstructions. It is not reliable where no other supporting evidence is at hand, however. Its validity decreases outside the range of 500 to 2,000 years.

While glottochronology has been much criticized, it appears that where data can be carefully controlled, as when there are closely related languages or dialects, it has some validity. The studies of Shoshone dialects in the Great Basin of the United States, for ex-

[19]See S. C. Gudschinsky, "The ABC's of Lexicostatistics (Glottochronology)," in D. Hymes (ed.), *Language in Culture and Society*, pp. 612–623, for a succinct discussion of the assumptions and procedures to be followed.

ample, show fairly conclusively a series of changes occurring within a time span of roughly a millennium.[20]

Lexicostatistics The statistical summations that reside in the glottochronological word lists may have yet another utility. Lexicostatistics begin to suggest hitherto unsuspected relationships between languages. To be sure, such relationships may be very ancient and one may be interested in the actual dating process. However, the problem of whether or not one language relates to another, easily resolved for Indo-European and other languages with a long written history, is less readily apparent among unwritten languages where historical depth must be inferred. Lexicostatistic similarities (cognate words) shed some light on the matter.

We said that a treelike scheme can be used in formulating linguistic relationships. However, this is an older way of viewing language history, and, in the light of lexicostatistical formulations, such a pattern seems in some measure subject to rethinking. Morphological features, syntactic elements, as well as cultural items of the lexicon may spread by a process of diffusion. The suggestion that there is a parallel between diffusion of language and diffusion of culture has some further application. A language can assimilate new elements from without, whether these are in lexicon, element of sound, or element of structure. It is known that this happens to such an extent that some languages appear to take on the apparent structure of neighboring but unrelated languages. The linguist Morris Swadesh has formulated the concept of a "mesh principle," showing that diffused or convergent patterns may be operative among unrelated languages over wide areas. The reverse may also be true. Languages may remain apparently distinct from each other.

Yet when compared lexicostatistically, using the basic word lists, relationships are beginning to be found between languages where previously none were thought to exist.

SUMMARY

Language is a distinctly human system of communication that is symbolic and oral. It must be learned, and it is an aspect of culture. Other animals beside man can communicate, and some, in controlled laboratory situations, appear to be capable of limited symbolic associations. But only man is able to abstract and to form complex symbolic vocal combinations in the highly structured way that we identify as language. This human achievement apparently came about as a result of a fairly sudden genetic breakthrough or "tipover" in Lower Pleistocene times.

Every language is a complete system, wholly adequate to all human situations. Thus, although there are thousands of languages spoken by primitive peoples, we cannot say that one language is more or less primitive, more or less developed than any other. Vocabularies vary in richness by stylistic and pragmatic criteria—not by primitiveness.

Although so-called primitive languages are unwritten, writing is not in itself an intrinsic part of language. Most languages have been unwritten, but any language can be put into writing.

As a total, self-contained system, every language has its structure that can be analysed much as an ethnologist analyzes a culture. The analysis of structure is the concern of *synchronic linguistics.* Structure begins with *phonemes,* the smallest units of sound on which a language builds. Sounds within a given language have regular patterns of arrangements that produce a *phonology.* The way phonemic units are combined constitutes the *morphology* or structure of a language, and *morphemes* are the basic units of structure. The patterned arrangement of

[20]Wick R. Miller, James L. Tanner, and Lawrence P. Foley, "A Lexicostatistic Study of Shoshoni Dialects" (*Anthropological Linguistics*, vol. 13, 1971), pp. 142–164.

morphemes in phrases and sentences makes up the *syntax* of a language. The range of variation in phonologies and syntaxes in the languages of the world is indeed tremendous. These are all linguistic problems. For the anthropologist as an anthropologist, the main language problem is one of *semantics,* or the meaning of meaning. What are the denotive and connotive intentions of speakers and informants? Major cultural communication takes place through language, and languages must *ipso facto* be understood, explicitly and implicitly.

The discovery of transformational grammars is one of the recent and potentially great developments of contemporary anthropological linguistics. Transformational grammar is concerned with meaning and structure as governed by the "deep" rules which determine syntactic ordering of word units and phrases.

The extent to which the syntax of a language preconditions, limits, and directs the thought patterns of the carriers of a given culture is the subject of the Sapir-Whorf hypothesis. We now realize that we think and perceive in the thought-grooves that the patterns of our own peculiar grammar set for us. Whether this is really a matter of linguistics or of the psychology of cognition remains a moot question.

Diachronic linguistics is concerned with the historic processes of growth and change in languages. The comparative method involves the compilation of vocabulary lists to establish genetic identities in languages and also traces patterns of phonetic shifts as dialects diverge and become new languages. On the assumption that basic vocabularies change at a fixed, determinable rate (analogous to the process of radioactive disintegration), *glottochronology* provides a method of determining the number of centuries which have passed since the speakers of two related tongues have branched apart. *Lexicostatistics* is a later development out of glottochronology. In this technique of the historical method, interest is shifted from time determinations to identification of statistical concordances which suggest historical affinities among languages which no longer have sufficient superficial similarities to be readily identifiable as related.

SELECTED READINGS

Birdwhistell, R. L., *Kinesics and Context: Essays on Body Motion Communication* (1970). Body signals as language adjuncts.

Bloomfield, L., H. Hoijer (ed.), *Language History* (1965). The modern classic, first published in 1933 as a part of Bloomfield's *Language,* now reprinted. Covers the basic principles by which historical derivation of languages is worked out.

Burling, R., *Man's Many Voices: Language in Its Cultural Context* (1970). The effect of the cultural setting on the whole process of communication. The emphasis is on the nonlinguistic factors which affect the use of language; linguistics with a strong cultural anthropological slant.

Carroll, J. B. (ed.), *Language, Thought, and Reality: Selected Writings of Benjamin Lee Whorf* (1956). Whorf's original essays in metalinguistics in a readily available form.

Chomsky, N., *Language and Mind* (1968). By the formulator of modern transformational grammatic methods.

Greenberg, J. H., *Anthropological Linguistics: An Introduction* (1968). A basic book.

Gudschinsky, S. C., *How to Learn an Unwritten Language* (1967). It will take more than this little manual to go about learning how to learn an unwritten language. Nevertheless, it is useful, and could be an eye-opener to the student who has had no linguistic training.

Hall, E. T., *The Silent Language* (1959). A popular and intriguing account of extralinguistic cues as they operate in cultural communications. Holds up for understanding what everyone acts upon but rarely is conscious of. Particularly helpful in its analysis of failure in cross-cultural communication because of unsophisticated awareness of meaning of cues on the part of business and public officials.

Hall, R. A., Jr., *Linguistics and Your Language* (2d rev. ed. of *Leave Your Language Alone!* 1960). A penetrating, easily understandable exploration of process and function in languages.

Hockett, C. F., *A Course in Modern Linguistics* (1958). A clear-headed introduction to the subject.

————, and R. Ascher, "The Human Revolution" (*Current Anthropology,* vol. 5, no. 3, 1964), pp. 135–168. A highly imaginative, hypothetical reconstruction of the origin of language during the transition from ape to man. Highly inferential and speculative, it is stimulating reading, but the thesis has not been discussed in this chapter because of its extreme tentativeness.

Lehmann, W. P., *Historical Linguistics: An Introduction* (1962). Covers the techniques of reconstruction of the "genetic" relationships of languages, in addition to some of the results of the method.

Smith, A. G., *Communication and Culture: Readings in the Codes of Human Interaction* (1966). Covering more than linguistics, this collection contains a number of interesting articles on communication in its broadest sense as written by outstanding thinkers.

Swadesh, M., and J. Sherzer (eds.), *The Origin and Diversification of Language* (1971). A posthumous publication by a highly original thinker in the field of historical linguistics. Contains a useful chapter on glottochronology (pp. 271–284), which Swadesh was the first to develop.

Tyler, S. A. (ed.), *Cognitive Anthropology* (1969). Essays on method and results in the study of how different people define and classify the world and experience and ideas.

Chapter 32

Art

The urge to artistic expression is one of the unique and most interesting characteristics of the human being. It is, as seen by Justice Oliver Wendell Holmes,

One of the glories of man that he does not sow seed and weave cloth, and produce all the other economic means simply to sustain and multiply other sowers and weavers. . . . After the production of food and cloth has gone on a certain time, he stops producing and goes to the play, or he paints a picture or asks unanswerable questions about the universe, and thus delightfully consumes a part of the world's food and clothing.[1]

Franz Boas saw this "glory of man" as an expression of a universal, human aesthetic quality. He wrote:

No people known to us, however hard their lives may be, spend all their time, all their energies in the acquisition of food and shelter, nor do those who live under more favorable conditions and who are free to devote to other pursuits the time not needed for securing their sustenance occupy themselves with purely industrial work or idle away the days in indolence. Even the poorest tribes have produced work that gives to them esthetic pleasure, and those whom a bountiful nature or a greater wealth of inventions has granted freedom from care, devote much of their energy to the creation of works of beauty.

In one way or another esthetic pleasure is felt by all members of mankind.[2]

[1] O. W. Holmes, Jr., "Law in Science and Science in Law" (*Collected Legal Papers*), p. 212.
[2] F. Boas, *Primitive Art*, p. 9.

Fig. 32-A   Carved ivory mask from Nigeria. (Courtesy of the Museum of Primitive Art.)

Man could survive without art; yet man, society, and art are inseparable. To be artless is to be dehumanized. Not without reason are the arts and belles-lettres known as the *humanities*. Yet, art, as we shall see, involves much more than aesthetic pleasure, essential as the latter may be to the essence of art.

From the point of view of the anthropologist, granted that the creative artist is moved by impulses and that he exercises skills not characteristic of the ordinary man, art is not to be approached solely through individual psychology. It must by now be obvious that art forms of various kinds are intricately meshed with all other aspects of life, although the manifestations vary from one society to another. We have observed weapons and tools, housing and temples, clothing and jewelry, cooking utensils and containers adorned far beyond the requirements of utility. Naming ceremonies, initiation rites, funerals, hunting and war parties, medicine and healing, government, religion, magic—all of these, we have seen, are conducted or presented in a rich mixture of ritual and pageantry which includes drama, dance, music, and, frequently, tangible art objects as well.

There is also art even more obscure:

the art that rarely or never reaches the museums . . . that is seen only by the most persistent of ethnographers . . . designs that are carefully made with dyed flour at Nsenga puberty ceremonies, and then danced on and destroyed in less than two minutes . . . the sand-drawings, the body-paintings [Figure 32–1], the scarifications that are seen only by a woman's husband. . . .[3]

What Is Primitive Art?

Before answering the question, "What is primitive art?" one must, of course, ask first, "What is art?" Definitions proffered by artists, art historians, aestheticians, philosophers, politicians, semanticists, and others are

legion. Not surprisingly, all these definitions "vary with the purposes of the definers,"[4] the artist stressing the creative impulse, the art lover emphasizing the emotional response, the Marxist official stressing the opinion-molding purpose of the art, etc. All definitions, by whomever given, cast valuable illumination on the fascinating, complicated behaviors involved in the creation of, and response to, the artistic process. Since we have already stated that art is to be perceived in the total cultural context, we shall concentrate on a few definitions offered by anthropologists.

Art Defined One working definition of art for anthropological purposes is given by E. G. Burrows in his work *Flower in My Ear: Arts and Ethos in Ifaluk Atoll:*

. . . art is any human activity or product (artifact) that emphasizes form beyond all requirements except those of a distinctive pleasure that the manufacture and contemplation of form can give. By form is meant a perceptible relation of parts to a whole. The distinctive pleasure it gives is here called "aesthetic experience."[5]

More simply, Herskovits states:

In the widest sense . . . art is to be thought of *as any embellishment of ordinary living that is achieved with competence and has describable form.* . . . [T]he student of culture must regard as art whatever a people recognizes as manifestations of the impulse to make more beautiful and thus to heighten the pleasure of any phase of living.[6]

R. Sieber feels that it is necessary to add that

[T]his embellishment of life . . . its beautification or adornment, can and, indeed, usually does sustain a level of meaning. In short, there are two basic aspects of art: its esthetic or presentational context comprised of form and skill and embodying style, and its meaning context comprised of subject and symbolic associations.[7]

[3]J. Blacking, "Comment on A. W. Wolfe, 'Social Structural Bases of Art'" (*Current Anthropology,* vol. 10, 1969), pp. 30–31.

[4]G. Mills, "Art: An Introduction to Qualitative Anthropology," in C. M. Otten (ed.), *Anthropology and Art,* p. 77.
[5]P. 11.
[6]M. J. Herskovits, *Cultural Anthropology,* p. 235.
[7]R. Sieber, "The Arts and Their Changing Social Function" (*Annals of the New York Academy of Sciences,* vol. 96, 1962), p. 653.

Regardless of differences in wording, certain basic elements are stated or implied in most definitions of art: there is a creator(s), a process, a medium, a product presented for public (sometimes limited) view, a content and meaning, and a response on the part of the beholder(s).

Art is a transformation. The beauty of nature may be aesthetically overwhelming—as a gorgeous sunset—but it is not art. Its transformation to a painting, a dance, a song, a poem is. However, some natural objects may become *art by metamorphosis;* that is, something that was not created with the intention of its being art is accepted as art. In most art, however, the human artisan intervenes more actively in the transformation process. This is *art by intention,* the outcome of a human creative process.

Art and Handicrafts   Many handicraft works may or may not be viewed as art. Jacques Maquet, in a penetrating analysis of problems in the anthropology of art, has clearly spelled out the distinction between the con-

cepts of *instrumental form* in relation to *noninstrumental* features. He suggests:

Let us take an example: a wooden bowl with some engraved marks. Its context is everyday life; it is used to serve food. Its shape is circular, its rim rounded, its bottom flat. These formal characteristics are instrumental; circular shape and rounded edge make cleaning easier; flat bottom prevents the vessel from being overturned. Some of the engraved marks are magical signs that keep the evil spirits away and prevent them from spoiling the food; they are instrumental too. But we notice also that the rim of the bowl is a perfect circle, which is not easy for a carver working with only adze and knife to achieve. The magical symbols are well balanced and elegant; and beside them there is an engraved pattern, which is just ornamental. These noninstrumental characteristics pertain also to the form. By revealing noninstrumental features, the bowl's form discloses its aesthetic quality.[8]

Figure 32-2 illustrates these principles as seen in a Trobriand Island ceremonial feasting bowl.

[8]J. Maquet, "Introduction to Aesthetic Anthropology" (*McCaleb Module in Anthropology,* 1971), p. 8. Quoted with permission of Addison-Wesley Publishing Company, Inc.

Fig. 32-1   Ephemeral art. Body paintings of adult male dancers in an Australian initiation rite. (Fritz Goro, Life *Magazine,* © *Time, Inc.)*

Noninstrumental expression is the embellishment of an artifact. Plains Indian moccasins were embroidered with dyed porcupine quills. Later, when traders made colored beads available, beadwork replaced quillwork. Basket makers found that variations in twilling produced interesting and pleasing designs within the structure of the basket. They discovered that the use of varicolored fibers made possible tasteful coil and twill work (Figure 15-13). Potters discovered that slips, painting, and sculptural detail made infinite variety a possibility in ceramic production. Clay vessels can be mere household articles, or, by attention to line and form, they can be transformed into objects of aesthetic contemplation. Rawhide boxes could have been left as crude and undecorated as our corrugated shipping cartons. But Plains Indians preferred to decorate them with geometric designs in color. A lime spatula could be a simple stick, but the natives of eastern New Guinea prefer to carve out a handle with painstaking skill. Northern Shoshones were content with roughed-out spoons of mountain-sheep horn, whereas Northwest Coast

Indians worked intricate totemic designs into their handles.

These are all examples of noninstrumental embellishment—modification in line, form, or color of useful articles—which is superfluous in the sense that such modifications do not contribute to the utilitarian effectiveness of the article. But they please their owner, impress his guests, and whet the acquisitive appetites of museum collectors.

A valid principle seems to be that as soon as a people solves the fundamental technical problems in the production of an artifact or tool, the artistic impulse begins to assert itself. The more aesthetically endowed individuals begin to play with the surface in an effort to increase the interest potentials of the object.

As a rule, instrumental technique must be mastered before art develops. Beyond mastery of technique, the more leisure the subsistence techniques and resources of a people's culture allow, the greater the likelihood of decorative embellishment. This must not, however, be taken as a bald assertion that leisure produces art. It may, or it may not. Surplus energies and time may be directed into other channels to satisfy other interests, such as war, trading, or games.

To take one more step with Maquet, the quality that makes the noninstrumental significant rather than just "useless" is *aesthetic contemplation*. If the added elements arrest the attention of a public for their own sake, if one sets aside other concerns for the sake of beholding the object for the interest evoked by its form (not its symbolic content), then that is aesthetic experience—good or bad.

Anthropologists agree that aesthetic sensibility is a universal human feature: "one of the few fundamental ways man relates himself to the world."[9] Man is, indeed, an aesthetic animal.

Primitive Art   What, then, is primitive art? Primitive art is simply the art of primitive peo-

Fig. 32-2   Instrumental and noninstrumental features in a carved Trobriand Island wooden bowl. The shape of the bowl is functionally instrumental, while the flexed snakes and small human figures wearing large plumed headdresses (at the ends of the bowl) may be considered to be symbolically instrumental. The small carved ridges and repeated indentations on the lip of the bowl itself are noninstrumental. (Private collection. Photograph by Don Breneman.)

[9]*Ibid.,* p. 9.

ples. It includes music, dance, myths and oral literature, religious ceremonies such as the sun dance (pages 653–654) and the Okipa (pages 566–571), decorative arts and crafts, religious icons, weaving, pottery, statuary, carvings, and painting. (The place of architecture and tools in both the "fine arts" and the "primitive arts" is somewhat in dispute.) Ideally, our discussion of art should perhaps give equal attention to all these media, but because of both the superabundance of graphic and plastic art objects and the greater ease of reproducing them on the printed page, we shall deal primarily with these permanent and visible products. It must be kept in mind, however, that any comment on their role and function in the particular societies from which they come is likely to pertain in one respect or another to all the other art forms as well.

An unfortunate semantic confusion arises over the term "primitive" in art discussions. The so-called primitivists in recent Occidental art stripped down their art forms to an essential simplicity but were not necessarily emulating primitive art, even though they may have been consciously influenced by the art of certain primitive peoples, especially African sculpture. On the other hand, the "American Primitive" school of art consisted of the untutored representatives of an American offshoot of the European cultural tradition. These painters, working in the early nineteenth century (and some, like Grandma Moses, more recently), had access to only a very limited history and knowledge of technique.

The inclination in art criticism to equate "primitive" with "crude" or "childish" is in part due to the fact that, when primitive art objects were first presented to European artists and connoisseurs (a presentation beginning several centuries ago, but accelerating rapidly in the nineteenth century), these objects were evaluated in terms of classical and traditional standards. "Everything was reckoned according to the degree it approached Judeo-Christian and Classical-Western concepts. Thus, art (meaning idealized nature) was beyond the achievements of primitive man. . . ."[10]

The art of primitive peoples runs a wide gamut from technical clumsiness to high skill, from childlike simplicity to impressive complexity, from naturalism and realism to conventionalized abstraction. Even when we eliminate the more florid forms of primitive art from our consideration and concentrate on the arts of the most primitive of known peoples, this is still true. Bushman art is naturalistic and full of vitality (Figure 32-3). Australian art is highly stylized and in certain forms is abstract and symbolic (Figure 32-4). Eskimo art is naturalistic and technically quite sophisticated (Figure 12-2). Shoshone art was almost nonexistent.

No qualities that universally characterize primitive art forms can be adduced from the art of primitive peoples, unless it is that no primitives ever solved the problem of perspective—with which most of them never dealt.

The Functions of Art

The very universality of art, its presence in all times and places where human societies are known, indicates a significant role and several profound functions in human life. This

[10]D. Fraser, "The Discovery of Primitive Art," in C. M. Otten (ed.), *Anthropology and Art*, p. 26.

Fig. 32-3   Bushman rock painting. The dancers.

we can say with some certainty. Exactly what these functions may be is more difficult to state.

Psychological Functions   It has been commonly assumed that one function of art is to release tensions by enabling the artist to externalize some of his emotions and ideas in an objective way. In the classical and Western view, the artist experiences "divine discontent" or "creative tension," which he expends or "sublimates" in a specialized "artistic process," which culminates in the production of a "work of art"—be it drama, music, dance, or a graphic art form. The release of the tensions brings satisfaction and pleasure to the artist. In their turn, the viewers of the art object, if it has meaning for them, are stimulated to sensuous perceptions that likewise produce emotional responses ultimately resolving into pleasurable feelings of euphoria and balance. This is not to deny, however, that the artistic experience may be highly disturbing and may even cause both

the artist and his audience great discomfiture while it runs its course. The expression of art begins in a state of tension, and the process of translating these feelings of tension into high artistic form is not an easy one.

Thus, even from the individualistic point of view, art never exists literally for art's sake alone. It exists for psychophysiologic reasons —at least in Western cultures. And because our scientific knowledge of the physiology of emotion is still crude, we understand little of the workings of the artistic impulses. Aesthetics, the study of beauty, remains almost entirely a branch of philosophy, for beauty is still subjective, as far as our understanding of it goes.

Societal Functions   But art may not be seen in its entirety if analyzed only from the individualistic point of view. Art is also a social expression, and inevitably exists as a part of culture. Since man is always a creature of society and the child of culture, art *ipso facto* serves social as well as individual interests

Fig. 32-4   Australian aboriginal bark painting: a kangaroo hunt. The style combines naturalism with a special focus of interest on the interior anatomy of the kangaroo, producing the so-called x-ray effect. (From New York Graphic Society, Australia, Aboriginal Paintings—Arnhem Land. *Courtesy of UNESCO.)*

and needs. Art is inextricably tied to religion and magic—and to politics. It cannot help expressing and reflecting social relations and systems. It can serve to sustain them, as Renaissance art so notably served medieval Christianity or as art in Russia is expected to evoke Socialist sentiments in Soviet citizens. It can also aim at their destruction, as has protest art at various times in recent history, and as does the contemporary anarchist art of those who hold modern civilization to be so false and meaningless that the artist can only ridicule it in the hope of bringing about its downfall.

In the words of Alan P. Merriam,

Through the humanistic elements of his culture, man seems to be making pointed commentary on how he lives; he seems in the humanities to sum up what he thinks of life . . . commenting upon himself and enunciating and interpreting his actions, his aspirations, and his values.[11]

In most primitive societies, art is an expression of world view and a handmaiden of religion.

The Functions of Art in Primitive Society   In the present age of individualistic romantic idealism in the West, the functions of art appear to be more antisocietal and countercultural than otherwise. The old world view is dissolving and the avant-garde is hurrying the process on its way.

Whereas the modern artist consciously creates or invents his own style in defiance of convention, "the primitive artist is . . . making works of art within a highly formalized, intensely local and very long established style, . . . he is probably largely unaware of the qualities of the style he follows; he uses it as he does his language, rightly, and without self-consciousness."[12]

In primitive societies the artist-creator, therefore, works from a clear set of social expectations, with traditional media, from agreed-upon values toward known and approved social ends. His personal satisfactions and achievements are incidental. What is important is that his product must satisfy the social needs of the occasion, must evoke the appropriate response, must fulfill the given social function. These social functions may be specific as with the Navaho artist who makes dry paintings (Figure 28-2) for both religious and medical functions "because art for the Navahos is intimately bound up with the maintenance of health and cosmic organization."[13] Or they may be generalized. The Okipa Maker must plan, cast, choreograph, rehearse, and present, with each part being played out correctly, the great Mandan myth in such a way as to reaffirm societal goals and reinspire moral and proper behavior.

The transcendent function, then, of primitive art, is to communicate symbolically the value scheme of the culture.

[T]he arts . . . are symptomatic of cultural values and . . . they are for the most part oriented positively, that is, toward man's search for a secure and ordered existence . . . [T]hey can be considered positive, integrated cultural manifestations, reflecting and reinforcing the basic values of the cultures that gave rise to them. . . . The arts at any time or place . . . evolve what might be called the "value image" that culture has of itself.[14]

In this regard, art in primitive societies is inextricably intertwined with politics, religion, world view—the entire complex of social institutions which seeks to bind each community.

The vital importance of art as social communication in primitive societies cannot be emphasized too strongly. The heterogeneous populations of complex civilized societies, with their plurality of backgrounds, values, and identifications; their geographic and social mobility; and their multiplicity of com-

[11]A. P. Merriam, *A Prologue to the Study of African Arts,* p. 14.

[12]R. Redfield, "Art and Icon" in C. M. Otten (ed.), *op. cit.,* p. 48.

[13]G. Mills, "Art: An Introduction to Qualitative Anthropology," in C. M. Otten (ed.), *op. cit.,* p. 68.

[14]R. Sieber, "The Arts and Their Changing Social Function," *op. cit.,* p. 655.

munications media (books, newspapers, periodicals, radio and television, movies, tapes, satellites) are dramatically different from the small, isolated, homogeneous, closely knit, stable (slow-changing) primitive societies. The function of art in the two types of societies, while sharing certain attributes, thus assumes an important quantitative difference. In primitive societies, art must carry a far greater burden in maintaining the society's cohesiveness than does modern art outside of Communist countries. Indeed, according to Charlotte Otten,

Here . . . lies the heart of the matter, and a crucial reason why we *cannot* validly equate the arts of nonliterate peoples with those of late civilizations in which writing has permeated the culture as the ordinary medium of communication and information storage. . . . In pre-literate or proto-literate culture, the art symbol *becomes* the fact; that is it simultaneously represents, defines, and manifests its referent. In such cultures, art objects and events serve as media for information storage, rather than books. . . .

Fig. 32-5   Naturalistic representation portrayed in an effigy jar from Mochica, Peru. (Courtesy of the American Museum of Natural History.)

Western . . . art only partially and sporadically carries this freight of prescribed symbolic meaning functioning simultaneously on many levels, reinforcing cultural values and at once enlarging, sensitizing, and unifying our perceptions.[15]

For the very same reasons, when a primitive society comes into contact with a civilization and starts to acculturate to it, one of the first things to go is its traditional art. It is not production for the tourist trade that destroys primitive art. It is the disintegration of the value system which the art had been originally produced to sustain.

Art as communication has an additional importance in our consideration in that artistic symbols provided the bridge to written language, and we have thus included art as transition to writing in this chapter (see pages 636–641).

Forms of Graphic Art: Style

Art forms may be *naturalistic* or *abstract,* with all degrees of transition between the extremes. A form is naturalistic if the transformation of the object results in a faithful representation of the original model (as in the Peruvian effigy jar shown in Figure 32-5). The form is abstract if the identifying attributes of the original object have been transformed by means of a symbolic identity which does not closely resemble the original form. The face and body of the ancestral figure painted on the facade of a Sepik River men's spirit house in New Guinea, as shown in Figure 32-6, is more abstract than naturalistic. The ideographic wall paintings from prehistoric Portugal, shown in Figure 32-17 (page 639), are wholly abstract.

Style   The term "style" means a departure from absolute naturalism. Artists always compose their creations to some degree. Documentary photography, as well as the snapshots of most amateurs, is not art. But by

[15]C. M. Otten (ed.), *Anthropology and Art*, pp. xiv–xv.

selective lighting, screening, and retouching, photography can be made to approach art. A textbook line illustration of an anatomical specimen is a scientific representation, but hardly ever art. Style denotes a standardized selective modification of the image in a way that produces an aesthetically effective and distinctive representation (Figures 32-7 and 32-8).

Style in Northwest Coast Art   One of the most distinctive of all primitive art styles is that which originates on the Northwest Coast of North America and is exemplified in the carving and painting of masks, totem poles, boxes, rattles, dishes, spoons, canoes, houses, and other objects. Exaggerations in representative art have led not to geometric design but to a unique stylization in which a body form can still be distinguished, in spite of the fact that it is greatly distorted in size and arrangement. All Northwest Coast art objects are utilitarian in intent, and therefore the decorative element is more or less subordinated to the object. This is definitely not free art.

The effects of this subordination of the art to the object are most interesting. The artist is given, so to speak, a decorative field that he must cover. He abhors blank spaces. He also wants all his decorative elements to represent some aspect of animal life. Hence, he is impelled to dissect, dismember, distort, and remold his creatures to fill the space whether it is the surface of a box, bowl, wooden hat, or rattle. Distortion becomes such that the representation is in the end a caricature.

Totemic symbolism   Design does not annihilate representation wholly, however, because the impulses of the Northwest Coast artist are not unalloyedly aesthetic. Totemic heraldry, with its rich mythology of clan and lineage origins from heroic animal ancestors, pervades most Northwest Coast art. The representative art portrays not just an animal but an animal that symbolizes some mythical or historic event in the social background of the artist. This interest in the art counter-

balances the tendency for caricature to get out of hand. The device by means of which this purpose is made effective is the standardization of certain immutable symbols based on one or a few outstanding anatomical traits of the natural creature portrayed. Thus, no matter how weird the distortion in the interests of design or in the flight of imaginative fancy, the message to be conveyed by the representation cannot be lost in meaningless form and line.

Fig. 32-6   Abstract of a human face and body, painted on the facade of a men's spirit house (Haus Tambaran), Maprik District, Sepik River, New Guinea. (Photograph by E. A. Hoebel.)

The marks of the beaver in Northwest Coast art are the most readily recognizable—his flat, scaly, mud-slapper tail and his efficient cutting teeth. These are always present in any artistic representation of the beaver. In Figure 32-9 we see a Haida Indian totem-pole beaver. He may be quickly recognized by his two great incisors and his crosshatched tail, which, since the pole is to be viewed from the front, is curled up between his legs, for otherwise it could not be seen. Since the beaver is a woodworker, he is often, but not always, shown with a chunk of a log in his paws. One other important landmark is the projecting ear. Although it will be observed that stylization of the face is in the direction of the human visage (all the mythological creatures talk, think, and act like human beings), the ears above the head are certain, distinctive evidence that a nonhuman animal is represented.

The bear in Figure 32-9 fills in a square design area. Again the ears prove him to be an animal. The teeth are bear teeth, but the most important mark is found in the long claws. Notice, too, that the bear looks as though he had been split down the back and then opened to fill out the flat space.

The best example of the use of this tricky device is in the treatment of the shark. The distinguishing shark features (Figure 32-9), which are all on the face, are (1) a large mouth, drawn down at the corners, (2) many sharp teeth, (3) gill slits on the cheeks, (4) large round eyes, and (5) a high, tapering forehead on which are drawn two circles like eyes and gill slits to form a pseudo subface. Since these features are all best seen from the front, the shark head is never shown in profile. Yet the side of the body must be shown in profile. In order that symmetry may be attained, the artist has split the fish down the back and folded the two sides out to the right and left of the head. What looks to us at first glance like wings are the outspread right and left sides of the shark's body. So that a large void is not left beneath the body, the pectoral fins are much enlarged; and then to

Fig. 32-7   A contemporary Trobriand Island statue combining naturalism and abstraction in its style. (Private collection. Photograph by Don Breneman.)

keep the whole within the rectangular decorative area, the split tail is turned down and inward at both ends of the body.

Thus we see how the Northwest Coast artist, with great skill and ingenuity, compromised and balanced in a sophisticated art style his hunter's interest in animal anatomy, his artistic interest in design, his abhorrence of blank spaces, and the totemic mythology which explained and reinforced his social systems.

Religion and Art

Religion and art are by no means inseparable, but for deep-rooted reasons they have a

Fig. 32-8 (right) Detail of carved and painted figures of facade of a men's spirit house (Haus Tambaran). Maprik District, Sepik River, New Guinea. (Photograph by E. A. Hoebel.)

Fig. 32-9 (below) Northwest Coast Indian art, Haida tribe. Top left, carved totem-pole beaver; top right, painted bear on a flat surface; bottom, painted shark or dogfish. (After Boas.)

strong affinity. In essence, religion is subjective—a matter of belief. Yet the covert concepts of religious belief need objectifying, and art is an outstandingly effective medium. By artistic embellishment, the paraphernalia of religion and magic may be lifted out of the realm of ordinary artifacts or activities to become endowed with the qualities of the unusual that should be associated with the supernatural—the sacred.

Yet even more important than the elaboration of religious paraphernalia is the representation of the spirits and gods. Gods are imaginative conceptions who exist in belief. If the belief can be translated into concrete form, it becomes more real and convincing. Paintings and statues objectify the subjective concepts of the divinities (Figure 32-10). The presence of a god at a ceremony is more directly felt by the majority of men if he is there in solid stone or wood looking out on the believers. The visual religious art of any primitive people communicates eloquently. Edmund Leach has stated it well:

It is intended to be understood. And in the ordinary way it will be understood by the audience for whom it is designed. For the audience for which a primitive artist works is composed of members of his own community steeped in the same mythological tradition as himself and familiar with the same environment of material fact and ritual activity; the primitive artist can therefore afford to communicate in shorthand; symbols have the same basic significance and the same range of ambiguity for artist and audience alike.[16]

[16]E. R. Leach, "Aesthetics," in E. E. Evans-Pritchard, *The Institutions of Primitive Society*, p. 32.

Leach goes on to observe that the European art critic who tries to understand primitive art is forced to concentrate on its form alone, without reference to its meaning; he is ignorant of the religious and mythic content of the object he is trying to analyze.

Masks and Rituals   Primitive religious sculpture is in the form of masks or statues—that is to say, idols. Without artists there can be no idolatry. The use of masks to portray supernatural beings is prevalent among primitive peoples in many parts of the world. Only Polynesia and Micronesia, in the Pacific, and the Plains and Basin areas, in the United States, are conspicuous in that masking is absent, or nearly so. In the religion of the Plains Indians, deities are of little importance; there is nothing much to mask. In Polynesia, although the pantheon is elaborate and deities are portrayed as statues, masking is abjured for reasons that are obscure.

In North America, the masks of the Northwest Coast attain a richness of variety and

Fig. 32-10   Sepik River statues. (a) Ancestral figure with body paint and grass skirt. (b) Mythic human head in which the characteristic pendant nose becomes the tail of a spirit bird. (Private collection. Photograph by Don Breneman.)

(a)

(b)

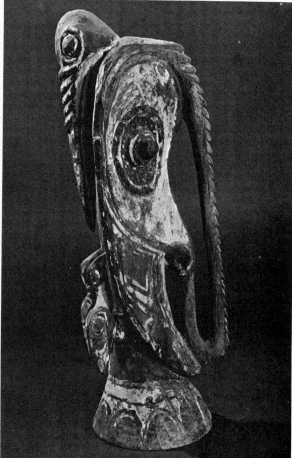

Fig. 32-11 (right)   Masked shaman of the Iroquois False Face Society in a sacred tobacco patch. (National Museum of Canada.)

Fig. 32-12 (below)   New Guinea masks. (a) Multicolored wood ancestral mask with pendant nose pierced with boar tusks. (b) Small clay mask modeled on a segment of tortoise shell, embedded with cowries and fringed with cassowary feathers, (Private collection. Photograph by Don Breneman.)

form that is rivaled only in parts of Melanesia. Many Northwest Coast masks, by means of hinges and strings, have movable parts that may be manipulated by the actor to heighten the dramatic effect. Some have an inner and an outer face to portray the dual character (animal and human) of the early mythological progenitors. The most important of the factors that have combined to produce the exotic elaborateness of Northwest Coast masks are (1) a social organization emphasizing hereditary status based in part on descent from mythological ancestral lineage founders, (2) elaboration of dance drama depicting the deeds of the mythical heroes, (3) technical mastery of the skills of carving, and (4) a vigorous creative drive to translate ideas and mental imagery into objective representations.

At the eastern end of North America, Iroquois masks as made and used by the False Face Society of curers are not so rich in variety or so elaborate as those of the Northwest Coast, but they bear the stamp of a grotesquely humorous realism designed to frighten away evil spirits (Figure 32-11). While the intent of the masks is serious, one cannot help feeling that the artist carves with his tongue in his cheek.

Masking associated with religious belief has generated rich art products in both Africa and Melanesia, but of the two areas, Melanesia has been the more prolific. (Figure 32-12.) Hence we shall briefly discuss its products. In Africa and Melanesia, the worship

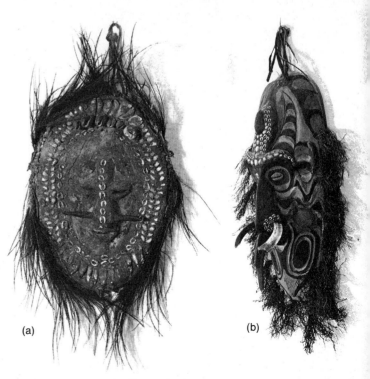

(a)   (b)

and veneration of ancestral spirits loom large in virtually all tribal religions. In Melanesia, particularly, the masks are representations of ancestors and are used in elaborate memorial rites. On the island of New Ireland, this complex reached its most elaborate expression in the ritual and art of the *malanggan.*

The Malanggan of New Ireland   The *malanggan* ceremonies of New Ireland, which lies northeast of New Guinea in the Southwest Pacific, celebrate the memory of the recently deceased, plus the initiation of adolescent boys. This system of festivals involves the production and use of intricately carved plaques and masks colored in red, yellow, blue, and white. They are impressive and spectacular (Figure 32-13).

The *malanggan* complex is Durkheimian (see pages 70–71) in nature, for it expresses the corporate immortality of the clan and its importance in tribal life and survival. "Thus malanggan may be viewed as a kind of replacement of dead members of a clan with new members reaching adult status."[17]

Each clan has a sacred spot in the bush where its guardian spirit dwells. As reported by Lewis, who observed a *malanggan* in 1954, when the time for the *malanggan* cycle was at hand, the men prepared a walled enclosure and planted special gardens in the vicinity. These provided dedicated foodstuffs. Shell money and currency were accumulated for gifts and exchange (see Chapter 17) and the rites, which covered the better part of a year, were underway.

The carving of masks, some of which were to be worn, others of which would crown the bodies of manufactured dummies, took weeks of secret activities, from which women and noninitiates were barred. Much planning and discussion went into the selection of mask forms and their execution by the carvers. It was in itself a highly social, albeit exclusive,

Fig. 32-13   New Ireland malanggan *ceremonial mask. (Courtesy of the Museum of Primitive Art.)*

undertaking. Meanwhile, the novitiates were receiving their bush school instruction.

When all was ready, the circumcision rites of the boys were carried out—in the seclusion of the *malanggan* enclosure.

Then it was time for the memorial services. "Art museums"—display halls for the masks and plaques—had been built within the compound, replacing the workshops and dormitory, which were torn down and thrown into the sea. Guests arrived from miles around.

The little initiates were brought out of the compound and returned to their families. Then a great, masked ancestral figure came forth to dance. "The crowd watched silently with great consternation."[18]

When the dance was over,

[T]he entire crowd, men, women, and children, filed in through the gateway. The malanggans were at the peak of their effectiveness, the paint was fresh, the green backgrounds of the display houses was [sic] not yet wilted, insects had not yet burrowed into the wood. . . . [T]his viewing time was a tense

[17]P. H. Lewis, *The Social Context of Art in Northern New Ireland* (Fieldiana: Anthropology, vol. 58, 1969), p. 45.

[18]*Ibid.,* p. 62.

and dramatic episode. The people would come forward to the display houses exclaiming in wonder and sometimes with tears in their eyes.[19]

Subsequently, the great pig distribution ceremonies and the final removal of the carved spirit figures from the compounds closed the ritual and disposed of its art representations.

The point to be made here is a reiteration of the theme that such art is *socially* meaningful and devoid of the individual self-centeredness which marks so much of contemporary Western art. Its import is to emotionalize the fact of social (in the case of the *malanggan,* clan) identity. It is not possible for the reader, who has not been raised in native New Ireland society, to sense what the masks actually convey in feeling to a New Irelander. Nor have we been able to convey more than a little of what it is about, for, as a German missionary scholar Augustin Krämer, has written:

The description of a malagan [sic] celebration in its separate parts and all of its variations would fill a whole book of considerable size, particularly if one would take into due consideration also the spirit which animates all. Everything must be interpreted, for a malagan is not merely external celebration, but a thoughtful act, whose ceremony, at least partly, contains a deep symbolic meaning.[20]

African Sculpture   Statuary as a medium of primitive religious art is common in Africa and Melanesia, and also in Polynesia and Central America. African statuary has had considerable influence upon modern European artists, beginning with Picasso. It possesses a living quality eagerly sought after by modernists. It embodies the people's hopes and fears; it terrorizes or delights them as it portrays the nature of the gods on whom they lean or before whom they prostrate themselves, not only in African sculpture, but also in Polynesian and Melanesian. The artist is close to his work, and his work is close to the interests and well-being of his people.

Mass, solidity, and plainness of surface are the impressive features of African sculpture, even though the figures are not usually very large. These qualities are induced partly by the nature of the material in which the artist works, and partly by his own inimitable style. The material is hardwood—mahogany, the aristocrat of timbers, and ironwood—tough, challenging material. No light-minded whittler can work the sculptor's transformation on such a block. The wood is close-grained and invites a high polish with dark lustrous tones. The glistening highlights of the smooth African skin are beautifully reflected in the finished statues. The wedding of subject matter and materials is perfect (see Figure 32-14).

African sculpture is characteristically disproportionate. The head is always large in relation to the torso; the legs are squat and sturdy. All the work is subject to the limita-

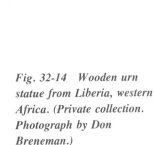

Fig. 32-14   Wooden urn statue from Liberia, western Africa. (Private collection. Photograph by Don Breneman.)

[19]*Ibid.,* pp. 62–63.
[20]Quoted and translated in Lewis, *op. cit.,* p. 71.

Fig. 32-15   Bakongo wood statue of mother and child. The large head and small legs, along with cicatrization on the upper torso, reveal common stylistic features of West African art. (Courtesy of the Museum of Primitive Art.)

tions of the mass of the block with which the artist works, which is to say that the African woodworker is no joiner. Since he cannot attach projecting pieces to the mass, the arms must be formed close to the body. The legs must be confined within the area of the original block. Such limitations contribute to the feeling of compactness that emerges from the art (Figure 32-15). Concentration of attention on the head of the statue, lineal elongation of the body, and dwarfing of the lower limbs are matters of stylistic choice in the African tradition.

Most African statues represent dead ancestors; they are created to house their spirits. The statue, when the spirit has taken up its abode, is in the true sense a fetish, an object possessing a supernatural quality. It is not just a work of art to be viewed objectively in a museum. It is a personage, alive with all the pulsating powers of the personality it represents—powers that are superhumanly potent because the personality it represents is no longer that of mere man but is godlike. As Maquet notes, contemporary Africans often protest with vehemence against the inclusion of their religious and political symbolic objects in European and American art museums. "They point out that these objects were not art for their forefathers."[21] They have become art by metamorphosis.

Art as Semantics

Throughout this entire book, but particularly in this section, we have emphasized the sym-

[21]J. Maquet, "Introduction to Aesthetic Anthropology" (*McCaleb Module in Anthropology,* 1971), p. 13.

bolic attributes of culture in the definition of world view, the infusion of meaning into life, and the generation of states of emotional commitment of the individual members of society to the groups of which they are members and to the society to which they are bonded. In addition to ritual and myth as aspects of religion, art, too, speaks a symbolic message. The message may be clear and explicit, as when a Tlingit totem pole presents the actors in a household mythic "history." Or it may be diffuse and ambiguous but nonetheless heard and sensed, as it is in contemporary junk art and the works of the counter-culture abstractionists, which give vent to the emotional instability, anxieties, irritation, free-floating anger, and frustrations so widely experienced throughout the modern world. What art communicates is not explicit but, rather, implicit.

The messages in Northwest Coast totemic art, for example, are clear and explicit only to the members of the tribe and clan who know the meanings of the "signs" in the art through knowing the myths, the specific forms (like the beaver's tail), and the symbolic referents of the different colors. Art as language speaks only to those who understand the language. It is particularistic and ethnocentric. Symbolic content is more important than the form. The form is conventionalized. The more the art is intended to convey a narrow and specific message rather than to evoke a generalized social effect, the greater will be the tendency toward economy of effort in the production of visible artistic signs and symbols. The movement in the development of visual language may be expected to be from naturalistic representation to simplified abstract representation. From such a process writing has developed. Hence, it will be treated here as the most specialized outgrowth of art.

Chiriquian Pottery Designs One of the best demonstrations of the process just introduced above is that advanced by W. H. Holmes in his discussion of Chiriquian pottery designs from pre-Columbian Panama.[22] Among the several design motifs discussed by Holmes, that of

[22]W. H. Holmes, *Ancient Art of the Province of Chiriqui* (Bureau of American Ethnology, Annual Report 6, 1888), pp. 171–186.

the alligator is most arresting. In Figure 32-16, some of the alligator designs are arranged to show progressive abstraction from stylized representations. In the upper left is seen the painted figure of an alligator with upturned snout and tail and dots to represent his scales. Below him is a conventionalized figure of an alligator that is almost unrecognizable, and at the bottom there appears a meandering abstraction that would be hard to identify as an alligator symbol if more realistic representations were not available for comparison. In the right-hand series is a simple curvilinear representation of an alligator that is progressively simplified through symbolic abstraction to become a mere curved line and a dot.

The two designs at the bottom of Figure 32-16 show a different way of symbolizing "alligator." The painting within the trapezoid is highly stylized and simplified, but not too abstract. To fill the bounded space, the artist has turned the head back over the body, which sags in the middle to make room for it. The tail is then turned downward and in, while two hooks at the bend of the neck represent the large dorsal scales. Next look carefully at the spiral figure in the circle to the right (at the bottom). It is another way of writing "alligator." It occurs on pottery of a type that is commonly decorated with alligators; it has the same in-turned hook of the tail; it has three semicircular protuberances (no more, no less), just as the alligator has three groups of semicircular legs and neck scales; and the inner loop of the spiral corresponds to the hooked loop of the alligator's nose. What looks like geometric scribbling is a meaningful symbol abstracted from a stylized representation of a real animal form.

Holmes was quite convinced that in the case of Chiriquian forms, a definite evolution from realistic through conventionalized to abstract symbols occurred. Critical objections have been raised to this thesis because it implies a temporal sequence from a typological classification, and Holmes had no proof that the realistic forms were actually earlier in time. Boas and others have pointed out that since in some known instances the evolution of an art style is found to have moved from geometric figures to realistic ones,[23] there is no justification for assuming priority of naturalistic forms unless there is stratigraphic or actual historical evidence implying such a time sequence.

Capsian and Azilian Picture Writing   In the cavern of Cogul, in Portugal, is a painted wall upon which prehistoric man of the Capsian culture left many paintings (Figure 32-17). One shows a man confronting a stag, not un-

[23]See F. Boas's study of Eskimo needlecases. Archaic geometric decorative elements are shown to have evolved into animal figures. *Decorative Designs of Alaskan Needlecases* (United States National Museum, Reports, vol. 39, 1908), pp. 221–344.

like the scene at Lascaux illustrated at the beginning of Chapter 9. On another part of the wall is a crudely conventionalized picture of a hunter who has just shot a large arrow at a stag. In yet another spot is a very queer figure, which by itself would be no more intelligible to us than the Chiriquian alligator symbols. We know, however, that the Capsian hunters were very much interested in dead deer, and with the more naturalistic examples before us, we can compare the number of prongs in the forklike projections on this figure with the prongs of the antlers in the naturalistic pictures. That a deer is meant is certain. Furthermore, since the four feet of the object are sticking straight up in the air, we may feel reasonably sure that this is the symbol for a dead deer, presumably a magic

Fig. 32-16   Conventionalization and abstraction of alligator designs on Chiriquian pottery. (After Holmes.)

hunting symbol to help the deerslayer. A Winnebago Indian has described in detail the working of such magic among his people. A vital fragment of his story was given in Chapter 9 (pages 186–187).

What took place at Cogul occurred elsewhere on the Iberian Peninsula. Obermaier, in arguing for a genetic relationship between the Azilian painted pebbles and the painted petroglyphs of the Spanish caves and rock shelters, prepared the comparative chart shown in Figure 32-18. Clearly, the Azilian ∧ symbolizes a squatting female, and the ⋒ is a male. Azilian man had apparently progressed from picture writing to the use of ideographs—drawn or written symbols that stand directly for things or notions instead of the sounds of words in the language of the users. Such is the first step in the evolution and origin of all systems of writing. The scribe is the intellectual offspring of the artist.

Chinese Ideographs On a much more elaborate level, the Chinese system of characters is fundamentally an ideographic picture writing which has become reduced to a set of timesaving brushstrokes and which is in some aspects also phonetic. Its ideographic quality may be readily discerned in the manner of writing such words as "prisoner," and "happiness." In the character for "prisoner," we see a man, 人 , in an enclosure, 囚 . "Happiness" is a woman (wife), 女 , with a son, 女子 . The earlier pictographic derivation of a number of Chinese characters may be seen in Figure 32-19.

The occurrence in all languages of words that are identically pronounced but have different meanings (*homophones*)[24] makes possible a ready extension of ideographic writing as soon as a people is able to make the mental leap of partially disassociating the picture from the idea and linking it to sounds as such. Thus the Chinese word for "horse," which is

Fig. 32-17 Three degrees of conventionalization in the representation of the stag in the Capsian art from Cogul.

Fig. 32-18 Probable female and male symbols on painted pebbles from Le Mas d'Azil (right) compared with female and male pictographs from Late Upper Paleolithic cave art in eastern Spain (left). (After Obermaier.)

---

[24]For example, *saw:* (1) past tense of *to see;* (2) a cutting tool with a serrated edge; (3) to cut with a sawlike tool; (4) to cut as if with a sawlike tool; (5) a sententious saying or proverb.

"mar," is represented by 𝐿. The Chinese term for "mother" used within the intimate confines of the family is sometimes "mama." Phonetically, then, it would be possible for the Chinese to write "mama" as 𝐿 𝐿. This, however, would be ambiguous, for unless the context made it clear, the reader would not be certain whether the symbol represented two horses or one mother. The Chinese get around this difficulty by first writing the symbol for woman, 女, followed by the homophone symbol for "mar." Thus they have produced a way of writing "mama" that is half ideogram and half phonogram. Because of its way of mixing ideograms and phonograms, Chinese writing is classed as a *transitional system,* a means of written communication which has gone beyond the more primitive forms of pictography but which still falls short of pure phonetic representation.

The ancient Egyptian, Hittite, Cretan, and cuneiform (Sumerian, Babylonian, Assyrian) script systems also developed out of picture writing by use of similar basic principles, although each evolved its own special forms. These and the Chinese, plus the Indic and Mayan-Aztec systems, are the only definitely known independent basic scripts invented by man. The transformation of art to writing is a supreme human achievement, so difficult that few peoples have done it on their own. Most men have achieved literacy through borrowing.

Alphabetic Origins Our own alphabet had its beginnings in Egyptian pictography. Its development from early Greek inscriptions is well known and, indeed, testified to by the very word by which we identify it: a compound of the first two words of the Grecian system, the *alpha* and *beta.* Beyond the Grecian alphabet, however, lies the Semitic from which it in turn is clearly derived: Hebrew, *aleph, beth, gimel.* Some Semitic symbols have clear derivation from Egyptian hieroglyphs; many do not. Known archaic Semitic inscriptions are few and far between, far too few to enable paleographers to advance well-founded reconstructions of the full history of the emergence of the alphabet. Although there are indications that parallel attempts at developing alphabetic systems were more or less simultaneously under way among several different Semitic peoples around the second millennium B.C., only one system (that of the Phoenicians) was finally perfected. From this, and this alone, all the extant alphabets of the world have descended. Here was a cultural triumph so difficult to conceive, and so perfect in form and function, that with minor modifications it could be adapted to any and all languages. It has superseded all other alphabetic systems; mankind has never again had either the need or the capacity to evolve a new system.

Of the Semitic symbols derived from Egyp-

Fig. 32-19 Pictographic derivation of some seventeenth-century Chinese characters. (After Brouner and Fung.)

Sun	Moon	Mountain
Child	Horse	Tree

tian hieroglyphic ideograms, the first letter of the alphabet will suffice for illustrative purposes. *Aleph,* in Semitic, means "ox." The Egyptian hieroglyph is ☞. On the Moabite stone, which presents a Semitic inscription of Mesha, king of Moab, in the ninth century B.C., the symbol is formed with three straight lines, ◁. In later Greek it was inverted on its horns, and became A. Similar transitions may be seen for *beta, gamma, delta,* and other letters. The Egyptian word sounds for "ox," "house," and so on were ignored by the Semitic scribes; what they succeeded in doing was to make pictorially derived symbols from Egyptian prototypes, which were subsequently associated with the separate consonants that went to make up their speech. The Semites never included vowels in their script, but wrote each word with only its consonantal sounds. The *aleph* symbol stood for the glottal stop, which is exceedingly important in Semitic speech. The Greeks had no use for the glottal stop, but they were able to represent the vowels of their speech in a way the Semites could not, and they completed the basic modern alphabet with the invention of vowel symbols. They converted the A to represent the first vowel and made other adjustments to take care of the rest.

The capstone was thus put on the transition from art to writing. The communication of generalized states of emotion and ideas through the aesthetic medium had at long last been transmuted to the communication of precise linguistic expression through phonetically representative symbols.

SUMMARY

What we call art is a universal feature of human culture, but art is a concept that does not necessarily exist in the minds of all people. The concept of art involves the transformation of an object or an idea into an objective form which has a noninstrumental attribute. Thus instrumental artifacts, or dance forms, or stories which are sufficient unto their ends and practical uses will not ordinarily qualify as art. But if noninstrumental embellishment is added, such extra creative effort is in the direction of art. If the object, because of its effect on the senses, stimulates a contemplative pause, an arresting, thoughtful, or feeling-laden consideration of it for its own sake, then it has evoked an aesthetic response. All art, it is held with Jacques Maquet, has this aesthetic attribute, and the aesthetic response is a universal feature of mankind—more or less highly sharpened according to culture and subcultures.

Most definitions of art imply or state a creator (art is a human product), a process of transforming a medium to a patterned form, a product which is publicly viewed, a content which is usually symbolic, and a response on the part of the beholder (the aesthetic experience).

The creator and the viewer are equally important to the concept of art. Much art is intended for ends that have nothing to do with art. The creator and his constituency may, as they indeed do in most cultures, have only instrumental ends in mind, ignoring the noninstrumental aspects of the object or action. But if in the act of creation the intent is to include decorative features for aesthetic contemplation which go beyond use and necessity, then we have art by intention. On the other hand, objects which were never intended as art by their makers or users can be converted into art objects by the connoisseur, native or alien, who responds to them with aesthetic contemplation. This makes the object art by metamorphosis.

Primitive art is simply the art of primitive peoples. It is not implicitly naïve or technically deficient—except for the lack of perspective in graphic art. It may be either naturalistic or abstract.

The primitive artist is rarely individualistic. He works within a stable style, in close communication with his tribal audience. The primary function of most art, especially primitive art, is to communicate the value scheme of the culture.

In form, art may be naturalistic or abstract,

with intermediate mixtures of the two. Style denotes a recurrent or standardized way of structuring the image in the transformation that is effected. Different cultures and ages produce their distinctive styles.

Because religions are symbolic systems, religion finds a ready expression in the objective forms provided by art. Masks are linked to religious expressionism at all cultural levels, while statues find their widest use in cultures other than those of hunters and foragers.

As systems of communication, art has much in common with language. When graphic art is developed to communicate particular, rather than general, messages, it tends to move toward simplicity of form and abstraction. Out of it comes ideographic representation and, finally, writing—a hallmark of civilization.

SELECTED READINGS

Boas, F., *Primitive Art* (1929). The classic work on the subject.

Breuil, H., *Four Hundred Centuries of Cave Art* (1950). The most comprehensive summary of Paleolithic art.

Buehler, A., T. Barrow, and C. P. Mountford, *The Art of the South Seas, Including Australia and New Zealand* (1962). Many beautiful color plates and numerous line drawings together with a very competent ethnography of Oceanic art.

Deringer, D., *The Alphabet* (1948). A detailed, but not too technical, discussion.

Dunn, Dorothy, *American Indian Painting of the Southwest and Plains Area* (1968). Illustrated with many handsome color plates. Especially interesting in its accounts of the development of modern Indian painting—a wedding of contemporary techniques and Indian cultural interests.

Herskovits, M. J., *Backgrounds of African Art* (1945). A useful survey of the major art styles of Africa.

Holm, Bill, *Northwest Coast Indian Art: An Analysis of Form* (1965). A study of the basic principles underlying the decorative art of the Northwest Coast.

Inverarity, R. B., *Art of the Northwest Coast Indians* (1950). A profusely and beautifully illustrated book on the distinctive aboriginal art of the Northwest Coast of North America.

Krieger, H. W., "Design Areas in Oceania" (*United States National Museum, Proceedings,* vol. 79, 1932), pp. 1–53. A good example of an ethnological study of stylistic distributions.

Kroeber, A. L., "Art," in J. H. Steward (ed.), *Handbook of South American Indians,* vol. 5, *The Comparative Ethnology of South American Indians* (1946), pp. 411–492. A comprehensive survey of aboriginal, including prehistoric, art in South American cultures.

Linton, R., and P. S. Wingert, *Arts of the South Seas* (1946). A well-illustrated and stimulating coverage of this subject.

Maquet, J., "Introduction to Aesthetic Anthropology" (*McCaleb Module in Anthropology,* 1971). A penetrating and beautifully reasoned formulation of a general anthropological theory of art.

Otten, C. M., *Anthropology and Art: Readings in Cross-cultural Aesthetics* (1971). Contains twenty-four well-chosen articles on theory and method in the study of primitive art, primitive artists, and art forms in relation to culture areas.

Redfield, R., M. J. Herskovits, and G. F. Ekholm, *Aspects of Primitive Art* (1959). Three lectures presented by three distinguished American anthropologists at the Museum of Primitive Art in New York in 1959.

Smith, M. W. (ed.), *The Artist in Tribal Society* (1961). An anthropological exploration of the roles and functions of the primitive artist by a symposium of experts convened by The Royal Anthropological Institute in London. The verbatim record of the discussions is particularly interesting.

Part 6   Anthropology Today and Tomorrow

Chapter 33

Culture Change

As we plunge into the Atomic Space Age, technological change and social transformations are the order of the day. Both are the products of the most far-reaching cultural revolution that man will have experienced in the two million years of his existence up to A.D. 2000. We have seen that culture is a system of learned behaviors.

Although human behaviors can become standardized as habits or social usage, behavior is always variable, even when it is habit-bound. Because of this propensity to variability, it is impossible to fix behavior absolutely so that it never changes. Since culturally patterned behavior is learned and not fixed in the organism, it is modifiable

Fig. 33-A   Agents of culture change. A missionary plane arriving among the Amahuaca Indians of the Peruvian rain forest. (Cornell Capa, Magnum.)

and flexible. Therefore, cultures are changeable. Rates of change vary from place to place and from time to time. Some cultures have grown and changed with great rapidity; others have remained relatively stable for hundreds of thousands of years. We have also seen that the changes in Stone Age cultures from generation to generation were minuscule and that it took tens of thousands of years to develop even so simple a thing as a chipped-stone hand ax. Yet the culture of Japan changed from that of a feudal-peasant society to that of a front-rank industrial society in less than one hundred years.

The problem of differential rates of culture growth intrigues and puzzles layman and scientist alike. Why did the Indians of North America not develop any culture comparable to that of nineteenth-century Europe? Why have African cultures lagged behind those of Asia? Truly satisfactory answers cannot yet be given, but certainly a start can be made. This is one of our recurring concerns in this book. At this point, let us consider the mechanisms of culture change and growth.

As they are the key concepts of anthropology, human biological and cultural adaptation, homogeneity and diversity in man and culture have been central themes running throughout this book. Structure, function, and symbolic representation in societal maintenance through cultural systems have also been given great weight. Now, before looking to the future (in our final chapter), there is need to survey the factors which are relevant to the understanding of culture change.

Culture grows by accretion of inventions and the modification or replacement of old ways. An individual culture changes and grows by acceptance of inventions devised by members of its own society or by acceptance of new ways invented elsewhere and brought to the attention of its members through diffusion and borrowing of ideas and behaviors.

Invention and Discovery

What is an invention? Does it differ in any way from a discovery? These questions are not merely of theoretical importance for analytical purposes. They are of tremendous practical significance in the operation of modern patent law, under which an invention is patentable while a discovery is not.

In the view of a United States District Court of Appeals, for example, a valuable patent on the process of irradiation of foodstuffs by exposure to ultraviolet light was invalid because it merely utilized a physicochemical process that has existed since life began. A distinction is drawn between the invention of a lamp for producing ultraviolet light and the discovery that exposure to ultraviolet rays increases the vitamin content of the exposed organic materials. The one is patentable—that is, subject to certain legal limitations; the other is not.[1]

A discovery is the act of becoming aware of something which has been in existence but which has not been previously perceived. Vitamins and sunspots were discovered, not invented.

An invention is an alteration in, or a synthesis of, preexistent materials, conditions, or practices so as to produce a new form of material or action. We must, therefore, deal with new patterns of action that are translated into concrete form (material inventions), and also with inventions that remain in the realm of nonmaterial action patterns solely. The latter are sometimes called *social inventions* or, by philosophers, *moral inventions.*

To illustrate the distinction between discovery and invention more fully, it might be noted that the first ninety-two elements, from hydrogen to uranium, were *discovered* by means of scientific perception. But the new transuranium elements, such as neptunium and plutonium, which have come into

[1]*Vitamin Technologists v. Wisconsin Alumni Research Foundation (Federal Reports,* 2d series, vol. 146, 1945), pp. 941ff.

being since 1940, are truly *invented* elements. They were not found to exist in nature; they were produced as a result of human ingenuity in the development of techniques for separating neutrons from their elemental nucleus and causing them to enter another elemental nucleus without producing fission. New combinations of protons, neutrons, and electrons were produced—hence, the new elements.

However, to invent or discover something (we are not here speaking of discovering a new continent or a mountain) involves a mental act, one which requires that two or more existing things be conceptually broken into parts and that one, or some, of the parts be modified or replaced or recombined so that a new structure exists. Homer Barnett, the anthropologist who has devoted more thinking and research to the problem of cultural innovation than any other in our time, uses the invention of producer gas as one example of this process:

Innumerable people have known that vapors emitted from crevices in certain parts of the earth are inflammable. About 1684, John Clayton verified reports of this phenomenon in Lancashire and then proceeded to produce such a gas himself. Conjecturing that there was a relationship between the gas, the earth's heat, and the coal deposits in nearby mines, he applied heat to coal placed in a retort . . . as a substitute for the earth. . . . Then, in a second step, he caught the released gas . . . in a bladder . . . formerly used for many . . . [other purposes], instead of letting it escape into the atmosphere. . . . He punctured the bladder with a pin, brought a candle flame near the vent, and so produced the precursor of gas lights and burners.[2]

Clayton *discovered* that a volatile, flammable gas is locked in a solid state in coal; he *invented* an artificial technique for releasing and capturing it. In each act, however, there is a common element. Invention creates a new material combination by synthesizing a new idea from previously disconnected ideas. Discovery involves a new perception of something that has been pres-

ent but unnoticed because preexisting ideas were not equipped to deal with it. Until such time as someone performs the mental act of separating and isolating the unnoticed event from its natural context and then recombining it with other things in a new way, it has no recognized significance; it remains undiscovered. This was the case, for instance, when ultraviolet rays were isolated from sunlight, artificially produced, and applied to cereals and milk.

Volitional invention of this order is a rational process of imaginative substitutions and recombinations. It represents the most sophisticated level of cultural modification. Such a process is characteristic only of highly complicated societies with a cultural bent toward dynamic change. Even among advanced civilized nations, relatively few include within their populations a great number of active, willful inventors.

Because invention is highly valued and richly rewarded in our culture, many aspiring minds struggle to find new relations as solutions to set problems. In the process of volitional invention, the inventor recognizes a need or thinks he sees an insufficiency in some form or function. He sets a problem for solution on the basis of this recognized need and proceeds from this point to attempt a rational solution in the form of a practicable invention.

Accidental Juxtaposition and Invention   In the primitive world, volitional inventiveness is truly a rare occurrence. Conscious tinkering with the social structure or with gadgetary improvement is not the order of the day. Most primitive inventions are nonvolitional. They result from what Greenman has called *accidental juxtaposition*.[3]

The operation of the principle of accidental juxtaposition on the crudest level may be illustrated by the activities of Sultan, one of Köhler's famous apes. Sultan was presented with a problem—how to get a banana. He was

[2]H. G. Barnett, "The Innovative Process" (*Kroeber Anthropological Society Papers*, no. 25, 1961), p. 32.

[3]E. F. Greenman, "Material Culture and the Organism" (*American Anthropologist*, vol. 47, 1945), pp. 212ff.

also presented with two hollow bamboo sticks, neither long enough in itself to reach the banana. They were so fashioned, however, that one could be snugly fitted within the other to make a stick long enough to meet the need. An invention was called for, and the means were at hand. Sultan strained his simian brain for a solution, but the best he could work out was to push one stick toward the banana with the other. This failed to capture the banana. At length, like many another disgusted inventor, he gave up. His efforts at volitional invention were a flat failure. He dropped the sticks and turned his attention to less frustrating activities.

As he roamed around his cage looking for amusement, his attention was once more directed to the sticks. He picked them up and began to play with them in a casual manner and entirely without interest in the elusive banana. Suddenly he found himself holding the two sticks end to end. He pushed the one into the other. Lo, he had it! Accidental juxtaposition had resulted in a new set of relationships, a synthesized combination that constituted an invention. At this critical point, his intelligence was equal to the occasion. He could recognize a useful relationship when he saw it. Immediately he went to the bars, used his tool, and swallowed the banana.[4]

We actually know very little of the precise steps by which most primitive inventions came into being. Long archaeological sequences such as those established for Old World and Southwest prehistory reveal the external form of the gradual steps by which many artifacts have been developed over generations of time. A less empirical method, of which earlier anthropologists were quite fond, was to reconstruct the inventive steps by mesological inference. This is a most intriguing pastime, but too often the result is more "just so" story than objectively substantiated analysis worthy of scientific attention.

The Cheyenne Indian account of the invention of the tipi is of this order. Grinnell recorded that:

The first lodge of modern shape is said to have been suggested by a man who was handling a large poplar leaf, and quite by accident bent it into the shape of a cone—that is to say, of a lodge, such as are used today. As he looked at the leaf it flashed into his mind that a shelter like it would be better than those they then had. He showed it to the people, and they made lodges in the shape of this leaf, and have used them ever since.[5]

Although it is extremely unlikely that any Cheyenne Indian invented the conical lodge in this manner,[6] the story illustrates quite perfectly the operation of the principle of juxtaposition. Sultan's invention was the result of the close juxtaposition of two objects, the sticks; the supposed invention of the Cheyenne tipi was the result of the juxtaposition of two mental images, the cone formed by the leaf and the potential house. The two accomplishments together exemplify Greenman's final definition of juxtaposition:

The creation of a new implement as the sequel to the establishment of a close spatial relationship between two or more objects, or of a close temporal relationship between the mental images of two or more objects, by natural or artificial means without foreknowledge of the result.[7]

In the technical field, therefore, the creation of a new type of artifact as a result of juxtaposition is a mental reaction to a stimulus in the environment. For the most part, "the progressive evolution of technical forms had to wait upon such accidental juxtapositions."[8]

Of course, accidental juxtaposition can lead to inventive errors as well as to beneficial creativeness. The heavy freight of shibboleths, nonsense tabus, and false dogma

---

[4]W. Köhler, *The Mentality of Apes*, pp. 130–133.

[5]G. B. Grinnell, *The Cheyenne Indians*, vol. 1, p. 50.
[6]The Cheyennes did not acquire the conical skin tipi until well into the nineteenth century. Other Plains and Woodlands tribes had it before them, so it is quite certain that the Cheyennes borrowed the idea.
[7]Greenman, *op. cit.*, p. 215.
[8]*Ibid.*, p. 218.

carried through the ages by mankind results from erroneous association of images in juxtaposition.

Furthermore, mere juxtaposition does not in itself automatically generate an invention. The use, meaning, and function of particular artifacts or social forms may be such as to block acceptance of new forms, uses, meanings, and functions that are proposed in conjunction with the new inventive ideas. Resistance to new inventions is proverbial, and inventors are by no means always heroes.

Any new idea or new form must find its first creation somewhere, and at a specific time. Therefore it would be the height of foolishness to deny all inventiveness to primitive men. Were they not inventive, cultures would never have changed. There would be none of the rich diversity in cultures which anthropology has discovered for us, nor would there have been any evolution of culture whatsoever through the ages. But the protracted span of the Old Stone Age—nearly two million years of hunting and gathering technology before the domestication of plants and animals—testifies to the rarity of innovation before the dawn of civilization.

The vast majority of human societies can claim relatively few inventions to their credit. Abundant evidence proves that most trait accretions occur through borrowing, and this leads us to a consideration of diffusion.

Diffusion of Culture Traits

When we find a particular trait or trait complex spread over a wide area and practiced by a number of different tribes, we are confronted with several theoretical possibilities. Each tribe may have invented the same trait independently; one tribe may have invented it, after which it spread to the others by borrowing; or several may have invented it separately, after which it spread over the area.

We can safely say that the first hypothesis is an impossibility. Historical observation establishes that all peoples are always borrowing from others. We know, for instance, that Indians did not invent the domestication of the horse, nor the art of riding, nor halters, bits, reins, saddles, or any of the other accouterments of riding. They were all adopted from the Spaniards, first by the tribes of the Southwest frontier, who passed them on to the north and east.[9] An interesting fact to note is that the Western saddle, horn-pommeled and deep-backed, was copied from the Spanish saddle, as was the Indian's. But the Eastern riding saddle is copied from the English type that made its first appearance in the New World on the Atlantic Coast. The McClelland army saddle is a fusion of the two types.

Even such simple matters as hide dressing are acquired by borrowing. According to Grinnell:

When the Cheyennes first found the buffalo, they had no knowledge as to how to dress hides. Later, the Sioux on the east side of the Missouri showed them how to cut hides in two, dress them, and sew them together again. These they used as robes. After they reached the Black Hills the Kiowas and Comanches taught the Cheyennes how to dress buffalo-hides in one piece, and also showed them the use of a mixture for softening the hide.[10]

The Diffusion of Material Culture Material culture and mechanical processes of technology are much more readily borrowed than ideas and abstract concepts.

No one has expressed this more impressively than the two missionaries to the Shipibo of the Upper Amazon, Fathers Girbal and Marques, who in 1792 wrote to their headquarters:

To reap it wholly and to bring to God all these heathens certain things are necessary, of which we are

---

[9]C. Wissler, "The Influence of the Horse in the Development of Plains Culture" (*American Anthropologist*, vol. 16, 1914), pp. 1–25; F. Haines, "Where Did the Plains Indians Get Their Horses?" (*American Anthropologist*, vol. 40, 1938), pp. 112–117; also "The Northward Spread of Horses among the Plains Indians" (*American Anthropologist*, vol. 40, 1938), pp. 429–437.

[10]Grinnell, *op. cit.*, p. 52.

in need and of which we shall be in need. Send them to us; God and our most blessed father San Francois will know how to acknowledge it. . . . You will find added to our letter a note of these requisitions. . . . 400 axes, 600 cutlasses, 2000 straight knives, 1000 curved knives, 4 quintos of iron, 50 pounds of steel, 12 books of small fish-hooks, 8000 needles, one case of false pearls, 500 flints and steels, 4 gross of scissors, 2 gross of rings, 3000 brass crosses, 1000 varas of calico to cover the skin of those who are naked, an assortment of colours to paint our church, a very immaculate Virgin and some ornaments. We also want two skins of wine, both for the celebration of the holy sacrifice and to stop diarrhoea and bloody flux among the infidels.[11]

Fathers Girbal and Marques sensed that if metal were first accepted, *then* these Stone Age gardeners might be ready to consider a new religion, the assumption being that a superior technology is the product of a more powerful mastery of the supernatural.

It does not take long to perceive the value of iron implements. Captain Cook, who was deified by the native Hawaiians in 1779, was later killed by them when he tried to recover one of his ship's longboats which had been stolen so it could be stripped of its metal parts. It was thirty years later that Hawaiians decided to abandon their old ideational order and social system for the culture presented by sailors and missionaries; they realized that the material and ideational aspects of that culture went together, and they wanted both—plus the fact that certain members of the Hawaiian royal family (especially the women) found the tabu and social class system increasingly onerous and repugnant.[12]

The Tiwi of Australia, according to Hart and Pilling,

. . . were first drawn out of their hostile insularity by curiosity and the desire for iron, the same factors which had attracted them toward the Portuguese a century earlier. Iron looted from shipwrecks, channel markers, and the camps of casual visitors to the islands was not sufficient; the Tiwi desired a permanent avenue by which they could obtain the metal. The oldest Tiwi in the early 1950's stated that during the 1890's the Tiwi began to feel that opportunity was passing them by as they noted ship after ship sail in and out of Darwin; the islanders therefore came to the conclusion that they wanted a permanent European settlement in their midst, like the earlier Fort Dundas, for only in this way could they be guaranteed an uninterrupted source of iron.[13]

It is much easier to establish a steel mill in a newly developing country than it is to diffuse the ideology and processes of democratic political culture—a simple fact, belatedly recognized by many who hoped for too much, too rapidly, from American foreign-aid programs.

The Diffusion of Nonutilitarian Culture
Complex nonutilitarian culture structures also spread through borrowing. In reconstructing histories of cultures, a number of similar traits are frequently found to have existed in two or more cultures. It is a canon of anthropological analysis that such similarities are the probable result of diffusion rather than of independent invention, especially if the group of traits has no inherent reason for existing as a complex.

Tylor was the first to formulate and apply this principle in a study of the diffusion of the ancient East Indian game of pachisi into prehistoric America, where it appeared among the Aztecs as *patolli* and in various other forms among other Indians.[14] Tylor undertook to prove the historical connection between the Asiatic and American forms of these games by "analysing such phenomena

---

[11]Quoted in H. Hoffman, "Money, Ecology, and Acculturation among the Shipibo of Peru," in W. H. Goodenough (ed.), *Explorations in Cultural Anthropology*, p. 266.
[12]W. Davenport, "The 'Hawaiian Cultural Revolution': Some Political and Economic Considerations" (*American Anthropologist*, vol. 71, 1969), pp. 1–20.

[13]C. W. M. Hart and A. R. Pilling, *The Tiwi of North Australia*, p. 100.
[14]E. B. Tylor, "On the Game of Patolli in Ancient Mexico, and Its Probable Asiatic Origin" (*Journal of the Royal Anthropological Institute of Great Britain and Ireland*, vol. 8, 1879), pp. 116–129.

into constituent elements showing so little connection with one another that they may reasonably be treated as independent. The more numerous such elements, the more improbable the recurrence of the combination."[15]

Myths The technique may be applied to any aspect of culture,[16] but there is a remarkable stability in myth complexes the world over.

Frazer's *Folklore in the Old Testament* is a fascinating study of comparative distributions of Old World myth complexes and is challenging reading. For our demonstration of the application of the principle of diffusion analysis by means of internal congruity of traits, we shall use the "Tale of the Wandering Animals."

This story is familiar to all readers of Grimm's *Fairy Tales* as the "Musicians of Bremen." The old donkey, the worn-out hound, the abused cat, the rooster destined for the pot, and other rejected, decrepit animals all joined forces to go to the fair port of Bremen to become *Stadtmusikantern*. Night closed in on them as they found themselves deep in the woods. Frightening a band of robbers out of a forest hut, they made themselves at home, each in his favorite spot—the cat on the hearth, the rooster in the rafters, the dog on the doorstep, the donkey on the dungheap. The robbers sent back a spy in the darkness. But when he lighted the fire, the cat flew in his face; the dog chewed his leg as he fled through the door; the donkey planted a kick; and the rooster crowed his doom. The weak and despised creatures frightened away the robbers, who are symbolic of those who normally rule and dominate "the little man," and lived prosperously ever after in the nice snug little hut in the woods.

In Southeast Asia and Japan an ancient story is told, which in its simplest outline runs as follows.

An egg, a scorpion, a needle, a piece of feces, and a rice mortar (or any hard, heavy object) came together upon a journey. They entered the house of an old woman during her absence, and in order to do her harm, they disposed themselves in different places. The egg lay on the hearth, the scorpion in the water basin, the needle on the floor, the feces in the doorway, and the mortar over the door. When the old woman came home in the evening, she went to the hearth to light the fire, but the egg sprang up and smeared her face. When she went to the basin to wash, she was stung by the scorpion. Seized by terror, she rushed from the house, but the needle stuck in her foot; she slipped on the feces and was upset, and the mortar fell on her head, killing her.[17]

Here is the "Musicians of Bremen" all over again. Aarne justifiably concluded: "The concurrences between the tales are so significant that in my opinion we must conclude that the stories stand in an interdependent relationship in their origin."[18] He traced the story through India, into South Russia, up through Central Europe, and into Germany, where it arrived in the late Middle Ages.

Now let us shift our attention to the Northwest Coast of North America. A favored story of the Northwest Coast Indians has now a familiar ring. It is "Raven's War on the South Wind.[19] Raven is the mythological culture hero of this area, and the South Wind often brings too much rain from the ocean.

The South Wind, so the story runs, was

[15]E. B. Tylor, "American Lot Games as Evidence of Asiatic Intercourse before the Time of Columbus" (*Internationales Archiv für Ethnographie*, vol. 9, supplement, 1896), p. 66. For a critical evaluation of Tylor's method, see C. J. Erasmus, "Patolli, Pachisi, and the Limitation of Possibilities" (*Southwestern Journal of Anthropology*, vol. 6, 1950), pp. 369–387.

[16]F. Boas, *Tsimshian Mythology* (Bureau of American Ethnology, Annual Report 31, 1916), pp. 393–558. This is the classic study of the reflection of a people's material culture and social organization in their mythology.

[17]A. Aarne, *Die Tiere auf der Wanderschaft* (Folklore Fellows Communications, no. 11, 1913), p. 100.

[18]*Ibid.*, p. 162.

[19]Eleven versions are recorded in Boas, *op. cit.*, pp. 79–81, 658–660.

blowing so incessantly that all the creatures had to stay in their huts. They could not hunt, and they were hungry. The smoke blew back down their smoke vents and made their eyes sore. At last Raven called a council of war to propose an attack on the Master of the South Wind. A special canoe was procured, and the war party made the journey to the home of the South Wind. They had trouble landing because the gale caused by the flatulence of the Master of the South Wind was so strong that they were nearly overcome.

But once ashore, Halibut and Flounder or Skate (all flat, slippery fish) arranged themselves according to Raven's orders just outside the South Wind's doorstep. Red Cod or the Wren went in and started a smudge (in another version, Mouse went in and bit the South Wind's nose). As the Master of the South Wind staggered from the house, he slipped on the fish and slithered down the beach, where the waiting animals tried to beat his brains out with clubs—which are as hard as a rice mortar or a donkey's hoof. The South Wind made a successful deal for

his life—four days of good weather to alternate with four days of bad.[20]

Here, then, is a basic plot in which pusillanimous animals overcome masterful human beings in their very houses by combining their own little natural aptitudes to undo mankind. No matter that men were the authors of the tale. It is the story of the little men triumphing over the big men who order their lives. Its appeal as a vicarious release of suppressed resentments is clear. The ludicrousness of the event provides an elemental sort of gusty humor. The story is too good to keep. It has a broad appeal because it meets a common need. From Asia it spread westward into Europe and northeastward into the northwest corner of North America. This, however, is not the end of its history. In post-Columbian times, variants of the "Musicians of Bremen" form of the tale were brought to the eastern American Indians by

[20]An analysis in full detail is given in E. A. Hoebel, "The Asiatic Origin of a Myth of the Northwest Coast" (*Journal of American Folklore,* vol. 54, 1941), pp. 1–12.

Fig. 33-1   Diffusion of the Asiatic "Tale of the Wandering Animals." A, Asiatic center of origin; B, the "Musicians of Bremen" version; C, "Raven's War on the South Wind"; D, "Big Turtle's War Party."

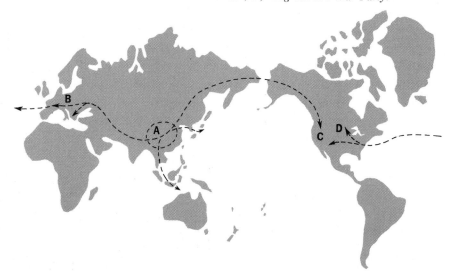

early trappers, and on the Plains and in the Woodlands these variants were adapted into a charming story known as "Big Turtle's War Party."

Thus, by word of mouth, crossing language barrier after language barrier, the "Tale of the Wandering Animals" has girdled the globe; penetrating North America from the west and from the east, it met itself along the rocky spine of the Western mountain area (Figure 33-1). Either by reliance upon historical data or by inferential reconstruction from distributional analysis, trait after trait may be followed through the course of its diffusion.

Dynamics of Diffusion: Selective Factors
Diffusion is no simple, straight-line process in which a people put an idea on wheels, figuratively speaking, and give it a shove to send it on its way around the world.

Every spreading trait or complex, as it moves from one society to another, must face the test of its acceptability in the culture of the receivers; and if it is accepted, it is invariably reworked in form, use, meaning, or function. No people take an alien trait without altering it to some degree.

The Sun Dance   The fate of the Plains Indian sun dance illustrates this clearly. The sun dance is a fairly complex ritual shared by a score of tribes in the western part of the Plains area. The ceremony is most elaborated and developed among the Arapaho and Cheyenne. From these tribes, according to Spier's classic analysis, the complex spread out among the other nomadic tribes.[21] In its core, the sun dance shows remarkable stability wherever it occurs. The fundamental form of the dance is universal within the area of its distribution. Nevertheless, considerable variation in content occurs from

tribe to tribe. As Spier observed, strong systematic selection was exercised.

Selection often works in subtle ways that we cannot determine *ex post facto*. Some of the more obvious determinants, however, may be quite clear. Thus, two features of the Arapaho sun dance are the use of medicine bundles and the special roles played by the military fraternity of the man who sponsors the dance. Among the Wind River and Idaho Shoshones, neither of these occurs in connection with the dance. The reason is simply that the limited culture of the Shoshones has no military societies within its social structure and no priesthood of bundle owners. The Shoshones stripped the complex ritual down to the structure of their meager social framework. As they adapted it, the sun dance became primarily a purification and curing ceremony, designed to bring general well-being to the entire tribe. For the closely related Utes, the function and meaning were quite similar, although details, such as an increased emphasis on dreaming, varied.[22]

The Crows used the sun dance to generate war power against specific enemies. Revenge was the motif; a scalp, the object; a war party, the follow-up.

The Cheyenne sun dance was, and still is, a world-renewal ceremony. In the Cheyenne world view, the energy of the universe is being continuously used up and must be annually recharged mimetically through the ceremonies. Although the dance is pledged by one individual, the entire renewal effort is directed toward the welfare of all members of the tribe.

There is one recorded instance where the dance was "borrowed" by a tribe, tried once, and forever dropped. Urged on by their "messiah" and in need of "war medicine," the Comanches presented one sun dance that was to endow them with immunity to bullets. Soon after, they were thoroughly defeated in

[21]L. Spier, *The Sun Dance of the Plains Indians* (American Museum of Natural History, Anthropological Papers, vol. 16, part 7, 1921).

[22]M. K. Opler, "The Integration of the Sun Dance in Ute Religion" (*American Anthropologist*, vol. 43, 1941), pp. 550–572.

battle. The ritual had failed in its desired function, and it is improbable that it ever developed any meaning for them.[23]

Thus, the function and meaning of the sun dance varied as it was worked into one tribal culture after another. For the buffalo hunters in the mid-nineteenth century, its chief function was that of tribal integration. The scattered bands that eked out the winter separately were brought together in early summer for a grand socializing prior to the communal buffalo hunt. For individuals, the dance functioned to relieve anxiety. It also expressed a subconscious submissiveness to the supernatural through self-imposed hunger and thirsting and bloody immolation of the self to gratify the spirit forces. It functioned to make more probable the acquisition of power through visions by means of heightened social suggestion.

As the sun dances are performed on the reservations today, they function mostly as reinforcers of tribal integrity in the face of all the surrounding forces of disintegration.

The selective effect of ideology, or meaning, on cultural diffusion and reinterpretation may be seen if we look at the celebration of the Fourth of July by the Crows and Cheyennes in the 1960s. On the Crow reservation, a large crowd gathers at a racetrack. The betting is as spirited as the horses, the latter ridden by Crow Indians splendid in colorful jockey costumes. The shouting is loud. The fireworks are deafening. There is no sun dance. For the Crows, the old sun dance is dead, and although a new form of the dance was borrowed from the Wind River Shoshones after 1941, it has not become a tribal ceremony of major significance.

At the Cheyenne reservation, a few miles away, an essentially traditional sun dance comes to its four-day climax. The dancers move through the ceremonial forms with somewhat weary dignity. The audience

watches quietly. A neatly lettered sign reads: "Quiet. No Fireworks Allowed."

Why such a difference between two tribes of Plains Indians, whose acquaintance stretches back over many years and who currently live boundary to boundary?

It is obvious that both groups are celebrating the Fourth of July and that as citizens of the United States, they recognize this date as a symbol of American identity. However, each group has recombined certain elements of the national rite in such a way as to produce two very different kinds of celebration. The Cheyennes, with their age-old emphasis on world renewal and group solidarity, seem not so much to be celebrating the birth of the nation as seeking to revivify it through their tribal efforts. The basic meaning of the dance has changed little, although its form has worn a bit thin. The time of the dance has been changed from early June to July 4, signifying tribal integration into a new and larger society. School vacations and work schedules make this a convenient and natural date. Perhaps, too, the selection of the national holiday indicates that they are sufficiently identified with the larger society to wish to proclaim their membership in it and help keep it strong and vital.

The original function of the Crows' sun dance, to bring success in scalp-hunting, has long vanished. The meaning of the dance was too specialized to permit adaptation to contemporary conditions. But gambling and horse racing, with their attendant noisy clamor, are ancient pastimes. It was natural for the Crows to seize on the festive aspect of July Fourth and to make of it a noisy carnival as they, too, proclaim their identity with the United States.

The Importance of Meaning   This fundamental anthropological fact—in cultural transference a trait or complex will be evaluated and rejected, or accepted and modified, in terms of the meaning it has for the receiving people—is one of the most difficult for pro-

[23]E. Wallace and E. A. Hoebel, *The Comanches*, pp. 319–326.

fessional civilizers to perceive and apply. This applies to teachers, Peace Corps volunteers, economic-development programmers, public health workers, and missionaries, whose numbers are steadily increasing. When this principle is ignored, the consequent mischief worked is often monumental.

Over one hundred years ago, a wise and not too doctrinaire Episcopalian missionary demonstrated his full recognition of this aspect of intercultural transference. Sensing the likelihood of misinterpretation of the Christian rite of communion by the Tsimshian Indians, among whom he was working, he was induced to omit the ritual from his services. Cannibalism among the Northwest Coast Indians, although quite different in meaning for the Indians, was too similar to communion in form and function. Not only in this but in other points as well did Duncan, the missionary in question, deliberately and as a matter of policy eliminate "many of the potential danger spots in Christian metaphysics for a native whose only basis for interpreting new belief was in terms of the old."[24]

Even with foresight, one cannot anticipate some consequences of interpretation of new phenomena in terms of old meanings. For example, the Dani tribesmen of the Balim Valley in western New Guinea (Irian) are active cannibals. American missionaries who entered the area in the 1950s discouraged the practice in their efforts to promote civilization and Christianization. As the Dani became familiar with eating canned goods, they quickly comprehended that a tin bearing a picture of beans on its label contained beans, that one picturing pears contained pears, and so forth. When one of the mission wives gave birth and cans of Gerber's baby food with pictures of healthy babies on the labels were flown in, the Danis' idea of the

eating habits of American missionaries need not be guessed.[25]

Commonly, in diffusion and culture growth, the form of a trait or complex will remain the same, at least initially. But the meaning is almost certain to be altered, and, possibly, the use and functions also. Thus, a highly technical artifact, such as a film spool or a light bulb when it has fulfilled its originally intended function, may be adopted for entirely different use, meaning, and function within another cultural context. The delight of the New Guinea girl pictured in Figure 33-2 is not at all unusual, as, confident of her beauty, she has converted burnt-out light bulbs into aesthetic objects of artistic ornament. The form of each bulb is unaltered but its use is as costume; its meaning is aesthetic and perhaps also magical; and its function, that of prestige enhancement and ego gratification in a ceremonial context. The bulb

[25]Personal communication from a member of the mission organization, 1962.

Fig. 33-2   Cultural significance of use, meaning, and function. A New Guinea girl converts burnt-out light bulbs into aesthetic objects of ceremonial costumery. (Courtesy of the American Museum of Natural History.)

[24]H. G. Barnett, "Applied Anthropology in 1860" (*Applied Anthropology,* vol. 1, 1942), p. 24.

is thus culturally acceptable because it readily fits into the context of the native culture in a positive way.

The Selective Consequences of Negative Meanings   Traits that have positive meaning in one culture may be blocked in diffusion because their forms are associated with negatively colored uses, meanings, or functions in the existing cultures of potential receivers.

At a Northern Cheyenne peyote meeting, the author once became interested in a decorative staff used in the ritual. It seemed to be carved with figures of bison quite similar to those of Franco-Cantabrian cave art. The thought was intriguing. Upon closer examination, however, the carved scenes proved to be of toreadors and charging bulls. There was also the Mexican eagle sitting on his cactus, but the snake in his claws had been scraped out with a knife. Black Wolf, the peyote leader, explained that the staff had come from Mexico, and he pointed out that the eagle is good medicine. The toreador confronting the bull suggested the vision-seeking Indian confronted by a bison. However, he said, "Those people down there worship snakes, but we don't. So we took the snakes out. We can't have any snakes in our ceremony." The Cheyennes, in point of fact, are not simply neutral with respect to snakes. In their mythology, the Horned Snake (or the Plumed Serpent) is a creature much to be feared and avoided.

Barnett has detailed a number of such rejections by several northern California tribes. When the bobbing of women's hair came into vogue, it met heavy resistance because that hair style was believed to cause death. Corsets and hairpins were rejected at first because they resembled the warrior's rod armor and the bone pins that he used in his hair.[26]

On a larger scale, the efforts of the Belgian administration in the Congo to make the Pygmies of the forest more economically self-sufficient by inducing them to take up gardening were rejected outright. A few Pygmies made the try on "model" plantations, and although they demonstrated the ability to cultivate, "they degenerated socially and physically at an alarming rate, losing all sense of individual or family responsibility and dying from sunstroke and stomach disorders."[27] These were merely symptoms; they were dying because they had accepted a new way of life utterly devoid of meaning. Other Mbuti "clearly see and state that once they abandon their nomadic forest existence they will cease to be Mbuti."[28]

For similar, though less drastic, reasons, as we have seen (Chapter 14, page 292), the Navaho have refused through a thousand years of contact with the Pueblo Indians to adopt Pueblo architecture, even though it is structurally "better." To give up the hogan, or earth lodge, for an apartment in a pueblo-type settlement would require the abandonment of basic values that the Navaho hold dear. Such housing would make it impossible to live as a Navaho. As a people, they have stoutly refused to shed their identity simply for a better home.

These examples demonstrate that the pre-existing biases of the members of a receiving society facilitate or block the accepting or borrowing of any new cultural possibility. The compatibility of a new way with the basic postulates and derived corollaries underlying the receiving culture is of vital importance (Figure 33-3). On the other hand, the acceptance of materials of apparently neutral significance but of demonstrated technical efficiency, such as iron or tractors, may ultimately lead to value and postulational disruptions that were never anticipated. The successful development of lunar and interplanetary rockets, for example, obviously

---

[26]Barnett, "Applied Anthropology in 1860," *op. cit.,* pp. 31–32.

[27]C. M. Turnbull, "The Mbuti Pygmies of the Congo," in J. L. Gibbs, Jr. (ed.), *Peoples of Africa,* p. 313.
[28]*Ibid.*

holds undreamed-of cultural consequences in store. Yet we seem quite willing to take our chances on what the penetration of space will mean for the future.

The Selective Consequences of Cultural Indifference   The selection of culture traits in accordance with their compatibility with a specific set of cultural postulates and related cultural values leads not only to negative rejection. It may also result in the neutral nonacceptance of alien possibilities because of indifference. A thing or an idea may be seen or encountered and yet not be borrowed, adapted, or even desired. It meets no felt need of a people; or its usefulness is not perceived by them; it rings no bell. Their interest is in other things or ideas. Loren Eiseley astutely comments of the Maya, who were capable of inventing such an abstraction as the concept of the zero, plus a hieroglyphic symbol to represent it:

These men who could predict eclipses never learned to weigh or to use the wheel for transportation, though wheeled toys were in use among their neighbors. No better example could be utilized to reveal that a given society has just so much energy and interest at its disposal, and that its intellectual achievements will move in the path of its deepest motivations. The Mayan intellect centered upon a divine mathematics that controlled the human world, just as different cultures, including our own, have pursued reality in other shapes and guises.[29]

Fig. 33-3   Diffusion of a culture trait. The memorial epitaph of European culture is adapted to a traditional type of Kwakiutl Indian grave post. In this carving, a frock-coated chief holds a representation of a valuable copper shield upon which is painted the English sentiment. (Courtesy of Robert Gardner.)

Ideology and Structure in Cultural Change

We have been discussing the acceptability and rejection of innovations in terms of their compatibility to preexisting cultural standards (ideal norms). Usually, however, this is not a clear and simple matter. Every innovation begins with the act of somebody. Who that somebody is and how he manages

the strategy of introducing his new idea in relation to existing patterns can make a great difference—as can, of course, the temper of the times.

The Role of the Individual   Values are never absolutely consistent and tensions engendered by alternative choices are always present. In no phase of human life is this more evident than in the area of conflict between the urges of individual sexuality and the standardized channeling of sex in social structure.

To take a Cheyenne case in illustration: Cheyennes (as we have seen on pages 551–

[29]L. Eiseley, "In the Beginning Was the Artifact" (*Saturday Review*, Dec. 7, 1963), p. 52.

552) viewed the energy quotient of the universe as limited, and they extended this view to sexual relations. Unlike their neighbors the Comanches, they did not allow for sexual competition among the males. The Comanches frequently stole one another's wives; the Cheyennes did not. But then a wily Cheyenne who wanted another man's wife schemed to alter the Cheyenne pattern. Here is how it went, as told by Blackwolf in 1935.

A war party was organizing. Walking Rabbit approached the leader with a question. "Is it true that you have declared we must all go afoot? If so, I would like to be able to lead a horse to pack my moccasins and possibles." The leader gave him an answer. "There is a reason for my ruling. I want no horses, that it may be easier for us to conceal our movements. However, you may bring one horse." Then Walking Rabbit asked for instructions concerning the location of the first and second nights' camps, for he would start late and overtake the party.

Walking Rabbit's sweetheart had been married only recently to another. "My husband is not the man I thought he was," she told her former suitor. So Walking Rabbit took her to join the war party. [The Cheyennes have a phrase describing the single man who marries a one-time married woman —"putting on the old moccasin."] In this way, it turned out that the "moccasin" he was packing was a big woman.

When they saw this woman there, the warriors got excited. The party turned into the hills and stopped. The leader opened his pipe. The leader's pipe was always filled before they left the camp, but it was not smoked until the enemy was seen or their tracks reported. Now the leader spoke. "When we take a woman with us it is usually known in the camp. Here is a man who has sneaked off with another's wife. Now what is going to happen?" That is what they were talking about.

The leader declared, "The only thing this man can do is return and make a settlement with the husband. Then he may follow us up."

One warrior was for aiding Walking Rabbit. "Why can't we let him stay?" was his proposal. "If we take any horses, we can give them to her husband." That was rejected.

The decision was that he had to go back. "If you had told us you wanted her so badly, we might have waited for you to settle for her. Then we could have taken her the right way. If you really want to go to war with us, you will be able to overtake us. We are afoot."

Then three or four warriors spoke up, each promising Walking Rabbit a horse to send to the husband. Everyone gave one or two arrows to be sent as well.

In the meantime Walking Rabbit's father had fixed it up with the aggrieved husband. Since he and his wife were incompatible, he was willing to release her. When Walking Rabbit came in and told his father the story of the soldiers' action, the father said, "Just let that stand. The thing is fixed. When those fighters come back they may want to give to the girl's parents. You go back after your party." But Walking Rabbit preferred to stay at home.

When Walking Rabbit did not go out, his closest relatives raised a big tipi. When they heard of the approach of the returning war party, everything was in readiness.

The warriors came charging in, shooting; they had taken many horses. The first coup-counters were in the van. Walking Rabbit's father had a right to harangue; he was a crier. "Don't go to your homes! Don't go to your own lodges! Come here to the lodge of Walking Rabbit, your friend!"

When they were all in this lodge the old man entered and told them his story. "I had this thing all settled before my son returned. You have sent arrows and promised horses. Now I have kept this girl here pending your return. I shall send her back to her parents with presents. I have waited to see what you are going to do."

The leader replied for his followers. "Yes, we will help you. We promised to help your son. When you send her back, we'll send presents with her." The men who had promised horses went out to get them. Others gave captured horses.

Sending her back with these presents was giving wedding gifts. Her relatives got them all. They gathered up their goods to send back. The war party was called together once more; to them this stuff was given. It was a great thing for the people to talk about. It was the first and last time a woman was sent home on enemy horses the day they came in.[30]

In this instance, which took place about

---

[30]K. N. Llewellyn and E. A. Hoebel, *The Cheyenne Way*, pp. 13–15.

1820, an innovation was rejected and, with ceremony and gift-giving, was made so memorable that the people could never forget it. What is more, the reinforced norm against wife-stealing stuck: from then until the end of the raiding days (1878), there were no more attempts by lovers to abscond with war parties. Walking Rabbit failed as an innovator. Cheyenne moral ideology was reaffirmed and reinforced.

Successful Innovation   On the other hand, a Kapauku schemer, who was wholly successful in abrogating the incest rules of his society, illustrates in fine detail some of the specific factors of motivation and action involved in cultural ideology and change of social structure. The case is reported in full, and analyzed, by Professor Leo Pospisil.[31]

The Kapauku are patrilineal gardeners living in western New Guinea. Awiitigaaj is a Big Man (*tonowi*), a village headman, and a leader of a political confederacy that links a pair of lineages and their several villages. Up to 1935, the penalty for incest within the lineage was death. Like Walking Rabbit, Awiitigaaj took a fancy to a forbidden woman and wanted to marry her. "I liked her; she was beautiful." So he ran off with her, the traditional death penalty notwithstanding. The formal reaction was right and proper. "The infuriated relatives of the couple pursued the lovers, and the girl's father, Ugataga, who was a coheadman of the Ijaaj-Jamaina sublineage . . . ruled that both his daughter and her lover must be executed by arrow according to Kapauku customary law. His decision was upheld by the head of the Ijaaj-Pigome Confederacy."[32]

Awiitigaaj knew, however, that when the girl's father's anger had cooled, he would realize that the execution would deprive him of a very large progeny price and an impor-

tant son-in-law—a serious conflict of public and private interests. So the couple hid out in the jungle, aided and abetted by Awiitigaaj's mother's brothers and other maternal kin, who were custom-bound to protect him regardless of his offense. Eventually, the upholders of law and traditional morality tired of beating about the bush. The outraged father of the bride continued to put on public temper tantrums and speeches, but under pressure from neutral leaders gradually agreed to settle for a progeny-price payment. In so doing, he accepted the legitimacy of the marriage. Eventually, because the members of the girl's sublineage became impatient over delays in the payment of the progeny price, they attacked Awiitigaaj's lineage mates with sticks. In a counter suit the latter were freed of the need to pay any progeny price whatsoever, whereupon they too publicly agreed to the acceptability of the marriage. The precedent became a new alternative. By 1954, 22 per cent of the marriages within the lineage were with previously forbidden lineage mates.

Neighboring lineages followed suit and a fundamental change in the postulates requiring sib-exogamy was clearly effected. A significant change in the social structure had been brought about by a skillful self-seeker who successfully manipulated a complex situation to achieve a change in ideology, kinship organization, and law. A change effected in the real culture brought about modifications in the ideal culture. In 1954, nearly two-thirds of the adult members of the village originally involved told Pospisil that they approved of the change.

Stimulus Diffusion   Culture contact generates culture change. Only isolated societies retain prolonged stability. Contact opens up new alternatives and unthought-of possibilities. In the two case studies just cited, the Cheyenne had the Comanche example to give him his idea, and Awiitigaaj knew of the existence of lineage endogamy among another population in a nearby region. In

[31]L. Pospisil, *Anthropology of Law,* pp. 214–232; also "Structural Change and Primitive Law: Consequences of a Papuan Legal Case," in L. Nader (ed.), *Law in Culture and Society,* pp. 208–229.
[32]L. Pospisil, *Anthropology of Law,* p. 216.

Fig. 33-4   The Tasaday, a Stone Age people surviving into the last third of the twentieth century, had no contact with the outside world until "discovered" on June 7, 1971. (Dolf Herras, Time *Magazine.)*

these instances the process is one which is known in anthropology as *stimulus diffusion.*

Stimulus diffusion occurs when the general idea of a culture trait or complex is transferred from one people to another without a transmission of the actual detailed content. The content of the pattern is more or less invented by the borrowers of the idea. Sequoya, the Cherokee inventor of the syllabary used by the Cherokees for writing their tongue, got the idea of writing from contact with whites, but he did not learn to write the English language. He took some alphabetic symbols directly from English, modified some, and invented others. His English symbols, however, bear no relation to the English phonetic system. He made them stand for Cherokee syllables. He took the idea, but not the form, of writing.

Stimulus diffusion as a process stands midway between independent invention and genuine diffusion. Awareness of a need or an inventive possibility is stimulated by con-

tact with a trait or a complex from an alien source. The stimulated people, who lack the trait, attempt independently to invent an equivalent of it.

Acculturation

Acculturation occurs when a society undergoes drastic culture change under the influence of a more dominant culture and society with which it has come in contact.[33] The acculturating society alters its culture in the direction of adjustment and (greater or lesser) conformity to cultural ideology and patterns of the dominant society. However, the acculturating society, although signifi-

[33]A standard definition of acculturation emphasizes "changes in the culture patterns of either or both groups"; R. Redfield, R. Linton, and M. J. Herskovits, "Outline for the Study of Acculturation" (*American Anthropologist,* vol. 38, 1936), p. 149. However, the concept as it is most frequently used applies to the process as we have defined it here.

cantly modified in its life-way, retains its discrete identity.

Acculturation is thus to be seen as a special form of culture change. The rapid spread of tobacco from the American Indians all around the world is a prime example of diffusion of a culture trait, but it would hardly be correct to say that tobacco-smoking Chinese became acculturated to the American Indians. To carry the point further, European Americans, as they built up the culture of the United States, borrowed many new traits from the American Indian: cultivation of maize, beans, and squash in hills; maple syrup and sugar production; snowshoes, toboggans, and canoes, to name only a very few items. The government of the United States built an elaborate legal subculture to accommodate to the presence of the many tribes within the federal legal system. There was indeed a good deal of culture change produced in response to the presence of American Indian tribal societies on the continent. But most white Americans were not acculturating to the Indian way of life. On the other hand, many American Indians were, over the decades, changing their ideologies and cultures in the direction of Westernized modes of life.

Differential Acculturation   Once again it must be emphasized that culture change occurs first in individual behavior. The change appears as a deviation from previous customary norms. It can be hailed with enthusiasm, be overlooked, be mildly disapproved and lightly sanctioned, or be rejected outright and heavily sanctioned. At any rate, it never takes place totally and instantaneously throughout any society.

Menomini Indian Acculturation   The most effective demonstration to date of the point of differential acculturation is found in the study of the psychology of Menomini Indians, living in Wisconsin, done in the early 1950s by

George and Louise Spindler.[34] By using a schedule of twenty-three sociocultural indices "for placing subjects on an acculturative continuum and defining explicit values associated with the native or American culture," plus autobiographies and intensive personal interviews over a period of seven seasons of fieldwork, the Spindlers arrived at a fivefold classification of the mid-twentieth century Menomini population in terms of degree of acculturation. In summary form, they are stated as follows:

A. *Native-oriented*—all members of the Medicine Lodge and/or Dream Dance group where the patterns of traditional culture survive to the greatest extent.
B. *Peyote Cult*—composed of participating members of the Cult and constitutes a unique variation of culture conflict resolution with the transitional position.
C. *Transitional*—consisting of persons in cultural transition who have participated in native-oriented religious activities and groups but have moved towards Catholicism and Western culture during their lifetimes, and are at present not clearly identified with either Western or native-oriented groups and values.
D. *Lower status acculturated*—persons who were born Catholic and maintained this identification, know little or nothing of native traditions, but who have acculturated to a laboring class standard.
E. *Elite acculturated*—composed of persons who participate regularly in Catholic services, are members of the prestigeful Catholic Mother's and Holy Name Societies, and, if male, occupy managerial or semiprofessional positions in the tribal lumber industry or agency.[35]

Figure 33-5 shows the relative positions of the Menomini groups on the continuum of acculturation from native to American, combined with degree of socioeconomic status

[34]G. D. Spindler, *Sociocultural and Psychological Processes in Menomini Acculturation* (University of California Publications in Culture and Society, vol. 5, 1955). L. Spindler and G. D. Spindler, "Male and Female Adaptations in Culture Change" (*American Anthropologist,* vol. 60, 1968), pp. 217–233.

[35]L. Spindler and G. D. Spindler, *op. cit.,* pp. 218–219.

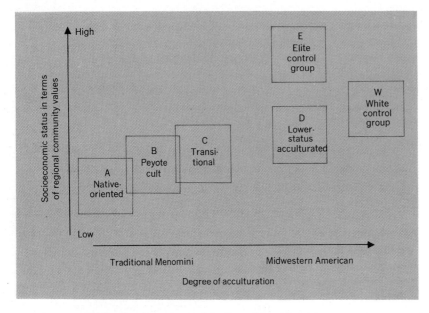

High

Socioeconomic status in terms of regional community values

E
Elite control group

W
White control group

D
Lower-status acculturated

C
Transi-tional

B
Peyote cult

A
Native-oriented

Low

Traditional Menomini   Midwestern American

Degree of acculturation

Fig. 33-5   Differential acculturation and socioeconomic status of Menomini Indians in relation to the larger American regional society. (Adapted from G. D. Spindler, "Sociocultural and Psychological Processes in Menomini Acculturation" (University of California Publications in Culture and Society, vol. 5, 1955, p. 118.)

within the larger, regional society of midwestern Wisconsin.

The most valuable and significant feature of the Spindler studies lies not so much in the explicit demonstration of differential acculturation in the external behavior but rather in the revelation of parallel differences in the deeper psychological adjustments which are characteristic of the different Menomini groups. This was achieved through sophisticated use of Rorschach's psychodiagnostic inkblot tests. Rorschach analysis shows that

. . . [T]he native-oriented group operate with deep internal controls over aggression. The people are inward-oriented, not achievement-oriented; they lack overt emotional responsiveness but are sensitive to the nuances of interpersonal relations; they are fatalistic in orientation, and exhibit quiet endurance under stress or deprivation, a pattern Louise Spindler has termed "latescent" . . . . There is no marked evidence of anxiety or internal conflict, nor a free-flowing spontaneity.

The Peyotists are a special case. They are highly committed to the ideology and ritual of Peyotism stressing rumination about one's self, sins, and salvation, attainment of power individually and through partaking of Peyote in an acceptant mood. There is significant relaxing of controls over emotions and overt expression of feelings,

with public crying during testimonials and rituals and bids for collective expressions of sympathy, which are offered freely.

The ungrouped transitionals are characterized by very uneven adjustments to the vicissitudes of transformational culture change. Some are striving for an orderly way of life, towards goals recognizable in the surrounding non-Indian community; others are withdrawn and mostly just vegetate; others go on destructive rampages, during or between drunks. Beating, murders, illegitimacy, dirt and disorder are a way of life for many in the latter group. The Menomini transitionals are like human populations everywhere who have lost their way; for them neither the goals of the traditional or the new culture are meaningful.

The acculturated, and particularly the elite, are radically different from any of the other groups. The roles they occupy demand punctuality, regular hours of concentrated work, orderly behavior and planning, pride in material possessions and economic status. The psychological data on them shows that they are emotionally open, but not disorganized. They utilize their emotional energy in the attainment of goals—personal success, material acquisition—approved of by middle-class persons in the surrounding communities. They are concerned about production and competition. They react to environmental pressures in a controlled but aggressive manner. They are also more anxious and tense than the native-oriented, but this anxiety is focused, rather than diffuse (as it is among the transitionals).

The acculturated Menomini deny their identity as Indians and specifically disclaim any relationship to "those Indians"—the members of the native-oriented group. Most of them do not speak their own language. The few who do rarely use it. Their homes and possessions are indistinguishable from those of Whites in nearby towns.

It is evident that the radical departure represented by the elite acculturated in the acculturative continuum of the Menomini occurs in both the manifest and psychological phases of adaptation. In order to "make the grade" on the terms of American middle-class culture the elite had to learn to stop being Menomini and learn how to be middle-class, achievement-oriented Americans. This reorganization occurred in depth and was not merely an overt adjustment.[36]

Finally, not only are the psychological characteristics of the male Menomini different according to degree and kind of acculturation, but Menomini women show much less psychological change than do Menomini men. In their more traditional roles as wives and mothers, less is demanded of them in acculturative adjustments. "They do not find the flux and conflict of rapid change as disturbing as do the males."[37]

To sum up: some Menominis have acculturated so completely that they are assimilated within Midwestern white society—behaviorally and psychologically. Some are in marginal transition. Some have sought a new type of adjustment in a "reactive movement," the Peyote Cult, which is neither white nor old Menomini, and a small handful cling to a residual belief in what is left of old Menomini ways.

Can one say that all the Menomini Indians are acculturated? No. Can one say that most Menomini Indians are significantly acculturated? Yes. Can one say that all Menomini

Indians have experienced significant culture change in the past 200 years? Most definitely. With variations in degree and forms, it seems probable that a Menomini-like model will hold good for all Eskimos and Indians who have survived in the Western Hemisphere—from Point Barrow to Tierra del Fuego, and in many other parts of the world.

Forced and Voluntary Culture Change
Throughout human history, trade and alliance have evidently provided the major pipelines of diffusion and cultural change. Traders bring new objects of material culture and news of people who have different life-ways. Traders are almost always welcomed (once the nature of their roles is perceived) and their technically superior or more easily acquired goods are quickly incorporated. This is as true of prehistoric and aboriginal traders as it is of the harbingers of civilization (see pages 355–359, on trade).

Intertribal alliances produce intermarriage and ceremonial visitations in which cultural forms may be copied or transferred. In the early 1930s, religious specialists from Taos pueblo, for instance, were invited to Santa Ana pueblo, in New Mexico, ritually to repair the roof of the mission church. In exchange, the Santa Anas taught them the songs and the steps of a dance, giving them the right to perform it thereafter. Such culture change is obviously voluntary.

In the modern economic context, the desire for money with which to buy today's goods quickly leads to many voluntary shifts in cultural practices and social structure in order to acquire that mystic token of economic value.

Slave taking from alien peoples is something else again. The forcible removal of individuals from their home societies and their injection into an alien one requires anguishing cultural readjustments on their part. Conquest and political subjugation, with or without slavery, has even greater acculturative effects, for the conquered must accommo-

[36]G. D. Spindler, "Psychocultural Adaptation," in E. Norbeck, D. Price-Williams, and W. M. McCord (eds.), *The Study of Personality*, pp. 329–330. (© Holt, Rinehart, and Winston, Inc. Quoted with permission.)
[37]L. Spindler and G. D. Spindler, *op. cit.*, p. 229.

date to the rule and presence of the conquerors in their own territory, often with little or no choice.

Settlers, missionaries, educators, medical and technological specialists, and even tourists and travelers all play their roles, as do medical and technological specialists. (See Figure 33-6.) Nor are we speaking only of the European expansion and colonial imperialism of recent centuries. The Indonesian archipelago was Hinduized by conquering Indian princes and priests beginning in the tenth century and continuing until overthrown by Muslim converts in the fifteenth and sixteenth centuries. Centuries before (600 B.C.), Greek traders and settlers Hellenized the Upper Indus Valley, and later, Greek teacher-slaves gave much to the intellect of Rome, while Rome transformed the barbarian world of Europe. For some hundreds of years, Arab slavers, traders, and teachers have pressed their cultural mark on the Africans of the Sudan. Acculturation is the product of response to militantly dominant cultures and/or those which offer more effective adaptive uses of physical environments and responses to the mysteries of life—i.e., the management of meaning and symbolic systems.

Fig. 33-6   Voluntary acculturation. African Bushmen learning to read and write their language from books prepared by missionaries. Smoothed earth serves as "writing boards." (George Rodger, Magnum.)

Culture Crisis and Reactive Movements

When value systems are out of joint because they are too inconsistent with existing realities, a condition of cultural crisis may build up. Culture crisis breeds reactive movements. Such movements are the product of the gap between present circumstance and dreamed-of expectancy. The reactive movement may present a reformed value code or it may propose drastic changes in the environmental condition or in the social system which is contributing to the sense of crisis. Or it may attempt to deal with all these possibilities simultaneously.

If the dominant aim of a movement is to raise up a depressed, pariah group which has long suffered in an inferior social standing and which has its own special subcultural ideology, the movement is called *millenarism*. Prophetic Judaism and early Christianity are examples.

If the movement aims to reconstitute a destroyed but not forgotten way of life, it is called *nativistic* or *revivalistic*. The Plains Indians' ghost dance is an example.

If the movement seeks to speed up the acculturation process in order to share more quickly and fully in the supposed benefits of dominant cultures, it may be called *transitional*.

Finally, if the aim of the movement is directed primarily to the ideological system and the attendant social structure of a cultural system from within, the movement is called *revolutionary*.

Millenarism   Although aspects of millenarism may be found in other parts of the world, it is particularly a Western phenomenon found in the Judaic, Christian, and Islamic cultural traditions. It is a form of religious utopianism based upon a firm conviction that the gap between the ideal in culture and the real in social life can be and will be closed—the Kingdom of God realized on earth. Man and life will be perfected according to the blueprints set forth by the prophets in a form of collective salvation for True Believers.

The Latin term *millenium* and its Greek equivalent, *chilias,* literally mean a period of a thousand years. According to the millenarian tradition, which is based on Jewish apocalyptic literature and the Revelations of St. John, Christ will reappear in the guise of a warrior, vanquish the Devil, and hold him prisoner. He will then build the Kingdom of God and reign in person for a thousand years. Those saints who have remained steadfast and who have given their lives for their faith shall be raised from the dead and serve as His royal priesthood. At the end of this period, Satan will be let loose again for a short while and will finally be destroyed. The victory will be followed by the general resurrection of the dead, the last judgment, and final redemption.[38]

Millenarism promises the absolute conquest of evil, symbolized in the person of the Devil, forever. "The new dispensation will bring about not mere improvement but a complete transformation and perfection itself . . . ultimate and irrevocable . . . revolutionary and catastrophic."[39]

Through the centuries, millenial cults have risen and fallen, often with a messianic leader as spokesman, often without. The means are always supernatural and mystic. The end is cultural perfection realized—at a stroke.

Nativistic Movements: The Ghost Dance
Wave after wave of crisis movements swept through the American Indian populations in the nineteenth century. Of these, the Ghost Dance Movement of 1890 is the most famous.

The last of the tribes had been subjugated by the United States, the buffalo were gone, measles and smallpox had decimated many tribal populations, most of their lands had been ceded and opened to white settlement, the religious powers on which their security rested had been proven pitifully inadequate. Destructive catastrophe had overwhelmed virtually all the tribes.

Visits to the Land of the Dead and return to the living were not uncommon aboriginal experiences among Indians of the Great Basin. In 1870, a Paiute named Taivo from western Nevada visited the "Great Spirit," who told him a massive earthquake was coming to destroy all whites and Indians; however, after three days all Indians would be resurrected in a state of plenty—with the whites destroyed forever. Later, the prediction was amended to include only "believing" Indians in the resurrection. Belief was attested in a Round Dance.

Twenty years later, a new prophet arose. Wovoka, "The Cutter," was his name. He had learned some Christian theology from the ranch family for whom he worked.

In a delirium of fever, he was lifted up to see God. Heaven was full of happy dead per-

---

[38]Y. Talmon, "Millenarism" (*International Encyclopedia of the Social Sciences,* vol. 10, 1968), p. 349.

[39]*Ibid.,* p. 351.

sons who would never grow old and who enjoyed pleasant work and games. Their idyllic life would be brought to all on earth in a grand reunion of dead and living, in a good life that would never end, God said, if living human beings would stop fighting, live in loving goodness, and dance the ceremony God gave to him. An earthquake or flood would wipe out the bad old earth in preparation for the new, but good people need not fear it.

At the news of the messiah, various tribes reacted variously. Since they would soon rejoin the dead, the Arapaho gave up shooting their horses and gashing their arms in mourning when someone died. To escape the flood, they should go to high mountains, leaving skeptics behind to turn to stone and the whites to be covered. On the new skin of the earth, game would once again abound. The Cheyenne said the Earth was getting old, grass and trees were worn out, and the people getting bad. Besides, the Earth was too small, so God was going to do away with heaven and remodel a bigger Earth for both living and dead. The Shoshone said a deep four-day sleep would come over all believers, and they would awaken on the fifth to a new world. Kiowa thought the new earth would slide from the west over the old one, bearing buffalo and elk upon it, and their sacred dance feathers would lift the faithful up onto the new world. Some Arapaho spoke of a wall of flame that would drive the whites back to their own country; sacred feathers would lift them over the fire and a twelve-day rain would subsequently extinguish it. The Walapai awaited a hurricane, the thunder of which would kill the whites and unbelievers. All these tribes believed the whites would be eliminated through supernatural means, and they bitterly blamed the warlike Sioux for later taking naturalistic means to this same end.[40]

A few Sioux, under Yellow Shirt, turned the Ghost Dance into an active resistance movement. They died at Wounded Knee.[41]

Transition Movements: The Cargo Cult In the South Seas, crisis cults first began in the

1870s and 1880s as nativistic movements, but by 1914 the emphasis shifted from overturning the white colonialists (so as to revert to "the good old days") to getting direct access to the largesse of European goods. Proper ceremony would bring in the cargo ships loaded with canned food, tobacco, cloth, lamps, axes, knives, and rifles. These were all material objects which the whites did not make (so far as the Melanesians could observe). Nor did most of the whites in the South Pacific know *how* to make them. Asked how to make glass for a window, could you tell a native? How about paper? A gasoline engine? If you want these things, how do you get them? You order them! The ships, and later, the planes, bring them. That is all there is to it, as any reasonable man can see.

"Ordering" is a form of ritual control over the remotely located, unseen beings who make the goods. Old aboriginal rituals are abandoned, masks destroyed or sold off to Europeans; fields may be abandoned, new ceremonies with new symbols introduced, marching drills abound. Wharfs are built to receive the ships and welcoming miniature air strips are hacked out on jungle mountain ridgetops to receive cargo planes far from the ocean.

A central idea among New Guineans is that their own spirit ancestors actually produce all the material goods, which are intended for them and not for the Europeans. But white men developed a magic (religion) to divert the goods to themselves. The new cargo cult religions will ritually rectify that.

World War II intensified the cargo cult movements in Melanesia. The thousands of American ships and planes which flooded the beaches and bases with seemingly inexhaustible supplies of goods, many carelessly tossed away or generously given to the Melanesians, confirmed the belief that all these things could be theirs—always—if only the proper compelling rituals could be invented. In 1967, the most ambitious cult, which developed among the inhabitants of

[40]W. LaBarre, *The Ghost Dance*, p. 230.
[41]J. Mooney, *The Ghost Dance Religion and Sioux Outbreak of 1890*.

the Sepik River Valley, proposed to dry up the river, after which a ribbon of concrete would unroll to form a superhighway up the river bed, along which fleets of trucks would flow, bringing cargo to the interior.

Transition cults reach out to the new. They may appear to be irrational and unrealistic when viewed from the outside, but they do have their own logic, in terms of the original world views and the limited knowledge of the total cultures with which the groups are confronted. And be it not forgotten that many Melanesians are learning the basic techniques of road building, truck driving, bookkeeping, malaria control, modern agriculture and marketing—fast.[42]

Revolutionary Movements: Cultural Max Gluckman has written with much insight on the social function of "rituals of rebellion" designed to "oust the incumbents of offices of power or influence without attempting to alter the nature of those offices or the claims of particular types of persons to be their incumbents."[43] Rebellions "throw the rascals out" and substitute another set, but there is no attempt to alter either the cultural ideology or the form of the social structure. In political revolution, attempts are made to seize the offices of power in order to change social structure, belief systems, and their symbolic representations. Political revolutions are usually turbulent, violent, and not long-lasting. A successful revolution soon moves to reestablish a stable, though changed, social structure; yet, "it has far-reaching political, social, and sometimes economic and cultural consequences."[44] Political revolution as a means of cultural change is largely a matter of recent centuries (the French, American, Russian, Turkish,

and Chinese revolutions are outstanding). Certainly, it is not characteristic of either primitive societies or preindustrialized civilizations. For them change has not been engineered through organized political parties.

Cultural revolutions, on the other hand, extend over centuries and decades. They are the cumulative product of culture change which has moved technologies and societies in a given direction which can hardly be discerned while the change is going on. Looking back, however, evolutionary leaps can be seen to have occurred. The quality of human living has been fundamentally and irrevocably altered. In human culture history, we have seen that the first such revolutionary change was the development of Paleolithic culture, when men learned toolmaking, controlled the use of fire, and developed speech along with belief and symbolic systems, organizing new patterns of social life. The second such revolutionary change was initiated in the Mesolithic Age when man forsook hunting and gathering for intensive foraging. It was established in the Neolithic urban revolution and the rise of civilization. It is just now being completed as the last of the globe's primitive peoples are being brought within the cultural network of civilization at the very time that civilization itself is completing its course. For civilization, as a phase of cultural evolution, is in the process of being replaced by new forms of culture expressive of the newly born Atomic Space Age. This will be the subject of our closing chapter.

SUMMARY

Cultures grow and change by accretions of discoveries, inventions, and borrowed traits. A discovery is an act of becoming aware of something which has been in existence but which has not been previously perceived. In an invention, on the other hand, preexistent materials or ideas are rearranged so as to produce a new material or form of action.

---

[42]For an overall view of cargo cults, see P. Worseley, *The Trumpet Shall Sound.*

[43]M. Gluckman, *Politics, Law and Ritual in Tribal Society,* p. 137.

[44]W. Laqueur, "Revolution" (*International Encyclopaedia of the Social Sciences,* vol. 13, 1938), p. 505.

Nonvolitional inventions often result from accidental juxtaposition. Two things happen to come together; somebody sees significance in the combination, and thereafter intentionally brings the two things together in order to repeat the new combination at will. In volitional invention, a person sees or feels a need and sets about creating the tool or mental artifact to fulfill the need.

Although invention is necessary to the growth and evolution of culture, most cultures grow by borrowing traits that have been invented elsewhere. The process is that of diffusion. Material culture diffuses much more rapidly than ideas and concepts. The utility of a steel ax when compared to one of stone is easier to sense than is belief in a particular spirit being, for example. Nonetheless, complex, nonutilitarian cultural structures, such as myths, ceremonies, and games, also spread through borrowing.

However, no people ever takes an alien trait without altering it to some degree. First, it must pass the test of acceptability in terms of a people's basic values. If it is accepted, it is invariably reworked in form, use, meaning, and function. The role of specific individuals as innovators may strongly influence how a given people evaluate a new possibility with respect to form, use, meaning, and function, as the Cheyenne and Kapauku cases illustrate. When a general idea is borrowed, but its specific form and other qualities are invented by the borrowers of the idea, the process is known as *stimulus diffusion.*

Acculturation occurs when a society undergoes drastic culture change under the influence of a more dominant culture and society with which it has come in contact. It is a special form of culture change. Within a society, acculturation proceeds at different rates, as illustrated by the Menomini Indians.

Culture crisis occurs when values cannot be realized. Culture crisis usually creates reactive movements. *Millenarism* is a movement based on the belief that a complete and perfect transformation of society will take place by the will of God and will last a thousand years, whereupon the forces of evil (those which frustrate the achievement of ideal goals) will be destroyed forever. *Nativistic movements,* such as the Ghost Dance, seek to reestablish an old way of life and to wipe out the forces which have altered or destroyed it. *Transition movements,* such as the cargo cults of Melanesia and the Peyote Cult of North American Indians, seek to establish a material or spiritual incorporation of new elements, derived from culture contact, within the context of old ideological patterns. Political *revolutionary movements* differ from rebellions in that the latter seek only to change office holders without seriously altering institutions. Political revolutionary movements attempt to seize the offices of power in order to change social structure, belief systems, and their symbolic representations. Political revolutions do not appear to be characteristic of primitive social systems, although rebellions may be.

Cultural revolution tends to be drawn out over decades and centuries, and has occurred on a grand scale but three times in human history: when man first learned toolmaking, developed speech and symbolic belief systems; when man domesticated plants and animals, and developed cities and civilization; when man produced industrialization and entered the atomic space age—now!

SELECTED READINGS

Arensberg, C. M., and A. H. Niehoff, *Introducing Social Change* (1964). Intended as a handbook for non-social scientists engaged in overseas programs of technical, medical, and social development, this book provides a readable and interesting introduction to the principles and processes that influence success or failure in projects in effecting culture change and development.

Barnett, H. C., *Anthropology in Administration* (1956). A leading anthropologist dissects the problems of making anthropological expertise effectively available to administrators in United Nations trust territories and in colonial governments.

————, *Innovation: The Basis of Culture Change* (1953). The most intensive effort so far at systematic analysis of the processes of culture growth.

Erasmus, C. J., *Man Takes Control: Cultural Development and American Aid* (1961). Rather like Goodenough's book (below), this first discusses cultural processes (with emphasis on economic systems), then describes and analyzes in detail a successful development program in northwestern Mexico.

Foster, G. M., *Applied Anthropology* (1969). What is the basic relationship between theoretical and applied science in general? How does applied anthropology as an agent of culture change fit into the general scheme? The author discusses the relevance of the flexible and adaptive research methods of applied anthropologists at work on specific problems.

Gerlach, L. H., and V. H. Hine, *People Power, Change: Movements of Social Transformation* (1970). Based on field studies of the Black Power and Pentecostal movements of social transformation in contemporary America, this fascinatingly written book spells out the individual and organizational factors at work.

Goodenough, W. H., *Cooperation in Change: An Anthropological Approach to Community Development* (1963). Two-thirds of this excellent book is devoted to a conceptual analysis of culture and culture change. The rest is given over to practical problems in community development.

Hodgen, M. T., *Change and History* (1952). Shows how technological advance within England varied by districts during the industrial revolution. Pinpoints the particular towns and parishes where technological innovation took place.

Hogbin, H. I., *Social Change* (1958). This book discusses change and acculturation in Africa and Melanesia with great acumen. A very worthwhile book.

Lawrence, P., *Road Belong Cargo: A Study of the Cargo Movement in the Southern Madang District, New Guinea* (1964). A truly excellent historical-functional in-depth study of reactive movements in a given area of New Guinea, extending from 1871 to 1950.

Mead, M. (ed.), *Cultural Patterns and Technical Change* (1955). Prepared as a manual by The World Federation for Mental Health, this book lives up to its claim of showing "how modern technological and scientific methods, if carefully related to the group's cultural values, can advance the well-being of . . . communities which have lived for centuries according to ancient hallowed patterns."

Mooney, J., *The Ghost Dance Religion and the Sioux Outbreak of 1890* (1896). The classic, firsthand study of the great nativistic movement among the Plains Indians at the end of the nineteenth century.

Moore, W. E., *Social Change* (1963). A compact introduction to a modern sociological view of social change; theoretical and conceptual.

Niehoff, A. H. (ed.), *A Casebook of Social Change* (1966). Highly recommended for its specific, detailed accounts of nineteen projects of planned community development, land reform, or eradication of disease in South America, Africa, the Middle East, and Asia.

Singer, S., E. J. Holmyard, and A. R. Hall (eds.), *A History of Technology,* 3 vols. (1954). Definitive. The most comprehensive summary of invention and the steps that have occurred in the development of material culture.

Worseley, P., *The Trumpet Shall Sound: A Study of "Cargo" Cults in Melanesia* (1957). A comparative study of reactive movements in the South Pacific.

Chapter 34

Beyond Civilization: What of the Future?

The study of man as it has been presented in this introduction to anthropology has focused on the ways of life which have dominated the human scene for more than a million years. Tribal life characterized the entire Pleistocene period. It evolved slowly and steadily into ever larger units of social organ-

Fig. 34-A   On the last frontier of primitive man, a United Nations Trusteeship Council Representative meets with two New Guinea highlanders. (United Nations)

ization, with more variations on the common themes of obtaining a living and of distributing goods, of organizing the family and kinship groups, of political determination of social goals, of ways of viewing the surrounding environment and the forces of the universe, and of giving symbolic expression to all these factors in language, art, myth, and religious ritual.

Then came the domestication of plants and animals followed by civilization with its explosion of culture linked to the life of cities. This was the first of man's great revolutions. Civilization, as we know, means "the culture of cities," the urban way of life. Like tribal culture before it, civilization has unfolded in a number of variations, with subsistence, kinship, government, and world view always present although manifested variously. Perhaps the most radical changes it produced, however, were a quantum leap in the amount of usable energy made possible by the domestication of plants and animals; the addition of writing, monumental architecture, and public buildings to art, myth, and religion as forms of symbolic expression; the decline of the kinship group in social importance; and the increasing dominance of controlling elites over the economic and political orders.

The task of studying and interpreting the course of civilizations has (except for New World archaeology) been largely the responsibility of historians, rather than anthropologists. Hence, it has been touched on only peripherally in this book. Nonetheless, anthropologists have been much concerned with what has happened to mankind in the transformation from primitive to civilized life. Civilization has been the great triumph of human achievement during the past six millennia. Now it is giving way to a new kind and level of culture. The task for anthropology is not only to complete the story of man's prehistoric past and to reveal the nature of all known and knowable social systems of yesterday and today, but also to clarify the transformations that so confuse our times and to help build a decent and rational life-way for all mankind in the future.

The Transformation of the Primitive World

The process of revolutionary culture change that is now overtaking civilization has recurred repeatedly in the world of primitive man as civilization overtook it. It involves great technological innovations, to be followed by far-reaching changes in ideology and social structure. The effects of the change are manifest in crises in what Redfield called the "moral order" within cultures.[1]

The Moral Order   The moral order is what generates the sense of social commitment in a people—the emotional sense of being a significant part of a community of human beings to whom one has obligations and duties and from whom one receives support, emotionally and socially. The moral order consists of shared understandings about individual and collective goals and their meanings. It becomes manifest as patterns of kinship, neighborhood, club, and work groups, and of recreational, artistic, religious, and community roles in social contexts in which the roles are performed with an accompanying sentiment of "rightness" and gratification. Obviously, the moral order may be closely related to the world view.

The Moral Order of Primitive Societies   The cultures of most preliterate societies have been

governed by their moral orders. Few primitive men have doubted the validity of their social systems. Their moral orders have sustained them from their early period of enculturation until death. Most primitive cultures are what Edward Sapir called "harmonious, or genuine," cultures:

The genuine culture is not of necessity either high or low; it is merely inherently harmonious, balanced, self-satisfactory. It is the expression of a richly varied and yet somehow unified and consistent attitude toward life, an attitude which sees the significance of any one element of civilization in its relation to all others. . . . The major activities of the individual must directly satisfy his own creative and emotional impulses, must always be something more than means to an end. . . . A culture that does not build itself out of the central interests and desires of its bearers, that works from general ends to the individual is an external culture. . . . The genuine culture is internal, it works from the individual to ends.[2]

Through selective adaptation in which symbolic integration and close personal relations are effectively developed, long-enduring cultures have always possessed effective and "genuine" (in Sapir's sense) moral orders.

We may follow Redfield further in his characterization of primitive societies as possessing certain general characteristics: (1) the community is usually quite small; (2) kinship relations and close, personal bonds extend throughout the community; (3) economic and social interests are homogeneous, and there are few specialists; (4) attitudes and behavior are dominated by religious-mystical assumptions about the nature of man and the outer world; and (5) suspicion of outsiders (nonkinsmen) commonly leads to a chronic state of warfare with some other groups.

As we know full well by now, the qualitative

[1]R. Redfield, *The Primitive World and Its Transformations*, pp. 20–25.

[2]E. Sapir, "Culture, Genuine and Spurious" (*American Journal of Sociology*, vol. 29, 1924), p. 410. Of course Sapir uses the words "genuine" and "spurious" in specific senses. All cultures are genuine in the sense that they exist.

expression of these traits varies among primitive cultures, but they characterize all small, primitive societies held together by the moral bond.

The Technical Order   A complement to the moral order within cultures is what Redfield called the *technical order:*

The bonds that co-ordinate the activities of men in the technical order do not rest on convictions as to the good life; they are not characterized by a foundation in human sentiments; they can exist even without the knowledge of those bound together that they are bound together. The technical order is that order which results from mutual usefulness, from deliberate coercion, or from the mere utilization of the same means. In the technical order men are bound by things, or are themselves things.[3]

The Technical Order of Civilizations   The rise of cities has repeatedly shattered the moral orders of the people who have been drawn into them. A city is rarely, if ever, the product of a local population that has stayed put and ''just growed.'' As far back as the time of Çatal Hüyük, trade was the lifeblood of the city, although it relied, too, on the food products of the surrounding country. All cities incorporate strangers, and in the initial phases of a city's life, the separate little moral orders, according to which the strangers have previously been organized in tribal lifeways, dissolve. New urban civilizations are held together mainly by reliance on technical order. Regulations, prescripts, and edicts set the formal patterns to be observed. Magisterial and priestly exactments drive or exhort men to obey. Religious spectaculars and civil carnivals are designed by the priests and rulers to substitute as symbolic integrators for the old tribal rituals. Soldiers, jailers, and executioners coerce the recalcitrants into behavior which they feel insufficiently committed to adopt for themselves. The dungeon and the prison are inventions of early civilizations.

[3]Redfield, *op. cit.*, p. 21.

This is the period in which the moral order becomes managed by an elite, or functional class, and in which the reflection and systematization accomplished by the literati have added a new dimension to the ethical and intellectual life. The moral order now has a public phase connected with deliberate policy. . . . Religion is now, in short, a way of making citizens.[4]

Civilization, the city way of life, is always marked by a new kind of social bonding. At the outset, the moral order of each urban culture in civilization is *managed* in contrast to the *self-maintaining* moral order of primitive societies. For the great civilizations of the past, such orders sufficed for long periods of time. Eventually, they declined in effectiveness as disintegrating forces dissolved their influence. Urban populations of antiquity acquired *proletarii,* which in Rome meant the lowest class of the city, who were regarded as contributing nothing to the state but children. Some urban populations became caught in a welter of conflicting beliefs that tended to nullify one another's influence. The reform religions of Christianity, Islam, and Buddhism each arose to provide foundations for new moral orders upon which new civilizations could be built.

In antiquity, the urban revolution churned up the old tribal world into a condition that was, apparently, both frightening and exhilarating. The Egyptians and the Aztecs, as we have seen, built on fear; the Greeks, on exhilaration. Medieval civilization in Europe was reconstituted on a feudalistic Christian moral order, and ultimately on an industrial Christian moral system that has proved to be tremendously effective down to the twentieth century.

Anomy and Civilization   Anomy[5] occurs when drastic change causes moral orders to lose their bonding and motivating effect, or when segments of the population are left be-

[4]*Ibid.,* p. 65.
[5]The French spelling, *anomie,* is also used by some American sociologists under the influence of Émile Durkheim, but the English word has been well-established for at least four hundred years.

hind—alienated because no satisfying place exists for them in the changing social structure. The resulting anomy is marked by

... the retreat of the individual into his own ego, the skeptical rejection of all social bonds. . . . It signifies the state of mind of one who has been pulled up from his moral roots, who no longer has any standards but only disconnected urges, who no longer has any sense of continuity, of folk, of obligations.[6]

Anomy is the disease of the disintegrating or reconstituting civilization—or of the shattered primitive society. Apathy and demoralization characterize many American Indian populations that have not become extinct or been absorbed into the civilization that has engulfed them. A contemporary journalist's description of anomy embraces much of Western society:

The sense of belonging, of place, of a shared heritage of memories, has disappeared in an anonymous urban sprawl, and each of us forages orphan-like in alien streets where all the dreams have died, armed with plastic credit cards that vainly protest our identity.[7]

A major task of applied anthropology today is to assist national planners and international development agencies in finding ways to promote modernization without causing the paralyzing disruption of ongoing moral orders before new and effective orders can replace them. This requires, in the first place, a genuine understanding of the moral orders by which people who are to be "modernized" now live. Even in city slums, the anthropological approach provides the understanding, in ways that otherwise seem to be overlooked. The work of Oscar Lewis in Mexico City, San Juan, Puerto Rico, and New York City is the prototype of what the new anthropology can offer to this end.

In Lewis's words:

One of the major obstacles to more rapid and sig-

nificant progress in the current war against poverty is the great gulf that exists between the values and way of life of the very poor and those of the middle-class personnel—teachers, social workers, health workers, and others—who bear the major responsibility in carrying out these programs. We know a great deal about the statistics and economics of poverty, but we are only beginning to understand the psychology and inner life of some of the very poor. In the case of the Puerto Ricans, many of whom have come from rural areas or urban slums, the obstacles to understanding are even greater because of the barrier of language and the differences between cultures. And while Puerto Ricans have been one of the most surveyed and studied groups, most of the studies have been of a questionnaire type and have told us too little about the intimate details of their lives and the conditions which have formed their character.[8]

Peasant Societies

Before we look at the next stage of cultural evolution, an overview of the place of peasant society in the scheme of things is in order.

Peasant societies are the tribal communities of the primitive world transformed into a special and long-enduring type of little community within the structure of civilizations.

A peasant society may be defined as a subsociety of a large stratified society which is either preindustrial or only partly industrialized. It is further characterized by most or all of the following traits: rural residence; familial agriculture on self-owned small land holdings or other simple rural occupations providing a modest or subsistence livelihood; the family as the centrally important social unit; low social status; economic interdependence in varying degree with urban centers; simple culture; and attachment to the soil, the local community and tradition.[9]

The peasant community is like the tribe in certain aspects of the quality of its moral

[6]R. I. MacIver, *The Ramparts We Guard,* p. 77.
[7]S. Hempstone, "Leaving Grandpa to Die by a Dry Waterhole" *(Minneapolis Tribune,* Dec. 5, 1971), p. 37A.

[8]O. Lewis, "Mother and Son in a Puerto Rican Slum; Part 1: Felicita" *(Harper's Magazine,* December, 1965), p. 72.
[9]E. Norbeck, "Peasant Society," in J. Gould and W. L. Kolb (eds.), *A Dictionary of the Social Sciences,* p. 490.

order; it differs in its lack of autonomy and independence and in other respects mentioned below. It is part of a larger social system in which it is related to and dominated by the cities of the civilization of which it is a part. "It required the city to bring it into existence. There were no peasants before the first cities. And those surviving primitive peoples who do not live in terms of the city are not peasants."[10]

Historically, the original peasants were Neolithic agriculturalists who were not sucked into the cities and retained a subcultural identity of their own. They lived in marginal and partial isolation upon the land they tilled. Their food and craft surpluses were taken through taxation, or traded or bartered in open markets located in the towns and cities, and fed into the exchange and consumption systems of the local states and empires of which they were part. Peasants adapted to the existence of cities but steadfastly remained apart from the cities. Usually illiterate, they could not master the arts and learning essential to knowing the mysteries of civilized life. Or if, as individuals, they did do so, they entered at first into the lower bureaucracy of the state and church systems, cutting off their peasant ties. Or they disappeared in time into the urban proletariat. Cities have always replenished themselves and nourished their own growth with migrants from tribal and peasant populations. The reservoir of peasants has been vast, for as observed by Daniel Thorner, ". . . [T]he peasantry has constituted the most numerous social group in all organized states, from ancient to modern times, that have rested on traditional forms of agriculture."[11]

During the eighteenth and nineteenth centuries, extinction was the fate of many tribes. In the twentieth and twenty-first centuries, except in the case of such marginal peoples as the African Bushmen, incorpora-

tion into post-civilizations, rather than extinction, will undoubtedly be achieved by most tribal groups. As populations, either they will be pulled into the industrial-surban complex, or they may retain a measure of group identity for a while through a transformation from a tribal to a peasant existence.

Yet, strangely, except as a source of anachronistic beliefs, looked upon as survivals in the writings of Tylor and Frazer, there was little study of peasant communities and social structure until after World War II. Then with a newly ignited interest in India and other Asiatic countries, along with the rapid acculturation of the remaining tribal populations in all parts of the world, anthropologists began to give attention to European, African, and Middle and South American peasantry, as well as Asiatic. Just when anthropologists have begun paying attention to peasantry as a special cultural manifestation, peasantry, like the civilization of which it is a part, is disappearing.

Qualities of Peasant Culture   The peasant has his own integrity and a clear sense of his own identity, but he is usually backward, unsophisticated, and underprivileged relative to the city dweller—and he knows it. He may resent his lowly and powerless position, but historically 'he has rarely revolted. He must pay tribute or taxes to landlords, middlemen, and the state; he and his wife go to market and touch upon the life of the city, but they are not of or in it.

The home village is the peasant's base of security; yet it is not a whole society, because of the presence of the city beyond the horizon. The peasant community has its own cycle of folk rituals and festivals, usually marking the high points of the annual cycle of crops and movements of the sun. Folk beliefs are thinly watered versions of the great religions which characterize each major civilization. The peasants' folk ceremonies may be colorful and boisterous enough, but they rarely seem to exhibit anything like the rich symbolic tapestry of many of the great

[10]Redfield, *op. cit.,* p. 31.
[11]D. Thorner, "Peasantry" (*International Encyclopedia of the Social Sciences*, vol. 11, 1968), p. 504.

primitive tribal rituals. For the peasant, world view expresses a limited segment of culture and society—and therefore a limited conception of the universe.

The Image of the Limited Good   In his limited and constricted corner of the great world upon which his experience impinges but rarely penetrates, the peasant adjusts to his marginal status with the "image of the limited good,"[12] as George M. Foster has labeled it. "Self-improvement," family advancement, and community betterment are not accepted as social goals. The peasant sees not an expandable universe but a fixed and immutably limited, closely bounded source of available resources. It is a "zero-sum" situation in which it is believed that if one gets more, another must get less. As expressed by Foster:

By "Image of Limited Good" I mean that broad areas of peasant behavior are patterned in such a fashion as to suggest that peasants view their social, economic, and natural universes—their total environment—as one in which all of the desired things in life such as land, wealth, health, friendship and love, manliness and honor, respect and status, power and influence, security and safety, *exist in finite quantity* and *are always in short supply,* as far as the peasant is concerned. Not only do these and all other "good things" exist in finite and limited quantities, but in addition *there is no way directly within peasant power to increase the available quantities.*[13]

The result, according to the reports of most anthropological field workers, is that peasants struggle desperately for survival with sweat, hard work, and resignation. A stroke of good luck may bring a windfall to a villager, but in the tight little village community this commonly brings with it "envy, gossip, criticism, and calumny."[14] Such cutting down

of the fellow villager is a functionally effective way of choking off competition for closely limited goods and minimizes the possibilities of disruption of the conservative, face-to-face social order. It also makes life niggardly.

Kinship Structure   An interesting feature of peasant social structure is that although peasant societies are strongly male-centered they do not develop patrilineages or patriclans. The most common residential unit of peasant societies has been found to be the patrilineal composite family. Of forty-six peasant societies analyzed by Walter Goldschmidt and Evalyn Kunkel, ten have virilocal "stem" families and eighteen are organized around virilocal joint families. In the stem families, one son continues to reside in his parents' household after marriage. Others move out when they marry. The stay-at-home son inherits the family farm as a unit. The estate is indivisible.

In peasant societies which are built around virilocal joint families, all (or most) sons stay on in the homestead when they marry, working the land jointly for a time but eventually each taking his separate share of the land. The estate in these instances is partible (divisible).

The stem family and indivisible estate exist where land is scarce, while the joint family and divisible estate occur where new farm land is, or has recently been, available.

In thirteen of the forty-six peasant societies studied, newly married couples establish independent households of their own with neolocal residence, and all sons and daughters inherit equally from their parents.

Finally, "peasant societies never show a preference for matrilineal land inheritance, and none consistently forms joint households on the basis of matrilocal residence."[15]

One may ask: "Why the male-centeredness of peasant society? And why have lineage and clan, which are so important to primitive

[12]G. M. Foster, "Peasant Society and the Image of the Limited Good" *(American Anthropologist,* vol. 67, 1965), pp. 293–315.

[13]*Ibid.,* p. 304.

[14]G. M. Foster, "Peasant Character and Personality," in J. M. Potter, M. N. Diaz, and G. M. Foster (eds.), *Peasant Society: A Reader,* p. 297.

[15]W. Goldschmidt and E. J. Kunkel, "The Structure of the Peasant Family" *(American Anthropologist,* vol. 73, 1971), p. 1061.

social systems, disappeared so completely in the peasant complex?" The answers seem to lie in the facts that peasant subsistence is agricultural, not horticultural (and agriculture is a predominantly male activity); that war is no longer an activity for kinship groups among peasants (it is the prerogative of the national state); that hunting lands are not open to exploitation by peasants; and that major legal crises with respect to land and homicide must be settled within the legal framework of the larger civilization in which the peasant segment is embedded. In other words, neither ecology nor the overall social structure provided the conditions which would give lineages or clans anything functionally significant to do. Therefore, they died out.

The Passing of Peasant Society   The advent of industrialization first sounded the death knell of the peasant way of life. The swelling factories of Europe and North America in the nineteenth and twentieth centuries were urban generators of a new form of life into which millions of European peasants were fed. Today, for a few brief decades, the same flight to the cities is occurring all around the world as industrial development takes root in South America, Asia, and Africa, while simultaneously, peasant society dissolves. For:

In the modern world peasant societies are anachronisms, and it is inevitable that they disappear. Peasants themselves have demonstrated time and time again that they prefer a different, and what they believe to be a better life. Poverty, illiteracy, oppression, disease and early death, and a backbreaking life of sweating over a piece of land, have little nostalgic value to peasants, a great many of whom will take every reasonable opportunity to escape to the new life of the city. Modern technology as well as human desires have conspired to hasten the end of traditional peasantry.[16]

Peasant societies are the little communities of the primitive world transformed into culturally marginal units of civilizations. They occupy a developmental position between tribal society and industrial urban society.

But urban society itself is now in the process of a great transformation. For today we are witnessing not only the passing of the primitive world and the demise of peasant society, but also the dissolution of civilization itself—"civilization" meaning the culture of cities.

The Atomic Space Age and Surbanization

Professor Leslie White has emphasized the close correlation between technology, the amount of controlled energy at the disposal of a society, and the evolutionary development of the nontechnological aspects of culture.[17] This theme, which has run throughout this book, is called the Energy Theory of Cultural Evolution.

Energy and Culture   The difference between the simple hunting society at the Paleolithic beginning of human social evolution and the vastly complex technological society of the twentieth century is a good deal more than the difference between a population of 100 persons as against 200 million for the United States or 700 million for China.

We have already touched on the qualitative differences in the moral and technical orders which characterize the two extremes in size and social structure. But underlying it all is the great difference in the amounts of energy directed to human use—a difference made possible by the technological aspects of evolving culture.

At the Stone Age end of the evolutionary

[16]J. M. Potter, "Peasants in the Modern World," in Potter, Diaz, and Foster (eds.), *op. cit.,* p. 378. (Quoted with permission of Little, Brown and Company.)

[17]L. A. White, "Energy and the Evolution of Culture" *(American Anthropologist,* vol. 45, 1943), pp. 335–356. See also W. F. Cottrell, *Energy and Society.*

continuum the potential daily average energy output of a healthy man is estimated to have equalled approximately 50 pounds lifted 1 foot in 1 second, or roughly 1/600 horse-power-hour. Taking into account infants, the sick, and aged or feeble adults who could do little or no work, the daily amount of energy available in the earliest societies was approximately 1/1,200 horsepower-hour per person. For a very primitive local group, this would amount to an energy utilization of no more than 1/24 horsepower-hour a day for the entire society. Not much could be accomplished with that. As long as man was restricted to such a level, the development of culture was destined to be limited regardless of other factors. This condition prevailed throughout the Old Stone Age and was characteristic of all societies before the development of hoe culture and the domestication of animals.

The great revolution of the Neolithic Age was wrought by the domestication of plants and animals. Domestication of plants increased man's control over solar energy, which is stored in plants. Domestication of animals made him an exploiter of animal energy. More efficient tools reduced energy waste, and new tools made possible new applications of energy. All culture expanded rapidly; the mode of life changed from that of hunters to that of gardeners and pastoralists. Old institutions and customs went down, and new ways had to be worked out. The savages became barbarians.

The Bronze and Iron Ages are but extensions of the Neolithic Age, which fulfilled its potential in the urban revolution. Metal was substituted for stone. Increased efficiency of tools, leading to stepped-up productiveness in handicraft industries and gardening, gradually expanded the cultures of the Old World.

The next cultural revolution awaited the harnessing of steam, the invention of the internal combustion engine, and the artificial production of electricity. With the Industrial revolution, feudalism gave way to modern capitalism. The reorganization of society and culture shook the modern world through and through.

To sense the significance of the energy increase brought about by the industrial revolution (prior to the atomic revolution), consider that the total horsepower capacity of all prime movers (work animals, automobiles, factories, mines, railroads, ships, aircraft, windmills, electric power generators, and farms exclusive of work animals) in the United States of America was 8,495 in 1850. At the beginning of the second half of the twentieth century (in 1955), it was 7,143,723.[18] Yet in 1955, the horsepower capacity of animals in use had dropped for the first time to a level below that of 1850.

In 1965, the actual electrical energy output and consumption of the United States was 1.5 billion horsepower-hours.[19] This is nearly ten billion times the total from all sources which is estimated for the typical Stone Age society—and the figure does not include automotive energy or fossil fuel energy used in steam and internal combustion engines in factories, ships, or airplanes.

Thermonuclear Energy In 1945, the most stupendous energy conquest of all time was accomplished. Einstein's theory of the equivalence of mass and energy ($E = mc^2$) indicates that 1 kilogram (2.2 pounds) of matter, if it could be converted entirely into energy, would release 25 billion kilowatt-hours of energy, or approximately 33 billion horse-power-hours. Splitting the uranium atom, as was first done in 1945, converted 0.1 of 1 per cent of the uranium mass into energy. Thirty-three million horsepower-hours of energy could then be released from one kilogram of uranium.[20] And this was but the beginning, for not only has the efficiency of techniques

[18]U. S. Bureau of the Census, *Historical Statistics of the United States, Colonial Times to 1957*, p. 506.
[19]*Britannica Book of the Year: 1968*, p. 364.
[20]H. D. Smyth, *Atomic Energy for Military Purposes*, pp. 2 and 224.

for splitting the atom been improved, but also we have learned since then how to release energy through fusion of the hydrogen atom.

By 1971 the efficiency of energy conversion by fission had been increased tenfold. In November, 1971, the U.S. Atomic Energy Commission tested a nuclear warhead deep in an underground shaft in Amchitka Island in the Aleutian Island chain off the coast of Alaska. It was described as a 5-megaton bomb, meaning that it had an explosive power equal to that of 5,000 tons of TNT. But what does this mean in terms of energy conversion? One way to illustrate the meaning is this: that single instantaneous conversion released 10^{10} (10 billion) horsepower-hours of energy, or nearly 500 million times as much as an entire Paleolithic society could put to work in an entire day. Nuclear bombs capable of releasing $2,000 \times 10$ billion horsepower-hours of energy stood ready for war use by Russia and the United States at the beginning of 1972.

In 1957, there were no atomic-powered electric plants at work in the United States. In 1970, thermoelectricity was just beginning to become a significant factor in the productive energy output, but still accounted for less than 1 per cent of the total productive energy used in the United States. What fabulous amounts of energy will be harnessed for human use in the next era of biocultural evolution is only beginning to be realized.

Space Exploration and Travel   On July 20, 1969, Astronaut Neil Armstrong, placing the first imprint of a human foot on the moon, uttered the prophetic words, ''That's one small step for a man, one giant leap for mankind.'' Meanwhile, several hundred space satellites were continuously orbiting the earth, some scanning the weather, others collecting atmospheric data, some serving as radio and television relays, some simply following their endless orbits, their recording and transmitting instruments played out.

At the end of 1971, after a ten-month flight through space, the U.S. Mariner IX was in continuous orbit around the planet Mars, nearly 49 million miles from the earth, and was sending back photographs. At the same time a Soviet spacecraft arrived to land the first human artifact on that far-off planet. Plans for the Mariner X project were already far advanced. A space laboratory was to be landed on Mars, a laboratory which would contain mass spectographs and other necessary equipment to do automatic chemical-physical analyses of the atmosphere of Mars, the mineral surface of the planet, and possible life forms. All data were to be radioed and televised back to the earth. Mars landings may be expected before the century is out, and other planets will also be probed.

Surbanization   The Atomic Space Age is, indeed, already here. The greatest cultural revolution of two million years of hominid experience is under way. Civilization is fast being relegated to obsolescence. By the end of this century, you will very likely have witnessed the passing of the last primitive tribe, the disappearance of most remaining

Fig. 34-1   Surbanization.   Continuous settlement sprawl marks the pattern of the near future. (Wide World Photos.)

peasant societies, and the dissolution of cities into residual nuclei within vast settlement sprawls covering hundreds of square miles (Figure 34-1). The Atlantic seaboard of the United States has already become one continuous residential, factory, and commercial complex from Virginia to Maine. From eastern Wisconsin, across southern Michigan and northern Ohio, and into western Pennsylvania, more than a quarter of what was farm land in 1900 has already been converted into "urban" land. The same process is well-advanced in England, where hopefully planned garden cities have been swallowed up and engulfed in the compact settlement pattern which is stretching out across the midlands to link Manchester to London. Indeed, the great planner Constantinos Doxiadis finds it impossible to form any idea of the sizes of cities of the future because, "all cities will be interconnected in major urban complexes where no distinction between large and small will be possible; they will all have become one"[21] (Figure 34-2). The terrestrial environment of the future is becoming noncity and noncountry.

Increasingly, social scientists and other future-oriented scholars have recognized that man's future way of life will be so vastly different from his past as to require a new nomenclature.

Kenneth Boulding was one of the first writers to coin a new term for the social system ahead, offering "post-civilization" as the appellation of the future.[22] Sociologist Daniel Bell suggested "post-industrial,"[23] while Doxiadis refers to the huge urban complexes of tomorrow as "ecumenopolis."[24] Toffler's choice is "super-industrial," a term "intended to mean a complex, fast-paced

Fig. 34-2   Surbanization. Superhighways provide mobile arteries through the industrial and settlement sprawl.

society dependent upon extremely advanced technology and a post-materialist value system."[25]

Other writers put forth other names, each endowed with special meanings and attributes by its creator. As Toffler comments, "There is, as yet, no widely accepted or wholly satisfactory term to describe the new stage of social development toward which we seem to be racing."[26] It is interesting to note, however, the frequency of the prefixes "post-," "beyond-," and "super-" in the various tentative labels. Interesting, also, is the common agreement that "civilization" (with its implication of "cities" surrounded by settled communities whether "suburban," or "rural," and "wilderness") will no longer be

[21]C. A. Doxiadis, "Ecumenopolis: Tomorrow's City" (*Britannica Book of the Year: 1968*), p. 26.
[22]K. E. Boulding, "The Death of the City: A Frightened Look at Post-civilization" (1961, mimeographed); also, *The Meaning of the 20th Century: The Great Transition.*
[23]D. Bell (ed.), *Toward the Year 2000.*
[24]C. A. Doxiadis, *op. cit.*

[25]A. Toffler, *Future Shock*, p. 491. See his discussion, pp. 490–491, of other terminology to describe the social system of the future.
[26]*Ibid.*, p. 490.

a satisfactory rubric. The sheer mass and concentration of people in the noncity, noncountry, nonanything-ever-before-known, plus the immediacy of the electronic-connectedness of all populations, makes the era ahead different not only in quantity, but in kind. This author's choice of term to describe the new social setting of mankind is *surbanization.* "Post-civilization," "post-industrial," "super-industrial," etc., attempt to define the future in terms of the admittedly outmoded past. The social setting that is to come (and that is already well on its way) must be recognized as that which has evolved *above and beyond the cities.* Why not, then, call it *surbanization,* a convenient contraction of sur-urbanization, and meaning "above and beyond the culture of cities?"[27] For the remainder of this book, the term will be so used. (If the reader has an alternate preference, well and good, so long as we keep in mind that we are speculating on the next stage in social development.)

The Transformation of Society   Surbanization, the society of the future, is not yet a historical fact. Nonetheless, without even suggesting that *futurology* is a discipline, to say nothing of its being an empirical science, let us read the outlines of future society insofar as past experience and current trends tell us what we may expect.

How long will it take mankind to work out the great transformation? How long before surbanization will be a reality? Whether the great transformation will be achieved in one hundred or five hundred years, no one can predict. A Third World War, with hydrogen bombs directed from outer space, could initiate a new Dark Age of retrogression around the globe in which cultural recovery could be held back for several centuries. Even without global war, there is serious danger that as the rejected values and societal structures of civilization progressively lose their

hold on men, more and more human beings will lose their holds on themselves, lapsing into apathy or raging in violent social destructiveness. If man lapses into apathy, the human energy to carry on the transformation will be lacking. If rage takes hold, the problem will be to survive in a world of anarchy. However it goes, the immediate future is bound to be beset with dissension, uncertainty, and swirling tides of controversy and disorder as new life styles vie for acceptance. Such turmoil is an inevitable part of the new cultural revolution into which we have been thrust with hurricane force. The scientific postulates which engendered the Atomic Space Age are not compatible with many of the assumptions of traditional world views. Religion, government, and science will be under continuous pressure to redefine, reformulate, and reshape new and viable postulates, values, and institutions. One cannot expect such a gigantic task to be easily or smoothly accomplished. Yet if two million years of human endeavor mean anything, we are probably safe in prophesying that most human populations will hold together, will retain their integrity. Enough realistic innovators and enough creators of culture will continue to work to achieve the breakthrough into the next higher order of human living experience. Many social ideas will be stillborn. Others will not meet the test of survival, even though they may prevail for some little time.

In the future, as in the past, men will require a social system. In the future, as in the past, we may expect that such social systems must fulfill certain basic functions if they are to prevail. Early in this book (page 34) six functional prerequisites for societal survival were introduced into our discussion. Let us restate them here and see how they relate to future possibilities. Each society must (1) maintain the biologic functioning of the group members; (2) reproduce new members for the group; (3) socialize new members into functioning adults; (4) produce and

---

[27]Sur-urbanization was first proposed in the third edition of this book, but even in the author's mind, the word proved to be phonetically too clumsy.

distribute goods and services necessary to life; (5) maintain order within the group, and between the group and outsiders; and (6) define the "meaning of life" and maintain the motivation to survive and engage in the activities necessary for survival.

Maintenance of Biological Functioning of Group Members This will be a simpler matter than ever before in man's existence. Mankind in the era of surbanization may be expected to live in a golden age of good health. Health, a basic concern of both primitive and civilized men, will no longer be a source of serious worry. Debilitating and death-producing diseases as we now know them will long since have been conquered, as have polio, tuberculosis, smallpox, and others in the present era. Hereditary defects in biological constitution will have been wholly eradicated through genetic engineering. Prenatal diagnosis of such serious genetic defects as may occur will almost certainly lead to selective aborting of fetuses. This, however, will be an outmoded negative action which will rarely be called upon. Far more likely will be the actual restructuring of the genetic codes of individual gametes so as to tailor living human beings for healthy functioning in the kinds of environments— physical and social—which will then exist. With tissue and organ transplants, it is predicted that life expectancy will rise to 100 or more years and that adults will look and feel young and vital for most of that long life span.

The only grave challenge to biological well-being might be found in overpopulation. The people explosion of the twentieth century could have serious carry-over effects for a long time to come. As of this moment, there is little hope of slowing down the current rates of population increase before the turn of the century. The year 2000 will see six billion people crowding the earth, and demographers do not expect to see the total stabilize there. They project a probable maximum

global population of twenty billion and a possible saturation of the earth's surface with fifty billion people. How well such numbers may be fed remains a dubious question. Certainly they will not be meat eaters, for animal raising will be too inefficient a method of energy conversion. Fish, synthetic foodstuffs, and distilled sea water will be the primary human energy-producing inputs.

Reproduction of New Members for the Group This, we may be sure, will be the least serious of all the societal maintenance problems for the surbanizations of the future. In the first place, when once the global population has been stabilized, the need for reproductive replacements will be minimal. A newborn replacement for each living person will be needed only at the rate of one a century or thereabouts. Babies will be relatively rare, children and young people small minorities. Adults will form the great majority, but they will remain "young" in body. And in spirit?

Sexual activity will be wholly obsolete— imagine that! Will it be retained for erotic amusement and an antidote to boredom? Or will it be eradicated as a bothersome nuisance? This much is certain, the actual sexual relation of male and female will be biologically unnecessary.

Bisexual reproduction, wholly or partly carried through in population-replenishment laboratories—with or without a female host —could well continue for purposes of experimental development of new variations of human types designed for new functions (such as life in space) or for specific characteristics (reduced sexuality, increased range of visual or auditory acuity) or for particular social niches (managerial, artistic, physical sports, or drone). But if the reproduction of new individuals directly from single body cells is accomplished, as sober biologists predict, then previously existing individuals could be reproduced over and over in genetically exact replications at will. Bisexual reproduction would be wholly passé, except for experimental purposes. Cloning would take care of most of the reproductive needs of surbanization. However, who is to decide who gets to be reproduced, when, in what type, in what numbers, for what purposes? This could be the major issue in political contests in the society to be. Would races be maintained? If so, in what proportions? Or would functional "specialist populations," different from others in intelligence, physical skills, and emotional affect, be produced according to plan? The latter is a good possibility.

Socialization of New Members   With the population replacement input at a low level, infant care and child training will be easily handled. Even though socialization will continue to be extremely important, it will be a relatively simple task which will take but a small part of the time of grownups. The specific techniques which may be utilized cannot be foreseen, but that they will be akin to operant psychology as advocated by Prof. B. F. Skinner today seems wholly feasible.[28]

The tantalizing question is: What will happen to the family and kinship? As anthropological evidence has so overwhelmingly demonstrated, the family has been the seedbed of socialization in all heretofore known cultures (except Nayar). The extended kinship group has been the supportive socializer of the young, the vehicle of physical and economic security, and the means of inheritance of property and statuses. Through marriage and the family, sex has been regularized so as to establish jural parents who are socially responsible for the nurture and enculturation of the young, thus preparing them to fulfill the statuses that will come to them through their kinsmen. The family has provided for complementary division of labor between the sexes in mutual maintenance of the unit and its members.

The signs are now clear that the family is

atrophying. Hair and clothing styles, women's liberation, equality in jobs and pay—i.e., the trend to unisex—plus the growing social acceptance of homosexuality, all bespeak the shrinking significance of the conjugal base of family structure. A continuing spread of governmental underwriting of economic needs (aid to dependent children, free and universal education, guaranteed basic income, Medicare, and old age security) with little private wealth left over for inheritance presages the disappearance of the economic functions of family and kinship. As for legal protection, kinship has long since been stripped of this one-time important function by the later civilizations. It will not be revived in surbanization.

But what of intimacy and the emotional support of close personal ties? Is interpersonal dependency a universal human requirement that will persist into the next stage of human living? Surely it is at the present time. The countercultural experiments of the 1960s and 1970s all bespeak it. Hippie communes extol love and sharing, calling themselves "families"; they speak the kinship ideology without the fact of kinship. Yet they may well be one variant of the residential groups of the future, once the generation gap has closed, as it certainly will when surbanization is achieved. Group life in innumerable variations will abound. Clubs, associations, and other manifold interest groups, including a revival of ethnocentric movements, will be the antidote to separateness, providing rich variety to the social fabric in co-residential "cells" of fictive brotherhood and enduring comradeship.

Production of Goods and Services   Subsistence needs will be no less important to the men of the future than they have been to primitive and civilized peoples. The earth and its atmosphere are not infinite; natural resources are not unlimited. Whether food production can be expanded to meet the survival needs of expanding populations is a

[28]B. F. Skinner, *Beyond Freedom and Dignity.*

moot issue. Whether the balance between world population and world subsistence resources is achieved at a level which provides enriched living for all or marginal subsistence for most will depend on the degree of success in population control and management. One thing is clear: very few workers will be engaged in basic food production. In precivilized societies, all able-bodied adults, even kings, were engaged in food production. In early civilizations, probably not more than 10, or at most 20, percent of a population could be freed from food production to serve as administrators, artisans, and soldiers. In the United States today, not more than 10 per cent of the population is directly engaged in agriculture. At the end of this century, it will be 3 per cent or less. The farmer is nearly as extinct as the dodo. In surbanization the family farm will be only a historical memory, and farming will be a large-scale industry. Most food production, however, will be synthetic.

It is not unreasonable to expect that the great free market economies of the world today will be displaced by managed systems of rationed distribution according to controlled allocation plans. The economy would then not be reciprocal, redistributive, or market, but would be distributive-managed and would operate without the use of money.

Power-generating, construction, communication, transportation, entertainment, health, and other personal service activities bid fair to be the central productive concerns of surbanization. Of these, only construction (for there may be much building and rebuilding), entertainment, health, and personal services may give occupation to many people.

In the view of G. S. Stent:

The will to power will not have vanished entirely, but the distribution of its intensity among individuals will have been drastically altered. At one end of this distribution will be a minority of the people whose work will keep intact the technology that sustains the multitude at a high standard of living. In the middle of the distribution will be found a type, largely unemployed, for whom the distinction between the real and the illusory will still be meaningful and whose prototype is the beatnik. He will retain an interest in the world and seek satisfaction from sensual pleasures. At the other end of the spectrum will be a type largely unemployable for whom the boundary of the real and the imagined will have been largely dissolved, at least to the extent compatible with his physical survival. His prototype is the hippie. His interest in the world will be rather small, and he will derive his satisfaction mainly from drugs or, once this has become technologically practicable, from direct electrical inputs into his nervous system. This spectral distribution, it will be noted, bears some considerable resemblance to the Alphas, Betas, and Gammas in Aldous Huxley's *Brave New World.*[29]

Stent's view of the nonproducing, sensate, consuming majority in the image of the hippie must not be narrowly construed. What he means to say is that the bulk of humanity in surbanization will be consumers with lots of time and little work. And what will they do for fun, for satisfaction, for fulfillment?

Maintenance of Order   Law, as we have found, has been a nearly universal feature of human cultures. Will it so continue in the new social order of surbanization? Presumably. The functions of law in society, as they were stated on page 507 above, are:

1. The definition of obligatory relationships between the members of a society, so as to assert which activities are permitted and which are ruled out and to maintain at least minimal integration between the activities of individuals and groups within the society. This involves the culture-building process in response to the imperative of selection.

2. The allocation of authority and the designation of the person who has the socially recognized privilege-right to initiate and carry through legitimate corrective actions leading to economic or physical sanctions

[29]G. S. Stent, *The Coming of the Golden Age*, pp. 137–138.

when substantive norms are violated, so that force is controlled and directed toward social goals.

3. The disposition of trouble cases as they arise; that is, to clean up social messes (tangled claims, squabbles and fights, killings and woundings) so that people may get on about their business of everyday living with reasonable certainty and security.

4. The continuing redefinition of relations between individuals and groups as the conditions of life change, to maintain adaptability and flexibility in both substantive and procedural law in response to shifting values and new technologies.

The imperative of selection in culture building will be intensified in its effects. Two factors, at least, will be responsible. Crowding and the heterogeneity of the masses of humanity which will have to be organized will require insistence on standard and predictable behavior in crucial areas of public interaction. A great increase in the intensity and scope of communications will enhance the frequency of personal and intergroup contacts. They will require increased regulation.

The instruments of power and social control will be so sophisticated in their effects that the allocation of legitimate power (the second function of law) will be of critical importance. Will this be determined through mass public participation (democracy) or by a self-perpetuating managerial elite? There is no answer at the present time. One thing is certain, however: throughout the transition decades (or centuries) which lie immediately ahead, the power struggles for legal and governmental control of the reshaping of social machinery will be waged with the greatest intensity.

Dispute settlement may shift from person against person, business against business, to the hearing and disposition of grievances against the great bureaucracy itself. This would certainly be the case if there were no longer much in the way of private property or free economic enterprise.

When once surbanization is achieved, society will be stabilized for a long future, as discussed below. The fourth function of law will then become less weighty. But between now and then, law will be put to such strains as it has rarely experienced in the past. Can the legal systems of mankind change and adapt rapidly and skillfully enough to contain criminal disorder, preventing destructive anarchy, while at the same time responding to shifting values and new technologies?

Three decades ago Karl Llewellyn and I wrote:

Each law-job, and all of them together, presents first of all an aspect of pure survival, a bare-bones. The job must get done *enough* to keep the group going. This is the brute struggle for continued existence. It is the problem of attaining order in the pinch at whatever cost to justice. But beyond this, each job has a wholly distinct double aspect which we may call the *questing-aspect*. . . . [which], on the one side . . . looks to more adequate doing of the job, just as a doing: economy, efficiency, smoothness, leading at the peak to aesthetically satisfying grace in the doing of it. On the other side, the questing aspect looks to the ideal values: justice, finer justice, such organization and such ideals of justice as tend toward fuller, richer life. It does no more to forget the barebones in favor of these things than it does to forget these things in favor of the barebones.[30]

The legal order of surbanization must solve the "barebones" issue for all mankind. This means at least a minimal world law and a multiplex global government. Failure in achieving these goals will mean that there will be no surbanization, no next higher level of human culture achievement. If they are achieved, then it is not too much to expect that the central concerns and creative energies of mankind will no longer focus on technology but will shift to the questing aspect of law and society: finer justice directed toward fuller, richer life for all.

[30]K. N. Llewellyn and E. A. Hoebel, *The Cheyenne Way*, p. 292.

Definition of the Meaning of Life Just as the breakdown of tribal moral orders in the rise of early civilizations was ultimately met by the emergence of universalistic religions —Zoroastrianism, Buddhism, Christianity, Islam—expressing enlarged views of the nature of man and the universe, and fixing mankind's relation to a "civilized" conception of the supernatural and social life—so new philosophies of life and life-ways will certainly emerge. Many competing attempts and movements, secular and religious, will vie for acceptance in efforts to provide viable moral orders in a society dominated by a supertechnical order.

What will be the world view of surbanized man? No one can yet tell. It may be quite matter of fact—profane, in the Durkheimian sense. Almost certainly this may be expected to be true of the managerial and technocratic specialists who will organize, maintain, and operate the automated production and computerized memory and problem-solving systems. Their world will of necessity be ordered and mechanistic. And since it will be central to the very lives and livelihood of the leisured masses, their outlook will most likely be dominant, if not universal.

The concern of the vast majority will not be with the mechanics of subsistence and the ordering of society, however. It will be with the finding of meaning in life in a planetary system in which there is little biological turnover (death rarely occurs), little child raising, and no work for the vast majority. Will men culturize masochism in order to sustain a contrast to endless horizons of hedonism? What prophets will speak to man? In what words? What symbolic drama, what forms of ritual, will vitalize his mechanical existence? Philosophers, artists, and playwrights will have their work cut out for them.

Social Equilibrium or Endless Innovation?

The final questions to be considered are: "What of evolution? Will it go on forever?" Many alarms have been raised over the potential unmanageability of rapidly increasing new knowledge. How can knowledge and technology—which together mean culture—keep on expanding indefinitely? Many scientists now hold that an inevitable slowdown in the expansion of the scope of science is near at hand. The era of exciting discovery is drawing to a close with the climax of civilization.

Bentley Glass, speaking as president of the American Association for the Advancement of Science on December 28, 1970, observed:

The great conceptions, the fundamental mechanisms, and the basic laws are now known. For all time to come, these have been discovered, here and now, in our lifetime. They can never be discovered again unless man loses his scientific heritage; and even so, they cannot be discovered again for the first time. They can only be reexhumed, refined, or modified.

The uniformity of nature and the general applicability of natural laws set limits to knowledge. If there are just 100, or 105, or 110 ways in which atoms may form, then when one has identified the full range of properties of these, singly and in combination, chemical knowledge will be complete. There is a finite number of species of plants and of animals—even of insects—upon the earth. We are as yet far from knowing all about the genetics, structure and physiology, or behavior of even a single one of them. Nevertheless, a total knowledge of all life forms is only about 2×10^6 times the potential knowledge about any one of them. Moreover, the universality of the genetic code, the common character of proteins in different species, the generality of cellular structure and cellular reproduction, the basic similarity of energy metabolism in all species and of photosynthesis in green plants and bacteria, and the universal evolution of living forms through mutation and natural selection all lead inescapably to a conclusion that, although diversity may be great, the laws of life, based on similarities, are finite in number and comprehensible to us in the main even now. We are like the explorers of a great continent who have penetrated to its margins in most points of the compass and have mapped the major mountain chains and rivers. There are still innumerable details to fill in, but the endless horizons no longer exist.[31]

[31]B. Glass, "Science: Endless Horizon or Golden Age?" (*Science*, vol. 171, no. 3966, 1971), p. 24.

Certain it is that scientific progress cannot and therefore will not proceed indefinitely. Concomitantly, although technical refinements may continue, technology may be foreseen as reaching a condition of relative stability.

Whether the mineral resources of the earth and other planets will be adequate to meet the material needs of surbanized society indefinitely, only the future can tell. If they are inadequate, then there will be no ultimate stability. If they are adequate, however, then a state of homeostasis in environment and technology may be realized. And if technical evolution slows to a halt, so too will social and biological evolution. Equilibrium theory will be the order of the day; progress will be a historical memory, rather than an expression of human aspiration. Man could live long generation after long generation on a "golden plateau," working toward an ultimate refinement of social life.

Anthropology and the future

Anthropology's great contribution is to the understanding of mankind by man. It has a vast task ahead. How great it would have been if anthropologists had been present to record and analyze the urban revolution as civilization was being born! How infinitely richer and more certain our understanding of the human enterprise would be, had that been possible. Today we are more fortunate; we can observe, record, interpret—and help guide—the greatest cultural revolution of all time, the dawn of the Atomic-Space Era of Surbanization.

SUMMARY

The evolution of culture produced a first widespread crisis in the moral orders of human societies with the rise of civilization. The moral orders of primitive societies bind the individual in personal relationships which extend from family and kin throughout his whole community. He is bound in a network of society-wide reciprocity of obligations and expectancies. He shares a common understanding of the nature of things and of the ends and purposes of life, in intimate communication with others.

With the advent of civilization a new type of social ordering—called the technical order—displaced the old moral orders for those who moved to the cities. Social convenience, rather than moral commitment, became the order of the day. Anomy is its complement.

Ancillary to cities and subordinate to them, civilization transformed rural populations from independent tribal communities into dependent peasant communities. The peasant society has its own moral order, but its relation to the city is wholly "technical" in that while peasants adapted to the existence of the city, they steadfastly remained apart from and marginal to it. Peasants have always outnumbered urbanites in pre-industrial civilizations; they have fed the cities but have themselves been but little nourished by civilized beliefs and arts.

In the final, industrialized phases of civilization, with mechanization of agriculture, the need for great numbers of factory workers, and the spread of universal education, the breakup of the peasant way of life is inexorable. It is rapidly dissolving in the great transformation which is now bringing about the dissolution of civilization itself.

The growth and increasing complexity of culture through time has been positively related to a progressive increase in the amount of controlled energy utilized by societies. The first great energy-controlling revolution came with the domestication of plants and animals. It laid the technological foundation for civilization, transforming men from hunters and gatherers to urbanites and peasants. The second great energy-controlling revolution began with the invention of the steam engine but moved rapidly into the generation of electricity and on to production of thermonuclear energy and space exploration. Man has just entered the Atomic Space Age in which surbanization will replace civilization.

Surbanization will be noncity, noncountry. Men will be distributed over vast areas in unbroken settlement sprawls. The society of surbanization will be made up of ten, twenty, or fifty billion human beings packed around the earth's surface.

The six functional prerequisites of societal maintenance may be expected to be met through far-reaching transformations of culture. Human beings will be long-lived, infants and the young few and far between. Sex will probably be treated as biologically obsolete, with reproduction selectively controlled and genetically managed. Socialization of the young will be simple and effective. Mutual interest groups may be expected to replace the family in providing some measure of social intimacy.

The production of goods and services will be largely automated and allocated by a directed distributive economy functioning without money. Few will work, and most of the population will be leisured consumers.

The great concentrations of people will certainly increase the need for social regulation and control, unless socialization produces passive conformers. During the transition to surbanization, however, the outlook is for an increase in conflict and crime, as old values lose their bonding effect and as civil and regional groups vie for dominance in the system. With a world ordering achieved, law can move from emphasis on technical order to the search for refined justice.

The ultimate problem is sure to be the most difficult: "How can life be made meaningful?"

SELECTED READINGS

Boulding, K. E., *The Meaning of the 20th Century: The Great Transition* (1965). One of the most imaginative contemporary social thinkers examines the barriers that are to be surmounted in reaching the new society of the era that is just opening. A brief and stimulating book that looks beyond civilization into the culture of the twenty-first century.

Glass, B., "Science: Endless Horizons or Golden Age?" (*Science,* vol. 171, 1971), pp. 23–29. A sober evaluation of where scientific technology may be taking us, presented as the presidential address to the American Association for the Advancement of Science in 1970.

Potter, J. M., M. N. Diaz, and G. M. Foster, *Peasant Society: A Reader* (1967). A compendium of articles by various authors presenting recent anthropological thought and studies concerning peasant society, economics, personality, and contemporary problems.

Redfield, R., *The Primitive World and Its Transformations* (1953). Primitive, peasant, and urban life-ways are reviewed to provide an overview of how urbanization has transformed man from the primitive to the civilized state.

Rosenfeld, A., *The Second Genesis: The Coming Control of Life* (1969). The potential of biological engineering presented and rationally explained.

Scientific American, "Energy and Power" (*Scientific American,* vol. 224, 1971). The entire issue is devoted to eleven articles, well illustrated, on all aspects of the physical, industrial, and social components of energy, earth, and man. A very valuable discussion.

Seidenberg, R., *Posthistoric Man* (1950). This author expects that the end of scientific advances will lead to the end of human striving. Society will settle down to a Golden Age of endless cycles of Elysial existence devoid of emotional feeling.

Stent, G. S., *The Coming of the Golden Age* (1969). Like Seidenberg, Stent predicts a static future for mankind but with more emphasis on the possibility of blissful freedom from the "divine discontent."

Toffler, A., *Future Shock* (1970). Discusses the social and individual disorientations of today which are the consequences of too much change coming upon us too rapidly; this best seller also suggests strategies for surviving into the future.

ab·u′sua The matrilineal clan in Ashanti society.

ac·cul″tur·a′tion The process of interaction between two societies in which the culture of the society in the subordinate position is drastically modified to conform to the culture of the dominant society.

A·cheu′le·an A culture of the Lower Paleolithic Age.

a·do′be An unfired, sun-dried clay brick.

af·fi′nal Related by marriage.

age class, age grade, age set An organized association that includes all the members of a tribe who are of a given age and sex.

ag′nate A kinsman related in the male line of descent, i.e., patrilineally.

a·lign′ment A series of standing stones (menhirs) arranged in rows.

al·lele′ One of a pair of genes which give rise to contrasting Mendelian characters and which have identical loci on homologous chromosomes.

al″lo·pat′ric Taking place in, or biologically relating to, different territories.

alter ego The soul, spirit, ghost, or other self of a person.

al·ter′na·tive A behavior pattern in which two or more permissible response norms occur for a given stimulus situation.

al′ve·o·lar arch The part of the jawbone in which the teeth are set.

am·bi·lin′eal Affiliation with either the father's or the mother's descent group, at the option of the individual.

am·bi·lo′cal *See* bilocal.

am′i·tate The complex of special behavior patterns governing relations between a child and its father's sister.

a·mok′ (to run amok) A form of psychotic behavior prevalent among Malayan peoples. It is characterized by inattention followed by a violent outbreak, often directed toward homicidal assault.

An″a·sa′zi The prehistoric and contemporary culture of the Pueblo Indians of the Southwest.

an″dro·cen′tric Centered about the male.

an″dro·crat′ic Ruled by males.

an′ga·kok″ An Eskimo shaman.

an′i·mat·ism The attribution of life to inanimate objects.

an′i·mism The belief in the existence of spiritual beings. (Tylor's minimum definition of religion.)

an″thro·po·ge·og′ra·phy The study of the effect of geographical factors upon man and society.

an′thro·poid Having the characteristics of the highest family (that of man and the tailless apes) within the primate order.

an″thro·pom′e·try The division of physical anthropology concerned with the measurement of man's bodily characteristics.

an″thro·po·morph′ism The attribution of human form to any object.

an″thro·poph′a·gy Cannibalism.

Ap″ol·lo′ni·an A configuration of culture that emphasizes restraint, moderation, and "middle-of-the-road" behavior in human conduct.

ar′ti·fact Any material object that has been "worked" or has been used as a tool. Also, an imaginary concept used in logical analysis.

as·so″ci·a′tion A social group specifically organized for the pursuit of special interests.

at′latl The Aztec name for a dart or spear thrower.

Au″rig·na′cian The second culture of the Upper Paleolithic Age in Europe; 28,000 to 22,000 B.C.

aus·tra″lo·pith′e·cine One of any of the varieties of fossil hominoids closely related to *Australopithecus*.

Aus·tra″lo·pi·the′cus af″ri·can′us A genus of fossil hominoid first found at Taung South Africa; Lower Pleistocene age.

Aus·tra″lo·pi·the′cus ro·bus′tus A heavy-bodied genus of fossil hominoid found in Africa; Lower Pleistocene age.

689

a·void′ance   The inhibition of social interaction, especially between affinal relatives.

a·vun′cu·late   The complex of special relations between a mother's brother and his sister's child.

A·yan′thi·an   A Lower Paleolithic pebble-tool culture of Burma.

A·zil′i·an   A culture that is transitional between the Upper Paleolithic and Neolithic Ages in Western Europe; usually associated with the Tardenoisian.

band   A territorially based social group that is less inclusive than the tribe.

bar′ba·rism   A classification of cultures possessing gardening, agriculture, or domesticated herds but devoid of written language.

bar′row   The English term for a burial mound.

bar′ter, dumb   Exchange of goods between hostile people without face-to-face contact and without the use of middlemen.

Bas′ket Mak′er   A prehistoric culture (or the people who produced it) widely spread throughout the southwestern parts of the United States and antecedent to the Pueblo cultures.

bast   The fibrous inner bark of certain trees.

ber·dache′ (ber·dash′)   An American Indian transvestite who assumes the social roles ascribed to women.

bi″fur·ca′tion   Separation into two branches or sections.

bi·lat′er·al de·scent′   The system of kinship structure in which an individual belongs equally to the kindred of both parents.

bi·loc′al   The practice in which a newly married pair establishes residence with or near the parents of either spouse. (*See also* ambilocal.)

blas′tu·la   A mass of cells, usually in the shape of a hollow sphere, resulting from the cleavage within an egg.

bo′lo   A weapon made of several stones, each encased in a leather pouch at the end of a string, and with the free ends of the strings joined together.

Bon′du   The women's tribal secret society among the tribes of Sierra Leone and Liberia in West Africa.

brach″i·a′tion   Use of the arms; in a special sense, movement through the trees by swinging from the branches.

brach″y·ce·phal′ic   Roundheaded; having a cephalic index of 81 or more.

broth′er e·quiv′a·lence   The classifying of brothers within a single kinship status.

broth′er·hood, blood   A pact of reciprocal assistance sealed by a ritual act of intermingling or drinking each other's blood.

bull′-roar″er   A flat board that, when whirled at the end of a string, makes a whirring noise.

bu′rin   An Upper Paleolithic flint blade, one end of which has a sharp-pointed, chisel edge.

ca·cique′   The Carib word for "chief"; often used for the sacerdotal head of a Pueblo Indian tribe or any Central or South American tribe.

cal·var′i·um   The skullcap, or upper portion of the cranium.

ca′nine fos′sa   The pair of small openings in the facial bones just below the eye sockets; the passage for the facial nerves.

Cap′sian   An Upper Paleolithic culture in North Africa and Spain.

car′bon 14   A radioactive isotope that provides the basis for a method of archaeological dating.

car′go cult   A reactive social movement intended to bring the material goods of civilization to an acculturating society.

car′i·nate   Having the form of a keel.

caste   An endogamous social group, usually linked with a specific occupation.

Cau·ca′sian race   The so-called "white" or European race.

celt   A polished stone ax head.

ce·phal′ic in′dex   A metric expression of the ratio between head breadth and head length:

$$\text{C.I.} = \frac{HB}{HL} \times 100$$

cer′vi·cal   Pertaining to the neck or cervix.

chal·ced′o·ny   A white, waxy "flint."

Chal″co·lith′ic Age   The Copper Age.

Châ″tel·per·ro′ni·an blade   An Upper Paleolithic flint blade with a curved cutting edge. The back edge is blunted by the removal of small flakes. Characteristic of the Châtelperronian culture, 32,000 to 28,000 B.C.

Chel·le·an The Lower Paleolithic "hand ax" culture.

chert An impure form of flint.

chief, peace A chief whose functions are concerned largely with the direction of civil affairs.

chief, talking In many societies the chief does not publicly address the people. A "speaker," or talking chief, does this for him.

cic″a·tri·za′tion Scar tissue produced by making incisions in the skin. Often done in patterns for ornamentation.

cire′ per·due′ *See* lost-wax method.

cist An individual, slab-lined grave.

civ″i·li·za′tion A classification of cultures possessing gardening, agriculture, or domesticated herds, and a written language.

Clac·to′ni·an flake A large Lower Paleolithic chopping flake.

clan A unilineal kinship group that maintains the fiction of common genetic descent from a remote ancestor, usually legendary or mythological.

cline A smoothed, curving line drawn on a map connecting geographic points having like numerical values for a given variable.

clon′ing The reproduction of plants or animals by propagation of individual body cells.

coc′cyx The hidden tail in man, formed of the last several rudimentary vertebrae at the end of the spinal column.

cog′nate A kinsman related through either the father (male filiation) or the mother (female filiation).

col·lat′er·al Kinship relations which are identified across a generation level rather than by lineal descent.

com·po·nen′tial analysis A method of determining the units of classification used in a cultural system.

con·cu′bi·tant A male who has the status of marriageability to a person without necessarily being married to that person.

con·di′tion·al curse A ritual declaration that if the facts are not as stated, or if certain conditions come to pass, ill fortune may strike the person cursed.

con·dyle The rounded ball head of a bone which fits into a socket in another bone to form a movable joint.

con·fig″u·ra′tion of cul′ture The distinctive and characteristic quality of a culture that derives from the special relationship of its parts to one another.

con·san′guine Kinsmen who are related by descent rather than marriage. Literally, "blood relatives."

con·ver′gence A process of cultural dynamics in which two or more cultures contain similar institutions or behavior patterns independently arrived at, i.e., without historical connection.

cop′ro·lyte Preserved or petrified animal feces.

cos′mic time All time prior to the formation of the earth.

coup An attested deed of valor among the Plains Indians.

coup counting The social practice of publicly reciting coups.

coup de poing A flint hand ax characteristic of the Chellean, Acheulean, and Mousterian cultures.

cou·vade′ The practice whereby a husband retires to bed upon the birth of his offspring and acts as though he had just gone through childbirth.

cow′rie shell A small glossy marine shell of the genus *Cypraea*, highly valued for decoration and use as a medium of exchange in the Pacific area and Africa.

cra′ni·al ca·pac′i·ty The interior volume of the cranium measured in cubic centimeters.

cra′ni·um That portion of the skull which encloses the brain.

Cro-Mag′non man A variety of *Homo sapiens* dominant in Western Europe during the last half of the fourth glaciation.

crom′lech A circular arrangement of standing stones.

cross-cous′ins Cousins whose related parents

are siblings of unlike sex. Offspring of a person's mother's brother or father's sister.

cult An organized system or a group, characterized by performance of supernatural rituals and ceremonies and possessing an underlying body of dogmatic belief.

cul·tur·al or″tho·gen′e·sis The relative overdevelopment of one aspect of a culture.

cul′tur·al relativism The view that culture elements and institutions should be evaluated in terms of their own cultural setting. (*See also* postulates, cultural.)

cul′ture The integrated sum total of learned behavior traits characteristic of the members of a society.

culture area A geographical territory within which the cultures tend to be similar in some significant aspects.

culture complex An integrated system of culture traits organized about some focal interest.

culture construct A selective and descriptive formulation of the modal or normal behavior characteristic of the members of a society.

culture, ideal A verbalized formulation of normative patterns for behavior as stated by the members of a given society.

culture pattern A normative form of behavior laid down by the consensus of the members of a society.

culture trait or element A reputedly irreducible unit of learned behavior pattern or material product thereof.

cus′tom A traditional norm of social behavior.

Cy″pro·lith′ic Pertaining to the Copper Age.

dead′fall″ A type of trap so constructed that a weighted lever, rock, or ceiling drops on the victim when released by a trigger.

de·mand′-right An individual's legally supported expectancy that another person behave in a certain way with respect to him.

deme (1) An endogamous community consisting of a single kindred. (2) A territorial political unit in Attica after the reorganization by Cleisthenes in 509 B.C.

den·ta′li·um shell An elongated, tubelike sea shell used as money and treasure among the Northwest Coast Indians of North America.

di·a·chron′ic Through time.

di″a·ste′ma A gap between two teeth.

dib′ble A pointed digging stick.

dif·fu′sion A process in cultural dynamics wherein culture elements or complexes spread from one society to another.

di·mor′phism, sexual A difference in bodily characteristics between the two sexes.

Di″o·nys′i·an A categorical label attached to cultures that emphasize sensate experience.

DNA Deoxyribonucleic acid, the molecular structure of which constitutes the hereditary determinants in genes.

dol″i·cho·ce·phal′ic Long- or narrow-headed; having a cephalic index of less than 75.9.

dol′men A structure formed of three or more slabs of rock set on edge and covered with a flat slab; hence called *table rock.*

dou′ble de·scent′ The existence of a maternal and a paternal descent system side by side within the same culture.

drive A state of neurophysiological tension that motivates an organism toward action.

drive, acquired or secondary A learned drive.

drive, basic A drive that is innate in the organism, the satisfaction of which is ultimately necessary to survival of the organism or the species.

Dry″o·pi·the′cus A genus of Miocene fossil ape from which man and the great anthropoids evolved.

dys″tel·e·ol′o·gy *See* vestigial remains.

earth lodge A house built wholly or partially of sod or made of a framework covered with dirt.

e·col′o·gy The study of the relationships between organisms and their total environments.

ec·u·men·op′olis The settlement pattern of surbanization which with interspersed parks will cover the earth as a continuous system forming a universal settlement. (Coined by Doxiadis.)

Eg′bo A secret fraternity identified with the leopard in certain West African tribes.

e′go (1) In kinship analysis, the person who is used as the reference point for identification of kinship relations and terms. (2) In psychoanalysis, the individual's concept of himself.

e′′go·ma′ni·ac A person whose self-centeredness reaches psychotic proportions.

Ek′pe *See* Egbo.

e·lec′′tro·pho·re′sis The movement of colloidal particles in an electrically charged fluid.

E′′le·men·tar′-ge·dank·en Elementary ideas. Cultural concepts that, according to Adolf Bastian, are universal because they are psychic responses to universal human experiences.

em′′bry·ol′o·gy The study of the embryo and its development.

em′ic The perception of a phenomenon as seen and felt by an inside participant.

en·cul·tu·ra′tion The process by which the individual learns and assimilates the patterns of a culture.

en′′do·cra′ni·um The inner surface of the cranium, or braincase.

en·dog′a·my The rule that requires a person to marry within a given social group of which he is a member.

E′o·cene The first period of the Cenozoic era.

e′o·lith A stone implement so crudely made that its shape is more fortuitously than purposefully determined.

ep′′i·can′thic fold An overlap of the upper eyelid.

Er′′te·bolle′ A local manifestation of Early Neolithic culture in Denmark.

eth·no·cen′trism The view of things in which the values and ways of one's own group are the center of everything, and all others are scaled and judged with reference to it.

eth·nog′ra·phy The division of anthropology devoted to the descriptive recording of cultures.

eth·nol′o·gy The division of anthropology devoted to the analysis and systematic interpretation of cultural data.

eth·no·sci′ence The systematic study of the cognitive systems, or ways of classifying the experienced world, which are implicit in cultures.

eth′′no·se·man′tics The study of meaning from the point of view of speakers raised in differing societies and speaking different languages.

eth·ol′ogy The biological study of behavior.

et·ic′ The perception of a phenomenon by an outside observer.

ev′′o·lu′tion, biological or **organic** The continuous modification of Mendelian populations through modifications in genetic composition.

evolution, cultural Modification of culture patterns in a given direction through persistent social change. *General evolution* purports to express modifications characteristic of all cultures at specific stages in their development. *Multilineal evolution* purports to express modifications characteristic only of like cultures. *Specific evolution* purports to express changes characteristic of specific cultures.

evolution, divergent or **radiating** The process of evolutionary development that results in several lines of progressive modification from an original common form.

evolution, unilinear The evolution of social forms in a universal and ordered sequence; a theoretical process.

ex·og′a·my Marriage outside a specific social group of which a person is a member, as required by custom or law.

fam′i·ly A bilateral kinship group.

family, conjugal-natal A social group consisting of spouses and their offspring.

family, extended A social group consisting of near relatives in addition to the mated pair and their offspring.

fa′ther·hood, sociological The institution whereby the adult male who is the husband of a child's mother is functionally the father to the child, regardless of his biological relationship.

felt′ing A cloth-making technique in which the fibers are matted together, not spun and woven.

fe′mur The thighbone.

fet′ish An object that is revered because it is believed to house a supernatural power.

fib′u·la (1) The long bone that, with the tibia

(shinbone), makes up the lower part of the leg. (2) A Bronze or Iron Age safety pin.

fil·i·a'tion The culturally determined tie between parent and offspring.

fo·ra'·men mag'num The "great window." The hole in the base of the skull through which the spinal cord leaves the cranium.

fo·ra'men men·tal'is The openings in the lower jaw through which nerves and blood vessels pass to serve the lower portion of the face.

fos'sil An organic object that has been transformed into stone or has left an imprint in stone.

fra·ter'ni·ty (1) An association of men. A men's society. (2) The children of a woman. *See* sibling.

func'tion·al·ism A theoretical and methodological approach to anthropology that emphasizes concern with the part each unit within a culture plays in the total existence of the culture.

ga'mete A sex cell.

gas'tru·la A stage in embryonic development in which the embryo consists of an outer layer of cells, enclosing a cavity and having an opening at one end.

gene The minimum part of a chromosome that (1) functions to control a single chemical synthesis in a cell, (2) alters just one trait of a cell when its own molecular structure changes (mutates), or (3) "crosses over" to the other chromosome in the pair in a reproductive cell.

gen''er·a'tion e·quiv'a·lence The classifying of relatives of different genetic relation, but within the same generation level, into a single kinship status.

gen'i·tor A biological parent.

ge'·no·type An organic specimen in which both the genes that determine a specific trait are dominant or recessive. The somatic characteristic therefore directly reflects the gene combination.

gens A patrilineal clan.

ge''o·log'ic time All time since the formation of the earth.

ger''on·toc'ra·cy A society dominated by the old (usually men in primitive societies).

ge''ron·to·mor'phism The tendency to domi-

nance of adult male characteristics in body build.

Ghost' Dance A nativistic reactive movement among western American Indians in 1890. The dance was intended to revive the dead and restore the Indians' old way of life.

glot'tal stop A phoneme produced by closing the glottis.

glot''to·chro·nol'o·gy A method of calculating the time elapsed since the speakers of two related languages separated from each other.

God, High The supreme deity in a polytheistic system.

gra·vette' blade An Upper Paleolithic straight-edged pointed flint blade, the back edge of which has been blunted by the removal of small flakes. Characteristic of the Gravettian culture, 26,000 to 20,000 B.C.

G-string A string or band of material worn between the legs and fastened around the waist.

half-life The amount of time required for a radioactive substance to lose one-half of its radioactivity.

har·i'jan caste The impure, therefore "untouchable," castes of India.

head'man A leader of a kinship or territorial unit who is not endowed with specific and determinative authority; less than a chief.

Hei'del·berg jaw A fossil mandible found in first interglacial deposits at Mauer, near Heidelberg, Germany; *Homo erectus heidelbergensis.*

het''er·o·zy'gous Having a dominant and recessive pair of alleles at a chromosome locus.

hi'er·o·glyph'' A highly conventionalized symbol developed from pictorial representation and used as an element in certain archaic writing systems.

ho'gan The Navaho dwelling.

Ho'ho·kam Pertaining to a prehistoric culture localized in the desert areas of central Arizona.

hom'i·nid (1) A primate who belongs to the order of Hominidae, or human beings. (2) Having the characteristics of a human being.

hom'i·noid Like a human being, but not fully qualifying as such.

Ho'mo e·rec'tus e·rec'tus   A Lower Pleistocene fossil species of man found in Java and Africa. Formerly called *Pithecanthropus erectus.*

Ho'mo e·rec'tus mau''ri·tan'i·cus   A Middle Pleistocene fossil variety of man found in North Africa.

Ho'mo e·rec'tus pe''ki·nen'sis   A Middle Pleistocene fossil species of man found in China. Formerly called *Sinanthropus pekinensis.*

Ho'mo e·rec'tus rho·de''si·a·nen'sis   An Upper Pleistocene fossil variety of man found in Rhodesia.

Ho'mo e·rec'tus so''lo·en'sis   An Upper Pleistocene fossil variety of man found in Java.

Ho'mo ha·bi'lis   A fossil hominid found in Bed 1 at Olduvai Gorge. It may be either an advanced form of australopithecine or the earliest known member of the genus *Homo.*

Ho'mo sa'pi·ens sa'pi·ens   Modern man. The sole existing species of the genus *Homo.*

Ho'mo sa·pi·ens stein''hei·men'sis   The Middle Pleistocene fossil precursor of modern man *(Homo sapiens sapiens),* found in Europe and represented by the Steinheim, Swanscombe, and Fontechevade fossils.

ho·mo·zy'gous   Having two identical genes at the same locus on a chromosome.

hu'mer·us   The upper longbone of the arm.

hy·per'ga·my   Marriage upward from a lower social class or caste into a higher one.

id   The Freudian term for all the innate, unmodified biological impulses of the human being.

id'e·o·graph''   A drawn, carved, or painted symbol which stands directly for an object or idea and which is nonphonetic in the language of its user.

id'e·o·lect   The uniquely individual choice of words and other language usages of a particular person.

id''i·o·syn'cra·sy   An aspect of behavior uniquely characteristic of an individual.

il'i·um   The broad, flaring bone which forms the upper side of the pelvis.

in'cest   Sexual contact between persons who are members of the same culturally defined kinship group.

in'dus·try (archaeological)   All the known objects, artificially produced or not, used by a group of prehistoric people in one area over a span of time.

in·fan'ti·cide   The killing of infants.

in''sti·tu'tion, social   A complex of behavior patterns organized about some dominant central interest.

in·ter·sta'dia   The intervals between glacial phases within a major glaciation.

in''va·lid'i·cide   The killing of invalids.

in·ven'tion, independent   *See* parallelism.

is'chi·um   The lower posterior bone in the pelvis.

jaj·mani'   The system of customary services between the members of a Hindu jati and a landlord.

ja'ti   A localized subcaste in India which is endogamous, named, and possesses a distinctive combination of culture traits.

Ja'va man   A Lower Pleistocene fossil man found in Java; *Homo erectus erectus* (formerly called *Pithecanthropus erectus*).

jok'ing re·la'tion·ship''   An institutionalized pattern of privileged familiarity or joking between persons of specific social statuses.

jur'al parent   The culturally defined adult from, or through, whom a child receives its kinship identity. The jural parent may or may not be a genitor.

K-A dat'ing   The long-range method of archaeological dating by measuring the degree of disintegration of potassium 40 into argon 40 that has occurred in geological materials.

ka·chi'na   The gods in certain Pueblo cultures, who are represented in ceremonials by masked dancers.

Ka·nam' man   *Homo kanamensis.* A purported species of modern man represented by a fossilized symphysis found in Kenya, East Africa.

kay·la'si   Adultery among the Trobriand Islanders.

kin'dred   A local group that is constituted of bilateral relatives.

ki·nes'ics   The study of gestures.

kin'ship, classificatory   The lumping, merging, or equating of relatives of differing genetic relationship into the same kinship status.

kinship system The customary complex of statuses and roles governing the behavior of relatives.

kinship terminology The set of names applied to the various statuses in a kinship system.

kitch'en mid'den A refuse heap.

ki'va A semi-subterranean ceremonial chamber, usually round, in the Southwest Indian pueblos.

ku'la ring The system of intertribal ceremonial exchange of shell armbands and necklaces in southwestern Melanesia.

Kul·tur'kreis A conception of large culture complexes that, in the theory of the culture historical school (*Kulturkreislehre*) of ethnology, diffuse en bloc over large areas of the globe.

ku'tu The judicial body among the Barotse of Zambia.

la'bret A plug worn through an incision in the lip.

lau'rel-leaf point A flint blade shaped like a laurel leaf and characteristic of the Solutrean culture.

law A social norm whose violation beyond permissible leeway evokes a formal procedural response initiated by an individual or group that possesses the socially recognized privilege-right of determining guilt and of imposing economic or physical sanctions upon the wrongdoer.

law, adjective The part of the law that governs legal procedure and the application of legal sanctions.

law, private Law that is normally enforced by the wronged party rather than by a public officer.

law, public Criminal law; that which is enforced by a public officer.

law, substantive The norms that define illegal activity.

le·ji'ma The nonlocalized maternal clan in Umor society.

le'mur A primitive type of primate that first emerged in the Eocene period.

lep're·chaun The fairy or elf of Irish folk belief, usually in the form of a little old man.

Le·val·loi'si·an A Lower Paleolithic culture characterized by a flint flake tool with a prepared striking platform.

lev'i·rate Brother-in-law marriage. The marriage of a woman to her deceased husband's brother.

levirate, anticipatory The practice in which a husband extends limited sexual privileges with his wife to his younger brother.

lex''i·co·sta·tis'tics A method of counting the frequency of cognate (related) words in basic vocabulary lists for dialects or languages in order to calculate how long ago the languages may have been one. (*See also* glottochronology.)

li·bi'do The Freudian term for the id energies.

lig'a A pile of heated stones used for baking taro in New Ireland, Melanesia.

lin'e·a as'pe·ra The longitudinal ridge on the posterior surface of the femur.

lin'e·age A unilineal kinship group that traces descent from a known common ancestor, who lived not more than five or six generations back.

lo'bo·la Progeny price among the Bantu-speaking tribes of South Africa.

loess Deposits of rock dust carried by wind from glacial moraines and outwash deposits.

lost-wax meth'od A process of casting metal objects in molds shaped about a wax form, which is then melted out.

mac''ro·ce·phal'ic Pertaining to an abnormally large head.

Mag''da·le'ni·an The final culture of the Upper Paleolithic Age in Europe.

mag'ic The control of supernatural forces by means of compulsive formulas.

magic, contagious A form of sympathetic magic. It operates on the principle that things once in contact with each other can exert a continuing influence upon each other.

magic, imitative A form of sympathetic magic. It operates on the principle that like influences like.

magic, sympathetic Magic that operates on the principle of homeopathic association, i.e., that one object can exert an influence upon others that have an identity with it.

Mag''le·mo'si·an A local manifestation of the Mesolithic Age in the Great Swamp of the Baltic Coast.

ma″·ka·ra′ta   A formal, regulated combat among the Murngin of Australia.

ma·lang′gan   A complex of memorial festivals in New Ireland, Melanesia.

ma′na   Supernatural power that does not occur in the form of a spirit being.

man′i·oc   A tropical plant of the genus *Manihot*, whose roots yield a nutritious starch; also called *cassava*.

ma′no   A grinding stone that is held in the hand.

mar′riage   The social institution that regulates the special relations of a mated pair to each other, their offspring, their kinsmen, and society at large.

marriage, affinal   Marriage to a spouse's relative. In-law marriage.

marriage, cross-cousin, asymmetrical   A pre‒ferred marriage form that is restricted to one type of cross-cousin only. Marriage of a man to his mother's brother's daughter is permitted, while marriage to his father's sister's daughter is prohib-ited or vice versa.

marriage, cross-cousin, symmetrical   Marriage in which either type of cross-cousin is permissible or preferred as a spouse.

marriage, extended affinal   Marriage to an affinal relative of a higher or lower generation. Marriage based upon an extension of the levirate or sororate principles.

mas′ta·ba   An Egyptian subterranean burial chamber that is prototypic of the pyramids.

mas′toid pro′cess   The bony downward projec-tion of the skull located immediately behind the ear.

ma·tai′   The titular head of a Samoan household.

ma′tri·arch″ate   A society distinguished by uxori-local residence and matrilineal descent.

ma″tri·lat′er·al   Pertaining to descent that is reckoned through one's mother's brother.

ma″tri·lin′e·al   Of or pertaining to descent through the mother; descended through the mother.

ma″tri·lo′cal   *See* uxorilocal.

mean, arithmetical   The average. That point in the range of variability of a phenomenon at which exactly equal quantities fall on either side.

me′di·an   The midpoint. That point in the range of variability of a phenomenon which falls exactly at the middle of the two extremes.

meg′a·lith   A large stone used as a marker, altar, or monument.

meg″a·lith′ic com′plex   A cultural system cen-tering about large stone monuments.

mei·o′sis   The process of reduction division in which the number of chromosomes in a gamete is reduced by half so that the doubling effect of fer-tilization is compensated for.

Mel″a·ne′si·a   The island area of the Southwest Pacific inhabited by dark-skinned natives.

Men·de′li·an pop·u·la′tion   A localized group of members of a species who interbreed mostly among themselves but occasionally with members of sister populations.

men′hir   An elongated standing stone raised as a monument or altar.

merg′ing (in kinship systems).   *See* kinship, clas-sificatory.

mes″o·ce·phal′ic   Medium-headed; having a cephalic index of 76 to 80.9.

Mes″o·lith′ic   The Middle Stone Age; charac-terized by intensive seed gathering and foraging.

mes″o·log′i·cal   Semilogical or quasilogical; applied to the method of reasoning used by the nineteenth-century lineal evolutionists, who by inference reasoned that beginning with assumed starting points, the successive stages of each form of social institution or material invention could be described.

me·ta′te   A flat or grooved grinding stone that functions as a mortar.

mi′cro·ce·phal′ic   Pertaining to an abnormally small head.

mi′cro·lith   A minute stone artifact made from fine flint flakes.

Mi″cro·ne′si·a   Small islands. The island area of the West Central Pacific.

mil·le′nar·ism   A reactive social movement based on the belief that the gap between the cultural ideal and the social reality will be closed (and will last for a thousand years).

mil′pa   The Maya Indian method of gardening, involving the slash and burn technique of clearing garden plots in the forest.

Mi′o·cene The middle, or third, period of the Cenozoic era.

mis″ce·ge·na′tion Interbreeding between two Mendelian populations.

Mith·ra′ic cult The religious system devoted to the worship of Mithras, the Persian god of light, upholder of the truth and the foe of evil.

mi·to′sis A form of cell division and reproduction during which chromosomes are duplicated.

mode The high point. That point in the range of variability of a phenomenon which occurs with the greatest frequency.

Mo″gol·lon′-Mim′bres A prehistoric Pueblo culture localized in the mountainous area of southeastern Arizona and southwestern New Mexico.

moi′e·ty Half. The social unit based upon kinship that occurs when the tribe is divided into two recognized units.

mo·nog′a·my Marriage of one man to one woman.

mon′o·lith A structure consisting of a single stone.

mon′o·the·ism The worship of one god.

moraine The debris of earth and rocks deposited along the edges of a glacier.

mor′pheme A minimal unit of language that has meaning.

mor·phol′o·gy The study of the form and structure of an organism or social manifestation.

Mous·te′ri·an The culture associated with Neandertal man during the third interglacial and fourth glacial epochs in Europe.

mul′ler A grinding stone held in the hand and rubbed over a metate.

mu·ta′tion An abrupt modification of the genetic composition of an organism.

na′sal in′dex The relation between the breadth and height of the nasal orifice. $N.I. = \frac{N.B.}{N.H.} \times 100$

na′si·on The intersection of the internasal suture with the frontal bone of the skull.

na·tiv·ist′ic movement A reactive movement which would restore a bygone culture.

Ne·an′der·tal man An extinct fossil variety of man dominant in Europe from the second interglacial epoch to the climax of the fourth glacial; *Homo sapiens neandertalensis.*

Ne·gri′to The "little Negro," or Pygmy, race.

Ne′groid Characteristic of Negroes.

Ne″o·an·throp′ic man A "modern" or *sapiens* type of man.

Ne″o·lith′ic The New Stone Age.

neo·lo′cal The practice in which a newly married pair establish a new household in a locality other than those of their parents.

neu·ro′sis A mild form of behavior disorder.

Ngbe *See* Egbo.

Ni·lot′ic Pertaining to or designating a people who live in the Nile Basin.

no·bil′i·ty A class or caste with hereditary status of high prestige and ceremonial or political power.

nor′ma·tive Relating to or inducing conformity to a norm.

no′to·chord A rod of cells that forms the beginning of the backbone in vertebrate animals.

nto′ro The patrilineal clan in Ashanti society.

oath A formal declaration that the facts are as stated. (Not to be confused with conditional curse.)

oc·cip′i·tal torus The horizontal bony ridge across the rear portion of the skull to which the back muscles of the neck are anchored.

oc′ci·put The bone that forms the rear and lower segment of the cranium.

Oed′i·pus com′plex A psychological state of a male characterized by sexual desire for the mother and antagonism toward the father.

o·ke·ya′me The talking chief in Ashanti society.

Old′u·wan cul′ture A Villefranchian and Early Pleistocene pebble-tool culture.

ol′i·gar″chy A state whose government is controlled by a small group within the larger society.

on·tog′e·ny The natural history of an individual, beginning with the fertilized egg.

or·deal' A ritual method of verification of testimony in which the litigants are subjected to a physical test designed to injure or kill the falsifier.

os·te·o·don''to·ker·a'tic An assemblage of bone, tooth, and horn artifacts.

Pa''le·o·lith'ic The Old Stone Age.

Pa''le·o·sim'i·a A genus of Miocene fossil ape ancestral to the orangutan.

Pa''le·o·zo'ic The third era of geological time.

pal''y·nol'o·gy The branch of science concerned with the study of pollen and spores. Prehistoric climatic conditions can be determined by counting the different kinds of pollen in soil samples.

pa·py'rus The Egyptian paper made from the pith of *Cyperus papyrus*, an Egyptian sedge.

par'al·lel-cous'ins Cousins whose related parents are of like sex. The offspring of a person's mother's sister or father's brother.

par'al·lel·ism The development of similar cultural forms through identical steps without historical interaction or contact.

Par''a·pi·the'cus A genus of fossil primate found in Oligocene deposits and believed to be ancestral to man, the apes, and monkeys.

par'fleche An oblong rawhide box made by Plains Indians.

pas'to·ral·ism A culture marked by a subsistence technique centered about the herding and husbandry of domesticated animals.

pa''ter·fa·mil'i·as The authoritarian father in the Roman family.

pa·tol'li The Aztec form of pachisi, a game played with dice.

pa'tri·arch''ate A society dominated by the father as head of the kinship group, characterized by patrilineal descent and virilocal residence.

pat''ri·lin'e·al Pertaining to descent through the father. Children belong to the kinship group of their father.

pat''ri·lo'cal *See* virilocal.

pa·tron'y·my The custom of giving children the name of their father's kinship group.

peas'ant A social type of rural farmer associated with preindustrial civilization, dominated by the city and its culture but marginal to both.

Pe'kin man A Middle Pleistocene fossil man; *Homo erectus pekinensis* (formerly called *Sinanthropus pekinensis*).

pem'mi·can A preserved cake of shredded dried meat and berry pulp.

per·cus'sion flak'ing The technique of shaping flint artifacts by removing flakes with blows of a hammerstone.

per''son·al'i·ty The sum total of behavior traits, overt and covert, characteristic of a person.

personality, basic structure The constellation of behavior traits and attitudes established in the members of a given society by their childhood reactions to the methods of child training characteristic of their culture.

personality, ideal type The construct of the personality configuration most highly emphasized in a culture.

personality, modal The personality configuration most commonly manifested by the members of a society or group.

pet'ro·glyph A symbol incised in rock.

pe·yo'te A variety of cactus (*Lophophora williamsii*) ingested by Indians (notably Plains Indians) to stimulate visions as a form of religious experience.

phae''o·mel'a·nin Black skin pigment that reduces sunburning.

phe'no·type The physically apparent expression of heredity.

pho'neme The smallest sound unit used in a language.

pho·net'ics The general study of spoken sounds.

phra'try A social unit consisting of two or more linked clans between which exists a special bond of unity as against clans joined in other phratries within the society.

phy·log'e·ny The natural history of a species or variety.

phys'i·cal an''thro·pol'o·gy The branch of anthropology concerned with the bodily characteristics of mankind.

pic'to·graph A simple picture, or series of pictures, intended to describe a situation or record an event.

pile dwelling A house raised from the ground or built over water on piling.

pit dwelling An earth lodge built over an excavated pit.

Pleis'to·cene The fifth period of the Cenozoic era. The glacial age during which man rose to dominance among life forms.

Pli'o·cene The fourth period of the Cenozoic era; a warm period during which early human types became differentiated from apes.

Pli'·o·pi·the'cus A genus of Pliocene fossil ape that is directly ancestral to the gibbon.

plu'vi·al A Pleistocene wet epoch outside the areas of glaciation.

pol'y·an''dry The marriage of a woman to two or more men simultaneously.

polyandry, attenuated The marriage relationship in which a married brother extends limited sexual privileges with his wife to his unmarried younger brothers. Also called *anticipatory levirate*.

polyandry, fraternal A polyandrous marriage in which the husbands are brothers.

po·lyg'a·my Any multiple marriage.

pol''y·gen'e·sis The evolutionary hypothesis which assumes that the several genera of prehistoric man have evolved from different species of Pliocene apes.

po·lyg'y·ny The marriage of a man to two or more women simultaneously.

pol''y·mor'phism The occurrence of a trait in variable forms in a Mendelian population.

Pol''y·ne'si·a Many islands. The area of the Central Pacific that falls within a triangle formed with Hawaii, Easter Island, and New Zealand as the apexes.

pol'y·the·ism Worship of many gods. A system of religion recognizing multiple gods.

pop·u·la'tion A group of individuals or of possible observations united by some common principle or principles.

pop''u·la'tion ge·net'ics The study of gene frequencies and changes in Mendelian populations.

Por'ro The men's secret fraternity in Sierra Leone and Liberia, West Africa.

pos'tu·late, cultural A basic proposition as to the nature of things (existential) or the desirability or undesirability of things (normative) which underlies a cultural system.

pot'latch The Northwest Coast Indian institution of ceremonial feasting accompanied by lavish distribution of gifts.

pref''er·en'tial mar'riage A form of marriage that is enjoined or preferred between two persons of specifically defined statuses.

pres'sure flak'ing The technique of shaping flint artifacts by removing fine flakes by means of steady pressure applied with a stick or bone.

priest A religious functionary whose supernatural authority is bestowed upon him by a cult or organized church, in contrast to the shaman, who derives power directly from supernatural sources.

pri'mate An order within the mammalian class.

prim'i·tive Pertaining to a culture or an aspect of a culture that is not characterized by the inclusion of a written language; also pertaining to an individual whose culture includes no written language. Therefore, nonliterate or preliterate.

pri''mo·gen'i·ture Inheritance by the first-born son or child.

pri'vi·lege-right The legal relation in which a person is free to behave in a certain way to another without legal prohibition or consequence.

priv'i·leged fa·mil''i·ar'i·ty A culturally permissive relation of free joking between individuals of certain statuses.

Pro·con'sul A Miocene hominoid from East Africa.

prog'e·ny price The wealth transferred by the kin of a groom to the kin of his bride in compensation for their release of claim to the children that are produced in the marriage; also known as *bride price* and *bride wealth*.

prog'na·thous Having a projecting jaw.

prom''is·cu'i·ty The absence of any social restraints limiting or regulating sexual behavior.

prop'er·ty The special and socially sanctioned

relation of a person or group to the utilization of some object.

property, communal Property that is owned by the entire community.

property, incorporeal Property that involves a nonmaterial object.

property, joint Property that is owned by a group smaller than the entire community.

Pro''pli·o·pi·the'cus A genus of fossil ape found in Oligocene deposits of Egypt. It is a prototype of the gibbon.

pro'tein A class of organic compounds composed of a number of amino (NH_2) acids.

Prot''er·o·zo'ic The second era of geological time.

prox·e'mics The study of the use of space (nearness and distance) in communication and social relations.

psy''cho·cul'tu·ral-or·gan'ic The level of natural phenomena that are not preset (instinctive) in the organism. Also called *superorganic*.

psy·cho'sis An extreme form of behavior disorder marked by relatively fixed patterns of maladaptive attitudes and responses.

pueb'lo A village constructed of clay bricks (adobe) or stones, characteristic of the Indians of the southwestern United States and northern Mexico.

Pyg'my *See* Negrito.

py'rite A mineral, such as flint, used for striking fire.

quern A grinding stone.

race A human population that is sufficiently inbred to reveal a distinctive genetic composition manifest in a distinctive combination of physical traits.

race, geographical A human population that has inhabited a land mass or an island chain sufficiently long to have developed its own distinctive genetic composition, as contrasted to that of other continental populations.

race, local A distinctive Mendelian population located within a continental land mass or island chain.

race, microgeographic An extremely isolated, tightly inbreeding small Mendelian population.

rac'ism A doctrine that assumes the inherent superiority of one or another race over others.

ram·age' A non-exogamous, extended corporate kinship group in which members get their identity by descent from a common ancestor traced either patrilineally or matrilineally, according to individual preference and convenience. It is thus ambilineal.

rel'a·tives, affinal Persons related through marriage.

relatives, genetic Biologically related persons.

re·li'gion A belief in supernatural beings and the attendant ways of behaving in consequence of such a belief.

Rho·de'si·an man *Homo erectus rhodesianensis.* An Upper Pleistocene fossil found at Broken Hill in Rhodesia, South Africa.

rite de pas·sage' *See* transition rites.

rite, fertility A ritual complex designed to promote genetic reproduction.

role The customary complex of behavior associated with a particular status.

sac''er·do'tal Of a priestly nature.

sa'crum The wedge-shaped bone formed by the joining of the vertebrae that form the posterior segment of the pelvis.

sag'it·tal crest A ridge running longitudinally along the roof of the skull.

sanc'tion Any social reaction operating to induce conformity to a normative standard of behavior.

sanction, legal A coercive penalty involving the use of physical force in threat or in fact, attached to the violation of a social norm, when the application of the sanction is considered legitimate according to the prevailing standards of the culture.

sa·rong' A loose girdlelike skirt originally made of bark cloth and worn by Polynesian women.

sav'age·ry A state of cultural development marked by the absence of gardening or agriculture and written language.

scap′u·la The shoulder blade.

scar″i·fi·ca′tion The process of mutilation of the body through the artificial raising of scar tissue. *See also* cicatrization.

schiz″o·phre′ni·a A behavior disorder marked by a replacement of the learned behavior systems with desocialized behavior dominated by private fantasy.

se·nil′i·cide The killing of the aged.

se·rol′o·gy The study of the chemical and physical properties of blood.

sha′man A religious specialist who has received his power directly from supernatural sources; synonymous with *medicine man, witch doctor, angakok* (Eskimo).

sib A unilateral kinship group; synonymous with *clan.*

sib′ling Brother or sister; a member of a sib or clan.

si′lent trade *See* barter, dumb.

sim′i·an Apelike.

Sin·an′thro·pus pe″ki·nen′sis See *Homo erectus pekinensis.*

Skhūl man A highly variable type of fossil man found in Palestine. It reveals both Neandertaloid and *Homo sapiens sapiens* characteristics.

slav′er·y The institution whereby persons are subjected to involuntary servitude, are denied the right of freedom of movement or action, and must place their productive efforts at the disposal of the master.

so′cial class A category of persons within a society who (1) hold a number of distinctive statuses in common, (2) receive differential rewards and privileges, and (3) have an awareness of their like interests and life-style in contradistinction to other social classes.

so′cial dis′tance A term covering the relative "spatial positions" of two statuses; generally used to emphasize limitations on social intercourse.

so′cial struc′ture The ways in which groups and individuals are organized and relate to one another.

so·ci′e·ty, human A spatially identifiable population, centripetally-oriented, acting in accordance with a distinctive culture, and emotionally bound through common language and symbolic experiences.

society, military An association of warriors.

society, secret A fraternity or association whose membership and activities are shrouded in secrecy. A tribal secret society embraces all adult males in its membership.

So′lo man An Upper Paleolithic human fossil type found on the Solo River, Java; *Homo erectus soloensis.*

So·lu′tre·an A culture of the Upper Paleolithic Age in Europe; characterized by the laurel-leaf point.

sor′cer·y The use of supernatural power as an aggressive instrument to further the interests of the sorcerer. *Magic* is a more neutral term.

so·ro′ral po·lyg′y·ny The simultaneous marriage of two or more sisters to one husband.

so·ro′rate The practice whereby a younger sister marries the widowed husband of her deceased elder sister.

sou·la′va The red shell necklaces exchanged in the Melanesian kula.

spe″ci·a′tion The genetic divergence of a species to produce two new populations that are no longer capable of gene exchange (interbreeding) with each other.

sta′di·a The minor advances of ice sheets interspersed with interstadia within a glacial epoch.

state The association within a society that undertakes to direct and organize social policy on behalf of and in the name of the entire society.

sta′tus The social position of an individual with reference to the other members of his society.

ste″a·to·py′gi·a Large accumulations of fat in the buttocks.

Stein′heim man A type of fossil man found in Middle Pleistocene deposits at Steinheim, Germany; *Homo sapiens steinheimensis.*

stim′u·lus dif·fu′sion The process of cultural dynamics in which one people receive the idea of a cultural invention from another but give a new and unique form to the idea.

stra·tig′ra·phy Analysis of geological deposits in terms of discernible layers. Derivative time sequences are inferred from the relative positions of the strata or layers.

sub''·in·ci'sion A surgical operation in which the urethra of the male sex organ is slit open; a mutilation performed as a part of the male puberty rites in certain Australian tribes.

suit'or ser'vice A substitute for, or equivalent of, progeny price, in which the potential groom works for his intended bride's kin.

su''per·or·gan'ic Pertaining to the phenomena, known as *cultural,* that occur on a level over and above the organic; i.e., they are not preset in the organic structure.

su''pra·or'bit·al ridge A bone ridge above the orbits, or eye sockets.

sur·ban·i·za'tion The culture of the future. That which is beyond civilization. The mode of life-to-be in the Atomic Space Age (author's term).

sur·viv'al In evolutionary methodology, a culture trait that is purported to have lost its original function. A conceptual equivalent to vestigial remains in biological evolution.

su'su The kinship group formed of a woman, her children, and her brothers.

su·va·so'va Breach of exogamy among the Trobriand Islanders.

Swans'combe man A fossil hominid found in Middle Pleistocene deposits in southern England; classified as *Homo sapiens steinheimensis.*

sym·bi·o'sis The living together of two or more species of organisms in which the relationship is not destructive of either and is necessary to the existence of at least one of them.

sym·pat'ric Pertaining to living forms that inhabit a common territory.

sym'phy·sis The line along which two bones grow together.

syn·chron'ic Existing at the same time.

syn'cre·tism The fusion of two distinct systems of belief and practice.

ta·bu' Prohibition of an act, violation of which is punishable by supernatural sanctions.

ta'pa Polynesian bark cloth.

tar'a·vad The joint-family household consisting of the members of a matrilineage among the Nyar

caste in Kerala on the Malabar Coast of India.

Tar''de·nois'·i·an A prehistoric culture of France representing the Mesolithic Age and characterized by microlithic flints.

ta'ro A staple food plant of the Pacific area.

Taung ape man See *Australopithecus africanus.*

tau''ro·dont'ism An enlargement of the pulp cavity and fusion of the roots in molar and premolar teeth.

tax·on'o·my The systematic classification of things according to scientific principles.

tek·non'y·my The practice of addressing an adult after the name of its child, and vice versa.

tel'e·o·lith'' A purposefully shaped stone.

tell In the Middle East, a mound built up by prolonged human occupation of a site.

than''a·to·ma'ni·a The depression of the will to exist to the point of death.

thau'ma·tur''gy Magic.

the·oc'ra·cy A social order controlled by religious specialists.

till A glacial deposit of unstratified rock and earth.

ti'pi A conical skin tent.

tort *See* wrong, private.

to'tem An object, often an animal or plant, held in special regard by an individual or social group.

to'tem·ism The institutional complex centering about a totem.

to·vo·dun' The deified ancestors in Dahomean religion. (*See also* vodun.)

tran·chet' A flaked core-biface stone artifact shaped rather like a modern ax head.

trans·hu'mance A mixed food-producing economy involving nomadism and gardening according to the season of the year.

tran·si'tion rites Ritual complexes associated with important changes in personal status, such as birth, adolescence, marriage, and death.

trans·ves'tite An individual who effects a transfer of sex roles, such as occurs when a male takes on the dress and roles of a female, or vice versa.

trau'ma A bodily or psychologic injury, or its effect.

trav′er·tine   A porous limestone; also called *tufa*.

tra·vois′   A carrying device that has two poles, like the tongues of a buggy, hitched to a draft animal. The free ends of the travois drag along the ground.

tribe   A social group speaking a distinctive language or dialect and possessing a distinctive culture that marks it off from other tribes. It is not necessarily organized politically.

Trick′ster   A character in mythology who alters the order of things by tricking men or animals into choices or circumstances that they do not expect or desire.

Tri′nil man   *Homo erectus erectus.*

troll   A mountain-dwelling giant in Scandinavian belief.

tu′mu·lus   A mound of earth covering a dolmen or burial chamber.

ul″ti·mo·gen′i·ture   Inheritance by the youngest son or daughter.

u″ni·lin′e·al   Pertaining to descent through one parent only.

u″ni·lo′cal   Relating to or designating the practice whereby a married couple regularly settles with, or close to, the parents of one of the spouses. *See also* uxorilocal; virilocal.

u″ni·ver′sal   A behavior pattern characteristic of all the members of a society.

u′su·fruct   The right to use an object of property without possessing title of ownership.

ux·or″i·lo′cal   Pertaining to the practice whereby a married couple settles in the domicile of the wife's family; synonymous with *matrilocal residence.*

var′na   The four mythically founded castes of India which emerged from the body of primordial man.

varve   A band of clay deposited annually in a glacial outwash.

ves·tig′i·al re·mains′   Organs whose physiological functions have been lost (as far as can be determined).

Vil·la·fran′chi·an   The early part of the Pleistocene, prior to the first glaciation, in which modern genera of animals appear for the first time.

vir″i·lo′cal   Pertaining to the practice whereby a married couple settles in the domicile of the husband's family; synonymous with *patrilocal residence.*

vo·dun′   A system of religious belief and practice developed by Caribbean Negroes and combining elements of Catholicism and African, particularly Dahomean, religions. Magic is only a minor element in the entire complex. It is called *voodoo* in the American vernacular.

wam′pum   Elongated beads drilled out of clamshells, used by Indians of the northeast woodlands.

warp   The parallel-lying foundation threads of a fabric.

weft   The threads woven at right angles through the parallel-lying foundation threads, or warp; also called the *woof,* or *filler.*

wer′gild   The money payment made by the kin of a murderer to the kin of a murdered man.

wick′i·up″   A beehive-shaped grass hut.

wife lend′ing   The custom whereby a husband extends to a household guest the sexual favors of his wife as a symbolic gesture of brotherhood.

wig′wam   A domed bark hut of the Algonkian Indians of the northeast woodlands.

wil′low-leaf point   A long, slender flint blade characteristic of the Solutrean culture.

win·di′go   A type of homicidal psychosis involving cannibalism in Ojibwa and other Algonkian Indian cultures.

woof   *See* weft.

wrong, private   An offense against an individual that is customarily punished by legal action instituted by the injured person or his kinsmen. Private wrongs make up the body of private law.

wrong, public   An offense against the social entity punished by the legal action of the group at large or by its official representatives.

wur'ley   A lean-to shelter built by Australian aborigines.

ye·pun'   The virilocal, patrilineal clan in Umor society.

yuc'ca   A plant belonging to the lily family and possessing long fibrous leaves. The sap of its roots produces suds in water.

Zin·jan'·thro·pus boi'sie   A form of *Australo-pithecus robustus* found in Bed I at Olduvai Gorge.

zy·go'ma   The cheekbone.

zy'gote   A fertilized egg (female sex cell).

Bibliography

Aarne, A., *Die Tiere auf der Wandershaft* (Folklore Fellows Communications, no. 11, 1913).

Aberle, D. F., "The Psychological Analysis of a Hopi Life-History" (*Comparative Psychological Monographs,* vol. 21, no. 107, 1951).

Adamic, L., *The Native's Return: An American Immigrant Visits Jugoslavia and Discovers His Old Country* (New York, 1934).

Adams, R. M., *The Evolution of Urban Society: Early Mesopotamia and Prehishpanic Mexico* (Chicago, 1966).

Aginsky, B. W., "An Indian's Soliloquy" (*American Journal of Sociology,* vol. 46, 1940), pp. 43–44.

—— and Rangi Hiroa (P. H. Buck), "Interacting Forces in the Maori Family" (*American Anthropologist,* vol. 42, 1940), pp. 195–210.

Aitken, M. J., *Physics and Archaeology* (New York, 1961).

Aldridge, A. O., "The Meaning of Incest from Hutcheson to Gibbon" (*Ethics,* vol. 61, 1951), pp. 309–313.

Allison, A. C., "Aspects of Polymorphism in Man" (*Cold Spring Harbor Symposium on Quantitative Biology,* vol. 20, 1955), pp. 239–255.

Almond, G. A., and J. S. Coleman, *The Politics of Developing Areas* (Princeton, N.J., 1960).

Amsden, C., "The Loom and Its Prototypes" (*American Anthropologist,* vol. 34, 1932), pp. 216–235.

——, *Navaho Weaving* (Albuquerque, N.Mex., 1949).

Anderson, A. J. O., and C. E. Dibble (trans. and eds.), Fray B. de Sahagún, *Florentine Codex: General History of the Things of New Spain* (10 vols., Santa Fe, N.Mex., 1950–1966).

Anderson, R., "The Buffalo Men, A Cheyenne Ceremony of Petition Deriving from the Sutaio" (*Southwestern Journal of Anthropology,* vol. 12, 1956), pp. 92–104.

Arellano, A. R. V., "Some New Aspects of the Tepexpan Case" (*Bulletin of the Texas Archaeological and Paleontological Society,* vol. 22, 1951), pp. 217–225.

Arensberg, C. M., and A. H. Niehoff, *Introducing Social Change* (Chicago, 1964).

Ashley-Montagu, M. F., *Coming into Being among the Australian Aborigines* (New York, 1938).

——, "On the Origin of the Domestication of the Dog" (*Science,* vol. 96, 1942), pp. 111–112.

——, *Man's Most Dangerous Myth: The Fallacy of Race* (2d ed., New York, 1945).

Atkinson, J. J., *Primal Law* (London, 1903).

Ayoub, M. R., "Parallel Cousin Marriage and Endogamy: A Study in Sociometry" (*Southwestern Journal of Anthropology,* vol. 15, 1959), pp. 266–275.

Bachofen, J. K., *Das Mutterrecht: eine Untersuchung über die Gynaikokratie der alten Welt nach iherer religiösen und rechtlichen Natur* (Stuttgart, 1861).

Bacon, E., "A Preliminary Attempt to Determine the Culture Areas of Asia" (*Southwestern Journal of Anthropology,* vol. 2, 1946), pp. 117–132.

Baker, P. T., "The Biological Adaptation of Man to Hot Deserts," in T. W. McKern (ed.), *Readings in Physical Anthropology* (Englewood Cliffs, N.J., 1966) pp. 174–185.

Balfour, H., *The Evolution of Decorative Art* (London, 1893).

Bandalier, A. F., "Final Report" (*Papers of the Archaeological Institute of America,* vol. 3, 1890), p. 284.

Banton, M. (ed.), *The Relevance of Models for Social Anthropology* (New York, 1965).

——, "Voluntary Associations: Anthropological Aspects" (*International Encyclopedia of the Social Sciences,* vol. 16, 1968), pp. 357–362.

Barnett, H. G., "The Nature of the Potlatch" (*American Anthropologist,* vol. 40, 1938), pp. 349–358.

———, "Culture Processes" (*American Anthropologist,* vol. 42, 1940), pp. 21–48.

———, "Applied Anthropology in 1860" (*Applied Anthropology,* vol. 1, 1942), pp. 19–32.

———, *Innovation: The Basis of Cultural Change* (New York, 1953).

———, *Anthropology in Administration* (Evanston, Ill., 1956).

Barnouw, V., *Culture and Personality* (Homewood, Ill., 1963).

Barrett, S. A., *Pomo Indian Basketry* (University of California Publications in American Archaeology and Ethnology, vol. 7, 1908).

Barth, F., "Father's Brother's Daughter Marriage in Kurdistan" (*Southwestern Journal of Anthropology,* vol. 10, 1954), pp. 164–171.

———, *Nomads of South-Persia* (New York, 1961).

Barton, R. F., *Ifugao Law* (University of California Publications in American Archaeology and Ethnology, vol. 15, 1919).

———, *Ifugao Economics* (University of California Publications in American Archaeology and Ethnology, vol. 15, 1922).

———, *The Half-way Sun: Life among the Headhunters of the Philippines* (New York, 1930).

———, *Philippine Pagans: The Autobiographies of Three Ifugaos* (London, 1938).

———, *The Religion of the Ifugaos* (American Anthropological Association Memoir 65, 1946).

———, *The Kalinga: Their Institutions and Custom Law* (Chicago, 1949).

Bascom, W., *The Sociological Role of the Yoruba Cult-Group* (American Anthropological Association Memoir 63, 1944).

Bauman, H., "The Division of Work According to Sex in African Hoe Culture" (*Africa,* vol. 1, 1928), pp. 289–318.

Beaglehole, E., *Property: A Study in Social Psychology* (London, 1931).

———, "Character Structure: Its Role in the Analysis of Interpersonal Relations" (*Psychiatry,* vol. 7, 1944), pp. 144–162.

Beals, R., P. Carrasco, and T. McCorkle, *Houses and House Use of the Sierra Tarascans* (Washington, D.C., 1944).

Beattie, J., *Other Cultures: Aims, Methods and Achievements in Social Anthropology* (Glencoe, Ill., 1964).

Bellah, R. N., *Apache Kinship Systems* (Cambridge, Mass., 1952).

Belo, J., "A Study of a Balinese Family" (*American Anthropologist,* vol. 38, 1936), pp. 12–31.

Bender, M. A., and E. H. Y. Chen, "The Chromosomes of Primates," in J. Buettner-Janusch (ed.), *Evolutionary and Genetic Biology of Primates* (2 vols., New York, 1963), chap. 7.

Benedict, R. F., *The Concept of the Guardian Spirit in North America* (American Anthropological Association Memoir 29, 1923).

———, "The Science of Custom: The Bearing of Anthropology on Contemporary Thought," in V. F. Calverton (ed.), *The Making of Man: An Outline of Anthropology* (New York, 1931), pp. 805–817.

———, *Patterns of Culture* (New York, 1934).

———, "Marital Property Rights in Bilateral Society" (*American Anthropologist,* vol. 38, 1936), pp. 368–374.

———, "Religion," in F. Boas (ed.), *General Anthropology* (New York, 1938), chap. 14.

———, *Race: Science and Politics* (New York, 1940).

———, *The Chrysanthemum and the Sword: Patterns of Japanese Culture* (Boston, 1946).

Bennett, J. W., "The Development of Ethnological Theories as Illustrated by Studies of the Plains Sun Dance" (*American Anthropologist,* vol. 46, 1944), pp. 162–181.

——— and M. M. Tumin, *Social Life, Structure and Function: An Introductory General Sociology* (New York, 1948), pp. 45–59.

Bennett, W. C., and R. M. Zingg, *The Tarahumara: An Indian Tribe of Northern Mexico* (Chicago, 1935).

Berlin, B., "A Universalist-Evolutionary Approach in Ethnographic Semantics," in A. Fischer (ed.), *Current Directions in Anthropology* (vol. 3, no. 3, part 2, 1970).

Berreman, G. D., "Pahari Polyandry: A Comparison," in P. Bohannan and J. Middleton (eds.), *Mar-*

riage, Family, and Residence (Garden City, N.Y., 1968), pp. 147–167.

Bielicki, T., "Some Possibilities for Estimating Inter-Population Relationship on the Basis of Continuous Traits" (*Current Anthropology*, vol. 3, 1962), pp. 3–20.

Birdwhistell, R. L., *Kinesics and Context: Essays on Body Motion Communication* (Philadelphia, 1970).

Blacking, J., "Comment on A. Wolfe, 'Social Structural Bases of Art'" (*Current Anthropology*, vol. 10, 1969), pp. 30–31.

Blackwood, B., *Both Sides of Buka Passage* (Oxford, 1935).

Bloomfield, L., in H. Hoijer (ed.), *Language History* (New York and others, 1965).

Boas, F., *The Central Eskimo* (Bureau of American Ethnology, Annual Report 6, 1888), pp. 399–669.

——, *Social Organization and Secret Societies of the Kwakiutl Indians* (United States National Museum, Annual Report, 1895).

——, *Tsimshian Mythology* (Bureau of American Ethnology, Annual Report 31, 1916), pp. 393–558.

——, *Primitive Art* (Oslo, 1929).

——, "Anthropology" (*Encyclopaedia of the Social Sciences*, vol. 2, 1930), pp. 73–110.

——, *Anthropology and Modern Life* (rev. ed., New York, 1932).

—— (ed.), *General Anthropology* (New York, 1938).

Bodmer, W. F., and L. L. Cavilla-Sforza, "Intelligence and Race" (*Scientific American*, vol. 223, 1970), pp. 19–29.

Bogoras, W., "The Chukchee: I, Religion" (*Jesup North Pacific Expedition*, vol. 7, 1904–1909).

Bohannan, P., *Justice and Judgment among the Tiv* (London, 1957).

——, *Social Anthropology* (New York, 1963).

—— and G. Dalton, *Markets in Africa* (Evanston, Ill., 1962).

Bordes, F., *The Old Stone Age* (New York, 1968).

Boulding, K. E., "The Death of the City: A Frightened Look at Post-civilization" (1961, mimeographed).

——, *The Meaning of the 20th Century: The Great Transition* (New York, 1965).

Bourguignon, E., and L. Greenbaum, *Diversity and Homogeneity: A Comparative Analysis of Societal Characteristics Based on Data from the Ethnographic Atlas* (Columbus, Ohio, 1968).

Bourlière, F., "Patterns of Social Groupings among Primates," in S. L. Washburn (ed.), *Social Life of Early Man* (Chicago, 1961), pp. 1–10.

Bowers, A. W., *Mandan Social and Ceremonial Organization* (Chicago, 1950).

Boyd, W. C., *Genetics and the Races of Man: An Introduction to Modern Physical Anthropology* (Boston, 1950).

——, "The Contributions of Genetics to Anthropology," in A. L. Kroeber (ed.), *Anthropology Today: An Encyclopedic Inventory* (Chicago, 1953), pp. 488–506.

Brace, C. L., "The Fate of the 'Classic' Neanderthals: A Consideration of Hominid Catastrophism" (*Current Anthropology*, vol. 5, no. 1, 1964), pp. 3–46.

—— and M. F. A. Montagu, *Man's Evolution: An Introduction to Physical Anthropology* (New York, 1965).

Braidwood, R. J., "Jericho and Its Setting in Near Eastern Prehistory" (*Antiquity*, vol. 31, 1957), pp. 73–80.

——, *Prehistoric Men* (3d ed., Chicago, 1957).

—— and G. R. Willey (eds.), *Courses toward Urban Life: Archeological Considerations of Some Cultural Alternatives* (Viking Fund Publications in Anthropology, no. 32, 1962).

Bram, J., *An Analysis of Inca Militarism* (American Ethnological Society Monograph 4, 1941).

Breuil, H., *Four Hundred Centuries of Cave Art* (New York, 1950).

Brew, J. O. (ed.), *One Hundred Years of Anthropology* (Cambridge, Mass., 1968).

Brinton, D. G., *Religions of Primitive People* (New York, 1897).

Britannica Book of the Year 1968 (Chicago, 1968).

Bronowski, J., and U. Bellugi, "Language, Name, and Concept" (*Science*, vol. 168, 1970), pp. 669–673.

Brouner, W. B., and Y. M. Fung, *Chinese Made Easy* (Leiden, 1935).

Brown, J., "A Cross-cultural Study of Female Initiation Rites" (*American Anthropologist,* vol. 65, 1963), pp. 817–853.

Buck, P. H., *Vikings of the Sunrise* (New York, 1938).

Buehler, A., T. Barrow, and C. P. Mountford, *The Art of the South Seas, Including Australia and New Zealand* (New York, 1962).

Buettner-Janusch, J. (ed.), "The Relatives of Man: Modern Studies on the Relation of the Evolution of Non-human Primates to Human Evolution" (*Annals of the New York Academy of Science,* vol. 102, 1962), pp. 181–514.

——, *Evolutionary and Genetic Biology of Primates* (2 vols., New York, 1963).

——, *Origins of Man: Physical Anthropology* (New York, 1966).

Bunzel, R., *The Pueblo Potter* (Columbia University Contributions to Anthropology, vol. 8, 1929).

——, *Introduction to Zuni Ceremonialism* (Bureau of American Ethnology, Annual Report 47, 1932).

Burgess, E. W., "Introduction," in E. F. Frazier, *The Negro Family in the United States* (Chicago, 1939).

Burling, R., "American Kinship Terms Once More" *Southwestern Journal of Anthropology,* vol. 26, 1970), pp. 15–24.

——, *Man's Many Voices: Language in Its Cultural Context* (New York and others, 1970).

Burrows, E. G., *Flower in My Ear: Arts and Ethos in Ifaluk Atoll* (University of Washington Publications in Anthropology, vol. 14, 1963).

Bushnell, G. H. S., *The First Americans: The Pre-Columbian Civilizations* (New York, 1968).

Busia, K. A., *The Position of the Chief in the Modern Political System of Ashanti: A Study of the Influence of Contemporary Social Changes on Ashanti Political Institutions* (Oxford, 1951).

——, "The Ashanti of the Gold Coast," in D. Forde (ed.), *African Worlds: Studies in the Cosmological Ideas and Social Values of African Peoples* (London, 1954), pp. 190–209.

Campbell, B., "Quantitative Taxonomy and Human Evolution," in S. L. Washburn (ed.), *Classification and Human Evolution* (Viking Fund Publications in Anthropology, no. 37, 1963), pp. 50–70.

Caneiro, R. L., "Slash and Burn Cultivation among the Kiukuru and Its Implications for Cultural Development in the Amazon Basin," in *The Evolution of Horticultural Systems in Native South America, Causes and Consequences—A Symposium* (Anthropologica Supplement No. 2, Caracas, 1961), pp. 47–67.

Cardozo, B. N., *The Growth of the Law* (New Haven, Conn., 1924).

Carpenter, C. R., *A Field Study of the Behavior and Social Relations of the Howling Monkeys (Aloutta palliata)* (Comparative Psychological Monographs, vol. 10, 1934), pp. 1–168.

——, "Societies of Monkeys and Apes" (*Biological Symposia,* vol. 8, 1942), pp. 177–204.

Carrol, J. B. (ed.), *Language, Thought, and Reality: Selected Writings of Benjamin Lee Whorf* (New York, 1956).

Carter, G. F., "Origins of American Indian Agriculture" (*American Anthropologist,* vol. 48, 1946), pp. 1–21.

Caso, A., *The Aztecs: People of the Sun* (Norman, Okla., 1958).

Catlin, G., in J. C. Ewers (ed.), *O-kee-pa: A Religious Ceremony and Other Customs of the Mandans* (New Haven, Conn., 1967).

Chang, K.-C., "The Beginnings of Agriculture in the Far East" (*Antiquity,* vol. 44, 1970), pp. 175–185.

Chard, C. S., *Man in Prehistory* (New York, 1969).

Childe, V. G., *The Dawn of European Civilization* (New York, 1925).

——, *New Light on the Most Ancient East* (London, 1935).

——, *What Happened in History* (London, 1942).

——, *Man Makes Himself* (rev. ed., New York, 1951).

Chomsky, N., *Language and Mind* (New York, 1968).

Christensen, J. B., *Double Descent among the Fanti* (Behavior Science Monographs, New Haven, Conn., 1954).

Clark, G., *The Stone Age Hunters* (New York, 1967).

———, and S. Piggott, *Prehistoric Societies* (New York, 1965).

Clark, J. D., "Africa South of the Sahara," in R. J. Braidwood and G. R. Willey (eds.), *Courses toward Urban Life: Archeological Considerations of Some Cultural Alternatives* (Viking Fund Publications in Anthropology, no. 32, 1962), pp. 1–33.

———, *The Prehistory of Africa* (New York, 1970).

——— and F. C. Howell (eds.), "Recent Studies in Paleoanthropology" (*American Anthropologist*, vol. 68, no. 2, part 2, Special Publication, 1966).

Clark, J. G. D., *Prehistoric Europe: The Economic Base* (New York, 1952).

———, *World Prehistory: An Outline* (Cambridge, England, 1961.

Codere, H., "Exchange and Display" (*International Encyclopaedia of the Social Sciences*, vol. 5, 1968), pp. 239–245.

Cohen, Y. A., *The Transition from Childhood to Adolescence: Cross-cultural Studies of Initiation Ceremonies, Legal Systems and Incest Tabus* (Chicago, 1964).

Cole, G. D. H., "Inheritance" (*Encyclopaedia of the Social Sciences*, vol. 8, 1932), pp. 35–43.

Cole, S., *The Prehistory of East Africa* (New York, 1963).

Comte, A., *Positive Philosophy* (H. Martineau, trans., London, 1893).

Cook, W. W., "Ownership and Possession" (*Encyclopaedia of the Social Sciences*, vol. 11, 1932), pp. 521–525.

Coon, C. S., *The Races of Europe* (New York, 1936).

———, *The Story of Man: From the First Human to Primitive Culture and Beyond* (New York, 1955).

———, *The Origin of Races* (New York, 1963).

———, S. M. Garn, and J. B. Birdsell, *Races: A Study of Race Formation in Man* (Springfield, Ill., 1950).

——— with E. E. Hunt, Jr., *The Living Races of Man* (New York, 1965).

Cooper, J. M., "Mental Disease Situations in Certain Cultures" (*Journal of Abnormal and Social Psychology*, vol. 29, 1934), pp. 10–17.

———, "Is the Algonquian Family Hunting Ground System Pre-Columbian?" (*American Anthropologist*, vol. 41, 1939), pp. 66–90.

———, "The Patagonian and Pampean Hunters," in J. H. Steward (ed.), *Handbook of South American Indians* (6 vols., Washington, D.C., 1946–1950), vol. 1, pp. 127–168.

———, "The Yahgan," in J. H. Steward (ed.), *Handbook of South American Indians* (6 vols., Washington, D.C., 1946–1950), vol. 1, pp. 81–107.

Cottrell, W. F., *Energy and Society: The Relation between Energy, Social Change, and Economic Development* (New York, 1955).

Curtis, E. S., *The Kwakiutl* (New York, 1919).

Dalrymple, G. B., and M. A. Lanphere, *Potassium-Argon Dating: Principles, Techniques, and Applications to Geochronology* (San Francisco, 1969).

Dalton, G., "Traditional Production in Primitive African Economies" (*Quarterly Journal of Economics*, August, 1962), pp. 360–378.

Dart, R. A., "The Predatory Implemental Technique of Australopithecus" (*American Journal of Physical Anthropology*, vol. 7, 1949), pp. 1–16.

———, *The Osteodontokeratic Culture of Australopithecus prometheus* (Transvaal Museum Memoir 10, 1957).

Darwin, C., *The Origin of Species by Means of Natural Selection; Or, the Preservation of Favored Races in the Struggle for Life* (Macmillan, New York, 1927).

Davenport, W., "Nonunilinear Descent and Descent Groups" (*American Anthropologist*, vol. 61, 1959), pp. 557–572.

———, "The 'Hawaiian Cultural Revolution': Some Political and Economic Considerations" (*American Anthropologist*, vol. 71, 1969), pp. 1–20.

Davidson, D. S., "Knotless Netting in America and Oceania" (*American Anthropologist*, vol. 37, 1935), pp. 117–134.

Dawson, J., *Australian Aborigines* (Melbourne, 1881).

Day, M. H., *Guide to Fossil Man: A Handbook of Human Paleontology* (Cleveland and New York, 1965).

de Jong, Josselin, *Lévi-Strauss's Theory on Kinship*

and Marriage (Mededelingen van het Rijksmuseum voor Volkenkunde, Leiden, no. 10, 1952).

de Lumley, H., "A Paleolithic Camp at Nice" (*Scientific American,* vol. 220, 1969), pp. 42-50.

de Montaigne, M., *Selected Essays* (D. M. Frame, trans., New York, 1943).

de Schlippe, P., *Shifting Cultivation in Africa: The Zande System of Agriculture* (London, 1956).

de Terra, H., J. Romero, and T. D. Steward, *Early Man in Mexico* (Viking Fund Publications in Anthropology, no. 11, 1949).

Densmore, F., "An Explanation of a Trick Performed by Indian Jugglers" (*American Anthropologist,* vol. 34, 1932), pp. 310-314.

Dirringer, D., *The Alphabet* (New York, 1948).

Dobzhansky, T., *Genetics and the Origin of Species* (3d ed., New York, 1951).

———, *Mankind Evolving: The Evolution of the Human Species* (New Haven, Conn., 1962).

———, "Evolution: Organic and Superorganic" (*The Rockefeller Institute Review,* vol. 1, no. 2, 1963), pp. 1-9.

Domenech, E., *Seven Years' Residence in the Great Deserts of North America* (2 vols., London, 1860).

Dorsey, G. A., *The Cheyenne: II, The Sun Dance* (Field Columbian Museum, Publication 103, Anthropological Series, vol. 9, no. 2, 1905).

——— and J. R. Murie, *Notes on Skidi Pawnee Society* (Field Museum of Natural History, Anthropological Series, vol. 27, 1940).

Douglas, D. W., and K. du P. Lumpkin, "Communistic Settlements" (*Encyclopaedia of the Social Sciences,* vol. 4, 1930), pp. 95-102.

Dowling, J. H., "Individual Ownership and the Sharing of Game in Hunting Societies" (*American Anthropologist,* vol. 70, 1968), pp. 502-507.

Doxiodis, C. A., "Ecumenopolis: Tomorrow's City," in *Britannica Book of the Year 1968* (Chicago, 1968), pp. 16-38.

Dozier, E. P., "Rio Grande Pueblos," in E. H. Spicer (ed.), *Perspectives in American Indian Culture Change* (Chicago, 1961), pp. 94-186.

Driver, H. E., and K. F. Schuessler, "Correlational

Analysis of Murdock's 1957 Ethnographic Sample" (*American Anthropologist,* vol. 67, 1967) pp. 332-352.

Drucker, P., *Indians of the Northwest Coast* (New York, 1967).

——— and R. F. Heizer, *To Make My Name Good: A Reexamination of the Southern Kwakiutl Potlatch* (Berkeley and Los Angeles, 1967).

DuBois, C., *The People of Alor* (Minneapolis, 1944).

———, "The Alorese," in A. Kardiner (ed.), *The Psychological Frontiers of Society* (New York, 1945), pp. 101-145.

Dumarest, N., *Notes on Cochiti, New Mexico* (American Anthropological Association, Memoirs, vol. 6, no. 3, 1919).

Dunn, L. C., *Heredity and Evolution in Human Populations* (Cambridge, Mass., 1960).

——— and T. Dobzhansky, *Heredity, Race, and Society* (rev. ed., New York, 1951).

Durkheim, É., *Elementary Forms of the Religious Life* (London, 1914).

Dyson-Hudson, R., and N., "Subsistence Herding in Uganda" (*Scientific American,* vol. 220, 1969), pp. 76-89.

Eggan, F., *Social Organization of the Western Pueblos* (Chicago, 1950).

———, "Social Anthropology and the Method of Controlled Comparison" (*American Anthropologist,* vol. 56, 1954), pp. 743-763.

——— (ed.), *Social Anthropology of North American Tribes* (2d ed., Chicago, 1955).

Eiseley, L. C., "In the Beginning Was the Artifact" (*Saturday Review,* Dec. 7, 1963).

Eisenstadt, S. N., *From Generation to Generation* (Glencoe, Ill., 1956).

Ekvall, R. B., *Fields on the Hoof: Nexus of Tibetan Nomadic Pastoralism* (New York, 1968).

Engels, F., *The Origin of the Family, Private Property, and the State in Light of the Researches of Lewis Henry Morgan* (London, 1885).

Epstein, A. L., *Politics in an Urban African Community* (Manchester, 1958).

Erasmus, C. J., "Patolli, Pachisi, and the Limitation

of Possibilities" (*Southwestern Journal of Anthropology,* vol. 6, 1950), pp. 369–388.

——, *Man Takes Control: Cultural Development and American Aid* (Minneapolis, 1961).

Erikson, E. H., "Life Cycle" (*International Encyclopedia of the Social Sciences,* vol. 9, 1968), pp. 286–292.

Erikson, J. M., *The Universal Bead* (New York, 1969).

Evans-Pritchard, E. E., *Witchcraft, Oracles and Magic among the Azande* (Oxford, 1937).

——, *The Nuer: A Description of the Modes of Livelihood and Political Institutions of a Nilotic People* (Oxford, 1940).

——, "The Nuer of the Southern Sudan," in E. E. Evans-Pritchard and M. Fortes (eds.), *African Political Systems* (Oxford, 1940).

——, "Nuer Bridewealth" (*Africa,* vol. 16, 1946), pp. 1ff.

——, *Kinship and Marriage among the Nuer* (Oxford, 1951).

——, *Social Anthropology* (Oxford, 1951).

——, *Nuer Religion* (Oxford, 1956).

——, *Anthropology and History* (Manchester, 1961).

——, *Essays in Social Anthropology* (Glencoe, Ill., 1963).

——, "Heredity and Gestation as the Azande See Them," in *Essays in Social Anthropology* (Glencoe, Ill., 1963).

—— and M. Fortes (eds.), *African Political Systems* (Oxford, 1940).

Ewers, J. C., *The Horse in Blackfoot Indian Culture: With Comparative Material from Other Western Tribes* (Bureau of American Ethnology, Bulletin 159, 1955).

Fagan, B. M., *Introductory Readings in Archaeology* (Boston, 1970).

Fallers, L. A., *Bantu Bureaucracy: A Study of Integration and Conflict in the Political Institutions of an East African People* (London, 1956).

Fenton, W. N., "Locality as a Basic Factor in the Development of Iroquois Social Structure," in *Symposium on Local Diversity in Iroquois Culture* (Bureau of American Ethnology Bulletin 149, 1951).

——, "J.-F. Lafitau (1681–1746), Precursor of Scientific Anthropology" (*Southwestern Journal of Anthropology,* vol. 25, 1969) pp. 173–187.

Firth, R., *We the Tikopia, A Sociological Study of Kinship in Primitive Polynesia* (London, 1936).

——, *Primitive Polynesian Economy* (London, 1939).

—— (ed.), *Man and Culture: An Evaluation of the Work of Bronislaw Malinowski* (London, 1957).

Fitch, J. M., and D. P. Branch, "Primitive Architecture and Climate" (*Scientific American,* vol. 207, 1960), pp. 134–144.

Flint, R. F., *Glacial Geology and the Pleistocene Epoch* (New York, 1947).

Ford, C. S., "The Role of a Fijian Chief" (*American Sociological Review,* vol. 3, 1938), pp. 542–550.

——, *A Comparative Study of Human Reproduction* (Yale University Publications in Anthropology, no. 32, 1945).

Forde, C. D., *Habitat, Economy, and Society: A Geographical Introduction to Ethnology* (2d ed., New York, 1937).

——, "Kinship in Umor—Double Unilateral Organization in a Semi-Bantu Society" (*American Anthropologist,* vol. 41, 1939), pp. 523–553.

——, "Applied Anthropology in Government: British Africa," in A. L. Kroeber (ed.), *Anthropology Today: An Encyclopedic Inventory* (Chicago, 1953), pp. 841–865.

—— (ed.), *African Worlds: Studies in the Cosmological Ideas and Social Values of African Peoples* (London, 1954).

Fortes, M., *The Dynamics of Clanship among the Tallensi* (Oxford, 1945).

——,(ed.), *Social Structure: Studies Presented to A. R. Radcliffe-Brown* (Oxford, 1949).

——, *The Web of Kinship among the Tallensi* (Cambridge, England, 1949).

——, "Structure of Unilineal Descent Groups" (*American Anthropologist,* vol. 55, 1953), pp. 17–34.

Fortune, R. F., *Sorcerers of Dobu: The Social An-*

thropology of the Dobu Islanders of the Western Pacific* (New York, 1932).

—— , *Manus Religion* (Proceedings of the American Philosophical Society, 1935).

Foster, G. M., "Peasant Society and the Image of the Limited Good" (*American Anthropologist,* vol. 67, 1965), pp. 293–315.

—— , "Peasant Character and Personality," in J. M. Potter, M. N. Diaz, and G. M. Foster (eds.), *Peasant Society: A Reader* (Boston, 1967), pp. 296–299.

—— , *Applied Anthropology* (Boston, 1969).

Franklin, B., *The Interests of Great Britain Considered* (Boston, 1760).

Fraser, D., "The Discovery of Primitive Art," in C. M. Otten (ed.), *Anthropology and Art* (Garden City, N. Y., 1971) pp. 20–36.

Frazer, J. G., *Totemism and Exogamy* (4 vols., London, 1910).

—— , *Folk-lore in The Old Testament: Studies in Comparative Religion Legend and Law* (abridged ed., New York, 1923).

—— , *The Golden Bough: A Study in Magic and Religion* (abridged ed., New York, 1941).

Frazier, E. F., *The Negro Family in the United States* (Chicago, 1939).

Freuchen, P., *Arctic Adventure: My Life in the Frozen North* (New York, 1935).

Freud, S., *Totem and Tabu* (reprinted in *The Basic Writings of Sigmund Freud,* New York, 1938).

Garfield, V. E., *Tsimshian Clan and Society* (University of Washington Publications in Anthropology, vol. 7, no. 3, 1939).

Garn, M. S., *Human Races* (Springfield, Ill., 1961).

Gayton, A. H., *Yokuts-Mono Chiefs and Shamans* (University of California Publications in American Archaeology and Ethnology, vol. 24, 1930).

Geertz, C., *The Religion of Java* (Glencoe, Ill., 1959).

—— , "Religion as a Cultural System," in W. A. Lessa and E. Z. Vogt (eds.), *Reader in Comparative Religion* (2d ed., New York, 1965), pp. 204–215.

Geertz, H., *The Javanese Family: A Study in Kinship and Socialization* (Glencoe, Ill., 1961).

Gerlach, L. P., and V. H. Hine, *People, Power,*

Change: Movements of Social Transformation* (Indianapolis, 1970).

Gibbs, J. L., Jr. (ed.), *Peoples of Africa* (New York, 1965).

Giffen, N. M., *The Roles of Men and Women in Eskimo Culture* (Chicago, 1930).

Gifford, E. W., *Tongan Society* (Bernice P. Bishop Museum Bulletin 61, 1929).

Gillin, J. L., and J. P. Gillin, *An Introduction to Sociology* (New York, 1942).

Gillin, J. P., *The Barama River Caribs of British Guiana* (Papers of the Peabody Museum of American Archaeology and Ethnology, Harvard University, vol. 14, 1936).

Glass, B., "Science, Endless Frontier of Golden Age?" (*Science,* vol. 171, 1971), pp. 23–29.

Gluckman, M., *Custom and Conflict in Africa* (Oxford, 1955).

—— , "How the Bemba Make Their Living: An Appreciation of Richard's 'Land, Labour, and Diet in Northern Rhodesia'" (*Rhodes-Livingstone Institute Journal,* June, 1945), pp. 55–67.

—— , *The Judicial Process among the Barotse of Northern Rhodesia* (Manchester and Glencoe, Ill., 1954 and 1955).

—— , *The Ideas of Barotse Jurisprudence* (New Haven, Conn., 1965).

—— , *Politics, Law, and Ritual in Tribal Society* (Chicago, 1965).

Goldenweiser, A., *Anthropology* (New York, 1937).

Goldfrank, E. S., "Socialization, Personality, and the Structure of Pueblo Society (with Particular Reference to Hopi and Zuñi)" (*American Anthropologist,* vol. 47, 1945), pp. 516–539.

Golding, W., *The Inheritors* (London and New York, 1955 and 1962).

Goldschmidt, W., and E. J. Kunkel, "The Structure of the Peasant Family" (*American Anthropologist,* vol. 73, 1971), pp. 1058–1076.

Goodall, J., "Tool Using and Aimed Throwing in a Community of Free-living Chimpanzees" (*Nature,* no. 201, 1964), pp. 1264–1266.

Goodenough, W. H., "Residence Rules" (*Southwestern Journal of Anthropology,* vol. 12, 1950), pp. 22–37.

———, "A Problem in Malayo-Polynesian Social Organization" (*American Anthropologist*, vol. 57, 1955), pp. 71–83.

———, *Cooperation in Change: An Anthropological Approach to Community Development* (New York, 1963).

———, "Rethinking 'Status' and 'Role': Toward a General Model of the Cultural Organization of Social Relationships," in M. Banton (ed.), *The Relevance of Models for Social Anthropology* (New York, 1965), pp. 1–22.

Goodman, M., "Man's Place in the Phylogeny of Primates as Reflected in Serum Proteins," in S. L. Washburn (ed.), *Classification and Human Evolution* (Chicago, 1963), pp. 204–234.

Goodwin, G., *The Social Organization of the Western Apache* (Chicago, 1942).

Goody, J. (ed.), *The Development Cycle in Domestic Groups* (Cambridge, Mass., 1958).

———, "The Classification of Double Descent Systems" (*Current Anthropology*, vol. 2, 1961), pp. 3–26.

———, *Death, Property and the Ancestors: A Study of the Mortuary Customs of the Lodagaa of West Africa* (Stanford, Calif., 1962).

Gough, E. K., "Changing Kinship Usages in the Setting of Political and Economic Change among the Nyars of Malabar" (*Journal of the Royal Anthropological Institute of Great Britain and Ireland*, vol. 82, 1952), pp. 71–87.

Gravel, P. B., "The Transfer of Cows in Gisaka (Rwanda): A Mechanism for Recording Social Relationships" (*American Anthropologist*, vol. 69, 1967), pp. 322–331.

Greenberg, J. H., "Historical Linguistics and Unwritten Languages," in A. L. Kroeber (ed.), *Anthropology Today: An Encyclopedic Inventory* (New York, 1953), pp. 265–286.

———, *Anthropological Linguistics: An Introduction* (New York, 1968).

Greenman, E. F., "Material Culture and the Organism" (*American Anthropologist*, vol. 47, 1945), pp. 211–231.

Grinnell, G. B., *The Fighting Cheyennes* (New York, 1915).

———, *The Cheyenne Indians: Their History and Ways of Life* (2 vols., New Haven, Conn., 1923).

Gudschinsky, S. C., "The ABC's of Lexicostatistics (Glottochronology)," in D. Hymes (ed.), *Language in Culture and Society: A Reader in Linguistics and Anthropology* (New York; Evanston, Ill.; and London, 1964), pp. 612–623.

———, *How to Learn an Unwritten Language* (New York, 1967).

Gulliver, P. H., *The Family Herds: A Study of Two Pastoral Peoples in East Africa, the Jie and Turkana* (London, 1955).

———, "The Jie of Uganda," in J. L. Gibbs, Jr. (ed.), *Peoples of Africa* (New York, 1965), pp. 159–196.

Haddon, A. C., *Evolution in Art* (London, 1895).

Haines, F., "The Northward Spread of Horses among the Plains Indians" (*American Anthropologist*, vol. 40, 1938), pp. 429–437.

———, "Where Did the Plains Indians Get Their Horses?" (*American Anthropologist*, vol. 40, 1938), pp. 112–117.

Haldane, J. B. S., "The Argument from Animals to Men: An Examination of Its Validity for Anthropology" (*Journal of the Royal Anthropological Institute of Great Britain and Ireland*, vol. 86, part 2, 1956).

Hall, E. T., *The Silent Language* (New York, 1959).

Hall, G. S., *Adolescence: Its Psychology and Its Relations to Physiology, Anthropology, Sociology, Sex, Crime, Religion and Education* (2 vols., New York, 1904).

Hallowell, A. I., "Bear Ceremonialism in the Northern Hemisphere" (*American Anthropologist*, vol. 28, 1926), pp. 1–175.

———, "Culture and Mental Disorders" (*Journal of Abnormal and Social Psychology*, vol. 29, 1934), pp. 1–9.

———, "The Nature and Function of Property as a Social Institution" (*Journal of Legal and Political Sociology*, vol. 1, 1943), pp. 115–138.

———, "Psychological Leads for Ethnological Field Workers," in D. G. Haring (ed.), *Personal Character and Cultural Milieu* (3rd rev. ed., Syracuse, N.Y., 1956), pp. 341–389.

———, "The Beginnings of Anthropology in America," in F. De Laguna (ed.), *Selected Papers from the*

American Anthropologist: 1888–1920 (Evanston, Ill., 1960), pp. 1–90.

Hambly, W. D., *Source Book for African Anthropology* (Field Museum of Natural History, Anthropological Series, vol. 26, part 2, 1937).

Hamilton, W. H., and I. Till, "Property" (*Encyclopaedia of the Social Sciences,* vol. 12, 1934), pp. 528–538.

Hammel, E. H., "A Transformational Analysis of Comanche Kinship Terminology" (*American Anthropologist,* vol. 67, part 2, no. 5, 1965), pp. 65–105.

Hammond, P. B., *Cultural and Social Anthropology: Selected Readings* (New York, 1964).

———, *Physical Anthropology and Archaeology: Selected Readings* (New York, 1964).

Haring, D. G. (ed.), *Personal Character and Cultural Milieu* (3rd rev. ed., Syracuse, N.Y., 1956).

Harrasser, A., *Die Rechtsverletzung bei den australischer Eingeborenen* (Beilegeheft zur vergleichende Rechtswissenschaft, vol. 50, 1936).

Harris, M., *The Rise of Anthropological Theory: A History of Theories of Culture* (New York, 1968).

Hart, C. W. M., "Contrasts between Prepubertal and Postpubertal Education," in G. D. Spindler (ed.), *Education and Anthropology* (Stanford, Calif., 1956), pp. 127–145.

——— and A. R. Pilling, *The Tiwi of North Australia* (New York, 1960).

Haury, E. N., "The Greater American Southwest," in R. J. Braidwood and G. R. Willey (eds.), *Courses toward Urban Life: Archeological Consideration of Some Cultural Alternatives* (Viking Fund Publications in Anthropology, no. 32, 1962), pp. 106–131.

Hawley, F. M., "Pueblo Social Organization as a Lead to Pueblo History" (*American Anthropologist,* vol. 39, 1937), pp. 504–522.

Hay, C., et al. (eds.), *The Maya and Their Neighbors* (New York, 1940).

Hays, H. R., *From Ape to Angel: An Informal History of Social Anthropology* (New York, 1958).

Heine-Geldern, R., "One Hundred Years of Ethnological Theory in the German-speaking Countries: Some Milestones" (*Current Anthropology,* vol. 5, 1964), pp. 407–429.

Heizer, R. F., and L. K. Napton, "Biological and Cultural Evidence from Human Coprolites" (*Science,* vol. 165, 1969), pp. 563–568.

Helm, J., *Pioneers of American Anthropology: The Uses of Biography* (American Ethnological Society Monograph 43, 1966).

Hempstone, S., "Leaving Grandpa to Die by a Dry Water Hole" (*Minneapolis Tribune,* Dec. 5, 1971), p. 37A.

Henry, J., *Culture against Man* (New York, 1963).

Herskovits, M. J., "Preliminary Consideration of Culture Areas of Africa" (*American Anthropologist,* vol. 26, 1924), pp. 50–63.

———, "African Gods and Catholic Saints in New World Negro Belief" (*American Anthropologist,* vol. 39, 1937), pp. 635–643.

———, "A Note on 'Woman Marriage' in Dahomey" (*Africa,* vol. 10, 1937), pp. 335–341.

———, *Acculturation: The Study of Culture Contacts* (New York, 1938).

———, *Dahomey: An Ancient West African Kingdom* (2 vols., New York, 1938).

———, *Backgrounds of African Art* (Denver, 1945).

———, *Economic Anthropology* (New York, 1952).

———, *Cultural Anthropology: A Study in Comparative Economics* (New York, 1952).

——— and F. S. Herskovits, *An Outline of Dahomean Religious Belief* (American Anthropological Association Memoir 41, 1933).

Hickerson, H., "Some Implications of the Theory of the Particularity, or 'Atomism,' of Northern Algonkians" (*Current Anthropology,* vol. 8, 1967), pp. 313–327.

Hiebert, P. G., *Konduru: Structure and Integration in a Hindu Village* (Minneapolis, 1971).

Hill, W. W., *The Agricultural and Hunting Methods of the Navaho Indians* (Yale University Publications in Anthropology, no. 18, 1938).

Hobhouse, L. H., G. C. Wheeler, and M. Ginsberg, *The Material Culture and Social Institutions of the Simpler Peoples* (London, 1930).

Hocart, A. M., "Kinship Systems" (*Anthropos,* vol. 32, 1937), pp. 345–351.

Hockett, C. F., and R. Ascher, "The Human Revolution" (*Current Anthropology,* vol. 5, 1964), pp. 135–168.

Hoebel, E. A., "The Sun Dance of the H3kandika Shoshone" (*American Anthropologist,* vol. 37, 1935), pp. 570–581.

——, "Comanche and H3kandika Shoshone Relationship Systems" (*American Anthropologist,* vol. 41, 1939), pp. 440–457.

——, *The Political Organization and Law-ways of the Comanche Indians* (American Anthropological Association Memoir 54; Contributions from the Laboratory of Anthropology 4, 1940).

——, "The Asiatic Origin of a Myth of the Northwest Coast" (*Journal of American Folklore,* vol. 54, 1941), pp. 1–12.

——, "The Comanche Sun Dance and Messianic Outbreak of 1873" (*American Anthropologist,* vol. 43, 1941), pp. 301–303.

——, "Fundamental Legal Concepts as Applied in the Study of Primitive Law" (*Yale Law Journal,* vol. 51, 1942), pp. 951–963.

——, "Anent Blood Relationship" (*Science,* vol. 103, 1946), pp. 600–602.

——, "Law and Anthropology" (*Virginia Law Review,* vol. 32, 1946), pp. 836–854.

——, "Eskimo Infanticide and Polyandry" (*Scientific Monthly,* vol. 64, 1947), p. 535.

——, "Underground Kiva Passages" (*American Antiquity,* vol. 19, 1953), p. 76.

——, *The Law of Primitive Man: A Study in Comparative Legal Dynamics* (Cambridge, Mass., 1954).

——, *The Cheyennes: Indians of the Great Plains* (New York, 1960).

——, "William Robertson: An Eighteenth Century Anthropologist-Historian" (*American Anthropologist,* vol. 62, 1960), pp. 648–655.

——, "Keresan Pueblo Law," in L. Nader (ed.), *Law in Culture and Society* (Chicago, 1969), pp. 92–116.

Hogbin, H. I., *Law and Order in Polynesia: A Study of Primitive Legal Institutions* (New York, 1934).

——, *Social Change* (London, 1958).

Hole, F., and R. F. Heizer, *An Introduction to Prehistoric Archaeology* (New York, 1965).

Holleman, J. F., *African Interlude* (Johannesburg, 1958).

Hollis, A. C., *The Nandi* (Oxford, 1909).

Holmes, O. W., Jr., *The Common Law* (Boston, 1881).

——, "The Path of the Law" (*Harvard Law Review,* vol. 10, 1897).

——, "Law in Science and Science in Law" (*Harvard Law Review,* vol. 12, 1899), pp. 443–463.

——, *McDonald v. Maybee* (*Supreme Court Reporter,* vol. 37, 1917), p. 343.

Holmes, W. H., *Ancient Art of the Province of Chiriqui* (Bureau of American Ethnology, Annual Report 6, 1888).

Homans, G. C., and D. M. Schneider, *Marriage, Authority, and Final Causes: A Study of Unilateral Cross-cousin Marriage* (Glencoe, Ill., 1955).

Hooton, E. A., *Up from the Ape* (rev. ed., New York, 1947).

Hostetler, J. A., *The Amish* (Baltimore, Md., 1964).

Howell, F. C., "The Place of Neandertal Man in Human Evolution" (*American Journal of Physical Anthropology,* vol. 9, 1951), pp. 379ff.

——, "Pleistocene Glacial Ecology and the Evolution of 'Classical Neandertal' Man" (*Southwestern Journal of Anthropology,* vol. 8, 1952), pp. 377–410.

——, "The Evolutionary Significance of Variation and Varieties of 'Neanderthal' Man" (*Quarterly Review of Biology,* vol. 32, no. 4, 1957), pp. 330–347.

——, "Potassium-Argon Dating at Olduvai Gorge" (*Current Anthropology,* vol. 3, no. 3, 1962), pp. 306–308.

——, "Observations on the Earlier Phases of the European Lower Paleolithic," in J. D. Clark and F. C. Howell (eds.), "Recent Studies in Paleoanthropology" (*American Anthropologist,* vol. 68, no. 2, part 2, Special Publication, 1966), pp. 88–200.

——, "Remains of Hominidae from Pliocene/

Pleistocene Formation in the Lower Ono Basin, Ethiopia" (*Nature,* vol. 223, 1969), pp. 1234–1239.

——— and F. Bourliere (eds.), *African Ecology and Human Evolution* (Chicago, 1963).

Howell, P. P., *A Manual of Nuer Law: Being an Account of Customary Law, Its Evolution and Development in the Courts Established by the Sudan Government* (London, 1954).

Howells, W. W., "Fossil Man and the Origin of Races" (*American Anthropologist,* vol. 44, 1942), pp. 182–193.

———, *The Heathens* (Garden City, N.Y., 1948).

———, *Back of History* (Garden City, N.Y., 1954).

———, *Mankind in the Making* (New York, 1959).

———, "The Distribution of Man," in Scientific American, *Human Variation and Origins: An Introduction to Human Biology and Evolution* (San Francisco, 1967), pp. 215–223.

Howitt, A. W., *The Native Tribes of South-east Australia* (New York, 1904).

Hrdlička, A., *The Neandertal Phase of Man* (Smithsonian Institution, Annual Report, 1928), pp. 593–623.

Hsu, F. L. K., *Religion, Science and Human Crisis* (London, 1952).

———, *The Study of Literate Civilizations* (New York, 1969).

———, *Americans and Chinese: Purpose and Fulfillment in Great Civilizations* (Garden City, N.Y., 1970).

Huang, S. S., and T. M. Bayless, "Milk and Lactose Intolerance in Healthy Orientals" (*Science,* vol. 160, 1966), pp. 83–84.

Hulse, F. S., *The Human Species* (rev. ed., New York, 1971).

Hutton, J. H., *Caste in India: Its Nature, Function, and Origin* (London, 1946).

Huxley, J. S., *Evolution in Action* (London, 1953).

Huxley, T. H., *Evidence as to Man's Place in Nature* (London, 1863).

Inverarity, R. B., *Art of the Northwest Coast Indians* (Berkeley, Calif., 1950).

Izikowitz, K. G., *Lamet: Hill Peasants in French Indochina* (Goteborg, 1951).

Jeffrey, M. D. W., "Lobola Is Child-price" (*African Studies,* vol. 10, 1951), pp. 1–40.

Jelínek, J., "Neanderthal Man and *Homo sapiens* in Central and Eastern Europe" (*Current Anthropology,* vol. 10, no. 5, 1969), pp. 475–503.

Jenks, A., *Wild Rice Culture of the Upper Great Lakes Region* (Bureau of American Ethnology, Annual Report 19, 1898).

Jenness, D., *The Indians of Canada* (National Museum of Canada Bulletin 68, Anthropological Series, no. 15, 2d ed., 1934).

Jennings, J. D., *Prehistory of North America* (New York, 1968).

——— and E. Norbeck (eds.), *Prehistoric Man in the New World* (Chicago, 1964).

Jhering, R. von, *Law as Means to an End* (translated from the German, New York, 1924).

Jocano, F. L., *Growing Up in a Philippine Barrio* (New York, 1969).

Jochelson, W., "Past and Present Subterranean Dwellings of the Tribes of North Eastern Asia and North Western America" (*Proceedings of the Fifteenth International Congress of Americanists,* Quebec, 1907).

Jolly, C. J., "The Seed-eaters: A New Model of Hominoid Differentiation Based on a Baboon Analogy" (*Man,* vol. 5, 1970), pp. 5–26.

Junod, A. H., *The Life of a South African Tribe* (2 vols., London, 1913).

Kaplan, D., "The Superorganic: Science or Metaphysics?" (*American Anthropologist,* vol. 67, 1965), pp. 958–976.

Kardiner, A. (ed.), *The Individual and His Society* (New York, 1939).

——— (ed.), *The Psychological Frontiers of Society* (New York, 1945).

——— and E. Preble, *They Studied Man* (New York, 1961).

Keesing, F. M., "Some Notes on Bontoc Social Organization, Northern Philippines" (*American Anthropologist,* vol. 51, 1949), pp. 578–600.

Kennedy, R., "Bark Cloth in Indonesia" (*Journal of the Polynesian Society,* no. 172, 1934).

———, *Islands and Peoples of the Indies* (Smithsonian Institution War Background Studies, no. 14, 1943).

Kenyon, K., *Digging up Jericho* (London and New York, 1957).

Kitching, J. W., *Bone, Tooth and Horn Tools of "Paleolithic Man"* (Manchester, 1963).

Klinger, H. P., et al., "The Chromosomes of the Hominoidea," in S. L. Washburn (ed.), *Classification and Human Evolution* (Chicago, 1963), pp. 235–242.

Kluckhohn, C., "Some Reflections on the Method and Theory of the Kulturkreislehre" (*American Anthropologist,* vol. 38, 1936), pp. 157–196.

———, "The Place of Theory in Anthropological Science" (*Philosophy of Science,* vol. 6, 1939).

———, "The Influence of Psychiatry on Anthropology in America during the Past One Hundred Years," in J. K. Hall et al. (eds.), *One Hundred Years of American Psychiatry* (New York, 1944).

———, *Mirror for Man: The Relation of Anthropology to Modern Life* (New York, 1949).

———, "Philosophy of the Navaho Indians," in F. S. C. Northrop (ed.), *Ideological Differences and World Order* (New Haven, Conn., 1949), chap. 17.

——— and W. H. Kelley, "The Concept of Culture," in R. Linton (ed.), *The Science of Man in the World Crisis* (New York, 1945), pp. 78–102.

——— and D. Leighton, *The Navaho* (Cambridge, Mass., 1946).

——— and O. H. Mowrer, "'Culture and Personality': A Conceptual Scheme" (*American Anthropologist,* vol. 46, 1944), pp. 1–29.

Knopf, A., "Measuring Geologic Time" (*Scientific Monthly,* November, 1957), pp. 225–236.

Köhler, W., *The Mentality of Apes* (New York, 1925).

Kortland, A., "Chimpanzees in the Wild" (*Scientific American,* vol. 206, 1962), pp. 128–134.

Kranz, G., "Brain Size and Hunting Ability in Earliest Man" (*Current Anthropology,* vol. 9, no. 5, 1968), pp. 450–451.

Krieger, A. D., "Early Man in the New World," in J. D. Jennings and E. Norbeck (eds.), *Prehistoric Man in the New World* (Chicago, 1964), pp. 23–84.

Krieger, H. W., "Design Areas in Oceania" (*United States National Museum Proceedings,* vol. 79, 1932), pp. 1–53.

Kroeber, A. L., "Classificatory Systems of Relationship" (*Journal of the Royal Anthropological Institute of Great Britain and Ireland,* vol. 39, 1909), pp. 77–84.

———, "The Superorganic" (*American Anthropologist,* vol. 19, 1917), pp. 163–213.

———, "Review of R. H. Lowie, *Primitive Society*" (*American Anthropologist,* vol. 22, 1920), pp. 377–381.

———, "Yurok Law" (*Proceedings of the Twenty-second International Congress of Americanists,* 1926), pp. 511–516.

———, "Caste" (*Encyclopaedia of the Social Sciences,* vol. 3, 1930), pp. 254–256.

———, *Cultural and Natural Areas of Native North America* (University of California Publications in American Archaeology and Ethnology, vol. 39, 1939).

———, "Stepdaughter Marriage" (*American Anthropologist,* vol. 42, 1940), pp. 562–570.

———, "Stimulus Diffusion" (*American Anthropologist,* vol. 42, 1940), pp. 1–20.

———, "Culture Element Distributions: XV, Salt, Dogs, Tobacco" (*Anthropological Records,* vol. 6, no. 1, 1941), pp. 1–20.

———, "Art," in J. H. Steward (ed.), *Handbook of South American Indians* (6 vols., Washington, D.C., 1946–1950), vol. 5, pp. 411–492.

——— (ed.), *Anthropology Today: An Encyclopedic Inventory* (Chicago, 1953).

———, "Critical Summary and Commentary," in R. F. Spencer (ed.), *Method and Perspective in Anthropology: Papers in Honor of Wilson D. Wallis* (Minneapolis, 1954), pp. 273–299.

———, "Preface," in W. Goldschmidt (ed.), *The Anthropology of Franz Boas* (American Anthropological Association Memoir 89, 1959), pp. v–vii.

———, *Style and Civilizations* (2d ed., Ithaca, N.Y., 1963).

——— and C. Kluckhohn, *Culture: A Critical Re-*

view of Concepts and Definitions (Anthropological Papers, Peabody Museum, no. 47, 1952).

Kuper, H., *The Swazi: A South African Kingdom* (New York, 1963).

Kurth, G. (ed.), *Evolution and Hominization* (Stuttgart, 1962).

Kwang-chih Chang, "New Evidence on Fossil Man in China" (*Science,* vol. 136, no. 3518, 1962), pp. 749–760.

LaBarre, W., *The Peyote Cult* (Yale University Publications in Anthropology, no. 19, 1938).

——, "Potato Taxonomy among the Aymara Indians of Bolivia" (*Acta Americana,* vol. 5, 1947), pp. 83–102.

——, *The Human Animal* (Chicago, 1954).

——, *The Ghost Dance: Origins of Religion* (Garden City, N.Y., 1970).

Lafitau, J. F., *Moeurs des sauvages américains comparées aux moeurs des premiers temps* (Paris, 1724).

Lambert, B., "Ambilineal Descent Groups in the Northern Gilbert Islands" (*American Anthropologist,* vol. 68, 1966), pp. 641–664.

Landes, R., "The Ojibwa of Canada," in M. Mead (ed.), *Cooperation and Competition among Primitive Peoples* (New York, 1937), pp. 87–126.

Lang, A., *Myth, Ritual, and Religion* (London, 1887).

——, *The Making of Religion* (London, 1898).

——, *Social Origins* (London, 1903).

Langer, S., *Feeling and Form* (New York, 1953).

Lantis, M., "The Alaskan Whale Cult and Its Affinities" (*American Anthropologist,* vol. 40, 1938), pp. 438–464.

Laqueur, W., "Revolution" (*International Encyclopedia of the Social Sciences,* vol. 13, 1968), pp. 501–507.

Lawrence, P., *Road Belong Cargo: A Study of the Cargo Movement in the Southern Madang District, New Guinea* (New York, 1969).

Leach, E. R., *Rethinking Anthropology* (London School of Economics, Monographs on Social Anthropology, no. 22, 1961).

——, "The Epistemological Background to Malinowski's Empiricism," in R. Firth (ed.), *Man and Culture: An Evaluation of the Work of Bronislaw Malinowski* (London, 1957), pp. 119–137.

—— (ed.), *Aspects of Caste in South India, Ceylon and North-west Pakistan* (Cambridge, 1960).

Leach, M. (ed.), *Standard Dictionary of Folklore, Mythology and Legend* (2 vols., New York, 1949).

Leakey, L. S. B., *Olduwai Gorge: A Report on the Evolution of the Hand-axe Culture in Beds I–IV, with Chapters on the Geology and Fauna by the Late Prof. Hans Reck and Dr. A. T. Hopwood* (Cambridge, England, 1951).

——, "A New Lower Pliocene Fossil Primate from Kenya" (*Annals and Magazine of Natural History,* vol. 14, 1961), pp. 689–696.

——, "East African Hominoidea and the Classification within the Super-family," in S. L. Washburn (ed.), *Classification and Human Evolution* (Chicago, 1963), pp. 32–49.

Leakey, R. E., "Early *Homo sapiens* Remains from the Omo River Region of Southwest Ethiopia" (*Nature,* vol. 222, 1969), pp. 1132–1138.

Lee, D. D., "Being and Value in a Primitive Culture" (*Journal of Philosophy,* vol. 46, 1939), pp. 401–415.

Lee, O., "Social Values and the Philosophy of Law" (*Virginia Law Review,* vol. 32, 1946), pp. 802–817.

Lee, R. B., and J. DeVore (eds.), *Man the Hunter* (Chicago, 1968).

Le Gros Clark, W. E., "Hominid Characteristics of the Australopithecine Dentition" (*Journal of the Royal Anthropological Institute of Great Britain and Ireland,* vol. 80, 1952), pp. 37–54.

——, *History of the Primates: An Introduction to the Study of Fossil Man* (4th ed., London, 1954).

——, *The Fossil Evidence for Human Evolution: An Introduction to the Study of Paleoanthropology* (Chicago, 1955).

—— and L. S. B. Leakey, *The Miocene Hominidae of East Africa* (British Museum Fossil Mammals of Africa, no. 1, 1951).

Lehmer, D. J., *Introduction to Middle Missouri Archeology* (Washington, 1971).

León-Portillo, M., *Pre-Columbian Literatures of Mexico* (Norman, Okla., 1969).

Lerner, J. M., *Heredity, Evolution, Society* (San Francisco, 1968).

Leslie, C. M., *Now We Are Civilized: A Study of the World View of the Zapotec Indians of Mitla, Oaxaca* (Detroit, 1960).

Lessa, W. A., *An Appraisal of Constitutional Typologies* (American Anthropological Association Memoir 62, 1945).

—— and E. Z. Vogt, *Reader in Comparative Religion: An Anthropological Approach* (2d ed., New York, 1965).

Lesser, A., "Levirate and Fraternal Polyandry among the Pawnees" (*Man,* vol. 30, no. 77, 1930), pp. 98–101.

Lévi-Strauss, C., *Tristes Tropique* (J. Russell, trans., New York, 1964).

——, *Structural Anthropology* (C. Jacobson and B. G. Schoepf, trans., Garden City, N.Y., 1967).

——, *The Elementary Structures of Kinship* (*Les Structures Élémentaires de la Parenté*) (rev. ed., J. H. Bell, J. R. von Sturmer, and R. Needham, trans., Boston, 1969).

Levy, M. J., Jr., "Notes on the Hsu Hypothesis," in F. L. K. Hsu (ed.), *Kinship and Culture* (Chicago, 1971), pp. 33–41.

—— and L. A. Fallers, "The Family: Some Comparative Considerations" (*American Anthropologist,* vol. 61, 1959), pp. 647–651.

Lewin, J., *Studies in African Native Law* (Cape Town and Philadelphia, 1947).

Lewis, I. M., "The Northern Pastoral Somali of the Horn," in J. L. Gibbs, Jr. (ed.), *Peoples of Africa* (New York, 1965), pp. 319–360.

Lewis, M., and W. Clark, *History of the Expedition of Captains Lewis and Clark: 1804–05–06* (Hosmer ed., 2 vols., Chicago, 1902).

Lewis, O., *The Effects of White Contact upon Blackfoot Culture, with Special Reference to the Role of the Fur Trade* (American Ethnological Society Monograph 6, 1942).

——, "Comparisons in Cultural Anthropology," in W. L. Thomas (ed.), *Yearbook of Anthropology—1955* (New York, 1955).

——, *The Children of Sanchez* (New York, 1961).

——, "Mother and Son in a Puerto Rican Slum: Part 1; Felicita" (*Harper's Magazine,* December, 1965).

Lewis, P. H., *The Social Context of Art in Northern New Ireland* (Fieldiana: Anthropology, vol. 58), 1969.

Lienhardt, G., *Social Anthropology* (Oxford, 1965).

Life, Editors of, *The Epic of Man* (New York, 1961).

Lindzey, G., *Projective Techniques and Cross-cultural Research* (New York, 1961).

Linton, R., "Culture Areas in Madagascar" (*American Anthropologist,* vol. 30, 1928), pp. 363–390.

——, *The Tanala: A Hill Tribe of Madagascar* (Field Museum of Natural History, Anthropological Series, vol. 22, 1933).

——, *The Study of Man* (New York, 1936).

——, "The Marquesas," in A. Kardiner (ed.), *The Individual and His Society* (New York, 1939), pp. 197–250.

——, "The Tanala," in A. Kardiner (ed.), *The Individual and His Society* (New York, 1939), pp. 251–290.

—— (ed.), *Acculturation in Seven American Indian Tribes* (New York, 1940).

——, *The Cultural Background of Personality* (New York, 1945).

—— (ed.), *The Science of Man in the World Crisis* (New York, 1945).

——, *The Tree of Culture* (New York, 1955).

—— and P. S. Wingert, *Arts of the South Seas* (New York, 1946).

Little, K. L., *West African Urbanization: A Study of Voluntary Associations in Social Change* (Cambridge, England, 1965).

Llewellyn, K. N., and E. A. Hoebel, *The Cheyenne Way: Conflict and Case Law in Primitive Jurisprudence* (Norman, Okla., 1941).

Lloyd, S., *Early Highland People of Anatolia* (New York, 1968).

Loeb, E. M., "Javanese Word Formation, High and Low" (*Journal of the American Oriental Society,* vol. 64, 1944), pp. 113–126.

—— and J. O. M. Broek, "Social Organization

and the Long House in Southeast Asia'' (*American Anthropologist,* vol. 49, 1947), pp. 414–425.

Lounsbury, F. G., "A Formal Account of the Crow and Omaha-type Kinship Terminologies," in W. H. Goodenough (ed.), *Explorations in Cultural Anthropology: Essays in Honor of George Peter Murdock* (New York, 1964), pp. 351–393.

Lowie, R. H., *The Northern Shoshone* (American Museum of Natural History, Anthropological Papers, vol. 2, 1909).

——, *Societies of the Crow, Hidatsa and Mandan Indians* (American Museum of Natural History, Anthropological Papers, vol. 11, 1913).

——, *Plains Indian Age Societies: Historical Summary* (American Museum of Natural History, Anthropological Papers, vol. 11, 1916), pp. 877–984.

——, *Primitive Society* (New York, 1920).

——, *Notes on Shoshonean Ethnography* (American Museum of Natural History, Anthropological Papers, vol. 20, part 3, 1924).

——, *Primitive Religion* (New York, 1924).

——, *The Origin of the State* (New York, 1927).

——, "Incorporeal Property in Primitive Society" (*Yale Law Journal,* vol. 37, 1928), pp. 551–563.

——, "Kinship" (*Encyclopaedia of the Social Sciences,* vol. 3, 1932), pp. 568–572.

——, *The Crow Indians* (New York, 1935).

——, "Lewis Henry Morgan in Historical Perspective," in *Essays in Anthropology in Honor of Alfred Louis Kroeber* (Berkeley, Calif., 1936), pp. 169–181.

——, *The History of Ethnological Theory* (New York, 1937).

——, *An Introduction to Cultural Anthropology* (rev. ed., New York, 1940).

——, "Property Rights and Coercive Powers of the Plains Indian Military Societies" (*Journal of Legal and Political Sociology,* vol. 1, 1943), pp. 59–71.

——, "Evolution in Cultural Anthropology: A Reply to Leslie White" (*American Anthropologist,* vol. 48, 1946), pp. 223–233.

Lucretius, T., *Lucretius, the Way Things Are: The Rerum Natura of Titus Lucretius Carus, translated by Rolfe Humphries* (Bloomington, Ind., 1968).

McClelland, D. C., *The Achieving Society* (Princeton, N.J., 1961).

McCown, T. D., and A. Keith, *The Stone Age of Mt. Carmel,* vol. II, *The Fossil Human Remains from the Levalloiso-Mousterian* (Oxford, 1939).

MacIver, R. M., *Society: Its Structure and Changes* (New York, 1931).

——, "Government and Property" (*Journal of Legal and Political Sociology,* vol. 4, 1946), pp. 5–18.

——, *The Web of Government* (New York, 1947).

McKern, T. C., *Readings in Physical Anthropology* (Englewood Cliffs, N.J., 1966).

McLennan, J. F., *Primitive Marriage* (Edinburgh, 1865).

——, *The Patriarchal Theory* (London, 1885).

MacNeish, R. S., "The Origin of New World Cultivation" (*Scientific American,* vol. 211, 1964), pp. 29–37.

Maine, H. S., *Ancient Law: Its Connection with the Early History of Society, and Its Relation to Modern Ideas* (3d American ed., New York, 1879).

Mair, L., *Primitive Government* (Baltimore, Md., 1964).

Malinowski, B., *Argonauts of the Western Pacific: An Account of Native Enterprise and Adventure in the Archipelagoes of Melanesian New Guinea* (London, 1922).

——, *Crime and Custom in Savage Society* (New York, 1926).

——, *The Father in Primitive Psychology* (New York, 1927).

——, *Sex and Repression in Savage Society* (New York, 1927).

——, "Culture" (*Encyclopaedia of the Social Sciences,* vol. 4, 1931), pp. 621–646.

——, *Coral Gardens and Their Magic: A Study of the Methods of Tilling the Soil and of Agricultural Rites in the Trobriand Islands* (2 vols., New York, 1935).

——, "Preface," in R. Firth, *We, the Tikopia* (London, 1936), pp. vii–xi.

——, *Freedom and Civilization* (New York, 1944).

——, *Magic, Science and Religion and Other Essays* (Glencoe, Ill., 1948).

Mallowan, M. E. L., *Early Mesopotamia and Iran* (New York, 1965).

Malthus, T. R., *An Essay on the Principle of Population: or, A View of Its Past and Present Effects on Human Happiness; with an Inquiry into Our Prospects Respecting the Future Removal or Mitigation of the Evils Which It Occasions* (London, 1798).

Mandelbaum, D. G., *Society in India* (2 vols., Berkeley, Calif., 1970).

———, G. W. Lasker, and E. M. Albert, *The Teaching of Anthropology* (Berkeley and Los Angeles, Calif., 1963).

Maquet, J., "Introduction to Aesthetic Anthropology" (*McCaleb Module in Anthropology,* Reading, Mass., 1971).

Marett, R. R., *The Threshold of Religion* (2d ed., London, 1914).

Marshall, G. A., "Marriage: Comparative Analysis" (*International Encyclopedia of the Social Sciences,* vol. 10, 1968), pp. 8–19.

Mason, O. T., *Aboriginal American Basketry* (United States National Museum, Annual Report, 1904), pp. 171–548.

Mauss, M., *The Gift: Forms and Functions of Exchange in Archaic Societies* (I. Cunnison, trans., London, 1954).

Mead, M., *Coming of Age in Samoa: A Psychological Study of Primitive Youth for Western Civilization* (New York, 1928).

———, *Growing up in New Guinea: A Comparative Study of Primitive Education* (New York, 1930).

———, *Sex and Temperament in Three Primitive Societies* (New York, 1935).

——— (ed.), *Cooperation and Competition among Primitive Peoples* (New York, 1937).

———, *And Keep Your Powder Dry* (New York, 1942).

———, "On the Implications for Anthropology of the Gesell-Ilg Approach to Maturation" (*American Anthropologist,* vol. 49, 1947), pp. 69–77.

———, *Male and Female: A Study of the Sexes in the Changing World* (New York, 1949).

———, *New Lives for Old: Cultural Transformation —Manus, 1928–1953* (New York, 1953).

———, "Some Theoretical Considerations on the Problem of Mother-Child Separation" (*American Journal of Orthopsychiatry,* vol. 24, 1954), pp. 471–483.

——— (ed.), *Cultural Patterns and Technical Change* (New York, 1955).

——— and M. Wolfenstein (eds.), *Childhood in Contemporary Cultures* (Chicago, 1955).

Meadow, R. H., "The Emergence of Civilization," in H. L. Shapiro (ed.), *Man, Culture and Society* (rev. ed., Oxford, 1971), pp. 112–167.

Meek, C. K., *Tribal Studies in Northern Nigeria* (2 vols., Oxford, 1925).

Meggitt, J. M., "Male-Female Relations in the Highlands of Australian New Guinea" (*American Anthropologist,* vol. 66, no. 4, part 2, Special Publication, 1964), pp. 204–224.

Meighan, C. W., *Archaeology: An Introduction* (San Francisco, 1966).

Mellaart, J., "A Neolithic City in Turkey" (*Scientific American,* vol. 210, no. 4, 1964), pp. 94–105.

———, *Earliest Civilizations of the Near East* (New York, 1966).

Merriam, A. P., *A Prologue to the Study of African Arts* (Yellow Springs, Ohio, 1962).

Métraux, A., "The Botocudo," in J. H. Steward (ed.), *Handbook of South American Indians* (6 vols., Washington, D.C., 1946–1950), vol. 1, pp. 531–540.

———, "The Tupinamba," in J. H. Steward (ed.), *Handbook of South American Indians* (6 vols., Washington, D.C., 1946–1950), vol. 3, pp. 95–133.

———, "Warfare, Cannibalism, and Human Trophies," in J. H. Steward (ed.), *Handbook of South American Indians* (6 vols., Washington, D.C., 1946–1950), vol. 5, pp. 383–409.

Middleton, J. (ed.), *From Child to Adult: Studies in the Anthropology of Education* (Garden City, N.Y., 1970).

Middleton, R., "Brother-Sister and Father-Daughter Marriage in Ancient Greece" (*American Sociological Review,* vol. 27, 1962), pp. 603–611.

Miller, N., and J. Dollard, *Social Learning and Imitation* (New Haven, Conn., 1941).

Millikan, R. A., "Science and the World Tomorrow" *Scientific Monthly,* vol. 49, 1939), pp. 212–240.

Mills, G., "Art: An Introduction to Qualitative Anthropology," in C. M. Otten (ed.), *Anthropology and Art,* pp. 66–92.

Mirov, N. T., "Notes on the Domestication of the Reindeer" (*American Anthropologist,* vol. 47, 1945), pp. 393–408.

Mishkin, B., *Rank and Warfare among the Plains Indians* (American Ethnological Society Monograph 3, 1940).

Mombert, P., "Class" (*Encyclopaedia of the Social Sciences,* vol. 3, 1930), pp. 531–536.

Mongait, A., *Archaeology in the U.S.S.R.* (Moscow, 1959).

Montagu, M. F. A. (ed.), *Culture Man's Adaptive Mechanism* (London and New York, 1968).

Mooney, J., *The Ghost Dance Religion and the Sioux Outbreak of 1890* (Bureau of American Ethnology, Annual Report 14, 1896).

Moore, W. E., *Social Change* (Englewood Cliffs, N.J., 1963).

Morant, G. M., "The Form of the Swanscombe Skull" (*Journal of the Royal Anthropological Institute of Great Britain and Ireland,* vol. 68, 1938), pp. 67–97.

Morgan, L. H., *Ancient Society, or Researches in the Lines of Human Progress from Savagery, through Barbarism to Civilization* (New York, 1877).

——, *Houses and House Life of the American Aborigines* (Contributions to American Ethnology, vol. 4, 1881).

——, *The League of the Ho-dé-no-sau-nee or Iroquois* (2 vols., New Haven, Conn., 1954).

Morley, S. G., *The Ancient Maya* (Stanford, Calif., 1946).

Morris, D., *The Naked Ape: A Zoologist's Study of the Human Animal* (New York, 1967).

Movius, H. L., Jr., *Early Man and Pleistocene Stratigraphy in Southern and Eastern Asia* (Papers of the Peabody Museum of American Archaeology and Ethnology, Harvard University, vol. 19, 1944).

——, "Old World Prehistory: Paleolithic," in A. L. Kroeber (ed.), *Anthropology Today: An Encyclopedic Inventory* (Chicago, 1953), pp. 163–192.

Murdock, G. P., "The Science of Culture" (*American Anthropologist,* vol. 34, 1932), pp. 200–215.

——, *Our Primitive Contemporaries* (New York, 1934).

——, "Comparative Data on the Division of Labor by Sex" (*Social Forces,* vol. 15, 1937), pp. 551–553.

——, "Double Descent" (*American Anthropologist,* vol. 42, 1940), pp. 555–561.

——, "Bifurcate Merging: A Test of Five Theories" (*American Anthropologist,* vol. 49, 1947), pp. 56–68.

——, *Social Structure* (New York, 1949).

——, "Family Stability in Non-European Cultures" (*Annals of the American Academy of Political and Social Sciences,* vol. 272, 1950), pp. 195–201.

——, "World Ethnographic Sample" (*American Anthropologist,* vol. 59, 1957), pp. 664–687.

—— (ed.), *Social Structure in Southeast Asia* (Viking Fund Publications in Anthropology, no. 29, 1960).

——, *Ethnographic Atlas* (Pittsburgh, 1967).

——, "The Current Status of the World's Hunting and Gathering Peoples," in R. B. Lee and I. deVore (eds.), *Man the Hunter* (Chicago, 1968), pp. 13–20.

Murphy, R. F., and L. Kasdan, "The Structure of Parallel Cousin Marriage" (*American Anthropologist,* vol. 61, 1959), pp. 17–29.

Myrdal, G. S., *An American Dilemma: The Negro Problem and Modern Democracy* (2 vols., New York, 1944).

Nadel, S. F., "The Kede: A Riverian State in Northern Nigeria," in E. E. Evans-Pritchard and M. Fortes (eds.), *African Political Systems* (Oxford, 1940), pp. 165–195.

Nader, L. (ed.), *Law in Culture and Society* (Chicago, 1969).

Napier, J., and N. A. Barnicot (eds.), *The Primates* (Symposia of the Zoological Society of London, 1963).

Naroll, R., and R. Cohen, *A Handbook of Method in Cultural Anthropology* (Garden City, N.Y., 1970).

Needham, R., *Structure and Sentiment* (Chicago, 1962).

Nelson, E. W., *The Eskimos About Bering Straits* (Bureau of American Ethnology, Annual Report 18, 1899).

Netting, R. M., *Hill Farmers of Nigeria: Cultural Ecology of the Kofyar of the Jos Plateau* (American Ethnological Society, Monograph 46, 1968).

Niblack, A. P., *The Coast Indians of Southern Alaska and Northern British Columbia* (Board of Regents of the Smithsonian Institution, Annual Report, 1890).

Niehoff, A. H. (ed.), *A Casebook of Social Change* (Chicago, 1966).

Norbeck, E., *Takashima: A Japanese Fishing Community* (Salt Lake City, 1954).

——, *Religion in Primitive Society* (New York, 1961).

——, "Peasant Society," in J. Gould and W. L. Kolb (eds.), *A Dictionary of the Social Sciences* (Glencoe, Ill., 1964), pp. 490–491.

Northrop, F. S. C. (ed.), *Ideological Differences and World Order* (New Haven, Conn., 1949).

Oakley, K. P., *Man, the Tool Maker* (Chicago, 1957).

——, "On Man's Use of Fire, with Comments on Tool-making and Hunting," in S. L. Washburn (ed.), *Social Life of Early Man* (Chicago, 1961), pp. 176–193.

——, *Frameworks for Dating Fossil Man* (Chicago, 1964).

—— and H. M. Muir-Wood, *The Succession of Life through Geologic Time* (2d ed., London, 1952).

Oberg, K., "The Kingdom of Ankole in Uganda," in E. E. Evans-Pritchard and M. Fortes (eds.), *African Political Systems* (Oxford, 1940), pp. 121–162.

Olearius, *The Description of the Journey in Muscovia* (Moscow, 1906).

Oliver, D. L., *A Solomon Island Society: Kinship and Leadership among the Siuai of Bougainville* (Cambridge, Mass., 1953).

O'Neale, L. M., "Weaving," in J. H. Steward (ed.), *Handbook of South American Indians* (6 vols., Washington, D.C., 1946–1950), vol. 5, pp. 97–138.

Opler, M. E., *An Apache Life-way: The Economic, Social, and Religious Institutions of the Chiricahua* (Chicago, 1942).

——, "Themes as Dynamic Forces in Culture" (*American Journal of Sociology,* vol. 51, 1945), pp. 198–206.

Opler, M. K., "The Integration of the Sun Dance in Ute Religion" (*American Anthropologist,* vol. 43, 1941), pp. 550–572.

——, *Culture, Psychiatry and Human Values: The Methods and Values of a Social Psychiatry* (Springfield, Ill., 1956).

Osgood, C., *Ingalik Material Culture* (Yale University Publications in Anthropology, no. 22, 1940).

Otten, C. M. (ed.), *Anthropology and Art: Readings in Cross-cultural Aesthetics* (Garden City, N.Y., 1971).

Paddock, J., "Archaeology and Indigenismo" (*América Indigena,* vol. 18, 1958), pp. 71–81.

Park, W. Z., "Paviotso Polyandry" (*American Anthropologist,* vol. 39, 1937), pp. 366–368.

——, *Shamanism in Western North America: A Study in Cultural Relationships* (Evanston and Chicago, Ill., 1938).

Parsons, E. C., *American Indian Life* (New York, 1923).

——, *Pueblo Indian Religion* (2 vols., Chicago, 1937).

Patai, R., "Cousin-right in Middle Eastern Marriage" (*Southwestern Journal of Anthropology,* vol. 11, 1955), pp. 371–390.

Paul, B. D., "Interview Techniques and Field Relationships," in A. L. Kroeber, *Anthropology Today: An Encyclopedic Inventory* (Chicago, 1953), pp. 430–451.

——, "Teaching Anthropology in Schools of Public Health," in D. G. Mandelbaum, G. W. Lasker, and E. M. Albert (eds.), *The Teaching of Anthropology* (Berkeley and Los Angeles, Calif., 1963), pp. 503–512.

Penniman, T. K., *One Hundred Years of Anthropology* (Cambridge, Mass., 1936).

Perrot, J., "Palestine-Syria-Cilicia," in R. J. Braidwood and G. R. Willey (eds.), *Courses toward Urban Life: Archaeological Considerations of Some Cultural Alternatives* (Chicago, 1962), pp. 147–164.

Pettitt, G. A., *Primitive Education in North America*

(University of California Publications in American Archaeology and Ethnology, vol. 43, no. 1, 1946).

Pfeiffer, J. E., *The Emergence of Man* (New York, 1969).

Piggot, S. (ed.), *The Dawn of Civilization: The First World Survey of Human Civilizations in Early Times* (New York, 1961).

Pike, K. L., *Language in Relation to a Unified Theory of the Structure of Human Behavior* (Glendale, Calif., 1950).

Pilbeam, D., *The Evolution of Man* (New York, 1970).

Polanyi, K., *The Great Transformation* (New York, 1944).

—— and A. Rotstein, *Dahomey and the Slave Trade: An Analysis of an Archaic Economy* (Seattle and London, 1966).

Pospisil, L., *Kapauku Papuans and Their Law* (Yale University Publications in Anthropology, no. 54, 1958).

——, *The Kapauku Papuans of West New Guinea* (New York, 1963).

——, "Structural Change and Primitive Law: Consequences of a Papuan Legal Case," in L. Nader (ed.), *Law in Society and Culture* (Chicago, 1969), pp. 208–229.

——, *Anthropology of Law: A Comparative Theory* (New York, 1971).

Potter, J. M., "Peasants in the Modern World," in J. M. Potter, M. N. Diaz, and G. M. Foster (eds.), *Peasant Society: A Reader* (Boston, 1967), pp. 378–383.

——, M. N. Diaz, and G. M. Foster (eds.), *Peasant Society: A Reader* (Boston, 1967).

Pound, R., "A Theory of Legal Interests" (*American Sociological Society Publications*, vol. 16, 1920).

Powdermaker, H., *Life in Lesu: The Study of a Melanesian Society in New Ireland* (London, 1933).

——, *Stranger and Friend: The Way of An Anthropologist* (New York, 1966).

Powell, H. A., "Competitive Leadership in Trobriand Political Organization," in R. Cohen and J. Middleton (eds.), *Comparative Political Systems: Studies in the Politics of Pre-industrial Societies* (Garden City, N.Y., 1967), pp. 155–192.

Prins, A. H. J., *East African Age Class Systems: An Inquiry into the Social Order of Galla, Kipsigis and Kikuyu* (Groningen and Djakarta, 1953).

Provinse, J. H., "Cooperative Ricefield Cultivation among the Siang Dyaks of Central Borneo" (*American Anthropologist*, vol. 39, 1937), pp. 77–102.

Radcliffe-Brown, A. R., *The Andaman Islanders* (Cambridge, England, 1922).

——, "The Social Organization of Australian Tribes (*Oceania*, vol. 1, nos. 1–4, 1930–1931; reprinted as Oceania Monographs, no. 1, Melbourne, 1931.)

——, "On the Concept of Functionalism in the Social Sciences" (*American Anthropologist,* vol. 37, 1935), pp. 394–402.

——, "Patrilineal and Matrilineal Succession" (*Iowa Law Review,* vol. 20, 1935), pp. 286–298.

——, *A Natural Science of Society* (Chicago, 1948).

——, *Structure and Function in Primitive Society: Essays and Addresses* (Glencoe, Ill., 1952).

—— and M. Fortes (eds.), *African Systems of Kinship and Marriage* (Oxford, 1950).

Radin, M., "A Restatement of Hohfeld" (*Harvard Law Review,* vol. 51, 1938), pp. 1141ff.

Radin, P., *The Winnebago Tribe* (Bureau of American Ethnology, Annual Report 37, 1923).

—— (ed.), *Crashing Thunder: The Autobiography of an American Indian* (New York, 1926).

——, *Monotheism in Primitive Religion* (New York, 1927).

——, *Primitive Man as Philosopher* (New York, 1927).

——, "The Mind of Primitive Man" (*New Republic,* vol. 98, 1939), p. 303.

Rasmussen, K., *Grønlandsagen* (Berlin, 1922).

——, *Across Arctic America* (New York, 1927).

Rattray, R. S., *Ashanti* (Oxford, 1923).

——, *Ashanti Law and Constitution* (Oxford, 1927).

Ratzel, F., *Anthropogeographie* (2 vols., Stuttgart, 1882).

Ray, V. F., *The Sanpoil and Nespelem: Salishan*

Peoples of Northeastern Washington (University of Washington Publications in Anthropology, vol. 5, 1932).

Read, M., *Children of Their Fathers: Growing Up among the Ngomi of Malawi* (New York, 1968).

Reay, M., *The Kuma: Freedom and Conformity in the New Guinea Highlands* (Melbourne, 1959).

Reddy, N. S., *Transition in Caste Structure in Andrah Presh with Particular Reference to Depressed Castes* (Lucknow, 1952).

Redfield, R., *The Folk Culture of Yucatan* (Chicago, 1942).

———, "Maine's Ancient Law in the Light of Primitive Societies" (*Western Political Quarterly,* vol. 3, 1950), pp. 574–589.

———, *The Primitive World and Its Transformations* (Ithaca, N.Y., 1953).

———, *The Little Community and Peasant Society and Culture* (Chicago, 1960).

———, *The Social Uses of Social Science: The Papers of Robert Redfield* (2 vols.; edited by M. P. Redfield, Chicago, 1963).

———, *Art and Icon,* in C. M. Otten, *Anthropology and Art: Readings in Cross-cultural Aesthetics* (Garden City, N.Y., 1971), pp. 39–65.

———, M. J. Herskovits, and G. F. Ekholm, *Aspects of Primitive Art* (New York, 1959).

———, R. Linton, and M. J. Herskovits, "Memorandum for the Study of Acculturation" (*American Anthropologist,* vol. 36, 1938), pp. 149–152.

Reichard, G. A., *Prayer: The Compulsive Word* (American Ethnological Society Monograph 7, 1944).

Ribeiro, D., *The Civilizational Process* (B. M. Meggers trans., Washington, D.C., 1968).

Richards, A. I., *Land, Labour, and Diet in Northern Rhodesia* (Oxford, 1950).

Richardson, J., *Law and Status among the Kiowa Indians* (American Ethnological Society Monograph 1, 1940).

Rivers, W. H. R., *The Todas* (London, 1906).

———, *Kinship and Social Organization* (London, 1914).

Roach, M. E., and J. B. Eicher, *Dress, Ornament, and the Social Order* (New York, 1965).

Robbins, M. C., "House Types and Settlement Patterns: An Application of Ethnology to Archaeological Interpretation" (*Minnesota Archaeologist,* vol. 28, 1966), pp. 1–25.

Roberts, J. M., "The Self-management of Cultures," in W. H. Goodenough (ed.), *Explorations in Cultural Anthropology: Essays in Honor of George Peter Murdock* (New York, 1964), pp. 433–454.

———, "Oaths, Autonomic Ordeals, and Power," in L. Nader (ed.), *The Ethnography of Law* (*American Anthropologist,* vol. 67, no. 6, part 2, Special Publication, 1965), pp. 186–212.

——— and B. Sutton-Smith, "Child Training and Game Involvement" (*Ethnography,* vol. 1, 1962), pp. 166–185.

Robertson, W., *The History of America* (2 vols., 1st American ed., Philadelphia, 1812).

Robinson, J. T., *The Dentition of Australopithecus* (Transvaal Museum Memoirs, no. 9, 1956).

———, "The Australopithecines and Their Bearing on the Origin of Man and of Stone Tool-making" (*South African Journal of Science,* vol. 57, 1961), pp. 3–13.

———, "The Origins and Adaptive Radiation of the Australopithecines," in G. Kurth (ed.), *Evolution and Hominization* (Stuttgart, 1962), pp. 120–140.

———, "Adaptive Radiation in the Australopithecines and the Origin of Man," in F. C. Howell and F. Bourlière (eds.), *African Ecology and Human Evolution* (Chicago, 1963), pp. 385–416.

———, and R. J. Mason, "Occurrence of Stone Artifacts with *Australopithecus* at Sterkfontein" (*Nature,* vol. 180, 1957), pp. 521–524.

Roediger, V. M., *Ceremonial Costumes of the Pueblo Indians: Their Evolution, Fabrication, and Significance in the Prayer Drama* (Berkeley and Los Angeles, 1961, reprint).

Rohner, R. P., "Parental Rejection, Food Deprivation, and Personality Development: Tests of Alternative Hypotheses" (*Ethnography,* vol. 9, 1970), pp. 414–427.

Romer, A. S., *The Vertebrate Story* (4th ed., Chicago, 1959).

Roscoe, J., "The Bahima" (*Journal of the Royal Anthropological Institute of Great Britain and Ireland,* vol. 37, 1907), pp. 93–118.

——, *The Northern Bantu: An Account of Some Central African Tribes of the Uganda Protectorate* (2 vols., Cambridge, England, 1915).

——, *The Banyankole* (London, 1923).

Rosenfeld, A., *The Second Genesis: The Coming Control of Life* (Englewood Cliffs, N.J., 1969).

Rowe, J. H., "Inca Culture at the Time of the Spanish Conquest," in J. H. Steward (ed.), *Handbook of South American Indians* (6 vols., Washington, D.C., 1946–1950), vol. 2, pp. 183–330.

——, "The Renaissance Foundations of Anthropology" (*American Anthropologist,* vol. 67, 1965), pp. 1–20.

Sahlins, M. D., and E. R. Service (eds.), *Evolution and Culture* (Ann Arbor, Mich., 1960).

Salmond, J. W., *Jurisprudence* (7th ed., New York, 1924).

Sapir, E., "Culture, Genuine and Spurious" (*American Journal of Sociology,* vol. 29, 1924), pp. 401–429.

Sauer, C., "American Agricultural Origins: A Consideration of Nature and Culture," in *Essays in Anthropology in Honor of Alfred Louis Kroeber* (Berkeley, Calif., 1936), pp. 279–297.

Sayce, R. U., *Primitive Arts and Crafts: An Introduction to the Study of Material Culture* (Cambridge, England, 1933).

Schaller, G. B., *The Mountain Gorilla: Ecology and Behavior* (Chicago, 1963).

——, *The Year of the Gorilla* (Chicago, 1964).

Schapera, I., *A Handbook of Tswana Law and Custom: Compiled for the Bechuanaland Protectorate Administration* (Oxford, 1938).

——, *Tribal Legislation among the Tswana of the Bechuanaland Protectorate: A Study in the Mechanism of Change* (Monographs on Social Anthropology, London School of Economics and Political Science, no. 9, 1943).

——, *Married Life in a South African Tribe* (London, 1950).

——, *Government and Politics in Tribal Societies* (London, 1956).

Schmidt, W., *The Origin and Growth of Religion* (H. J. Rose, trans., New York, 1935).

——, "The Position of Women with Regard to Property in Primitive Society" (*American Anthropologist,* vol. 37, 1935), pp. 244–256.

Schneider, D. M., and K. Gough (eds.), *Matrilineal Kinship* (Berkeley and Los Angeles, 1961).

—— and G. C. Homans, "Kinship Terminology and the American Kinship System" (*American Anthropologist,* vol. 57, 1955), pp. 1194–1208.

Schoolcraft, R. H. (ed.), *History of the Indian Tribes of the United States* (Philadelphia, 1860).

Schurtz, H., *Altersklassen und Männerbunde* (Berlin, 1902).

Schwabedissen, H., "Northern Continental Europe," in R. J. Braidwood and G. R. Willey (eds.), *Courses toward Urban Life: Archeological Considerations of Some Cultural Alternatives* (Viking Fund Publications in Anthropology, no. 32, 1962), pp. 254–266.

Scientific American, *Human Variation and Origins: An Introduction to Human Biology and Evolution* (San Francisco, 1967).

Scientific American, "Energy and Power" (*Scientific American,* vol. 224, 1971).

Seagle, W., *The Quest for Law* (New York, 1941).

Seidenberg, R., *Posthistoric Man* (Chapel Hill, N.C., 1950).

Service, E. R., *Primitive Social Organization: An Evolutionary Perspective* (New York, 1962).

Seward, G. H., *Sex and the Social Order* (New York, 1946).

Shapiro, H. L., "From the Neck Up" (*Natural History,* vol. 56, 1947), pp. 456–465.

——, *The Heritage of the Bounty* (New York, 1962).

Shapley, H. (ed.), *Climatic Change: Evidence, Causes, Effects* (Cambridge, Mass., 1953).

Sharp, L., "People without Politics," in V. Ray (ed.), *Systems of Political Control and Bureaucracy* (Seattle, Wash., 1958), pp. 1–8.

Sharrock, F. W., *Prehistoric Occupation Patterns in Southwest Wyoming and Cultural Relationships with the Great Basin and Plains Cultural Areas* (University of Utah Anthropological Papers, no. 77, 1966).

Sieber, R., "The Arts and Their Changing Social Function" (*Annals of the New York Academy of Sciences,* vol. 96, 1962), pp. 653–658.

Simmons, L. (ed.), *Sun Chief: The Autobiography of a Hopi Indian* (New Haven, Conn., 1942).

——, *The Role of the Aged in Primitive Society* (New Haven, Conn., 1945).

Simons, E. L., "The Earliest Apes" (*Scientific American,* vol. 217, 1967), pp. 28–35.

Simpson, G. E., "The Vodun Service in Northern Haiti" (*American Anthropologist,* vol. 42, 1940), pp. 236–254.

Simpson, G. G., *The Meaning of Evolution* (Oxford, 1950).

——, *Principles of Animal Taxonomy* (New York, 1961).

——, "The Meaning of Taxonomic Statements," in S. L. Washburn (ed.), *Classification and Human Evolution* (Chicago, 1963), pp. 1–31.

Singer, M., "Culture: The Concept of Culture" (*International Encyclopedia of the Social Sciences,* vol. 3, 1968), pp. 527–543.

Singer, S., E. J. Holmyard, and A. R. Hall (eds.), *A History of Technology* (3 vols., Oxford, 1954).

Skinner, B. F., *Beyond Freedom and Dignity* (New York, 1971).

Skira, A., and G. Bataille, *Prehistoric Painting: Lascaux or the Birth of Art* (Switzerland, n.d.).

Smith, A. G., *Communication and Culture: Readings in the Codes of Human Interaction* (New York, 1966).

Smith, G. H., "J. B. Trudeau's Remarks on the Indians of the Upper Missouri, 1794–95" (*American Anthropologist,* vol. 38, 1936), pp. 565–568.

Smith, M. G., "Secondary Marriage among Kadara and Kogow," in P. Bohannan and J. Middleton (eds.), *Marriage, Family, and Residence* (Garden City, N.Y., 1968), pp. 109–130.

Smith, M. W., "The War Complex of the Plains Indians" (*American Philosophical Society Proceedings,* vol. 28, 1938), pp. 425–464.

—— (ed.), *The Artist in Tribal Society: Proceedings of a Symposium Held at the Royal Anthropological Institute* (New York, 1961).

Smith, R. T., "Family: Comparative Structure" (*International Encyclopedia of the Social Sciences,* vol. 5, 1968), pp. 301–312.

Smyth, H. D., *Atomic Energy for Military Purposes: The Official Report on the Development of the Atomic Bomb under the Auspices of the United States Government, 1940–1945* (Princeton, N.J., 1946).

Solecki, R. S., "Prehistory in Shanidar Valley, Northern Iraq" (*Science,* vol. 139, no. 3551, 1963), pp. 179–193.

Solheim, W. G., II, "Reworking Southeast Asian Prehistory" (*Paideuma,* vol. 15, 1967), pp. 125–139.

Southall, A. W., *Alur Society* (Cambridge, England, 1956).

——, "Stateless Society" (*International Encyclopedia of the Social Sciences,* vol. 15, 1968), pp. 157–168.

Southwick, C. H. (ed.), *Primate Social Behavior: An Enduring Problem—Selected Readings* (Princeton, N.J., 1963).

Speck, F. H., "The Family Hunting Band as the Basis of Algonkian Social Organization" (*American Anthropologist,* vol. 17, 1915), pp. 289–305.

Spencer, H., *The Principles of Sociology* (3 vols., London, 1887–1896).

Spencer, R. F., "The Arabian Matriarchate: An Old Controversy" (*Southwestern Journal of Anthropology,* vol. 8, 1952), pp. 478–502.

—— (ed.), *Method and Perspective in Anthropology: Papers in Honor of Wilson D. Wallis* (Minneapolis, 1954).

——, "Language," in J. Gould and W. L. Kolb (eds.), *Dictionary of the Social Sciences* (Glencoe, Ill., 1964), p. 377.

——, "Spouse-Exchange among the North Alaskan Eskimo," in P. Bohannan and J. Middleton (eds.), *Marriage, Family, and Residence* (Garden City, N.Y., 1968), pp. 131–144.

Spicer, E. H., *A Short History of the Indians of the United States* (New York, 1969).

Spier, L., *The Sun Dance of the Plains Indian* (American Museum of Natural History, Anthropological Papers, vol. 16, part 7, 1921).

——, *Havasupai Ethnology* (American Museum of Natural History, Anthropological Papers, vol. 29, 1928).

——, *Plains Indian Parfleche Designs* (University of Washington Publications in Anthropology, vol. 4, no. 3, 1931).

——, *Yuman Tribes of the Gila River* (Chicago, 1933).

—— and E. Sapir, *Wishram Ethnography* (University of Washington Publications in Anthropology, vol. 3, no. 3, 1930).

Spier, R. F. G., *From the Hand of Man: Primitive and Preindustrial Technologies* (New York, 1970).

Spindler, G. D., *Sociocultural and Psychological Processes in Menomini Acculturation* (University of California Publications in Culture and Society, vol. 5, 1955).

——, *The Transmission of American Culture* (Cambridge, Mass., 1959).

——, "Psychocultural Adaptation," in E. Norbeck, D. Price-Williams, W. M. McCord (eds.), *The Study of Personality: An Interdisciplinary Appraisal* (New York, 1968) pp. 326–347.

Spindler, L., and G., "Male and Female Adaptations in Culture Change" (*American Anthropologist,* vol. 60, 1958), pp. 217–233.

Spuhler, J. N. (ed.), *The Evolution of Man's Capacity for Culture* (Detroit, 1959).

Srinivas, M. N., *Religion and Society among the Coorgs of South India* (Oxford, 1952).

Steggerda, M. G., "Physical Measurements on Negro, Navajo, and White Girls of College Age" (*American Journal of Physical Anthropology,* vol. 26, 1940), pp. 417–431.

Stent, G. S., *The Coming of the Golden Age* (Garden City, N.Y., 1969).

Steward, J. H., "A Uintah Ute Bear Dance, March, 1931" (*American Anthropologist,* vol. 34, 1932), pp. 263–273.

——, "The Economic and Social Basis of Primitive Bands," in *Essays in Anthropology in Honor of Alfred Louis Kroeber* (Berkeley, Calif., 1936), pp. 331–350.

——, "Shoshoni Polyandry" (*American Anthropologist,* vol. 38, 1936), pp. 561–564.

——, "Ecological Aspects of Southwestern Society" (*Anthropos,* vol. 32, 1937), pp. 82–104.

——, *Basin-plateau Aboriginal Socio-political Groups* (Bureau of American Ethnology Bulletin 120, 1938).

—— (ed.), *Handbook of South American Indians* (6 vols., Washington, D.C., 1946–1950).

——, "Cultural Causality and Law: A Trial Formulation of the Development of Early Civilization" (*American Anthropologist,* vol. 51, 1949), pp. 1–27.

——, "Evolution and Process," in A. L. Kroeber (ed.), *Anthropology Today: An Encyclopedic Inventory* (Chicago, 1953), pp. 313–326.

——, *Theory of Culture Change: The Methodology of Multilineal Evolution* (Urbana, Ill., 1955).

Stewart, G. R., *Ordeal by Hunger* (Boston, 1960).

Stewart, O. C., "Fire as the First Great Force Employed by Man," in W. L. Thomas (ed.), *Man's Role in Changing the Face of the Earth* (Chicago, 1956), pp. 115–133.

Stewart, T. D., "A Physical Anthropologist's View of the Peopling of the New World" (*Southwestern Journal of Anthropology,* vol. 16, 1960), pp. 259–273.

Stirling, M. W., *Historical and Ethnographical Materials on the Jivaro Indians* (Bureau of American Ethnology Bulletin 117, 1938).

Stocking, G. W., Jr., *Race, Culture, and Evolution: Essays in the History of Anthropology* (New York, 1968).

——, "Tylor, Edward Burnett" (*International Encyclopedia of the Social Sciences,* vol. 16, 1968), pp. 170–177.

Stoll, N. R., et al., *International Code of Zoological Nomenclature* (London, 1961).

Stow, G. W., *The Native Races of South Africa: A History of the Intrusion of the Hottentots and Bantu into the Hunting Grounds of the Bushman* (London, 1905).

Sturtevant, W. C., "Studies in Ethnoscience," in A. K. Romney and R. G. d'Andrade (eds.), "Transcultural Studies in Cognition" (*American Anthropologist,* vol. 66, no. 3, part 2, Special Publication, 1964), pp. 99–131.

Sumner, W. G., *Folkways: A Study of the Sociological Importance of Usages, Manners, Customs, Mores and Morals* (Boston, 1913).

Swadesh, M., *The Origin and Diversification of Language,* edited by J. Sherzer (Chicago, 1971).

Swanton, J. R., "The Social Organization of American Tribes" (*American Anthropologist,* vol. 7, 1905), pp. 663–673.

Swartz, M. J., V. W. Turner, and A. Tuden (eds.), *Political Anthropology* (Chicago, 1966).

Talmon, Y., "Millenarism" (*International Encyclopedia of the Social Sciences,* vol. 10, 1968), pp. 349–362.

Tax, S., "From Lafitau to Radcliffe-Brown: A Short History of the Study of Social Organization," in F. Eggan (ed.), *Social Anthropology of North American Tribes* (2d ed., Chicago, 1955), pp. 445–481.

——, "Some Problems of Social Organization," in F. Eggan (ed.), *Social Anthropology of North American Tribes* (2d ed., Chicago, 1955), pp. 2–32.

——, L. C. Eiseley, I. Rouse, and C. F. Voegelin (eds.), *An Appraisal of Anthropology Today* (Chicago, 1953).

Taylor, G. R., *The Biological Time Bomb* (New York, 1968).

ter Haar, B., *Adat Law in Indonesia* (translated from the Dutch and edited with an introduction by E. A. Hoebel and A. A. Schiller, New York, 1948).

Thomas, E. M., *The Harmless People* (New York, 1959).

——, "The Herdsmen" (*New Yorker,* May 1, 8, 15, and 22, 1965).

Thomas, W. I., *Primitive Behavior* (New York, 1937).

Thompson, D. F., "The Joking Relationship and Organized Obscenity in North Queensland" (*American Anthropologist,* vol. 37, 1935), pp. 460–490.

Thompson, J. E. S., *The Civilization of the Mayas* (Field Museum of Natural History, Anthropology Leaflet 25, 4th ed., 1942).

——, "A Survey of the Northern Maya Area" (*American Antiquity,* vol. 2, 1945), pp. 2–24.

Thompson, L., "The Culture History of the Lau Islands, Fiji" (*American Anthropologist,* vol. 40, 1938), pp. 181–197.

——, *Toward a Science of Mankind* (New York, 1961).

—— and A. Joseph, *The Hopi Way* (Lawrence, Kans., 1944).

Thompson, S., *Tales of the North American Indians* (Cambridge, Mass., 1929).

——, *The Folktale* (New York, 1946).

Thorner, D., "Peasantry" (*International Encyclopedia of the Social Sciences,* vol. 11, 1968), pp. 503–511.

Thurnwald, R., *Banaro Society* (American Anthropological Association Memoir 3, no. 4, 1924).

——, *Economics in Primitive Communities* (Oxford, 1932).

Tilney, F., *The Brain from Ape to Man* (2 vols., New York, 1928).

Titiev, M., "The Influence of Common Residence on the Unilateral Classification of Kindred" (*American Anthropologist,* vol. 45, 1943), pp. 511–530.

——, *Old Oraibi: A Study of the Hopi Indians of the Third Mesa* (Peabody Museum of American Archaeology and Ethnology, Harvard University, vol. 22, no. 1, 1944).

Tobias, P. V., "The Kanam Jaw" (*Nature,* vol. 184, no. 4714, 1960), pp. 946–947.

——, "Early Man in East Africa" (*Science,* vol. 149, 1965), p. 27.

de Tocqueville, A., *Democracy in America* (New York, 1945; translated from the French, first published in 1835).

Toffler, A., *Future Shock* (New York, 1970).

Trowell, M., and K. P. Wachsman, *Tribal Crafts in Uganda* (Oxford, 1953).

Tuden, A., and L. Plotnicov (eds.), *Social Stratification in Africa* (New York and London, 1970).

Tumin, M. M., *Caste in a Peasant Society: A Case Study of the Dynamics of Caste* (Princeton, N.J., 1952).

Turner, V. W., "Myth and Symbol" (*International Encyclopedia of the Social Sciences,* vol. 10, 1968), pp. 576–582.

Tyler, S. A. (ed.), *Cognitive Anthropology* (New York, 1969).

Tylor, E. B., *Researches into the Early History of Mankind* (2 vols., London, 1871).

———, *Primitive Culture: Researches into the Development of Mythology, Philosophy, Religion, Language, Art and Custom* (2 vols., New York, 1874).

———, "On the Game of Patolli in Ancient America and Its Probable Asiatic Origin" (*Journal of the Royal Anthropological Institute of Great Britain and Ireland,* vol. 8, 1879), pp. 116–129.

———, *Anthropology: An Introduction into the Study of Man and Civilization* (London, 1881).

———, "On a Method of Investigating the Development of Institutions; Applied to the Laws of Marriage and Descent" (*Journal of the Royal Anthropological Institute of Great Britain and Ireland,* vol. 18, 1889), pp. 245–272.

———, "American Lot Games as Evidence of Asiatic Intercourse before the Time of Columbus" (*Internationales Archiv für Ethnographie,* vol. 9, supplement, 1896), pp. 55–67.

Tyrell, J. B. (ed.), *David Thompson's Narrative of His Explorations in Western America, 1784–1812* (Toronto, 1916).

Underhill, R., *Ceremonial Patterns in the Greater Southwest* (American Ethnological Society Monograph 13, 1948).

UNESCO, *The Race Concept* (Paris, 1952).

———, *African Worlds: Studies in the Cosmological Ideas and Social Values of African Peoples* (Oxford, 1954).

U.S. Bureau of the Census, *Historical Statistics of the United States: Colonial Times to 1957* (Washington, D.C., 1970).

Vaillant, G. C., *Aztecs of Mexico: Origin, Rise and Fall of the Aztec Nation* (New York, 1941).

Vallois, H., "Néanderthal-Néandertal" (*L'Anthropologie,* vol. 55, 1952), pp. 557–558.

van Gennep, A., *The Rites of Passage* (M. B. Vizedom and G. L. Caffee, trans., Chicago, 1960).

Vavilov, N., *Studies on the Origin of Cultivated Plants* (Bulletin of Applied Botany and Plant Breeding, Leningrad, 1926).

Vercors, *You Shall Know Them* (Boston, 1953).

von Frisch, K., "Dialects in the Language of the Bees" (*Scientific American,* August, 1962), pp. 3–7.

Waitz, F. T., *Anthropologie der Naturvölker* (6 vols., Leipzig, 1859–1871).

Wallace, E., and E. A. Hoebel, *The Comanches: Lords of the South Plains* (Norman, Okla., 1952).

Waln, N., *The House of Exile* (Boston, 1933).

Warner, W. L., "Murngin Warfare" (*Oceania,* vol. 1, 1940), pp. 457–477.

——— and P. S. Lund, *The Social Life of a Modern Community* (New Haven, Conn., 1941).

Washburn, S. L., "The New Physical Anthropology" (*Transactions of the New York Academy of Sciences,* series II, vol. 13, 1951), pp. 298–304.

———, "Tools and Human Evolution" (*Scientific American,* vol. 203, 1960), pp. 62–75.

——— (ed.), *Social Life of Early Man* (Viking Fund Publications in Anthropology, no. 31, 1961).

——— (ed.), *Classification and Human Evolution* (Viking Fund Publications in Anthropology, no. 37, 1963).

Waterbolk, H. T., "The Lower Rhine," in R. J. Braidwood and G. R. Willey (eds.), *Courses toward Urban Life: Archeological Consideration of Some Cultural Alternatives* (Viking Fund Publications in Anthropology, no. 32, 1962), pp. 227–253.

Watson, W., *Early Civilization in China* (New York, 1966).

Wax, M., and R. Wax, "The Notion of Magic" (*Current Anthropology,* vol. 4, 1963), pp. 519–533.

Webster, H., *Primitive Secret Societies: A Study in Early Politics and Religion* (New York, 1908).

Weidenreich, F., "Some Problems Dealing with Ancient Man" (*American Anthropologist,* vol. 42, 1940), pp. 375–383.

——, "The Skull of Sinanthropus pekinensis: A Comparative Study on a Primitive Hominid Skull" (*Paleontologia Sinica,* n.s., D, no. 10, 1943), pp. 1–484.

——, *Morphology of Solo Man* (American Museum of Natural History, Anthropological Papers, vol. 43, part 1, 1951), pp. 205–290.

Weiner, W. S., and B. G. Campbell, "The Taxonomic Status of the Swanscombe Skull," in C. D. Ovey (ed.), *Swanscombe—A Survey of Research on a Unique Pleistocene Site* (London, 1964).

Weltfish, G., "Prehistoric North American Basketry Techniques and Modern Distributions" (*American Anthropologist,* vol. 32, 1930), pp. 454–495.

Westermarck, E., *The History of Human Marriage* (3 vols., London, 1925).

Wheeler, M., *Civilizations of the Indus Valley and Beyond* (New York, 1966).

White, J. P., "New Guinea: The First Phase in Oceanic Settlement," in R. C. Green and M. Kelly (eds.), *Studies in Oceanic Settlement,* vol. 2 (Pacific Anthropological Records, no. 12, Bishop Museum, Honolulu, 1971), pp. 45–52.

White, L. A., "A Problem in Kinship Terminology" (*American Anthropologist,* vol. 41, 1939), pp. 566–570.

——, "Energy and the Evolution of Culture" (*American Anthropologist,* vol. 45, 1943), pp. 335–356.

——, "The Symbol: The Origin and Basis of Human Behavior" (*Etc.: A Review of General Semantics,* vol. 1, 1944), pp. 229–237.

——, "'Diffusion vs. Evolution': An Anti-Evolutionist Fallacy" (*American Anthropologist,* vol. 47, 1945), pp. 339–355.

——, "The Expansion of the Scope of Science" (*Journal of the Washington Academy of Sciences,* vol. 37, 1947), pp. 181–210.

——, *The Evolution of Culture* (New York, 1959).

Whiting, B. B., *Paiute Sorcery* (Viking Fund Publications in Anthropology, no. 15, 1950).

—— (ed.), *Six Cultures: Studies of Child Rearing* (New York and London, 1963).

Whiting, J. W. M., "Effects of Climate on Certain Cultural Practices," in W. H. Goodenough (ed.), *Explorations in Cultural Anthropology: Essays in Honor of George Peter Murdock* (New York, 1964), pp. 511–544.

—— and I. L. Child, *Child Training and Personality: A Cross-cultural Study* (New Haven, Conn., 1953).

——, R. Kluckhohn, and A. S. Anthony, "The Function of Male Initiation Ceremonies at Puberty," in E. E. Maccoby, T. Newcomb, and E. Hartley (eds.), *Readings in Social Psychology* (New York, 1958), pp. 359–370.

Whitman, W., *The Pueblo Indians of San Ildefonso* (New York, 1947).

Whorf, B. L., *Language, Thought, and Reality* (Cambridge, Mass., 1956).

Willey, G. R., "Archeological Theories and Interpretations: New World," in A. L. Kroeber (ed.), *Anthropology Today: An Encyclopedic Inventory* (Chicago, 1953), pp. 361–385.

——, *An Introduction to American Archaeology:* vol. 1, *North and Middle America* (Englewood Cliffs, N.J., 1966).

Wilson, G. R., *The Hidatsa Earthlodge* (American Museum of Natural History Anthropological Papers, vol. 33, 1934).

Wilson, M., *Good Company: A Study of Nyakyusa Age-villages* (London, 1951).

Wissler, C., *The American Indian* (3d ed., New York, 1938).

Wolf, A. P., "Adopt a Daughter-in-law, Marry a Sister: A Chinese Solution to the Problem of the Incest Taboo" (*American Anthropologist,* vol. 70, 1968), pp. 864–874.

——, "Childhood Association and Sexual Attraction: A Further Test of the Westermarck Hypothesis" (*American Anthropologist,* vol. 72, 1970), pp. 503–515.

Wolf, E., "Closed Corporate Peasant Communities in Mesoamerica and Central Java" (*Southwestern Journal of Anthropology,* vol. 13, 1957), pp. 1–18.

——, *Sons of the Shaking Earth* (Chicago, 1959).

Worsley, P., *The Trumpet Shall Sound: A Study of "Cargo" Cults in Melanesia* (London, 1957).

Yerkes, R. M., and A. W. Yerkes, *The Great Apes: A Study of Anthropoid Life* (New Haven, Conn., 1929).

Index

Page numbers in *italics* indicate illustrations or charts.

CULTURE AREAS:

I. North Africa
    A. Mediterranean Coast
    B. Egypt
II. Sahara
III. Sudan
    A. Western Sudan
    B. Eastern Sudan
IV. Guinea Coast
V. East Horn
VI. Cattle Area
    A. Eastern Cattle Area
    B. Western Cattle Area
VII. Congo
VIII. Khoisan
    A. Bushman
    B. Hottentot
IX. Madagascar

TRIBAL GROUPS:

1. Dogon
2. Wolof
3. Mano
4. Hausa
5. Kpelle
6. Tallensi
7. Nupe
8. Ashanti
9. Dahomeans (Fon)
10. Yoruba
11. Ibo (incl. Ibibio)
12. Tiv
13. Azande (Zande)
14. Pygmy Tribes—Twa (Batwa)
15. Herero
16. Bushman
17. Hottentot (incl. Nama, Bergdama)
18. Lozi (Barotse)
19. Ba-Ila (Ila)
20. Zulu
21. Tswana
22. Swazi
23. Bemba (Babemba)
24. Nyakyusa
25. Chaga (Tschagga)
26. Ankole (Banyankole, incl. Bahima and Bairu)
27. Sukuma
28. Watussi (Tussi)
29. Nyoro (Banyoro or Bakitara)
30. Alur
31. Masai
32. Nuer
33. Dinka
34. Tanala-Betsileo
35. Sakalava

Scale at equator
500   0   500
Miles

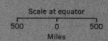

AFRICA

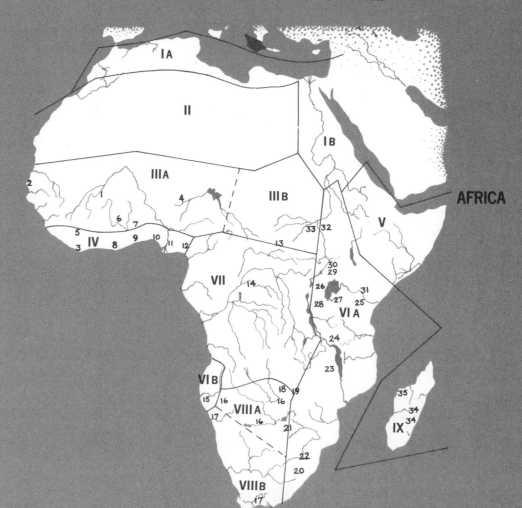